A Library
of Literary
Criticism

A Library of Literary Criticism

VOLUME 1
Abouzeid to Etcheverts

MODERN WOMEN WRITERS

Compiled and edited by

LILLIAN S. ROBINSON

A Frederick Ungar Book
CONTINUUM · NEW YORK

1996
The Continuum Publishing Company
370 Lexington Avenue
New York, NY 10017

Printed in the United States of America

Library of Congress Cataloging-in-Publication Data

Modern women writers / compiled and edited by Lillian S. Robinson.
    p.   cm. — (A library of literary criticism)
  "A Frederick Ungar book."
  Includes bibliographical references and index.
  ISBN 0-8264-0823-0 (set). — ISBN 0-8264-0813-3 (v. 1). — ISBN
0-8264-0814-1 (v. 2). —ISBN 0-8264-0815-X (v. 3).—ISBN 0-8264-0920-2 (vol. 4)
    1. Literature—Women authors—History and criticism.
  2. Literature, Modern—20th century—History and criticism.
  3. Women authors—Biography. I. Robinson, Lillian S. II. Series.
PN471.M62 1996
809'.89287'0904—dc20   94-43197
                                        CIP

INTRODUCTION

Modern Women Writers. It's more of a problem—or a set of them—than a title, for each of the three words provokes insistent queries about what it means. How recent is modern? Who counts as a woman writer? What kinds of writers? More temperately expressed, does "modern" refer to period or style? That is, are the writers included here contemporary or modern*ist*? And what are the boundaries of the "contemporary" period? Does "women" designate all members of the sex or only those who address gender issues? Are the included writers all feminists or, on the other hand, are they all authors of what used to be called "women's books"? And who counts as a "writer," anyway? Are only literary authors included or are there journalists, pamphleteers, and diarists among them? I hope that starting with some of the questions suggested by the title itself will help to explain the purposes of this collection, its uses, and its limitations.

These volumes are part of Continuum's Library of Literary Criticism series. Each component of this series—covering, so far, modern American, Arabic, Black, British, Commonwealth, French, German, Irish, Latin American, Romance, Slavic, and Spanish and Portuguese literatures, as well as modern dramatists and modern science fiction, fantasy, and detective writers—comprises selections from critical writings about the authors included. For the entire series, "modern" is understood to denote the twentieth century, from the beginning to the date of that particular volume's publication. Supplements have updated *Modern American Literature, Modern British Literature,* and *Modern Black Writers,* adding new authors, as well as new material on those already listed.

Following this pattern, *Modern Women Writers* presents criticism of women writers who lived and worked in this century, whether they were authors who created, participated in, ignored, deplored, or altered the literary trends that characterized their times. Writers whose careers began in the nineteenth century are included if they also published work in the twentieth. I had expected a few iffy cases to arise, where I would have to determine whether someone whose oeuvre straddled the century mark really belonged in spirit to the modern age. In practice, however, I ended up excluding no one on this basis, although I did not go as far as the editors of *Modern American Literature,* who bent the century division so far back as to include Emily Dickinson (1830–86), presumably on the grounds of her very real modern affinities and influence, as well as extensive posthumous publication. When the rubric is *women* writers, after all, there are a great many authors of the past whose work is receiving initial publication or enthusiastic reissue in the late twentieth century.

The only generalization that can safely be made about the authors discussed in *Modern Women Writers* is that they are members of the female sex. Their work may concentrate more (and more respectfully) than that of men on female experience, but it does not do so exclusively. And there is no uniformity of attitude or approach. No claim is being made, here, for the existence of a single tradition that unites twentieth-century women writers across regional, national, ethnic, racial, ideological, sexual, and stylistic boundaries. Not only are these writers not all feminist, they are not all *any* one thing.

With all these negative disclaimers, why compile a collection on modern women writers and why consider it a feminist project to have done so? I believe that twenty-five years of feminist criticism has taught us, above all, that gender is a significant category in literary history, as it is in social history. It affects the experience of the writer all the way from whether she gets to write at all to her relationship to language; it also has an impact on the content and form of her text, its connection to other texts, and the experience of the reader. This means that, because human experience is so heavily gendered—although differently so in different cultures—there is a gender dimension to what leads women to write, what they write about, how they do so, and how their work is interpreted.*

---

*For a general introduction to the viewpoint of feminist criticism and an overview of key works in the field, see Lillian S. Robinson, "Feminist Criticism," *Encyclopedia of World*

Recognition of gender as a legitimate category in literary study means that grouping women writers from around the world is, in itself, an act of inquiry, a marking off of territory, rather than a definitive statement about what these writers have in common. The social construction of their common gender creates the category, much as the social constructions of nation and language do for other volumes in this series, but articulation of the category suggests questions, rather than answers.

So, yes, although "feminism" is a far from monolithic term, some of the writers included here are or were consciously involved in the struggle for recognition of women's full humanity. Many others were not feminists according to even this most flexible of definitions. A few were militantly antifeminist. Because the grouping of women writers has often meant relegating them to a secondary status, some of the authors included here have resisted identification with such a category. "I am a writer," they will say, or "a poet." Not a *woman* writer, a *woman* poet. This collection is not intended to ghettoize women writers, much less to dismiss them. In this, as in other areas, the approach is not "either-or," but "both-and." Authors discussed in *Modern Women Writers* are women writers *and* participants in a national or ethnic tradition, women writers *and* experimental poets, women writers *and* proletarian novelists. Reading them through the clarifying lens of gender is meant to add another dimension to the interpretation and situate each author in at least implicit relation to the others.

The women included here are primarily literary writers, authors of novels, short stories, poems, and plays. Most of their work inhabits the secure realm of "art." But, since feminist criticism has deliberately challenged the stratification of culture, there are also many whose work was addressed to a mass audience, often through popular genres like the detective novel, science fiction, or juvenile literature, to which women have made notable contributions. Feminist criticism has also expanded our definitions of literature to embrace forms like the autobiography, the diary or journal, and the letter that were the sole or principal outlet for many women. Some of the women included in this collection are called "writers"

Literature in the 20th Century, volume 5, Steven R. Serafin and Walter D. Glanze, eds. (New York: Continuum, 1993), pp. 221–23.

only according to this expanded definition of what constitutes literature. (Although I defy anyone to convince me that Auschwitz memoirist Charlotte Delbo and political organizer Emma Goldman were *not* writers.)

These definitions of "modern," "woman," and "writer" represent choices that may be controversial, but that are the defining characteristics of the collection. I suspect that there will be even more challenges to specific inclusions and omissions of authors and critics. Explaining the process of selection will, I hope, speak to some of these objections, although differences of opinion—some of them founded on taste, some on readers' special knowledge and interests—will undoubtedly remain.

The decision to make the collection as international and multicultural as possible led to most of the choices likely to prove problematic. The relative importance of any writer within her own national tradition is subject to debate, and the argument heats up considerably when the frame of reference becomes global. If the rationale for this project holds true, the category "twentieth-century women writers from around the world" constitutes a congenial or at least an interesting context in which to consider a particular author's work. But how to determine which authors should figure in that context?

Of the more than 570 writers discussed in these volumes, I doubt if as many as 10 percent would appear on everyone's list of *inevitable* inclusions. To date, eight women have won the Nobel Prize for Literature: a Swede, a Norwegian, an Italian, a Chilean, two Americans, a South African writing in English, and a German Jew who spent the last three decades of her life in Sweden. This scanty information may not suffice to enable even the knowledgeable reader to identify, respectively, Selma Lagerlöf, Sigrid Undset, Grazia Deledda, Gabriela Mistral, Pearl S. Buck, Toni Morrison, Nadine Gordimer, and Nelly Sachs, and I suspect that not all of them would appear on that combined "must" list.

If not even the Nobel Prize is a reliable guide to "world class" stature, how were selections to be made? How does one decide between the claims of, say a much-anthologized but no longer fashionable white American poet (when there are dozens of other American poets of all races already included), a Balkan poet whose compatriots are the only ones who can read her work, but whose inspiring words thousands of *them* know by heart, and the first daring woman to publish a work of fiction in a recently independent Third World nation with distinct ethnic languages and cultural traditions, but where the only national language is the one imposed by the former colonial power? These descriptions are of archetypes rather than actual writers, but the dilemma was real enough. In what follows, I shall try to describe my method of selection, as well as the principles that guided its implementation.

I knew I would be comparing literary apples and oranges, but first I had to assemble them for the fruit salad. For those national literatures that are the subject of earlier volumes in the Library of Literary Criticism, a ready-made list of nominees existed, which could then be supplemented from other sources. For the parts of the world not yet covered by another volume in this series, chiefly Scandinavia, Asia outside of the Indian subcontinent, and those Middle Eastern countries (Israel, Turkey, Iran) whose literature is in a language other than Arabic, I had recourse to compendia like Continuum's *Encyclopedia of World Literature in the 20th Century,* which was revised through a supplementary volume in 1993, and the *Bloomsbury Guide to Women's Literature,* published in 1992. Reference guides to particular literatures or to women writers in those literatures, as well as the journal *World Literature Today* also provided useful summaries of major trends and figures in unfamiliar cultures.

Toward the end of my nearly eight years' work on the project, colleagues were continuing to suggest new names for consideration. By this time, I was able to express with confidence and irony the (admittedly inconsistent) standard that had evolved through practice: if your candidate were a Bulgarian instead of an Englishwoman, she would have a better chance. This does not, of course, reflect an intrinsic preference for Bulgarian writers, but rather the vast differences in the pools available to select from. Inevitably, authors of work in the principal international languages or of work that is widely translated are likelier to appear in the collection.

The volumes in A Library of Literary Criticism are selections from *criticism,* not anthologies of literature. In order to be included, an author has to have attracted a "critical mass" of commentary, from which, generally speaking, at least three pieces can be chosen. The politics of language on the global scale and the limitations of my knowledge and resources, on the personal one, forced certain choices. For those non-English languages I am able to read, all of which are European (French, Italian, Spanish, Portuguese, and German), I could skim an article and decide which selections were to be translated. For all other languages, the piece would have to be translated in its entirety *before* I excerpted it, which restricted me to short critical articles. In selecting Chinese, Japanese, and Israeli writers, therefore, my attention was most insistently directed to those who have won attention abroad, and my list may therefore not always correspond to one that an informed native critic would make. (Even here, however, there may be a kind of critical "uncertainty principle" at work, for specialists have pointed out that translation and consequent recognition abroad often boosts a Chinese writer's reputation at home.)

Since much of my own theoretical and polemical writing over the past dozen years has criticized the processes of canon formation and the canon(s) it has established, it is particularly ironic that, in *Modern Women Writers,* I should seem to be making a canon myself. For better or for worse, however, editing this collection did not really put me in a position to influence which writers were considered "important." The severest limitation on dramatic innovations in the list of writers derived from the amount and availability of useful criticism. Although the result seems to confirm a consensus, this is a field where, in fact, no general agreement yet exists, and where the apparent consensus is actually the sum of a great many small individual judgments.

When I mentioned "useful criticism," just now, I was referring to the standards I applied in compiling each entry to meet the needs of those likely to consult these volumes. Where I had a choice, I selected criticism that represented the range of an author's work and the range of critical opinion about it. Excerpts are often arranged in such a way as to suggest the outlines of the debate. If there is feminist criticism on a particular author, I have included it among the excerpts, but in no case are the excerpts limited to feminist readings. In some cases, I have included criticism that is consciously or unconsciously antifeminist, because such excerpts help explain the context within which women writers do their work and women's literature develops. At the beginning of the project, I would probably have enunciated it as a principle of selection that the only criticism to be excluded was stupid criticism. But, as the work progressed, I came to understand that even criticism I consider stupid—a category that certainly includes a narrow or stereotyped view of gender roles and possibilities—can have its educational uses. The "stupid" excerpts are not so labeled, but those readers who are just starting to work with critical sources—high school students and undergraduates, for example—should be reminded that not every statement that appears in print is equally trustworthy, much less true, and that, when you cite criticism, you are expected to exercise your own critical judgment as to its validity.

For those writers included in previous Library of Literary Criticism collections, the earlier entry served as a basis for the one here. Usually, I have added to it critical excerpts published more recently. Sometimes, a few of the earlier excerpts have been omitted in the interest of balance between old and new material; more rarely, an excerpt from earlier criticism has also been added. The only female authors included in previous Library of Literary Criticism volumes who do *not* appear in *Modern Women Writers* are those about whom I could find no suitable recent criticism. In a few cases, I have fleshed out an entry by including as the third item an excerpt from a biographical and critical reference guide. There are even a few instances where an entry contains only two items, normally because, although more criticism exists, it was linguistically or materially inaccessible to me. Most of the excerpts for each author-entry are in chronological order, by date of publication. I have occasionally deviated from this pattern, however, when an excerpt, or several excerpts, would serve to introduce the reader in some important way to the career of the author under consideration.

Changes in the arena of world history have had a surprising impact on the development of this project. When my work began in 1988, the Soviet Union, Czechoslovakia, and Yugoslavia were each one country, Germany was two. Now, in 1996, the political situation and even the map of Eastern Europe are different, and the consequences for literature and for women remain unclear. But this collection already contains entries on Russian, Rumanian, and Bulgarian writers whose names could not have appeared on the preliminary list of contents compiled eight years ago. If the project were delayed another few years, when the entire twentieth century could be surveyed, I suspect there would be a much larger representation of varied and lively voices from that part of the world.

Geopolitics also creates problems about the national labels to be applied to certain authors. The earlier components of this series tended to solve these problems by including an author whose nationality might be disputed in more than one volume. Thus, several writers appear in both *Modern British* and *Modern Irish,* and Doris Lessing in *Modern Commonwealth* as well as *Modern British.* For *Modern Women Writers,* however, these authors do have to be assigned a nationality, and the labeling is not always satisfactory or consistent. Doris Lessing, for example, was born of British parents in Persia, now, of course, called Iran, but not particularly significant for her future development as a writer. Her childhood and young adult years were spent in what was then Rhodesia, now Zimbabwe, and Africa does figure largely in her work, most of which, however, was done in England, where she has lived for nearly fifty years. For a number of reasons, I am far from contented with the description "Zimbabwe–Great Britain" that I used as her national affiliation, although I am unable to come up with a formula that would adequately summarize her history.

Such dual identification also applies to writers who immigrated from one country or another or who spent some period as refugees or exiles. The Nobel Prize Committee identified Nelly Sachs's "country" as Sweden, but I think my label for her, "Germany–Sweden" helps introduce what the critical extracts have to say about the language and the themes of her poetry. Another German-language Jewish poet who survived the Holocaust, Rose Ausländer, presents a knottier geopolitical case. Not only did horrific world events force her geographical displacement, but her native region, Bukovina, has belonged to four different countries in this century, and her native city, in whose literary history she is an important figure, has changed its name almost as often, from Czernowitz to Cernauti to Chernovtsy. The poet herself spent some time in America and her last years in Germany, where her literary reputation continues to grow. As a label, "Bukovina–Germany" reflects this complex history, but does not begin to convey it. For natives of the former Yugoslavia, where conflicts continued, though a fragile peace has been reached as I write, I have allowed an author's language to suggest a nationality, but this may have led to grim mistakes in some instances.

In the heading of each entry, I have usually adhered to the spelling of the author's name used in the *MLA Bibliography*. But, particularly for transliterations from systems of writing other than the Latin alphabet, different versions may appear in different critical excerpts. (Russian poet Marina Tsvetaeva, for example, is Cvetaeva in the library catalogue I consulted and in some of the critical extracts, Tsvetayeva in others.) I have deviated from the MLA usage only where *all* the critical excerpts I chose happened to use the variant spelling.

The four volumes of *Modern Women Writers* are arranged in alphabetical order, rather than by country, region, or language. Given the problems entailed in assigning a suitable geographical label to many writers, the advantages of the alphabetical organization are obvious. When a writer is a member of an ethnic group or linguistic minority in her country, that fact and its significance almost always come up in the critical excerpts. For the United States, where there are so many minority writers of so many ethnicities, the listing in Authors Included identifies them as African American, Asian American, Cuban American, Mexican American, Native American, and Puerto Rican authors. *Modern Women Writers* also includes an Index to Critics.

One way I imagine this collection will be used—by students, in particular—is as a starting point for research. From that point of view, the entries lay the groundwork for bibliographies of both texts and criticism. Some critical excerpts provide a general survey of the writer's work; others focus on one or more particular works. In the case of specific works mentioned, the original titles are provided, along with English translations, where necessary. In addition, each item supplies a full reference to its source, so the reader will finish the entry with the beginnings of a critical bibliography. Consulting the book, article, or review excerpted here not only provides a longer discussion of the author's work, but directs the reader to the critic's full approach and (it is hoped) to other works of criticism, as well.

I know I am not the only researcher who finds it impossible to look up something in a reference book, even a dictionary, without getting sidetracked by some of the other entries. The very randomness of the alphabetical arrangement in this collection produces some intriguing juxtapositions, and I hope reading around in *Modern Women Writers* will arouse interest in other modern women writers. These four hefty volumes contain a great deal of criticism, but the major critical work still lies ahead of us, as we— this collection's readers, along with its contributors—come to increasingly deeper understandings of the connections between gender, language, expression, and narrative as these have been manifested in women writers around the world in our century.

*   *   *

In addition to the acknowledgments for reprint permissions at the end of volume 4, I owe personal thanks to the many institutions and individuals who have helped me put this collection together. The libraries at Stanford, University of California at Berkeley, University of Texas at Austin, Virginia Tech, and NYU were primary sites for my research; I am particularly indebted to the Interlibrary Loan and Humanities Reference staffs at Virginia Tech's Newman Library. Thomas F. Staley, director of the Harry Ransom Humanities Research Center at the University of Texas, Austin, whose own critical and editorial commitments are reflected in a number of selections in *Modern Women Writers,* provided me with an institutional home for the period of most intensive work on the collection. I relied heavily on advice about authors or critics offered by Charlotte Armster (German), Miriam Cooke (Arabic), Shelley Fisher Fishkin (American), Jane Marcus (British), and Shoshana Milgram (British and Russian). Gloria Feiman Waldman and Jane Marcus generously gave me access to material of theirs that was not yet published. Barbara Kennedy turned ponderous German critic-speak into readable English prose.

More than a decade ago, I acknowledged Greg Robinson's research efforts on another project of mine by referring to his serving as my "eyes, legs, and occasionally wits" at distant libraries. His contribution to *Modern Women Writers* was even more significant. Alex Robinson-Gilden's clerical assistance began with the unexpected nonclerical feat of scaling a wall and climbing into a window. On that occasion, he was substituting for Douglas Michael Massing, the research and clerical assistant who has been with me almost since the start of the project, and whose contribution to the accuracy and consistency of the contents—not to mention my own sanity—cannot be overestimated. These three men, my nephew, my son, and my friend, have joined an army of women and my incomparable editor, Evander Lomke, in keeping me and my work going through a difficult time.

Lillian S. Robinson
Greenville, North Carolina

AUTHORS INCLUDED

Volume 1

Abouzeid, Leila	Morocco
Acker, Kathy	U.S.
Adcock, Fleur	New Zealand
Adnan, Etel	Lebanon–U. S.
Aguirre, Mirta	Cuba
Agustini, Delmira	Uruguay
Ai Bei	China
Aichinger, Ilse	Austria
Aidoo, (Christina) Ama Ata	Ghana
Akhmadulina, Bella	Russia
Akhmatova, Anna	Russia
Alegría, Claribel	Nicaragua–El Salvador
Aleramo, Sibilla	Italy
Aliger, Margarita	Russia
Allen, Paula Gunn	U.S. (Native American)
Allende, Isabel	Chile
Allfrey, Phyllis Shand	Dominica
Alós, Concha	Spain
Anderson, Jessica	Australia
Angelou, Maya	U.S. (African American)
Anhava, Helena	Finland
Anzaldúa, Gloria	U.S. (Mexican American)
Ariyoshi Sawako	Japan
Arnow, Harriette	U.S.
Ashton-Warner, Sylvia	New Zealand
Astley, Thea	Australia
Atencia, María Victoria	Spain
Atwood, Margaret	Canada
Ausländer, Rose	Bukovina–Germany
Avison, Margaret	Canada

Bâ, Mariama	Senegal
Ba'albakkī, Laylā	Lebanon
Bachmann, Ingeborg	Austria
Bagryana, Elisaveta	Bulgaria
Bainbridge, Beryl	Great Britain
Bambara, Toni Cade	U.S. (African American)
Banti, Anna	Italy
Baranskaya, Natalya	Russia
Barker, Pat	Great Britain
Barnes, Djuna	U.S.
Baynton, Barbara	Australia
Beattie, Ann	U.S.
Beauvoir, Simone de	France
Bedford, Sybille	Great Britain
Belli, Gioconda	Nicaragua
Benešová, Božena	Czech Republic
Benmussa, Simone	France
Bennett, Louise	Jamaica
Bennūna, Hanata	Morocco
Benson, Stella	Great Britain
Berberova, Nina	Russia
Bing Xin	China
Bishop, Elizabeth	U.S.
Blais, Marie-Claire	Canada
Blandiana, Ana	Rumania
Blume, Judy	U.S.
Bogan, Louise	U.S.
Bombal, María Luisa	Chile
Bosco, Monique	Canada
Bottome, Phyllis	Great Britain
Boucher, Denise	Canada
Bowen, Elizabeth	Great Britain
Bowles, Jane	U.S.
Boye, Karin	Sweden
Boyle, Kay	U.S.
Brittain, Vera	Great Britain
Brodber, Erna	Jamaica
Brøgger, Suzanne	Denmark
Brooke-Rose, Christine	Great Britain

Brookner, Anita	Great Britain
Brooks, Gwendolyn	U.S. (African American)
Brophy, Brigid	Great Britain
Brossard, Nicole	Canada
Brouwers, Marja	Netherlands
Brunet, Marta	Chile
Bryher (Winifred Ellermann)	Great Britain
Buck, Pearl S.	U.S.
Bullrich, Silvina	Argentina
Burgos, Julia de	U.S. (Puerto Rican)
Burke, Fielding (Olive Tilford Dargan)	U.S.
Burnett, Frances Hodgson	U.S.
Busta, Christine	Austria
Cabrera, Lydia	Cuba
Calisher, Hortense	U.S.
Campobello, Nellie	Mexico
Campos, Julieta	Mexico
Capécia, Mayotte	Martinique
Cardinal, Marie	France
Carter, Angela	Great Britain
Cassian, Nina	Rumania
Castellanos, Rosario	Mexico
Castillo, Ana	U.S. (Mexican American)
Cather, Willa	U.S.
Cederna, Camilla	Italy
Cervantes, Lorna Dee	U.S. (Mexican American)
Cespedes, Alba de	Italy
Chacel, Rosa	Spain
Chang Ai-Ling (Eileen)	China
Chauvet, Marie	Haiti
Chedid, Andrée	France–Lebanon–Egypt
Chen Jo-Hsi (Ruoxi)	China
Chen Yuan-Tsung	China
Chopin, Kate	U.S.
Christensen, Inger	Denmark
Churchill, Caryl	Great Britain
Cialente, Fausta	Italy

Duncan, Sara Jeannette	Canada
Duranti, Francesca	Italy
Duras, Marguerite	France
Ebner, Jeannie	Austria
Edgell, Zee	Belize
Edmond, Lauris	New Zealand
Ekman, Kerstin	Sweden
Emecheta, Buchi	Nigeria
Enchi Fumiko	Japan
Engel, Marian	Canada
Erb, Elke	Germany
Erdrich, Louise	U.S. (Native American)
Espina, Concha	Spain
Esteves, Sandra Maria	U.S. (Mexican American)
Etcherelli, Claire	France
Etcheverts, Sara de	Argentina

AUTHORS INCLUDED

Volume 2

Falcón, Lidia	Spain
Farrokhzad, Farūgh	Iran
Fauset, Jessie Redmon	U.S. (African American)
Fell, Alison	Great Britain
Ferre, Rosario	U.S. (Puerto Rican)
Field, Michael (Katherine Harris Bradley and Edith Emma Cooper)	Great Britain
Fleisser, Marieluise	Germany
Forché, Carolyn	U.S.
Fornés, María Irene	U.S. (Cuban American)
Frame, Janet	New Zealand
Franklin, Miles	Australia
Freeman, Mary E. Wilkins	U.S.

Hareven, Shulamit	Israel
Harjo, Joy	U.S. (Native American)
Harrower, Elizabeth	Australia
Harwood, Gwen	Australia
Hayashi Fumiko	Japan
Hazzard, Shirley	Australia
Head, Bessie	South Africa
Hébert, Anne	Canada
Hellman, Lillian	U.S.
Henley, Beth	U.S.
Herbst, Josephine	U.S.
Hernández, Luisa Josefina	Mexico
Hill, Susan	Great Britain
Hirabayashi Taeko	Japan
Hodge, Merle	Trinidad
Holtby, Winifred	Great Britain
Hopkins, Pauline Elizabeth	U.S. (African American)
Howard, Elizabeth Jane	Great Britain
Hoyos, Angela de	U.S. (Mexican American)
Huch, Ricarda	Germany
Hulme, Keri	New Zealand
Hurston, Zora Neale	U.S. (African American)
Hyvrard, Jeanne	France
Ibarbourou, Juana de	Uruguay
Idström, Annika	Finland
Jackson, Shirley	U.S.
Jameson, Storm	Great Britain
Jansson, Tove	Finland
Jellicoe, Ann	Great Britain
Jennings, Elizabeth	Great Britain
Jewett, Sarah Orne	U.S.
Jhabvala, Ruth Prawer	Poland–Great Britain–India
Johnson, Pamela Hansford	Great Britain
Johnston, Jennifer	Ireland
Jolley, Elizabeth	Australia
Jong, Erica	U.S.

Jordan, June M.   U.S. (African American)
Jorge, Lídia   Portugal
Joubert, Elsa   South Africa

Kahana-Carmon, Amalia   Israel
Kaschnitz, Marie Luise   Germany
Kaye-Smith, Sheila   Great Britain
Keane, Molly (M. J. Farrell)   Ireland
Kennedy, Margaret   Great Britain
Keun, Irmgard   Germany
Kilpi, Eeva   Finland
Kincaid, Jamaica   Antigua–U. S.
Kingston, Maxine Hong   U.S. (Asian American)
Kirsch, Sarah   Germany
Kobylyanska, Olga   Ukraine
Kogawa, Joy   Canada
Kolb, Annette   Germany
Kollontai, Alexandra   Russia
Kolmar, Gertrud   Germany
Königsdorf, Helga   Germany
Koroleva, Natalena   Ukraine
Kossak, Zofia   Poland
Kostenko, Lina   Ukraine
Koziol, Urszula   Poland
Kunewicz, Maria   Poland

Lacrosil, Michèle   Guadeloupe
Laforet, Carmen   Spain
Lagerlöf, Selma   Sweden
Lagorio, Gina   Italy
Langgässer, Elisabeth   Germany
Larsen, Marianne   Denmark
Larsen, Nella   U.S. (African American)
Lasker-Schüler, Elsa   Germany
Laurence, Margaret   Canada
Lavant, Christine   Austria
Lavin, Mary   Ireland
Leduc, Violette   France
Lee, Vernon (Violet Paget)   Great Britain

Le Fort, Gertrud von	Germany
Le Guin, Ursula K.	U.S.
Lehmann, Rosamond	Great Britain
L'Engle, Madeleine	U.S.
Lessing, Doris	Zimbabwe–Great Britain
Le Sueur, Meridel	U.S.
Leutenegger, Gertrud	Switzerland
Levertov, Denise	U.S.
Lewis, Janet	U.S.
Li Ang	China
Lidman, Sara	Sweden
Lindgren, Astrid	Sweden
Linhartová, Vera	Czech Republic
Lisnyanskaya, Inna	Russia
Lispector, Clarice	Brazil
Livesay, Dorothy	Canada
Loranger, Françoise	Canada
Lorde, Audre	U.S. (African American)
Lowell, Amy	U.S.
Loy, Mina	Great Britain–U.S.
Loy, Rosetta	Italy
Luft, Lya	Brazil
Lynch, Marta	Argentina

AUTHORS INCLUDED

Volume 3

McCarthy, Mary	U.S.
McCullers, Carson	U.S.
Macaulay, Rose	Great Britain
MacEwan, Gwendolyn	Canada
Maillet, Antonine	Canada
Majerová, Marie	Czech Republic
Maksimović, Desanka	Serbia

al-Malā'ika, Nāzik	Iraq
Mallet-Joris, Françoise	Belgium
Manicom, Jacqueline	Guadeloupe
Manning, Olivia	Great Britain
Mansfield, Katherine	New Zealand–Great Britain
Manzini, Gianna	Italy
Maraini, Dacia	Italy
Markandaya, Kamala	India
Marshall, Paule	U.S. (African American)
Martín Gaite, Carmen	Spain
Martinson, Moa	Sweden
Mason, Bobbie Ann	U.S.
Matute, Ana María	Spain
Mayröcker, Friederike	Austria
Medio, Dolores	Spain
Meireles, Cecília	Brazil
Menchú, Rigoberta	Guatemala
Mew, Charlotte	Great Britain
Meynell, Alice	Great Britain
Meynell, Viola	Great Britain
Miles, Josephine	U.S.
Millay, Edna St. Vincent	U.S.
Millin, Sarah Gertrude	South Africa
Minco, Marga	Netherlands
Mistral, Gabriela	Chile
Mitchison, Naomi	Great Britain
Mitford, Nancy	Great Britain
Miyamoto Yuriko	Japan
Moix, Ana María	Spain
Montero, Rosa	Spain
Moore, Marianne	U.S.
Moore, Olive (Constance Vaughn)	Great Britain
Moraga, Cherríe	U.S. (Mexican American)
Morante, Elsa	Italy
Morejón, Nancy	Cuba
Morgenstern, Beate	Germany
Morgner, Irmtraud	Germany
Morrison, Toni	U.S. (African American)
Mugo, Micere Githae	Kenya

Mukherjee, Bharati	India–Canada–U.S.
Munro, Alice	Canada
Murdoch, Iris	Great Britain
Naidu, Sarojini	India
Nalkowska, Z fia	Poland
Naranjo, Carmen	Costa Rica
Nasrallah, Emily	Lebanon
Naylor, Gloria	U.S. (African American)
Neera (Anna Radius Zuccari)	Italy
Nemes Nagy, Ágnes	Hungary
Nin, Anais	U.S.
Njau, Rebecca	Kenya
Noailles, Anna de	France
Nogami Yaeko	Japan
Norman, Marsha	U.S.
Novak, Helga	Germany
Nwapa, Flora	Nigeria
Oates, Joyce Carol	U.S.
Ōba Minako	Japan
O'Brien, Edna	Ireland
O'Brien, Kate	Ireland
Ocampo, Silvina	Argentina
Ocampo, Victoria	Argentina
O'Connor, Flannery	U.S.
Odio, Eunice	Costa Rica–Mexico
O'Faolain, Julia	Ireland
Ogot, Grace	Kenya
Okamoto Kanoko	Japan
Oldenbourg, Zoe	France
Olsen, Tillie	U.S.
Onwueme, Tess	Nigeria
Oreamuno, Yolanda	Costa Rica–Guatemala
Ortese, Anna Maria	Italy
Owens, Rochelle	U.S.
Ozick, Cynthia	U.S.

Paley, Grace	U.S.
Panóva, Vera	Russia
Pardo Bazán, Emilia	Spain
Parker, Dorothy	U.S.
Parra, Teresa de la	Venezuela
Parra, Violeta	Chile
Parun, Vesna	Croatia
Pawlikowska-Jasnorzewska, Maria	Poland
Peri Rossi, Christina	Uruguay
Petrushevskaya, Ludmila	Russia
Petry, Ann	U.S. (African American)
Piercy, Marge	U.S.
Piñon, Nélida	Brazil
Pitter, Ruth	Great Britain
Pizarnik, Alejandra	Argentina
Plath, Sylvia	U.S.
Plessen, Elisabeth	Germany
Pollock, Sharon	Canada
Poniatowska, Elena	Mexico
Porter, Katherine Anne	U.S.
Portillo del Trambley, Estela	U.S. (Mexican American)
Potter, Beatrix	Great Britain
Poulin, Gabrielle	Canada
Pozzi, Catherine	France
Prichard, Katherine Susannah	Australia
Pritam, Amrita	India
Prou, Suzanne	France
Pujmanová, Marie	Czech Republic
Pym, Barbara	Great Britain
Queiroz, Rachel de	Brazil
Quiroga, Elena	Spain
Raab, Esther	Israel
Raine, Kathleen	Great Britain
Rama Rau, Santha	India
Ratushinskaya, Irina	Russia
Ravikovitch, Dalia	Israel
Rawlings, Marjorie Kinnan	U.S.

Redmon, Anne	Great Britain
Reinig, Christa	Germany
Renault, Mary	Great Britain
Rhys, Jean	Dominica–Great Britain
Ribeiro Tavares, Zulmira	Brazil
Rich, Adrienne	U.S.
Richardson, Dorothy	Great Britain
Richardson, Henry Handel (Ethel F. Robertson)	Australia
Riding (Jackson), Laura	U.S.
Ridler, Anne	Great Britain
Riley, Joan	Jamaica–Great Britain
Rinser, Luise	Germany
Roberts, Michèle	Great Britain
Robinson, Marilynne	U.S.
Rochefort, Christiane	France
Rodoreda, Mercè	Spain (Catalan)
Romano, Lalla	Italy
Rose, Wendy	U.S. (Native American)
Roth, Friederike	Germany
Roy, Gabrielle	Canada
Rukeyser, Muriel	U.S.
el-Saadawi, Nawal	Egypt
Sachs, Nelly	Germany–Sweden
Sackville-West, Vita	Great Britain
Sagan, Françoise	France

AUTHORS INCLUDED

Volume 4

Sahgal, Nayantara	India
Salisachs, Mercedes	Spain
Sanchez, Sonia	U.S. (African American)
al-Sammān, Ghāda	Syria

Sandel, Cora (Sara Fabricius)	Norway
Sandoz, Mari	U.S.
Sarraute, Nathalie	France
Sarton, May	U.S.
Sata Ineko	Japan
Sayers, Dorothy L.	Great Britain
Schoultz, Solveig von	Finland
Schreiner, Olive	South Africa
Schwarz-Bart, Simone	Guadeloupe
Sebbar, Leila	Algeria
Seghers, Anna	Germany
Seidel, Ina	Germany
Senior, Olive	Jamaica
Serao, Matilde	Italy
Sexton, Anne	U.S.
al-Shaykh, Hanan	Lebanon
Shange, Ntozake	U.S. (African American)
Shen Rong	China
Sidhwa, Bapsi	Pakistan
Silko, Leslie Marmon	U.S. (Native American)
Silva, Clara	Uruguay
Sinclair, May	Great Britain
Sitwell, Edith	Great Britain
Slesinger, Tess	U.S.
Smedley, Agnes	U.S.
Smith, Pauline	South Africa
Smith, Stevie	Great Britain
Södergran, Edith	Finland
Somers, Armonía	Uruguay
Somerville and Ross	Ireland
Sono Ayako	Japan
Sontag, Susan	U.S.
Soriano, Elena	Spain
Sow Fall, Aminata	Senegal
Spark, Muriel	Great Britain
Stafford, Jean	U.S.
Stark, Freya	Great Britain
Stead, Christina	Australia
Stein, Gertrude	U.S.

Stern, G. B.	Great Britain
Stockenström, Wilma	South Africa
Storni, Alfonsina	Argentina
Struck, Karin	Germany
Suckow, Ruth	U.S.
Swenson, May	U.S.
Szymborska, Wislawa	Poland
Tafdrup, Pia	Denmark
Taggard, Genevieve	U.S.
Tan, Amy	U.S. (Asian American)
Taylor, Elizabeth	Great Britain
Teasdale, Sara	U.S.
Teliha, Olena	Ukraine
Telles, Lygia Fagundes	Brazil
Terry, Megan	U.S.
Thirkell, Angela	Great Britain
Thomas, Audrey	Great Britain
Thorup, Kirsten	Denmark
Tikkanen, Marta	Finland
Tlali, Miriam	South Africa
Tolstaya, Tatiana	Russia
Traba, Marta	Argentina
Treadwell, Sophie	U.S.
Triolet, Elsa	Russia–France
Trotzig, Birgitta	Sweden
Tsushima Yuko	Japan
Tsvetaeva, Marina	Russia
Tūqān, Fadwā	Palestine
Tusquets, Esther	Spain
Ty-Casper, Linda	Philippines
Tyler, Anne	U.S.
Tynan, Katharine	Ireland
Ukrainka, Lesya	Ukraine
Under, Marie	Estonia
Undset, Sigrid	Norway
Uno Chiyo	Japan

Valenzuela, Luisa	Argentina
Vega, Ana Lydia	U.S. (Puerto Rican)
Vilalta, Maruxa	Mexico
Villanueva, Alma	U.S. (Mexican American)
Villemaire, Yolande	Canada
Vorse, Mary Heaton	U.S.
Voznesenskaya, Iulia (Julia)	Russia
Waciuma, Charity	Kenya
Waddington, Miriam	Canada
Wakoski, Diane	U.S.
Walker, Alice	U.S. (African American)
Walker, Kath (Noonuccal, Oodgeroo)	Australia
Walker, Margaret	U.S. (African American)
Wang Anyi	China
Warner, Sylvia Townsend	Great Britain
Warner-Vieyra, Myriam	Guadeloupe
Watson, Sheila	Canada
Webb, Mary	Great Britain
Webb, Phyllis	Canada
Weil, Simone	France
Weldon, Fay	Great Britain
Welty, Eudora	U.S.
West, Jessamyn	U.S.
West, Rebecca (Cicily Isabel Fairfield)	Great Britain
Wharton, Edith	U.S.
White, Antonia	Great Britain
Wickham, Anna	Great Britain
Wilder, Laura Ingalls	U.S.
Williams, Sherley Anne	U.S. (African American)
Wilson, Ethel	Canada
Wiseman, Adele	Canada
Wittig, Monique	France
Wohmann, Gabriele	Germany
Wolf, Christa	Germany
Woolf, Virginia	Great Britain

Wright, Judith	Australia
Wylie, Elinor	U.S.
Xiao Hong	China
Xi Xi	China–Hong Kong
Yamamoto, Hisaye	U.S. (Asian American)
Yang Jiang (Chiang)	China
Yezierska, Anzia	U.S.
Yosano Akiko	Japan
Young, Marguerite	U.S.
Yourcenar, Marguerite	France
Zamora, Bernice	U.S. (Mexican American)
Zardoya, Concha	Spain
Zelda (Zelda Shneúrson Mishowsky)	Israel
Zhang Jie	China
Zhang Kangkang	China
Zhang Xinxin	China
Zhu Lin	China
Ziyadah, Mayy	Lebanon–Egypt

ABOUZEID, LEILA (MOROCCO) 1950–

Leila Abouzeid's novel published in the early 1980s is both similar and different from other novels by men. *Year of the Elephant* deals with Morocco's
struggle for independence and its aftermath, but through the experience of
one working-class woman. And though it is like Ben Jelloun's work about
men and women and the roles into which Arab men and women are socialized,
the perspective throughout is that of the woman, not the man. The style is
more immediate than dreamlike, the tone more ironic than cynical. . . . *Year
of the Elephant* addresses three inter-related problems of the new generation:
the issue of history, the issue of a national language and the issue of
feminism. . . .

The author gives the Moroccan struggle depth in Islamic history by
comparing it to an important battle in early Islam, when foreign tribes riding
elephants march on the sanctuary at Mecca. The battle of "Year of the Elephant" was won, not by arms and superior numbers, but by the support of
small and unimportant elements: flocks of birds which miraculously appeared
and so bombarded the elephants with clay pellets and rocks that the mighty
animals were forced to turn back in defeat.

Leila Abouzeid is clearly giving credit to ordinary people for the success
of the Moroccan battle of independence; Zahra becomes one of the "flock"
of small and unimportant people who made the difference in the undeclared
war against French rule: the blacksmiths, the housewives, the spice merchants, the rug merchants, the lorry drivers. To those who in the history
books are called simply "demonstrators" or "protestors," the author gives
faces and names. We come to know the spice merchant with "a sixth finger
like a tumor," the cheerful blacksmith; the women who hide fugitives in their
storehouses; the one-legged veteran of Dien Bien Phu. . . .

Leila Abouzeid writes her novella and short stories in what is called
modern standard literary Arabic, but her dialogue is written in a modified
vernacular. Hence the Arabic used in this novella is also an important innovation, as Arabic reviews indicate. . . .

The novella forces us to ask difficult questions about feminism. What is
the relationship between women's political and economic activity and
women's independence? What about the relationship of the woman to her
kin group? What are the events that force a woman to a new kind of consciousness, a desire for change? What is the role of religion in such change?
Is it a force for reform or for reaction? Does true independence imply larger
participation, a measure of the world's wealth and happiness? And finally, is
Zahra's choice a feminist choice?

The answer to the last question must be both yes and no. Zahra becomes an independent, self-sufficient woman, but in a narrow limited way few feminists East or West would totally accept. And Zahra's experience clearly does not conform to that of most Western feminists. She is not a Western woman, but a Moroccan woman, a Muslim woman who finds comfort in her religious faith. She is the product of a different history, a different expectation. That difference is illuminated by Leila Abouzeid in her successful effort to relate Zahra's independence and the problems associated with that independence to the wider issue of national independence and its problems. One woman's experience becomes a metaphor for society, a view that has less to do with Western ideas of individualism than it does with Middle Eastern ideals of the value of the group. The novel does not make an ideological statement, but rather presents in fictional form the real life situation of a real woman, the data that all ideologies must take into account.

Year of the Elephant offers insights into the specific situation of Moroccan women. As the first novel by a Moroccan woman written in Arabic to be translated into English, it suggests new directions within Moroccan literature, the increasing choice of Arabic over French in national writing, and the participation of a growing number of educated women as well as men in literary endeavors.

As a woman's perspective on the tumultuous events of recent Moroccan history which led to independence, the novella is unique. No patriotic rhetoric is found here, no self-justification, although there is no doubt that the author takes great pride in the achievements of her country. A certain sense of realism is present, a recognition that there are no easy solutions to the troubles of nations—and peoples. . . . Leila Abouzeid's brief novella, in Barbara Parmenter's fine translation, opens a small window through which Western readers may glimpse not only an aspect of the realities of Moroccan women's lives, but also an aspect of the rich historical heritage and the complex reality—political, economic, linguistic—that in itself constitutes Morocco in the late twentieth century.

Elizabeth Warnock Fernea. Introduction to
Leila Abouzeid. *Year of the Elephant: A
Moroccan Woman's Journey toward
Independence, and Other Stories.* Austin:
University of Texas Center for Middle
Eastern Studies, 1989, pp. xii–xiii, xvii, xxi,
xxv–xxvi

This book presents to English readers a translation of *'Am al-fil,* together with eight short stories by Leila Abouzeid. In an informative and useful introduction, Elizabeth Fernea terms it "the first novel by a Moroccan woman written in Arabic to be translated into English," although elsewhere in the introduction she also terms it a novella. While we need not dwell too long on the appropriate term to apply to this work . . . this particular piece of fiction does raise other questions regarding the assessment of literary value.

Like many other works of modern Arabic fiction, this work appeared for the first time (in 1983) as episodes in a newspaper, *Al-Mithaq,* published in Rabat. It was produced in book form . . . in Morocco in 1984; it immediately sold out and was reprinted. A further edition was published in Beirut . . . in 1987. The contents of the story may perhaps provide a clue as to the source of this instant popularity: a female narrator gives the reader her perspective on the events in the final phase of Morocco's struggle for independence. . . . The process of linking this work of fiction to the events of recent history is further underlined by the comments of the author in the preface: "The main events and characters throughout the whole collection are real. . . . I have not created these stories. I have simply told them as they are."

The narrative endeavors to link together two areas of tension. On the one hand, are the activities of the men and women involved in the independence movement: the smuggling of freedom fighters and weapons to different locations within the country; burning the shops of those who cooperate with the French; and, in the case of the narrator in particular, visiting her arrested husband in prison. All this culminates in the magical moment when independence is declared and the sultan returns. . . . On the other hand are the narrator's references to the tensions within her own family, before and after marriage, that have resulted in her being divorced by her husband. This requires that she leave the house, "along with her papers and whatever the law provides," to quote the bland official phrase that reflects the callous treatment accorded those women who share her fate. Her husband, the freedom fighter whose struggles and accompanying dangers she has shared and whom she has visited in prison, has become a senior figure in the postindependence regime. This new status has brought with it a palatial new home, servants, and—for her husband—a secretary with whom he has formed a liaison. Even Faqih, the colleague of her husband whom she has smuggled out of danger by sharing a bus ride with him disguised in women's clothing, acknowledges that her husband "no longer respects anyone."

This brief analysis of the events of the narrative makes it clear, I believe, that the subject matter gives the work an immediate appeal, not least because the first person narrator has provocative things to say about the role of women in society in general and her attitudes towards her own family in particular. . . .

The eight stories included in this collection are brief vignettes of the "slice of life" variety. They are concerned with settings (although, apart from place names, there seems nothing intrinsically "Moroccan" about them) and incidents. In other words, they seem to be in the form of tales that are short rather than examples of that structurally complex and linguistically taut genre of "short story," of which Arab authors have in recent decades provided so many wonderful examples. The stories of this collection are described in the introduction as being "experimental" (p. xi), but, to this reader at least, they merely join a host of other examples of this type, most of which belong to a period in the modern development of the genre that is long since over.

Roger Allen. *International Journal of Middle Eastern Studies.* 23, 1991, pp. 678–79

The publication of the translation of Leila Abouzeid's 1983 novel *Year of the Elephant* is a happy event for many: for Anglophones interested in contemporary Moroccan literature; for world-literature critics bemoaning the unavailability of women's texts from the South; for the feminist and peace-studies scholars looking for literary elaborations of women's experiences in situations of conflict. Elizabeth Fernea's full introduction places the work into its historical and political context so that issues of biculturalism and Morocco's special relationship with outsiders in the past are brought to bear on the text itself. Fernea also highlights the sensitive issue of feminism in a society that does not allow for its manifestation in a way that Westerners can recognize.

The title *Year of the Elephant* succinctly conveys the message of the novel: just as the seemingly insignificant flocks of birds were able to vanquish the prophet Muhammad's enemies on their elephants, so the unexceptional populace in Morocco was able to bring defeat to the mighty French. Carefully distancing herself from her narrator, a sixty-year-old illiterate urbanized woman, Abouzeid traces through the life of a woman whom circumstances threw into military activism during the Moroccan resistance of the early 1950s. The reader shares the excitement of participation, the danger of hiding guns, and the satisfaction of smuggling fugitives, but also the disappointment at the betrayal of the revolution, as those who thought "left" quickly accommodate to living "right."

The novel is not a blatantly feminist text. The narrator's divorce which kicks off the story is not the centerpiece. This is not another version of Fanon's version of the Algerian Revolution, in which the women fought and sacrificed and were rewarded with a neotraditional system. On behalf of the resistance Zahra risks all that she has gained, loses it all through divorce, but then realizes that her experience has given her the strength to survive. Her survival as a cleaning woman in the French Cultural Center may not represent an ideal, yet more than the room of her own in her native town, to which she returns briefly in despair, it provides an outlet and a means for achieving autonomy.

Abouzeid situates Zahra's struggle within a long line of Muslim women's activism that has gone unnoticed in the greater annals of history. She depicts a woman who is not so simple that she does not notice how her husband, the erstwhile activist, has sold out to the extent of needing everything *à la mode française,* including a new-model wife. She accuses him of being worse than the colonizers. Abouzeid portrays a society in which the oppressed do have recourse—sometimes to one another, sometimes to religion. Hers is a world that is not closed but which offers a modicum of opportunity for those who trust enough to find it.

At a time when there is growing interest in the intersections between gender and war, *Year of the Elephant* provides an unself-conscious enterprise of self-affirmation.

Miriam Cooke. *World Literature Today.*
65, 1991, p. 173

ACKER, KATHY (UNITED STATES) 1948–

In her very interesting *The Adult Life of Toulouse Lautrec by Henri Toulouse Lautrec,* Acker focuses with particular intensity upon the larger socio-political structures which affect the subject, ranging from capitalism in general to the art world as culture business, and touching with particular intensity the problematic nexus of desire, love, and woman almost as a microcosm of the trace effects of "the system" upon "the individual." Acker's "Henri" lives in the emotional desert which the patriarchal myth of selfhood prescribes for a woman who attempts to avoid her role in its ritual.

From one perspective the novel is a reflexive anthology of discursive genres including a M. Poirot mystery, art history, fables, adolescent exempla, porn, the movies, Hollywood tabloid, economics, and crime biography, to name the extended examples. Much of the fun as well as the effect of the novel is the interplay among these genres and the full range of assumptions which they introduce into the narrative. The focal "I" modulates with these genres indexing textual sources for consciousness: to represent a subject, it would seem, is to track the cultural elements of which it is composed. Hence the narrative takes quite seriously the social construction of identity by transforming its characters' time, place, gender, and circumstances. The protagonist, Henri Toulouse Lautrec, is female (as her narrator says in another novel, "I always get my sexual genders confused"), Van Gogh's daughter transforms into the nine-year-old Janis Joplin, Scott the architect is sometimes known as James Dean the movie star (having an affair with Janis), and the novel ends with the life of Johnny Rocco (who subsumes the novel's males, as the victimized "dame" does the females). The "he" and "she" of these shifting narrative situations thus represent the imaginary of two genders emerging from the various popular genres included in the novel.

From another perspective, the novel studies closely how capitalism, in reifying all manner of social forms from popular culture to subjectivity itself and all manner of institutions from crime to politics to the art world, distills within gender its special blend of violence, exploitation, and disruption of forces peripheral to its own productive ends. These two perspectives, I think, allow us to see the complexity of the vision Acker offers us of the American present, a vision in which neither a simply semiotic nor a purely ideological model of the contemporary subject suffices.

Robert Siegle. *Literature and Psychology.*
33:3–4, 1987, pp. 46–47

It is important to emphasize the intellectual contexts of the work of Kathy Acker because her work does not feel quite "literary," despite her frequent adaptations (appropriations, plagiarisms and cannibalisms) of literary works from Shakespeare to Beckett. Although her works are writerly, Acker eschews the rhetoric of ambiguity so valued among literary critics, particularly since the advent of modernism. Her surfaces are almost antiliterary, despite their allusiveness, deliberately assaultive and overt. She hopes to make the abstract material, physical. In "Empire of the Senseless, she pleads, "It seemed to me that the body, the material, must matter. My body must matter to me." She makes explicit her treatment of the body as a desiring and desirable "text": "If my body mattered to me, and what else was any text: I could not choose to be celibate." Her works offer many justifications of this position. Through the words of her female Don Quixote, for instance, Acker proffers one explanation of her emphasis on the body: "All the accepted forms of education in this country, rather than teaching the child to know who she is or to know, dictate to the child who she is. Thus obfuscate any act of knowledge. Since these educators train the mind rather than the body, we can start with the physical body, the place of shitting, eating, etc., to break through our opinions or false education."

The language of the body in Western culture is taboo, therefore not as thoroughly constructed by the cultural powers as the mind.

Thus, the body, particularly the female body, becomes the site of revolution. In this regard, Acker, perhaps more directly than many other women writers, creates the feminine texts hypothesized by Hélène Cixous in essays such as "Castration or Decapitation?" Feminine writing, according to Cixous, should be rooted in the woman's experience of her body, her sexuality. . . .

In *The Newly Born Woman,* Catherine Clément argues that "every society has an imaginary zone for what it excludes," a zone located on the "fault lines" of the culture. She and Cixous, her collaborator on the book, propose that "women bizarrely embody [that] group of anomalies showing the cracks in the culture" through which the silenced of culture exerts its pressure, makes itself known—the cracks through which the repressed returns. In Acker's political translation and transformation of this idea, the repressed is embodied by figures and concretized as acts outside the social code—outlaws, outcasts, taboos—that threaten it. In unlikely partnership with Emily Dickinson, she says madness is divinest sense: "No to anything but madness." She sees the culture in the same position as the dying animal whose leg is caught in a trap: in order to escape, it must chew through its leg. Similarly, for a chance to transform contemporary culture from the deadly trap it is, Acker cautions you must "eat your mind," which has been so completely constructed by the phallus, so thoroughly written by society's metalanguages, that there is no room, in her terms, to truly name oneself. Acker's narratives, in their subversive appropriations of master texts, their aggressive assertions of criminal perspectives, their relentless interrogations of art, culture, government, and sexual relations, are designed to be jaws steadily devouring—often to readers' horror and certainly to their discomfort (which is part of the strategy)—the mindset, if not the mind, of Western culture.

Ellen G. Friedman. *Review of Contemporary Fiction.* 9, 1989, pp. 39, 47–48

Acker's habit of disclaiming authorship by attributing authorship to her titular subject has the effect of placing the entire work in quotation marks, creating an invincibly ironic "as if" which crucially skews the reader's attempt to interpret, logically or emotionally, the extreme states of mind represented in the book. The "author" of the novel is a part of the title, a part of the "made up"; where then is the "real" Acker in this fiction? Is the entire narrative to be read as parody? The covers of any book are, in a sense, quotation marks, delineating the boundaries between what someone—traditionally, the author—"said" and a larger context, a world, in which that statement is made and has meaning. But mimetic fiction encourages us to experience the book as both a world in itself and a pure representation of "the" world, rather than a controvertible statement about an idiosyncratic experience. Acker's authorial impersonations emphasize the derivativeness of all texts, their me-diated, unreliable and quite probably falsified status, and remind us that only a fool expects to encounter some author, some great soul, some "reality" in a work of fiction.

Acker's technique of quotation and cross-quotation equally forbids us to identify with her fictional characters. What are we to make of a female narra-tor named Henri Toulouse Lautrec who recounts the life of her brother Vin-cent Van Gogh while searching through Paris with Hercule Poirot for clues to the murder of Melvyn Freilicher, a real person documentably alive in the "real" world of documentation? What of the whore Giannina's erotic reminiscences of the American poet Ron Silliman? This undifferentiated use of figures from history, literature and contemporary literary circles merges all realms of language in which meanings reside, and thus destroys meanings by destroying the contexts which focus them. Brought into forced conjunc-tion, these irreconcilable contexts split open and spill their constituent parts into a formless intertext.

Despite the seemingly illimitable license of Acker's pornographic imagi-nation, one senses always a "holding back" in her habit of quotation and plagiarism, an unwillingness to own—in the sense of admission as well as of possession—her work.

Naomi Jacobs. *Review of Contemporary Fiction.* 9, 1989, p. 51

A fairly recent and paradigmatic literary anecdote might be: Kathy writes a quote for my novel *Haunted Houses*. I receive a phone call from a copy editor or fact checker at Simon & Schuster (my imprint's "parent") who says, adamantly, "Kathy Acker is not the author of *Don Quixote*." I respond, with assurance, "Yes she is and so is Cervantes." There's a long pause. The woman asks, "Well, what else has she written?" *"Great Expectations,"* I say.

Lynne Tillman. Review of Contemporary
Fiction. 9, 1989, p. 70

Unfortunately, much of the critical response to Acker's work has not gotten very far beyond these first comments of my more conservative students. As Acker commented to me, most accounts "have left some or many concerns out, usually the political, and most fetishize the sexual." She knows that the culture works on its members most subtly and most profoundly by colonizing the libidinal aesthetics, turning desire into the most productive means of channeling, normalization, and, even if by pure distraction, social control. Much of her work does confront directly the sexual material of the culture in order to carry out her most basic project. "[T]he center of my writing, if there is a center, is a search for value, or lack of value," she wrote me, and the play between "search" and "lack," between "center" and the iffiness of the very idea of a structure with center, is precisely what is finally at stake in Acker's fiction. Trying to understand a pathological culture and to locate some potential for freeing the body from the hold of that culture means confronting sexuality but also all the concerns that mainstream American writing typically prefers to omit. . . .

Pure writing, the direct connection, the interaffiliation between the sexual and the political, and the desire to "see society in a different way"—these utopian impulses play constantly alongside the most devastating narrative critique of Western culture to appear in American literature. The resulting mix of the sacred and the profane, the utopian and the despairing, carries us far beyond the titters and thrills of the first-time reader to a profoundly moving, detailed, and instructive analytical critique of the cultural processes precisely at the point from which they are experienced by the Other of the culture—children, women, the poor, the trapped. Acker's work moves steadily toward an imaginative demolition of the oppressive dimension of our cultural machinery. . . .

Acker's work taken as a whole carries its central importance not only because she was among the first downtown writers and remains the most extreme one, but also because of what her work achieves. It is a postmodern narrative *Being and Time* with a streetwise poststructural footing. Her phenomenology is that of bodily experience rather than Germanic speculation; her *Alltäglichkeit* is not Heidegger's anesthesia but a predatory death cult; her dasein is confused by complexly interlocking forces of history, economics, politics, media, and gender, rather than by the business of life distracting her from her true Being; and her focus is less on Being-toward-death than on a Being-for-life. But however different her assumptions, she is as serious as Heidegger in understanding the worldness of the world, dispersing the active force of traditional thought, exploring "care as the being of *dasein*," and recognizing Understanding as the fullness of ways in which we live rather than as some kind of knowledge either apart from the world or compartmentalized within some particular discipline. Acker matches wits with the most brilliant of contemporary theorists and leads us through a career whose stages reprise the intellectual revolution that the last two decades have wrought in our thinking about Being and history.

After some survival time during the radical politics of the sixties, Acker produced a trilogy of novels pushing the limits of appropriation to document the plagiarized Being to which we are consigned. To look in detail at these novels is to identify the starting assumptions from which this entire revolution in narrative takes off. Indeed, the first of these, along with Constance De-Jong's *Modern Love,* struck with tremendous impact a generation that had not yet begun to find its own narrative voice. Her books take, as she puts it in talking with Vitale, "the society as a series of texts. . . .

And using new additions, new renderings in the texts to attack the society. First of all to find out how it works and then attack it." Hence we must look closely at *The Childlike Life of the Black Tarantula by the Black Tarantula* [completed 1973], the first volume of the trilogy, and at the also important *The Adult Life of Toulouse Lautrec by Henri Toulouse Lautrec* [1975]. The middle volume is *I Dream I Was a Nymphomaniac Imagining* [1974]. In *Kathy Goes to Haiti* [1978] and *Blood and Guts in High School* [completed in 1978], Acker turns the language of the body against hegemonic forms and institutions of every description. Building upon the earlier works' appropriation tactics, these two books offer a bruised and bruising portrait of coming of age. In the early eighties a pair of works, *Great Expectations* [1982] and *My Death, My Life* [1983], both now also published by Grove Press, rethinks the problem of language as it affects Acker's enterprise to work beyond the theoretical impasse of the radical writer working within the culture's sign systems. Finally, in *Don Quixote* [1986] and *Empire of the Senseless* [1988], Acker carries us to a profound vision of the contradictory nomadic life she prescribes for those who desire more than "the grey of yuppy life." At midlife, in other words, Acker has already achieved a career of major proportions, both in its ambitions and accomplishments. . . .

Robert Siegle. *Suburban Ambush:
Downtown Writing and the Fiction of
Insurgency* (Baltimore: Johns Hopkins
University Press, 1989), pp. 47–50

Sad but not funny, and only as deep as the nearest gutter, is Kathy Acker's encounter with Lust. Acker, the biggest "name" among the contributors to [Alison Fell's collection] *The Seven Deadly Sins,* takes this only sin traditionally personified as female and turns the virgin/whore dichotomy on its ear in a self-consciously bizarre and ugly story. Lust is a male prostitute who spends half the story wandering the streets of Berlin, picking up "sadistic and masochistic drifters," until finally he strangles a sailor named Joachim. Inexplicably, the story then moves to St. Mark's Church in the Bowery, where a poetry reading is in progress. The audience consists of "ugly old men" poets, students and bums. "The students weren't yuppies, but revolutionary radicals and nonrevolutionary radicals who aspired to the radicalness of bums. . . . No one gave a damn about the reading."

What Kathy Acker does so well in novels such as *Sex and Death in High School,* where she creates a pornographic novel told from the point of view of the exploited woman; in *Don Quixote,* where DQ is not only an American but a woman as well; and in *Great Expectations,* where the narrator changes both identity and gender, doesn't work here. The pornography ceases to be anarchic commentary, fervid reaction; rather, it becomes simply what it appears to be.

Carolyn Cooke. The Nation.
January 22, 1990, p. 100

In Alison Fell's *Seven Cardinal Virtues* seven feminist writers, Kathy Acker the best known among them, offer satirical takes on the seven virtues: charity, chastity, generosity, fortitude, humility, justice and patience. Acker's biting drama, "Dead Doll," deconstructs humility, and while it is the best of the lot, the others do not lag far behind for emotional impact. "Dead Doll" reveals the propriety and pettiness that dominate over the written word in book publishing, forcing authors into a deferential age.

Penny Kaganoff. Publishers Weekly.
September 14, 1990, p. 120

According to [Robert] Siegle, "'pornography' is Acker's device for desublimating the content of all the media transformations of her pornographic kernel.". . . Like Airplane, women are torn between a desire for power, to be "hard," and a desire to make others "like them" at the same time. Acker quite literally exposes the pornography of the patriarchal script; however, in doing so, she is not according to Siegle "really" writing "pornography"—it just looks that way to the unreflective reader. Acker simulates pornography to expose the simulation. This move is in keeping with Baudrillard, who argues, for instance, that the "scandal" of Watergate was "constructed" precisely in order to cover the fact that politics itself is scandalous. . . . Acker, parodying pornography, intends to prevent the patriarchy from establishing pornography as something other from itself. . . . Yet despite her radical assertions, Siegle's conclusions about Acker are essentially conservative, speaking literarily. In direct contradiction to Baudrillard, Siegle sees the culture's best writers as those able to distinguish between simulation and reality; what is read is what is tactile, what is painful, what reminds us of the body—the inscribed upon rather than inscription.

Colleen Kennedy. *American Literary*
History. 4, 1992, pp. 181–82

ADCOCK, FLEUR (NEW ZEALAND) 1934–

Lately, we have heard much . . . of Japanese haiku as a mode and a model. However remote or conscious the influence, I do not think we can fail to be aware of it in Fleur Adcock's "Lines Written by a Seashore":

> We threw stones into the harbor
> Yours went far, but mine fell close to the shore.
> A mist rose over the sea,
> And at our feet the grass rustled.
> You looked across at the silent hill;
> I gazed down at the water.
> Now I stand again on the stony bank.
> The evenings are becoming shorter:
> Soon it will be too dark to see the hill.

This is not one of the strongest or most typical of the poems in Miss Adcock's first collected volume *(The Eye of the Hurricane),* but it does indicate her remarkable ability to isolate the occasional incident, drop her poetic pebble, and let the ripples enlarge.

Behind the lyric—that personal cry of wonder, joy or pain—must often lie the tiny irritant, the small incident of common life that has some exquisite or intolerable private bearing. Men, who have monopolized most of our Western lyrical poetry, are seldom content with the bare incident: by nature or training they are prone to exaggerate its importance, to wrap it around with tragic or noble thoughts. Women (it is their recompense for having escaped over-education) are more responsive, more honest about their own emotions, and a good deal less moral. So while the number of women poets may be relatively small, I think it is true that they generally render their own experience more faithfully, with a more convincing actuality—compare, for example, William and Dorothy Wordsworth. Women poets *can,* of course, strike attitudes, play the pythoness or the philosopher; but then they are seldom at their best. It is the domestic side of Emily Dickinson, not the cosmic, that is immortal.

Fleur Adcock, who has intelligence and a nice taste in classical irony as well as sensibility, is sometimes drawn towards the gnomic: there are touches of the pythoness, more minatory than consoling, in "Advice," "Always," "A Thought for the Sphinx," and the last section of "Flight, with Mountains." These rare gestures, however, are always controlled, and admirably managed. The verse is flexible or firm at need, as in this formulation of the renewal of post-coital hostility:

> And the salt and indrawn savor
> Is not of sweat but of such choking
> Tears as darkly teased Jocasta
> Who, cast down beside her lover,
> Turned from riddles not worth asking,
> Knowing more than the mere answers,
>
> And hid her cold breasts from that stranger.

In these poems I have named, and more strikingly in the "Note on Propertius I. 5" (here marred by a misprint), one is gratefully aware of a talent for synthesis rarely met with in modern verse. There are other pieces, more lightly textured, in which nursery rhyme or fairy tale provide a starting point for wry observation; there is a timeless witch (with male clients), and one hate-poem—"Instructions to Vampires"—which really frightened me.

Yet the most striking feature of this collection is the number of poems written directly out of moments of physical or emotional intimacy, with the kind of self-revealing candor that I associate with an Oriental rather than a Western tradition. The incidents they record are not falsified; they are neither blown up to screen size, nor deliberately dehydrated in the prevailing English manner, but transcribed with an immediacy of feeling that is sometimes entirely convincing. Fleur Adcock is a "we-poet" rather than an "I-poet"; she prefers dialogue to soliloquy, and it is in the interdependence of the closest human relationships—wife to husband, woman to lover, mother to child—that her sensibility finds its truest expression. This is tricky material, if overdramatization on the one hand, or sentimentality on the other, are to be avoided. It helps, of course, if the writer has a natural command of pure diction, and a sense of form and cadence that can clarify and compress into the short lyric the strange stuff with which the heart is burdened, in these moments of penetration or agonizing reappraisal.

Of the poems in this kind, the more ambitious—like the title poem, "Knife-Play," and "Night-Piece" (the account of a love affair from the woman's viewpoint, distanced by a biological dream and then sharply returned to actuality)—seem to me vivid and interesting, but less effective poetically than shorter pieces—"Incident," "Wife to Husband," "Cold Moon Shining"—in which a greater concentration on the mood and the moment is achieved. Most completely successful of all, perhaps, are the conversation poems with children. At the risk of suggesting the *The Eye of the Hurricane* is a much nicer book than it is, I must quote one of these in full. "For a Five-

year-old" originally appeared in *Landfall* this year; it was a pleasure to meet
it again more recently in the English *Listener.*

> A snail is climbing up the window-sill
> Into your room, after a night of rain.
> You call me in to see, and I explain
> That it would be unkind to leave it there:
> It might crawl to the floor; we must take care
> That no one squashes it. You understand,
> And carry it outside, with careful hand,
> To eat a daffodil.
>
> I see, then, that a kind of faith prevails:
> Your gentleness is molded still by words
> From me, who have trapped mice and shot wild birds,
> From me, who drowned your kittens, who betrayed
> Your closest relatives, and who purveyed
> The harshest kind of truth to many another.
> But that is how things are: I am your mother,
> And we are kind to snails.

There is only one word here that is even faintly self-conscious and stiff: for
the rest, the delicate balance is faultlessly maintained.

For the range of human feelings Miss Adcock explores so candidly, and
for the deftness of her treatment of it in verse, we can only be grateful. This
is a modest but courageous first book: without fuss or feminism, it reclaims
in poetry some territory which has hitherto largely remained in the male
prerogative. It establishes its author as an accomplished writer in a number
of lyrical modes, and—apart from the Audenesque invocation, an honorable
failure—it seems to me that Fleur Adcock has a clearly recognizable voice
and music of her own.

James Bertram. *Landfall.* 18:4,
December, 1964, pp. 369–72

There are three other poems which don't fall into any distinct category but
which deserve special mention. "Country Station" is a beautifully successful
poem which will speak best for itself:

> First she made a little garden
> of sorrel stalks wedged among
> some yellowy-brown moss-cushions
>
> and fenced it with ice-lolly sticks
> (there were just enough); then she
> set out biscuit crumbs on a brick

for the ants; now she sits on a
deserted luggage-trolley
to watch them come out for dinner.

It's nice here—cloudy but quite warm.
Five trains have swooshed through, and one
stopped, but at the other platform.

Later, when no one is looking
she may climb on the roof of that
low shed. Her mother is making

another telephone-call (she
isn't crying any more.)
Perhaps they will stay here all day.

"Against Coupling" is the comic counter-statement to the love poems—
wry, frank, witty, not in the least cynical. "A Surprise in the Peninsula" is a
fantasy or dream poem (or perhaps it merely seems so). I had the peninsula
firmly in mind as Coromandel until I noticed the "bitter local coffee," which
might suggest Greece, or nowhere. The protagonist arrives home and finds
the skin of a dog nailed to her wall, a coarse map of the "peninsula" singed
in the fur, "the town" marked by a bullet hole that goes right through the
wall. Literalness and understatement (as in so much of the book) are the
qualities of the style:

It seemed freshly killed—
There was blood at the edges. Not
my dog: I have never owned one,
I rather dislike them. (Perhaps
whoever did it knew that.) It

was a light brown dog, with smooth hair;
no head, but the tail still remained.

A balance is maintained on a fine line between terror and the absurd: hysteria
is just out of the picture, giving it its sharpness and point.

With such a transparent style, a good deal of any poem's interest will
depend on its subject matter, or on (to return to my opening) the personality
of the poet. If there is anything lacking in this collection it is certainly not
accomplishment. It is true that poets whose intelligence and sense of decorum are as highly developed as Miss Adcock's sometimes suffer at their own
hands. Careful selection can look like meanness, and control like lack of

feeling. But to complain of it would be to do the injustice of asking Miss Adcock to be another poet than the one she is.

C. K. Stead. *Landfall.*
December, 1971, pp. 234–37

A satisfying feature of the last decade has been a rise in the number of women writing good verse. . . . Fleur Adcock has been publishing over a much longer period, and she like more recent women poets records incidents involving mother and child, woman and husband, lover, friend. Her verse, supple and assured, has continued to delight since she first staked her claim to our attention with that urbane testimony to a classical education, "Note on Properitius I.3." In 1965 she said: "I tend to admire poetry which can wear a formal dress lightly and naturally." In an apt verse tribute to her second volume, *Tigers* (1967), Charles Brasch wrote (in "Saying a World") of the "grace and crispness" of her "detached, distinct" voice, in "saying-songs that talk/People, animals," poems "Disclosing a tiger-cool/Simulacre of mind and being." Her manner is always equable and decorous, but may be astringent, and many poems are tense with intuited menace, their composure holding nightmare at bay. In her latest collections her "saying-songs" fall mainly into syllabics or freer forms. A poem such as the beautiful "Kilpeck," so exact in its delineation of complex feeling through a faultless selection of external details, she considered in 1977 "typical of the way I now work." Yet in the last section of "The Soho Hospital for Women" she reverts to a most effective use of rhyme.

Macdonald P. Jackson. Macdonald P.
Jackson and Vincent O'Sullivan, eds. *The
Oxford Book of New Zealand Writing since
1945* (Auckland: Oxford University Press,
1983), p.xxx

ADNAN, ETEL (LEBANON–UNITED STATES) 1925–

The works of Etel Adnan . . . reveal a deep involvement with the fate of her country and of the Palestinians, and she is able unerringly to put her finger on the mechanisms of repression which are employed against women, the poor and other weak members of society. The apocalyptic tone of her political poems is in strong contrast to the gentleness with which she sings of love.

Hilary Kirkpatrick. In Mineke Schipper, ed.
*Unheard Words: Women and Literature in
Africa, the Arab World, Asia, the
Caribbean, and Latin America* (London:
Allison and Busby, 1985), p. 79

Etel Adnan. . . was the only child of a Greek mother from Smyrna and a Syrian father who was old enough to have fought as an officer in the Battle of the Dardanelles. She went to the USA in the 1950s to complete her study of philosophy, begun at the Sorbonne, at the University of California at Berkeley and at Harvard University. She writes only in English and French, since as a child in Lebanon she had been punished whenever she spoke Arabic. This linguistic constraint bred a frustration that she tried to ease by writing "with the intention of being translated into Arabic.". . .

Today she retains a lively interest in Arabic, but has come to terms with the fact that when in France she writes in French, when in America in English. However, painting offers an unsullied expression of her origins and continued loyalty. What she said during the Algerian War of Independence remains true today: "I painted in Arabic. I signed my name in Arabic, because I couldn't stand to use the colonizers' language."

Although painting was important, it was writing that integrated her into a society in which she had previously felt herself to be a stranger. Writing defined her "first total identity." In 1947, she wrote her first poem, "Book of the Sea," and in 1970 she wrote "Beirut-Hell Express," a long poem that anticipated the civil war. This poem first appeared in the cultural pages of *L'Orient-Le Jour* in 1971. She also intuited the war in *L'Apocalypse Arabe,* a collection of French poems that she began in February 1975 and completed in August 1976, after the fall of the Palestinian camp of Tall Zaatar. Her next work was a French novel, *Sitt Marie Rose* (1978). It was based on the true story of a Syro-Lebanese woman. Marie Rose Boulos was a Lebanese citizen married to a Lebanese. She taught in a school for mentally retarded children, but was murdered in 1977 as a Lebanese citizen for her support of the Palestinian cause. Adnan also wrote the texts for two documentaries on the war, and illustrated the sleeve of a recording of Nadia Tueni's last anthology, *Archives Sentimentales d'une Guerre au Liban* (1982).

Etel Adnan did not give up hope or faith in Lebanon until two years after the Israeli invasion. As the anarchy persisted, and international manipulations became increasingly evident, she at last decided that after thirty years out of Lebanon she would take up American citizenship. . . .

Women could dream, could create new realities, but not outside their heads. Those who chose to stand alone and to demand their rights had a tough battle against entrenched attitudes. Etel Adnan's novel *Sitt Marie Rose* demonstrates the difficulty of a woman's rebellion. The four Christian murderers could not stand the ignominy of one of their women going over to the enemy. She had to pay for her foolishness and, at the same time, serve as an example to others who might be tempted to such rashness. Sitt Marie Rose's loyalties and disloyalties did not really concern them, for after all she was only a woman, her treachery was due to her weak womanly nature. Only men are properly prepared for life's challenges. When entering a desert, one of the murderers told her:

> You have to strike out on your own, find your own trail with nothing but a map and compass to really see it. You, you'll never be able to do that."

This was the men's attitude, but it was also the women's. Sitt Marie had not thought that her sympathies and loves could be matter for political concern. She had not known that the war had made her actions politically visible. War, the great leveller, had focused attention on a woman, and beyond her on other women. Their actions mattered:

> She [Sitt Marie] was also subject to another great delusion, believing that women were protected from repression, and that leaders considered political fights to be strictly between males.

War had politicized gender and men were taking note:

> Yes. It's taken nearly a year of civil war, hundreds of dead every day in Beirut, and an upsetting of the old alliance between heaven and earth for me to conceive of a woman as a worthy partner, ally or enemy. But I am one of the few that would admit it.

Yes, the war was creating a different kind of woman, one who defiantly challenged the system. But Sitt Marie acknowledged that "a woman who stands up to them and looks them in the eye is a tree to be cut down, and they cut it down." The defiant woman alone could not survive.

Miriam Cooke. *War's Other Voices: Women Writers on the Lebanese Civil War* (Cambridge: Cambridge University Press, 1988), pp. 9–10, 141

Sitt Marie Rose by the Lebanese poet Etel Adnan is an ethnographic novel that is outstandingly subjective. Reviewed as a feminist novel, winner of the France-Pays Arabes award, *Sitt Marie Rose* was first published in 1978 in French (the second language of Lebanon) by Des Femmes, Paris. The Post-Apollo Press, Sausalito, California, produced the English translation by Georgina Kleege in 1982, and the novel has appeared also in Arabic, Dutch, and Italian.

The work certainly deserves the term feminist novel, for it is about a woman who becomes a sacrificial victim when she breaks the rules of the Mediterranean code of honor. But it is also an anti-war novel, an antireligious novel, and, above all, it is an ethnographic novel, conveying information about the persistent, troubling conflict in Lebanon while giving us a sense of what that conflict feels, smells, and looks like to the people of Lebanese society. Through Etel Adnan's artistry, form and substance, content and style are joined, thus achieving the goal of all imaginative literature, as well as the recently stated goal of the new, experimental ethnographies (Marcus and Cushman 1982).

The dust jacket of the novel states that *Sitt Marie Rose* is "the story of a woman abducted by militia during the Civil War in Lebanon and executed."

Marie-Rose is in her early thirties, divorced, Christian, and the mother of three children. She has been living for seven years with a young Palestinian doctor, who is high in the councils of the PLO, and this has brought a good deal of criticism upon her from the rich, upperclass Christian community of which she is a part. She has been involved in community and charitable causes, we are told, and teaches in a school for deaf-mutes. One morning on her way to work, she is abducted at a checkpoint while crossing from the Muslim zone into the Christian zone of the divided city. Her capture arouses indignation and concern since she is known in both zones for her nonsectarian humanitarian service.

> The news of her capture had the impact of a submarine missile in the camps. . . . Even in families accustomed to tragic news that was repeated with the monotony of weather reports, there rose a kind of death-rattle.

Intercession with her captors is unsuccessful. She is interrogated, tortured, and finally killed.

The facts of this tale, not unusual in what is left of Lebanon today, unfold in a most unusual manner. The heritage of Scheherazade, the Arab storyteller par excellence, retreats into the dim past as Etel Adnan tells her story, not in traditional linear, narrative form, nor even in the *lozenge* form ascribed by folklorists to the tales of the East, but in a charged composite of many different forms of discourse: conversation, news bulletins, participant observations, monologues, life histories, interviews, and commentary. Within this multilayered text are found character, action, plot, fantasy, and prophecy, those aspects of the novel so gracefully delineated by E. M. Forster in 1927, but in combinations that Forster might not have recognized as novelistic. Etel Adnan utilizes techniques of ethnographic description as well as artistic forms from the oral and written literary tradition, and also draws upon narrative conventions from journalism and film. The influence of the distinguished Arabic poetic tradition, of which she herself is a part, is also evident. . . .

If the novel were analyzed as an experimental ethnography, one might suggest that the author uses the short pieces, the voices, in the same way that an ethnographer uses quotations from interviews and field notes to give the reader not only the sequence of events in the society, but also the reactions of individual informants to those events. Stylistically, the quick shifts back and forth between voices, and the short, choppy paragraphs like jump cuts in film serve to reinforce the sense of terror, urgency, and horror associated with the war; they help convey the human emotions of the moment, the immediacy of different individual experiences, and the texture of the time, place, and events.

Another quality of experimental ethnographies found here is the placing of the ethnographer's or the informant's personal thoughts about the text within the text, the statement of self-conscious awareness that the ethnographer or the informant is part of the text. Fouad says:

> I didn't position artillery on the hills of the city to get myself mixed up in some story about a woman. I did it to blow up things. . . . They said to me, You Fouad, you're an anarchist.

If one turns the analysis around, however, one can see a major element than traditional social science would criticize, but that is allowable in imaginative literature: the expression of value judgments, based on subjective opinions. . . .

In the final analysis, *Sitt Marie Rose* is less important as a feminist novel that as a document of social history, an ethnographic novel that chronicles not only feminist concerns, but also the end of a class—the urban Maronite Lebanese Christians, who were placed in power fifty years ago by colonial France. *Sitt Marie Rose* was a best seller in Paris as well as in Beirut. The author, Etel Adnan, teaches her audience both East and West through her highly charged combination of many forms of discourse. . . . Given the challenges of a new Arab world, she has responded with a literary *bricolage,* a new kind of novel, that is ethnographic in terms of our response as much as because of the way it is written.

Sitt Marie-Rose, the focus of the novel, was a real person. The novel's extraordinary intensity is a result of the poet-author's careful observation, faithful detailing of everyday life, and a genuine concern for human beings— the characteristics of good ethnography and a basis for good imaginative literature.

Elizabeth Fernea. In Philip A. Dennis and
Wendell Aycock, eds. *Literature and
Anthropology* (Lubbock, Texas: Texas Tech
University Press), 1989, pp. 154, 156, 160,
162–63

[Adnan] now writes in English, after having composed in French for many years (she also divides her time between California and Paris). At the same time, she is unquestionably an Arab writer. How, then, can one come to an easy definition of Adnan? Is she a Lebanese writer, a French writer, an American writer, a woman writer?

Her example also throws into relief the narrowly defined and often exoticized category of Arab women's writing, a body of literature that American readers are only beginning to familiarize themselves with. . . .

As well as being a novelist, essayist and poet, Adnan is also a painter, a fact that constantly informs her work, particularly her two latest books, *Paris, When It's Naked* and *Of Cities & Women (Letters to Fawwaz).* Of the connections between language, image and origins, Adnan has written that she can only express herself in Arabic through painting. Despite the multiplicity of her cultures and endeavors, these books provide an excellent introduction to her unique blend of acute observation, emotional integrity, political clarity and philosophical speculation.

Paris, When It's Naked is the testimony of a lover whose conscience is stricken, whose awareness has been pierced by the fruit of other knowledge and experience. The lover is Adnan herself, the object of her desire is Paris and the forbidden fruits are her past and present allegiances.

Where *Paris, When It's Naked* delves into the accumulated layers of the self, *Of Cities & Women* is more concerned with the nature of race itself, its definition and redefinition, through philosophical speculation, observations on the relations between artists and their ostensible subjects, between women and cities, between women and men. As Adnan writes: "It is no longer a question of clarifying the distinction between the feminine and the masculine, but of redefining the human species."

Adnan goes about thinking through this redefinition in many guises: through an incident in the red-light district of Barcelona; the tale of a "disturbed" single woman on [a] Greek island who had been taken to a mental asylum; the death of a close friend in Beirut; her obsession with "what Cézanne and Picasso can reveal about women, about the way women are looked at." The passages on "these two sacred monsters," in addition to representing some most revelatory writing on the two painters, are also among the most striking sections in the book. . . .

Here. . . as in two other key works, *Sitt Marie-Rose* (1982) and *The Arab Apocalypse* (1989). . . Adnan embodies the role of both visionary and chronicler, seeing what is to come by unveiling accepted ways of receiving and recording the past.

With what . . . Juan Goytisolo, has called the "memoricide" of cultural pluralism taking place in the heart of Europe, as fundamentalist warlords obliterate not only the people but the material, spiritual and cultural inheritance of Bosnia, we would do well to take cognizance of Adnan's insistence on remembering, on her insistence that difference is memory, and this fact sustains the survival of the species. . . .

By never losing sight of the primal and contradictory impulses that motivate human behavior, Adnan serves as an essential guide to a world bent on obliterating even the traces of unsanctioned existences, a world where, as a friend of hers in Beirut says, "Our memories don't have any future."

Ammiel Alcalay. The Nation.
March 7, 1994, pp. 311–13

Sitt Marie Rose's story links the fate of the nation, whose phantasmatic unity is figured as a maternal body, to women's claims to self-determination. The "impossible mutation" represented by Sitt Marie Rose's defection to the enemy breaks the natural bonds of filiation to create new forms of political affiliation and thereby redefines the status of the mother. In response to her refusal to reproduce existing social relations, "le corps social affolé dégage ses anticorps dans un mécanisme aveugle et automatique" [the political body releases its antibodies in a blind automatic process.] As "antibodies," the militiamen attempt to erase Sitt Marie Rose's claims to being the subject of her own desires and to narrating her own body, for example, by choosing to live with a Palestinian doctor. . . .

At the end of the novel, when the "deaf-mute" children respond to the violence of the war and the murder of their teacher, Adnan suggests an alternative to the choice between modernization on Western terms and a return to tradition. The children make an ironic comment on the failure of the Committee of National Dialogue's last-ditch effort to reconcile sectarian disputes in Lebanon before the outbreak of the war. Walid Khalidi describes the committee's meetings as degenerating "into a dialogue of the deaf," who "may not have heard one another but . . . could not have failed to hear the rising din of bursting mortar shells and machine-gun fire outside." The figure of the "deaf-mute" children thematizes the question of what would constitute a national dialogue or a national dialogism. These children provide a reminder of the difficulties involved in the construction of a radically democratic public sphere, one that would not systematically silence whole groups of citizens.

The passages in which the "deaf-mute" children are paradoxically represented as collectively "speaking" also enact the necessity of communication across the boundaries that define cultural identities. . . .

The formally dialogic character of Adnan's novel is violently foreclosed in the social setting that the novel represents. But the possibility of translating textual practices into social ones can be prefigured. At the end of the novel "les sourd-muets se lèvent et, soutenus par les rythmes transmis à leurs corps par la terre martelée à nouveau par les bombes, ils se mettent à danser" [the deaf-mutes rise, and moved by the rhythms of falling bombs their bodies receive from the trembling earth, they begin to dance]. The students are able to experience the violence of the war in their bodies, to survive that violence, and to transform it, in the same way that their "mains . . . reconnaissent la musique" [hands recognize the music] when "posées sur les radios" [pressed against radios]. . . .

Sitt Marie Rose's death literalizes her position outside the militiamen's nationalist narrative of woman's "place" and marks the empty space of political possibilities that cannot be thought within the dialectic of colonialism and nationalism, where it is assumed that the liberation of colonized peoples requires a repetition of the historical trajectory of European national formation. *Sitt Marie Rose* suggests that those new political possibilities are inseparable from the emergence of women's movements capable of asserting sexual difference as a historical problematic within nationalist thought.

Adnan's critique of the desire for an internally homogenous national space is also relevant, however, to the relation of Western readers to postcolonial histories and the relation of male readers to women's histories. If Adnan's novel can be fully understood only within Arab intellectual traditions, it also problematizes any attempt by Western readers to situate themselves outside the story and to reduce it to an object of study. In a similar way, the novel problematizes any attempt by the male characters to reduce the narrative to "some story about a woman" that they simply happened "to get . . . mixed up in." Like the character whose name it bears, the novel refuses its readers the comfort of such "clean and definitive" boundaries.

Thomas Foster. *PMLA*.
110 (1995), pp. 69, 71

AGUIRRE, MIRTA (CUBA) 1912–80

In the most highly rated poems in the only collection of her poetry that she has published so far, *Presencia interior,* immediately transcending some external resemblance to Lorca and Neruda, Mirta Aguirre offers a direct, economical and acute poetic voice. Through her self-absorbed tone, through her independent energy, there appear social concerns that are as intense and profound as her lyrical states of grief or solitude. For this reason, Juan Ramón Jiménez, referring to the "revolutionary" tendency within Cuban poetry in 1936, described Mirta Aguirre as "the one who has bestowed its noblest accent upon it." Another direction pursued in this book is the use of forms suggested by Spanish popular traditions, which were subsequently to enrich poems like *Cantares del mal de amores,* also a good example of her delicate handling of language.

Cintio Vitier. *Cinquenta años de Poesia
Cubana (1902–52),* (Havana: Editorial de
Cinquentario, 1952), p. 280

Mirta Aguirre's "Cancion Antigua" for Che Guevara, which evokes the French *chanson de geste* and that Pierre du Terrail, or Lord Bayard, the paragon of medieval knights, whose legend (*sans peur et sans reproche*) pervades the poem, is not, as its title and formal elegiac treatment might imply, a homogeneous composition that simply compares Che to a hero who has become legendary, however singular his fascination might have been. We should remember that Ignacio Agramonte was also called the ideal of bravery, the "Bayard of Camaguey." The word "Bayard" itself calls up images of gallantry and moral superiority that fit Che perfectly. Yet the question must be asked, "Perfectly? A Che in the trappings of a medieval courtier? Che as Bayard?" The comparison needs only be made for the differences to appear. . . . It is the apparent contradiction between title and contents that suggest a futile task, that of explaining a poem which, like all poems, either explains itself or cannot be explained at all.

Fina García Marruz. *Union* (Havana).
14:2, June, 1975, p. 129

The collection *Ayer de Hoy* has established Mirta Aguirre's poetry as an indispensable moment and voice in the creative process of Cuban literature. Nonetheless, a good deal of the poetry that she wrote remained unpublished until now. Her poems had slept the best of all dreams. . . . The culmination of her poetry was, as we see from this collection, a sacred action very much of a piece with what Mirta meant with regard to her condition as a Sunday poet.

Although I believe that her role as a writer was qualitatively larger, no one can deny the seriousness and the strict dedication shown by her poetic style. Moreover, this natural spontaneity that every image, every line emits, is not only owing to certain gifts that any poetic work requires, but also the joyous exercise of a discourse that has always paid attention to the rules, as well as—very wisely—to free will.

The first book that Mirta Aguirre published, *Presencia interior*, dates from 1938. In it, we perceive an unusual and powerful universe whose form was nurtured in the most exquisite Spanish tradition and, at the same time, with the rhythms of free verse, following models that influenced Latin American poetry from Darío to Neruda. Mirta also learned much from the way that the Spanish poets of the generation of 1927 expressed their gifts (especially Lorca and Alberti), modes of expression appropriate for the exercise of a certain dramatic quality born of specific social and—why not?—political urgency.

The impact that *Presencia interior* had on the national literary scene was more than considerable, it was symptomatic. It was the great Spanish poet Juan Ramón Jiménez who, during a brief stay in Havana, described the relevance of Mirta Aguirre's early poems. The fact of having had Juan Ramón among us was codified in the famous anthology of our poetic work of that time, where the most important elements of the most representative authors of the period were enshrined. There, the author of *Piedra y cielo* had pointed out the "noble accent" that already distinguished Mirta's style. We must agree with Juan Ramón's prescient eye in discerning a literary talent that was already giving out sure signals. The Spaniard's words naturally had their positive and negative aspects. There is, paradoxically, both praise and doubt in his appreciation of the qualities of the poet's work. . . .

No one nowadays would question the value of these poems, which do not only pay attention to the delights of rhyme or the subjects provided for the poet by the light of her inner fire or her surroundings. In the case of Mirta Aguirre the adaptation of form to content is noteworthy. And, since we have reached this crucial point in the debate around poetry, it must be acknowledged that without control of form there is no poetry possible, be it called old or new. . . .

There is one poem that deserves our special attention. It is "Vayamonos," which Mirta includes in a book only now and which Juan Ramón anthologized in 1935. For many of us, "Vayamonos" seemed liked part of *Presencia interior,* but it was not. What happened was that already in 1936, this poem expressed the attitude of an entire generation. The social and political ambience that reigned in the country as a result of the abortive revolution of 1933 marked a whole generation. "Vayamonos" gives shape to the anxieties of the young revolutionary intellectuals of that time. Having left the hosts of modernism behind, along with a certain religious spirituality or a certain declamatory tone, this poetry stripped of all rhetoric had already entered into territory that other poets would take to deeper levels years later. . . .

In his *Contemporary Cuban Poetry,* Roberto Fernández Retamar recognized something very special about Mirta Aguirre. In describing the distinct directions that our socially oriented poetry has taken, Fernández Retamar indicated those personified by Regino Pedroso and Manual Navaro Luna, while he reserves for the so-called black poetry whose chief ornament was Nicolas Guillen most of the burden of social expression. In fact, both lines, which are examplararily integrated in the universal work of Guillen, are complementary and were the two sides of a single coin. The third option, as hindsight shows us, definitely lives in the poetry of Mirta Aguirre who "intends to reconcile interior poetry with the social," as is the case with almost all the poems that she has written since *Presencia interior. . . .*

Already in the thirties our poetry had undergone essential transformations. These were transformations of such scope that the poetic language of *Presencia interior,* in its encounter with a philosophical-social ambition, makes use of a discourse that above all else is an instrument of allusive power, language that is above all the compilation of resonant equivalences. Mirta Aguirre's poetry, then, entails "that artistic health that comes from breathing the air of one's time, that masterly conjunction of the social and the lyrical, with full lungs.". . .

With the rest of her poetic output collected in the section *Otras poemas (1935–1947)* and *Poemas de amor,* the reader will experience a discovery and a reaffirmation that have evolved from what had been established in aesthetic terms in *Presencia interior.*

The poet with whom we are concerned today is the living example of the harmony between intention and ability. . . . Consciously involved in working with the expressive idols dearest to the Spanish language from time immemorial—that is, both Spanish-American and Spanish—she has also been sensitive to certain forms of French poetry. This is reflected in *Ayer de Hoy* in the very short and beautiful poems grouped together under the title of "Chansons." Similarly, another discovery and a definite joy will be the love poems written in the thirties, in which the author has succeeded in refining her instrument to such an extent that she is able to let varied and rich possibilities of very contemporary feeling be manifested in the eternity of poetry. Faithful to the emotions of her "I" and its time, Mirta Aguirre has been able to leave us a poetic oeuvre stripped of artifice, precise in its construction, beautiful in its aim of depositing in each human being sensitivity so indispensable at this time, to exist and construct a better universe.

Nancy Morejón. *Case de la Américas.*
21, 1980, pp. 128–32

Many Cuban intellectuals have found their work as critics—whatever the frequency—to be a veritable crucible in which to develop the (by no means simple) capacity to make judgments. This was the case with Mirta Aguirre who, starting in 1944 and for several years thereafter, ran a varied cultural section in the newspaper *Hoy* (an organ of the Popular Socialist Party), which was an example of timely criticism whose value transcends the limited historic moment in which it developed. . . .

The film criticism Mirta Aguirre wrote for this section, opposing the dangerous invasion of North American movies, was important for two reasons: first of all, its appropriateness with respect to the issue itself, to the critic's role, as it took into account the existence for several decades of a creative movement in the popular taste; and secondly because it did not fall into the obvious facile traps, avoiding risks such as denying certain facts that attracted us to this cinema or extolling the cinematographic products of Cuba or other Latin American countries, which were evidently of low quality, lacking in subject matter and weak in formal values. Her intention was simply to open the readers' eyes to this issue. . . .

Other frequent topics in Mirta Aguirre's criticism were theater and music, through work that took place within the national setting, although in the case of music there were also reviews of foreign artists who performed in our country.

Being aware of the needs of our national culture and the inadequacy of government support and funding, Mirta turned her criticism gradually toward a sustained effort on behalf of certain groups that had the unimaginable goal of developing our theater, our music, and our other art forms. . . .

The points mentioned above may provide a general idea of the timely nature of the work accomplished by Mirta Aguirre in relation to her historic moment. But they do not suffice to illustrate what we believe to be their enduring quality with respect to the dialectical relationship between critic and audience: her language, perfectly accessible to a range of readers, her absence of intellectual prejudice in the exercise of judgment, her breadth of topics, her sincerity, her constant reference to the reader, her absence of "maternalistic" condescension to the audience or author, her consideration of all factors, including the recreational, present in the work of art, her respect for all serious artistic work over and above their possible inadequacies, her use of criticism as a vehicle for aesthetic ideas so as to educate the reader. . . .

All the critical work accomplished by Mirta Aguirre over several years in the 1940s was highly stimulating in its time for cultural creativity and for groups that were making serious efforts toward Cuban artistic development in the midst of conditions that were hardly propitious for it; for the audience, which was not dealing with a distanced or infallible critic, but one that was alien to all facile rhetorical disruptions of communication and was, despite the rigor of her ideological and aesthetic points of view, entirely down to earth.

At the present time, with the demands and needs of our revolutionary process and its principal protagonist, the people, it is far from useless to turn back to consider, for our present critical function, those earlier experiences that Mirta Aguirre's criticism offers us.

Mirta Pernas Gomez. *Universidad de la Habana*. 230, Summer, 1987, pp. 93–100

AGUSTINI, DELMIRA (URUGUAY) 1886–1914

Critics are haunted by the need to find traces of influences in literary works, and the need has caused some to find in Delmira's poetry influences of Darío, D'Annunzio, Baudelaire, and Poe. Should I affirm it or deny it? It may be that she read them and that she slept with their books beneath her pillow. But I suspect that if this were so, she was nonetheless inspired first by an intellectual fervor and then by a physical fervor toward those men who moved her sensitivities and whom she undoubtedly wanted to encounter along the way, encounter them really, in the flesh. In any case, if they in part nurtured the deep roots of her inspiration, it is difficult to recognize the contribution of each one, for a genius knows how to incorporate all sources without showing them.

Of course, it is true that Delmira followed the dominant tastes of her age . . . and she could be classified with the decadents. But she was no slave to line or rhythm, nor did she trap her verses in the bonds of meter. . . . When she attempted to find her own door to passion, fearful that all would be lost, she found a violent escape, like any unprincipled girl, through the window. And she did not find her escape from the tower down medieval stairways or drawbridges, or even in secret; she fled wildly out into the open, shouting aloud, demanding from life what she had expected of it. Drunk with herself— "I am a bacchante, I am a bacchante"—she ran yelling down the road and then brought it all to her poetry. She was as sincere in the way she lived as in the way she wrote. Her "originalities" scandalized the Uruguayan bourgeoisie to which Delmira belonged, and that bourgeoisie looked askance at her. So much the better for her: she ceased to have anything to do with dull people. She limited her daily life to her family circle and gained enough time and space to develop her mind.

E. Labarca. *Atenea*. 110, August, 1934, pp. 314–15

The renovation that the women poets brought to modernism included the appearance of themes that had not yet been developed in [Latin] American poetry. Not only are personal, romantic feelings exalted; the women poets bare their souls and embrace as frequent themes overwhelming passion, disenchantment, the unrealized life. . . .

Delmira Agustini was one of the most representative figures of this period, which I, echoing Federico de Onís, would label post modernism. If we examine [four traditional poetic subjects—God, nature, love, death] in the poetry of Agustini, we will note that she does not develop the theme of God, perhaps because of her secular cultural background. And nature does not attract this poet. When she does describe it, she describes not real nature but rather a nature that belongs more to the realm of visions, raptures, or ecstasies, one which, in any case, has no correspondence with surrounding reality. This fact can be explained by her naturally introverted nature.

On the other hand, love and death, above all love, are frequent themes. Love . . . is her dominant theme, the lyrical expression of a sexual pantheism. For Delmira Agustini, the poem is nothing more than an obligatory form, an inevitable ordering, given her necessity to contemplate her own feelings. She seeks after lyrical expression because it is the form that best lends itself to that exaltation which is most private, individual, and feminine—Agustini herself. To this extent, the short lyrical form, which reveals the significant details briefly, which condenses the emotion in them, is the genre most suitable to the presentation of erotic themes.

Roberto Bonada Amigo. *Delmira Agustini en la vida y en la poesía* (Montevideo: Librería Técnica, 1964), pp. 53–54

[Agustini's] intellectual—we could say philosophical—intuition . . . became apparent, in the introspective mystery of her solitude, when, shut up in her room, "La Nena" [the little girl] transformed herself into a poet, like the chrysalis into a butterfly—but one that became a chrysalis again the next day, when it came into contact again with real life, with the daily reality of a middle-class young lady and a spoiled child. This distinctly poetic intuition, which she expressed exclusively in a language of images, symbols, allegories, and dreams, became intensified in the poems in her second book [*Morning Songs*], written between 1907 and 1910. She overcame a certain literary ingenuousness present in her first book [*The White Book*], and she descended, so to speak, from the platonic region in which she moved to a consciousness of carnal reality now quite a bit more painful, and at times more somber. She was evolving toward her third book [*The Empty Chalices*], in which we find originality and the brilliant fusion of sexuality with thought, of the physical side of the erotic with the abstract side of the conceit. But she achieved this without losing her purely poetic nature and language. On the contrary, she increased her powers of vision and symbol, which is, as has been recognized, what makes the erotic poetry of Delmira both unique and valuable, different from all other examples of erotic poetry: its transcendence, its sense of the beyond.

And all of this occurred without her ever ceasing to be, on the exterior, in her daily life, the young middle-class lady and the spoiled child who wrote idiotic letters and in whose "favorite, homey little look" (as her own family put it) she played mother to that doll that we have seen [in a picture]: blonde, dressed in baby-blue satin, with its porcelain smile, looking like Delmira herself.

Clara Silva. *Genio y figura de Delmira Agustini* (Buenos Aires: Editorial Universitaria de Buenos Aires, 1968), p. 32

[My] purpose [in] this study [is] to examine the poems of *La Alborada* (1896–1904), *El libro blanco* (1907), *Cantos de la mañana* (1910), *Los cálices vacíos* (1913), and the two posthumous works *Los astros del abismo* and *El rosario de Eros* (1924). The specific focus of this formalistic analysis is the theme which unifies Delmira's total poetic output, her ardent and never-ending quest for transcendence. Delmira's quest for transcendence centers around her poetry, her dreams, love and death, and, while the early works are basically optimistic, the later poetry becomes increasingly pessimistic as her desire to reach the *más allá* is not satisfied. . . .

In her quest for transcendence Delmira turned at an early age to writing poetry. In various poems she gives her definition of poetry and the poet. She believes the poet to be a seer and one who brings light, and she considers the labor of the poet divine. She also thinks that the poet is superior to the ordinary human being and that he suffers greatly from solitude, envy and hate.

In addition to her definition of poetry and the poet, Delmira also expresses some of her own poetic theories. She feels that poetry must have music, light, color, force and beauty, but, more important, it must have thoughts. She introduces many of her theories in poems on the muse. Some of these theories are that poetry should have qualities of dream, fantasy and mystery and that the antithetical elements of life should be fused in poetry. She does not prefer any one style of poetry but wants variety and contrasts.

While writing poetry brought Delmira intense pleasure, it also caused her great pain. In several of her poems she describes the pain caused by her efforts to express herself poetically and the magnificent pleasure that the achievement of such expression brings.

Because writing poetry was not enough to satisfy her desire for the *más allá*, Delmira turned to dreams. In her poems her quest for transcendence through dreams centers around her indications of how to reach her imaginary world and her descriptions of the world itself, characterized by its mystery, magic and light. Although Delmira is frequently able to escape into her world of dreams, at times she is forced to confront reality, and, at other times, she cannot distinguish between the imaginary and the real. This confusion of dreams and reality can best be seen in the poems which treat the theme of the dream lover, the most significant of the inhabitants of Delmira's imaginary world.

Doris T. Stephens. *Delmira Agustini and the
Quest for Transcendence* (Montevideo:
Ediciones Geminis, 1975), pp. 203–5

The surprise occasioned by the sincerity of . . . female voices [in Latin American poetry] was enormous, especially as concerns Delmira, who was the earliest of them. She was too young and beautiful—and womanly—to be so intelligent and so cultivated. . . .

Delmira longed for total union with the Nietzschean superman, a union for which she appeared to be ideally endowed, physically, as well as intellectually. She did not achieve the desired Pascalian interpenetration with another being, the illusory sense of being a single entity, one organism with two parts that functioned beyond the bed, because it is inseparable and complete. If a play on words is allowed, comparison with Teresa of Avila is valid, because, while Teresa succeeded in making mysticism an erotic experience, Delmira made eroticism a mystical experience. . . .

Her poems are too passionate and their sensuality too open for their time. . . . Some men were shocked by her, but others saw her in their dreams as the ideal lover, the perfect combination of beauty and intelligence, of sensual and spiritual ardor, able to share experiences on the basis of an equality that their socialization made impossible for the vast majority of women of her time. These experiences perhaps did not exist outside the confines of her imagination, but they embody her image as the ideal lover.

Dolores Koch. *Revista Iberoamericana.* 51,
July–December, 1985, pp. 724–25

Delmira Agustini published three books: *El libro blanco* (1907), *Cantos de la mañana* (1910), and *Los cálices vacios.* The first of these books contains fifty-one poems; the last seven poems, which are love poems, appear under the subtitle *Orla rosa.* The second of Delmira's books is shorter. It contains nineteen poems and three short prose poems. The author's last book is her most important because Delmira not only presents twenty-one new poems in it, but also a complete reprinting of *Cantos de la mañana* and thirty poems from *El libro blanco,* including those of *Orla rosa.* This anthological impulse seems to mean that Delmira was indicating she saw her work as a unity or a single cycle. Although an author's objective intention is not sufficient to establish the unity of her work, it may nonetheless serve to suggest that such unity is possible.

Another interesting aspect of *Los cálices vacios* is that the arrangement of the poems is the reverse of their chronological order of composition. The book begins with poems in Eros and ends with those of *El libro blanco.* The order that Delmira imposes on *Los cálices vacios* would seem to indicate that the author wanted this book to be read as the description of a process that culminated in Eros, emphasizing once more the unitary structure of the work as a whole, whose central metaphor would be Eros.

Eros is truly the central metaphor of Delmira's work, but this work does not deal with love, sex, life, death, or dreams. Although these elements appear in the work, they are not its themes, as many critics have claimed. . . . Neither is it the expression of a feminine soul or testimony to a fundamental failure on the part of its author in her search for something impossible to achieve, as other critics have maintained. . . . The subject of the work . . . is the life and nature of art and imagination, for which Eros is the central metaphor.

Imagination appears in three ways in Delmira's work. First, it is the subject of the work, what it defines, explains, and develops. Specifically, the work reveals the process of creation from the point of view of both the creator and the created form and of the relations between the two. The work therefore represents a divided or double consciousness that observes and studies itself to create and/or be created. Second, imagination is the structural principle of the work, that which governs its organization and development. The imagination—acting in accordance with its own particular logic—is thus what establishes the boundaries of Delmira's poetic universe, what governs the development and evolution of the images and the structure of its symbols. Finally, imagination is the theme of the work, which is to say, the meaning if its overall structure.

> Nydia Loureiro de Renfrew. *La imaginación*
> *en la obra de Delmira Agustini*
> (Montevideo: Ediciones Letras femeninas,
> 1987), pp. 14–15

For Agustini, the winged spirit is essentially female, most often without the light airiness proposed by Rodó. Her winged creatures include, as well as the famous bleeding swan she creates in "Nocturno," winged vampires, Iris, and bats, as well as butterflies and doves.

Critics and biographers of Agustini have warned her readers of the likely dangers of misjudging her poetry. Over and over again they warn us to separate the "eternal" from the "worldly reflections" of her overly heated, decorated, and decadent epoch. And more, we are to be taught to avoid the dangers of naively trusting in her overtly erotic expressiveness, "redeemed," in the eyes of Zum Felde, by her "dramatismo." Sylvia Molloy, however, has outlined very clearly the materialization and explicit erotic force of Agustini's swan in Agustini's writing. She points out her rewriting of Dario's work, where her unmistakable subject position of *female* enunciator leaves no doubt as to the sexual suggestiveness of the classical encounter.

My focus here is another: Agustini's apparent "unfinished" technique. Did she choose a freer style, as many critics have said, because of her childish lack of discipline or training in poetic form? Or, as others have said, is it her innate femininity, her spontaneity of desire that impedes her chiseling perfect

Parnassian forms? All we know for sure is that she is no representative of
formal perfection. She leaves her sonnets unfinished at times (reminding us
of Darío's haunting "Nocturno"), and rhymes repetitively and often trivially,
even "moka," "loca," "boca." Augmentative techniques contrast with the
foreshortened ones. Anaphora can produce an incantatory effect, as in "Las
alas," but its combination with exclamation sometimes thunders on too heavily. She uses a kind of shorthand to set a scene: "Diríase" or "Se diría crisálida
de piedra," prefiguring its use in more recent verse (e.g., Vallejo). Her use
of the ellipse perhaps best characterizes her technique. In Agustini, this has
been seen as lack, although it is recognized in later poets as the fine cutting
of the ironic edge, the intrusion of doubt and silence that unanchors a logocentric universe.

Gwen Kirkpatrick. Romance Quarterly. 36,
1989, pp. 310–11

AI BEI (CHINA) n.d.

Let me warn the reader. In Ai Bei's stories, you won't find any tales with
happy endings, no easy reconciliation with the world. In fact, I would guess
that her stories are not what either Chinese or American audiences would
consider "easy reading." There are no stories about the mild malaise of
middle-classdom, boring marriages, uncomfortable family reunions, dead-
end lifestyles and the like. The so-called themes and style contain none of
the spare, carefully controlled or understated traits that this country's reviewers prize so much in current literature—the drop-dead scene and the narrator's non-reaction to it.

I also think reviewers would be hard-pressed to describe Ai Bei's fiction
as resembling any kind of style, school of literature, or genre. To be sure, her
fiction concerns life in a dirty realism sort of way—at times. But then there
are the dark surrealistic images of the mind, providing counterpart to daily
existence. And her fiction is certainly suffused with the most lush, sensual
and sexual prose I have seen coming out of recent China. But I would say
this is merely one quality of her voice, not the dominating aspect of her
themes. And certainly there are moments—dialogue and images—punctuated
with sharp humor and wry observations.

If you pushed me to the wall and forced me to say which American
writer I thought Ai Bei's literary voice most resembled, I would have to say
Allen Ginsberg—but only in the tone of her voice. In Ai Bei's stories, you
get an immediate sense of her "presence," a strong and distinctive voice. Her
voice has an edge to it. The anger is explosive. She gnaws on the anguish.
She writes stories, as if her life depended on it.

And in fact, that is what her three stories and one novella are about: difficult issues about existence—the self in conflict with both society and the self that society has created. From the very first sentence of "Bala's Dream," you sense the narrator's disgust at the moral decay that arises from self-ambitions—a husband who fakes love for an old Swedish woman to secure his future, a beggar who fakes an oozing sore for charity, and the narrator herself who has faked a righteous moral good when it was really her ego at stake. And so the narrator goes off for a pilgrimage to mythical places of innocence, beauty, and pure passion—perhaps to purge herself, perhaps to destroy the last of her illusions. She shows off a tough exterior, a street-smart savvy about the ways of the world and its façade. And—just as she suspected—the mythical places have turned into tourist traps, film locations, and clichéd artist retreats. She presses on, walking with her guide. She reaches the primitive village of Bala's Dream—and the unexpected happens, something that leaves her vulnerable again.

I won't tell you the ending, only say that it raises the question: Will the dream you think can save you ultimately destroy you in the end?

The other stories in *Red Ivy, Green Earth Mother* are just as rich, just as powerful. It is the self in conflict with the world. The stories raise questions about the odds for or against existence and survival of the individual.

In looking at any translated work, it's always difficult to provide any casual comparison or critique of style or theme, technique or literary intent. Even with the best of translations, the author's voice, words, and rhythms change—necessarily so to make it accessible to readers of another culture. So much can be lost in translation. So much can be excised by wary editors on both shores. In fact, I have often wondered in reading current literature arriving from the PRC, "How much has been left out?"

This anthology represents a possible first: fiction by a Chinese writer that is published in this country in its entirety—unexpurgated, uncensored. In fact, I am told that some of these stories, which were published in literary magazines in Beijing, had been edited extensively; politically or sexually provocative passages were trimmed out. Ai Bei has chosen to restore her stories to the original.

Amy Tan. Foreword to Ai Bei. *Red Ivy,*
Green Earth Mother. (Layton, Utah:
Peregrine Smith, 1990), pp. x–xii

Three stories and a novella are the first of this writer's works to be translated into English and offer a good introduction to a startling new voice. Ai Bei's female protagonists come from all ranks of contemporary Chinese society—intellectuals, prison guards, latrine cleaners—but each strives equally hard to define herself, both to herself and to the people around her. To capture the complexities of a milieu in which people mouth modern sexual platitudes but act according to old ones, Ai Bei slips back and forth between realism, stream-of-consciousness and a kind of hallucinatory superrealism. In "Bala's

Dream," a city woman in search of a "purer" culture is led up a mountain by a scornful travel guide and narrowly escapes rape in a village mating ritual. In the novella, "Red Ivy," a prominent Party member's niece finds employment in a women's prison; life there is vicious yet not as alienating as on the outside, where women work next to men but bow to their double standards. Ai Bei's stories are not about blame or the lack of it; her characters, female and male, are trying to pick their way through a cultural landscape changing so fast that it's different every time they look at it.

Penny Kaganoff. *Publishers Weekly.* August 24, 1990, p. 58

Three short stories ("Bala's Dream," "Green Earth Mother," and "The Final Myth") and one novella ("Red Ivy") make up this thin volume. All the stories deal with women's difficulties, especially with men. Some are rather overblown, surreal fantasies, some realistic, but all portray the seamy, unpleasant side of life in China. Although the style is often engrossing if overwrought, the emotionally charged characters seem remote and strange despite their hypersensitivity. Popular in China before she became a dissident, Ai now lives in exile in the United States. She is an important contemporary stylist who deserves to be heard.

Kitty Chen Dean. *Library Journal.* August, 1990, p. 136

Red Ivy, Green Earth Mother is the first single-author volume in English by one of the many really fine writers who began to emerge in the Peoples Republic of China around 1984. Here is a book of fiction by a Chinese woman writer that teachers of Chinese literature in translation will not have to apologize for. The stories have everything we expect from good fiction: imagination, style (especially lush, evocative imagery), emotional honesty and intensity without sentimentality, and serious social commentary that does not degenerate into jejune didacticism. They are stories for adults by a woman with an adult sensitivity to the highly ambiguous moral climate of contemporary Chinese life.

As Amy Tan points out in her foreword there are no happy endings in the selections of *Red Ivy*, "no easy reconciliation with the world." The fictional worlds of the three short stories and one novella are not ones with which any strong-minded person would want to be reconciled. From the first twenty-seven-line sentence of a two-sentence paragraph, beginning with the word *if*, we at once recognize that we are in the presence of a genuine talent who understands and expresses the reality of the mainland China many of us have experienced. The rest of the book is just as artistically translated as the marvelous "if sentence" with which it begins.

The protagonists of the four works are all women, women seeking and not really finding some escape from modern and contemporary China's particularly restrictive social reality. "Bala's Dream" begins with a realistic description of a trip to an isolated village of that name in exotic Xishuang Banna and ends with a shocking, surrealistically achieved, and totally unexpected . . . shall I say, climax (and leave the rest for the reader to discover). "Green Earth Mother" is the tragic and often-repeated story of a young bride's defeat at the hands of a strong mother-in-law and a weak husband; but seldom has such a story been told this way, replete with multicolored natural imagery, sexual passion, and mythic metaphors. "The Final Myth" is the myth of love; its theme: "Someone in love is consigned to hell." "Red Ivy" is complex and finely plotted story of several women imprisoned both in jail and in society at large; thematically it asks the question: "Did these criminals destroy the beauty of society and create flaws in it, or were they the products of a flawed society." The answer the story gives would not be pleasing to the guardians of the criminal "justice" system in the PRC. All the women who suffer most in this highly realistic, even naturalistic narrative do so for reasons that readers will certainly feel to be unjust. But then, as the narrator speculates near the end, "Maybe the lifelong trials of being a woman had made suffering commonplace to them." In context, this line appears utterly plausible despite its unadorned message.

The messages of the stories of *Red Ivy* are important, but it is the artistry that will make one want to read them again. I strongly recommend them for courses in comparative literature, women's studies, and literature in translation. Watch for a forthcoming book of Ai Bei's stories on completely different themes.

Michael S. Duke. *World Literature Today.*
65, 1991, pp. 361–62

AICHINGER, ILSE (AUSTRIA) 1921–

Miss Aichinger is concerned with the tragedy of the human situation, which is evident behind the pathos and irony of her stories. A little boy mistrusts grown-ups when his mad tutor is dragged away. . . . A little girl is left barren when her practical friends deny her the angels, and the bound man welcomes his bondage and fears his freedom. There is even a woman who fades away the minute she takes off her sun glasses. The author also has a sense of humor, and if it has the bitter taste of irony it is because it rises from the irony of the human situation.

Patricia Donegan. *Commonweal.* 1956,
p. 354

Aichinger has frequently been characterized as a disciple of Kafka, certainly with good reason. Aichinger's characters, like Kafka's, are frequently symbols rather than human personalities who exist in a world which bears but slight resemblance to our world of reality. Aichinger's stories share with Kafka's an intriguing undercurrent of allegory so elusive as to defy definitive interpretation. Yet the great difference between the two authors is that while Kafka's works have an oppressive, nightmare quality, Aichinger's have a lyrical, dreamlike atmosphere. The pessimism which predominates with Kafka is totally missing in Aichinger. Nowhere is the contrast more marked than in passages dealing with death. For Kafka, death is at best an escape from the horror of existence, always a miserable, degrading transition. Aichinger's hero dreads the coming of death, but discovers that it really presents a new beginning and a freer one.

Carol B. Bedwell. *German Quarterly.* 1965,
p. 37

If one wants to classify Ilse Aichinger's narrative style under a critical rubric, surrealism is the closest. . . .

In surrealist literature . . . the image takes on an extraordinary importance. . . .

In her latest story, *Eliza Eliza,* Ilse Aichinger renounces any rational or even merely psychological development. Instead, images suddenly crop up, at first glance without any obvious motivation. In the course of the narrative one image transforms itself into another, often by means of a hardly perceptible change of perspective. . . .

What happens within the story defies description. Just as clouds in the sky in their unceasing motion continually produce new variegated images, the created images *(Imaginationen)* in the narrative are transformed one into the other. What the author fails to give in the way of explanation, she demands from the reader's associative ability. One is inclined to describe the narrative text no longer as prose, but as *poésie* in Sartre's sense. . . . The word is no longer meaning but substance. . . .

Except for a minimal residue, the author has eradicated all descriptive language—which was still prevalent in her early prose pieces. . . . Instead, things and events speak, *i.e.,* the images themselves. The storyteller has withdrawn completely into the background; her interpretive explanations have made way for concrete images. As a result, the narrative stands on its own feet, has seemingly slipped the storyteller's curb bit, and has taken on a peculiarly organic quality. It draws, as it were, its life from within itself, giving birth to its own symbolism. Necessity has replaced narrative freedom; the story is revealed as myth.

Rainer Lübren. *Neue Rundschau.* 1965,
pp. 627–28, 635–36

The spoken word is of great importance in Aichinger's work. Already in *Herod's Children* there are long passages that assume a dramatic character. The author herself considers the "stage-setting" of language, the gestures, as significant as speech itself. Not only the word, but the underlying speech act is essential for the interpretation in context. Of course, dialogues and the aural plays that develop from them are genres that reach all within ear-shot, but nondramatic texts contain discussion and dialogues that imply a listener or audience through questions, indirect quotations, responses, interjections.

Accordingly Aichinger's poetry benefits from being read aloud. The author herself is by far the best reader of her texts. Through the modulation of tonalities and departures from the printed text . . . a vocal quality and an accessibility are conferred upon texts that at first glance appear hermetically sealed, e.g., "Doubts on the Balcony" or "Dover." Aichinger's reading makes it clear that the content of her texts, rather than deriving from the connection of images with material words, stems from the semantic and syntactical structure of her sentences. Her stressed passages establish a network of meaning that reflects back on the actual text and within which the rather formal syntax is the connecting link. Behind the logic of language there is a meaning that is not grasped through it, but is built up from the succession of impressions. The superficial structure of the text and the underlying significance do not often create a unity.

Aichinger's own spoken language is very close to her texts. In conversations with her, it becomes clear that, especially in writing her later pieces, she is not aiming at a fixed, secure literary language. The same intense imagery characteristic of her writing, the same formal elements—wordplay, aphorisms or adages, double meanings and puns—also characterize her speech. Her tone of voice often betrays the intended nuance—humor, derision, bitterness, or amusement—as the texts give the verbal utterance a stylistic competence, wit, and lightness, without sacrificing seriousness and gravity in the process. The transition from discursive speech to poetry is fluid. Aichinger's sentences can turn spontaneously into "stories," her own term for her prose.

As Aichinger says, she writes spontaneously. Her descriptions form into sentences, she writes, until her strength fails her and the "right sentences don't come any more." She exercises only a limited control over the process. Sentences and words, in her opinion, are a law unto themselves. . . . The predisposition as the author calls it, especially the strength, that develops spontaneous creations dependent on a psychic state, puts the aspect of actual writing in the context of a meditative form. . . .

The author has no "message"; her work, which is not based on any particular ideology, bears witness, rather, to the search for a point of view standpoint. The writings come from this quest. . . . Dissatisfactions with what is, with the actual physical world, underlie her work. . . . External realities and language impose such constraints that "one cannot escape."

Aichinger's sensitivity to prejudice and injustice enters her life as a writer through the construction of antiworlds that are expressed from an antiperspective. The exception establishes the rule. Through that exception that is visionary material, the everyday conditions of existence mature out of strength, as a whole or in part. In her portrayal of reality things are possible that are closed off in everyday life. The unexpected becomes the possible, categories get turned around, exchanged, metamorphoses are consummated from one state of being into another. The hierarchy of phenomena can shift. The grotesque can be joined with the ordinary, the everyday with the sublime, the ridiculous with the tragic, so that a world emerges from all the elements in which our basic judgments are no longer valid.

Dagmar C. G. Lorenz. *Ilse Aichinger*
(Königstein: Athenäum, 1981), pp. 26–27

Aichinger's works first evoked notice in the United States after publication of the German edition of her collection *Der Gefesselte (The Bound Man)*. A 1954 review in *Books Abroad* applauds Aichinger's "convincing style of symbolic realism" and ranks her "in the forefront of the rich crop of poets, novelists, and playwrights which appeared in Austria after the Nazi tide subsided." *Books Abroad* is for the "literary immigrant" a sort of Ellis Island. Authors and works mentioned there must "come ashore" to be really in America. That happened in Aichinger's case with the publication two years later of *The Bound Man* in simultaneous U. S. and British printings of Mosbacher's translation. They were immediately discussed in the standard review journals and in literary sections of major newspapers. *The Saturday Review* lauds her as "an astonishing new talent." She is said to excel "in a form usually considered the domain of Anglo-Americans: the tale of the supernatural, of chilling poetry, of horrors not quite grasped. The light playing over her world is both bright and impenetrable, and wherever it appears to unveil the outlines of a face, a character, a destiny, it conceals the truths it pretends to disclose."

U. Henry Gerlach. *Modern Austrian*
Literature. 20, 1987, pp. 96–97

The publication of the volume *Kleist, Moos, Fasane* (1987) brings together some of Ilse Aichinger's recent prose-texts difficult of access, and it provides material that fills out aspects of her biography not generally known. It also includes at least one previously unpublished text that takes her experiments with language a stage further than those in the volume *Schlechte Wörter* (1976). This article will examine Aichinger's published works since her volume of poetry *Verschenkter Rat* (1978; and as a Taschenbuch, 1981), with special reference to the most recent volume and to three dialogues of the 1980s.

The title *Kleist, Moos, Fasane* refers to the first item in the volume, originally published as childhood memories in *Atlas* (1965). Together with autobiographical texts from the 1950s and 1960s, it gives an insight into her relationship with her unhappy grandmother. There is a harmonious interaction between the atmosphere of her grandmother's kitchen and the child's imagination of the first section, shattered by the contrast between the discipline of parts of schooldays and the still naive coziness of the children in the second. The third part records the timelessness of the countryside during long summer holidays, a feature of the writer's memories that lingers as a mystery and is focused on the berries she went to pick, so the text ends with words that sum up Aichinger's relationship with her past in general. . . .

Vor der langen Zeit recalls Christmas 1938 with its harsh contradictions between the message of Christ's birth and the threats of deportation and war, the two Aichinger sisters listening with horror by night to the lorries moving towards the East while glimpsing the tinsel of Christmas decorations in their room. By the time of the next text, *Der 1. September 1939,* Ilse was helping younger children to escape to freedom, while older relatives were trying to avoid deportation. This previously unpublished piece and the next *(Hilfes-telle)* show just how close to her own experiences were the details of the novel *Die größere Hoffnung* (1948). The search for visas, feelings of guilt and insufficiency, interest in maps to point out distant places of hope and the labyrinthine world of the ghetto where rumors flourished and relationships were at their most raw—all are relativized in the previously unknown text *Nach der weißen Rose* with its evocation of hope embodied by the Munich resistance group led by the Scholl family. Never before had Aichinger made public her feelings when she went in 1950 to help found the Academy of Design in Ulm with Inge Scholl. . . .

In *Von gestern,* as in her famous *Spiegelgeschichte* (written in 1948), the structure, direction and apparent simplicity of the vocabulary and sentences become a complex web of interrelated signs in retrospect. A pattern of the unexpected followed by an explanation builds up a banal set of happenings, only the final sentence giving them interrelationship and an extra level of personal meaning. Not until that final sentence does the eight-times repeated paragraph-opening "Gestern" sound like a death-knell. Typically for Aichinger, there is no other clue offered, and we are left as in a parable with the statement that the writer died yesterday. Taken literally, there is nothing more to add, except that the writer saw yesterday as one of revelation, a time of uncertainty, disharmony and decay. Taken metaphorically, the "Ich" that died was one that spoke too much. . . . By implication the new "Ich" will have less to say. . . . .

Aichinger's insistence on concentration in order to find what her true self can grasp is an essential component of her writings—hence for instance on one level the deliberate choice of particular "Ich"—narrators with their restricted perspectives (a mouse, a rejected doll, the daughter of a man of straw—all from the volume *Eliza, Eliza* (1965). Those final two sentences project the reasons for the structure of *Spiegelgeschichte* among other stories. Refashioning boundaries as contours would also be applicable to many of the texts in *Schlechte Wörter.* Already here in an early entry there are ideas that are worked out in detail later. . . .

Aichinger's recent works, including the few poems published since the collection *Verschenkter Rat,* show that she clings to certain moments and situations where she has felt most authentically herself. She mistrusts the world and the human heart, and she registers sets of signs that protect and point the way forward. They also show less certainty, as if she was increasingly aware of the fragile and temporary quality of all statements about life.

Brian Keith-Smith. *German Life and Letters*. 41, July, 1988, pp. 504–5, 509–11

AIDOO, (CHRISTINA) AMA ATA (GHANA) 1942–

Miss Christina Ama Aidoo's play, *The Dilemma of a Ghost* . . . was performed by Theatre Workshop of Lagos from January 26th to 28th. This play takes off where Lorraine Hansberry's *Raisin in the Sun* left off, with Assegai the African on the brink of marrying an American Negro girl. That play has given a glimpse of the extraordinary vision of their "homeland" prevalent among less informed American Negroes. This vision was the result of little knowledge and much romance.

Miss Aidoo's play explores the situation in which an American Negro bride returns "home" with her Ghanaian husband, to find herself a complete stranger, colour not withstanding. The agonising situation is portrayed with the kind of humor that is next door to tears. The crux of the play is the differing attitudes to childbearing. . . .

Miss Aidoo displays a gift—very useful to a social dramatist—of showing both sides of the coin at the same time. She shows the reverence of African village society towards motherhood while at the same time exposing the inherent cruelty of a system which makes the childless woman utterly miserable.

The play has a hopeful end. Not the rather doubtful hope that black people, whatever their background, can always understand each other, but the more universal one that there is common underlying essential humanity, which, given certain conditions, can come to the surface. In this play, motherhood, suppressed in one person, gratefully welcomed by another, and agonisingly unavailable to a third, is the unifying link.

Eldred Jones. *The Bulletin of the Association for African Literature in English*. 2, 1965, p. 33

Since she has only one play and two short stories so far published, it is perhaps too early to herald [Aidoo] as a pathfinder; but she clearly represents a movement that is gathering force among the younger writers. In her story "No Sweetness Here," published in the *Black Orpheus Anthology,* she describes with tenderness and compassion a woman's love for her child. To an American or European reader, this story might seem charming if not particularly unusual in form. In African writing, however, the story is quite unique, for it explores with convincing legitimacy the intensity of individual emotional experience. Now, to show that she can turn to wider issues, Miss Aidoo has given us *The Dilemma of a Ghost,* a play that has already been performed in Accra, Lagos, and Ibadan. . . .

The Dilemma of a Ghost is a delightful piece of writing, simple, delicate, and containing much wisdom. The dialog has authenticity, as well as sparkle and wit, though there are occasional failures in the use of American slang. It is less successful as a play, because Miss Aidoo lacked an experienced stage director to help her work out a final version before publication. In this she suffers the same lack as all dramatists in West Africa, where there is no professional English-language theater group. . . .

Since Miss Aidoo wrote *The Dilemma of a Ghost* when she was still an undergraduate at the University of Ghana, it may seem churlish to draw attention to weaknesses in the dramatic construction. On the other hand, she is an artist exploring new realities with skill and distinction, and a patronizing accolade would be out of place. We look forward to seeing developments in Miss Aidoo's dialectic skill and personal insight, for she is among the first of a growing literary line of Africans unbu⁻ ⁻ned, at least in part, by the problem of the color line, beneath which has always lain the problem of the culture line. And there are many more ghosts needing this kind of exorcism.

C. J. Reay. *African Forum.* Summer, 1965,
pp. 112–13

The play *Anowa* cries out to be performed. The story is simple enough, of the life of a girl in "the state of Abura" in the 1870s, a strange girl, too advanced for her time, whose father felt should perhaps have been a priestess. Instead, being a progressive woman, Anowa chooses her own husband, Kofi Ako, and they go to the coast where the husband grows rich on the palm oil trade. But Anowa is barren, and slowly becomes ghost-like, trying to persuade her husband to take another wife. The climax is a great quarrel between the two, following which they both commit suicide. Although there is a certain Greek starkness about it, the language switches easily from the folksy-conversational to the apocalyptic. . . .

The short stories [in *No Sweetness Here*], like the play, are simple and direct, being concerned with the real problems of ordinary people. There is a certain social consciousness, in some of them, a burning desire to point a lesson, such as in the tale of the woman who worries that her sister is the mistress of a politician. With the coup she hopes the situation will change, but then her sister comes home with a highly-placed army captain. Ama Ata writes with transparent honesty: behind it there is the feeling, the same as in the novels of Ayi Kwei Armah, of being near to tears. She and Armah are in the front rank of the literary talents that have come to the fore in recent years in Ghana.

K.W. *West Africa.* Jan. 30–Feb. 5, 1971,
p. 133

[In *No Sweetness Here*] Ama Ata Aidoo celebrates womanhood in general and motherhood in particular. She stands up for the woman who must go and protect her own; who must go through "pregnancy and birth and death and pain, and death again." There will always be a fresh corpse and she will weep all over again. The woman who, even while she is nursing an infant, must lose her husband to the south, where there will be better money for one's work. And it will still be the woman—the mother—who must receive the news first that her son is going to leave his wife and child. . . . The woman who watches over a sick child. . . . The mother who waits for the man who never returns—son or lover or husband. . . . The mother who knows that she is giving birth for the second time when she launches her son on the road to higher education. . . .

The men in Miss Aidoo's fiction are mere shadows or voices or just "fillers." Somewhere, quietly, they seem to be manipulating the woman's life or negatively controlling it or simply having a good time, knowing that they are assured of something like a divine top-dog position in life. Given this premise the woman, without worrying about her traditional place, simply gets up on her feet and asserts not her importance in relation to the male, but her motherhood.

> Ezekiel Mphahlele. Introduction to Ama Ata
> Aidoo. *No Sweetness Here* (Garden City,
> New York: Doubleday, 1972), pp. xix-xx

Various African writers have depicted the conditions and quality of life of traditional and modern African womanhood. . . . Still, it seems to me that the Ghanaian writer Ama Ata Aidoo is unique for she almost exclusively rivets attention on black African womanhood of the village and the city. And because she is a woman, Miss Aidoo is able to view the plight of African women from a natural and familiar vantage point.

In *No Sweetness Here,* a collection of eleven short stories, the male characters generally play a peripheral role. They are frequently in the background, usually managing directly or indirectly to bring about the suffering of women. In those allusions to life in Accra and other urban centers of Ghana Miss Aidoo depicts the moral failings of young women who become prostitutes or mistresses of wealthy men in order to enjoy the material opportunities offered in a city. On the other hand, the stories set in villages do not offer a particularly pleasant alternative for the African woman, especially if she is the least respected wife in a polygamous household. In such a case the wife asserts her identity as a woman through her love of her children. A tragic situation occurs if she can have no children or her single child dies. Such is the case in the title story "No Sweetness Here." . . .

Does Miss Aidoo offer a solution to the dilemma of the modern urban African woman? Not directly. However, she does suggest that education offers a chance for a woman to develop herself independently of the pressures placed upon her by men. Otherwise she must be content to exploit her body and be exploited.

Donald Bayer Burness. *Studies in Black
Literature.* 4:2 Summer, 1973, pp. 21, 23

As students of African literature we usually deal with the African woman as a topic in that literature, but very seldom as a contributor. The neglect of the African woman as writer results, in part, from the invisibility, or near invisibility, of women writers in general; but that universal problem has been compounded, in this instance, by the relatively short supply of women writers in Africa. Ama Ata Aidoo of Ghana has managed to survive this double handicap, if one may judge, not by the number of studies of her work (for these are rare), but by her continuing popularity in the accepted arenas of public attention—anthologies, reprints, and mass circulation interviews. She has attracted some attention as a dramatist, but it has been as a short-story writer that she has been most prolific. And it has been in the short-story medium that she has been most successful in developing narrative techniques that are integrated with those thematic perspectives which she derives from the traditional situation and the contemporary experience of the African woman. In other words, Aidoo's art as a short-story writer combines her narrative materials and structures with narrative points of view which, in turn, reflect a variety of insights into the situation of Aidoo's women. Briefly, there is a general tendency to use traditional story-telling techniques (from the African oral tradition) as the media for traditional viewpoints in a rural society. And, in turn, a more self-consciously Western style or structure is the medium for a Westernized female consciousness, or at the very least, for the insights of a Western education, into the ambiguities of female roles in both traditional African and contemporary Western societies. . . .

The focal point . . . is . . . the woman's role. The urban woman's relatively unrestricted sexuality arouses the male narrator's possessive puritanism; but, simultaneously, it stirs the erotic self-consciousness which challenges that masculine puritanism. Moreover, the archetypally "liberated" woman of the city represents a broader cultural challenge to the older African order, from a brash alien lifestyle. For if the coherent family structure (which is emphasized by the narrator's asides to uncles, brothers and his mother) represents a stable, conventional tradition, then the "bad" women of the city are symbols of a new uprootedness that is both exhilarating and destructive. But above all, the woman of the city bears a radically subversive image precisely because she can no longer be perceived or described within a conventional, familiar context: she is no longer a woman of the family, and quite apart form the morality of her sexual choices, this uprooted condition is "bad" (i.e., disturbing, menacing), from the settled communal [experience].

Lloyd W. Brown. *World Literature Written
in English.* 13:2, 1974, pp. 172, 175

Ama Ata Aidoo, . . . is perhaps best known for her collection of short stories, *No Sweetness Here,* but she has also written two plays, *The Dilemma of a Ghost,* written and staged in 1964 and published in 1965, and *Anowa,* published in 1970. I intend in this paper to examine her two plays, with special emphasis on her deft use of language.

Speech, in Aidoo's plays, is an index of social class, age, and background; it is also a vehicle for characterization. John Millington Synge, the Irish dramatist, said in his Preface to *The Playboy of the Western World,* "Every speech should be as fully flavoured as a nut or an apple." Miss Aidoo's speeches certainly have this quality. Her success in creating levels of language, in matching literary grace with veracity of characterization, in suiting, for the most part, the action to the word, the word to the action, is commendable in such a young dramatist.

Looking closely at *The Dilemma of a Ghost,* one can identify six levels of language: the American English of Eulalie Yawson, the educated African English of Ato Yawson, the stylized poetry and prose of the Prelude, the childlike talk of Boy and Girl, the chit-chat in verse of the 1st Woman and the 2nd Woman, and the language of Nana, Akyere, Petu, Mansa, Akroma, and Monka. . . .

The fifth and sixth levels are of especial interest. Although "transcribed" into English by a dexterous dramatist, there is every reason to believe that these speeches are made by characters who speak a Ghanaian language, probably Fanti, and Aidoo (like Synge *vis-à-vis* the Gaelic-speaking characters—as opposed to his English-speaking characters—in his Anglo-Irish plays) wants us to believe so. . . .

The levels of language in *Anowa* do not parallel those six levels discussed with regard to *The Dilemma of a Ghost.* The society in the later play has had a uniform pattern of exposure. There is no evidence that any member of the community has had a Western education: the nearest one comes to this possibility is Anowa's carping remark to Kofi in Phase 3, suggesting that he has "learned the ways of white people." There is no concrete evidence of "schooling" in the Western tradition. . . .

What seems the most likely explanation, is that the playwright is dealing with a situation different from that she was confronted with in *The Dilemma of a Ghost:* here she is dramatizing an old Ghanaian legend for the benefit of present-day audiences and readers, and since the society is homogeneous, a laborious creation of levels of language might not have recommended itself to her. This is not to say that there is no individuation in the speeches of the different characters.

In these two plays, then, Ama Ata Aidoo has shown how dexterously language can be manipulated to serve dramatic ends. She has a gift both for the sparse economical language of sadness and despair and for the gaiety, rollicking boisterousness, and acid wit of comedy, satire, irony, and parody. Aidoo's use of language is an indication of how educated dramatists can portray with veracity and accuracy the different generations and levels of education in present-day Africa.

Dapo Adelugba. African Literature Today. 8,
1976, pp. 72, 82–83

The Ghanaian Ama Ata Aidoo has written not only stories but a number of plays as well. One of them, *Anowa* (1970), is based on a familiar story from the oral tradition. A willful young beauty refuses all the marriage partners proposed by her parents because she wants a man of her own choice. Later it becomes clear that she is married to a devil. The moral of the story is of course that a woman must conform to the rules, otherwise she will come to a bad end.

Ama Ata Aidoo chose to situate the old familiar tale in a nineteenth-century context. Against her parents' will Anowa marries a trader in hides who has become rich by exploiting his slaves. Anowa's mother represents the conventional feminine code of conduct and her ideals contrast sharply with those of her headstrong daughter. . . .

Anowa proves to be just as stubborn a wife as she was a daughter. She is against the principle of slave labor and in the end she is proved right. It is against the will of the gods, and they punish her and her husband with childlessness. Anowa is unhappy because her status prevents her from working. The play ends in a double suicide: Anowa drowns herself and her husband Kofi shoots himself. Aidoo's themes broach relevant social questions, the language is impressive and the role of Anowa is completely credible.

Aidoo's short stories too are dramatically sound, due in part to the extensive use of dialogue, and several of them have been successfully adapted as radio plays. In her sole novel, *Our Sister Killjoy* (1977), she relates her experiences in Europe, as so many Africans have done of late. "Been-tos" is the name given to people who have been to the metropolis. As a been-to she observes the strange ways of the Westerners and their reactions to Africans. The heroine Sissy records her impressions of life as a grant student in Germany and she is not sparing in her criticism of that curious culture. European readers will find the views of the African been-tos on Western society most enlightening.

Mineke Schipper, ed. Unheard Words:
Women and Literature in Africa, the Arab
World, Asia, the Caribbean, and Latin
America (London: Allison and Busby, 1985),
pp. 42–44

Ama Ata Aidoo, Ghana's fine female writer perfects [Charity] Waciuma's [feminist] approach in her collection of short stories *No Sweetness Here* and novel, *Our Sister Killjoy*. In those works, the problems of the African woman are expressed as integral parts of the problems of colonial and post-colonial Africa. Aidoo's feminist concerns are not treated in isolation from Africa's political instability, the new master complex of the so-called elite, the atavistic problems of the rural African at the cross-roads of history, the fury and impotence of the radical African, the lure of the Western world, and so forth. Such problems are all neatly slotted into a cultural matrix often evoked successfully by the writer's rich personal experience.

There are eleven stories in the *No Sweetness Here* collection. Despite the diversity in themes, all the stories are products of an intense involvement not just in the problem of women but the problem of the Black race as a whole. Aidoo herself justifies her involvement in these words: "I cannot see myself as a writer writing about lovers in Accra because, you see, there are so many problems."

Aidoo's plethora of problems is projected by various narrative voices in shifting perspectives. What this approach accomplishes is to make us accept the author as a detached and neutral observer advancing cases for all the underprivileged in society instead of being a solicitor for any special interests. Consequently we are compelled to suspend our own partisan prejudices and look at all the problems from a fresh and correspondingly neutral vantage point. We trust the "unseen" author and concentrate and rely on her created mouthpieces. . . .

The three major sections of *Our Sister Killjoy* merge into each other in whorls. The concerns are the same and the examples used to support those concerns are similar as we shift from one geographical focus to the other. In the final major section, there is greater introspection because of the literary approach—a confrontational "love letter" from Sissie to an imaginary male partner. The letter suggests a way out of the morass—communication between man and woman. The same kind of self search and dialogue is endorsed for similar problems in Ngugi's *A Grain of Wheat*. Such dialogue based on a mutually comprehensible language would then form the secret springboard for the solution of *all* the spiritual and material problems bedeviling the Black world.

Aidoo has dealt with women's problems with arresting wisdom and grace. The conservative dissenter and the radical sympathizer will probably find her approach stimulating. Aidoo's forte is her tremendous *feeling* and honesty of sentiment in expressing those issues. Her works ring like the unimpugnable scold of a justly aggravated parent. "Although writers of both sexes have written about Mother" assesses McCaffrey "the woman writer naturally identifies with her female characters." Aidoo's identification extends beyond "underprivileged womanhood and the arrogance of manhood" to include a variety of social problems across geographical boundaries. Without doubt, like her feminist mouthpiece in her play, *Anowa*, Aidoo has learnt and heard that "in other lands a woman is nothing." Despite that knowledge, "everything counts" in the way she assembles her materials in her short stories and novel, *Our Sister Killjoy*, to register a feminism reasonably in tune with social realities.

Certain problems remain apparent in spite of Aidoo's strengths. It is still difficult to avoid some degree of prejudice and presumption when dealing with issues concerning men and women especially in African societies. We still have to deal with psychological and cultural questions many of which do not appear within the scope of Aidoo's discourse. It is not enough to indicate that if human beings have values placed on their heads, "boys" are always more "costly" than girls. We must be willing to deal with certain root fears and desires. For instance, the predominantly African assumption that women eventually marry and leave their birth families to assist in building their husbands' families. That cultural attitude and the African love for large families still make polygamy possible in so-called modern African societies. We have to deal with the desocialization of traditional African males who still cling to the chauvinistic guns of the past despite changed and changing social relations. We must also extend our attention to certain rural circumstances where social relations remain affected by taxing agrarian occupations which restrict women to specific economic and social positions. Finally, the past is a valid reference point for understanding present reality and projecting future directions. The key to a means for resolving our problems is a reasonable degree of honesty in facing all of those problems. This is where Aidoo takes the lead among other African women in search for social justice through creative literature.

Chinalum Nuankwo. In Carole Boyce
Davies and Anne Adams Graves, eds.
*Ngambika: Studies of Women in African
Literature* (Trenton, New Jersey: Africa
World Press, 1986), pp. 152, 158–59

AKHMADULINA, BELLA (RUSSIA) 1937–

Bella Akhmadulina, unlike Yevtushenko, has written hardly any poetry on political themes. Nor does she hold her readers with striking verse forms, play of words, or sharp dissonances as does Andrei Voznesensky. Bella stands closer to tradition in this respect. And yet her clear, lovely measures are so moving, so fresh, that they seem newly discovered, not at all derivative.

Readers are drawn to Akhmadulina's "everyday life" verse, as they are to the work of other new generation poets, because it has something new to say and new and fresh ways to say it.

Feeling is primary in her poetry. Her verses break from her irresistibly, like molten lava. She likes to write about the intricacy of simple things and the simplicity of intricate things. She does not write with cool objectivity.

Her lines come straight from a young and impassioned heart. They are spontaneous, moving, fashioned with innate artistry. . . .

Akhmadulina also has her excesses. Infatuated with a "newsy" quality in poetry, she sometimes slips into bookishness. In some of her verses there is an overly fond contemplation of feminine weakness and too much in musical phrases and somewhat tired similes. She then has visions of "roving sails," "an ancient park," "a black swan," "the pilgrim at the gates of a temple," the reckless rider who does not heed the woman crying "Love me!"

It is not without reason, therefore, that the critics have taken Akhmadulina to task for a chamber-music quality, a certain "defenselessness" that threatens to vitiate her poetry.

Evgeni Dvornikov. *USSR: Soviet Life Today*. March, 1963, p. 62

In Bella Akhmadulina's love lyrics, the note of despair, at times verging on anachronism, is coupled with a quite old-fashioned pride. And even though she does not yet write as if a lover were looking over her shoulder all the time, there is at least no representative of the Writer's Union. Her small but distinguished body of work shows that she is one of the most promising poets. . . .

Verbiage spoils Bella Akhmadulina's prenatal autobiography just as glaringly. With her Italo-Tartar lineage, this talented poetess could hardly have failed to do something dashing. Not yet an architect, Akhmadulina works unevenly, untidily in spots, and in this long piece, "My Genealogy" ["Moya rodoslovnaya"], attempts to hang the story of her ancestors on a tricky, false, and unnecessary nail of contingency. But the good outweighs the defects. There is a boisterousness about this uneven poem, a bubbling wonderment about life and self, an innocent incestuousness in her intrusion into the matrimonial beds of her interesting grandparents. The lack of fit between design and detail does not spoil the poem. What does is the pomp and falsehood of the inevitable conversation with the reader.

Vera S. Dunham *Slavonic Review*.
March, 1965, pp. 62, 68

Some poets acquire range first and only later master the formal incarnation. Only in some rare cases do both achievements come together. Bella was too young to have any range in her knowledge of the world. She lacked the personal suffering to feel with her own skin "the tragic essence of the world." Of course, she did feel something instinctively, but that did not blend in her with the intimate experiences of a large-eyed girl, with a Komsomol badge and schoolgirl's plaits. But instead she began seriously to study form. In the instability of her gifted sentimental lines something concrete and concise started to appear. Endowed with an amazing poetic ear, Bella grasped the inner law of freshness of rhyme, resilience on rhythm, and delicacy of epithet, and that is one of the most important components of real poetry. She managed to master in only one year as much as I did in at least ten. She learned the charm of grammatical incorrectness which creates a special air in a poem. She understood that sentimentality and metaphors alone cannot get her very far if there is a lack of tension and compactness in her poems. Out of her sleeves, like an enchantress from a Russian fairy tale, she produced a sparkling shower of epithets, rhymes, intonations, images. Formerly her verses merely rustled. Now they started to ring. However, the compactness of the form, still combined with the poverty of the content, as yet could not command faith in her future in the minds of many serious people, although it did raise some hopes.

Her name became known among readers, but for the sake of honesty one has to admit that this was due not to her poems, but to some kind of promise which was contained in them, as well as to her participation in the general wave of Soviet poetry and to other accompanying circumstances.

> Yevgeny Yevtushenko. Introduction to Bella
> Akhmadulina. *Fever and Other New Poems*
> (New York: William Morrow, 1969), p. 3

In Pavel Antokosky's Introduction to her 1975 collection he speaks of Akhmadulina's "strong masculine talent. . . . I don't mean in the craftsmanship, or technique . . . but where it really matters, at the root; in the moral tension of a human being who is growing, even as we look. She is a poet, not a poetess." Many voices would join him in that; and it is, I believe, no accident that it is Bella Akhmadulina who has most boldly taken upon herself the inheritance of her great women predecessors, Anna Akhmatova and Marina Tsvetayeva. Yevtushenko dates her maturity as a poet from the moment she first acknowledged that weight upon her, and singles out particularly her poem "I Swear." From that point on, he says, her own nerves became "the nerves of her age." That poem he claims was "an inner Rubicon . . . after which she felt herself nervously responsible for everything that was, is and shall be." "I Swear" is a poem in which Akhmadulina personified the murderous forces of bureaucratic pettiness as a fairy-tale monster, to which she gives the name Yelabuga, the town where Marina Tsvetayeva took her own life. When she spoke about the poem to me in 1977, she was at pains to point out that the inhabitants of that particular town were of course innocent.

At her finest, Akhmadulina combines a fierce, comic invention with her most passionate utterance: she turns her wit upon herself (as in "Fever"), or upon the complacent materialism of the worldly (in "A Fairy Tale of Rain"), with equal ferocity. Her voice often recalls that of Tsvetayeva in "Praise to the Rich." In many of her poems the figure of the poet is compelled to behave in ways that bring the contempt of more conventional people upon him. . . .

At the center of "A Fairy Tale of Rain," another heroine who feels herself to belong to a world of values ignored in her society finds herself pursued by Rain, which takes many shapes, but always suggests the playful fertility of the human spirit. Whether rain is the gift of poetry or poetry itself, its one determination is to prevent the heroine making a peaceful adjustment to the arid materialism she feels on every side. She has an invitation to a party at a house of considerable splendor, where she knows she will meet hidden disapproval, precisely because she cannot be trusted to behave conventionally. She will be tolerated only because she has a certain fashionable reputation. But the discomfort is mutual. The heroine senses something sinister in the beauty of this house; a corruption in its very perfection of taste. When at last she rings the bell and appears, soaked by the rain, the guests try to bring her close to the fire to dry out. Akhmadulina imagines in their invitation an echo of that medieval hatred and fear of the strange that once had led people to burn witches. Akhmadulina often works best within the context of an extended metaphor. Although many of her short lyrics are tender, she needs space and length to let her voice rise to its true pitch, as it does in the climax of "Rain."

Elaine Feinstein. Introduction to *Three
Russian Poets* (Manchester: Carcanet, 1979),
pp. 13–15

Akhmadulina['s] poetry is not unlike that of Akhmatova in the interesting and original use she makes of concrete things, sometimes very obvious things like aspirin or a motorcycle. Some of her lines give the impression of a carefully controlled and metrically perfect hysteria, a quality not unlike the nervous agitation of Tsvetayeva. One of her best poems was written many years ago and is called "A Fairy Tale about the Rain." In that poem the poet is in conflict with philistines and her inspiration ("the rain") splashes the floors in their fine houses. The "Fairy Tale" is a masterpiece in the tense, high-strung expression of contempt and scorn for the safe, the comfortable, and the obvious. She has a strong sense both of language and structure, and she delights in intricately unusual end-rhymes, some of which have the effect of neat puns. Every line of hers seems a spontaneous *bon mot*.

E. J. Brown. Introduction to Mary
Maddock, ed. *Three Russian Women Poets*
(Trumansberg, New York: Crossing Press,
1983), p. 12

Akhmadulina [like Akhmatova and Tsvetaeova] has had to deal with silence, but coming later she has fared better than earlier poets, for the main terror has perhaps abated. She, at least, has been allowed to publish, although she has been able to join the Writer's Union only as a translator and not as a poet because of her apolitical stance. Her first volume, *Struna (String)*, published in 1962, was criticized by Soviet authorities for being too close to the decadent verse of Akhmatova, whom Akhmadulina admired. The silences with which she has had to deal have been primarily creative; the poet who loses her own voice.

In "Zhaleyka" Akhmadulina expresses her sense of weariness, although she cannot understand its origins. She only knows that it has dried up her creativity: "Forgive me, zhaleyka, / for not singing. / I'm sick and worn out, / I don't know why."

Similarly, in "The last day I live in a strange house," she speaks of an untraced source of sorrow. She should be happy, yet she tells us, "I ache and have no words."

Most often, when Akhmadulina speaks of silence, she speaks of the silence of her Muse. In "Muteness" Akhmadulina tells us of the disappearance of her poetic voice: "I shout, but muteness,/ like vapor, leaves my mouth and curls around my lips." In "Snowless February," Akhmadulina writes, "My handwriting is eaten up and mute./I can't write as I want/ and to write as I can—what good is it?" But her silence, symbolized in this poem by the absence of snow, is broken when the snow finally comes, her life falls into place, and she regains her poetic voice.

Clearly, by contrast with her besieged predecessors, Akhmadulina's problems of speech are neither tragic nor final. She has had the privilege of silences which is the artist's rightful problem, and she has survived, and unlike Akhmatova and Tsvetayeva she has enjoyed an apparently secure popularity in her own country.

Mary Maddock. Introduction to *Three Russian Women Poets* (Trumansberg, New York: Crossing Press, 1983), p. 16

The latest collection of verse by Bella Akhmadulina *Tajna: novye stixi* (Secret: New Poems), typifies the artistic development of this poet, both in terms of presenting her most cohesive collection to date and in terms of unveiling the arena for the second stage of her lyric persona's artistic creation. Observing a degree of continuity with the preceding poetry, the collection features at least fifteen poems from previous collections. Fourteen of the poems are found in the collection *Sny o Gruzii* (Dreams of Georgia), the most extensive collection of Akhmadulina's work. While the opening poem in *Secret* expounds on the secret, the illumination of which occupies a great deal of the collection, it, like the remaining pieces, bears no such title.

As it stands, the collection is intricately interwoven thematically. Some poems are linked openly and sequentially, with their titles clustering around a given theme, such as the moon, space, or the bird-cherry tree. In others the coda of one poem frequently anticipates the subject of a subsequent one, and often the theme enters following its appearance as a motif. . . .

The collection centers on poetic creation, a leitmotif which is no novelty for Akhmadulina; however, in her first stage (the period preceding *Secret*). . . . only certain poems focused on it. Now an entire collection scarcely departs from it. Still, the real newness lies in the direction of the leitmotif's development. Previously, in poems of poetic creation the garnered impressions, experiences, and observations from the energetic, multicolored summer ambience were contemplated with the onset of autumnal rain and the flu. This helped the poet to withdraw temporarily from her friends and obligations to absorb summer impressions. In winter all the colors of nature merged into their all-encompassing color—white—through the arrival of frost, the freezing of water and the restriction of mobility in winter. The color white harbored within itself all the possible colors of the rainbow, which made available their intense exploration. The persona-poet crafted her poetic images, encased, as in a cocoon, in a warm snowbound house with a cricket for "artistic" company, as well as for literary continuity with Pushkin, and a candle for tangible continuity with the heritage of the past. Love lyrics were conspicuously absent in the early thematic cycle of poems on poetic creation, and what had been a trend for a specific cycle now encompasses the entire volume.

> Sonia Ketchian. In Anna Lisa Crone and
> Catherine V. Chvany, eds. *New Studies in*
> *Russian Language and Literature*
> (Columbus, Ohio: Slavica, 1986), pp. 183–84

AKHMATOVA, ANNA (RUSSIA) 1889–1966

The ideology of Anna Akhmatova's *Chetki* [The Rosary] is not clearly thought out. The poetess did not figure herself out, did not, to unite her experiences, place at their center some external fact that does not refer to something understood only by her. In this, she is different from the symbolists. On the other hand, her themes are often not realized within the limits of the given poem. Much in Akhmatova seems unfounded because it is unproven. Moreover, as is the case with the majority of young poets, Anna Akhmatova often utilizes the words "pain," "grief," and "death." This pessimism, so natural and therefore beautiful and youthful, had been until now the property of a "proving pen"; in Akhmatova's poems pessimism has found its place in poetry for the first time. . . .

Akhmatova's book seems exciting and dear to people . . . who are controlled by a deceptive memory and who are wrangling about each stage of the heart they have experienced. It contains the hitherto mute voice of various beings; women who have fallen in love, who are cunning, dreamy, and ecstatic, speak at last in their real and, at the same time, artistically convincing voice. That connection with the world, which I have mentioned before, seems to be the fate of each genuine poet. It is almost attained by Akhmatova because she knows the joy of contemplating the external world and is capable of conveying this joy to us.

> Nikolai Gumilyov. *Apollon.* 5, 1914, p. 36

Akhmatova's diction is characterized by a conscious effort toward the simplicity of colloquial speech and everyday words far removed from the narrow circles of lyric poetry; her syntax gravitates toward the freedom of a living word, not a written one. . . . But this colloquial style never lapses into prosaic expressions but always remains artistically effective. It shows Akhmatova's great artistic mastery; her striving for a pristine simplicity of words; her distrust of unjustified poetic exaggerations, excessive metaphors, and worn-out paths; and her clarity and deliberate precision of expression.

One of the most important characteristics of Akhmatova's poetry is its epigrammatic quality. In this, one can see both an affinity with the French poets of the eighteenth century (as well as French classicism) and a sharp distinction from the musical and emotional lyrics of the romanticists and symbolists. A subtlety of observation and correctness of view, an ability to generalize in a short verbal formula, a completeness of verbal expression— these traits, sharply contrasted to the musical lyricism of the old and new romanticists, are indispensable conditions of the epigrammatic style. Yet there is an important difference between Akhmatova and the French; where in the latter there is only a general judgment—antithetically sharpened and expressed in the form of aphorism employed everywhere and on all occasions independent of the conditions that brought it about—in Akhmatova one could hear the personal voice and sense the personal mood even in the most general aphorisms.

Viktor Zhirmunski. *Russkaya mysl.*
December, 1916, pp. 34–35

Akhmatova, employing the purest literary language of her time, applied with utmost determination the traditional forms of the Russian—and the universal—folk song. In her verses there is no psychological fragmentation at all, but rather the typical parallelism of the folk song, with its strong asymmetry of the two adjacent theses, according to the following scheme: "In the kitchen-garden there is an elder-tree, and in Kiev an uncle." Hence a two-leaved stanza, with the unexpected thrust at the end. Her verses resemble the folk song not only in structure but also in essence: they seem invariably to be lamentations. The poet's purely literary vocabulary, muttered through clenched teeth, makes her especially interesting and allows us to divine a peasant woman in a literary Russian lady of the twentieth century.

Osip Mandelshtam. *Russkoe iskusstvo.*
January, 1923, p. 79

Akhmatova's subject matter is altogether individualistic. The range of her poetry is limited to squalor; it is the poetry of a frenzied lady, dreaming about the boudoir and the chapel. Basic with her are amorous and erotic motifs, intertwined with motifs of sorrow, yearning, death, mysticism, and doom. The feeling of being doomed, an understandable feeling for the social consciousness of a dying group; the gloomy tones of a deathbed hopelessness; mystical experiences, coupled with eroticism—such is Akhmatova's spiritual world, a splinter from the old culture of nobility, the "good old times of

Catherine," which has passed into eternity, never to return. She is not exactly a nun, not exactly a harlot, but rather nun and harlot, with whom harlotry is mixed with prayer. . . .

What has this poetry in common with the interests of our people and state? Exactly nothing. Akhmatova's creative genius is a matter of the distant past; it is alien to the modern Soviet actuality and cannot be tolerated in the pages of our journals. Our literature is not a private enterprise calculated to please the varied tastes of a literary market. We are in no way obliged to provide a place in our literature for tastes and tempers that have nothing in common with the ethics and qualities of Soviet people. What instruction can Akhmatova's works give to our youth? None, besides harm. These works can only sow despondency, low spirits, pessimism, the inclination to turn away from the burning questions of social life and activity for the narrow little world of personal experiences. How is it possible to turn over to her the upbringing of our youth? And yet Akhmatova has been published with great readiness . . . even in separate collections. This is a crude political error.

Andrei Zhdanov. *Zvezda*.
July–Aug., 1946, pp. 10–13

Akhmatova's poetry, particularly in *The Rosary,* has also another peculiarity. It is these unexpected but convincing, illogical but fine psychological transitions from words of emotion to words of description, from the soul to nature, from feeling to fact. She assembles artistically the particulars of a given moment which are often unnoticeable to others; she notices everything anew so that her internal world is not merely framed by the external world, but they combine into one solid and organic wholeness of life. "Her poems are her life." She often compares the present with the past, and the recollections of her youth create nostalgic moods. . . .

Akhmatova is essentially an urban poet, a poet of St. Petersburg. The spring's twilight—"the white nights"—with its melancholy and dreaming on the islands, where the Neva rolls her waves into the sea and where calm and serenity reign; the autumn winds round the Winter Palace, when smoke from the chimneys dances a wild witchdance in the air and the steel grey Neva roars with hidden fury, streaming over the parapet into the streets where disaster awaits the citizens of the capital of Peter the Great; or the cold winter brings down masses of snow from the grimy sky, covering the pavements with a white eider-down over which horse-drawn sleighs glide noiselessly— such are the settings of Akhmatova's poetry. But occasionally her muse carries her to the countryside.

Leonid Strakhovsky. *ASEER*. May, 1947,
pp. 6–7

The subject matter of Anna Akhmatova is feminine, and feminine her attitude toward it. It is almost entirely love, for even when her subject is the absence of love she treats it in terms of love. It is hardly ever happy love, and it is never love in the abstract. It is all occasional; some of her nymph, but of a pious Christian woman, or of a modern, bourgeois lady, simple and direct. She finds love beautiful and terrible for being an all-day reality, an everyday thing: the most intimate of all habits, the daily bread of the soul. The poetess savors the experience of love in all its recurring phases, meeting and separation, distance and absence, desire and longing, jealousy and remorse. Each one of these feelings or events is projected outside, within the visible, objective world and finds forever a local habitation and a name in the place to which it is still connected in the poetess' memory, which turns that place into a kind of private shrine.

Renato Poggioli. *The Poets of Russia*
(Cambridge: Harvard University Press,
1960), pp. 231–32

As a poet Anna Akhmatova combines three qualities: classical austerity, lyrical intensity, and a marked gift for precise and concrete language. The combination of these three qualities is rare if not unique in modern Russian poetry.

Classicism is, as a rule, a cold and generalized affair, dealing in allegories and disdainful of the shapeless variety of life. Nor is lyricism necessarily concrete. Blok, for instance, can rarely be pinned down as to the time, location and sequence of events he describes. Again, realism rarely goes hand in hand with classical simplicity. In Akhmatova all three are effectively combined in one powerful, highly idiosyncratic poetic personality.

The epithet "classical" has nothing self-consciously archaic in Akhmatova's case. The language she uses is the ennobled everyday speech of an educated Russian. So, of course, is Pasternak's poetic language. But there is a clear distinction between Akhmatova's speech and that of Pasternak and Tsvetaeva. These two poets reflect the earthy and folksy Moscow ambience. Akhmatova's restraint and reserve are in the Petersburg tradition. On her own testimony her three masters were Derzhavin, Pushkin, and Annensky— three Petersburg poets from three successive centuries. Primeval chaos is as firmly controlled in Akhmatova's poetry as the Neva is by her granite banks. Her diction is austere and distinct. There is a definite Latin sonority about her verse—surprising as this is in the case of a highly feminine poet. Yet this reserve co-exists with great lyrical passion. In fact it requires all Akhmatova's inborn sense of form and proportion to control the passions fighting their way into her lines.

Victor S. Frank. *Survey*. July, 1966, p. 97

Anna Akhmatova writes about herself, and if her poetry gives us a picture of her country and her epoch, it is through herself that they are seen—an undistorted image, because her vision is clear, her perceptions straight and honest, her sense of actuality very keen. . . . She is her own theme, a Tolstoyan heroine writing of herself, and like a Tolstoyan heroine, responding with tremulous sensitivity to what occurs to her and around her. Her poems are a wonderful self-portrait, drawn from moment to moment, recreating, like a nineteenth-century novel, each scene and event, evoking its atmosphere, and reviving the emotion at its core; but because she is a lyric poet and not a novelist, she is never circumstantial. And she does not distort or exaggerate. In her laconic, understated way, she tells a poignant story of unhappy love, resignation, and profound grief. It is a record of emotions that shape each scene and every event, but are never analyzed or spelled out, never explicitly given but are implicit in details etched on the memory—of a room, an action, a gesture. . . .

Akhmatova has a gift for recreating the painful drama of baffled love, and then of resignation, when her voice strikes a deeper note, and in telling herself that life is easier without love, because insomnia has gone and the pointer that marks the hours on the tower clock is no longer an arrow that threatens death, she is actually underscoring the depth of her loss. Many moods accompany unhappiness, and the love that seemed dead is always there; memory keeps it alive, and there is jealousy, and long, slow, empty days, and the useless question: what did I ever do to have been punished so? Such are Akhmatova's early poems—full of pathos, though not weakness. They are the work of a woman strong enough to be undeceived and of a clear-eyed artist entirely in command of herself, who with a steady hand engraves the image of her unhappiness in lucid, sparse, deep lines.

Helen Muchnic. *Russian Review.*
January, 1967, pp. 17–18

The attitude of the prerevolutionary critics toward Akhmatova's poetry differs from that of the critics after the Revolution. Similarly, in the Soviet period the critics looked upon the poet differently before and after Stalin's death. Outside the Soviet Union the critics, both Russian and foreign, differed sharply with Soviet critics in their evaluation of Akhmatova's contribution to Russian literature. All these differences and changes were brought about not so much by changes in Akhmatova's poetry, of which to be sure there were some, as by the different vantage points of, and changes in, the critics themselves. As is often the case with Soviet writers, their purely literary achievements were accepted or rejected for nonliterary reasons. . . .

While prerevolutionary references to [Akhmatova] are mainly concerned with her new, strong talent and have a relatively easy task because of the single theme of her poetry, later critiques differ sharply in their basic approach. The opponents of the regime tend to see in Akhmatova a victim and a martyr; the proponents of the regime at first reject her, then condescend to accept her into the family. But no matter how all these critics differ in their evaluation of Akhmatova's views or themes, they agree that she is a master of her craft and of the language and that she has decisively contributed to Russian literature. The prerevolutionary critics and those immediately following the Revolution (especially the Formalists) pay much more attention to her purely artistic qualities, while the later critics, both Soviets and émigrés, allow political considerations to govern their judgment and to overshadow their examination and presentation of her works as literary art.

> Vasa D. Mihailovich. *Papers on Language and Literature*. Winter, 1969, pp. 102–3, 110–11

Anna Akhmatova . . . one of the major poets of the century was a contrast to her contemporaries, the symbolist Blok and the futurist Mayakovsky. Her verses when they first appeared in 1912 took deliberate issue with symbolist poetics, rejecting a mystical vocabulary in favor of constituting in poetry the body and texture of real things, their concrete olfactory, visual and auditory existence. She was a contrast to Mayakovsky both in the private, feminine locale of her poems and in the mixed register of her voice. As Chukovsky put it, "Akhmatova is shrouded in silence, in whispered, almost inaudible words. Mayakovsky shouts like a thousand-throated public square." She offers herself as a contrast and corrective both to "otherworldliness" and to the raucous "macho" make believe of Mayakovsky.

> E. J. Brown. Introduction to Mary Maddock, ed. *Three Russian Women Poets* (Trumansberg, New York: Crossing Press, 1983), p. 11

Anna Akhmatova endured two long periods of official silence in her career: 1923–1940 and 1946–1951, during which she was not allowed to publish her work. After a period of acceptance during World War II, she was expelled from the Writer's Union, the organization to which Soviet writers must belong to be recognized and published. In 1946 a party edict condemned her verse on the grounds that it was autobiographical, intimate and emotional. The personal quality of her lyrics, so out of place in an impersonal revolutionary regime, made them, Zhdanov claimed, "decadent and capable of corrupting Soviet youth." He stated that her work was "devoid of substance and alien to the Russian people."

For much of her life, Akhmatova lived in internal exile. Her room and telephone were monitored; she was isolated from friends and family and was constantly watched by the secret police. Her son, Lev, was imprisoned on three separate occasions as a result of Stalinist purges. Yet despite efforts to silence her, Akhmatova continued to write if not publish, regardless of repression and the efforts of her second husband, V. K. Shileyko, who burned her poems and forbade her to write. It was not until 1958, when she was rehabilitated, that Soviet audiences could again read the works of this essential twentieth-century poet.

The silences recorded in Akhmatova's poetry are not only political but also personal. At times, she chooses silence. More frequently, a violation of friendship imposes silence upon her, as in "On a White Night," when her lover fails to come. The silence at the core of human nature is often her theme: our loneliness and essential isolation, despite emotional and physical closeness. "In intimacy," she tells us, "there's a secret place/even passion cannot penetrate."

Mary Maddock. Introduction to *Three Russian Women Poets* (Trumansberg, New York: Crossing Press, 1983), pp. 13–14

The subject of religion in Akhmatova's poetry has been under discussion for most of the sixty or so years since she began to publish her poems, and it has proved to be highly contentious. "If literary criticism lacked example for striking diversity of opinion on a single subject, the peculiar religiosity of Akhmatova's poems would provide an excellent one," writes Sam Driver. And indeed, it is impossible to read Akhmatova's poems without reflecting on the role of religion within them. As Driver remarks, "even in frankly religious verse, such an abundance of Biblical and liturgical images might seem extreme." Almost immediately after the appearance of Akhmatova's first book of poems in 1912, critics took up the challenge of defining the place and type of religion in her work. . . .

Most of [her early] poems constitute fragments of the heroine's speech, mainly in the form of monologue. However, Akhmatova sometimes introduces dialogue as well, reproducing, for example, conversations between the heroine and her lover, or remarks made to the heroine by Nature, or even by inanimate objects. The overall effect is of reading extracts from the heroine's diary or from her private correspondence, and no doubt it was the combination of narrative and conversational style which led Pasternak to speak of the grains of prose in her poetry, and Mandelshtam to emphasize Akhmatova's debt to the tradition of the nineteenth-century Russian novel.

At the center of the monologue stands the heroine herself. Details of her appearance and past history are supplied, but the heroine never speaks about her feelings. These we intuit from her words, from her tone of voice, from descriptions of her movements and gestures, and from what we understand to be the significance of her physical surroundings. As Gumilev writes, "she almost never explains, she shows." She is, therefore, both present and absent at the center of the account which is, in Zhirmunsky's words "spiritually severe and chaste," devoid of self-pity.

The subject matter of the poems is the heroine's inner world, to which we penetrate through her accounts of various events in her life. Each individual poem recounts one incident in her search for love, though it is never related in its entirety, for we are shown only one particularly agonizing moment, the pain of which can be judged from the fact that the words spoken imprint themselves on the heroine's mind with such clarity that she can report them verbatim. The moment of crisis consists in an emotional conflict, and thus it sheds light on the hero and heroine, but thanks to the incomplete narration, light is shed only to the degree that Akhmatova chooses.

The heroes of the poems are described only by the heroine, in relation to her, and in terms of her feelings about them. Their qualities are ascribed to them by the heroine, and they have no independent or continuous existence. Symptomatically, they have no names. When they speak with the heroine, the conversation is invariably dislocated, and hero and heroine misunderstand and contradict one another. Their words given an impression of tension, sometimes of tragedy: hence the conflicts and crises which punctuate the poems.

These conflicts and crises are all much alike, but otherwise similar incidents are differentiated by the settings in which they occur. The material objects concerned have exactly the same circumscribed existence as the heroes, but by virtue of their association with some critical moment in the drama, they come to symbolize its emotional content, or even the complete event.

Some of the feelings connected with the central incident are transient, and others are lasting, and the complexity of its perception is maintained in the poem. The moment is shown both as it happens, and as something which is already in the past—hence Akhmatova's intricate use of tenses. Rather than unfolding the course of the action, the poem superimposes one view of it on another, usually with the heroine's commentary on what is shown.

This structure has clear consequences for the tone of the narrative, which combines emotional speech with more restrained narration. The underlying tone is often tragic, and the gradations of tone are always subtle: Akhmatova avoids emotional outbursts.

Her narrative method is also refined. It is often not clear to whom the heroine's words are addressed, in what tone of voice she is speaking, or what role is being played by the hero. Indeed, Vinogradov calls Akhmatova's poetry "a poetry of hints, of emotional reticence, of vague indications." It is as if the heroine were describing events for those who are close to her and who do not, therefore, require explanation of details: the reader, overhearing, as it were, remains uninitiated. The heroine remains reserved, and is well defended against the reader's intrusion into her private world, even though she ostensibly reveals it to him. . . .

The poems are the heroine's attempt to make sense of lived experience. They are quiet statements of partial and isolated insights into the meaning of existence. They proceed through a constant variation of the theme of the heroine's unhappiness in love, gradually elaborating a system of symbols, and investing each with new depths of meaning.

> Wendy Rosslyn. *The Prince, the Fool and*
> *the Nunnery: Religious Themes in the Early*
> *Poetry of Anna Akhmatova* (Avebury,
> England: Avebury, 1984), pp. 5, 22–24, 28

The poetry of Anna Akhmatova contained in the three short works *Beads, The White Flock,* and *Anno Domini* creates the impression of a single volume. It can all be held in the hollow of one's hand like a bird whose heartbeat thumps against the palm.

Over there an entire generation was entranced by her verses. For that generation—now dispersed and decimated—poetry was a kind of noble craftsmanship. What united the youth of St .Petersburg—more headstrong than ardent—was not a literary society, but a mastership, guild.

The master craftsman was Nikolai Gumilev, the poet murdered by the Cheka, and he ruled his guild with an iron rod. Subordination, disciplined effort, and intellectual clarity were the staunch virtues the proprietor exacted from his labor of poetic renewal.

In this versification factory . . . among the twenty-year-old academicians (who were more punctilious than precocious), Anna Akhmatova represented inspiration plain and simple, that priceless contraband prohibited by their doctrine. . . .

Not a single cerebral constraint interfered with her inspiration. She was free in the sense that she obeyed only her impulses. And, by turns, she was whimsical and plaintive, sensual and penetent, Siren and Beguine, vampire and victim, that is, nothing other than a woman giving vent to her amorous sorrows. . . . To explain [the poems] is to undo them. Remarks about prosody and lists or statistics of imagery only misrepresent a poem by arbitrarily fragmenting an indissoluble whole. . . .

Akhmatova writes in Russian. In order to examine her poems they must be translated, that is, rationalized by placing all the sense on the significance, by substituting logically ordered references for mysterious incantations ripe for discussion, by calling intelligible that which is more suggestive than anything else. And in so doing, the poetic mood is not only decreased, but deformed. . . .

Thus, having renounced an examination of verbal expression, we are left to enumerate the themes of her poems, to describe the anxiety that pours forth, and to count the beats of the heart via those of the rhyme. To say "themes" is perhaps excessive. Let us say "the" theme, the one and only theme from Sappho to Akhmatova: love. And for love there exists but a single, sorrowful epilogue: the lament of the forsaken. . . .

The blood that gushes from her torn breast and colors her pale lips blends—in her verses—"with that of others," spilled on her account. Her muse is both a sweet companion with golden tread and a black beggar. Her soul vagabonds throughout the granite parapets above the Neva in St. Petersburg—that city of glory and sorrow—and along the golden shoal of the Crimean Sea where she spent her childhood. She extolled the "vagrants and sinners" of Russian bohemia at the famed cabaret the Stray Dog in St. Petersburg, a phantom city built on a marsh where one has but to descend a few paces to be swallowed up forever. And, to rouse the chimes of the white orthodox churches, she finds the tones of angels.

Her name itself sounds strange. Is she a Russian poet or a Tatar horsewoman? Everything about her has a double meaning, right up to her appearance. Her excessively thin waist and her acrobatic suppleness give way more and more to a monastic rigidity. Her aquiline nose, the pale greenish tint of her hollow, drawn face—are these the features of a witch ready for the pyre or a deaconess ready to don a hair shirt once again? Only her verses contain a clue about the contents of the labyrinth in her flat, cavernous breast. And I cannot quote them! For a calque will not allow us to breathe the perfume of this plague-stricken flower.

André Levinson. *Chicago Review.* 34, 1984,
pp. 74–76, 78

ALEGRÍA, CLARIBEL (NICARAGUA–EL SALVADOR) 1926–

Claribel Alegría was born in 1926. A year later, Augusto Cesar Sandino initiated what became, in 1961, the Sandinista movement. Sandino, outraged at the willingness of some of his compatriots to collaborate in the subordination of their country to business enterprises of the United States, gathered together a small band of peasants and began a six-year campaign which ended, as he had promised, when the last Marine left Nicaraguan soil. Official United States documents began by referring to him as a "bandit," ended by calling him a "guerilla fighter."

Alegría's poetic and political consciousness, which did not find its way into print until the 1950s, emerged from the experience of exile in her childhood. When she was nine months old, her father was forced into exile. The family moved to El Salvador, her mother's birthplace, where she grew and took up citizenship. Her Nicaraguan origin, nevertheless, shaped her identity. The times through which she has lived, her travels, and her literary work have led her to an internationalism of a revolutionary Hispanic cast. After the triumph of the Sandinistas, she and her husband, Darwin Flakoll, spent six months traveling throughout Nicaragua, gathering information and seeing and hearing from people firsthand, for a five-hundred-page book they are now writing.

Alegría's exile and return runs parallel to the history of *Sandinismo,* that is, the Sandinist resistance movement. One of the short poems entitled "Time," in *I Survive* can be seen in that light:

> I walked around
> my past
> my future
> and suddenly my present
> took fire.

This almost lifelong exile taught perseverance and gave perspective. From her experience, Alegría fashioned an epic vision whose sweep encompasses pre-Columbian myths and finds in geography and landscape sources for interpreting the grotesque reality of contemporary Latin America. In "Estelf," she describes the harshness and bitterness of this reality in a poem about Estelf, the town where she was born, and its river:

> your channel has been filled.
> With mud and blood
> it has been filled
> with empty cartridges
> with shirts
> pants
> and corpses
> sticking like algae
> to the rocks.

An encompassing mythic and social vision characterizes "Flowers of the Volcano." Like the political poetry of Pablo Neruda and César Vallejo, of León Felipe and Ernesto Cardenal, and like the murals of José Clemente Orozco and David Alfaro Siqueiros, "Flowers of the Volcano" is eclectic and panoramic, ethical and impure. It conjoins the pre-Columbian past and our postindustrial epoch of Toyotas and televisions; the masses of men, women, and children who descend in a red wave assert the continuity of humanity and its primacy. Specific historical and geographical references both serve as backdrop and stand in high relief: Central American history has been dramatically affected by its geography, and geography becomes a metaphor for historical events.

From the craters of the volcanos fiery lavas have erupted as have social upheavals. Alegria's description of the children sent from their hideout homes in the volcano to sell flowers and deliver messages to clandestine workers in towns and cities reveals the tenacious spirit of resistance inspired by Sandino which the Somozas never succeeded in crushing. Alegría sketches Latin America's history of imperialist devastation. She tempers the drama with ironically humorous treatment of the hurricanes and earthquakes that make Central America tremble.

The deaths caused by the Somoza carnage are made bearable and comprehensible only by analogy. Alegría explains the price of the inevitable victory of a long-suffering people through the myth of Chac and Tlaloc. In the myth, the yearly ripening of crops and the renewed lease on the planet depended on the sacrifice of human blood. (The lunar calendar carved in stone reflects the cyclical concept of time held by many indigenous groups. Each one hundred years, the earth was to come to an end; permission for another cycle had to be assured through human sacrifices.)

I Survive, the collection that includes "Flowers of the Volcano," asserts the strength of human life and mourns human suffering. The title refers both to the daily act of surviving and to the miracle and the guilt of surviving in our times. Alegría has felt in her flesh and in her verse the death of more than forty thousand of her compatriots. When writing her earlier books, her anguish about Central America was perhaps too close; she turned to Auschwitz and Hiroshima as symbols and intimations of present horrors and those to come.

"Flowers of the Volcano" and six other poems in *I Survive* draw directly on Spanish American politics, reminiscences of family, exile, and death. "Sorrow," the longest poem—dedicated to guerilla-poet Roque Dalton—evokes with chilling immediacy the murdered, the imprisoned, the tortured, and the "disappeared." These themes are underscored by quotations from García Lorca, Antonio Machado, Miguel Hernández, Pablo Neruda, and a popular Argentine tango.

Alegría's earlier poetry established an approach to personal themes still visible in her work, a distilled and abstracted simplicity, as in "I Expected to Spend my Time." This simplicity now allows her to interweave powerfully complex historical and personal themes. Nine of the twenty-three poems in the book are composed of fewer than eight lines:

> I expected to spend my time
> loving
> and being loved.
> I began to realize
> that I spent it shattering
> while I in turn was
> sh
> at
> ter
> ed

Through her poetry, Alegría demonstrates how hard survival is, how enmeshed her life has been with the lives of those who must persevere removed from the immediate ongoing struggle.

Electa Arenal. *Feminist Studies.* 7, 1981,
pp. 20–23

Claribel Alegría has published nine books of poetry to date, but the early ones (ingenuous lyricism with traditional rhythms and forms) certainly did not anticipate the dense and original expression that begins to mature starting with *Huesped de mi tiempo* (1961) and *Via unico* (1965) and that reaches fulfillment in *Pagare a cobrar* (1973), *Sobrevivo* (*I Survive*, 1978), and the unpublished (or hitherto uncollected) poems that appear at the end of this collection *(Suma y Sigue).* . . .

Evidently, in most of the poems, the poet starts from a personal anecdote (or one incorporated into her memory) that she does not recount; at best she condescends to give some hints. She begins to write starting from a supposition: that the reader knows the truth or should know it or perhaps guesses

it. In this way, her poems are lyrical or psychological or metaphysical commentaries on episodes or faces or landscapes that remain outside the common
reader's range of inquiry. For this reason, starting from each poem, the reader
can construct his or her own, that is, his or her own interpretation.

Claribel Alegría's hermeticism is different from other hermeticisms in
that it does not always appear as such; on the contrary, it allows the reader
to make his or her own key and become the possessor of the secret. Nonetheless, certain signals do come through the feelings. Feelings, in this poetry,
are sort of road signs that lead to the nucleus of inspiration, to the human
and female being who offers the existential raw materials to an intellect that
desires to become essential but that fortunately does not succeed. . . .

Her people, this extraordinary Salvadoran people that unbelievably
struggles and dies and is reborn and returns to the struggle for its liberation,
she has not just turned into the irreplaceable rationale for her rich days
(Claribel is certainly one of the Salvadoran intellectuals who participate most
actively in the indispensable task of explaining to the world, in all sorts of
forums, the causes and goals of this rebellion with a cause, this struggle
without quarter), but also the principal subject of her poetry.

Poems like "Desde el puente" or "La mujer de rio Sumpal" could not
have been written without this strong linkage, without this deep understanding of a divided sound, and the reader of this collection can surely verify that
neither political denunciation nor solitary gesture have marred the formal
rigor or the strictly poetic level of this unique work. Unexpectedly, the poet
has retained much of the fervor, the energy, the original impetus that illuminated her poems of twenty years back. Claribel, who was always able to
transcribe the constancies of love and life, now also succeeds in reuniting
and revealing them in her transcendental patriotic ceremonial.

Mario Benedetti. Introduction to Claribel
Alegría. *Suma y sigue* (Madrid: Visor, 1981),
pp. 9–11, 15–16

"I have no *fusil* [rifle] in my hand, but only my testimony." Her hands sculpt
her language as she speaks. . . . "I was asked what I would have done if we
[writers] had been issued rifles. I explained that I could not take up the gun,
that I would not be good with a gun. I would have asked for bandages and
medicines instead—this is one thing I know how to use. The other is the
word."

The ink of memory washed in blood, clouds that are wrapped around
the open wounds of the *Cordillera*. Claribel Alegría is a poet who has called
herself a cemetery, willing to provide herself as a resting place for those
whose bodies have never been recovered, the friends whose flesh has been
mutilated beyond recognition. They are the dead who have become "too
many to bury," who do not cease to exist and who seem to besiege surviving
poets with pleas to witness on their behalf, to add their names to a litany
and, in so doing, illuminate a senseless brutality.

These poems are testimonies to the value of a single human memory, political in the sense that there is no life apart from our common destiny. They are poems of passionate witness and a confrontation. Responding to those who would state that politics has no place in poetry, that expressions of the human spirit in art should be isolated in aesthetics, she would add her voice to that of Neruda's: *we do not wish to please them.*

In her poems, we listen to the stark cry of the human spirit, stripped by necessity of its natural lyricism, deprived of the luxuries of cleverness and virtuosity enjoyed by poets of the north. It is enough that the poet succeed in denying herself any justifiable indulgence.

In translating the work of contemporary Latin Americans, it is marginally possible to reproduce essential content, but in altering substance, there are always precipitates: those of music and atmosphere specifities of tone. . . .

But in these we are not talking about the real difficulty—that of translating the human condition, the reality of one world, so that it may be intelligible to those of a world which has been spared its harshness.

Claribel Alegría's memory is suffused with death, the recurring vision of a young poet whose waterlogged body never washed ashore. She echoes the primitive wisdom: *there are lies more believable than the truth.* The cries of those who vanish assail her with accounts of torture and disappearance. . . . Her poetry fills with verdant jungles, volcanos, the glow of their craters, the spillage of black rock; with olive trees twisted by time, trees that are wisely neglected to assure that their fruit will be moist and firm. We are immersed in memories of crumbling aristocratic elegance: French wines, leather-spined books, English roses that have since been supplanted for her by flowers splashing down the volcanos in the arms of *campesino* children.

She carries within her the heavy, ancient blood of the Pipiles and laces her language with a mestizo richness, words like the stones of a land where mystery is still palpable. She is attentive to her dreams, trusting them for news of her homeland, and she is comfortable with the deceased, with the powers of amulets and herbs and the gift of understanding the language of coincidence and omen. . . .

In these poems, we have her account of her search for the grave of Garcia Lorca in Andalusia, undertaken while Franco was still alive. An impossible search. We are invited to explore the candlelit village of Santa Ana where she spent her childhood, a place stripped of hope now, strafed by DDT and altered by the calm history of disintegration. We glimpse condors, tangos, the smoke of *copal,* a particular kind of light, *izote,* the constant presence of death, the face of an assassin transformed by traffic lights until he is seen as one of the many faces of his kind.

The poet is finally silenced herself, taking on the persona of the imprisoned, where she continues her poem "with tears, with fingernails and coal—the poem we are all writing."

Carolyn Forché. Preface to Claribel Alegría.
Flowers from the Volcano (Pittsburgh:
University of Pittsburgh Press, 1982),
pp. xi–xiv

Claribel Alegría's report on the condition of women in El Salvador offers a detailed and highly informative picture of the phenomenon. . . . [of] how, where poverty and injustice reign, women are the most victimized. Girls sent to make a living in the city where, seduced at an early age, they have no alternative but to become prostitutes, daughters deprived by their fathers of an education which might enable them to become economically independent, until the day they get married, passing from one system of patriarchy to another, are both the product of the process of oppression which generates more oppression. It is the same social situation which is exemplified by the last episode of Rosario Castellanos's story "Modesta Gomez." At the lowest level of this system of hierarchy is the mother who repeats the centuries-old rite of clitoridectomy on her baby daughter so that she will be less likely to go off with a man at an early age and will, instead, be prepared "to work harder." Thus, woman perpetuates the tradition of female victimization.

Claribel Alegría, whose commitment to the cause of women is clearly revealed in her report, is also a poetess and prose writer. In her book *El detén,* published in 1977, figure three women; a nun, Sor Mary Ann, Natalia, a divorcee sexually infatuated with Mark, and Karen, her 15-year-old daughter. Karen is studying in a convent where she has been sent by her father so that her education can be carried out without overburdening his responsibilities and, at the same time, away from the dangerous influence of Mark. It is through the perspective of the adolescent's feverish imagination that we are acquainted with the events which take place around her. "There can be many realities; besides the one we touch there is also the one we dream and the one we invent," states Karen.

The girl's mischievous manipulation of the people around her and her insight into the multiple levels at which they exist create a disturbingly lucid portrayal of the psychology of adults and of their relationships. We see how Mark takes advantage of Natalia's passionate attachment to him and revels in being cruel and in tantalizing her by his attentions to Karen, whose budding womanhood stimulates his sexual appetites; and how the tight-lipped nun, to whose special care Karen has schemingly entrusted herself, is both shocked and excited by the episodes which the girl narrates with apparent candor: "What did you feel when Mark touched you?" she morbidly asks. "Men are like animals. . . ."

At the end of the book, both Natalia and the nun have reached a state of moral disintegration: Natalia utterly subjugated by her lover, the nun totally corrupted by the desire which the recounting of the girl's experiences has awoken. While a fleeting vision of the adolescent's future reveals the traumatic and warping effects of her early exposure to Mark's corrupting influence; Mark, on the other hand, appears to survive unscathed.

Claribel Alegría, though born in Nicaragua, was brought up in El Salvador, with which she feels closer emotional links. Now resident in Mallorca, she has returned to her country of adoption and become involved in its people's struggle for justice and freedom, as shown by her report on women. The oppression of the government and the exploitation and persecution of the peasants on behalf of the military now trained and supported by the US Army are the themes of some of her later poems. "La mujer del rio Sumpul," for example, describes at length the ordeal of a peasant woman who, having lost husband and sons in the battle, escapes from the guards and hides herself and her two youngest children by the water of the river Sumpul; her wounds are bleeding, her babies on the verge of crying and alerting the soldiers, while vultures fly low over their heads. The poetic language flows easily, like the waters of the river, like the language of the people sharing the fight of the guerrilla movement, whose life (as the history of all mesoamerican nations) blends with myths. A mythology of fierce gods and of angry volcanoes, a history of aggression and rebellious resistance which like pouring lava silently invades the "pueblo incandescente" (the aroused people).

Elsewhere, we read a brief poem, "Por las noches," in which Claribel Alegría evokes in her sleep the images of dead friends and wonders upon awakening whether they also have dreamt of her. Again, as in *El detén,* we find the allusion to realities beyond our perception; but the barrier between living and dead is broken, for the dead awake and share the dreams and aspirations of the living.

Psiche Hughes. In Mineke Schipper, ed.
Unheard Words: Women and Literature in Africa, the Arab World, Asia, the Caribbean, and Latin America (London: Allison and Busby, 1985), pp. 239–42

In a poem in her 1978 book *I Survive,* Claribel Alegría characterizes her writing as "a collection of ghosts." In another poem, the dead populate the discourse as if it were a cemetery. . . .

In this collection of poems [Letras de emergencia (stuffed with the dead)], the title suggests that incorporating or inscribing death is a way to survive. . . .

In *I Survive,* this sociocritical deconstruction of the subject is incorporated, but, far from providing an alternative to the alienating nature of death that could motivate the dissolution of the subject, it functions as a fetishizing negativism that turns the subject into a sort of desensitized similacrum before the "stench of dispossession" that institutionalized terror and consumer exude. . . .

Only in a recent documentary narrative—*They Won't Take Me Alive: The Salvadoran Woman in Struggle* (1983), where the woman becomes conscious of the situation and joins with a popular struggle, do the conditions exist for turning the dissolving or disappearing subject into the emerging subject. The solitary alienation of *Via unico* and the similcrum of "des/pe/da/za/do" in *I Survive* are transformed into the commitment to solidarity in the face of death in *They Won't Take Me Alive.*

They Won't Take Me Alive thus encounters a narrative articulation appropriate to overcome the dead ends in the earlier poetry collections and narratives. Before the emptiness of Carmen, who is the reflection of an alienated and alienating society and family, Eugenia opens up her own space in the struggle to de-alienate society, to create new forms of social organization, to inspire the development of an emerging subject. This is also the feeling and the function of Claribel Alegría's "emergency letters," which thereby take an active part in the struggle for power of a free and unalienated people.

George Yudice. *Revista Iberoamericana.* 51, 1985, pp. 53–64

ALERAMO, SIBILLA (ITALY) 1876–1960

The making of Sibilla Aleramo was, in the beginning, the work of Giovanni Cena (1870–1917). A poet and a novelist whose *Gli ammonitori* (1904) would win the ecstatic praise of Maxim Gorky and gain him a wide international reputation, Cena wielded a powerful influence in Italian literary life as editor in chief of the *Nuova Antologia,* beginning in 1902. He had met Aleramo in 1899 when she was Rina Pierangeli Faccio, editor of a Milanese feminist journal, *L'Italia Femminile.* At twenty-three she was ravishingly beautiful, with literary gifts that any aspiring writer might envy. She was also suffering acute depression over a loveless marriage to a man who had raped her at fifteen and later had gotten her with child. Scarcely more than a child herself, Rina sustained a double shock from this brutal attack: not only were her romantic sensibilities about love violated and permanently injured, but the ensuing marriage plunged her, a Piedmonteste by birth, into the primitive world of the Italian Marches. In 1887 her father had moved the family from Milan to Porto Civitanova on the Adriatic coast, near Porto Recanati, where he managed a glassworks. Enlightened and iconoclastically progressive by late-nineteenth-century Italian standards, he imparted his advanced views to the adored Rina. Even after the removal to Porto Civitanova, she continued to live in an oasis of northern Italian culture and values. Marriage to the man who had raped her, one of her father's local employees, deprived her of this parental shelter, and direct exposure to provincial mores chilled her soul. . . .

A Woman is an artistic rendering of Rina Pierangeli Faccio's escape from the graveyard of her fears to freedom. The symbol of that transition was a name change: Sibilla Aleramo. . . .

Hardly had Aleramo left home than she began to write about why it had been necessary for her to leave. *A Woman* took shape around this necessity. . . .

Cena aided her through the entire literary process, from outline to published book. She never forgot him for this, or forgave him, either. True, "he had made opportune observations, indicating . . . where it was necessary to abbreviate and to develop," but Cena was also responsible for a decision that she regretted for the rest of her life. He prevailed upon her to change the ending of *A Woman.* She had originally closed the book with a candid confession of all her motives in leaving home, including the love affair with Damiani. However, Cena sensed correctly that the moral force of *A Woman* would be diminished if public attention were distracted by the all-too-familiar device in Italian fiction of an adulterous triangle. He strongly urged her to end the novel on a lofty moral tone, revealing the "naked relentless conscience of a woman facing herself, with a duty toward herself." Aleramo yielded to her lover on this point with extreme reluctance, remembering in 1939 that "by mutilating the truth" she had experienced a sense of committing a sin. In her old age she preferred to believe, with her usual spite toward ex-lovers, that Cena was only interested in protecting his male vanity because he wanted no one to know his mistress had loved anyone before him. In reality, however, the enormous success of *A Woman,* together with its continuing worldwide appeal, suggest that Cena the critic never gave any writer better advice than he did his reluctant protégée.

Richard Drake. Introduction to Sibilla
Aleramo. *A Woman* (Berkeley: University of
California Press, 1980), pp. vii, xiii–xiv, xvi

In the case of *A Woman,* the story presents the contemporary reader with a situation that we may define as that of an unhappy marriage, a situation to which the reader is quite familiar and which she hears discussed all the time without the dramatic tone that such a subject could still evoke only a few years ago. . . .

In short, feminism has reached a stage of diffusion *as a problem* (it's not up to us here to discuss its theoretical results and history) that is without precedent in history for the way its tentacles have reached into every home, every school, every public and private debate. . . .

Sibilla Aleramo's *A Woman* would not have been written, perhaps, without the first wave of women's struggle for emancipation, their first resistance to social inequality. Nonetheless, we must not assume that feminism at that time was as widespread and significant as a cultural phenomenon as it is in our time. In the literary realm at that time, the heroines of novels bore very little resemblance to Ibsen's Nora who was, nonetheless, Aleramo's principal model for her first novel. . . .

Its austere language, "passionate" but at the same time restrained, its flat narrative with scrupulous attention to chronology of an experience that was all the more bitter and painful in that it was *not* extraordinary made *A Woman* a document, a manifesto, the testimony of a conscious martyrdom lived outside of all rhetoric, something, therefore, very different from the romanticized, pastel-colored story that the pulp repertoire offered vis à vis the phenomenon of female emancipation.

It can be said that *A Woman* is the story of a bad marriage entered into in order to escape the loneliness of another bad marriage, that of the parents. The author underlines the fact that the case is *not* accidental or isolated, but rather a link in a very particular chain: a procession of women who have sacrificed everything for the family passes before the reader's eyes from the novel's first page to its last. The sense of solidarity is gradually cemented in the protagonist, and, in the process, the distant, unfocused image of the mother takes on its clear outlines through a series of identifications, first on the emotional level (the protagonist, in the moments of greatest suffering in her married life, finds herself calling on her mother rather than the father whom she loved so much in childhood) eventually thought-out and rational (she finds a letter in which her mother indicates she is planning to leave the family for the good of all concerned, a decision that only the daughter will actually implement as we know, at the end of the novel).

Along with her identification with her mother, there begins a process of personality integration for the protagonist, whose result, however, is neither repetition of the same destiny of passivity and self-negation nor the purely liberatory desire of adolescence. This mother who is within us, the author seems to be saying, this being who has been weakened by oppression and blinded by the ideology of sacrifice, *must be loved.* The indifference that her young daughter shows to her mother during adolescence seals both of their dooms.

Perhaps her daughter's understanding would have prevented the mother's madness, and a mother capable of intention and volition would not have allowed her daughter to set out on the series of mistakes caused by her isolation. It is nonetheless clear that the play of identification between mother and daughter is not limited to these pragmatic considerations of practical interaction ("I will advise you and you will be my staff in old age"), but has a far greater symbolic weight. Integration of the personality becomes for Aleramo integration, as well, of her own situation into the historic female condition: once more the personal and the social tend to become one and to constitute, together, the basis for struggle.

Maria Pia Pozzato. Il Castoro. 161, May,
1980, pp. 45–47, 54–55

Within Sibilla Aleramo's literary output, the two volumes of her diary, the first of them published by Tumminelli in 1945, when the author was still alive, and the second turned over to Feltrinelli in 1955 in exchange for a pension that at last gave Sibilla a certain economic security and published [after her death] in 1978, deserves some separate discussion, if only in the expository sense. The second volume, "the ideal sequel to *A Woman,*" as the critics basically defined it, achieved great public success (more than five thousand copies sold within a few months), which would certainly have made up to Aleramo for the bitterness of the scant recognition that, after the first novel, her work received, particularly from official literary circles.

Even if the renewed interest in the writer is chiefly marked by the revival of *A Woman,* which has been adapted for television and reprinted to attract a female readership, these connections only confirm the contemporary nature of her literary and ideological notions of the interpenetration of art and life.

Obviously, when discussing an author who passed away only a few years ago and who was very active artistically and politically up to the end, it is not appropriate to speak of a rediscovery; it seems to us more properly to be an observation of the new perspective that characterizes the reading of her work, so as in a sense to do justice to Sibilla's own aspirations, even though it is an expression of a cultural and ideological situation that is profoundly different from the one in which Sibilla lived her experiences as woman and writer.

And the autobiographical nature of all her work seems to us one of its most contemporary features, since it is characteristic of so much literary discussion and debate, mainly though not exclusively as an expression of the feminist movement, which was the first to identify the "personal" as a locus of reflection and struggle in contrast to more traditional ones. . . .

By using history to explain or simply to "accompany" the contemporary flowering of "telling one's life," maintaining as a basis the now-historical thinking of Aleramo and *her* contemporaries, we can trace the modalities of the emergence of the "I" as an object of the discourse of the recent philosophic and literary past. We can find within it an "ideological" rendering of romanticism, a scientific basis in Freud, an artistic sanctification in Proust. But the discourse would become too broad, necessarily generic, demanding.

What seems more interesting to us is a brief reflection on the "need for truth," the "passion for the real" that characterizes the approach devoted to everything that in some way "reproduces" that which exists—all in a game of mirrors that is hard to unravel and whose signs include . . . the kind of success ordained for books like Sibilla's *Diary*.

Its "contemporariness" has been identified above all as residing in the relationship it constantly attempts between dailiness, "life," always marked by passion, and the need to make writing, "art," out of it.

Isabella Pezzini. Il Castoro. 161, May, 1980,
pp. 9–10

Yes to the Earth represents, in our opinion, the moment of Sibilla's poetic maturation. In this collection, the phoneticolinguistic aspect of the work runs parallel to a current that is pregnant with meaning. . . .

Sibilla's lyric inspiration, which became increasingly pressing and inclusive over time, now brings forward universal themes. Nature with its multifarious aspects is included as a whole in an Earth with a capital E, which in turn is set within the astronomical system. . . . The lyrics are centered once more on a dialogue whose participants are the human soul, accessible and effusive as Sibilla's soul always was, and the Earth, as indifferent as her cruel lovers were. . . . The verb "to laugh" serves to express the evocation of a serene and joyous nature, but also to illustrate the irreconcilable contract between our unhappy destiny and occasional—if buffoonlike—moments of splendor.

Maria Federazioni. *Il Castoro*. 161, May, 1980, pp. 103–8

The events described in the novel do not vary significantly from those in Aleramo's diaries and other autobiographical works. Although the book is partly the tale of Aleramo's contact with extensive social and cultural changes which took place at the turn of the century, [*A Woman*] draws mainly from the author's personal sphere, from the facts of her childhood and adolescence, marriage, maternity, and subsequent separation from husband and son. Aleramo describes, in a first person narration, the painful transitions and disappointments a young, nameless protagonist experiences and her floundering attempts to be freed from family ties to an overbearing father, a provincial industrialist in the Marche, and a distraught mother, who has been forced to accept the humiliation and pain of her husband's adulteries. By defending her mother, the young woman loses the love of the father she idolizes and who had overseen her liberal education. Alone, she accepts the courtship of a young man in her father's employ. The first part of the novel portrays the protagonist coming to terms with "un'esistenza tragicamente mutata," the sudden, violent loss of her virginity, and her growing abhorrence of what has happened to her when she is forced to marry the clerk after a year. The narrative takes on an anxious, claustrophobic quality as she describes her solitude, her husband's violent jealousy, and her growing repulsion and fear. Unable to accept this life, the protagonist begins, in the second of three sections of the novel, to overcome the external and internal obstacles to a self-consciousness which proves her salvation. Reading and writing are her tools for spiritual survival, and she barely manages to preserve her manuscripts from the rampages of a husband. . . . The protagonist chooses to abandon her husband and son, and flees to Rome, where she becomes a writer and social activist.

Regarding the subject of woman and writing, even a bare outline of the book's contents shows that Aleramo understands her writing to be an instrument of a larger, social and feminist enterprise capable of promising women a new dignity. . . . The literary portrayal of "l'anima femminile" hinges on the protagonist's efforts to uncover that soul through an arduous process of self-consciousness through writing. . . . Despite the suffering it provokes, writing links the individual to other readers and thus to the larger society, while reading the works of others produces a liberating catharsis capable of transfiguring individual experience. . . .

Although the thematic elements linking writing to activism, self-consciousness, and catharsis are frequent and important in the work, if one were to take into account only thematic considerations the individual self in [*A Woman*] might appear to be absorbed into larger patterns. The "autos" of the autobiography might seem to fade into the background. Similarly, if the reader were to judge the book solely from the dramatic nature of the events narrated, the "autos" would appear subordinated to the "bios," or, to use the terminology of Benveniste, discourse would appear subordinated to history. This is not the case in [*A Woman*], though, for the individual "mark of style" to which Starobinski referred reveals the forceful, nearly overwhelming nature of the "I" of the writing.

In [*A Woman*], the potential dichotomy between an "I" who is the subject of past, tumultuous events, and the present narrating "I" is averted by the author's constant efforts to incorporate the past in the present. . . .

Over the span of the novel . . . Aleramo gradually turns the emphasis away from the events of the narration to the voice of the "I," and, indeed, something like a lyric-ecstatic mode dominates the final chapter. As the supposed moment of transcription nears, the author progressively drops the past tenses, and portrays her protagonist's decision to desert her family in a series of tenseless infinitives and exclamations dictated by the recitation of strong emotions. . . .

The protagonist's last words . . . express faith that the book will bridge the gap between the new and past self. The latter was distinguished mainly for having fulfilled the female biological role by producing a son. In Aleramo's paradoxical scheme of things, it is only through the loss of the son (his father has legal custody) that her protagonist achieves the new self, "una donna" (a woman). The title may imply that one woman's tormented existence can stand for that of all others ("*una* donna"), but it also suggests that the protagonist has become a true woman ("una *donna*"), true to herself and her greater destiny. She has gained a new life by following a *via crucis*—she has saved her soul, the embryo of the new life ahead. The book constitutes a record of and link to the past "I," and the rescued soul, or nucleus of selfhood, can be equated with powerful "I" of the novel, with the voice which has escaped the holocaust of events and lived to tell them. The text's words will "reach" the son, and unite him to his mother, at least in purpose, turning the destruction to their separation into salvation for both. The subject of the spiritual transformations of womanhood, the metamorphoses of "l'anima femminile," dominated Aleramo's lyric poetry and much of the rest of her writing career.

Keala Jane Jewell. *Canadian Journal of Italian Studies*. 7, 1983, pp. 149–52

"My youth was free and joyous. To revive it in memory, make it shine once more before my consciousness is a vain effort"—this incipit to *A Woman*, Sibilla Aleramo's first book, which appeared in 1908, begins her confession with a vehemence that corresponds to the fullness of life what she wants to underscore in order to draw a more effective contrast between the hopes of a happy adolescence and the long humiliation that followed it. The author devotes this rigorously autobiographical novel to the recovery of the first twenty-five years of her own life, from her brief childhood to the act that signaled the definitive breach with her world of wife and mother and began her career as a writer. The act's motivations, internal and external, are recorded in a narrative detail that concentrates on analyzing interior conditions in the light of the discoveries that the years gradually deposited within the protagonist's consciousness. The idea of a book that would document the truth of a representative female condition in the society of the time came to Sibilla Aleramo through the influence of reading about the movements for women's emancipation in England and Scandinavia and the suggestive power, for her, of Ibsen's play *A Doll's House,* whose author Sibilla would consider a guide and almost a master throughout her life. But the bent for writing had revealed itself in her in an even more confused and tempestuous form at the most dramatic moments of her life as a woman when she asked sorrow itself "if it could become fertile." Although *A Woman* remains a unique experience in Aleramo's long career, connected to a climate and a naturalistic period whose characteristics she freely elaborated, with precision but also with limpidity and lyricism, it also reveals the content of her future work: the extended autobiography, the myth of youth, her intellectual fervor and desire for knowledge, and, above all, the constant attention to the moments of her own inner life that will constitute the basic theme of her entire oeuvre.

Olga Lombardi. *Belfagor.* 41, 1986, p. 525

ALIGER, MARGARITA (RUSSIA) 1915–

Aliger came to fame in the Soviet Union with the fiercely patriotic poetry she was writing at the outbreak of the Second World War. An epic poem called "Zoya," about the sufferings of a girl tortured to death by the Nazis was particularly well-known. . . . She was . . . brave enough to fly into Leningrad at the height of the siege and report the horrors of it and she spent little time at home. . . . Aliger has lived through, and understands at first hand, one of the most cruelly difficult periods of Soviet history. In 1976 she said to me that in spite of all the hardships she endured then she had probably been happiest during the Second World War, because "It was the time when all our people were together, and knew they were fighting an enemy *outside* that was evil."

Aliger was on the same train as Akhmatova, traveling towards Chistopol in 1941. She remembers someone commenting on the beads Anna Akhmatova was wearing round her neck. "That was a present from Marina," Akhmatova said. And everyone fell silent, appalled by the knowledge of Tsvetayeva's suicide two months earlier, in the little town of Yelabuga, on the river Kama. The question of guilt preoccupies Aliger. In her memoir of Akhmatova, she tells the story, and wonders whether it is possible to ask who is guilty. Aliger, with Tsvetayeva's daughter Alya, and Ilya Erenburg, has been among the most hard-working of the Commission set up to reestablish Tsvetayeva's reputation (and indeed publication) in Russia. Quite recently, Aliger's long brooding over Tsvetayeva's suicide brought her to write one of her own finest poems: "House in Meudon."

All though her life, Aliger has seen the writing of poetry as primarily a means of sharing the experiences of pain and joy with other people. In her most recent poems her conversational manner has become more terse and even more direct. The political changes that have affected her life most deeply over forty years of writing are now most movingly expressed in poems of love and mourning.

Elaine Feinstein. Introduction to *Three Russian Poets* (Manchester: Carcanet, 1979), pp. 9–11

Margarita Aliger published her previous book *Sinij Cas* (Dark blue hour) in 1970. Here, I hold in my hands the little volume of lyrics that was published eleven years later. What accompanied this long, protracted interruption? The reader received the book of memoir prose *Tropinka vrzi* (Path in the wheat) which called forth a broad, grateful response. Published posthumously, the collection of poems of Leonid Pervomajskij *Vcera i Zavtra* (Yesterday and tomorrow) was superbly translated by Margarita Alǵer.

And what of her own lyrical lines? They were saved up in the period of a decade, so that almost at once they appeared in the journals *Znamija, Novij mir, Druzba narodov, Oktjabr', Literaturnaja gazeta,* and *Sovetskaja rossija,* and then were put into a book. . . .

Cetvert' veka (A quarter of a century): having given such a name to a book the author sharply defines her borders in time. But by reading, these set boundaries involuntarily expand. You remember the poems written by Alǵer in the thirties and forties which are not included in the book, but are invisibly present in it. In the cycle "The 1970's" a few pages, bright and bitter, were born (of) the journey to southern Spain.

"I'm glad. I'm glad. I'm glad that the heart aches over the past . . . that there is still courage in my veins and that the word 'Madrid' is like a password, that for all that I still have the strength to cry over Puerta del Sol." These words are blending together in my consciousness with the poem "Xota—Dance of the Basques." Aliger wrote it in 1939, after a meeting with Spanish children who came to us (in the USSR) after the burning of Bilbao. "The foreign women, silently crying, hugged the orphans."

This is a return to what was said earlier—the essential subject of the book. But perhaps most important in it is the deep inner unity. It is most visible in those instances when the poet turns not only to an event, to journeying, to a meeting, but to the very self, when . . . today's day has been survived while yesterday's we perceive with today's perception. With this mixing of points of veiw arises a stereoscopic clarity of thought and color, which not only opens up the chronicle of the decades that have past, but also a chronology of the soul. . . .

With her whole being, Margarita Aliger was prepared for all of the ordeals that social duty thrust on her, for those burdens and losses that touched her personally. She was prepared in order to write "To Zoya" and the bitter confession of a soldier's widow: "With a bullet in my heart, I live in the world."

No complication of path, no kind of pause prevented her after the war from returning to that which had brightly burned in her soul in her youth. The poem "Reading Thomas Mann" is dated 1979. It absorbs in itself the eternal and contemporary alarm, seizing the world again: "From the time of Abraham-Jacob without distinction of length or breadth, they cried in the world, always the same, generations of widows and orphans."

Iakov Khelemski. Znamya. 9, September,
1982, pp. 228–29

Margarita Aliger, who is among the best-known poets of the generation born just after the Revolution, comes from a poor assimilated-Jewish family in Odessa. Her father played the violin well, and knew four languages; her mother read classics of Russian poetry to her. Aliger found recognition as a poet early enough; but her life has been hard and bitter. Her first husband was killed in the Second World War, her first child died of meningitis at eight months. She is now a short, frail dark-skinned woman of about sixty, who lives alone in a gracious flat opposite the Tretyakov gallery. Recently Yevtushenko wrote a poem about her called "Poet in a Market," in which he described her going to buy honey for her elder daughter who was in that year very ill, and has since died. He saw in her frail figure standing among "the cabbages and the lard" unrecognized by other shoppers

> the pure light
> and pride of
> someone who was both Jewish woman
> and Russian poet.

. . . The war was not only a time of horror and loss and the demands of courage for Aliger. It was also the time when she was closest to Fadaeev; and it is to their relationship so many of her best poems refer. Fadaeev was a novelist who acted as Secretary of the Writers' Union from 1939 to 1953. During the last years of his life, when he and Aliger were estranged, Fadaeev began drinking more and more heavily. In 1956 he killed himself. It was in the autumn of that year that Aliger wrote "Two," a short sad lyric, which fixed (as Akhmatova might have done in her early period) on a single moment, like a perfect still:

> Once again they've quarreled on a tram
> shamelessly indifferent to strangers.
> I can't hide how much I envy them.

I can't take my eyes off their behavior.

They don't even know their good fortune,
   and not knowing is a part of their luck.
Think of it. They are together. Alive.
And have the time to sort things out and make up.

Regret sounds a stronger note than loneliness here, and there are other lyrics in which the main preoccupation is the unhappiness of being a survivor. It is a theme which has a peculiar poignancy whenever Aliger reflects on the gap between her own generation and that of Yevtushenko and Akhmadulina, a gap she feels separates her even more strongly from the younger poets springing up after them whose lives have been so much easier and who cannot understand how it was in the thirties. "It was not so simple as they think now," she once said to me. In Aliger's poem to Lermontov (a poem I much admire) she is writing not only about the difference in fate between her life and that of the great poet who died young, but offering the apology of a survivor, who feels that the price of survival has been to live through more than anyone could be expected to endure.

Elaine Feinstein. In Mary Jacobus, ed.
Women Reading Women's Writing (Oxford:
Oxford University Press, 1986), pp. 141–43

ALLEN, PAULA GUNN (UNITED STATES) 1939–

Laguna mother, Lakota grandfather, Lebanese father, life on the margins of mainstream and Indian: Paula Gunn Allen lives somewhere between American norms and Native American closures. She writes in the shadows of visions, "fingering silence and sound" with a poet's touching measure. She sings of desire and grief, confusion and rage over a horizon note of loss. *Shadow Country:* that marginal zone of interfusions, neither the shadower, nor the shadowed, both and neither, in liminal transition. "I looked about me and could see that what we then were doing was like a shadow cast upon the earth from yonder vision in the heavens, so bright it was and clear," Black Elk remembered. "I knew the real was yonder and the darkened dream of it was here."

Paula Allen grew up in the halfway house of mixed ancestry. This woman lives not so much in a given tribe as working to articulate her sense of the tribal, without rhetorical claims. She chooses Native American definitions, defining Native American *in* her life. Her Laguna origins come mixed. Ruth Underhill sees the Laguna Pueblo in *First Penthouse Dwellers of America* as "a refugee town of Spanish days" back many centuries, a mixture of Keresan,

Shoshonean, Tanoan, and Zuñian influx with Navajo, Spanish, and immigrant Anglo settlers. Edgar Hewett elsewhere describes this settlement as "an old aggregate of tribes and clans brought more or less together by acculturation and intermixes."

Both part of and apart from Laguna, Allen knows only too well the tribal sense of alienation, the corresponding necessity for mutual assimilation. She lives America *and* Native America. And fall is always back of the country, under dreams of spring. Allen sees a changed America, unknown to her now, remembered lyrically as "native" for indigenous peoples. In "Tucson: First Night" she recalls,

> "the Road," we said,
> implying that time had no changing.
>   (Like Plato in our innocence)
> clouds that were there
> are here. Now. My mind and the sky,
> one thing on the edge of surmise (sunrise).

Paula Allen rediscovers old traditions and records new Indian adaptations. Her poems shatter stereotypes of blood warriors and demure squaws. *Shadow Country* gives voice to the polychromatic shock of Indian modernism as, for example, visualized in Fritz Scholder's paintings: cowboy Indians slouch with cigarettes and dark glasses, Coors beer cans and American flag shawls, ice cream cones and flared umbrellas on horses. Scholder's "Portrait of a Massacred Indian" portrays an image of bow and plains buckskin, the warrior's head a blurred acrylic palette. "Indian Power" silhouettes a naked red torso on a lunging purple pony, Kafka not far away.

Paula Allen experiments with personal quests through poetic forms and subjects. A mood or technique carries her an uncharted distance through open forms; on the way she sets her own standards of honesty and love. The poet's body is her receptor, mind her tool, spirit her courage. Allen's *impress*ion leads toward thought; she follows a sentiment diversely, wherever it goes, without compulsion to answer or solve the problems encountered. Her poetry accepts a common "negative capability": the aloneness, irresolution, even tragedy a person lives out honestly and struggles to voice.

Allen explores a woman's self-images and self-esteems, with a girl-child's sensitivity to pain. Men stand in the distances, women foregrounded. . . .

Paula Allen writes with the complete and myriad sensitivities of a woman with children, with a husband, in love, out of love, marriage, divorce, redefinition: old women with weavings and potteries, new women with separations and self-definitions.

Kenneth Lincoln. *Native American Renaissance* (Berkeley: University of California Press, 1983), pp. 214–15, 219

The way in which Allen balances the diverse elements of her heritage with her own voracious inquiry into all systems of human thought—religious, philosophical, and political—is well illustrated in *Coyote's Daylight Trip*. At a first reading the poems seen unconnected to each other, but a careful study of the book's major themes reveals a process of learning documented by the various poems. At first we find nostalgic idealism and longing for the kind of community the poet intuitively believes once to have been in existence at Laguna Pueblo. Then comes a realization that she must identify with contemporary fragmentation and loss. With identification comes the possibility for transformation of the pain found in urban streets, and finally the poet knows she is creating not only poems but the actual patterns for a new way of life.

The entire process implies a belief in the mythic foundations of metaphor and poetry giving language what N. Scott Momaday has called "its deeper and more vital context" than is usually taken into account. Poetry that so directly relates to myth is written in order to function as myth does in society, establishing structures (or metaphors) that not only make the world intelligible and help people see it in a new way but also teach people about the creative powers of the universe. Belief in these powers is part of the religious tradition of all tribes. Creating poetry that is a contemporary realization of the powers of mythic processes is a quite different matter from merely using myth as a source of imagery or allusions. While the content of specific poems may reflect specific American Indian myths, a poem does not have to include overt reference to anything Native American to show how the energies dramatized in ancient myths can still shape life in today's city streets. Following through her book Paula Gunn Allen's vision of how myths function today can be for the reader a remarkable experience of seeing previously unimagined facets of American life. . . .

When Paula Gunn Allen writes in her poem "Paradigm" that "life here is here," she is acknowledging the oneness she describes in her prose. As we read the essay, we tend to imagine the rural landscape of the reservation as it once was, forgetting or perhaps not knowing that today Laguna Reservation includes a huge uranium mine. Few readers go beyond the mine-pocked reservation scenes of the southwest to imagine an urban skid row or even a middle-class suburb as one part in the "land/people" entity described by Allen. Yet in *Coyote's Daylight Trip*, the "here" which the poet must accept is a city in turmoil. How then does this "larger being" find renewal? The answer to that question is given us bit by bit throughout the rest of the book of poems.

Using the strings of poetry to mend the fragile fabric of life is the work and goal that drives many American Indian women to delicate but strong lines. With their intuitions of a mythic order in which their own forms partake, American Indian women like Paula Gunn Allen are exploring various directions toward a future that is hurtling toward us "with the speed of light." Reading these women can be a richly comforting experience as we sense the truth of Allen's statement, "perhaps when the worst has happened one can accept life sanely."

Elaine Jahner. In Helen Winters Stauffer and Susan J. Rosowski, eds. *Women and Western American Literature* (Troy, New York: Whitston, 1982), pp. 312–14, 325

Much of Allen's work is a search for meaning, an attempt to understand natural harmony and to place the individual in that fusion of person, land, and spirit. Each moment is placed on a web of history, natural harmony and traditional understanding. Through this perceptive act, the moment is given significance such as in the poem "Jet Plane/Dhla-nuwa," where the flight on the plane is seen in scientific historical terms, personal historic terms and in mythological terms or, as in "Affirmation," where Grandmother Spider's webs and thoughts are seen throughout the world and the narrator sees "each journey retracing some ancient myth."

Allen's stance is a highly meditative one wherein she forges connections between mundane and mythic space. Making these connections is frequently referred to as "going home," for we see the physical journey often combined with the mythic journey and the personal search. However, as in the poem "Displacement," we see a world today where "nothing stays in the any sense where it belongs," and home is, consequently, hard to find.

Allen's work is personal in the sense that it often is initiated by her emotional reactions to the mundane world's lack of mythic space. This barren world is America today, but it is where most of America places its values. In poems like "Surfacing in Private Spaces," "The Last Fantasy," and "The Kerner Report on Camp Creek Road," we see the average American reader lost as he/she searches for control, for certainty, for meaning where he/she can find none. All that remains are the tentative solutions on the mundane plane and the despair and dissatisfaction which must follow. Perhaps Allen has followed some of these paths herself: "Our private search for meaning, / for certainty, for a silver peg / to hang ideals on." Because of her understanding of herself and modern America, she can perceive the significance imparted by a vision of the mythic space; she can penetrate the illusions. Frequently, as in the poem "Hanging out in America," the narrator seems like a ghost, a shade wandering the paths of America, outside the process but watching the "alien ways empty." She knows Americans are "dead to the visions / that could give us life."

Allen's initial perceptual impulse is to look inward first, to follow her emotions and perceptions, to seek truth there, then to move out. "I play it close to my chest, look down/and out, look inside, in city, in street, in body, both/ways before I move." She may act physically or write poetry to create an image to aid perception of mythic space. She will make the connections for herself first, then write so as to help others make them. A good example of this process is in the poem "The Turning Point." In this poem, another person's desire to find the origin of mankind in another time—millions of years ago and on another continent—is internalized by Allen as a personal journey into herself and there to find a personal/mythic understanding. . . .

The narrator must relinquish the things she has learned of America: she must seek inside herself the ancient power, the origin, the source of life. The poem ends with the narrator—unafraid, knowing the steps, the chain of spirit—asking for the ancient power of life to be restored to her. Only through this personal completion can any action on the human plane with other beings be meaningful and effective.

The poet may recoil from this formidable task, but as in the poem "Nos Vemos," there is always the sense in Allen's work that the earth and spirit are working to reunite their harmony and that the mythic and mundane space will be inevitably reunited at some point in the future. Mythic space has always been here and always will be. It is what gives meaning to life. The holistic fabric of meaning is like an old rug; the poet merely mends the holes in the ancient creation. If the poet doesn't, then someone else will because the rug—the fusion of person, spirit, and land which creates mythic space— is valuable. It is all we have. In the poem "Grandmother," Allen speaks of Grandmother Spider's efforts in creating bright, complete life, and of the poet's task.

>   after her,
>   the women and men weave blankets into tales of life,
>
>   memories of light and ladders,
>   infinity-eyes, and rain.
>   After her I sit on my laddered rain-bearing rug
>   and mend the tear with the string.

It is this fusion, this blending of mythic and personal, that creates the perfect harmony. The old informs, strengthens the new, as in the poem "Womanwork," where present-day women remember "The Mythic Woman" and use that understanding to strengthen themselves much as old pottery fragments are used to strengthen new pieces. The women's lives are informed by the mythic space and they celebrate it.

Jim Ruppert. *American Indian Journal.*
7, 1983, pp. 32–35

Allen's novel, *The Woman Who Owned the Shadows,* is about a journey to healing—a journey back to the female center. At the beginning of the novel, the central character, Ephanie Atencio, is a half-breed who has lost the sense of who she is; she is isolated and fragmented as a human being, belonging neither to the Pueblo community nor to the non-Indian community. Ephanie has a fragmented self from an inner war. As a half-breed Guadalupe woman,

Ephanie is caught in the erosion of the traditional place of honor and respect in which a Guadalupe woman is held by her tribe and in the stereotyped and patriarchal view from which she is viewed by non-Indians. She is surrounded by forces which work to destroy whatever link she has to the traditional culture in which the women were central figures. The reader follows her struggle to regain her sanity as she sorts out her childhood and her tribal beliefs and connections, marries a second-generation Japanese-American man, and deals with the death of one of their twins. She joins a consciousness-raising group, goes to a psychiatrist, studies the old traditions, and tries to commit suicide, but it is only when she is able to synthesize what she has learned from all of this, see its connection to her tribal traditions, and reaffirm the importance of the female, especially the importance of the "amazon tradition," that she is healed.

The Laguna society to which Allen's mother and maternal grandmother belonged and in which she places her character was matrilineal (descent recognized through the female line) and matrilocal (ownership of houses held by women). Allen says in *The Sacred Hoop* that her "mother's Laguna people are Keres Indian, reputed to be the last extreme mother-right people on earth." Women also controlled and cared for the ceremonial objects . . . and the power to conduct ceremonies came from both men and women. . . . According to Allen, one of the problems with Christianity is that it attempts to use "male power" only. Women also owned the crops while men did the farming. The primary deities were Thought Woman (Tsitstinako) and her sisters, Corn Woman (Iyatiku), and Sun Woman (Nautsityi). For Allen, "womanness . . . is preponderant; it is the source of human male and human female, the giver and bestower of life, ritual, afterlife, social power, and all that is sacred." Because the Laguna society in which Allen places her characters has lost this central importance of the female, both the Laguna and Euro-American society need balancing. The old stories are not effective in acting as curing ceremonies because they do not account for the influence of Euro-American culture.

Allen's main character in *The Woman Who Owned the Shadows* illustrates the isolation and fragmentation which occur if individuals pull away or are left out of the community and their experience or "story" cannot be seen as part of the whole. As a mixed-breed person who lives apart, Ephanie is unable to fit into the old ways; there are no stories for her experiences. Only when she makes sense of the old stories by seeing the continuities in them and how she fits into those continuities can she be healed, for the Laguna believe that everything that has happened will happen again only in a different form. . . .

By allowing the reader to participate in the curing ceremony of the novel by following the main character in her own restoration of balance, Allen seeks to restore balance to the community-at-large. Through this the reader is reminded of the power of storytelling and the responsibility of each human to the community. Further, if, as Judy Grahn says in her comment on the back cover, "you come with an honest heart," the novel enables the non-Indian reader to begin to see from a non-Euro-American perspective. To begin to change the Euro-American vision of disconnectedness to one of connectedness would be a "curing" indeed. As Williams notes, a most important function of curing is a "healing of the mind." Although the novel ends with Ephanie's understanding of her connection to her heritage and although the reader does not see how it will affect her life, Allen's novel is also an important offering to Native American lesbians. She has shown a connection that present-day lesbians might make to a special spiritual heritage and role which such women played in Native American cultures. As Allen says, "It all has to do with spirit, with restoring an awareness of our spirituality as gay people." . . .

More generally in the novel, the healing of the main character occurs when she is able to reconnect with the female principle which is exemplified in Thought Woman and her sisters and consists particularly of life and strength—she recovers the ancient qualities of woman who was seen as "strong and powerful," balancing the ancient qualities of man who was seen as having "transient or transitory" qualities. . . . This balancing of qualities where "woman-ness is not of less value than man-ness" . . . allows both the individual and tribe to continue and prosper. The telling of the story allows the listeners/readers to visualize how their experiences fit into the great web of being, the patterns of life. The story and the experiences become one, leading to harmony and healing. By using this journey as a model, we can begin to see how to reclaim our female deities and "the wholistic, pacifistic and spirit-based." . . . principles of our grandmothers in order to bring together mind/spirit and body, inanimate and animate, to insure continuance of the earth as well as the individual.

> Annette van Dyke. In Karla Jay and
> Joanne Glasgow, eds. *Lesbian Texts and*
> *Contexts* (New York: New York University
> Press, 1990), pp. 342–43, 351–52

Paula Gunn Allen always shapes her aesthetic and critical work to mediate between Native American and white experience. For example, in the poem "Hoop Dancer" Allen begins by empathizing with the white reader's difficulty in ever understanding the mental space of the Native American:

> It's hard to enter
> circling clockwise and counter
> clockwise moving no
> regard for time, metrics
> irrelevant to this place
> where pain is the prime number
> and soft stepping feet
> praise water from the skies

The difficulty, however, goes beyond confrontations between cultures; in "this place" of ceremonial time and significance, even metrics are "irrelevant" as even the white man's aesthetic formulae fail to encompass the integrating and empowering vision of the Native American. For the Native American's space, in Allen's vision, is one of balance and timelessness, always sought, rarely recovered. . . .

While Allen's imaginative landscape is rich in authentic detail of the American West within and without the reservations, she is far more concerned with the effects of translocation and dislocation than with the meanings of actual lands and creatures. Where Allen registers her strongest Western literary key is in the shade and movement of her hymns to the sacred in Native American experience. By discovering her own mode of American sacred, Allen creates her own myths; she reinvokes primordial sacred time with a contemporary profane time in order to recover and remake her self. That restored, renewed self suggests in symbolic terms a revival within Native American experience as a whole. Like Allen's own vision of self, contemporary Native Americans exist not in a romantic past but instead in a community which extends through the whole of American experience.

Yet the revival Allen addresses in her works of art and criticism also creates inextricable tensions and paradoxes. Like the "breeds" of American literature—Thoreau's Joe Polis, Melville's Queequeg, Hemingway's Prudie/Trudie, and Faulkner's Sam Fathers—the perspective of the figure on the margin is acutely responsive and must respond to sensitive, even radically conscious circumstances. But it is within these lightning rod beings between two worlds that the essential paradoxes within America's heterogeneity are most clearly faced and understood. It is the "breed" who is compelled to deal with two cultures as his or her daily bread. It is the "breed" who may understand two cultures, quite diverse in themselves, and may live to tell the tale. It is the "breed" who knows that Native Americans may learn something of the world view of whites and whites may learn something of the cultures of Native Americans, but neither can be fully judged by the norms of the other. In her criticism and in her creative writings Allen provides a gloss on Native American experience and literature, but more even than that, she offers a particular telescope through which we may explore the whole range of classic American fiction. In her vision and art she stimulates scholars and students of American literature to see the canon through new eyes. . . .

The mediative role Allen assumes in her criticism of Native American literature is meant to act as a catalyst to new inquiries into perhaps the most crucial of all questions in American Studies: what is an American? The complex dialogue among white Americans engaged in struggle with the American continent, a dialogue so fully explored by Melville, Thoreau, Hawthorne, Mark Twain, and Faulkner, is illuminated and complicated by the voices of Native Americans such as Allen's. Main Street American literature leads to Indian territory, after all, but now the white man's Indians can speak for themselves.

Elizabeth S. Hanson. *Paula Gunn Allen*
(Boise, Idaho: Boise State University
Western Writers Series, No. 96, 1990),
pp. 40–41, 43–45

ALLENDE, ISABEL (CHILE) 1942–

Isabel Allende's first novel, *The House of the Spirits,* in only three years of existence, is already as much a landmark for the critic as for the reader. This work has already had twelve editions in Spanish and has been translated into French, German, Italian, and Norwegian. Publication of the English translation is scheduled for the Spring of 1985.

This novel appears to have been concocted by a delicate and benevolent witch, like its central character, Clara del Valle. Isabel Allende herself, speaking about her novel, says that "it was born marked with the sign of good fortune" and adds, "a few months ago, when it was published in Spain, it was in a bookshop for the first time. It was stuck shyly in a corner. I was afraid for my novel. I felt that it didn't belong to me anymore, that I couldn't do anything to help it. But with the passage of time, I have calmed down and now I believe that there really is a spirit watching over it."

To enter into the magical and enchanted space of *The House of the Spirits,* to become acquainted with Clara, most brilliant and clairvoyant, with her white tunics, imagining her rising up from the pages and playing beautiful melodies on the locked piano and seeing her at a red wooden table noting things down in the notebook of her life, is to belong to that invisible circle where the uncontrolled imagination joins with a lucid and truthful story.

This novel *is* the imaginary cosmos of its picturesque characters, like Esteben Trueba, the dreaded but benevolent patriarch with his uncontrolled sexuality; the Mora sisters, with their scent of lavender and lemons, harbingers of bad tidings. It is the story, as well, of a Latin American country lashed by a monstrous dictatorship. The country is not named, but we know that it is Chile, with its implacable mountain ranges and seas and earthquakes that besiege this hidden corner of the planet. In her pages, Allende, with the mastery of an experienced writer, guides us through the intricate labyrinths of Chilean history from the turn of the century to the present time.

Within the pages or, better yet, upon reading, we recognize the control of the land by the age-old oligarchs, the first hints of land reform in the sixties, the victory of Salvador Allende and his deliberate destruction by the forces of the opposition and foreign intervention. Chilean history appears in all its detail in these nearly 400 pages, from the great landlords to the revolutionaries who end their lives in cells, driven by fear, injustice, and powerlessness.

The House of the Spirits provides a double textual reading. On the first level: the story of the Trueba family and its unforgettable components, both legitimate and illegitimate. On another level, the novel brilliantly outlines the political and social history of Chile from the turn of the century to the present time.

Among the most interesting characters, we may identify the sweet Clara, who chose silence for nine years, not as an act of passivity or fear, but rather as the only possible means for imagining a space molded out of secret signs and three-legged tables that could levitate, just like her.

Beyond Clara's clairvoyant alchemies, she is the center of a group of women devoted to helping the dispossessed. Clara gives warmth and food to all the impoverished beings who parade through her huge house and, by extension, through the whole country.

The woman-centered nature of the central characters, who are the central texts of this reading, and not its pretext, is one of the striking and disquieting aspects of the book, from the first pages on. The author has written a women's saga comparable to others in the genre, like Thomas Mann's *Buddenbrooks,* Gabriel Garcia Marquez's *One Hundred Years of Solitude,* or Leon Uris's *Trinity.* It is the women who, through the writing, the disordered imagination, and clairvoyance, represent the history of a country from the beginning of the century to our own day.

Marjorie Agosin. *Revista Interamericana de Bibliografia/Inter-American Review of Bibliography.* 35, 1985, pp. 448–49

In the words of Vivien Forrester, "women's history of women in history, depending on the categories used, has been one of stagnation, exclusion and silence." And Virginia Woolf adds that "little is known about women. History . . . is the history of the masculine line." *The House of the Spirits* turns this premise around as the chronicle of a Chilean bourgeois family over the last fifty years of the country's life. History becomes family history, and the masculine line passes before the female gaze. In the process, the microcosm reflects and refers to the sociohistoric macrocosm in which the family group is inscribed.

The feminine vision determines the narrative universe as well as the discourse that generates it, because the women, apparently situated within the paradigm of irrelevance and passivity that the social contract/system imposes upon them, find the form in which to transcend the father's history; by making use of the very values, attitudes and images that the adjective "feminine" ascribes to them, they are able to break the dominant vision of power, whose representative in the novel is Esteban Trueba, the male figure in whose attributes (father, employer, oligarch, Conservative Party senator) an entire history of dominance is identified.

The women's version presents an unmasked story of reality as the collective memory of a "before" in which appear, with almost mythic implications, characters like the Poet, the eternal Candidate and late President, as male figures who open up the option to an alternative history and who, by the same token, are also silenced by the nightmarish archetype of Power that is the Dictator. From the fascinating past to a tragic present, the facts begin to be recorded through Clara, the material and magical center of the Trueba family.

Rene Campos. In Marcelo Coddou, ed. Los libros tienen sus proprios espiritus (Vera Cruz: Universidad Veracruzana, 1986), p. 20

The House of the Spirits is an especially good illustration of a new phase of female experience represented in a kind of writing that embraces more aspects of life. As with other contemporary Spanish-American women writers—Peri Rossi, L[uisa] Valenzuela or Albaluca Angel—politics and the family are thematic nuclei in these new explorations. Allende shares another trait with Angel and Peri Rossi that distinguishes them from the women writers of the past: humor and a freer attitude with regard to sexuality. The richness of Allende's novel is manifested not only in the wider thematic and spatial horizon that it covers (the country, the city, the rich and the poor) but also in the abundant variety of human types, male as well as female.

In contrast, nonetheless, to these other writers and many other *cosoeurs* from other parts of the world, especially the United States, who, in their efforts to unmask socioeconomic structures, blame the women for being such good transmitters of them, Allende constructs her world by revalorizing certain of the traits that feminism has tended to devalue. (In this sense, she belongs to the last feminist tendency that Jonathan Culler reviews in his "Reading as a Woman.") But she enriches them with new strengths, opened up by experience. For example, many feminists see the spirit of sacrifice instilled in women by the culture as one of the major obstacles to the assertion of the female "I." Whence an entire narrative strain centering on "bad mothers" exposed as the best followers of the traditional social pattern of what a woman "should" be. Allende shows us various modalities of sacrifice in her novel, which results in an examination of positive and negative forms of actualization. As with the spirit of sacrifice, there are other characteristics that Allende uses to create her characters, who follow or break the traditional molds of conduct for the two sexes. . . .

When I chose sacrifice as an example in the previous paragraph, I did so with the idea that it is related to solidarity, which, in my opinion, is the basis of the worldview that the book espouses. It is a solidarity that unites all the women, especially, breaking the traditional mold of rivalry that according to psychological studies divides them. In the novel, mothers and daughters, mistresses and servants, political prisoners are linked by strong bonds of solidarity. This solidarity goes beyond the material aid that they can give one another: it deepens into an understanding of acts and persons, the acceptance of differences.

The chain binds mothers and daughters of the Trueba family together because it presents an egalitarian relationship of loyal friends, as opposed to the more distant and hierarchical relationship of older tradition. It seems obvious that the author is trying to project behavioral metaphors through the medium of these women, whom she has given names synonymous with light and clarity (Nivea, Clara, Blanca, Alba).

Gabriela Mora. In Marcelo Coddou, ed. *Los libros tienen sus proprios espiritus* (Vera Cruz: Universidad Veracruzana, 1986), pp. 71–72

At first reading, *The House of the Spirits* has a great deal in common with *One Hundred Years of Solitude*. Although history is translated geographically from a rural environment (the estate of the Three Marias) to an urban one (the capital of a country whose name is never given but which it is not hard to identify with the author's native land) and a constant contrapuntal back and forth throughout the narrative, its axis also turns about a family: that of the Truebas. In the novel, we watch the unfolding of the experiences of Esteban Trueba, aged landholder and senator, and those of an interesting intergenerational quartet of female characters: his mother-in-law Nivea, his wife Clara, his daughter Blanca, and his granddaughter Alba. Some of the characters display unusual peculiarities, much like the inhabitants of Macondo. Rosa "the beautiful," Clara's older sister, has a disturbing fascination as mysterious as that of Remedios the beautiful. Alba examines the writing in her grandmother's notebook with the same mystical ecstasy with which several of the Buendias treat the description of the gypsy Melquiades's parchment scrolls. . . . The social and political flaws of Latin America are denounced with the same vehemence as in *One Hundred Years:* for example, corrupt electoral practices, the neocolonial presence of foreign railroads, formerly North American and now English. . . . Some of the Truebas appear to have inherited the Buendias' globe-trotting instincts, like Nicolas, Blanca's brother, who "spent a year as a beggar, following the yogas' road on foot, on foot through the Himalayas, on foot through Katmandu, on foot through the Ganges, on foot through Benares."

To measure these superficial resemblances, which are part of *The House of the Spirits*'s "reproving" strategy and confuse Isabel Allende and García Márquez would mean making a mistake comparable to considering Cervantes as a continuator of the chivalric romances. *Don Quixote* is not an imitator of *Amadis* but rather its parodic sepulcher. The historical experience and the generational perspective of the Chilean novelist are visibly different from those of her Colombian colleague. Isabel Allende, forty years younger than García Márquez, also wrote her novel in exile, but under far worse conditions.

During the fifteen years between 1967 and 1982—publication dates, respectively, of *One Hundred Years of Solitude* and *The House of the Spirits*—the Spanish American world witnessed a series of historicopolitical tragedies that included the Tlatelolco massacre in 1968, the Uruguayan and Chilean military coups in 1973 and, later, the Argentinian coup that began the shameful period of the "trial" in 1976, which obviously left their marks on this very rich production of the "post-boom" fruit of the desperate exodus that, in addition to Isabel Allende's novel, includes the narratives of her compatriot Antonio Skarmeta, the Argentinians Mempo Giardinelli, Osvaldo Soriano and Luisa Valenzuela, and the Uruguayan Saul Ibargoyen, to mention only a few.

> Juan Manuel Marcos and Teresa Mendez
> Faith. In Marcelo Coddou, ed.
> *Los libros tienen sus proprios espiritus*
> (Vera Cruz: Universidad Veracruzana,
> 1986), pp. 62–63

The novels of Isabel Allende not only make no attempt to breach the mimetic contract, they postulate themselves as the bearers of suprareferentiality. Their attachment to the historical context has the function of being a voice of warning, a call to attention to the danger implicit in human existence. In a writer like her, this is translated into a determined testimony, a genuine compromise of sociopolitical projects with those that she wants to bring into her work. She has said:

> Latin America is experiencing a tragic period in its history. In our land, fifty percent of the population is illiterate, but writers are honored and respected, for they are the voice of those who suffer. . . . All of us who write and have the good luck to be published must take on the responsibility of serving the cause of freedom and justice.

The narrator of her first novel fulfills, through her writing, the same function that the grandmother, Clara, assigns to her "notebooks for taking notes on life," that is, seeing things in their real dimension and getting the best of a bad memory. Clara's notebooks, Alba's text, Isabel Allende's novel are all responses to this mimetic intention; they are trying to replicate or duplicate reality. And it seems to me that this has to be understood in the sense that Aristotle used the term mimesis: reality is not the idea in itself—as Platonic postulates would have it—nor the concrete and specific, but rather the dialectical process through which the idea acts upon the concrete and the concrete acquires meaning through the idea or form that operates upon it. . . . Isabel Allende's realistic poetics thus accepts a specific mission for mimesis: to be conscious of reality, insofar as one's object is to imitate it as an essentially imaginative process. The mimesis, then, becomes a means of cognition and provides privileged access to the totality of the real and its meaning. Mimesis in fiction . . . [means that] the truth presented should not be understood as a correspondence, but rather as a consistency, a coherence. . . .

It is not hard to prove that in *The House of the Spirits* we are confronted with many facts that constitute historic reality on our continent, especially in Chile. As might have been imagined, this is what provoked the greatest efforts at denigration of the work on the part of critics subservient to the regime in power in the country that is the fiction's point of reference. Very common ways of dehistoricizing the text have consisted of limiting the critical act to "structural" or stylistic analysis, with the goal of establishing its formal character, envisaged as a mere "aesthetic" function, separate from its nature as an instrument for transmitting a particular view of the world, of "this" world. Dehistoricization also occurs when there is an attempt to insert *The House of the Spirits* into the literary currents of the hegemonic discourse, with little or no attention to the specifically Latin American character of the current into which such a work is inserted. The obsession with tracing the influence of García Márquez in Isabel Allende seems to me a variant of the same intention. . . . Under conditions of ideological immobility in which a society is subjected to harsh control and repressive mechanisms operate with the greatest effect, all critical discourse is constituted and manifested in marginality. But the phenomenon is not so simple: censorship or exile—decisive points of understanding Isabel Allende's work—do not automatically mean either silence or absence. The political novel (which is the basic nature of the two published by Isabel Allende) is marginalized by official criticism, which when it condescends to refer to, it proposes a markedly ideological reading. . . .

I believe that the novels of Isabel Allende, by calling profoundly into question the darkness that covers the recent past in Chilean society, have accomplished the double task that characterizes all fiction that is close to history: describing the relevant facts and converting them into historical facts. And this is the way that alternatives, challenges to the hegemonic projects, take root.

Marcelo Coddou. *Literatura chilena: creación y critica*. 39, 1987, pp. 11–12

ALLFREY, PHYLLIS SHAND (DOMINICA) 1915–86

This is a familiar prelude to the experience of the West Indian writer and its source is not provincial amateurism but the legitimate and hungry need for a solid context of endeavor. Hawthorne, after all, did have his ancestors. The West Indian writer has only the disparate fragments of his own and his society's experience and an immense burden of responsibility that is not the necessary lot of the artist. At the same time his own society is not likely to welcome his work. It might want to but it doesn't know how to. His work has the occasional and partisan support of government. If the writer himself has the appropriate social contacts he might be accorded a warm sense of belonging. But the real terms of comprehension and dialogue do not exist. The writer, for example, at public meetings is likely to be asked to comment on the extent to which he is West Indian. Because the West Indies is not merely in a tragic sense isolated from world history—it is also isolated from world literature. It easily supposes, for example, that local writing is calculatedly vicious and depraved. It confuses satire with sarcasm and supposes that irony is another name for patronage. It is willing to believe that its writers, especially those long resident abroad, are engaged in some form of conspiratorial treachery with English reviewers and publishers. It is likely to endorse the work of those writers who either endorse the cliché of a fifth form taste for romantic poetry, or who offer their writing as a weapon in an ill-understood political conflict. Significantly the only important ironist the West Indies has yet produced, V. S. Naipaul, appears to have taken up permanent residence in England and has refused to be identified as a West Indian writer. And Naipaul's irony is often elaborately defensive.

Within the society itself there is no coherent class structure with a fertilizing mobility. There are simply the maginot lines of color or affluence; and behind those lines the self-conscious groups of intellectuals. The only West Indian novel which provides an analysis in depth of a society is Phyllis Allfrey's *The Orchid House*. The novel is set in Dominica, a society frozen into its pasts. With rich and careful nostalgia, and a penetrating but unobtrusive symbolism, Mrs. Allfrey establishes the society and the attempt of three young people both to understand it and break away from it. In political terms her society supplies the means of its own betrayal. And the meaning of her three central characters is only available to them abroad.

W. I. Carr. *Caribbean Quarterly.* 11: 1–2,
March–June 1965, pp. 76–77

Three novels by white West Indians relate to West Indian society in more interesting ways. *The Orchid House, Christopher,* and *Wide Sargasso Sea* differ in narrative technique and theme, and while the first two are set in the twentieth century, Jean Rhys's work is located in the immediate post-Emancipation period. But the elements of continuity between them are remarkable: the attitudes of the white characters to landscape and to the Negro masses; the functional presence of long-serving Negro nurses, and of obeah-women; the occurrence of dreams, nightmares, and other heightened states of consciousness; and references to an outer socio-economic situation that is recognizable as the fall of the planter class. These elements of continuity arise not from the authors' knowledge of one another's work, but involuntarily from the natural stance of the white West Indian. With differing degrees of intensity, the three novels reflect a significant, but in these days forgotten, aspect of West Indian experience. . . .

The Orchid House is narrated in the first person by a peripheral character, Lally—the long-serving Negro nurse of a white family in a fictional island modeled upon Dominica. Lally's memory spans three generations. It is part of the author's purpose to convey a particular sense of the decline of the class to which the planter family belong and to comment on the emergence of the new economic and ruling forces. . . .

Mrs. Allfrey uses the experience of the First World War as the immediate cause of the present Master's state of shock and dope addiction, but that this is only an intensification of something pervasive is readily apparent: Lally describes the Old Master's habit of insulating himself for "hours and hours" in the strange shapes, scents and colors of his orchid house at L'Aromatique; and Andrew, the cousin of the Master's three daughters, is given as dying slowing of consumption, without the will to live, in a retreat called Petit Cul-de-Sac. The malaise in the novel thus spreads from the time of the Old Master to his grandchildren's day.

When the three sisters, Stella, Joan, and Natalie, return after many years abroad, to visit their parents and their native land, they find that a strange entente has been established between the elderly virgin Mamselle Bosquet and their mother, both of whom love and are ministering to the Master; and as the three sisters visit Andrew who lives in concubinage with their colored cousin Cornelie, the reader discovers that each of the girls is in love with Andrew, as he is with them. To the sense of withdrawal we must add sexual inbreeding (a feature of enclave life which appears fleetingly in *Wide Sargasso Sea* and in *Christopher,* where the boy's aunt turns out to be in love with her sister's husband). The effect of the land on all this is more than implicit.

Just as their father on his return from the war expresses his sensuous feel for the native place, so each sister indulges nostalgically in the sounds and sights of a clinging land:

> In Stella's sick dreams of home the island had been a vision so exquisite that she was now almost afraid to open her eyes wide, lest she might be undeceived and cast down, or lest confirmation would stab through her like a shock. Treading the black damp earth of the bridle-path, brushed by ferns and wild begonias, experiencing the fleet glimpse of a ramier flying from the forest floor through the branches into the Prussian Blue sky, it was impossible not to look and look and drink it in like one who had long been thirsty. *It is more beautiful than a dream, for in dreams you cannot smell this divine spiciness, you can't stand in a mist of aromatic warmth and stare through jungle twigs to a spread of distant town, so distant that people seem to have no significance: you cannot drown your eyes in a cobalt sea, a sea with the blinding gold of the sun for a boundary.*

In *The Orchid House,* the sensuously felt land is a function of the characters' nostalgia (and incidentally that of the author) but nostalgia is only one component of the author's view made explicit at another point:

> Beauty and disease, beauty and sickness, beauty and horror: that was the island. A quartering breeze hurried eastward, over cotton clouds; the air was soft and hot; colour drenched everything, liquid turquoise melted into sapphire and then into emerald.

It is a weakness of *The Orchid House* that Mrs. Allfrey's language is not equal to the sensuous task she sets it: there are too many labored passages of passionate declaration and too few which involve us dramatically. But the "beauty and sickness" view of the island is the source of the novel's peculiar difference from *Wide Sargasso Sea* and *Christopher.* Reflecting on her period of service with the family, Lally (the embodiment of the traditionally devoted Negro servant) contrasts her past with her present outlook:

> When I was nurse to the little girls, I had no time to fall ill or to see how beautiful everything was. And anyhow, when you are working for white people whom you love, you can only think of those people and their wants, you hardly notice anything else. I did not even pay any attention to my own people, the black people, in those days, but now I am observing them and seeing what is happening to them. I am seeing how poor they are, and how the little babies have stomachs swollen with arrowroot and arms and legs spotted with disease.

Kenneth Ramchand. *Journal of Commonwealth Literature.* 7, July 1969, pp. 9–12

Phyllis Allfrey's novel is a memorable one in several ways. Not the least of these are the absence of self-conscious West Indian detail and her refusal to purvey the clichés of race, color, and class. Instead she offers something more subtle and enduring, a sustained and sensitive analysis of Dominican Society. She pursues her theme with a single-mindedness which does not exclude the feeling for a whole society, economically caught in the rich metaphor of her prose.

The society, emblematized by the Orchid House itself, is already decaying, though it still remains aloof from the new forces which are stirring and must ultimately sweep it away or leave it stranded. The central impulse in the novel is to preserve, incorporate, and render meaningful to the present what it felt to be valuable in the past. But the tone is one of regret, arising out of helplessness before irreconcilables.

Likewise the central characters are felt to be part of what is almost oblivion, are activated by their desire to ward off the present, or, attempting to give the present meaning through recollection, experience a frustration which finalizes their exile. Past and present are woven together in the figure of the old nurse Lally. She is the center from which the major contrasts of the book operate. But she herself is caught in the change, and dying of a tumor, "nurses her complaint." Her winding, retrospective rhythms dimly restore what has gone, but fail to give meaning to the present.

The Master, shattered by his experiences in the First World War, flees the present. Having hurled his medals and the puppy "Flanders" from the window he has retired into drug-sustained reminiscence, maintained by the sinister Lillipoulala, the embodiment of escape. The Master takes with him the two women who love him. His wife and Mamselle ally themselves for his protection. Mamselle, who after her visit to Europe prided herself on her elegant French and fashionable clothes, now speaks patois and her clothes are faded and démodés.

It is against this that the three daughters returning from exile are matched. Each one demands change. Stella arranges the death of Lillipoulala and thus makes certain the inevitability of change or destruction. The two women continue to shelter the Master, who eventually learns that his means of escape from the present has ended, but cannot respond. Stella leaves the island maimed, suspended between past and present, unable to act any further. Joan, bringing with her the ideals of English socialism, seeks to alter the social and economic structure of the island, but is frustrated by the Catholic Church and the vested interests of business. It is Stella's act which has given these two conservative forces the means to frustrate her intentions, but she has sown the seeds for the future in Baptiste and returns to a meaningful relationship with her husband. Nathalie has no respect for ghosts and both destroys and preserves. Her money wins where everything else has failed. The past, however, cannot be altered completely in a moment, and the Master is killed while at best his son Andrew can make only a partial [recovery.]

Beyond the House there are the poor and the underprivileged whose grievances are only beginning to be articulated. . . .

The new order evolves, based not so much on whiteness, but on money, while still appealing to the values of a white elite no longer to be reckoned with.

This change Phyllis Allfrey partly locates and reflects in the relationship of Andrew and Cornelie. The position of Cornelie, the brown-skinned, illegitimate daughter of Rufus, has altered as the society has readjusted. She embodies the middle-class qualities of respectability and acquisitiveness. Lally warns Stella that it would be a mistake to treat her as "no account," to think of her "as someone Master Andrew might leave." The interest of the Catholic Church allied to the respectability of the Brown middle class is pressing her to marry Andrew. She wishes to remove the final barrier to the recognition of her position. She is contemptuous of Joan, who is involved with the black lower class, and fears Stella, who involves Andrew in nostalgic retrospection. Yet in all this Phyllis Allfrey is concerned to show that something beautiful and desirable is being superseded, that the relationship of the House and its occupants with the rest of the island can be symbiotic and not parasitic. The parasites are the wealthy coloreds now evolving in the island. They continue the exploitation begun by colonialism. The House has that which any society, especially West Indian, needs: grace and beauty. But while the evils it once represented are transferred and maintained what will become of its values?

Such themes are made compelling and vivid by the consistent evocation of an over-ripe beauty, containing the seeds of its own destruction and a constant reminder that the loveliness of the islands has made even more perplexing their history of inhumanity and violence. "Beauty and sickness, beauty and horror" characterize this world. Here the great whale pants to death on the beach, the restless humming-bird dashes itself to death against the window-pane; "Beauty grows like a weed here so does disease."

Thus we return to one of the central motifs of the novel, the orchid. This beautiful flower needs a living organism to grow upon, but does not suck life from that organism; instead it beautifies. It derives its moisture from the air because the roots never penetrate the earth. The emerging society might have its roots in the land and produce a flower as beautiful and more permanent. Hence the tragedy of the people of Orchid House. Their relationship with the islands is epiphytic. They are people who embellish with their beauty, are made tragic by their transience, are not of the land, are part of a moment, in flux.

The world of *Orchid House* has a metaphorical intensity and is convincing because it is all-pervasive. It enlarges our understanding of human frailty. There is nothing hackneyed, no comment, no moralizing, no bitter flourish. Instead there is quiet pathos for people matched against an inscrutable and inexorable historical process.

Barrie Davis. *World Literature Written in*
English. 11, 1972, pp. 81–83

Here is an island whose very nature expands the imagination. It so informs *The Orchid House* (and *Wide Sargasso Sea*) that in commenting upon the setting of Allfrey's novel years before he visited Dominica, Louis James in his introduction to *The Islands in Between* fused the atmosphere of the novel and that of the island which inspired it: "The house at the center of the action is called L'Aromatique. The island around it is drowsy with humming-birds, heat-dazed green and the glow of jewelled flowers. It is fascinating and diseased. Disease is a sweet sickly image recurring through the book." In short, Allfrey's novel is a rendition into prose of Dominica's combined danger and beauty. The physical atmosphere that Allfrey evokes in *The Orchid House* and Rhys in *Wide Sargasso Sea* is authentic, and not simply the romantic recollections of two women trying to recapture a bygone time and place. . . .

L'Aromatique or the Orchid House, so named for its attached conservatory where the exotic blossoms native to the island are nurtured, is a neglected estate in the mountains of what must be Allfrey's own Dominica. The master of the estate—he remains nameless in the novel—sequesters himself in the shadows of L'Aromatique, hoping to heal the mental wounds inflicted during his service in the First World War. "The Master" first returns from the war to the town house "Maison Rose," but he retreats soon after to L'Aromatique, further into psychological withdrawal, and finally into death. Metaphorically, what Allfrey depicts is the gradual disappearance of the last of the West Indian colonizing fathers.

While the men of L'Aromatique fade into enfeeblement—the master through his drug-induced dependency, the cousin Andrew through tuberculosis—the women summon the courage to survive. Lally, the feisty old nurse who acts as narrator, is the primordial survivor—not unlike Faulkner's Dilsey in *The Sound and the Fury*. L'Aromatique is, as Lally calls it, a house "empty of men." It is a "house of women" with Madam directing its daily functioning, Mamselle teaching its children, and Christophine preparing meals for all its inhabitants and hangers-on. The daughters of L'Aromatique bring additional survivor skills to the beleaguered household. Stella brings charm and passion; widowed Natalie brings her money to help the family through its numerous crises; Joan brings her political skill and energy to revitalize both the family and the island's economy.

Phyllis Allfrey has attempted to identify herself with the wonderful old nurse Lally although it is actually Joan who best corresponds to Allfrey's own character. . . .

Allfrey's retirement from active politics has encouraged her to return to literature, and a new novel, *In the Cabinet,* nears completion; its title promises a continuation of Joan's Orchid House story.

Elaine Chamberlain. Introduction to
Phyllis Allfrey. *The Orchid House* (rpt.
London: Virago, 1982), pp. viii–x, xiv

ALÓS, CONCHA (SPAIN) 1929–

[Concha] Alós began as a social realist, preoccupied with injustice and inequality in society, and is concerned in her fiction with exposing and denouncing inequities, most particularly as they affect women. In addition to novels, she writes short stories and occasional television script.

Los enanos (1963; The dwarfs) describes life in a pensión in a large Spanish city, a run-down boardinghouse whose inhabitants exist on the fringes of poverty. With neonaturalist touches in the style of Baroja, it combines somber and sober, direct observation of life with an anguished existentialist view of the human condition. Following Darwin (and Baroja), life is a jungle in which the strongest survive, and in this vein, most human beings are dwarfs (while society is a giant). . . .

In her second novel, *Los cien pájaros* (1963; A hundred birds), Alós depicts the sexual and social awakening of Christina, a working-class girl in a provincial city (perhaps Valencia). . . . Insecure and romantic, Christina has a short-lived affair with the married brother of her pupil, a playboy who gives her expensive presents, rents a villa for their meetings, and tires of her even before she learns she is pregnant. Barely eighteen, she decides to have her child, leaving home to spare her parents, and resisting the temptation of marriage to the working-class boy who loves her. The conclusion is no solution; the novel ends as she boards the train for Barcelona to face uncertainty and seek independence as well as existential acceptance of responsibility for her own actions. This is laudable, from a feminist viewpoint, but realistically very risky and impractical, unlikely even to be feasible in the Spanish society of that day.

Las hogueras (1964; Bonfires), which won the Planeta Prize, pictures the atmosphere of a Majorcan village where a wealthy foreign couple's somewhat parasitic existence is contrasted with the background of poverty and frustration characterizing the lives of the peasants. The foreign couple consists of a self-centered ex-model, Sibila, and the older husband she has married for security, a middle-aged businessman. . . . All of the characters seem suffocated by passion or frustration, a notion reinforced by the leitmotiv of the fish out of water, gasping for breath. Existentially, however, they are inauthentic, and their barren souls are symbolized by the bonfires of the title, a reference to accidental summer fires and the barrenness they produce.

El caballo rojo (1966; The red horse inn) is based upon the refugee experience of Alós and her parents as they fled Castellón and the approaching Franco forces. In spite of this point of departure, Alós employs a seemingly objectivist technique in a narration that aspires to impartiality. The characters are a heterogeneous group of Republican sympathizers temporarily brought together when one of their number manages to obtain a job as waiter in "El caballo rojo," which becomes a meeting place for refugees. A dominant note is *costumbrismo,* a depiction of local color and customs, and as is typical of the genre in Spain, character development is minimal and somewhat stereotypical. Much in the fashion of Dolores Medio's *El pez sigue flotando,* the narrative moves from one character to another, in a plotless portrayal of collective sufferings, discomforts, hunger, sorrows, and longings experienced by a group of refugees. Lacking a protagonist, the narrative reveals the gap between optimism, dreams or hope, and harsh realities.

Alós's second novel, which deals more or less directly with the Spanish Civil War, is *La madama* (1970; The madam), whose time frame is slightly before that of *El caballo rojo,* covering the early months of the conflict. Also utilizing a third-person narrative perspective, this novel possesses greater unity—implicit in the title, which appropriately calls attention to the ascendancy or predominance acquired by an individual, much as the title of *El caballo rojo* signifies the collective or generic nature through its focus upon a group meeting place. Instead of the many families that appear in the earlier novel, *La madama* portrays only one, the Esprius, a formerly wealthy, bourgeois unit whose members falter under stress. . . . The two narrative planes— prison and beleaguered city—are fused by the repetition of similar motifs signifying degeneracy, suffering, degradation, anguish, and despair.

El rey de gatos (Narraciones antropófagas) (1972; King of cats, Cannibalistic tales) contains nine short stories with a wide variety of themes. "La otra bestia" (The other beast) relates how a woman murders her unfaithful husband, although it may also involve her suicide. In the title tale, a strange man who becomes progressively more antisocial retires to an isolated cabin with untold numbers of cats, and one day nothing is left but the cats. All of the stories suggest the world of fantasy or madness which is just beyond the touch, the mirror, the door or wall that limit everyday reality. Frequently narrated in first person, the stories explore themes such as the war between the sexes, identity crises, alienation, fear, jealousy, and the loss of the mysterious something that separates human from animal.

In *Os habla Electra* (1975; Electra speaking), a Freudian study of mother-daughter relationships, Alós moves further from the surface plane of . . . realism toward psychological analysis and the re-creation of myth. Characters and the atmosphere around them are studied in detail, and the narrative fuses past and present, real and fantastic, memories and that which never was. *Os habla Electra* signifies a change in style and technique for Alós, who concentrates upon the dichotomy between fertility and the threat of destruction. References to the Electra myth occur primarily in the tragedy of the characters, rather than in specifics of the plot, as Alós sketches the struggle between patriarchal and matriarchal modes with the female (Electra, singular and plural) striving to regain identity or androgynous wholeness. Combining oneiric imagery and fragmented structure, Alós transcends the limits of social realism that defined her prior novels.

Something of the mythic atmosphere remains in *Argeo ha muerto, supongo* (1983; Argeo's dead, I suppose) in which the novelist explores the invisible bounds between the fantasy world of childhood and the secrets of adulthood. Autobiographical in format (a first-person, linear narrative), the story develops the themes of childhood as Paradise Lost, the loss of illusion, and the loss of first love. The narrator-protagonist Jano struggles with reconciling reality and the dream world as she attempts to cope with fragmentation of personality and frustrated passion for her foundling brother, Argeo. Infantile mythology includes the capability of transcending barriers and convention, and while the enchantment lasts, the youthful heroes achieve their greatest adventures. But time passes, and as happens with other animal "species" human beings are subject to a life cycle: the magic of childhood disappears and communication with it, and then the only solution is introspection.

Alós's most recent novel is *El asesino de los sueños* (1986; The assassin of dreams). Written in alternating sequences of second-person, familiar (tú), and third-person, objective narration, *El asesino de los sueños* presents the aspirations of the mother (coinciding with the norms of conventional society) and contrasts them with her reality ("fallen woman"). A novel of complex intertextuality—mythological allusions, the principals of *Othello,* Melibea and Polyphemus, Ortega, Tennessee Williams, Sophocles, Camus, *Ulysses,* Dumas, and others—the narrative is set in the Balearic Islands and Barcelona. . . . *The Assassin of Dreams* is both experimental and literarily mature.

Janet Perez. *Contemporary Women Writers of Spain* (Boston: Twayne, 1988), pp. 110–14

The novelistic trajectory traced by Concha Alós has been a stylistically varied one, from the social realism of early novels such as *Los enanos* (1962) to the non-chronological, dreamlike scenarios of *Os habla Electra* (1975) and *Argeo ha muerto supongo* (1982). Yet throughout more than two decades of creative production, a primary concern expressed in her work has been woman's marginal position within a restrictive, patriarchal society. In *Os habla Electra* this preoccupation assumes mythic proportions as a first person narrator/protagonist seeks to recreate a green world of feminine power and autonomy which has fallen prey to the destructive influences of man and his patriarchal culture. Central to this now extinct paradise is the figure of the narrator's mother, Electra, who recalls the archetypal Great Mother in her symbiotic relationship with the natural world and her independence from societal norms. Opposing this repository of matrilinear power is Madame la baronne, a patriarchal agent who invades Electra's green-world paradise, establishes ascendancy over it, and initiates a systematic extermination of the area's wildlife and natural resources.

The movement from green-world freedom to patriarchal confinement delineated by the narrator closely approximates the green-world archetype and its negation, the rape/trauma archetype, identified by Annis Pratt in *Archetypal Patterns in Women's Fiction.* A similar parallel can be seen in the transition of primitive matrilinear cultures to patriarchal systems, as described by cultural anthropologists such as J. J. Bachofen, Helen Diner and Robert Briffault. The tension maintained throughout the novel between the feminine principle and its patriarchal response may be linked to two specific mythological frameworks, the Greek legend of Electra and the Demeter/Kore archetype, thus supporting Pratt's identification of such correspondences as "signals from a buried feminine tradition that conflict with cultural norms and influence narrative structure."

Lucy Lee-Bonano. *ALEC.* 12, 1987, pp. 95–96

In the fictional world created by Concha Alós, woman appears as the central figure. The author strongly denounces the political, social, and economic circumstances that keep women in an inferior position with respect to men in contemporary Spanish society.

The modus operandi employed for the analysis of women's condition as Alós presents it in her novels is based principally on three aspects of the author's literary creation. In the first place, there are . . . her themes, which run from absence of love to sexuality. Then there is . . . Concha Alós's system of values as reflected in her novels, as well as . . . the author's own world, where life experiences, which are closely related to her work, contribute a great deal of authenticity to its aspects as a sociological and witness-bearing document. . . .

Although her themes center on the condition of the modern Spanish woman, some of them, like the absence of love, failure of communication, and isolation, transcend that specific condition and acquire universal tonalities. As for Alós's system of values, her novels reflect a negation of the majority of Spain's traditional values, with their emphasis on formulaic religion; instead, there is an affirmation of dignity, of life and the vital necessities of being.

Concha Alós's treatment of woman's condition in Spanish society assumes an explanation of the problems that women have faced in the past and continue to face today. It assumes, moreover, a clearer view of its causes, as well as a conviction that her political, social, and economic inferiority is not due to her sex's own actual inadequacy, but is rather imposed from without. This explanation evokes a greater sensitivity in the reader to woman's problems and a greater sympathy for her condition.

In addition, Alós offers partial solutions and responses to the condition of the Spanish woman, among them rebellion against unjust sociopolitical structures, rebellion against a rigid and antiquated morality, the importance of woman's education for a profession, and the liberation of the instinctual or animal side of woman's nature.

Fermin Rodriguez. *La Novelistica de Concha Alós* (Madrid: Origenes, 1985), pp. 13–14

ANDERSON, JESSICA (AUSTRALIA) n.d.

A work which responds to a variety of critical approaches, the action of *Tirra Lirra* takes place in the mind of a central character, Nora Porteous, who has returned as an old woman to her empty family home in Brisbane, having spent her adult life in Sydney and London. Jessica Anderson, too, was born in Brisbane and lives in Sydney, but although it is tempting to draw easy equivalences between the author and the narrating voice, a feeling of distance between the two, even of dislike, is established and carefully maintained.

Further, the sense of place in the novel is very diffuse. This is not an Australian novel like David Malouf's *Johnno* which explores and explains authorial identity through a retrospective recreation of a particular time and place; Brisbane is identifiable only by occasional references to humid heat, poinsettias, a mango tree, the joy of eating a pawpaw in the place in which it was grown, houses on stilts, and nebulously, by the fact that Tennyson is a suburb of Brisbane, creating a quirkish connection with the title.

Nora's search for a sense of self, established as her memory ranges back over her life, depends less on conflict between an individual and a particularized, hostile environment, a subject of much Australian literature, than on a rejection of any environment which is ugly to Nora, in either its human or its inanimate aspect. Continually oppressed by self-limiting, middle-class gentility—her only, older sister Grace sends Nora "an exhortation to duty, unselfishness and common sense" and a warning not to cry for the moon, "which has always been your big drawback, Nora"—and correspondingly confining surroundings, Nora withdraws, reacting psychologically and physically in ways which seem typically feminine, prompting another kind of analysis, trendily feminist.

Written by a woman, and exclusively and self-consciously concerned with an individual female experience, *Tirra Lirra* can be seen as part of a tradition of literature by and about women. Nora's withdrawal is on the one hand aesthetic: faced by a physical world which is inimical to her, she creates her own space, developing, according to Virginia Woolf's famous injunction, a room of her own. That these literal spaces are small and domestic assertions of self establishes a recognizably feminine life pattern.

Delys Bird. *Westerly.* 25, December, 1980,
pp. 78–79

During the 1979 National Book Council Awards, Jessica Anderson's *Tirra Lirra by the River* was given special mention as an "Australian novel of considerable merit." However, although the author's previous books were well received, she remains largely an enigma, receiving temporary exposure with literary awards and reviews.

Tirra Lirra by the River traces the life of Nora Porteous over most of the twentieth century. The action moves from Brisbane to Sydney to London and back again, involving both an inner and an outer journey by the central character. For many years Nora fights for the right to work and independence. It is interesting that Nora Porteous's first male friendships are with homosexuals. For some women of this generation, such friendships may have provided the only possible alternative to Australian stereotyped masculinity and mateship. It is interesting that this novel, more than any other, has been taken up by the women's movement as a book that reflects the lives of Australian women. *Tirra Lirra by the River* has much typical women's experience, such as the imprisonment of marriage, abortion, sexuality, liberation, and ageing.

Anderson's most recent novel, *The Impersonators,* which in 1981 won both the Miles Franklin and New South Wales Premier's Award, also traces a woman's return from Europe, but Sylvia Cornock is a young woman called home because of the impending death of her father. She returns to a family separated by class and age barriers. It could even be said that the Cornock family is a microcosm of Australian life in the 1970s—diverse, separated, aggressively affluent, or poor as their various branch lines indicate. In their interactions, polite manners save the day while, beneath the surface, petty jealousies and recriminations assert themselves. Anderson conveys most of this tension in brilliant passages of dialogue, where people talk without listening to one another.

Against the family network, Anderson conveys the city of Sydney. In one sequence she describes the lunchtime jog of two of the novel's central characters—one moves as if part of the city, the other jogs with a tension that pits himself against the city as if he must bring his will to bear on Sydney despite the level of personal cost. The central persona, Sylvia, as she walks through the Domain, sees the environs in yet another way that understands both the jarring bold beauty of Sydney and the avariciousness of climbing in a new land. The three central characters move through the same landscape at the same time, but all have different relationships to it. The passage's perception of male and female consciousness is acutely sensitive.

In *The Impersonators* the lives of women are shown to be lonely and victimized; they are sometimes saved by their solidarity with one another or in rare instances, as with Sylvia herself, by the sensitive support of a man. As the novel progresses, Harry emerges as the new breed of man—the male that exists in some women's writing as a counterbalance to traditional men trapped by conservative history.

Margaret Smith. In Carole Ferrier, ed.
*Gender, Politics and Fiction: Twentieth
Century Australian Women's Novels*
(Queensland: University of Queensland
Press, 1985), pp. 205–6

The conflict between the desire for flight and the desire for security is highly visible in *Tirra Lirra by the River* and *The Impersonators,* explored primarily through Nora and Sylvia, and as in *The Fortunes of Richard Mahony,* houses are prominent among the outward manifestations of these conflicting desires. To live in someone else's house may be to find oneself in a trap, as the young Nora discovers in the house of her mother and later her mother-in-law, and ownership of "the best home in the street" is not enough to save Dorothy Rainbow from despair and madness. But at best, a room of one's own can be both a sanctuary and an outlet for artistry. Even in London, where Nora changed her dwelling place many times, she "never once lived in an ill-proportioned room." The twin aspects of sanctuary and artistic expression are in Nora's mind as she considers the possibilities of the old family home in Brisbane, made available by Grace:

> In whatever circumstances I have found myself, I have always managed to devise a little area, camp or covert, that was not too ugly. At times it was a whole room, but at others it may have been only a corner with a handsome chair, or a table and a vase of flowers. Once, it was a bed, a window, and a lemon tree.

After a lifetime of living in flats, rooms, buildings shared with others, Nora is "no longer used to space," and like her sister plans to use only part of the house. One remembers her habit of regarding only part of Sydney, London, as "hers."

When Nora first sees her mother-in-law's house in Sydney, "a red-brick house in a big flat checkerboard suburb, predominately iron-grey and terra-cotta in color," she tells her husband "If I had to live here I would die." Faced with a similar prospect in Coventry, she clearly reaches the same conclusion.

> From the window I could see the rectilinear pattern made by straight streets and a hundred neat rooms. Iron-gray and terra-cotta. Who would have thought that at my age I could feel it again—the old oppression, the breast breaker?

That evening, Nora decides to return to Australia.

There are many shared experiences between the expatriate protagonists, Nora and Sylvia. Both leave home by ship, a definitive way of marking change of country that is now generally lost to us, like the raising of the curtain in the theater; both women, returning by plane, have on the flight vivid involuntary memories. For Nora, it is the house of her childhood, "no blob now, but *it,* the real house, a heavy wooden box stuck twelve feet in the air on posts," and for Sylvia, her mother and father, "two shapes in confrontation, the one towering, massive, slow, the other thin, shrieking, volatile, with bits of moving glitter about her dress." Both are enabled to return by the legacy of a dead woman. London, Europe—this was where one escaped to broaden one's existence; but for these two women, it has imperceptibly narrowed. For Nora, life has contracted into the sanctuary of number six, while outside the "villages" of London "were now meshed by the flow of traffic into one huge hard city, whose constant movement confused us, and whose noise beat upon our brains." Sylvia, who has always wandered further than Nora, and is a young woman when she leaves Europe, is less confined, but she too has become "a lover rather than an explorer, returning to places she knew instead of seeking new ones" in order to "protect herself against rawness and incoherence."

The Impersonators is a more diffuse book than *Tirra Lirra by the River.* It has a large cast, focusing on each group in turn; the characters are loosely linked by their family connections and by the way most of them, as the title suggests, are in a sense "impersonators," playing a role, wearing a protective mask. It would take more space than I have available here to chart the permutations of these impersonations, from Molly's pretence that she can read to Ted and Rosamond's marriage, supported by the legend that they have "remained in love." Greta attempts to move away from the long-established impersonation that falsifies her relationship with Sylvia, her step-daughter; but Sylvia will not permit it. Sylvia is also more comfortable with "the old act" she shares with her father: "Now that there is no question of anything but falsity, she dropped easily into chatter." It is possible that Jack Cornock becomes, unpleasantly, "more fully himself." After his stroke, and perhaps Ted also, in his open dishonesty after the crash of his firm and his passion for Jackie Tonn. The book is sharp-eyed rather than satirical about this fragmented, largely self-absorbed segment of Sydney society, in the year 1977; Jessica Anderson is an observer rather than a judge.

The second and sometimes even more overt interest of *The Impersonators* is expatriation, explored not only in character and action but in open debate: Europe versus Australia, "the consolation of the old" versus the raw discontinuity of the new; and whether there is a moral imperative for Australians who have been abroad to places where culture is more securely consolidated to "come home and use what they've learned." Sylvia, in contrast to Nora, is not an artist, so that the debate of *The Impersonators* of necessity differs from that of *Tirra Lirra by the River*. The resolution, however, is surprisingly similar. Both Nora and Sylvia are initially irritated, critical, alienated from their homeland; both come to accept the country and the culture to which they were born, an acceptance reflected in the comment of the homecoming narrator in Barry Hill's story "Lizards": "We come home in order to be real again.". . .

The city of Sydney, or part of it—primarily the area around the harbor, the North Shore, and Burwood—is splendidly conveyed. Houses are very important; in contrast to the houses of *Tirra Lirra* they tend to be possessions rather than sanctuaries, and indices of how much money you have, or have lost. Stewart is a knowledgeable up-market estate agent, but not surprisingly, the women are more sensitive to houses than are the men. For Hermione in particular a house may be a work of art; but the book raises the diverse possibilities that she fantasizes about houses she cannot afford, that houses are an expression of her first concern, status, that she is a genuine perfectionist, painfully holding out for excellence. Greta's garden seems an outlet for artistry very like Nora's rooms, corners, that were "not too ugly." The city is seen primarily through the eyes of the characters, the eyes being most frequently Sylvia's. Quite simply, the characters *notice* their surroundings. In spite of the bitumen, Wynyard ramp, suburbs which are either too sprawling or too ordered, *The Impersonators* sounds frequently like a love song to Sydney, and in particular to its harbor and gardens. The pace by pace description of Sylvia, Steven and Ted jogging their separate but seemingly synchronized ways round the Domain is gently amusing in its precision. The image which Sylvia uses to argue that Australia is not a classless society is that of passengers waiting, back to back, on the adjoining Platforms 3 and 4 of Wynyard Station: "the westbound on 3, and the northbound on 4."

In this Sydney setting *The Impersonators* occasionally breaks, in minute fractures, from the exclusive concentration on Europe/Australia which has become characteristic of Anderson's fiction. There is a Japanese container ship coming into the harbor, a mainland Chinese vessel is anchored in Woolloomooloo Bay which is observed by several characters, and sails out again presumably taking with it the five sightseeing Chinese sailors first observed by Sylvia in the Domain, and frequently thereafter as they wander through the book, sightseeing. Sylvia and Harry go to a Vietnamese restaurant in Oxford Street; the call girl with whom Harry falls hopelessly in love is a Vietnamese, Jackie Tonn. Though Sylvia has intended to settle in Rome, instinct tells her, when she realizes she may inherit some money from her father, that "now she would be able to go to India, China, anywhere." This is still a Europe-Australian centered book, but the East, like the five sailors, is quietly, peripherally, briefly present.

Arlene Sykes. Southerly. 1986, pp. 67–71

Nora herself draws the connection with the poems of Tennyson, not only by mention of *The Idylls of the King* and "The Lady of Shallot," but by her explicit correlation between the world of Camelot with the curse on the Lady, and the interior world of her mind with the spell cast by her vision of the imaginary landscape. . . .

Here, . . . at the very beginning of the novel, we have an affirmation about art—the kind of art in which Jessica Anderson believes. It is not the art of sensation, of shock, of attempts to make us experience horror or ugliness by rubbing our noses in it. The novel contains several incidents which invite sensational treatment—Nora's experience at the abortionist's, her attempted suicide, her failed face-lift, Dorothy Rainbow's massacre of her children and subsequent suicide; yet these are related in an almost off-hand way. The novel affirms that, despite modern assumptions and fashions in art and film, we do not understand things better by experiencing them at the white heat of passion and intensity, but only by distancing ourselves from them, by reflecting on them and, through the process of artistic creation, transforming them. Nora tells us how she used to walk by the real river, "broad, brown and strong," but she "hardly saw it and never used it as a location for [her] dreams." Instead her dreams are of beauty. "I was in love with beauty" she says, in the same paragraph in which she describes the "raw, ugly, sprawling suburb" in which she lived, the pile of excrement from the carthorse and the stench of the nightcart. . . .

Thus Nora parallels both the Lady of Shallot and the author of the novel and thereby, in her dual role as weaver of tapestries and recorder of her life, emphasizes the similarity of artistic and literary creation. In this regard, it is both significant and intentional that Nora should be portrayed as a character

with whom the reader is not allowed to identify too closely. We are deliberately distanced from her as, by her apparent sense of superiority, she has
become isolated from most of her family and friends. . . . This *Verfremdung-
seffekt* is consonant with the theory of art implicit throughout the novel at
the several levels I have indicated and is reaffirmed explicitly on the last page
which concerns that experience of such intense sorrow in her past that Nora
has suppressed the memory all her life. The grief has been made bearable by
the distancing effect of the funeral ceremony. The words of the unnamed
person at the funeral, "A very fine ceremony, madam! A verry fine ceremony!," are not, as we might at first think, repeated here ironically to show
the insensitivity of the speaker. On the contrary, like James McAuley, Nora
and, I think, Jessica Anderson, endorse the concept of ceremony which distances, makes bearable and transforms into art, those intense experiences in
life which would otherwise be intolerable. . . .

Here, as in the skilful employment of diverse word connotations, *Tirra
Lirra by the River* displays a considerable sophistication in its drawing of
implicit parallels between the various aspects of art, reflection and reality
and in its use of structure and characterization as meaning. When one becomes aware of these levels of subtlety and of the pervasive and consistent
affirmations about the nature of art and reality, one is ready to forego the
more fashionable elements of realism—shock, passion, intensity and the cult
of ugliness—for the art of reflection.

Roslynn D. Haynes. *Australian Literary
Studies.* 12, 1986, pp. 319–20, 322–23

It has taken some years and several novels for Anderson to speak through
that authoritatively confessional and female voice for which she is now
praised. Her early novels in hindsight appear to represent a search for a voice
that is neither colonially nor gender prescriptive and they are, in consequence, full of dialogic tension. Instead of being typically first-novel autobiographical, the first two novels not only are clearly non-biographical, but they
also focus on a male central character who is at the same time the reluctant
subject and the upholder of latter-day imperial superiority through a self-
chosen profession, and whose speaking position is continually threatened by
equivocality of the female voice.

This essay therefore will concentrate on *An Ordinary Lunacy* (1963) and
The Last Man's Head (1970) in order to illustrate how the dialogic imperative
is the source of a particular type of narrative tension in her early work; I
conclude with the last and just published *Taking Shelter,* in which this tension
is now muted through the more equally balanced dialogism of the confident
Australian and female discourse.

In *An Ordinary Lunacy* and *The Last Man's Head* the impact of political,
cultural and sexual colonization is implied throughout the highly charged
emotional encounters which control and focus the sequential energy of each
novel. Each novel attempts to cede authority to the subsidiary discourses,

to establish them in a position of dominance, but with only dubious success. Dialogism in these novels therefore issues a challenge; it fulfills its etymology; it is confrontational; by foregrounding the other, it becomes the site of conflict because the colonized discourse is channelled through male authority figures who are both overtly representatives of old-world colonial dominance, while the female moves within an ill-defined and potentially unregulated space which encompasses both the new and the old worlds: Daisy in *An Ordinary Lunacy,* the interior decorator whose cultural references are wholly European; Sophie, Australian born but with "foreign intonations . . . owing to her sparse and intermittent education having been received mostly in France and Spain"; and Isobel, who "had travelled the world, and remembered its landscapes, buildings, and peoples only as a confused and dreamlike background against which she and Richard Purdy had played out their selfish yet self-losing drama of love and hatred."

Dialogic interaction underscores the difficulty of speaking back, of successfully enunciating an authentic speaking position. In both novels the male Australian voice appears to dominate at the expense of the female deracinated voice. The victory, however, is quite clearly shown to be Pyrrhic; a profounder signification derives from the unvocalized moments in what will develop as a pattern of enforced silences throughout her work. . . .

In both early novels [*The Impersonators* and *The Last Man's Head*], Anderson's main characters, both male authority figures, metonymically become the site of the dialogic struggle, David as barrister, Alec as detective, and it is through demonstrating the tenuous authenticity of the male Australian voice that Anderson moves towards the authoritative female voice in her later novels. I would like to see this progression as a deliberate one, but there is a tentative air about her sense of the need for speaking back in these two novels which somehow belies confidence and certainty. . . .

While we can see *The Commandment* (1975) representing a positive and final writing out of the male figurehead of the colonial system with Patrick Logan's death, *The Last Man's Head* does this in that modern setting of Sydney which is most readily identifiable as the Anderson world. If both Alec and Robbie can be regarded as the bitter subject of the London nursery rhyme which supplies the title, then Alec's submission to the power of his daughter and the female is indicative of a change in Anderson's concerns at the end of the novel:

> When the women saw him drop suddenly into the chair lately vacated by Agnes, and put his head on Esther's breast, and stay in that position as if struck dead, Miss Torpy and Trixie looked in alarm at each other, and then at Agnes for an explanation. But Agnes's affronted stare was fixed on Alec's red neck, over which, as she watched, Esther's hand slid.

No longer is the male imperial voice dominant. Both novels have demonstrated the weakness of that lingering post-colonial position, and her subsequent work evinces no difficulty with the centrality of the female voice in its various guises which is able to speak confidently yet still dialogically through a variety of narrative positions—nostalgia, memory, dreams and tale-telling.

In Anderson's recently published novel *Taking Shelter,* the Australian experience is authenticated through dreams and tale-telling, in which the fictive and the fabulous are all associated with old Europe. At the center of the novel is Beth, the Scheherezade and *trompe-l'oeil* artist, and her memory of a childhood incident in Rome when she met Marcus, another transplanted Australian child, in some museum cloisters, making a list of the animals in the stonework: "I went on with that list all over Rome. Ran out of real animals, and started on the fabulous ones. Griffin and satyr and so on." This incident, which is related in its wholeness as the short story "Changing the Tune," published in 1987, is played with by Anderson as she weaves it in and out of Beth's and her tale. In this weaving process the subtle symbolism of the only part of Marcus's list the young Beth is able to catch a glimpse of, *"And the rhino has ivy growing out of his mouth,"* is gradually focused on the male/female relationships:

> Beth hoped it was not too late to keep her childish little Roman adventure to herself, and that it had not been too much distorted by its presentation, first to Doctor Gelthartz, then, selectively, for the amusement of Miles and Clem and Conrad. She shut her eyes and conjured up the rhino's head, clearly delineated against the blue sky, glossy ivy spilling out of its mouth. It seemed intact. Miles said, "I think you ought to drive this last bit, Beth."

In this latest novel the two central female voices, Beth and Juliet, both confront the dialogically powerful interplay between illusion and reality. They each play with illusion. Beth through her tales and visually through her murals which valorize the Australian experience (the bush gas station, the cinema entrance, the projected Captain Cook scene); and Juliet with the analysis and transcribing of her sexually potent dreams to which she adds "a little punctuation," and in which the reader reads more than Juliet is consciously willing to. At the end of the novel the painting and the dream merge; in the young Beth and the old Juliet the images of angel and caryatid are fused— those old-world artifacts, which in a new-world setting are a problem for the "list of fabulous creatures." Nita's final throwaway words "Plus some other stuff . . . that I've forgotten," are discounted by the reader's prior knowledge of the rest of the mural and Juliet's projections of the future, in which she will once again buy a house in the country and re-form the group which is now ironically united by Aids as much as by sophisticated interests. As in

The Last Man's Head the search for the mother—Beth is a watcher of real mothers—is rendered unnecessary by the imminent birth of Beth's child.

It is in this final novel, then, that the dialogic tensions in the old- and new-world speaking positions are resolved in the authoritative female voice of the dreamer and the tale-teller.

Barbara Garlick. The Journal of
Narrative Technique. 21:1, Winter, 1991,
pp. 74–76, 80–82

ANGELOU, MAYA (UNITED STATES) 1928–

In [the] primal scene of childhood which opens Maya Angelou's *I Know Why the Caged Bird Sings,* the black girl child testifies to her imprisonment in her bodily prison. She is a black ugly reality, not a whitened dream. And the attendant self-consciousness and diminished self-image throb through her bodily prison until the bladder can do nothing but explode in a parody of release (freedom).

In good autobiography the opening, whether a statement of fact such as the circumstance of birth or ancestry or the recreation of a primal incident such as Maya Angelou's, defines the strategy of the narrative. The strategy itself is a function of the autobiographer's self-image at the moment of writing, for the nature of that self-image determines the nature of the pattern of self-actualization he discovers while attempting to shape his past experiences. Such a pattern must culminate in some sense of an ending, and it is this sense of an ending that informs certain earlier moments with significance and determines the choice of what experience he recreates, what he discards. In fact the earlier moments are fully understood only after that sense of an ending has imposed itself upon the material of the autobiographer's life. Ultimately, then, the opening moment assumes the end, the end the opening moment. Its centrality derives from its distillation of the environment of the self which generated the pattern of the writer's quest after self-actualization. . . . Her genius as a writer is her ability to recapture the texture of the way of life in the texture of its idioms, its idiosyncratic vocabulary and especially in its process of image-making. The imagery holds the reality, giving it immediacy. That she chooses to recreate the past in its own sounds suggests to the reader that she accepts the past and recognizes its beauty and its ugliness, its assets and its liabilities, its strength and its weakness. Here we witness a return to and final acceptance of the past in the return to and full acceptance of its language, the language a symbolic construct of a way of life. Ultimately Maya Angelou's style testifies to her reaffirmation of self-acceptance, the self-acceptance she achieves within the pattern of the autobiography.

Sidonie A. Smith Southern Humanities
Review. Fall, 1973, pp. 366–67, 375

I Know Why the Caged Bird Sings creates a unique place within black auto-biographical tradition, not by being "better" than the formidable autobiographical landmarks described, but by its special stance toward the self, the community, and the universe, and by a form exploiting the full measure of imagination necessary to acknowledge both beauty and absurdity.

The emerging self, equipped with imagination, resourcefulness, and a sense of the tenuousness of childhood innocence, attempts to foster itself by crediting the adult world with its own estimate of its god-like status and managing retreats into the autonomy of the childhood world when conflicts develop. Given the black adult's necessity to compromise with prevailing institutions and to develop limited codes through which nobility, strength, and beauty can be registered, the areas where a child's requirements are absolute—love, security, and consistency—quickly reveal the protean character of adult support and a barely concealed, aggressive chaos. . . .

A good deal of the book's universality derives from black life's traditions seeming to mirror, with extraordinary intensity, the root uncertainty in the universe. The conflict with whites, of course, dramatizes uncertainty and absurdity with immediate headline graphicness. What intensifies the universalism still more is the conflict between the sensitive imagination and reality, and the imagination's ability sometimes to overcome. Maya and her brother have their reservoir of absurd miming and laughter, but sometimes the imagination is caught in pathos and chaos.

The major function of the imagination, however, is to retain a vigorous dialectic between self and society, between the intransigent world and the aspiring self. Through the dialectic, the egos maintain themselves, even where tragic incident triumphs. In a sense, the triumph of circumstance for Maya becomes a temporary halt in a process which is constantly renewed, a fact evident in the poetic language and in the mellowness of the book's confessional form. . . .

The uniqueness of *I Know Why* arises then from a full imaginative occupation of the rhythms flowing from the primal self in conflict with things as they are, but balanced by the knowledge that the self must find its own order and create its own coherence.

George E. Kent. *Kansas Quarterly.*
Summer, 1975, pp. 75–78

When Maya Angelou speaks of "survival with style" and attributes survival to the work of artists, she is talking about a function of art similar to that described by Ralph Ellison. . . .

Such an affirmation of life, a humanizing of reality, is Maya Angelou's answer to the question of how a Black girl can grow up in a repressive system without being maimed by it. Art protects the human values of compassion, love, and innocence, and makes the freedom for the self-realization necessary for real survival. Her answer, like Ellison's, skirts the reformer's question: is "the cost of that style" too high? In this sense she and Ellison are religious writers rather than social ones, for their ultimate concern is self-transcendence. It is unlikely that either would deny the practical value of the past twenty years' progress toward attainment of Negroes' full citizenship in America. But ultimately, as artists, their concern is with the humanity which must survive, and even assimilate into its own creative potential, such restrictions as these writers have encountered. For if this humanity cannot survive restriction, then it will itself become assimilated to the roles imposed upon it.

Myra K. McMurry. *South Atlantic Bulletin.*
41: 2, 1976, pp. 110–11

And Still I Rise is (Maya) Angelou's third volume of verse, and most of its thirty-two poems are as slight as those that dominated the pages of the first two books. . . . On the other hand, a good Angelou poem has what we call "possibilities." One soon discovers that she is on her surest ground when she "borrows" various folk idioms and forms and thereby buttresses her poems by evoking aspects of a culture's written and unwritten heritage. "One More Round," for example, gains most of its energy from "work songs" and "protest songs" that have come before. . . . The idea of somehow binding "work" and "protest" forms to create new art is absolutely first rate, but the mere alternation of "work" and "protest" does not, in this instance, carry the idea very far.

Other poems, such as "Willie," cover familiar ground previously charted by Sterling Brown, Langston Hughes, and Gwendolyn Brooks. Indeed, Angelou's Willie, despite his rare powers and essences . . . approaches becoming memorable only when he is placed in that pantheon where Brooks's Satin-Legs Smith and Brown's Sportin' Beasly are already seated. Similarly, "Through the Inner City to the Suburbs," "Lady Luncheon Club," and "Momma Welfare Roll" bear strong resemblances to several poems of Brooks's pre-Black Aesthetic period in *Annie Allen* and *The Bean Eaters.*

Up to a point, "Still I Rise," Angelou's title poem, reminds me of Brown's famous "Strong Men," and it is the discovery of that poem that helps us define Angelou's particular presence and success in contemporary letters and, if we may say so, in publishing. The poetic and visual rhythms created by the repetition of "Still I Rise" and its variants clearly revoice that of Brown's "strong men . . . strong men gittin' stronger." But the "I" of Angelou's refrain is obviously female and, in this instance, a woman forthright about the sexual nuances of personal and social struggle. . . . Needless to say, the woman "rising" from these lines is largely unaccounted for in the earlier verse of men and women poets alike. Most certainly, this "phenomenal woman," as she terms herself in another poem, is not likely to appear, except perhaps in a negative way, in the feminist verse of our own time. Where she *does* appear is in Angelou's own marvelous autobiographies, *I Know Why the Caged Bird Sings* and *Gather Together in My Name.* In short, Angelou's poems are often woefully thin as poems but they nevertheless work their way into contemporary literary history. In their celebration of a particularly defined "phenomenal woman," they serve as ancillary, supporting texts for

Angelou's more adeptly rendered self-portraits, and even guide the reader to (or back to) the autobiographies. With this achieved, Angelou's "phenomenal woman," as persona *and* self-portrait, assumes a posture in our literature that would not be available if she were the product of Angelou's prose or verse alone.

R. B. Stepto. *Parnassus*. Fall/Winter 1980,
pp. 313–15

If it was stated earlier that [in her autobiographies] Maya is a static figure, this should not be taken to mean a deeply rooted one. "Moved from place to place—from the South to St. Louis, back to Arkansas, then to California— she develops no sense of stability," complains Rayson about Maya in *I Know Why the Caged Bird Sings*. This restless movement foreshadows the later autobiographies: in *Gather Together in My Name,* Maya travels from San Francisco to Los Angeles, to San Diego, to Stamps, Arkansas, back to San Francisco, to Stockton, and to Oakland. In *Singin' and Swingin' and Gettin' Merry Like Christmas,* she travels with the *Porgy and Bess* company from Montreal . . . to Italy, France, Yugoslavia, Egypt, Greece, Israel, Morocco, Spain, and Switzerland; at the end of the book, she is in Hawaii. In *The Heart of a Woman,* she is drawn from New York to London, then to Alexandria in Egypt, and finally to Ghana. Angelou organizes the various places in her narrative—somewhat in the form of a travel diary, a form that her account of the *Porgy and Bess* European tour is not the only section to approach. . . . Rayson is right to criticize Angelou's rootlessness, but she considers it only from the point of view of a critic of autobiography. Whereas she insists on the unity of these countless episodes, the splitting up of the narrative structure through "horizontal displacement" and "vertical social stratification" is the identifying mark of the picaresque narrative. The reliability of the narrative "I" in the autobiography is vitiated not only through rootlessness . . . but in a very fundamental sense through the distortion of the narrative's central object.

Susanne Mayer. *Die Sehnsucht nach den
anderen: Eine Studie zum Verhältnis von
Subjekt und Gesellschaft in den
Autobiographien von Lillian Hellman,
Maya Angelou und Maxine Hong Kingston*
(Frankfurt: Lang, 1986), pp. 135–36

Early in her memoir [*I Know Why the Caged Bird Sings*], Angelou presents a brief but rich *biographia literaria* in the form of a childhood romance: "During these years in Stamps, I met and fell in love with William Shakespeare. He was my first white love. Although I enjoyed and respected Kipling, Poe, Butler, Thackeray, and Henley, I saved my young and loyal passion for Paul Lawrence Dunbar, Langston Hughes, James Weldon Johnson, and W. E. B. DuBois's 'Litany at Atlanta.' But it was Shakespeare who said,

'When in disgrace with fortune and men's eyes.' It was a state with which I felt myself most familiar. I pacified myself about his whiteness by saying that after all he had been dead so long that it couldn't matter to anyone any more." Maya and her brother Bailey reluctantly abandon their plan to memorize a scene from Shakespeare—"We realized that Momma would question us about the author and that we'd have to tell her that Shakespeare was white and it wouldn't matter to her whether he was dead or not"—and choose Johnson's "The Creation" instead. This passage, depicting the trials attending those interracial affairs of the mind that Maya must keep hidden from her vigilant grandmother, raises the question of what it means for a female reader and fledgling writer to carry on a love affair with Shakespeare or with male authors in general. While the text overtly confronts and disarms the issue of race, the seduction issue is only glancingly acknowledged. But this literary father-daughter romance resonates quietly alongside Angelou's more disturbing account of the quasi-incestuous rape of the eight-year-old Maya by her mother's lover, Mr. Freeman—particularly by virtue of the line she finds so sympathetic in Shakespeare, "When in disgrace with fortune and men's eyes."

[After Mr. Freeman's death], Maya breaks her [year-long] silence when a woman befriends her by taking her home and reading aloud to her, then sending her off with a book of poems, one of which she is to recite on her next visit. We are not told which poem it was, but later we find that the pinnacle of her literary achievement at age twelve was to have learned by heart the whole of Shakespeare's *Rape of Lucrece*—nearly two thousand lines. Maya, it appears, emerges from her literal silence into a literary one. Fitting her voice to Shakespeare's words, she writes safe limits around the exclamations of her wounded tongue and in this way is able to reenter the cultural text that her words had formerly disrupted. But if Shakespeare's poem redeems Maya from her hysterical silence, it is also a lover that she embraces at her peril. In Angelou's text, Shakespeare's Lucrece represents that violation of the spirit that Shakespeare's and all stories of sleeping beauties commit upon the female reader. Maya's feat of memory signals a double seduction: by the white culture that her grandmother wished her black child not to love and by the male culture that imposes upon the rape victim, epitomized in Lucrece, the double silence of a beauty that serves male fantasy and a death that serves male honor. The black child's identification with an exquisite rape fantasy of white male culture violates her reality. Wouldn't everyone be surprised, she muses, "when one day I woke out of my black ugly dream, and my real hair, which was long and blond, would take the place of the kinky mass that Momma wouldn't let me straighten? My light-blue eyes were going to hypnotize them. . . . Because I was really white and because a cruel fairy stepmother, who was understandably jealous of my beauty, had turned me into a too-big Negro girl, with nappy black hair, broad feet, and a space between her teeth that would hold a number two pencil." Maya's fantasy bespeaks her cultural seduction, but Angelou's powerful memoir, recovering the history that frames it, rescues the child's voice from this seduction by telling the prohibited story.

Christine Froula. *Signs: Journal of Women in Culture and Society.* 11 Summer, 1986, pp. 634, 636–37

ANHAVA, HELENA (FINLAND) n.d.

Reading the poems of Helena Anhava is like having a long talk with a wise, middle-aged, somewhat melancholy woman. In her latest volume of poetry, *Valoa* (Light) Anhava describes everyday life and such familiar environs as her home, garden, summer cottage, and the nearby forest. The poems are reflective, sometimes aphoristic. Her subject is often the mother who thinks about children and childrearing. Here the children have already left home, but still the mother hears their voices: "Somebody calls mother in the back yard / and anxiety goes through your mind before you remember: / nobody calls this mother anymore." The implication is that maternal instincts last forever. The poet also feels continual responsibility for young people, with much talk about development and growth. Still, the educator, though trying to do her best, cannot help but be insecure: "Education, double face. / Joyfully talking, cheerfully / you lead by hand / the trusting child straight to the mouth of the wolf, to school, / to the world."

Anhava's poems are often minimalist, containing only a few words or a single stanza, as in this aphorismlike example: "Once again a day / through the mind drive / crushing carriages." Even the imagery frequently consists of such small things as a leaf, an apple left on a tree in winter, a bird, a butterfly, a daisy. Her minimalism continues a tradition that began in Finnish poetry during the 1950s (Anhava herself debuted in the 1970s) and is practiced today by Risto Rasa, among others. Sometimes Anhava creates portraits of ordinary people such as Kreeta-Liisa Isokorpi, a hardworking mother who dies at an early age under the heavy pressures of childrearing, since the father of her children focuses only on his work.

Anhava's verse is often gloomy, and she writes frequently about the wounds left by life, its pain and anxiety. There is no self-pity, however. Nature is her living power, and in nature death is part of both life and beauty, as in the line "Beautifully falls the dying leaf."

Sinikka Tuohimaa. *World Literature Today.* 64, 1990, pp. 160–61

Poems 1971–1990 contains six previously published collections and a new series of poems, "After the Storm." The poetry is quiet, intimate, reflective, and often aphoristic. The earlier collections react to the committed verse of the sixties and seventies, the later ones perhaps to the speculation and materialism of the eighties. Helena Anhava's lines are strewn with flowers, wild and garden. They are peopled by small creatures, weasels and wagtails, moving among modest trees like the rowan and the alder. They are clear, deceptively easy. They deal with everyday life, with the world of woman— life's common laborer, the world of corsets and cosmetics, of children and their upbringing. She often tells us proverbial truths: "It's easier to decide what a child needs / than to listen to the child." She gives abundant advice: "You must learn to live with yourself, as with a difficult illness." She tells us how to write as we speak and breathe, different days, different ways; she warns us against becoming "a certain age."

This, like Eeva Kilpi's verse . . . is the poetry of the no longer young, of middle age, "as if one had come / from a long journey / home." If we were a misled generation, she tells the young Finn, make sure you are not one as well. Middle age brings resignation and a certain conservatism, but the poet sees her middle-aged, middle-class world with irony and questions its values as much as she does those of the radical young. In the seventies she was openly in opposition to her times: "There always have to be those you can spit on: / Reds, Jews, Gypsies, / now's the turn of the individualist." Today her criticism of society is less obvious but still apparent.

Sometimes it is difficult to decide whether Anhava's aphorisms are wise or trite, as when one is faced with a line like "Writing is a dialogue with life." Or is she being purposely trite? Often the simple statement gathers echoes or ripples around it, or it has a rightness of its own. . . . There are few incidental images in her verse; the image is in the total expression.

The general impression conveyed by *Runot 1971–1990* is of one who has thought long and deeply about the world she lives in and has worked painstakingly and honestly to polish her thoughts to a sharp, durable edge. The poet should be an "ear," Anhava has said. Her ear is certainly acute, but the quiet tones of her voice too are distinctive. Her poetry has been rewarded by a steady popularity among Finnish readers that more conspicuous poets have sometimes failed to achieve.

Philip Binham. World Literature Today. 65,
1991, pp. 153–54

ANZALDÚA, GLORIA (UNITED STATES) 1942–

The universe of discourse Gloria Anzaldúa's 1987 work *Borderlands/La Frontera* entered was, to some extent, one that she had helped to shape in key ways. An earlier text, the award-winning anthology *This Bridge Called My Back: Writing by Radical Women of Color,* edited by Anzaldúa and Cherríe Moraga, appeared in 1981, was reissued in 1983, and sold more than

35,000 copies. It also helped pave the way for Anzaldúa's virtuoso 1987 experiment. Anzaldúa's contributions to the earlier book—her introduction, her essay, "Speaking in Tongues: A Letter to Third World Women Writers," her story, "La Prieta," her interview with Luisah Teish, and her foreword to the second edition—show some signs of things to come. . . .

In *Borderlands/La Frontera*, Gloria Anzaldúa merges two narrative realms: that of the poet and that of the nonfiction writer. While moving between Spanish and English (in addition to Nahuatl and a range of other languages) with the skill of the poet, Anzaldúa lays out the facts of her subject with the care of the historian or social scientist. The result is a book unlike any that had gone before. It is Anzaldúa's artful movement between Spanish and English that makes the book a groundbreaking experiment in American nonfiction narrative. . . .

Anzaldúa . . . explains the switching of linguistic codes that will take place in the book:

> The switching of "codes" in this book from English to Castillian Spanish to the North Mexican dialect to Tex-Mex to a sprinkling of Nahuatl to a mixture of all these, reflects my language, a new language—the language of the Borderlands. There, at the juncture of cultures, languages cross-pollinate and are revitalized; they die and are born. Presently this infant language, this bastard language, Chicano Spanish, is not approved by any society. But we Chicanos no longer feel that we need to beg entrance, that we need always to make the first overture—to translate to Anglos, Mexicans and Latinos, apology blurting out of our mouth with every step. Today we ask to be met halfway. This book is our invitation to you—from the new mestizas.

She will not translate at every turn, or apologize with every step: sometimes she will translate directly, sometimes she will paraphrase, and sometimes she will refuse to translate at all. The final word of Anzaldúa's preface, "mestizas," is unitalicized: it is English. The lack of italics reminds the reader of the cross-pollination that has already taken place between English and Spanish, and reminds us that we already inhabit a place where "two or more cultures edge each other."

The borderlands Anzaldúa charts in *Borderlands/La Frontera* are legion: that between Chicano and Anglo, Mexican and Anglo, Mexican and Chicana, Mexican and Chicano, Chicano and Chicana, Chicana and Chicana, Anglo and Indian, Indian and Mestizo, Spanish and Indian, Spanish and Mestizo, male and female, female and female, male and male, heterosexual and homosexual, rich and poor, urban and rural, spirit-world and real world, articulate and inarticulate, and so on. All of us, as we soon realize, inhabit many borderlands. Anzaldúa invites us to enter hers, in empathy and imagination; and

she invites those who already inhabit that borderland to understand, appreciate, and reclaim it with the same passionate concentration that yielded her
art. "I am a border woman," Anzaldúa writes. "I grew up between two cultures, the Mexican (with a heavy Indian influence) and the Anglo (as a member of a colonized people in our own territory). I have been straddling that
Tejas–Mexican border, and others, all my life. It's not a comfortable territory
to live in, this place of contradictions. Hatred, anger and exploitation are the
prominent features of this landscape."

Anzaldúa's book is comprised not only of multiple linguistic codes, but
also of multiple genres. Her first chapter, a powerful essay embracing autobiography, history, journalism, and social science, starts with two extracts and
a poem. The first extract, in Spanish, is a quote from *"Los Tigres Del Norte,"*
which the footnote identifies as a *"conjunto* band." The second extract is
from a book. It identifies *"The Aztecas del norte"* as "the largest single tribe
or nation of Anishinabeg (Indians) found in the United States today. . . .
Some call themselves Chicanos and see themselves as people whose true
homeland is *Aztlán* [the U.S. Southwest]." We move from self-identification
of *"el otro Mexico"* by the *conjunto* to a scholar's discussion of Chicano's
identification of themselves and their homeland to Anzaldúa's own statement
on the subject—the first harsh and lyrical poem of many such poems the
reader will encounter in the volume, one filled with striking images:

> 1,940 mile-long open wound
>   dividing a *pueblo,* a culture,
>   running down the length of my body,
>   staking fence rods in my flesh,
>   splits me   splits me

Even before Anzaldúa begins the narrative prose that comprises the bulk of
this chapter, she has set the stage for the idea that borders are complex,
elusive constructions that may bring to mind gashes, cuts, and deep painful
wounds—images that are stark, fresh, and surprising. . . .

One of Anzaldúa's key themes is the difficulty of translating your life
into a language that cannot express it. While she wants to communicate the
difficulties of living on linguistic borderlands, she also wants to communicate
the richness it entails—not only for those who live there already, but, potentially, for the rest of us. She pursues these goals with two complementary
strategies. On the one hand, the book is filled with highly evocative, clear,
and readable passages . . . that move back and forth between Spanish and
English in an apparently seamless flow, minimizing the difficulty of translating
from one realm to the other; these passages give the reader a sense of what
it feels like to live in two languages, in a world where the borders between
languages are fluid. On the other hand, the book is also filled with slyly
evasive "nontranslations"—passages that might appear, on the surface, to be
translations, but which turn out, on closer view, to be nothing of the sort—

complex passages that paraphrase, amplify, contradict, extend, or contract the passages that precede them, doing everything, in fact, but "translating" them. These passages underscore for the reader the poverty of one who does not have a mestiza consciousness of language. Anzaldúa's goal, of course, is to teach the reader to appreciate and value precisely the fecundity of imagination and expression that *"la consciencia de la mestiza"* can yield. The book is interesting and readable on any terms, but for the reader who can approach the mestiza's linguistic awareness, it holds special secret luminous riches. . . .

Anzaldúa wants to do more than simply validate her language or her vision: she wants to reclaim and celebrate dimensions of the experience they embody. Anzaldúa will settle for nothing less than wrenching from her own experience as an outsider—as a Chicana, as a mestiza, and as a lesbian—the guideposts of a new way of being in the world. Anzaldúa universalizes the particulars of her own experience by forging a powerful link between those particulars and the creative process itself. She makes a strong case for the idea that the sense of disruption, discontinuity, dislocation, ambiguity, uncertainty, and fear that living on cultural, social, linguistic, and sexual borders entails can be a positive force for the artist. For while living with constant fear (of humiliation, of deportation, of hundreds of unnamed terrors) can paralyze, it can also produce a heightened sensitivity to one's environment, or what Anzaldúa calls *"la facultad."* Born of the fear that comes from paying intense attention to "when the next person is going to slap us or lock us away," this supersensitive "radar" that yields subtle and complex data about emotions and people gives "the one possessing this sensitivity" the sense of being "excruciatingly alive to the world." "Another aspect of this faculty," Anzaldúa writes, is that "it is anything that breaks into one's everyday mode of perception, that causes a break in one's defenses and resistance, anything that takes one from one's habitual grounding, causes the depths to open up, causes a shift in perception . . ." And while the disruption, dislocation, and ambiguity produce enormous tensions, the individual who learns to manage those tensions develops extraordinary capacities to forge new creative syntheses, to thrive in what Anzaldúa calls "the *Coatlicue* state." *"Coatlicue,"* a concept drawn from early Mesoamerican fertility myths, "is a rupture in our everyday world . . . a synthesis of duality, and a third perspective—something more than mere duality or synthesis of duality." Like Anzaldúa herself, *"Coatlicue"* is a symbol of the fusion of opposites.

Anzaldúa wants to share with the reader that sense of breaking through one's "everyday mode of perception." She wants to take her reader beyond her "habitual grounding"—whether that reader is a Chicana who is ashamed of her language, a lesbian who is afraid to express her love of women, an Anglo who may suspect the words "Chicano culture" to be an oxymoron, a poet who thinks history should be left to the historians, or a man who takes women's silence as tacit assent. . . .

The hundred pages of poems that follow the hundred pages of prose in the book serve as a reprise, chanting the themes the first section introduced in new and different keys, with subtle variations, all the while reaffirming their-basic message. Anzaldúa reclaims ancient myth, recent history, contemporary conditions, and the timeless patterns of nature, and weaves them into a stunningly coherent paean to the anguish and beauty of life. "To survive in the Borderlands," Anzaldúa writes, "you must live *sin fronteras* / be a crossroads." It is to these crossroads that Gloria Anzaldúa's "new mestiza" will lead.

> Shelley Fisher Fishkin. In Norman Sims, ed.
> *Literary Journalism in the Twentieth Century* (New York: Oxford University Press, 1990), pp. 160–70

Gloria Anzaldúa's *Borderland/La Frontera,* an elaboration of her own feminist theory . . . examines the dynamics of race, class, gender, and sexual orientation. For Anzaldúa, feminism emerges as the force that gives voice to her origins as "the new mestiza." This "new mestiza" is a woman alienated from her own, often homophobic, culture as well as from the hegemonic culture. She envisions the new mestiza "caught between *los intersticios,* the spaces between the different worlds she inhabits." Anzaldúa's feminism exists in a borderland not limited to geographic space, resides in a space not acknowledged by hegemonic culture. Its inhabitants are what Anzaldúa calls *"los atravesados . . . :* squint- eyed, the perverse, the queer, the troublesome, the mongrel, the mulatto, the half-breed, the half-dead. . . ." By invoking racist, homophobic epithets, Anzaldúa obliterates the power that the dominant culture holds over what is "normal" or acceptable.

Whereas the earlier works of women like Angela de Hoyos articulate Tejana feminist issues, Anzaldúa makes the leap from the history of colonization by the United States to the history of colonization as a *mestiza,* a Native American woman. And although some Chicana critics reject the internal colony model because, as Maria Linda Apodaca states, "when the land was conquered, the Mexican population in the Southwest was small given the total land mass," the specific history of the Tejano/Tejana urges us to remember that there is not one monolithic Chicano/Chicana experience in the United States. Apodaca's assumptions neglect to acknowledge the historical specificity of the Tejanas/Tejanos who were forced to live under a reign of terror in post-1848 Texas. . . .

Anzaldúa's text is itself a *mestizaje:* a postmodernist mixture of autobiography, historical document, and poetry collection. Like the people whose lives it chronicles, *Borderlands* resists genre boundaries as well as geopolitical borders. The text's opening epigraph is an excerpt from a song by the *norteño* conjunto band Los Tigres del Norte. But if Anzaldúa's historical ties are closer to the *corrido* tradition than to the historical imperatives of postmodern theory, hers is the new *corrido* of the mestiza with a political analysis of what it means to live as a woman in a literal and figurative Borderland. She tells us that "the U.S.-Mexican border *es una herida abierta* [is an open wound] where the Third World grates against the First and bleeds. And before a scab forms it hemorrhages again, the lifeblood of two worlds merging to form a third country—a border culture". Through issues of gender politics, Anzaldúa locates personal history within a history of the border people. Legitimacy belongs to the Anglo hegemony; the indigenous population is nothing more than an aberrant species. To the white power structure, the *mojado* (wetback) is the same as the *mexicano de este lado* (Mexican from the U.S. side). As she chronicles the history of the new mestiza, Anzaldúa explores issues of gender and sexual orientation that Chicano historians have not adequately addressed. . . .

Anzaldúa's project threatens further still the traditions of Chicanismo, when, as a lesbian Chicana, she forces the homophobes of the Chicano community to see their prejudice. If the heterosexual Chicana is ostracized from her culture for transgressing its rules of behavior, for the Chicana lesbian, "the ultimate rebellion she can make against her native culture is through her sexual behavior." She makes the "choice to be queer" and as a result feels the ultimate exile, cultural as well as geographic, from her homeland. She transforms the bourgeois concepts of safety and home to concepts she can carry with her along with her political commitments. And, as a Chicana "totally immersed" in her culture, she can choose to reject the crippling aspects of traditions that oppress women and silence homosexual men and women. Her refusal to "glorify those aspects of my culture which have injured me and which have injured me in the name of protecting me" signals the agenda for the new mestiza, the border feminist. The border feminist that Anzaldúa presents is a woman comfortable with new affiliations that subvert old ways of being, rejecting the homophobic, sexist, racist, imperialist, and nationalist. . . .

In the poem "To Live in the Borderlands Means You" Anzaldúa sums up her definition of the new mestiza, the feminist on the border. She is one who "carries five races" on her back—not Hispanic, Native American, African American, Spanish, or Anglo, but the mixture of the five which results in the mestiza, mulata. She's also "a new gender," "both woman and man, neither." While not rejecting any part of herself, Anzaldúa's new mestiza becomes a survivor because of her ability to "live *sin fronteras* / be a crossroads."

While Anzaldúa transgresses aesthetic boundaries in her text, transgresses gender boundaries in what she names her "choice" to be a lesbian, transgresses ethnicity and race in her formulation of the new mestiza combining Indian, Spanish, African, and even Anglo blood to form a *mestizaje,* her project is nonetheless articulated within the vital history of the Texas Chicana. If history is what forces Anzaldúa's escape into what Jenny Bourne has called "identity politics" in her essay "Homelands of the Mind," it is because the only history for the Chicana is the history of the mestiza's colonization by both the Spanish conquerors and the Anglo-American imperialists in their conquest of South Texas. . . .

The Chicana feminist's methodology is ideological analysis and material-ist, historical research, as well as race, class, and gender analysis. Her theory is never an ahistorical "politics of equal oppressions," because Chicana femi-nism develops from an awareness of specific material experience of the his-torical moment. Unlike the feminism of sisterhood, "feminism which is separatist, individualistic and inward-looking," Chicana feminists look inward in moments of self-exploration and see themselves as daughters of nonwest-ern indigenous tribes. Anzaldúa's feminist discourse leads her to look inward for a deeper understanding of a larger, erased history.

> Sonia Saldívar-Hull. In Florence Howe, ed.
> *Tradition and the Talents of Women*
> (Urbana: University of Illinois Press, 1991),
> pp. 295–302

In *Borderlands/La Frontera: The New Mestiza,* Gloria Anzaldúa traces a childhood on the borders between two cultures, Anglo and Mexican, in prose and poetry in three languages. Her history fades back into the legends of the Aztecs and forward into the movements of migrant farmworkers and lesbian feminists. Yet even in a work of such sociohistorical richness, Anzaldúa ap-peals to an artistic "self" that has all the trappings of romanticism. She writes of her art as an hierophantic—even chthonic—rite:

> I sit here before my computer, *Amiguita,* my altar on top of the monitor with the *Virgen de Coatalopeuh* candle and copal incense burning. My companion, a wooden serpent staff with feathers, is to my right while I ponder the ways metaphor and symbol concretize the spirit and etherealize the body. The Writ-ing is my whole life, it is my obsession. This vampire which is my talent does not suffer other suitors. Daily I court it, offer my neck to its teeth. This is the sacrifice that the act of creation requires, a blood sacrifice.

Although Anzaldúa elsewhere claims that "my people, the Indians, did not split the artistic from the functional, the sacred from the secular, art from everyday life," this desublimation of art is not evident here. Her testimony to the difficulty and pain of genius does not differ from similar expressions throughout the annals of canonical male literature. Anzaldúa considers that Western "objectivity"—the splitting off of self from others and the world to make objects of them—is "the root of all violence," and she deplores white anthropologists' historical objectifications of people of color. Yet she partici-pates in dualistic thinking in her stance as artist—an autonomous self imper-vious to external environment and conditions: "I had to leave home so I could find myself, find my own intrinsic nature buried under the personality that had been imposed on me."

Regenia Gagnier. *Feminist Studies.*
17:1, Spring, 1991, p. 138

I am speaking, here, of Gloria Anzaldúa, a Texan woman, and her efforts to maintain a balance between the positive images of her three identities. And she has another, as well, she is a lesbian, which further complicates the situation. In general, Anzaldúa, as in her book *Borderlands/La Frontera,* deals more with the positive images of the Chicana-woman-writer-poet (I do not say poetess because the term traditionally means poetry on the margins of *poetry*). Her prose is almost a stream of consciousness . . . with quotations from the poetry of others, songs, etc. Her poems include more of her lesbian identity. . . .

Anzaldúa presents images of strength and power through three elements: the serpent, the word, and the generational chain of women. Anzaldúa's work is not only very visual in her images, but it is also full of linguistic significance. Semiotics functions on two levels to encounter its messages. The three elements establishing the images of strength and power are represented with words in the feminine gender: *la* serpiente, *la* palabra, *la* cadena, which gives the reader highly visual signals.

The serpent is Anzaldúa's personal symbol (her animal identity as she explains in chapter 3 of her book, "Entering into the Serpent").

What is important in the motif of the serpent is the nexus that it represents with Indian culture. . . . Anzaldúa explains the native religion in detail and establishes a balance between the two cultures, showing pride in her indigenous ancestors; the Chicana can take a double ration of strength and power from her two cultures. The woman is associated with the goddesses, Coatlicue, Tonantzin, Tlazotleotl, Ciuhuacatl, and with the serpent in its various forms. . . . These were the creators, the mothers of all. It is obvious that the goddesses represent power and the poetic for the woman. There also exists the natural aspect of the serpent, the shedding of its skin, which represents birth. The serpent not only symbolizes birth and the creative function through its divine aspect, but also offers hope for the future. . . .

Traditionally, the acts of speaking and writing have represented acts of taking control, the assumption of strength and power. For the Chicano, the word, spoken or written, also has a political dimension. Bilingualism and especially "interlingualism" represents a balance between the two cultures and an experience of power. Anzaldúa speaks of this in chapter 5, "How to Tame a Wild Tongue," with her practice of code-breaking . . . frequently in the same sentence. And if control of the language is an image and a form of power for the group as a whole, it is all the more so for the woman and the poet. . . .

The image of the generational chain in Chicana literature has many functions: as a connection with the Indian ancestors, as a source of the oral tradition in *la raza,* and as a persistence of the ability to survive. But, in addition to being a Chicano sign, the chain also represents the woman: grandmother, mother, sister, daughter. It is not a question of negating the existence of a male chain, but rather of signalling the enormous and positive force of the female one.

Debra D. Andrist. In Aralia López-Gonzalez
et al., eds. *Mujer y literatura Mexicana y
Chicana: Culturas en contacto,* vol. 2
(Mexico City and Tijuana: Colegio de
Mexico and Colegio de la Frontera Norte,
1990, pp. 244–46

ARIYOSHI SAWAKO (JAPAN) 1931–84

[In *Hananka Seishu Tserra,* The Doctor's Wife], Ariyoshi's fictionalized version of Seishū's story centers on the relationship between the doctor's wife Kae and his mother Otsugi as they vie with each other for primacy in relation to him. Their conflict—and conflict between a mother and her daughter-in-law is a staple of Japanese expectations—is played out by each of them offering herself as subject for his experiments with anesthesia. Each is eager to be the first one granted permission to be made unconscious in his service. Kae is eventually blinded as a result of these experiments, but they are ultimately successful: the doctor's first use of his anesthetic is to operate on a breast cancer.

The achievements of these women is in something that might be termed "aggressive submission": neither, of course, has any possible world of achievement outside the Hanaoka family. The doctor's achievement is not to be disparaged; nonetheless it is made clear that it was attained by the sacrifice of the women in his family. Not only his wife and mother, but his two unmarried sisters, labor to educate him, then to run his household: the sisters both die young of illnesses that he cannot yet treat. Seishū assumes as a new family crest the depiction of a knot his wife Kae learned from a samaurai-stock grandmother, and used to tie her legs for the experiments so that in unconsciousness she would not thrash about in an unseemly way.

This short and selective description perhaps makes the novel sound unduly heavy-handed; however, the symbols of unconscious submission and physical restriction are quite clear. The only tools of expression these women had were their physical beings, and they made full use of them. Although "Seishu himself was never reluctant to emphasize the tremendous support he had received from his mother and Kae," the final acknowledgment they receive is indicated in the final paragraphs of the book:

> When [Kae] was laid to rest in the Hanaoka cemetery by the Iris Pond, her tombstone appeared one size larger than the one behind her which belonged to Otsugi—a difference due perhaps to the increased prosperity of the family. Her stone, which over-shadowed Otsugi's, was inscribed simply with her posthumous Buddhist name. Even larger than twice the size of the two women's tombs combined is that of Seishu, who died six years after his wife. . . . If you stand directly in front of Seishu's tomb, the two behind him, those of Kae and Otsugi, are com-pletely obscured. It is that big.
>
> Amy Vladek Heinrich. *Proceedings of the Xth Congress of the International Comparative Literature Association* vol. 2 (New York: Garland, 1985), p. 611

Traditionally the Japanese have followed the Confucian ideal of filial piety, of respect toward elders, and the image persists that Japan is a society in which the old have a special, revered place. In modern Japanese literature, however, the Confucian ideal has been challenged by writers who have called attention to the growing number of elderly and the problems of caring for them. One such work is Sawako Ariyoshi's 1972 novel *Kōkotsu no hito (The Twilight Years)*. Composed in graphic, naturalistic detail, the novel was a sensation in Japan, selling over a million copies in less than a year. . . .

The extended narrative of the novel form gives Ariyoshi the luxury to develop characters and issues through detailed incidents. From the beginning Akiko Tachibana, dutiful and hardworking, is an appealing figure. Told of the lifelong self-absorption of her father-in-law, the eighty-four-year-old Shigezō, and his unkind treatment of Akiko over the years, the reader is in complete sympathy with her and her distaste for ministering to the old man, for whom she has full responsibility. When she considers an institution for the rapidly deteriorating Shigezō, she is made to feel guilty by the social worker, who advises her to keep him at home and berates contemporary attitudes toward caring for the old: "These days young people no longer have feelings of filial piety. The general trend among the young is to do whatever they can to live in separate households. This is the problem we are confronted with at present." . . .

One purpose of the novel is to show unflinchingly Shigezō's decline into senility and decrepitude. . . .

Ariyoshi uses Shigezō's state of mind to raise questions about senility, particularly through a secondary character, a neighbor and contemporary of Shigezō. Though she becomes physically dependent later in the novel, Mrs. Kadotani remains mentally alert. At first she is quite taken with the still-handsome Shigezō, accompanying him to the local senior citizens' center and then spending days with him in his cottage. Though she flirts with him boldly, her effort is wasted, since he neither is interested in her nor remembers who she is. She finally becomes disgusted with him and embarrassed by his vacancy, blaming his condition on inertia and self-absorption.

> Senility is a state of mind. They all say that Mr Tachibana became senile because he didn't exercise his mind or his body. They also say that he was probably lazy. . . . People used to think that men deteriorated physically while women became senile. It's not true! Women rarely become senile, because they have to use their brains—whether they're sewing or doing the laundry.

Because Ariyoshi's novels deal with strong women, it is not surprising that she has Mrs. Kadotani utter the lines above or that she shows old women in the novel as lively and alert.

In its focus on the relationship between adult children and aging parents, *The Twilight Years* can be called a novel of generations, and as in Ariyoshi's other novels of generations, such as *The River Ki* and *The Doctor's Wife,* time is a subject of considerable thematic interest for her. Time is pervasive in *The Twilight Years:* the treatment of historical time; the coordination, or lack of it, between personal experience and objective time; and especially the idea of time as identity.

Celeste Loughman. *World Literature Today.*
65, 1991, pp. 49–50

One characteristic of Ariyoshi's writing is that, unlike other Japanese women writers, she is not known for her love stories. As a professional writer she believed that there were too many issues more important than love. Indeed, she wrote about a great many subjects: racial and other social prejudices, environmental pollution, caring for the elderly, the role of women in society, among other topics. Although her early short stories about artists and artisans dedicated to their craft are of interest, she will probably be best remembered for her social-problem novels. "Kiyu no shi" (1962; the death of Kiyu) describes a prostitute who commits suicide rather than becoming the mistress of an American merchant; Ariyoshi attempts to trace the beginning of Japanese prejudice against Caucasians in this short story. In *Hishoku* Ariyoshi has as her main character a Japanese war bride married to a black American. While living in Harlem, the heroine observes for herself the racial prejudice toward blacks and Hispanics in the U.S.

Ariyoshi lived through a remarkable period in the modern history of Japan, and she thought deeply about the social problems that many industrial nations are facing. Her approach, however, was unique in that she focused on the victims of a social problem, be it radiation disease, caring for the elderly, or environmental pollution. She was deeply sympathetic to the less fortunate in the strictly stratified Japanese society—the pariahs and under-privileged, those who are not blessed with an impressive pedigree and fine upbringing, and she saw clearly the bigotry and prejudice of the Japanese toward these and other outsiders. Whether they are victims of the U.S. atomic-bomb blasts of August 1945 or victims of environmental pollution, they will be affected for generations.

As a divorced woman with a daughter to raise and educate, Ariyoshi thought deeply about the position of women in Japanese society. She wrote about prostitutes and princesses, housewives and old women. Because, as a rule, women have had to struggle harder than men, they emerge as final victors in many of her stories. In Ariyoshi's works, none of them typical "love stories" or unrelentingly gloomy autobiographical works so characteristic of other Japanese woman writers, Ariyoshi makes her characters come alive. . . .

Ariyoshi's works have a wide appeal to readers of all age groups. She often spent years planning and doing research for a particular work, whether it was a historical novel or a work treating a modern social problem. Her works have been translated into Chinese, English, and a number of European languages. Ariyoshi will doubtless be remembered as a unique writer who admirably contributed to the great tradition of outstanding Japanese women writers in our time.

Mildred Tahara. In Steven R. Serafin and Walter D. Glanze, eds. *Encyclopedia of World Literature in the 20th Century* (New York: Continuum, 1993), pp. 44–45

ARNOW, HARRIETTE (UNITED STATES) 1908–86

That Harriette Arnow will go down in the American literary chronicle as a major figure is, at this point at least, highly improbable. Four conventionally written novels—in a time, unfortunately, when such have not been readily accepted by critics and scholars as being on the cutting edge of creativity—are hardly enough to establish her in the major category. As an artist, how-ever, she certainly needs no defense. A Realist who rejects such things as experimental forms, complex plots, sentimental themes, the pyrotechnics of sex, and the contemporary mania for neurotic protagonists, she combines in her work a penetrating and sensitive insight into the human condition with a lean prose style—a combination that has been responsible for a literary out-put that, though thin in quantity, is abundant in quality. . . .

In her writing, . . . Mrs. Arnow has been content to be a simple story-teller, attempting to record honestly the nature of human experience as she conceives it. Her mountain fiction, for example, goes beyond the mere local-color approach that marked that genre for so long. More than just presenting the sights, sounds, beliefs, customs, institutions, and such of the area and its people, she brings out the tragedies and ironies engendered in a severely isolated and circumscribed way of life. In the same way, she casts a hard light on the environmental and social conditions that limit her characters in urban settings—a housing project in *The Dollmaker* and an exclusive suburb in *The Weedkiller's Daughter*. . . .

Of Mrs. Arnow's characters, the women stand out as the strongest and the most fully developed. Other than Nunn [Ballew] in *Hunter's Horn,* no male character is developed to any real degree. The reason for this lack of significant male characters is not that Mrs. Arnow is unable to portray men, because as her treatment of Nunn illustrates, she can project herself into the male psyche as well as into the female one. Perhaps it is engendered in her feeling that American literature has exhibited a paucity of truly substantial women characters. In an interview with Evelyn Stewart of the *Detroit Free Press* in 1958, she remarked that she hated to "emerge from the Eighteenth Century" because "life was better for women way back then." Though women did not have to compete with men then, they had, in Mrs. Arnow's mind, more power than now. "And the men didn't hate women then, the way they do now," she went on. "Men and women were yoke-mates, pulling together. Now they're pulling different ways, each trying to manipulate the other and run the other's life." No better example of this view, perhaps, can be found in her own fiction than in the conflict between Gertie and Clovis Nevels in *The Dollmaker.*

Mrs. Arnow's characters, more often than not, are trapped by social restrictions and environmental forces from which they cannot escape. In *Mountain Path,* Chris Bledsoe seeks violence and revenge because they are part of the code under which he has grown up. Louisa knows the potential that is within Chris, but she also knows that it can never be realized in Cal Valley. Time for him has run out, and all that remains is for Louisa to build her future in light of what she has learned.

In *Hunter's Horn,* Milly, Nunn, and Suse—all three—are limited by conditions which they do not fully comprehend. Milly stoically accepts her lot with a fatalistic "Oh, God, it's hard to be a woman." Nunn and Suse both try to escape: Nunn, through chasing King Devil; Suse, through dreaming of a life in the outside world. When Nunn's chase is finished, he, too, is in a sense finished. By condemning Suse, he has reverted to a viewpoint common enough among his neighbors, but which he for a time had escaped. Suse has never tasted the pleasures nor felt the opportunities of the outside world, but she knows that somewhere there exists a place better than Little Smokey Creek—a place where excitement abounds and where love is possible. She doesn't really learn from Lureenie's experiences that the outside world also has its relentless forces that can grind one to the ground.

In *The Dollmaker,* Gertie Nevels learns firsthand of such forces in the world away from the mountains. She sees her family come apart: Reuben rejects Detroit and returns home; Clytie and Enoch drift away from the old traditions amid the pressures to conform; and Cassie is killed because she is unable to express her own innocent version of love and affection in a world that will not understand. More than learning about city life, Gertie experiences a kind of revelation. Her creative spirit that flourished so freely in Kentucky is crushed in Detroit, but in return she achieves an understanding of humanity that was not available to her before. Whether the price she pays is too great is left for the reader to decide.

In *The Weedkiller's Daughter,* Susie Schnitzer serves as a contemporary illustration of the theme of the individual versus the human condition. She is Louisa Sheridan, Suse Ballew, Gertie Nevels embodied in a teenaged girl. Wise beyond her years and clever almost beyond belief, Susie rejects everything that militates against her being herself. She triumphs—at least temporarily. In doing so, she is not so much a real person as she is a symbol of what Mrs. Arnow has been driving at all along—that only when one searches out and nourishes his own natural yearnings and only when he learns humility and compassion can he truly be an individual.

All of Mrs. Arnow's fiction reflects an ironic approach. While she may be simply a storyteller, she does not oversimplify; for life is not to be explained in simple terms or easy philosophies. She knows, and her characters learn, that life is full of contradictions as well as harmonies and that good and evil are not always clearly discernible, but often overlap or fuse. Moreover, while she does not have an uncritical faith in human nature, she does not take a stance of superiority over her characters. She sees them as human beings—often cruel, often kind, and often bewildered by the world in which they live. Nor is she the obvious iconoclast or preacher with regard to human institutions and beliefs. She may, for example, draw devastating pictures of fundamental religion, be it of the Kentucky Protestant variety or of the Detroit Catholic variety, and of the right-wing bigotry of such people as Susie Schnitzer's father; but she does not let thesis impinge upon art. Rather, her characters and their actions speak for themselves—and often eloquently.

Closely related to Mrs. Arnow's ironic point of view is her treatment of nature. Throughout her stories runs the idea that nature, timeless and bigger than man, is the ultimate reality; but it, too, has its ironies. While in all the novels Mrs. Arnow sees an affinity between natural life and moral life, she does not flinch from the threatening aspects of nature. Indeed, the relationship between man and nature is not a reciprocal one so much as it is a one-sided one. It is man that must adapt to nature, for only in a correct adaptation can he find real sustenance; and this lesson is what many of Mrs. Arnow's characters either know or learn. Nunn Ballew, for example, discovers the folly of making nature (the fox in his case) a symbol of something more than it is. King Devil is neither good nor evil but merely a fox trying to stay alive in the world in much the same way that Nunn is. Nunn, by attributing malice to the fox, suffers from an intellectual and moral misconception of the way things are. He does not understand what Susie Schnitzer does—that man's dignity comes not from a foolhardy defiance of nature but from a recognition and acceptance of its beauty and power. And the same may be said for a recognition and acceptance of a man's worth—what Gertie Nevels learns.

Thus, while most of Mrs. Arnow's stories could not be said to have unqualified happy endings, they do not hum the umbra's note to the extent that the works of so many contemporary American authors do. She is not, to be sure, a rear-guard romanticist, but neither is she one who has lost hope in the present and future of man. She recognizes that human plans do not always coincide with the way things go. She also recognizes, however, that man has within him a certain indomitable spirit that, though occasionally stifled, can never be permanently erased. Nitro Joe in "Marigolds and Mules," for example, may be blown to bits in an ugly oil field, but the genuine love he had for pretty flowers is no less real. And the world may defeat Suse Ballew, but her counterpart, Susie Schnitzer, at least for the moment, prevails.

William Eckley. *Harriette Arnow* (Boston: Twayne, 1974), pp. 125–27

"What possible difference," Tillie Olsen asks (in *Silences*), "does it make to literature whether or not a woman writer remains childless—free choice or not—especially in view of the marvels these childless women have created"? Answering her own question, Olsen supposes that there would have been "other marvels" as well, or "other dimensions" to the enduring works they have created. She suspects that there might have been present "profound aspects and understandings of human life as yet largely absent in literature."

The Dollmaker testifies to the correctness of Olsen's suspicions. Its depiction of family life—the entangled bonds between parents and children, brothers and sisters—is unparalleled in modern American fiction. Especially affecting is the loving relationship between mother and daughter shared by Arnow's heroine, Gertie, and five-year-old Cassie. Skillfully and movingly the novel depicts fictional children as original and as realistic as any child the reader has known. It also makes the joys and the pains of motherhood as heartbreakingly palpable as any vicarious account can suggest.

More than just employing fresh subject matter, *The Dollmaker* dramatizes the frequently skirted conflict between a mother's attempt to be both true to her art and watchful of her children's welfare and happiness. Gertie Nevels, a hulking Kentucky hill woman with a talent for carving in wood, grapples with the distractions and obstructions that interfere with her sculpting a human figure out of a cherished man-sized piece of wild-cherry wood. The cherry-wood figure is more than an art object: carved during moments of hope, sorrow, regret, and then despair, it reflects the nature and the toughness of Gertie's moral fiber. The aesthetic and moral quality of the figure thus takes on singular importance in Gertie's life, for she is as much creating and discovering her destiny as she is demonstrating and assessing her talent.

More than anything else, Gertie's motherhood is responsible for the cherry-wood figure's reflecting her sympathies with suffering humanity and for its remaining unfinished. Her children are the source of Gertie's sympathy and compassion—the material for her art and the cause of its doom. Thus mother-hood at once inspires Gertie's creativity and condemns it to destruction.

The Dollmaker embodies, as well as dramatizes, the mother-artist's struggle to create a masterwork. The novel is Arnow's man-sized wild-cherry wood: weighty, skilled, ingenious, penetrating, and also somewhat unfinished. In some ways it is as rough and unhewed as Gertie's block of wood. However recognizable the novel is as a masterwork—Joyce Carol Oates calls it "a legitimate tragedy, our most unpretentious American masterpiece"—it lacks the streamlining and the polish that come only from sustained concentration, a luxury Harriette Arnow seldom had during its writing. For as Gertie was demanding to be written, Mrs. Arnow was responding to the more immediate demands of her own two children, both young during the early fifties, when their mother awoke at three or four o'clock in the morning to answer Gertie's "compelling pull" before her sleeping children could begin to exert theirs. Arnow's masterwork reveals the same moral probing evinced in Gertie's—the practical and spiritual conflicts that bedevil both the artist and the mother, and perhaps most unrelentingly she who is both.

Glenda Hobbs. *Georgia Review.* 33, Winter,
1979, pp. 854–55

To depose the God of wrath, Gertie creates a humanistic vision of God as love. She names her youngest son Amos, after the prophet who preached that God is benevolent and just, and would lead his Children of Israel to their promised land. She envisions a Christ very different from that of her mother's apocalyptic being. Gertie sees him as a workingman, a carpenter like herself, who loves music and children.

For years she has treasured a block of cherry wood from which she intends to carve the figure of her vision of Christ. She can never, however, capture her image of his face because, like her daughter's imaginary play-mate, Christ cannot and does not exist in Gertie's world, the slums of Detroit.

So, the face of Gertie's carving begins to take on the aspect of Judas instead of Christ, just as Gertie herself becomes a Judas to her own art, carving and finally mass-producing for sale in the alleys of Detroit ugly painted puppets and tortured Christs on crosses. She literally and figuratively sells both Christ and herself. But her Judas is as much her own creation as her Christ. She explains that her carving is, "Not Judas with his mouth all drooly, his hand held out fer th silver, but Judas given th thirty pieces away. I figger . . . they's many a one does meanness fer money—like Judas . . . But they's not many like him gives th money away an feels sorry onct they've got it."

The novel ends, seemingly, with the ultimate self-betrayal, the destruc-tion of the cherry wood. Gertie, desperate for money to feed her children and husband, splits the great block into the fragments with which she will manufacture more puppets and crucifixes to sell. She thus betrays her vision of the impossible loving Christ, her own art, and perhaps her very soul. . . .

All women in *The Dollmaker* are both Judas and Christ, suffering and selling themselves because this is the necessity in their world. The God of wrath *does* exist for Arnow in this novel, and his universe is a depressingly fatalistic one. The excellence of Arnow's work, comparable to the best examples of literary naturalism, lies in this portrayal of the barrenness of life and the futility of the human predicament.

The only meaning, Arnow says, is to be found in human relationships. The women in the alley form a kind of sisterhood in which all of them tend each other's children, mutually help to fill the emotional "holes" in their lives, and somehow preserve for themselves and for each other a human dignity. When Sophronie is drunk and naked, Gertie and the others hasten to cover her nakedness. When Mrs. Daly's daughter enters a convent and rejects the trousseau her mother has spent years collecting and caring for, Gertie and her neighbors provide comfort and sympathy. When Gertie is near insanity with grief at her daughter's death, the women of the project rally to care for the surviving children and to help Gertie recover.

For Arnow, it is individual relationships and human dignity that make survival desirable, even in Gertie's Detroit. And, Arnow writes, these things exist and have value, not because of God and society, but in spite of them.

Barbara Rigney. *Frontiers*. 1, Fall, 1975,
pp. 83–85

In *The Dollmaker* Arnow anatomizes the sources of tension in the polyglot and multi-ethnic urban world of her novel. Like Homer Anderson, a minor character in the novel who is writing a doctoral dissertation on "The Patterns of Racial and Religious Prejudice and Persecution in Industrial Detroit," Arnow describes in detail instance after instance of racial and/or religious prejudice: the Irish Catholic Dalys frequently quote their spiritual leader, the fascistic Father Moneyhan, probably a fictional representation of the notorious Father Coughlin, a priest who openly preaches hatred of Protestant heathen, Jews, Communists, and Blacks; the "Polock foreman" is said to "hate everything and everybody that ain't just like hissef," including "niggers," whom he calls "shines" and to whom he assigns the "meanest jobs"; and a big Ukrainian fellow in the munitions plant "hates everything, niggers, hillbillies, Jews, Germans, but worsen anything, he hates that Polock foreman."

Into this strife-ridden urban world come Arnow's protagonist, Gertie Nevels, a "hillbilly" from Appalachia, and her family. The first part of the novel describes the homogeneous rural community from which the Nevels originated. Arnow then contrasts this community with the urban community in Detroit to which they move during World War II. The Nevels are shown to be as alien in Detroit as are any of the immigrants who are their neighbors. Like the "greenhorns" found in Abraham Cahan's *The Rise of David Levinsky* or Anzia Yezierska's *Bread Givers,* the Nevels must learn to adapt their customs to the customs of the majority and to learn to speak what virtually amounts to a new language. When Gertie Nevels asks her son's teacher, for example, whether she "recollects" which child her son is, the teacher replies, "Does that mean 'remember'?" Very quickly the Nevels children, exposed to the mockery of the children at school and in their housing development, become ashamed of the speech patterns of their parents. Realizing this, Gertie Nevels understands why Michael Ospechuk's mother looks so frightened at the school's open house. "Maybe she had older ones who didn't like the words she used and told her what to say," Gertie thinks. Though the teacher of Gertie Nevels' youngest child, Cassie, is amused when she overhears Cassie telling a classmate from Mexico that her own country is Kentucky, Arnow emphasizes the fact that for the Nevels Detroit *is* another country, one in which the epithet "hillbilly" is pronounced with as much derision and hatred as are the words "nigger," "wop," "Polock," and "Jew."

The women in the novel are not free of the racial and religious prejudice that characterizes the behavior of the males. . . .

Yet despite these instances of hostility among the women characters that are cited in the novel, it is their mutual support for one another rather than their antagonism that Arnow emphasizes.

Charlotte Goodman. MELUS. 10, Winter,
1983, pp. 49–51

Aside from specialists in American literature and women's studies, few people have heard of Harriette Arnow, and fewer still know any of her novels except *The Dollmaker.* Writing about hill people from her native state of Kentucky, she is alternately labeled a "woman" or a "regional" writer. While it is generally conceded that the former tag is pejorative, few have considered the assumptions behind the term "regional." It is, I suspect, employed as condescendingly as the qualifier "woman": a "regionalist" can be "good" but only in a limited sphere. . . .

Perhaps *The Dollmaker* is better known than Arnow's previous two novels because it is less obviously "regional," and has been spared the unfortunate blemish of the misused word. Three-fourths of the novel takes place in wartime Detroit, where the Nevels family migrates so the father can work in a factory and contribute to the "war effort." Arnow's first two novels, *Mountain Path* (1936) and *Hunter's Horn* (1949), are set entirely in rural Kentucky, and both describe hill people struggling with a barren, gully-ridden land, with a vestigial fundamentalist fatalism, and with their own tribalism. While enthusiastic critics lauded both novels, unknowingly they undermined their own praise and relegated the works to obscurity when they categorized them as "regional." Some, mistaking necessary descriptions for decoration, meant "local color"; others, assuming that any work rooted firmly in rural Kentucky must have only a limited appeal, used "regional" to mean folksy, and therefore of minor importance.

Mountain Path established Harriette Arnow as a writer whose gift was her poignant evocation of a poor but starkly beautiful "Appalachia." The story of a city-bred college student who goes to a remote "hollow" to board with a hill family and teach in a one-room school, *Mountain Path* dramatizes the young woman's emotions as she learns to appreciate their familial devotion, their intimacy with the land, and their unique brand of justice. . . .

Arnow does not write about Kentucky any more than Twain wrote about Missouri. These writers create art from experiences that include details of memory and observation, but their backgrounds are more important for the ideas and attitudes that have evolved over generations. A writer cannot deny her heritage. Living in a close-knit community gives the writer a special focus—what Arnow calls "a sense of belonging"—and creates a world of moral choice the characters accept or protest against. Arnow's fiction demonstrates her belief that character is more important than setting: "I had to have some setting because the people were either at one with the setting or rebelling against it.". . .

Harriette Arnow's first three novels should no more be read because they are "regional" than because she is a "woman writer." Her contribution to literature is her harshly moving portrayal of people struggling to maintain their integrity in an oppressive, often hostile environment, wherever they find it. But citizens of any world will find her novels more gripping because her characters' dilemmas grow out of the "habits of blood" they acquired from generations in the Kentucky hills. Attempts to break those habits—Reuben's carrying a knife, or Cassie's talking with her imaginary playmate Callie Lou— are met with deep and often fatal resistance. Perhaps Arnow will begin to receive her due acclaim when critics realize that she has gone far beyond local color. Labels like "regional" do not trouble Arnow's readers, who find it difficult to recover their own worlds once they have entered hers.

Glenda Hobbs. In Emily Toth, ed.
Regionalism and the Female Imagination
(New York: Human Sciences Press, 1983),
pp. 83–84, 89–90

ASHTON-WARNER, SYLVIA (NEW ZEALAND) 1908–84

Sylvia Ashton-Warner's *Spinster* is a rather formless novel (although it does trace a story of success, it ends by a sheer act of author's will) in a full romantic tradition. The story is told in the first person by Anna Vorontosov, an infant mistress in a largely Maori school in New Zealand. Madame— as she is addressed by her colleagues—is a somewhat sentimental, often tremulously hysterical woman, who is also witty, defiant, and self-amused. If she recalls Chekov's Ranevskaya in her cherry orchard, she is also a woman of audacity and persistence who contrives a new way of teaching reading to Maori children. For Madame is constantly transforming her blocked passion into an inspired search for communication with her many children. She fights with them and for them, insists that they be allowed and also required to become their own selves. The language of the children runs through the book, sounding anxiety, wonder, aggression, and love. . . . This is the "true voice of feeling" which Madame tries to release.

What makes Miss Vorontosov most impressive is her readiness to accept the whole range of experience, to face whatever she finds in herself as well as the children. She struggles with the help of brandy to transmute self-pity and frustration into a power of sympathy and an art of perception. There is the familiar romantic agony in her isolation, touchiness, and histrionic self-protection, but it produces a work of art, the reading books she composes of the words that voice the children's deepest feeling and of the pictures those feelings have shaped. The novel is written in a rapid, fluid, often brilliant style.

Martin Price. *The Yale Review.* June, 1959,
pp. 600–601

From the point of view of descriptive artistry, this novel [*Greenstone*] is a gem. Descriptions of the New Zealand locale—the atmosphere, the flowers, the birds, even the rain—are beautifully executed. Characterization is vivid and realistic. The parents and the numerous children come to life as they progress through their daily routines. Despite the number of personages, each one retains his identity and has a niche in the total picture of this at times difficult group.

The story centers around the once famous Englishman, Richmond Considine, a now hopelessly crippled victim of rheumatoid arthritis, and his shrewish wife, who by necessity becomes the teacher-breadwinner, housekeeper, shopper, cook and general factotum for the family. Stark poverty and inability to make ends meet make this a pretty depressing tale. Children who are for the most part uncooperative and buck-passing don't make it any less so. The remnants of decency, culture and past grandeur, plus the mother's highly motivated zeal and ambition for her children somewhat alleviate the situation. But the atmosphere of hopelessness is lifted only at the end by a near miracle rescue by their older children. (It's a little too sudden.) . . .

This novel is different. Its biggest drawback is the excessive use of Maori chants and terms. The glossary of these terms at the end is a help, but constant reference to that section makes for a lack of fluidity. The story is for adults, and perceptive enthusiasts for description, at that. It has a certain charm, but is for a limited audience.

Catharine D. Gause. *America.* March 26,
1966, p. 423

The absurd poses of [Ashton-Warner's] heroines can be frightening in their unreality, until one comes to realize that through the histrionics and quivering sentiment appear a genuine emotion and a more than fragmentary truth. If her first novel, *Spinster,* could be described as a dramatized treatise on educational theory and racial understanding interrupted by an embarrassing interior monologue, and her second, *Incense to Idols,* as a mental and emotional melodrama of the sex-obsessed and God-intoxicated, these inadequate descriptions would at least indicate the difficulty of accepting either as a great novel or dismissing both as inferior entertainments. *Teacher* sets out to provide more substantial documentary evidence for the teaching scenes of the earlier novel, but becomes as much an exercise in imaginative realism as a stimulating textbook for teachers; and *Bell Call* returns to the theme with a bizarre romance of Tarl Pracket's search for her Shangri-La and her attitude to freedom of the mind, living in the Everlasting Now and schools as "Institutions of Force with Someone in Charge." . . .

She is a highly fanciful rather than a deeply imaginative writer. Reality and dream are not used as they are by Janet Frame to reveal and explore the complexities of the human situation, but to embroider material in which the authentic merges into a world of make-believe. She tends to exploit her mannerisms as well as her manner in such a way that an impression of overstrained and slightly wilful romanticism is left; but she often succeeds in surrounding characters and scene with an atmosphere that more properly belongs to myth or legend. "The line between reality and fantasy has escaped them," she writes of the Considine family in *Greenstone,* and when later she observes that among its members "reality is unacceptable and seldom used as workable fact" she is, perhaps unconsciously, betraying one of the secrets both of her strength and her weakness as a novelist.

H. Winston Rhodes. *New Zealand Fiction*
since 1945 (Dunedin, New Zealand:
McIndoe, 1968), pp. 40, 42–43

Sylvia Ashton-Warner's report [*Spearpoint*] of her experience in an "open" primary school in Colorado is delightful, literate and personal. She knows she is a good teacher; she is openly pleased or displeased with herself and with others, or with the whole shebang; and she unselfconsciously and meticulously records her teaching triumphs and failures.

But the book is more than a record of her slow and sometimes impatient progress toward order and discipline in the face of their opposites (a colleague advises her not to talk of "discipline" but of "guidance") and toward the development of a teaching that is successful, to the degree that it is also a learning. Working "organically" with the children, she is also aware of the organic tie between the American classroom, or whatever it may be called, and the great American outside. Indeed, as a New Zealander, she may sometimes be too eager to find connections in America, but she readily indicates how some clues may confuse or mislead. . . .

In spite of [her] emphasis on and exploitation of uniqueness, Miss Ashton-Warner, like any teacher, is tempted to make generalizations to ease her work. Every so often she looks for a ready umbrella under which to crowd her charges. She suggests, for example, that the failure of her children to question her on occasion comes from their watching television so much and having to accept everything they're told by the tube since, obviously, they can't answer back or question back. That's just not right: I've heard children talk back to sets, and I certainly used to have to answer myself for something said or shown on the screen.

This very occupational failing underscores Miss Ashton-Warner's thorough professionalism. Unexamined teaching, she has learned, is unfulfilled teaching; her experience has taught her the importance of always probing one's own teaching powers, even when the probing is inadequate. Throughout the book she can therefore be found pausing to reflect on the whole process of teaching, sometimes simply, sometimes with implications that illumine larger human encounters.

Morris Freedman. *The New Republic.*
September 23, 1972, p. 30

Perhaps the role of the woman is the most widely discussed subject in Sylvia Ashton-Warner's work. This is a question of national importance in New Zealand where emancipation is a fact but where many Victorian attitudes remain. In such a social environment a woman artist's problems are twofold and either her life or her art must suffer. If her life as wife and mother retains priority then her art will be regarded as a genteel pastime for the moments of leisure she may be fortunate enough to glean. Yet, if her art dominates, her daily life may be ruined by its demands. Reflecting this conflict, Sylvia Ashton-Warner's heroines are often reduced to silence and a form of paralysis. Indeed, although her most successful artists are women, the act of creation is often associated with men; Tarl in *Bellcall,* Anna in *Spinster,* Germaine in *Incense* to *Idols* have a certain artistic potential, although it is not expressed. They are to be compared with Angela in *Bellcall* and Angelique in *Three* (the similarity of their names can hardly be fortuitous), who are stereotypes of femininity: Angela is the ideal mother, devoted to the upbringing of her family to such an extent that her own intellect stagnates so that her judgements are based on principles rather than reflection, and Angelique seems devoid of any thought. Fixed values are a source of comfort for these women; Tarl finds them inhibiting. "We are not happy in civilized places," she explains to Angela. Convention, society and its laws, suffocate this eccentric until she violently breaks free to circle round the enclosed, claustrophobic world. Tarl's attempts to escape are accompanied by visions of flight, of retreat to a primitive world, in this case, that of the Maoris.

Such images of flight are frequent in Sylvia Ashton-Warner's world. When she discusses the contrast between reality and fantasy and reality and utopia, the idea of crossing the barrier, whether it be physical, for example the river in *Greenstone,* or mental, for instance with the story time in *Spinster,* poses the problem of relationship. In fact, "flight" completely destroys the normal barriers of time and space and opens the way to the idea of a complete, three-dimensional freedom. Even so, these outward flights are usually controlled by the necessity to "come back to base." The characters, having once attained their desire are inexorably attracted back to the environment from which they were attempting to escape.

This is possibly the result of the author's introduction of a matriarch system within her work. She often puts matriarchal and patriarchal law into conflict: on the whole, the male characters represent respectable restraint, even inhibition, while the main women characters demand freedom for themselves and for their children to develop naturally.

Carole Durin. *World Literature Written in English.* 19, 1980, pp. 105–6

The self that Ashton-Warner presents (but scarcely analyses) is one with strong emotional needs: on the one hand the need for emotional self-expression, on the other the need to love and, more important, to be loved and to be given attention. That self's means of attempting to meet these needs are in potential conflict: on the one hand, the pleasure principle, a kind of self-indulgent dreaming by which "whatever [she] wanted very much and didn't have [she] simply supplied it in mind"; on the other hand, the reality principle, the discipline which can become "shelter like a roof over you." What she was searching for was a way to integrate these needs and means into a whole person, something that New Zealand society made very difficult with its distrust of emotion, its lack of respect for the aesthetic, its restriction of opportunity and accomplishment for women, and its authoritarian control of non-conformity—"the steel straight-jacket [*sic*] of tradition clamped upon the souls of the wild ones with penalties for variation." Such a "staid, sedated and timid society" discourages artistic expression, oppresses women, gives no recognition to original accomplishment, and even discourages the kind of psychological knowledge that might help one to cope with the stresses it causes:

> I was assembling quite a fair picture of how things were behind the eyes, which is known to most students today but to me, way back there in the stale air beneath the crinoline over the country, the respectability, righteousness and morality, the revelations came as simply shocking.

Thus Ashton-Warner's struggle was a long one in which she never fully achieved what she sought. As a teacher with an original method, she never overcame "PSBMEH—the Permanent Solid Block of Educational Male Hostility." She achieved recognition and status overseas, especially in Canada, but not in her own country. As Stuart Middleton has said, ". . . there exists in the education system an almost unlimited capacity to scorn and reject the work of this writer/teacher." In music and art she had searched for a way to "break cover from conformity, to get out from under the crinoline" by finding something "that could say the unsayable things inside you," but only in writing could she bring together the various aspects of self:

> unruly native imagery found a channel through which to surface, clearing out on its way the delirium of both music and paint to enrich the main stream. Writing siphoned off the effervescence of dreaming, the constant opposition party, and there was discipline required for that.

However, she still encountered a block of male hostility, for the New Zealand literary world, dominated by male rebels against their society, did not grant this female rebel status. More than Robin Hyde, who had at least an equivocal place on the edge of the male literary world, she was on the outside, for many years isolated from other writers in rural Maori communities and, even after she had achieved world attention rare for a New Zealand writer, ignored in New Zealand literary journals. The one substantial attempt to come to terms with her work, an article by Dennis McEldowney in *Landfall* in September 1969, was attacked by Brasch in a letter in the next issue in which he denied that her work deserved "serious consideration," implying that it would not have merited an article under *his* editorship. At the end, all passion spent, she could say "I understand my country and forgive her all" and could accept that "whatever my disasters in this country . . . these islands turn out to be the one place where I would wish to be," but, ironically, it was only with the publication of *I Passed This Way* that she achieved one of New Zealand's major literary awards.

The perspective from which Ashton-Warner tells her story is Provincial, with the usual dualism between a hostile society (with more emphasis on its rejection of non-conformity, less on its sexual puritanism or philistinism) and the alienated artist. The artist as Woman Alone is presented in more self-dramatizing terms than are used by Sargeson or Brasch:

> I was in the wilderness myself, having fallen into the hands of the philistine who, on that high plateau of boundless horizons, had ambushed me and hurled me over a cliff upon the rocks below where I'd broken every bone in my heart.

But she also presents the artistic benefits of being Woman Alone:

> Isolation is the best condition for procreation as lovers will agree, ostracism the best sperm for conception, silence the best womb for the idea-fetus, persecution the best of incubators, and austerity the best education; all of which the white cloud supplied with profligacy, tossing up one large mind after another.

The imagery in these two quotations points to the most striking difference setting Ashton-Warner off from Brasch and Sargeson, her way of telling. McEldowney has ranked Ashton-Warner with Robin Hyde, Janet Frame, and other women writers in that her "discoveries have been made not so much through intellectual contemplation as through intensity of feeling," while C. K. Stead has compared her to Katherine Mansfield and Frame in the way in which "the raw, untrammelled, human personality and intelligence is overlaid with very little and breaks out easily into full abundant self-expression. Both critics point to her place in the "feminine," subjective, impressionist tradition. This is evident in *I Passed This Way* not so much in the narrative organization (roughly chronological, although framed by a prologue and epilogue, with a shifting present-time perspective) as in her metaphorical, emotionally expressive style. Even descriptions of external place are put in metaphorical, subjective terms, so that the Wanganui River at Pipiriki is described as "lying on her back on the floor of the valley like a woman besottedly in love, forever desiring the forest above her reflected in her eyes," while the contrasting landscape of Waiomatatini is seen as having "the blanched face of nightmare when the artery of love is severed." The metaphors are even more profuse (with nature as vehicle rather than tenor) in the evocations of internal states:

> Juices flowed like sap in the spring, and the spring pushed on and on, round corner after corner, up steep hills and down the gullies, beneath overhanging cliffs. You forded frequent floods of passion or they'd swallow and sweep you away.

Thus, for example, the thought of sexual touch is described as "rocking the mindscape so that clay banks on the wayside split and crumbled, streams changed course and raw horizons reared." This style, like her mode of drawing and painting, is for emotional, expressive purposes, like one of her metaphorical paintings a way "to escape from the representational and to speak in uncluttered symbol." It is the expression of an inward focus. While *I Passed This Way* tells of a career . . . the career is important primarily as part of an attempt to meet inner needs. Ashton-Warner's "Selah," the place from which she creates her art, is more physical than Hyde's "Home," more akin to Sargeson's bach, but it is more symbolic than the bach, finally, as Stead puts it (speaking of the earlier *Myself*) becoming an image of "the freedom of the creative spirit, the making of a space, a privacy in which it can live and breathe."

Lawrence Jones. *Ariel.* 16:4, October 1985, pp. 139–42

ASTLEY, THEA (AUSTRALIA) 1925–

It is possible to see Thea Astley, in her four published novels, searching for a form capable of keeping the recalcitrance of life within the definition and completeness of an art, and the loosest of arts, at that. She tries first the shifting kaleidoscope of impressions: an ordinary mind is touched to memory by the day's most credible proceedings, in the hope that time and the novel may finally stand as one and a whole history be fulfilled. Or she tries to restrict her novel carefully within the life she has known and to make that life a microcosm. Or ties herself to completeness in the whole life of her hero. None of these devices set her free again. But they allow her to approach her fourth novel with a firmer trust in the mercy of more traditional means, where character and events are involved in a plot still able to convince and please, not least by bringing the novel towards artistic ends.

Her first novel, *Girl with a Monkey,* was published in 1958. The heroine is setting off in the evening on the Brisbane train, and the novel has to find form and unity from this fact. As a limiting condition to work in, it is a good choice, and it leaves some impression of completeness on the mind. In the process of reading, however, as the heroine, Elsie, tidies up in this Queensland town and remember what happened to her there, the fluctuations in time have little power over the reader.

Thea Astley observes very precisely, and with nicely judged detachment and irony, the things that happen to us, the places where they happen, and the uninvolved good-humored juxtaposition of others while events are happening. She has, nevertheless, nothing but a shifting style of life to observe so neatly. The towns are not communities, to her or to anyone. People exist in them, smoking one cigarette after another. They have no tradition beyond petrol, a grilled steak, an empty glass, and who is doing it, no matter with whom. If life cannot mean, it is no wonder that the novelist should take the train away, or escape into the esoteric world of recherché quotation, far-fetched metaphor. . . .

The sliding, impressionist presentation of character suits the novel, the times, and Thea Astley, but it is an iceberg way of writing. What the characters do must be all the more convincing and inevitable to them just because we are allowed to see only fractures of them. "Elsie! Elsie! Here's some fruit I brung yer" has at once the capacity to surprise and is right for the good-natured, ill-bred, feckless "monkey" on whom she has focused her discontents and from whom she is escaping. But some of the surprise springs from a certain demur. The gift comes from a very sozzled man chasing the train out of the station and out of the book. We are asked to assent that this hardy, self-assertive type can be flung out of the train by his faceless rival without any obstreperousness and with an impulse to buy flowers and a pigeon's ability to deliver them at the proper window at twenty miles an hour on a platform full of people. Life imitates art, but if this happened it doesn't quite authenticate it in a novel, which must carry its own convictions. . . .

[Her] fourth novel, *The Slow Natives*, returns to the earlier impressionism with room and proportion for the fleeting disorder of modern life but the plot is stronger and so, perhaps, for the first time in her work fulfils its function of holding the novel together.

Most emphatically of all the novels, *The Slow Natives* opposes Catholicism to the permissive tolerance of modern society. For three-quarters of the book the permissiveness is seen to loosen the Catholicism, so that one is inclined to ask: Why is the novel Catholic? It is otiose and peculiarly effete to have a religious insistence where there is no belief to back it. The religion becomes a parade of its forms. . . .

It is unevenness that mars Thea Astley's novels, and it is caused chiefly by straining after effect to catch a suspected loss of attention—an application of zeugma, or bizarre metaphor, poetical fine writing, willful flashback, thought impressions by means of a mockery of cliché, the escape of any character in exigency into cultural parade, or of the plot into sensation. But she is mastering these faults and in *The Slow Natives* integrates theme, plot, character, dialogue and narration with impressive assurance and promise.

J. M. Couper. *Meanjin.* October, 1967,
pp. 332–33, 336–37

Over the six novels Miss Astley experiments both with the kind of individual and the nature of the personal stance that, together, will be most capable of enduring life in the eye of the storm; a life, that is, in which beleaguered men and women are conscious simultaneously of the elaborate spiritual and psychological defences they are building and tortuously renewing against a nameless, imminent anarchy, and of their own desperation, the inevitability of their ultimate capitulation. In *Girl With a Monkey*—the very title prefigures the book's close attention to the psyche of one individual—we experience an almost oppressively close and continuous contact with Elsie's consciousness as the attempts to cope with "a complete island of twenty-four hours." That no other character in the book develops much beyond having certain distinguishing features and traits is attributable to this intense focussing upon Elsie. It is not simply a matter of one emphasis being to the detriment of another: it is a strategy, a condition of Elsie's existence that she should keep relationships, overtures, events at a distance as it were, where, without commitment, they are analysable, controllable. Such a strategy throws the emphasis very heavily upon the analyzing intelligence and withdraws emphasis somewhat from the things analyzed. The latter tendency is carefully reinforced by certain consistent metaphoric references: images of water, for example, are frequent, but generally of a kind that isolate or distance the heroine. She is enisled, she hears as through water, she wakes to a room that is like a "green aquarium" with the light filtering slowly through and "her soul struggling to the surface through washings of shapeless ideas;" and so on. But Elsie is happiest in this insulated state; it is because she cannot maintain it, because she subconsciously senses the anarchic character of love and of Harry's love in particular, that she lives in such tension, such alternations of dissociation and involvement. From the dangerous calm she sees the storm encroaching. It breaks when Harry sprints pathetically down the platform, chasing her train, desperately stretching out to her his pitiable gift; Else has failed hopelessly to control her emotional life—it has slipped away from her ordering and analysing consciousness into chaos. Like several other Astley novels, *Girl with a Monkey* leaves us not with a tidy ending but with the implicit question: where can it possibly end?

Brian Matthews. *Southern Review* (Adelaide,
Australia). June, 1973, pp. 151–52

[If] Astley were to turn her hand in a moment of what would for her be eccentricity to the writing of detective novels, horror stories and other thrillers, she would probably make a lot of money. Her gift for the creation of an atmosphere of unease which progresses through suspense to menace is apparent even in her extraordinary first novel *Girl with a Monkey,* in which the reader's sympathy and growing concern for the central character is expertly manipulated right to the end. Just as we feel that disaster has been averted, there comes a piece of dialogue more violent in its effect on the reader than any punch-up; it elicits a massive shift in reader sympathy and makes the meaning of the novel's title finally, entirely clear.

After this psychic violence at the end of her first novel, however, there's almost always climactic physical violence of one kind or another in her subsequent books, whether it's the large-scale mayhem of the hurricane in *A Boat Load of Home Folk* and the massacre in *A Kindness Cup,* or the mutilation and/or death of various characters in *A Descant for Gossips, The Slow Natives, The Acolyte,* and *An Item from the Late News.* There's something almost Gothic about Astley's imagination, and in this her writing is reminiscent of short stories by women writers of the American South. Flannery O'Connor, in her relentless retributions, and Eudora Welty, in her knowledge of small-town life and her delight in the physical texture of any given day, are the two names which spring most readily to mind. . . .

I suspect that Astley would hate to be taken up by a certain kind of mainline feminist academic almost as much as Christina Stead did; like Stead, however, she is nevertheless fully attuned to (and sometimes joyfully savage about) women's lot. . . .

In her fiction Astley can (and, repeatedly, does) turn a horribly ruthless eye on human specimens of both sexes, but while her demolition of her female characters' characters is usually of the flip throwaway variety—the disposable insult is a form she has under total control—her male characters expose themselves by their own behavior. . . .

It will be interesting to see what Astley does next; her last two books have been respectively the lightest-hearted and the grimmest of all that she's written. *Hunting the Wild Pineapple* has some outrageously funny moments (the scene in "The Curate Breaker" in which the priest's father keeps calling his son Father renders any ordinarily intelligent reader deeply helpless), while *An Item from the Late News* is not only graver in tone, more preoccupied with the nature of evil, than any of her previous writing; it doesn't even have the witty narrator who, unhappy or not, saves a lot of *The Acolyte* from being excessively grim. On the contrary, the narrator of *An Item from the Late News* is a fairly humorless, fairly neurotic character the use of whom to tell the tale was a brave, and must have been a difficult, thing to do. The story "Traveling Even Farther North" (subtitled "David Williamson You Must Have Stopped at the Border") in *Meanjin* 4/1982, in which the narrator gives up trying to eat her plastic chips and smokes them instead while quoting snatches of English, French and German poetry to herself as she watches the passing parade, suggests that Astley has taken off at some surreal tangent to what most of us sadly acknowledge as the real world.

Kerryn Goldsworthy. *Meanjin*.
December 1983, pp. 479–80, 484

Astley's work has long run a course of its own far outside the mainstream of Australian writing. Astley has never been exact enough in her representation, mundane enough in her prose, to fit the school of realism that still dominated Australian fiction when she started writing. Nor has she taken up popular causes, such as Marxism, feminism, or nationalism, which have at times shaped some Australian storytelling. Neither has she relied on warmed-over metafictional techniques, now so self-consciously fashionable in much Australian work. Instead, Astley's writing stands by itself, as surely as that of Patrick White and Randolph Stowe, as that of Judith Wright, all of whom in the 1950s beheld Australia in a new way: wrote the parish—the Australian landscape, people, experience, history—and extended into metaphysical dimensions the metaphors they discovered.

Just as Astley's individualistic and original body of work adds to the possibilities of Australian literature, it also belongs fully to international writing in English. After all, a prime characteristic of the fiction emanating from the defunct Empire is its adherence to the parish, whether it be Africa or Canada or India or New Zealand, or wherever the English and their language spread; and the exotic locale has long been part of the literature's appeal. Still, no matter how farflung the parish or how exacting its representation, fiction based solely on distance and faithful rendering constitutes little more than rarefied regionalism, a limitation from which the body of writing once called colonial literature sometimes suffered. In such instances, the writers failed to extend the metaphor when making fictions out of the preoccupations that characterize international literature in English, whether from the colonial or postcolonial era.

In the past those preoccupations have been the multiple dilemmas created by colonialism itself, the response to an alien landscape, the evolutionary process of language, and the quest for the center. Now that the word colonialism most often carries a prefix, usually "neo" or "post," the controlling subjects have shifted but not changed altogether. For the imperial residue yet lingers, the landscape continues to intrigue, the English language keeps on evolving. And, most importantly, the center still beckons: In the past it was "Home," the metropolis, England; then the "heart of darkness" in the new land; finally a grasp of self in a postcolonial setting. Such is the stuff from which a writer like Thea Astley extends her metaphors when writing the parish of her Australia. . . .

Thea Astley has sought to write the parish and extend the metaphor into the elusive center of being; that her characters with the "sore fruit" of their souls will—except rarely—remain outsiders outside the truth, "the smallest of points" beyond the redemptive circle.

> Robert L. Ross. *International Literature*
> *Written in English: Essays on the Major*
> *Writers* (New York: Garland, 1991),
> pp. 594–95, 600–601

ATENCIA, MARÍA VICTORIA (SPAIN) 1931–

María Victoria Atencia, whose books have not been readily available due to their exclusive editions, but who has been hailed by both Vicente Aleixandre and Jorge Guillén as one of the most authentic and promising voices among Spain's poets today, is now offering a more easily accessible compendium of her work in the handsome volume *Ex Libris.* She began to publish in 1953 and after the first few books imposed total silence upon herself for fifteen years. Since 1976 she has brought forward samplings of her work at an accelerated pace. *Ex Libris* represents a partial "complete works," with very scant representation of the earlier poems but with complete reproduction of every book since 1976. The poems in the last part, in the meantime, have been grouped together in two new books, *Compás binario* and *Paulina,* both published in 1984.

Even the earliest poems show great mastery of form and the serene determination which makes Atencia's poetry so unique in today's poetic panorama. Her voice is poised; her gait, almost majestic. Most of the poems are very short and dense. Her preferred meter, the *alejandrino blanco,* permits intricate rhythmic modulations without calling attention to form. Most of her work is a dialogue with things and beings surrounding her, or with the mute witnesses of past times—without nostalgia, rather recalling their splendor and joy. In her affirmative attitude, condensed faith, and preference for the present, and in the dynamic tension underlying the imposed control of form, Atencia shows some affinity with Jorge Guillén. Hers is a very personal voice, surging apart from fashions or groups. Possessing perfect mastery of the verse and of all stylistic devices, she prefers to draw the reader's attention to the mysteries they veil/reveal, often proceeding by allusion and leaving the reader floating between two worlds, while she herself ascends toward light and the ultimate truth.

Fernando Ortiz has referred to Atencia as "the only woman who writes like a woman in Spain": delicate sensibility, barely noticeable eroticism, great capacity for compassion expressed in forceful, almost sculptured verse. Hers is a voice which will have to be listened to carefully in the future; she already writes like a classic.

Biruté Ciplijauskaitè. World Literature
Today. 59, 1985, p. 574

María Victoria Atencia, although not widely anthologized, deserves to be recognized as one of the most interesting poets writing in Spain today. The Mainstay Press volume is the first selection of her verse available in English translation. Guillermo Carnero, one of the main figures of the last generation of Spanish poets, has pointed out that Atencia's poetry is an exercise in indirect expression. Her poems grow out of the tension that exists between the major problems of human existence, as they are faced by the poet, and the serenity that is required for poetic expression—what Carnero calls (in his preface to Atencia's *Ex libris* . . . "the tension that exists between saying and not naming."

Tension and *serenity* are the best terms to define Atencia's verse. An example can be seen in the poem "December 1st." There the tension between beginning and end (the first day versus December, the last month) and life and death (animals in heat, broken toys, fish by the shores, or the irony of roofs greening—that is, having the tiles broken) in the first stanza is removed in the second, where serenity is achieved through images of moderated melancholy: sorrow did not increase; willows did not weep. Although referring to a "chilling" premonition of death, the last two lines of the poem attenuate this sensation—ironically, of course—in the routine of serving afternoon tea. Additional examples of Atencia's mastery can be seen in poems such as "Epitaph for a Girl," "The World of M.V.," "Vigil of Venice," and "Tribute to Turner," or in the poem "English Painting," where the aforementioned serenity is obtained by projecting the voice of the poet in an image, specifically the figure in a painting: "There is neither pleasure nor pain: a stillness / Learnt from centuries remains in her face."

Although a selection is by definition limited, the thirty-two poems included in the present book are representative of Atencia's production, and Louis Bourne has provided a good translation.

Ignacio-Javier López. World Literature
Today. 62, 1988, p. 635

It is possible to perceive in the poetic trajectories of Atencia and Maria Sanz a progressive submission to the patriarchal model of female identity. Gradually an "I" of one's own, open and more authentically that of a woman, is silenced. In the first books that Atencia wrote after fifteen yeras of silence, *Marta y Maria* [Martha and Mary], *Sueños* [Dreams], and *El mundo de MV* [The World of MV], a female voice may be heard facing the sorrow of living without an identity of one's own, but in later books, the "I" is diluted and is hidden among monuments, works of art, landscapes, and objects. It is common to describe this evolution of Atencia's work in terms of an enhancement of intimacy and an approach to culturalism. . . .

In the work of Sanz and Atencia, more than one phase may be identified. Their poetry reflects not only submission to the artistic models and social roles defined by the dominant culture that we indicated, but also signs of discontent. They are protests in a low voice, in no way ironic or powerful like those that are beginning to be heard in the work of poets who are more fully representative of the feminist phase in the development of women's literature. . . . In the poetry of Sanz and Atencia, together with the feminine and the feminist, there coexist characteristics typical of the third phase of women's writing. Several of their texts contain sketches, however faint, of a new female identity.

The feminist traces in Atencia's poetry are principally to be met with in the books of her second stage, especially in *Marta y Maria* and *El mundo de MV*. In these volumes, there are poems in which the poet-speaker bemoans the desperation of not being, thus connecting with other contemporary women poets . . . who express the tragic absence of the "I". . . .

A constellation of words associated with domestic limitation and women's clothing establishes the woman as the central focus of the poem: "dress," "bread," "collar," and "needles." But these nouns do not appear in a neutral form. Immediately, the use of verbs and adjectives makes any positive association with feminine space impossible: the dress "is tearing," the bread is "hard," the collar is "frosty," and the needles "rusted." The last lines of the poem '1 de diciembre" [December 1st] are another example of the feminist voice in Atencia's poetry. The speaker protests against the effect of domestic routine imposed on the woman that freezes her spirit. But because she sees no way out of the oppressive situation, she continues serving tea at the right time. . . .

The title *Marta y Maria* embodies the internal conflict of the poet-speaker. As a woman, she lives with a divided I. Martha, the perfect housekeeper and doer, represents the imposed identity, and Mary, the dreamer, represents a more authentic but suppressed identity. Various poems in the volume have as a theme this division between a known life that suffocates and an unknown one that terrifies.

Sharon Keefe Ugualde. *Revista Canadiense de Estudios Hispanos*. 14, 1990, pp. 514–16

ATWOOD, MARGARET (CANADA) 1939–

Margaret Atwood is, perhaps, three writers: the Canadian poet whose first real book, the 1966 *Circle Game,* won the Governor General's Award, whose pioneer *Journals of Susanna Moodie* evoked Canadian history, whose *Power Politics* and *You Are Happy* continue to attract international scholarship, and whose *Selected Poems II, 1976–1986* has just appeared. Margaret Atwood is also the internationally read, translated, and critiqued fiction writer whose six novels, from the 1969 *Edible Woman* through *Surfacing, Lady Oracle, Life Before Man,* and *Bodily Harm* to the 1985 *Handmaid's Tale,* have established her as one of the . . . best women writing in English, and one of the world's most original contemporary novelists. Margaret Atwood is also the forthright critic whose thematic guide to Canadian literature, *Survival,* has survived, [a] brief but intense 1973 controversy, as Canada's best-selling and most influential work of literary criticism, and has become, as a side effect, a key guide to her own work; and whose collected 1982 *Second Words* [covers topics] from Canadian poetry and women's writing to international human rights.

And, as George Woodcock presciently saw, in 1969, the connections between Atwood's diverse genres are capillary; the works correspond and resonate with one another, so that the serious reader is drawn, book by book, further into Atwood's allusive and metamorphic territory.

> Judith McCombs. Introduction to *Critical Essays on Margaret Atwood* (Boston: G. K. Hall, 1988), p. 1.

The title poem of Margaret Atwood's book, *The Circle Game,* describes the children in a ring-game moving in an expressionless trance without joy, and with no other meaning or purpose than in "going round and round." It is a symbol which accrues meaning as the book develops. The world of the first part of the book, apparently in the Maritime Provinces of Canada, is a world of stifling conventionality, a "district of exacting neighbors." There are only slight traces of the crumbling of this ordered circle dance into panic, but deep beneath the surface lie cruelty and brutality, "the voracious eater/the voracious eaten." The middle section of the book describes the same joyless circle game of propriety in the narrower circle of the poet's marriage, as she accuses her husband of playing this game, while she is driven by the pressures of her tense frustrations into gestures of cruelty and bitterness, full of hatred and self-pity. These poems are themselves a part of the "circle game," although it is not clear that the poet sees them that way. . . . The poems in the final section of the book are white to the earlier poems' black. They are truly liberated from the pattern of frustration and cruelty with its narrow focus on self into a broad and selfless search for "the other."

> Samuel Moon. *Poetry.* June, 1968, pp. 204–5

Margaret Atwood's second book *[The Animals in That Country]* is one of the most interesting I have read in a long time. There is nothing "feminine" about the poems, which are unmetered and unrhymed, pruned of any excessive words; some of them present a sequence of uninterpreted details, but these are intriguing enough to beguile the reader into an attempt to penetrate their mystery (unlike many a poem written by many another poet in this mode). Miss Atwood frequently uses the old device of a final line's being given extra drama by spacing it further from the rest of the poem, sometimes with great success (as in "A Foundling"), sometimes with total failure (as in "The Animals of That Country"). There is a complete avoidance of the trite or the familiar, in both attitude and image.

What interests me is the compulsive subject of these poems: a distrust of the mind of man, the word, the imagination, even the poem. To Miss Atwood the world is a sacred mystery which can suffer death by the imagination, and man's every conceivable way of dealing with his world is a "surveying," "dissecting," "mapping," "anatomizing," and "trapping" of it, an "invasion" and a "desecration." A pencil, even in the hands of a poet, is a "cleaver"; what is completely captured by the poem dies. In the hands of a critic it is conceived to be "reducing me to diagram," threatening a hidden self. Yet there is a fascinating ambivalence.

Mona Van Duyn. Poetry. March, 1970, p. 432

Atwood's first four major collections of poetry defined her essential vision during the first decade of her career; they dwelt on the private interior journey, the source of her poetic power. With the 1970s came both continuity and shifting emphasis, as Atwood asserted a tone both more sharply political and, alternately, more compassionate, humane, and affirmative. Having staked out her territory, she continued to exploit its key images, but in ways that coincided with changes in her personal relationships, with her role as public advocate of Canadian cultural nationalism, with her taking up residence on a farm near Alliston, Ontario, with her giving birth to her first child, and with her increasingly vital interest in political terrorism and torture, manifested by her affiliation with the worldwide human rights organization Amnesty International. This varied and disharmonious mixture—of the joys of parenthood and the torments of political horror—may be a clue to the radical shifts in tone in her work during the 1970s and early 1980s: a reflection of an ever more compelling need to counter human brutality with a vision of hope and endurance, to see in the otherwise harsh milieu of *Power Politics,* for example, a "tenacity" in the human spirit that goes "beyond" futile assertions of "truth" that often serve merely as one more weapon of the hostile surrounding world. . . .

Atwood's novels and short stories show her to be a skilled and versatile stylist capable of working with success in a variety of genres. Some early reviewers, stressing her poetic style, thought differently. They seemed indignant that this poet had dared enter the world of prose fiction, had dared map out a literary journey for which she had not been intended. One critic noted that *The Edible Woman* contained "a clutter of inessentials through which the reader must dig"; another observed that "the poetry-ridden prose" of *Surfacing* (1972) "is a shame, for we can hardly hear through it what Miss Atwood is genuinely trying to say." And yet one more, who felt he could hear what Atwood was saying but preferred to hear it in her poems, asserted that her novels were "auxiliary to the poetry," merely a reduction of its themes "for the wider fiction audience."

Those critics who appreciated Atwood's fiction found her poetic craft and her venture into prose to be a happy combination. "Its poet–author," one writer said of *The Edible Woman,* has created a novel "exceptional for its finely textured prose and . . . cuttingly ironic perception"; "Margaret Atwood," observed a reviewer of *Surfacing,* "is a Canadian poet, one of the best, and this is a poet's novel." It could be argued that even these positive reactions to Atwood's fiction suggest ambivalence, pointing as they do to her known strengths as a poet. Yet, with the subsequent publication of *Lady Oracle* in 1976, *Life Before Man* in 1979, and *Bodily Harm* in 1981, Atwood's prose writing became a literary presence that critics would have to reckon with on its own merits.

Jerome H. Rothenberg. *Margaret Atwood*
(Boston: Twayne, 1984), pp. 62, 95–96

In Margaret Atwood's fiction the human body is often a war zone, a "prairie" of flesh ravaged by disputes between the self and a variety of invasive influences including disease, other people, and culture in general. In *Lady Oracle* (1976), for example, the once obese protagonist, Joan Delacourte Foster, reports: "by [the] time [I was thirteen] I was eating steadily, doggedly, stubbornly, anything I could get. The war between myself and my mother was on in earnest; the disputed territory was my body." Atwood's preoccupation with the experience of the body becomes evident at many textual levels—thematic, stylistic, rhetorical, and structural. Indeed, even the titles of some of her novels—*The Edible Woman* (1969) and *Bodily Harm*—reveal this preoccupation. The protagonists in these and other works generally come from prudish Victorian families exhibiting various degrees of fear, disapproval, and denial of the body. *The Edible Woman,* Marian, has grown up in a community of people who peer out at their neighbors from behind the proverbial "lace curtains." Her own family, relieved when she decides to marry, has long dreaded the unfeminine consequences of her university education; she might "undergo some shocking physical transformation, like developing muscles and a deep voice." In *Surfacing* (1972) the narrator's parents are less narrow-minded, but the attitudes of her small rural community have left an impression: "Shorts were against the law, and many [women] lived all their lives beside the lake without learning to swim because they were ashamed to put on bathing suits." In *Lady Oracle* Aunt Lou's job at a sanitary napkin company cannot be discussed, while in *Bodily Harm* the protagonist learns to judge human "decency" in terms of the amount of flesh covered by collars, sleeves and hems.

Coming from such backgrounds, the female characters in Atwood's novels unsurprisingly suffer troublesome relationships with their own bodies. They exhibit an array of physical and body-related psychological ills: eating disorders, disturbed body image, rational and irrational fears of infestation, mutilation, and amputation. At crucial periods in their lives they are apt to develop actual hatred of physical embodiment, a feeling expressed at its most extreme in the desire to be invisible. Such a problem is inevitably augmented by cultural stereotypes of feminine beauty that demand thinness (little embodiment) and spirituality (disembodiment) on the one hand, and sexuality and motherliness (flesh and physical nurturance) on the other.

The conflicts which Atwood's characters face, however, consist of more than surface results of oppressive feminine stereotypes. Each of her female protagonists evinces a fundamental difficulty in negotiating the boundaries between self and world. In their struggle toward emotional, psychological, and physical integrity, these characters appropriate either too much of the world (Joan in *Lady Oracle* is fat and, to vex her mother further, tries to be even more imposing by wearing loud clothes), or too little of the world (Marian in *The Edible Woman* becomes anorexic but feasts her eyes on others as they eat). Moreover, their means of appropriating or rejecting the world are not limited to obviously body-related activities such as wearing clothes, eating, or looking; their struggle to draw boundaries between self and world involves the use of language as well. For Atwood's characters language becomes another, probably the most troublesome, means of assimilating and distancing the world. In *The Edible Woman, Surfacing, Lady Oracle,* and *Bodily Harm,* human conflicts which at first seem to concern only the body begin to reveal a fascinating linguistic dimension. In the struggle to settle "disputed territory," the elusive area of demarcation between self and not-self, Atwood's characters go through similar developmental stages. Basic to this pattern is the concept of war waged not only in terms of the body but also in words: "Words [are] not a prelude to war but the war itself, a devious, subterranean war that [is] unending." In one of Atwood's more humorous passages dealing with language as related to corporeal battles, Ainsley Tewce *(The Edible Woman)* declares that in Quebec many people suffer from constipation owing to "the strain of the language-problem" combined with a diet heavy in potatoes.

Mary Catherine Drinkwater. In Beatrice
Mendez-Egle, ed. *Margaret Atwood:
Reflection and Reality,* Living Authors
Series no. 6 (Edinburg, Texas: Pan
American University, 1987), pp. 14–15

The Edible Woman is Margaret Atwood's first novel. It was not well received; its strangeness bewildered, and reviewers dismissed what they could not understand. A summary of its plot from a *Saturday Review* review suggests the nature of this reception:

> Marian MacAlpin becomes engaged to Peter, a "nicely pack-aged" conservative young lawyer. . . . [She] picks up a graduate [student] named Duncan, who finds ironing soothing and tells Marian . . . [she is] "just another substitute for the laundro-mat." . . . As Marian's wedding day approaches, she begins to lose her appetite. . . . A party at Peter's apartment is a disaster, and so is a night in a cheap hotel with Duncan. Eventually Marian bakes a sponge cake and molds it into the shape of a woman. She feeds it to Peter, telling him, "You've been trying to assimilate me." Her engagement broken, she feels better, and manages to eat some of the cake herself.

This reviewer concludes, "in a world where books filled with drama, passion, humanity, humor, fantasy, challenge, or even love are galloping into print, forget it." Another reviewer describes the material as "thin" but "padded with tedious, irrelevant detail," and the characters as "essentially uninteresting": "There's no reason to purchase *The Edible Woman*."

It is true that this novel does not deliver the customary satisfactions of popular fiction, but a writer as critical of "consumption" as Atwood is could hardly be expected to offer a "consumable" text fit for readers addicted to "stale popcorn," to use her term in "Power Politics." This is not (in Roland Barthes's term) a text which allows the reader to be a passive consumer. Although the novel was—as Atwood herself says—"conceived by a twenty-three-year old and written by a twenty-four-year-old," it is witty and original. In fact it is "witty" in the seventeenth-century sense of the word, in that it centers on a "conceit," an extended metaphor or series of metaphors. It offers an original combination of Dickensian social satire and black comedy, with a Marxist feminist view of human relations under capitalism. Its charac-ters are caricatures rather than characters because Atwood is making a point about the impossibility of transcending "the system."

The originality of *The Edible Woman* is in a "lyric" construction. Though Atwood's imagery is actually more "witty" than lyrical, more like that of a metaphysical than a lyric poem, "what the novel is about" is expressed in its texture of images and ideas—in the development of a conceit (an implicit pun on "consume") from which radiates a series of images (relating to hunting and sex) to create a vision of women under capitalism. This is a novel about a person to whom nothing happens, to whom nothing can happen, because in conforming to her society's ideal of "femininity," Marian is paralyzed. In the end Marian does summon herself to act, and her action "embodies what the artist means"—but baking the cake lady is effective mainly as a symbol, as a witty conceit whose very outrageousness suggests Atwood's difficulty translating vision into event.

The novel thematizes two kinds of "consumption." "Consuming" is a physiological process, the ingesting and digesting of food, as in Marian's reference to "her body's consumption"; and it is a socioeconomic process, the purchases and use of commodities, in which Marian is implicated both by being a young woman on "the market" (to use her term for sexual availability) and by her work as a market researcher. As the title *Edible Woman* suggests, the idea of eating is central. Numerous scenes take place over lunch, dinner, drinks; food metaphors are everywhere, as though the novel has been written by a starving person who can think of nothing but food— which is indeed what Marian becomes when her body stops "consuming." The two meanings of "consume" are suggested by Duncan's word play on "system," when he offers his explanation for Marian's inability to eat: "You're probably representative of modern youth, rebelling against the system"; though it isn't considered orthodox to begin with the digestive system" and it is he who makes the pun explicit when, at the end, he welcomes her back "to so-called reality" as "a consumer." Duncan's term "consumer" implies both physiological and socioeconomic meanings, both eating and participating in the social system. Atwood's analogy between the digestive and the socio-economic "systems" ("machines and mouths," in Ainsley's term) suggests that a society that makes "consumption" the top prority of life—a "consumer society"—makes us prey on one another and finally "consumes" us.

Gayle Greene. In Beatrice Mendez-Egle,
Margaret Atwood: Reflection and Reality,
Living Authors Series, no. 6 (Edinburg,
Texas: Pan American University, 1987),
pp. 95–98

I read a great many novels, a fair number of which I find interesting. A few I find extremely interesting and worthwhile. And occasionally, very, very rarely, I come across a novel which will continue to inhabit my head, a novel so striking that I become evangelical about it. Margaret Atwood's second novel is such a book. It is excellent in so many ways that one cannot begin to do justice to it in a review. It has to be read and experienced. . . .

The dust jacket of *Surfacing* contains a curious sentence, saying that the novel ends on "an unexpected note of hope." Personally, I did not think that the note of hope (and it is a very qualified hope) was unexpected at all. No one, I would have thought, who knows the meaning of rites of passage or who has read even fragments of *The Golden Bough, Beowulf,* or, somewhat more recently, Amos Tutuola's *The Palmwine Drinkard,* to name only a few out of zillions, could think so. For it is the ancient Quest which is the journey here, the descent into the dark regions, where some special knowledge is gained, some revelation, before the return to the world of known creatures. The woman does return, and will go back to the world of humans, but she has been given a knowledge of her own power, a power which had frightened her and which she had therefore denied, and a knowledge of her previous willingness to be a victim, a willingness which had of course also victimized others. She has also, I think, been given another knowledge—the ancient gods of forest and land are by no means dead; they are there, and attention must be paid.

The woman's journey will, of course, be seen by the others as a breakdown in response to the discovery of what happened to her father. The "American" hunters, ironically enough, have in their bulldozer fashion also discovered what happened, and must publicize it, bring everything out, literally, in a detestable fashion. But even this violation of the spirit of the dead cannot in the end damage the woman's newfound self, for the truth is that she has gone into the deepest places, the deepest lakes of the mind, and has surfaced.

The skillful language of this novel reminds one of the beautifully sparse language and many-layered quality of Margaret Atwood's poetry. It is an incredibly short novel (192 pages) to convey so much. The images of animals, birds, fish, trees, water, act on several levels simultaneously—yes, as symbols, but as symbols rooted in living breathing things.

The themes are many, and the nature of reality is one of the most interesting. Some of the themes concern our most burning contemporary issues—the role of women, the facts of urban life, and most of all, the wounding and perhaps killing of our only home, Earth. Margaret Atwood is one of the very few novelists writing today who can deal with these issues without ever writing propaganda. Perhaps she has been able to do this partly because she has interwoven all these themes with the theme which is central to our mythology, our religions, our history and (whether we know it or not) our hearts—humankind's quest for the archetypal parents, for our gods, for our own meanings in the face of our knowledge of the inevitability of death.

Margaret Laurence. *Quarry.* Spring, 1973,
pp. 62, 64

Margaret Atwood's earliest volumes through *Power Politics* and the first part of *You Are Happy,* published in 1974, question and anatomize the traditional nature of love between men and women. Atwood is searching for what Marge Piercy in another context calls "Doing it Differently." Usually in Atwood's poetry and novels, her lovers hack away at each other, clad in their social roles; interaction becomes a war, and sexual involvement causes pain to the women and shatters their selfhood. This warfare occurs because the restrictions on women in traditional sexual roles create the anger which infuses Atwood's women and causes them to resist what their lovers offer. The men seem to emerge unscathed, hardly aware that they gouge their lovers. Yet relations between men and women cause women pain by definition. . . .

The men don't see the need for change—because they aren't hurt by being in power. But Atwood's women fight, their anger ferociously funny and defiant, to retain their individuality, their rage, and their special selfhood.

Power Politics ends with the questions raised but still unanswered. The "Circe/Mud Poems" of *You Are Happy* represent a real advance, for in them Atwood uses women's anger to create new possibilities for love, for Circe is forced to imagine a new world in which love might consist of equality and compassion. Circe and Odysseus, divided at first, transcend harrassing anger. Their love flows into warmth and trust and becomes a union of equal adults. At the end of the cycle, the imagined island wherein a new kind of love is possible establishes the space in which occurs the final section of *You Are Happy*, "There is Only One of Everything."

Jane Lilienfeld. *Worcester Reviews,* Spring, 1977, pp. 29–30

Margaret Atwood's first three novels (*The Edible Woman,* 1969; *Surfacing,* 1973; *Lady Oracle,* 1976) focus on the quest for unified female selfhood. In each narrative, problems related to ego boundaries, merging, and separation form a cluster of psychological issues that are ultimately clarified for the protagonist as she comes to understand her relationship to her parents (particularly her mother), with a man, or both. *Life Before Man* (1979) moves closer to a kind of existential reality: the void is not just the inner vacuum that precedes autonomy or follows separation from the parents. Rather, it is the void in which we are all suspended as part of our solitary humanness; one becomes more acutely aware of it in direct proportion to one's sense of separateness and isolation from others.

The author's most recent novel, *Bodily Harm* (1981), develops these thematic concerns in even more global dimensions, in both figurative and geographical senses. On the one hand, it is Atwood's most politically feminist novel, immediately concerned with such issues as body image, female sexuality, male-female relationships, and male brutality in a patriarchal society. One might even conclude that the novel is an angrily anti-male work. In a certain sense it is so, although the object of Atwood's anger is less the male sex per se than the patriarchal establishment and value system that continue to endow it with excessive privileges and powers, both personal and political.

On the other hand, *Bodily Harm* is a deeply existential novel, focusing on the relation of the individual woman to society: her sense of connectedness to the major moral conflicts of her time, to the issues of power and powerlessness; the illusion of exemption from evil; and the necessity for being politically and personally engaged. Additionally, it examines the nature of moral responsibility for both the individual and the group in a world they never made. The novel is what I would term a truly feminist existentialist text: a novel about "power politics" that not only connects the female world meaningfully to the real structures of power but insists that they cannot be understood separately. Thus, male aggression and female passivity are seen not only in their immediate, private forms but also through their major consequences upon political or public reality—and vice versa. The body politic is the form writ large of the individual body, in this instance the female body; bodily harm in one domain is directly felt in the other.

Roberta Rubenstein. Journal of Canadian
Studies. 20 Spring, 1985, p. 120

Politics, Margaret Atwood once said, means "who is entitled to do what to whom, with impunity; who profits by it; and who therefore eats what." *The Handmaid's Tale* proves that Atwood is among the most telling political writers in the West today. Simply put, *The Handmaid's Tale* is a feminist dystopia. Atwood transmogrifies the Cambridge, Massachusetts, of the late twentieth century into the capital of a monotheocracy, the Republic of Gilead, a nasty piece of work. Its fundamentalist founders have pulled off a bloody coup d'état. They have replaced the Constitution with the overweening patriarchal principles of Genesis. Gilead expels Jews and blacks. It compels rigid gender roles. White women have no money, education or civil rights. However, ladies of the elite get to lord it over the household. They decide who watches what on television. . . .

A superb storyteller, Atwood riskily interweaves the narrative threads of the protest novel, the psychological novel, and the bedroom farce. [The handmaid] Offred's tale is a scholarly reconstruction, assembled some two centuries later from tapes she dictated while living in a safe house in Bangor, Maine. History fails to record whether she ever reached freedom in Canada or England. Her stone in the graveyard of time is but half-inscribed. . . .

The central figure in Atwood's territory is a woman. Atwood Woman is young, educated, white, middle class, invariably heterosexual. She has a job—as an illustrator, scientist, journalist. She has had her share of sexual experience. Her men are often weaker than she. She is urban, but the wilderness is usually the site of her most profound moral and psychological education. In flight from her day-to-day life, she discovers the meaning of survival, a key word in Atwood's vocabulary. She is Marian in Atwood's comedy of manners, *The Edible Woman;* the nameless narrator in the quest novel, *Surfacing;* Joan, the Gothic fraud, in that wonderful romp, *Lady Oracle;* Lesle and Elizabeth in the somber chamber piece, *Life Before Man;* Rennie in a second quest novel, set in the Caribbean rather than in Canada, *Bodily Harm.* Now she is Offred.

Flanking Atwood Woman are two other sorts of women, both of whom influence her. One is her contemporary, often more raucous or audacious than she. The second sort of woman is older. She is Atwood Woman's landlady, employer, aunt, mother, neighbor. Reactionary and manipulative, she strips the world of sensuality and spontaneity. Terrified of the naked, she nevertheless denudes her environment. Her ideals are decency, respectability. Acting on them, she commits moral indecency after moral indecency. She enjoys watching the wormings and turnings of another's submission. Frequently these toughies, in their hats, gloves and woolen underwear, represent provincial Anglo-Canadian society. In *Bodily Harm,* Rennie says sardonically of Griswold, Ontario, her hometown: "In Griswold everyone gets what they deserve. In Griswold everyone deserves the worst."

Gilead is Griswold gone wild. The Aunts, who pump iron (but never irony) into the body politic of technological Calvinism, represent Atwood's most disdainful depiction of the petty female boss. Wearing electric cattle prods on leather belts, they control, reward and punish other women. Like certain of Brecht's characters, they are at once sinister and funny. Atwood achieves a triple effect—she makes her dystopic state even more frightening because it issues cattle prods to such ordinary figures. Yet she also manages to domesticate totalitarianism, because she shows it peopled by such ordinary figures. The state becomes even more frightening, because its monstrosity seems normally absurd, absurdly normal. Finally, Atwood reminds her reader of the political function of satire: to weaken the grip of the cruel and foolish by sending them up witless. . . .

As Atwood's politics have deepened, her ideas about language have altered. Her writing still has the energy and clarity of a swift river. It is limpid without being limp; clever without being silly; controlled without being stilted; precise without being pedantic. She is a rhetorical marvel. In 1975, praising Adrienne Rich, Atwood might have been describing her own style: "mercilessness, of a desirable kind. . . . Language is honed down, decoration trimmed off." She is equally capable of showing the shore of a northern wilderness lake, its fronds and waves and rootlets, and of skewering a frivolity or booby. In *Life Before Man* an Atwood Woman, Elizabeth, goes to bed with William. His devotion to the environment does not redeem his dull devotion to himself. The experience is "like sleeping with a large and fairly active slab of Philadelphia cream cheese."

Paradoxically, like Rich, Atwood also distrusts language. In part she pays an obligatory homage to the weary modern awareness of the gaps between the word and the thing; sign and meaning; culture and nature. Welcoming the death of syntax, Atwood is also paying the now equally obligatory homage to a distrustful postmodern awareness of the ability of the powerful to control discourse. The surprising end of *The Handmaid's Tale* is a parody of academic style. Atwood invents the partial transcript of the Twelfth Symposium on Gileadean Studies, in June 2195. The transcript contains the major paper about the handmaid's tale, which reassures us that Gilead has fallen. However, the transcript does nothing to dispel the fear that pompous, sniggering academics will still be labeling reality in centuries to come.

Yet, Atwood's politics demand that the writer use language to say who is doing what to whom, with impunity. In "Notes Towards a Poem That Can Never Be Written," Atwood insists that the writer see "clearly and without flinching"; that the writer bear "witness." She must speak for the woman "on the wet cement floor" who herself is "silent and fingerless." That woman's death must become another woman's syntax. . . . In *The Handmaid's Tale*, Offred talks into a tape recorder, to an unknown audience. Of course, her story is not true. It is, though, imaginatively plausible. For Atwood, no one can ignore that plausibility with impunity.

Catharine R. Stimpson. The Nation.
May 31, 1986, pp. 764–67

Atwood teaches mostly through negative example: her protagonists are not very heroic heroines in the beginning of their adventures and sometimes not even at the conclusion. They are not totally reliable narrators; they may lie to the reader as they sometimes lie to themselves, or in some instances, they are even a bit mad. They are often fragmented, isolated, "seeing poorly, translating badly." All are, in varying degrees, failed artists like those meta-phorically paralyzed and amputated authors whom Atwood describes in *Survival,* cut off from tradition, bereft of audience and of social or political relevance. All of Atwood's writer/artist protagonists share a curious ambiva-lence towards their craft: they often use their fictions for the evasion of reality rather than for confrontation; they create illusion rather than transform reality. Much like Atwood's mirror images, so central to all her novels and poems, art can function, as it does for these heroines, as a way to lose the self in a vision of the self, to establish a conflict between the "I" of the self and the "she" of one's fiction, to become object rather than subject, to create polarities where none should exist. Like Alice in Wonderland, Atwood's hero-ines often move through mirrors and through their own self-deluding fictions into worlds of myth, where it is possible to lose the self and where they flounder amidst the ruins of traditional roles and obsolete images of women. But Atwood is always intent to state that, also like the mirror, art can and should function as an agent of truth, a means to knowledge and confrontation. Those of her heroines who resolve this basic conflict of illusion versus reality, who ultimately discover truth in and through art, also discover their own identities and their own humanity. In the refutation of the fantasy of the self as little-girl-lost, as innocent victim, they assert their own maturity as powerfully creative agents—as artists.

Atwood's "maps" for the arrival at such a destination are often complex and sometimes difficult to read. There is always more than one way to get there from here, and "here," in Atwood's psychic geography, is sometimes the greatest enigma of all. . . .

The role of the artist, particularly in contemporary society, is, for At-wood, shamanistic, even though she indicates throughout her work a realiza-tion of the dangers for the artist herself that are implicit in such a distinction. There is the inherent moral obligation to use one's art to create life rather than reduce it to artifact, to avoid the misuse of art which is the curse of "the girl with the Gorgon touch" and of the female Frankenstein, both of whom appear throughout Atwood's fiction and poetry. . . .

Atwood derives her mythic metaphors from diverse sources: classical accounts of metamorphoses (particularly in the "Circe/Mud Poems"), gothic horror stories, the ghost tales of Henry James, Christian concepts of martyrdom, Canadian folklore, and fairy tales for children. . . . But always her use of myth is a deconstructive one; she disassembles the myth to reconstruct it in terms of the modern female psyche and the special circumstances of the contemporary female *kunstlerroman*. Her protagonists are always explorers through tradition and myth in search of a new identity and in search of a voice, a tongue, a language, an art, with which to proclaim that identity.

Particularly in this sense, Atwood can be seen as a "feminist" writer: she is concerned for the psychological and physical survival of women, and she sees this in terms, not merely of individual survival, but of sisterhood. Almost always there is a sister-figure in Atwood's fiction, a secondary character, sometimes a confidante, who often aids the protagonist, even if the protagonist solipsistically refuses to recognize her value. Women friends, being subject to the faults of the rest of humanity, may turn out to be as treacherous as men, as is the case with Ainsley in *The Edible Woman* and with Anna in *Surfacing*, but they may also serve as unconditional supporters and faithful allies in a way that men never do. Moira in *The Handmaid's Tale* and Lora in *Bodily Harm*, for example, are more heroic figures than are the heroines themselves.

Too, Atwood frequently incorporates the theme of the rediscovered mother, a pervasive concern in feminist literature as a whole, from *Jane Eyre* to Adrienne Rich. . . .

Atwood has grown up with the contemporary women's movement and, like most of the best writers today, she has transcended its infancy along with her own. From what Atwood herself has termed in *Second Words* the "protofeminism" of *The Edible Woman*, her work has developed into an increasingly revolutionary vision of women's place in a profoundly political world, a vision based on women's humanity and their potential acceptance of human responsibility, for evil as well as good. Like many other feminist writers, she is concerned most specifically with the role of women as artists and with the political implications of that role. More than men, women artists are subject to role prescriptions and the necessities of the mundane; as the speaker/artist complains in "Small Poems for the Winter Solstice," "You think I live in a glass tower / where the phone doesn't ring / and nobody eats? But it does, they do / and leave the crumbs and greasy knives" (*True Stories*, 33). Childbirth and artistic creativity may be metaphorically linked, but in a practical world they may also represent a conflict: "and I wonder how many women / denied themselves daughters, / closed themselves in rooms, / drew the curtains / so they could mainline words." . . .

But perhaps finally we must categorize Atwood's most recent work (if such categorization is desirable at all) as something like "radical humanism." From her early disclaimers of aspiration to a political voice, her frequent statements that "books don't save the world," she has moved steadily towards a firm commitment to human rights and the conviction that if books, in fact, don't save the world, then nothing else can, either. From early essays reprinted in *Second Words* we infer that Atwood's philosophy was one of reservation, that there is "a questionable value of writers, male or female, becoming directly involved in political movements of any sort: their involvement may be good for the movement, but it has yet to be demonstrated that it's good for the writer." . . . Later, however, particularly as manifested in *Bodily Harm, True Stories,* and *The Handmaid's Tale,* that sentiment has changed, perhaps due to Atwood's discovery of Amnesty International and her growing recognition that we live in an increasingly violent and power-oriented society. The facts and political realities, atrocities committed in the name of ideology, terrorism and brutality, become crucial for Atwood, "not because the writer is or is not consciously political but because a writer is an observer, a witness, and such observations are the air he breathes." . . . Politics, which Atwood defines in deceptively simple terms as "who has the power," becomes a matter, not of choice, but of human responsibility for which both novel and poem become the vehicle.

Barbara Hill Rigney. *Margaret Atwood*
(Houndsmill: Macmillan Educational, 1987),
pp. 1–2, 7, 10–12, 16

Most reviewers have emerged from their reading of *Cat's Eye* to report, whether in disappointment or relief, that the Witch of the North has failed to bring it off this time around. Instead of the nightmare of a whole future society, they tell us, Atwood gives us "merely" the present and the past of one woman artist. Words like *Bildungsroman* and *Künstlerroman* are bandied about as if they said it all, and the new ground she breaks, the *female* artist's life, is revealed as a tedious whine. . . .

Cat's Eye does provide the materials from which to document a single character's experience of growing into the particular woman and artist she is. . . .

But it is not only time that distances Elaine [Risley] from her own development as a female in postwar North American culture. There is a sense in which women's traditional destiny has always been more of a spectacle than an experience to her. For one thing, rigid sex roles and conventional relationships are an alien subject matter Elaine has to begin learning at age eight, when her family abandons a roving life of collecting botanical specimens in northern Ontario and moves to a Toronto suburb. Although on a certain level Elaine is so eager to fit in with the neighborhood girls that she mutilates her own personality in the attempt, she nonetheless views their ways with a bemused combination of detachment and agony, rather like an anthropologist captured and prepared for the table by cannibals she had thought would only be the subjects of study. . . .

Because it is the girls and women of Toronto who give Elaine her first harsh lessons in female reality, growing into her own identity becomes a process, for her, of growing away, not only from their precept and example, but from women in general. Similarly, it is the feminist movement, represented here by a group of militant women artists, that helps Elaine to her first recognition as a painter, as well as to the elements of a raised consciousness. But we meet her in the 1980s as someone who has grown away from feminism—at least feminism as the social analysis of private suffering—and we find out in the course of the novel that she never really identified with the women's movement. Elaine takes a dim view of the hip young woman reporter who interviews her before the opening because she feels that no one now in her twenties can know what it was like to be a woman in *her* time. But it is actually Elaine Risley who has missed out on both extremes of female experience, the deepest pain and the highest sisterhood.

If that were all, *Cat's Eye* would still be chiefly a Bildungsroman and a Künstlerroman, and my problem as a reader would be whether my impatience with the heroine was strong enough to overpower my appreciation of the brilliantly realized details of life in the 1950s and 1960s. But the story of Elaine Risley's maturation as a woman and, for that matter, the story of those decades, are situated in a larger context. In the conventional disclaimer where she specifies that this first-person narrative is not an autobiography but a novel, Atwood also states that "space and time have been rearranged to suit the convenience of the book." It turns out to be significant that concepts as portentous as space and time are introduced into an explanation of how a work of fiction departs from a recitation of facts. On her acknowledgment page, she expresses her indebtedness to a number of well-known physicists and cosmologists whose subject matter she says she has "sideswiped" in this novel.

One of the intellectual turning points in *Cat's Eye* comes when Elaine's brother, while both are still teen-agers, interrupts one of their father's dinner-table lectures about species extinction on the earth, to point out the impermanence and insignificance of our sun itself in the greater order of things. Physics overcomes biology and ecology as the son out-machos the father. Elaine's quest—and, through it, Atwood's—is to bring the new, implicitly masculine, vision of space and time, of the multiplicity of dimensions, into the framework of her life as a woman and an artist. Thus, one of the newest paintings in her Toronto show is titled *Picoseconds,* while another is called *Unified Field Theory.* Both pictures use concepts from the world of physical and cosmological speculation to make sense of the artist's own history. . . .

World War II is not long over when Elaine's family moves to Toronto, and its cultural mark is still palpable. In the 1980s, Elaine tells the young interviewer that there is a division between those of us who remember that war and those who do not. Later, she observes that the war seems not to have ended after all but only to have fragmented and spread out into an ongoing series of smaller wars. But Atwood endows Elaine with no curiosity as to what those multiple wars have to do with, say, the changing economic and demographic face of Toronto, the condition of women or the destruction of the environment—although these are all pieces of history that do affect her. Even when Elaine's physicist brother is shot dead by terrorists, which brings the new war almost as close to home as it can get, Atwood deliberately keeps her ignorant of the hijackers' cause and even their faces. These people's history thus becomes as random as their tactics, and it looks as if it is Atwood who is saying that a Third World struggle (whatever it may happen to be) is without meaning—in general and in her narrative.

At the end of *The Handmaid's Tale,* the lecturer who is presenting that novel's . . . [tape-recorded] memoir of a woman's life within a totalitarian nightmare utters some pompous footnotes instead of telling us what happened to Offred. After which he concludes the novel with a final piece of pedantry, asking, "Are there any questions?" Well yes, there were and there are. This next novel raises some I already had in mind and some new ones as well. *Cat's Eye* ends with Elaine mourning the future that she will never share with Cordelia—"two old women giggling over their tea"—and then turning to look at the stars in a moonless sky, describing them in terms informed by both art and astronomy: "It's old light," she concludes, "and there's not much of it. But it's enough to see by." Maybe, but I'm still here in the political science lecture room with my hand raised and some unanswered questions on the tip of my tongue.

Lillian S. Robinson. *The Nation.* June 5,
1989, pp. 776–79

AUSLÄNDER, ROSE (BUKOVINA–GERMANY) 1907–88

Silent words, fish words are exchanged, and with one's own breath, mill wheels are set in motion. Rose Ausländer has . . . no fear of beautiful images. Those who are long lost live in castles in the air, on myrtle paths, and drowned companions swim with gifts of seashells to the shore. But she also has the courage to see her "parents, young inside the red velvet album" and herself, old in the spotted mirror. She speaks of a time when Austria does not exist, a time with no bushes or birds, and of a new "clean-shaven" earth where the children no longer return home from the fields, where she herself is trapped inside the rotating, prattling clock with no way out.

There are no longer any still brooks in which a Narcissus could reflect his image; Rose Ausländer's "drawing water through a sieve" represents many fruitless efforts, and worldwide want enables us to understand that her mill wheels no longer grind grain, but hunger. In the poem "Fragebogen" (Questionnaire,) she still movingly reports her fate, but the life-long "bearing of the casket" is then again a short testimony, a completely scant image.

The poet must seek her way between the sharks, and she feels herself tense up before the wheels of the clock; she chews again and again at the word peace, and it never sates her. In the poem "Your House," the sun, the rain and the dust speak to her in that extreme desolation that scarcely any lyric poet in our day beside Rose Ausländer dares to express. In such desolation, she speaks in the company of Nelly Sachs, Georg Trakl, and Käthe Kollwitz, observing the black-tongued poppy-flower that stands on the grave of her fellow countryman, Paul Celan.

Only the shadow of her own self protects her from the dog-day heat; it is indeed this Own Self that keeps her alive, her ability to speak, this daring and sad voice. Relations with friends, even the dead ones, are replaced in the long run by relations with faces and voices; other signs appear in the heavens and cheerful fantasies appear like that from "The End of Time," where people in mutual understanding go walking down the street of shells together. Here it also seems possible that, beyond death, "heritage continues to write itself as poetry." Israel rises up behind the Wailing Wall, the Age of the Phoenix has begun, new like Jerusalem. Even in the hospital, she sets out on a journey, past the obstructed bed, on into a land free of goals, and out of her—our—feelings of suffocation emerges the "Litany of the Air": her—our—yearning for perfection originates in the "Miracle of the Word."

"From my dead mother's sleeve I fetch the harp, a wind in the shepherd's field to the east strokes the strings": these are her words in a memory poem. But Rose Ausländer has outgrown mere personal recollection. It is of our privations, our fears that she speaks.

Marie Luise Kaschnitz. *Frankfurter Allgemeine Zeitung*. February 16, 1974

Rose Ausländer comes from the Jewish community in Czernowitz which produced several German-speaking poets, including Paul Celan. She managed to survive the Holocaust in her native land and in 1946 emigrated to the United States, where she was to remain for eighteen years before she returned to Europe, settling first in Vienna and, a year later, in Düsseldorf. The various stages of her life—the disillusioning return to Germany, the years of exile, the persecutions and, very rarely, the lost idyll of the distant past—are reflected in her melancholic verse.

A few poems deal specifically with one of these stages. There are some excellent Holocaust poems in *Ohne Visum;* and two in *Andere Zeichen,* "Fragebogen" and "Wandlung," perfectly capture the dilemma of the Eastern European Jewish poet who exchanges the exile of New York for that of postwar Germany. But the major emphasis is placed on the general condition of alienation and not on autobiographical details. In most poems the act of the speaker's sense of homelessness is more important than the historical causes. An effective, restrained, elegiac tone is maintained throughout both volumes. The individual is at the mercy of the dictates of fate, the whims of chance and the malice and callousness of his fellow man.

One of the principle techniques used to create the depersonalized world of these poems and the impression of the omnipresence of the forces of evil and destruction is the blurring of distinctions between subject and object, between the individual and the environment. Things are often personified, taking on—especially in *Andere Zeichen*—a human role and acting upon the speaker, who is at their mercy. Solace is sought in poetry, "im Wunder des Worts"; but the promise must remain unfulfilled, for the word, like the speaker, is "verwundet" and "entwurzelt." "Bekenntnis," the strikingly affirmative concluding poem of *Andere Zeichen,* reflects the poet's determination to assert her belief in the value and dignity of human life, in spite of— or perhaps because of—the absence of any justification of such affirmation.

Jerry Glenn. *Books Abroad.* 50, 1976,

pp. 154–55

The publication of a handsome volume of new poems by Rose Ausländer follows relatively closely behind a volume of her collected poetry. *There's Still Room* is the title of her most recent work. Hans Bender writes a brief epilogue. If it is applicable to state that writing, and in particular the writing of poems, is something like a affirmation of being alive, then this is true in the case of the poet Rose Ausländer. It is at the same time a form of survival: "You write and write / you will never / finish writing / From the afterlife you will dictate / your syllables to the grass."

Much is as blunt, concise and simple as are these lines (the poem is called "Writing"): the author, in poem after poem, takes up a conversation with herself, with the "possibility of mastering the past and the present." It is precisely that "Who am I / if I am not / writing" that keeps her verses in disquiet, in context with her other writings, in interdependency with each text and the next.

The vocabulary necessary for doing this has on the whole become more limited, much to the advantage of each individual poem, its clarity, and yes, the concision of the imaginative fantasies it elicits. In this volume, as already in the earlier works, we find key words, catch phrases, word motives: these are at once imaginably simple, humane and atmospheric; I and you, the wind, the air, all ever returning in this manner in Rose Ausländer's poems, along with her memories and visualizations. She includes them in her gestures of escape, as well as in her recollected landscapes of Bukovina, Southern France and Tessin.

An urgency, free of impatience, is perceptible in many of her new works, as well as a passionate directness, an openness, an embracing of her surroundings, of other people, of "you and you and you" as expressed in her poem "Contract" ("Vertrag"). Key words are no longer encoded, pregnant with mystery, or cryptic, no longer Celan-like ventures in the Word. Only rarely do momentary opportunities for comparison arise ("Young word" or "In the Rose Gomorra the Thorn-Poem," as well as the previously cited "Syllables from the Afterlife"). Rose Ausländer's vocabulary distinguishes itself now not only through its concision, but also through its increased permeability, its airiness. One of her poems bears the characteristic title "Lands of Air," and another ("Everything that Breathes") reads: "The air says / I am air / Everything that breathes / breathes me in and out / belongs to me / I belong to you all for a while." The self-evident manner with which she employs her favorite words has a freeing quality. At the same time, more clarity, intensity and immediacy is gained.

The poems establish contact by virtue of their simple message and their plainest of realizations. They are completely economical poems, for they include not a single word too many. The metaphoric darkness, and also the metaphorically dark beauty that was observable in the author's earlier works, dissolve into these lines, which are as succinct as they are confessional. Of course Rose Ausländer's poems are now and will continue to be beautiful poems. Still, it is no longer a complicated and artistically irritating beauty that we recognize, but rather one that is latently melodious. Conspicuous is the complete absence of decor. If such a thing as programmatic poetry could exist with this poet, then "Sentences" would have to be an example. As transparent as it is, it expresses that which is characteristic of nearly all the poems in this volume: "Crystals / irregular /compact and translucent/ behind them the things / recognizable / This searching / for words that connect / sentence to sentence / reaching ever further / into the familiar / incomprehensible world."

Undoubtedly, the concretion of the poems in *There's Still Room* has become more stable, more convincing, more resistant. And the "searching for words that connect" is an expression of the searching for connection, intimacy, and ultimately for the "you and you and you," a search that is frank and unreserved.

Karl Krolow. *Frankfurter Allgemeine Zeitung*. January 17, 1977

Rose Ausländer—the name is already an omen—belongs with certainty today to the most important women poets of the German language. Having escaped attention most of her life, she has become known in the last few decades, but has yet to become famous. Her lyric poetry, though not voluminous, is nonetheless poetically exact, and its special quality derives from the fact that it never ran aground in the darkness of grief, as did the poetry of Celan and Nelly Sachs. "Behind the Wailing Wall / the age of the Phoenix / burns": these, her words in another poem on the same theme. Transformation and new figuration are clearly a theme for her.

Horst Kruger. *Frankfurter Allgemeine Zeitung*. July 29, 1978

Rose Ausländer's utopia looks back. Looking back, she takes up archetypical images for her poems, which signify an arresting of the fight for life, even an abolition of longing: self-denial as the ultimate ratio of loyalty. The dimensions to which the seventy-two-year-old is bound: deliverance from desire, the standing still of time, the end of death, peace, sleep, night, paradise; the principle of Nirvana not as death, but as life. Imaginary resting points in the apocalyptic whirlpool of time. They symbolize a state of being which nears and is equally far from life and death, yet not bound to either: "Dissolved / the years flow / to the time-drowned shore." And: "I shall / live / even under the earth / It receives me / holds me / in its breath / We grow / together." Rose Ausländer and her vision of writing poetry:

> Seven hells
> to pass through
>
> Heaven
> is pleased
>
> go ahead it says
> you have nothing
> to lose

She writes her life in poems. Reality becomes poetry experienced.
Jürgen Serke. Afterword to Rose Ausländer.
Im Atemhaus Wohnen (Frankfurt: Fischer,
1981), pp. 147–48

It seems a miracle that a woman whose life was disfigured by the violations of this century: emigration, Holocaust, eternal loss of homeland, a woman, who in old age is not spared the isolation of illness, can write: "My breath is called Now," "The layers of the past formed me, I inherited the future / My breath is called Now." Others who preceded her, Nelly Sachs and Paul Celan, did not escape their persecutors, even though they too tried to bring the persecutors to silence through the gesture of the word, through the divining-rod of remembrance.

The miracle of consolation can not be explained, and Rose Ausländer's struggles with the teachings of Buddha also prove nothing, for seeking and finding are conditionally dependent. We may speak then of a strength whose roots she fostered within herself, the strength that has grown out of the long history of her people's suffering, that we find in the Chassidic faith, in the mirth amid the misery in the *stetl,* in the Chassidic music, in the rich literary tradition.

In contrast with Nelly Sachs, Rose Ausländer has not struggled with the tradition, for she coped with it as a matter of course on the Pruth, in the city of her birth, while Nelly Sachs, born in Berlin, first had to overcome the cruel failure of Jewish emancipation before, deeply shaken, she experienced the Jewish diaspora as her own history.

A gift of grace, that which is heavy and difficult can become weightless— or so we Christians interpret such an experience. Yet Job of the Jewish tradition experiences a similar gift of grace.

So it really must be a part of mankind's miracles of consolation that the knowledge of one's own impermanence superimposes itself over the knowledge of cruelty, of misery. For the knowledge of one's own impermanence reflects back onto one's own experience of unreality in dreams.

Ingeborg Drewitz. *Die Hören.*
145, 1987, p. 157

AVISON, MARGARET (CANADA) 1918–

Winter Sun is an appropriate title for the first book of collected poems by Margaret Avison, a Canadian poet of already considerable standing. The title, like so many of the poems themselves, is not merely what it seems. One might, at first glance, take it as a hint about the prevailing mood of the contents, and it does indeed evoke the bleak somber bareness of the Toronto watery-sunlight winters that provide material for much in the book. But although Miss Avison's light is a winter light, it is still the sun: a particular sun which is capable of rendering immediate appearance transparent as the glass of a lens.

One always runs the danger, when speaking of a poet's "reality beyond the finite," of branding the poet as a floaty-footed and cloudy-headed mystic whose vision, although it may be directed upwards, tends to encounter nothing but fog. (In Toronto, of course, the fog has at least some relation to actual experience.) To identify Miss Avison with this cliché would be sticking the label on the wrong bottle. She has her feet firmly on the ground (usually the "cinder mash" or "cool tar" of the city poems); her vision is always focused to, and through, specific concrete reality rather than past it. Again, if one praises a poet's descriptive powers, one risks conveying the image of a housewife cooking up a poem (of the Oh Beautiful Sunset or Hooray For Autumn variety) by applying adjectives to an object like icing to a cake, with the same result: if one swallows much of it, one feels a little ill. But Miss Avison never slathers her poems. Her use of descriptive words is not only precise and striking, but so precise and striking that the words do not just describe the object but *are* the object: there are other tennis players in both art and life, but *her* tennis players, "albinos bonded in their flick and flow," are the only ones of their kind.

She pares her works to the core, and throws out all extraneous and diluting verbal peelings. The result of this critical cutting and sorting is a highly condensed poetic texture which demands a lot of conscious concentration on the part of the reader. For example:

> The even-bread
> Of earth smokes rainbows. Blind stars and swallows parade
>   the windy sky of streets
>   and cheering beats

> down faintly, to leaves in sticks, insects in pleats
>> and pouches hidden
> and micro-garden.

Winter Sun is not a chocolate-covered poetic pill, guaranteed to taste nice, go down easily, and eliminate all need for effort. Such sweetness would be useless in its universe:

> Nobody stuffs the world in at your eyes.
> The optic heart must venture: a jail-break
> And re-creation.

Miss Avison portrays consciousness as an attempt to encounter and to form a relationship with the external; the ultimate locus of such an encounter is the individual human mind, which makes its ordered cosmos out of a chaos which includes bits of society, scraps of sense perception, snips of science, moments of history, chips of myth, and the elbowings of the insistent self, as well as the phenomena of the natural universe. Her ordered structure is built of various poetic forms, among them simple lyric stanzas, unconventional sonnets, blank verse, and highly disciplined irregular lines which avoid the free and all-too-easy idiom of the contemporary common denominator. Her verbal wit is considerable, but never coy; her humor subtle, sometimes ironic, but always wise; her human warmth (a warmth which is connected with a strong sense of nostalgia) is most evident in the last, longest, and most definitely not least poem, "The Agnes Cleves Papers."

In the last analysis, the poetic eye sees its own world, a world which both reflects and transcends the formlessness of the finite world outside, and reality becomes internal:

> Gentle and just pleasure
> It is, being human, to have won from space
> This unchill, habitable interior
> Which mirrors quietly the light
> Of the snow, and the new year.

Winter Sun is a book not to be read, on any account, just once.

Margaret Atwood. Acta Victoriana. 85,
January, 1961, pp. 18–19

Margaret Avison is a poet difficult to fault. Her new volume, *The Dumbfounding* confirms my belief that she is a highly professional writer with unusual resources of tact and poetic intelligence. Nothing here is exaggerated or faked, every insight is earned. . . .

The vitality of the language owes much to Hopkins, as does the concern for the exact adjective and the precise detail. As we react to such description, however, we become aware that it requires an intellectual, as well as a sensuous, response. A process of evaluation is implicit in the presentation of scene or situation; it arises out of contexts, out of an awareness of the way each new image qualifies the preceding ones. Avison is a poet of perspectives and points of view, acutely aware of the modes by which we see and understand. Even her titles suggest this: "Natural/Unnatural," "Meeting Together of Poles and Latitudes (in Prospect)," "Walking Behind, en Route, in Morning, in December." When she presents a scene (as in "Twilight"), it is usually with a keen sense of how the mood of the viewer controls the selection of detail; when she tells a story (as in "A Story"), there are, characteristically, several frames of reference, a story within a story within a story. She is remarkably versatile in the techniques of establishing multiple points of view, and her poetry is full of voices, monologues, dialogues, and asides by the narrator. She handles sequences (spatial and geometrical, or temporal) with great care, and she gives a significant role to such elements of typography as italics, parentheses, and line arrangement. She explores the epistemology of saying things in a manner reminiscent of that in which some contemporary painting is concerned with the epistemology of sight.

This is cerebral poetry, but no mere academic exercise. Control, self-conscious order, and quiet wit are employed in the exploration of themes that are urgent, deeply moving, and often violent. The basic situations tend to be frightening—isolation, drowning, tyranny, blindness, crucifixion. Scenes of beauty frequently contain something ominous or disturbing within them. Even the more purely descriptive poems explore sensation in a manner that is disquieting in its lack of sentiment. There is a steadfast refusal of the heroic gesture and the stock response. . . .

Those familiar with Avison's earlier collection, *Winter Sun,* may be surprised to find that the new volume contains many poems on religious themes. The title poem, "The Dumbfounding," is itself a meditation on the life of Christ and the meaning of the Incarnation. Again, Hopkins points the way:

> lead through the garden to
> trash, rubble, hill,
> where, the outcast's outcast, you
> sound dark's uttermost, strangely light-brimming, until
> time be full.

The religious pieces are successful because they are poetry before they are devotion. They introduce a new note of commitment into Avison's work, and this at times brings with it a new lyrical freedom. It will be interesting to see how fully her characteristic techniques (with their emphasis on diversity) can be adapted to the new vision (with its emphasis on unity).

Hugh MacCallum. *University of Toronto
Quarterly.* 36, 1967, pp. 354–59

Under the scrutiny of her intellect the world sometimes becomes austere, but the poems are never unfeeling. "Thought" *becomes* "feeling," and Romanticism is thus inverted—not to find its values valueless, or to praise the social world as the best of all possible, but to find another expression for a metaphysical sensibility by which "that" world of understanding and "this" one of perception can be brought together. The brief moment for which this may be possible is still stable, and by being, it becomes part of the future experience, or field of vision, of the poet-perceiver. Sensitivity to word and sound is not irrelevant to this pursuit, but rather the key. The very momentariness of perceptions, and the continuous shifting in point of view, are communicated to our understanding when they are rendered in sound: the multiple meanings inherent in puns immediately suggest this flux, which is the medium in which Margaret Avison looks for a self, and for both release and illumination. . . .

Since 1966, Margaret Avison has published no poems, but as she is a writer who labors over her work before bringing it into print—and does not revise after that—we can hope that another volume is in the making, one that will introduce us to a new group of finely wrought poems and another stage in the development that has already made her an important writer. "The Agnes Cleves Papers," at the end of *Winter Sun,* held within it much that was to be developed in *The Dumbfounding;* "The Unspeakable," at the end of *The Dumbfounding,* indicates that Margaret Avison has accepted the traditional poet's task of celebration. But of what?. . . .

Margaret Avison would have us praise, but continue to fear as well, knowing our place as we see it from instant to instant. *The Dumbfounding* as well as *Winter Sun* reminds us that "When day and life draw the horizons / Part of the strangeness is / knowing the landscape." In coming to know it, we discover the "unused"—which is not formless, but should not be governed by preconception either. So, paradoxically rejoicing in a frightening prospect of swimmers' moments, we continue to perceive the world, eschewing an imposed system of geometry, and discovering form and content together. And so perhaps in discovering the various forms of the unused, lies the direction for Margaret Avison's new-found self, sight, and freedom.

William H. New. *Twentieth Century*
Literature. 16, July, 1970, pp. 187, 201–2

"The Agnes Cleves Papers" portrays one woman's "experience of living" in a manner that recalls Coleridge's "Rime of the Ancient mariner." In it, an old woman tells a lovely, young woman—a wedding guest, the opening stanza suggests—the story of her life. "The need to tell you is exciting / And very bleak," she confesses, like the ancient mariner who is compelled to tell his tale to certain people who are compelled to listen. Her tale is a "compressed epic" that sets out from a "windy harbor," ends with a "late sail out beyond the gap," and leads through the perilous seas of her life on a quest aptly described by the epigraph to Coleridge's poem:

> About such matters the human mind has always circled without attaining knowledge. Yet I do not doubt that sometimes it is well for the soul to contemplate as in a picture the image of a larger and better world, lest the mind, habituated to the small concerns of daily life, limit itself too much and sink entirely into trivial thinking. But meanwhile we must be on watch for the truth.

Agnes Cleves's mind circles through images of her past in a quest for knowledge of a larger and better world that she hopes to discover, not by transcending the small concerns of daily life, but by confronting and assimilating them in a vision of the truth. It is a redeeming vision, which will knit her chaotic life into a whole that is significant, dramatic, and that can save her from the wintry chill of solitude, "venom and timidity." It is a vision that, like her "exhibition rocket," is outside time because it surveys and justifies her entire lifetime. Unlike the ancient mariner, however, she has not yet mastered her story, learned its truth, or accepted her guilt. We observe her in the act of constructing her tale, searching through her life for a pattern and a meaning. In this respect she is like Hagar Shipley, the heroine of Margaret Laurence's *The Stone Angel*, who at one point compares herself to the ancient mariner. Both old women find their memories untrustworthy and erratic: sometimes "pink-striped" in "garish colors"; sometimes softly tinted in "aquamarine and ocher"; sometimes formed like "clay figurines" that are perfect but lifeless; sometimes obscurely "scarfed in dreadful mist." Moreover, Agnes Cleves does not trust the very words with which she tells her tale ("There ought to be a word cognate with love"), and though she wishes to speak "in plain words," she is constantly drawn into circumlocutions, analogies, and paradoxes. She must develop her own language, a task which, Margaret Avison suggests in an essay on "Poets in Canada," she shares with all Canadian storytellers:

> Any Canadian writer, for example, is aware of a scuffle to find his own words, his own idiom. . . . In trying to find his language-level, then, a Canadian poet is trying to assert both an identity and an aesthetic.

To assert her identity, Agnes Cleves must devise an aesthetic: as she discovers, "for my secret I would have a universe." The effort of understanding her life and so defining her secret self is the effort of narrating her life and so setting her world in order.

J. M. Kertzer. *Concerning Poetry.* 12:2,
Fall, 1979, pp. 17–18

[W]hen it is not unusual for poets to produce a volume a year, she waited six years before publishing her second volume, *The Dumbfounding*. This volume is, by common consent, even better than *Winter Sun,* and one critic called *The Dumbfounding* the most original book of modern poetry in Canada. Twelve years later, we have *sunblue.*

Whether this volume will result in a further fillip to work on her is uncertain, but few poets can have had so much critical and academic attention with only two volumes of verse totaling some 190 pages. . . .

If Miss Avison is one of Canada's most distinguished poets, she is also one of the most intelligent if not the most difficult. She shapes for herself a unique and demanding vocabulary and approach. A masterful logopoeia and unexpected images explode like crackers against the night sky. The pyrotechnics, the agility of voice, the trapeze show is memorable, if stunning. It can safely be said that none of the poems in her first two volumes can be understood, let alone mastered, before several readings. Some of them are reminiscent of crossword puzzle clues. This is not to deny their emotional power, it is only to define her particular sensibility which feels by thinking.

That echo of Eliot's views of seventeenth-century poetry is not accidental. She belongs to the line of strong, socially and spiritually concerned and intensely felt poetry that runs from Donne and Herbert to Gerard Manley Hopkins and T. S. Eliot. There is the same wide-ranging curiosity, and awareness of current issues, the same massive and stimulating intellectual quickness and power, the same concern with artistic detail as well as structure.

Her differences with these poets are firstly that she is Canadian and Presbyterian rather than English (or American) and Anglican. Her Presbyterian background leads her to sympathy with the prosaic worker in the factory, and opens her up to inspiration from each order of creation, however lowly. And Miss Avison is distinctly, unmistakably, perhaps even proudly, Canadian. Born in Galt, Ontario, in 1918, she spent her childhood in Western Canada which, with its spaciousness and peculiar quality of light, was to deeply inform her artistic vision. It is not just that landscape and light and a seeing eye are central to her work, as they are to so much Canadian literature. She shares with other Canadians a concern with survival. Her work rises to epic or at least heroic stature precisely because nature is transfigured rather than domesticated in her work. Travel, and trains, loom large in her poems, but do not reduce man to insignificance as in, say, Purdy's best work. While she shares the sameness and rationality of Donne and Eliot, Miss Avison does not discount the non-rational (witness "Stone's Secret" in *sunblue*). This links her not merely with the medieval mystical tradition but also with such contemporary Canadians as Margaret Laurence and Morley Callaghan. In the work of these three, as in so much Canadian literature, myth and reality commingle and interpenetrate, revitalizing mind and heart and hand.

A second way in which Miss Avison differs from her forbears, however, is in her variety of form, tone and voice. Donne was always unmistakably himself, whether the love he was celebrating was divine or profane. But there was a greater concern with clarity of form as well as of meaning after his conversion—a process more distinctly noticeable with Eliot. Avison's work has always been marked by a multiplicity of method and content: but it is perhaps not surprising if there is a greater proportion of the lucid in her latest volume. . . .

Her independence ought not to be confused with a retreat into a private world. Indeed, never has it been so clear that she is fully aware of contemporary developments—science and technology, pollution and ecology, poverty and Vietnam, earthquakes and comets, throng these poems. The SKETCH'es show her equally aware of her more immediate surroundings, and she captures them with all the warmth of Hogarth.

Eleven of the sketches are the first eleven poems in the book and the twelfth one is the second last of the collection. In a sense, the whole volume is a collection of sketches. There is a remarkable sense of thematic and poetic continuity and unity in the volume, and the overall impression left by it is that of the abundance of multi-facetedness of life—life in the great brightness of a sunlit world. For a woman now well into retiring age (though hardly in retirement!) that is quite an achievement. I suspect, however, that *sunblue* will be disregarded in academic and critical circles till a fourth volume makes clear the direction of the changes in her poetic vision and style. Those who have the adventurousness to change their skin must be patient with the more cautious and conservative of critics. If what *sunblue,* after twelve years of silence, adds to Miss Avison's stature is yet unclear, it can be thoroughly recommended as one introduction to a challenging, contemporary, and consummate Canadian poet.

Prabhu S. Guptara. *The Literary Criterion.*
16, 1981, pp. 42–45

All of Margaret Avison's poetry is marked by a persistence in self-questioning, by a desire for honesty that goes beyond the merely intellectual, but which is profoundly intellectual in character. This alone would set her apart from many of her contemporaries. From the point of view of her poetic, in which "Prelude" is the central early document, this means that she is continuously subjecting to scrutiny not only history and the world but also the virtues of language, metaphor, the conventional forms of poetry, even her very vocation as a poet. "Butterfly Bones" (*Winter Sun*) is in this sense more than a principled questioning of the high traditional artifice of the sonnet, but a disturbing query concerning the value to perception of trophied language—even, perhaps, of any language. Avison is not primarily concerned here with the atrophy of poetic idiom, I take it, but rather with the failure of language as an instrument, and so expresses her consistent worry that poetry, like criticism, might become "the kind of story that kills what it conveys." This line ought to be read in the context of Avison's growing concern, from the early poetry on, to see poetry as means and not as an end. Just as light for her is the means whereby the world is known, so poetry, as an experience of light, is to be valued in proportion as it illumines. The final question of this sonnet:

> Might sheened and rigid trophies strike men blind
> Like Adam's lexicon locked in the mind?

is thus a question of profound concern not only for her poetic but for poetic language as well.

David Lyle Jeffrey. In David Kent, ed.
*"Lighting up the Terrain": The Poetry of
Margaret Avison* (Toronto: ECW Press,
1987), pp. 138–39

BÂ, MARIAMA (SENEGAL) 1929–81

Mariama Bâ is Senegalese, an educated Senegalese, a member of several associations interested in enhancing the female position in a predominantly Moslem, male-oriented society. Her western education notwithstanding, she would like to be considered as an "average Senegalese woman," "a woman of the house." *So Long a Letter* is her first novel and it is filled with autobiographical elements, expressing as it does the novelist's desires and dilemmas, tracing her life in a society caught between the established order of the past and the exigencies of the present. A traditionalist at heart, Bâ aspires to be a revolutionary. A maternal retiring figure through and through, she aspires to be a pioneer in female emancipation. Her family upbringing and the Koranic training have imbued her with the absolute law of "divine wish": man is woman's overlord. Added to that is Bâ's fatalism. Destiny is a fixed reality, impossible to avoid.

> Destiny seizes whoever he wants, when he wants. If his desire tallies with yours, he brings you an overabundance of bliss. But most often, he unbalances and brings conflict. You can only submit yourself to his laws.

However, such fatalistic tendencies are contradictory to the tenets of the white man's school where Bâ learned how to manipulate the French language. Submissiveness in the face of suffering is discouraged and the victim is told to demand total reform of the social order. Her "letter" is written in the form of a notebook kept by the heroine named Ramatoulaye. Married for thirty years to Modou by whom she has twelve children, Ramatoulaye has been separated for five years from her husband who repudiated her and left her for a much younger woman. Her "letter," ostensibly addressed to a bosom friend, a divorcee working as an interpreter in the Senegalese embassy in New York and due to return home very soon, is written immediately after Modou's death. It is a reflection of life in a psychological ghetto of mental torture and social disorder, where woman is a slave and a beast of prey. Divorce is a rarity but separation and infidelity are common. The life of the couple, far from being a haven of contentment and consideration, is a hell of conniving criminals and common cretins. According to Bâ, two camps are precisely delineated: the victimizer, the slave master, the ruler of this hell on earth, is Man; the victimized, the slave driven at times to the point of mental exhaustion, is Woman.

Femi Ojo-Ade. *African Literature Today.* 12,
1982, pp. 72–73

So Long a Letter is a radical novel which adopts the form of a long letter. Through a series of reminiscences Ramatoulaye shows how she is able to retain her sanity and dignity in the difficult situation created by the death of her husband. She records her loneliness, grief, display of courage in the face of great odds, her internal striving for a more secure life, her social inadequacies and achievements. The novelist skillfully puts together a rambling collection of episodes built around matters of national and universal significance. Through this she mobilizes public opinion in favor of women's liberation, freedom of action for the individual and a total rejection of all unprogressive ideas and attitudes.

At the center of the work is a consideration of the place of the woman in a Muslim society. . . . Ramatoulaye is an embodiment of all that is noble and dignified in a woman. As an activist she is endowed with a lot of physical and mental energy which she puts to good use. She finds herself taking on different kinds of responsibilities and she performs admirably. On her own she solves all the problems that confront her, even though these weigh her down occasionally. That she remains so mentally alert and accomplishes so much in the unhappy situation in which she finds herself is no mean achievement. She is meant to be an attractive example of how brilliantly a woman can perform when the use of her talent and ability is not obstructed by restrictions and taboos. It is by such constructive achievements, rather than by empty sloganizing, that women can prove their mettle and establish a place of honor for themselves in a male-dominated world. Ramatoulaye's activities and achievements put a woman's enormous capabilities and resilience beyond doubt. She expects that her contribution will result in the glorification of womanhood.

> I am not indifferent to the irreversible currents of women's liberation that are lashing the world. This commotion that is shaking up every aspect of our lives reveals and illustrates our abilities.
>
> My heart rejoices each time a woman emerges from the shadows. I know that the field of our gains is unstable, the retention of conquests difficult: social constraints are ever-present, and male egoism resists.

Although much has been accomplished, much remains to be done. Total success can only be recorded if the struggle continues relentlessly and the battle is waged with great intensity.

The novel deals with other areas of life where women have been effective or require help—education, politics, home and family life. The author is forthright in her assertions on these matters. Education is the means of achieving "a rapid social climb" and of contributing maximally to the good of society. It is a continuing process in which teachers play a crucial role. A teacher herself, she deals at length with the nobility of the work of the teacher.

> Each profession, intellectual or manual, deserves consideration, whether it requires painful physical effort or manual dexterity, wide knowledge or the patience of an ant. Ours, like that of the doctor, does not allow for any mistake. You don't joke with life, and life is both body and mind. To warp a soul is as much a sacrilege as murder. Teachers—at kindergarten level, as at university level—form a noble army accomplishing daily feats, never praised, never decorated. An army forever on the move, forever vigilant. An army without drums, without gleaming uniforms. This army, thwarting traps and snares, everywhere plants the flag of knowledge and morality.

Politics should not be the exclusive preserve of men. Women should be encouraged to participate in the art of government and decision-making. They help in laying a sound foundation for society in the home and are therefore eminently qualified to get involved in national affairs.

> Women should no longer be decorative accessories, objects to be moved about, companions to be flattered or calmed with promises. Women are the nation's primary, fundamental root, from which all else grows and blossoms. Women must be encouraged to take a keener interest in the destiny of the country.

On pan-African solidarity she regrets the breaking up of regional groupings like the French West Africa Organization which provided a strong link for the Francophone peoples of the area. This "made possible a fruitful blend of different intellects, characters, manners and customs. . . . We are true sisters, destined for the same mission of emancipation."

So it becomes obvious that Ramatoulaye uses her long letter to Aissatou only as a medium of putting forward her radical views on several issues, many of them related to the elevation of the status of women in society. Even so, she succeeds, through her style of direct narration, in retaining the intimacy which a private letter from one friend to another demands. She frequently emphasizes the bond between her and her friend.

> We walked the same paths from adolescence to maturity, where the past begets the present. . . .
> Yesterday you were divorced. Today I am a widow.

and talks of the superiority of friendship over love.

> Friendship has splendors that love knows not. It grows stronger when crossed, whereas obstacles kill love. Friendship

resists time, which wearies and severs couples. It has heights
unknown to love.

Her husband may disappoint. But the friendship between her and Aissatou
is reassuring. This is why she is, as it were, emptying her heart to her friend
in the hope that she will get some comfort and pleasure by so doing. The
novelist has thus used the letter form to carry out not only a public obligation
but also a private duty. This is the unique achievement of this work.

Odalele Taiwo. *Female Novelists of Modern
Africa* (New York: St. Martin's Press, 1984),
pp. 17–21

Abandonment in the novels of Mariama Bâ is predominantly a female condition. It is both physical and psychological, and it transcends race, class,
ethnicity, and caste. Hence the unity of the universal cry of the woman subjected to this condition. The forces in society that set in motion the process
that culminates in abandonment and the resultant impact of such a process
on the abandoned female are conceived by Mariama Bâ to be enormously
out of proportion to each other. The whim or accidental fancy of the male
and the calculated machinations of a female elder, translated into reality
either willingly or reluctantly by the male, place upon the female a burden
infinitely heavier than the cause of that burden. The response to this unexpected burden takes one of two forms: reluctant surrender and bear the burden while lamenting and exposing social and other kinds of ills, or categoric
refusal to shoulder the burden and opt for freedom through various means.
In either case, the female will and determination to live and to retain the
integrity of her moral principles usually predominate. Herein lies the faith
and confidence of Mariama Bâ in a better future for women in particular, and
humankind in general.

Posed in this manner, the problematic of abandonment in the novels of
Mariama Bâ begins to take on the characteristics of a power struggle in which
both sides, male as well as female, invoke canons of indigenous traditions as
well as adopted nonindigenous values (conceived of as "universal") to justify
or contest attitudes, beliefs, and actions. More specifically, the novelist concentrates on the question of the misuse and distortion of power and privilege
in a sociocultural milieu in which one segment of the population—male, acting independently or under pressure from outside forces (usually revenge or
profit-motivated parents)—readily acknowledges but selfishly and deceptively perverts privileges bestowed upon it by tradition to the detriment and
disadvantage of the female segment. The two possible responses to this selective adherence to tradition—selective because it acknowledges privileges yet
shirks responsibilities and obligations that come with such privileges—defines the nature, the intensity, the parameters, and the outcome of this power
struggle. In light of this, one can right away dismiss the stereotype of the
docile traditional African woman who mutely and passively surrenders to

the whims and dictates of the African man. The very idea of a response suggests some measure of consciousness, consciousness which, in the case of Mariama Bâ's heroines, is translated into various kinds of concrete actions designed, in most cases, to counteract the potentially devastating condition of physical and psychological abandonment.

Power struggle, then, is to be seen not so much in terms of victory/defeat, since it is the kind of struggle that yields a no-win situation, but it is to be looked at from the perspective of the impact of the experience on the individual and the latter's ability to examine, articulate and utilize the transformative capabilities of such an experience of struggle. . . .

If Mariama Bâ is not the first African writer to treat the problematic of abandonment and if she is not the pioneer of the epistolary form in African literature, she is, however, regarded as the first female African writer to offer, according to Abiola Irele, "a testimony of the female condition in Africa, while giving that testimony a true imaginative depth." She is the first African writer to systematically utilize and adapt the widest range of the potential of the letter as artistic form and narrative vehicle in order to enhance this female imagination, a kind of imagination that is immaculately distilled and refined to capture and articulate the fear, the weakness, the hope, the strength, the resolve, the resilience, and the sense of mission of the African woman, in particular. The originality of her work resides in the studied manner in which she adapts and uses an Islamic religious and juridical precept in *Une Si Longue Lettre* and a Wolof cultural concept in *Un Chant Ecarlate* to inform and, to a large extent, even generate the narrative content as well as the structure of the respective novels. Both of these—narrative content and structure—combine to graphically manifest the central problematic of abandonment that underlies both novels, hence their thematic uniformity.

Mbye Baboucar Cham. *Current Bibliography on African Affairs.* 17, 1984–85, pp. 30–32

Mariama Bâ's discourse . . . while never questioning the fundamental precepts of Islam, stemmed deliberately and convincingly from a dynamic conception of society, a strong belief in social and political change and progress. At first glance, each of her two novels seems to center around one specific topic: the evils of polygamy in *Une Si Longe Lettre* and the failure of a racially mixed marriage in *Un Chant Ecarlate* (A scarlet song), her second novel, published posthumously. However it is my contention that despite their apparently different foci, there is one underlying theme that runs through both novels, and that is the theme of personal happiness. . . .

One could be tempted to conclude that Mariama Bâ's novels were nothing but pleas against polygamy. But that would be definitely superficial. Mariama Bâ's central preoccupation in these novels was more the pursuit of happiness than an outright attack on polygamy. And when Rama praises her friend Aïssatou and calls her "pionnière hardie d'une nouvelle vie" (daring pioneer of a new life), she was indeed expressing her admiration for her friend's courage in continuing her search for true happiness without any compromise with polygamy or any other binding traditions. However, although she did not embark on an outright diatribe against polygamy, Mariama Bâ was convinced that happiness—and not just women's happiness, but men's as well, a whole society's happiness—must be based on a monogamous marriage. And in the modern context, for her, monogamous marriage meant a close association between two equals, and the sharing of pains, joys, hopes, disappointments and successes. The foundation stone of this happiness is without doubt in the couple, a concept, an ideal that is clearly new in Africa. . . . While both Memmi and Sembène treated the couple as a central and exalting entity, Mariama Bâ was the first African writer to stress unequivocally the strong desire of the new generation of Africans to break away from the age-old marriage customs and adopt a decidedly more modern approach based on free mutual choice and the equality of the two partners.

Edris Makward. In Carole Boyce Davies
and Anne Adams Graves, eds. *Ngambika:
Studies of Women in African Literature*
(Trenton, New Jersey: Africa World Press,
1986), pp. 272–73, 278

One of the key concepts that emerges from Mariama Bâ's novels is that of choice. This is most striking in *Une si longue lettre* where the recurrence of words like *le choix, choisir, j'ai choisi, j'ai décidé, ma décision, j'ai voulu, je n'ai pas voulu,* (the choice, to choose, I have chosen, I have decided, my decision, I wished, I did not wish to) is in itself indicative of the importance of choice for Mariama Bâ. In *Un chant écarlate,* even though words pertaining to choice are less recurrent, crucial choices are constantly being made throughout the novel. The act of choosing is shown as being pivotal in human experience. It is indeed a powerful act which gives shape and direction to human existence. . . .

It is possible to say that in *Une si longue lettre* Aïssatou and Ramatoulaye have made different choices in similar situations. However, what is important is that the choices have been made. For too long a time women have been denied [the right] to choose the course of their lives, even though choice is at the center of what gives significance to human existence. In this novel Mariama Bâ shows clearly that women do have a deep consciousness of the options opened to them and that they are willing to make the choices that will make their lives more wholesome, no matter what the consequences might be. There is also a strong intimation that the generation of Daba (Ramatoulaye's daughter) will go even further in their choices and will deal with that concept in a more radical way.

In *Un chant écarlate* Mariama Bâ widens the scope of the concept of choice by showing how all human beings, female and male, Black and white deal with that concept and the consequences that choice can have on the self and on the human community.

After a long silence, women like Mariama Bâ have chosen to talk. Their voices have sprung up to revive the role that women have traditionally played as storytellers. They now tell their "modern stories" through the medium of the written word. Using their female sensibility, they approach women's issues from within, offering a female way of looking at the world. This is indeed a choice that needed to be made.

Irene Assiba d'Almeida. In Carole Boyce
Davies and Anne Adams Graves, eds.
*Ngambika: Studies of Women in African
Literature* (Trenton, New Jersey: Africa
World Press, 1986), pp. 161, 171

In both [of her] novels, Mariama Bâ examines the issue of intercaste, intercultural, and interracial marriage and relationships, and she raises questions on whose satisfactory resolution will depend the stability and viability of much of the moral, political, social, economic, and cultural fabric of her society. This issue is increasingly becoming a focal point for a number of African artists concerned about the nature and implications of personal and social relationships within and between societies in Africa, in particular. This is the case with a number of recent African films.

Although Mariama Bâ does not look at the currently topical issue of female excision and infibulation in these novels, her concern with the general issue of inequality puts her in the mainstream, if not the forefront, of contemporary feminine and African thought. In spite of awesome odds, her heroines are champions of change and justice and they inspire other women and people to live and carry on.

This affirmative attitude toward life that the novelist invests in her heroines and that she wants to inspire in all women is conveyed in a language and form that have few parallels in African literature. One of the distinguishing features of Mariama Bâ's language is its poetic majesty which effortlessly expresses the emotion and thoughts of her characters in ways that could come only from the imagination of an accomplished woman artist. The novelist is at her best in those instances when she takes us deep into the mind and feelings of mothers disappointed with the choice of mate of their offsprings, of mothers and other women scheming to undermine one another, of mothers on the joys, pains and challenges of motherhood, of women confiding in other women, of women concerned with the political and economic health of society, and of men trapped in a quagmire of vanity, lust, and deception.

Mariama Bâ's use of the letter form is unparalleled in its method and system in African literature. *Une si longue lettre* is entirely in the form of a letter while *Un chant écarlate* makes use of intermittent letters as part of the narrative technique. Letters are used to continue the love affair between Ousmane and Mireille and at the same time to give an account of sociopolitical activities and information. Letters announce the marriage of Ousmane and Mireille to their respective parents, and it is an anonymous letter that exposes Ousmane's deception to Mireille. In *Une si longue lettre,* the novelist even uses the technique of a letter within a letter, as is the case when Aissatou writes Mawdo to inform him of her decision to leave. Such refined use of the epistolary form invites appropriate comparison with the recently acclaimed epistolary novel of Alice Walker. *The Color Purple.*

Culture, argues Léopold Senghor, is the bedrock of development. Culture, says Ngugi wa Thiong'o, is much more than just folklore. It encompasses the entire spectrum of relations and activities in any given society. Consequently, any movement in or of society must have its feet firmly rooted in healthy cultural grounds if it is to be of any lasting and meaningful value to the welfare of individuals and society at large. And a healthy culture, in Ngugi's terms, is a culture of equality, a culture free of all forms of exploitation, and above all, a culture rooted in the true traditions of the people. In *Une si longue lettre* and *Un chant écarlate,* Mariama Bâ uses the strength, the maturity and finesse of her imagination and artistry to reinforce this fundamental notion of culture and society. In her work, technique is combined with a sharp sense of human and social detail to capture the soulbeat of a society in the midst of a historic effort to balance its weakness and strength for a healthier future. Too bad that this female visionary left this world after writing us only one long letter and singing a beautiful song for all.

Mbye B. Cham. In Eldred Durosimi Jones,
Eustace Palmer, and Marjorie Jones, eds.
Women in African Literature Today
(Trenton, New Jersey: Africa World
Press, 1987), pp. 99–101

BA'ALBAKKĪ, LAYLĀ (LEBANON) 1936?–

I Live is the story of a young girl who introduces herself to us as she knows herself. She also takes us into unknown recesses of herself, areas she does not know but wants to find out about. We set out on a journey of discovery inside the world of a young virgin, an unknown world in which the author assumes the role of an experienced guide, one who shares with you everything such girls know and feel, and who then goes on to join in investigating the things they do not know or find impossible to understand. There is no attempt to suppress what the guide knows or to claim to know things that are not known, as is the case with guides in museums and at monuments!

In this novel Laylā Ba'albakkī declares open revolt, the revolt of girls of the Middle East against their present reality. She rebels against the emptiness of life . . . and everything that is tawdry about our social relationships and the way people think. She rebels against her colleagues who fool around with no sense of direction, who lust after money and look for it wherever they can. She rebels against young men in the Arab world, even those who have been educated and have gone to university, young men who cannot think about girls without seeing a bed in their mind's eye. Finally, she rebels against the home because it is a prison even though the bars may be made of gold; it seems to be a home for her family but not for herself. . . .

Laylā Ba'albakkī is a tremendous talent. We will not term her (as some have) the "Arab Françoise Sagan" because we do not want her to be that, but simply Laylā Ba'albakkī. We want her to achieve her potential as a citizen and a writer, a young girl who may fall in love or dream of so doing; who may marry or dream of marriage. But along with that, she should produce ideas, art, or literature too. We need more works like *I Live,* and better works at that. . . . so let her persevere and continue her literary production. She should think of herself as being at the beginning of the road. If she thinks she has achieved her goal, she will in fact be finished without ever reaching that goal or pinnacle in her career.

Anīs Sāyigh. *Al-Ādāb.* May, 1958, pp. 59–61

In [the short-story collection *Spaceship of Tenderness to the Moon*] we encounter the personality of Laylā Ba'albakkī along with the same basic constituents that appeared in *I Live.* There is also a tangible advance in poetic sensibility, in use of imagery, in style, and in the attainment of maturity during the inevitable and necessary crisis through which the author goes.

The pivot of her "problem"—if the expression can be used—is the relationship of Middle Eastern women to men, linked to the development of their selves and their search for freedom within the current social and moral ambience. However, this problem (which can be characterized as a "general" one) loses its general status and any abstract intellectual framework it may have. With Laylā Ba'albakkī it takes shape in the personality of an individual with her own feelings, someone who lives with the outside world. . . . The various strands in the personality of this author are embodied in a kind of dialectic of opposites found in society, and, in fact, in the individual as well, and in every single aspect of nature, with its varying seasons.

In the stories of *Spaceship of Tenderness to the Moon* the author dwells on the internal events and concentrates on the self, with its tragic problems and willful attempts to escape, to break loose. We see that she has tried to combine this internal drama, in which she may be either angry or submissive, and the external drama, where all this effusion of life either meets or separates, harmonizes or clashes . . . an effusion that divides into two streams, one of despair and pain, the other of optimism and happiness. . . .

With her nervous, sensitive, poetic, colorful style, full of imagery, this writer has thrown some light on the limits of the problem. Her story goes on a journey with her, on a nighttime adventure. It stays close by her when she looks at a mist and a beautiful scene in nature, when she trembles at a sudden encounter with a face in the crowd or probes the depths of banal reality with a rapid glance. We can say that she is herself the pivot of her story and the focus of the enigma it contains.

Hānī Abū Sālih. *Hiwār*. 8, 1964, pp. 133–34

The novel *Disfigured Gods* by the Lebanese writer Laylā Ba'albakkī treats the idea of past and future on the level of personal relationships. What is it that brings together Mīrā, the young girl of twenty-two, and Nadīm, the history professor who is over forty. It is just that they live in the same building; the older man feels a craving for youth, while the young girl discovers an obscure feeling of ease in consorting with a man who is her father's age. Both of them are fighting devils from their past. Mīrā lives with the thought of her father, who died of a heart attack; she believes that she will die the same way. The dead man is still the master of the house, which he rules from a picture hanging on the wall. Her mother sits by the picture every day and talks to it any time something serious happens, as though she is the priestess of some idol god. Nadīm lives with the idea that his wife left him. He has led a life full of women and has grown tired of it all. Now he dreams of a modest house and a faithful woman who will not invite men to come and visit her because he will be able to satisfy her every need and desire. He likes to imagine himself as a happy father with lots of children. But 'Ā'ida, his wife, let him down; she was not a virgin.

Each of these characters needs the other. The young girl restores a sense of youth to the middle-aged man, while he in turn releases her from slavery to her own father. Then the abandoned wife becomes pregnant. She has taken advantage of a drunken moment when Nadīm is raving about Mīrā in a stupor, taken him to bed, and held him in her arms "like a sick baby." The young girl, meanwhile, has been cured of her fear of "the violet cloud" which, she fears, will carry her away as it did her father. She has come to know happiness. She falls in love with a young man of her own age and they decide to get married. . . .

However, while life opens its arms to the young girl, who manages to obliterate the image of the past from her imagination, oblivion and languor envelop the middle-aged man, who remains bound to his past, its passions and disappointments. 'Ā'ida has died during childbirth, the baby has been put into an oxygen tent, and Mīrā has left the building. All that is left for Nadīm is the bottle so that he cannot open his eyes and see the light.

Shukrī 'Ayyād. *'Ālam al-fikr*. October–December, 1972, pp. 637–38

The defiant mood of Lina—the protagonist of Laylā Ba'albakkī in her novel *I Live* (1958)—is deeply rooted in her egoistic assertion of her individual freedom. Her strong feelings and ideas spring from a point of view which focuses on her ego to the almost total exclusion of social reality. What is at issue for her is her personal problems. [Georg] Lukács' characterization of modernist literature applies here. He points out that the process of negation of history takes "two different forms in modernist literature. First, the hero is strictly confined within the limits of his own experiences. There is not for him . . . any preexisting reality beyond his own self. . . . Second, the hero himself is without personal history. He is thrown into the world: meaninglessly, unfathomably." Lina proudly proclaims her separation and self-sufficiency by contemplating the following analogy: "I am a luxurious palace. . . . It has everything necessary for the sustenance and reproduction of life; it needs no help from the outside world. . . . the wall around it is high and separated from the road by a moat. I am an autonomous world whose course of life is not influenced a bit by any outside event which does not spring from my ego." Being preoccupied with her self to the point of narcissism and almost totally engaged in the nurturing of her ego, Lina pays little attention to others, "to those strange creatures who slide on the outer surface of my life." It is consistent with such a view that she has no interest in politics: "I simply confess that I do not have the mind to find a solution to the problem of Palestine, Kashmir, or Algeria. What worries me . . . is how to walk for the first time with my shoes that raise me seven centimeters above the ground. Will they break as I rush into the streets?" Let no one be tempted into believing that the author's intention here is simply to expose Lina's trivialities. The intent is to shock and defy the society. That is, without doubt, the crux of the matter. The defiance is most intense when directed against the family. Lina despises her father and his wealth, and shows ambivalence (reflected in feelings of pity and disgust) toward her mother.

> Halīm Barakāt. *Visions of Social Reality in*
> *the Contemporary Arab Novel* (Washington,
> D.C.: Center for Contemporary Arab
> Studies, 1977), pp. 23–24

The public prosecutor of the Court of Appeals called the author, Laylā 'Alī Ba'albakkī, in accordance with item 532 of the criminal law, accusing her of harming the public morality in her book recently published under the title *A Space Ship of Tenderness to the Moon*. The public prosecutor of the Court of Appeals, Mr. Sa'īd al-Barjāwī, assigned the case to the court in charge of monitoring publication (Makhamat al-Matbū'āt). The trial of Miss Ba'albakkī was ordered to begin. Under item 532 the public prosecutor demanded the imprisonment of Miss Ba'albakkī for a sentence of one to six months plus a fine of ten to one hundred liras. . . .

The author's purpose and intention. Now the court proposed to examine in some detail the stories in the defendant's book *A Space Ship of Tenderness to the Moon* in order to determine whether the author's intention was serious, or whether it was simply to divert the reader and to arouse his sexual desires and thus harm the public morality. First, let us consider the defendant herself, Laylā 'Alī Ba'albakkī, the daughter of a conservative Lebanese village family, who left her home and traveled to Paris, where she remained for some time, in an environment totally different from that of her own people. As she lived in this strange environment, she observed the people's life styles, their confusions, their troubles, their silences. Each day she tried to learn more about this new society, to discover its particular truths. Trained from childhood in letters, coming from a tradition which used words to express enlightened thoughts, Laylā 'Alī Ba'albakkī was moved to put down on paper the things she had seen and felt in her real and her subsequent imaginary trips to the strange society in Paris, and thus she wrote the book in question, *A Space Ship of Tenderness to the Moon.* . . .

Therefore, after all these points have been considered, the court views the defendant Laylā 'Alī Ba'albakkī and her book *A Space Ship of Tenderness to the Moon* as follows: Her intention was to portray, realistically and truthfully, her characters as she saw them moving on the bare stage of life. She gave to acts and emotions their accurate names in order to dramatize the idea which she was presenting. Just as a human being exposes his real self in front of a mirror in order to see clearly, and hopefully improve, its faults and its uglinesses, so does the book in question use realism to help the reader see life more clearly. The stories in question do not arouse sexual instincts or harm public morality. The work is to be seen rather as a serious creative effort, a call to set people free from their narrow environments, a call for all of us to face the naked truth and its ramifications, to see good and evil and to learn to choose between them, not with eyes closed with the trachoma of tradition that has woven a veil of ignorance around us, but with eyes wide open toward the light.

And therefore, the court finds that, since such efforts do not constitute a crime which is subject to punishment, the court's judgment is that all procedures against the defendant, Laylā 'Alī Ba'albakkī, should cease immediately. [August 23, 1964]

> Court decision. In Elizabeth Warnock
> Fernea and Basima Qattan Bezirgan, eds.
> *Middle Eastern Muslim Women Speak*
> (Austin: University of Texas Press, 1977),
> pp. 280–81, 287–89

In 1958, Ba'albakkī published her novel *Anā ahya* (I live), which signaled a bold rebellion against the hypocrisy and injustice of a society that considers women to be sex objects. Lina Fayad rebels against her family and goes to work and to university. At the university she meets a young Communist, with whom she falls in love. Illusion soon gives way to reality, as it becomes clear that ideology is only skin-deep. In despair at her discovery of this stereotypical chauvinist, Lina decides to kill herself, but her society will not allow her such control. As she is about to throw herself under the wheels of a passing truck, she is saved by a friendly passerby. In her next novel, *Āliha mamsūkha* (Deformed gods; 1960), Ba'albakkī, like al-Malaika in Iraq and Venus Khuri in Lebanon and Paris, protests against a society that demands unimpeachable modesty and chastity of women and mandates that men fulfill their manhood by displays of sexual prowess. The heroine may protest, but she is at the mercy of her society's expectations.

Miriam Cooke. *World Literature Today*.
Spring, 1986, p. 214

[T]wo approaches can be distinguished in the work of [Arab] women writers. One is inspired by concern for the individual and society as a whole and treats the position of women as one of a number of important themes, while the other is a product of a particular concentration on the oppression of women in Arab society which pretty well excludes any other themes. This second approach was forcefully exemplified in one of the first Arabic novels to be written by a woman, *I'm Alive!* by the Lebanese Laylā Ba'labakkī. This book caused a sensation when it appeared in 1958 and it is still cited as the most remarkable expression of feminist literature in Arabic. The title suggests the writer's individualism and her violent protest against the values of the Lebanese bourgeois milieu in which women can merely be decorative. The main character looks for a job, breaks away from her parental home and begins a stormy, passionate friendship with a student who is a Communist. In the end she has to face the impossibility of living independently of her family. The book is written in a staccato, nervous style well suited to the atmosphere of challenge and self-affirmation which the author seeks to express. No wonder that it excited a storm of protest in the Arab world when it was published; no woman had ever dared to accuse society in this way in black and white. Laylā Ba'albakkī has published a few other works since, but she withdrew from literary life some years ago.

Hilary Kirkpatrick. In Mineke Schipper, ed.
*Unheard Words: Women and Literature in
Africa, the Arab World, Asia, the
Caribbean, and Latin America* (London:
Allison and Busby, 1985), p. 82

BACHMANN, INGEBORG (AUSTRIA) 1926–73

The autonomy and literal meaning of the prose in Ingeborg Bachmann's stories is always maintained. Like Ilse Aichinger, her primary interest is not in the detailed exposition of plot but the possibilities of extreme situations. In reacting to the demands of such circumstances, the fictional characters are forced to convey a sharpened portrait of human nature. The images and symbols she has adopted from lyrical expressionism, however, function allegorically in her stories, and she employs all the means of descriptive and psychological narrative to interpret them precisely. The surrealistic images in Ilse Aichinger's prose exist only in a dream world, but Ingeborg Bachmann connects them directly with the object by which they have been ignited. They are decoded and their meaning confirmed through the plot.

Kristiane Schäffer. *Monat.* August, 1962,
p. 72

Ingeborg Bachmann's poems are a testimony to her unconditional . . . courageous readiness to meet her destiny. She chooses the lonely road although it is beset by fear and terror; . . . she dares to raise unanswered questions. . . . She describes, freshly and in their totality, the first initiation into love, the destruction and loss of love, and violent beauty hardly to be "endured." In hymnlike song, the poetess proclaims her readiness to accept life wholly. . . .

In formal terms, what prevails is a free, heavy, flowing rhythm. Occasionally, strict rhyme schemes are inserted. The imagery, drawn largely from nature but also from the world of myth and fairy tale, mirrors man's states of mind and his historical situation. Verses of the most tender poetic melody, immediately accessible and in their language equally palpable and striking, occur side by side with wild and impenetrable lyrical passages. The occasional and unexpected slips into contrived and pompous language are always redeemed by a great, free-flowing poetic power.

Charlotte Nennecke. In Hermann Kunisch,
ed. *Handbuch der deutschen*
Gegenwartsliteratur
(München: Nymphenburger, 1965),
pp. 63–64

When preparing to read this prose one should not expect stories, descriptive action. Information about events or characters in the accepted sense is no more to be expected than harsh assertions. A voice audacious and lamenting. A voice speaking honestly about its own experience of things certain and uncertain. And, when the voice fails, an honest silence.

Neither speaking nor remaining silent without reason, or taking a stand on the ground either of hope or despair. She has scorned lesser reasons for speaking.

Audacity? Where should we seek it—in an admitted retreat before superior powers, in admitted powerlessness against the increasingly alien world? In the admissions themselves? Without doubt, since they are not routine admissions made lightly or willingly. But even more in resistance. She does not retreat without a struggle, or fall silent without a word, nor does she abandon the field in resignation. To admit what is true—to make true what should be true. Literature has never been able to set itself a higher aim.

Lament? Not about small things, and never plaintive lament. About the approaching lack of words, about the threatening disintegration of the links between literature and society that faces every writer in a bourgeois environment. About the prospect of being left alone with words ("the word will only draw other words after it, the sentence a sentence"). About the haunting temptation to join hands—through conformity, blindness, acceptance, habit, illusion or treachery—with the deadly dangers to which the world is exposed.

Courage? She is surprised but not defeated, full of sorrow but without self-pity, and not enamored of suffering. One is confronted by a battlefield. Sees the forces gathering. Lyric poetry, prose and essay all move in the same direction: from the unquestioned to the questionable, from the usual to the unusual, from the uncommitted to the committed, and allegiance, too, from the inexact to the authentic. "Follow me, words!" A kind of battle cry, brave enough, dignified enough.

Representation? The poet as representative of his day? Ingeborg Bachmann, shy but also proud, ventures to make this claim. She is bound to arouse offense, because representation has been abandoned in the literature of the moderns. She goes further. "To the writer who wishes to change things how much is open and how much not?" she asks, as if it were agreed that writers wish to change things and not violently disputed amongst them. Is the writer—in her day and in the country in which she lives—still master of the effects he wishes to produce? She has no illusions about this, she remains incorruptible: "Nothing stirs, only this fatal applause." Nothing moves. So the writer has spoken in vain? Can the blunting of his readers, produced by the "many playful shocks" administered to them in the course of years, be beyond recall? But what must writing be like if, before all else, it is to change this?

Christa Wolf. *The Reader and the Writer*
(New York: International Publishers, 1977),
pp. 83–84

Caution seems to be in order when confronted by the large number of women who emphatically and desperately demand their own feminine language and their own kind of literature and thought that is often seen as represented in the works of Ingeborg Bachmann, a woman writer who has only recently become timely again in the literary and scholarly establishment. Thus, there are good reasons why feminist literary scholars in America, among others, are studying Ingeborg Bachmann, her literary development, individual works, dominant motifs and themes, and finally her own conception of herself as a woman writer.

Ingeborg Bachmann's statement in her *Frankfurt Lectures* of 1959 has a paradigmatic quality to it: "If we had the words, if we had the language, we would not need the weapons." What seems like linguistic euphoria in this sentence, like the utopian conception of a poetic language that can prevent war, belongs in this case to a context that is in no way optimistic and not at all utopian. On the contrary, this context thematicizes scepticism, the fundamental discord in the experience of writing and of poetic existence. Both experiences are equally characteristic and fateful for Bachmann.

As a poet, she began with poems that announced the new beginning and turning point in a political and intellectual position that is commonly designated by the catchwords "Demolition" *(Kahlschlag)* or "Zero-Hour" *(Nullpunkt)*. In 1954, with the picture caption "Poems from the German Ghetto," *Der Spiegel* declared her a new discovery of the Group 47. Not only Ingeborg Bachmann the poet, but also Ingeborg Bachmann the radio playwright and feature writer, the storyteller and novel writer made headlines. Unlike any other post-war woman author, Bachmann's extraordinary literary talent was acknowledged, and she was patronizingly and priggishly advised to abandon prose and novel writing because—according to one of the West German popes of criticism—her writing here showed signs of "frivolous exaggeration."

Finally, there was also Ingeborg Bachmann the literary object, the subject of Max Frisch's and Uwe Johnson's works, the "poetess in the professor's chair" and [the] authoress who lectured in Frankfurt on "Questions of Contemporary Poetry," and who had to allow—how could it have been otherwise for a woman?—her demeanor, her speaking style, her clothing and her smallest habits to be publicly analyzed. It was not Ingeborg Bachmann herself, but the press which continually sought such headlines about her; and scholars and literary critics remain to this day preoccupied with her in the strangest ways.

Irmela von Luhe. New German Critique.
Fall, 1982, pp. 31–32

The fairy-tale motif of the water-sprite Undine as an elemental spirit has been of great interest to German writers since the end of the eighteenth century. A comparison between the original myth and Ingeborg Bachmann's use of it brings into focus Bachmann's break with tradition. A textual analysis of "Undine geht" discloses that Bachmann extends the motif of the watersprite to bring it into the context of existentialist thinking. Central to existentialism is the question of one's own existence, one's identity, and the relationship between the Self and the Other. My interpretation of Bachmann's story will elucidate the relationship between Self/Undine and Other/Hans as one of estrangement. A careful reading of the text reveals that Bachmann uses the theme of alienation also to symbolize women's self-discovery or unification with self, which requires a negation of the self as other (as male defined) and thus constitutes a withdrawal from male-dominated culture. . . .

While Bachmann alludes to the fairy-tale motif by juxtaposing love and the desire for unification with separation and loss, she uses the theme as a point of departure to underscore an existential concern: the gap that exists between men and women, their separateness, and their inability to communicate with one another. The lack of communication is evident in fragmented speech and in terse soliloquies that express Undine's introspection, her self-assessment, and her condemnation of men. Undine's monologue displays her vulnerability, her anguish, and the void she feels for lack of contact in a mutually satisfying relationship. When Undine attempts to make contact with an Other by rising to the surface of the water, men hear her call as ghostly music. Her laughter is a "gurgelndes Gelächter" that terrifies. The allusions to terror, anxiety, and lack of communication illustrate Bachmann's break with the romantic tradition by viewing the relationship between Self and Other as one of alienation and estrangement rather than of unification.

Renate Delphendahl. *Modern Austrian Literature.* 18:3–4, 1985, pp. 195–96

The prose of Ingeborg Bachmann is informed by a tension between surface and subtext. Beneath the realm of appearances the surface "reality" of the narrative, lies a subliminal world which, much like the pre-or subconscious in the human psyche, is always present and intermittently manages to swell to the surface. It expresses itself in gestures and body language, dreams and hallucinations, in names, silence, and Freudian slips, and in the poetic images, analogies, and allusions of the narrative. The highly allusive and encoded nature of her prose has seldom been stressed by Bachmann scholars. Behind or beneath the figures and events of the surface narration lies a thoroughly constructed fabric of parallels and models taken from the realms of myth, music, and other literary works. A decoding and analysis of these allusions is crucial to an understanding of Bachmann's writing. . . .

In the case of Bachmann's female characters, living under oppressive patriarchal conditions, the counterpoint is striking. Against the backdrop of stories about women who are destroyed or self-destruct in various ways—often while protecting the men in their lives from the unpleasant reality of their situation, often while unaware themselves of the reality of their situation—Bachmann projects images of women who do exist, have existed, or could exist as authentic subjects. On the surface level the women suffer disfiguration, sensual reduction (e.g., loss of hearing or eyesight), convulsions, nausea, nervous breakdown; they are raped, murdered, and commit suicide, while on the subtextual level, they emerge as princesses, goddesses, saviors, prophets, and similar self-defining subjects from Moses to Faust. Out of the tension between the two contexts arises the critique of a culture which systematically destroys its women. Whether Bachmann intended her women as specifically gendered or merely as epitomizing individual human suffering is not the question here. The issue in no way dilutes her depiction of both the real (in the "Todesarten" fragments) and the symbolic destruction of women (in the *Simultan* stories, written at the same time as *Malina,* even though they appeared a year later). . . .

Within Bachmann's work . . . , one finds examples not only of fairytale motifs taken over unaltered, but also of role reversals and total reworkings as well as mythopoetic fantasies which she has created herself. While the sources themselves do not in most cases offer utopian visions, they function in the text to provide either glimpses of an alternative reality or an insight into the actual situation; either they transcend the real limits to suggest another "truth" about the characters, events, or relationships obtaining in the text, or they serve to redefine the real situation and bring it into sharper focus. In drawing from fairytale sources Bachmann has consistently rejected or reworked material which shows woman's "otherness," while salvaging those extant bits and pieces which have resisted patriarchalization and thus still provide a glimpse of female authenticity and responsible selfhood.

Karen Achberger. *Modern Austrian Literature*. 18:3–4, 1983, pp. 211–13

The division of the self in "Undine geht" reflects the text's underlying dualistic model of reality, built upon and incorporating the polarity of masculine and feminine, and apparently deeply experienced by Bachmann. Her admission in an interview that she aligned herself with the world of Hans rather than Undine, moreover, testifies to an ambivalent but persistent identification with the values and achievements of the male order. Bachmann had recognized this identification with what she called "das männliche Ich," and acknowledged, "daß ich nur von einer männlichen Person aus erzählen kann." With her choice of a feminine-masculine "Doppelgänger-Ich" for the protagonist-narrator of *Malina* Bachmann thematized this conflict and explored whether and how the two halves might co-exist. But the novel also showed why, as she put it, "dieser männliche und ihr überlegene Doppelgänger, also dieses denkende Ich" must finally destroy its feminine, feeling counterpart. The difficulty of imagining a whole female self that is not tragically split into two opposing sides, then, remained a fundamental problem for Bachmann, and became if anything the more acute with her increasing awareness of it.

Perhaps because the pattern of polarity is so deeply set, "Undine geht," despite its multiple deconstructions of the traditional material, never explicitly challenges the dualism that pervades it. On the contrary, by hypostasizing the traditional dichotomies into female and male figures it reaffirms a dualistic model. The oppositions of culture and nature; rationality and feeling; logical discourse and poetic utterance; social order and ecstasy of freedom; and masculine and feminine are assumed as given, and by their eloquent embodiment gain new power. A similar dilemma is also inherent in the project of the French feminists to "speak the feminine." Wishing to valorize a concept of woman based on assumed common biological and psychological qualities, they also risk perpetuating traditional categories that prescribe and limit women's actual possibilities. But so long as the underlying dichotomous structure itself is not questioned, our thinking, like Undine's, will remain caught in the "logic" of these categories, and we will be faced with unacceptable choices such as that between self-denying male-identification and a marginalized, mystified feminine Other.

Ritta Jo Horsley. *Modern Austrian Literature*. 18:3–4, 1985, pp. 233–34

BAGRYANA, ELISAVETA (BULGARIA) 1893–1991

Bagryana nourishes her spirit through traveling. In this way she escapes the cramped cage of obligation, the constantly repeated, boring situations. The change of scenery; the new adventures offered by change; the expectation of something that has not happened before—all this means great, affecting, beautiful experience for her. She is fused, united, with a strange world, not because she has fled from her native land but because she is eager to experience more, to feel the pulse of contemporary life from closer up. Her wayward blood impels her toward activity, and her thoughts and feelings search for new nourishment and new, unexpected impressions. She rushes to travel in new lands, dreams continually of the unknown, praises what she sees with a poetic power that pervades every detail.

Speed of movement makes her happily intoxicated. This feeling is no less strong than love's torment, inasmuch as it also contains the unexpected, an element of the whirlwind mindlessness of the cosmos. A change in situation means a break with tradition, a liberation of the personality from involvement with the known. Movement and change are synonymous with joy and freedom. With all her being—spiritually and physically—Bagryana feels united with the speed of a train, with the velocity of an airplane. . . . Bagryana was the first in our poetry to proclaim this new feeling, which arises from progress in technology and the dizziness of speed. To be in the morning in the Balkans, in little Sofia, and then in the evening to be amidst the brilliant liveliness of Paris or the silence of a frigid northern climate, at the foot of frozen Scandinavian mountains—how wonderful this is, how great, and unusual. . . .

Bagryana gave back to our poetry spiritual values that were lost in the ethereal lyrics of the symbolists. In her work language becomes a vital and youthful creator both of ecstasy and of burning tragic passion. Her work concretizes the dream of experiencing, grasping, getting to know the world.

Bagryana also brought clarity back into our poetry. She began to train our ears to hear precise assonances and alliterations, without depriving them of the larger impressions of sound. . . . She does not use broken syntax, asymmetrical constructions; she avoids indefinite sound textures. . . .

Bagryana has taught us to accept her poetry as both confession and action. In her work everything is a process of becoming, of being achieved. . . . She is a great poet not only within the confines of our literature but also on the scale of world poetry, a poet such as few nations on earth have had.

Panteley Zarev. Literaturna misŭl. 4, 1968,
pp. 20–21, 40–41

In [Bagryana's] poetry we hear the voice of a person who is able to rejoice in life and the world, because she feels at one with it. Full of the feeling that the world is hers, her whole being trustfully inclines itself toward life; every moment she expects new wonder from it. She is able to take delight in the moment, to be dissolved entirely in its currents. The shadows of the past, the torments of thought—everything recedes before the strength of the living moment, full of beauty and promise. . . .

Woman in Bagryana's poetry is free and bold. Her ability to take flight destroys the barriers of convention and prejudice. Nothing can stop her elemental drive. She is not interested in what others say; she is not afraid to brook tradition, to be the first to venture along an unknown path. She is ready to take all the risks her passions encourage, to sacrifice peace and prosperity for her right to live according to her own will. Her eyes are wide open to the world. . . . Her pulse beats with the rhythm of a new age. She knows the intoxications of height and speed; shivering in the face of danger is pleasant for her. . . . Simultaneously, her psyche is limitlessly feminine: in her there speaks the heart of the "last and first woman." . . .

In Bagryana's poetry love is the eternal fellow-traveler of woman, her spirit, her way of life. Therefore, she is as rich as life itself, evolving through different phases, understanding the different nuances of feeling.

Without making psychological problems out of immediate experience, Bagryana introduces us to a rich scale of amorous emotions, to the psychology and rules of love. In her markedly earthy and natural world love is also an immediate and primary feeling, part of the laws of nature, authoritative and irrevocable like them.

Milena Tsaneva. In Tikhomir Tikhov, ed.
Ochertsi za bŭlgarski pisateli vol. 3 (Sofia:
Bŭlgarski pisateli, 1970), pp. 98–99, 103–5

What above all attracts me to Bagryana's poetry? The simplicity and charm, the vivid beauty of the form, the impetuous dynamics, the astonishing wealth, the varying rhythms. . . . The musicality of Bagryana's verse is inseparable from the picturesqueness of her descriptions, from her very real, concrete perception of the world. Or, better stated, the concrete impression, the experience, firmly relegated to the memory of mind and heart, dictates the rhythm, the music of the verse. . . .

Her poem dedicated to the town of Sliven, in which she was born and in which her jubilee was celebrated (this is the Bulgarian tradition—to celebrate in the native town), is also based on direct, concrete impressions. In this town all is blue: blue cliffs, blue water, blue sky. At times a destructive wind blows here. Once, when she was a very small girl, the wind lifted her and knocked her down painfully against the stones of the town square. This episode arose surprisingly clearly in her memory when, after many, many years she visited her home town; it is engraved in this verse.

Bagryana loves her suburban home in Boyana very much: the white house at the foot of the mountain, her green oasis fragrant with roses and irrigated by a spring so pure that its water is as clear as a mirror. She built this house together with her husband. When the house was completed, her husband died, and she entered the home alone. Her "Boyanski tsikl" [The Boyana Cycle] of poems was created out of solitude and loss, together with an understanding of the eternal, holy beauty of nature. . . .

B. Brainina. *Novy mir.*
July, 1971, pp. 249–50

Among the foremost attainments of Bulgarian lyric verse between the two World Wars is the poetry of Elisaveta Bargyana. Both Bulgarian critics and foreign critics who are familiar with Bulgarian literature agree on this point. Reviews of Bagryana's poems appeared long before her first book of poetry was published. One year after the first edition of *Vechnata i svjatata* [The Eternal and the Sacred] (1927) appeared, Ivan Meshekov devoted a whole book to the young poetess. Bagryana's lyrics today are considered classic. At the time of her literary debut, however, they shocked readers with their sincerity and pristine quality. As with all great poetry of the twentieth century, Bagryana's verse mingles different styles, different systems of versification and various emotional moods. It is a poetry tuned to the tension between these elements of poetic technique. On occasion the author does not hesitate to introduce plot into a lyric poem, to introduce an epic element, and thus an event becomes a pretext for spinning out a lyrical or philosophical reflection. . . .

It seems that the main problem for Bagryana—indeed it is a matter of life and death—is love. It is the measure, it is the gauge of woman's liberation. The true liberation of a woman is her equality in love, her right to approve or disapprove of anybody's feelings, her right to live together with whomever she wants to, but also her right to terminate the relationship when she herself feels fatigue and discouragement in a lasting relationship. In confrontation with contemporaneity the poetry of Bagryana withstands the test of time and is modern above all expectations—it still sounds fresh, it rouses admiration by its apt observations and its novelty. An especially fine feature of this poetry is its unusually subtle description of various stages of emotional links between woman and man: the beginning of love, a woman's devotion, passion, jealousy, cooling of the emotion, the tragic end of love, reminiscences about time spent together—all these tremors of human feelings find in Bagryana's poetry their own unique expression. They display wisdom and unusual psychological shrewdness, which place her on the roster of the greatest love-poets of modern world literature. In her eagerness for the full emancipation of woman Bagryana does not hesitate to question the validity of such a time-honored institution as marriage.

Edward Možeko. In Charles A. Moser, ed.
*Conference on Twentieth Century Bulgarian
Literature* (Washington, D.C.: Office of
Education, Institute of International
Education, 1972), pp. 54–55

The Bulgarian poet Elisaveta Bagryana has recently turned ninety; amid much celebration, in the course of a gala organized in her honor at the National Theater in Sofia, she received the award of "Hero of the Bulgarian People's Republic" from the Council of State, for both her literary work and her social and political commitment. . . .

While she was still a high school student sensitive to both Bulgarian and foreign poetry, she had cultural contacts with Bulgarian writers of the period. From 1921 on, after several of her poems had been published in *The Women's Newspaper,* she was regularly invited to contribute to publications of a literary nature.

After an initial period characterized by an elaborate symbolism in her poetry, Bagryana refined the expression of her feelings, a refinement that amounted to the reevaluation of a woman capable of claiming her own specificity. On the Bulgrian poetry scene of the time, this was an innovation. For the first time, lyrically, a woman was proudly exalting love, the sorrow of separation, the pride of passion that burns the body and torments the spirit, allowing the woman who loves to enter emotional terrain unknown and closed to others. It is the pagan feast of the flesh, the exaltation of the enchantments of love, that recall the singers of antiquity. . . .

Slowly, there grows and takes shape in the poetry of Elisaveta Bagryana the problem of the future of the planet, the ephemerality of existence, the possible or perhaps unacceptable decline. In 1969's "Counterpoint," the poet sings with different and varied accents, but she also offers the absolute values of life, so insignificant and yet so great. Thus, she has declared . . . that the most valid expression in all of human experience is love between two people, steadfast love, an existence lived profoundly, mutually, until the last breath.

Pavle Petrov. *Balcanica.*
2:2, June, 1983, p. 153

BAINBRIDGE, BERYL (GREAT BRITAIN) 1934–

Perhaps because she writes of mean people in drab places, perhaps because her plot devices are at times so deceptively sensational that her fiction is confused with crime stories—whatever the reason, Beryl Bainbridge has been scandalously neglected. On the evidence of *The Secret Glass,* she is an author of extraordinary power whose touch is at once steel-hard and delicate. Indeed, she is a more remarkable, far more original writer than Lessing or Murdoch or Spark.

The time of *The Secret Glass* is World War II. In a working-class district of dank and murky Liverpool two unmarried middle-aged women, the dress-maker Nellie and her younger sister, Margo, have been rearing their niece, Rita, in oppressively genteel poverty. Nellie, a woman of ramrod determination and sobriety, fusses over her dead mother's furniture like an obsessive nursemaid. Her sister Margo, once briefly married, is flighty, sexy, easily distracted and disheveled, a soft and disorderly contrast to Nellie's stern, hard-working responsibility and spinsterly propriety. Trouble comes in the form of an American GI, stationed at a nearby camp, with whom foolish, romantic Rita falls in love. Ira is a crass, hard, illiterate scoundrel who breaks Rita's heart and stirs a fire of vengeful hatred in Nellie that leads to disaster.

But the plot of this domestic tragedy is less important than Miss Bainbridge's precision, the quiet perfection with which she renders the quality of life in this suppressed, anguished household, and her wit, which has Nellie sitting down to her Singer "like the great organ at the Palladium cinema before the war." When Rita brings the American to tea with her aunts, Margo knows instantly what sort of man he is, and Miss Bainbridge defines the menace of his heartless, animal greed by means of a bleak spareness that only a superbly gifted writer can manipulate with such awesome resonance.

So intense, pure and unsentimental is the feeling Miss Bainbridge draws from these lives of proud desperation, of pleasureless obedience to unquestioned imperatives of convention, that a great stillness comes over the reader. As we follow Nellie and Margo and Rita and Ira to their catastrophic climax, our involvement in their experience—through the novelist's brilliant shaping—becomes an act of uncluttered concentration and total assent. Judgment is there—it must be there—yet it is tempered at every point by Miss Bainbridge's knowledge and humor, her affection and pity, her unique and wholly arresting talent.

Pearl K. Bell. New Leader.
September 2, 1974, p. 18

Binny (or Binnie, as the blurb [of Injury Time] prefers to call her), mother of three, husbandless, in her mid-forties, is not the first Beryl Bainbridge heroine to be afflicted with an indignant sense that her life is not under control—her own or anyone else's. . . .

The passing of standards causes her a good deal of grief, especially as she is aware that they have gone inside her as well as out in the world. The schools, it seems, have taught her children nothing, but she cannot control them or educate them either, or keep her house clean, or conduct a reasonable marriage or love affair. Even her devices for giving pleasure go wrong: the table-tennis table blocking her bedroom had once been intended to keep the children off the streets. Now she is ready to bribe them to go out. Alison Lurie's War between the Tates established forever the way in which the small, gentle lovers of the nursery awake one morning transformed into vicious monsters, and Beryl Bainbridge's children are of the same breed. They despise and abuse but depend on their mother. Brutal of tongue and habit—except, she concedes, that they don't torture animals—they seem unlikely ever to leave the nest they foul. Binny, once a liberal parent in her view, suddenly realizes she has veered to the right: "Only the other day her son had called her a fascist pig. It was true she didn't want to share anything any more, particularly not with the children." . . .

We know by now the deadly striking power of the Bainbridge sentence, the exactness of her social horror show. This is as good as ever: the jokes are funny in the "I could have died" style. Indeed, "I could have died" lurks inside each of the overburdened, slightly malfunctioning frames she has given her middle-aged characters. I'm not entirely carried away, though, by the move towards plot—or perhaps it is a device for turning a novella, just, into a novel. Binny, Edward [her lover] and their friends are thrust into real adventure, risk and violence: "I could have died" begins to look like an outside threat, as a group of gunmen invade the house, pursued by the police. Of course it gives her a chance to have some satirical fun about television sociologists' attitudes to criminals, and her local effects are as sharp as one could wish.

Claire Tomalin. *The New Republic.*
November, 1977, pp. 57–58

Beryl Bainbridge evokes, in this apparently simple relation of everyday life [*A Quiet Life*], the frightening unpredictability of people and events, so that every character in the novel is in a constant state of flux and uncertainty, never behaving as we expect them to. Although one sometimes feels the author stretches the license of this uncertainty a little too far, the novel remains an exciting, yet at the same time moving, exploration of human relationships.

A Quiet Life is an engrossing and stimulating novel, if somewhat disturbing. It centers around a series of episodes (or, more accurately, non-episodes) in the life of Alan, an adolescent boy in a middle-class home. The characters are almost frighteningly vivid and human—the near paranoia of Father, the socially orientated but basically vulgar Mother, and, most important of all, Alan's sister Madge. . . .

The paralyzing dullness of their lives is emphasized by the atmosphere of sordid decay present throughout the novel. The cramped, airless houses, the nondescript streets and the steady mediocrity of the weather, all contribute to a sullen feeling of seediness which perhaps reaches a climax when Father, furiously trying to burn the armchair which to him represents his failure, drops his false teeth in the fire and has to stamp about frantically trying to save them. This kind of semi-comic, semi-tragic incident (for Father *is* broken by his sense of failure) enhances the underlying tension present throughout; the novel pulses with suppressed violence and climactic unease. Of course, as in real life, the climax is never reached; nothing startling, unique, or rewarding happens, and one is left with a bitter sense of futility.

When measured against its perception and depth, the novel's brevity and the concision of its prose arouse one's admiration for Miss Bainbridge's powers of economy and precision, coupled perhaps with a certain reluctance to believe fully in the horrors of middle-class life as she portrays them. As was not the case in her earlier novel, *The Bottle Factory Outing,* the plot and characterization here are largely credible, making *A Quiet Life* far more memorable for this particular reader.

Karen Worthy. *The Anglo-Welsh Review.*
Autumn, 1977, pp. 123–24

Winter Garden is another of those teasingly slight black comedies by which Beryl Bainbridge has made her name. The chilling accuracy of detail, the sharp, loaded, pithy prose and the cunning awareness of the precise moment at which ordinary experience tilts into farce, and of the precise agent to transform that farce into horror, are once again devastatingly combined. In one sense *Winter Garden* is a hilarious sub-Kingsley Amis account of a mild Admiralty lawyer's awful official visit to Russia with awful companions in awful weather amid awful confusion. At this level Bainbridge is as adept as Amis. A combination of weary distaste, nervous unease and absurdist glee permeates every line. Her characters are in the grip of a ruthless, savagely comic, capricious, implacable fate. The laughter *Winter Garden* provokes, however, is the sort that chokes rather than rocks the reader. There is a grim undertone of madness to Douglas Ashburner's increasingly futile attempts to make sense of his Russian trip which leaves many of Bainbridge's sallies, such as Ashburner's realization that the Russian artist is part of the machinery of state, resting "like a fishbone in the gullet." Ashburner's mistress Nina disappears; we never find out what has happened to her. He is convinced that she has been murdered, and the faces of those around him mutate into hers without warning. He even sees her, in a condensed passage of exceptionally deft writing, undergoing a brain operation at which a characteristic muddle over his identity has forced him to be a spectator. His desperate attempt to keep track of life is echoed in the jerky, horribly logical narrative line, which resists the sinuous, ordered development of the conventional novel. Only a willfully obscure ending mars a book that manages to be both entertaining and thought-provoking.

Neil Philip. *British Book News.* February,
1981, p. 117

Bainbridge has turned a reviser's hand very successfully to *Another Part of the Wood* (as well as adapting it for television) and now does the same for *A Weekend with Claude,* trimming it scrupulously to the Duckworth-Bainbridge house-style, and so completing a ten-novel cycle.

Bainbridge's major achievement is as chronicler of the lives and neuroses of that sprawling mass of desperate Englishness inadequately known as the lower middle classes. The comedy she extracts from their cavortings is as painful as that of a Mike Leigh improvisation. Her minor, status-seeking characters are made to reveal themselves mercilessly, their blundering desire for success and respectability often violently at odds with obstinate personal eccentricity. Billie, for instance, in *A Weekend with Claude,* professes distaste for Lily's bohemian grubbiness, yet with his seemingly unsheddable checked coat, his gift of a toffee boxed like a jewel, and other peculiarities, he is hardly Mr. Average himself.

Bainbridge's main characters are also divided, torn between their search for love and the rigidities of correctness on which they have been raised. Ann, for example, in *Sweet William,* has a mother she is still anxiously trying to propitiate, though she cannot resist the intensity of a more honest and threatening relationship with the amoral William. Lily (Maggie in the original *Claude*) is also in this mold, though a little further down the road to anarchy. Such characters (often, though not always, female) express, with the fragile authority of the wounded, the ravenous need of love that underlies adult pretensions and ideals. Like the women characters of Jean Rhys, they have the power to move us because they are yes-sayers, troupers; despite their suffering they go bravely into the limelight, feeling everything, shrinking from nothing. . . .

Even with . . . judicious and elegant revision, *A Weekend with Claude* is perhaps a little less emotionally engaging than some of its successors, primarily because the reader has less opportunity to identify with a single tragi-comic character. Moreover, the problems are offered us, so to speak, in retrospect: we feel, at a relatively early stage, that things can't have turned out too badly after all. The novel has a little less in the way of crackling dialogue than, say, *Injury Time* or *A Quiet Life,* though some very pleasing inanities are proferred, "in between the acts," by the desk-purchasing man and his wife. The book is nevertheless an extremely lively and incisive piece of entertainment, and to compare the two versions is an object-lesson in the novelist's craft.

Carol Rumens. (London) Times Literary
Supplement. September 11, 1981, p. 1031

BAMBARA, TONI CADE (UNITED STATES) 1939–96

A title with a religious allusion may seem inappropriate for an essay on the works of Toni Cade Bambara since religion, i.e., Christianity, as it is often depicted in the works of Black writers with their depictions of hair straightening, signifying in church, and preacher men—sometimes more physically passionate than spiritually—is conspicuously absent here. In fact, many of the usual concerns, about color and class, frequently found in the writings of other Black women prosaists, are absent. Bambara appears less concerned with mirroring the Black existence in America than in chronicling "the movement" intended to improve and change that existence. Like a griot, who preserves the history of his or her people by reciting it, Bambara perpetuates the struggle of her people by literally recording it in their own voices.

Her three major works of fiction, *Gorilla, My Love* (1972), *The Sea Birds Are Still Alive* (1977), and *The Salt Eaters* (1980), trace the civil rights movement in America from its inception, through its most powerful expression, to its loss of momentum. Each uses language to particularize and individualize the voices of the people wherever they are—on a New York City street, crossing the waters of the Pacific, amid the red salt clay of the Louisiana earth—and to celebrate their progress as they think, feel, and act in their struggle to be free.

But, paradoxically, while Bambara uses language to capture the speech patterns of the characters she idiomatically places in their time and space, Bambara eschews language, words, rhetoric, as the modus operandi for the people to attain their freedom. For Bambara, an innate spirituality, almost mystical in nature, must be endemic to the people if they are to have success. Her works juxtapose the inadequacy of language and the powers of the spirit, which needs no words to spread its light among the masses.

> Ruth Elizabeth Burks. "From Baptism to Resurrection: Toni Cade Bambara and the Incongruity of Language." In Mari Evans, ed. *Black Women Writers* (Garden City, New York: Doubleday, 1984), pp. 48–49

Ultimately the genuinely modern writer "assumes a culture and supports the weight of a civilization." That assumption connects the present moment both to an immediate and to a remote past. From such a writer, we learn that whoever is able to live completely in the present, sustained by the lesson of the past, commands the future. The vitality of the jazz musician, by analogy, is precisely this ability to compose, in vigorous images of the most recent musical language, the contingencies of time in an examined present moment. The jam session, the ultimate formal expression of the jazz musician, is, on one hand, a presentation of all the various ways, past and present, that a tune may be heard; on the other, it is a revision of the past history of a tune, or of its presentation by other masters, ensuring what is lasting and valuable and useful in the tune's present moment and discarding what is not. Constructing rapid contrasts of curiously mingled disparities, the jam session is both a summing up and a part-by-part examination by various instruments of an integrity called melody. Now a melody is nothing more or less than the musical rendition of what a poet or a historian calls theme. And a theme is no other thing than a noticeable pattern occurring through time as time assumes its rhythmic cycle: past, present, and future. *The Salt Eaters* of Toni Cade Bambara is a modern myth of creation told in the jazz mode.

A narrative which opens with a direct question—"Are you, sure, sweetheart, that you want to be well?"—evokes from us an immediate response. In a time of ubiquitous pollution, unless we are head-buried geese, we answer: Yeah! By leave of our spontaneous response to an irresistible call (the mode of the jazz composer), we enter the improvising, stylizing, re-creative, fecund, and not-so-make-believe world of *The Salt Eaters*. That world, called Claybourne, Georgia, is in a state of definition and transition: "Claybourne hadn't settled on its identity yet. . . . Its history put it neither on this nor that side of the Mason Dixon. And its present seemed to be a cross between a little Atlanta, a big Mount Bayou and Trenton, New Jersey, in winter." But we enter Claybourne during its preparation for spring festival, and there we discover what resembles a splendid community marketplace: "Tables, tents, awnings, rides, fortunetellers, candy booths, gymnasts with mats, nets, trampolines, oil drums from the islands, congos from who knew where, flat trucks, platforms, pushcarts and stalls of leather crafts, carved cooking spoons, jewelry . . . flower carts, incense peddlers . . . kids racing by with streamers and balloons. . . . Folks readying up for the festival" scheduled to begin when "Hoo Doo Man broke out of the projects with a horned helmet . . . and led the procession through the district to the Mother Earth floats by the old railroad yard." We discover that during festival, "People were supposed to write down all the things they wanted out of their lives—bad habits, bad debts, bad dreams—and throw them on the fire." Claybourne is in preparation for the rites of spring renewal. Yet in the midst of "the fugue-like interweaving of voices" resonant in the streets, we hear the voice of a street-corner preacher admonishing:

> History is calling us to rule again and you lost dead souls are
> standing around doing the freakie dickie . . . never recognizing
> the teachers come among you to prepare you for the transforma-
> tion, never recognizing the synthesizers come to forge the new
> alliances, or the guides who throw open the new footpaths, or
> the messengers come to end all excuses. Dreamer? The dream
> is real, my friends. The failure to make it work is the unreality.

The ominous cry of the street preacher, urging the community to recall its history, manifest its destiny, and heed its loas, intones the themes of its spring celebration: transformation, synthesis, and renewal.

As the community must engage its history in order to decipher the meaning of its own rituals—the rhythmic movement toward its destiny—so the individual self must engage its history in order to be well (whole); for if it does not, it hazards the loss of all that makes it whole. That loss is unaffordable and dread; it abates the power of regeneration.

The voice of the street preacher merges with the voice which has opened the narrative. That voice, its music "running its own course up under the words" is the Ebonic, mythopoeic voice of Minnie Ransom, "fabulous healer" of Claybourne, directly addressing Velma Henry, her patient, the celebrant, who enacts the meaning of the ritual that the entire community prepares to celebrate. It is through Velma's consciousness that we hear and observe everything that we know of Claybourne; it is Velma's personal transformation that we experience and that figures in the possibility of the community's renewal; it is through Velma's negation and acceptance of the actual and her pursuit of the possible that we learn the identity and enormous re-creative powers of those who have eaten salt together and who have learned to reconcile both the brine and the savor of life. . . .

Modernity, a jam session constructing rapid contrasts of curiously mingled disparities, is at once an extension of the past and a conduit of some future balancing of the best and worst of human possibilities. Thus, the child, also a passenger on the boat of refugees, snuggling close beside her mother as they grope their way topside to the deck searching a seat, is directed: "the passengers along the way grabbing the small hand and leading the child to the next hand outstretched." This child, like lil' Hazel and baby Jason and Raymond and Ollie and Manny and Patsy and Sylvia and Rae Anne and Horace and all the little girls becoming women and boys becoming men and the communities of the stories in *Gorilla, My Love* and *The Sea Birds Are Still Alive,* lives amid the scheme of oppositions played out in the great conjugation of past and present time mediating future possibilities.

It is this conjugation of time along with its referent—the salient features of a journey into experience conducted by a people who wrenched from a coherent past cast refugee upon a sea of circumstance confront incoherence and give it form—the Afro-American paradigm of creation—which *The Salt Eaters* evokes. Its cast of characters so far consummate the Bambara canon. Velma and Obie of the cast of *The Salt Eaters* are the energy of our possibilities while Campbell, Ruby, Jan, and company are the resources of our strength. Fred Holt, the bus driver of *The Salt Eaters,* is our worst choices able to be redeemed, while Dr. Meadows represents our ability to choose. The entire community of all of them is sufficient to defy the agents of destruction aligned around the malign power plant which seems to tower in their world. The valiant and gorgeous people of *The Salt Eaters* portray the strength of our past, available in the present, able to move our future.

As story, *The Salt Eaters* is less moving tale than brilliant total recall of tale. It is no blues narrative plucking the deep chords of the harp of our soul; no tale of anguish, struggle, lust, and love inspiring and conducting us toward mastery of the spirit and therefore mastery of the demon blues (and whites). It is not a declaration; rather it is an interrogation. It is not indicative in mood; rather it is subjunctive in mood. The novel, which is less novel than rite, begins with a question. It moves around a central word, *if. If* we wish to live, *if* we wish to be healthy, then we must *will* it so. *If* we *will* it so, then we must be willing to endure the act of transformation. *The Salt Eaters* is a rite of transformation quite like a jam session. The familiar tune is played, reviewed, and then restated in a new form.

In the tradition of fiction from which she works, Toni Cade Bambara's first novel faces fabulous first novels. Some among that rich opulence are William Wells Brown's *Clotel,* Du Bois's *Quest of the Silver Fleece,* James Weldon Johnson's *Autobiography of an Ex-Colored Man,* Jean Toomer's *Cane,* Langston Hughes' *Not without Laughter,* Zora Neale Hurston's *Jo-*

nah's Gourd Vine, Richard Wright's *Native Son,* Ann Petry's *The Street,* James Baldwin's *Go Tell It on the Mountain,* Ralph Ellison's *Invisible Man,* Gwendolyn Brooks' *Maud Martha,* Paul Marshall's *Brown Girl, Brownstone,* Ishmael Reed's *The Free-Lance Pallbearers,* Toni Morrison's *The Bluest Eye,* and Charles S. Johnson's *Faith and the Good Thing.* All of these she knows and knows well. *The Salt Eaters* gestures to these and more. Many of these books belong to the company of the best ever written; all are global in their implications. More in the style of the zany brilliance of a Reed and the cultural ecology of a Johnson, *The Salt Eaters* does not pretend toward the simple splendor of the high elegant blues tradition. Though the work matches the encyclical inclusiveness of single works within that tradition, it dares a wrench. It subdues story, eschews fiction, not for fact but for act. It challenges us to renew and reform our sensibilities so that the high mode—the conquering healing power of main-line Afro-American fiction—can reemerge and become again our equipment for living—for life.

Eleanor W. Traylor. In Mari Evans, ed.
Black Women Writers (Garden City, New
York: Doubleday, 1984), pp. 58–60, 68–69

Although everyone knows instinctively that Toni Cade Bambara's first novel, *The Salt Eaters,* is a book that he or she must read, many people have difficulty with it. They get stuck on page ninety-seven or give up after muddling through the first sixty-five pages twice with little comprehension. Some cannot get past chapter one. Lost and bewildered, students decide that it is "over their heads" and wonder what made their teacher assign it in the first place.

There are compelling reasons for studying the novel. It is a daringly brilliant work that accomplishes even better for the 1980s what *Native Son* did for the 1940s, *Invisible Man* for the 1950s, or *Song of Solomon* for the 1970s: It fixes our present and challenges the way to the future. Reading it deeply should result in personal transformation; teaching it well can be a political act. However, Toni Cade Bambara has not made our job easy. *Salt* is long, intricately written, trickily structured, full of learning, heavy with wisdom—is, altogether, what critics mean by a "large" book.

At its literal-metaphoric center, Velma Henry and Minnie Ransom sit on round white stools in the middle of the Southwest Community Infirmary. "The good woman Ransom," "fabled healer of the district," is taxing her formidable powers with Velma, who has lost her balance and attempted suicide. The novel radiates outward in ever-widening circles—to the Master's Mind, the ring of twelve who hum and pray with Minnie; to the music room cluttered with staff, visitors, and assorted onlookers; to the city of Claybourne surrounding the Infirmary walls—a community which itself is composed of clusters (The Academy of the Seven Arts, the cafe with its two round tables of patrons, La Salle Street, the park); to the overarching sky above and the earth beneath steadily spinning on its axis. From the center, the threads web out, holding a place and weaving links between everything and everybody. At the same time, this center is a nexus which pulls the outside in—setting up the dialectic of connectedness which is both meaning and structure of the book.

Of the huge cast, certain characters stand out. There is M'Dear Sophie Heywood, Velma's godmother, who caught her at birth and has protected and praised her ever since. Now, she is so incensed with Velma's selfish nihilism that she has imposed silence upon herself and exited the circle/room, thinking back on her godchild as well as her deceased mate, Daddy Dolphy; on her son and Velma's almost-husband, Smitty, who was turned into an invalid by the police in a violent anti-war demonstration; and on her own bitter memories of being brutally beaten in jail by her neighbor, Portland Edgers, who had been forced to do so by guns and clubs. There is Fred Holt, the bus driver, "brimming over with rage and pain and loss" (and sour chili). Married as a youth to Wanda, who deserted him for the Nation of Islam, he now has a white wife Margie, who gives him nothing but her back. His misery is completed by the death of his best friend, Porter, a well-read conversationalist who was the only bright spot in Fred's days. Other important characters are Velma's husband Obie, whose "image of himself [is] coming apart"; Dr. Meadows, a conscientious young M.D. who is pulling together his "city" versus "country," his white westernized and ancient black selves; and a traveling troupe of Third World political performers called the Seven Sisters.

The rich cross section of variegated folks also includes less prominent characters such as Butch and Nadeen, two teenage parents-to-be; Jan and Ruby, activist women sharing a salad and organizing strategy; Donaldson, the inept FBI-CIA informant; and the list goes on. Some of these people appear onstage *in propria persona;* others are offstage fragments of memory. Some are quietly dead; others are roaming spirits. In many ways, these distinctions are false and immaterial, for everyone we meet takes up essential space, and there is no meaningful difference between their various states of corporeality / being / presence (a fact which confuses readers trying to keep the characters "straight"). Old Wife, Minnie's "Spirit Guide," is as "real" as Cora Rider grumbling in the music room. When Obie muses about his younger brother Roland, incarcerated in Rikers Island prison for raping a forty-six-year-old black woman, mother of four, Roland's voice and the woman's mopping up her own blood are as clear as Palma and Marcus hugging in the rain. And, like Velma, all of the major figures who need it undergo a healing change. . . .

Two versions of the future are given. One is an in-process sketch of a humanitarian society newly evolving from the death of "the authoritarian age." The other is a nightmarish glimpse of "everyone not white, male and of wealth" fighting for burial grounds, of radioactively mutant kids roaming the stockaded streets killing "for the prize of . . . gum boots, mask and bubble suit" needed to breathe the contaminated air. Yes, there are "choices to be noted. Decisions to be made." This ultimatum is the burden of the question that Minnie repeatedly puts to Velma: "Are you sure, sweetheart, that you want to be well?"—for health entails taking responsibility for the self and the world we live in. Years after her healing, Velma "would laugh remembering she'd thought *that* was an ordeal. She didn't know the half of it. Of what awaited her in years to come."

Concern for a viable future explains the emphasis which Bambara places upon children, the succeeding generations. Unfortunately, they, too, are suffering from the vacuity of the age:

> there was no charge, no tension, no stuff in these young people's passage. They walked by you and there was no breeze of merit, no vibes. Open them up and you might find a skate key, or a peach pit, or a Mary Jane wrapper, or a slinky, but that would be about all.

They want a sweet, easy life, and they fight each other. Like their elders, they, too, have to be saved from and for themselves, for, as Old Wife declares, "The chirren are our glory."

As a self-described "Pan-Africanist-socialist-feminist," Bambara not only cares about children, but manifests a political consciousness which makes her a socially committed writer. It was quite some time, she says, before she "began to realize that this [writing] was a perfectly legitimate way to participate in struggle." Now she fulfills what Kalamu ya Salaam defines as the "responsibility of *revolutionary* Third World writers": "to cut through this [mass media] crap, to expose the cover-ups and ideological/material interests inherent in these presentations, and . . . to offer analysis, inspiration, information and ideas which . . . work in the best interest of Third World defense and development."

Gloria T. Hull. In Marjorie Pryse and
Hortense J. Spillers, eds. *Conjuring: Black
Women, Fiction, and Literary Tradition*
(Bloomington: Indiana University Press,
1985), pp. 216–19, 228–29

The question of identity—of personal definition within the context of community—emerges as a central motif for Toni Cade Bambara's writing. Her female characters become as strong as they do, not because of some inherent "eternal feminine" quality granted at conception, but rather because of the lessons women learn from communal interaction. Identity is achieved, not bestowed. Bambara's short stories focus on such learning. Very careful to present situations in a highly orchestrated manner, Bambara describes the difficulties that her characters must overcome.

Contemporary literature teems with male characters in coming-of-age stories or even female characters coming of age on male typewriters. Additional stories, sometimes written by black authors, indeed portray such concerns but narrowly defined within crushing contexts of city ghettos or rural poverty. Bambara's writing breaks such molds as she branches out, delineating various settings, various economic levels, various characters—both male and female.

Bambara's stories present a decided emphasis on the centrality of community. Many writers concentrate so specifically on character development or plot line that community seems merely a foil against which the characters react. For Bambara the community becomes essential as a locus for growth, not simply as a source of narrative tension. Thus, her characters and community do a circle dance around and within each other as learning and growth occur.

Bambara's women learn how to handle themselves within the divergent, often conflicting, strata that compose their communities. Such learning does not come easily, hard lessons result from hard knocks. Nevertheless, the women do not merely endure; they prevail, emerging from these situations more aware of their personal identities and of their potential for further self-actualization. More important, they guide others to achieve such awareness.

Bambara posits learning as purposeful, geared toward personal and societal change. Consequently, the identities into which her characters grow envision change as both necessary and possible, understanding that they themselves play a major part in bringing about that change. This idea approximates the nature of learning described in Paulo Freire's *Pedagogy of the Oppressed,* in which he decries the "banking concept," wherein education becomes "an act of depositing, in which the students are the depositories and the teacher is the depositor." Oppressive situations define the learner as profoundly ignorant, not possessing valuable insights for communal sharing.

Although many of Bambara's stories converge on the school setting as the place of learning in formal patterns, she liberates such settings to admit and encourage community involvement and ownership. Learning then influences societal liberation and self-determination. These stories describe learning as the process of problem solving, which induces a deepening sense of self, Freire's "intentionality."

For Bambara the community benefits as both "teacher" and "student" confront the same problem—that of survival and prospering in hostile settings, without guaranteed outcomes. The commonality of problems, then, encourages a mutual sharing of wisdom and respect for individual difference that transcends age, all too uncommon in a more traditional education context. Bambara's characters encounter learning within situations similar to the older, tribal milieus. The stages of identity formation, vis-à-vis the knowledge base to be mastered, have five segments: (1) beginner, (2) apprentice, (3) journeyman, (4) artisan, and (5) expert.

Traditional societies employed these stages to pass on to their youth that information necessary to ensure the survival of the tribe, such as farming techniques, and that information needed to inculcate tribal mores, such as songs and stories. Because of Bambara's interest in cultural transmission of values, her characters experience these stages in their maturational quest. In her stories these levels do not correlate with age but rather connote degrees of experience in community. . . .

Toni Cade Bambara's stories do more than paint a picture of black life in contemporary black settings. Many writers have done that, more or less successfully. Her stories portray women who struggle with issues and learn from them. Sometimes the lessons taste bitter and the women must accumulate more experience in order to gain perspective. By centering community in her stories, Bambara displays both the supportive and the destructive aspects of communal interaction. Her stories do not describe a predictable, linear plot line; rather, the cyclic enfolding of characters and community produces the kind of tension missing in stories with a more episodic emphasis.

Her characters achieve a personal identity as a result of their participation in the human quest for knowledge, which brings power. Bambara's skill as a writer saves her characters from being stereotypic cutouts. Although her themes are universal, communities that Bambara describes rise above the generic. More fully delineated than her male characters, the women come across as specific people living in specific places. Bambara's best stories show her characters interacting within a political framework wherein the personal becomes political.

Martha M. Vertreace. In Mickey Pearlman,
ed. American Women Writing Fiction
(Lexington: University Press of Kentucky,
1989), pp. 155–57, 165–69

The nationalist–feminist ideology in *Seabirds* is not solely generated by depictions of characters. It is reinforced by narrative texture and form. As a body of race- and gender-specific narratives, these stories draw on various Afro-American cultural practices—the oral storytelling tradition, the use of folklore, and the reinscription of Afro-American music forms. The incorporation of these practices is evident in the narrative structure, point of view, and semiotic texture of the stories.

Bambara has spoken and written extensively on the influence of Afro-American music on her work. What is most striking about her appropriation of jazz in *Seabirds,* however, is its role in emphasizing and reinforcing the ideology of the text. Jazz performances generally begin with a statement of theme, are followed by improvisations or extreme variations, and conclude with reiteration and resolution. An analogous pattern structures each of the stories in this collection. In "The Apprentice," for example, the narrative begins with the narrator's anxiety about her mission, moves to an encounter between a young Black man and a white policeman, then moves to a senior citizen's complex, and finally to a Black restaurant. It then refocuses on the narrator's concerns and reveals her resolution to remain committed to political engagement. In "Witchbird," each fleeting reflection of Honey's extended blues solo constitutes a comment on some aspect of her life—her career, her past relationships with men, and her overall perception of herself. And in "Christmas Eve at Johnson's Drugs N Goods," Candy begins by reflecting on Christmas and a possible visit from her father, moves on to individual episodes largely focused on characterizations of the store's customers, and concludes with accepting Obatale's invitation to a Kwanza celebration.

This mode of narration serves a significant ideological function. In its highlighting and summarizing, as well as its glossing over certain episodes, the text produces its ideological content largely through clusters of events. Hence, in "Broken Field Running," the renaming process by which Black children discard their "slave names" and appropriate African names to define themselves with the context of Black culture, the police harassment symbolized by the police car cruising in the Black community, and the destructive effect of ghetto life depicted in the criminal activities of Black males form a montage, a cluster of images each one of which might be said to encode a particular aspect of ideology.

The narrative perspective, particularly as it reveals the narrator's relationship to the text's ideology, also contributes to the ideological construct. In *Seabirds,* as in *Gorilla,* the dominant narrative strategy is the apparently unmediated response of characters to the world around them. . . .

Gorilla and *Seabirds,* . . . while produced at historically different moments, are both structured by the desire to synthesize contending ideologies of Black cultural nationalism and feminism. With its submerged text, its positioning of girls and women as primary narrators, its eruption of women-defined issues and strategies of marginalizing Black males, *Gorilla* disrupts the apparent unity of the world it seems to represent: an idyllic inner world of the Black community in which intraracial strife is minimal or nonexistent.

Seabirds identifies itself with the emergent feminist movement even in its dedication. The women in these stories possess a keen political awareness; the young girls have expanded their political consciousness; and Black male figures are even farther on the margins than they were in the earlier work. Tensions between nationalists and feminists are concretely presented in *Seabirds,* and the indeterminancy of the text is in the foreground.

The Salt Eaters, a work that bears all the traces of postmodern textual production, radically rewrites and displaces these earlier works. . . . [Its] central representations of madness and disillusionment, the increased antagonism between the sexes, and the triumph of an alternative culture displace the ambivalence of the earlier works and project a vision that is both dystopian and utopian.

Elliot Butler-Evans. *Race, Gender and Desire: Narrative Strategies in the Fiction of Toni Cade Bambara, Toni Morrison, and Alice Walker* (Philadelphia: Temple University Press, 1989), pp. 119–20, 122

BANTI, ANNA (pseud. LUCIA LOPRESTI) (ITALY) 1895–1985

In order to categorize, albeit provisionally (for Banti's own history continues and one can never be sufficiently perspicacious, as far as future work is concerned), those directions that have gradually emerged as narrative choices (containing all the others) and summarize them appropriately, we must necessarily take into account her progressive distancing from anything in the "autobiographical" mode, in the sense of an imperious need to objectify the narrative substance, especially after identification of her own destiny and others' time had become increasingly concrete. In tracing this continuous straining toward objectivity, we cannot identify irreversible stages; in other words, the majority of the development of Banti's poetics was "anticipated" right away, already apparent in that thematic prelude constituted by *Paolina's Itinerary*. We find there the themes of the sin of Eve, the latent taste for the "bitter" and, along with them, the absolute imperative to narrative, a right and proper play of appearances, accepted and repeated (all of Banti's characters love to tell themselves stories and dream different lives, even while they are living and not only when their eyes are closed). . . .

Essentially, Banti's turning point involves a flight towards the past, which has led her step by step to rediscover a present without measure, static, hieratic, pictorial . . . a present without boundaries and without end, with a precise consciousness of being immobilized at the center of time's "differing repetition"—which is unique for all and different for each—artificially joined together. . . . All too perceptible in her "sea of objectivity" is the force of Banti's irony that passes from the fleeting smile commenting on unfunny jokes at the expense of the characters she loves best, like Artemisia and Cecilia . . . ultimately, the historical poetics is also an assault on the great project of objectivity, to the extent that this becomes, besides being the site of the greatest freedom, also the means to actuate that analysis *of* analysis toward what Banti has always tended.

Enza Biagini. Anna Banti (Milan: Mursia,
1978), pp. 178–81

In 1968, drawing a comprehensive critical profile of Anna Banti, Gianfranco Contini located her narrative output around the central poles of the problems of women and the historical novel, indicating that the writer's best results came from the interaction of the two elements. . . . Criticism along this line obviously privileged, within Banti's varied oeuvre, the exquisitely evocative flow of *Artemisia* and *Lavinia in Flight*. . . . Despite the diverse experiences brought to maturity in *Bastard, Golden Flies,* and *We Believed,* Banti's reputation rested, as late as 1968, on the complex relationship between historical evocation and female character, as was the case with *Artemisia* and its contemporaries.

More than the preference expressed for a given portion of Banti's narrative—the one, after all, generally privileged by all criticism—Contini's remarks are of interest because of the connection he astutely establishes
between the author's self-control and the indefiniteness of her object, between the pathos contained and the necessity of historical distance, which
makes any fortuitousness in the relationship between female character and
history impossible to maintain. In fact, in the light, as well, of recent data that
emerged from her 1973 novel, the hypothesis of a Banti who was interested in
the female condition, on the one hand, and the problem of the historical novel,
on the other, interweaving them by chance, becomes entirely inadequate and
certainly not confirmed by the author's own ideological and literary positions.

> Anna Nozzoli. *Tabù e coscienza: La*
> *condizione femminile nella letteratura*
> *italiana del novecento* (Florence: La Nuova
> Italia, 1978), pp. 85–86

When Anna Banti died in Ronchi di Massa at the age of ninety on September
2, 1985, she was remembered and honored above all as the author of *Artemisia.* "Addio, Artemisia" ran the headline in *La Nazione,* the daily paper of
Banti's native Florence. To be sure, Anna Banti—the literary pseudonym of
Lucia Longhi Lopresti—had written other novels, as well as short stories,
art criticism, and drama. The recipient of various prestigious literary awards,
she was also for many years the editor of *Paragone,* the review founded by
her husband, the art historian Roberto Longhi, and was president of the
Foundation for the Study of Art History "Roberto Longhi" (Fondazione di
Studi di Storia dell'Arte "Roberto Longhi"). It was Banti's fictionalized biography of the real seventeenth-century painter Artemisia Gentileschi, however, that established her literary reputation and remained her most enduring
achievement. In *Artemisia,* Anna Banti brought to life and celebrated this
"woman painter of excellent abilities, one of the few whom history remembers." Artemisia Gentileschi was, moreover, as Banti tells us in her introduction, "one of the first women to uphold through words and achievement the
right to fulfilling work and spiritual equality between the two sexes."

Banti's construction of the painter's life and character is interwoven
with her account of the novel's genesis. The work begins with the author-
narrator in the Boboli Gardens, seeking refuge from the exploding mines and
machine-gun fire accompanying the German retreat from Florence in August
1944. In the midst of the disasters of war, her imagination conjures up Artemisia as a living presence who is eager both to console and to be consoled.
"Don't cry"—the first words of the novel, spoken by the hallucinated protagonist to the author-narrator, set the tone for the narrative that is to follow,
which is marked, structurally, by a dynamic interchange between protagonist
and author–narrator and, thematically, by the rejection of despair. . . .

Banti's choice of a great woman painter as fictional protagonist distinguishes her narrative from the tradition of the realistic (above all, nineteenth-

century) novel on several grounds, the most obvious of which, as previously noted, is the documented authenticity of Artemisia Gentileschi. Conventions of the realistic novel required that its protagonist be a fictional creation, unknown to history. Where actual historical figures appear in the nineteenth-century novel (as, for example, in Manzoni or Stendhal), they play, as Lukács long ago pointed out, minor rather than major roles. Moreover, traditional novelistic heroes may be exemplary only to the extent that they remain typical, or at least broadly representative. However much greatness of spirit they may possess, they are invariably limited by constraints of custom and opportunity—time and place—and, usually, by flaws of their own characters as well: hence another of the realistic novel's underlying conventions, that even potential greatness can never result in great achievement.

Banti's Artemisia, then, triumphing against overwhelming odds and not forgotten by history, belongs only in part to the tradition of the realistic novel, diverging from her literary predecessors as much because of her substantial artistic achievement as because of her historical prototype. Still, Banti's fictionalized historical heroine may be more fully appreciated if we pause to reflect on the familiar limitations of the traditional relation between women and painting in literature, from which Banti's character so conspicuously departs. Certainly, in the novel, as in the history of painting, women have frequently served as models, muses, or the symbolic embodiment of an art form itself, for the male artist. Additionally, women in nineteenth-century novels are often presented as pursuing drawing and painting as dilettantes, as if the skill were one item in a package of feminine "accomplishments" that were supposed to distinguish the properly educated young lady. Even more serious fictional treatments of women's creativity tend to focus on the meaning of their artistic efforts as a key to the psychological depths and complexity of their souls or as a reflection of a certain inner liberation, rather than on their work as substantial objective achievement, as independent, self-justifying artifacts.

Probably the most notable break from the dominance of this fictional tradition (which in turn reflects a broader cultural one) comes with the creation of Lily Briscoe in *To the Lighthouse* by Virginia Woolf, an author admired by Banti. . . . [H]ere, some two decades before *Artemisia*—we find an earlier and kindred treatment of a woman painter, which also evokes and subverts older, more entrenched expectations. Lily's canvases, however, exist chiefly as verbal suggestion, in terms of a professed theoretical goal; they are not described in great detail. On the other hand, the extraliterary existence of Artemisia Gentileschi's paintings adds a new kind of dimension to Anna Banti's narrative. At the same time, reverberations of earlier literary treatments of women and painting help enrich the significance of her climactic discussion of Artemisia's boldly innovative portrait of a woman painter.

In addition, Banti takes a radically innovative step in choosing to present this painting—so repeatedly designated as self-portrait and the art of painting—instead as a portrait, from memory, of another woman, one Annella de

Rosa. In the novel, Annella is a gifted younger artist whom Artemisia meets in Naples, a battered wife whose early death will prevent her from fulfilling her promise. In a briefly sketched episode that becomes significant only retrospectively, Annella rejects Artemisia's overture of friendship, causing her to speculate at the time on the impossibility of friendships between women in a world created by men for their use and convenience. Yet Artemisia's later painting of the younger artist emerges as a triumphant affirmation of female solidarity. Earlier, during her painting of Judith, Artemisia had refused the female intimacy based on shared fears and hatreds that the court ladies offered her. Here, at last, as an accomplished artist, she realizes the ideal of female friendship through a painting that celebrates the creative spirit in another woman. "That a woman achieves honor, honors her as well."

As the author's Artemisia, in celebrating Annella and giving her life, finds that another woman's honor also becomes her source of pride, so too Anna Banti, in celebrating and resuscitating Artemisia, finds honor for herself in another woman's creative achievement. Thus, the novelist-narrator commemorates Artemisia Gentileschi, the woman painter whom history remembers, by imagining her as commemorating Annella de Rosa, the woman painter whom history has forgotten. This vision returns us to the initial mirroring of narrator and protagonist, so crucial to the novel's structure. The fundamental truth of this reciprocal relationship remains, even if Banti's fanciful redesignation of the painting as a portrait of Annella is fiction: "Portrait or not, a woman who paints in 1640 constitutes an act of courage; this applies to Annella and to at least a hundred others, down to today. 'It applies to you, too,' concludes a brusque, dry sound, by candlelight, in a room darkened by war. A book is closed, abruptly." Contemplating the painting, the narrator decodes a vital message for herself. Through her undying work of art, Artemisia reaches out from her century to ours, to teach and inspire Banti—and through her, her readers—by her enduring, shared affirmation of female courage and achievement.

Deborah Heller. In Santo L. Aricò, ed.
*Contemporary Women Writers in Italy: A
Modern Renaissance* (Amherst: University
of Massachusetts Press, 1990), pp. 45, 56–58

BARANSKAYA, NATALYA (RUSSIA) 1908–

The novella *A Week Like Any Other* is a remarkable work that evoked widespread reaction when it first appeared in 1969. It remains significant today, for its account of the daily frustrations of a Moscow working mother is as accurate now as it was two decades ago. The heroine of the story, the scientist Olya, races through life with too little time for everything: her family, her research, and herself. *A Week Like Any Other* is not as stylistically or thematically sophisticated as works by contemporary writers like Tatyana Tolstaya or Liudmila Petrushevskaya. Its force derives instead from the compelling case its realistic first-person narrative makes for a heightened feminist consciousness among Soviet women and men, a consciousness that even under *glasnost* shows few signs of emerging. Traces of irony and subtle humor alleviate what might otherwise be a picture of unrelieved gloom.

The author of *A Week Like Any Other* is not the youthful radical one might expect. Born in 1908, Natalya Baranskaya spent many years engaged in museum work before embarking on a second career as a writer of fiction when she was nearly sixty. Her own experience, which resembles that of many women of her generation, undoubtedly made her particularly sensitive to the problems inherent in juggling family and work, given the unfavorable conditions created by Soviet society; as a young mother, she lost her husband during World War II and subsequently struggled with the difficulties of single parenthood.

Many of the other stories in the collection reflect concerns similar to those explored in *A Week Like Any Other,* although none so effectively. One of the best is "Lubka," originally published in 1977, which describes the public haranguing of a teenager who angers her neighbors by refusing to behave like a model young Soviet citizen. In the course of the story an accumulation of poignant details reveals that Lubka has retained a dynamic personality and a kind spirit despite the dual burden of a fatherless childhood and an alcoholic mother. Unlike *A Week Like Any Other,* "Lubka" has an upbeat ending, as the heroine finds happiness and more conventional stability with the Komsomol member Mikhail.

A Week Like Any Other has been translated before, but not in a widely available form. The majority of the stories in the collection appear here in English for the first time. Pieta Monks is an experienced and accomplished translator who renders well Baranskaya's unadorned style. The volume should prove to be a welcome addition to the small but growing number of contemporary Soviet literary works by and about women available in translation.

Margaret Ziolkowski. *World Literature Today.* 64, 1990, p. 660

In November 1969, Natalya Baranskaya's novella *A Week Like Any Other* was published in the prestigious literary journal *Novy Mir.* (It has just been published in English, along with several of Baranskaya's short stories, by Seal Press.) Written in the form of a week's diary entries, it details the nightmare of one woman's daily life: food shortages, endless lines, poor health care and day care, the lack of basic household services and a husband who buries himself in the TV or newspapers and never lifts a finger. When he suggests to Olga, a young scientist, that she top working and stay home to take care of the family (a familiar proposal these days), she is appalled:

"You want to shut me in here for the whole year! How could we live on your salary! . . . All this boring stuff is for me alone, and the only interesting things are for you!" Olga's story touched a raw nerve; Baranskaya received hundreds of letters from grateful women thanking her for telling the truth about their lives.

Katrina vanden Heuvel. *The Nation.* June 4, 1990, p. 775

[Baranskaya is] a writer who has recently become famous in the Soviet Union but is not yet widely known in this country. The U.S. critical establishment has not rushed to talk about Baranskaya; were she a dissident writer (especially a male dissident writer) her work would already be available from the major New York presses. But this collection of three long and four short stories does not fit the Western stereotype of an Eastern European writer. Baranskaya is extremely political, but her focus is on relations between the sexes rather than among nations. In the world of her characters, socialism is simply a fact, a realism American commentators find unpalatable, if not incomprehensible. Her stories focus on conflicts of power, but these conflicts take place in the areas where most people have to deal with them, in the family, the neighborhood, and most of all, for Baranskaya, in the workplace.

The title novella was hailed as a contemporary classic when it first appeared in the Soviet Union. A day-by-day "diary" of a week in the life of a working mother, the story presents the rush and grind of her life with such detailed intensity that it produces in the reader a kind of horror. Careful dramatic heightening focuses our attention on inequalities which the narrator herself takes for granted. All through the week, Olga Nikolaevitch works at her job as a laboratory statistician and translator, stands in line at the shops, and fights the weather and the crowded buses to get home and cook and care for her children. At stray moments, she makes plans to read in her professional journals or repair the belt loop on one of her garments, but the time is never there. Her husband, who, as she points out during an argument, has the same degree as she and works at the same kind of job, contributes in only token ways to the shared labor of the household; both take for granted that while Olga is washing and cooking, he should read in his journals so as to advance his career.

Olga feels that something is desperately wrong with her life, that somehow she should have some time for herself, but is too tired really to try to figure it out. Time and again, she almost breaks through her internalized conditioning, but the very grind she is subjected to leaves her no time for epiphany. Baranskaya's handling of this theme becomes more and more compelling as Olga staggers on through the week, raising a diary of "undramatic" events to the pitch of tragic art.

This story has a documentary quality, not unlike Chekhov's "The Peasants" and Solzhenitsyn's "One Day in the Life of Ivan Denisovich." Olga's situation is the same as that faced by the working mothers of all the industrial nations; in the United States, the situation is worse, on the whole, since our society refuses to acknowledge working parents' need for day care, maternity leave, and so forth, and since our divorce rate is so much higher.

In the second long story, "The Petunin Affair," the focus is once again on the politics of the workplace, though the narrator is a not-altogether-convincing male voice. The story is narrated in flashback by a writer at a provincial television station who has been transferred because of a conflict with a new, efficient manager brought in from Moscow. The new manager has mounted a campaign against alcoholism, a social problem which in the Soviet Union is given the prominence of crack wars in this country. The campaign becomes more and more theatrical and sensationalistic, and the protagonist objects.

This story has some interesting turns, but is in the end unsatisfying. Part of the conflict has to do with a woman admired by both the narrator and his enemy, but this relationship is not extensively developed, and in closure the story shifts to a romantic happy ending which lacks drama.

In the other long story, "Lubka," the romantic ending is much more effective. Lubka is a high school dropout and party girl who gets in trouble with the neighborhood council for her concupiscence. Most of the story consists of the council's hearing, an exercise in a kind of communal democratic socialism that western readers tend to think has vanished from industrial countries. The story counterpoints the public apparatus of the council with Lubka's internal monologue, which shows that she is goodhearted but has trouble paying attention to anything earnest. Her change of character at the end of the story, triggered by her attraction to a coworker and her sudden realization of the monotony of her life, is convincing and satisfying. This story is the most successful character study in the book, though once again a political subtext is prominent: the council's attack on Lubka is clearly the product of sexual double standards.

The four shorter stories are haunting and effective, brief impressionistic pieces of a type not often published anymore in this country outside of *The New Yorker*. "The Purse" is about a woman's discovering the freedom and importance of writing. "A Delicate Subject" and "The Woman with the Umbrella" are about sexual double standards: in the first a woman is criticized for her relationships, and in the second a woman is ridiculed for being a "spinster." Perhaps the best of the short stories is "At Her Father's and Her Mother's Place," a sensitive study of a child of divorced parents trying to make sense of the differences in the two households between which she moves.

This is a solid, memorable collection from a gifted writer who shows us not only her own imaginative world but the world of a foreign culture as well.

Gail Regier. *Southern Humanities Review.*
25, 1991, pp. 295–97

BARKER, PAT (GREAT BRITAIN) 1943–

Union Street, Pat Barker's first novel, is a product of the grim wasteland of England's industrial northeast. It is the hard winter of 1973; a miner's strike amplifies a landscape of gray drizzle, physical and spiritual impoverishment. Against this background seven women enact their individual rites of passage. They range from eleven-year-old Kelly Brown, who is violated into sudden maturity, to Alice Bell, who struggles to avoid the workhouse and die with dignity. Yet this bleak synopsis does no justice to a novel that is much more than the sum of its parts. When it was published in Britain it was called feminist, proletarian, socialist-realist; Lawrencian, Osbornian, Sillitoe-esque. It has even been compared with Stella Gibbon's mock-gothic laugh riot, *Cold Comfort Farm.*There are those who've found it too grim and gritty, and those who've called it "the undiluted gospel of the distaff side."

But Pat Barker's work sits squarely in the tradition of Willa Cather. Both began publishing late (thirty-nine when their first novels appeared); both had written mannered "literary" works before they found genuine material in their own backgrounds, in each case through the example and advice of older, established women (for Cather, this was Sarah Orne Jewett; for Barker, Angela Carter). Barker's working-class world of shabby, burnt-out buildings and daily work in the cake factory calls to mind the arid, provincial small towns of Willa Cather's shoreless plains, the "iron country" from which there is no escape. . . .

Union Street reaches into human truths that are older than the sad historical milieu in which they are acted out; these women's lives are not wasted in history. They are, rather, gathered up in images of startling intimacy and concreteness, like that of the dying woman, Alice Bell, encountered freezing on a park bench by Kelly Brown. . . .

Union Street, written in prose that is spare, transparent, exacting, redeems and salvages the lives of these women, who are simultaneously specific, real, and Everywoman. Pat Barker's creative vision is as in touch with the psychologically primordial as Melville's; she might have entitled her book *Moby-Jane.*

J. S. Harper's. October, 1983, p. 76

The man who wasn't there [in the novel of that title] is Colin's father. "Shot down," says Viv, his mum; "Buggered off," thinks Colin. He noticed on the first day at school his birth certificate was shorter than everyone else's. Now that he can read he's not going to wait till he's twenty-one to be told about his father, as Viv says he must. Next time Viv goes out to serve as waitress in a nightclub, he rifles the old handbag in the wardrobe till he finds the certificate. Against the space for his father's name is a blank.

Colin is twelve, smart, cheeky, always in trouble at school. Colin fills the vacuum left by the absence of his father by creating an ongoing B-movie, a ham adventure set halfway between *Boy's Own* and occupied France. Co-lin's film stars himself, alias Garçon, a twelve-year old parachuted into France because of his uncanny fluency with the language. He is surrounded in the film by the people who inhabit his real life, only they're French, in cafes and stations. He tries out stories of espionage, betrayal, torture, and confession. When Colin's friends say "My dad says," all that Colin has to counter with is images from films. His own film is funny, sometimes unwittingly; it is a retreat as well as an exploration.

Pat Barker's talent is for people, period, and dialogue, and in Colin she perfectly creates the mood of a 1950s twelve-year old, a latchkey kid. The war years, the time of Colin's birth, were the time of his mother's life. Her current boyfriend is the married owner of the nightclub where she works. To this romance Colin puts a quick and expert end. Pat Barker's community is made up of real people, tolerant and abrasive. It is they, and their dialogue, who make this book, with their matinees and outings, seances and beans on toast. The plot is slightly confusing; there is an uncertainty as to the identity of "the man in black," a character from Colin's imagination who becomes real. Is he real? Is he Colin's father? A ghost? Is he Colin's future?

Kathleen Jamie. (London) *Times Literary Supplement.* April 14, 1989, p. 404

Women, surprisingly, scarcely feature in Pat Barker's latest novel. Perhaps because she is bored to tears with being described as the feminist chronicler of northern, working-class womanhood, *Regeneration* is almost entirely con-cerned with middle-and upper-class men.

More predictably, Barker has lighted on another excellent story: a true story, an old one, but rich in present-day literary potential. In 1917, Siegfried Sassoon, poet and decorated war hero, was bundled away into Craiglockhart hospital, ostensibly to be cured of "shell shock," but in fact to be dissuaded from his recent, vociferous protest against the war.

In Barker's Craiglockhart, the wards are screaming with those who have wasted their sanity, but the core of her novel is the dialogue that develops between Sassoon and his doctor, an elderly, doubt-prone, intelligent man called Rivers. Between them, the two try to tease out the meanings of cour-age, duty and masculinity, while underneath their debates a flourishing father-son relationship extends the book's exploration of manhood.

So far, so engrossing. The problem is that none of it is pushed to its imaginative limits. No matter how theoretically disturbing, in practice the book remains resolutely nice: as though, in her pity for the damaged young men, Barker has decided to return them to the safety of a wholesome and sexless *Jennings* school story, a land where the worst nightmares can be soothed by matron's protective hand. The novel is far too compassionate and serious to dislike. It is also, I should add, very readable, with one alarming passage of odd beauty and a number of interesting, semi-developed ideas.

The one that had lodged in my mind is Dr. Rivers's suggestion that the trenches drove so many young men insane not because they were dangerous, but because they subjected the soldiers to a helpless *passivity:* a state, in other words, not far removed from that which, in peacetime, drives so many women to breaking point.

Harriett Gilbert. *New Statesman and Society.* May 31, 1991, p. 37

Craiglockhart, with a population of Royal Army officers consigned to it with the diverse symptoms of what was hesitantly and still suspiciously termed "shell shock," is the primary setting for Pat Barker's absorbing historical novel *Regeneration.* . . .

The story is taken up as Sassoon is admitted there, in mid-1917, with the war verging on the muddy destructions of Passchendaele, and with no one in command able to articulate the principles that separated one side from the other. Sassoon, an early volunteer, decorated for bravery, had issued a public declaration "of willful defiance of military authority," in which he denounced his country's political motives and refused to return to service. Speaking as a soldier and for the sake of soldiers, he called for a clarification of England's war aims, and wrote that he hoped to destroy "the callous complacence with which the majority of those at home regard the continuance of agonies which they do not share, and which they have not sufficient imagination to realize."

Sassoon's statement, reproduced whole, leads off Barker's first page, and her novel is a tracing of its consequences, which were neither as public nor as clear as its valiant author had wished. . . .

To label *Regeneration* an antiwar novel—which it is, in part—suggests a didacticism that figures no more than it should in this richly storied and peopled amplification of events. Nor is the book a dark journey into Bedlam, despite the evident pain and potential horror of the subject. The animated and diverting life of Craiglockhart—"that living museum of tics and twitches"— contains comedy as well as tragedy, and it is not the chill black comedy of the Joseph Heller tradition (or, indeed, of the Siegfried Sassoon tradition, which is its distant ancestor) but, rather, comedy flushed with warmth. . . .

Few historical novelists can have had such ample and minutely detailed sources to draw upon as Barker. . . .

Sassoon went on to publish six autobiographical volumes, chronicling his years up to and through the war, and, along with Graves and Edmund Blunden, he makes up a trio that Paul Fussell christened the war's "classic memoirists." Barker depends on all three, and more besides, and it is perhaps ironic, given the degree of self-confessed fiction present in the memoirs, that only in Barker's novel are the real names of all the principal figures restored. . . .

Although *Regeneration* is essentially a moral drama, it is never static, never weighty. Barker is an energetic writer who achieves much of her purpose through swift and easy dialogue and the bold etching of personality—effects so apparently simple and forthright that the complications of feeling which arise seem to do so unbidden. The vivid immediacy of her style is perhaps better suited to situation and speech than to the processes of thought however; the shifting interior lights by which doctor and patient gradually adjust their positions are a little too clearly outlined, too artificially legible. . . .

It has been Pat Barker's accomplishment to enlarge the scope of the contemporary English novel. A woman of working-class background from the industrial North, she was educated in London but has kept to her roots. . . .

The documentary realism of Barker's first novel, *Union Street,* a harshly elemental book about the interwoven lives of a group of extremely poor women, won from the British press the honorific—or the brand—of "working-class masterpiece." Set amid unemployment and scrimping and alcohol and pride in a Northern coal-mining city devastated by the policies of Thatcherism, *Union Street* is an unsparing book, and its scenes of the imperative biology of these women's lives—sex, childbirth, abortion—are fully as harrowing as the men's traumas of war recounted in *Regeneration.* Indeed, this seems to be part of Barker's point: the two subjects are counterparts. . . .

Barker's second novel, *Blow Your House Down,* was a deliberately blunt and even brutal work about a group of prostitutes stalked by a killer in an actual 1970s case in England.

There are many battles being fought in *Regeneration,* and the war, for some, may not always be the hardest to face. Preparing to return to his regiment, Sassoon feels cheerful: "Exactly the same feeling he had had on board ship going to France, watching England slide away into the mist. No doubts, no scruples, no agonizing, just a straightforward, headlong retreat towards the front." Barker does not follow her characters to their separate fates; it is the moment of mutual touch and transformation which concerns her. *Regeneration* is an inspiriting book that balances conscience and the vitality of change against a collapsing world—a book about voyages out.

Claudia Roth Pierpont. *The New Yorker.*
August 10, 1992, pp. 74–76

[*The Eye in the Door,*] Pat Barker's sequel to her dazzling and disturbing *Regeneration* (1991) has as much scope as that book, greater buoyancy and an equally impressive ability to anchor major issues in the experience of her real and invented characters. Set in the spring of 1918, it shows the English psyche under pressure after four years of war. The first lines give the tone:

In formal beds beside the Serpentine, early tulips stood in tight-lipped rows. Billy Prior spent . . . moments setting up an enfilade, then . . . seized an imaginary machine-gun and blasted the heads off the whole bloody lot of them.

Myra stared in amazement. "You barmy bugger."

There is a bleak joke here for, while metaphors do lurk among the tulips, Myra, unknown to herself, has hit home. Prior has been close to insanity and has practiced buggery, and public attitudes to both are threatening factors in *The Eye in the Door,* whose master theme is cracking-up.

Like the minds under scrutiny, the prose here is rarely innocent, so one stays alert and, sure enough, some lines further on, the sunlit twigs which glow like "live electric filament" recall the electrodes applied in *Regeneration* to the throats of shell-shocked soldiers suffering, as Prior did in that novel, from mutism. He was spared this treatment thanks to Dr. William Rivers, who features here again, though the central role is now Prior's. Like Rivers in *Regeneration,* he is faced by a moral dilemma arising from the war.

Rivers's trouble was that when he cured officers who had been driven mad by their experiences in the trenches—they were sent back to those trenches. Prior's quandary is more elusive. Of working-class origins, he is an officer and "temporary gentleman." He hates the war from which he was invalided home, but feels solidarity with the men at the front and works for the Ministry of Munitions Intelligence Unit. Discomfort sharpens when he is sent to visit Beattie, who looked after him as a child. She is a pacifist who has been imprisoned on a trumped-up charge of trying to kill Lloyd George, and Prior's superiors hope to use his old friendships to lead them to wanted pacifist leaders. Class is only one of the fault lines along which his conscious-ness is liable to crack, so when Beattie asks if he even knows on whose side he is, he doesn't answer. Mutism again? Worse follows when he starts to experience fugue states during which he does things he cannot afterwards recall. Meanwhile, in nightmares, the eye painted on the spy hole of Beattie's cell door fuses with the eyeball of a dead man which Prior remembers picking up when he was at the front. Noting the connection between eyes and spies, he begins to fear that his aberrant self may have betrayed him.

Homosexuality, so dangerously akin to soldierly comradeship, is the ob-ject of a witch-hunt which threatens other patients of Rivers, including Charles Manning, with whom Prior has a sexual encounter. What is intriguing about this scene is that its vibrancy comes as much from class antagonism as from sex. Englishness, so often dimmed or diluted by irony in English fiction, is here presented in all the vigor of its flayed, cocky virulence. Prior is a marvelous creation: familiar off the page and plausible on it. Pat Barker's triumph is that she makes us understand and therefore care about him, just as she makes us care about Rivers's other balky patient, Siegfried Sassoon. Painfully proud, Prior has suffered more, and his lively mind, riven by the cleavages afflicting society, embodies society's ordeal while remaining viv-idly particular.

Barker draws on a battery of skills: historical intelligence, a sense of how people from up and down the social scale feel and talk, a risky readiness to freight that talk with ideas, plus an anthropologist's eye for detail. Her narrative glints with graphic bits of social lore which lighten and enlighten our apprehension of the whole.

Julia O'Faolain. (London) *Times Literary Supplement*. September 10, 1993, p. 21

BARNES, DJUNA (UNITED STATES) 1892–1982

No one need be entirely unhappy this fall with such a book as *Ryder* newly come into the world—no one, at least, with a clear head and a stout stomach. Here are nimble wit, gay humor, trenchant satire, and, above all, a grandiose imagination creating a robustious world of loose-tongued, free-living characters such as have hardly ventured on paper for a century. . . . *Ryder* is certainly the most amazing book ever written by a woman. That much abused word "Rabelaisian" . . . is here perfectly in place. In fact, *Ryder* is more "Rabelaisian" than Rabelais himself.

Ernest Sutherland Bates. *Saturday Review of Literature*. November 17, 1928, p. 376

If genius is perfection wrought out of anguish and pain and intellectual flagellation, then Djuna Barnes's novel *Nightwood* is a book of genius. In language, in philosophy, in the story it unfolds, she has woven a dark tapestry of spiritual and emotional disintegration whose threads never outrage each other in clashing disharmony. No gayety and no light falls upon her pattern, which is not to say that her pages are devoid of laughter or humor. For humor she has in abundance but it runs deep in hidden places and the laughter it evokes is tragic. If she has been ruthless and cruel to herself in writing this book out of the rich essence of her knowledge and her thinking and her experience, she has the compensating reward of compelling the thoughtful reader into attention to what she has to say and her manner of saying it. Her prose is lyrical to a degree where it seems of another age and another world but at the same time it does not lose kinship with the earthiness of humans.

Rose C. Feld. *New York Herald Tribune*. March 7, 1937, p. 4

The Antiphon is unmistakably the work of a mind of distinction and stature. I was not so much moved as shaken by the spectres it raises. But is it, as a work of art, successful? Is it really comparable with Webster, or is the style a sham Jacobean, or a sham Eliot-Jacobean make. . . . The speeches of the characters are never, in the true sense, dramatic, shaped by a living emotion.

For all the sombre violence of imagery, they are aggregates of fancy, not imaginative expression proceeding from an inner unity of condition and thought.

Kathleen Raine. *New Statesman and Nation.* February 8, 1958, p. 174

It is virtually impossible to speak of an ethic of Djuna Barnes's view of human situations, because that view rests on a total psychological determinism. Man is subject to the dictates of his unconscious nature even in his revolt against that nature itself. The courses of all the relationships in *Nightwood* are inevitable once chance has initially brought the characters together at certain particular places at certain particular times. . . . No ethical principle can aid the hero who enters the world of the night through love or disorientation; the only dictum which can be directed to the ordinary person who is spared this suffering is a warning to pay homage to the dark gods for continued preservation from a destruction which it is finally beyond the individual's power to prevent. . . .

Safety is the reward of moderation; but for man in his highest state of consciousness, which comes only in aspiration and revolt, destruction is inevitable. Pain increases in direct proportion to consciousness. Thus conscious life seems to be a mere freak of nature, or at most a register through whose tormented search for unity and permanence the inhuman universe is made aware of its own disorder and flux. Yet in this situation Djuna Barnes finds a basis for attaching a tragic value, which extends beyond stoicism, to human aspiration and suffering. Love, in that it seeks to heal fragmentation, to overcome solitude, and to deny mortality, is man's most perfect act of revolt; and in love man himself, by the force of his own suffering, of love as spiritual death, invests the loved object's existence with a value which it, as a meaningless freak of creation, did not possess before it was loved.

Alan Williamson. *Critique.* Spring, 1964, pp. 64–65

[Barnes's] world is a world of displaced persons—of an Armenian country boy on the lower east side of Manhattan, of Russian emigrés in Paris, Berlin, Spain, or New York, of Scandinavians or English in American farmland. They have abandoned national, racial, and ethical traditions; their human contacts are laceration. They lack even the integrity in isolation that comforts the characters of Hemingway or the early Faulkner, for they are estranged against themselves. Their aborted and ineffectual attempts to find meaning, order, or love are the subjects of the stories. Technique, as well as subject, marks the stories as extraordinary.

Readers who find the verbal pyrotechnics of *Nightwood,* or of the 1927 novel, *Ryder,* or of *The Antiphon* too often merely talky and falsely rhetorical will discover in most of the stories a fusing of experience and idea. Economy is especially characteristic of the revised versions collected in the *Selected*

Works, where verbal fat has been pared away, and objects, persons, and actions flash out with chilling precision. This is not to say, of course, that the stories are easy to read; on the contrary, like those of Katherine Mansfield and Katherine Anne Porter—which technically many of them resemble— they retain their meaning in a very dense texture, where each detail is significant and essential to the whole. And in spite of *Nightwood's* relatively wide circulation they are generally unknown today.

Suzanne C. Ferguson. *The Southern Review.*
Winter, 1969, p. 27

Djuna Barnes's middle vision comes to its fullest expression in *Nightwood;* that . . . immaculate novel is indeed a masterpiece. To let it stand alone as representative of a full career, however, is to deprive the novel of a good share of its merit. *Spillway* and *The Antiphon,* rather than being blind thrusts in new directions, follow from *Nightwood* in a precise and logical way. It may even be argued that *The Antiphon* is a work of comparable value insofar as it gives final shape to Miss Barnes's central themes. Certainly both companion volumes to *Nightwood* in *The Selected Works* greatly amplify the themes and stylistic attainments of their predecessor. Likewise, the uneven and sometimes flawed work before *Nightwood,* if seen with attention to the emergence of qualities that finally cohere in the novel, may reveal merits that have been overlooked. Even the early popular journalism, seeming hardly to bear upon a cryptic and subjective novel of 1936, may suggest something of what was to follow. . . .

In all, *Nightwood* is Djuna Barnes's central work, if not her only achievement of distinction. The book's trans-generic mode enables Miss Barnes to focus the themes and stylistic techniques that had been forming for years into a cohesive whole. It is completely consistent with the earlier work in form and themes, only more concentrated and intricately worked within its selective range. It brings the aims of the novel perhaps as close as possible to those of poetry, particularly with respect to the poetic image. It remains to be seen whether or not *The Antiphon,* a similar attempt in the genre of verse drama, is as successful. But *Nightwood* is a masterful work architecturally and linguistically, comparable to the works of Joyce and Eliot among the moderns, and to those earlier writers quoted or echoed in the novel itself. Like Malcolm Lowry's *Under the Volcano* and William Gaddis's *The Recognitions,* equally neglected works of similar merit, nearly every phrase in it is distinctive and functional, essential to the whole.

Louis F. Kannenstine. *The Art of Djuna*
Barnes: Duality and Damnation (New York:
New York University Press, 1977),
pp. xviii, 126

Barnes's reputation rests essentially on *Nightwood* (1936). A powerful novel of marriage, adultery, and betrayal, it should not be mistaken for a domestic narrative in the Updike manner, where failures can be comprehended and new beginnings achieved. Focusing on bogus aristocrats and American expatriates in Europe during the 1920s and 1930s, this is a nightmarish world, off kilter and surreal. Its inhabitants lose the object of their love, Robin Vote, and are unable to find an outlet or spillway for their anguish. Almost like puppets, they are set into frenetic motion and new behavioral patterns by forces from within their unconscious. These include sudden transvestism and bisexuality, metamorphoses of personality, and schizophrenia, all placed against juxtaposed times and swift changes in setting. Complex techniques such as these, along with eccentric characters, have led critics to associate Barnes with experimental forms and especially with anti-realism. But she is not a one-book author, and therefore she should be examined in the larger context of other important works. Though more traditional, they still reveal characters and conflicts that are the foundation of *Nightwood,* as well as her dexterity in using vastly differing styles. *A Book* (1923) and *Night among the Horses* (1928) consist of short stories, poems, and one-act plays that, unlike *Nightwood,* are concise and even traditionally narrated. But it is here that themes such as the severed self and the atomized self are introduced. . . .

Whatever the techniques—traditional or experimental—Barnes's work is concerned with ways of being reconciled to life's random misfortunes. In the stories of *Spillway* there is often an emotional "spillway" that rechannelizes feelings of helplessness and isolation. Its specific form may not be pleasurable, yet still it exists as an alternative to the completely isolated personality. For some characters who are whirled about by stimuli they never quite understand, the spillway is passivity or acquiescence, while for others it is a private fantasy, endless travel, or psychological regression. Whatever the case, the suffering begins with detachment from origins.

Miriam Fuchs. *The Hollins Critic.* June,
1981, pp. 2–3

Its author calls it a "slight satiric wigging" (even as she sets it next to Proust); its 1972 publishers claim she regarded it as "a simple piece of fun, in no way to be considered among her serious works." Its original, anonymous, and private publication, though in a foreign tongue, was so threatening that its distributor withdrew and the book was sold by its author's friends on Paris streets. It has confounded critics, intimidated readers, enticed feminists, outraged conservatives, and delighted for decades the people it parodies. But mostly it has been unnoticed and unread: only now is *Ladies Almanack* beginning to assume a place of distinction is the complicated corpus of Djuna Barnes and the differently complicated intertext of lesbian literature. In both canons, *Ladies Almanack* stands apart, posing a challenge to questions of writing, reading, and authorship.

It is at once a book that reaches forward and a book intimately tied to time (1928) and place (expatriate Left Bank). Barnes's slim volume is the most audacious of a body of texts produced by and about the lesbian society that flourished in Paris between the turn of the century and World War II. *Ladies Almanack* was allegedly created for the amusement of Barnes's lesbian friends, who persuaded her to publish it and financed the venture. Its actual and implied readers were its own cast of characters: the circle of Natalie Clifford Barney, *l'Amazone* whose Paris salon was a center of culture in the first decades of the century. The Barney whom Barnes creates is a savior of women, pictured in Barney's favorite of the drawings "carrying a pole" and "stepping out upon that exceedingly thin ice to which it has pleased God, more and more, to call frail woman, there so conducting herself that none were put to the chagrin of sinking for the third time!" This "wonderworker" becomes the centerpiece of a bawdy *discours à clef* that eludes classification and inscribes a world in which the lesbian is normative. And though Djuna Barnes was apparently unwilling to associate herself with the women's movement of the 1970s and 1980s, the vision of her *Almanack* finds it surest resonance in contemporary lesbian-feminist wit. . . .

Ladies Almanack is finally an extraordinary text in the Barnesian chronicle (as in all its canons—lesbian, female, modernist), sharing theme and form with other works, yet far more radical in its politics, far more gynocentric in its consciousness. As such, *Ladies Almanack* suggests the power of a moment—of an intersection of cultural circumstances—virtually to overpower personal "identity" in shaping the voice and vision of a text. There is finally no authorization from Barnes herself—from her public statements, her private correspondence or her published works—for the radical implications of *Ladies Almanack,* no moment in Barnesian discourse that matches the vision of this text. And had Djuna Barnes been presented with the political implications of her work as I have drawn them here, she might well have disavowed them entirely.

Barnes may finally, then, have been articulating a universe less of her own desire than of the desires of those who were at once her friends, readers, and characters. Such a concept challenges notions of the unitary writing subject and traditional images of the nature of writing in relationship to authorial identity. We may then have to account for the radical vision of *Ladies Almanack* in the euphoria and daring of a cultural moment of which Barnes found herself the articulating voice. And if context is able so profoundly to shape discourse, virtually to generate its vision, then the notion of "author" becomes inconceivable or irrelevant apart from "text." The problem lies, then, not in attempting to reconcile the historical Barnes with the textual voice of *Ladies Almanack* but in having thought the two equivalent. It is within the freedom of this more complex vision of reading and writing, of *Ladies Almanack* and Djuna Barnes, that one may discover the pleasures and perils of speaking in tongues.

Susan Sniader Lanser. *Frontiers.* 4, 1979,
pp. 39–40, 46

Most critical discussion of *Nightwood* has centered on questions of genre, style, and structure. Barnes's use of caricature and her virtuosity of language invite us to trace the patterns of imagery and allusion that are clearly central to *Nightwood's* meaning. But this is also, as Andrew Field has demonstrated, an intensely personal book, and its "necessary excesses," in Louis Kannenstine's words, constitute a strategy of disguise as much as a "rhetoric of lamentation," as Kenneth Burke has suggested. This ambivalence between disguise and revelation makes *Nightwood* both intriguing and problematic. In showing that female experience, specifically lesbian love, proves false our assumptions about both love and gender, it promises a new form of meaning, but it then denies the possibility of making meaning.

Nightwood is distinctively modern not only in its subject and form, but in its consideration of what our concepts of masculine and feminine imply. It has become a truism that the opposition between masculine and feminine shapes our conceptions of identity and meaning. Masculine and feminine are metaphysical constructs, categories with which we organize and interpret the differences we perceive in the world. Because we live in a patriarchal culture, we tend to label as masculine those aspects of our experience and those qualities that are closest to the existing forms of power (autonomy, reason, speech, culture), and we tend to label as feminine what cannot be accommodated by, is contrary to, or threatens the existing forms of power (passivity, emotion, silence, nature). These abstractions are, as Djuna Barnes was aware, inseparable from our psychosocial experience. We tend to formulate our values and to define our assumptions about the world in terms of the meanings we have invested in masculine and feminine. In our cultural mythology, therefore, sexual difference represents the primary experience of our individual difference.

In *Nightwood* Djuna Barnes treats this mythology ironically. In portraying the inversion of experience, depicting a world of darkness, irrationality, and degeneration, she tells four "anti-fairy tales" in which she caricatures the qualities opposed in masculine and feminine to show that they are inherently incompatible. In addition, she deconstructs the opposition between masculine and feminine because it does not define the most fundamental experience of difference: the difference between the identity one imagines (the self as Subject) and the identity one experiences in relationship with someone else (the self as Other). In defining this difference, central to the experience of women, in terms of the opposition between mother and child, Barnes raises the possibility for a new figuration of female identity.

Judith Lee. In Mary Lynn Broe, ed. *Silence and Power: A Reevaluation of Djuna Barnes* (Carbondale: Southern Illinois University Press, 1991), pp. 207–8

Djuna Barnes's great Rabelaisian comic epic novel, *Nightwood* (1936), is beginning to excite the critical attention it deserves. As a contribution to that effort this essay is a feminist interpretation that argues, among other readings, that *Nightwood* is a brilliant and hilarious feminist critique of

Freudian psychoanalysis and a parody of the discourse of diagnosis of female hysteria. . . .

Nightwood, in its original title of "Bow Down" and its continual reference to submission and bowing or lowering of the self, is a study of *abjection,* and . . . that by its concentration on the figure of The One Who Is Slapped, the downtrodden victim, it figures by absence the authoritarian dominators of Europe in the 1930s, the sexual and political fascists. . . .

I maintain that Barnes's portraits of the abject constitute a political case, a kind of feminist-anarchist call for freedom from fascism. Looking at Nikka's tattoo as a defiance of the Levitical taboo against writing on the body, I see the body of the Other—the black, lesbian, transvestite, or Jew—presented as a text in the novel, a book of communal resistances of underworld outsiders to domination. Its weapon is laughter, a form of folk grotesque derived from Rabelais and surviving in circus.

With Bakhtin's *Rabelais* as model methodology, I see *Nightwood's* extravagant language and imagery as a direct descendant of medieval "grotesque realism" (as *Ladies Almanack* is certainly a descendant of the Rabelaisian almanac hawked about in Paris street fairs). In this "reversible world" or "world turned upside down," Barnes moves from high to low culture, from opera to circus, and even expands Bakhtin's categories from their base in the material to include the mystical and mental grotesqueries that he excluded.

I would also argue that the status of *Nightwood* as a lesbian novel or a cult text of high modernism has obscured the ways in which it is a French novel, indebted as much to Victor Hugo and Eugène Sue as it is to Rabelais. My purpose in reviving *Nightwood* is political. Strangely canonized and unread, it cannot function as a critique of fascism. The revision of modernism in which this essay participates is an effort to read race, class, and gender back into the discussion. Unlike most expatriate writing from this period, *Nightwood* paints the Paris underworld and demimonde with its own colors, not a specifically American palette. Its characters are Barnes's modern "misérables," brothers and sisters to the hunchback of Notre Dame. *Nightwood,* like modernism itself, begins in Vienna in the 1880s. Freud, fascism, Hitler, "high art," and the lumpen proletariat haunt the text as a potent "political unconscious." *Nightwood's* hysterical heteroglossia is a perverse and almost postmodern fold-text in which language and its possibility for figuration is as potent and explosive as it is in Shakespeare or Joyce.

Jane Marcus. In Mary Lynn Broe, ed.
*Silence and Power: A Reevaluation of Djuna
Barnes* (Carbondale: Southern Illinois
University Press, 1991), pp. 221–22

BAYNTON, BARBARA (AUSTRALIA) 1857–1929

In these days when pain is fashionable Barbara Baynton is widely admired for writing accurately about the terrible lives endured by women in the bush. She is commended for having fractured the rose-colored lenses through which Australians peered reverently at their pioneer mothers. However understandable this version of Barbara Baynton may be, it is also highly ironic. The woman herself was no truth-sayer. Her grandson H. G. Gullett put the matter charitably: "she was a highly imaginative woman with no strict regard for truth. She told her children many conflicting stories of her early years and of her parents, and it rather seems as if the truth to her was what she chose to believe it ought to be at any given moment, and of course it would vary with her moods." Such a woman makes a strange feminist icon.

It is not just the impulse towards falsifying that makes her difficult to come to terms with, but the direction that impulse took. She seems to have spent the second half of her life pretending away the experiences which made possible the writing of *Bush Studies* and *Human Toll*. . . . As Mrs. Baynton, Barbara had come in from the cold and for the rest of her life she would remain warmed by the fires of the wealthy and the socially respectable. Surely no one can pass moral judgment on her for that. Literary judgments are another matter, and here the evidence is clearcut: she wrote best when she was writing about people left out in the cold.

Her sensitivity to their plights even lends imaginative force to "A Dreamer," with its mawkish plot characteristic of soppy fiction written for women's magazines. Here the central figure is a young pregnant woman left out in the cold quite literally. She has arrived late at night in a one-street country town to pay her mother a long overdue visit. Finding no one at the station to meet her, she walks three miles through a storm. After almost losing her way in the dark bush and nearly drowning in a flooded river, she gets home only to find her mother dead. The rank melodrama of the plot spreads out to infect the prose. Breathlessness abounds. Exclamation marks are everywhere. The natural world is treated as personally vicious. Even the ordinarily gentle willow trees have branches animated to become antagonists threatening death:

> The wind savagely snapped them, and they lashed her unprotected face. Round and round her bare neck they coiled their stripped fingers. Her mother had planted these willows, and she herself had watched them grow. How could they be so hostile to her!

Such overstated gestures abound. Yet, in a story clogged with literary trivia, with outmoded language and discredited fictional devices, there is genuine insight and power. The story is a remarkable rendering of a rarely treated subject: a woman's struggle to come to terms with feelings she has for her own mother at a time when she is about to become a mother herself.

The struggle engenders psychic disarray. The woman's passage through the storm becomes a metaphoric journey through a landscape experienced as nightmare. The physical world is shaped by a dreamer's fears, not by the laws of nature. The "feel" and the logic of the story belong to the world of nightmare. This is why willows are more than willows; they are personally hostile antagonists. To animate nature as if it were an extension of the perceiver is an epistemological fallacy in a waking mind (and the pathetic fallacy when it invades literature). For the dreaming mind, however, such animation is the arena of psychological truth, and this is why "A Dreamer" is truthful, against all literary odds. The narrative achieves insight into the confused state of a woman for whom motherhood is an issue compounded of violence, guilt and sentimentalized love. . . .

"Squeaker's Mate" is an angry story of a woman who will not accept defeat. Its emotional contours surely found their genesis in Baynton's life with Alexander Frater among the selectors of the Coonamble district. Being displaced as wife by another woman in the same household, particularly by a servant, would have been mortifying, whatever contempt Barbara may have felt for Frater. Like the mate, she refused to turn her face to the wall and conveniently die. Fury maintained self-esteem. Barbara Frater left the demeaning bush life and took her children to Sydney. As Barbara Baynton, she could extract through her fiction the revenge of the tigress.

Barbara Baynton certainly took her revenge on the bush. Never for a moment in *Bush Studies* does it seem a genuinely desirable home for a woman. Everywhere the experience of the housekeeper in "Billy Skywonkie" is underlined:

> A giddy unreality took the sting from everything, even from her desire to beseech him to turn back to the siding, and leave her there to wait for the train to take her back to civilization. She felt she had lost her mental balance. Little matters became distorted, and the greater shriveled.

Bush life threatens to overwhelm the self. Barbara Baynton's problem as a writer was an inability to push beyond this insight. She needed pain to impel her imagination. Without pain, she seems to lose focus, as she does in most of *Human Toll,* or to write sentimentally, as she does in most poems and the later stories. In "Trooper Jim Tasman," for example, the cause of neither soldier nor mother is well served when the narrator intones piously:

> I saw those silent bush women. Early pioneers, who had left father and mother, and sister and brother and friends, to face the great unknown as mate to their man, and of silent courage had bred those Anzac heroes.

The tough-minded prose of "Squeaker's Mate" has vanished. Without pain, and pain personally felt while objectively rendered, both truth and imaginative vividness are lost. Security and an easeful existence served the *grande dame* well, but not her fiction.

Lucy Frost. In Shirley Walker, ed. *Who Is She?* (New York: St. Martin's Press, 1983), pp. 56, 59–60, 68–69

When critics of Australian literature focus on the writers of the *Bulletin* school of the 1890s in terms of a tradition of democratic nationalism, they seldom mention women. A. A. Phillips however, in his 1966 revised edition of *The Australian Tradition,* includes a new chapter on Barbara Baynton, author of *Bush Studies* (1902). Phillips applies the label "dissidence" to the character of Baynton's writing, along with that of Miles Franklin's *My Brilliant Career,* Norman Lindsay's *Redheap,* Arthur Adams's poem, "The Australian," and some of the short stories of Henry Lawson, like "The Union Buries its Dead." He writes that they exhibit an "undercurrent of revolt against the barbaric fate of being an Australian." The issue is not woman's fate, but that of "being an Australian." Nonetheless, the manner in which this so-called dissidence is approached has relevance in the light of contemporary theoretical questions concerning the relationship between narrative and gender. Phillips's remark concerning Baynton's dissidence is relevant to both the production of "woman's place" in the annals of Australian literature and to the processes of naming through critical exigesis. An examination of Barbara Baynton's short story, "The Chosen Vessel," an abridged version of which originally appeared in the *Bulletin* in 1896 under A. G. Stephens's title, "The Tramp," and its critical reception by Phillips and others will serve to illustrate the nature of the problem. Focusing on the place of woman as sign in the short story and critical commentaries, keeping in mind the question of women's dissidence, I will trace the ambiguities of meaning within the original text and its more singular "truth" as represented by the critical tradition.

This was the only story by Barbara Baynton to appear in the *Bulletin* (December 1896). A. G. Stephens, editor of the Red Page, thought her work "too outspoken" for an Australian audience, but praised it for its realism. Six of her stories, including "The Chosen Vessel" were first published in England under the title *Bush Studies* in 1902. Like "The Chosen Vessel," all convey a hostile image of the bush as perceived by its victims—the old, the weak, the women. But the stories have been read in terms of the way in which they reflect the Australian tradition. Censorship of the stories to fit their assumed context began with first publication. Stephens cut the entire third section, concerning the Catholic voter horseman, and he retitled the story "The Tramp," possibly even changing Baynton's neutral pronouns for the man as "he" into "the tramp." Baynton offered the title "What the Curlews Cried," but it was rejected. Thus, from the outset, the religious theme of section three, which unites the sexual with the symbolic, the bush mother with the Virgin Mother, the silenced with the spoken theme, is censored. And the title was changed, thus shifting reader interest away from the murder, evoked on several levels of the text, and on to the male character, called a "tramp," *not* bushman or swagman, by Stephens.

When A. A. Phillips writes of the story he comments that Stephens's judgments were "sound" in these matters and suggests that even more could have been peeled away. He cites the opening episode, in which the text evokes a harsh image of the husband (not to mention the wife), as unnecessary as well. We only need to know, he says, that the husband was absent. The extra details are examples of Baynton's "subjective obsession" about man's cruelty forcing its way into the incidental details of the story. Phillips is clearly bothered by Baynton's "obsessions"; "grim prepossessions" he calls them in another place. . . .

An analysis of Phillips's discourse on Baynton reveals a myriad of ways in which the writer is literally blind to women as writers/characters except as they reflect or challenge the bush ideal. The category "woman" is empty and filled by shifting significations which mirror the place of woman in what might be called the Australian Imaginary (in the Lacanian sense of what we take to be real but is imagined with reference to a patriarchal symbolic order). The woman, herself, does not exist; she is absent from the discourse. For example, when Phillips delineates what he sees as Baynton's major themes, he says that they convey: "the most intense effect . . . of the image of a lonely bush hut besieged by a terrifying figure who is also a terrified figure." In "The Chosen Vessel" we recall that it is not the hut, but the woman in the hut, who is besieged. And the terrifying figure is certainly not "also the terrified figure." Here Phillips repeats Stephens's trick of shifting emphasis from victim to attacker. The second theme Phillips mentions is "the fierce power of the maternal instinct."

Still there is no mention of the woman who possesses it. But later the text reads "the possessor of the maternal instinct is usually the victim of evil, which wreaks at a terrible destruction." The evil, we are assured, is "essentially weak," while the maternal force "has lasting strength." So "woman" as a central character, motif, theme in Baynton's fiction, has thus far been displaced as (1) the bush hut, (2) the terrifying figure of her attacker, (3) the maternal force, (4) the possessor of the maternal force, (5) the victim of evil, (6) the survivor (child or dog) which endures as the maternal representative. Where is the woman? Absent. How is she portrayed? Objectified into the unproblematical motif of "the maternal." . . .

Phillips's analysis aligns the maternal force, or instinct, or power, or what have you, with a "bitter insistence on man's brutality to women." He writes, "One feels, perhaps without logical justification, that the two themes beat together in the pulse of Barbara Baynton's intuitions." In this sentence the reader can begin to detect the workings of Phillips's imaginary, and the discursive transference to the symbolic order, in his juxtaposition of the logical with the intuitive. "Perhaps without logical justification," for whom?

The conflation of referents which blend literal and figurative meanings denying as they uphold the "fierce power of the maternal," exist together, at every point of text. But they work most explicitly with reference to the third section—that which both A. G. Stephens and A. A. Phillips deemed unnecessary to the unity of plot, character, action. In the third section a doubling takes place. The main action is repeated in a way that transforms murder into redemption, revolt into acquiescence, the absence of woman into the insistence of the maternal power, the transference of the literal into the figurative, the imaginary into the symbolic. If one reads through the contradictions, woman is not guilty at all—she is wholly absent. She takes no part in the actions of the story except to represent male desire as either Virgin or whore. Her "lack," disguised as maternal power, enables "him" (husband, son, horseman, priest) to attain or maintain an identity. She has been named, captured, controlled, appropriated, violated, raped and murdered, *and then* reverenced through the signifying practices of the text. And these contradictory practices through which the "woman" is disseminated in the text are made possible by her very absence from the symbolic order except by reference to her phallic repossession by Man. Baynton's text, in its deliberate irony, calls attention to these facts while it calls into question the idealization of the bushman as the embodiment of the Australian personality. . . .

Through our examination of Baynton's text as it attempts to deconstruct the place of woman we can register her dissidence, not only as interpreted by A. A. Phillips as that which denies the legend but also, and more fundamentally, as imagined by Julia Kristeva in her insistence that woman is the perpetual dissident. "Woman is here to shake up, to disturb, to deflate masculine values, and not to espouse them. Her role is to maintain differences by pointing to them, by giving them life, but putting them into play against one another." This surely has been one of the functions of Baynton's short story, "The Chosen Vessel." Its representation here, by way of this analysis, may help to restore to the vessel a richness and multiplicity of meanings which have been lost through repeated critical attempts at phallic mastery.

Kay Iseman. Australian Literary Studies.
11:1, May, 1983, pp. 25, 27–29, 36–37

Although Barbara Baynton's short stories have attracted considerable critical attention, her novel *Human Toll,* first published in 1907, but largely inaccessible to modern readers until Krimmer and Lawson's *Barbara Baynton: Portable Australian Authors* in 1980, is usually either disregarded or dismissed as a flawed anti-climax to the controlled savagery of the stories of *Bush Studies.* . . . The novel fulfills the expectations of classical realism: it is bleak and pessimistic, it portrays the sordidness of working class life as a realistic novel ought to do, and it certainly gives that impression of verisimilitude which results from the use of realistic visual and social detail and of the vernacular. The geography of the selection Merrigulandri with its key reference points—the homestead, the wim, the hut with its broken roof and the ominous graves beneath the myall trees—is accurately realized, as is the layout of the small town with its flour mill beside the river:

> as if purposefully linking the mill with Fireman Foreman's dwelling on the opposite side . . . But now, in the unillusioned light and broody quiet of a Sabbath morn, the cold, silent mill, shorn of its nebulous halo, looked old and worn—an aged actor off the stage.

Baynton's vivid miniatures, such as that of the "dawn-rising Chinamen" who "shogged with nimble bare feet under their yoke-linked watering-cans" add to the realism:

> These busy brethren, meeting sometimes on the same narrow track, would pause, ant-like, seemingly to dumbly regard one another and their burdens, then, still ant-like, pass silently to their work.

while her rendition of the church service and the dance at Stein's are masterpieces of social reportage. The use of the vernacular, though sometimes labored, conveys a vivid sense of the idiom of the bush—of "Pat the dry sixpence" and the property "Gi' Away Nothin' 'All"; of a man "too slow to trap maggots" or another, Hugh Palmer, who resembles "the bull on Keen's mustard" and acts like one. Given Baynton's undoubted mastery of the techniques of pictorial and social realism, it is safe to assume that the digressions of the first two chapters and the circumlocution of the final two are less a failure of form on her part, than a deliberate experiment; an attempt in the former to set the scene in symbolic as well as literal terms, and in the latter to capture a different kind of realism, the psychological realism of disintegration. . . .

Modern readers immediately perceive that *Human Toll* is an exciting and disturbing text; exciting for its range of response to bush experience, for the passion of its presentation, and for the outrage of its tone. It is clearly a dissident text; one which challenges through a woman's experience the whole ethos of the 1890s—of mateship, of bush community and of Australian nationalism. *Human Toll* is also an exciting technical experiment. If we view it not as a realistic novel which fails because of a lack of control, but rather as a protomodernist text where a variety of techniques, many of them far in advance of their time, are employed in order to create a powerful account of the physical and psychic destruction of a young female in an Australian bush town and in the bush itself, then we may come to a clearer appreciation of Baynton's achievement. In these terms, for instance, Baynton's persistent use of the melodramatic is not a return to the tropes of Victorianism, but a means of conveying, by excess, the suffering and despair of her heroine and of condemning the spiritual poverty of bush society. Moreover, the incoher-

ence of events and the impressionism of certain sequences can be seen as a
totally appropriate means of portraying the disintegration of personality
under extreme stress. It will be shown that this text is a subversive text,
both thematically and structurally, in that it consistently utilizes conventional
modes, forms and techniques, only to circumvent them in order to demonstrate that disintegration which is its major theme. . . .

The text is modernist . . . in its use of wasteland themes. There is no
incompatibility between these themes and the melodramatic for, according to
Brooks, melodrama "marks the final liquidation of the traditional Sacred"
and "comes into being in a world where the traditional imperatives of truth
and ethics are questioned," and this is certainly the case in *Human Toll*.
Baynton's themes are those of the twentieth century; of a secular world
deprived of love, of the failure of spirituality and the rejection of all traditional
sources of spiritual comfort. In this sense the theme of maternity denied is
all-important, for the bush township has cut itself off from all values except
materialism and has perverted its religious heritage. The move to the bush
itself, the natural world which Eliot was later to use to signify his existential
wasteland, is significant too. The arid yet overgrown bush provides Baynton
with wasteland imagery of drought and thirst, of burning sand instead of life-
giving water, and of an overgrowth of foliage which threatens, impedes and
"shuts out heaven" when it should nurture and protect. Meanwhile the track-
lessness of the bush images its existential meaninglessness as well as the
inner circling of the solipsistic consciousness which seeks spiritual refuge
there and finds none. It is this search for a spirituality which has disappeared
from the land—projected in Ursula's vision of the blind and crucified Christ
upon the gum-tree—which confirms the orientation of *Human Toll* toward
the twentieth rather than the nineteenth century. . . .

The mixture of modes and techniques and the excessive experimentation
of *Human Toll* possibly detract from its success, even for the most dedicated
of readers. However the novel should be seen, not as a deviation from the
Australian literary tradition from which its springs, but as a proto-modernist
text which is well before its time.

Shirley Walker. Southerly. 49:2, June, 1989,
pp. 131–33, 144–48

It is difficult to imagine a fiction more haunted with evocations of defiled
maternity than that of Barbara Baynton. Indeed, the human toll, in the novel
of that name, is death by childbirth. Considering Baynton's own experience
of motherhood—her first child born to her in a lonely bush hut without any
witness whatsoever, the second aided by a midwife who referred to the child
as "another little bit of flesh" and told her of "unbelievable horrors, of pregnant women, exhausted from overwork, dying alone in labor and being found
with "wild pigs eatin' her as I come along," the third followed by finding her
husband in bed with her niece who in turn was driven mad by childbearing—
it is scarcely surprising that ambivalence toward the maternal haunts Bayn-

ton's fiction. All around her she saw the toll of motherhood, the sacrifice of women undergoing "a coded, fundamental perverse behavior, ultimate guarantee of society."

Baynton's only novel, *The Human Toll* is specifically concerned with motherhood; indeed motherhood is "the human toll." It is a fate that Ursula, the orphan protagonist of the book, struggles to evade. Troubled by her own sexuality—her attraction to Andrew—she asserts her determination to be a writer and separate herself from corporeal process. However, throughout the novel she is beset by evocations of abjection—of defiled maternity—which operate as emblems of female guilt toward the mother for choosing writing instead of loving, for preferring the s/ word of the father to the womb of the mother. Indeed Ursula's desire to escape the body and write leads to a nightmare confrontation with "the maternal." . . .

Baynton's stories are similarly mother-haunted. Ambivalence toward the maternal and longing for archaic maternal love exist side by side. In "A Dreamer" a young woman is driven back to the home of her girlhood; it is a nightmare journey of return impelled by the woman's own pregnancy, a reminder of the girl's pre-oedipal dependence on the maternal body. . . .

Although "Squeaker's Mate," through masculine identification, has gained the mastery necessary to censor all trace of dependence on the maternal body, she is crushed by a falling tree and brought back to a grim caricature of the female condition: confinement and sexual subordination, the conditions of maternity which "both create and emblematize the condition of women.". . .

"The Chosen Vessel" is centrally concerned with the negation of the maternal body. Articulated as pure virginal Madonna to make her fit cohabitate for the clean and proper self, woman in her corporeality is brutalized and negated. With only her "Mother's brooch" for protection—"it was the only thing of value that she had"—the young mother is violated and murdered, her body returned to fundamental abjection of the corpse.

Kristeva's formulation of social classification rooted in an extreme fear of the generative power of the mother has extraordinary explanatory power in its application to Australian culture, in particular the literature of the abject which it has produced. A society like Australia, formulated under the regulation of a powerful, punitive external law—a penal system based on rigid hierarchical arrangements—has remained particularly resistant to intermixture, to the erasing of differences and to the threat of undifferentiation. There is a fierce belief in the principle of identity without admixture, the exclusion of anything that breaks boundaries, a fierce need to maintain symbolic oneness, and a fierce condemnation of hybrids and migrant beings; but above all there has been a particular resistance to the feminine—to woman and the maternal. The idea of the self most commonly articulated in Australian literature bears strong resemblance to Kristeva's borderliner, who lives in a fortified but empty castle; unwilling to experience his own vulnerability, he remains a prisoner in the tower of his own identity, projecting his own abjection onto others and violently punishing them for it.

It is the power of writers like Baynton to provide a powerful critique of this virulent form of patriarchy in Australian culture and to chronicle the fate of the maternal in its context. In confronting the abject, she prepares the ground for what Kristeva refers to as "the first great demystification of Power (religious, moral, political, verbal) that mankind has ever witnessed."

Joan Kirkby. *Westerly.* 4, December, 1989, pp. 114–15, 123–24

BEATTIE, ANN (UNITED STATES) 1947–

Something of Updike's attentiveness to ordinary human encounters distinguishes Ann Beattie's *Chilly Scenes of Winter,* a fine first novel which records the reluctant passage into adulthood of a twenty-seven-year-old survivor of the Woodstock generation. The novel incorporates characters and situations Beattie had treated earlier in her *New Yorker* stories, nineteen of which have been gathered under the title *Distortions* and released as a companion to the novel. But the novel is a more interesting and significant performance, richer in psychological nuance and in documentary power. Though there are many isolated passages in *Distortions* that exhibit Beattie's descriptive care and her talent for truthful dialogue, only one of the stories, "Snake's Shoes," has the sustained authority of the novel. One reason for the novel's superiority is that it is less tendentious than the stories, less confined by neo-absurdist attitudes toward contemporary experience. The novel is thus less somber than the stories and registers on every page a lively, generous alertness to the antic or comic in human relations. The characters in *Chilly Scenes* are respected more consistently than their counterparts in the stories, and although their vivid idiosyncrasies are always comically before us, what is odd or distinctive in their behavior belongs to their personalities, is rooted in Beattie's powers of observation and dramatic representation. Too often in the stories, in contrast, one feels the pressure of a surrealist program, the influence of Barthelme and Pynchon, behind the author's choice of details or in the often schematic resolution of her plots.

Chilly Scenes is written in the present tense and relies heavily on dialogue and on a purified declarative prose not unlike good Hemingway, but much funnier. This disciplined young novelist takes care to differentiate even her minor characters, and one of her most memorable cameo players declares herself only as a voice through the telephone—a nervous, guilty mother trying to trace her wayfaring daughter in two brief conversations that momentarily distract the protagonist during this final winter of his prolonged adolescence. The hero himself is wonderfully alive: a gentle bewildered man, extravagantly loyal to old friends and to the songs of the 1960s, drifting through a final nostalgia for the mythologies of adversary selfhood he absorbed in college and toward an embarrassed recognition of his hunger for such ordinary adventures as marriage and fatherhood. The unillusioned tenderness that informs Beattie's portrait of her central character is a rare act of intelligence and mimetic art.

David Thorburn. *The Yale Review.* Summer,
1977, pp. 585–86

I can think of no other American writer save Thomas Pynchon who has found so wide and respectful an audience so early in her career. No one who has a serious interest in contemporary fiction can fail to be aware of Beattie's abrupt and alarming stories. Their publication in book form [*Distortions*] marks, I believe, a genuine event in the national life.

I suppose that one first feels struck by Beattie's consummate technical virtuosity. Her frigid prose, the shocking inexorableness of her humor and narrative designs, the macabre and spare efficiency of her thought, conspire to project her tales as actual—if rather awful—occurrences of modernist existence. I have called Beattie's prose cold: but one must read this most wicked and witty writer very closely indeed. It is true that she assembles as subjects a grotesque community of dwarfs, fats, gargoyles, and sluts, a bizarre collection of the lonely, the disoriented, and the dispossessed. Never, though, does she permit her figures to seem merely apathetic or aimlessly malcontent. Nor does she ever dismiss them as freaks. Beattie constructs her stories from within a soft and subtle sensibility of sympathy, participation, and hopefulness. She understands that, however capricious or queer, her characters' pains have their origin less in the morasses of individual neurosis than in the insipidity of the culture at large, the withering vapidity of the historical processes which envelop one and with which one must manage to coexist in some sort of emotional relation. It is the sign of her extraordinary intelligence and gentleness that Beattie considers her fictionalized people to be as human as their author; that she regards her own suffering as conterminous with that of her roughly satirized characters.

Beattie comprehends, this is to say, that we are driven into our misery and peculiarity because, appropriately, we cannot accommodate the abstraction and absurdity which surround us. Her characters fervently want to feel; especially they long to love. But the rapidity and monstrousness of contemporary history, the dearth of external supports for even the minimal impulses of human life, seem to the stories' people to invalidate the very possibility of achieving affective experience.

Peter Glassman. *Hudson Review.* Autumn,
1977, p. 447

The characters who populate [*Secrets and Surprises*] came of age during the 1960s. They are, on the whole, a nice-looking bunch of people who have never suffered from any of the basic wants. Most of them, for reasons often unexplained, share a mistrust of passion and conversation. . . . They exist mainly in a stateless realm of indecision and—all too often—rather smug despair. . . .

Frequently, in these stories, things are substitutes for the chancier commitment to people; things people buy or live with or give one another are asked to bear the responsibility of objective correlatives, but too often they become a mere catalogue of trends. The reader is left holding an armful of objects and wondering what emotional responses they were meant to connect him with.

Perhaps the best level on which to enjoy these stories is as a narrative form of social history. Miss Beattie has a coolly accurate eye for the *moeurs* of her generation. . . . But a sharp eye for *moeurs* doesn't add up to a full fiction any more than the attitude of irony can be said to represent a full human response.

Gail Godwin, *The New York Times.* January
14, 1979, p. 14

To say that Ann Beattie is a good writer would be an understatement. Her ear for the banalities and the petty verbal cruelties of the late 1970s middle-American domestic idiom is faultless, her eye for the telling detail as ruthless as a hawk's. She knows her characters inside out, down to the very last nastiness and snivelling sentiment, and she spares us nothing. The characters themselves are representative rather than exceptional: both halves of a splitting marriage, the husband enraged because he feels he married the wrong woman and had the wrong children, the wife obsessed, for lack of anything better, by her dead dog; their children, whose mutual hatred mirrors that of their parents, the boy fat and unhappy, the girl despising everything except Peter Frampton; the husband's young lover, the lover's ex-lover; the ex-lover's lover. There are loose connections among them, but part of Beattie's point is the looseness of the connections.

All could be illustrations for Christopher Lasch's *The Culture of Narcissism,* demanding love and commitment from those around them but unwilling to give it. They feel that their lives are entirely out of control, that they lack power and cannot be expected to take responsibility for the consequences of their actions. Their dominant moods are anger and self-pity, and we find their triviality enraging until we come to see them not as minor sadists but as drowning people clutching each other's throats out of sheer panic. Adrift in a world of seemingly pointless events, bombarded with endless media flotsam, trapped in a junkyard of unsatisfactory objects, plugged into the monologues of others who appear to be deaf to their own, these characters cry out for meaning and coherence, but their world hands them nothing more resonant than popular song titles and T-shirt slogans.

Despite it all they remain yearning romantics. What they want from each other is nothing less than salvation, and Beattie's vision is ultimately a religious one. With religion having been designated as uncool, however, they're stuck in Middle Earth. Heaven is being in love, and stoned too if you can manage it, and Hell is a family barbecue. In fact, not just Hell but the entire cosmology is other people. "Save me," says Cynthia, as she falls into the arms of her just-returned lover Spangle. We know he can't.

The only answer for these glutted but spiritually famished people would be God or magic. God appears only as a T-shirt slogan—"God Is Coming And She Is Pissed"—and magic is represented by a third-rate party magician who gets a crush on Cynthia in a laundromat. He's a fraud, but he does represent magic of a kind: his love for Cynthia, unrequited though it is, is the only bit of disinterested altruism in the book. He doesn't want to possess her, he wants to wish her well, and it is through his magic binoculars that Cynthia sees her vanished lover as he finally appears again. It isn't much, but in view of the odds, it's a tiny miracle.

The society Beattie depicts is chaotic and random. Things happen to these characters, they change, but there is no plot in the traditional sense of the term. The major event, the shooting of the husband's daughter by his ten-year-old son, is an accident, and the general reaction to it is stunned disbelief. "Things just fall into place," says one character, commenting on *Vanity Fair.* "Maybe things just fell quickly because of gravity," thinks another, "and when they stopped, you said they were in place." Which is a comment also on Beattie's particular art. Sometimes the reader feels caught in an out-of-control short story, sometimes in a locked train compartment filled with salesman's samples and colossally boring egomaniacs, but most of the time, thanks to Beattie's skill, her novel not only convinces but entrances. The details are small, but the picture of our lives and times built up from them is devastating.

Margaret Atwood. *Washington Post Book World.* May 25, 1980, pp. 1, 9

Miss Beattie has a real subject, and a highly interesting one. Her subject is the fate of her own generation, the generation that was in college and graduate school in the late 1960s and early 1970s. This generation, as everyone knows, grew up in the shadow of the Vietnam war, and it was the first to have a free hand with sex and drugs, to know splendor both in and on the grass. I recall, in the middle 1960s, a *Partisan Review* symposium, those occasions on which intellectuals are invited to say things they are sure to regret later, in which nearly all the participants had a good word for the young. Everyone agreed that this was to be a generation of great promise. The members of this generation felt that they were promising, too, but they also felt that they were, in some odd and never quite defined way, promised. Promised what! Because of their own intrinsic superiority, moral and intellectual, they felt they were promised a freer and richer and happier life than any known before here in America and possibly on earth.

But the world of the 1960s ended neither with a bang nor with a whimper but, it would seem from Ann Beattie's fiction, with an album, "Rachel cried when she heard Dylan's *Self Portrait* album, because, to her, that meant everything was over." In the story "The Lawn Party" from the collection *Secrets and Surprises* (1979) we read: "When Janis Joplin died Elizabeth cried for six days." A character in Miss Beattie's first novel, *Chilly Scenes of Winter* (1978), remarks of his sister: "You could be happy, too, Sam, if you were nineteen in 1975, and you hadn't had your eyes opened in the 60's." In the same novel another character says: "Everybody's so pathetic. What is it? Is it just the end of the 60's?" And a character in *Falling in Place* (1980), Miss Beattie's most recent novel, remarks: "There were a lot of things for which graduate school did not prepare you." One of them being, the reader is tempted to answer, the rest of life.

About all of Ann Beattie's fiction there is something of an after-party atmosphere. Her stories begin after the 1960s binge is done and gone. No mention is made of the Democratic convention of 1968, of the marches and protests, of any other of the momentous happenings of those years. In one of her stories a maimed Vietnam veteran appears, in another a woman's brother is mentioned as having been killed in Vietnam, and in yet another a veteran is said to be unable to stop talking about Vietnam. Yet Miss Beattie does not hammer away at Vietnam or speak of politics except obliquely, though a foul air of things gone wrong hovers about her characters and their world. Anxiety, disappointment, despair, these are the pollutants in the Beattie atmosphere, and both characters and readers are made to choke on them.

Already in *Distortions* (1976), her first book of stories, the general pattern of Ann Beattie's fiction is set. *Distortions* is very much a young writer's book, and hence rather more experimental than the more mature Ann Beattie's fiction will be. The book's opening story is about a marriage of dwarfs. Another story is done in short takes, rather like blackout sketches. . . . But the less experimental Ann Beattie's stories are, the better. Taken by themselves, some of the straighter stories are quite impressive—"Wolf Dreams," for example, written when Miss Beattie was only twenty-six. Nearly all the stories show a high degree of professional polish. The dialogue always feels right; the interior monologue, too, seems on target. The flat style, a Beattie trademark, is already in use in *Distortions*. . . .

"The important thing," one character in a story in *Distortions* advises another, "was to know when to give up." Here is a note Ann Beattie has held through all her books. The first story in *The Burning House* ends thus: "What Ruth had known all along: what will happen can't be stopped. Aim for grace."

Amazing grace. If grace is what Ann Beattie's characters aim for, very few achieve it. But then they don't aim very carefully. Not much in life interests them. Politics doesn't—though they are all convinced that America is hopeless—neither conventional politics nor emotional politics. "There aren't any answers," says a Beattie character. "That's what I've got against woman's liberation. Nothing personal." Although people have love affairs, once a couple moves in together, the end is in sight. Sex is no big deal. Miss Beattie rarely describes it. Detailed description tends to be reserved for getting stoned. Few relationships endure. Work is pointless. Things fall apart; the center, hell, in Ann Beattie's fiction not even the fringes seem to hold.

Joseph Epstein. *Commentary*. March 1983,
pp. 55–56

Beattie is perhaps the first and the finest laureate of that generation of Americans born to a society built on quicksand and doomed to a life in the long, ambiguous shadow of the 1960s. The characters in her stories are left over from that abandoned decade, hung over with its legacy, saddled with hand-me-down customs that have gone out of style. Usually in their early thirties, they stand for all those who were neither incapacitated by Vietnam nor unhinged by drugs, but unsettled only by their innocence of both extremes. Sprung loose from certainties without being swept up by revolution, old enough to have witnessed turmoil, yet too young to have joined or beaten it, they find themselves stranded in that famous space between two worlds, one dying, the other powerless to be born. Yes, they routinely—if not religiously—smoke dope, crash on sofas, sing along to Bob Dylan, shack up, and hang out; but they also think of ardor, passion, change itself as cobwebbed anachronisms. For there is resolution in revolution; and if the 1960s were a time of decisiveness, however reckless, or wayward, or violent, the 1970s recoiled into hedged bets and hesitations. In the world of Beattie's people, conviction has followed convention into premature retirement; commitment is a dirty word. . . .

Beattie has always crafted metaphors that precisely reflect such off-balance lives slipping out of control. One of her latest novels is titled *Falling in Place;* stories in this collection are called "Learning to Fall," "Gravity," "Waiting," "Afloat," and "Like Glass." They are preoccupied with weightlessness and drifting, with water and air. Characters do not sink or swim; they float, or—as the modish phrase has it—they go with the flow. It is the unspoken irony of the title story that nothing seems to be "burning"; on the contrary, Beattie marked out the frosty and fragmented terrain that has become her own with the title of her first novel—*Chilly Scenes of Winter*. . . .

Her parched, exhausted stories themselves seem numb. Her wan sentences and neutral cadences follow one upon another with sharp, chill clarity. Wandering like their characters' days, her anodyne stories have no resolution—in part because their people can't make sense of life, in part because nothing ends in any case. As if to invert the eventful frenzy and clamorous manic swings of the world according to television, a Beattie story is naked of explosions or emphases. It has neither strain, nor looseness; neither lyricism, nor radiance, nor rhythm, nor hope. Reading it is like driving for mile after mile down a straight road through a snow-covered desert. . . .

It cannot be denied that Beattie's stories are perfect mirror images of the protagonists and predicaments they describe. But that may be their problem. They surrender to diminished expectations; they change location and little else; they loiter and go nowhere. Because her theme so rarely varies or evolves (save for on gay and giddy *jeu d'esprit* called "Happy," an exception to prove the rule), Beattie's tales seem almost massproduced. . . .

[U]ltimately, these stories may best be regarded as a collection of photos in an album: each records a situation, revives a memory, and redeems nothing. Considering them is like consulting a doctor's X ray of contemporary America. But unless he is impeccably sterilized, a doctor is vulnerable to the very diseases he treats; just so, the closeness of Beattie's manner to her matter can be dangerous. Privy to anomie, her stories become party to it; faithful to the details of the world, they seem treacherous to the energy and heroic idealism that are her country's saving grace. Her disciplined, level-headed realism—exemplary of the meticulous tradition she upholds—finally passes on to the reader, as if by contagion, a melancholy torpor that suffocates. And so, having paid one's respects to the tasteful and well-ordered room of her fiction, one yearns only to escape, or to fling its windows open and admit the wild, fresh air of possibility.

Pico Iyer. Partisan Review. 50, 1983, pp. 549–53

Beattie's 1980 novel, *Falling in Place,* typifies the general sense of discontinuity, emptiness, and boredom pervading her world. The novel focuses on the unhappy members of a suburban Connecticut family and the people around them. Although we are presented with family, lovers and friends, no one is fully connecting with anyone else. If the Knapp family is a unit, it is bound only by the accidents of birth and a mutually felt anger and frustration. The characters not only fail to understand each other, they cannot understand; they cannot understand, much less control, their own real feelings or the patterns that their lives have taken. John Knapp tries to express his exasperation to his children: "Don't you think I might already realize that my existence is a little silly? Do you think I had visions of working at an ad agency dancing in my head like sugarplums? Everybody I work with . . . is stoned on Valium all day." Knapp's bored, aloof daughter, Mary, responds: "I haven't finished the book but that's what *Vanity Fair* is like. Things just fall into place." Knapp thinks this is a remarkable insight and wonders how his daughter could be failing English. He also realizes, though, that if she truly thought this from reading the book or "from what she knew of life," then why should she make the effort to succeed? "Of course, if that was what she thought, then there wasn't much point in her trying to organize her life or in any of the things he had believed about getting ahead, the necessity of getting ahead, when he was her age." Many of Beattie's characters cannot imagine a future that they have a role in shaping; they cannot think through the consequences of their actions or, as a result, feel any meaning or purpose in their present lives.

In Beattie's first novel, *Chilly Scenes of Winter,* the sense of futility and empty boredom is best exemplified by the daily encounter between the central character, Charles, and a blind man who runs a concession stand. Charles routinely picks up a candy bar and the blind man routinely asks, "What have you got?" At one point Charles reflects, "What have you got?" The blind man there every day to remind him that, at the close of the day, he has nothing. It adds insult to injury to have to answer, "A peanut butter cup." The last line is typical of Charles's, and Beattie's, ironic, self-deprecating humor. Yet the humor has a bitter edge and irony always implies a distance from its subject. Charles's detached self-reflection is characteristic of the general sense of detachment the novel conveys, a detachment the characters feel from one another as well as from themselves. Life for Charles is as predictable and meaningless as his daily routine with the blind man. "Predictable. Everything is predictable," he thinks, and the thought becomes a motif that runs throughout the text. His stepfather, Pete, accuses him of never having done anything exciting in his life and Charles replies, "There's not much exciting to do." Life, excluding his obsession with his unattainable former girlfriend, Laura, holds no meaning or promise; the world, like the blind man, is a blank presence that cannot recognize or affirm his existence and that can offer nothing more than a peanut butter cup.

In *Love Always,* one character quits the job that had defined his life for several years and videotapes himself cleaning out his office: "Everything might have been anyone's. Looking at the videotape, he was convinced, long before it was over, that he had never been there at all, in spite of all the things he saw himself lugging away." . . . The title *Love Always* refers to the closing of an ambiguous love letter one of the characters receives. The letter's recipient, Lucy, ponders whether the words are flippant or sincere, finally feeling "unsure of what was or ever had been true" about their relationship, about her lover's feelings or about her own. . . .

Barbara Ann Schapiro. *Literature and the Relational Self* (New York: New York University Press, 1994), pp. 145–47

BEAUVOIR, SIMONE DE (FRANCE) 1908–86

In the novels of Jean-Paul Sartre . . . it is the individual who receives the chief emphasis. . . . But in the novels of Simone de Beauvoir the focus is kept chiefly upon a conflict of free beings and the problems which they encounter as they struggle to achieve an authentic co-existence. The problem raised in *L'Invitée* is how one can preserve his uniqueness as an individual while participating in collective relationships. . . . In *Le Sang des autres* the problem is whether an individual has the right to involve anyone in a conflict or cause which may or may not succeed and which may cost the one involved his life. . . . For her characters, liberty is not a pursuit but a state of living . . . ; it is not an abstraction, but is realized by the individual only as he participates with others in the affairs of their common existence.

Gwendolyn Bays. *Yale French Studies*.
Spring-Summer, 1948, pp. 106–7, 111

Simone de Beauvoir's characters [in *The Blood of Others*] are practicing existentialists, literally mouthpieces for the basic tenets of the philosophy. It would seem that she has succeeded where Sartre has failed. She violates some of our conceptions of good narrative writing, true; but she has written the real thesis novel in an economical, sometimes flat style which conceals a remarkably sustained note of suspense and mounting excitement due to the sheer vitality and force of her ideas.This is perhaps the way a novel of ideas should be presented, not loosely sprawled all over the place, trying to appeal to three or four levels at the same time.

Richard McLaughlin. *Saturday Review of
Literature*. July 17, 1948, p. 13

The Second Sex, by Simone de Beauvoir, is one of the few great books of our era. It flows from a quality men often deny to women: genius—at least by my definition of that lofty capacity. Genius, I think, is the ability to discover or to create a new *category* or a new *dimension* of human knowledge, human understanding, or human experience. Simone de Beauvoir has finally succeeded in adding that much insight to the subject of woman and the twice-larger subject of human sexuality. That is why I feel no one can leave her book unread and still be considered intellectually up-to-date. It makes a fresh contribution to awareness that cannot be missed any more than the contribution of Freud, say, or Einstein or Darwin—without the onset of a private cultural lag.

Philip Wylie. *Saturday Review of Literature*.
February 21, 1953, p. 28

There are so many things I want to say about [*The Second Sex*]. First, that it is a great book, a book that will be read long after most works which have been written on the subject will have been forgotten. Second, in its qualities of analysis, restrained eloquence, and the influence it is bound to have upon human thought and conduct, it ranks next to John Stuart Mill's *Subjection of Women* (1869). Third, one cannot help being impressed by the skill with which the author has avoided the pitfalls into which so many others have fallen in discussing such thoroughly misunderstood institutions, for example, as matriarchy. Fourth, the balance, good common sense, and profound insight of the author constitute a most refreshing and illuminating experience in an area in which the discussion is usually tendentious and biased. Fifth, the

book is beautifully written in all senses of the word. And sixth, while the
book could have been written by a man, it took a woman to do it. . . .

Woman, as the author points out, is brought up without ever being impressed with the necessity of taking charge of her own existence. Men have
taken it over, and have oppressed women; as oppressors they cannot be
expected to make a move of gratuitous generosity. It will be up to the women
of the world fully to emancipate themselves. Some men will help, but for the
present women will largely be forced to do the necessary work for themselves. Meanwhile, Simone de Beauvoir's *The Second Sex* may serve them
not only as a breviary but also as a call to action.

Ashley Montagu. *Saturday Review of*
Literature. February 21, 1953, p. 29

Just as all the men [in *The Mandarins*] are alike, the women are varied and
autonomous, simultaneously real and fictional. . . . As soon as a woman—
whatever her character may be—steps into a narrative by Simone de Beauvoir, and as soon as the question of love is raised, everything becomes firmer
and brighter. Simply from the narrative related by Anne—indeed, simply
from those fragments in her account that concern her brief love affair in
America with Lewis Brogan—one can extract one of the most striking love
stories ever written by a woman. This story contains everything—the sudden
and heart-rending revelation, the wonder of the first night, the great fire of
happiness, the ashes of the separations, the anguish of the silences, the alternations between hope and doubt, the ambiguity of the reunions. . . . At the
end of the novel, having lost her lover and feeling certain that neither her
daughter nor her husband nor her friends need her any more, Anne comes
very close to doubting that there is meaning in anything. Yet it is she who,
through the passion for life she radiates, makes the novel pulsate. Nothing
escapes her; she does not lie about anything. . . .

The novel's universe is one in which nobody else lies either. The women
especially are ferociously honest; even the unbearable Nadine plans her evil
deeds openly. The reader shudders to see Anne so willingly recognize the
face she will have in ten years in the faces of other women; and also to see
her recognize that saying so is a more subtle way of maintaining her self-
esteem as a woman. It is certain that this particularly feminine keenness,
toughness, and shrewdness constitute a great deal of the power of *The*
Mandarins.

Dominique Aury. *Nouvelle Revue Française.*
December, 1954, pp. 1082–84

By writing [in *The Mandarins*] about men corroded by their inner life, perpetually busy reconciling irreconcilables—their ideals, their private lives, and
political reality—she has written the most humane novel that has appeared
in France in recent years.

Humane, for there can be no more representative description of man than one that presents intellectuals forced by their very craft to harmonize the happenings of their lives and the dictates of consciences. It is also a novel that is true in the purest sense of the term, for Simone de Beauvoir, a philosopher, cannot handle fiction otherwise than by describing step by step things she has experienced.

Madeleine Chapsal. *The Reporter.*
January 27, 1955, p. 16

What a course has been traversed between *The Guest* and *The Mandarins!* . . . The remarkable fact is that the most recent novel has all the qualities generally found in a first novel: spontaneity, rich inner life, and many varied characters. One obtains from reading it the impression of vigor and youth, and at the same time the impression that an experience has been revealed in its totality, as happens in those first books in which the author tells everything.

Everything flows naturally, and everything seems matured in this novel. The reader may prefer *The Guest* because of its classical strictness and its philosophical basis, or *All Men Are Mortal* because of the originality of its theme and the existential anguish that emerges from it. But *The Mandarins* has much richer resonances. The multiplicity of the themes, the vigorous tone, and above all the emotional sensitivity revealed in Anne's story make this novel perhaps Beauvoir's masterpiece. It is undoubtedly not by chance that the heroine of the book, unlike Beauvoir's other heroines, is a married woman and a mother (and even soon to be a grandmother!). . . . She calmly accepts the limitations imposed by her sex. . . .

As different as they may be, all of Beauvoir's female characters accept their condition as women. . . . But until the great achievement of *The Mandarins,* there was still something cerebral and slightly artificial in the portrayal of these women, who had only a distant relationship to their creator. It was in *The Second Sex* that Beauvoir had put all of herself.

Geneviève Gennari. *Simone de Beauvoir*
(Paris: Éditions Universitaires, 1958),
pp. 76–77, 80

Two themes may be distinguished in Simone de Beauvoir's writings, that receive particular attention and to some extent account for the specific quality of her work. These are *womanhood* and *the role of the intellectual.* . . . Simone de Beauvoir is indeed speaking of herself, when she offers us the example of a woman who has rejected the conventional paths trodden by womanhood, but this individual example may acquire the force of a principle. It is a principle which she submits to ceaseless examination. Not only in her life but in her books also. And when she defends the "second sex," she speaks of all women to all women. She speaks to them of a woman's rights, of her right to choose her own life, to assume responsibility for her own destiny and to refuse what society would thrust upon her.

And a like responsibility is involved—this time on the political plane—when she portrays the French "mandarins" of the post-war years. Just as a woman can no longer be satisfied to be attractive and nothing more, similarly the intellectual cannot continue to play the seer, enveloping himself in a timeless purity and timeless responsibility.

Jacques Ehrmann. Yale French Studies.
Spring-Summer, 1961, pp. 26, 32

Mme. de Beauvoir's existence has always been governed not by Heideggerian *angst*, as orthodoxy demands and as earlier writings seemed to indicate, but by a relentless drive to *happiness*. . . . Her capacity for absorbing what she calls "happiness" is truly frightening. And the salvation she pursues is typical of our age, insofar as it is a strictly individual one; she must build her happiness all alone, *toute seule, sans secours.* . . . How can we save ourselves, concretely, in the absence of God, if not by surpassing our fellow human beings in all sorts of worldly endeavors? . . . Mme. de Beauvoir is the voice of all the other feminine first-prize winners. She reinterprets the traditional culture of France from the perspective of the career woman; she expresses a viewpoint entirely novel to the French social set-up in a language worthy of a long intellectual past.

René Girard. Yale French Studies. Spring-
Summer, 1961, pp. 41–43

The characters in *The Guest* lack any "moral sense." They do not find good and evil in things. They do not believe that human life, by itself, makes any definite demands, or that it follows a self-contained law as trees or bees do. They consider the world (including society and their own bodies) as an "unfinished piece of work"—to use [Nicolas de] Malebranche's profound phrase—which they question with curiosity and treat in various ways.

It is not so much their actions which bring down censure on these characters. Books, after all, are full of adultery, perversion, and crime, and the critics have come across them before this. The smallest town has more than one *ménage à trois.* Such a "family" is still a family. But how is one to accept the fact that Pierre, Françoise, and Xavière are totally ignorant of the holy natural law of the couple and that they try in all honesty—and without, moreover, any hint of sexual complicity—to form a trio? The sinner is always accepted, even in the strictest societies, because he is part of the system and, as a sinner, does not question its principles. What one finds unbearable in Pierre and Françoise is their artless disavowal of morality, that air of candor and youth, that absolute lack of gravity, dizziness, and remorse. In brief, they think as they act and act as they think. . . .

True morality does not consist in following exterior rules or in respecting objective values: there are no ways to *be* just or to *be* saved. One would do better to pay less attention to the unusual situation of the three characters in *The Guest* and more to the good faith, the loyalty to promises, the respect for others, the generosity and the seriousness of the two principals [Pierre and Françoise]. For the value is there. It consists of actively being what we are by chance, of establishing that communication with others and with ourselves for which our temporal structure gives us the opportunity and of which our liberty is only the rough outline.

> Maurice Merleau-Ponty. *Sense and Non-Sense* (Evanston, Illinois: Northwestern University Press, 1964), pp. 38–40

In *Old Age* Simone de Beauvoir has written an extraordinary, altogether engrossing, large work on growing old. I cannot take issue with it since in its sweep I have learned all that I know about the matter. Personal experience and observation are confirmed and enriched at every point by the learned intensity of the book and the generosity of the feelings. A fluent use of history and literature, the portraits of great and humble persons who were given long life, the lessons of philosophy and the power of social indignation—these come together in a prodigious outburst of energy and imagination. . . .

About our life today, *Old Age* is a fierce indictment of society's indifference and cruelty toward old people. The degradation, the hatred of the elderly are scarcely recognized and their plight, shrouded not so much in ignorance as in the determination to ignore, is harsh beyond all necessity. . . . The only way to give old age decency is, in the author's view, to give "value to the life of others, by means of love, friendship, indignation, compassion." The huge space between those privileged, either by talent or class, and the great body of mankind is at its most dishonorable and unjust in the case of the old. Millions of people are literally abandoned, "scrapped," as if while still breathing they were already dead, buried alive.

The ruins of time—a tragic, inescapable subject.

> Elizabeth Hardwick. *The New York Times.* May 14, 1972, pp. 1, 42

The death of Simone de Beauvoir's mother is the most detailed of all the encounters with death [in her work]. It is the only death to which an entire book is devoted although it might be said that the memoirs are, in fact, about the death of Simone de Beauvoir. This book [*A Very Easy Death*], in which there is more mother and less I, is perhaps Simone de Beauvoir's best. Neither fiction nor memoir, *A Very Easy Death* is a *récit-reportage* [short-narrative-journalism] shorter in length and more tightly constructed than Simone de Beauvoir's other writings. . . .

The reader who is familiar with the three volumes of Simone de Beauvoir's memoirs is familiar, too, with the figure of Françoise de Beauvoir. Simone de Beauvoir portrays her mother as a rather attractive but silly woman, a willing victim of the Catholic milieu to which she belonged and enthusiastically adhered. The reader shares Simone de Beauvoir's resentment of the innumerable prejudices that clogged Françoise de Beauvoir's mind and heart and that restricted her capacity to feel and see. Simone de Beauvoir is quite explicit about her own preference for her non-conformist father. She was never very close to her mother, and one senses that her revolt against the despicable bourgeoisie is, in part, an outgrowth of her revolt against Françoise de Beauvoir. . . . [But] what she thought she felt about her mother does not coincide with what she feels during the long agony.

The pity, horror, and helplessness the reader of *A Very Easy Death* feels, corresponds both to the author's central emotion and to the underlying theme. No attempt is made at any moment in the main body of the *récit* to transcend the facts of dying or the sentiments, gestures, and words of the woman who is dying and the daughters who are watching her die. The irony of both the Dylan Thomas quotation which is used as an epigraph, "Do not go gentle into that good night," and of the title is continued throughout the book in a courageous desire to break through some of the simplistic left-wing ideology that often replaces intelligent analysis in her other books. When the bourgeois Catholic images which she had so firmly and so conveniently affixed to her mother are displaced, a human being begins to die, and Simone de Beauvoir begins to suffer for someone other than herself. Sartre is absent from all but two scenes in the *récit,* and this significant absence helps to explain Simone de Beauvoir's ability to sustain, for so long a time, an excruciating lucidity.

Elaine Marks. *Simone de Beauvoir:*
Encounters with Death (New Brunswick:
Rutgers University Press, 1973), pp. 100–102

In *The Second Sex,* de Beauvoir expands the analysis of oppression, freedom, and morality she began in *The Ethics of Ambiguity.* "Every time transcendence falls back into immanence, stagnation, there is a degradation of existence into the 'en soi'—the brutish life of subjection to given conditions— and of liberty into constraint and contingence. At one time, in early civilization, there were material reasons for men becoming the dominators and women the dominated, but these reasons have long been obsolete. This downfall represents a moral fault if the subject consents to it; if it is inflicted upon him, it spells frustration and oppression." Women who want to be the subject of their lives as much as do men, are confined to immanence, to being an object: "What particularly signalizes the situation of woman is that she—a free and autonomous being like all human creatures—nevertheless finds herself living in a world where men compel her to assume the status of Other." Unable to reach out toward new liberties through projects in the world, women live unduly tied to their bodies, their physiology; through narcissism, they make projects of themselves, but they thereby only increase their situation as the Other. . . .

Unfortunately, . . . this enormously creative project of determining women's "moral inventiveness" within the framework of oppression is only unevenly accomplished. (In fact, more than thirty years later, the project awaits furthering by any writer.) Instead, *The Second Sex* has a lumpiness, in which oppression is described with great vigor for paragraphs or pages on end, and only at times interspersed with sections in which one sees how women choose or act upon their (greatly constricted) freedom, pushing it beyond its previous borders. Of course, the overweighting of the oppression side of the dialectic has also been emphasized in the English edition (and in the most current French edition, as well) by the omission of the lives of fifty French painters, writers, soldiers, doctors, etc., who pushed beyond the borders of their world and so created greater freedom for themselves and others. Still, the integration of freedom and oppression doesn't work perfectly on every page. One can imagine de Beauvoir in the Bibliothèque Nationale. She had begun the project, she says, not out of being a feminist, but merely to try to understand what it meant to be a woman. The impressions caused by her reading must have bowled her over! It must have been hard to remember the sense of freedom and choice she had sought to keep alive.

Simone de Beauvoir's pleasure in her memoirs when inner freedom and necessity seem contained within each other show both that she (like most others) finds comfort in being in harmony with herself, and that in her youth and early adulthood this inner harmony seemed most likely to be produced by loving someone who gave her life direction. Yet her life has not been one geared toward comfort; on the contrary, she had often sacrificed the least of the known in order to think and act in ways that grant herself and others greater freedom. If there is the anguish of this discomfort in her fiction and later memoirs, it is an honest anguish—of the price that everyone must pay.

Carole Ascher. In Alice Kessler-Harris and
William McBrien, eds. *Faith of a (Woman)*
Writer (1984; rpt. Westport, Connecticut:
Greenwood Press, 1988), pp. 176–79

Simone de Beauvoir's only play, *Les Bouches inutiles,* was first produced on the Paris stage in November 1945. Although it is a major work exploring the relationship between gender and power predating *The Second Sex* by about four years, unfortunately it has been almost completely neglected by critics and scholars of her work. However, in 1945, critic Marc Beigbeder wrote of *Les Bouches inutiles,* "It has been a long time since we have seen a play of as great scope as that of Simone de Beauvoir, alongside it even *Caligula* and *The Flies* appear to be bourgeois psychological dramas." Simone de Beauvoir herself recalls the play in several brief passages of her memoirs in which she gives it short shrift, depreciating the play's originality and ground-breaking themes. She records in *Force of Circumstance* that Genet sat next to her for one of the performances and kept whispering, "This isn't what the theater's about! This isn't theater at all. . . ." In the end, she dismissed the play (though not, she added, without reservation), saying, "My mistake was to pose a political problem in terms of abstract morality." In spite of this early and seemingly categoric dismissal, a reading of *Les Bouches inutiles* today raises serious philosophical and political issues which are of growing concern in our nuclear age. The themes of war, gender, and society are conjoined in a situation far more poignant and realistic than the legendary *Lysistrata*. Simone de Beauvoir's play poses the following questions: in a world of scarce resources, in a crisis of political legitimation where the stakes appear to be life or death, how shall people govern themselves? How is power defined and established? How is power shared? How are societal values determined? Are some persons seen as having more intrinsic worth than others? On what basis? What does it mean to be useful or useless to society? How do the governed consent to their rulers? Can they participate in their fate to ameliorate it? Or is it only possible to perpetuate a democracy at the intervention and the decision of the governing? . . .

   Les Bouches inutiles is remarkable in that it was and is a very contemporary play. Feminists of the 1980s find dramatized the issues of comparable worth and the continuing struggle for democratic justice. But we also find a parable of the betrayal we experience if we accept to be governed by the principles of the New Right. If we trust that men will recognize our worth and grant us equality, we will be disappointed, for recognition will be achieved only with our collective struggle. A few enlightened men under certain conditions may be reasoned with, but government is illegitimate if women cannot participate. Projected into the past rather than the future, the play does not present radical solutions because it fails to present new, collective action by women. Its unsettled ending is, however, conscious of these flaws. Simone de Beauvoir's theoretical achievement here is nonetheless significant. She sensed that male alienation from reproduction affects political decision making and is thus a crucial issue for feminism to address. Attempting to present the dilemma and choices of an entire town, she used the theater as a medium for exploring gender relations in society rather than the plight of a single "hero." Simone de Beauvoir thus began a critique of subjectivity and legitimacy in government which is continued in her later work. In so establishing the terms of "the woman question," *Les Bouches inutiles* is a powerful forerunner to *Le Deuxième sexe*.

Virginia M. Fichera. *Yale French Studies.*
72, 1986, pp. 51–52, 64

Myth, mystification, mystique: all of these words have been used to describe the aura with which the modern world has suffused the idea of motherhood. From early childhood, Simone de Beauvoir resisted this mystique, insisting on imagining that her dolls were her pupils rather than her children. Her fictional works served to some extent as a testing ground for her very strong feelings about the societal pressures which had for centuries propelled young women into an unthinking acceptance of the role of wife and mother. For the first time in history, women of the mid-twentieth century had access to safe methods of controlling their fertility. Simone de Beauvoir's fiction seems designed to make sure that, for her readers, motherhood will always be a conscious choice rather than a passive yielding to tradition.

In the characters Simone de Beauvoir created, she explored the extremes of varying approaches to the raising of children. She worked through her ambivalence about the mixture of love and domination with which her own mother brought her up as well as her rage at the manipulative possessiveness of Zaza Mabille's supposedly well-intentioned mother. She observed with a clinical eye the effect of an overabundance of maternal devotion on the self-respect and sense of identity of mature women. Manipulative, long suffering, perfectionistic, seductive: Beauvoir's fictional mothers are eloquent spokeswomen for the author's repeated warnings about the dangers of concentrating all of one's energy on one's husband and children. Along with *The Second Sex* and the volumes of her autobiography, Simone de Beauvoir's novels and short stories constitute a giant step toward the demystification of motherhood.

Yolanda Astarita Patterson. Yale French
Studies. 72, 1986, p. 105

BEDFORD, SYBILLE (GREAT BRITAIN) 1911–

The reader who expects a book about Mexico [*The Sudden View*] to be a Catholic threnody or a proletarian paean will be disappointed. Nobody else will. Quadrilingual, Mrs. Bedford writes with delicate grace an English prose admirably adapted to record her highly personal impressions of that extravagantly beautiful, bloody country. Her decision to go there was determined by a chance reading of Madame Calderon de la Barca. . . . In Mrs. Bedford's company . . . nothing is obvious, everything is new. . . .

Written without indignation or Laurencian twitchings of the solar plexus, with a detachment at once ironic and sympathetic, these sections [of travel routes] still do not reveal Mrs. Bedford at her best. The most remarkable part of her book is entirely original. Others have written well on Maximilian and Carlotta, but nobody else, at least nobody who can write, has stayed with Don Otavio on one of the remoter shores of Lake Chapala.

John Davenport. New Statesman and
Nation. March 28, 1953, p. 374

So that this shall not appear as a notice of unrelieved, and therefore perhaps rather dubious, praise, let me state at once where it seems to me to fall short of extreme excellence. There is a certain clumsiness in the telling of the story [*A Legacy*] that reveals the unpracticed hand. The time sequence is unnecessarily disturbed. . . . There is a descent, rather past the middle, where we have too much talk between Sarah and Caroline, as though the author had taken a deep, unaccustomed draft of Henry James and become momentarily intoxicated. There is, to my mind, a slight improbability in the mechanics of the final catastrophe. There is some theological uncertainty. . . . But when these few blots have been noted there remains a book of entirely delicious quality. The plot is intricate and admirably controlled. The theme is not superficially original; two families vastly dissimilar, the one Jewish, inartistic millionaires, the other slightly decadent Catholic aristocrats, become joined in marriage. That sort of situation has been employed often enough before. But here everything is new, cool, witty, elegant, varying in range from the horrors of Prussian military education to the farce of monkeys in the Kaiserhof Hotel. The scenes of the baptism of the Jewish heiress are uproariously funny and totally free of offense to either religion. There is no hint of (odious, cant word) nostalgia in the book. The loveable, civilized "hero" is ruthlessly stripped and exposed. Only Gottlieb, the butler, maintains his ascendancy uncompromised. The rest are "all, all of a piece throughout"; frauds and failures and each event in the elaborate structure has a direct causal connection with the revelation of them.

We know nothing of the author's age, nationality or religion. But we gratefully salute a new artist.

Evelyn Waugh. *The Spectator.* April 13,
1956, p. 498

A Legacy appears to be only the second book written by Sybille Bedford, her first being a record of a Mexican journey. The evidence is that this is her first novel. If so, she is a writer of extraordinary power. Her book is unconventional, bold, experimental, but not always easy to follow, and unmistakably sincere in spite of some eccentricity. It has considerable faults and is probably not a masterpiece for that reason, but it is written with genius. By that I do not mean that is as good as Shakespeare, but that it is manifestly written throughout from a deep inner impulse. The reader never doubts that the observation is the result of firmly grasped experience. A more practiced hand at novel-writing would have arranged some of the experience in a way which made it accessible to more readers, for sometimes quite simple events require concentrated study of Miss Bedford's prose before they become clear; but no novelist could convey with more decisiveness a "vision" of how life moves in certain conditions.

Christopher Sykes. *Encounter.* June, 1956,
p. 93

This [*The Trial of Dr. Adams*] is an extraordinarily exciting book. The excitement it arouses is of two kinds, on two quite different levels. As the factual report of a famous trial for murder, it reads like a good thriller, tightening the life-and-death suspense to the point where we can feel the hangman's knot. And as an exposition of human justice at its careful best, the book is a catharsis we take with a sigh of mixed emotions—relief, yes; also disappointed curiosity; also gratitude and hope and quiet applause.

It may seem an odd subject for a writer like Sybille Bedford to have tackled. But she is an original, and can be expected never to turn up twice in the same place.

T. S. Matthews. *The New York Times.*
March 1, 1959, p. 6

Chiseled and economical in the paragraph, it [*A Favorite of the Gods*] is yet leisurely and discursive in the whole: a gentle stroll through a classical landscape in which the characters do not seem to be participating in action so much as creating a flavor of life.

While this does not give it quite enough body for a novel it is agreeable enough as a memoir of the sort of life available to cultivated young women with cash and connections in the earlier part of this century. Anna, the American heiress, makes an unsuccessful marriage with an Italian prince; her daughter Constanza repeats the pattern. Unhappiness is relative; I found I could face their well-cushioned difficulties with equanimity and very little involvement. Interest is also lured away by the settings—by Mrs. Bedford's disciplined nostalgia for a world in which the grand European express trains sweep the privileged from one little oasis of grace and intellect to another.

Andrew Leslie. *The Manchester Guardian*
Weekly. January 17, 1963, p. 7

Sybille Bedford's *Aldous Huxley* strikes one as in fact both unlikely and extraordinary: unlikely that it should ever have been brought off, most extraordinary in its achievement.

Here again the mystery was no doubt at the bottom of things, for Sybille Bedford seems to have been destined to write this great book. All her life and all her work seem almost to have been designed to acquire the skills, the techniques, the knowledge, and the experience which, directed by a peculiar genius, could produce this one-of-a-kind book—virtually a genre unto itself. But though the *Huxley* is generically unique, and a major triumph in its discovery of the exact form to recreate the moral odyssey that was Huxley's life, it is also the logical culmination—in retrospect, the predestined, foreseen, necessary climax—of all of Sybille Bedford's earlier works: on the one hand, the three volumes of fiction—a fiction deeply committed to memory and to a memorial reshaping and recovery of the past; and, on the other hand, the three volumes of observation, speculation, reportage, moral journalism, exploratory nonfiction—whatever we are to call *The Sudden View. The Faces of Justice,* and *The Trial of Dr. Adams.* Perhaps it would be more just, however, and certainly truer to one's sense of *Aldous Huxley,* to speak not of Sybille Bedford's life and work alone as having been shaped to this end but of Huxley's wildly improbable and extraordinary life also as having been destined to provide the subject for this book. In *Aldous Huxley* we have something like the perfect symbiosis of artist and subject matter. Sybille Bedford living that life necessary to write just this biography, Huxley living that life necessary to provide her with the requisite stuff of her art. Working from both ends toward this culmination, a conspiracy of mysterious powers— the ways of art being as "unutterably mysterious" as the ways of life—has here brought together the ideal artist and her ideal subject.

James Olney. *South Atlantic Quarterly.*
Summer, 1975, p. 378

Like [Graham] Greene, Sybille Bedford is concerned with ethics, with human conduct, with the nobler hypothesis again. *A Legacy* is a very full book on both national and personal levels. Though it suggests rather than prescribes solutions, it deals with ethical actions some of which are of great importance to readers, particularly those whose history goes back to World War II. It is in this double sense that we are talking about here a very fine book indeed, one that has been too little read and underappreciated.

Sybille Bedford's two other novels, *A Favorite of the Gods* and *A Compass Error,* also treat ethical problems, problems of human conduct, but without the same historical skeleton as *A Legacy.* They are more personal books, and indeed they are so charming (and so fluffy) that it is again easy to mistake the deeper meaning—or to miss the point. . . .

If we put the two books together and make of them one long novel dealing with major themes of the times, they are a considerable accomplishment. What Sybille Bedford considers essentially is ethical action, what principles amount to, what right principles, perhaps, are, and how we should come through our own sentimental education to recognize them. These are important subjects for a novelist, and her accomplishment is considerable. Sybille Bedford is a novelist of absolute integrity bent on telling her readers the truth. That she clothes it in delightful European scenes, in many comic incidents, in allusions to a broad reading in several languages should only make the novel better, not conceal its true value, but the reviews have hardly done better with *A Favorite of the Gods* and *A Compass Error* that they did with *A Legacy.*

Many of the techniques she uses in *A Legacy,* particularly those which gain economy in writing, appear again in the later books (and indeed in her non-fiction). There are few new devices, but the texture is perhaps even richer in the later books. In *A Favorite of the Gods,* for example, we hear of Mr. Asquith, Keir Hardie, Winston Churchill, and Lloyd George only a few lines away from Cézanne and Picasso, Stravinsky and Debussy, almost on the same page with Bernard Shaw, H. G. Wells, and D. H. Lawrence, E. M. Forster, Marcel Proust, Eliot, the Sitwells, Pound, Gerard Manley Hopkins, and even d'Annunzio. The texture is loaded with contemporary European culture, in itself a strong plus value for the reader.

Who is to say how time will deal with the novels of Sybille Bedford? She is very different from most contemporary English novelists. Her canvas is so much larger. Her ethical considerations more reminiscent of Conrad (or Tolstoy) than of Iris Murdoch or Muriel Spark or Doris Lessing. She tends to deal in life in a larger sense than, say, Muriel Spark does in *The Prime of Miss Jean Brodie,* but she can be quite as ironical, just as funny, and as delightful to read. She deserves a revival. If I sound complimentary, it is deliberate.

Roberto Evans. *Studies in the Literary Imagination.* Fall, 1978, pp. 75–78

BELLI, GIOCONDA (NICARAGUA) 1948–

Gioconda Belli was born in 1948, when iron-clad silence surrounded a decimated, but never extinct resistance [in Nicaragua]. The Marines had left in 1933, but were replaced by Anastasio Somoza and his military-terrorist arm, the National Guard. Somoza ordered the assassination of Sandino, with the approval of the North American ambassador. The brutal excesses of the Somozan regime and its unabashed seizure of almost one-half the nation's wealth and land gradually forced even relatively apathetic and conservative citizens to support the Sandinista Liberation Front.

Belli's brief comment on her political awakening serves as an example of the extent to which the ideology of oligarchic despotism blinded the affluent. As a student, she had started writing; she won a university prize for poetry and began associating with artists and writers who taught her that "things were not as they should be in my country." [Claribel] Alegría, the daughter of an exile, had grown up with that knowledge. Belli had to learn it where deception reigned. . . .

In the 1970s, Belli's engagement with words became inseparable from her political collaboration. The courage to become a militant grew almost naturally once her eyes were opened to the outrages. . . . She became well-versed in the language and ideology of resistance and revolution. The year of her most active militancy coincided with the publication of her first book of poems, *Sobre la grama* (On the grass).

By 1974 she had joined those organized in cadres. She was assigned to "clandestine intelligence," and participated in plans to attempt to free political prisoners by taking a well-known Somoza official hostage during a large formal party. Through her contacts, she was able to obtain blueprints of the mansion where the party was to be held. But she was discovered, pursued, and in 1975, forced into exile in Costa Rica. She traveled to Puerto Rico to encourage support of the FSLN (*Frente Sandinista de Liberación Nacional*); she worked in offices, waited, and wrote. Out of this experience and out of personal relationships with Sandinista men, the poetry of *Firing Line* developed.

Línea de fuego (Firing line), a collection of fifty-five poems, is divided into three sections: "Patria o muerte" (Homeland or death), dedicated to her comrades of the Sandinista Liberation Front; "Acero" (Steel), dedicated to Comandante Marcos-Eduardo Contreras Escobar, who fell in Managua, November 7, 1976; and "A Sergio" (To Sergio) . . . "who gave me the rainbow."

In half the poems, the speaker articulates the revolutionary struggle as a participatory "I." She is a woman of action and sorrow, a mother wrenched from her children to fulfill a larger mothering role in clandestine activity and exile. The poems illustrate the marches, hunger strikes, and mourning rituals devised as tactics of motherly militancy by Latin American women.

The other half are love poems in which a woman affirms her erotic sensuality amidst the strife. In these poems, the male beloved becomes the intermediary for the poet's relationship to rebellion and to self. He could be termed "muse," inspirer of revolutionary ardor and poetic expression. Given the circumstances of the anti-Somoza challenge, this muse—in the poems of other Nicaraguan women poets as well—at times is also the martyred guerrilla. . . .

In these poems, popular heroism is manifested in the will to sacrifice. Sandinista political strategy itself is a theme of "Strike," "Dressed in Dynamite," "Evasion," and"We Shall Beget Children." Unshakable in their belief that "El pueblo unido jamás será vencido" (The people united shall never be defeated), Nicaraguans were willing to affirm that they would beget children to replenish the ranks—for every one of us you kill, many more shall be born. The clear focus on a vision of the future allows the guerrilla to live in daily contact with violence.

In "Strike," Belli communicates the life-preserving impetus found in the writing of many women. She anticipated the total halt that accompanied Somoza's bloody leave-taking. Although women are conventionally grouped with doves, flowers, and children, the poem becomes, through its integral vision, a call for everyone to strike on every level against the larger threat to life.

Electa Arenal. Feminist Studies. 7, 1980,
pp. 23–25

The poet's first book, containing an extensive introductory essay by José Coronel Urtecho, and illustrated with sketches of Belli, *Sobre la grama* significantly establishes the young poet as an important voice in Latin American literature. Despite the preponderance of love poems in the collection, Belli does not wallow in sentimentality but rather imbues her lyrical statements with a strong sense of self. The pieces to her young daughters are exceptionally tender, documenting their birth and early years, her sense of joy and fulfillment, as well as the realistic demands of motherhood. She exults in being a woman: "Y Dios me hizo mujer"—the leading piece in the anthology, which was later combined with "Tengo," a shorter work, to make an extraordinary statement about the female condition. . . .

Línea de fuego, . . . winner of the 1978 Casa de las Américas prize for poetry, [has its] fifty-five poems divided into three sections, "Patria o Muerte," "Acero," and "A Sergio," reflecting the themes of revolutionary fervor, pervading nostalgia for Nicaragua, and frank expressions of sexual desire and fulfillment. Added stylistic interest is provided by eight prose-poems and one work combining both genres. The most incisive pieces deal with new roles for revolutionary women, as well as the traditional ones in new guises which they must play. An admixture of real and surreal, powerful imagery, inventive metaphor and true poetic vision create incisive statements. . . .

Miriam Ellis and Elisa Davila. In Diane E. Marting, ed. *Women Writers of Spanish America.* (Westport, Connecticut: Greenwood Press, 1987), p. 38

One of the most interesting Greville Press publications is Gioconda Belli's *Nicaragua Water Fire.* It consists of the title poem about her home country—"my love my little raped girl / rising to her feet adjusting her skirt / stalking the murderer"—and *New York,* a contrasting diatribe against that city's "unintelligible graffiti /signs of those who don't know what to say." The work is remarkable for treating poetry's reduced battle lines (specificity, exclusively) as if they didn't exist and going for the all-out assault: "The peasant keeps Agrarian Reform titles in a wooden box / let the devils go round announcing the good news of forgiveness / to those who saw huts go up in flames." Her decision to go ahead and put everything into a poem, regardless of the rules of good behavior, make them hard to like in the way that one "likes" the little book one keeps in the lavatory, but perhaps it is appropriate if the subject is a country. . . .

Her Scotch Tape, shanty town approach to writing poems works well enough when she is speaking from inside her subject; in *Nicaragua Water Fire* she has earned the right to sweep it all up into a ball. But the poem about New York comes across as a collage of old clichés and paranoias, made even more corny by its disjointed syntax: "country of mad enlightened poets painters / floods of light dance schools," although one would have to say the same about Ginsberg, who is partly responsible. Having visited both countries, I can confirm that "tiny poor coffee-exporting countries drink watery coffee / so that in New York we may go past shops / where coffee saturates the smell of the entire street." But that glaring "we" gives lie to Belli's ambiguous status as a privileged traveling Nicaraguan. Where is she standing exactly? She gets into worse trouble when she identifies with "Nicaragua my little girl" who "goes off in planes to tell her story / talks till it's coming out of her ears / to newspapers in incomprehensible languages." Her charm is that she doesn't give a damn.

Her friend Salman Rushdie has said that "in Belli's kind of public love poetry she comes closer to expressing the passion of Nicaragua than anything I have yet heard." . . .

As part of a BBC film crew, I had thought I would be an exception to the rule that "nobody passes through Nicaragua without something happening to him." I realized later that I was wrong. I had met Gioconda Belli, she of the beautiful warlike smile. I had been driven round Managua by a poet who had driven cars for *clandestinos*. It occurred to me that her poetry had earned its right to inclusivity.

Hugo Williams. (London) *Times Literary Supplement.* December 20, 1991, p. 14

BENEŠOVÁ, BOŽENA (CZECH REPUBLIC) 1873–1936

[Benešová's] is a world of northern sadness, a world portraying the deep crises of a lonely heart straining to break through the blinding mists yet unable to immerse itself in a world of alien spirits. It is a world of ironic fates, ruled by the grotesque conversion of yearning into its very opposite, of a dream into its ironic analogue, a world in which a vain battle for redemption assumes ominously eccentric forms. Benešosvá is the poet of this human isolation and yearning for redemption from egotism.

Her strength lies in her vivid portrayal of the impenetrability of the human heart. She excels in perceiving the grotesque contrasts in man's inner being, the ironic tangling of an ardent heart and fanatical reason, the darkness of a spirit that is desperately impotent because it lacks inner balance and self-confidence. And Benešová herself, as a writer, possesses this burningly cold outlook. . . . A strong intellect is evident in all her writing. It is not cool reason but passionate thought, a fanatical brain speaking here. In short, dissonance and reflection are the sources of her art. . . .

When reading Benešová, I always feel a strangely cold glow, the fever of a sober. . . . one might almost say, a prescient madness of the intellect. These are not the most enviable qualities for a writer to have. Her work tends to be labored, because, in raising her characters to the higher spheres of fate. Benešová is obliged to use some degree of force. With its dissonant source, her art does not lend itself to be melodized into a natural epic stream.There is no naïveté in it. On the contrary, nothing comes easily to her. Whatever she has gained has been dearly paid for in pain, labor, suffering, and intense effort. In brief, she represents a poetic type in the great tradition of the [German] dramatist Hebbel.

František Götz. *Básnicky dnešek* (Prague: Václav Petr, 1931), pp. 89–90

The fiction of Božena Benešová, which reached maturity during the world war—often inspired by the events and their consequences in that period— nevertheless has its roots in the preceding period. Indeed, it bears witness in a remarkably truthful manner to how, in the bosom of Moravian middle-class society, a courageous woman's spirit refracted the ideas of realism and progressive movements as remedies for nihilistic skepticism and desperate illusionism.

Most fruitful in nourishing her thinking was ethics. Flaubert, her first teacher, was overshadowed by the stronger influence of Dostoyevski. Her predominantly analytical approach and the restless stylistic impressionism of her early works, when she was under the influence of [Růžena] Svobodovà, also bear a prewar stamp.

She fought these influences, however, through her strict formal discipline, leaning, for a time, toward the neoclassical novelists, until she achieved a synthesizing presentation and a typifying characterization—these, too, being indicative of the striving for objectivity that always accompanied her writing. These qualities brought [her] closer than any other Czech woman writer since [Teréza] Nováková to the type of writing represented by Karolina Světlá, whereas all the Czech women impressionists derive their style from Božena Němcová.

> Jan V. Novák and Arne Novák. *Přehledné dějiny literatury české* (Olomouc: R. Promburger, 1939), p. 1034

[*Člověk* (Man)] deals with man's responsibility for the life entrusted to him, and represents Benešová's closest approach to Dostoyevski's ideology. The theme of humiliation and degradation, as well as the construction and technique of this novel, which is set in Vienna and Southern Moravia, were also inspired by Dostoyevski. Benešová overcame the skepticism and false illusions of the pre-1914 middle-class generation by depicting unselfish submission to the enigmatic omnipotence of God in the spirit of the Russian author.

Her trilogy dealing with events of World War I in her native region is less well-rounded: *Úder* (1926; The stroke) describes the outbreak of war and pan-Slavic aspirations: *Podzemni plameny* (1929; Underground flames) deals with the problems of the Czech middle class; the final volume. *Tragická duha* (1933; Tragic rainbow), reflects the divided attitudes of the Czech people at the end of the war.

> Otto Tureček. In Wolfgang Bernard Fleischmann, ed. *Encyclopedia of World Literature in the 20th Century* (New York: Frederick Ungar, 1967), pp. 118–19

BENMUSSA, SIMONE (FRANCE) n.d.

Simone Benmussa's theater revels in the mysteries and pleasures of illusionism even as she queries its processes. Her work is not a rejection of the theater of representation but a reading of it—to be explicit, an adaptation of it. To adapt (from *adaptare,* "to make fit") refers to an arrangement between unequal partners, the original work, which is fully present, and its adaptation, that which modifies the original "to fit" a new medium. The adaptation exists independently, but never replaces the original—the French *adapté d'après* marks the temporal spacing between the two. The text of adaptation, then, as Brecht well knew, dismantles the presumption of textual authority. But Benmussa goes further: she insists on her belatedness. In *Appearances,* for example, whole passages from Henry James's "Private Life" occur not only in the dialogue of the characters but in the italicized stage directions, conventionally the space where the author speaks directly to the reader, Who, then, is the author?

In Benmussa's text authorship loses authority; the single becomes double, a scandalous hybrid. Moreover, rather than masking the authority of her model, Benmussa playfully deconstructs it. That is, she dismantles the presence-absence binary (which assures the power of the absent author) by putting the author's name in circulation. "Henry James" appears as a character in *Appearances;* an unseen voice called "George Moore" penetrates and directs the action in *The Singular Life of Albert Nobbs;* "Freud" moves through Dora's painful dream world in *Portrait of Dora;* and the recorded voice of Nathalie Sarraute becomes the interlocutor for the actress who embodies one of the narrative voices of *Childhood.* A Benmussa production dramatizes its belatedness; it is always already a deferral from the immediacy of an original, never a copy of it. If representation is tied to the reproduction of the same, adaptation, by definition, proposes difference and deferral—and, consequently, alternative modes of theatrical inscription. . . .

Using texts from "elsewhere," Benmussa herself remains elsewhere, a "place" French theorist Luce Irigaray valorizes in "The Power of Discourse." Given that patriarchal thought tends to "reduce all others to the economy of the Same [the self-representing masculine subject]," women need "to listen (psycho)analytically to its [philosophy's] procedures of repression, to the structuration of language that shores up its representations, separating the true from the false, the meaningful from the meaningless." The strategy for the female inserting herself into patriarchal discourse is, for Irigaray, "mimicry," a "playful repetition" which might uncover "a possible operation of the feminine in language." What makes this a tantalizing proposition is that feminine mimics can repeat without becoming recuperated. Says Irigaray: "They also remain elsewhere."

Benmussa's adaptations might be called subversive mimicries of the tightly woven discourses of representation. In a carefully written performance text of light, sound, image, word, and gesture, she dislodges the actor from her "character," time from chronology, and space from its bondage to the present. Her actors seem to move through a dense medium, embodied at one moment, then blurred; they appear, leave traces and visual echoes, then disappear before reappearing once more. . . . The "obviousness" of something that is not there (the quotation marks refer to a comment by Freud) recalls the teeming domain of the unconscious which is there and not there in the deferred, scrambled, and fragmentary writing of dreams, jokes, and slips of the tongue. The hand, the profile are like the "nodal points" in Freudian dreamwork, on which an indeterminate number of dream elements converge, and by such image fragments the spectator follows the traces of unrepresentable desire. In Benmussa's theater, the awareness of "reading" visual and verbal traces becomes an integral part of spectatorship. The introduction to *Benmussa Directs* refers constantly not to the truth of performance but to the complexity of reading and writing. The "levels of memory, of the real, of the dream, and of fantasy" in *Portrait of Dora* "must always remain readable"; moments must be "legible." But this readable performance text is not, as Barthes would say, "readerly"; it does not close on a signified. Rather, the movement of the signifier in Benmussa's text, as in Barthes's text, can be understood only in its "connections, overlappings, and variations."

In the textuality of her productions, with their "nebulous zones" and oscillating desires, Benmussa's adaptations both focus on and make problematic a particular cultural and historical moment: bourgeois society from the mid-nineteenth to the first decade of the twentieth century, when social awareness of the "new woman" converged with the new science of psychoanalysis, and when the technologies of photography and film would soon suggest new ways of reading and expressing human desire.

> Elin Diamond. In Enoch Brater, ed.
> *Feminine Focus: The New Women*
> *Playwrights* (New York: Oxford University
> Press, 1989), 66–69

While George Moore's narrator was the fictional anonymous "I," Benmussa nominates her narrator "Moore" and circulates his voice through the episodic events which constitute the life of Albert Nobbs. Moore, aggressively omniscient, is everywhere: he opens and closes Albert's story, speaks for Albert in the first scene with Mrs. Baker, articulates Albert's unconscious in the dream sequence, speaks contemptuously of Albert's appearance, just as though the Albert we see were absent from her own story, a mere diegetic description. And of course the woman concealed under the name "Albert" is representationally absent; her costume, says Benmussa, is not only her disguise but becomes her prison, then takes over her body. Moore's voice which penetrates her mind, and which utters the narrative that contains her, becomes identified with the shackles of the gender code.

Throughout *Albert Nobbs* the collision between the "here" of theatrical representation and the elsewhere of narration produces a play of signifiers that makes it impossible for the audience to consume a unified image of feminine identity. One is tempted to call the textual intersections in *Albert Nobbs* an instance of intertextuality, the transposition of one signifying practice into another. But this would be to misuse Kristeva's neologism. Intertextuality, by Kristeva's definition, means a "transposition" of signifying practices that opens up new possibilities of articulation. What is crucial in Benmussa's text is that narrative is coercive; it will not be transposed. Moore's disembodied voice is the voice of phallic power for whose privileges, sanctioned and perpetuated by history, Albert sells her sexuality. She gains no new powers of enunciation, but merely assumes the gender markings appropriate to the status quo: that of a male. By refusing to grant Albert a status outside Moore's narrative, Benmussa semiotizes the patriarchal narrative that determines Albert's position. All characters are trapped, as Beckett's Hamm says, by the dialogue, but Albert Nobbs is trapped in a "true" history that refuses to symbolize her; in both stage and fictional narratives, Albert remains an old perhapser.

By foregrounding narrative, Benmussa exposes the audience's own narrativity—our desire for order and closure. The final stage image shows Albert in her death posture (which was also her life posture), seated holding her napkin and a pair of unshined shoes, tokens of her servitude while Hubert Page, her double and foil, muses on the impossibility of reversing her own gender change. (The doubling of Albert and Hubert is made thematically explicit when the latter announces that she, too, is female and when each, at different times, thinks of the other as a spouse.) Hubert decides that to resume her female identity would mean to cast herself once again into economic servitude. At this point Benmussa has Alec intervene, hungry for more details, and we spectators, because we partially share his stance, become implicated in his simple narrativity. Alec decides that Hubert could easily render her last years as a fairy tale because no one would believe that a woman could marry another woman and live happily with her for fifteen years. Such a woman is not "natural," says Alec, by which we infer that her story cannot be inscribed in a patriarchal symbolic that represents woman only as man's natural opposite.

Alec's dismissive treatment of Hubert's story illustrates the teleological and exclusionary pressure of the narrative form: Alec forecloses Hubert's story, insisting that it cannot be told. However, in Benmussa's stage directions, Hubert, in her man's clothes, sits "dreaming." After the closure of narrative, does the female subject dream of a discursive space accessible to female experience? Perhaps she dreams because this "space" is unknowable and resists knowing in the symbolic order as well as in narrative history. Benmussa's achievement in *Albert Nobbs* is to induce narrativity in the audience while insisting on the coercive effects of a male narrative that (inevitably) refuses or diminishes and distorts the experience of female subjects.

Albert's story—or rather Moore and Alec's storytelling—indicts the practice of enacting or telling any woman's story, including those cultural myths and histories that women and men "naturally" consume, inhabit, and perpetuate.

Elin Diamond. Theatre Journal. 37, October,
1985, pp. 281–83

The creator's art is to take metaphors literally and to see that set formulas, repeated without thinking, are never innocent. Like intonations, they are indices. Whether it is Freud she brings to the stage (*Portrait of Dora*), Nathalie Sarraute, or Henry James, not to mention George Moore (*The Singular Life of Albert Nobbs*), Simone Benmussa adopts this procedure herself: generalized suspicion, patient interrogation of the *blinding* evidence of the image Realization/Unrealization *by* the image. As for suspicion, let us listen to Freud, stealthily advancing: "These events are announced, like a shade, in dreams. They often become so distinct that you think you can seize them palpably, but in spite of that, they escape a definitive clarification, and if you are not very smart and careful in how you proceed, you can never decide if such a scene actually took place." As for making metaphor concrete, it is Henry James who does it most subtly. It is said that a presence "haunts" a place, so he takes this idea seriously and makes a subtle ghost in whom you *almost* believe, it is "as if" you believed. In *The Jolly Corner,* which could serve as an apologia to Simone Benmussa's work, a man returns to an empty house after thirty years and finds the house haunted by his own double, the person he would have been if he had stayed there. But who is "he"? That is where perception gets confused. In *Appearances* (*The Private Life*), the marginal fable that Simone Benmussa had translated into theatrical images was the following: a writer (Clare Vawdrey) is a double character—the one who writes, whom one never sees, and the one who is seen and who is nothing but the author. By contrast, a man of the world (Lord Mellifont) exists only in public; outside his representations, there is such a total intermission that he ceases to exist. Already in *Portrait of Dora,* the actors were accompanied by their double in the form of holograms. A character left a trace of his presence on stage, or he appeared furtively even before his presence materialized: as when someone's presence is *evoked.* There are *degrees* of presence, the stage images and the "visual echoes" were saying. In *Appearances,* an English actress, Susannah York, played an English actress, Blanche Adney. For this, she must to some extent become her own hologram, "become unreal to herself," as Sartre said of *The Maids.* A character and his or her double occupy the same theatrical space: luminous to the point of transparency, opaque to the point of enigma. Stage writing has as its function to make the vacillations of perception *visible.* As if by magic, but the magic hangs by a hair, an invisible thread: the meticulous precision of scenography.

Marie-Claire Pasquier. Cahiers Renaud-
Barrault. 115, 1988, pp. 93–95

George Moore's short story "Albert Nobbs," contained in his collection of short stories, *Celibate Lives,* recounts the true story of a woman who spent her life as a man in nineteenth century Ireland. Reading the story, Simone Benmussa felt that Moore's interest in Albert was too clinical, that of an outsider simply commenting on Albert's celibate existence, "a man telling a woman's story."

In her stage adaptation, Benmussa creates a feminist reading of Albert's life. While she does not significantly alter the text of the short story, the stage pictures and visual spectacle that she creates are distinctly new. The visual rhetoric of the play intersects, interrupts, and even occasionally contradicts the narrative spoken by Moore. A new discourse is established that distances the viewers from the narrative voice and asks them to consider the social, sexual, and economic implications of Albert's fate.

Nevertheless, George Moore remains central to Benmussa's play. His is the first voice that the audience hears, that of an offstage narrator who relates Albert's story to Alec, a young man of Asian descent and lower-class status. Through the narration (physically and ideologically distant from the on-stage characterization of Albert), the audience learns of Albert's cross-gender disguise. Moore views Albert unsympathetically as a cultural aberration, as Other. His narrative voice places the action in the past as an historical event. On the other hand, the visual rhetoric of the play places Albert sympathetically before the audience in the present. According to Elin Diamond, the male narration "refuses or diminishes and distorts the experience of the female subjects." The audience must, therefore, consciously separate what they hear from what they see.

Benmussa places not only Moore but the other two male characters, Alec and Joe Mackin, offstage as well. Yet even in their absence, the men are a controlling force. Joe Mackin, an unseen voice from the kitchen, urges the kitchen maid, Helen Dawes, on in her scheme to exploit Albert's naiveté. The non-appearance of the men, in conjunction with their heard voices which surround the stage, signifies powerfully to the audience the invisible confines of the patriarchal system, limiting the social mobility of the onstage, visible women.

The absence of the men also shifts the dramatic focus to the lives, experiences, and behavior of the women. When Albert first appears on stage, she is shown as part of a trompe l'oeil backdrop of painted hotel guests and hotel rooms. She is merely another anonymous two-dimensional face on the backdrop. Within the context of this backdrop and her onstage life, the woman who is Albert has no real identity. The two-dimensional image of Albert serves as a visual metaphor for Albert's position within the narrative provided by Moore. Denied the right to speak for herself, she is just a representation, the embodiment of Moore's vision.

As the stage lighting separates Albert from the backdrop and makes her three dimensional, it reveals her seated in a chair that rests on the landing between the first and second floors of the Morrison Hotel. This is her place, her work station. The placement of Albert on the landing between floors symbolizes her cross-gendered existence: Albert is literally neither upstairs nor downstairs. As Jill Dolan puts it, Albert is "caught in the discrepancy between her sex and her gender." Hubert Page, the only person in whom Albert confides the truth about her sex, calls Albert "A perhapser, neither man nor woman." The visual rhetoric inherent in Albert's positioning onstage emphasizes the conflict that is central to Benmussa's feminist reading of Moore's story.

Through the representation of Albert, Benmussa wants the audience to understand that gender is, as Janelle Reinelt argues in "Feminist Theory and the Problem of Performance," "a field of experience, socially constructed, constantly changing." Because Albert easily adopts the masculine gender, gender can not be seen as a biological reality but merely as an economic necessity. The character Hubert Page reinforces this viewpoint. Page, like Albert, is a woman who has chosen to disguise herself as a man. She has left an abusive heterosexual marriage and dresses as a man in order to succeed in the exclusively masculine field of house painting. Together Page and Albert convey the idea that gender is an external attribute almost as changeable as one's clothing. . . .

Through Benmussa's play the audience recognizes the isolation and re-pression that gender distinctions can foster. By creating a visual rhetoric juxtaposed with the narrative voice of George Moore, Benmussa calls on the audience to question gender roles not only in Victorian times but today as well. The historical setting allows not only for distance but for reflection. The past informs the present in *The Singular Life of Albert Nobbs*.

Harry J. Elam, Jr. *Text and Performance Quarterly.* 11, 1991, pp. 313–14, 317–18

Perhaps in response to the dearth of desirable vehicles for female performers in drama, women have been increasingly turning to other forms of literature and art—the short story, poetry, paintings, and epistolary collections—to create their own theater pieces. One such contemporary stage adaptation of great interest to feminist critics is Simone Benmussa's *The Singular Life of Albert Nobbs,* based on George Moore's short story, and first performed in Paris in 1977. Set in Victorian Ireland, "Albert Nobbs" is the tale of a poor woman who lives disguised as a male waiter in a large hotel in Dublin in order to secure economic freedom. Encouraged by a chance, brief meeting with another disguised woman (Hubert), Albert decides to court Helen, a hotel maid, in order to add companionship to her lonely life. But the courtship ends when Albert is unable to disclose her sex, and she lives the rest of her life in the Morrison Hotel and dies alone.

Critic Ruby Cohn points out that Benmussa retains much of the original story's narrative and, indeed, that she seems attracted to this narrative pre-cisely because it is in the past and, therefore, "ill at ease" with the present, which is, of course, the material of the theater. Benmussa herself states that she found a dialectic between "the distance implied by narration" and the "identification with the characters demanded by the theater," an identification created by the very sentience of the actors, by their living existence. This "collision" between the here-and-now of theater and the "elsewhere" of narration in *The Singular Life of Albert Nobbs* is viewed by Elin Diamond as "forcing the audience to understand female identity as a historical and cultural construction whose causes and consequences constitute the drama being enacted." Diamond emphasizes the "foregrounding of narrative" in Benmussa's text as "coercive" and clearly identifiable with the "shackles of the gender code.

What is missing however, is an analysis of the actual fabric of Benmussa's adaptive art. In *La jeune née,* Hélène Cixous has maintained that if the phallocentrism which "funds" our system of thought were challenged, "Then all the stories would have to be retold." But how can Benmussa "retell" Albert Nobbs's story if she maintains most of George Moore's original script? Like feminist Madeleine Gagnon, Benmussa is "snatching this language that is foreign to [her] and turn[ing] it about in [her] fashion"; she is "translating . . . self by quoting all the others." And the transforming medium through which Benmussa filters the "elsewhere" of Moore's patriarchal language is the "here and now" of the theater.

Simone Benmussa creates a set for *The Singular Life of Albert Nobbs* which frames the space with two revolving doors which often revolve of their own accord. Benmussa stipulates that the doors be isolated and operate in the "void." These doors are clearly reflective of Albert's entrapment in a world not of her own creation. She can leave this world through the swinging doors, but they always return her to the inside; they never function as exits or modes of escape. It is on the outside of this frame that the controllers of her society exist.

And it is on the outside of the frame that Benmussa places her male voices: they exist only on tape or as offstage voices. The play opens with the disembodied voice of George Moore telling his friend Alec the story of Albert Nobbs, and it is clearly this voice that controls and "sees" all of the action. Benmussa makes this point skillfully from the beginning by moving slowly to Nobbs' own voice. At first we hear only Moore talking *of* Albert, *then* we see Albert frozen in conversation as George Moore literally speaks *for* her. Not until the second scene does the actress playing Albert Nobbs actually speak in her own voice. . . .

Jacques Derrida argues that the text must be overthrown to allow creativity in the theater. Paradoxically, in her adaptation of George Moore Simone Benmussa *uses* that very tyranny of the presence of the narrative . . . text to *overthrow* and, thus, *deconstruct* the text. In so doing, she clarifies position of women in the stifling patriarchy of late nineteenth century . . . society. The abundance of text and narrator underlines the "invention of 'woman' in a patriarchal society and transforms George Moore's story into an "ideotextual mise en scène" in which "It is not so much the text itself that is staged as the political, social, and psychological subtext.

Simone Benmussa's *The Singular Life of Albert Nobbs* has moved critic John Simon angrily to denounce the play by observing that the "extremely interesting" George Moore did not have his "cause advanced by Simone Benmussa's stage adaptation of his story . . . a work that positively cries out *not* to be so adapted." But Benmussa did not intend to further Moore's "cause," nor yet to discredit his considerable talent in storytelling. Her adaptation, instead, *transforms* his text, through the medium of the theater, into a clear and critical look at a patriarchal society, and one that positively cries out *to be* so deconstructed.

Sharon Ammen. *Text and Performance Quarterly.* 11, 1991, pp. 308-9, 311–12

BENNETT, LOUISE (JAMAICA) 1919–

The work of Louise Bennett is unique. Whether in the field of the Jamaican theater where she has found form and living purpose, or in the field of literature where she is yet an unheralded guest among some of the literary establishment, she presents problems—problems of classification and of description. This in a way is her greatest asset, for she is original and of her own kind. It is not in Miss Bennett's nature to make any special claims for herself. As an artist she knows what is exactly the proof of the pudding and she makes the authenticity of her dialect verses speak for itself. Her belief in people as they *are* comes out when she declared that if the Jamaican dialect were to become a standard language in her lifetime, she would "still write in the free expression of the people"—that is, to use her own words, "a manner of speaking unhampered by the rules of (Standard English) grammar, a free expression—a dialect."

In a quarter of a century she has carved designs out of the shapeless and unruly substance that is the Jamaican dialect—the language which most of the Jamaican people speak most of the time—and has raised the sing-song patter of the hills and of the towns to an art level acceptable to and appreciated by people from all classes in her country. Yet not all are agreed on just what she is or stands for on the cultural scene. In the post-independence period when many Jamaicans are asking themselves questions about who and why they are, Miss Bennett has taken on new and important dimensions. One poet committed himself to paper on the subject of reading Louise Bennett seriously and another verbally gives the edge to Miss Bennett as the "only poet who has really hit the truth about the society through its own language." These are justifiable—and unselfish—tributes. But there are others who would feel it improper to endow her with the name of poet, though they would generously crown her as the leading entertainer in Jamaica's comedy-lore whether on stage, television, or radio. And those who indulge her rumbustious abandon and spontaneous inducement of laughter will sometimes forget that behind the exuberance and carefree stance, there are years of training—formal and informal—as well as this artist's own struggles to shape an idiom whose limitations as a bastard tongue are all too evident. Then there is the view, sometimes barely conceded, that Miss Bennett has given to Jamaica "valid social documents reflecting the way we think and feel and live."

As poet, Miss Bennett must first be seen against the background of her society. This is imperative. One critic (a Jamaican emigré) in London, on hearing Miss Bennett render her poems at the Royal Court Commonwealth Poetry Festival thought that her "unpretentious monologues . . . went a long way towards proving that a large part of the job of poetry in a new nation is not to make or break images, but to tell the truth so that it sounds true." One must assume that all Jamaican poets have at one time or another understood that challenging role of their art, but as Morris himself suggests not many of them have quite found out how to realize it. Miss Bennett went to the basics and grasped the fact that she lived in an oral tradition where people talked and listened, cross-talked and reported and possess, almost to a fault, a high propensity for words—"bad" words, new words, archaic words, "big," long and sonorous words. The Bible, the Sankey hymnal, the folksong and the memory gems form the background to these propensities. To Louise Bennett who had the benefit of schooling, the ballad-form, the oldest form of English poetry, would probably have come as the nearest basis of comparison and in her early years it could even have been a conscious model. For many Jamaicans of Miss Bennett's generation were exposed to, in fact saturated with, *Sir Patrick Spens,* which is an established ballad, and *The Rime of the Ancient Mariner,* Coleridge's literary invention. Indeed, most of Miss Bennett's stanzas do take the conventional structure of iambic quatrains with an *abab* rhyme scheme and with stresses of 4 and 3 in alternating lines. But even the iambic rhythms are natural to the Jamaican drawl. Conscious aping of a poetic form is no guarantee of success, however, and one must look to Miss Bennett's own individual use of balladic and other poetic attributes to measure her success. . . .

Miss Bennett is a performer, accomplished and unrivaled. If on the printed pages her poems appear to be dated frozen jingles, in the renditions she gives of them they take on vitality and meaning—capturing all the spontaneity of the ordinary Jamaican's joys and even sorrows, his ready poignant and even wicked wit, his religion and his philosophy of life. *Miss Bennett is indeed a poet of utterance.* With her experience and skill she exploits the complex intonation contours of the Jamaican dialect and turns out pieces which are at once fresh, vital and entertaining. The charm of her winning personality is essential in all this and she uses it with unqualified success. It has won her the applause of foreign audiences whose ears must be ill-attuned to the dialect. What she sometimes does is to manipulate the tonal range of the language, setting the poems almost to music as she patters along. The punchline technique of music-hall comedy is liberally utilized and her audience participates with laughter at the end of many a stanza. Her play on the infinite nuances of meanings of a single word or phrase reminds us that she is involved in the art of words and when some 60,000 souls flock to the Ward Theatre in Kingston three months each year to see her in the annual folk-musicals, they go to indulge Jamaica's own entertainer speaking and singing in Jamaica's own language.

It must not be forgotten that Louise Bennett wrote many of her poems for performance and even those published weekly in the *Sunday Gleaner* throughout the forties were read in tenement yards all over the country—probably by the one literate person in each yard. Many listened. Today her poems are "recited" by many school children who give the dramatic monologues new interpretations and even new sounds, and many more are listening. No one should worry that many of these poems will have to be performed in order to survive. But to those who believe that all that these poems need are stentorian vocals and tireless gusto, the truth is soon revealed. For they are capable of subtle interpretation and demand the careful modulation of tones and pitch in order to communicate honestly and vividly. Above all, they demand an understanding of and a feel for the language. For understanding and feeling are among Miss Bennett's greatest attributes, resulting in the delightful intermingling of "those qualities of head and heart which we term wit and humor—wit which illuminates and humor which reveals," as Philip Sherlock once aptly put it.

It is as performer that the *personae* created by Miss Bennett come to life, whether they be matriarchs, of which there are a-plenty in her society, higgler, samfie man, political demagogue, or quashie. It is through her performances that she has proven herself relevant to the society about which she writes, and it is through her performances that the sanity and generosity of spirit which Mervyn Morris commends becomes evident. This sanity and generosity of spirit is the occasion, not the cause, of her artistry. For as a poet of utterance, she has had to be sane and generous for the nightly confrontation which a live and living audience demands of any performing artist. The safe distance of the published writer she never enjoyed. But, in any case, she was using the normally *spoken* language, not the normally *written* tongue. . . .

Jamaica has indeed seen many crusaders against "bad speaking" ever since it was established that a command of "Standard English" was a passport to status and class in the island. There has developed genuine academic interest in the Jamaican dialect, which has been carefully studied by reputable scholars, but it is still the target of middle-class snobbery. Although it has been accepted for entertainment largely through the efforts of people like Louise Bennett, and even though its literary merit is conceded by some, it still carries with it the stigma of ignorance and nonsophistication. Louise

Bennett has often been the target of attack and the fact that *Bans O' Killing* was written in 1944 near the beginning of her career, gives the reader some insight into Miss Bennett's early sense of purpose and literary courage. That the earlier criticisms are far less applicable today is to the credit of Louise Bennett, who has never doubted the power of the language she uses to express the essential passions of her people's hearts.

Her inspiration came, and still comes, from the everyday happenings around her. She is acutely sensitive to these occurrences and finds in them a thousand wonders—wonders easily concealed from those of us who have been too long conditioned to seeing the worth of human experience only in the deeds of kings and conquerors. She may not have bothered to ask in explicit terms about the ends of existence. Nor did she labor on the fears that men have about their inevitable mortality. Instead she concentrated on the immediacy of the task of having to survive. An uprooted, poor, but proud people are primarily concerned about surviving, having found themselves alive. They make the best of it with an intelligent optimism which is the occasion of Miss Bennett's bright-side-of-life humor. Humor becomes, as it were, the expression of a people's will to live and Miss Bennett recaptures this will with understanding, compassion and truth. What more should one ask of her?

> Rex Nettleford. Introduction to Louise
> Bennett. *Jamaica Labrish* (Kingston,
> Jamaica: Sangster's Book Stores, 1966),
> pp. 9–11, 23–24

[T]he metaphoric structure of Bennett's poetry is actually an imitation or reflection of the essential creativeness of the unlettered folk's sophisticated use of language. This explains why so little, if any, of her "topical" materials are ever dated. The wartime poems, for example, are as fresh and as striking as when they were first performed because by virtue of their style their focus is less on the specific topics of the 1940s (food shortages, high prices, the war itself) and more on the continuing modes of perception and communication which they dramatize. . . .

This is also a two-way process. For if the war in Europe supplies grist for local Jamaican concerns, the war itself is also reduced to its essential obscenity by being subjected to the outrageously irreverent puns of the non-literate whose style reflects an acute understanding of European language and civilization. In "Perplex," for example, the speaker professes to be confused by it all, comprehending only that that madman Hitler had appropriately called himself a "Naasy" (that is, "nasty" and "Nazi"). Clearly the European's wars have been seized upon to dramatize another continuing conflict—that between black identity and the Westerner's Eurocentric notions of culture and civilization. Thus that age-old self-defense by blacks in a white world—the feigned inability to understand the other's language—is also a form of subversiveness, particularly when the Europeans' internecine (as well as interracial) violence raises questions about the humaneness of their vaunted civilization. . . .

Given the immediate significance of talk and oral style in the lives of Bennett's speakers it follows that they are acutely sensitive to the function or dysfunction of the outsider's language. . . . Altogether, the distrust of a narrowly intellectual wordiness must be traced to the duality which Bennett perceives in her folk traditions. And if her oral mode encourages a distrust of pretentious literacy, the converse is also true: the folk's admiration of, and loyalty to, a Western middle-class ethic of achievement encourages a frank admiration for foreign "twang" and for "big words" used in a certain way. . . .

The point is not that Bennett's poetic vision is itself insincere or hopelessly inconsistent. More pertinently, as a highly disciplined artist she subordinates the authorial voice completely to the cultural personality and values described by her art. Hence the primary function of her art is to reproduce in all its self-revealing details, the Jamaican's national consciousness as it shifts and varies from one Jamaican to another, or as it wavers within any single individual. The aim is not to offer an overview of a collective consciousness deduced from her cultural ambience, or even created by the poet herself. Instead the objective is to portray a variety of attitudes among her wise collection of personalities, and to express the contradictions, self-conflicts and uncertainties within any single personality. And in doing this the artist consistently allows free rein to her speaker.

Lloyd W. Brown. *West Indian Poetry*
(London: Heinemann, 1984), pp. 111–15

In the poem "Jamaica Oman," the Louise Bennett persona employs an earthy metaphorical proverb to expose, with obvious relish, the jinnalship (resourcefulness) and fortitude of the Jamaican female:

> Oman luck deh a dungle,
> Some rooted more dan some,
> But as long as fowl a scratch dungle heap
> Oman luck mus come!

In that body of Jamaican folk wisdom transmitted in proverb, Anansi story and riddle, is the genesis of an indigenous feminist ideology: the paradigm of a submerged and fated identity that must be rooted up, covertly and assiduously. The existential dungle, the repository of the accumulated waste of the society, becomes in the folk iconography the locus of transformation. It is the dungle, and the dehumanizing social conditions that allow it, which is the enemy of woman. Cunning, rather than overt male/female confrontation, is the preferred strategy for maintaining equanimity.

This proverbial cunning of the Jamaican woman is one manifestation of the morally ambiguous craftiness of Anansi, the Akan folk hero transmuted in Jamaican folklore into Brer Nansi, the archetypal trickster. Folktales of the mighty outwitted by the clever proliferate throughout the African diaspora: the shared history of plantation slavery in the Americas consolidates within the psyche of African peoples in the hemisphere, cultural continuities, ancestral memories of sabotage and marronage, systemic resistance to servitude. It is within this broader tradition of neo-African folk consciousness— the Anansi syndrome—that Bennett's elaboration of the Jamaican female sensibility can be best understood.

Carolyn Cooper. *Race and Class.* 29:4,
Spring, 1988, pp. 45–46

[T]he symbolic opposition of male strength to female weakness, so alien to earlier literary presentations of the Jamaican woman . . . suggests that a new view of female character had become the norm in Jamaican society.

Development can be noted in the poetry of Louise Bennett. Though Bennett maintains the old view of the working-class woman as more than a match for her oppressors at the level of language, her poems tend to show women using men as surrogates for their aggression and, at a first glance, she seems to follow the bias of Jamaican men in her presentation of women as apolitical. In "Uriah Preach" for example, Bennett recounts the vicarious pleasure taken by a Jamaican women in the accomplishments of her children and especially in her son's ability to use his occasional ascent to the pulpit to lambast the family's enemies. . . .

The woman's pride in the poetic justice of her son's scriptural attacks on her enemies is a comic version of the religious escapism expressed earlier in the poetry of Marson and Bell. In "Me Bredda," an irate woman who has failed to get a job as a domestic servant forces her would-be employer to placate her with two weeks' wages by threatening to call in her imaginary brother to settle the matter physically. . . .

Here again the woman shifts the responsibility for physical confrontation to a male figure, implying that the woman herself no longer considers the threat of her own action sufficient to terrify the housewife she abuses.

Though Bennett often works through apolitical female figures who are more likely to react to the cut of a politician's clothes than what he says, she often expresses a womanist perspective on topical issues and her poems take note of social reforms intended to improve the position of women. In "Bans of Oman," for example, she celebrates the founding of the Jamaican Federation of Women in the 1940s aimed at bringing together women of all classes, describing the clothes and social status of the women who flock to support it as "high and low, miggle suspended." Poems like "Solja Work" show the consequences of a local military presence for Jamaican women.

Bennett is one of the first creative writers to register the increase of female oppression which was one of the consequences of the male assertion of racial and political power during the nationalist movement of the 1940s and 1950s. Her poem "Pinnacle" satirizes the new chauvinism of men towards women as it manifested itself within the Rastafarian movement, which in other respects has had such a profound and in many ways beneficial effect on Jamaican attitudes to language, race and spiritual values. Written after the brutal destruction of one of the first Rastafarian communities by the Jamaican government, the poem delights in the humiliation of one of the male members of the sect who had formerly used his Rastafarian convictions to terrorize his woman. . . .

Bennett's satirical resources however are limited to what she can authentically express through the resonances of a specific social reality and way of speech, so that in her dramatic monologues she can only be as positive about women as she thinks the character through whom she speaks is in real life. In a more recent poem she has described what she considers the philosophy of the Jamaican woman:

> Jamaica Oman know she strong,
> She know she tallawah,
> But she no want her pickney dem
> Fi start call her "pupa."
>
> So de cunny Jamma Oman
> Gwan like pants-suit is a style,
> An Jamaica man no know she wear
> De trousiz all de while!
>
> So Jamaica Oman coaxin
> Fambly Budget from explode
> A so Jamaica man a sing
> "Oman a heaby load!"

This presentation of the female point of view elucidates Bennett's own method in the early poems, by which she is able to assert a sense of female strength under the guise of using male surrogates and seeming to acquiesce in ideas about female weakness. The fact that she feels constrained to work through such masks, however, gives an indication of the extent to which the attitude to women in Jamaican society had become that expressed in the song she quotes in her poem on Jamaican women: "Oman a heaby load!"

Rhonda Cobham. In Carole Boyce Davies
and Elaine Savory Fido, eds. *Out of the
Kumbla* (Trenton, New Jersey: Africa World
Press, 1990), pp. 217–19

BENNŪNA, HANATA (MOROCCO) 1940–

The Moroccan woman writer Khannathah Bennūna appears on the literary scene in the mid-1960s with several collections of short stories: *Li-Yasqut al-Ṣamt* (1965), *al-Nar wa-al-Ikhtiyar* (1968), *al-Ṣurah wa-al-Sawt* (1975), *al-Aṣifah* (1975), and more recently, a full-length novel, *al-Ghad wa-al-Ghadab* (1981). Bennūna is currently a school principal and many of her writings draw upon her experiences as a student at the university. Although never explicitly autobiographical, her work echoes the questionings and rejections of her generation. Her first collections carry these seeds of estrangement of the individual from his society and his bewilderment at the hypocrisy inherent in it. Her characters' lack of heroism is by itself a statement of her loss of faith in the society of the forefathers. Bennūna is a writer whose impulse is turned inward rather than outward. The reality she depicts is not observed and then re-created in a sociological manner, but rather is set as a mirror which reflects the drives, the flaws, and the deep anxieties of a society at large. Her men and women are constantly depicted as probing, meditative characters beset by doubts, guilt-ridden and, in general, insecure antiheroes. These people seem helpless in arbitrating their destinies. They are men and women who grope for happiness and rarely achieve it. More importantly, they seem to encapsulate the anguish and defeats of a whole generation of Moroccans in crisis.

To give expression to this special world, Hanata needed as it were to create a new medium of the Arabic language to present systematically her philosophical and psychological probings. She is more interested in the Arab consciousness than the material, external surroundings of Moroccan society. She is more preoccupied with what her characters *think* than with what they *do*. For this purpose she seems to have created a new level of the language, an "agonized prose.". . .

Bennūna's orientation is the future—the specific future of her generation. She religiously believes that the writer must make a politically and socially conscious commitment, a commitment ultimately aiming at the liberation of both men and women. In a story entitled "Suqūṭ al-Intiẓār" (The downfall of waiting), a woman lawyer who is absorbed in mundane petty cases dreams of heroic feats: "I wish I could give of myself to every hungry and destitute human being, to every possible change." Her sense of utter inability to bring about any change is a condition that constantly haunts her and underlines her sense of loneliness and alienation. This perhaps leads her to self-delusion, to believing that she can serve humanity at large in small ways by tending to their problems and litigations. Yet she is never totally deluded. Her gnawing realization that she is ultimately helpless is further seen in her comments about her circle of friends who have succeeded in dismissing the whole question of responsibility and engagement *(iltizam)* by convincing themselves that they are mere puppets, insignificant moments in history enveloped in a cloud of numbness and lethargy.

Bennūna's characters, particularly the women, are constantly challenged to choose for themselves within the limitations of their circumstances. In some sense they are faced with the dilemma of opting for either total freedom—choosing one's actions and bestowing whatever value one chooses upon one thing rather than the other—or total responsibility. Her men and women are intellects who perceive separate, disjointed states, and more often than not are powerless to control their environment. The tension is caused by the intellectual desire to achieve liberty and to end the state of paralysis.

The characters in the stories are both spectators and actors. They watch themselves live self-consciously. The danger they run is the possible failure of their attempt to turn mind into action and intellect into passion. Bennūna's characters are eternally theorizing about their own lives. In her most recent work, the novel *al-Ghad wa-al-Ghaḍab* (1981; Anger and the future), she attempts to treat some of the criticisms that have been directed at her treatment of form and content. She quite successfully attempts to merge two narratives that intertwine in time and space, while she develops her characters within a more traditional linear evolvement of plot and action. As she herself says in a postscript to the work: "I have (attempted) to fulfill the multiplicity of voices, diversity of backgrounds, angles of vision, that interlock and separate until they merge in unison when thought and action are merged in a dialectical relationship reflected in collective action that seeks Change."

> Mona Mikhail. *Arabic Literature in North*
> *Africa: Critical Essays and Annotated*
> *Bibliography—Mundus Arabicus* Annual,
> (Cambridge, Massachusetts: Dar Mahjar,
> 1982), pp. 54–55, 58–59

At the moment there are two women writers in Morocco who are fairly well known. Rafīqa aṭ-Ṭabiʿa has published three collections of short stories and Hanata Bennūna also has three books of stories to her name, as well as a novel which appeared in 1981. Both women teach and are presently employed as headmistresses of girls' schools. . . . Hanata Bennūna's work has philosophical undertones and everything she writes echoes a deep involvement with the political situation in the entire Arab world. She has an exceptional style, which Mona Mikhail refers to as "agonized prose." . . .

Although Bennūna's "mirror" also reflects the fate of the less fortunate members of society, women among them, this image is supplanted by a flow of ideas emanating from the main characters, who are laboring to express their individual dissonance with the surroundings and the political situation.

The most prominent woman in the field of Moroccan emancipation . . . Fatima Mernissi. . . . replied to the critic whose extensive review of Bennūna's novel appeared in the Moroccan newspaper *al-ʿAlam*. She exposes his review as a sample of typical male thinking. "You are still the master and you conduct yourself as master, as one who understands nothing of women, who does not listen to her words and cannot accept her writings." In her article she stresses her own responsibility, and that of every woman who is capable of expressing herself on paper, to communicate to the opposite sex some understanding of feminine nature.

Lourina de Voogd. In Mineke Schipper, ed.
*Unheard Words: Women and Literature in
Africa, the Arab World, Asia, the
Caribbean, and Latin America* (London:
Allison and Busby, 1985), pp. 94–95

Starting from her first moments as a writer, nationalist commitment, assuming the very particular form of "the Palestinian question," could be seen reflected in all her works in more or less explicit form, to the point of constituting one of the fundamental axes of her narrative production, as well as the motivation that impelled her to take up the pen.

Although totally aware of what was happening in Palestine—a place that, since her childhood, she had considered "her dreamed-of spiritual home-land"—the face to face encounter with the bitter reality caused her to experience a profound shock that turned her entire being around. This shock was so decisive a moment in her life that I would go so far as to say that it was at this exact moment that Bennūna the teacher was transformed into the writer Hanata Bennūna. . . .

The second constant around which many of her narratives center is concern for the social deterioration that Morocco is undergoing—in her own words—through the underdevelopment, third-worldization, immobility, and oppression suffered by its people. Such accusations, although rooted in conditions in her Moroccan homeland, extend to the whole Arab world. . . .

Female consciousness in struggle—in all areas and aspects of life—is another of the constants of her literary production. Her fervent desire to be involved in the intellectual formation of woman inspired her, in 1965 and by overcoming a large number of obstacles, to found *Suruq* (Dawn), a magazine explicitly devoted to the problems of women.

If we focus on her narrative work, it may be readily observed that her position on the problem of the Moroccan woman and of the Arab woman in general is reflected in it. With reference to her first book (*Li-yasqut al-samt*), the writer herself commented that this collection "was a revolution against the situation experience by the young woman in a traditional society that considers the female a precious object in an exhibition hall."

In Hanata Bennūna's works there is a predominance of female protagonists who . . . are frequently determined women who reject the dominant stituation in the world around them.

Guadalupe Saiz Muñoz. *Miscelanea de
estudios arabes y hebracios.* 37, 1988,
pp. 245–48

BENSON, STELLA (GREAT BRITAIN) 1892–1933

Mundos acknowledges a debt to Mrs. Woolf. . . . Apart from that, a posthumous novel is always a disappointment, partly because the inflation which publicity now ensures a living author is matched by a corresponding intensity of oblivion when he is dead . . . and partly because there is usually a good reason why the posthumous work was not previously published. *Mundos* is both unfinished and a not very good example of the work of the author. . . . Miss Benson was highly gifted and sometimes wrote exceedingly well. *Mundos* is often readable and amusing, but on the whole reveals only the faults of cleverness—the affectation, the febrility, the pretentiousness of a clever woman showing off. . . . The publishers explain that Miss Benson left a wish that none of her half-finished work should be published after her death, and that they thought otherwise.

Cyril Connolly. New Statesman and Nation.
April 27, 1935, p. 594

It is a significant fact that Stella Benson regarded her diary, which she stipulated was to remain unpublished for forty years after her death, as more important than any of her published novels—significant because it raises the problem as to how far she may be considered an artist at all, how far a sociological specimen. "The pretender," she wrote in *Worlds within Worlds,* "who cannot sufficiently buttress up his secret throne with lovers and friends would do well to keep a diary. . . . Diaries are like dreams, an inward consolation to the outwardly humiliated." Now this is an extremely revealing quotation with reference both to Stella Benson's life and to her work; though of course it does not necessarily follow that she had not many of the qualities that any serious artist ought to have.

To a point, she really was sensitive and intelligent—to the point, at least, of being a misfit. And it is not merely that she was forced to live so long among people "whose highest idea of wit is a joke about being drunk and whose only outlet for intelligence is Bridge"; her conviction was as passionate as that of her old Mrs. Cotton that America and all it stood for was worse than death. . . .

Stella Benson saw through the pretensions of the contemporary world with a bright bird-like form-prodding intelligence, she impaled the Tams and Daleys of society with devastating finality. Yet all the time she half longed to be of them; her mocking toughness arose from an agony of self-humiliation, which is the peculiar ant-like impetus from which her art springs. . . . Lawrence said somewhere that to break a heart was to break the spontaneous flow of communion between people, and in this sense Stella really had a broken heart. One of the main themes of her books, which became more urgent as she grew older, was the impossibility of communion between people, all of whom live segregated in "distinguished and divided worlds." It is in this respect that she most obviously differs from E. M. Forster with whom, as a "feminine counterpart," she explicitly invites comparison. Like him she was intelligent about people and she was a whale for sensitiveness (consider the celebrated description of the birth of the foal in *Tobit Transplanted*), yet what is the use of being intelligent and sensitive if these qualities don't help you to live more adequately? They conspicuously helped Stella Benson to nothing more than a consciousness of failure for she could not believe, as Forster passionately believed though he too knew the difficulty of communication, in human relationships. For other people and for herself she at most had pity, at worst contempt, and so complete a deficiency in belief implies a deficiency in vitality too—an inadequacy as an artist. . . .

In the earliest fairy books there is a too patent juxtaposition of fantasy and realism combined with an insufferable archness, as in Forster's *Celestial Omnibus* stories, though naturally more feminine and kittenish. But in the last of these books, *This Is the End,* the Secret Friend, the House of Living Alone, the other props to the separateness of the individual, are relinquished in favor of a stiff-lipped resignation.

"Now I know that growing up is like going through a door into a little room; and the door shuts behind one." In her very first book Stella Benson had written "sometimes I pose, but sometimes I pose as posing" and isn't she here "posing as posing"? At any rate the only comment one can make on the sort of growing up that *This Is the End* represents is that it is precisely the reverse—a symptom of protracted adolescence, a disease from which she never quite recovered, for it is present not only in her persistent twinklebud-isms, her private canine language, the pet names for her pleurisy, for motor cars and hot water bottles, and in the groups she uneasily mingled with, but in the tenor of her works as a whole. Even in her best, her funniest, most destructive books, *The Poor Man* and *Good-bye Stranger,* I suppose the "dazzling" wit—genuinely the product of an agile mind netting the butterflies of unexpected relations—cannot be reckoned as aesthetically "serious"; though her pernickety masochism told her of the temptations to which the "intelligent and sensitive" are exposed. . . .

The scope and sanity of Stella Benson's vision were limited not by her having a personality but by her inability to escape a personal manner, to separate the woman who "suffered" from the creative mind. Whether you regard the inability as a deficiency of character or of civilization makes little odds, but beside it even Mr. Forster's most ambiguous whimsicality seems curiously untrivial . . . failing a Forsterian conformity with "the liberal tradition," her escape from the ignominy was not much more unacceptable than the average—than that, say, of Mrs. Woolf herself or of Peter Warlock except insofar as these two had a streak of genius compared with her modest share of talent, and possibly just because she was less of an artist she was a more representative figure.

W. H. Mellers. Scrutiny. September, 1939,
pp. 221–25

"It is simple and human," Stella Benson once wrote, "to pose a bit and not know you are posing. When you try to know yourself too well you devastate yourself." She herself was the last person to act upon that piece of kindly wisdom. Forever striving to know herself down to the last unexplored corner of her brain (in the secret places of her heart she took much less interest), she would not let herself off the necessity for facing up to anything and everything that she might find in her explorations, and the result would have been devastating to her sensitive nature had it not been for her saving humor. Though she analyzed herself and other people so acutely she took nobody entirely seriously, least of all Stella Benson. A curiously individual wit plays over all her books, not least *The Poor Man,* and makes tolerable a bitterness that could not otherwise be borne. And the very acuteness of her analytical mind has compensations. At times you may wriggle unavailingly beneath the probing knife but at others you cry out for pleasure at the unexpected and delightful accuracy of her description of your symptoms. Time and again you exclaim, "Yes, of course, that is true; that is how *I* feel. But no one else has ever noticed." Take for instance her revelation of that harmless but carefully concealed oddity, the habit of inventing private signs and omens. "He made up little tests to find whether she would come. 'If the sunlight reaches the chin of the man opposite before a tram goes by outside I shall know that she will not come.'" Again, being slightly deaf herself, she knew and took the trouble to note down that curious and compensatory freak of nature by which the partially deaf often hear remarks infinitely more interesting and beautiful than the words actually spoken. Incidentally, Stella Benson's deafness probably explains her preoccupation with the theme of shyness and embarrassment, her constant reiteration of the difficulty of making contact between person and person. . . .

Wit and perception help to lessen the acid taste of *The Poor Man,* and descriptive passages of a curious beauty act as a relief to the general bitterness of the novel. In Stella Benson's earlier books the descriptions are all too obviously purple, but in *The Poor Man* they have a lyrical character that contrasts oddly with their setting of satire. . . . Brilliant though *The Poor Man* may be the fire of its brilliance burns with a cold flame that can never warm the heart. Stella Benson does not quite succeed in blending her strangely assorted ingredients into a satisfactory whole; the mixture lacks the essential touch of humanity. The same criticism applies to *Good-bye Stranger* and *Pipers and a Dancer,* two books in which she makes a not entirely successful attempt to combine the "fairy" manner of her earlier novels with the satire of *The Poor Man.* Then in 1931 she published *Tobit Transplanted,* and with this book came to the full height of her stature as a novelist. Hitherto she had not found a wholly satisfactory medium of expression; even the best of her previous books had been in the nature of promise rather than performance, leaving the reader with a sense of pleasurable expectancy as to what she might one day produce. In *Tobit Transplanted* promise is fulfilled, expectancy satisfied. The novel tells the Apocrypha story of Tobias and the

Angel transposed into modern times and imagined as taking place among a colony of White Russians in Manchuria. The limits of the fable set a pattern for the story, a convention exactly suited to Stella Benson's talent, which was inventive of bypaths, but not particularly happy when confronted with the necessity of constructing a plot. Here at last she has combined comedy and romance, wit and lyricism into a harmonious whole, lit with understanding and sympathy for poor human beings in whose lives humor and tragedy are so inextricably mixed. The book met with great success, winning the Femina Vie Heureuse prize, but it is doubtful whether it was, or is likely to be, generally popular, in spite of the plaudits with which it was greeted. *Tobit Transplanted* is that rare thing, a witty novel, and there is nothing that the British and American public distrust more than wit, as opposed to humor, unless it be a story with an exotic setting. . . .

Stella Benson asks to be judged as an artist and nothing but an artist.

Her place in literature is hard to determine because she left behind her so little work that can be called mature. She was only forty-one when she died. Jane Austen died at forty-two, Charlotte Brontë at thirty-nine, Emily at thirty, and among the moderns, Katherine Mansfield at thirty-five, yet all these authors, even Emily Brontë, are far more easy to assess than Stella Benson. They had already found the right expression for their particular gifts at an age when she was still experimenting with her material. Coming late to artistic maturity she only "found herself" with *Tobit Transplanted.* A direct line of succession can be traced from *Northanger Abbey* to *Persuasion,* but no such kinship exists between *Tobit* and *I Pose,* and the unfinished *Mundos* gives ample proof that *Tobit* was only the beginning and not the peak of her possible achievement. If she is to be judged on the greater part of her work she must be counted an entertaining, original writer, but no more; if it is possible to assess her only on her performance in *Tobit Transplanted* and her promise in *Mundos* she attains to a small but secure place in the front rank of modern novelists.

A comparison inevitably arises between Stella Benson and her contemporary Katherine Mansfield, a writer who was perhaps unduly praised in her own day and who is certainly unduly neglected now. The circumstances of their lives were curiously similar. Both had a natural talent for painting and for music as well as for literature, both were dogged by ill health, both were obliged to spend a great part of their lives separated from their husbands and to forego that normal home life for which they craved, both were childless to their great sorrow, both died young. They never met in the flesh, but they knew and appreciated each other's work. Judging only from her books Katherine Mansfield described Stella Benson as "a very attractive creature," adding, however, that "she seems to me just to miss it." (It must be remembered that this criticism is written twelve years before the publication of *Tobit Transplanted.*) Stella Benson was greatly influenced by Katherine Mansfield's Letters and Journal, recognizing in them the mind of a writer who appeared to attain that integrity which was the goal of all her own effort. Higher than anything else in life or in art both of these writers valued truth.

Georgina Battiscombe. *The Nineteenth Century.* April, 1947, pp. 209–11, 214–15

Stella Benson believed her conscious identity more significant than her biological identity—that she was a writer was more significant than the fact that she was a woman—as a writer, not a woman writer, she should be judged. And it was as a writer that David Daiches judged her in 1958. He described Stella Benson as "a highly original novelist whose tragic view of life is artfully disposed behind a facade of remarkable comic wit." Benson recognized the difficulty of bringing to term the joy latent in life, and her work recognizes the frequent failure of the imagination, but she never lost sight of the continuing presence of potential. Her wit and imagination contradict the intellectual message of tragedy in the factual world.

Tobit Transplanted is a clear descendent of *I Pose* and *The Poor Man.* These three novels seem to anchor themselves firmly in the real world. All three suggest that there is an external world of verifiable fact by which we must judge ourselves. All three have central characters with clear objectives and practical activities in the external world. The suffragette in *I Pose,* unmarried by chance, has dedicated herself to achieving something more than what society has allotted her. She wants to consider the situation in the world around her and improve the lot of women. Emily in *The Poor Man* seeks emotional fulfillment with a married man and has traveled as his secretary to accomplish her objective. Tanya in *Tobit Transplanted* has sought to avoid emotional responsibility by maintaining her status as daughter. Each of the three women must adjust either her objective or her activities.

Faced with conflicting desires, the suffragette chooses to give up the need for choice. Although she wants the comfort of a husband she will not narrow her vision to include only domestic life. Drawn toward marriage by desire though not by choice, she elects to remove herself completely from a world in which she cannot reconcile conflicting roles. Emily in *The Poor Man* refuses to settle for any man just because he is a man. Faced with loneliness and the certain knowledge that her affair with Tam is over, she nonetheless chooses to be alone rather than accept Edward Williams as a lover. She exercises a positive choice which does not bring immediate happiness but allows her the dignity of independent action. Finally, Tanya, as she realizes that her desire for freedom from responsibility will be thwarted by her father's insistence that she become what he believes she should be, chooses another sort of invisibility when attracted to a man who seems to share her respect for life. Although she takes on the responsibility of a husband and the emotional support that requires she will gain a new kind of transparency. She will fulfill the expected role of wife and will be freed from criticism of her "unnatural" nature. These three novels all deal with women who have an idea of what they are and what they want, and the novels follow the women as they do or do not attain their objectives. These novels are fundamentally traditional in conception and development. There is a romantic interest, there is a male protagonist of importance at least equal to—and in the case of *The Poor Man* greater than—that of the female central character. Even *I Pose,* with its feminist bent, its unnamed protagonists, and its dramatic rejection of marriage is far more traditional in tone and perspective than *This Is the End* with its nearly conventional ending or *Pipers and a Dancer* with its absence of any hint of magic.

Tobit Transplanted offers depth of characterization and greater realism than *I Pose,* but the singular accomplishment of that first novel should not be overlooked. *I Pose* makes a clear and unambiguous statement about the frustration and actual hardship suffered by women imprisoned by stereotypes and self-serving masculine prejudice. Serving strictly moral ends *I Pose* is armed with witticisms shooting truths home to an enchanted reader.

As the narrator of *I Pose* points out, "Imagination seems to be a glory and a misery, a blessing and a curse. Adam, to his sorrow, lacked it. Eve, to her sorrow, possessed it. Had both been blessed—or cursed—with it, there would have been much keener competition for the apple." It is the glory and the misery of the imagination that Benson demonstrates in *This Is the End; Living Alone; Pipers and a Dancer;* and *Good-bye, Stranger.* Most reviewers appreciating these books comment on the wit and the feeling of magic in them. What has not been sufficiently stressed is the fact that their real power comes from the clear creation of a tangible reality against which the insubstantial world of the imagination wavers. . . .

Reginald Johnson said in response to Benson's first three novels that she was a woman writing for women. He was only partially correct. Stella Benson was a woman writing *about* women, but she was writing *to* all people prepared to try to look anew at themselves and the world around them. As it happened, Benson wrote about the isolation of women who live restricted by what society deems appropriate for them. But as women increasingly insist on the freedom to be persons, all people, men and women, are pushed toward a new freedom, a demanding freedom in which each must decide for himself or herself which possible self he or she will pursue.

Most critics have agreed that *Tobit Transplanted* is her best work, but perhaps some readers' evaluations have depended too heavily upon what they were comfortable with. With *Tobit Transplanted* many readers could enjoy in comfort a novel with a clear story line, vivid imagery, consistent characterization, friendly humor, and perceptive observation. It is, as Benson herself described it, a friendly book, and there is no doubt that it is a remarkable literary achievement. But the familiarity and safety of *Tobit Transplanted* with its positive ending has unfortunately tended to overshadow her earlier accomplishments. If *Tobit Transplanted* is lit by the bright light of the sun, Benson's other novels seem to glimmer with ethereal magic in the light of the moon. Although *Tobit Transplanted* is Stella Benson's most widely acclaimed book, it is not on that novel alone that her reputation must rest. *I Pose,*

Pipers and a Dancer, Good-bye, Stranger, and *Tobit Transplanted* are all worthy results of artistic effort. Benson's exploration of isolation and defeat is developed through her understanding of the frustrating position of women. Her message, though, is not for women only. Painfully aware of life's cruelty and humanity's weakness, she sought to strengthen the soul through gaiety and to train the eye to see beauty. All the while she reminded the intellect that the world could be better. . . .

Benson's novels are witty and haunting. Her poetry complements them in its seriousness. Her accomplishment is original and significant. Christopher Morley once said that lazy and contented people will never appreciate her work. That is probably true, but for those who dare the disarming challenge she waits to be appreciated.

R. Meredith Bedell. *Stella Benson* (Boston: Twayne, 1983), pp. 122–25

BERBEROVA, NINA (RUSSIA) 1901–

Nina Berberova numbers among those rare creative individuals for whom advancing years seem to intensify rather than slacken productivity. . . .

From what is presently available in English, Berberova's book, *The Italics Are Mine* ranks among her greatest literary achievements and will no doubt be her legacy in the history of émigré literature. Although written in Russian during the years 1960-65, it was the English translation which appeared first in 1969 from Harcourt Brace. This memoir-autobiography is much more than a chronicle of events experienced and people met: Berberova's recreated dialogues and richly descriptive passages give life to these events and people. Her prose is forceful and dynamic, reflective and poetic. The irony and humor leave no room for self-pity. Berberova was excited by life and interesting people; hers is a story of a commitment to live life to the fullest. Berberova's keen sense of detail (selective detail) revives Kerensky, the Merezhkovskys, Bunin, Gorky, Khodasevich, Nabokov and scores of others who were the luminaries during the 1920s and 1930s among the émigrés in Paris. Obviously, the book is controversial: Berberova's opinions and impressions are of a very personal nature.

Berberova, relatively early on in her career, relegated poetry writing to second place among her interests. She was also the first to concede that the novel was not the genre best suited for her talents. But in short fiction, she was a prodigious and successful writer. Her interest in the genre developed in the 1920s, while she was on the staff of *Poslednie novosti.* She was casting about for a backdrop, or *fon,* for her experiments in short prose; she felt that she needed a unifying setting. She neither knew, nor was interested in writing about Old Russia: she felt that there were enough émigré writers in Paris who were living in the past, reminiscing about tsarist Russia. She did not identify with France or the French language, and she was not yet ready to write about herself.

In 1927, Berberova became acquainted with life in Billancourt, and this proved to be fertile ground for the series of highly popular stories which became known as "Biiankurskie prazdniki." Billancourt, a suburb southwest of Paris, was at that time the site of the Renault automobile works which began to grow rapidly after the first World War. Workers were in great demand and the French found a ready and eager labor force in the legions of the white army who were scattered about in northern Africa, Bulgaria, Serbia and other countries. In addition to Renaults, these thousands of workers were also building a new life on French soil, recreating an ersatz Russia, striving to preserve past customs to give their life in Billancourt a modicum of familiarity and stability.

The Billancourt stories are interesting reading at many levels. From the historical and sociological points of view, the stories were the first to depict the day-to-day life of these uprooted masses who had no hope of returning to their homeland. For the linguist, there is a wealth of material to investigate in the émigrés' most obvious link to their past—the Russian language. And while their language had lost its roots and chances of its survival in France were precarious at best, one senses both a public and private struggle among these half-educated, hard-working émigrés who had come together from all parts of Russia to keep it alive.

Murl Barker. Russian Literature
Triquarterly. 22, 1988, pp. 241–42

Le mal noir (The black sickness) the sixth of Nina Berberova's works to be translated into French, focuses on the pain of love and exile. Via a pair of earrings which the protagonist felt impelled to pawn in order to pay for a ticket that would take him to the United States, readers are introduced into a delicate world constellated with symbols, images, and ellipses. Never does the author overtly state situations or events or depict people; to increase suspense, rhythms slacken, nuances burgeon, a play of phonetics and phonemes is intertwined in the prose along with asides, all of which impose their presences in the dialogic interchange. Only through subtle references, analogies, and innuendoes are readers introduced to the very personal and poignant domain of the Russian émigré who narrates the tale.

Via the world of objects, such as the exquisite depictions of a dancer's costume or the banal world of any traditional rented room, and of financial difficulties experienced by the narrator, Berberova discloses a whole hidden dimension within which character traits can be subsumed, sensed, felt: the agony of solitude, of feeling exiled from the world and from oneself by an emigrant who left his native Russia to live in France and, after his friend has died in a bombardment while they were making love, decides to make his home in the United States. So much is left unsaid; so much is inexplicable for those exiles who spend their lives wandering about attempting to find—something, but exactly what? *Le mal noir* is alive within the archetypal protagonist and has been for a million years! Short and gripping, Berberova's tale is a small gem.

Bettina L. Knapp. *World Literature Today.*
64, 1990, p. 480

The name Nina Berberova brings to mind a rich and varied career in Russian émigré literature: poet, novelist, journalist, short story writer, translator, memoirist, cultural historian, critic and teacher. . . .

Berberova is, above all, a survivor and she admires survivors. She would be the first to disavow any truth to the old chestnut that "we love others for their weaknesses, not their strengths." In real life and in her fiction, Berberova is drawn to individuals who possess either a tangible or an intangible source of strength for survival. Physical strength, robustness, good health, good looks: her admiration for these qualities is obvious. But equally important, or indeed, if not more important in her view is that inner strength, the *centrum securitatus* that is a vital aid in the struggle, or rather, the will, to survive. It may take many forms: a governing idea (that goodness will triumph over evil); a renewal through the appreciation of beauty; the power of love. But above all, both in Berberova's life and in her fiction, she is drawn to individuals who think, who are mentally active, who have created their inner legend that neither historical events nor any other individual can destroy.

Murl Barker. *Selecta.* 11, 1990, pp. 69–70

Berberova's indifferent attitude toward the past endows her foray into autobiography with an uncommon sense of immediacy. "For me," she declares, "even my own past is not worth as much as the present." She indulges in no false nostalgia for history's "artificial charm," nor does she yearn for some Messianic future. Rather, she translates yesterday into a sensuous, satisfying experience for today. It all makes exhilarating reading.

One characteristic that critics have often noted in Berberova's fiction is its utter lack of sentimentality, verging on heartlessness. So it is with her memoir. She recalls that, as a small girl, she horrified her mother by suggesting that she and a schoolfriend exchange families in order to learn about each other's existence. From childhood on, Berberova has detested the "nesting" convention. She regards solitude as humanity's natural and loveliest condition. The whole "spirit of family," she suspects, is a "civilized" drapery obscuring the confrontation of death, which is necessary before movement, change and growth can take place. . . .

As a refugee, Berberova may have had little opportunity to publish. Nonetheless, *The Tattered Cloak,* a collection of novellas written between the 1930s and the 1950s, was brought out last and warmly received. Now, with the U.S. appearance of *The Italics Are Mine,* we can see she has satisfied all her priorities. Beyond ably detailing the exploits of her fellow Russian émigré writers, Nina Berberova has fulfilled her quest for personal growth. Her memoir records a response to life that I think readers will find inspiring.

Freema Gottlieb. *The New Leader.*
July 13–27, 1992, pp. 17–18

BING XIN (CHINA) 1900–1988

[After 1927] writers like Bing Xin turned to humanism and love as the remedy for social turmoil; others shook themselves out of a lethargic, cynical stupor and began to question seriously their reasons for writing. . . .

Bing Xin too made a comeback into the realm of political realism in the 1930s with such stories as *Miss Winter,* a lively and witty portrayal of a poor Peking girl who ignores the moral and ethical dictates laid down for her sex by setting up her own business after her father abandons mother and daughter. She defies the reckless bullying of soldiers stationed in her "territory" and even plays a few roguish tricks upon them much to her mother, the narrator's consternation. The story flows with positive energy: if one can withstand poverty and the pillaging of starving restless soldiers, then the future holds bright possibilities. Miss Winter takes on the task of family protector and makes a better success of it than her father did, for as she says to her mother, "If we two look after each other then we'll be better off than before when he was around, won't we now?"

Jennifer F. Anderson and Theresa Munford.
Introduction to *Chinese Women Writers*
(San Francisco: China Books and
Periodicals, 1985), pp. xvii, xix

The older generation, indeed the first generation, of women writers, represented here by Ding Ling and Bing Xin, grew up at this time and, like their fellow students, threw themselves into the May 4th Movement. They were both unusual in that they came from families that encouraged their education; the opposite of the suicidal bride's. . . .

For Ding Ling and Bing Xin, the short story in the vernacular was a new form, a product of the movement towards the vernacular and of translations. The short story had flourished in the seventh and eighth centuries but written in classical language; expressions of emotion existed in Chinese literature but expressed, often with subtle indirectness, in the same classical language. The vernacular was a new language without the constraints of tradition; Bing Xin translated Tagore, amongst others, part of the wave of literature from the outside world that was there for exploration, ingestion or incorporation in the search for new forms. . . .

The subject matter of women's fiction is immensely varied; their work is perhaps characterized by a refusal to automatically write "as women." It is not uncommon for them to choose a man as narrator, perhaps to deflect easy interpretation. One of Bing Xin's early works was called *About Women,* a first-person narrative in which the narrator was a man; it is a very amusing lightly satirical piece, very different from her sensitive (some would say over-sensitive) stories and poems. Yet problems specific to women, the exploitation of professional women, the near-impossibility of reconciling the demands of home and work and the double standard, expecting virtue from women and accepting less from men, preoccupy the group of middle-aged women writers.

Frances Wood. Introduction to *One Half of the Sky: Stories from Contemporary Women Writers of China* (New York: Dodd, Mead, 1987), pp. viii–ix

Bing Xin's early collections, *A Maze of Stars* and *Spring Water,* are interesting and important for a number of reasons: because of their position in the history of modern Chinese poetry; because of their relationship with non-Chinese literature, specifically the work of Tagore; because of their influence on later Chinese poets; and, not least, for their intrinsic worth.

Bing Xin began—shyly, reluctantly—to take her place as a pioneer of radical changes in the very nature of Chinese poetry during the period immediately following the May 4th Movement. She was in her late teens. Bing Xin had a long-standing involvement in traditional poetry and felt instinctively that its characteristic combination of formal beauty and traditional themes constituted the essential Chinese poetry. From her writing about her early collections, it is clear that she was less certain about the status of her own work and that of other writers using the vernacular in a poetic mode and it is also clear that the very idea of the "New Poetry" caused her some anxiety. In any case, she was primarily a writer of short pieces, mainly fiction, and this remained her first love. She did, however, have confidence in the quality and worth of many fragments she had been collecting for some years. Once she had been exposed to certain types of foreign literature which had acknowledged authority and which seemed to have a marked formal similarity with some of the things that she was writing, she began to publish. Her work was soon seen in terms of the so-called "mini poem" and she is credited by some with the virtual creation of the genre. This she chooses to deny in her own accounts. Instead, she suggests that many writers experimented with fragments as the literary revolution extended to poetic writing. Certainly the form became instantly fashionable. It was seen as a modern correlate of the brief (most often twenty or twenty-eight syllable) traditional Chinese quatrains *jueju* . . . with some influence from Japanese *tanka* and *haiku.* However, all these earlier forms are clearly highly structured in traditional ways. It is fair to suggest that the mini poem was something of an easy way out for the writer faced with formal problems in trying to use the poetically immature medium of the vernacular. We can admire Bing Xin's honesty in resisting the tendency to apply the word "poetry" to a form of writing at this stage of its development. Besides, when we look at the antecedents of her collections in particular, we can see that their relationship to poetry is itself somewhat problematic. . . .

Despite her claim that she was uncertain about the poetic status of Tagore's fragments and despite her later assertion that she was anxious about her supposed contribution to a new poetry, it is interesting to note that Bing Xin's verses have more of the "structured" look of Western poetry than either Tagore's originals or Zheng Zhenduo's translation. . . .

The influence of Bing Xin on younger Chinese poets will have been moderated by her limited poetic output—a function of her later concentration on prose—and also, for the new generation of writers in the post-Mao era, by her having been an early revenant towards the end of the Cultural Revolution. Still, she must be given some credit for the fact that the "mini poem" form has survived in the new Chinese poetry and recently, moreover, experienced a revival and revitalization in the work of certain so-called "obscure" or *menglong* poets. *A Maze of Stars* and *Spring Water* constituted a popular and authoritative collection of what might otherwise have become mere poetic trifles: diversions or mistaken turnings on the road to the development of a true vernacular poetry in Chinese. As contemporary Chinese poetry now opens itself up to world literature in ways which have been unheard of since the time of the New Culture Movement, there are signs of a reassessment of the poetic pioneers and early translators. Bing Xin will find a vital place in any such reassessment. Her work contained the "translation" of a partially foreign sensibility, one which appears as relatively individualistic and aesthetic when set against that underpinning the bulk of modern Chinese poetry. However, pervading this individualist expression there is the undeniable sense of a subtle, poeticized patriotism and a social and political engagement. This is an early romantic precursor of a position and sensibility which has only just become once more a public possibility for those post-Mao poets who are consciously moving away from the obligation to subordinate their poetic intentions to politics. . . .

Bing Xin's fragments can be read with pleasure in translation. They are not great poetry, as the poet herself would have been the first to admit. They openly declare a specific Western model for their form, but avoid becoming merely derivative because they have been created out of personal observation and experience. There is certainly no question of simply following a literary fashion. They are engaged with the events of their times, but this engagement is subtle and individually felt. It is an engagement which accords, more easily than other work from socialist societies, with liberal Western ideas of the way the writer expresses his or her social and political concerns. What a Western reader finds most difficult in these poems is their sometimes extreme sentimentality, their emotional attachment to childhood and filial affection. Often, even Tagore seems too saccharine for our present sophistication, focused too softly to convey the harder edges of his vision. Bing Xin is "sweeter" still. But they can both surprise us with a coolness and intellectual engagement which is enough to keep us on our toes and make us return gratefully to the otherwise overly sentimental beauty of their natural images.

John Cayley. *Renditions*. 32, 1989, pp. 118-20, 122-23

BISHOP, ELIZABETH (UNITED STATES) 1911–79

Elizabeth Bishop is spectacular in being unspectacular. Why has no one ever thought of this, one asks oneself; why not be accurate and modest? Miss Bishop's mechanics of presentation with its underlying knowledge, moreover, reduce critical cold blood to cautious self-inquiry. . . . With poetry as with homiletics tentativeness can be more positive than positiveness; and in *North and South* a much instructed persuasiveness is emphasized by uninsistence. . . . At last we have someone who knows, who is not didactic.

Marianne Moore. *The Nation*. September 28, 1946, p. 354

The best poems in Elizabeth Bishop's *North & South* are so good that it takes a geological event like *Paterson* to overshadow them. "The Fish" and "Roosters" are two of the most calmly beautiful, deeply sympathetic poems of our time; "The Monument," "The Man-Moth," "The Weed," the first "Song for a Colored Singer," and one or two others are almost, or quite, as good; and there are charming poems on a smaller scale, or beautiful fragments— for instance, the end of "Love Lies Sleeping." Miss Bishop is capable of the most outlandish ingenuity—who else could have made a witty mirror-image poem out of the fact that we are bilaterally symmetrical?—but is grave, calm, and tender at the same time. It is odd how pleasant and sympathetic her poems are, in these days when many a poet had rather walk down children like Mr. Hyde than weep over them like Swinburne, and when many a poem is gruesome occupational therapy for a poet who stays legally innocuous by means of it. The poet whom the poems of *North & South* present or imply is as attractively and unassumingly good as the poet of *Observations* and *What Are Years*—but simpler and milder, less driven into desperate straits or dens of innocence, and taking this Century of Polycarp more for granted. (When you read Miss Bishop's "Florida," a poem whose first sentence begins, "The state with the prettiest name," and whose last sentence begins, "The alligator, who has five distinct calls: / friendliness, love, mating, war, and warning," you don't need to be told that the poetry of Marianne Moore was, in the beginning, an appropriately selected foundation for Miss Bishop's work.) Miss Bishop's poems are almost never forced; in her best work restraint, calm, and proportion are implicit in every detail of organization and workmanship.

Instead of crying, with justice, "This is a world in which no one can get along," Miss Bishop's poems show that it is barely but perfectly possible— has been, that is, for her. Her work is unusually personal and honest in its wit, perception, and sensitivity—and in its restrictions too; all her poems have written underneath, *I have seen it.* She is morally so attractive, in poems like "The Fish" or "Roosters," because she understands so well that the wickedness and confusion of the age can explain and extenuate other people's wickedness and confusion, but not, for you, your own; that morality, for the individual, is usually a small, personal, statistical, but heartbreaking or heartwarming affair of omissions and commissions the greatest of which will seem infinitesimal, ludicrously beneath notice, to those who govern, rationalize, and deplore; that it is sometimes difficult and unnatural, but sometimes easy and natural, to "do well." . . .

Randall Jarrell. *Partisan Review.* 13:4,
September–October, 1946, p. 4

Geography III is a magnificent book of ten poems whose power and beauty would make it seem gross to ask for more of them. Its epigraph is a catechistic geography lesson quoted from a nineteenth-century textbook, claimed for parable in that seamless way of allowing picture to run into image that the poet has made her own, in this instance, by her own added italicized questions about mapped bodies—of land, of water—and about direction, following the epigraph in its own language but now become fully figurative. The opening poem of Miss Bishop's first volume, *North & South,* is called "The Map"; in all the work that has followed it, the poet has been concerned with mappings of the possible world. More generally, she had pursued the ways in which pictures, models, representations of all sorts, begin to take on lives of their own under the generative force of that analogue of loves between persons which moves between nature and consciousness. We might, somewhat lamely, call it passionate attention. Its caresses, extended by awareness that pulses with imagination, are not only those of the eye and ear at moments of privileged experience, but rather at the times of composition, of representing anew. The mapmakers' colors, "more delicate than the historians'," are as much part of a larger, general Nature as are the raw particulars of unrepresented sea and sky, tree and hill, street and storefront, roof and watertank. Much of the praise given Miss Bishop's work has directed itself to her command of observation, the focus of her vision, the unmannered quality of her rhetoric—almost as if she were a novelist, and almost as if love of life could only be manifested in the accuracy and interestingness of one's accounts of the shapes which human activity casts on nature.

Robert Lowell. *Sewanee Review.* 53,
Summer, 1947, pp. 497–98

She never moralizes. She is not interested in the abstract truth at the end of the road, but in the concrete truths that lie along the way—the shape of a tree, the look of gently broken water in the morning sunlight, or the appearance of an old fish half-in half-out the boat. Her truths are the truths of a bowl of peaches by Cézanne, a wheat field by Van Gogh, a lady playing the lute by Ter Borch. The reader must therefore be interested in the manner in which she selects or "filters" her subject, in the tonality she achieves, in her massing of the details into significant form. Her best poems do reveal moments of vision, but she inserts them so unpretentiously amid carefully and skillfully selected objective details that a careless reader easily misses them. Her vocabulary, too, is so utterly free from pomposity that its accuracy and suitability to the occasion is not at first apparent. Only rarely is she obscure, but on these rare occasions it is an obscurity arising from reticence rather than from a desire to mystify or to conceal lack of thought. She never forces a poem beyond its limits, nor herself to assume a pose that is unnatural. In this lies her strength, a strength with limitations.

James G. Southworth. *College English.*
February, 1959, p. 214

Elizabeth Bishop is modest, and she is dignified. Because she is modest, she has not presumed to assign to her artistic sensibilities an importance incommensurate with their value. Hers may be a minor voice among the poets of history, but it is scarcely ever a false one. We listen to it as one might listen to a friend whose exceptional wisdom and honesty we gratefully revere.

Because Elizabeth Bishop is dignified she has been reluctant to fling her troubles at the world; she prefers always to see herself with a certain wry detachment. As a result, her poems are occasionally artificial; there is sometimes a coy archness which undermines the strength of her deeper perceptions. On the other hand, her tone savors more good manners than of mannerism. She would not insult us as she tells us the often unflattering truth. . . .

Elizabeth Bishop is a realist, but she sees miracles all the time. In her poems it is as if she were turning again and again to say to us: "If man, who cannot live by bread alone, is spiritually to survive in the future, he must be made to see that the stuff of bread is also the stuff of the infinite." The crumb which becomes a mansion in "A Miracle for Breakfast" is more than a clever poetical conceit. It is a symbol of hope in a world which can be bearable—for some mysterious reason—in spite of its evils.

Anne Stevenson. *Elizabeth Bishop*
(New York: Twayne, 1966), pp. 126–27

On the surface, her poems are observations—surpassingly accurate, witty and well-arranged, but nothing more. Sometimes she writes of a place where she has lived on the Atlantic Coast; at others, of a dream, a picture, or some fantastic object. One is reminded of Kafka and certain abstract paintings, and is left rather at sea about the actual subjects of the poems. I think that at least nine-tenths of them fall into a single symbolic pattern. Characterizing it is an elusive business.

The structure of a Bishop poem is simple and effective. It will usually start as a description or descriptive narrative, then either the poet or one of her characters or objects reflects. The tone of these reflections is pathetic, witty, fantastic, or shrewd. Frequently, it is all these things at once. Its purpose is to heighten and dramatize the description and, at the same time, to unify and universalize it. In this, and in her marvelous command of shifting speech-tones, Bishop resembles Robert Frost.

In her bare objective language, she also reminds one at times of William Carlos Williams; but it is obvious that her most important model is Marianne Moore. Her dependence should not be defined as imitation, but as one of development and transformation.

John Hollander. Parnassus.
Fall, 1977, p. 359

One hopes that the title of Elizabeth Bishop's new book is an error and that there will be more poems and at least another *Complete Poems.* The present volume runs to a little more than 200 pages, and although the proportion of pure poetry in it outweighs many a chunky, collected volume from our established poets (Miss Bishop is somehow an establishment poet herself, and the establishment ought to give thanks; she is proof that it can't be all bad), it is still not enough for an addict of her work. For, like other addicting substances, this work creates a hunger for itself; the more one tastes it, the less of it there seems to be.

From the moment Miss Bishop appeared on the scene it was apparent to everybody that she was a poet of strange, even mysterious, but undeniable and great gifts. Her first volume, *North & South* (1946), was the unanimous choice of the judges in a publisher's contest to which 800 manuscripts were submitted. Her second won the Pulitzer Prize. One of her poems is enough to convince you that you are in expert hands and can relax and enjoy the ride; in the words of Marianne Moore reviewing *North & South,* "At last we have someone who knows, who is not didactic." Few contemporary poets can claim both virtues.

Her concerns at first glance seem special. The life of dreams, always regarded with suspicion as too "French" in American poetry; the little mysteries of falling asleep and the oddness of waking up in the morning; the sea, especially its edge, and the look of the creatures who live in it; then diversions and reflections on French clocks and mechanical toys that recall Marianne Moore (though the two poets couldn't be more different; Miss Moore's synthesizing, collector's approach is far from Miss Bishop's linear, exploring one).

And yet, what more natural, more universal experiences are there than sleep, dreaming and waking; waking, as she says in one of her most beautiful poems, "Anaphora," to: "the fiery event / of every day in endless / endless assent." And her preoccupation with wildlife and civilized artifacts comes through as a exemplar of the way we as subject feel about the objects, living or inert, that encircle us. We live in a quandary, but it is not a dualistic conflict between inner and out reality, it is rather a question of deciding how much the outer reality is our reality, how far we can advance into it and still keep a toe-hold on the inner, private one, "For neither is clearer / nor a different color / than the other," as Miss Bishop says.

This strange divided singleness of our experience is a theme that is echoed and alluded to throughout Miss Bishop's work.

John Ashbery, *New York Times Book Review.* June 1, 1969, p. 8

The poems in *Questions of Travel,* and some of the new poems first printed in *The Complete Poems* are so clear they seem spoken by someone fresh from dreams, just awake. Many of them describe a country where the truth is almost as strange as dreams and to which the forms of legend and ballad ("The Riverman"; "The Burglar of Babylon") seem entirely appropriate. Humble figures are described in an understated, humorous fashion, and yet take on a mythical air, like the tenant Manuelzinho or the seamstress who grows to be like one of the Fates, Clotho nourished in their midst. But nothing is overdone or beyond the daily exercise of composing oneself. Here, I think, is the point at which Miss Bishop's poems are most provocative. Finally their technique is the opposite of the poetic journal, Lowell's latest urgent attempts at registering character in verse. Registering, transmitting, is the *Notebook*'s strongest effect, these poems which end in blazing nightmares, clear vision frayed by underground warnings. Miss Bishop's instinct—from which so much of the modern poetic interest in character derives—is something else: without ever abandoning the feelings of the moment, continually aware, constantly using verse to master the flood of the particular, she writes poetry to compose rather than expose the self. Doing that, her *Complete Poems* makes us alive again to what poetic *composition* is—both something private and something shared.

David Kalstone. *Partisan Review.* 37:2, 1970, p. 315

What is the color, the temperature, the tone, the quality of Elizabeth Bishop's voice? Is it obscure, sharp, profound, luminous? Where does it come from? Like the voice of any authentic poet, her voice comes from there, from the other side, which can be anywhere and anyplace. The voice the poet hears she does not hear in the oracle's cave but in her own room. Yet as soon as poetry occurs, "suddenly you're in a different place / where everything seems to happen in waves," one side of the buildings glistens like a field of wheat, and in the taxi "the meter glares like a moral owl." The poetic act frees things from their habitual associations and relations; on walking along the beach we see "a track of bid dog-prints," and at the end of the poem we discover that "those big, majestic paw-prints" were but those of the "lion sun, a sun who'd walked the beach the last low tide. . . ." In the poetry of Elizabeth Bishop things waver between being what they are and being something distinct from what they are. This uncertainty is manifested at times as humor and at other times as a metaphor. In both cases it is resolved, invariably, in a leap that is a paradox: things become other things without ceasing to be the things they are. This leap has two names: one is imagination, the other is freedom. They are synonymous. Imagination describes the poetic act as a gratuitous game; freedom defines it as moral choice. The poetry of Elizabeth Bishop has the lightness of a game and the gravity of a decision.

Octavio Paz. World Literature Today. 51,
1977, pp. 15–16

Elizabeth Bishop's poems in *Geography III* put into relief the continuing vibration of her work between two frequencies—the domestic and the strange. In another poet the alternation might seem a debate, but Bishop drifts rather than divides, gazes rather than chooses. Though the exotic is frequent in her poems of travel, it is not only the exotic that is strange and not only the local that is domestic. (It is more exact to speak, with regard to Bishop, of the domestic rather than the familiar, because what is familiar is always named, in her poetry, in terms of a house, a family, someone beloved, home. And it is truer to speak of the strange rather than of the exotic, because the strange can occur even in the bosom of the familiar, even, most unnnervingly, at the domestic hearth.)

Helen Vendler. Part of Nature, Part of Us
(Cambridge: Harvard University Press,
1980), p. 97

Bishop was not a believer; her use of the word "spiritual" is largely secular, as an equivalent for "significance." Nonetheless, much of Bishop's childhood was lived in an atmosphere of traditional Protestant faith. She spent formative years with her maternal grandparents in a Nova Scotia village. Her grandfather was a deacon; her aunts sang in the Baptist choir; and Bishop described herself as "full of hymns." Bishop's secular interest in the relationship of the seen to the significant does have a religious dimension: her tendency to "read" the world for signs of truth reflects the traditional Christian view of nature as God's second book. At the same time, her inability to find such signs, her insistence that "finding" them is not a matter of discovery but of subjective imposition, undermines all religious and metaphysical systems.

Several poet-critics testify to the religious tenor of Bishop's work, including her frequent use of such religious materials as miracles, revelations, Bibles, feast days, and hymns. Yet each observer also thinks that Bishop would have firmly repelled any description of herself as a "religious" poet. As Richard Wilbur says, "she had no orthodox convictions, and wondered at such certainties in others." In an interview, Ashley Brown asked Bishop if she thought it "necessary for a poet to have a 'myth'—Christian or other-wise—to sustain his work." The response was one Bishop gave elsewhere when faced with questions she found either too incisive or too abstract: "It all depends—some poets do, some don't." When pressed, she replied, "Some people crave organization more than others—the desire to get everything in its place."

Perhaps Bishop did "crave organization" less than others. Surely she subscribed to no religious or other comprehensive "myth." But it may be more accurate to say that although she craved organization a good deal—not least because of the disruptions and dislocations of her early family life—Bishop was less willing than most to force the particulars of experience to fit a satisfying or comforting pattern.

> Guy Rotella. *Reading and Writing Nature:*
> *The Poetry of Robert Frost, Wallace*
> *Stevens, Marianne Moore, and*
> *Elizabeth Bishop* (Boston: Northeastern
> University Press, 1991), p. 188

Bishop has been highly valued by critics and fellow poets but is too often overlooked by literary historians. Her style is understated, and as a result, historians have tended to overlook her not inconsiderable contribution to the development of contemporary poetic idiom. Bishop's work is not only large and complex but coherent and powerful. She responds with imagination, wit, emotional honesty, and keen intelligence to problems that have haunted the contemporary imagination: isolation, emotional loss, rootlessness, and the limits and possibilities of fiction. Self-pity, arguably the most pernicious of contemporary spiritual diseases, is her central subject. In poem after poem, self-pity is entertained but given no quarter. She vanquishes it to such a degree that one acute reader, the poet Mark Strand, was moved to say, in only partial error, "There is no self-pity in Elizabeth Bishop's writing." She is so subtle that some of her closest students can feel the major effect of her work (the purgation of self-pity) without quite recognizing its cause.

Bishop was not a world-historical figure, like Yeats, Eliot, or Lowell. Instead, she was one of those startlingly individual lyric voices who vex the historian, a voice as fresh and unique as Gerard Manley Hopkins, Emily Dickinson, or her own beloved George Herbert. As with them, complete recognition has taken time. Her historical importance rests, not on her imme-diate impact on her day, although that was greater than has been measured—she contributed importantly to the idiom of Robert Lowell and many of her younger contemporaries—but on the uniqueness and lasting value of her poetic creation.

> Thomas J. Travisano. *Elizabeth Bishop: Her*
> *Artistic Development* (Charlottesville:
> University Press of Virginia, 1988), pp. 4–5

Separated as she is from Dickinson both by time and temperament, Elizabeth Bishop nonetheless faces an allied if somewhat extenuated version of the Emersonian Sublime, and, once again, the crux of the poetic problem relates to gender. But Bishop, even more than Dickinson, defends against the challenge to her poetic autonomy by usurping the very terms in which it is made. In other words, Bishop compensates for the recognition of her loss of poetic authority in Emersonian terms by an erasure of the sexual dialectic upon which his vision fundamentally depends. Although Dickinson experiments with a similar strategy, substituting the male for the expected female pronoun or referring to her youthful self as a boy, she moves beyond gender only at intervals; it remains for Bishop to provide a sustained rhetoric of asexuality in order to find an adequate defense against the secondariness to which the American Sublime would sentence her. What distinguishes Bishop's work from the canonical American Sublime, I would suggest, is a loss equivalent to restitution, the enactment of Bishop's "I" as the eye of the traveller or the child, able to recapture an innocence that only apparently evades intimate sexuality or the assertion of gender. One finds in Bishop's poems a map of language where sexuality appears to yield to an asexual self, making possible a poetry that deceptively frees her from the gender-determined role into which she would be cast as a female descendant of the American Sublime. Bishop evades being diminished, exiled, or isolated from the tradition by sidestepping the distinctions imposed by Emerson and his agonistic disciples. Her poems' prevailing absence of the overtly sexual Whitmanian self, the apparent dismissal of heterosexuality, becomes a means of reestablishing woman's unmediated relationship to the world she would make her own. Thus, her poems are a kind of brilliant compensation, a dazzling dismissal of the very distinctions that might otherwise stifle her.

Joanne Feit Diehl. In Harold Bloom, ed.
Elizabeth Bishop: Modern Critical Views
(New York: Chelsea House, 1985), p. 178

Elizabeth Bishop concerned herself, throughout her career, with questions of mastery—artistic, personal, and cultural. Her poems portray both the desire for mastery and the dangers and illusions to which such desire is prone. Throughout Bishop's poems we find a strong urge for order and dominance confronting a recalcitrant world and volatile inner life. Bishop sometimes expresses dismay, even aristocratic disdain, over an untidy or barbaric world. But the same poet forces herself and her reader to encounter the mess of life, at times even to exhilarate in it. How much imaginative, cognitive, or political control can we have over a diverse and changing reality? What are the pleasures of relinquishing control? What limited forms of mastery remain necessary and viable? Bishop is a profoundly visual poet with an eye for the particular and mutable. Thus these questions of mastery promote new ways of seeing in time.

The traditions—devotional, romantic, and modern—out of which Bishop wrote often made the image a means of unifying experience and transcending time. Visual schemata might reveal a higher spiritual authority or concentrate experience in a unified aesthetic moment. Bishop's work responds to a broad and dynamic tradition of seeing and beholding—imitating, revising, challenging its claims and techniques. Her visual experience and the spatial and visual poetry which communicates it do not resist history and diversity but rather disclose it, challenging her position as a detached creative subject. She sets her eye not on the transcendental fade-out or on the modernist fixed object, but on the panorama and minutiae of a changing world which she tentatively orders and interprets.

Critics have long appreciated Bishop's visual accuracy and the spiritual and psychological expressiveness of her images. They have admired her skill in turning description to the task of mapping an inner life. "Everything has written under it—'I have seen it,'" wrote Randall Jarrell. John Hollander, on the other hand, calls Bishop's images "tropes of psyche, not mere reports from the psyche." What has not been sufficiently explored is the complex, unresolved relationship in this poet's images between observation and metaphor. To read Bishop's poetry is to be caught up in its descriptive vitality and its psychological and philosophical wisdom. But it is also to find the balance between them shifting and unstable. This fluency between description and trope relates . . . to the questions of mastery that pressure her imagination.

Bonnie Costello. Elizabeth Bishop:
Questions of Mastery (Cambridge: Harvard
University Press, 1991), pp. 2–3

BLAIS, MARIE-CLAIRE (CANADA) 1939–

Marie-Claire Blais was 20 when her first novel, *La belle bête* (Mad shadows), was published. She has survived the *réclame* of that novel and the stir it caused in her native Quebec, and also the inevitable comparison with Mlle. Sagan, who has set such a premium on precocity. Now, a full 22, Miss Blais has written her second book, and it shows an increasing maturity, primarily in a less evident desire to shock. *Tête-Blanche* (Whitey) is a story of childhood and the author writes it with the understanding of one who has survived the experience of being a singular child, but is still young enough to remember the pain.

Tête-Blanche, seen here mostly through letters and a diary, is a delinquent. At the beginning of the brief novel he is 10, and at the end he is only 15, but in the years he has learned all about cruelty, something about love and enough about "the others"—the world outside—to fall into despair. . . .

Miss Blais was a Quebec City stenographer when her first novel was published. The general reader may be surprised to learn that *La belle bête,* an earthy first novel, was published through the intervention of a priest. It got a mixed reception and one critic spoke of its "boozy, tumescent prose." This second novel is written without rhetoric or sentiment, and its plainness gives it power. Charles Fullman has supplied an unobtrusive translation, occasionally sacrificing idiom for accuracy. The stark unchildishness of *Tête-Blanche* may jar the reader, but reading it is not an easily forgotten experience.

Walter O'Hearn. *The New York Times.*
February 4, 1962, pp. 4–5

In approaching the novels of Marie-Claire Blais, there is one widely current assumption that it is important to dismiss from one's mind: the supposition, that is, that her work has anything in common with that of Françoise Sagan. . . . Mlle. Blais had published her first book at nineteen. Otherwise, she and Mlle. Sagan could hardly have been more different. Mlle. Sagan is a highly sophisticated Parisian, who goes in for fast cars and destructive drugs and complicated love affairs. . . . Mlle. Blais, on the other hand, comes out of a bleak bigoted Quebec. . . .

In *Une saison dans la vie d'Emmanuel,* the writer has made a definite new departure. The clairvoyant's crystal ball that revealed the diminished, remote and somewhat mysterious visions englobed in the early novels has the actual French Canadian world with the squalor and the squirming life that swarms in the steep-roofed cement-covered houses of the little Canadian towns. . . . Though the material of *Une saison dans la vie d'Emmanuel* is that of an actual milieu in all its prosaic and sordid detail, it is not presented prosaically nor even, in spite of its horrors, sordidly, but infused—and sometimes a little blurred—by the fantasies of adolescence, saturated with the terrors and appetites, the starving and stifled aspirations of these young people in their prisoned overpopulated world. . . .

The author of *Une saison dans la vie d'Emmanuel* has in the past sometimes been the subject of exacerbated controversy; but one now gets the impression, in reading the reviews of Mlle. Blais's latest book, that her compatriots—who are now so zealous, in their struggle against the English-speaking ascendancy, to put forward their cultural claims—are becoming proud of this young writer. Certainly, to the non-Canadian, the appearance of such a book as this—so far, it seems to me, much the best of Mlle. Blais's novels and the best I have read from French Canada except some of those by André Langevin—would seem to show that French Canadian literature, after producing a good deal of creditable work of merely local interest, is now able to send out to the larger world original books of high quality.

Edmund Wilson. Introduction to
Marie-Claire Blais. *A Season in the Life of
Emmanuel* (New York: Farrar, Straus &
Giroux, 1966), pp. v–ix

The Manuscripts of Pauline Archange begins by characterizing some Canadian nuns as "the chorus of my distant miseries, ancient ironies clothed by time with a smile of pity, though a pity that faintly stinks of death." At once we recognize a translation from the French. The first three sentences slowly unroll, almost filling two pages, like parodies of Proust. The length of the sentences is extended by the repetition of similes—each nun has "slim brown boots glimmering like furtive breaches of propriety" and a forehead "betraying like some secret frivolity its dark lock of thick hair"—by unnecessary adjectives and adverbs, and by rambling parentheses. . . .

The extravagance of the language may be partly the responsibility of the translator—who certainly offers some extraordinary dialogue. . . . But the extravagance of the incidents must be intended. In this Canadian town, torture is the main preoccupation: cats are skinned alive and children beaten until their eyes bleed. Meanwhile, a Genetesque priest makes love to a boy murderer with a vague, cruel smile. As a criticism of a Catholic upbringing, it is too nightmarish to carry weight. It reads like a child's crude fantasies, worked up by an over-literary adult. Its sensuous appreciation of pain, cruelty, and guilt is so unrestrained as to be finally ludicrous.

D. A. N. Jones. *New York Review of Books.*
October 22, 1970, pp. 38–39

It is worth noting that the structure of *The Day Is Dark,* a somewhat Gidean structure, is the same as that of *The Unsubmissive Woman.* In both Blais novels characters speak in turn, and each interior monologue forms a separate section of the book. The monologues add to or alter our feelings about the speakers created by the monologues of the other characters. In *The Day Is Dark* the characters' unbalance becomes evident even sooner than in *The Unsubmissive Woman.* . . .

Why are Blais's characters marked by misfortune and virtually fascinated by it? The answer is that they are all "unsubmissive.". . . What else is there to be said? They might be called metaphysical: they rebel against an eternal order of things (or at least against an order that has thus far been eternal)—the order of life, and therefore of time, and therefore of death. Very complex, secretive, and tormented, these characters have a romantic thirst for the absolute and the impossible. They want only to do good, and they lose their clear-sightedness in the process; they test their courage and do wrong, contrary to their intentions. With a shock of pain, they are made to face their imperfect and tragic condition—which is, moreover, governed by time. From the first page to the last of these short novels, death is an immortal bird spreading its black wings.

Yves Berger. Preface to *Marie-Claire Blais.*
L'insoumise (Paris: Éditions Bernard
Grasset, 1971), pp. 8–10

If in *The Unsubmissive Woman* Mlle. Blais indirectly explored the unrealized potential for good in the life of handsome, athletic, generous Paul Robinson, in [*David Sterne*] she investigates ugly tormented youth's capacity for evil and despair. The seminarian, Michel Rameau, is brilliant but frigidly rational. He believes that the only freedom in life lies in choosing one's own death. Sick and sensual David Sterne falls under his influence and together they conduct experiments in homosexuality, rape, theft, and prostitution. These are cold and lonely experiments which provide no enjoyment, not even the satisfaction of revolt, not even a sense of solidarity in evil, for the two "friends" find no challenge in corruption and eventually grow callously indifferent to one another. Compared to the unrelieved, driven decadence of these two, Jean-Le Maigre's and Number Seven's dabbling in crime and perversion [in *A Season in the Life of Emmanuel*] seems robust and innocent fun. Francois Reine, the human torch and the most likable of the three, in turn falls under David Sterne's influence and, despairing of his feeble attempts to help the poor or to save or even reach David, finally chooses self-immolation.

In *David Sterne* Marie-Claire Blais is working close to the bottom of her murky imagination. Obsessed as always by the existence of evil and by what François Reine calls "the problem of lost souls," she engages the problem less in pursuit of a solution than as an observer on a one-way trip down the vortex of despair. She does not judge her miserable characters; she hardly attempts to account for their misery; she simply assumes it and tries to give it dramatic expression. In doing so she refuses the novelist's conventional all-seeing, all-knowing privileges and attitudes and presents her subject from the inside. So intense is her effort of sympathetic identification that her style, freeing itself from the rather mechanical control of *The Unsubmissive Woman,* breaks away into the lyric disarticulation of *The Day Is Dark,* though this time it carries much more violence and terror.

Philip Stratford. *Marie-Claire Blais*
(Toronto: Forum House, 1971), pp. 50–51

A book which bears the same relation to these themes—the acquiescence in one's role as victim, the obsession with death—that, for instance, Cohen's *Beautiful Losers* does to Indians-as-victims and Gibson's *Communion* does to animals-as-victims is Marie-Claire Blais's *A Season in the Life of Emmanuel.* Again we find the poverty-stricken rural family, the mother drained by too-numerous babies, the coarse male figures who brutalize those weaker than themselves, the dying child, the daughter who elects to escape by becoming a nun. But the *willing* participation of the characters in the perpetuation of their own misery is here rendered explicitly. . . .

Two other themes which haunt Quebec literature are focused here also: the theme of thwarted incest (in a literature so family-centered, there are few other available love-objects) and the theme of total entrapment. The plight of English Canadian characters trapped by their family ties seems mild compared with that of the French Canadian ones: in Quebec, it seems, you can't leave home *at all,* and if you do you'll want to go back, no matter how miserable home was when you actually lived there. Jean-Le Maigre, dying in the infirmary, has a hallucination in which he's trying to escape from the seminary in order to return home. His hallucination ends in death, and in fact many escaped characters, when they or even their thoughts turn homeward, suffer a similar fate: Philibert, for instance, has been thinking of going home just before his fatal car crash. In the Quebec novel, the family is a claustrophobic inferno, but freeing yourself from it emotionally and returning to it once you've technically made your getaway are equally impossible. No wonder coffins seem preferable.

Margaret Atwood. Survival (Toronto:
Anansi, 1972), pp. 225–27

There's nothing phony or specious about *St. Lawrence Blues.* It's a marvelous tour de force that Blais sustains from the unbelievable beginning to the amazing end. And in her unflagging blaze of energy, in her inexhaustible fund of folklore, in her wild comic turns, her bitter local satires, she is nourished, supported, and enhanced all the way by a translator who is fully equal to her in energy, ingenuity and the love of language.

The story tells about the adventures of Ti-Pit as he lives his life in a parochial culture (Quebec) in all its boisterous detail. But behind the narrative voice of Ti-Pit is the voice of Blais, and it is anything but parochial; and behind Blais's voice is the translator [Ralph] Mannheim's voice with all its verbal intuitiveness and emotional intelligence. For me, as a reader, there's nothing left except to read the novel in the original French to see how he accomplished the impossible. To translate [the dialect] *joual* so that you are hardly aware of reading a translation is to perform a miracle. Thus a priest is a sky pilot, winter driving is to set sail in the snow, a poet is a scribbleroo, and so on from one richness to another. Blais presents us with an immense windblown tapestry of poor people—students, prostitutes, homosexuals, prurient landladies, red-nosed snow shovelers, oily lawyers, soft-hearted ambulance drivers; anyone who has ever known Montreal and loved it, will find more reason for it in these pages.

Miriam Waddington. Books in Canada.
November, 1974, p. 5

In some ways, *St. Lawrence Blues* is the first book in which Blais has attempted to bridge the gap between the old Quebec and the new one, to show representatives of both encountering each other, disputing, reacting. As such it's a very ambitious work, wide in scope, swarming with characters, aiming for breadth as well as depth. Blais has done many detailed studies of single characters, but *St. Lawrence Blues* is populous and many-faceted.

It's a fresh departure for her in other ways as well. She has always been amazingly versatile, switching with ease from romantic fantasy to novels of ideas to psychological studies to carefully drawn social chronicles. But *St.*

Lawrence Blues is none of these. The predominant note is satire. It's not a totally new element for Blais, as her previous work has often contained satirical and even humorous interludes; but these were asides, whereas in *St. Lawrence Blues* the tone is constant. . . .

Blais brings all the elements of her broad social canvas together at the end of the book in a giant demonstration against social injustice, which is supposed to be heroic but instead turns into a combination of farce and tragedy. The groups of demonstrators, including nuns, prostitutes, students, fishermen, homosexuals, and even some disgruntled policemen who feel the public is not grateful enough, wallow about in the ever-present snow, exchange insults, scuffle and shout each other down until the police break up the march with needless viciousness, killing a student in the process. Only then can the bewildered and injured treat each other with anything resembling kindness and humanity. For Blais, ideology separates, suffering unites. . . .

Reading *St. Lawrence Blues* is like listening to the many voices of Quebec arguing among themselves. It's a domestic argument, and as such, parts of it are not totally comprehensible to an outsider. There are private grudges, puns on names and titles, snide references, innuendos and complicated ingroup jokes. But like all domestic arguments, it provides more intimate and in many ways more accurate insights into the personalities of those concerned than their polished official facades would ever give away. This is the book of a culture laughing at itself; though as befits a colonized culture, the laughter is not totally lighthearted, not without bitterness and a characteristic Quebecois sense of macabre irony.

> Margaret Atwood. Introduction to
> Marie-Claire Blais. *St. Lawrence Blues*
> (Toronto: Bantam, 1976), pp. 9–11

In the first published novel of Marie-Claire Blais. *La Belle Bête,* a daughter sets fire to her mother and throws herself under a train, leaving her own daughter to wander off alone. In sharp contrast to this image of female hostility, two of Blais's most recent novels, *Les Nuits de l'Underground* and *Le Sourd dans la ville,* end with a younger woman's effort to bring an older woman back to life. And her most recent work to date, *Visions d'Anna,* concludes on a note of reconciliation between mothers and daughters, a reconciliation which promises to bring salvation to both.

In her novels Blais has recorded the disintegration of an outdated vision of the family and of the mother-figure who was traditionally at its center. Moving beyond this critique of existing social structures, she has begun to work out a new model of human interaction based on the very relationships among women which she had earlier seemed to reject. In Blais's recent work, this model—based on the reciprocal caring of mothers, daughters, sisters, friends, and lovers—offers the only hope of human survival in the violent climate of the modern world. . . .

In the novels where Blais recorded the breakdown of the traditional family and the tragic isolation of the individual, she showed herself to be conscious of the larger context of social reality within which these changes were occurring. Similarly, she sees the work of reconstructing relationships between individuals as essential to the reestablishment of a new form of social order, an order in which human concerns would once again provide a check to pervasive violence and destruction. Thus, in the relationships she describes in her recent fiction, Blais sets up a model of "feminine" caring, capable of combatting the "masculine" autonomy and violence which dominate the surrounding culture. In her emphasis on the connection between the personal and the social, and in her attempt to extend the relational capacities possessed by women to the society as a whole, Blais shares in a more general movement in contemporary feminist thought. . . .

It is somewhat ironic that, in her effort to define a new mode of human relationship, Blais has placed at the center of her vision the qualities of compassion and concern explicitly identified with the mother—the very mother she had rejected and even killed in her early novels. But Blais had long perceived in her maternal figures—even an ambiguous one like Grand-Mère Antoinette—a positive value which provided the hope of human continuity. Liberated from the repressive role which had been assigned her in the patriarchal system, the maternal figure, as Blais now sees her, has become free to exercise her essential capacity for caring—a capacity which may be shared by all women, mothers or not, and which is capable of animating an entire network of human relationships. As the life-giving mother had been the symbol of survival for her people in the world of nineteenth-century Quebec, it is the model of maternal nurturance and compassion which now, in Blais's twentieth-century vision, holds out the hope of survival for us all.

Mary Jean Green. In Paula Gilbert Lewis,
ed. *Traditionalism, Nationalism, and
Feminism: Women Writers of Quebec*
(Westport, Connecticut: Greenwood Press,
1985), pp. 126, 137

BLANDIANA, ANA (RUMANIA) 1942–

This selection of [Ana Blandiana's work *The Hour of Sand*] was about to be printed when the Revolution occurred; there is a tactful and tight-lipped Introduction using such phrases as "circumstances beyond her control," and an outspoken "Postscript" written after Rumania's transformation and casting light on the "circumstances" in question.

The poems themselves appear detached from the increasingly repressive conditions under which they were written, although a darkening of tone in the later pages betrays their author's mood. Blandiana is a more gentle, delicate poet than [Nina] Cassian; Rumanian critics have stressed the "purity" of her writing, with its slightly old-fashioned lyricism and its drowsy, haunting world of sleep and dreams, inhabited by angels, hermits, souls, stars and lovers. Poem after poem in the early parts of the book (the arrangement is chronological) speaks of sleep: "I pass through one life into another / Lightly stroking / The mane of the sleep-lion . . ."; "Perhaps someone is dreaming me . . ."; "Crickets make their music only in sleep . . ."

Blandiana is a Romantic poet, in the tradition of her great nineteenth century predecessor Eminescu, but there's nothing mushy about her poetry (or very little: "you can hear the grass / Tickling the stars in laughter" is an example of the whimsical note which occasionally creeps in). Her language has a tensile strength which keeps it from lapsing into flabbiness, in spite of the material she chooses to write about. In the later part of the selection, in poems taken from her 1985 collection *Star of Prey* and the subsequent one (not yet published in Rumania) the images become tougher—an eye "clenches its eyelashes like teeth"—and the tone is harsh and despairing, expressing a sense of being trapped and powerless. The last poem, "Ballad," refers to the legend of the master-builder Manole who was told in a dream that the monastery he was building would never be finished unless a living creature was walled up in it; the first to appear next morning was his wife Ana, whom he had to sacrifice for the sake of his vow. Her namesake, the poet, sees herself as comparably walled-in by events: "I have no other Ana / And myself even / Less and less often / Do I have."

The Rumanian text of this poem is printed facing the translation, which—as may be gathered from the somewhat un-English word-order—follows the original very closely. Jay and Cristofovici are scrupulously accurate translators, highly sensitive to the subtle pace and movement of Blandiana's language and to the shapes of her poems. The results are mostly admirable; only occasionally does their insistence on preserving the original punctuation (sometimes not entirely helpful in an English context) and their preference for the original order of lines and phrases lead to minor ambiguities, such as a noun which looks like a verb. At least we can be sure, though, that they are not distorting the content for the sake of effect: what they give us is, as nearly as possible, Blandiana's own poetry, and it's well worth having.

Fleur Adcock. *Poetry Review.* 80, 1990, p. 23

The latest book offered by Anvil Press in their excellent series on Rumanian poetry in English translation is the work of a poet whose name was often mentioned during the revolution in Rumania. Ana Blandiana belongs to a generation of Rumanian writers who came into full maturity in one of the most tragic periods of Rumanian history. In recent years she has been banned for her protest poetry. Due perhaps to the editors' intention to communicate, through this poet's work, something about poetry and the strategy of survival in such times, and together with the fact that some poems suffer translation better than others. . . . *The Hour of Sand* seems to serve best certain aspects of Blandiana's work, whereas other aspects are less well represented. The editors' selection makes her appear mostly as a voice of her later poems, a voice corrugated with anger, rendered harsh and adamant by the despair of witnessing. The theme is often disintegration and fear: "Twins in the uterus of fear / Inhabitants of the same cell / Blind and dumb / In the darkness savagely resonant / Only with the nourishing pulse." Humanity is "sentenced to birth, alone and impotent," and "the future life brews in the mother's body as if in a grave." Her latest poems furiously dismantle and cancel life's glory while their imagery borrows elements from the condition of womanhood: words like *fetus, uterus, blood, pregnancy,* and *delivery pains* return obsessively, as if to emphasize the supreme absurdity and waste of giving life amid defeat and destruction. The poems are shorter, as if, compressed by adverse forces or by the urgency of the issue at stake, the poet cannot afford to waste words or time any longer. At times the poems become almost fables, a form possibly dictated by the necessity to escape the watching eye of censorship.

Still, the feeling of a progressive darkening of mood that Blandiana's work began projecting throughout her ten books of poetry should not be exclusively attributed to the particular fold of history in which she has lived and worked. What happened between the debut of the adolescent girl who watched "the trees, vegetal satyrs / tossing round their hips their growth rings / headlessly dancing the hoola hoop" and her latest work was the life of a woman and a poet who, poem by poem and verse by verse, was moving closer to lucidity. The political and social themes are only part of the earnest questions which begin surfacing early in her verse: a search for purity, the struggle to remain faithful to a certain set of values in all circumstances, the responsibility toward her gift. In the headiness of youth Blandiana discovers her own "vulnerable heel," the title of her second collection of poems. Poetry becomes—and will remain throughout the poet's work—a grave self-interrogation, a search for one's own cardinal points, a severe scrutiny of life. The poet's progress toward lucidity is made painfully, with zones of delays and regrets, with nostalgia, with returns to a time of remembered innocence. One of her memorable poems on time and the rites of passage, "Portrait with Cherry Earrings," is born out of just such a zone. Unfolding like a dance of death on a medieval stained-glass window, adjusting the quality of its light to the succession of ages in a woman's life it depicts, the poem offers one of the best glimpses at the intimate sources of Blandiana's art. Its absence from the collection is regrettable.

Other important themes in Blandiana's earlier work—sleep and death and the way they intersect and borrow from each other—are also insufficiently represented. More than a retreat from the world, for Blandiana sleep is a state of grace and a time of creative bliss, holding the sleeper at its center. Along with poems of minor personal epiphanies of a particular charm, Blandiana also has poems of breath-taking perspectives, like "Genealogy" (also missing from the present collection), where "The first master / Of sleep, the one who sleeps, / At the foundation of the worlds" dreams the universe as a giant pyramid of sleepers who, in turn, are dreaming one another, "each one a tender link / in the chain without beginning." We recognize that mysterious energy, the creative power the dream holds in the world of legends, of spells and folklore myths, where heroes asleep receive guidance in their dreams, a place where imagination commands reality, a world familiar to this poet, raised and educated in a family with strong ties to the imaginative tradition of the village.

Despite its omissions, *The Hour of Sand,* with its skillful and respectful translations, is a successful effort of interpretation. In addition, the postface, rushed to the printer shortly after the December 1989 revolution, communicates to the reader something of the nightmarish conditions in which poetry survived in Eastern Europe while poet and reader sustained each other.

Marguerite Dorian. *World Literature Today.*
65, 1991, p. 103

Though her poems appeared in *Tribuna* from Cluj as early as 1959, Blandiana could not publish her first volume until 1964, after the process of de-Stalinization had started. *Persoana întîia plural* (First person plural) surprised critics with its fresh, uninhibited treatment of subjective emotion and exuberant imagery. Her second volume, *Călcîiul vulnerabil* (1967; The vulnerable heel), toned down the youthful rhetoric, introducing a more reflexive, self-questioning style that was to become Blandiana's distinctive feature. By the end of the decade, Blandiana was the acknowledged leader of a group of women poets who had made essential contributions to the "poetic revival of the 1960s." While Blandiana has never allowed herself to be categorized as a "woman poet" ("poetry, like truth, like freedom, cannot be categorized into great and small, good and bad, male and female"), her poetry balanced from the start existential and sociocultural concerns, an imaginative exploration of individual experience with an emphasis on broader sociophilosophical issues such as women's lot and experience.

Blandiana's subsequent volumes of verse, *A treia taină* (1970; The third enigma), *Cincizeci de poeme* (1970; Fifty Poems), *Octombrie, noiembrie, decembrie* (1972; October, November, December), and *Poezii* (1974; Poems), deepened and darkened this twofold concern. Very little of Blandiana's earlier expansive rhetoric survived in these poems: The reflection is internalized or impersonal—the motifs of sleep, silence, inner reflection predominate—the line is terse and nervous, devoid of "ornaments." Sentimentality is here refused in favor of an austere, detached mapping of essentials; poetry is no longer a transcription of emotional states, but an intense scrutiny of life, an act of skeptical cognition. Feminine themes are present—maternity, feminine sexuality, woman's spiritual needs—but they are broached from a transpersonal perspective that allows important moral and philosophical questions to be asked. The main emphasis is on cosmic "spending," on existential and poetic dissipation. And yet Blandiana's vision remains hopefully dialectic, highlighting alternatives, redefining the boundaries between nature and spirit, love and death, individual desire and norm. The competing terms are often described by striking oxymorons: Death is "clear," despair is "happy" and "gentle," light is "ferocious," darkness is "clean" and "tender," "loneliness is a happy town." Blandiana's deliberately ambivalent, antipoetic style calls into question traditional literary discourse, its problematic claims to truth. Words become the poet's necessary "adversaries" in a lucid dialogue about the limitations of art.

Blandiana's recent poems continue to reevaluate critically the relation of literature to existential and social truth. *Somnul din somn* (1977; The sleep in sleep), *Ora de nisip* (1983; The hour of sand, 1990), and *Stea de pradă* (1985: Predatory star) are underwritten by a sterner moral and metaphysical perspective, but also by a clearer understanding of a time of great personal and national crisis. Blandiana's sparse, thinly veiled imagery denounces collective compromises as in the famous lines that got an entire editorial board fired after their publication: "I believe we are vegetal people / How otherwise to account for this compliant / Shedding of our leaves." By and large, Blandiana's poetic evolution parallels the broader course of contemporary Rumanian poetry: expansive and lyrical in the early 1960s; philosophically skeptical and self-ironic in the 1970s; politically engaged and questioning in the 1980s.

Blandiana's prose reflections published over the years in two short columns have been collected in *Calitatea de martor* (1970; rev. 2nd ed., 1972; The mark of a witness) and *Eu scriu, tu scrii, el, ea scrie* (1976; I write, you write, he, she writes). These pages of an ongoing "antidiary" gloss with aphoristic crispness Rumania's recent cultural history, exposing its social and moral faults. Blandiana's gift for sharp observation and controversy is also reflected in *Convorbiri subiective* (1971; Subjective dialogues) and *O discuţie la masa tăcerii şi alte convorbiri subiective* (1976; A discussion around the silent table and other subjective colloquies)—two collections of spirited interviews coauthored with her husband, Romulus Rusan.

> Marcel Cornis-Pope. In Steven R. Serafin
> and Walter D. Glanze, eds. *Encyclopedia of
> World Literature in the 20th Century* (New
> York: Continuum, 1993), pp. 77–78

BLUME, JUDY (UNITED STATES) 1938–

Judy Blume, forty-four, godmother of upscale adolescent realism. Nineteen million of Blume's fourteen teen tales are currently in paperback. She tackles social and sexual mores with sprightly straight talk. In one of her books, a group of twelve-year-old girls stare at the centerfold in a copy of *Playboy,* marveling at the model's breasts. Exclaims one flat-chested admirer: "Look at the size of her! They're huge!"

In Blume's *Deenie,* the thirteen-year-old narrator faces disease and ignorance in Elizabeth, N.J. Suffering from scoliosis. Deenie must wear an ugly, uncomfortable back brace. The experience helps her overcome the primitive adolescent fear of being different. But Deenie represents up-to-date psychology as well. Could her curvature of the spine have been caused by occasional masturbation? Set straight by a briskly efficient gym teacher named Mrs. Rappoport, Deenie muses: "I never knew there was a name for what I do. I just thought it was my own special good feeling. Now I wonder if all my friends do it too?"

Blume explores both the spirit and the senses. In *Are You There God? It's Me, Margaret,* the twelve-year-old protagonist must choose her religion. Margaret's father is Jewish, her mother Episcopalian. The girl also fears that she will be the last of her clique to menstruate. Prays Margaret: "I'm going to be the only one who doesn't get it. I know it, God. Just like I'm the only one without a religion. Please . . . let me be like everyone else." . . .

She keeps her highly praised ear for dialogue in tune through the two thousand letters that she receives each month from youthful admirers. Asked one twelve-year-old: "Do you write your books from your mind, or do you use a kit?" Blume hardly needs a blueprint. Says she: "I don't have a teenage audience in mind when I write. I try to get inside the mind and skin of a kid, and let the book find its own audience." One nine-year-old requested, "Please send me the facts of life in number order." Blume replied, "Ask your parents." She hates to see her explicit novel of first love, *Forever,* on the shelves next to books for younger children. The bittersweet romance, however, is the volume most requested by teens in the New York Public Library.

J. D. Reed. *Time.* August 23, 1982, pp. 65–66

In my first exposure to Blume, a few years ago, I turned out to be immune to Blume fever. Her realism struck me as shallow, and I was put off by her knack for observing unpleasant details. Recently, I read her again, determined to find her magic formula. . . . [and] I am now ready to amend my . . . [views]. In a Judy Blume book, realism is everything. . . . True, she includes unpleasant details—things we all notice but usually don't mention—yet they increase the credibility that is the source of her magnetic power. Blume's technique might be compared to *cinema vérité,* she writes as though filming the landscape of childhood from the eye level of a child. She focuses on nearby objects and immediate events with a child's intense gaze, picking out details that evoke instant recognition. As in a play, dialogue carries the story along. It is colloquial, often funny, and always revealing. Blume doesn't mince words. Her stories are told in the first person—sustained soliloquies that are prodigies of total recall. Each novel begins on a note of candor. We have the feeling of reading a secret diary—something the writer intended only for himself. Thus, it seems natural when usually private matters are included.

Often, they are things that have to do with the dawning of sex, and though most are quite innocuous it is a shock to see them suddenly exposed in print. The effect is a mesmerizing intimacy, which convinces Blume's readers that she writes the whole truth about what kids think and feel.

The heroine of *Are You There God? It's Me, Margaret* is nearly twelve. Her overriding concern is that she won't mature as fast as her friends, though her head is also filled with thoughts about school, the boy who mows the lawn, the question of whether to be Jewish, like her father, or Christian, like her mother, and new social experiences, which include a first party where kissing games are played. As Margaret confides in God (a device that rubs me the wrong way but that I learned to put up with), she gives Him a running account of events during this suspenseful time. She is conscientious, relating everything she deems important. Each detail has meaning. . . .

Her realism serves well for comic effect in *Tales of a Fourth Grade Nothing,* the swallowed-turtle book. Kids always find breaking taboos and mentioning embarrassments immensely funny. *Fourth Grade Nothing* is a slapstick comedy of family life in which nine-year-old Peter is a victim of circumstance. His hitherto comfortable life comes unhinged when his parents produce a second child, nicknamed Fudge, on whom they foolishly dote. For Peter, life with Fudge is a series of indignities and inconveniences. His view of his little brother is unclouded by sentimentality.

Peter's account of family follies is continued in *Superfudge,* in which he is further burdened by a baby sister. *Superfudge* is a compendium of small-boy humor. The high point may be an episode concerning a lady who is willing to pay Peter for collecting worms. She offers five cents a worm. Peter and his partner in the worm business speculate on what the lady does with them. Worm soup? Worm stew? Worm-and-cheese sandwiches? By the time they get to worm ice cream, they are doubled over with laughter. Worm jokes are not new, but they're surefire, and Blume seems to have a limitless store of similar touchstones of childhood. However, *Superfudge* is better than a mere joke book. The fun lies in Peter's dry wit, yet beneath his veneer of cynicism the reader can detect a warm emotional message as Peter unconsciously reveals his growing fondness for both little pests.

No report on Blume is complete without a look at *Forever,* the book for which some critics have not forgiven her. *Forever* is the case history of a teenager's affair, in which Katherine, seventeen, deludes herself that she is truly in love and sleeps with [Michael]. The description of what Katherine and Michael do in bed, and what Katherine feels, is a carefully worded answer to questions hygiene manuals fail to address. The affair ends when Katherine falls out of love and realizes emotions can be unreliable. I found the encounter one of the dullest on record, but it is easy to see that a naïve reader must find it fascinatingly revealing. It is equally obvious that such a book would kick up quite a storm.

Without the revelations of *Forever* and the small, stunning shocks that Blume sprinkles through her other books like nuts in a brownie, she might not have lured so many millions of readers, but she has also won her audience through honest work, superior craftsmanship, and a talent for recreating an evanescent period of life—the years from nine to thirteen. She writes about the loneliness of being young; about youthful secrets—fear, anxiety, longing, guilt. It is rough being a kid, she often says. Her kids are swept along by capricious currents. They struggle to keep their sense of humor, and to keep their heads above water. At the end of the story, they find their feet for a moment of equilibrium as they contemplate the next stage of life. I sympathize with the librarians who hate to see *Tom Sawyer* and the rest of the books we have all loved shoved off the shelves, but the times, not Blume, are to blame for that. I find much in Blume to be thankful for. She isn't scary or sick. She writes clean, swift, unadorned prose. She has convinced millions of young people that truth can be found in a book and that reading is fun. At a time that many believe may be the twilight of the written word, those are things to be grateful for.

Faith McNulty. *The New Yorker.*
December 5, 1983, pp. 193–94, 198–201

Judy Blume's considerable gifts of humor, readability and child appeal mask her other vocation as a teller of moral tales. In *Iggy's House, Then Again Maybe I Won't* and now in *Blubber* she has dealt with questions of prejudice, conformity and cruelty. Although her heroes and heroines are never surrounded by a heavenly light, her bad guys and bad girls tend to be old-fashioned villains in that they are evil to the core.

The author has no illusions about children. In *Blubber* her kids pick their noses, pass gas, urinate on hedges and generally perform all the physical acts that most children do and most children's writers ignore. Judy Blume's children are also sophisticated, self-centered, often nasty and generally suburban American.

They speak right up for themselves. This time, it's Jill Brenner, a fifth-grader who relates how the kids in her class go after Linda Fischer and, led by the savage, unremittingly wicked Wendy, enjoy themselves as she devises new and crueler torments. Because Linda gives a report on the whale and because she is fat and ungainly, Wendy dubs her *Blubber,* and *all* the kids go along with the nickname and the gang-up.

Unlike other stories about victims, Judy Blume's sympathies do not particularly lie with Blubber. We never really get to know much about her, and when, suddenly, Wendy and her followers select Jill as the new victim, Blubber (now Linda again), joins the wolf pack enthusiastically. The author's focus then is not on the victim as it is in Taro Yashima's *Crow Boy* or on differences as in Eleanor Este's *The Hundred Dresses* or even on non-conformity as in Robert Cormier's *The Chocolate War.* This book, instead, focuses on the dormant, indiscriminate cruelty of the mob and the absolute evil of any leader who uses her powers to direct that cruelty against a victim. Mrs. Blume is also saying that nobody should *allow* herself to be victimized and that Blubber's helplessness is also responsible for the gang-up since she "lets everybody walk all over her . . . she looks for it."

It is possible to disagree with this latter point of view but not with Judy Blume's concern about cruelty and injustice. *Blubber* will be read by many children who love her books and who, I hope, will absorb her message.

Marilyn Sachs. *New York Times Book Review.* November 3, 1974, p. 36

Blume's writing has been criticized from every angle. Although few critics have come forward to support Blume's writing, because Blume dares to write about sensitive subjects, she has been attacked by many conservative authorities in the field of children's literature.

To understand this widespread critical assault, it is necessary to examine Blume's place in the field of young adult literature. To begin with, Blume is a writer of realistic fiction. *Time* magazine writer J. D. Reed aptly dubbed her the "godmother of upscale adolescent realism." Then there is the difficulty of distinguishing the realistic novel from the problem novel. Blume's characters clearly do have problems. Her books do not become problem novels because the stories do not focus on the problem but on the protagonists' resolution of the problem. Characters are the essential ingredient in a Blume novel. As Richard Jackson notes, "Each of her main characters faces a problem, but none of her books is about the problem; each is about a kid or kids in a real situation, facing it in his or her own way." Norma Klein observed in an article entitled "More Realism for Children": "Whenever you say you are interested in realistic fiction which deals with modern themes, people assume you mean something grim, what has come to be known as 'problem' books. That very term is revealing; it shows the extent to which we still regard any aspect of sexual development as negative, perforce a 'problem.'" Even renowned children's author Beverly Cleary has explained that she does not write problem novels: "I'm more interested in writing about people than problems. *Dear Mr. Henshaw* is about a boy that had a problem, not a problem that had a boy. I don't search for a new problem.". . .

Blume is not a narrative writer. We come to know the characters and their surroundings through their dialogue. Jackson says, "The British reviewers go crazy because there's no description. Judy doesn't like description. I asked her in *Tiger Eyes* to describe the ocean. She wrote it and she hated it and we cut it. It is not something she does with any comfort, nor does she believe it's necessary." Again, Blume shows through dialogue rather than tells. Her readers seem to find that seeing and hearing what happens is certainly more interesting than being told what is happening.

"The triviality of her thinking is matched by the sheer shoddiness of her English," says David Rees of Blume's style. "She employs the usual sub-Salingerese American first-person narration, but so unmemorably that it makes Paul Zindel's use of the technique look like startling originality. There is absolutely nothing in Judy Blume's style that defines it as specifically hers."

R. A. Siegal, in an article entitled "Are You There God? It's Me, Me, Me" in *The Lion and the Unicorn,* praised Blume's style on the one hand— "Blume's most characteristic technique and the key to her success is the first-person narrative. . . . All her books read like diaries or journals and the reader is drawn in by the narrator's self-revelations"—and damned it on the other— "Since all her books are told through the voice of a child narrator, the vocabulary is necessarily limited and the sentence construction basic and repetitious." . . .

Blume's characters fill out, not only physically but emotionally as well, until they are quite will rounded. Deenie and Davey, in particular, grow and change in the course of their stories. Her father's love is a positive force in Deenie's life, and Wolf, the young college student, helps Davey see that life is worth living. Essentially, however, both Davey and Deenie find an innate strength within themselves. Blume's characters may not suffer the poverty and cruelty inflicted on the characters in a Dickens novel, yet they do suffer the helplessness of youth. Critics who claim that Blume's protagonists do not experience pain are like Tony's mother who says, "What problems? A thirteen-year-old boy doesn't have any problems!"

Blume's heroes and heroines depict the powerlessness of childhood. Decisions are made without their input—decisions about jobs, new babies, and relocation of the family. However, they are not abandoned by their loved ones, as Saku Repo in *Canadian Dimensions* would make them out to be. "The children of Judy Blume are alone in a much more profound sense than orphan Anne Shirley ever was at the lowest point in her life. They can count on nothing but their own resources in figuring out how to survive with some integrity." This is simply not true. Even in the worst family situations—*It's Not the End of the World,* for example—Karen has a best friend that she can count on, and she has a younger sibling who needs her, and those two people are essential to Karen's survival. "The parent-child relationships," says Richard Jackson, "are always very interesting. All of her books contain very sustaining family situations—even the ones that are falling apart."

There is a vigorous sense of caring and kindliness in Blume's fiction that is not present in the work of other writers. Big sisters comfort younger siblings in *Just as Long as We're Together, Tiger Eyes* and *It's Not the End of the World.* Katherine, in *Forever,* tells her parents that she is keeping an eye on her younger sister at camp. Katherine's parents, too, are loving and understanding. Jill's mother, in *Blubber,* listens and gives astute advice. Blume has been criticized for not dealing with moral issues. What could be more virtuous than a warm, caring family relationship? Blume has said, "I expect to write about those subjects that are important to me. And what is especially important are human relationships." . . .

The debate over literary value may continue for as long as Blume's works are in print. Teachers and librarians and parents have to decide whether to take advantage of the popularity of the books or to attempt to undermine their impact. Even Blume's harshest critics may conclude that these books can at least be used to lead youngsters to more traditional material. Philomena Hauck has proposed this compromise: "Instead of ignoring the books or being ultra-critical of them, teachers and librarians will have to adopt a different stance. They should become thoroughly familiar with the Blume books. . . . Then they can talk to young people about them and gradually lead their young charges to become more critical and perceptive. . . . They can take them from where they are to other similar books which will bring greater insight and satisfaction." Don Gallo has advised teachers that "We do our students as well as ourselves a disservice if . . . we dismiss Judy Blume as a shallow writer because she writes as kids talk, uses one-dimensional characters, and deals with topics previously considered taboo by proper people." Many other critics, including Faith McNulty, are grateful to Blume for having "convinced millions of young people that truth can be found in a book and that reading is fun."

In more than twenty years the Blume titles have garnered more criticism than books by any other author of books for children and young adults. Teachers and librarians and critics may debate the pros and cons of Blume books, but youngsters continue to read them. As Ursula Nordstrom has so wisely said, "The children are new, though we are not." Richard Jackson quotes Blume as saying, "There will always be fear and hope, love and hate, jealousy and joy . . . because feelings belong to everyone. They are the link between the child of today and the children we were."

Maryann Weidt. *Presenting Judy Blume*
(Boston: Twayne, 1990), pp. 114–21

BOGAN, LOUISE (UNITED STATES) 1897–70

Under a diversity of forms, Miss Bogan has expressed herself with an almost awful singleness. . . . One can be certain that experience of some ultimate sort is behind this writing, that something has been gone through with entirely and intensely, leaving the desolation of a field swept once for all by fire. But the desolation is not vacancy or lassitude. The charred grass is brilliantly black, and the scarred ground is fascinating in its deformity. There still is life, hidden and bitterly urgent.

Mark Van Doren. *The Nation*. October 31,
1923, p. 494

The poet of the present age, in order to free himself from the handicap of the philosophical misconceptions of the age, has, I believe, to turn metaphysician in a profound and serious way if he is not to be victimized by false emotions, as most of our contemporaries in at least a measure are; or, if he is not to be, as Miss Bogan in some degree is, limited rather more than some of his more fortunate forefathers. Very few contemporary poets seem aware of the difficulty or seem willing to make the effort. I am thoroughly convinced that the effort need not be, as Mr. Allen Tate seems certain that it is, fruitless. The least—and the most—that one can demand of it is that it clear the air once and for all of a great deal of nonsensical doctrine and belief, along with the attendant feelings, and that it justify, and make it possible to assume with a measure of ease, a normal and more or less classical dignity of attitude toward human destiny and human experience, an attitude that at least *seems* natural to Hardy but that is achieved by only a few contemporaries (Miss Bogan among them) and by most of them (Miss Bogan included) only with a good deal of effort, suspicion, and trembling. The means to this end may strike the innocent bystander as unjustifiably complicated, but it is still the only means that will accomplish the end in a thoroughly satisfactory fashion. The short cuts invariably end in bogs, and the avoidance of the labor ends either in bogs or in insecurity.

Yvor Winters. *The New Republic.*
October 16, 1929, p. 248

There are bitter words. But they are not harassingly bitter. . . . There are paralleled series of antithetical thoughts, but the antithesis is never exaggerated. . . . There are passages that are just beautiful words rendering objects of beauty. . . . And there are passages of thought as static and as tranquil as a solitary candle-shaped flame of the black yew tree that you see against Italian skies. . . . There is, in fact, everything that goes to the making of one of those more pensive seventeenth century, usually ecclesiastical English poets who are the real glory of our two-fold lyre. Miss Bogan may—and probably will—stand somewhere in a quiet landscape that contains George Herbert, and Donne and Vaughan, and why not even Herrick?

Ford Madox Ford. *Poetry.* June 1937,
pp. 160–61

The virtues of her writing which have been most often spoken of are, I should suppose, firmness of outline, prosodic accomplishment, chiefly in traditional metrics, purity of diction and tone, concision of phrase, and, what results in craft from all these, and at bottom from a way of seizing experience, concentrated singleness of effect. . . . A large part of their moral force derives from the refusal to be deluded or to be overborne. The learning of the unwanted lesson, the admission of the hard fact, a kind of exhilaration of rejection, whether of the scorned or the merely implausible, the theme appears in the earliest work. . . . It is an art of limits, the limit of the inner occasion and of the recognized mode.

Léonie Adams. *Poetry.* December, 1954,
pp. 166–69

The body of her complete poetic work is not great, but the "range," both emotional and geographical, is much wider than might be expected from a lyric poet. There is the brilliant (and exact) imagery of her New England childhood; there is also the highly formal world of Swift's Ireland; the rich and baroque background of Italy called up in the evocative "Italian Morning." And, of course, her beloved Austria. Her best lyrics, unlike so much American work, have the sense of a civilization behind them—and this without the deliberate piling up of exotic details, or the taking over of a special, say Grecian, vocabulary.

Invariably these effects are produced with great economy, with the exact sense of diction that is one of the special marks of her style. Even out of context, their power, I believe, is evident. . . .

The imagery in some of the last poems is less specific, yet still strongly elemental; we have, I think, what Johnson called the grandeur of generality. They are timeless, impersonal in a curious way and objective—not highly idiosyncratic as so much of the best American work is. Her poems can be read and reread: they keep yielding new meanings, as all good poetry should. The ground beat of the great tradition can be heard, with the necessary subtle variations. Bogan is one of the true inheritors. Her poems create their own reality, and demand not just attention, but the emotional and spiritual response of the whole man. Such a poet will never be popular, but can and should be a true model for the young. And the best work will stay in the language as long as the language survives.

Theodore Roethke. *On the Poet and His Craft* (Seattle: University of Washington Press, 1965), pp. 133–34, 148

Theodore Roethke, who learned a great deal from her, has written the best-known tribute to Miss Bogan. He distinguishes her from other women poets who hide "from the real agonies of the spirit," who refuse "to face up to what existence is." *The Blue Estuaries* is the portrait of a remarkable sensibility, one free from what Ezra Pound called "emotional slither," one whose constant attempt is to define and dramatize what Roethke himself called "the cold fleshless kiss of contraries" ("Her Becoming") and "the dreary dance of opposites" ("What Can I Tell My Bones?"). In Bogan life is neither all one thing or another. The life force giveth and the life force taketh away. Here is a poetry of meditation. Where to stand in a changing world, a world in which both our desires and the objects of our desires change?—this is the question. I keep going back to "Short Summary" as one of the poems most representative of her stance and voice, and also as one of the poems that best illustrate how in Miss Bogan's work repeated readings yield layers of meaning. . . .

The great strength of Louise Bogan's poetry is its compression. No poet has been more adamant that she in demanding the uncluttered line and the precise image.

William Heyen. *Prairie Schooner.* 43, Fall, 1969, pp. 323–35

It is [a] constant conflict between will and authority that shapes Bogan's poems. Because she herself unconsciously represented some of the strictures her spirit rebelled against, only form and symbol can express the tight, concentrated emotion of the unconscious struggling with the conscious. Although she strove always to make her poetry something beyond the narrowly personal and to cast out "small emotions with which poetry should not, and cannot deal," to be objective (a note on the worksheet indicating the poems to be published in the volume *The Sleeping Fury* says ". . . they must be as objective as possible"), it is often the personal emotion of the poet that informs the poem and gives authenticity to it. The emotion which is distanced by formal structures, sometimes distanced to the point of a "mask," a male persona, operates to illustrate the inherent conflict that the poem is really about. . . .

Her use of lyrical stanzas with second and fourth lines of rhyme or slant rhyme link the intellectual content of the poem with the subjective response to rhythm and sound. The appeal is to both the conscious and unconscious, and the imagery is of both: the images of the conscious of the first two stanzas and the images of the unconscious in the last two ("whispers in the glassy corridor" is especially wonderful in combining sound, imagery, and meaning). The tone is one of unhappy questioning rather than of being "contented with a thought / Through an idle fancy wrought." Her poem wonders about the human state that, by implication, is ruled by the same "forms and appetites" as the rest of nature, but aspires to more and therefore suffers. . . .

Louise Bogan once made the comment that highly formal poetry has always been obscure because the universe is difficult. Her own formal poetry is an acknowledgment of that difficulty, that obscurity, and of the complexity of modern truth.

Jacqueline Ridgeway. Women's Studies. 5:2,
1977, pp. 141, 147–48

Louise Bogan was a poet who matured during the first half of this century and who embraced traditional forms, masks, and mythologies. Compared to contemporary women poets, she is neither direct, personal, or particular. Yet buried under the metrical decorum, the masks, the symbols, and the reticence of her poetry is a person who is painfully aware of her situation as a woman, and who tries to escape it. . . .

The strongest desire in Bogan's poetry has Emersonian overtones: she wants to recover a sense of wholeness in the face of the human passion for destructive analysis. Bogan dislikes anything that the human mind superimposes on the world because human interpretations or analyses are distortions of the unity of nature and experience. Her clearest expression of this dislike is in "Baroque Comment." . . .

"Masked Woman's Song" is extremely oblique and can only be understood by sifting it through the motifs in her other poems. . . . In Bogan's poetry men are always threatening or betraying. They try to pin women to words in "The Romantic," try to trap women in those forms "Coincident with the lie, anger, lust, oppression and death in many forms" in "Baroque Comment," and try to reduce women to heartless, emotionless servants who "return, return, / To meet forever Jim home on the 5:35," in "Evening in the Sanitarium." . . .

In ["Masked Woman's Song"] . . . Bogan writes that men have overthrown the constructive values of life, like freedom and love, and have forced women to live, out of fear, at a distance, masked from the varieties of experience and the wellsprings of life. But such an interpretation must be made between the lines: Bogan's attitude toward men, as ever, is obscured by her restrained and elliptical style. Her true feelings are blurred by symbol, distanced by masks, muted by form.

Today, needless to say, such a style is rare, if not impossible, in a feminist poet. Where free verse is the exception in Bogan's poetry, something like a sigh of relief in a wasteland of anxiety and repression, most contemporary women poets use free forms as a matter of course, for their spontaneity, directness, and freedom from objectification and unwanted literary associations. But contemporary women poets have much less to fear than Bogan did; feminism is more secure now and support groups abound. Yet Louise Bogan was one of the earlier women poets who pointed to a way out of the strangling forms and mentalities of traditional verse. If for no other reason than that, her life and her poetry deserve our interest and attention.

Patrick Moore. In Janet Todd, ed. *Gender and Literary Voice* (New York: Holmes and Meier, 1980), pp. 67–69, 78–79

Louise Bogan is a modernist with a difference—she is a woman. A formalist, she writes from female experience: Her integration of a glassy poetic surface and female subject matter have confused formalist and feminist critics alike. Assumptions about formalism and female subject matter have hindered access to the critical tools that would help us understand the work of Louise Bogan. This idea of "limitation" links form and subject matter as it suggests a relationship: The white woman poet must define herself in terms of two traditions, the female and the male. In Bogan's work, this negotiation led to an "aesthetic of limitation," or a strict idea of what a woman poet could and could not permit herself. A self-taught literary historian and the poetry critic of the *New Yorker* for thirty-eight years, Bogan absorbed modernism's formal lessons, using its standards of compactness and control to rein in "female emotion"; yet her subjects were women's subjects, heterosexual love and disillusionment and breakdown and an uneasy peace with the self. Her work is an extreme example of a woman's internalization of male ideas of the woman poet. The limits Bogan imposed on herself and the creative limits that were placed upon her are identical. Her oeuvre is contained in the one hundred five poems of her final collection, *The Blue Estuaries: Poems 1923– 1968*. Out of this self-censorship came perfectionism and, inevitably, silence.

Yet paradoxically, as she encapsulated male strictures, Bogan created a peculiarly female idiom, thus adding to and transforming the female tradition of poetry. . . .

Those anthologies of poetry by women that we welcomed in the 1970s inevitably included poems with "female" or "woman" in the title; thus, among feminists Louise Bogan is best known for her poem "Women." And "Women," we should not be surprised to learn, has been read as a "self-hate," and thus a "woman-hating," poem. . . .

We need to understand that Bogan at once includes and excludes herself from this indictment. "Women," published in her first book, when she was twenty-six years old, reflects her famous ambivalence about women in general and thus about her own gender. Mary de Shazer and Cheryl Walker think the change in syntax in the final couplet ("As like as not. . .") reflects a sympathy for women and an understanding of our position in the world; Louise Bogan herself set special store by the poem early in her career since she had it reprinted for private distribution in 1929. Years later, in a reading of the poem at the Library of Congress, she said that over the years she had learned to appreciate, admire, and value women. It is this complexity of ambivalence that we find registered in Bogan's oeuvre. In fact, "Women" deserves to be read, not as an isolated poem in an anthology, but in the context of a lifelong quest for expression. Louise Bogan is at times contemptuous of women, and herself; at times appreciative of us, and capable of self-love. What one can always expect from her is an art that is as brutally honest as it is perfectionist. At the heart of her work and life is a terrible balance— that precarious tightrope position between the female and male traditions of poetry, between psychic health that made creativity possible and breakdown that ended it, between love that nourished and love that destroyed. "It is no small thing to know, as precisely as Louise Bogan did, what it is to be a woman," wrote Ruth Limmer in her introduction to the letters. In the end, if closely read, the poetry that seems to conceal in fact reveals worlds— probably much more than even Louise Bogan knew.

Gloria Bowles. *Louise Bogan's Aesthetic of Limitation* (Bloomington: Indiana University Press, 1987), pp. 1–2, 4–5

BOMBAL, MARÍA LUISA (CHILE) 1910–80

María Luisa Bombal's first novel, *La última niebla,* was published in 1935 in Buenos Aires. Her second novel, *La amortajada,* appeared in 1938. In 1947 she published *The House of Mist,* a novel in English based on *La última niebla.* These three books and a few short stories are all that she has written. In 1963 she was supposed to be working on another novel, *El Canciller,* which had originally been written in English in 1953 and was called *The Foreign Minister.*

María Luisa Bombal was chosen for this study because her treatment of alienation and loss of self seen in *La última niebla* represents two fundamental possibilities of the theme. She shows alienation, as a human experience, arising from personal, internal forces. Cedomil Goić states: "The world exposed in *La última niebla* has as its only base the personal existence of a woman reflectively turned upon her own destiny. This novel is distinguished by its personal structure." This evaluation is not completely accurate. Although the personal element is predominant, there are social conditions, secondary in nature, that are important in terms of alienation. These will be examined later.

Bombal's literary treatment of the theme is its other fundamental possibility; the mode of presentation, development, and structure is poetic. Amado Alonso in his introduction to *La última niebla* emphasizes this: "The natural and direct form of narration is due, if I am not mistaken, to the sure knowledge of having a poetic concept to present. Thus the nature and function of the imagery will be central to an examination of alienation and loss of self. It will be seen that concrete entities are used to symbolize and give poetic value to the alienated state. In addition, literary or thematic devices serve to distance the reader from the material, again creating a poetic experience of alienation.

Amado Alonso and Cedomil Goić both consider the date of publication of *La última niebla,* 1935, to be important because it marks a change in Chilean literature. Novelists up to then had been writing under the influence of naturalism, but around 1935 literature in Chile began to reflect surrealism and other contemporary movements of world literature. Goić says: "When María Luisa Bombal begins to write, she does so completely within the system of preferences of the new sensibility. She belongs to a younger generation than the surrealists; she moves with comfort and surety of means within the new rules imposed on the contemporary novel."

Although the emotional states described in *La última niebla* are of great complexity and artfully constructed, the overall emotional trajectory of the protagonist is quite simple; starting from an unhappy marriage, the protagonist moves away from the real world into herself, through a process of increasing fantasy, and then is forced to retreat from this created world to face the realities of aging and emotional barrenness. Her interior movement is the focus of the novel.

However, there are exterior social dimensions that, although they never come into the foreground, provide a hidden influence that tends to push all Bombal's women into themselves, giving them a feeling, frequently not expressed, of lack of control over their lives. The position of women in the society described in her novels is the most outstanding of these forces, in that it makes marriage the central issue of their lives. On the emotional level, the most important one within Bombal's works, this position gives men the power of choice as opposed to women's relative helplessness, turning men into an external alienating force.

M. Ian Adams. *Three Authors of Alienation: Bombal, Onetti, Carpentier* (Austin: University of Texas Press, 1975), pp. 15–17

Alienation—defined as powerlessness, meaninglessness, isolation, normlessness and self-estrangement—is fundamental in these novels. The transference of these sociopsychological categories from the domain of industry to that of marriage is warranted by the asymmetrical power structure between the male and the female in marriage, which gave rise to Engels' still apt observation, "Within the family he is the bourgeois, and the wife represents the proletariat."

Frustrated expectations perpetuate female powerlessness. This is especially obvious in the case of the nameless protagonist of *La última niebla* and of Teresa in *Chilena, casada, sin profesión,* women whose husbands keep themselves aloof. At the psychological level neither woman can exert any influence whatsoever to change this situation, and at the material level there is no possibility of self-determination. . . .

In *La última niebla* the only alternative to marriage for the narrator would have been to remain a "solterona arrugada" (a wrinkled old maid), and Blanca Ordóñez recalls that "Pensar que Teresa y yo no soñábamos más que con casarnos. ¿Qué otra cosa se hubiera podido hacer?" (To think that Teresa and I didn't dream of anything other than getting married. What else could one have done?) The narrator's sense of powerlessness is so overwhelming in *La última niebla* that she no longer functions as an autonomous entity, for her loss of will and self-direction reduce her to the behavior of a robot as she follows her husband. . . .

The rupture between the individual and her role expectations gives rise to a sense of isolation, formulated in similar metaphors. Detached from a solid familial identity, Blanca Ordóñez finds herself "tan sola y alejada como si fuera un velero fantasma, sacudiéndose en su rada" (as alone and distant as though she were a phantom sailboat, flapping its sails in its bay), and Teresa admits that "a veces sueño con que me dejan sola en un desierto o en un mar, no sé, y despierto sin haberlo sabido; en la pesadilla todos se van sin mí" (sometimes I dream that they leave me alone in a desert or in a sea, I don't know, and I awaken without having known it; in the nightmare they all leave without me). Although such symptoms of alienation—powerlessness, meaninglessness, normlessness, isolation—are not necessarily sex-linked, self-estrangement *is* directly related in these novels to the protagonists' being-in-the-world as females. It is connected, therefore, with the usage of the term "alienation" in existentialist philosophy.

The clearest indication of the insecurity of these characters is their obsessive concern with the mirror. They subject themselves to an interminable self-scrutiny, resulting not from narcissism but from the endless assessment of their desirability to a man. The body, meaningful only as a synthesis, is fragmented into separate parts of erotogenic significance as these women observe themselves as outsiders, adopting the male point of view.

Marcia L. Welles. In Beth Miller, ed.
Women in Hispanic Literature: Icons and Fallen Idols (Berkeley: University of California Press, 1983), pp. 282–85

The work of María Luisa Bombal is, in the opinion of many, representative of a typically feminine literary corpus. Its sentimentality and poeticization mask the dark continent of the body, and its passive female characters, who appear unaware of historical process, are consonant with the ontological and behavioral models assigned to women by society. Notwithstanding, in the margin of these texts that the critics of the time applauded as "a subtle expression of the mysteries of the feminine soul," María Luisa Bombal strategically demonstrates a part of the forbidden fruit by inoffensively transgressing against a literary norm and giving voice to a silenced historical reality. The key to understanding her work, then, lies precisely in this confluence of that which is accepted by masculine values and that which is marginal, which expresses the repressed areas of femininity.

The absence of a real questioning of the system is the key aspect for understanding the ideology and the message of María Luisa Bombal in all its complexity. The assumption that it is the nature of women that makes the man always the center of her life implies a conception of "the feminine" and "the masculine" as innate, static attributes constituting what Roland Barthes called a myth—that is, a process of conceptualizing and signifying the world that is motivated by the need to maintain the dominant order that presents itself as the natural order. That is, the myth of intuition versus intelligence, fragility versus virile strength, feminine sentimentality versus rational power. Conceptualizations that in our Western culture have deliberately masked the fact that "the feminine" and "the masculine" are social categories, susceptible of modification by history.

A surprising fact for anyone who studies the work of María Luisa Bombal is to recognize that the author had a very conservative ideology, that her version of the sexes reflected an internalization of these values. . . .

The work of María Luisa Bombal . . . suggests that the confluence of the marginal and the conventional culminates in hermeticism. . . . And the categories of this version of the world so appropriately reflected in a . . . tension-laden configuration are similarly related to the historic situation of women in Latin America who, in the 1930s, did not even have the right to take an active part in politics. Probably, apart from this hermeticism, there is also a hollow zone, a silence, where the repressed negative, that is, the anger, the rebellion, and the body of a real woman, is masked in wrappings of shame and euphemism imposed on the women's literature of the time.

Lucia Guerra-Cunningham. *Revista Chilena de Literatura*. 25, April, 1985, pp. 90, 98–99

La última niebla is not included in the canonical corpus of Latin American criticism among the founding texts of our modern literature, that is, what was recognized and accepted as "new" in the mid-1960s and that perhaps we shall soon be calling "classic." Nonetheless, María Luisa Bombal's first book, published in 1935 as the *Universal History of Infamy,* reflects certain characteristics similar to those of the other founding texts of modern Latin American literature in this century, and these characteristics were recognized very early in a number of works. . . .

In his 1976 book devoted to the author, Hernan Vidal proposed that *La última niebla* be included among the works that, in one way or another, showed a subversive attitude with respect to the bourgeois epic spirit of the earlier narrative. Calling attention to the poetic quality of Bombal's prose has been a commonplace of criticism; the homogeneity of the discourse, without gaps between the "real" and the "unreality" of dream, fantasy, or obsession *(La última niebla),* or between life and an intermediate state between life and death *(La amortajada)* have placed the writer in the avant garde marked by surrealism. . . .

The hiatuses between the juxtaposition of episodes are repositories of significance in the novel; in these blank spaces the variegated voice of the narrator appears to echo, a voice of what is missing from the outside world. . . . The breakdown of the protagonist of fiction says little about the female essence. Beyond showing that woman "lives for the affective life of the soul" (Amado Alonso); beyond having its origin in her "imaginative and dreamy nature" (Cedomil Goić), the breakdown exemplifies *the situation in which the woman is placed* (or was placed in a Latin American country at the beginning of the twentieth century) who transgresses the male norm to elevate herself to the (masculine) acts of imagining and writing.

María Luisa Bastos. *Revista Iberoamericana*. 51, 1985, pp. 557–58, 564

Although the era in which María Luisa Bombal wrote has passed, the intrinsic value of her work endures, because it reflects a debate of vital interest in her time and in ours, the condition of woman in her time and in relation to the opposite sex. . . .

Her work is notable for the human thematics that vibrate in it, distilling through her stories and novels the evil consequences of a society regulated by worn-out forms of behavior. . . .

The women that María Luisa presents belong to the traditional type: passive, domestic, and not aggressive. They are, generally speaking, wives, sisters, daughters or lovers. But the writer pays greatest attention to the role of wife.

There is usually a rift between the woman and her husband. . . . Brigida in "El Arbol," Ana Maria in *La amortajada,* or the protagonist of *La última niebla* represent the continuity of the same problem: being part of a marriage that is falling apart, because the grounds on which it was based are wrong is a theme that interested Bombal enormously, that she analyzes from all angles, because she sees it as an insuperable obstacle to equality between the sexes.

In marriage as she represents it, women experience frustration, unhappiness, lack of common interests, lack of sexual and mental communication. All of them enter the married state for reasons other than love, false motivations, whether they were looking for social position, economic security, or protection. It is therefore in the affective area that their greatest disillusionment occurs. . . .

From her exploration of humanity and with the goal of reestablishing the marital equilibrium by transforming it, Bombal tries to protest the system. How can society be changed? What roles should men and women assume to improve their relationships?

In this search, the idea of change arises, a change that is tacitly expressed in the creation of the imagined life, endowing the imagination with the principal and specific function of sublimating and healing reality in the face of the absence of satisfaction or gratification in the outside world. . . .

As the most important Chilean writer of the 1930s and as a woman she is admired because she gave shape to her ideas in a world that was not yet capable of understanding them.

Gloria Gálvez Lira. *María Luisa Bombal:*
Realidad y fantasía (Potomac, Maryland:
Scripta Humanistica, 1986), pp. 95–97, 102

BOSCO, MONIQUE (CANADA) 1927–

Poststructuralist criticism has eagerly seized upon Gide's concept of "mise en abyme," a phrase he borrowed from heraldry where the inner design of a shield repeats the overall pattern. Modern critics have extended this synecdochic relationship to include the image of two mirrors facing one another thus creating infinite reflection, repetition, or vertigo such as might be experienced on the edge of an abyss. This sense of vertigo appears as an important characteristic of Quebec fiction in general, and more specifically, the "mise en abyme" effect seems central to the novels of Monique Bosco. The present study seeks to explore some varieties of "abyme" that inform Monique Bosco's writing, as her characters lose themselves in bewildering labyrinths of obsessive repetition, from which they emerge only to find themselves reeling on the brink of an abyss. Repetitive thoughts, actions, and language that preoccupy her protagonists and narrators reveal dilemmas paradigmatic of modern fiction.

Un amour maladroit (An awkward love), (1961) winner of the American first-novel award begins with . . . lines [in which] Bosco announces her obsession with lamentation: repetitive tears in front of repetitive walls that connect her to her ancestors. In her claustral universe "walls" play a central role, occasionally pierced by windows or mirrors that, instead of offering relief or escape, merely intensify the sense of endless repetition and incarceration. Immediately following the poem about Jerusalem's Wailing Wall or psychological ghetto walls, the narrator "reflects" upon her existence. . . . Through her looking glass the narrator perceives a doubling confirmation of her internalized identity, a vision confounded by domestic labyrinths. . . . By the end of the novel she has resolved the question posed at the outset of how to grasp her life as she returns to her mirror. . . . Where earlier she had sought "le miracle d'une metamorphose," she now resigns herself to confronting a reality unchanged by flattering mirrors.

Like all self-reflexive mirrors, the windows in *Un amour maladroit* offer no outward escape, for they serve only to isolate Bosco's young protagonist from society. She addresses the shop window separating a little girl from toys: "Un meme mur, invisible comme une paroi de verre, se dressait toujours entre la vie et moi" (The same sort of wall, invisible as a sheet of glass, always stood between me and life). This self-proclaimed masochist finds no outlet at her window which reminds her only of the happiness of others. . . . While others rush forward, she remains alone, static, petrified at her window. . . . Not unlike Anne Hébert's heroines, Monique Bosco's protagonists find themselves stationed at windows peering into vacant external worlds, or surrounded by walls that enclose an equally internalized emptiness.

Michael Greenstein. Canadian Literature.
99, 1983, pp. 48–49

In the wake of Monique Bosco's poetic oeuvre, one wonders if one can ever draw from it the same substance as from her fiction. One is right to wonder, but the question arises in other terms. Let us say that the same substance could be human misery. This is a hypothesis. One will find this misery in both the novels and in the poems, but the latter will translate it into the very quick of language, while the novel will modulate it through characters in situations. The changes of form will have modified this substance so much that they themselves will be what replaces it: unassimilable language fields.

Let us understand, as well, that Bosco's poetry has not, hitherto, obtained the recognition that it deserves. *Schabbat* speaks more softly than *Un amour maladroit; Jericho* does not arouse the same echo as *Charles Levy, M.D.* . . as *New Medea,* or as *La Femme de Loth* (Lot's wife). Certainly. The poems published in periodicals perhaps do not exist. There's a challenge there to pick up. It can always be argued that this poetry has presented its strangeness more than its similarity. A limpidity and a restraint, a timidity and a sincerity that the institution has not known what to make of. . . .

The eighteen poems that appeared in *Ecrits du Canada français* in 1963 . . . modulate in their way, which is rapid and direct, the unhappy confidences already given in her first novel, *Un amour maladroit* (1961). It is the revelation of a life of splits and tearings-away, a route of wanderings and sojourns as only Jewish destiny has known and still knows. But here it is a woman speaking. . . . I do not see how this 1963 series of poems could have received the "critical" reception that it deserved or how it could have been harmoniously integrated into the Quebecois literary context, given the ideological violence that marked the passage of Quebecois poetry from the nationalist to the revolutionary stage . . . and given, as well, the historic silence of women. How could wandering Jewry have nailed down its corner into sedentary Quebec-itude? . . . On top of this, in Quebec as elsewhere, one might mention the oppression of a patriarchal system that mystified, deformed, or distorted women's words. Bosco in theory had nothing going for her. It is the patience of the woman writer, novelist and poet, that in the long run conquered general apathy. A more receptive time has come that now gives us access to this body of work.

Joseph Bonenfant. Voix et Images. 9, 1984,
pp. 13–14, 16

The sensitive, fragile reader does not descend without discomfort into the tragic universe of Monique Bosco. Like [her] Charles Levy in the caves of Bellamar, "au coeur même de la noirceur et des entrailles du monde" (in the very heart of blackness and the entrails of the world), he is seized by anguish in this cavern of mother earth, decorated by monstrous phalluses. "La, en bas, c'est la mort" (There, down there, is death) while at a distance, very high up, in "ce faible rais de lumiere, d'un bleu blafard, c'est la vie, c'est là, dehors" (this feeble ray of light, of a blinding flue, is life, there, outside) out of reach. Primordial scene. All of Monique Bosco's work, whatever the modulation of the descent to hell may be, gives over the floor to the cry of the being between Life and Death.

The tragic is born of this original contradiction. Whether the fault line is located in the experience of birth and the earliest years that differentiate the image of the I from that of the Other, or whether it is sublimated on the metaphysical plane, in the divorce between gods and men, matters little, for it comes back to the same thing. The tragic cry is always born in the panic of a lost oneness. . . .

Tragedy, "pure act," is born of this primordial stage-setting. . . . The exasperation of passion without results, the destructive monstrousness of the character "purges" us of our violences, in pity and terror, the nerves of all tragedy. And the effectiveness of this catharsis is permitted by the austere and diversified alternation of tones and voices. . . .

Nonetheless, all the works of Monique Bosco, by the fact, first of all, that they are monologues, theatricalize passion in a crescendo of tears, cries, and words, of madness, silence, and death.

Jeanne Goldin. *Voix et Images*. 9, 1984,
pp. 23, 27

The first time that I read the title *Un amour maladroit* (An awkward love), the adjective spontaneously functioned as the second term of a metaphor, but at the moment when I finished reading the text of the novel, its literal sense was retrospectively imposed. In fact, at first contact with the title, obeying a certain habit of reading or the habit of reading a certain literature, the reader confers upon the awkwardness of this love in question a spiritual value, and sees in it the expression of a certain discordance at the level of affective relations, whereas, once the novel is finished, the same reader becomes aware that the awkwardness, before being of a spiritual or affective nature was first and foremost of a physical nature. For the amorous failure to which the title refers constitutes nothing other than the last sequence in the history of an uncoordinated body, is only the conclusion in other words of the failed apprenticeship of a body as social object, the last act of its lacking socialization. . . .

At the end of *Un amour maladroit* there is a sentence to remember, for it has close ties with Bosco's third novel, *La Femme de Loth* (Lot's wife):

> I love this insidious malady that is slowly, inexorably trans-
> forming me into a pillar of salt.

The bridge that this allusion creates to the fate of Lot's wife establishes between the first and third novels of Monique Bosco's does not represent a simple filiation, for *La Femme de Loth,* both by its form and its content, allows itself to be readily reduced to a sort of "remake" of *Un amour maladroit*. . . .

Beyond [certain] superficial resemblances, these two novels come together chiefly at the level of the form of their content. In each of the novels, a woman, retrospectively, explains the relation of her body to the world, in unction, not of deliberate choices, but of precise affective and physiological determinisms. Hélène and Rachel are not like sisters, even Siamese twins, but like two masks behind which, so to speak, a single character appears. . . . The changing of the decor, the modification of details, do not mask the identity of the two stories. . . . Between these two novels, so similar, Monique Bosco published *Les Infusoires* (The infusors) in 1965. . . .

Without plot complications almost, so to speak, without action, *Les Infusoires* limits itself to presenting one by one, chapter by chapter, each of the characters whose psychological attitude and behavior are connected in a relation of causality, as happens in *Un amour maladroit* and in *La Femme de Loth,* to the situation that they had to undergo as children. Although narrated in the third person, the story is only exceptionally taken on by the narrative instance, since each character in turn assumes the point of view of the narrative. . . .

Written by a woman, with their principal characters all women, the first three novels of Monique Bosco that we have just examined would, nonetheless, I fear, be judged rather severely if they had to be judged in the light of today's feminism. They could, however, also be presented as so many examples of woman's alienation in a world where the phallus imposes its domination. Bosco's novels would then serve as counter examples.

François Gallays. *Voix et Images.* 9, 1984,

pp. 35, 39–40, 42, 44

Iconoclasts are not forgiven if they become part of a herd. Or if they destroy only idols already condemned by fashion. Never if they attack head-on icons that have barely been discovered and those that wait in oblivion. Still less if these iconoclasts are women. Monique Bosco is one of these, always against the grain, against the times, against everything, but also in reverse-time, in double-time. . . .

Le Portrait de Zeus peint par Minerve (The portrait of Zeus painted by Minerva) is a very good example of this. For, voluntarily burning all bridges, it leaves no room for ideological criticisms, nor for any sort of co-optation. . . .

If Monique Bosco's "fiction" often has the rhythm or the harmonies of poetic prose, while presenting itself as narrative, but without being a novel, nor poetry, it is no less attached to the new writing, which would be hard to find any definition of whatsoever. The sentence, aside from a few fantasies in the punctuation line and some purely typographical effects, remains classic, the game of the signifier, much more moderated than in *Charles Levy, M.D.* No acrobatics of style, few semantic games. A translucid word, deployed like a wave covered over by the sands of time, an obsessive and repetitive phrase, like that movement of advance and retreat of the rising tide.

Le Portrait de Zeus peint par Minerve is that of a god, a father, a man who is dying interminably, under the gaze by turns rebellious, incredulous, suspicious, demanding, vengeful, pitying, disenchanted, hateful, passionate, and tender of a Minerva asking herself about the death of the gods, but also about life without the Father.

Gloria Escomel. *Voix et Images.* 9, 1984,

pp. 47–48

Monique Bosco's *Clichés,* concentrates on social and cultural questions—primarily those connected with growing old. Throughout the collection, the author evokes the fear, the loneliness, the intolerance and the sense of waste and loss that seem to be inherent in this inevitable process. The ten stories of this collection often seem clichés, as the title indicates: clichés of the aging process (everything we suspected turns out to be true), and clichés in the other French meaning of the word—portraits of people growing old.

Comme les gens de mon age le savent bien, nous avons été manipulés facilement, nous les ignorants, les non-instruits says the retiree who has just signed up for further education. His confession then merits him the unwanted attentions of an older widow and he soon finds himself married again. In another story the medical secretary wonders how to best understand *la peur de la vieillesse, l'inflexible et solitaire vieillesse des célibataires*. There is a pervasive feeling of helplessness, powerlessness and a wasted existence.

Bosco's approach is moralistic. Though she offers the victims of *vieillesse* a certain sympathy, she condemns society's creation of and response to this phenomenon of gruesome solitude and indifference: *tout cela [se passait] dans l'indifférence totale des voyageurs regardant pudiquement par la vitre.* . . .

These are not light, amusing anecdotes; only one story is an exception in this string of depressing accounts of *l'âge d'or*. In "L'Histoire du petit homme et des deux obeses" the nasty little bilious and shriveled man is frightened to death by the obese couple that has repeatedly been subject to his intolerance and his insults. Finally someone has discovered the power of agency.

Luise von Flotow. *Canadian Literature*. 130,
Autumn, 1991, p. 156

BOTTOME, PHYLLIS (GREAT BRITAIN) 1884–1963

It should be said that on her own level Miss Bottome is one of the most readable of contemporary novelists. If she dashes on the local color with a fine, free hand and is inclined to use the word "diaphanous" like a Homeric invariable adjective, the total impression is one of vivid and lively narrative [*Under the Skin*].

John Raymond. *New Statesman and Nation*.
July 22, 1950, pp. 105–6

Of the numerous possible reasons for the silence of literary history about the novels these women [anti-Nazi novelists] wrote, lack of quality is not one. The novels are more readable and in many ways more profound and less flawed than numerous other 1930s novels whose titles are stitched in anthologies, histories, and encyclopedias of English literature. Bottome's *The Mortal Storm* (published in Britain in 1937 and in the United States in 1938) is a family or domestic tragedy. Considered a well-written, effective treatment of a serious subject, the novel was widely reviewed in both England and the States, reprinted thirteen times within ten months in the United States and turned into a 1940 Hollywood movie with the same title. Unlike the film version and the numerous examples of "alarmist 'next war fiction'" that Martin Ceadel examines in "Popular Fiction and the Next War, 1918–1939," Bottome's novel is not a thriller, neither a battle of the "bad guys" versus the "good guys" nor a science-fiction vision of the destruction of civilization. The novel is not a romance, though much radical fiction by women gets dismissed as such when its protagonist is a woman. Rather, it is a study of character and society, a twentieth-century novel of manners in which marriage does not provide the conclusion.

Set in Munich, *The Mortal Storm* relates what happens to the Roth family during the years 1932–34. . . . Even though the Holocaust, that nightmare of nightmares, could not yet have been envisioned in its enormity and profound evilness, Bottome, through the psychologically well-defined characters she creates, succeeds in helping us to understand how the unthinkable could happen there or, for that matter, here. . . .

Bottome's psychological insights (she was a student of Alfred Adler, to whom the book is dedicated) include identifying the appeal of Hitler for women who have never known freedom. . . .

A few of the reviewers thought the novel was too rhetorical, and the novel is at times discursive, like nineteenth-century novels in which narrators comment on the action or in which the commentary is provided by the thoughts or dialogue of one or another of the characters. But the novel is not a tract, even though the speeches of the characters occasionally seem too long. While Bottome's characters discuss the ideologies of nazism, communism, Judaism, and feminism, the novel directs our attention to the practice of those ideologies. Ideas are explored through situation and character, both of which are compelling. Bottome depicts Communists, Jews, liberated women, and those who join the Nazi Party as human beings, all of whom are likely to become victims of an ideology that preaches war and hatred and fails to understand that, in Bottome's view, freedom belongs either to all or to none. The novel continues to offer those of us who read it today an understanding of how political philosophies and ideals become the motivations for very private acts that transform the daily lives and relationships of ordinary, caring individuals and families.

Barbara Brothers. In Angela Ingram and
Daphne Patai, eds. *Rediscovering Forgotten
Radicals: British Women Writers, 1889–1939*
(Chapel Hill: University of North Carolina
Press, 1993), pp. 251–52

BOUCHER, DENISE (CANADA) 1935–

The desire for liberation from traditional roles, by now a standard motif in Quebec women's theater, reappeared as the major theme of Denise Boucher's *Les Fées ont soif* (1978). *Les Fées* became a *succès de scandale* when the Greater Montreal Arts Council tried to block its performance. Despite the loss of a $15,000 subsidy from the Arts Council, the Théâtre du Noveau Monde decided to go ahead with the production, refusing to give in to what it considered an attempt to censor artistic expression. Writers, artists, civil libertarians, and feminists supported Boucher and the TNM with demonstrations, petitions, and protest letters to newspapers. Although the Arts Council claimed that its decision was based on objections to the play's language and depiction of *québécois* culture, many people believed that it was motivated by the presence on stage of a living statue of the Virgin Mary.

In fact, the play's three characters—the statue of the Virgin, Marie the Mother, and Madeleine the Prostitute—are simply three faces of the same archetypal woman, the Virgin Mary. The play then is essentially a monologue by three voices with an occasional dialogue. Boucher wrote *Les Fées* to exorcise the terribly repressive model of the Virgin, the woman who cannot enjoy sex. This archetype is the product of man's (especially priests') fear of sexuality, according to Boucher. All three characters feel imprisoned by their roles. "Moi, je suis une image. Je suis un portrait / J'ai les deux pieds dans le plâtre. / Je suis la reine du néant," says the statue. "Entre le poêle et le réfrigérateur / Entre le réfrigérateur et le poêle / je t'attends et je prends ma pilule / . . . . Les murs se resserrent sur moi," says the mother. "Moi, je comprends Marilyn Monroe. . . . / Je suis comme elle. . . . / En quête de toutes les qualités de la / séduction. . . . / Et en même temps il faudrait que je sois inatteignable. . . . / transpa- / rente. / Virginale," cries the Prostitute. Together in the "Chanson d'errance," they proclaim their status as silenced, beaten, alienated, violated, demented, lost women. Together they express their fears of madness, solitude, ugliness, emotions, and sexuality. But finally they decide they have had enough: the time of victims is over. Marie drops her apron and leaves her kitchen; Madeleine drops her whore's boots and leaves her alcove; the Statue drops her rosary beads and breaks out of her plaster cast. Having exorcised the stereotypes and accepted their own carnality, the women are now ready to love and be loved by men.

Jane Moss. In Paula Gilbert Lewis, ed.
Traditionalism, Nationalism, and Feminism:
Women Writers of Quebec (Westport,
Connecticut: Greenwood Press, 1985), p. 289

Denise Boucher is a feminist author who actively rejects the Church's teachings. She focuses her revolt on the figure of the Blessed Virgin Mary, who has long been used by the Church as a model of feminine chastity and humility. Boucher considers the Virgin to be a wholly unsatisfactory role model for women. She also evokes Mary Magdalene, a complex figure around whom many myths have been constructed which either idealize her or demean her. For Boucher, Mary Magdalene is important because she reveals the ambivalent attitudes of men toward women. In *Les fées ont soif* Boucher demythologizes the Virgin and Mary Magdalene and dramatizes the liberation of women from society's stereotypes. . . .

In *Les fées ont soif,* Denise Boucher emphasizes the merging of Mary Magdalene the "holy harlot" with Mary the Virgin and mother. These three women constitute a female trinity, resembling the biblical Trinity in that they, too, are one in essence—unable to take pleasure in their own sexuality. Boucher considers them to be virgins. The play dramatizes their collective metamorphosis, through solidarity and sisterhood, into modern Eves who reject the confining image society has imposed on them and seek to rebuild the garden and begin again.

What will replace the old patriarchal system when its symbols and myths die? Boucher's play ends with the message, "Imagine." She invites us to reconstruct the world according to new principles. There is no need for an external authority figure, male or female; men and women are encouraged to seek divinity within themselves and to love the divinity in each other. We find this idea in Ntosake Shange's "choreopoem" *for colored girls who have considered suicide/when the rainbow is enuf;* one of the characters says, "i found god in myself/& i loved her/i loved her fiercely." In *Les fées ont soif,* La Statue, Marie, and Madeleine find the god/dess within themselves and learn to love her and to rely on her strength. Denise Boucher adds her voice to the chorus of women seeking to break down stereotyped images of women to make way for new, positive images based on love and respect.

Elaine R. Hopkins. *American Review of Canadian Studies.* 14:1, 1984, pp. 63–66, 70–71

The contemporary city frequently functions as one of the primary textual generators in recent writings by Quebec women. Paradoxically, this new attention to the urban milieu as a creative site for the generation of new fictions is occurring at a time when women writers are also expressing a growing ambivalence toward the high cost of modernization. And yet, it is precisely this confusion over contemporary urban life that has placed the city at the center of woman's search for identity. But more important, the city has gained a special significance because for many of Quebec's women writers the modern metropolis is a telling example of how the male establishment apportions space in order to assure maximum profits and safeguard its political control. Accordingly, the city is often associated with the economic exploitation of women in particular. . . .

With her own singular irony, Denise Boucher . . . translates the boredom and repetition of women's place in the consumer-oriented city in her theatrical bombshell *Les fées ont soif* (1978). But more than economic exploitation, the city represents the *lieu par excellence* of masculine identity and dominance over women. The city is thus a "foreign" place, the space of the Other. As a result, women are often portrayed as bewildered outsiders. . . .

Finally, as the defiled Madeleine bitterly informs us in *Les fées ont soif,* the city may also become a space of violation in which women are paralyzed and held prisoner of their darkest fears. . . .

Many of the texts of Quebec women writers bear witness to the disturbing effects of city life on female characters: loneliness, dehumanization, frustration, defenselessness, imprisonment. In virtually every text that develops the theme of the city, we note how the city defines women on its terms, in other words, in terms that were never invented by them.

Karen Gould. *American Review of Canadian Studies.* 12:1, 1982, pp. 3–4

BOWEN, ELIZABETH (GREAT BRITAIN) 1899–1973

Miss Bowen certainly does not let *her* inability to describe the passage of time dictate the theme. Her latest novel, *The House in Paris,* covers a period from before the birth of an illegitimate child until he has reached the age of nine. The popular novelist would have described every one of those years, however dull to the reader the accumulation of trivialities. Miss Bowen has simply left them out with the merest glance backward; we may believe that she has been forced to omit, but she has made of her omissions a completely individual method, she has dramatized ignorance. How with so little known of the "backward and abysm" can she convey her characters with any clearness? It is impossible, but her consciousness of that impossibility proves her great value as a novelist. She makes it the virtue of her characters that they are three parts mystery; the darkness which hides their past makes the cerebration which we are allowed to follow the more vivid, as vivid as the exchanges of people overheard talking on a platform before a train goes out. It is an exquisite sleight of hand: the egg was in the hat, now it is being removed from the tip of a robust woman's nose. We must fill in for ourselves what happened between; the burden of that problem is passed to the reader. To the author remains the task of making the characters understand each other without our losing the sense of mystery: they must be able to tell all from a gesture, a whisper, a written sentence: they have to be endowed with an inhuman intuition as James's characters were endowed with an inhuman intelligence, and no writer since James has proved capable of a more cunning evasion. Unable to convey the passage of time, she has made capital out of the gap in the records; how can we doubt the existence of a past which these characters can so easily convey to each other?

Graham Greene. *The London Mercury*.
October, 1935, pp. 563–64

Miss Bowen's scope of reference has a wider variety than Miss Compton-Burnett's, but whatever she writes of she knows. It is the same world—that of highly educated, civilized people—but altered and extended by the general loosening up and overlapping that have taken place in the last thirty years. . . .

Just as Miss Compton-Burnett is essentially an *ear,* Miss Bowen, despite the unquestionably real quality of her dialogue, is above all an *eye*. Her business is with the complexities of the heart, light with perceptive wonder, or heavy with some burden of unwelcome knowledge. But always the visual accompaniment of emotion is what gives to that emotion its force and color, and so fixes it in our minds. The scene, however fleeting, is always *set,* the characters may not give voice to their thoughts, but a sudden sunbeam, a shape of cloud, a sly look, a door ajar, a smoldering cigarette—these speak for them.

Like Miss Compton-Burnett, then, Elizabeth Bowen exhausts her material, but in pursuit of a very different theme. This—to put it roughly—is the conflict between Innocence and Guilt (using those words in the Christian sense). It is the same theme which fascinated Henry James in so many stories, from *The American* to *The Wings of the Dove* and *The Golden Bowl*. I say "conflict," but "attraction" better describes this most poignant of all situations; and it is in the corruption of guileless persons by those who simultaneously love and hate them that Miss Bowen finds her clue. Innocence is not the prerogative of girls, but although she has portrayed at least two innocent males (Colonel Bent in *The House in Paris,* Major Brutt in *The Death of the Heart*), it is natural that women should be her main target. Intense feeling—perhaps the most intense *personal* feeling he ever knew—kept Henry James at a respectful distance from Daisy Miller, from Milly Theale and Maggie Verver. Miss Bowen takes the analysis a step further, into the dead center of the personality, exploring that distressful limbo which rings with the faint cries of those whose trust has been betrayed. She is adept at conveying to us the fateful calm in which, at the outset of her novels, the heroine waits for something to happen. And it is always the worst that happens—the humiliation that injures the soul so much more directly than physical rape. Portia *(The Death of the Heart),* Emmeline *(To the North),* Lois *(The Last September),* Karen *(The House in Paris)*: these fine-grained creatures—*jeunes filles en fleur* trembling on the brink of "life"—are the descendants of Mignon, but for them fate is less foreseen. They all experience the heartbreak which is not (save in one instance) irreparable, either through the insouciance of philanderers (Portia, Emmeline, Karen), or through the selfish conventionality of their immediate surroundings (Lois). Evil, as a motive, has not in these novels the impersonal, terrifying power, working *from outside,* that it acquires in the work of François Mauriac or Graham Greene; but its precipitation in the alembic set a-boil by a chance encounter is the measure of Miss Bowen's seriousness as a critic of life, and of her importance in the history of English fiction. For it should be noticed that her most characteristic creations are distinctively English: one would not expect to find Portia or Emmeline or Lois in a Latin country, nor yet in the America of today.

As if to defend the subtlety of her theme, Elizabeth Bowen's plots are usually simple and well defined; unlike Miss Compton-Burnett's they are impossible to forget or to confuse one with another. Uninterested in complexity for its own sake, she never attempts a sub-plot, and the many subsidiary lives which surround the object of attention are not allowed to engage too much of the reader's interest. Nevertheless, the air in these books is easier to breathe than that of Miss Compton-Burnett's secret sessions. Miss Bowen enjoys a large cast: her people and places are open on all sides. There is a general air of busy-ness, of work in the background; light and space surround her characters, even in their tenser moments. These novels are full of movement, in the literal as well as the figurative sense, and this is perhaps why we never feel crowded out of the page—as we sometimes do in a novel by Miss Compton-Burnett.

Though true of all her books, the above assertions need to be modified in the case of what I consider Miss Bowen's finest achievements: *The Last September* and *The House in Paris.* The first of these is an idyll, and therefore more static than, for instance, *To the North.* The setting has some of Miss Compton-Burnett's enclosed quality. But the discursive style, light and quick as a dragonfly, dispels any sense of difficulty. Perhaps because this is an early book, a slight self-consciousness mars the surface; but the picture of an Anglo-Irish country house, spellbound in the lovely autumnal calm that precedes its extinction, could hardly be better done. The double tragedy, with which the book ends, completes the structure without weighing it down. Miss Bowen's debt to Jane Austen shows here (more clearly than in her first novel, *The Hotel,* which happens to be lighter in tone) in an uncommon ability to treat tragedy on the same level as comedy. "People do not feel as much as you want them to." Miss Bowen would not agree to that, and in her most artistically successful—her most mysterious and poetical—novel, *The House in Paris,* she gives us the full range of her subtle imagination. In this extraordinary and very beautiful book, the innocent and the guilty are less sharply distinguished than elsewhere in Miss Bowen's work, and the atmosphere is more sinister. Although there is plenty of movement, the dark little house of Mme. Fisher dominates the whole book and casts its ambiguous shadow across the Channel into the sunlit, spacious, everyday world of the Michaelis family, which is the author's natural milieu. . . .

The House in Paris is Miss Bowen's largest, most far-reaching novel to date. It was eclipsed in public esteem by the later *Death of the Heart,* which is more direct, more scathing, and more consistently amusing. In a sense it is its author's most *spirited* book.

Edward Sackville-West. *Horizon* (London)
June, 1946, pp. 378–81

The mere thought of criticizing Elizabeth Bowen's work makes one feel like one of the disaffected scoundrels in her novels who induce the death of the heart. The temptation to think of this author as she thinks of her heroines is almost irresistible. Her sunny reputation invites the cheerful, impressionistic remark; disinclination is rude; the air here is mild, polite, congratulatory. (She's not so perfect as Jane Austen, nor so original as Virginia Woolf, but how glad we are, etc.) Miss Bowen inspires confidence: the popular novelist, recently elected a Companion of the British Empire, with a London home in Regent's Park and a family house in County Cork, a sensitive, careful writer whose fineness of feeling is neatly ruffled with wit and laced with snobbery. E. Sackville-West speaks of her cleverness, her fresh and startling style; V. S. Pritchett thinks of her as a poet.

To go on from there is much more difficult. First, there is the well-bred woman of sensibility, moderately elegant, sensitive to differences in class, moralistic about taste, courtesy and fidelity; but there is another Elizabeth Bowen, a sturdy, determined writer, a romantic feminist who serves up a perennial dish: the tragedy of the Fine Girl and the Impossible Man. These are obviously women's books. The surface is urbane and complex, but unusually evasive, as though it were in some kind of secret struggle with the franker soul which has devised these stories of an innocent woman's maltreatment by the reprobate, the mysterious man, the weak or unfaithful lover. This theme, this bold heart throb, perhaps contributes to the popularity of her novels, and no doubt the decorative writing, the slow, oblique presentation of character are peculiarly necessary—without the latter adornments the sophisticated reader might reasonably question the whole matter. The style— Henry James, Virginia Woolf, and Katherine Mansfield—is extraordinarily fluent and diverting; one hardly notices, under its spell, the bias of the content, the oppressive tidiness of the values. In these novels, love's prerogatives are real; ambivalence is wicked, a moral and also a social failure, for the conflicts are somehow a part of the class struggle and the author appears to be a conservative of nostalgic temperament.

The opinion, or sentiment, that occurs again and again in Elizabeth Bowen's fiction and which seems to have commanded the labors on her ancestral chronicle, *Bowen's Court,* is that to know *who* you are, to be close to your past, to feel the pride and obligations of family and place, are, if not the most exquisite and difficult attainments, a great source of personal and national virtue. These warm, sustaining emotions are found most frequently in the gentry and upper class; the disloyal, the insincere and unreliable are the homeless, the shapeless nobodys, the complacent, vapid middle class, the mysterious foreigner, the restless, self-loving *arriviste.* . . .

As a sort of subhead to hereditary class, there occurs the abstract notion of Home, representing familiarities, allegiances, duties, and affections; under Home there is a particularity, the actual house in which the character lives. From the Home or lack of it, one's house, enriching or blighting the senses and manners, Elizabeth Bowen creates a fantastic environmental psychology, as implacable, materialistic, and mortifying as the verdict of a property assessor. For those who pass the test, and it is character that is at stake, the images are loving and generous.

The Heat of the Day is a curiously sentimental and confused reflection on a deplorable family with a stunted sense of the emotional value of property; and that this is the true theme is elaborately and tediously acknowledged by the subplot, which has to do with an estate in Ireland inherited by Stella Rodney's son. As a political novel, or a commentary on the English middle class, or a character novel, except for the engaging treatment of Stella Rodney, it is too impalpable to be held in the mind. . . .

The most striking thing about Miss Bowen's novels is that the attitudes and generalities which establish the tone, the more weighty reflections on status and character, either contradict or have nothing to do with the action. This author, as Mme. de Sévigné said of herself, is often very far from being entirely of her own opinion. Her typical heroines . . . are described as well-bred, calm, honest, and attractive; they represent class and family virtue, and yet we can understand their actions only in terms of bohemia, that land no parent, relative or property owner ever enters. . . .

The men are complex, ambiguous, dissatisfied—qualities Miss Bowen looks upon with finicky contempt. At the best, this contempt gives a structure to the story and a resolution to the plot. Elizabeth Bowen's novels *end,* usually in the death of the man. . . . One cannot help but see these concluding immolations as the "woman's revenge," condign punishment for male weakness, hesitation, and disingenuousness. And if there is something chilling and merciless in these finales, no one can doubt they give prodigal relief to both feminine sentiment and womanly outrage.

Since Miss Bowen's purest talent is for the simple love story, she seems to me at her best in *To the North,* a harsh, terrifying, and unaffected book. Even the title avoids the sentimental disguise of the other novels and candidly indicates the zero temperature at which these love affairs end. . . .

Just where Elizabeth Bowen "belongs" I cannot say. Readable, gifted, the very equanimity of her work makes criticism difficult. In a relaxed mood, she offers one the satisfaction of unabashed tears, an emotional evening in which love retains all its old sovereign rights, and the final pleasure of witnessing the bad end to which the inconstant come. As in an opera libretto you must take the roles on faith—a grunt of satire or a shiver of commonsense on the spectator's part, would be enough to disrupt the performance and bring the pretty scenery down upon the soprano's head.

Elizabeth Hardwick. *Partisan Review.*
November, 1949, pp. 1114–16, 1118–21

One does not normally think of Elizabeth Bowen as a historian of her time. Yet never has the sense of a particular place at a particular time been rendered more completely than in her *The Heat of the Day;* when the reader a century ahead wishes to know what life in London was like during the war years, the years of the air raids especially, it will assuredly be to this novel that he will turn. The time, indeed, is almost a character in *The Heat of the Day.* And never have Elizabeth Bowen's great talents been more generously displayed than here; her prose has a richness, a subtlety, a texture as of poetry which seems to me incomparable in the contemporary British novel. And her keen eye—we think of her now as a poetic novelist, but she began as and to some extent remains a social satirist—is as remorseless as ever. No novel, it seems to me, of all published in the year more repays study or bears more frequently repeated reading. One says this knowing that in some measure the novel fails. Miss Bowen's gifts are fused together as never before, yet she does not succeed in making her plot credible. She has always been interested in the theme of betrayal, but in the thriller element in *The Heat of the Day,* subdued though it is—the heroine discovers that her lover is a traitor while she is being pursued in love by the agent on his trail—she appears to me to have gone outside her range. It is the index of her achievement that, despite this fundamental failure, one reads and rereads *The Heat of the Day* with increasing excitement and fascination.

Walter Allen. *The Year's Work in Literature 1949* (London: British Council/Longmans, 1950), p. 33

Sensibility is . . . a kind of medium through which the world can be apprehended more clearly and significantly, just as the features of a landscape will stand out more sharply when seen in a particular kind of light. In other words, Miss Bowen uses her sensibility (which is without question exquisite) as an instrument, merely, for producing the particular effects at which she is aiming in her novels and stories.

What are these "particular effects" which distinguish her work from that of her fellow writers? What is it that one chiefly remembers when one has finished a book by Elizabeth Bowen? She herself has compared her specialized use of sensibility with the light which reveals the beauties of a landscape, and her simile, perhaps, was not quite accidental: for landscape, in the wider sense, is of the first importance in her work, and I think her vivid apprehension of the visible world is, above all else, what makes her writing so memorable. . . .

Miss Bowen has admitted that many of her novels and stories had their genesis in the vision of a particular place—a compelling, insistent vision which seemed, as she says . . . to "draw one into itself." Only at a much later stage would the characters and their actions emerge, as it were, from the middle distance into the foreground—and note that I say "emerge," for there is no question, with Elizabeth Bowen, of grafting a story arbitrarily upon an imagined scene; the *dramatis personæ*—and the drama itself—are already there, implicit in the landscape of which indeed they form an essential part, though they have yet to be picked out, as it were, by the camera eye of the novelist's vision. . . .

It is interesting, in this connection, to learn that Miss Bowen did, in her early youth, intend to be a painter. Another possible source for this pictorial quality in her work—and especially for her sensitivity to light—is the fact that Miss Bowen has spent much of her life in Ireland, where light is an extremely important factor in the landscape, and can, as Miss Bowen herself has said, "determine one's mood, one's day, and one's entire sense of the world." Each of her novels and stories seems, in retrospect, to be lit by its own particular radiance—one remembers, for instance, the ripe, late-summer sunlight of *The Last September,* the bleak, wintry afternoons on the south coast in *The Death of the Heart,* the blanched London moonlight of *Mysterious Kôr.*

This preoccupation with the visible world suggests a further comparison—not with painting, in this case, but with the work of another distinguished woman novelist of a slightly earlier generation than Miss Bowen's: I mean Virginia Woolf. In Mrs. Woolf's novels one finds the same acute awareness of outside things, the same almost pictorial intensity of vision; yet Mrs. Woolf tended, I think, to become preoccupied with the thing seen *for its own sake,* whereas, in the case of Miss Bowen, the landscape—however important—is never allowed to swamp the figures who inhabit it. . . .

In 1929 appeared Miss Bowen's second novel, *The Last September,* and with it she emerges for the first time as a mature and entirely original novelist. Many of her admirers consider it her best novel, and I am almost inclined to agree; Miss Bowen herself has a particular affection for it, and this is understandable, for *The Last September,* more than any of her other books, seems to have been written from the heart; it has, indeed, a quality which can only be called lyrical: the descriptions of the "Great House" and its demesne linger in the memory with an extraordinary persistence, so that in retrospect the story seems to belong to some far-distant, half-forgotten phase of one's own life.

Jocelyn Brooke. *Elizabeth Bowen* (London:
British Council/Longmans, 1952), pp. 5–7, 13

Elizabeth Bowen's fiction at its best is conscious, intelligent, even austere. One can say relatively little about the relationship of her art to that of her contemporaries, for her debts to them are either explicit and self-evident, or so oblique as to be nonexistent. She has always read widely in literature (poetry as well as prose) of all periods, and is fully aware of the debts she owes to past and present for the body of literary experience on which her own art draws. It is pointless to draw attention to the concerns her fiction does *not* dramatize, in domestic and professional life, in social classes other than her own. The world one could construct from all her novels and stories would seem "narrow" indeed, compared with that of almost any other major novelist. As [Sean] O'Faolain notes, for instance, anything "elemental" is usually circumscribed—not for the sake of "elegance" (as he implies) or prudery—but simply because she has always been cognizant of what any writer's language cannot do, and of the limits of her own powers.

It is certainly a measure of Elizabeth Bowen's stature as a novelist that these powers are used unremittingly in the dramatization of events that are important, in giving a unique form of life to propositions that are essential. What is at stake in her fiction one must call, for lack of less pompous terms, a sense of reality: in any world, the intelligent, imaginative person cannot make things of people and survive with integrity, cannot crudely substitute art for life and live with sanity. Yet one must in some way (her novels consider many) make art of life in order to live, for to deny the risk of imagination, inherent in its ability to expose the sensibility, is to abandon one's self to imagination's revenge as chaos and fantasy. This moral proposition her art repeatedly sets; but because these terms, like those of a parable, are extensive, her fiction is rarely repetitious.

To speak of any writer's success "within limits" usually implies denigration, even if one adds that the limits are "deep if not wide." Spatial metaphors used for evaluation too often introduce irrelevant nonsense. What a reader *can* say of Miss Bowen's achievement in the art of the novel can only be said of the greatest: that she has kept going a worthwhile continuity without submitting to nostalgia; that she has attempted honestly to assign importance to the elements of the world she and her readers share, without resorting to clichés of material or attitude; that she has given to her age and to her culture an image of art within which life can go on with relative fullness and sanity. Because she accepts and comprehends the work of those who have preceded her, thus giving her own art a role in a tradition, and because she has adapted what has gone before to a contemporary world, Elizabeth Bowen's novels, at their best, have the quality she herself has called (in a different sense) the most difficult to achieve: relevance.

> William Heath. *Elizabeth Bowen: An Introduction to Her Novels* (Madison: University of Wisconsin Press, 1961), pp. 158–59

[Bowen's] heroines want a "modern" sense of living without sacrificing the continuity or stability won by those who consolidated the values of a landed aristocracy with success in commerce. Where novelists of the 1920s often disdain the past and industrial society, she sees no future in flights to the Alps or islands off the coast of Africa and little sustenance in elite London coteries of fellow intensives. Miss Bowen's most thorough critic, William Heath, sees society as a rude limiter of the sensitive will, but her adults actually love-and-hate commercial civilization. She speaks for those adaptable aristocrats who moved the old furniture into the town house and got rich in the advertising business. And she knows what made them leave the farm. Over and over she shows the purposelessness, ineffectiveness, eccentricity, and insanity remaining in the less adaptable. Her heroines want to maintain or even construct continuity, but they do not foresee giving up London for a return to agriculture. (The author's part-time return to Ireland in later life may say something different.) Miss Bowen's best novels show imaginative energy so confined as to express only a small part of itself and ask, is this enough? They show, too, a resentment at situation so great as to make looking for new worlds—or old ones—impossible. But the sensitive will operates in contemporary circumstances *by choice*. To eliminate the taste for Regent's Park or even the rented flat would be to eliminate reality. Miss Bowen's heroines want to stay and complain.

The force behind this scene of an enlarged continuity comes from superimposing upon it a revolutionary scene—the twentieth-century shift in women's aspirations. Two of Miss Bowen's best novels express dissatisfaction with the role of wife and mother; her heroines find themselves inadequate to it and it inadequate to them. Her third important novel tests the possibility of free woman, man's comrade but not dependent. The books are not *about* this problem; they use it as a given condition for restlessness. And Miss Bowen pictures society's part in the conflict not as rules, but as feelings bred in by people whom the heroine respects, likes, and wants to please. Inner and outer merge—and have merged since birth. Women are expected to be sensitive and warm; they are also expected to make correct choices in marriage. Only a woman novelist realized fully the discrepancy in these prescriptions and put so directly the question that gives Miss Bowen a great part of her historical importance: is sensibility practical?

James Hall. *The Lunatic Giant in the*
Drawing Room: The British and American
Novel since 1930 (Bloomington: Indiana
University Press, 1968), pp. 18–19

Perhaps it is wrong to attempt to place authors too carefully—wrong . . . to try to sort them into first, second, third, and fourth divisions. But even if wrong it is a natural desire, and I can think of few novelists who more arouse the desire and more successfully frustrate it than Elizabeth Bowen. What, after all, is she up to? Is she merely the highly elegant, dazzlingly intelligent star of the psychological thriller class, or is she a serious contender for a place in the great tradition? And what, anyway, would be the distinctions—of genre, of talent, of purpose?

Her new novel, *Eva Trout,* is certainly a most impressive book. It creates a world so engrossing, so fully imagined in its own terms, that when interrupted while in the middle of reading it I would look up, vaguely, no longer quite sure where I was. This kind of creation is in itself a rare gift: one shared by Iris Murdoch, who also shares some of Miss Bowen's other eccentricities. Their worlds, in fact, are not dissimilar: the background of *Eva Trout* is one of Gothic castles, vicarage gardens, expensive hotels and restaurants, feminine institutions, suicidal homosexual passions. . . .

The theme—corruption, wealth and innocence—is worthy of Henry James, whose name is indeed invoked by the writer herself. . . . As well as the theme, as an additional benefit, there are those marvelous passages of description, for which Elizabeth Bowen is so justly famous: the prose, always elegant even when—or perhaps most when—tortuous, achieves a number of effects that are breathtaking. . . . She is also witty: several of her puns are really most satisfying. . . .

With all these qualities, it would seem grudging to complain. And yet finally one must, because there is something about the book that cheats the very seriousness with which the reader wishes to take it. The ending is symptomatic. It is crude, melodramatic, improbable—despite the careful plotting of the revolver and the constant premonitions of violent death—and it is at once facile and contrived. Worst of all, it makes one look back through the book at things which had seemed solid, and question their substance. . . .

Also, it is a pity that some of the characters should be so insubstantial. . . . Miss Bowen is magnificent when she writes about conspiracy, duplicity and ambiguity, and her achievement—despite her final cutting of the Gordian knot—is extremely impressive. But with the simple, with the world of common sense, she does not cope. Though perhaps in that (for good or for ill, see it as one may) she is merely the closer to Henry James.

Margaret Drabble. *The Listener.*
February 13, 1969, pp. 214, 216

If it is true that every author has only one story to tell and seeks repeatedly for its ideal form, then Miss Bowen's essential narrative begins with the destruction or delimiting of a woman's ideal desires, with her expulsion from a self-defined Eden. She is then confronted with, in Robert Frost's phrase, "what to make of a diminished thing." What she evolves is a mode of living which provides sufficient drama, or occasion to involve and satisfy her lunatic feelings, but which runs no risk of emotional involvement at a level which might entail further disappointment and frustration. This creative activity, which is not engaged in, of course, simply by the protagonist, Miss Bowen terms "art."

A considerable portion of the archetypal Bowen novel is devoted to examining variant forms of this protective artistry. In being defensive and in involving "playing about" to a considerable measure, these created roles remain essentially selfish. In seeking to give an idealistic girl some insight into the whole practice, an older man in *The Death of the Heart* tells her: "What makes you think us wicked is simply our little way of keeping ourselves going. We must live, though you may not see the necessity. In the long run, we may not work out well. We attempt, however, to be more civil and kindly than we feel." . . .

A danger to which most of these life-denying art forms are susceptible is the condition of stasis, or to what may be termed "the comfort principle." Once acclimatized to a relatively undemanding role, an individual is content to perpetuate it. Life may not be truly satisfactory, but it is adequate and that suffices. Unlike many fictional protagonists of the last twenty years, Miss Bowen's are not incapacitated by aimlessness; they have a sense of the game they must play in order to survive—and most of them, within its limitations, play it quite well. But their expertise is part of the trouble: it calls for too little effort from them. Several Bowen novels actually commence with their protagonists emotionally more dead than alive.

The Bowen novel begins by attacking youthful emotional ignorance or extravagance, but it concentrates its full force against the twilight security of the pleasure principle. And in this assault Miss Bowen turns the century's mutability to an advantage. Conditions refuse to stay settled for her characters, and sooner or later the unexpected ambushes them. Most of her novels and stories culminate with a moment of shock, a disclosure, or an experience which is sufficiently disturbing to the heroine's emotional being that her formalized role is cracked, increasing the likelihood of a richer, more responsible comportment with life. Miss Bowen stops short of showing the better life, for the achievement of enlarged comprehension and of honest assessments suggests the inevitability of an improved existence—and she will guarantee nothing more.

A. E. Austin. *Elizabeth Bowen*
(New York: Twayne, 1971), pp. 21–22

Elizabeth Bowen is the adult author-narrator in her novels, and she is also still the Anglo-Irish only child, for one grows up but one does not after all outgrow being an only child. Sometimes one senses in her attitudes about her art the feeling that the world of her writing is a new demesne where she can be again, as her ancestors had been, a rather detached, preoccupied Anglo-Irish landlord, where she can make patterns of her adolescent crises for her lonely characters. To go back even further, it is a return to that Eden where fact and fiction are the same, perfect and clear as a bubble. . . .

Miss Bowen seems to have dealt with, if not resolved, her identity confusion by remaining between being Anglo and Irish, only child and grown-up in a form of accommodation achieved in her role as writer. Elizabeth Bowen the novelist was the only adult Elizabeth the only child could trust. As an adult she knew she was lying, and as a child she knew she was being lied to, but the needs of both were fulfilled in the fiction, as before she and her parents had accepted the fictions of their future while her mother was dying of cancer and they all knew it, and as the Anglo-Irish landlords accepted the fiction of the eternality of their country-house world while it was being threatened from all sides. If, especially after the experience of World War II, the death of her husband at Bowen's Court in 1952, and the loss and final destruction of Bowen's Court itself in 1960–63, life came to mean—as it does for one of her child characters—"waiting for something awful to happen and trying to think of something else"; and if her life as a writer was all a lie, a precarious bubble world for a lonely child sick midway between Holyhead and Kingstown, it was a life and a lie that allowed her to say with characteristic toughness and candor, "it is not only our fate but our business to lose innocence, and once we have lost that it is futile to attempt to picnic in Eden." Her limitations were her strengths; she could and did act as though she believed in her own illusions because she had to, but she also knew and accepted them for exactly what they were. This was the achievement of her life and art.

Edwin J. Kenney, Jr. *Elizabeth Bowen*
(Lewisburg, Pennsylvania: Bucknell
University Press, 1975), pp. 37–39

Elizabeth Bowen has not written a short story as totally impressive as Lawrence's "Odour of Chrysanthemums" or Joyce's "The Dead," but she has produced the most consistent and extensive body of work in this form by any author writing in English. Unlike Joyce's and Lawrence's, her stories are not over-shadowed by her novels. "The Demon Lover" at least rivals *The Heat of the Day* in its imaginative response to war-time London. Yet she has never been fully assimilated to the canon of modern English literature, and this failure of judgment on the critics' part is intimately connected with her mastery of the short story form.

The ultimate and lasting impression which this entirely welcome collection [*The Collected Stories of Elizabeth Bowen*] will create is of Elizabeth Bowen's supremacy in responding to the civilian dimension of the Second World War. In contrast to *The Heat of the Day* such wartime stories as "The Happy Autumn Fields" are faultless embodiments of concentrated perception and intelligence. The novels after 1946 fall away, and it is strikingly evident from this present collection how little Miss Bowen wrote in the short story form after that date. The war provided her with the circumstances and symbols in which her art flourished: there was little thereafter to be said.

This centrality of the war in her career reminds us paradoxically of her Irishness; Louis MacNeice and Samuel Beckett (so different in every way) similarly found the war to identify a chasm in their own experience. For Elizabeth Bowen was not Irish in Joyce's sense; she was Anglo-Irish, her identity revolving around a hyphen, a linking minus. Meaning for such a writer involved the acknowledgment of two frequently hostile realities. "Mysterious Kôr," one of her finest stories, sets up the remote and deserted city as antithesis to spectral London. This kind of fiction, closer, at times to a self-effacing allegory than to the classic mimetic novel, is illuminated more successfully by reference to Yeatsian masks than to the practice of the Greenes or the Murdochs. . . .

It seems pointless then to insist on Elizabeth Bowen as one who "brilliantly portrayed classically English, reticent, emotionally secretive characters." Her real strength as a writer of fiction lay in the external perspective in which she presented character and the emotional grammar with which she deployed character.

These stories trace the growth of a remarkable writer who transformed uncertainties of origin, and limitations of convention and form, into a body of work uniquely (because tangentially) English. Fiction of the 1920s and 1930s, so often reduced to the *illuminati* of Bloomsbury and Eastwood, or inflated into a tired continuum of Huxleys and Greenes, might be very astutely approached by way of a reassessment of Elizabeth Bowen. This collection provides the very best starting point.

W. J. McCormack. The New Statesman.
February 13, 1981, pp. 19–20

If there ever was a writer of genius, or near-genius—time will decide—who was heart-cloven and split-minded it is Elizabeth Bowen. Romantic-realist, yearning-skeptic, emotional-intellectual, poetic-pragmatist, objective-subjective, gregarious-detached (though everybody who resides in a typewriter has to be a bit of that), tragi-humorous, consistently declaring herself born and reared Irish, residing mostly in England, writing in the full European tradition: no wonder all her serious work steams with the clash of battle between aspects of life more easy for us to feel than to define. It is evident from the complex weave of her novels that it can have been no more easy for her to intuit the central implication of any one of those conflicts—she never trod an obvious line; nor easy for her to express those intuitions in that felicitous language which, more than any other writer of her generation, she seemed to command as if verbally inspired. But that suggestion of inspiration lifts a warning finger of memory. Once, when one of her guests at Bowen's Court, I inadvertently interrupted her when she was, as I at first thought, tapping away fluently at her desk. She turned to me a forehead spotted with beads of perspiration.

And yet these thematic conflicts in her novels can sometimes seem quite clear in the first couple of pages. It is only a seeming: the sinuosities are waiting in ambush. See, for example, the later of her two masterpieces, *The Death of the Heart.* (The other, and for some readers the even finer novel, was *The Last September.*) If we again open it and read its first two pages to peer through the first wisps of its smoke of battle in search of the central theme, it is there as plain as an opened diary. The "catch" is, as old lovers of this poignant, funny, passionate story will at once remember, that this first open declaration carries with it a complexity of themes and subthemes: among others, Innocence versus Worldliness, Youth versus Maturity, Romantic dreams versus cruel Actuality, Love's illusions and delusions, the frailty of Ideals, the clash of the Generations, Society versus the Individual, and, this above all (it is a constant Bowen theme song), the lust to do the heroically honest thing when one does not know what the hell the heroically honest thing to do is in a socially "edited" world. On that terrible adjective we may pause for a long time. It throws the clearest and coldest beam of its presiding author's mind, and perhaps her final capital judgment on those cool conventions, those prophylactic artifices, with which, with the best of intentions, every organized society devitalizes the instincts of the "unedited" heart. It was very much a theme of the 1920s and 1930s. . . .

How on earth did Elizabeth Bowen succeed in conveying so many emotional variations in so large a cast of characters held together by one consistent discipline—that is, by her personal *manière de voir,* her rational view of life? The answer is too obvious to have any meaning—by her technique. . . .

Hermione Lee, in her indispensable, scholarly, penetrating, and sympathetic study of Bowen's work, puts her finger on the tap-root of her author's powers when she says that her "best work was done in the 'subjective,' 'personal' novels and stories of the 1929–1945 period, and not in the more cryptic 'distanced' last work. It is as a subjective writer that she is either praised or denigrated." So, if we airily say that she "does it" by her technique, what we are really saying is that she has some cryptographic, occult way of her own of using images, words, grammar, even punctuation, to communicate in her own personal style her own personal reaction to life. But is there, actually, a recognizable Bowen style, as there is, say, a recognizable Jamesian style? One single style for so complicated, so protean a personality? She has to employ half a dozen styles to suit her varying responses to her various occasions. There are the familiar Domestic Style that we all use, the Hectic Style that uses all of us when we get over-excited, the Sibylline which we whisper over a coffee, glancing about lest the victim overhear, the Impressionist style that is only for the most delicate artist to employ, the Waggish which only a few command, the Moody Style with which we address ourselves when alone and overcome, the Social which requires a great deal of cold, or amused, observed experience, the Grand Duchess which can also be disrespectfully called the Fortnum-and-Mason, or the Bond Street, or the Ritzy Style, unless those places have all been taken over by Lord Forte within the last couple of weeks, or, of all her styles that one which I feel she held most close to her heart, and which, again disrespectfully, I call the Bowen 707 or the Take-Off Style, which lifts her into the skies of her poet's imagination. For her essential nature is not, as has been so often asserted, that of the social critic, but of the visionary [idealist].

Sean O'Faolain. London Review of Books.
March 4, 1982, pp. 15–16

Although all Elizabeth Bowen's fiction has a sense of place, an appropriateness of background detail, her short stories differ from her novels in that geographical setting is not always specific. Her characters speak and behave for the most part as one might expect upper-class English or Anglo-Irish characters to speak and behave (exceptions are the young woman on the park bench in "Tears, Idle Tears" and the distraught source of the monologue of "Oh, Madame"), but the reader is not always told whether their dining rooms, sitting rooms, and bedrooms are in England or in Ireland. Even when the setting is specifically English, so alike are the speech and behavior patterns of the Anglo-Irish educated in England and the native upper-class English, and so often do the Anglo-Irish move back and forth between Ireland and England, that the exact background of specific characters may not be determined. Nor does it really matter. In fact, the very sense that on the surface these well-behaved people maintain their composure and relate to one another in the predictable ways prescribed by social class, the very sameness of their manners and chitchat, heightens the contrast between what they appear to be and what they are. It is in this contrast that the power of Elizabeth Bowen's short fiction may be found.

In eight stories, however, published in *Elizabeth Bowen's Irish Stories* (1978), setting is clearly and identifiably Irish. A ninth, "The Happy Autumn Fields," is also included in this volume, despite the fact that its Irish setting is not identified, because . . . the author herself had written in her preface to *The Demon Lover and Other Stories* that it was, for her, "unshakeably County Cork." Given this flimsy basis for selection, a tenth title could have been included: the story-within-story of "The Back Drawing-Room" also has an Irish setting. In these ten tales, Elizabeth Bowen's descriptive passages are more vividly rendered, more painterly in style, more nostalgic in mood, than those usually found in her short fiction. None of the so-called Irish stories, however, is useful in analyzing Elizabeth Bowen's impressions of or attitudes toward Ireland. For these the reader must turn to other sources: her only Irish novel, *The Last September;* her two histories, *Bowen's Court* (1942) and *The Shelbourne: A Centre of Dublin Life for More Than a Century* (1951); her essays, reviews, and autobiographical writings.

Janet Egleson Dunleavy. In James F. Kilroy,
ed. *The Irish Short Story: A Critical History*
(Boston: Twayne, 1984), p. 157

The Heat of the Day is one of the greatest English novels of the piety of home, the religion of place, of the setting and stability essential to humane life. Its achievement lies partly and most obviously in the thoroughness of its critique of English middle-class life and moral attitudes of the 1920s and 1930s. However, it has another and deeper claim to distinction. It possesses one of the most important marks of the great, as opposed to the merely competent and pleasing, in art. This is its awkward integrity, its avoidance of the neat synthesis, the readiness with which it faces the bold and jarring fact which is thrown against the whole drift of the novel. *The Heat of the Day,* above all, does not balk the problems innate in any "conservative" philosophy of the moral life, any emphasis on place, roots, and inheritance. Condemnation of the deracinated present, however justified and imaginatively presented, might well have been accompanied by an easy nostalgia for some largely imaginary "organic society" where wholesome relationships grew as naturally as the leaves on the trees. The love of order, which Elizabeth Bowen sees as innate to man *does* have those dangers.

John Coates. *Renascence.* 39, Summer,
1987, pp. 497–98

BOWLES, JANE (UNITED STATES) 1917–73

My feeling is that Mrs. Bowles has developed—and exploited—her own brand of lunacy and that she is, perhaps fortunately, unique. . . . To attempt to unravel the plot of *Two Serious Ladies* would be to risk, I feel sure, one's own sanity. . . . What does, however, link both the "Two Serious Ladies" and the other characters in the book is their mad, their wayward, their bizarre aberrations, in which they indulge with so reasonable an air. . . . *Two Serious Ladies* is intermittently funny and certainly original, but I also felt that it strains too hard to startle and to shock and that it all too often is just merely silly.

Edith H. Walton. *The New York Times.*
May 9, 1943, p. 14

There is nothing propagandistic or topical in Jane Bowles's *In the Summer House,* . . . which is not the only reason I prefer it to most of the plays I have seen this season. Its author has an original writing talent and a not at all stock sensibility. It may even be deemed a paradox that I like the earlier or wackier part of the play better than the last part, in which the characters are resolved with the aid of a little off-the-cuff psychoanalysis. . . . The aimless dialogue, the sadly abstract atmosphere of the first part of *In the Summer House,* is lovely, colorful and strangely evocative: it spins a melody of the trivial and "pointless" which emanates from the semi-consciousness of rather ordinary folk with a primitive directness that is essentially poetic.

Harold Clurman. *The Nation.*
January 16, 1954, p. 58

Mrs. Bowles has fashioned a work of intricate and seductive beauty, harmonious and subtle in its impact on the sensibility as a musical composition. And like a piece of music, it is accessible to criticism largely in terms of its modulation and coloring, its sensuous texture and expressive content. . . . It is Mrs. Bowles' special distinction to have rendered as faithful a justice to the external reality of her characters as she has to their interior substance: she is not in collusion with their psychic discomfort; one never feels of *In the Summer House* that it is but another gratuitous portrait of the debilitated sensibility.

Richard Hayes. *Commonweal.*
February 5, 1954, pp. 449-50

Surrounding Mrs. Bowles's art is an effluvium of chic despair which will alienate many readers. On the other hand, her work can easily be overvalued since it combines proud idiosyncrasy with a rather startling prescience (her novel, *Two Serious Ladies,* . . . forecast the current vogue of comic goth-icism). When that book first appeared here, reviewers could damn it with a clear conscience: modernism had not yet become an obligatory mass fash-ion. . . . Today in the United States, where the cultivated reader feels duty-bound to be affronted, Mrs. Bowles's controlled derision is likely to seem the definitive force of civilized disgust.

Surely her indictments have an easy inclusiveness. Like her husband Paul, Mrs. Bowles writes tight little anecdotes about the pull of bestiality, an unexpected form of self-fulfillment. Like her husband's stories, hers pit the weak against the strong, the righteous against the sensual, only to record a general rout. Though her tales lack his intellectual clarity, they have greater charm.

Charles Thomas Samuels *New York Review of Books.* December 15, 1966, p. 38

I saw *In the Summer House* three times . . . because it had a thorny wit, the flavor of a newly tasted, refreshingly bitter beverage—the same qualities that had initially attracted me to Mrs. Bowles's novel, *Two Serious Ladies.* . . . And yet, though the tragic view is central to her vision, Jane Bowles is a very funny writer, a humorist of sorts—but *not,* by the way, of the Black School. Black Comedy, as its perpetrators label it, is, when successful, all lovely artifice and lacking any hint of compassion. Her subtle comprehension of eccentricity and human apartness as revealed in her work require us to accord Jane Bowles high esteem as an artist.

Truman Capote. Introduction to *The Collected Works of Jane Bowles* (New York: Farrar, Straus & Giroux), 1966, pp. viii-ix

But Mrs. Bowles makes what might seem just strange into something wonder-ful—both haunting and witty—by her unsentimental feeling for these lost creatures, and the odd elegance of her writing. The atmosphere of almost all the works is overwrought or overheated, at times reminiscent of Tennessee Williams or even Ronald Firbank; but through all this miasma, the characters tend to speak to each other (and themselves) with the clarity and decision of people in Lewis Carroll. As you can imagine, this effect alone is extraordi-nary. Her writing is funny or sad or sharp or mysterious, but always arresting.

Roderick Cook. *Harper's.* January, 1967, p. 98

It is to be hoped that she will now be recognized for what she is: one of the finest modern writers of fiction, in any language. . . . Mrs. Bowles's seemingly casual, colloquial prose is a constant miracle; every line rings as true as a line of poetry, though there is certainly nothing "poetic" about it, except insofar as the awkwardness of our everyday attempts at communication is poetic. This awkwardness can rise to comic heights, and in doing so evoke visions of a nutty America that we have to recognize as ours. . . .

In her later stories Mrs. Bowles has played down the picaresque local color she used to such effect in the novel. . . . As in all her work, it is impossible to deduce the end of a sentence from its beginning, or a paragraph from the one that preceded it, or how one of the characters will reply to another. And yet the whole flows marvelously and inexorably to its cruel, lucid end; it becomes itself as we watch it. No other contemporary writer can consistently produce surprise of this quality, the surprise that is the one essential ingredient of great art. Jane Bowles deals almost exclusively in this rare commodity.

John Ashbery. *The New York Times.*
January 29, 1967, pp. 5, 30

It is difficult to imagine—especially in these days of celebrity-authors—a writer who would actually *prefer* a limited readership, but then Jane Bowles is not like other writers. She is original to the point of being unnerving, and it seems entirely possible that she wrote as much with the intention to exclude as to include. She is fated to remain a specialized taste because hers goes beyond a mere idiosyncrasy of style, an identifiable semantic tic like Donald Barthelme's or William Gass's. One is tempted to make comparisons—to Ivy Compton-Burnett for the entrenched habit of irony, to Carson McCullers for the use of the grotesque—but they don't really hold up: she is both more human than the former and less sentimental than the latter. Bowles's voice is an uncompromisingly independent one and it bespeaks a vision of life so unflinching as to challenge most of our assumptions.

To read *My Sister's Hand in Mine* is to submit to a demanding presence. Jane Bowles is one of those writers who can truly be said to inhabit a country of her own making. Although the specific geographical location might change, the emotional terrain is characteristically depleted, and one comes away with an unsettling image of projected solitude. . . .

Jane Bowles is a capricious weaver of spells; her stories often end as though they were about to begin again somewhere else—now you see the magic, now you don't. Perhaps that is because her fiction is conceived at such a rarified altitude; her characters are living in domesticated penal colonies. . . .

There is a persistent mystery at the heart of Jane Bowles's fiction. What is amazing, finally, is that fiction so intentionally whimsical, even perverse, should reverberate the way Bowles's does, igniting sparks of recognition on every page.

Daphne Merkin. *The New Republic.*
February 11, 1978, pp. 30–31

If there is one common denominator in Mrs. Bowles's work, it is women's relentless search for autonomy and self-knowledge, for release from all conventional structures. And a demonic, frenzied search it becomes in Mrs. Bowles's hands. . . .

Of the twentieth-century novelists who have written most poignantly about modern women's independence from men—Colette, Lessing, Kate Chopin, Jean Rhys, Jane Bowles come immediately to mind—the last three are consummate artists who have each spent several decades buried in oblivion. . . . As for Jane Bowles, whose oeuvre also concerns a redefinition of female freedom, a considerable silence has attended her work since the production of her play *In the Summer House* twenty-five years ago, notwithstanding the critical acclaim she has received. . . .

The theme of women's independence, and its frequent coefficients of solitude and potential destruction, have more often than not been limned with Lessingesque earnestness in a socio-realistic setting. So Mrs. Bowles's oeuvre is all the more unique because of its Grand Guignol hilarity, its constant surprises, and a blend of realism and grotesqueness that occasionally recalls Ronald Firbank. There is extraordinary tension between the sturdy, supernormal physical world she describes and the gloriously unpredictable, fantastic movements of the eccentric personages who inhabit it. . . .

Their gloriously uninhibited carousing, their voluptuous liberation from all male discipline . . . has much more to do with a return to the permissive sexual androgyny of juvenile bonding than with any sexual preference. It is this very childlike playfulness that gives Mrs. Bowles's work its fey power and its luminous originality, and that may disconcert readers fond of predictably "female," "mature" heroines. . . .

In Mrs. Bowles's work, the traditional novelistic struggle between weak and strong characters ends inevitably in a draw. The rigorous pursuit of autonomy, and a rueful acceptance of its often tragic consequences, is the only heroic goal. For even the strongest are unmade by their failure to take into account "the terrible strength of the weak," and follow an equally drunken downward path to wisdom. There is a severe avoidance of all moralizing. It is left to the individual reader to determine whether Mrs. Bowles's heroines were better off in the shelter of their repressive marriages and inhibited spinsterhoods than in the anarchy of their libertinage.

Francine du Plessix Gray. The New York
Times. February 19, 1978, pp. 3, 28

From the time she was a child Jane had had the sense of sin—a sin that she could never define except to say that it was hers and original, that which separated her from others. Her life had been spent in the doubleness of the knowledge of that sin and the evasion of the knowledge. She had been obsessed by Elsie Dinsmore and yet had mocked Elsie's obedience to her father and her even greater obedience to Jesus. She had read Simone Weil's work over and over, feeling an identity with her, but then she had laughed and said,

"But I have a sensual side too." For years she had spoken about sin and salvation—no one understood it. Most people thought it was Jane being funny, as when she'd said, "Most of all I want to be a religious leader," and then laughed and said, "But of course I'm not."

That sin which she took to be her destiny was inseparable from her imagination. Her writing became both the evidence of the sin and also—by some turn within her—the religious sacrifice that was its expiation. In her work, from the beginning, the themes of sin and salvation were unrelenting: in the words of Miss Goering as a child, baptizing Mary, "Dear God . . . make this girl Mary pure as Jesus Your Son"; in the words of Miss Goering at the end of her journey, " . . . is it possible that a part of me hidden from my sight is piling sin upon sin as fast as Mrs. Copperfield?"; in the words that tell of Sadie's life, "She conceived of her life as separate from herself; the road was laid out always a little ahead of her by sacred hands. . . ."

If in the earliest works there was a double edge—the sense of belief and the other side of belief, both present and united by her wiles—as the years went on, as her work became only unfinished work, the voices of sin and salvation became more urgent. "My life is *not* my own," Bozoe Flanner screams at Janet Murphy. "Have you missed the whole point of my life?" And of a woman in an unfinished play, Jane wrote: "She believes that she has a second heart and because she believes this she can accept a lie and protect it—Her wild clinging to this false trust is a result of her not wishing to discover that she has only one heart after all. . . . She guards her false trust in order not to fall into her single heart—The single heart is herself— it is suffering—it is God—it is nothing. . . ."

Millicent Dillon. A Little Original Sin: The Life and Works of Jane Bowles (New York: Holt, Rinehart and Winston, 1981), pp. 414–15

When I wrote the biography of Jane Bowles, I went into great detail about her anguish at not being able to go on, an anguish that she took to be a punishment for some nameless sin. The anguish went on for years and finally became punishment through the instrumentality of a stroke that afflicted her when she was forty. In fact, she never did complete another work after she began *Out in the World*.

Since the publication of the biography in 1981, I have begun to have other thoughts about what she felt to be her "block." I have come to look at those fragments in another way, as a mode of expression that was attempting to manifest itself through her but that she could not accept. The cast of her mind and feelings was expressing its intention in this form—through fragmentation and repetition—but she took the result to be only failure. If it is true that her work was psychically blocked, it is also true that had she been able to view this fragmentation as a valid expression of her own narrative vision, the fragmentation could have led her to further development—which may say something about the nature of "blocks." So that while I in no way discount Jane Bowles's own conviction of the continual disintegration of her capacity to work, I now see the history of her later writing as a flight from the form that she was being impelled toward by her very nature.

Toward the end of *Two Serious Ladies,* Mrs. Copperfield acknowledges that this is what has happened to her: "'True enough,' said Mrs. Copperfield, bringing her fist down on the table and looking very mean. 'I *have* gone to pieces, which is a thing I've wanted to do for years. I know I am as guilty as I can be, but I have my happiness, which I guard like a wolf.'"

But Mrs. Copperfield's going to pieces, the disintegration within her of moral choice, is counterbalanced in the novel and thereby controlled through the character of Miss Goering and through the formal aspects of their duality. There is no such counterbalance in *Out in the World.* Contained tension has given way to fragmentation. Plot begins to go wild. The willingness to go further and further into the characters without the safety of distancing ends in disorder. At the same time, the need to justify oneself becomes more and more insistent. And the only justification Jane Bowles can find is her own oddity, a judgment she pronounces upon herself.

So *Out in the World* was never finished. All of its cries were never uttered. But enough, nevertheless, was written to tell us what was at stake. Reading, almost forty years later, one does not have to make the judgments of oddity Jane Bowles pronounced upon herself. One can value the individual fragments and respect the form that was trying to appear. The world has, after all, changed. We have grown more able to bear our own experiments and others'. We are privileged to entertain new possibilities. We no longer have to discount their importance.

> Millicent Dillon. In Ellen G. Friedman and
> Miriam Fuchs, eds. *Breaking the Sequence:*
> *Women's Experimental Fiction* (Princeton:
> Princeton University Press, 1989),
> pp. 140–41, 146–47

BOYE, KARIN (SWEDEN) 1900–1941

From youth on, Boye's life and work were dominated by tensions generated through the conflicting aspects of her personality: hypersensitivity and aloof intelligence, instinct and a sense of duty. Her best volume of poems, *Moln* (1922), bears the traces of a recently undergone religious crisis which led her from Christianity to a "faith in life"; its form is still classical and obviously influenced by Ekelund. In 1925 she joined the "Clarté group," which was made up of young radicals who had responded to Barbusse's appeal for a world renewal of socialism. A growing interest in Marxism and psychoanalysis as well as a bluntly anti-Christian attitude are reflected in the poems (*Härdarna,* 1927) and essays of this period. By 1931, when Boye helped to found the "modernistic" journal *Spektrum,* she had already completed the shift toward expressionism in her poetry. Her autobiographical novels *Kris* (1934), and *Kallocain* (1940), expressive of a "negative Utopia," which made her known abroad, are more significant as tragic *documents humains* than as full-scale literary achievements.

Boye's poetry reaches its height in her posthumous volume, *De sju döds-synderna* (1941), in which her fears, feelings of loneliness and guilt, and her faith in life and yearning for God (for according to V. Svanberg "she was a secret Christian") find authentic expression.

> Joris Taels. In Wolfgang Bernard
> Fleischmann, ed. *Encyclopedia of World*
> *Literature in the 20th Century* (New York:
> Frederick Ungar, 1967), pp. 158–59

Karin Boye . . . describes in her autobiographical novel *Kris* (1934) how at the age of twenty she felt compelled to break with the high ideal of Christian obedience in favor of her own truth. Like Almqvist, she chooses as an artist, and what she chooses is the principle of beauty and free uninhibited growth. In some sense, the notion of *choice* is inaccurate, for she speaks of an inner necessity. . . . In *Kris* the object of her adoration is beautiful and serene, but there were to come times when she fell under the spell of demonic attractions, which she followed compulsively in the belief that ultimately, when all things stand revealed, they, too, would be seen to be another side of the Divine. . . .

Boye was a fighter. It is no accident that Gullberg called his memorial poem to her "Död amazon." Her own poem "Sköldmön" in *Gömda land* (1924) speaks of a valkyrie, of blood, fire, roses, and death in battle. It is immediately apparent that this imagery is a mixture of the erotic and the martial, and she was indeed divided, the male and female sides of her personality were both strong and contradictory. On the one hand she was femininely intuitive and vegetative, something strikingly brought out in the poem "Kunskap" in *För trädets skull,* in which seekers on a beach with long-handled fishing nets are laughed at by the sea, because knowledge can never be caught or owned, whereas if you fall into the sea as a drop of water ready to be transformed, then you will *be* knowledge. . . .

The longing to be known and revealed as we really are lies at the heart of Karin Boye's remarkable novel *Kallocain* (1940). It is a vision of a totalitarian state in which the individual counts for nothing and only the power organization which rules the collective is of any consequence. The narrator Leo Kall, loyal citizen and inventor of the truth drug Kallocain, has always seen life as a staircase in which each successive landing represents a further stage in his career. But his drug reveals that fellow citizens, although outwardly and of necessity conformists, inwardly are full of passionately held but repressed hopes and fears and dreams. In particular there is a group of people who make up a brotherhood whose members meet for human fellowship and the singing of strange songs (poetry, which the State had dispensed with), the clasping of hands in archaic greeting (discontinued by the State as unhygienic), and the placing of a ritual unsheathed knife beside themselves as they lie down defenseless beside it, as a sign of trust. Now although Kall fiercely denies to himself that he envies them, he dreams of the brotherhood's deserted city and of being beckoned into the ruins of a cellar open to the sky, with tendrils of green and grass growing between the stones under a clear sun, where he is greeted and embraced by a woman.

He discovers clear water, the wellspring of life, running across the earthen floor and is filled with indescribable gratitude. The contrast between the staircase leading up into a sterile block on the one hand, and the open cellar on the other is unmistakable. The State is built of stones while the brotherhood grows from inside, like trees, explains a member; being organic, she says, they need no organization. . . .

In her essay *Språket bortom logiken* Karin Boye stresses the role of the irrational and unconscious in human life and art. . . . Her poetic diction came increasingly to make use of images derived from the subconscious and dreams—an example of which is "Min hud är full av fjärilar" in *För trädets skull,* where superficial sensations seen as butterflies are juxtaposed against the pain of captive eagles confined within the poet's veins and marrow. Her best-loved poem with the general reading public is "Ja visst gör det ont" in *För trädets skull,* which has the most crystalline and accessible imagery. It is about the fear of growing, of the new and unknown—all marvelously translated into the pain felt by buds before they burst the trembling of glittering drops on a twig before they fall.

Karin Petherick. In Irene Scobbie, ed.
*Essays on Swedish Literature from 1880 to
the Present Day* (Aberdeen: University of
Aberdeen Press, 1978), pp. 141–43

Boye's early collections of poems, *Moln* (1922; Clouds) and *Gömda land* (1924; Hidden lands) are pleasing but vague and influenced by Vilhelm Ekelund.

In all her work a tension exists between rigid moralism and spontaneous instinct. In *Härdarna* (1927; The hearths) her disillusion with Christianity and embrace of "faith in life" together with a painful knowledge of being different are articulated.

In *För trädets skull* (1935; For the sake of the tree) form and point of view are influenced by psychoanalysis in the manner she postulates in the essay "Språket bortom logiken" (Language beyond logic). The symbolic language both confesses and hides her tragic personal split. Boye reaches equally high in the posthumously published *De sju dödssynderna* (1941; The Seven Deadly Sins), particularly in the short, simple poems about love and death.

Boye's best prose fiction is the negative utopia *Kallocain* (1940; trans. 1966), inspired by fears of nazism and communism.

Boye's lyrical production was fastidious, but cut short. Her finest poems have an original rhythm and a religious seriousness that fully express her "faith in life" and assure her rank among the great.

Margareta Mattsson. In Virpi Zuck, ed.
Dictionary of Scandinavian Literature
(Westport, Connecticut: Greenwood Press,
1990), p. 80

BOYLE, KAY (UNITED STATES) 1903–92

Anyone . . . whose standards of the short story are not the standards of the correspondence school will appreciate that the work of Miss Boyle, for simple craftsmanship, is superior to most of that which is crowned annually by our anthologies. Anyone with an ear for new verbal harmonies will appreciate that Miss Boyle is a stylist of unusual taste and sensibility. It is time, therefore, to cease to regard her as a mere lower case révoltée and to begin to accept her for what she is: more enterprising, more scrupulous, potentially more valuable than nine-tenths of our best-known authors.

Gerald Sykes. *The Nation.*
December 24, 1930, p. 711

Gertrude Stein and James Joyce were and are the glories of their time and some very portentous talents have emerged from their shadows. Miss Boyle, one of the newest, I believe to be among the strongest . . . . She sums up the salient qualities of that movement: a fighting spirit, freshness of feeling, curiosity, the courage of her own attitude and idiom, a violently dedicated search for the meanings and methods of art. . . . There are further positive virtues of the individual temperament: health of mind, wit and the sense of glory.

Katherine Anne Porter. *The New Republic.*
April 22, 1931, p. 279

Her short stories and her novels deal with the distress of human beings reaching for love and for each other, under the cloud of disease, or the foreknowledge of death. Her daring lies in an extravagance of metaphor, in roguishness, in ellipses. The short stories particularly revive for us the painful brilliance of living. Here is poison—in the small doses in which arsenic is prescribed for anaemia. . . . The author has a deep distrust of the false clarities which destroy overtones and mystery, since actions are the solid but not too significant residues of what goes on in heads and hearts.

Evelyn Harter. *The Bookman.*
June, 1932, pp. 250–55

Imagistic prose, stemming from the stream-of-consciousness, is a natural mode to people highly keyed to sensuous perception. But it varies in kind. In Virginia Woolf, where the approach is intellectual as well as sensuous, it is derived, an imagism of what the mind knows, a subtle and sophisticated play. If the balance is decidedly in the other direction, as in Waldo Frank, we have a feverish, almost physiological imagery. In Kay Boyle, at her best, the balance is nice—emotional, but with the perception swift and right. Where others clothe feeling in a bright array of words, she gives it the exquisite body in which it lives.

Myra Marini. *The New Republic.*
July 13, 1932, p. 342

Somewhere on the church at Gisors there is a wanton efflorescence of the latest Gothic which reaches its most intricate virtuosity only a stone's length from the pure and simple lines of the earliest Renaissance. In the tangle of the exquisite carving, figures of a brilliant precision are half hidden in a lush overgrowth of tortured stone wreathing into meaningless shapes. The grace of a detail catches the breath, the whole is a nullity, a confusion of motives eluding form.

Kay Boyle's writing is like that. . . . The carving hides the design, the figures are blurred by it.

Henry Seidel Canby. *Saturday Review of*
Literature. November 4, 1933, p. 233

She is one of the most eloquent and one of the most prolific writers among the expatriates; her work is always finished in the sense that her phrases are nicely cadenced and her imagery often striking and apt; her characters are almost always highly sensitized individuals who are marooned or in flight in some foreign country, banded together in small groups in which the antagonisms often seem intense beyond their recognizable causes. . . . It is noteworthy how much Kay Boyle gets out of the casual coming together of her people, what untold dangers and mysterious excitement she finds in their first impressions of each other—out of the tormented relationships and the eventual flight.

Robert Cantwell. *The New Republic.*
December 13, 1933, p. 136

Kay Boyle is Hemingway's successor, though she has not that piercing if patternless emotion which is what we remember of Hemingway at his best. It is significant that both writers received their literary training in Paris, as did Henry James, that they are familiar with deracinates and those casual sojourners in Paris whose search is for the exciting and the momentary. Each has the observational facility of the newspaperman, with the poet's power of meditating on life; their work stands out from any other type of fiction written in any other country, in both content and technique.

Mary M. Colum. *Forum*. October 1938,
p. 166

To my mind, the chief defect in Miss Boyle's equipment as an artist is to be traced to her lack of a subject which is organically her own; and by an organic subject I mean something more tangible than a fixed interest in certain abstract patterns of emotion and behavior. Being in possession of an elaborate technique and having developed disciplined habits of observation, Miss Boyle seems to be able to turn her hand to almost anything. As a result one feels all too often that she is not really involved with her themes, that she has not conceived but merely used them.

Philip Rahv. *The Nation*.
March 23, 1940, p. 396

Never in my life have I come across such descriptions of mountains. Never. . . . And I say this as a mountain-man. Her sentences about mountains go up and up to snow-peaked beauty almost unbearable, just as great mountains do, or swoop down like glaciers and snowfields, or are close and warming and exciting like snow in a village. Never have there been such descriptions of mountains.

Struthers Bart. *Saturday Review of
Literature*. January 15, 1944, p. 6

Kay Boyle . . . is one of the shrewdest stylists in the language and something of a mystic no matter what material she makes momentary use of . . . . The best thing she does is to transform the mundane detail and wring some spiritual essence from it; quite literally she can make (at her best) silk purses out of sows' ears, and you watch her writing as you would some marvelously deft machine performing this miracle, holding some scene or some person still while she outlines in space the nature of its, or his, meaning. And even when the miracle doesn't come off . . . even when the gears turn and the music soars, yet nothing is revealed but the fine hands of the operator, still the process is an exciting thing to behold. Miss Boyle can so compel us with symbols that we are lulled almost into accepting them as the stuff of life.

Nathan L. Rothman. *Saturday Review of
Literature*. April 9, 1949, p. 13

She has written of love in all of its possible phases. . . . She has written of all people and of their virtues, their sins, their crimes, their loves. There is also a deep love of nature, of mountains, snow, and forests. Even in stories the theme of which may be marital maladjustment, the devotion to the country in which the drama is played exceeds the author's concern with the drama itself. A preponderant part of her writing is descriptive, although she does not conceive of scenery merely as background. In her character portrayals a kind of compassion permits Miss Boyle to enter into the life of others with an intensity as violent as if the life were her own. This compassion gives a moving quality to her skillful portrayals of the blight of Nazism and fascism in Europe.

Harry R. Warfel. *American Novelists of Today* (n.p.: ABC, 1951), p. 45

Miss Boyle achieves her characteristic force by showing us a vision of humanity in need of pity and understanding, a central idea that does not make for light reading but one which accounts for the realism and effectiveness we inescapably feel as we read through her work. While probably not the end result of a reasonable philosophy, it is a telling and significant attitude toward life that makes of her writing much more than a pretty toy or a tract. Miss Boyle is not simply *interested* in people; she is vitally *concerned* with people and profoundly moved to write about their struggle with themselves and with their dreams.

Richard C. Carpenter. *The English Journal.* November 1953, p. 427

In her best work, it seems to me, her style is never noticeably brilliant; it is always subdued, always subservient to the creation of scenes and characters. One seldom feels, either, that Miss Boyle's stories or novels have been carpentered to fit a carefully worked out thesis. The best of her fiction is convincing and lifelike; the "meaning," seldom forced or imposed, rises—or seems to rise—naturally out of characters and actions, as though the author had actually observed the people and events just as she writes about them. . . . [S]he appears to be deeply committed to some ideal of social equality, personal freedom, universal tenderness or love—it is difficult to label what is usually subtle and complex—and she sees in the world about her the brutal violation of those who embody these ideals. Again and again in her fiction we are shown sensitive individuals, who respond to life feelingly rather than conventionally, attacked and defeated by tough, well-insulated barbarians flying the banners of custom and tradition.

William Stuckey. *The Minnesota Review.* Fall, 1960, p. 118

Kay Boyle has added eighteen poems from the last ten years to her earlier work in verse that culminated in the long 1944 poem *American Citizen;* these *Collected Poems* are elusive but—as always in the poetry of a writer whose characteristic achievement is in prose—they offer a reliable thematic index to Miss Boyle's preoccupations over the years: she aspires to be, doubtless is, a good European, the kind of person who knows the right café to sit in front of, the interesting wine to order, a hard ski slope to descend, an easy man to love. Her landscapes, both American and European, are made into emblems of the wild heart, the behavior of her animals likened to the actions of men. It is not entirely fair, by the way, to refer to her "earlier work in verse," since so many of these difficult pieces are experiments in mixing verse with extended prose passages; indeed, however obscure it may be, such prose is always firmer and, if not more deeply felt, then more dramatically honed than the verse, which in even the very latest poems is without much spine or spring, though Miss Boyle has spirit and to spare.

Richard Howard. *Poetry.* July, 1963,
pp. 253–54

Put simply, Kay Boyle's theme is nearly always the perennial human need for love; her design is woven from the many forms the frustration and misdirection of love may take. Her style and the care with which she limns a setting are, as they inevitably must be with a creative artist, but vehicle and adjunct for her central meaning. Although on occasion she may have forgotten the artistic obligation in exchange for sheer virtuosity (always a danger for the virtuoso), using her style to bedazzle rather than to aid vision, or letting exotic setting obscure the human situation with which she is dealing, in her better fiction, style, setting, and theme form a seamless web in which all the threads are held under a precise tension.

Richard C. Carpenter. *Critique.*
Winter, 1964–65, p. 65

She is the author of thirteen novels, some of them very good, but she is not quite a major novelist. Her major medium has always been the short story and the novelette. (And it is typical of this aristocrat, whose earlier work lay in the tradition of Edith Wharton and Henry James, not to use the fashionable word *novella.*) But even here, she was in the early 1930s, a writer of superior sensibility—or so I thought—using a foreign scene more successfully than her native one, and belonging, in essence, both to the expatriate line of James and Wharton and to that later "lost generation" of the 1920s.

What this new collection of Miss Boyle's short stories and novelettes does prove is that while all of the speculation above is somewhat true, none of it is really true, or profoundly true. She has all these elements in this new collection of her mature work. But, as in the case of every first-rank writer, she rises above the disparate elements in her work or in her temperament, to become something else. What *Nothing Ever Breaks Except The Heart* proves, in short, is that Kay Boyle has at last become a major short-story writer, or a major writer in contemporary American fiction, after three decades of elusiveness, sometimes of anonymity, almost of literary "classlessness," while she has pursued and has finally discovered her true metier. . . . To her earlier vision of sensibility, she has added what every first-rate writer must have, a standard of human morality—and the fact that human morality is usually, if not always, related to a specific social or historical context.

It is this familiar concept, missing in so much current and "new" American fiction that is embodied in the magnificent stories of her maturity.

Maxwell Geismar. *The New York Times.*

July 10, 1966, pp. 4, 16

With the publication of *Fifty Stories* in 1980, the republication of *Three Short Novels* in 1982 and *Being Geniuses Together* in 1984, and the appearance of three new books in 1985—a translation of René Crevel's *Babylon, Words That Must Somehow Be Said: Selected Essays of Kay Boyle 1927–1984,* and *This Is Not a Letter and Other Poems*—Kay Boyle's work is becoming increasingly accessible. For some reason, however, she has not received the wide recognition that her contemporaries of the 1920s and early 1930s assumed would be her due. Today, while her name is mentioned in many of the myriad memoirs and studies of the expatriates, it most often appears without elaboration as one of the "other" writers in Paris in the 1920s. The oblivion is undeserved. In the face of growing interest in women's studies and the widening awareness that women's contributions to literature have too long been underrated or ignored, Kay Boyle is a prime candidate for "rediscovery."

From her earliest short stories to her latest novel, *The Underground Woman* (1975), she has written of the power of women. Often a strong, spirited woman will play opposite a man made weak by egotism, narrow-mindedness, and petty possessiveness. Most of these men are nearly as pathetic for their limitations as they are despicable for their attempts at domestic tyranny. . . . In much of her fiction, Kay Boyle endows women with extraordinary power. It is a power that many men fear, and in order to preserve their own delicate concepts of themselves, they often attempt in her stories to reduce woman through a simplistic definition of her nature. "They're mothers or *putains,*" claims a young soldier in her 1949 novel, *His Human Majesty.* "There's nothing in between." In *The Underground Woman,* the 1975 novel based on the author's own arrest and imprisonment for demonstrating at the Oakland Induction Center in 1967, a nun comes to a stunning realization while in prison for protesting the Vietnam War. She tells her companion: "I knew that for centuries bishops and priests and abbots and popes were so afraid of the energy of women that they closed them all away. But I never wanted to say to myself, 'yes, this is true,' and now I can." She knows now that women were "taken away from life and cloistered in silence" because the men in the church hierarchy "were afraid that we might bring Christianity back on earth."

Sandra Whipple Spanier. In Alice Kessler-
Harris and William P. McBrien, eds. *Faith
of a (Woman) Writer* (1984; rpt. Westport,
Connecticut: Greenwood Press,
1988), pp. 60–62

BRITTAIN, VERA (GREAT BRITAIN) 1893–1970

It has been the common fate of feminists in the past to be first ridiculed, then ignored, and finally consigned to total obscurity. Outstanding among those whose work has in recent years been at least partially rescued from oblivion is Vera Brittain (1893–1970). Vera Brittain's early life has been the subject of a successful television series, *Testament of Youth;* several of her books, including *Testament of Youth, Testament of Experience,* and *Testament of Friendship,* have been reissued in both England and the United States; and her early war diary has been published under the title *Chronicle of Youth.. . .*

A prolific writer, Vera Brittain issued a steady stream of works. When she died in 1970 she left, in addition to innumerable journal articles, twenty-nine books including novels, poetry, autobiographies, biographies, and sociological and political studies. Of these, *Testament of Youth* (1933), which describes her experiences in World War I, will certainly prove to be her most lasting achievement. But her five novels, *The Dark Tide* (1923), *Not Without Honour* (1924), *Honourable Estate* (1936), *Account Rendered* (1945), and *Born 1925* (1948), although almost completely unknown today, have considerable significance in that they record some of the major events and ideas of the time.

Brittain contended that a principal function of the novel is to reveal the impingement of public affairs on private lives. While acknowledging that her closeness to the events depicted prevented her from seeing them in their final perspective, she nevertheless presented in her novels a picture of the main upheavals of the century. Drawing on her own experiences, often modeling her characters on real persons and tracing always the course of actual history, she rooted her novels firmly in fact. But their importance does not lie simply in their historical accuracy. Brittain conceived of these novels as further weapons in her campaign for women. In them, as surely as in her journalism, she wrote to analyze the existing conditions of society and to indicate the directions which future progress should take. She states her theory of the novel in the foreword to *Honourable Estate,* where she declares: "If large areas of human experience—political, economic, social, religious—are to be labeled inadmissible as subjects for fiction, then fiction is doomed as organic art." The novels, then, provide a detailed statement of the concerns and principles common in feminist thought during the decades following the attainment of the vote. . . .

Like all serious thinkers, Vera Brittain approached political and sociological issues from a moral perspective, and the value of her novels springs from the honesty and clear-sightedness with which she probed the moral problems underlying contemporary events. This is the source of both their strengths and their weaknesses. Admittedly Vera Brittain is sometimes more concerned with theories than with people. Her characters do not always come to life, and too often they are mouthpieces for her personal philosophies. But the preoccupation with ideas is also one of Brittain's strengths. Her novels are written with passionate conviction, and they affirm her deep-felt faith in human progress and her belief that human beings do grow in sympathy and understanding. This belief was one which she first formed as a history student at Oxford when she studied the great nineteenth-century treaties, and neither the economic disasters of the 1930s nor the world war of the 1940s could obliterate it. A true intellectual herself, she saw reason and intellect as the means by which human beings can transcend suffering and evil, put an end to injustice and oppression, and begin to establish a better order of life. Socialism, feminism, and pacifism were in her view all ways by which human society can advance from its primitive state to enlightenment. For her a recognition of women's rights was not the least significant indication of the development of the human spirit towards full civilization.

Muriel Mellowan. *Tulsa Studies in Women's Literature.* 2, 1983, pp. 215–16, 227–28

In her autobiography, *Testament of Youth* (1933), Vera Brittain wrote that it has often been said by pacifists "that war creates more criminals than heroes; that, far from developing noble qualities in those who take part in it, it brings out the worst. If this were altogether true the pacifists' aim would be, I think, much nearer of attainment than it is. . . . Our task is infinitely complicated by the fact that war, while it lasts, does produce heroism to a far greater extent than it brutalizes. Between 1914 and 1919 young men and women, disastrously pure in heart and unsuspicious of elderly self-interest and cynical exploitation, were continually rededicating themselves—to an end that they believed, and went on trying to believe, lofty and ideal. . . . Undoubtedly this state of mind was what anti-war propagandists call it—'hysterical exalta-tion' . . . but it had concrete results in stupendous patience, in superhuman endurance, in the constant re-affirmation of incredible courage. To refuse to acknowledge this is to underrate the power of those white angels which fight so naïvely on the side of destruction."

Since *Testament of Youth* is in print again and, in addition, was drama-tized on television, what is the point of now publishing Vera Brittain's earlier *Chronicle of Youth: The War Diary 1913–1917,* some of which appeared in *Testament?* At first I thought that it would only contribute another romantic text to nostalgia for war. The *Testament* was not the result of emotion recol-lected in tranquility, but of emotion recollected in a state of high anxiety, with the political force of Brittain's later pacifism, feminism and socialism standing over her shoulder like a bronze angel of justice and justification. What leaps off the pages of *Chronicle of Youth* is, to use her own phrases, the voice of a young woman "disastrously pure in heart," and afflicted with the "hysterical exaltation" of a whole nation. From a larger perspective, it is the story of a generation of young Englishwomen who came of age in World War I, whose experience of loss—husbands, brothers, lovers, fathers, cousins and all their young friends—has never been better told. And it records the voice of those white angels fighting naively on the side of destruction.

This diary forces us to come to terms with wartime "heroine-ism." While boys were taught in public schools to aspire toward the honor and glory of death on the battlefield for their country, the first generation of young women was modeling itself, not on the heroines of Jane Austen and George Eliot, but on Lyndall, the feminist heroine of Olive Schreiner's *Story of an African Farm*. Brittain was lucky that her teacher at St. Hilda's had given her Schreiner's radical novel, and that her lover, Roland Leighton, shared her passion for this book. Since she had played out the novel's tragedy in her diary as she lost her lover in the trenches, Brittain then took up Schreiner's feminism, pacifism and socialism in a lifetime of creative antiwar work. *Testament of Youth* is one of the great autobiographies of all time, as morally exhilarating as St. Augustine's, as painfully personal as Rousseau's, but the war diary stands in relation to it like raw liver to paté.

Do not mistake me. I wept over this book—and so will you. But it is too bloody and organic, too raw in feeling and experience, to stomach in its primal state. Brittain knew it, as she struggled to make a novel out of it, then to publish the diary itself. Abandoning both projects, she wrote autobiography as social history, capturing her class, her sex and her generation, freeing herself at last from the grip of patriotism and the torpor of nostalgia for war by getting a firm grip on her passion for peace. The difference between the diary and *Testament of Youth* is not merely one of genre. The *Testament* is what it says, a will or legacy for the next generation, bearing witness to the waste of war, and a compact, not with God, but with women and the working class, to whom Brittain devoted the rest of her distinguished writing life.

Because if originated in real experience, *Chronicle* comes through as a more passionate "indictment of a whole civilization." Brittain wears her patriotic heart on her sleeve, falling in love, playing tennis, struggling to enter Oxford, losing lover and brother at the front, and then, one by one, all the young men she knew, becoming a volunteer nurse, reciting the poems of Rupert Brooke and Wilfred Owen. The anguish of wartime casualty lists, of psychological wounds fostered by death and dying, is immediate and real. She was saved from despair by finding heroines, real ones like her teachers at Somerville College, Oxford, and literary ones like those in the novels of Olive Schreiner.

No heroine could be more aptly named than Vera Brittain. But she would not have wanted her life limited to the nostalgic, ghoulish glamour of the war nurse. After the war, Brittain chose women (particularly the novelist and critic Winifred Holtby) as the emotional focus of her postwar life, though she made a marriage of convenience for the purpose of having children, who might help rebuild England. The work her daughter, Shirley Williams, did for the Labor Party was a fulfillment of Brittain's legacy.

The examination question set for Vera Brittain's entrance scholarship for Somerville was to explicate Thomas Carlyle's crusty patriarchal pronouncement that history is the biography of great men. Her iconoclastic essay was the beginning of a writing career that would turn this assertion upside down and inside out. Her kind of history chose heroines who championed the liberty of women and of the working class.

Virginia Woolf told Ethel Smyth that she stayed up all night to read *Testament of Youth,* and she wrote in her diary that she devoured it "with extreme greed," though she felt in contact with "a stringy, metallic mind": "A very good book of its sort. The new sort, the hard anguished sort, that the young write; that I could never write. Nor has anyone written that kind of book before."

This diary is destined for the same classic status, being even more raw and bloody, stringy and metallic, than the autobiography, which was "an attempt to write history in terms of personal life." Whether we meet Vera Brittain in her diary or her autobiography, what we find is a social history of self-conscious heroineship. a plea for an end to naïve white angels.

Jane Marcus. *New York Times Book Review.*
January 30, 1983, p. 12

Brittain's autobiography was to some extent a response to the already published memoirs of Blunden, Sassoon, and Graves. All four of these books were written so long after the war that the authors had had time to assimilate their experience to traditional literary patterns. At the moment of occurrence, the traumatic incidents must have been chaotic for eyewitnesses, who needed to exert the pressure of the mind and of the years in order to reduce them to some kind of meaning. Paul Fussell has pointed out that Blunden's *Undertones of War* is patterned on the pastoral elegy, Sassoon's *Memoirs of a Fox-Hunting Man* on the pastoral romance, both relying on the juxtaposition of literary form and war experience to make an ironic contrast. In Graves's *Goodbye to All That* the ironic function is explicit, for the memoir takes the form of a farce, a Comedy of Humors as in Ben Jonson. Graves himself was highly aware of this function: his memories, he said, presented themselves as caricature scenes Brittain's *Testament of Youth* is built on the structure of romantic comedy, ending, after the years of grief and isolation, in the traditional comic conclusion of marriage.

Each of these texts has a distinctive surface metaphor for society. Blunden, the shepherd's solitary watch; Sassoon, the fox hunt; Graves, the public school; Brittain, the dinner or tea party. All of them, however, are informed by what Fussell calls "binary vision." The habit of dividing the world into "us" and "them" carried over from the trenches so that "they" were others besides the Germans. "They" might be at the base instead of up the line; indeed, "they" might well be the entire civilian population. In short, the image of the battlefield underlies all four memoirs and provides a common metaphor.

How much, then, did this binary vision affect the world view of Vera Brittain, who came to adulthood just as the war began? I suspect that it affected her view not only of the war and of subsequent years, but also her memories of the years leading up to them. The very first sentence of *Testament of Youth* mentions the effect that the war had on her. All the childhood incidents she recalls point forward to those events, particularly the death of Roland, that determined the course of her life. Thus the image of the battlefield shadows her entire autobiography. This binary vision structured not only the way she perceived herself in opposition to her father, to the administrations of Oxford University and of the VAD, but also her understanding of the contrast between her youthful outlook at the time when the events took place and her mature outlook at the time of writing.

With her dichotomizing vision strengthened, if not actually caused, by the war, Brittain felt a strong competitive urge when she came to write her autobiography. The male memoirists were already in print before she visualized her plan, so her work clearly stands in a dialectical relationship to theirs. Unlike the men, who said very little about the opposite sex, she took pains to detail her relationships with a number of male figures, thus establishing a dialectic within the book as well as between it and the memoirs already published. Her disagreements with her father and with Roland were pronounced, but because her overriding feelings for these figures were affectionate, as they unambiguously were for Edward, her real battle was against the tradition of authority, and this she waged regardless of whether the seat of power was occupied by man or woman.

Although she tried to indicate her youthful outlook by including letters, diary entries, and poems, her outlook at the time of writing predominates. The battlefield had become, as for her contemporaries, an image which structured the way she looked at the world. The battle she perceived between the claims of the private life and the public life, which I take to be the overall concern of *Testament of Youth,* was powered by the psychological mind set imprinted on her entire generation.

Jean Pickering. *Women's Studies.* 13, 1986,
pp. 75–77

In tracing Brittain's struggle with war from 1914 to 1950, we discover not a straight line to pacifism or feminism but a series of backward and forward movements. If we attempt to understand Brittain's ambivalence and the discourse that expressed it, we may uncover a relation between women and war. Brittain's prowar sentiments and her desire to be active in the war seem part of her professed desire to be a man. Although Brittain had declared herself a feminist as early as 1913, almost all of her role models during her adolescence and young adulthood were men. She borrowed her abstract rhetoric of patriotism and heroism from male friends and the male establishment. More than once, she cursed having been born a woman and more than once she showed a lack of respect for women. And more than once she wished Roland might be wounded so that she could nurse him and gain the sense of importance and usefulness that was only accorded men.

But it was love for Roland and the victims she nursed that finally brought Brittain into touch with her suppressed female identity. If we believe Carol Gilligan and others, who have argued that women, unlike men, see relationship as an essential part of self-development, then we might say that Brittain's personalization of the war, which eventually vanquished her tendency to prowar abstraction, involved a shift from male to female identification. She began nursing out of love for Roland and compassion for other women with sons and lovers at the front. Through love and nursing, she learned empathy even with those who daily endangered the life of her loved ones. Before the war, all her intimates were men; afterward she found friendship with a woman, Winifred Holtby.

Brittain's road to pacifism was inextricably intertwined with the passage from abstraction to relationship, which included the shift from a self-concerned to an empathic feminism. The final form of her pacifism was buttressed by a Christian rhetoric not much less abstract than her previous patriotic rhetoric. But, of the two voices with which she spoke, it was the voice embedded in relationship and then universalized that had the last word, the word for peace.

Lynne Layton. In Margaret Higgonet, et al.,
eds. *Behind the Lines: Gender and the Two
World Wars.* (New Haven: Yale University
Press, 1987), pp. 82–83

One way of describing the process between Brittain and Holtby is to see it as the mutual creation of acceptable fictions. These fictions are versions of each other and the other's world compatible with images of the self that each is able to live with. As Patrocinio Schweickart says, women "are most concerned in their dealings with others to negotiate between opposing needs so that the relationship can be maintained." Women also authorize each other in a third way, then, by making authors of each other. Brittain and Holtby did this in a literal sense, of course, since they encouraged each other to write. Their conversation, their attempt to reach consensus, took place on the page; they defined themselves through their written texts. This female friendship is thus not merely paradigmatic of the reading process but a literal illustration of it.

Elizabeth Abel has pointed out that "the clearest emphasis on a collaborative relationship that echoes the dynamics of female bonding occurs in reader-response criticism." Basically, reader-response theorists see reading as a meeting between the reader and the text that depends as much upon the nature of the reader as upon the nature of the text. The reader is thus an active agent in the creation of the text. This transaction parallels the personal interaction of friendship and like it involves the meeting of the self with a second self, a character or characters in a novel, for example.

In the case of Brittain and Holtby, who are both writers, the reader of one text becomes the author of another text, which is a rewriting of what she has read. In particular, fiction, with its imaginative license not to have to pretend to be the truth, becomes the opportunity to rewrite each other in relation to the self, to construct a reading of the other compatible with an acceptable version of oneself. Thus each becomes the other's subject and each the other's author—"you're the person who's made me," writes Holtby to Brittain—as well as being each the other's reader (in the sense also of being the work's intended audience or implied reader). As a reader each necessarily compares her own view of herself, of a shared experience, of an idea, with its presentation in the other's text and in turn reflects this response in her own rewriting. So, for example, Holtby's *The Crowded Street* can be read as an answer to Brittain's *The Dark Tide,* Brittain's *Not without Honour* as a comment on *The Crowded Street.*

> Jean Kennard. *Vera Brittain and Winifred*
> *Holtby: A Working Partnership* (Hanover:
> University of New Hampshire Press, 1991),
> pp. 17–18

BRODBER, ERNA (JAMAICA) 1936–

In structure and novelistic technique, *Jane and Louisa Will Soon Come Home* is quite different from [Merle Hodge's] *Crick Crack Monkey* and [Zee Edgell's] *Beka Lamb.* Yet there is the similarity of focus on childhood experience and the quest of the protagonist for positive selfhood. Central again is the internal struggle of the young protagonist to balance conflicting worldviews. For Nellie of *Jane and Louisa Will Soon Come Home,* the search for selfhood is a complex, integral, and lifesaving need because without a successful redefinition and unification of selfhood, she will return to her alienated, dysfunctional existence that led to a mental breakdown.

Through the fragmented sketches of her childhood which the novel offers, Nellie's upbringing by solid Jamaican peasant stock in a tightly circled rural community accounts for her distraught adult personality. Nellie must reconcile and resolve misguided attitudes toward individual and community relations, women's roles and sexuality, and family lineage and heritage. She develops these attitudes primarily from the influence of her Aunt Becca, who is determined to eradicate all vestiges of her peasant class origins. . . .

Nellie wants both oneness with the community and the affluence of the middle class but cannot reconcile the conflicting values representative of the two. As a child and later as an adult, Nellie wrestles with the conflict between the community's values which allowed human worth and importance to be determined by the person's life and deeds, with Aunt Becca's which judged people according to their class and material possessions. As an adult, she finds forming superficial relationships surrounded by an intellectual guise to be an easy way to escape the conflict; her education helps to facilitate this escape. . . . Nellie grows up to become a college-educated, sexually repressed, and intellectually alienated woman. She exists within a "kumbla," which is the symbolic representation of her alienation which Brodber uses throughout the novel. In order for Nellie to withdraw from the kumbla, from her protective enclosure which her middle-class aunt has so carefully taught her "how to wear," she must form real human bonds. She does form two: the first is with Baba Ruddick, her childhood friend who, in saviorlike white attire, destroys her self-deceiving role of secretary of a group of alienated pseudoradical intellectuals. The second important bond is formed with her Aunt Alice, and it is the one which effectively saves her life.

Establishing the healing bond with Aunt Alice is logical since Aunt Alice is the only grown woman Nellie knew who was never burdened by "it." In Nellie's consciousness, "it," menstruation, is the primary representation of the burden of female sexuality, which is responsible for the downfall of so many women in the community and for the need to be "cleansed" which Nellie so consistently feels.

Aunt Alice is oblivious to the conflicts caused by unwed motherhood and female sexuality, just as she is unaware of those created by class perspectives and arbitrary human bias because while she was still a child, "it had become crystal clear that little Alice was not quite right in the head."

The mental journey through the history of her father's family, starting with the white ancestor, the great-grandfather and his common-law wife, Tia Maria, who "did everything to annihilate herself. . . her skin, her dress, her smell," is what makes Nellie whole again. Recapturing the family history through the aid of a woman who is outside the realm of society's pressures and biases, allows Nellie a full perspective of her origins in the community. It gives her the material to piece together the social and psychological origins of her Aunt Becca's worldview. It also provides Nellie with the strength and courage to emerge from her "kumbla." Building upon the warmth and friendship that her Aunt Alice offered her as a child, Nellie actually reestablishes communication with her self, the self which has been buried, confused and denied by Aunt Becca's teachings and society's contradictory messages about women's roles. . . .

Erna Brodber's novel offers a possible solution for the woman, who unlike Beka, could not develop selfhood through positive self-definition while an adolescent. The solution which Nellie embraces—redefinition of the self through establishment of a sense of historical continuity and oneness and rejection of self-deprecating values—appears very plausible in the world of Brodber's novel because of her portrayal of Nellie as an alienated intellectual.

Yakini Kemp. SAGE. 2, 1985, pp. 26–27

The landscape of Erna Brodber's *Jane and Louisa Will Soon Come Home* is largely that of rural Jamaica, a setting in which family ties are complicated by the sinuous bonds of color and class; a context within which an oral tradition of long-time story, family history, and pure gossip flourishes along-side the world of books and distant town. Brodber's narrative method exemplifies an interpenetration of scribal and oral literary forms: a modernist, stream-of-consciousness narrative voice holds easy dialogue with the traditional teller of tales, the transmitter of anansi story, proverb, folk song, and dance.

Brodber's experiment in form is underscored by the writer's deliberately ingenuous assertion that *Jane and Louisa Will Soon Come Home* was not conceived as a novel: she set out to write a case study in Abnormal Psychology. But literary critics have appropriated the work, recognizing in its dense patterns of allusive imagery, its evocative language, and its carefully etched characterizations, the sensibility of the creative writer. The "functionalist" intention of the social psychologist appears divergent from the "structuralist" analysis of the literary critic. But, Brodber's "faction" can be categorized within a Neo-African folk aesthetic of functional form: literature as word-hoard, the repository of the accumulated wisdom of the community, the creative medium through which the norms of appropriate social behavior can be elaborated metaphorically.

The Afro-Jamaican folk ethos of *Jane and Louisa Will Soon Come Home* is evident in the organizing metaphors of the work, derived from the folk culture, and in its primary theme: the healing of the protagonist Nellie, who travels to "foreign" to study, and returns home to a profound sense of homelessness, from which she is redeemed only when she comes to understand the oral accounts of her fragmented family history, and the distorted perceptions of female identity and sexuality that she has internalized in childhood. The therapeutic power of the word is the subject and medium of Brodber's fictive art.

> Carolyn Cooper. In Carole Boyce Davies
> and Elaine Savory Fido, eds. *Out of the*
> *Kumbla: Caribbean Women and Literature*
> (Trenton, New Jersey: Africa World
> Press, 1990), pp. 279–80

As a work of West Indian fiction, *Jane and Louisa* is attempting to do what I think the works of Harris and Brathwaite also do—reclaim the past, reassess its values, and utilize its survivals and syncretisms as lessons, guidelines for contemporary life. In this novel, the quest is at once convincingly personal and female and, at the same time, communal and asexual. While we are explicitly told, "You'll find no finger posts to point you to our place," no hard and fast rules are given for how to go forward after the processes of historical and personal reconstruction are completed, the prevailing mood is one of progress, of optimism. The dream-image of the fish Nellie carries within her suggests the Christian fish symbol of surviving faith, a secret message of brotherhood and hope for the entire (religious) community. While this positive symbol is not *yet* "born," we are given to understand that "It will come"

(p. 147). So the novel ends with a farewell to the reclaimed ancestors and a reiteration of a positive future, not just by the central character, but by an entire West Indian generation:

We are getting ready.

Evelyn O'Callaghan. In Edward Baugh and
Mervyn Morris, eds. *Progressions: West
Indian Literature in the 1970s* (Kingston,
Jamaica: University of the West Indies,
1990), p. 242

BRØGGER, SUZANNE (DENMARK) 1944–

"As far back as I can remember I have believed I knew everything about sex." Thus at the outset Suzanne Brøgger, who insists she has never had doubts about herself because no one else has, establishes the theme and the mood for a long succession of repetitious rehearsals of erotic behavior. If she were not so disposed to excess and rationalization, the reader might be more convinced by her advocacy to dissolve ethical, social and civil mores—marriage, family, school attendance—but sophistry and exaggeration detract from persuasiveness.

There are distinct similarities between this book [*Crème fraîche,* Fresh cream] and the earlier "Deliver Us from Love." Both concentrate on the anomalous and the lurid, on seduction and copulation, and both evade, confuse and/or otherwise muddy the issues of good and evil in the interrelationships of the sexes. They are bold works from the pen of a Danish journalist, a would-be revolutionary, a devotee of Henry Miller and Douglas Johns, a feminist radical bent not so much on changing the world as on discarding it.

The autobiographical narrative takes us to remote locations and introduces us to more consorts than we can keep in mind. We learn of the narrator's parentage, childhood and education in Denmark. We share her experiences as a reporter in Vietnam, Lebanon, Jordan, Thailand and other countries and a visitor in London, Paris, New York, Hollywood and elsewhere. Fellow writers, painters, professors, sculptors, designers and all manner of men and women make up her world; but Max, the French diplomat, figures more prominently than the rest. Frequent allusions to literary, theatrical and political celebrities also contribute to the international flavor, but the relevance in context is not always clear.

There is, of course, something admirable to be said for an author's openness, chronological orderliness, vividness and fluent prose, and perhaps Suzanne Brøgger does not propose to stimulate imaginations or to stretch minds.

Whether the title is intentional mockery or serious intimation, "Fresh Cream" is a misnomer for so unsavory a volume.

A. Langemo. *World Literature Today.*
53, 1979, pp. 516–17

Suzanne Brøgger is at her best when she intimately and painstakingly details brief historical moments, infinitesimal clips of reality in which a universal significance comes forth. Her best work to date, the autobiographical *Crème fraiche* (1978) was written in this manner. Readers of Danish literature can now experience this same extraordinary literary style in a new collection of essays. . . .

One of the most outstanding and recently written essays, however, is that on Karen Blixen (1980), better known in the United States as Isak Dinesen. In a critical attempt to analyze Blixen's essay on marriage ("Modern Marriage and Other Considerations") Brøgger assumes a different attitude than that of previous Blixian scholarship. She concludes in one instance that Blixen's ideas of free love had more to do with the circumstances surrounding her distant relationship to Denys Finch Hatton than they did with a more general, well-thought-out concept of free love.

"Dorothy Parker" (1971) is of similar thematic material: an essay on a woman writer in a predominantly male writer's milieu, and the direction her life takes as a result of that circumstance. Whereas the former article deals analytically with Blixen's near-hypocritical relationship between what she wrote and why she wrote it, the latter is a touching, powerful account of Dorothy Parker and destruction—she had become a victim of the literature that made her famous. Brøgger's depiction of similar topics from the detached-intellectual and engaged-tragic perspectives demonstrates the extent of her versatility. As an essayist she is capable of responding to various and changing situations while her literary style maintains a high degree of intelligence and creativity.

Suzanne Brøgger has the uncanny ability of presenting the reader with material of concentrated density and eloquence that reveals interesting peculiarities in all societies, to say nothing of the peculiarities of life and culture in her native Denmark. This collection gathers the author's most illuminating essays and represents the best of that ability.

Scott de Francesco. *World Literature Today.*
55, 1981, pp. 682–83

When Suzanne Brøgger in the title story "No man's land" evokes the utopian idea of a female identity, she talks about a genesis, a movement out into the border area of patriarchal institutions, into a new space, where a new language comes into existence and where changeability replaces hierarchy, power and the phallic order. . . .

The choice of words in Brøgger's text is reminiscent of the French theoretician Luce Irigaray and her attempts to deconstruct the male norm, mainly by linguistic means, in order to clear the ground and find a new space. . . .

[But the notion of] solidarity is a red rag for the loner Suzanne Brøgger, who is attempting to renew women's roles mainly by refusing to adjust to them herself. . . . Brøgger quite consciously mingles polemic with lyrical prose, and does not distinguish between politics, life and fiction. . . .

Linguistic skepticism in this sense, or even ironic subversion, is a characteristic trait of all the authors represented here (with the possible exception of Elsa Gress). Brøgger attempts persiflage through games on words and through twisting meanings around.

> Annegret Heitmann. Introduction to *No
> Man's Land: An Anthology of Modern
> Danish Women's Literature* (Chester
> Springs, Pennsylvania: Dufour, 1987),
> pp. 1–3, 5, 7

The writings of Suzanne Brøgger are created as a mixture of genres, both fiction and nonfiction. Her own life is the object of reflection in these books. Yet the public display of her private life does not necessarily lead to a lack of political commitment or existential insight. Relating everything to herself, she at the same time distinguishes herself from everything, thereby eliminating the border between the public and private spheres. She presents her own personal life as an alternative to the traditional life of women with its inherent contradictions. She works through this alternative in her writings, trying to dissolve the contradictions that are present in women's literature elsewhere, including the conflict between work and love. The character "Suzanne Brøgger" in her works has decided once and for all that she does not want to work, in the traditional sense of the word. This means that she does not look at writing as a kind of work. Writing is a way of life. As the title of her first novel, *Fri os fra kærligheden* (1973) (Deliver us from love) (1976), indicates, the subject of her books is not personal love. Instead she describes a larger, expansive community of people whose relationships to one another are based on Eros. Her books express an attitude that fears stagnation and stasis and encourages change and creativity. The dynamics of change become an existential principle: "Now I will tell you the best way to live is like a fish in the water or a bird in the air. It is best to live in motion."

The reflective essay is her characteristic genre. This is a natural manifestation of the fact that she is expressing a personal attitude in her works. Her lifestyle is the result of a conscious moral choice. She reenacts her own life in fiction. Moments of weakness, anxiety, loneliness, and inadequacy, which permeate the more confessional writings in women's literature, are conspicuously absent in Brøgger's works. This means that the author's will to enact the alternative has become one with her literary intent.

Crème fraiche is a kaleidoscopic journalistic description of the author's own international escapades, a gigantic world tour that includes visits to both Eastern and Western capitals, including Saigon, Bangkok, New York, and London. Her visit to New York includes conversations with Henry Miller, her much-admired "mentor" who, like herself, advocates an anti-bourgeois lifestyle. Again she depicts her frightening closeness to life, love, pain, and death. Her own words serve best to illustrate the style of *Creme Fraiche:* "I'm not a poet, but a choreographer. I choreograph the movement that already *is* in order to make it more obvious, illuminating, attractive and frightening. It is not the goal of this movement that is important, it is the dance itself."

Her most critically acclaimed work, the epic poem *Tone* (1981), is about characters from the street whose lives are intense and passionate, characters who break with habit and with the bureaucratic and patriarchal organization that we call society. The heroine, Tone, lives life in the streets, full of intense happiness and closeness to life and death. *Tone* is about life as creativity and desire. It is about choosing to live a life of risk by exposing one's soul, thus rejecting stagnation, which is synonymous with death. This is Brøgger's most complex work. It reveals many of the same images and themes found in her early works, but these are treated more seriously, less superficially, in a characteristic interplay of styles that break with and underscore each other.

Jody Jensen. In Virpi Zuck, ed. *Dictionary of Scandinavian Literature* (Westport, Connecticut: Greenwood Press, 1990), pp. 89–90

"Carbon Monoxide" (or perhaps "Chokings") is a collection of thirty-six essays written by Suzanne Brøgger over a ten-year period. The volume is divided into six main sections, with single longer essays punctuating the beginning, middle, and end of the volume: "The Imagination" (or "The Female Fabricator"?), "the Crippled Nude Dancing Girl," and "The Inner Bag Lady."

Brøgger, by now a world traveler and a ceaseless voyager in the difficult and differing worlds of sexual mores, views herself as someone who no longer "acts" on behalf of desires and needs, but rather as one who "observes" and "manipulates." This is a loss of innocence. She declares that she was formed by the thinking of the 1950s to the 1980s: "duty" was the opposite of "desire," and one's "conscience" was replaced by a "solidarity" with others. In New Radicalism the law was considered to be petit bourgeois, and "internationalism" replaced old-fashioned concepts of morality. One needed be truly open only about sex. She has come to use her life to find out who she is, where she can learn, and where she belongs.

With wit, insight, and charm, Brøgger describes places, people, and problems. The places include Oman, Tibet, Thailand, Brazil, Argentina, the USA, Greenland, and Uganda. Among the people considered are the Dalai Lama, Borges, Colette, Robert Irwin, Ronald D. Laing, Alexandra David-Neel,

Karen Blixen (Isak Dinesen) and Aage Henriksen, David Bohm, Jacobo Timerman, Germaine Greer, and Marie Curie. Some of the problems discussed are poverty, terrorism, the status of refugees, population control, the loss of "belonging" to the desire for liberation, a future of isolation through egoism, and the need to analyze sexual roles as cultural expression.

Perhaps Brøgger's most important (and recurrent) themes are those that connect sexuality and death ("The Love of Death") and that link both to writing. Sexuality, like poetry, demands a form, and formlessness is death. Some forms of sexuality cannot last, and when form breaks, one "sort of" dies and love appears in no-man's land. One source of insight for Brøgger has been Colette, who maintained that women who are most known for cultivating love in reality are the most indifferent to it. Nevertheless, Brøgger maintains that the background for all art—and misery—is to be found in failed love. In the unending myth or dream one can assume many roles, for fiction allows all to compose along with the author, to dream, whereas biography forces the reader to compare realities.

It is in the treatment of the Danish self-biographical and polemical writer Elsa Gress that Brøgger half-unwittingly seems to turn the serrated blade of her irony against herself. She deems the heretic and polemicist to be someone wishing affection and esteem from, and acceptance by, society itself. Brøgger always seems to plunge into the subject of death, but that is a condition so unfathomable that the wonder and amazement she brings to life seem to float away—until she pops up once more, the "inner" bag lady borne up by her bags of life's leftovers.

Faith Ingwersen. World Literature Today. 66,
1992, p. 141

[A] turning-away from militant positions can be noticed in [Danish] women's literature, which after 1968 launched provocative attacks—fictive and nonfictive—on a male-dominated and oppressive society. Initially, a series of documentary reports were issued, such as *Kvinder på fabrik* (1971; Women in factories) or *Kvindernes bog* (1972; Women's book), which were succeeded by more personal, subjective accounts, such as Suzanne Brøgger's *Fri os fra kærligheden* (1974) (Deliver us from love) (1976). Brøgger provides an excellent example of the development of Danish feminist literature, maturing into discussions of gender roles and moving from semidocumentary or autobiographical accounts, such as the kaleidoscopic *Crème fraîche* (1978; Sour cream), toward pure fiction, such as the highly acclaimed epic poem *Tone* (1981; Tone). Brøgger's continued, unorthodox attempt at orienting herself in the contemporary world is also, mixed with religious elements, reflected in her latest work, *Den pebrede susen* (1986; The peppery soughing).

Sven Hakon Rossel. In Steven R. Serafin
and Walter D. Glanze, eds. Encyclopedia of
World Literature in the 20th Century (New
York: Continuum, 1993), p. 160

BROOKE-ROSE, CHRISTINE (GREAT BRITAIN) 1927–

It [*A Grammar of Metaphor*] is certainly lively. Indeed the book's combination of liveliness and rigor may make it the *Seven Types of Ambiguity* of its generation. If this happens, we shall soon have poets mindful that the possessive adjective is the least satisfactory way of introducing the Simple Replacement metaphor, calculating their Three-Term Formulae or hazarding a Double Genitive Link—just as long ago (and to the great enrichment of English poetic) they meditated a pretty Epanorthosis or a careful Hyperbaton.

J. I. M. Stewart. *The London Magazine.*
June, 1959, p. 82

Novelists love their time machine, however often it comes to pieces in their hands. . . . In *The Dear Deceit* Christine Brooke-Rose uses a method so simple and so logical that it is bound to seem audacious in the extreme.

She simply throws her time machine into reverse. Her story starts at the end, moves steadily to the middle, comes to the beginning, and stops. Thus the dominating mythology of our age is curiously challenged: If it is true that the child is father of the man, that as the twig is bent the tree will grow, that our goose (so they say) is already cooked in the egg, then in an intolerably damned and dreadful way we really do live backwards. Miss Brooke-Rose's hero is damned all right. . . .

It is in the humanity rather than the horror, I think, that the mystery lies. Perhaps the writer is trying to tell us that the important part of us is the part *not* made by our biography; or it may be as simple as that her hero has succeeded in getting away. At any rate there is a bad letdown at the end. It is not enough to strip away veil after veil, and finally reveal a rather corrupt infant. Short of some shattering experience at nursery level, which it would take a Henry James to accomplish, the author is inevitably left holding the baby. It is a psychological detective story, without a solution, a novel without a climax. But a novel that deserves to be read.

Norman Shrapnel. *The Manchester
Guardian Weekly.* October 27, 1960, p. 11

The jacket tells us that *Such,* Christine Brooke-Rose's new post-James Joycean novel, is about "A physicist turned psychiatrist for a university radio-astronomy unit." Certainly it's useful to know before one starts reading the book, because it's difficult to tell after. Through the stream of scientific "hithering thithering of," one glimpses Miss Brooke-Rose grappling with the theory that our individual natures are particulate—a theory arrived at by inference, I imagine, from the theory (which underlies Joycean writing) that our experience of living is particulate. As the latter theory is not borne out by experiment, it's understandable that she gets into difficulties with the former. However, it's possible that we're supposed to take it that "all is in the writing"—not in the content. On this level her stream of scientific terms used with an engagingly learned air in metaphor that doesn't figure, and simile that can't relate is fun, a sort of nonsense poetry. What seems to me the danger Miss Brooke-Rose may not have foreseen is that it asks to be taken as 110 per cent serious by people who fancy their chance as highbrows. It would be a sad and inappropriate fate for her, a clever and gifted artist, to find herself acclaimed their queen.

William Cooper. *The Listener.*
October 20, 1966, p. 583

Christine Brooke-Rose's *Between* makes an immediate appeal to the reviewer on two counts: its brevity and its remarkably pretty dust-jacket. The novel itself, a contribution to the French *nouveau roman* rather than to any English tradition, is the stream of consciousness of a simultaneous translator; flying hither and thither, seated in her aircraft as though in a church aisle, lying alone (a vicarious relief, I must say) in almost identical hotel bedrooms, attending gibberish conferences anent This and That, speaking, seeing, hearing a multitude of languages, her consciousness is recognizably of our time. You too, surely, have sat and said to yourself: "The label on the bottle says VICHY ETAT—Eau Minérale Naturelle." The point is that if this is not quite the sort of novel we are used to reading, it depicts very imaginatively the kind of life many people are perfectly used to living (not just the thousand simultaneous translators, but travelers of all sorts). It is almost, I suppose, a small bit of soc./psych., but what a difference from the usual: as if your story about the accountant were told by the accountant in the form of a tax-return.

Henry Tube. *The Spectator.*
November 15, 1968, p. 702

Miss Brooke-Rose [in *Go When You See the Green Man Walking*] is concerned with visual details, using the *nouveau roman* technique of repetitive, precise, objective descriptions, lists of contents (a fantasist spinster's trousseau for the girl-baby Messiah she believes she's chosen to bear) and the metronomic beat of incantatory phrases which suggest obsession—one of the most effective stories is "told" by the amputated foot of a model girl who's suffering phantom pain "related to a central excitatory state with emphasis on the internuncial pool of the spinal cord . . . afferent proprioceptive.". . .

Miss Muriel Spark's reputation was launched by a collection of stories: the wit, eccentricity, and graceful virtuosity in this collection deserve to do as much to widen public appreciation of Miss Brooke-Rose.

(London) *Times Literary Supplement.*
November 20, 1970, p. 1347

Bilingual from early childhood, Ms. Brooke-Rose demonstrates a keen sensitivity to both the peculiar nuances of the English language and the often perversely flattening effect of its clichés and jargons. Her wit is nowhere more evident than in dialogue, perhaps most spectacularly in *Such,* when a man of cosmic proportions who is undergoing an interstellar operation converses with a "girl-spy" out to help him. One is tempted to say that all of Ms. Brooke-Rose's characters, like those of Henry James, speak alike—but then, the goal in the creation of such odd beings is certainly not typicality or verisimilitude but rather a choice and somewhat bitter mélange of high irony and comic cunning.

Her special gift is the ability to pinpoint and explore those aspects of narrative language that are generally taken for granted by other novelists. Her fictions abound, for example, with the dubious assertiveness of negative statements, as when, in *Between,* "No one comes offering anything not ordered." Positive assertion is, in fact, a rarity in this work. For every proposition, there exists an alternate possibility. A sort of multiple-choice structure seems to lie not far below the surface, so that "at any minute now some bright or elderly sour not, young and buxom chambermaid in black and white. . . . Or a smooth floor-steward in white" will place something beside "the green or perhaps blue washbasin. . . ."

The phantasmagoric opening of *Between,* like a jet age version of the Proustian bedroom and place-name catalogues, seems built around a series of simple substitution exercises, like those one encounters in the audiovisual method of language-learning. Somewhat in the manner of Robbe-Grillet's shifting perspectives and deceptive dissolves, a curtain over an oval airline window acts as pivot in the change of scenery by becoming a hotel room curtain; a bathroom door doubles for both airplane and hotel scenes.

Ms. Brooke-Rose's fascination for the odd surprises that language can hold is not, of course, an accident. Though insisting that she's only an "amateur," she is thoroughly immersed in both structural and generative linguistics, the theories of which she implements in her courses at the Université de Paris VIII, Vincennes. . . . It should not be surprising that the most outstanding characteristic of her work is its mixture of discourses: scientific, legal, medical jargons, advertising lingo, conferencese, English, French, German, Spanish, Romanian, Russian, etc.—all these have their appointed yet oddly nondelimited place in her novels. Nor should it be surprising that her latest work, *Thru,* published this year by Hamish Hamilton, goes further into idiolect by integrating the writings of French theoreticians like Barthes, Greimas, and Kristeva into the very texture of the novel. What *is* surprising is that her novels have yet to find an American publisher. *Thru,* a text that, as she explains, progressively destroys itself as it is read, may well spark a long-deserved recognition, within all the English-speaking world, of Christine Brooke-Rose's unique and rewarding talent.

David Hayman and Keith Cohen.
Contemporary Literature.
Winter, 1976, pp. 1-3

The problem of narration in *Thru* . . . is a very complex one. The "floating I" in fiction—a first-person narration in which the "I" that narrates sometimes refers to one character and sometimes another—has been a recognized possibility since the publication of Alain Robbe-Grillet's *La maison de rendez-vous* in 1965. Much of *Thru* is told in the first person, and often the "I" is either Larissa or Armel. Both characterizations are extremely fluid. Larissa and Armel are both listed as instructors of university-level courses in literature. The first time the reader is sure that an "I" refers to Armel, he is writing a letter to Larissa while attending a faculty meeting. Later we come across a letter from Larissa to Armel in which she is a graduate student writing a dissertation on his poetry and hoping to meet him. . . . Occasionally the master of Diderot's *Jacques le fataliste* takes over the narration, sometimes in his own right and sometimes as Armel. Midway through the novel he decides that "it looks mightily as if [Larissa] were producing this [novel] and not, as previously appeared, Armel," which, as he tells Jacques, transforms their relationship, since Jacques's master is being changed into a mistress. In addition, it often appears as if the novel were being written by a creative-writing class, perhaps by Larissa.

The confusion in Brooke-Rose's method of illustrating the untrustworthy nature of the role of the narrator in contemporary fiction, the "absently unreliable or unreliably absent narrator," as she terms him, or "a speaking head on a platter, narrating yourself to an earful of crabs at the bottom of the ocean or shouting in the wilderness with a mouthful of locusts and wild honeybees." . . .

Yet Larissa and Armel both are clearly aspects of the author. Brooke-Rose has spoken of talking to herself in French, of addressing herself either as "je" or "tu" ("I" or "you"); in similar fashion Armel refers to Larissa as his "second person singular." The two characters complement each other. We are told, reversing the stereotype, that Larissa's "mental diagrams seem to be also a good deal more complex than [Armel's] though his emotional ones seem more complex than hers." Elsewhere Larissa tells Stavro (who may be Armel), "you have your list of women, children and languages, I have my list of publications." Just as the two pairs of eyes in the opening image are the reflection of one person, Larissa and Armel together (the one intellectual, the other emotional) seem to form one complete human being, perhaps in many respects Brooke-Rose herself.

Writing is a creative endeavor, and Brooke-Rose is not the first to describe it in sexual terms. She does, however, stress it throughout the text, in addition to providing both a male and female narrator for the novel. The "winedark sea of infratextuality" recurs some fifteen pages later as the "wine dark sea of infrasexuality." Plagiarism is described as a form of false "paternity." Linguistics is defined in terms of sexual relationships, "the double standard" for male and female adultery, she tells us, "is useful even in semiotics." There are several references to "heterotextuality," a term that seems perfectly coined to describe the fictional creation of this piece of fiction. *Thru* is a generative textasy.

Emma Kafalenos. *International Fiction Review*. 7: 1, 1980, pp. 44–46

That there is an unspeakable to be transformed into discourse is the result of a deliberate move, which is both a social and an aesthetic strategy: it implies the woman writer's need to find that mode of expression that, by being divergent, will both emphasize and validate the otherness of women artists. In the case of Brooke-Rose, the experimentation supersedes an immediate concern with feminism while not in any way canceling it from her awareness; she is, in the first instance, an experimental writer and secondly, a woman experimental writer and as such, she is concerned with "the fusion of different discourses."

Nevertheless, such arbitrary classification of an author is insidious; the experimenter and the woman cannot be so neatly disjoined. In what follows I shall continually be presupposing Christine Brooke-Rose the experimentalist and (perhaps) less insistently inferring her persona as a woman—it would be more sensible, maybe, simply to take her on her own terms as someone who eschews labels and thus pays the price of, as she herself points out, belonging nowhere. Consideration of her as an experimenter implies the acceptance of the opinion that such a view includes the dilemma of recognizing that experimentalism "is at once a stepping stone to something else and is gratuitous." It is, in fact, the "something else" beyond the stepping stones that I hope to be able to clarify. For any investigation of the nature of Brooke-Rose's experimentation will inevitably reveal her particular contribution to feminist literary discourse.

Christine Brooke-Rose's 1984 novel *Amalgamemnon* is "a polygonal story," essentially many-angled, a story illuminated from many different directions, many stories brought together within a multisided frame of polynarration. There are contemporary narratives of, for example, a university teacher of the humanities made redundant by the proliferation of technology, of fleeting surface relationships with would-be "helpful" men of conventional ideas and prejudices, a venture into pig farming, dialogues with students and friends, an encounter with a band of terrorists. Then again, each individual narrative gives birth to further narratives, which in turn intermingle with classical myths, legends, history, and fairy tale in a maze of paratactical juxtapositioning in which each segment of fragmented narrative is as important as the next. The novel is held together by a pattern of structural repetitions and planned echoes: "the rhetoric of repetition will protect me." . . . Not only does the repetition of structures, and thus of information, make for clearer reception, but words by engendering further discourses themselves become redundant, in both a social and a narrative sense, having served their purpose. . . .

Within the context of *Amalgamemnon,* the dominant female strategy is contained in a set of puns culminating in the verb "to mimagree"—to mime agreement. Redundancy is both an accepted aspect of the text, implying generation, and of female-experienced reality, so that as the novel closes, it is possible to state:

> The characters . . . will perhaps indulge in the secret vice of reading redundant textual sources of redundant psychic sources in redundant humanistic animals. . . . Secret cabinet sources will refuse to comment on these shadow-figures and I shall mimagree, how should I not?

This statement puts the critic in his or her place. Having commented on the shadow-figures of Brooke-Rose's novel, one is all too aware of the redundancy of one's own remarks. Should one have refused to comment?

Richard Martin. In Ellen G. Friedman and
Miriam Fuchs, eds. *Breaking the Sequence:
Women's Experimental Fiction* (Princeton:
Princeton University Press, 1989),
pp. 177–78, 188

BROOKNER, ANITA (GREAT BRITAIN) 1928–

In Miss Brookner's first novel, *The Debut* [*A Start in Life*], the heroine was induced by a literary tradition of filial duty to give up all claims to a personal future and settle dismally into the role of faithful daughter. In *Look at Me,* an unmarried librarian befriended by a glittering Beautiful Couple was eventually dropped, abandoned to a lonely middle age. In *Providence,* a woman in love with a professor discovered that the professor did not love her back, and the story ended abruptly with her disillusionment. The final mood has always been bleak, even accusatory—a sort of "Why me, God?" that left the reader slightly alienated.

But in *Hotel du Lac,* Miss Brookner's most absorbing novel, the heroine is more philosophical from the outset, more self-reliant, more conscious that a solitary life is not, after all, an unmitigated tragedy. Edith Hope receives two proposals of marriage during the course of the story. Both would-be husbands are flawed—one is too dull, one too pragmatic—but the earlier heroines, we suspect, would have settled for one or the other nonetheless. Edith ends up accepting neither. Ironically, it is she, the producer of pulp novels ("a writer of romantic fiction under a more thrusting name"), who is the first of Miss Brookner's heroines to arrive at a nonromantic, wryly realistic appreciation of her single state.

Anne Tyler. *New York Times Book Review.*
February 3, 1985, pp. 1, 31

There is a wealth of women novelists in the twentieth century who have only recently been revalued, from Edith Wharton, Kate Chopin, and Willa Cather (in America) to Rose Macauley, Jean Rhys, Rosamund Lehmann, Elizabeth Bowen, Barbara Pym, and Elizabeth Taylor. They have inherited many of the qualities of Jane Austen: superb structuring, delicacy, restraint, common sense and devastating social judgements. . . .

Brookner shares with these writers (particularly Edith Wharton and Elizabeth Bowen) the ability to represent the social frustrations and intimate thought processes of gifted, undervalued women. They understand the suffering of women morally alone, the vulnerability of the ingenuously affectionate in a scheming, conventional society. "Innocence so constantly finds itself in a false position that inwardly innocent people learn to be disingenuous, to exist alone."

Brookner displays, like Bowen and Lehmann, what might be termed a "feminine" sensibility in the subtle descriptions of appearance, textures, social nuances. They are gifted at linking character and background, representing the restrictive effects of environment on a girl's psyche. They possess the power to render the external world so that it becomes itself a character, rather than a setting. . . .

From eighteenth-century women's novels Brookner has taken a polishing of form, excluding extraneous themes. She believes "It's form that's going to save us." Like her forebears in both the eighteenth and nineteenth centuries, she shows us what it *feels* like to be a certain kind of isolated woman. Like many of their heroines, a Brookner protagonist turns exasperation against herself in the form of self-annoyance, unhappiness, even illness. Brookner can therefore be studied in the way Showalter and similar feminist critics study nineteenth-century women's literature. They see it as mirroring life, as conveying the suppressed frustrations of the author. . . .

Brookner's images represent women limiting the notion of themselves from within. Our images create the world for us; they shape our consciousness. The English novel since the eighteenth century has shown images of women in a private domestic world. Brookner continues this association between women and private feeling. She explores eighteenth- and nineteenth-century concepts of femininity and finds many of them still valid. She leaves the reader to ponder how far they are inculcated by upbringing (nurture), how much by heredity (nature).

Brookner wryly asserts, "I write out of a sense of injustice. In some curious way only fiction-writers are telling the truth." There is a twentieth-century awareness of contradictions in Brookner's double vision of the function of fiction. Like feminists, she realizes the damage it can inflict by purveying limited views of women, emphasizing cultural conditioning. Yet her heroines are lecturers or art historians, interpreting and molding their material into presentable forms. The very act of writing offers possibilities for shaping one's life, reworking incidents, giving them a more satisfying form. "Novels are the chance to examine within the limits of a structure.". . .

Brookner's six skillfully crafted brief novels survey aspects of femininity and romance today. Her first, *A Start in Life* (1981), brilliantly restructures elements of autobiography, centering on the unhappy life of Ruth, repressed by selfish parents. The opening sentence throws us into a central preoccupation, wittily and succinctly: "Dr. Weiss, at forty, knew that her life had been ruined by literature." The literature is the nineteenth-century novel, particularly Balzac's *Eugénie Grandet*. Eugénie loved in vain, too unpretentious and unattractive to win the man she adored. Such books have imbued Brookner's protagonist with role models that make her incapable of adapting to the changed ethos of the twentieth century.

Brookner's second novel, *Providence* (1982), examines the suffering of etiolation such inadaptation causes the individual woman. There is little overt experimentation with language or form, though a mastery of subtle expression and structuring. *Look at Me* (1983) begins and ends with notions of the circularity of time and memory. It is a scrupulous, passionate study of an unsuccessful, obscure protagonist—which is how she sees herself. Like *Jane Eyre* Brookner's heroines long for intellectual and emotional fulfilment through one man, while fearing frank sexuality. The novels are 140 years apart, yet exhibit a similar tension between longing and restraint, instinct and reason. Brookner, like Rebecca West, represents similar protagonists condemned to loneliness because their upbringing has repressed spontaneity, culture has cramped instinct.

Brookner's fourth novel *Hotel du Lac* (1985) won her the Booker prize and established her reputation. It concentrates on a writer of romantic novels, Edith Hope, banished temporarily to Lake Geneva. She had, in wry self-protection, told her taxidriver to drive away when she sighted her uninspiring fiancé on the registry steps. "Then she saw, in a flash, but for all time, the totality of his mouse-like seemliness."

Hotel du Lac was awarded the Booker prize as a "work of perfect artifice.". . .

The protagonist's life and thoughts bear a painfully close resemblance to Brookner's. "There were five novels, to prove she had not spent her time gazing out of the window like the Lady of Shalott. It was, she recognized, a tortoise existence, despite the industry. That is why she wrote for tortoises, like herself.". . .

Brookner's sensitive discourse for place and mood represents restricted lives. The almost unhappy endings provide a critique of the moral attitudes which circumscribe women. "How like a lingering illness sentiment can be," the matriarch remarks in *Family and Friends* of her rejected daughter.

Brookner's vision is disturbingly paradoxical. Contemporary society allows some intelligent women to enter hitherto male professions, such as lecturing, with their attendant demands. On the other hand, our society still places too high a value on romantic love. Even when her grasping, sexy women get their men, they are not happy because reality breaks in, in the form of adultery or old age. One key to apprehending her protagonists is the ironic contrast between what Brookner (and we) know and perceive, and their own often limited, naïve, tragicomic struggles. These women have to learn, through their suffering female self, that emotional fulfillment is often frustrated by intellectual achievement.

The creator is most in control in her latest novel *Family and Friends* (1985). Brookner uses a wedding photograph to distance herself and shows us the family with the eyes of an art historian: "Sofka stands straight and stern, her shoulders braced, her head erect in the manner of two generations earlier." This saga is based on her own family, seen through art; through style which can vivify the appearance but reify the personality.

Olga Kenyon. Women Novelists Today (New York: St. Martin's, 1988), pp. 149–54, 156–57

Family and Friends, Brookner's. . . . version of a family album novel written seven years later, strikes a careful balance: it assiduously avoids excess or outrageousness, but neither is there any mistaking the novel's fictiveness for documentary. A slice of Austen and James pared severely with contemporary skepticism and a minimalist style, the novel is a stylistically tight, gently sardonic look at a successful industrial family whose matriarch—Sofka Dorn—comes from the old world of Continental Europe. Events are neither striking nor dramatic: the neuroses, however debilitating, are understated.

The book takes for its interest the emotionally pinched lives of the over-bred and the well-moneyed. Behind the understatement of the opening—"Here is Sofka in a wedding photograph"—we discover . . . what does not show in the photograph, in this case, a family's tensions, jealousies, mean-spirited disapprovals, and discontent. In the way that cinema sometimes "releases" action from a still, Brookner unfreezes the narrative from the wedding photograph to record the ruptures and decline of the Dorns' monolithic nineteenth-century family structure. Twentieth-century culture and "lifestyle" intrude: one of Sofka's daughters, Betty, moves to New York and then to California to live pool-side, empty-headed, oppressed by a sexist movie magnate—Brookner's not very imaginative idea of America as a metaphor for moral, intellectual, and esthetic laxity. Mimi, Sofka's other unmarried daughter, agrees to a loveless marriage with a loyal, reliable foreman of the family. A baby who dies and future barrenness are, apparently, the penalties which she pays. Frederick and Evie, her son and daughter-in-law, remain distant in Europe and send telegrams when they are not speeding about on their mopeds. Alfred, another son, remains unmarried and childless.

The photographs described in the course of this narrative constitute stilled moments of unsatisfactory respite from the scattering and fragmentation in the face of which Sofka clings to a fragile power as an anachronistic matriarch. The novel ends just as it began, with a description of another wedding photograph: "Here they all are, family and friends, in the wedding photograph. It is the last one in the album.". . .

Brookner's novel . . . charts the dismantling of a family. Her characters represent a twentieth-century diaspora of a nineteenth-century family. . . . Brookner's fictional . . . family [is one] in exile: the wedding photos described in *Family and Friends* are gestures of composure and coherence, a stiffening in the face of family disintegration—cons to unity. As Jefferson Hunter says in regard to all family photos, they mitigate separations and keep the dispersed together." Abbreviated, fragmentary, incomplete, elusive, even misleading, the family album nevertheless provides a measure of security in a world of contingency.

Brent MacLaine. Mosaic. 24, 1991,
pp. 145–47

The novels of [Anita Brookner] may be divided without undue distortion into equal sets of three. The first group . . . are all closely modeled on previous literary texts: Balzac's *Eugénie Grandet (A Start in Life),* Constant's *Adolphe (Providence),* and—less explicitly—Proust's *À la Recherche du Temps perdu (Look at Me).*

Not even *A Start in Life* (1981), however, should be regarded as a simple critique of Balzac. It also has significant links with Dickens, reflected not simply in a shared indebtedness to the tradition of the *Bildungsroman,* but in a common use of the *leitmotiv* of food. *A Start in Life* announces, moreover, what will become Brookner's running engagement with the themes and conventions of popular romance. The major emphasis of the present reading nevertheless remains the "French Connection.". . . The second group of narratives. . . . are marked by a greater interest in technical experiment: this appears most obviously in the now more extensive application of *mise en abyme* in *Hotel du Lac* (1984), widespread "literary framing" in *Family and Friends* (1985), and a new comprehensive iconography in *A Misalliance* (1986). . . .

The admittedly less homogeneous third group of novels . . . draws on divergent meanings of the word "return": the sense of "profit" or "gain" as much as "regression" or "reversal." All three novels show Brookner capitalizing on her previous exercises in formal experiment, even as she falls back on earlier narrative patterns: the bifurcation or splitting of the characteristic Brookner heroine *(A Friend from England),* new thematic emphasis on otherwise familiar male voices *(Latecomers),* or the knightly quest and hitherto most explicit parody of Romance *(Lewis Percy).*

John Skinner. The Fictions of Anita
Brookner (New York: St. Martin's, 1992),
pp. 14–18

BROOKS, GWENDOLYN (UNITED STATES) 1917–

Two sections of [*A Street in Bronzeville*], including the one that gives it its title, represent rather unexciting vignettes of sentiment and character. They have, however, something of the spice and movement which many of the better Negro poets commonly lend to their work. No doubt a great bulk of the proficient and marketable poems written by poets of whatever color deal with such sure-fire or easy-mark situations as those in these groups. The good child envies the bad. Dreams are hard to sustain amid onion fumes or where red fat roaches stroll up one's wall. God must be lonely. The hunchback speculates on heaven. Yet even these sketches are somewhat safeguarded in the present case by some actuality of detail, freshness of image, dryness of angle or flexibility of tempo. . . .

All in all, despite the fact that this first book has its share of unexciting verse, there are considerable resources evidenced for future work. Miss Brooks, to use one of her own phrases, "scrapes life with a fine-tooth comb." And she shows a capacity to marry the special quality of her racial experience with the best attainments of our contemporary poetry tradition. Such compounding of resources out of varied stocks and traditions is the great hope of American art as it is of American life generally.

Amos N. Wilder. Poetry. December, 1945,
pp. 164, 166

The work of this young Chicago poet never fails to be warmly and generously human. In a surly and distempered age one is genuinely grateful to Miss Brooks for the lively and attractive spirit that sallies forth from her poems. In contrast to most of her contemporaries, she is neither ridden by anxiety nor self-consumed with guilt. There is in her work a becoming modesty. Though the materials of her art are largely derived from the conditions of life in a Negro urban milieu, she uses these incendiary materials naturally, for their intrinsic value, without straining for shock or for depth, without pretending to speak for a people. In reading this second volume [*Annie Allen*] by the author of *A Street in Bronzeville* I have been impressed by how little of the energy that should go into the building of the work has been diverted to the defense of the life.

Stanley Kunitz. Poetry. April, 1950, p. 52

Miss Brooks is a very accomplished poet indeed, often boiling her lines down to the sparsest expression of the greatest meaning, sometimes almost to a kind of word-shorthand that defies immediate grasp. Less simple and direct than the poems in her initial volume [*A Street in Bronzeville*], those in *Annie Allen* give, upon careful reading, as much interest and emotional impact. The book is a mood story in varying poetic forms of a girl's growth from childhood to the age of love, marriage, and motherhood.

There are sharp pictures of neighborhoods, relatives, friends, illnesses and deaths; of big city slums, cafes, and beauty shops. To me the third section, containing about half the poems in the book, "The Womanhood," is its most effective. The qualms, the longings, the love of a poor mother for her child is here most movingly expressed. . . .

The people and the poems in Gwendolyn Brooks's book are alive, reaching, and very much of today.

> Langston Hughes. *Voices.* Winter, 1950,
> pp. 55–56

The fact that Miss Brooks displays an excellent knowledge of form, whether in the versatile handling of types of forms of poetry included in *Annie Allen* or in the metrical variations in the volume, can be readily seen as proof of [the] new emphasis upon conventional form. She skillfully handles a number of stanzaic forms including couplets, quatrains, the Italian Terza Rima, and even in "The Anniad," the difficult rime-royal or the seven line stanza named for Chaucer. . . . In addition to these conventional forms she includes several poems written in free verse, as well as occasional lines of blank verse. In regard to types, she includes short lyrics, ballads, and sonnets written with veteran aplomb.

As a whole, *Annie Allen* is a fine delineation of the character of a young Negro woman from childhood through adolescence to complete maturity, but with slight racial exceptions it could apply to any female of a certain class and society. The entire volume is tinged with a highly sophisticated humor and is not only technically sure but also vindicates the promise of *A Street in Bronzeville.* Coming after the long hue and cry of white writers that Negroes as poets lack form and intellectual acumen, Miss Brooks's careful craftsmanship and sensitive understanding reflected in *Annie Allen* are not only personal triumphs but a racial vindication.

> Margaret Walker. *Phylon.* 11:4, 1950,
> pp. 351–52

With a few exceptions when straightforward narrative takes over, [*Maud Martha*] is presented in flashes, almost gasps, of sensitive lightness—distillations of the significance of each incident—and reminds of Imagist poems or clusters of ideograms from which one recreates connected experience. Miss Brooks's prose style here embodies the finer qualities of insight and rhythm that were notable in her two earlier books of poetry (her *Annie Allen* received the Pulitzer Prize), and gives a freshness, a warm cheerfulness as well as a depth of implication to her first novel. In technique and impression it stands virtually alone of its kind.

> Hubert Creekmore. *The New York Times.*
> October 4, 1953, p. 4

There is every indication in *Maud Martha* that poetess Gwendolyn Brooks is capable of well rounded characterizations of which her heroine Maud is a finespun, fractional specimen. For what Miss Brooks presents in this slender volume are bright glimpses of a world turning upon Maud's soft meditations. Writing with the quiet charm and sparkling delicacy of tone which brought Emily Dickinson's bird down the walk to drink a dew, Miss Brooks has begat a kind of beauty upon ugliness by lighting up the· humanity of her creation against the background of a Chicago slum area. . . .

Maud has not accepted herself with that unconscious assurance which makes her male counterpart, [Langston Hughes's] Jesse Simple, so articulate in his easy living with hard conditions. She finds herself too often wishing to be what her husband Paul, absorbed as he is in surface values, believes he wants her to be. For all practical purposes, this is as it should be, for what the author is dealing with from the inside of her creation are those very human hopes which grasp straw values in reaching very hungrily for real ones. In all this, Miss Brooks maintains a kind of subtle, close-lipped control over her style which so heightens its rich suggestiveness that one is led to believe he understands more for being told less.

Henry F. Winslow. *Crisis.* February, 1954,
p. 114

When many of us think of protest poetry we tend to recall the fiery lines of "If We Must Die," written by McKay during those exciting days of the New Negro Movement. Moreover, we have somehow come to expect the same kind of bitterness and defiance in all poetry of this kind. But Miss Brooks's protest poems, written in an integration age, are usually quite different in spirit and approach from those of the New Negro generation. She has subtle irony, a quiet humor, and oftentimes a sense of pity, not only for the black victims of prejudice but also for the whites who are guilty. But her works as a rule are not fiery or defiant, and they are seldom bitter. . . .

When one compares Miss Brooks's racial problems with those of an earlier generation of Negro writers, he finds this significant difference. In most of the earlier poems, regardless of the bitterness expressed, there is an implied faith in a better day which will come either through the fulfillment of the American Dream or through the workings of a Just God. In these earlier works, there was also on occasion the kind of self-abasement one finds in [James David] Corrother's lines: "To be a Negro in a day like this—/Alas! Lord God, what evil have we done?" There is no self-pity in Gwendolyn Brooks's racial poems and precious little optimism. She doesn't seem to have much faith in either the American Dream or a Just God. Expressing neither hope nor fear, she is content to describe conditions as they are in Bronzeville. She seems to be saying: these things are so, and they are bad; but modern men, white or black, are not heroic. One can't expect too much.

Arthur P. Davis. *CLA Journal.*
December, 1963, pp. 120, 125

Gwendolyn Brooks's *Selected Poems* contain some lively pictures of Negro life. I am not sure it is possible for a Negro to write well without making us aware he is a Negro; on the other hand, if being a Negro is the only subject, the writing is not important. Unfortunately, Miss Brooks too often says the obvious, in the easiest way. . . . Miss Brooks must have had a devil of a time trying to write poetry in the United States, where there has been practically no Negro poetry worth talking about. She deserves to be praised for her seriousness, and to be criticized into writing more poems on the order of her "The Bean Eaters."

Louis Simpson. *New York Herald Tribune.*
October 27, 1963, p. 25

Gwendolyn Brooks does the thing that so few poets anywhere can do, and that is to take a really spoken language and make it work for her. Most everyone writes a "writing" language, but in her work, there are all the familiar cadences and sounds of speech, right down to the bone-hard rhetoric of the 1960s. . . . I say that her technique is really useful to her because in addition there is visible a whole person behind her poems, and you always feel that she "writes committed." She is one of the very best poets.

Bruce Cutler. *Poetry.* March, 1964,
pp. 388–89

It's too soon to say anything definitive about the work of Gwendolyn Brooks. Perhaps she hasn't yet written the poems that will stand out a hundred years from now as her major ones. But she has already written some that will undoubtedly be read so long as man cares about language and his fellows.

There have been no drastic changes in the tactics and subjects she has dealt with over the years. It's doubtful if future critics will talk about the early and the late Brooks, not unless she strikes out into much different territory after 1969. What one observes is a steady development of themes and types.

Her poetry is marked by a number of central concerns: black experience; the nature of greatness; the way in which man expresses his needs, makes do, or lashes out. Ordinarily the view is one of delicate balance, that of a passionate observer. The poems strike one as distinctly those of a woman but always muscled and precise, written from the pelvis rather than the biceps. [1969]

Dan Jaffe. In C. W. E. Bigsby, ed. *The
Black American Writer* (Baltimore: Penguin,
1971), p. 93

When you view Gwendolyn Brooks's work in the pre-1967 period, you see a poet, a black poet in the actual (though still actively searching for her own definitions of blackness), on the roadway to becoming a conscious African poet or better yet a conscious African woman in America who chose poetry as her major craft. However, Gwendolyn Brooks describes her poetry prior to 1967 as "work that was conditioned to the times and the people." In other words, poetry that leaped from the pages bringing forth ideas, definitions, images, reflections, forms, colors, etc., that were molded over a distance of many years—her poetry notebook started at the age of eleven—as a result of and as a reaction to the American reality. And for black people, regardless of the level of their perception of the world, the American reality has always been a battle, a real alley fight. . . .

Gwendolyn Brooks's post–1967 poetry is fat-less. Her new work resembles a man getting off meat, turning to a vegetarian diet. What one immediately notices is that all the excess weight is quickly lost. Her work becomes extremely streamlined and to the point. . . .

We can see in the work of Gwendolyn Brooks of 1972 positive movement from that of the sayer to the doer, where she recognizes that *writing is not enough* for a people in a life and death struggle. For so few black writers to reflect the aspirations and needs of so many (there are about three hundred black writers who are published with any kind of regularity) is a responsibility that should not be taken lightly. Every word has to be considered and worked with so as to use it to its fullest potential.

Don L. Lee. Preface to Gwendolyn Brooks.
Report from Part One (Detroit: Broadside,
1972), pp. 13–14, 22, 29

The world of white arts and letters has pointed to [Gwendolyn Brooks] with pride; it has bestowed kudos and a Pulitzer Prize [for *Annie Allen*]. The world of black arts and letters has looked on with mixed emotion, and pride has been only one part of the admixture. There have also been troubling questions about the poet's essential "blackness," her dedication to the melioration of the black American's social conditions. The real duality appears when we realize that Gwendolyn Brooks—though praised and awarded—does not appear on the syllabuses of most American literature courses, and her name seldom appears in the annual scholarly bibliographies of the academic world. She, it would seem, is a black writer after all, *not* an American writer. Yet when one listens to the voice of today's black revolutionary consciousness, one often hears that Miss Brooks's poetry fits the white, middle-class patterns that LeRoi Jones has seen as characteristic of "Negro literature.". . .

Gwendolyn Brooks represents a singular achievement. Beset by a double-consciousness, she has kept herself from being torn asunder by speaking the truth in poems that equal the best work in the black and the white American literary traditions. Her characters are believable; her themes are manifold; and her technique is superb. The critic (whether white or black) who comes to her writing seeking only support for her ideology will be disappointed, for as Etheridge Knight has pointed out, she has ever spoken the truth. And truth, one likes to feel, always lies beyond the boundaries of any one ideology. Perhaps Miss Brooks's most significant achievement is her endorsement of this point of view, for from her hand and fertile imagination have come volumes of verse that transcend the dogma on either side of the American veil.

Houston A. Baker, Jr. *CLA Journal.*
September, 1972, pp. 24, 31

Report from Part One is a seemingly chunk and hunk assemblage of photographs, interviews, letters—backward glances on growing up in Chicago and coming of age in the Black Arts Movement. It is not a sustained dramatic narrative for the nosey, being neither the confessions of a private woman/ poet or the usual sort of mahogany-desk memoir public personages inflict upon the populace at the first sign of a cardiac. It is simply an extremely valuable book that is all of a piece and readable and memorable in unexpected ways. It documents the growth of Gwen Brooks. Documents that essentially lonely (no matter how close and numerous the friends who support, sustain and encourage you to stretch out and explore) process of opening the eyes, wrenching the self away from played-out modes, and finding new directions. It shows her reaching toward a perspective that reflects the recognition that the black artist is obliged to fashion an esthetic linked to the political dynamics of the community she serves. . . .

Like the younger black poets, Gwen Brooks since the late 1960s has been struggling for a cadence, style, idiom and content that will politicize and mobilize. Like the young black poets, her recent work is moving more toward gesture, sound, intonation, attitude and other characteristics that depend on oral presentation rather than private eyeballing. It is important to have the poet herself assess these moves in her own way so as to establish the ground for future critical biographies. But "change" and "shift" may be too heavy-handed, somewhat misleading; for in rereading the bulk of her work, which *Report from Part One* does prompt one to do, we see a continuum.

Toni Cade Bambara. *The New York Times.*
January 7, 1973, p. 1

[Gwendolyn Brooks's] *A Street in Bronzeville* and her *In the Mecca,* in all seriousness, could be used as reference works in sociology. Her *Annie Allen* quietly demonstrates the wealth of her observation of normal, not abnormal, psychology. She is at home with fact. Her alert mentality gathers in the evidence presented to the senses. But she is at home, also, with reflective thought. She sees not only the bare circumstance. She sees also its place in a rich context of fine relationships. Her craftsmanship is careful. Miss Brooks belongs to the school of writers who do not believe in wasting a single word. Selection and significance—one can divine in her diction how she has brooded over them, how every word has been chosen with due regard for the several functions it may be called upon to perform in the dispensation of a poem. But the brooding goes deep and it affects not only words. The words must be put together. And the principle of dire economy which governs her choice of diction disciplines severely all of her poetic maneuvers. Terseness, a judicious understatement combined with pregnant ellipses, often guides the reader into an adventure which permits a revelation of Miss Brooks's capacity for sensitive interpretations of the human comedy.

She never writes on "big" subjects. One finds on her agenda no librettos for Liberia [like Tolson's], no grand excursus into history like [Hayden's] "Middle Passage." *Annie Allen* typifies her method, the study, as it were, of the flower in the crannied wall. In such a method her genius operates within its area of greatest strength, the close inspection of a limited domain, to reap from that inspection, perhaps paradoxically, but still powerfully, a view of life in which one may see a microscopic portion of the universe intensely and yet, through that microscopic portion, see all truth for the human condition wherever it exists.

Blyden Jackson. In Blyden Jackson and
Louis D. Rubin, Jr. *Black Poetry in America*
(Baton Rouge: Louisiana State University
Press, 1974), pp. 84–85

Beckonings exemplifies Brooks's movement toward her new style, which is characterized by a struggle between her normal tendency to make each word bear its full measure of weight and suggestion and an insistence upon directness and simplicity of diction. Actually, despite her reputation for complexity, there are already many poems across the body of her work which are simple and direct. *A Street in Bronzeville* contains a large number of simple poems, some of which become favorites with readers. I would suppose the main difficulties for the uninitiated readers in some earlier poems would be the presence of irony and understatement. *Beckonings* reduces the element of irony and often goes into direct statement. . . .

"Five Men against the Theme 'My Name is Red Hot. Yo Name Ain Doodley Squat'" and "Sammy Chester Leaves 'Godspell' and Visits *Upward Bound* on a Lake Forest Lawn, Bringing West Afrika" use older techniques in a new way; that is, the unusual junction of words, the coinages, the sudden contrasts, and repetitions, remain within the bounds of a simplicity which is accessible to the pause for thought. There are other poems which make such combinations, and still others which move close to direct statement. "A Black Wedding Song" is a good example of this group.

The poems are evidence that the newer techniques will not sacrifice the complex rhythms of existence in their attempts to reach a wider audience.

George E. Kent. *Phylon*. Spring, 1976,
pp, 110–11

The silencing of Maud Martha occurs both within and without the text. Despite Gwendolyn Brooks's status as a Pulitzer Prize winning poet, no one in 1953 had more than six hundred words to say about the novel. The reviewers of [Ralph] Ellison's *Invisible Man* (published just the year before when Ellison was relatively unknown) suffered no such taciturnity and devoted up to 2,100 words to Ellison's novel. The *New Republic, Nation,* the *New Yorker,* and *Atlantic* magazine contained lengthy and signed reviews of *Invisible Man.* Wright Morris and Irving Howe were called upon to write serious critical assessments of Ellison's book for the *New York Times* and the *Nation.* In contrast, the *New Yorker* review of *Maud Martha* was included in their "Books in Brief" section—unsigned—suggesting that the real "invisible man" of the 1950s was the black woman. Critics called the main character "a spunky and sophisticated Negro girl;" Ellison's character was called a hero or a pilgrim. Brooks's character was never held up for comparison to any other literary character. Ellison's nameless hero was not only considered "the embodiment of the Negro race" but the "conscience of all races": the titles of the reviews—"Black & Blue," "Underground Notes," "A Brother Betrayed," "Black Man's Burden"—indicate the universality of the invisible man's struggles. The title of Brooks's reviews—"Young Girl Growing Up" and "Daydreams in Flight"—completely deny any relationship between the protagonist's personal experiences and the historical experiences of her people. Ellison himself was compared to Richard Wright, Dostoevsky, and Faulkner; Brooks, only to the unspecified "Imagists." Questions about narrative strategy, voice, and methods of characterization asked of *Invisible Man* were obviously considered irrelevant to an understanding of *Maud Martha* since they were not posed. Most critical, Ellison's work was placed in a tradition; it was repeatedly described by reviewers as an example of the "Picaresque" tradition and the pilgrim/journey tradition. *Maud Martha,* the reviewers said, "stood alone." Not one of these reviewers could place *Maud Martha* in the tradition of Zora Neale Hurston's *Their Eyes Were Watching God* (1937) or Dorothy West's *The Living Is Easy* (1948), or Nella Larsen's *Quicksand* (1928). Is it because no one in 1953 could picture the questing figure, the hero with a thousand faces, the powerful, articulate voice, as a plain, dark-skinned woman living in a kitchenette building on the south side of Chicago?

If Brooks's novel seems fragmentary and incomplete it is no doubt because the knowledge of one's self as a black woman was fragmented by a society that could not imagine her. With no college degrees, no social standing, lacking the militant or articulate voice, denied the supports black men could claim from black institutions, Maud Martha is the "invisible woman" of the 1950s. Shouldering the twin weights of racism and sexism, Maud showed with unsparing and brutal honesty, the self-doubt, the sense of inadequacy, the fears that black women lived with—and sometimes triumphed over. Brooks takes Maud to the edge of consciousness and out there to those edges of psychic extremity which most of us are afraid of. Maud takes the risks that allow her a rare self-awareness. "The poetry of extreme states," writes Adrienne Rich, "can allow its readers to go further in our awareness, take risks we might not have dared. It says, 'Someone has been here before.'" The vulnerability Brooks allows Maud Martha as she exposes the inferiority she feels before the white world is an act of courage which necessarily precedes growth. Brooks makes us follow Maud through the subterranean passages of her life, makes us attend to her interior life: the sense of being devalued at an early age, the uncovering of rage, the disillusionment of marriage, the discovery of vitality in black traditions, and finally, that brave search for a voice to express these feelings are the real autobiographical "facts" of the life of Maud Martha.

The thirty-four vignettes that make up the novel present the life of Maud Martha from the age of seven until she is grown and married with one daughter and pregnant with a second child. Maud grows up in the urban North— on the south side of Chicago to be exact—in the 1930s and 1940s. These vignettes, ranging from one and a half to seventeen pages in length might be described as a psychological portrait of Maud. The quite unremarkable and ordinary incidents in her life are used to reveal a profound inner reality. But Maud's quiet reflections and mute reactions, while they are the rich resources of a sensitive spirit, are also inadequate responses to sexism and racism; and no one is more aware of this powerlessness than Maud: "There were these scraps of baffled hate in her, hate with no eyes, no smile and—this she especially regretted—not much voice."

The strange experimental style and the relentless interiority of the novel place heavy demands on the reader. There is no sustained narrative connecting events, nor is there any attempt to establish cause and effect, to supply motivation, nor to develop complex characterizations of the people in Maud's life. Brooks does not lead us by plot, conflict, and resolution to her appointed conclusions. A chapter ends and a new one begins with no connecting devices, as though Brooks stripped away all externals in order to distill the essence of Maud's interior development. Maud does not "explain her explanations"; she simply admits us into the chambers of her psyche and lets us explore and experience her anger, her vulnerability, her pride, and powerlessness, and because we are so tightly locked in with her, there is no escape into action; we must suffer with her the weight of her accumulated pain, not as observers but as fellow analysands. The meaning of Maud's life derives from the absolute fearlessness with which she confronts her own psyche. The inner reality Brooks faithfully crafts through tone, image, and gesture constantly challenges the explicit assumptions of a world outside her—a world so deeply racist and sexist that we must marvel at the sense of wholeness Maud finally achieves at the end of the novel.

Mary Helen Washington. In Elizabeth Abel
et al., eds. *The Voyage in: Fictions of
Female Development* (Hanover: Dartmouth
College Press, 1983), pp. 271–74

BROPHY, BRIGID (GREAT BRITAIN) 1929–

In framing a new morality [*Black Ship to Hell*] the author goes by way of a vindication of "Sigmund Freud, Bernard Shaw . . . and Lucretius." But it is Freud who gets the lion's share of the vindication. Her exposition of the nature of our destructive impulses is so confusing, irritating, and occasionally absurd that those who are unfamiliar with her material may be excused if they take this book as good evidence for dismissing it out of hand; her solution to the problems of our self-destructive tendencies—that man can happily be employed in making love and in creative artistic activity—is quite acceptable, but this book will not, one fears, stimulate either of these activities to any great extent.

The author's approach is massively Freudian and other disciplines are virtually excluded. . . . And yet Miss Brophy can write interestingly and well. Sometimes her phallic arrows are well-directed; her section on religion is one of the best, but a reader is nonplused when he finds that nicest of animals, the harmless amoeba, dragged in for us to recognize both his Eros instinct and his Thanatos instinct. . . .

We need investigations of this nature and, if this particular attempt must be considered a failure, Miss Brophy's broad classical knowledge, together with her deep interest in the human species, will stand her in good stead when she next sets sail.

(London) *Times Literary Supplement.*
February 23, 1962, p. 119

No point, surely, in sending up "the most exclusive finishing-school on the French Riviera," and *The Finishing Touch* is perhaps just an exercise in how to write well without disclosing any point at all. In its few elegant pages the girls have names like Fraise du Bois, food is pineapple and passionfruit conserve, the headmistress has lesbian meditations ("How essentially moist the girls were") and even the bad jokes about sex and Catholics are perfectly calculated. A faint story is provided by the arrival of "royalty" among the girls. It's astonishing that it would be done without dire offense: but its language is so skillful and charming that it gives quite innocent joy.

Robert Taubman. *The New Statesman.*
August 16, 1963, p. 199

"People (even those who do not mean to be rude) often ask me whether my journalism interferes with my serious writing. As a matter of fact, my journalism *is* serious writing." Thus Brigid Brophy by way of foreword to her new collection of previously printed essays and reviews [*Don't Never Forget*], and I for one will call "Amen." For whatever else may be said of them every one of these pieces, which range from oral homilies of some length down to brief thriller notices, is scrupulously and seriously written round a point which is of serious import—to Miss Brophy if nobody else. I am sorry that it is necessary to qualify in this fashion; but I have to say at once that, while most of these pages are as full of sweet reason as a honeycomb is full of honey, there are occasional passages (among them some of the most intense in the whole book) of a dottiness almost beyond belief.

There are, it seems, two hands at work here. One, let us say, is that of Brophy, an intelligent writer of clear and masculine prose, sensitive indeed to every shade of meaning and every twist of moral subtlety, but in the sum tough, incisive, and direct; while the other hand is that of Brigid, a faddy and finicking prig. . . .

Taking a four-square eighteenth-century stance, Brophy deposes that what distinguishes man from the animals is his ability to adapt nature, that terrifying and incommoding old bore, to his own taste and convenience. Man makes light to banish nature's darkness; he tunnels under, flies over, or even lays flat the mountains which nature has set up as barriers; he drains nature's pestiferous marshes, irrigates nature's dreary deserts, and sets up magnificent cities to which nature is admitted only in the form of seemly and disciplined parks. It is therefore ridiculous, Brophy goes on, to praise the "natural" man or to make a song and dance about the "natural" way of life. The triumph of man lies in his civilization . . . and in his artificiality.

Simon Raven. *The Spectator*.
November 25, 1966, p. 685

In its encyclopedic knowledge of Firbank's life and its unqualified admiration for his work, Brophy's book [*Prancing Novelist*] will be eagerly devoured by Firbankians. She has investigated every odd nook of his mind and fiction, and no detail of either is too trivial to escape a torrent of exegesis and speculation. But those not already committed to Firbank will hardly be encouraged to sample him by the tendentiousness and irresponsibility of much of this book. Nor will they be persuaded by the self-conscious, at times exasperatingly cute prose. The archness of language and design running throughout *Prancing Novelist* continually intrudes between the reader and Firbank, undermining the cause the book is trying to serve. All too often our attention is focused on Brophy's antics—leaving Firbank, I am afraid, bloated and alone, still obliged to pay his own publication costs.

Michael Rosenthal. *The New York Times*.
July 22, 1973, p. 4

Since 1953, when her first volume was published, Brophy's output has been extensive: six novels, two collections of short prose fiction, one play, four nonfiction works, a critical collection written in collaboration with Michael Levey and Charles Osborne, and numerous articles. Her best-known novels are *The King of a Rainy Country* (1956), *The Finishing Touch* (1963), and *In Transit* (1969). *Black Ship to Hell* (1962), her first nonfiction work, is a lengthy treatment of Freudianism and rationalism which, combined with her classicism, are the underpinnings of her critical stance.

Her essays, both topical and critical, treat issues and the arts from a psychological and rational standpoint. In England Brophy is known both for her fiction and as a proponent of human and animal rights who writes and speaks out in favor of vegetarianism, birth control for animals and birds, prison reform, freedom from censorship, and a change in attitudes toward marriage and divorce. Her essays are both whimsical and penetrating: she has analyzed Mickey Mouse as a modern folk hero and animated phallic symbol.

What Brophy considers to be the best, or most representative, of her articles are collected in the nonfiction volume, *Don't Never Forget* (1966). An allusion to a phrase in one of Mozart's letters (written, in broken English, to an English-speaking friend), the title reflects Brophy's love for Mozart's music and her eclecticism. To varying degrees, her works all evince a continuing emphasis upon art, in the broadest sense. She uses musical patterns and shifting tempos, cinematic or photographic effects, and architectural images—most notably, baroque—to enrich the texture of her fiction.

Although her approach to fiction and concern with human and animal rights have remained fairly constant, her works are not all of a piece, which, she thinks, may be one reason for her not being well-known, especially in the United States. *Hackenfeller's Ape* (1953) explores a number of themes, among them original sin, the romantic viewpoint, and experimentation on animals for scientific purposes; *The Burglar* (1968) treats sexual puritanism and society's attitudes toward criminals; *The King of a Rainy Country* concerns a young boy and girl who undertake a literal and figurative search for a woman who represents their mother; and so on. Her most recent work, *The Adventures of God in His Search for the Black Girl,* subtitled *A Novel and Some Fables* (1968), indicates her debt to Shaw, as do the preface to, and stage directions for, *The Burglar.* Equally influential on Brophy's style and aesthetics is Ronald Firbank, the subject of her nonfiction work, *Prancing Novelist* (1973), and the stylistic model for *The Finishing Touch.*

Leslie Dock. *Contemporary Literature.*
Spring, 1976, pp. 151–52

Brigid Brophy's book [*Palace without Chairs*] opens with an appeal on behalf of Public Lending Right, and since the blurb is that part of a volume most studied in public libraries, it may not be irrelevant to note that the present blurb is exceptionally literate and composed by someone who has obviously read the book. Only one proposition in it would I quarrel with: its claim that the court of Evarchia has more in common with Kafka than with Anthony Hope. Miss Brophy's entertaining Ruritania has more in common with Nancy Mitford than with either Anthony Hope or (certainly) Kafka, for it shows the fading of the aristocracy, by processes both chosen and imposed, into the light of common day.

Evarchia, part of which was once in Dacia or perhaps Thracia, has a small Roman wall, presumably built to keep out "hordes of barbarian dwarfs," and appears to abut upon Bulgaria. The "most precariously placed national state in Europe," it has a sick king, a Most Catholic and Pre-Canonical Majesty, and also a canonical Communist Party. It has a Winter Palace, but, given the king's five children, four archdukes and one archduchess, the palace suffers from an insufficiency of chairs. The central symbol, to which one is graciously—and sensibly—alerted in the title, is of course that of throne *v.* chair.

"Every peasant cottage contains some chairs," says the Archduke Balthasar, whose name is consistently misspelt in the national press, and the shortage is alleviated and eventually resolved in the course of the story by means both natural and unnatural—whether death in its different kinds (a junior archduke is assassinated in place of the undersized crown prince by a lunatic who reasons that the tallest is the eldest: "anyone can work that out") or emigration or, indeed, lesbianism. The Archduchess Heather, a stout young republican, remarks en route to England, the land of equal opportunity: "I never let myself be beguiled by the attractiveness of air hostesses. They are invariably heterosexual." Her tone is scarcely that of a fairy-tale princess.

One is persuaded that Miss Brophy actually enjoyed writing this book, free from those major constraints and obligations which writers hang on themselves in the hope of disguising a minor talent . . . [Its] language and [its] allusions, indicative of the author's contained amusement, will elicit the obvious remark that she is writing "mannered" fiction. In fact, the prose is not so much mannered as well-mannered, being for the most part precise, open (or seemingly so) and cheerful without familiarity. . . .

[The book] is much less "artificial" than its subtitle, "A Baroque Novel," suggests—being neither "grotesque," as things go, nor particularly "whimsical," and certainly not "florid." And, though one would not wish to speculate on its accuracy as a case study in royal families, it is distinctly less unreal or Ruritanian, less of an extravaganza, than [Shaw's] *The Apple Cart,* a work at which the blurb glances discreetly. Miss Brophy makes gentle fun of myth, even while lightly penciling in its outlines. When you cannot beat the Zeitgeist, you can always laugh and cry a little over it. If the past is seen to be subject to mortality and change, then the chances are that the future will be likewise subject.

But there is a lot of civilized enjoyment to be had from the novel—even in such unlikely contexts as pigeons or separatism or the position of the writer vis-à-vis the state—and perhaps one should just be grateful for that and resist the itch to interpret.

D. J. Enright. *The Listener.*
April 27, 1978, p. 552

BROSSARD, NICOLE (CANADA) 1943–

In *Un livre,* Brossard lays out her theory of the text. This essay with a narrative dimension plays on two discrete levels. The fiction/narration displays elements belonging to the order of being, not that of doing, thus abolishing any narrative dynamic. But the fiction/narrative is cut up by a discourse on the text, in which Brossard develops a challenge to narra*tive,* parallel with a valorization of "scriptural desire." Between the two levels is created the writing space, the textual space wherein the thousand-and-one byways of negativized narrative words and discussable words driven mad by their superfluity plung in. *Trop* (too much) is undoubtedly the overdetermined word of this text, along with "entre" (between), "silence," "hors texte" (extratextual), and "rien" (nothing).

The word *trop,* the challenged illusion, affirmed and then destroyed, ends up abolishing the text and, beyond the words, leaving a blank page at the disposal of the reader. . . . The formal movement of *Un livre* goes back and forth between elements set out and then challenged (the characters), between elements affirmed and then immediately thrown back into this "nothing" of silence, of the blank page, of the space between the lines.

Irène Duranleau. Études Littéraires. 14:1,
April, 1981, pp. 111–12

From the standpoint of the boldness, audacity, and specificity itself of the project of writing, it may be concluded that Nicole Brossard's positions are ambitious since, from the beginning—taking only her prose into account, here—it has been a question, for her, of a transformation *of* the language and, if one believes in the revolutionary power of words, of a transformation *through* language.

On this level, Nicole Brossard's work has been read by critics (I think especially of the analyses of *Sold Out*) as completely recapitulating the observations of Jean Ricardou and his students on the text. All this independently of whether such intertextuality was or was not intended by Brossard. . . .

I am intentionaly citing relatively old novels by Nicole Brossard *(Un livre, Sold Out, French Kiss),* for my working hypothesis concerns precisely what has been called a progressive *deviance* in Nicole Brossard's prose, deriving from the growing importance granted, from one novel to the next, to what has been called "feminist engagement." Indirectly, the "new Québecois writing," given the central role Nicole Brossard has played in it, is also supposed to be marked by this deviance.

Louis Milot. Voix et Images. 11:1,
Fall, 1985, pp. 58–59

Nicole Brossard was one of the first here to affirm—with lucidity—the necessary interaction between theoretically oriented reflection, with its inevitable formal categorization, and textual practice, which is to say, with the exercise of the imaginary. All creativity implies theoretical postulates, given if not made, while all abstract reflection is impracticable without a certain creativity. Her texts . . . proclaim this interaction, this fusion. . . .

There is a problematic of signs and of modernity, because the specifically Québecoise tendency within feminism is characterized by such questioning—not to say that it was based on it, identifying in signs, those of language in particular, its locus of inscription and criticism, the terrain of choice. . . .

Certainly, during the 1970s, at the beginning of today's feminism, a good part of the Québecois intelligentsia defined itself by means of problematizing relations with language. Moreover, in Quebec, for various historical reasons, French, before being the official language, was the mother tongue. The woman was at home in it, on her own turf. And the woman of Quebec traditionally—and still today—occupies a place at least equal to that of men in writing, as literary history attests.

Language is the site *par excellence* of the symbolic, a site of power. It was thus inevitable that the feminist discourse of taking power would be born in and through writing.

Jean Fisette. Voix et Images. 11:1,
Fall, 1985, pp. 63–64

In the mid-1970s, Nicole Brossard was continuing her collaboration with women within the community of Quebec, . . . women who were in the process of effecting radical socio-cultural change. She and France Théoret, also an extremely exciting feminist writer and member of the original *Têtes de Pioche* group, organized the creation and production of a six-woman collective dramatic performance, *La Nef des sorcières,* which was presented in 1976 at Quebec's most established theater, Le Théâtre du Nouveau Monde. In real as well as symbolic terms, this was a major occupation by women of one of patriarchy's central spaces.

In her own text for *La Nef des sorcières,* "L'Ecrivain," Nicole Brossard offers the monologue of a writer reflecting on the creative process, aiming to find the ardent center of her creative force. She sees the strength which comes from knowing that other women are exploring their inner space, and she expresses violent anger against all that continues to alienate, suppress, and divide women. She finds her energy and her strength in knowing that women are taking a clear and lucid look at their own private experience, and that they are touching themselves and each other in so doing. Such acts are radically political and promise to alter the course of the history of humanity drastically. . . .

Of particular interest for the study of the political theme in her work are the five books of prose. They are exciting explorations of woman's space and the dynamic, explosive power of language. These books of prose successfully synthesize poetry, the genre in which she began her writing career, the novel, and theory in an active, imaginative process of creating the text, a process which remains open and unfinished. In them Brossard works out the various aspects of her writing which this essay has attempted to discuss. She has called the synthesis of poetry, novel, and theory "theoretical fiction" and has identified this approach as central to her work for the past several years. In these novel-length prose works, she refuses to use linear discourse to demonstrate theory directly or to represent reality; she refuses equally to fragment herself and her reader through an acceptance of the mind/body dichotomy. And so her books must be both understood and experienced: they must be read actively, imaginatively, and creatively. As an author she uses words for the purpose of creating her own autonomous universe, in whose organic, unfolding process she is lucidly and ardently involved. She makes a strong appeal to the freedom of the reader to join her in the creative process and so to share her revolutionary purpose. The space which takes form in her texts and in which she finds her being may be, singly or simultane-ously, the streets of Montreal or another large city, the material realm of her woman's desire, the field of motherhood, the imaginary space of the writer/reader.

> Louise H. Forsyth. In Paula Gilbert Lewis,
> ed. *Traditionalism, Nationalism, and*
> *Feminism: Women Writers of Quebec*
> (Westport, Connecticut: Greenwood
> Press, 1985), pp. 167–68

From the beginning, the works of Brossard have functioned in opposition to commonly accepted notions of space and reality. Her poet's awareness of the domains of all that has not yet been spoken and her particular sensitivity to motion and energy as essential components in the experience of space have led her to oppose vigorously all systems which dictate that the paths which have been followed in the past must be followed in the future. She is a whirl-ing, free-floating figure, an explorer using words to mark the fresh lines of each new trajectory. On the one hand, poets and seers posit inner space: that of the imaginary, of spirituality, of memory. In such space the inner eye receives its vision, the body touches immediately the source of energy, and the spirit, feeling in concentration its harmony with universal forces, knows its great power and autonomy. Brossard has evoked the limitless territories of such inner space and the vital sources of energy they contain, from the time of her first texts right up to her latest novel: "[. . .] quiconque sent sa folie sourdre dompteuse arrogante et surtout jamais rassasiée, à l'écoute de toutes les célébrations. la folie fertile qui [. . .] explore dedans la source vive des séjours intérieurs" *(La Partie pour le tout)*. Since by definition the fields of inner space are not normally visible, offering mere *traces* for the eye to see and the other senses to recognize, this spectacle which becomes visible through the looking glass—the *"scène de l'autre côté de la rive"* ("Enoncia-tion [. . .]")—can be reached only by moving through the fissures in the world of appearances and by responding to the inaudible vibrations picked up by the one's own energy: "Celle qui écrit dans la spirale entend alors à même sa propre énergie des ondes inaudibles en temps normal de la réalité, des ondes qui parcourent l'espace des maisons en prenant d'autres formes que celles qu'on imagine" *(Le Sens apparent).*

On the other hand, a commonsense notion has it that essential reality is constituted by the visible physical world, as structured, interpreted, and rendered meaningful by social discourse produced by the systems of intellectual and cultural traditions. Brossard's texts show that she has consistently found the structures and values inherent in such a notion of reality unacceptable for a variety of reasons: they deform experience and place undue emphasis on reason and logic over imagination and dream. Such reason is less objective than is claimed. In their emphasis on order and continuity, these structures and values are immobile and without fluidity, denying the vital energy of flux and motion. In their insistence on clarity, using various forms of maps and charts in order not to lose their linear direction, many things in human experience are left unseen or are passed over in silence. As the systems function according to their inescapable logic, power passes away from individual centers of energy. The inevitable, although not always recognized, *ideological* basis of the structures and values underlying the forms of dominant notions of *real* physical space leads to an abuse of power by those who exercise control in the system and in whose interest it is to perpetuate the notions on which it is based.

> Louise A. Forsyth. In Shirley Neuman and
> Smaro Kamboureli, eds. *A Mazing Space*
> *Writing Canadian Women's Writing,*
> (Edmonton: Longspoon, 1986), p. 335

Since *Aube à la saison* (1965) and especially since *L'Echo bouge bien* (1968), it has often been said that Nicole Brossard has marked the Québecois literary universe with an entire body of writing sustained by the search for "thought and emotion as motive and motivation," where it is basically a question of making the rounds of herself. In the course of the work, the passion has become distinct, integrating itself with the text, arising as enigma and energy, as the voice of a desire for beauty.

Even though it has always observed the state of the world and more particularly the condition assigned to women, with, among others, essays like *La Lettre aerienne* (1985), collections like *Le Centre blanc* (1970, *Double Impression* (1984), and *Amantes* (1980), prose works like *Amer ou le Chapitre effrité* (1977), *Picture Theory* (1982), and *Le Desert mauve* (1988), on through *Installations* (1989) and *A tout regard* (1988, for the two of which she received the Grand Prize for Poetry of the Fondation Les Forges, this work never has anything about it of the blocked writer or the depressive, has never wasted its time emphasizing "the defeat of thought" or "the era of the void," the decline of the modernist empire. Rather, she exults.

And the fleshly intelligence, this dynamism, which place her at the cutting edge of retreat and deployment, inscribes beauty in the multiple networks of the narratives, not as a "devouring force" but as a faith in the unexplored.

Gérald Gaudet. *Lettres Québecoises.* 57,
Spring, 1990, p. 11

Nicole Brossard has spent the last decade-and-a-half engaged in a multifaceted project to evacuate the space occupied by Woman, a male fantasy that hangs over our heads "like a threat of extinction," and whose images are scattered through the artifacts of Western culture. The first volume of her lesbian triptych, *These Our Mothers or the Disintegrating Chapter,* begins with a declaration of hostility: "It's combat. The book. Fiction begins suspended mobile between words and the body's likeness to this our devouring and devoured mother." The writer struggles between a language that excludes female and particularly lesbian subjectivity, produced by a discourse that reduces woman to biological functions and oppressive roles, and a vision she tries to generate through her writing. "Fiction" has a double aspect for Brossard; it is alien (patriarchal) scenarios ("fantasies [that] made her lose her sense of reality"), and a "fictive theory" the author is elaborating. Reconstruction begins with the alphabet, with words, with the body, with desire.

This leads us to the second movement in Brossard's texts, the creation of a space for the woman/lesbian subject of writing to articulate her desire, to refigure/revalue her self-apprehension. A revised subjectivity inclines us toward the "essentielle," inflected in the feminine. Combining "essence" or ontological status and the female pronoun "elle" (she), *essentielle* becomes a sign in Brossard's texts for an ideal or "aerial" woman, a figure to orient her desire and focus her vision. Michèle Causse calls this last project a "psychic parthenogenesis," in which we would given birth to ourselves, and which she sees as preliminary to an "ontogenesis," that would grant woman genuine access to "human" being. . . .

Although only in her mid-forties, Nicole Brossard has produced well over twenty volumes. Using the tools developed by postmodern textuality, which she adapted to her own purposes in *A Book,* (1970), *Sold-Out* (1973) and *French Kiss* (1974), she turned her attention after the mid-seventies to the inscription of a specifically lesbian desire. She experiments with the lexicon, with syntax, grammar, and graphesis in order to emphasize writing and book production, as well as to problematize the inherited terms for our experience, our reality, our self-perception and our bodies. She has left no word unturned, no image or concept unchallenged in her ongoing project to create a just future for the woman or more precisely the lesbian subject of writing. Her poetry, prose, and fiction theory that defy generic definition project a new space of the imaginary and of the symbolic. Brossard makes no excuses for the difficulty of her texts: all revolutions require intense discipline, intelligence, and vision. But unsuspected treasures await readers who are not intimidated by the praxis of experimental texts. . . .

For Brossard, there are words that seek us out just as we are searching for them. Certain words have an irreducible aura; they set off a chain reaction. Like the body, we cannot circumvent them. "Lesbian" becomes a "hologram of desire," where reading and writing, memory and utopia are fused in a creative symmetry ("Memory"), playing in the neural pathways of our minds. Brossard's latest writing insists on a double momentum of the body ("anterior and virtual") and a dual function accorded the sounds of the language (a "distinct pronunciation" and "sonorous form" of desire of/for her). Concentrating to maintain our equilibrium as we follow the complex steps of this lesbian *tango,* we surrender totally [*éperdument*] to an unedited music as we follow the voice in the text that inscribes it. "The reality is rounded out" ("Eperdument"). At the outer limits of signs, we read, "the tongue turns without respite to the unthought"; the words dance and the knots of memory come untied. "Deep in the brain the image comes alive" and makes its way into the vocabulary. Charged with emotion the image tells us that beyond the monsters and crumpled paper we can write of "cities, mirrors and the absolute." We merge with the image that gently replaces the subject. The fever Brossard describes is contagious, and we too desire such an image (of writing/reality/ourselves) as in "a spiral of love." Since her journey as an artist and her interventions as a radical lesbian feminist are far from complete, we expect her "virtual" woman and differential equations to lead to many more discoveries. The *Mauve Desert,* we find, opens on to a mauve horizon.

> Alice Parker. In Karla Jay and Joanne
> Glasgow, eds. *Lesbian Texts and Contexts:*
> *Radical Revisions* (New York: New York
> University Press, 1990), pp. 304–6, 326

BROUWERS, MARJA (NETHERLANDS) 1948–

One Dutch critic has written that Marja Brouwers's novel *Havinck* can be read as "an attack on the spiritual poverty of the bourgeois lifestyle" (review of *De feniks, De Volkskrant,* 4–10–85). Brouwers herself has said that she is concerned with the powerlessness of women in a world run by men. Although Brouwers does not ally herself with outspokenly feminist writers such as Hannes Meinkema and Renate Dorrestein, certainly her first two novels (her third was just published) are nevertheless profoundly feminist in the conflicts they chronicle as well as in their implicit and sometimes explicit criticism of male attitudes. Both *Havinck* (1984) and *De feniks* (1985) assert a causal link between patriarchal values and personal alienation: for in each novel male adherence to an ethic that stresses individual enterprise, self-sufficiency, and rationalism at the cost of feelings and human relationships ultimately produces emotional and spiritual isolation. The similarity of theme is the more striking because the structure and narrative techniques of the novels are so dissimilar: *Havinck* is a third-person narrative told entirely from the (male) title character's viewpoint, whereas *De feniks* consists of two first-person narratives told alternately by two different female characters. One of Brouwers's subtly brilliant achievements in *Havinck* is the reader's gradual loss of sympathy with the narrator, which results not from the perceptible worsening of Havinck's character, but on the contrary, from the slowly and as it were involuntarily emerging truth about what he has always been and intends to remain: a profoundly—and conventionally—selfish man. . . .

The short-circuited relationships portrayed in Marja Brouwers's novels are not the product of a society that is too free and too fast, as some reviewers have suggested, but on the contrary of one still encumbered with rigid ideas about gender and sexual roles and a male terror of vulnerability.

Nancy L. Chadburn. *Canadian Journal of Netherlandic Studies.* 11, 1990, pp. 81, 84

In recent years a large number of new women writers have emerged in the Netherlands; many have received positive reviews and a fair amount of media attention. Their presence on the literary scene has however as yet done little to alter the relatively small number of women writers whose works are discussed in influential literary journals and included in university courses. I believe the reluctance of Dutch critics and scholars to take women writers seriously has its basis in a complex of prejudices and assumptions about women, feminism, and literature that virtually precludes unbiased reviewing of books by women. [This thesis can be illustrated by] analyzing instances of gender bias in . . . reviews of Marja Brouwers's first novel, *Havinck* (1984). The categories of bias . . . include (1) anti-feminist sentiments, (2) an indulgent view of Havinck, the male protagonist, (3) a hostile and in some cases sexist attitude toward the female characters, and (4) the tendency to discuss new women writers together solely on the basis of their sex, and sometimes in order to compare one unfavorably with another. . . .

The issue [has] not been whether or not women writers receive positive reviews: indeed, all of the nine reviews [I have] examined contain more praise than criticism of Marja Brouwers's novel. The problems here are both more fundamental and more subtle ones: resentment of and lack of respect for feminism and feminist-informed literature; assumptions about male and female behavior that distort the perception of characters and narrators; and the maintenance of a separate and far from equal place for women writers— most especially those who do not follow established (male) rules about subject matter and narrative presence. Feminist ideas have had a profound impact on contemporary women writers: they have changed the way women understand and write about the world and their roles in it. Writers with a feminist consciousness do not set out to show that there are more loathsome men than loathsome women in the world, but rather that the structures of society allow and encourage men to oppress women. The Dutch literary establishment will only be able to evaluate women writers fairly and accurately when it recognizes the real disadvantages under which all women labor, and adopts a serious attitude towards women's and men's attempts to improve this situation. Characters like Havinck offer a glance into a mercilessly honest mirror for many men, including those who review books: it is time to drop the special pleading for such characters and face the issues raised by their creation in fiction. Women writers and women's issues, finally, must no longer be marginalized or ghettoized, for they concern all literate persons. Until Dutch critics and scholars recognize these facts, their willful failure of imagination will continue to do a disservice not only to women writers, but to Dutch literature itself.

Nancy L. Chadburn. Dutch Crossing. 42,
1990, pp. 96, 102

Six years ago Marja Brouwers made an impressive debut with her first novel, *Havinck,* which was subsequently made into a film. Now her third work, *De lichtjager* (The lighthunter), has been published in the Netherlands to considerable critical acclaim. The central character is Paul de Braak, just returned to Holland after fifteen years in America teaching art history at a university in Evanston, Illinois. He leaves behind him a broken marriage, as he had left behind a broken first marriage when he first departed Holland. The novel tells the story of his attempt to shape a life for himself in Holland, and his failure to do so.

De lichtjager is a dense, carefully constructed, and very readable work, told entirely from the point of view—and often in the words—of the characters themselves. A central theme is Paul's repeated failures in his dealings with women, and the outside views of him that we get are mostly those of the women in his life: his languid, blond first wife Lea, with whom he renews a relationship on his return to Holland; his tormented second wife Michal, full of hatred and rage; and his plump, officious half-sister Timna. The novel pivots on its central section, told in the first person by the American second wife Michal, who—in one of the novel's complexities—we discover (though not at once) is black. Paul sees her as undisciplined and wholly dependent upon him to complete her doctorate, yet one of the other characters toward the end discovers a book she has written on the effects of the loss of myth in modern urban culture. These two characters are linked, as Paul himself points out, because they both are in some sense outsiders in American life.

Brouwers, who spent a year as a visiting writer at the University of Minnesota, is especially perceptive about the not-always-smooth course of Dutch-American interrelations, and about the endless and at times annoying misconceptions a Dutch resident of the United States must endure. Another of the novel's subjects is the failure of an emigration, a sensitive topic in a nation which has produced so many emigrants. The main character here is a man who feels at home nowhere. Paul is essentially a man who does not know himself, as the views of the women in his life confirm, although no one of them sees him completely. He is an alcoholic full of barely repressed hostility, and his life is marked by incidents of irrational violence. His failure at marriage in two countries is paralleled in each case by an arrest for a violent act. The novel does not psychoanalyze its characters but instead shapes them for us, and this procedure makes them seem all the more solid. . . .

Marja Brouwers, with her intricate and finely crafted novel, demonstrates that she is one of the most accomplished newer writers on the contemporary Dutch literary scene. If her subject is not a cheerful one, her treatment of it is compelling and very satisfying. Her sense of the murkiness of human motives and the skill with which she weaves together a coherent story out of the diverse strands she uses as her material make *De lichtjager* one of the most effective recent novels in Dutch.

Fred J. Nichols. *World Literature Today.*
65, 1991, p. 313

BRUNET, MARTA (CHILE) 1897–1967

Commenting on an article . . . on "male poetesses" the publisher Nascimento stated that there are only two male writers in Chile: Gabriela Mistral and Marta Brunet. All the others were women writers. . . . In fact, both give evidence of a rare vigor that would be called virile if men ever possessed this quality.

Montaña adentro, her first and best work revealed her armed with all the weapons and able to compete victoriously with the master of the Creole art. It describes the land of the South, echoes popular speech, and colors typical scenes admirably without the slightest error in detail. Everything is in the foreground and medium shades and mental life are less important; it seems ready for the theater. . . . Its dialogue agile, its expression lapidary and pure, very Spanish in its regionalism, *Montaña adentro* appears like a little masterpiece, bold and perfect in its composition. If its breadth equaled its intensity, it would be identified not only here but all over the continent as an achievement of the first rank.

Hernán Díaz Arrieta. *Panorama de la
literatura Chilena durante el siglo XX*
(Santiago: Nascimento, 1931), pp. 147–48

The Creolism of Marta Brunet's early novels ignores the poetic, idyllic vision of the landscape and the detailed, insistent description of local customs. In her first creative moment as a novelist, Marta Brunet was looking for subjects and characters that could embody the conflicts that her themes develop in the Chilean rural environment. This kind of Creolism that goes beyond environmental limits, projecting toward general human concerns, where observation of external human conduct leads human beings to internal self-scrutiny, has been called neo-Creolism.

Marta Brunet, as she went forward with her publications, extended her writing to more transcendent concerns, even though several of her late novels take place in small towns in southern Chile. . . . Nonetheless, she always directs her attention towards hidden, powerful, predestined forces in the complex theater of the social conventions that act on man, whether he be a rough peasant or a refined urban intellectual.

Marta Brunet's subject matter is not wide. Her interest centers on human concerns and urgencies in the face of external circumstances. This human interest on the part of the novelist leads her to repeat her characters a great deal. Apparently, the characters rise as images latent in the author's imagination. The characters embody the subject matter that repeats the same concerns: fate, routine, the common life, identity, and solitude.

Marta Brunet's narrative does not directly make moral or religious statements as does the traditional realistic novel of manners. Despite her direct intervention in her early works, she does not insist on moralizing directly. Marta Brunet rejects disloyalty and the lack of human solidarity. Her novels embody the search for human authenticity on the part of individuals subjected to social conventions, stuck in provincial Chilean towns. The novelist's goal is not to preach a morality based in social conventions or in the specific external ideas of religion, but rather what concerns her is man in his responsibility and his need to know and accept himself as he is, man's obligation to live in sincere communication with his neighbor, always in touch with his natural inclination toward love and brotherhood.

Consistently with the novel's presentation of man and society, social conventions push man to live in constant pretense and hypocrisy and deprive him of the natural and sincere expression of personality. Marta Brunet underscores the internal conflicts that these claims of convention arouse in one's feelings. Marta Brunet's characters are beings who are desperately struggling to save themselves, and if they do not succeed socially, they attempt it mentally. Usually, they fail. . . .

In her work, narration receives greater attention than description; Marta Brunet's restraint in the use of any literary element that might detract from the narrative thrust should always be underscored.

In her development as a novelist, Marta Brunet reveals how close she is to the new technical foci of the modern novel: stream of consciousness, counterpoint, indirect characterization, the artful handling of time, and a style cleansed of recourse to merely decorative rhetorical devices.

Esther Melón de Díaz. La Narrativa de
Marta Brunet (San Juan, Puerto Rico:
Ediciones Universitaria, 1975), pp. 254–56

María Nadie presents the case of a girl who through her education, social position, and ideas could have reached relative security if she had done what ninety-nine per cent of the girls in her position did: stay at home, work until a husband came along, and then repeat the same cycle as her parents—respectability and mediocrity as a "decent woman" for the rest of her life. If her marriage were not perfect nor her dreams realized, at least her social group would have supported her to the extent that she would never feel completely alone. Family, friends, relations, subordinate classes, and superior classes form a typically Latin American symbiosis which lends itself well to the changing of her name from María Lopez to María "Nobody." But the author has shown another alternative and also the price María must pay for her independence. Since she is young and beautiful it is easy for her to obtain the attention of men and the rivalry of women. María wants to rebel against the middle-class prejudices of her parents and falls prey to her illusions. She wants to have full confidence in the man she loves, but common sense tells her that this man is not worthy of her and only exploits her emotions. She feigns indifference—both are free to come and go—but she feels that she wants to give herself exclusively to him as long as he does likewise. Although she is reasonable in her spending and in her daily activities, she has one extravagance: she wants to confront the world with a child that is "completely hers." When Gabriel tells her "you must be sensible and do things as they ought to be done" she rebels. In spite of her middle-class upbringing and knowing the social pressure against a "single mother," she wants to raise her child, even if it means losing her job and having to do menial tasks in order to feed it. She does not even consider the possibility that Gabriel will set her up in a house and will support her and the child, since she is now convinced that he is irresponsible and seeks sexual pleasure and nothing more. There is no communication between them. For her, physical pleasure is not sufficient to keep them together and yet she is not strong enough to break off the relationship completely. Only after his brutality and the abortion does she decide to flee, changing her name beforehand to María Nadie.

There are two other women in the novel who are very different from María but who are also victims of masculine instability. Reinoso's wife Ernestina is from the same social level as María. When they were married following the conventional courtship she was still a virgin. He too was sexually ignorant and after their first child he no longer loves his wife because she does not provide that "incomparable happiness described in novels." He begins to make up for lost time with every woman he meets while she, with the passivity of the escapist, exclaims "as long as he leaves me alone." When Reinoso falls platonically in love with María, he "continually enjoyed his intimate thoughts full of humiliations, interminable monologues referring to the young woman of the golden hair . . . without her ever finding out about it." Petaca's situation is much more bitter. She, in spite of working in the kitchen, maintained her virginity until her wedding night with Lindor. When she realizes that he is always looking for sexual adventures with other women she develops a tremendous hatred for both sexes. About men Petaca says: "You unclean, hollow shells of men . . . you only know how to talk about

whores. Beasts, worse than beasts." In general, the author has a very pessimistic view of the relationship between the sexes. In her other novels we find
machismo, homosexuality and feminine aggressiveness, as well as many other
facets of human behavior displayed by those who do not know how to resolve
their bitter unhappiness.

Lucía Fox-Lockert. *Women Novelists in
Spain and Spanish America* (Metuchen,
New Jersey: Scarecrow, 1979), pp. 200–201

A generation older than Rosario Castellanos, the Chilean Marta Brunet already had attempted to break with the literary traditions which bound women
writers and denounce the social conventions which enslaved her sex. Her
novels and short stories, depicting the life of her people, are free from the
detailed descriptions of places and situations traditionally expected within
that type of narrative, and concentrate instead of the psychological realization
of the characters, mainly women, who retain their intrinsic identity through
their independence at the cost of becoming social misfits. Marta Brunet's
language, a pure Castillian inherited from her Spanish mother, presented her
readers with a style both rigorous, strong and logical, such as "only men
could equal." What, however, mostly caught the attention of her critics was
the audacity of her stories and the frankness of their erotic details.

   Among the many characters of her fictional world recurs that of young
Marisol, "Solita," the daughter of a middle-class family, who cannot reconcile
herself to living within the conventional environment of her family and com-
plying with the standards expected of her. Her mother, a beautiful, gentle
and totally spineless creature, lives in a world of adorable distractions; her
father, strict and authoritarian, insists on his daughter not having an alarm
clock, "for the subconscious must remind her of her waking hour, so as to
extend his discipline even to the realm of sleep." . . .

   María Lopez, the heroine of the novel *María Nadie,* is another rebel
against the family structure in which she has grown up and against the values
it stands for. Being already an adult, she breaks away from it and chooses to
live alone and work for her living. But she has to pay a heavy price for her
independence; the loneliness she has chosen "is a mould tightly enveloping
her body until it suffocates it." This is why she becomes "María Nadie," a
nobody, while the people of the town where she has come to live, resentful
and suspicious of her aloofness, turn against her, and call her "Mala Pájara"
(Evil Bird). Love seems to come to her rescue in the form of an attractive,
pleasure-seeking extroverted man with whom María knows moments of bliss,
but also the agony of uncertitude, for he refuses to commit himself to any
arrangements which will limit his freedom. After a tormented pregnancy
which ends in miscarriage, she realizes that it is ultimately better to live
alone, than to be condemned to the "Servidumbre de un amor" (Slavery
of love). . . .

The spirit of independence of Marta Brunet's heroines, the revelation of the existence of a private world within the feminine mind, of an untapped well of sensuality, excluding the investigation and control of man, coupled with the classical form of her writing and the forceful directness of her style, which permitted no accusation of womanly sentimentality, proved a considerable challenge, unbearable at times, to her reading public. This reaction saddened the author and embittered her relationship with her own people. Breaking out of the literary molds to which women's writings were expected to conform and exploring the secrets of the female mind, Marta Brunet can be said to have pioneered the movement of contemporary female authors in Latin America.

Psiche Hughes. In Mineke Schipper, ed.,
*Unheard Words: Women and Literature in
Africa, the Arab World, Asia, the
Caribbean, and Latin America* (London:
Allison and Busby, 1985), pp. 233–35

BRYHER (pseud. WINIFRED ELLERMAN) (GREAT BRITAIN) 1894–1983

Winifred Bryher is among the few novelists of the present generation who have given renewed vitality and meaning to incidents of the past. Her historical novels are short, highly charged analogies to situations and problems that bedevil our days and nights. She has the perceptions of a poet, an extraordinary poet, who with fine discrimination selects an illuminating moment of action, and recreates it as a metaphor that may be applied to situations of the twentieth century.

Her latest novel, *Gate to the Sea,* revives an incident of the fourth century B.C. The scene is the port of Paestum, a town known for the beauty of its rose gardens, a Greek colony on the west, shores of the boot of Italy, then recently subjected to the tyranny of new and barbarous invaders, the Lucanians. . . .

Bryher's art . . . is one of understatement; no incident . . . seems theatrical or contrived, yet each has the strength of quietly exerted power, and that power is related to the quality of Bryher's prose: it is clear, taut, free of rhetorical gestures; it is poetic, yet austere—and many miles away from the pitfalls of the "mandarin style." No one living today writes prose with more quiet, unstressed authority than Bryher's. In telling the story of her heroine's decision to change her mind, to escape from Paestum, to carry the Poseidonian relics to a shrine beyond the reaches of barbarian conquerors, Bryher unfolds a dramatic narrative with high moments of action without once losing poise or clarity.

Horace Gregory. The New York Times.
September 14, 1954, p. 5

Those who know Bryher's historical romances will be surprised that *Beowulf* is a contemporary war novel, about the bombing of London in World War II. Despite its contemporaneity, however, this novel is as "historical" in its theme as Bryher's other novels, demonstrating her special gift for evoking the spirit of an age, for capturing a pattern of life that is no more. Yet the concern of *Beowulf* is not so much with memorable events and characters as with the larger historicity of things: the weaving together in time of the strands of human experience, every one unique, into the vast, repetitious tapestry called history.

There is really no plot to *Beowulf.* It is simply a brief record of what it was, for very ordinary men and women, to live in London under the shadow of the blitz. Death and horror could never be quite forgotten, in those days, but for the most part war to the Londoner was a thousand minor harassments and privations—shortages, rationing, the tyranny of forms and coupons, bad food, cold rooms, overcrowding, and overwork. It meant the bombs, too, but even bombing soon became part of a wretched, wearisome routine, with the cold and damp of the shelters more palpably menacing than the bombs. . . .

With all its epic overtones, however, *Beowulf* retains its modesty and humor. It is a slight piece of work, intelligent, ingenious, beautifully and subtly written, and completely without pretension. The closing affirmation of England's dauntless spirit is made by Selina Tippett, bewildered spinister of uncertain age: "Oh dear," she said . . . "I do think it is very embarrassing to be bombed."

R. T. Horchler. Commonweal.
October 12, 1956, p. 52

Bryher's previous novels have, each, revived an incident in history, symbolic of the free spirit overpowered but unconquered: the Battle of Hastings, the execution of Raleigh, the fall of Rome, the London blitz. Of them all, *Gate to the Sea* is the most compactly vivid and expertly absorbing—a masterpiece.

We can scarcely say with Paul Valéry that "poetry is to prose as dancing is to walking," T. S. Eliot feels, since some prose is poetry; and certainly poetry has taken to prose in Bryher's *Gate to the Sea.* "The path ended suddenly in the middle of a dune." Is not this typical of Greek seacoast? And could the sea be personified better than in this passage: "There was something friendly about the rush of water. Poseidon would be kind to them. . . . She clung to the seat [of the boat] as they soared up and forward . . . rode down into a hollow, rolled again, and rose upon a shieldlike surface of blue sea." The personalities portrayed are made to matter; the pulse of the predicament beats in the mind. Best of all, patriotism and ancient piety here "infuse belief."

Bryher is an invigorator. Faith, virtue, and freedom are her Ulysses—her Odyssey—enhanced by Paestum's scarred columns and porches, her pines and their shadows, as photographed by Islay de Courcy Lyons.

Marianne Moore. *Poetry*. February, 1959, p. 320

With a refreshing willingness to acknowledge early literary influences, Bryher dedicates this book to the memory of G. A. Henty, whose story for boys, *The Young Carthaginians* first awakened her interest in Hannibal. Since then she has read widely about Carthage, Sicily, and North Africa: reports of archaeological discoveries, Freeman and Flaubert, Greek and Latin histories of the Second Punic War. After these studies she is still as firmly in favor of Hannibal as ever, and has made her view of events into an entertaining and well-written novel.

Of course *The Coin of Carthage* is that. Anyone who sees the author's name on the title page will know as much. Bryher is a very good craftsman indeed. But it is not quite a masterpiece, not quite in the class of *Salammbô,* and this for two main reasons: the author takes a perverse view of the war itself, and the main characters do not quite come alive to the reader. . . .

As a novel this book is weakened by a multiplicity of leading characters who divide the reader's interest, and even more by the similarity between two of these characters. They are a pair of wandering peddlers, mongrels of mixed Greek and Italic descent from southern Italy. . . . Events are seen either through the eyes of Dasius or Zonas, but they are so much the same kind of man that a reader must continually glance back to remind himself which of them is speaking. It is hard to mind deeply what becomes of either of them. . . .

In short, this is not a bad effort to recreate the past, but in other books Bryher herself has done it better.

(London) *Times Literary Supplement.* January 23, 1964, p. 72

BUCK, PEARL S. (UNITED STATES) 1892–1973

She is entitled to be counted as a first-rate novelist, without qualification, for the exotic and unique material in which she works. . . . This is the elemental struggle of men with the soil.

The design is filled out with richness of detail and lyric beauty. If now and then there is a straining for effects of biblical poetry, more often there is poignancy in the simple narrative of simple, rude events. . . . Most of all there is verity.

Nathaniel Peffer. *New York Herald Tribune.* March 1, 1931, p. 1

Such a novel as *The Good Earth* calls at once for comparison with other novels of the same general design—novels of the soil on the one hand and novels concerning Oriental life on the other. Any such comparison brings out the fact that despite Mrs. Buck's very good narrative style, despite her familiarity with her material, her work has a certain flatness of emotional tone. . . . Mrs. Buck is undoubtedly one of the best Occidental writers to treat of Chinese life, but *The Good Earth* lacks the imaginative intensity, the lyrical quality, which someone who had actually farmed Chinese soil might have been able to give it.

Eda Lou Walton. The Nation.
May 13, 1931, p. 534

It ought to be very moving to a Western reader. There is only one difficulty. Romantic love is a fake center of psychology to ascribe to the typical Oriental man or woman, reared in the traditional bondage to quite different ideals. Although romantic love is second nature to the Western woman, trained to it by the traditions of a thousand years, it would not even be understood by an old-fashioned Chinese wife. By placing the emphasis on romantic love, all Confucian society is reduced to a laughable pandemonium. . . . *The Good Earth,* though it has no humor or profound lyric passion, shows good technique and much artistic sincerity. Thus, it is discouraging to find that the novel works toward confusion, not clarification. . . . Mrs. Buck, the daughter of a missionary, refuses from the start of her book to admit that there is such a culture as Confucianism.

Younghill Kang. The New Republic.
July 1, 1931, p. 185

Mrs. Buck is clearly not the destined subject of a chapter in literary history, and would be the last to say so herself. . . . (But) *The Good Earth,* the first volume bearing that name, not the trilogy, is a unique book, and in all probability belongs among the permanent contributions to world literature of our times. . . . It is a document in human nature, in which questions of style—so long as the style was adequate, and of depth—so long as the surfaces were true and significant—were not important. It did not have to be as well written as it was, in order to be distinguished. . . . We do not wish to be unjust to Mrs. Buck. Her total achievement is remarkable even though it contains only one masterpiece.

Henry Seidel Canby. Saturday Review of
Literature. November 19, 1938, p. 8

Although *The Good Earth* was among the most popular books of the 1930s—ranking just after *Gone with the Wind* and *Anthony Adverse*—and although it has received more prizes and official honors than any other novel in our history, there are still literary circles in which it continues to be jeered at or neglected. . . . It is the story of Wang Lu, a poor farmer who becomes a wealthy landlord, but it is also a parable of the life of man, in his relation to the soil that sustains him. The plot, deliberately commonplace, is given a sort of legendary weight and dignity by being placed in an unfamiliar setting. The biblical style is appropriate to the subject and the characters.

Malcolm Cowley. *The New Republic.*
May 10, 1939, p. 24

It is a quarter of a century since Pearl Buck wrote a novel which, perhaps more than all earlier books combined, made the outside world China-conscious. In *The Good Earth* millions of Westerners first met the Chinese people as they really feel and think and behave. . . . Before 1930 many Americans pictured the Chinese as queer laundrymen, or clever merchants like Fu Manchu, or heathens sitting in outer darkness; few believed they could greatly influence our own fate. Since then historical events have taught us otherwise—and among those "events" Pearl Buck's book might well be included. Her more than two dozen novels, translations, and non-fiction books interpreting traditional and revolutionary Asia have fully justified the early award to her of the Nobel prize in literature.

Edgar Snow. *The Nation.*
November 13, 1954, p. 426

There is a firm unity in her work which makes its component parts not easily distinguishable, . . . an identification with one's characters so complete and so well sustained is rare in fiction. . . . The language in which Mrs. Buck presents this material . . . is English—very plain, clear English; yet it gives the impression that one is reading the language native to the characters. . . . Mrs. Buck never, I think, uses a word for which a literal translation into Chinese could not be found. . . . Whether any novelist can be in the very first flight who depicts a civilization other than his own, I do not know. . . . But we may say at least that for the interest of her chosen material, the sustained high level of her technical skill and the frequent universality of her conceptions, Mrs. Buck is entitled to take rank as a considerable artist.

Phyllis Bentley, *The English Journal.*
December, 1935, pp. 791–800

Throughout her writing life, Pearl Buck has been building bridges of understanding between an old and a new civilization, between one generation and another, between differing attitudes toward God and nationality and parenthood and love. Not all of Miss Buck's bridges have withstood the weight of problems they were designed to bear. But *The Good Earth* will surely continue to span the abyss that divides East from West, so long as there are people to read it.

Virgilia Peterson. *The New York Times.*
July 7, 1957, p. 4

Mrs. Pearl Buck has been enveloped in a kind of critical and popular literary personality which has very little to do with what she actually writes. To the professional critic, she is suspiciously prolific and somewhat single-minded. To the political extremists, she is subversive just because she has been so prescient to Asian affairs. Her sense of Asian politics and society results in such accurate predictions that it is, by the logic of the extremist, a clear-cut evidence of her advocacy of what has happened.

The Living Reed will confirm both the critic and the extremist in their views. To a wide public, it will be the most powerful and informative book Mrs. Buck has written in some years. The Living Reed retains Mrs. Buck's sense of tradition, her deep commitment to the family scanned over several generations as a microcosm of larger social configurations, and her almost visceral feel for how the civil Leviathan can crush the bones of mere mortals.

Eugene Burdick. New York Herald Tribune.
September 15, 1963, p. 5

The reason Miss Buck has refused to keep pace with modern techniques is not far to seek. She is following the old-fashioned Chinese story practice of emphasizing event and characterization. And yet there is a dichotomy even here. In the 1930s her best fiction was objective, and the didactic element was usually muted or subordinated. When written in this vein, her work takes on force and meaning. After 1939, however, she breaks away from objectivity; didacticism becomes a dominant feature, and the quality of her work declines. If she had followed the same form of imitation of the Chinese novel type in her post-Nobel Prize writing, her work after 1939 might have reached the significance of her earlier productions. Increasing humanitarian interests brought a lack of *vraisemblance* and demonstrated the inadvisability of distorting what Thomas Hardy calls "natural truth" for the purpose of stressing didactic points. A growing sentimentalism also makes itself felt more and more in her later writing, and this attitude is detrimental to the highest artistry.

Paul A. Doyle, Pearl S. Buck (New York:
Twayne, 1965), p. 151

Written about a quarter century ago, around the time when Pearl Buck's The Good Earth was winning a Pulitzer, and, with her other work, a Nobel award, this novel [The Time Is Noon] was once set in type, only to have publication canceled with her approval—because, supposedly, it was "too personal." . . .

The parts that ordinary novelists do well stump this author, unfortunately; the parts that stump the others she handles wonderfully. Her villains are completely unbelievable—as if, in fact, she never really knew one. The minister father who steals the money hoarded by his wife, the farmer-husband and his doltish family, the scoundrel of a church organist are right out of dime novels. But her good people, customarily skimped or short-changed in fiction, often come touchingly, dramatically alive. . . .

W. G. Rogers. The New York Times.
February 19, 1967, p. 44

My Several Worlds begins with a statement of Buck's intentions. Characterizing her enterprise as an incomplete autobiography, which comprises a happy private life and the "age into which I am born. Never, or so it seems to me as I read history, has there been a more stirring and germinal period than the one I have seen passing before my conscious eyes," Buck sets out to sketch an eyewitness account of the transformation of China from a feudal society to a Communist state, with all the years of civil war and attempted reform in between.

Buck then backtracks to her childhood, presenting a panorama of incidents that are viewed from the present of writing; the past is given a retrospective significance that leads right up to Buck's adult identity as intermediary between East and West. . . .

When Buck's humanistic mission reaches its ultimate substantiation in Buck herself, the writing of *My Several Worlds* and Buck's large body of predominantly cross-cultural fictional works becomes a phenomenological act of cultural understanding as Buck sets herself up as the ambassador of both East and West.

It is at this level of cultural apprehension that domination is most complete. As Buck's personal history of intimacy with China becomes the legitimizing factor for her self-appointed role as its special friend, Buck's "voice," whether in her humanitarian works, fiction, or autobiography, attains the undisputed authority of historical/anthropological seriousness. From the reaction of her American readers who rebuke her for speaking too frankly about human life or inquire why she did not include what they know to be Chinese habits and customs to that of some offended Chinese who accuse Buck of distorting the image of China in *The Good Earth*. Buck's fiction, both in intention and reception, takes its place as a genre of writing about cultural experiences that claims more than mere entertainment value. . . .

Buck's love for China never extends to a recognition of the superfluity of her own position; the idea that the Chinese may not want to explain themselves to her and America is inconceivable to her, and it is on this basis that she rejects Communism for China.

Gìanna Quach. *Tam Kang Review*. 24:1,
1993, pp. 94–95, 101, 104

BULLRICH, SILVINA (ARGENTINA) 1915–90

Silvina Bullrich was born in 1915 in Argentina. Her literary production is quite abundant. Her first novel, *Su vida y yo,* appeared in 1941; later came *La redoma del ángel* (1943), *La tercera versión* (1944), *Bodas de cristal* (1952), *Teléfono ocupado* (1955), *Mientras los demás viven* (1958), *Un momento muy largo* (1961), *El hechicero* (1961), *Los burgueses* (1963), *Los salvadores de la patria* (1965), *La creciente* (1967), and *Mañana digo basta* (1968).

Bodas de cristal is the first short novel of a collection of three. The narrator is "the wife" for whom no other name appears, which alone signifies the importance of her matrimonial role. She is completing fifteen years of marriage—her "crystal" anniversary. She rejoices at having to resign herself to the infidelities of her husband. She also rejoices at being ten years younger—he is already forty-five—since she remains relatively attractive. The third and most important reason for her rejoicing is that she should always be pleased with her role of "legitimate" wife, given that even though her life is "full of surprises of men and women lying in ambush who could destroy our laboriously maintained edifice," she still has the hope that she and Luis will be united as the other women tire of awaiting a separation. This is because divorce, even though an alternative to a bad marriage, is in their case too full of problems, both of them being too conventional to risk their home and child by extraconjugal pressures. . . .

This novel presents one of the most incisive studies of the Hispano-American "conquistador," from his sociological causes to an explanation of his perpetuation in the system. The novelist presents various approximations of the conqueror to the conquered, and of her to him. For the first time, wife and lovers appear to be tacitly united above the traditional animosities. It is as if the author is focusing on the novel from the point of view of a "sisterhood" of understanding. One woman is like all women, in that one is not the triumphant and the other the conquered; all are bleeding and suffering for the same man. The wife is an extremely intelligent woman for not blaming anyone, but rather analyzing the circumstances and the typical development of the occurrences. She modestly says: "By chance I am saved by my lack of initiative, my lack of effectiveness in confronting life. Now I know that when the woman is too effective the home is endangered." Her case is typical of the many resigned women who must live in the system. She is not certain that Elena, or Susana, or her cousin Gloria—who is her confidante—are better than she, since they are opposite in every way: starting with the implied sentence of imprisonment to those who love them. The true ineffectualness of all these women is the same weakness which is common to all of them: their need to love in order to have their lives acquire meaning. All of them come from the upper class—with a few economic differences—or the upper middle class. All of them have been indoctrinated with love, marriage and children as their reasons for existence. The great emptiness that Luis fills in all their lives—with the exception of Isabel—has little to do with Luis, who is egotistical and vain. The emptiness is the result, as the wife illustrates, of being a small part of a machine and of finding oneself without any usefulness outside of that machine. Even Susana, who appears so modern, so independent, so dynamic, needs to believe that it is not worth living if there is only the possibility of dishonest love affairs, and if there is not a true passion between a man and a woman. Susana kills herself because she feels the emptiness of the system that has formed her. The inequality, the double standard, the uselessness of all her activities appear in the hypocrisy and in the injustice of the established order, and she is not able to adapt herself to an order that has deceived her.

Lucía Fox-Lockert. *Women Novelists in
Spain and Spanish America* (Metuchen,
New Jersey; Scarecrow, 1979), pp. 182–83

Jean-Paul Sartre treats as natural and inevitable the alienation occasioned by a subject's awareness of his own objectivity in the presence of another. The polemical implications of this phenomenon are discussed by Simone de Beauvoir in her definition of woman as the "second sex." Woman is a being who exists as "Other" in a world in which man is the "Subject." She becomes an object, even to herself. Thus, in the novels under analysis, the characters experience a strange detachment of consciousness. Blanca Ordóñez does not recognize her *self* in the mirror, where she sees "Casi el rostro de una mujer que no era ella" (Almost the face of a woman who was not herself). The dissociation between the consciousness and the body is acute in moments of sexual intimacy. In *Mañana digo basta* Alejandra remembers her body reacting to caresses, "mientras yo, la *verdadera* yo, librada de mi estructura terrestre, miraba irónicamente a esa pareja cincuentona que fingía tener ganas de hacer el amor" (while I, the *real* I, freed from my terrestrial structure, looked ironically at that pair of fiftyish-year-olds that was pretending to feel like making love). Blanca Ordóñez so removes herself from her body during copulation, described as the "acto mecánico y ritual" (mechanical, ritualistic act), that she wonders if she is not slightly schizophrenic. . . .

The clearest indication of the insecurity of these characters is their obsessive concern with the mirror. They subject themselves to an interminable self-scrutiny, resulting not from narcissism but from the endless assessment of their desirability to a man. The body, meaningful only as a synthesis, is fragmented into separate parts of erotogenic significance as these women observe themselves as outsiders, adopting the male point of view. . . . [T]he thirty-five-year-old protagonist of *Bodas de cristal* notes that "ya mis pechos, menos rigidos, no levantaban con tanta insolencia la seda de camisón" (my breasts, less taut, no longer raised the silk of my nightgown with such insolence). The judgment is sometimes favorable, as when Blanca Ordóñez says of herself "Buena cintura, buenos pechos, hasta las pantorrillas que mamá calificaba de fornidas resultaron ser un buen par de piernas" (Good waist, good breasts, even the calves that mother regarded as robust turned out to be a good pair of legs). Usually, however, the reaction to the alien body is negative, as occurs to Teresa: "Mientras se desvestia, sintió también repugnancia de sí misma, du su cuerpo, de su ser. . . . Por primera vez se odió" (As she undressed, she also felt repugnance toward herself, toward her body, toward her being. . . . For the first time, she hated herself). . . .

The body is thus a sign, an indictor of a woman's being-in-the-world as an object valued for its erotic attraction and fertility. For all these women one pathological consequence of the objectification of the body is its metonymic reduction.

Marcia L. Welles. In Beth Miller, ed.
*Women in Hispanic Literature: Icons and
Fallen Idols* (Berkeley: University of
California Press, 1983), pp. 284–86

The theme of the fragment "Cuando eras chica" in the novel *Los Burgueses* belongs to the Demeter/Kore archetype of rejuvenation of the mother in the personality of the daughter and the daughter in the personality of the mother. It is a descriptive narrative in which the mother recalls to the daughter that from the time she was a little girl what she liked best was to listen to scary stories that frightened her. It is the mother, a tutelary figure, who stimulates her daughter with a method for self-illumination, a process by which fear is overcome. . . . But fear is the liberation from the hypocritical bourgeois world that the narrative voice and the author are seeking, just as, according to the author, being a feminist limits the participants to their situation as men or women. As soon as fear saves them—brings to birth a "miraculously fertile world"—it is their inspiration to pass from one stage to another, going back down to their past and approaching self-illumination.

The daughter . . . never meant to unleash fear; she saw angels instead of the devil. Nonetheless, the theme of fear will unite mother and daughter, because the latter will constantly plead for its presence through the stories of the former, and in this way she will overcome what she finds incompatible with her nature. The mother, for her part, succeeds by way of a daughter who creates stories for her. The *Bildung* of the two of them advances by means of mutual influence. . . . The philosophical curiosity on the daughter's part complements the faith in the imagination on the mother's part. Her perspicacity rejuvenates the mother in the daughter and the daughter in the mother, although the movement of this discourse that reflects the external impulses of the two is toward self-illumination and will ultimately signify a distancing of the mother/mentor/hero.

Julia Kushigian. *Inti.* 29–30,
1989, pp. 212–13

BURGOS, JULIA DE (UNITED STATES) 1914–53

Intuitive lyrical depth, dynamism, and unity are the keynotes of Julia de Burgos's poetry. Dense lyricism of the spirit and not of the letter. . . .

If Julia de Burgos had to be classed within some literary movement, it would be in vanguardism, along with other poets who had a great influence on her poetry, like Federico García Lorca, Rafael Alberti, Miguel Hernandez, and Pablo Neruda. She shares with the vanguardist tendencies their radical and profound lyricism, the essentially intuitive dynamic conception of the poetic image, and the complex but substantial synthesis of the "contemporary spiral." To these factors are joined elements of the Spanish lyrical tradition, modernism, and the Juan-Ramonist cult of "an essential, naked, intimate poetry."

Generally speaking, Julia de Burgos retains a great deal of form from the tradition. In her poems, she alternates the use of the alexandrine and rhyming assonance with free forms. She cultivated the romance and the sonnet, albeit sporadically, and, in her poem "Las voces de los muertos" she attempts the slope of the epic. . . .

There persists in this poetry the romantic thrust, embodied in the emotional intensity of the expression: bare, dense, with a gradual though precipitous fall in the *being* and essence of the world.

Whence the unity of her poetry. . . . The unitary nature of this poetry is manifest in the subject matter as much as in the style. Love is the vital axis that orders reality, communicating feeling to it, and that determines the poetic world. In it converge her other major themes: the individual and death, making a thematic trajectory that goes from knowledge of one's own-being to love and from there to sorrow-death.

> Yvette Jiménez de Baez. *Julia de Burgos,*
> *Vida y Poesía* (Rio Piedras, Puerto Rico:
> Editorial Coquí), pp. 199–200

A common trend among critics is that of classifying the literary production of a country based on generational groups. This division, often problematic, is nonetheless an effective method of initiating the study of an author at a particular moment. One of the generations to have caused the greatest impact in Puerto Rican literature is that of the Generation of 1930. Constituting this generation is a large number of renowned twentieth-century Latin American writers. Among these are, for example, Luis Palés Matos who, along with Nicolás Guillén, is one of the top figures in Afro-Antillean poetry; Antonio S. Pedreira, who opened a still existing controversy on Puerto Rican society with the writing of his work *Insularismo;* Enrique Laguerre, who is one of the best known novelists of the century on the island and certainly the most prolific; and Clemente Soto Vélez, who is one of the founders of the Atalyista movement and the Puerto Rican Avant-Garde.

Julia de Burgos has been classified as a member of this productive generation. By the time of her death in 1953 in New York City, she had already won great recognition from the critics for her collections *Poemas exactos a mí misma* (1937), *Poemas en veinte surcos* (1938), *Canción de la verdad sencilla* (1939). Upon the publication of these works, the poet Luis Lloréns Torres extolled de Burgos as one of the great promises for Latin American poetry. . . .

Josefina Rivera de Alvarez in her *Literatura puertorriqueña—su proceso en el tiempo* makes reference to the "altos vuelos ideológicos en la poesía de de Burgos"; Lloréns Torres, in the previously mentioned article, even when praising the "abstracciones kantianas" in the work of the Puerto Rican poet, adds that this is connected to "la más limpia vibración emocional," thus falling once more into the typical reduction to which the poetry written by Puerto Rican women has been subjected—stressing the sentimental and personal aspects. Y. Jiménez de Baez, in the lengthiest study done on the poet, *Julia de Burgos—vida y poesía,* restricts herself, as the title indicates, to the life and work of de Burgos.

On the other hand, the considerable literary production of this poet would appear to be reduced to merely two of her poems: "Rio Grande de Loíza" and "A Julia de Burgos" since, according to the line of reasoning engaged in by critics until now, the first of these poems is seen as a representation of her childhood and adolescent remembrances of living near the aforesaid river, and the second poem has been viewed as an anti-bourgeois manifestation in favor of the social revolution in her country. . . .

In contrast I would suggest the existence of a complete level of meaning as well as language which alludes to the creative activity in the collection *El mar y tú.* In Julia de Burgos this language is hermetic but consistent and reveals a progression in the poetry of this collection. This metapoetic interpretation may serve to revise de Burgos's previous poetic work and reclassify her among the poets of her generation as someone who created more that "sentimental," "autobiographical," or "patriotic" poetry; she left us with a poetics of poetry.

> Luz Maria Umpierre. In Elizabeth and
> Timothy Rogers, eds. *In Retrospect*
> (York, South Carolina: Spanish Literature
> Publications, 1987), pp. 85–86, 93

Julia de Burgos's poetry is a testament and legacy of intense life experiences being potentiated through literature. . . .

The recurrent themes in Julia's poetry substantiate the interaction and tension of confluent forces: social history and individual life history. Julia struggled to authenticate a woman's voice. The search for authentic self-definition, affiliation, and intimacy is noted in the psychological literature as a process giving meaning to women's relational experiences. Various Puerto Rican writers have noted the salience of this search in Julia's poems. Julia's life and poetry embodied a struggle to legitimize a creative singular voice that could denounce social inequities and articulate her ruminations on sorrow, love, and death, and that would give form to her repeated inquiries about her identity in relation to the world. She says of herself, "I, Multiple / like in contraction / tied to a sentiment without limits / that alternatively united and disunites me / to the world." Julia could not be as society wanted her to be, she asserts: "I wanted to be like a man wanted to be: an intention of life / a game of hide and seek with myself / but I was made of the present / and my feet which touched promising ground / would not walk backwards." And as if conscious of what she was manifesting, she wrote, "Already defined my present path, I felt that I was an outpouring of all the earth's land . . . of all peoples . . . of all epochs." As such, Julia represented women's emancipatory strivings, while she denounced social and political injustices. She denounced hunger, colonialism, racism, fascism—oppressive forces that she had in some way known. She sided with human emancipation and affirmed this in a poem: "I live in that new person that struggles in each front / free from want and with justice of ideas." She spoke out and said, "Let us announce the cry of the present / We are closed fists!" Julia's consciousness had no borders; she was transnational; she was concerned with justice for all humanity. As Umpierre (1987) well put it, "it is through poetry that de Burgos confronts the challenge of society, it is in poetry where she finds her expression. Julia's poetry was her praxis, her life action. She conveyed and consolidated her internal subjective experience of objective social realities into a concrete form. José Emilio González (1976) said, "there is no discrepancy between the person and its expression. Reading her poems, we know Julia. That's why she is so alive amongst us.". . . [He] observed that Julia had a "strange capacity to integrate and assimilate in her own existential sphere, all that came into contact with her" and she does this with poetic lyricism.

This analysis illustrates how the contradictions and dualities she lived were objects of her inquiry, of her verses, and how her interiorized childhood and social experiences are forged in her poems. Within these, Julia could articulate sentiments of love, disillusion, and despair. Her journey into love, as expressed by her second book, *Canción de la Verdad Sencilla,* exquisitely expresses these sentiments. She wrote, for example, "And here you see me stars / spread out and tender with his love upon my breast." She exalts love, the loved one, and her need to express herself: "I wanted to say within the secret of my sorrow / but my soul can't reach the silence of a poem without words / and it jumps out through my lips made into dust of intimate throbbings." But as she could articulate love feelings, so she could express feelings of utter sorrow and despair and ruminations on death. She wrote, "I will discard paths that are burrowed within me like roots" and "I am also going to lose stars / and dew / and small streams"; and, as if foretelling her future, she asked, "Tell me, what is left of the world, what?" Julia commented on her anguish and in verses prognosticating her death, she offered us a message of how to view her, of her true meaning. She wrote, "How will I be called when the only memory is a rock on a deserted island? . . . they will call me a Poet." Julia affirms her truest identity and what gives her legitimacy; she lives in verse, her praxis is her poetry, and she left for posterity this legacy of dialogue.

Iris Zavala-Martinez. In Cynthia T. Garcia
Coll and Maria de Lourdes Matei, eds. *The
Psychosocial Development of Puerto Rican
Women* (New York: Praeger, 1979),
pp. 21–23

The personality of Julia de Burgos as a writer must be understood on several levels. In the first place, she is a woman coming to consciousness of the dualism that exists in Hispanic society. The typical contradictions of Hispanic society try to indoctrinate and subject her. . . .

In the second place, Julia de Burgos is a woman who accepts her restless and adventurous temperament. . . . In affirming her aggressivity and the dynamic nature of her personality, she rejects the traditional passivity that had been considered normal for the good woman in Hispanic society.

In the third place, it is through love and sexual passion that she believes she can affirm a free existence, without prejudices. The choice on the level of passion is what reveals not only her rebellion against the society, but her existential freedom, as well. . . .

In the fourth place, in her own being, she observes the profound contradictions between her sensuality and her spirituality.

Lucía Fox-Lockert. *Letras Femeninas.*
16:1–2, 1990, pp. 122–23

BURKE, FIELDING (pseud. OLIVE TILFORD DARGAN) (UNITED STATES) 1869–1968

Fielding Burke is not the first who has taken the industrial conflict in the textile industry in North Carolina a few years ago as material for a novel. He [*sic*] is the first who has given that conflict interpretation, not in the form of drab economic propaganda written in swift journalese, but in a powerful story of men and women, dimensional and vital because Mr. Burke has a true understanding of the people involved in that conflict and the rural life behind them. Unless we are facing a very happy year in literature there will be few books written in 1932 in so rich a spirit or about so moving a theme as his first novel, *Call Home the Heart*. A book, wealthy in flaws, it is wealthier still in its indigenous story of the last of the old, hard-struggling rural America engulfed in the new bitterness of the barren town which held out promise of escape from the barren land.

For Mr. Burke, the strike in Winbury (Gastonia, N.C.) is not fundamentally important. It is not a single bayonetting, a single sadistic beating of a striker by a deputy sheriff, which has caught the imagination of Mr. Burke. He is writing not about a strike but about a people. No mere industrial propagandist would have dug to such deep roots. No mere Communist would have given more than half of his book to building the rural life of the North Carolina mountains and in particular the woman's life of farm and house labor which has driven the stream of laborers into the mills. In the first 177 pages of the book there is no hint of economic propaganda, only a picture of mountain life with a sensitive appreciation of its beauty and an equally sensitive appreciation of its poverty and the hopelessness of young aspiration against Nature and the land.

Mr. Burke makes wholly understandable Ishmalee Waycaster's flight from Cloudy Knob and her husband, whom she loves, with another man into the "big happy world." What she finds is Winbury. And Winbury is physical and spiritual starvation, enlivened by the excitement of movies and ten cent stores and vulgar peep shows. She finds the people of Winbury cheap, raw material, used quickly and cruelly. There is nothing abstract or theoretical about Winbury as Ishmalee learns it in gradual bitterness and sympathy. It is concrete in individual human lives, as concrete as pellagra, as the "stretch out" system and scabs in the mills, as concrete as old, hopeless children and hopeless, childish men and women.

This picture of a North Carolina mill town is so unhappily veracious that many will see in it only a part of Mr. Burke's anti-capitalistic propaganda. Yet the picture is scarcely, if at all, overdrawn. The towns are heartrending in ugliness; the people are heartrending in their sodden helplessness. In his picture of the mill town just complaint might lie against Mr. Burke not as a propagandist who has falsified his scene but as an artist who has let his righteous indignation lead him into a betrayal of his art. This is true in spite of the fact that he seems to be writing Communist propaganda and that he is guilty of very nearly all the faults which generally pervade the single view-point novel of the economic conflict. The poor are good; the rich are evil. The hero and the heroine, the liberal doctor, the Communist leader, are all drawn in sentimentality. Life is perpetually dark under capitalism and the promise of perfect life lies in the reign of the proletariat. Yet the book is never just a preachment.

Very definitely Mr. Burke flies unsatisfied from his own propaganda just as does his heroine who fought and then fled back to her mountains. That flight probably marks for Mr. Burke the beginning of escape from forthright indignation into the truer perspective of the artist. In this book, despite the sentimentality and hard indignation with which he draws his opposing characters, they are alive, and the world in which they live, both in mountain and town, is vivid, true, and important. Here is rich promise. Here is better than promise, for with all its faults *Call Home the Heart* is perhaps the best novel yet written of industrial conflict in contemporary America. And how long we have needed it!

Jonathan Daniels. *Saturday Review of Literature.* February 20, 1932, p. 537

The recent *Call Home the Heart,* for instance, is, for the first half of its considerable length, one of the finest of American novels. It has pity, passion, elevation, a long list of characters clearly and plausibly realized; as you read it you are carried along on the current, completely surrendered to the illusion—and when you suddenly find yourself absorbing a communist mission-ary sermon that lasts for eight solid pages you feel as if the second act of

Tristan has been embellished with a long interpolation by a Salvation Army band. Thereafter the missionary sermons overshadow the story to such an extent that you are doubtful, for a while, whether this is communist propaganda or a not very skillful parody of communist propaganda. But it seems to be intended seriously; and it goes on and on till the very end, when the author, apparently not without shame for her weakness, permits herself a relapse into art. Her mountain heroine, descending into the plains and embracing the new faith, finally goes back to the mountains; her faith is firm, but she is too weak to labor in the vineyard; she can preach communism, but her blood revolts against physical contact with a negress (and its corollaries in communist doctrine). But despite this revulsion she seems able to swallow preachments that have wearied the reader long before.

The lady who calls herself Fielding Burke is an enthusiastic convert to the faith, but she cannot help looking backward occasionally toward the City of Destruction. She believes in the infallible Marxian Scriptures, and her criticism of truth is as strictly dogmatic as the most rigid of the faithful could ask; but when it comes to beauty she has some deplorable falls from grace. For she is an artist and she has not been able to rid herself altogether of an unregenerate weakness for bourgeois standards of beauty and proportion—even for bourgeois virtues. The chapters dealing with a Carolina mill town bring an authentic proletariat into the story; and Miss Burke commits the pretty nearly unpardonable offense of treating them as individual human beings and not as a mass. But her spirit is willing enough even if the flesh is sometimes feeble; she is ready to pluck out her right eye if it offends her, and the bourgeois reader can only be grateful that the left eye somehow escaped the same fate.

You will have to go a long way to find a more flagrant example of the disastrous consequences of a headlong collision between faith and art. The tolerant liberal will say, of course, that an author has a right to use her work as propaganda for her point of view. True enough; but the bourgeois ideology requires an author who does that to justify her faith by her works. A work of art aims at producing what may be called an illusion, in default of a better word; if the propaganda (or anything else) shatters that illusion, the novel has been spoiled by bourgeois standards of taste and the propaganda—also by bourgeois standards—becomes unconvincing.

So long as Miss Burke keeps her argument within the framework of the illusion and permits her doctrine to be inferred from what happens to the people in her story, the propaganda is powerfully effective. She knows her Carolina mill hands, and it may be presumed that she reports correctly what she has seen in a Carolina mill town. By mere presentation of what that means in its effect on the lives of human beings, she makes you feel that any social order which permits this sort of thing is self-condemned, that nothing could be worse. . . .

As an artist Miss Burke is highly sensitive to pain and cruelty; as a communist she knows that the only thing to do with people who disagree with her about the most effective method of improving the lot of the human race is to shoot them. Before the class struggle runs away with the story all the characters are realized with justice and insight; but the mill owner's wife is a figure from a comic strip and the professor who is set up as the intellectual champion of capitalism is a venal hireling aware of his own baseness and deliberately shutting his eyes to the true light. Moreover, Miss Burke is careful to give him only such arguments as could be knocked over by any bright pupil in a communist kindergarten. And, true to the faith, she reserves her bitterest scorn for the socialists. The mill owner and his daughter, if not his wife, are permitted some trace of human decency; but there is no redeeming merit at all in the characters who happen to be Marxians of a schismatic sect.

This is not only bad art from a good artist, but ineffective propaganda from a writer who has shown that she can produce good propaganda. It can be rationally explained only on the theory that when the hallelujah urge gets hold of her Miss Burke forgets everything but the ecstasies of the sawdust trail. It is argument by assertion such as can be heard every Sunday from Fundamentalist pulpits, and it springs from the same state of mind; it would be unimportant if it were not the work of the remarkable woman who wrote the first two hundred pages of *Call Home the Heart*. . . .

Historical parallels are never quite parallel, and the obvious resemblance between contemporary communism and early Christianity, in their relation to world society, can easily be pushed too far. Nonetheless, each of them professes to be a transvaluation of all previous values; in the case of Christianity the majority influence, for centuries, was against profane learning; and what the Church preserved of ancient truth and beauty, though it is pretty nearly all that was preserved at all, is considerably less than what Christianity destroyed. The present tendency of communism is in the same direction, and we are indebted to Miss Burke for furnishing, in the first and second halves of her book, an object lesson in the difference between bourgeois and proletariat art. If communism eventually gets the upper hand, what has hitherto been called literature is likely to be supplanted by something more on the order of the lives of the saints.

Elmer Davis. Saturday Review of Literature.
April 16, 1932, p. 662

"A gal she must marry, and a wife she must carry." Ishma Waycaster, the restless heroine of this novel, fulfills both lines from the mountain ballad— and more. Still pregnant, she descends to the North Carolina piedmont with another man, and is soon engaged actively on the side of the workers in a textile-mill strike. After a time, however, the mountains call her back, and she returns to her husband. Too many elements have entered her story to allow it a firm artistic line; but it is the expression of a warmhearted and distinctively American romanticism. The book is topically interesting, moreover, for what it reveals of mountain life and of labor conditions like those at Gastonia.

The New Republic. May 18, 1932, p. 27

In 1932, when Olive Tilford Dargan was sixty-three years old and had already published nine works under her own name, her first novel, *Call Home the Heart,* appeared under the pseudonym Fielding Burke. Dargan had deliberately sought a pseudonym "like a sword fresh from the scabbard . . . [to] stick in the public mind," a name no one "would jump on." Only a week after the novel appeared, however, a critic betrayed the identity of the novelist in his review in the *New York Sun.* Exhilarated by high praise—even from those who deplored her novel's politics or polemics or both—Dargan forgave the critic's indiscretion. . . .

Dargan's art was strengthened by her engagement in the struggle for survival on behalf of her mountain neighbors. She recognized the importance of joint projects in gaining the confidence of the wary mountain people and wrote repeatedly of new tasks that demanded her attention. In *Highland Annals* (1925), a collection of literary pieces concerning mountain people she had known, Dargan demonstrated her gift for a new medium. The liberating acquaintance with mountain storytellers, whose tales recalled the stories of her childhood, had engaged her latent narrative talents, and she found herself recording and transforming their stories in an effort to capture a way of life already disappearing. By the time she finished *Highland Annals,* Dargan had a model for the heroine of *Call Home the Heart.* . . .

Although there is no doubt that Dargan's strategic problems in presenting Ishma's character and her own political vision alienated both radicals and reactionaries alike, the novel caught on and seemed about to offer its author her first substantial taste of literary prominence. Neither of her subsequent novels, however—*A Stone Came Rolling* (1935) and *Sons of the Stranger* (1947)—met with the reception of the first. . . .

Dargan stopped predicting revolution with assurance after 1947, observing, "I've done my best to 'stand to,' I hope not forgetting art." She left the front lines to others who were younger. When a literary agency in Prague applied for translation rights to her novels, she decided that any publicity was dangerous. "God send another day!" she wrote, "I myself am adopting the discretion of an oyster." In 1955 she wrote of the "shock of having my last and best novel wiped from the public slate . . . [a shock] . . . so cruel and deep that I have not been able to recover from it." Later, she added, "I don't think the inhibition from the fate of my last novel will leave me until I am free of this world." Though she continued to write doggedly, receiving awards for her last volume of poetry, *The Spotted Hawk* (1958), and seeing a final collection of stories, *Innocent Bigamy* (1962), in print at the age of ninety-three, Dargan, like other authors of the 1930s, suffered the loss of her audience and of the conviction and courage necessary to sustain achievement. She died in 1968 at the age of ninety-nine.

Anna W. Shannon. In Biographical
Afterword to Fielding Burke. *Call Home the
Heart* (rpt. Old Westbury, New York:
Feminist Press, 1983), pp. 441–43

Olive Tilford Dargan's *Call Home the Heart,* originally published in 1932, was based, like five other contemporary novels of the early 1930s, on the events that occurred during a strike of cotton mill workers in Gastonia, North Carolina, in 1929. . . .

However, only Dargan, in *Call Home the Heart,* imagined a transcendent, symbolic confrontation that explored vividly the historical situation at Gastonia but was not dominated by it: a clash between intelligence and emotions, principle and prejudice, that the author does not pretend to resolve in any convenient final synthesis.

Dargan wrote out of a long-standing commitment to the power of rationality and science as the best means of reforming the human condition. As early as 1912 she had written a play attacking the horrors of capitalism, and she later used one-act dramas to investigate the evils of child labor and the place of scientific visionaries in the modern world. However, she had also an intimate knowledge of the non-rational propensities and folkways of the Southern mountain poor whites, whose lives she used as the basis for her *Highland Annals* in 1925. In Ishma she created a heroine conscious and worthy of the superhuman task before her, but who is finally driven by the all-too-human passions of love and hate to retreat from the revolution back to her beloved mountains and husband. Though Ishma's personal cup of happiness seems full at the end, she is no less aware than the reader of the sea of human misery that she has abandoned for the call of her heart. The greater satisfaction for Ishma of the triumph of principle is left for a later and less successful sequel to *Call Home the Heart, A Stone Came Rolling* (1935), in which the revelation of the meaning of Ishma's name, "waste," sheds an interesting light on the conclusion of the earlier novel. . . .

A false sense of a conversion of Ishma's personality in the novel led a number of reviewers of the first edition of *Call Home the Heart,* in 1932, to assert that it shifted from art to propaganda as the setting changed from rural to urban, only to be redeemed into art again by the final return to nature. The assumption seemed to be that Ishma was only truly herself in the "artistic" setting of rural poverty, embellished with Indian folklore, pretty scenery, humor, and ballads, while on the mill hill, in the ugly monotony of ten-cent stores and vulgar peep-shows, she became a tendentious tool of propaganda. Yet Ishma's essential character remains unchanged as she moves through these different environments. She is certainly given a drastically telescoped education in communist ideology after she meets Derry Unthank and becomes involved with union activities, and this undoubtedly contributes to a didactic element in the novel, but it can surely be considered neither obtrusive nor irrelevant: what Ishma finds in communism is a philosophical framework for her previous personal and untutored observations. Her private rebellion is given scope and coherence in the writings of Henry George, Bebel, and Marx, and when, in Winbury, Ishma finds that the logic of these ideas sometimes runs counter to her innate prejudices (against blacks, for example), we are well prepared for the consequences of just such a clash, having already seen it repeatedly on Cloudy Knob. The first reviewers of the novel had perhaps more justification in their criticism of the rather rigid endorsement of the contemporary communist line against the AFL, socialists, and liberal academics, all of whom are the objects of at least as much hostility as the capitalist exploiters. However, of those critics who justifiably mocked the formulaic left-wing rhetoric and stereotyped villains, not one objected to Dargan's application of a rather more time-worn formula at the end of the novel, when the reunion of Britt and Ishma is brought to a more powerful emotional climax by having it be the culmination of a conventional trail of lovers' misunderstandings about their true feelings. The provocative politics tended to get a much harsher scrutiny than the satisfied love affair.

Few of the critics of *Call Home the Heart* in 1932 commented on what is likely to be one of the most striking elements in the novel for the modern reader, namely, the pattern of feminist thinking that forms one of the strongest bridges between the rural and urban sections of the book. . . .

For Dargan, the feminism of *Call Home the Heart* belongs to a pattern of awakening class-consciousness, aided by a scientific revolution, whose beneficiaries will be all future generations, men and women alike. Any animus between the sexes in the novel is seen as the result of economic exploitation and blind tradition, not as the innate and inevitable result of biology.

Ishma's personal experience in Winbury convinces her of the harmony between her own sense of women's problems and the union's communist attitude toward them. Such convergence is not the case, however, on the question of racial solidarity, where Dargan again squarely confronts a controversial issue that caused a great deal of turmoil in the actual historical situation. . . .

In *Call Home the Heart,* Dargan attempts to present simultaneously both the anti-racist arguments of the communists and the depth of irrational resistance they are likely to meet, even in so sensitive and intelligent a woman as Ishma. Dargan is also able to subsume the particular issue of racism to the larger moral allegory of the novel, since Ishma's defection on race represents a rebellion of her instinct against her painfully won intellectual conviction. . . .

While the novel is . . . not unscathed by Dargan's application of her contemporary understanding of communist ideology in the early 1930s, it also derives much of its power from the sense of commitment that led her to explore and vividly recreate a complex urban environment—itself a radically new, and long overdue, setting for Southern literature. The painter Matisse has said that all art bears the imprint of its historical epoch, but that great art if that in which this imprint is most deeply marked: in *Call Home the Heart* it is the immediacy and detail of the fictional milieu of mountain and mill town that give life to the ideas that form the political element of the book.

> Sylvia J. Cook. In Critical Afterword to
> Fielding Burke. *Call Home the Heart* (rpt.
> Old Westbury, New York: Feminist Press,
> 1983), pp. 447–48, 454–55, 457–58

Call Home the Heart was Dargan's first novel. In the *New Masses,* it was given extensive treatment and judged among "the pioneer novels in the literature of the American working class." Robert Cantwell found Dargan "breaking new ground" in fiction but faulted the novel for poorly presenting the strike as a "dramatic conflict in itself." Cantwell attributed the shortcomings of *Call Home the Heart* to the lack of an articulated theory of proletarian fiction. *The New Republic* found the novel guilty of a "distinctively American romanticism" even though it was too cumbersome to quality as a work of art. Only the *New York Times* addresses the heroine herself, pointing out the struggle between her longings to "see more of the world" and the inescapable realities of her social and economic condition.

The *Saturday Review of Literature* praised *Call Home the Heart* for finally dealing with Gastonia "not in the form of drab economic propaganda . . . but in a powerful story of men and women." Sylvia Cook identifies a typical Dargan theme in the novel—the undermining of societal causes by the love between a man and a woman "which constantly threatens their loyalty and concentration." There is a "whole pattern of feminist discontent" in *Call Home the Heart,* moreover, which eluded contemporary critics and which is the unifying theme in the novel. . . .

Dargan views Ishma's brush with Communism and Communist ideology in general with a critical eye, unlike the treatment of Communism in the other novels. What Ishma wanted most of all in life was "to count, to be a part of something real," namely, the emergence of Communism as a force among workers. Communism, a rally speaker proclaims, "is a great mother, calling us to peace and plenty." Ishma pursues the "great mother" by studying world history and Marxist ideology and going to work for a union organizer, Amos Freer. Ultimately, however, Ishma cannot become a Communist due to her latent American racism. When her activities force her into close proximity with Negroes (she is hugged by a black woman after saving the woman's son), a revulsion sweeps over her, and she flees back to the mountain. Dargan was not about to accept the pretensions of contemporary Leftists who claimed to have the answer to the American race problem.

Sylvia Cook claims that Ishma's venture presents the feminist point that there will never be a Communist state without a prior change in the relations between men and women. While this is certainly a valid inference, it is not Dargan's strongest statement. . . .

Ishma's main struggle is not with Britt (he actually defends her right to leave him and pursue her dream when he pummels the preacher who speaks out against her), but with herself. After Vennie, her child, is dead, and after Rab falls in love with another woman, Ishma is completely free. With her new freedom she pursues an active life in the Communist movement, but ultimately fails due to her revulsion toward Negroes. Finally getting herself to a point at which she believes she is emancipated, Ishma discovers yet another obstacle, racism. In this sense, then, the novel is intensely individualistic, suggesting that progress lies in personal catharsis rather than political panacea, and denying there is any such thing as freedom. In other words, before assuming that simple "independence" will free her to effect social change or participate in radical politics, the individual woman must reach an understanding of herself which is conscious of all the oppressive distinctions handed down to her by the patriarchal social order. Dargan's feminist emphasis is not upon heterosocial relations so much as upon the self-knowledge and self-understanding of individual women.

Joseph R. Urgo. Minnesota Review. 24,
Spring, 1985, pp. 76–78

BURNETT, FRANCES HODGSON (UNITED STATES)
1849–1924

In 1892, almost at midpoint in a fifty-five-year career, a celebrated writer of popular fiction paused to write a childhood memoir in which she described how she "spent her early years in unconscious training, which later enabled her to make an honest livelihood" with her pen. In *The One I Knew the Best of All: A Memory of the Mind of a Child* (1893), Frances Hodgson Burnett, who had earlier portrayed the fictional paragon Little Lord Fauntleroy, now re-created her own childhood until the day when at age seventeen she sold her first story. . . . Frances Hodgson Burnett's memoir . . . provides evidence that this popular fiction writer's early training was significantly oral and formulaic. Because of Burnett's childhood training and her use of oral composition and reading as a mature writer, scholars interested in the relationships between oral and popular narrative would do well to study the use of stylistic and plot formulas in her work and other similar writers.

Burnett's career proved to be productive and lucrative as well as long. The fifty-five titles listed by her recent biographer include five bestsellers, one every decade from the 1880s through the 1920s; thirteen of her stories and novels saw stage production in England or America, and two were made into popular films; her writing earned her celebrity status and an expensive international lifestyle. The financial need of her fatherless English family transplanted to Tennessee had prompted her to submit her first story to an editor. After it was published in *Godey's Lady's Book* in 1868, she spent several years selling formulaic love stories to a wide variety of American magazines before she graduated to novels. Some of these, novels of the working-class and political life such as *That Lass o' Lowries* (1877), *Louisiana* (1880) and *Through the Administration* (1883), earned her critical recognition as a serious artist. American reviewers compared her work favorably with George Eliot's and placed her in the front rank of American fiction writers, alongside George Washington Cable, William Dean Howells and Henry James.

   Little Lord Fauntleroy (1886) established Burnett's reputation as a popular writer. Intended primarily for children, the book became a best-seller in English and was soon translated into more than a dozen languages. Burnett's stage version was popular in England, France and America, where it ran on Broadway for four years and toured the country with road companies almost as numerous as those producing *Uncle Tom's Cabin* and *Ben Hur*—in 1924 Mary Pickford starred in a film version. Burnett's literary creation immediately became a merchandising phenomenon, as Little Lord Fauntleroy set a fashion in dark velvet suits and lent his name to a variety of products from playing cards to candy. After this success, Burnett wrote more books for children, two of which continue to find an appreciative audience, *A Little Princess* (1905), made into a 1939 movie starring Shirley Temple, and *The Secret Garden* (1911), considered a juvenile classic. The books which found their way onto annual lists of bestsellers, however, were novels of fashionable social life for adults, *A Lady of Quality* (1896), *The Shuttle* (1907), *T. Tembarom* (1913), and *The Head of the House of Coombe* (1922). Before she died in 1924, Burnett had lost critical appreciation as a serious artist, but she never lost the assurance of a receptive audience; in fifty-five years of writing, she boasted, she had never had a story rejected except for reasons of length.

Phyllis Bixler. Journal of Popular Culture.
15:4, Spring, 1982, pp. 42–44

In 1890, there were few, if any, writers working specifically in child drama, so producers looked to writers in other realms to fill the void. The novelist Burnett, who had offered the American public *Little Lord Fauntleroy* in 1886, was . . . [an ideal] candidate for this activity; *The Little Princess* had first appeared in fictional form in *St. Nicholas* magazine in the late 1880s. The sentimental story of the orphan princess Sara lent itself well to dramatization and Burnett spared no theatrical devices in underscoring the melodramatic nature of the play.

   The Little Princess is the story of the wholesome and exuberant young Sara, who is left by her father in the care of Miss Minchin, a mistress of a school for girls. She is treated like royalty by Miss Minchin, who covets the rewards promised by the Crewe family fortune. But when Miss Minchin discovers that Sara's father has died after losing the family fortune, Sara is relegated to an attic garret, and is made to serve as a scullery maid to Minchin and the other girls in the school. In spite of these trials, Sara retains her good humor and optimism. Just as Sara's fortunes appear at their lowest and there seems to be little hope that she will be rescued, a startling series of coincidences occurs that brings about her salvation. A kind neighbor comes to her assistance, and a family friend arrives to tell Sara that the fortune is, indeed, intact. In the end, good is rewarded, evil is punished, and the audience is assured that Sara will live happily ever after.

While Sara may not originally have been created for the stage, she embodies much that was typical of this first important era in the development of dramatic literature for children in this country—an era when the majority of the plays produced were adapted from other mediums. She is a frankly one-dimensional character. In the true tradition of the Victorian age, Sara reflects all that was considered proper for children. She is obedient, trusting, good-humored, and intelligent; but Burnett does not allow us to see any other facets to her character. Sara's importance rests more on her function within the dominant, melodramatic plot structure than on offering truthful insights into human behavior. As in many plays of this era, plot supersedes all other elements. The characters align themselves in clearly defined factions: either "good," as represented by Sara, or "bad," as represented by Miss Minchin. The essential element of the play is not Sara's character development as she suffers through her ordeal (for she does not change), but, instead, the suspense created by her increasingly precarious predicament. Although the sequence of events in the play is highly improbable, it effectively builds suspense and leads the audience to the startling reversal of fortunes—an essential element of melodrama.

The Little Princess is moralistic, insisting that "good" will win in the end; but it is no more moralistic than most plays of the time. It is not altogether believable, but in the tradition of melodrama, it is exciting. And as adult theater-goers of the period were themselves entertained by a steady diet of such plays, it is not surprising that they would consider *The Little Princess* appropriate for their children.

Sara Crewe was one of the first characters in the literature whose popularity has transcended the age in which she was originally created. From a contemporary perspective, the character—and the play as a whole—are highly romanticized and artificial, but Sara is no less interesting now than she was eighty years ago. Because of Burnett's skill at creating melodrama, contemporary audiences can still be moved by the play, and can still become emotionally involved with Sara's plight.

Roger L. Bedard. Children's Literature Association Quarterly. 9:3, Fall, 1984, p. 103

In her preface to *A Little Princess* (1905), entitled "The Whole of the Story," Frances Hodgson Burnett explains how, in the process of adapting *Sara Crewe* (1887) for the stage, she discovered much that she had failed to hear and thus had left untold. The result of her more careful listening was an elaborate retelling; in fact, *A Little Princess* is three times the length of *Sara Crewe*. But Burnett's preface, even as it assures the child reader that the story is now both fully accessible and complete, invites the critic to guess at what remains hidden between the lines. For even if all the secrets of *Sara Crewe* have now been told, the new version may well possess secrets of its own, secrets that it—like its predecessor—is keeping even from the author herself. . . .

Phyllis Bixler has recently described how Burnett, after the phenomenal success of *Little Lord Fauntleroy,* turned more and more to popular romances for both children and adults, forsaking the working-class interest of *That Lass O'Lowries* (1877) and the social realism of *Through One Administration* (1883). The very title of *Sara Crewe or What Happened at Miss Minchin's,* written soon after *Fauntleroy* and before Burnett became a confirmed romance writer, leads us to expect a realistic account of boarding school life. On the other hand, the title of *A Little Princess,* written seventeen years later, emphasizes the way in which Sara's conception of herself as a little princess, her ability to romanticize her exile in the attic, sustains her through the ordeal. As Bixler has observed, "The frequent references to fairy tales and magic make it difficult to mistake *A Little Princess* for a realistic novel of child life." It is as though Burnett, on reconsidering *Sara Crewe,* saw how the story could be made to justify her own romantic imagination and the turn that her career, a commercial but no longer a critical success, had taken. Yet the heightened romanticism of *A Little Princess* is accompanied by a subtle psychological realism, a realism also characteristic of *The Secret Garden.* This realistic strain, I would argue, betrays the very ambivalence toward romance that Burnett is attempting to conceal even from herself. Had she had the ear to hear it, she might well have written still another version of Sara's story. . . .

Burnett, by making Sara a more imaginative child in *A Little Princess* while retaining the realistic episodes of *Sara Crewe,* does not succeed in sistifying her own and the Small Person's determined preference for sun-warmed peach but rather Sara's conversion from sun-warmed peach to raw turnip. But the later version, by dramatizing Sara's conflict between her romantic imagination and the facts of reality, constitutes a far more complex and truthful story than the memoir and thus a successful argument for works of the imagination. As Burnett suggests in her preface, "the whole of the story" never can be told: "Between the lines of *every* story there is another story" (my emphasis). For as the connection Burnett makes between lying and storytelling indicates, every story, by falling short of complete disclosure, is a kind of untruth. *A Little Princess,* in that its author tries to get us to believe in "magic," is a story in this pejorative sense; it is at best a partial truth. But if every story is less candid than it purports to be, it is also more revealing. *A Little Princess,* in that it allows us to read between the lines and discern the ordinary human traits that enable us to bear reality without denying its existence, is a triumph of the imagination. Burnett did not really want to give us the whole of the story, but she did give it in spite of herself. This, as she recognized, is what storytellers do.

Elizabeth Lennox Keyser. In Francelia
Butler and Richard Rotart, eds. <i>Triumphs of
the Spirit in Children's Literature</i> (Hamden,
Connecticut: Shoestring Press, 1986),
pp. 230–31, 241–43

Frances Hodgson Burnett's *The Secret Garden* . . . is probably on everyone's list of classic children's books in English; it has an assured place in that canon. Marghanita Laski described it as the "most satisfying" children's book she ever read, whatever that means. John Rowe Townsend is sure he knows: it has, he says, a "powerful effect on children's imaginations" in part because it speaks to their "instinctive feeling for things that grow," in part because it feeds their "longing for real, important, adult-level achievement." My own conclusions are rather different: this paper could be described as an attempt to show how it is "satisfying" but also what the limits are to the satisfaction it offers. The main characters of *The Secret Garden* are two children—Mary and Colin. Mary is an orphan whose parents have died during a cholera epidemic in India. As a consequence she is adopted by her uncle, Archibald Craven, the Master of Misselthwaite, and moves to Yorkshire in England. Colin, the heir of the Manor, is also an orphan of sorts: his mother died in childbirth and, secondly, he has been rejected by his grieving, constantly absent father. Initially both Mary and Colin are unlikeable children. Mary with the assistance of a robin, a cantankerous old gardener, and a Pan-like young boy, Dickon, and under the influence of the beneficent Yorkshire spring, changes from "the most disagreeable-looking child ever seen" to a pretty child who will be "like a blush-rose when [she] grows up." Her central act in the narrative is to be, in turn, the instrument of Colin's cure: to get him to the garden where the nurturing spirit of his dead mother returns him to both physical and psychic health. Their adventure therefore is more spiritual than physical—no dragons are slain, no family treasure restored—even if the representation of the manor itself is a minor gothic masterpiece, the site of fortunately unrealized perils.

What is disturbing about this fantasy is that its ideology is more than commonly masked for most of its course by the very charm of the narrative and the presentation of childish sensibilities, only to be revealed at the conclusion as the point to which it has been travelling all the while. The power of a Victorian neo-feudal social structure, which has been cancelled for most of the adventure, is firmly in place at the end. Dickon is clearly the figure of greatest authority throughout the tale; he is described at one point by an admiring adult as equally fitted to life in Buckingham Palace or down in the mines. However, in the most casual fashion the book finally, inevitably, denies him any opportunity to take possession of power, the kind of adult power that is measured out in privilege and largesse. It would be a waste of effort to try to describe a possible future for him: he is consigned in effect to his past as "a common moor boy." On the other hand, Colin is all future, when the novel ends appropriately enough, definitively indeed, with the two words that also constitute his title, his right to power, "Master Colin." As for Mary, whose name actually begins the story, who has been the true quester through most of the adventure, her future is really what this paper is all about. . . .

The Secret Garden bears the traces of the ideology which gave structure to Freud's culture as well as Mrs. Burnett's. For all her personal talents and accomplishment Frances Hodgson Burnett was no more able to construct a literary system that does other than grant privileged status to the male than Freud was in his theorizing of psychoanalysis. Equally the book clearly promotes a conception of motherhood as power of a sort: the power of fecundity, of giving; ostensibly it honors the mother, but never observes that this is actually a cultural procedure by which women are subordinated and consumed. The curtain is drawn, and drawn again; presence becomes absence; lack and desire form an endless chain that stretches beyond the generic joy of romantic endings.

The limits of this story of Burnett's, then, the point at which it stops being her story and becomes her culture's, are to be found in language itself. The instrument of colonial Mary's acculturation in Yorkshire is a discourse that enacts an exchange from free subject to object of consumption, for both the reader and those who inhabit the world of the text. When she is finally beaten in a race by Colin she is reduced to the level of synecdoche—a general signifier. . . .

As a text in its world, as a children's classic and therefore, in Foucault's phrase, inhabiting "an element of power," The Secret Garden, despite its energetic fantasy of inversion and reversion, all too completely images the power and the ideology of the late Victorian ruling class (with which, we should remember, Mrs. Burnett was only too happy to be familiar), including its consumption of women as signs of its own preeminence. Unquestionably this novel does possess to a degree what John Goode calls fictional coherence, in contradistinction to the ideological: it does play with romance form in such a fashion as to bring some sort of light to bear on its governing ideas about class and social relationships. Nevertheless this coherence equally clearly does not hold for a feminist reader: Burnett, having invited boys into a girl's story, never even notices that she has given the story away.

Claudia Marquis. Journal of the
Australasian Universities Language and
Literature Association. 68, November, 1987,
pp. 164–65, 184–86

The Secret Garden, [is] the first book which deeply affected me with joy, hope, and a sense of transcendence. As Madelon Gohlke pointed out when she wrote from the perspective of an adult critic of her profound experience as a child with The Secret Garden, "powerful response to a reading, even on the part of a child, acts as a sign of engagement, or what Iser would call the reader's 'entanglement' with a text." I too can affirm the power of the book on the imagination of my child self. The summer I was eight I discovered the book in my grandmother's basement and for several summers thereafter made a ritual of unpacking the book from storage, rereading it, and returning it to the basement at the end of my vacation. . . .

Many children's books which inspire hope do so, at least partially, because they create a time-out-of-time, transcending the instant and making it possible for the child protagonist and reader to live, however briefly, in that "'span' of time" which integrates past and future in the present. Because the stories I focus on are not fantasies but "realistic" novels, their characters live in clock time, but those stories also put readers in touch with sacred time, that decisive, ontological time when, as Madeleine L'Engle says, we will be known not by "some cybernetic salad at the bottom left-hand corner of a check, or [a] social security number or [a] passport number. In *kairos* [we] will be known by [our] name[s]," that is, by our "isness," our essence. . . .

Norman Holland speaks directly to the necessity that any integral criticism take cognizance of the transaction between the reader and the text, frankly acknowledge, accept, and use the critic's role in her own experience. Reading *The Secret Garden,* recalling few of its details but vividly remembering the aura of the enclosed garden, a secret and a saving place for two abandoned children, I was able to recognize it as a story of regeneration. Rereading *The Secret Garden* now with the same satisfaction, I see that the book does indeed incorporate a ritual of status reversal, does recover Eliade's mythic time and Macquarrie's span of time. Perhaps, indeed, it is *The Secret Garden*'s retrieval of primordial time which renders it timeless: an acknowledged children's classic in continuous publication; a perennial favorite among child readers, with the power to evoke a spark, even a blaze, of emotion among adult readers when they recollect their earlier "entanglement" with the book.

Mary Lennox finds a garden, the archetypal symbol of life and growth, which has been shut up for ten years; all but dead, it is described as a world of its own: "It was the sweetest, most mysterious-looking place anyone could imagine. The high walls . . . shut it in"; "it was different from any other place she had ever seen in her life." "Everything was strange and silent and she seemed to be hundreds of miles away from any one, but somehow she did not feel lonely at all. All that troubled her was her wish that she knew whether all the roses were dead." Mary's concern for the roses is significant, for the rose traditionally symbolizes the essence of completion, consummate achievement, perfection. Discovering that "even if the roses are dead, there are other things alive," Mary, in an act of reverent recreation, kneels down and, with a sharp stick, digs and weeds, making "nice little clear places around" the "green points pushing their way through the earth. 'Now they look as if they could breathe,' she said."

As the garden, including the roses, blooms, so do Mary and her frail cousin, Colin, whom Mary has unlocked as she has the garden itself. One fresh morning when Mary had "unchained and unbolted and unlocked" the door and bounded into the greening, "uncurling" world, "she clasped her hands for pure joy and . . . felt as if she must flute and sing aloud herself and knew that thrushes and robins and skylarks could not possibly help it. She ran around the shrubs and paths toward the secret garden." After Colin has been introduced to the garden, "he looked so strange and different because a pink flow of color had actually crept all over him—ivory face and neck and hands and all"; "'I shall get well!' he cried out. . . . 'And I shall live forever and ever and ever.'" . . .

Before the story is complete, the characters name the power at the center of their cosmos. In mythic cultures, to recognize, to know, the sacred power is primary. Knowledge of the power is symbolized by the ability to name it. What one can name, one has power over, for naming indicates knowledge of the essence. Mary and Colin do not call the power God; perhaps because they recognize it as "Mystery" but yet inherent in nature, they call it "Magic," and Colin plans to grow up to analyze it scientifically, to have power over it in another way. By whatever name, however, the reader recognizes the power as life transcendent and creative. . . .

This book ends with the return of Mr. Craven and the recreation of at least a partial family in which the children are parents to the man. Mary's, then Colin's, discernment of the regenerative force in physical and human nature has fostered an independence which will empower them to use their awareness of "Magic," the sacred immanent in the world, to change the stunted futures which seemed to lie ahead for themselves and Mr. Craven at the beginning of the book. Through the characters, readers, too, are put in touch with kairos and recognize in themselves, no matter how weak or contrary, the potential for moving into a mode of living where they also can shape their futures toward their dreams. For the reader, as for Mary and Colin, kairos, with the changing seasons, subsumes chronos in hope.

But Mary and Colin are privileged children. The fictional world of *The Secret Garden,* unquestionably class-bound, is pastoral, portraying poverty like that of the Sowerbys as picturesque, nurturing, and compensated by common sense and love for nature, physical and human. The seemingly stable world of the book is threatened only by disease and accidental death; personal griefs are eventually overcome by discoveries within the setting of home, discoveries that generate rebirth, growth, and reunification of the family.

M. Sarah Smedman. *Children's Literature.*
16, 1988, pp. 95–98

BUSTA, CHRISTINE (AUSTRIA) 1915–87

Christine Busta seems at present to be in a blind alley. Her *Scheune der Vögel* [The Barn of the Birds], which follows the rules of traditional melody and emotion, is most appealing at the points where not sibylline pathos but simpler, primitive experience is expressed—*e.g.,* "Schnee im Advent" [Snow at Advent]. One can ask too much of a talent, even one such as this poet possesses.

Claus Pack. *Wort und Wahrheit.* 1959, p. 212

In her *Sternenmühle* [The Mill of the Stars], Christine Busta has given us poems "for children and her friends" as a present (here the phrase is really in place), framed in naively colorful, childlike, clover-sweet pictures by Johannes Grüger. "Die Sternenmühle" is, like "Die Scheune der Vögel," a synonym for heaven, in which Christine Busta is more at home than on earth. Never has the validity of her claim to citizenship in that realm appeared so pure and convincing as here.

Wieland Schmied. *Wort und Wahrheit.*
1960, p. 211

. . . One of the greatest although least pretentious figures of the present lyrical generation is Christine Busta, born in 1915 in Vienna, whose work fortunately does not lack the recognition it amply deserves. She is, in my opinion, the most genuine, the most natural member of the triad of "Austrian sybils"—a slightly ironical and derogatory term applied to them by a German critic—the others being Ingeborg Bachmann and Christine Lavant.

To be sure, she is a visionary, but not of the Cassandra type. She is modest, but her Christian humility is not masochistic, and she has a wonderful sense of humor, which is amazing if one considers her hard life. There are chthonic shudders in her lines but they are more often melodious and balanced, and she can make a gnomic quatrain deeply symbolic but simple at the same time. The breath of silence becomes word here and not an unintelligible shorthand which can be deciphered only by a few initiates. . . . We feel the tragic basis of our existence, the anguish of our cataclysmic age, the roots of pain and sorrow out of which poetry always sprouts, but there is nothing to remind us of the fashionable nihilism, the futility and frustration, and her poems grant us something which has become a rare treat nowadays—compassion and consolation.

Ernst Waldinger. *Books Abroad.* 1961, p. 136

Christine Busta, who was honored with the Trakl Prize, transforms Trakl's rigid world of fate, which she approaches from the feminine polarity, into a cave of refuge. What in his work is hard and cutting becomes in hers soft and soothing. A poem, inspired by a Chagall painting, has the softened glow of a magic cave of the world. One is tempted to say that this is the real tone of the poetess. . . . Why the selfless magic, the rigidity, the metallic coldness precisely of Trakl? A deeper, more penetrating study of the poems suggests that this very coldness, this rigidity, this block of ice at some time or other gave birth to her lyric expression and that the warm world, the cave, encloses this block as its unfathomable nucleus. . . . Trakl's fate—or fate in general— in Christine Busta's poems is the alienating principle that surrounds the inner space with reversed pictures of life.

> Karl August Horst. *Kritischer Führer durch*
> *die deutsche Literatur der Gegenwart*
> (München: Nymphenburger, 1962), p. 251

For Christine Busta, a Viennese of the 1915 generation, the experience of time and history in the city of Vienna takes on a symbolic quality: the home of a glorious past becomes the object of melancholy contemplation. . . . Her basically Christian orientation finds it difficult to overcome sadness, sense of guilt, and melancholy. What is left are prayers for the dead, the memory of a childhood rooted in faith, and the hope of the Christian Jerusalem as the "happy city" where love will have triumphed.

> Albert Soergel. In Curt Hohoff, ed.
> *Dichtung und Dichter der Zeit* (Düsseldorf:
> August Bagel, 1963), p. 869

While strongly metaphorical poetry can create a hermetic world to which access is—often intentionally—obscured, . . . Christine Busta's later poetry is a message intended for the reader. For Busta, one of Austria's "metaphorical poets," poetry is a dialogue, a communication between the poet and an observed nature, between the poet and those to whom she has dedicated individual poems, and between the poet and her readers. Certainly Busta's work has found the audience she seeks, as is shown by her unusually large readership in Austria and abroad, and by her steadily growing critical acclaim. The multiple printings of her books of poetry also attest to her exceptionally wide appeal.

Busta's need to address an audience with her poetry is apparent in the personalized voice throughout her work and the tone of intimacy it creates.

In its totality man's existence includes for Busta both the physical and the transcendent dimensions, a fact which explains her poetic process, the development from the concrete-visual to the fundamental-spiritual. Just as the specific inspiration for "Oktoberabend in Venedig," the traveler's view of the city in the evening light, suggests symbols of man's spirituality to her, everything we see around us and can know through our senses gives testimony of a higher order; man's physical presence as well as his accomplishments symbolize a meaning in life that is known through direct experience. The dialogue that the poet creates with her readers includes a characteristically modest invitation to join in rediscovering the half-concealed spiritual dimension within contemporary existence.

Marilyn Scott. *Modern Austrian Literature.*
18:1, 1985, pp. 83, 90

Christine Busta ends *Salzgärten,* her 1975 collection of poetry, with a seemingly radical proposal for a poet: she suggests the unraveling of the threads of written language and proposes the transformation of all paper back into primeval forests. For then the poet, freed from the constraints of the written word, could compose in the pure language of physical experience, like the eloquent time rings on trees, which she calls "die kosmische Urschrift für Analphabeten." Spoken language is Busta's means of overcoming the estrangement she senses in modern society, here signified by the isolating act of reading the printed page, to establish an elusive kinship between people. The poem therefore contains this directive: "Die *gesprochene* Sprache knüpfen/ von Mensch zu Mensch und durch Dasein reden,/ wie die geduldigen Dinge es tun."

For Busta poetry itself is communication, the shy hand that reaches out to one's neighbor in the darkness. Much of her poetry is dedicated to specific friends, to fellow poets and artists, as well as to children. And it is apparent from the frequency of the pronouns "du" and "wir" in her work and from her use of the direct address, "mein Freund" or "mein Kind," that Busta is writing for an intimately familiar audience. But for her the ideal way to experience poetry is to say it aloud, just as she hears the lines when she writes them. Busta's closeness to the word spoken or sung also makes clear why she, as we have seen, often uses folksongs in order to parody them for other, often irritating effects. Since the original texts are part of her audience's heart and soul, the *Verfremdung* affects listener and reader even more strongly.

In dedicating *Die Sternenmühle* and *Die Zauberin Frau Zappelzeh* to "Kinder und ihre Freunde" the poet presupposes the kind of reception that she might choose for all of her work: an enthusiastic sharing of her poetry by reader and listener, here parent and child, so that the enjoyment of poetry in itself becomes a bridge from one person to the next.

This desire of Busta provides a fuller context for the dedication of the two books. We have seen that the poet expects children and adults alike to find pleasure in the childlike form and content of *Sternenmühle* and *Zappelzeh.* But the phrase "für Kinder und ihre Freunde" may also imply some deeper dimension for Busta, a Christian poet with oftentimes religious messages. Perhaps Busta is implying here that we can enter the "kingdom of poetry" most easily through the gate of its earliest stage, *Kinderlyrik.* After all, to see and to enjoy the world and its mysteries again through the eyes of children prepares both those readers and listeners who are still children and those who are not children for more "adult" poetry. In Busta's work, at least, the other poetry to which we gain admittance through the children's poetry is often revelatory in nature as well.

Marilyn Scott and Petrus Tax. *MLN*. 101:3,
April, 1986, pp. 654–55

CABRERA, LYDIA (CUBA) 1900–

Lydia Cabrera . . . [has] accomplished the artistic manipulation of reality in the realm of the imaginary, making possible, once more, the memesis of which Aristotle spoke and that has been so badly misinterpreted so many times. Lydia Cabrera, who entered the field of literature with her book *Cuentos negros de Cuba* (Black tales of Cuba) first published in Paris in 1936, based her literary fictions on materials derived from her research into black Cuban cultures. . . .

Cabrera wrote her first book within the orbit of the avant-garde. She has indicated more than once that it was no accident that, in 1936, Gallimard published her *Cuentos negros* and Miguel Angel Asturias's *Leyendas de Guatemale;* the black and Indian experiences in the work of these authors, respectively, left their mark on the avant-garde school. Lydia Cabrera's long years—more than forty—of research on the culture of black Cuba provides the raw materials for her works of fiction: *Cuentos negros de Cuba, Porqué Ayapu, cuentos de Cuba,* and other narratives recently published but not yet collected in book form. In the prologue to *El Monte,* probably the most important of her scholarly works, she tells us that the blacks were her "living source" and that she studied "the profound and living footprints that they have left on this island, Cuba: magical and religious concepts, the beliefs and practices of the blacks who were imported from Africa over several centuries of uninterrupted slave trade." She goes so far as to say that the blacks, her blacks, are the real authors of her books. . . . [providing] real experiences that, in her works of fiction, are transfigured by virtue of poetic alchemy, into the sphere of the imaginary. . . .

The raw materials, the same ones that were the basis of her scholarly books . . . have been poetically transformed, becoming fictionalized, in her imaginative books, to acquire, in the process, "a certain autonomy in the face of historical events, an autonomy which, by removing them from the flow of time, preserves and protects them.

Rosario Hiriart. *Circulo.* 7, 1979,
pp. 125–26, 128

In Cuba, the wealth of material hidden in these folk tales was ignored for many years, and it was only in the 1930s, with the rise of interest in the Negro and his culture that their literary value was recognized. A group of writers became involved in the study of legends and myths brought to the island by the Negro slaves from Africa during the colonial period. They devoted their time and talent to this task, and in a few years, four collections of these stories were published. *¡Oh mio, Yemayá!* (1938) by Rómulo Lacha-tañeré, *Cuentos y leyendas negros de Cuba* (1942), by Ramón Guirao; and *Cuentos negros de Cuba* (1940) and *¿Por qué?* (1948) by Lydia Cabrera.

Lydia Cabrera is by far the most accomplished of the three authors and has distinguished herself as one of the writers who, after Fernando Ortiz, has made the greatest contribution to the field of Afro-Cuban studies. This paper deals with the technical and artistic development of Lydia Cabrera's narrative in relationship to the African heritage.

Lydia Cabrera, born in Havana in 1900, has devoted her entire life to the study of the African cultures which were brought to Cuba. She has assembled stories of myths, legends, superstitions, customs and ancestral rites which were transmitted orally and has collected this heritage which was in danger of disappearing, giving it artistic form but at the same time remaining always faithful to the original culture.

Surrounding this author are a series of circumstances which contributed to her early understanding of the African heritage, such as her birth in a country where black influence reaches all social classes and permeates all facets of daily life: her close contact with numerous black servants and friends during childhood and later, her residence in France from 1922 to 1939, a period in which there was a strong ethno-aesthetic feeling for the African world. While in Paris she carried out studies in Oriental civilizations where she encountered similarities with African folklore and she therefore renewed her interest in this field which lead her to write her first stories, published in Paris in 1936.

Since that time she has dedicated herself to investigative studies of live sources, the living heirs of an oral tradition, a labor which was to produce eight books in which folkloric documents are united with poetry, the fantastic and the real with the "costumbrista," and investigation with creation. Even today in exile she continues to move closer to the blacks with sympathy and love and she has been able to penetrate not only their past but also their idiosyncrasies, and both of these elements have served to sustain her literary work.

Lydia Cabrera uses the black heritage in a twofold manner: sociologically, which has given rise to books such as *El monte, La sociedad secreta Abakuá, Anagó, Refranes de negros viejos* and *Otán Ivebiyé;* and aesthetically. In this latter manner she does not merely reproduce old themes, but she elaborates upon them artistically and has created sixty-nine stories, gathered together in three collections: *Cuentos negros de Cuba, ¿Por qué?* and *Ayapá: Cuentos de Jicotea.*

In those stories in which the gods intervene, Lydia Cabrera has re-elaborated a series of basic myths common to all cultures but which have reached her strongly tinged with African characteristics. This long list of myths as well as the presentation of a well-organized pantheon, illustrate that the Lucumis and the Congos brought to Cuba a very rich mythology whose influence still endures.

The animal stories form a very important part of world folklore and especially of that of the African. In these stories the author preserves the African characteristics which have been altered by living on the island for more than three centuries, but at the same time she instills in her characters a psychological depth which neither the original Africans nor those of any other country ever possessed.

In the course of the migration from the Old World to America the heroes of these stories suffered changes; in each region there is a preference for a specific one. In Cuba the preferred animal is the "jicotea," or turtle, a weak but wise figure in whom the black saw his own situation reflected and whom he endowed with his idiosyncrasy. In these animal tales, reinvented by Lydia Cabrera, what stands out is the author's ability to create comic situations and to demonstrate her understanding irony toward the feelings of these animals which are representative of man.

In the stories which revolve around the world of man one encounters his loves, his hates, his cleverness, his stupidity, his battles against others, but above all, his struggles against destiny and his dependence upon unknown forces which reside within and outside of him. These men move in an atmosphere in which there is no separation between reality and magic, a world which can be called "marvelously real."

In the elaboration of this magic realism Lydia Cabrera alternates the supernatural with "costumbrista" sketches which are detailed with great realism; therefore, in each story there are two distinguishable planes: the real, with which it begins, and then the sudden step to super-reality when the marvelous circumstance emerges. In the portrayal of these human characters the author displays a very well-developed literary technique. . . .

Upon studying these stories of Lydia Cabrera one can be assured that the African heritage serves her as a pivot to create works of high literary quality and that the role she has played is not that of a simple collector, even though she may have brought them from an oral to a written form. By means of these creations the author has attained an outstanding place in the period of contemporary literature, which is marked primarily by modernist echoes and vanguardist associations which are reflected in her stories. Like the writers of the Lorquian generation and the poets of the movement known as Afro-Cuban—Nicolás Guillén, Ballagas, Carpentier, Pales Matos, etc.—to whom Lydia Cabrera is tied by contemporaneity and common tastes and influences, she wished to elevate the popular, represented in this case by the black, to an aesthetic level and she has fully achieved this by concretizing the African heritage which is preserved in Cuba in enduring artistic works.

> Rosa Valdes-Cruz. *Proceedings of the*
> *Seventh Congress of the International*
> *Comparative Literature Association*
> (Stuttgart: Erich Bieber, 1979), pp. 327–30

In her books *Cuentos negros de Cuba, ¿Por qué?* and *Ayapú,* the author immortalizes the poetry, the music, and the world view of the primitive manifestations of a disappearing civilization.

In other books like *El Monte, La sociedad secreta Abakua, Anagó, Ana-faurana: Los símbolos de la sociedad secreta Abakua,* and others, Lydia Cabrera has collected the anthropological, religious, and cultural essentials of the Afro-Cuban heritage.

But it is in her literary work, more than in her anthropological work that we delight in the poetic, musical, and marvelous world of the writer that Guillermo Torre called . . . the "black Aesop" of her generation. . . .

[Unlike other members of the Paris avant-garde] Lydia Cabrera had no interest in looking for "magic" in European or Oriental occultism. It was enough for her to collect the black world of her country of origin, which is infinitely richer in poetic possibilities than the astrology of the dream and the collective mythic mentality. . . .

More than Breton's doctrines, surrealist painting had an impact on Lydia, probably because of the pictorial impulse that we see in her own very vivid descriptions. . . .

Lydia Cabrera, although influenced by the avant-garde, surrealist tendency of her time, belongs more to a group of writers who use the surrealist energy to encounter a plane of reality in which reality and dream converge, in order to create in their writings a different focus on the reality of the blacks and Indians of America. . . .

The relationship that exists between the fiction of her stories and daily reality is that of all super-realistic work. Or rather, the fiction of Lydia Cabrera is a "new" reality, through the discovery of new spheres of reality and the implications of these experiences and interpretations of reality. Her fiction gives space to irrationality, hence to ambiguity, to myth, to dream, to the absurd. Narrative time will not be chronological, external, objective, but rather will be time specialized for various cases, interior and subjective.

The world of fiction is a marvelous reality, credulous and without mystification; a reality that belongs to the contemporaneous experience of imaginative invention. With this statement in mind, we can say that Lydia Cabrera's narrative reveals the authenticity of telluric force, the primitive religion, and the extraordinary.

Lydia Cabrera is one of the most multifaceted authors Cuba has produced, because of her bringing together separate identities as anthropologist, ethnographer, writer, and above all interpreter and preserver of the rich Afro-Cuban treasure.

We owe the presence of the magical Afro-Cuban world to Lydia Cabrera and her *Cuentos negros, ¿Por qué?* and *Ayapú.* She was one of the first writers to penetrate into this world, through a desire to return to her own, having already penetrated the mysterious East. . . .

In these tales, we encounter a wealth of sensuality, originality, plasticity, and color. It is a dynamic narrative, rich in folkloric popular elements. The abundant use of images and metaphors as onomatopoeic phonemes and sounds produces the sensory and rhythmic effects desired.

These stories reveal the ethnic multiplicity of Cuba. . . . In a Creole and nationalistic tone, she presents the indigenous child of the Cuban land, the telluric individual. Her social protest dimension lies within the ideals of collective betterment that inspires the Cuban people, evoking a profound feeling of human solidarity.

The literary manifestation is of great value, not only because of the aesthetic pleasure that it produces, but also because of the social sensitivity it demonstrates in defending the African man from exploitation, humiliation, discrimination, and social injustice, evoking in its readers a vein of sympathy that leads them to understand the complex problems of the African people in greater depth. These are stories told by a white woman writer, but one very capable of feeling and internalizing the heritage of African origins and hence of integrating it into the Cuban literary tradition.

Sara Soto. *Magia y historia en los Cuentos*
negros, ¿Por qué?, y Ayapú de Lydia
Cabrera (Miami: Ediciones Universal, 1988),
pp. 8–9

The intellectual presence of Lydia Cabrera in Cuba and Spanish America is marked by some twenty-two titles of works that focus on Afro-American themes. These books may be categorized under broad and various headings: fiction, linguistics, and folklore. But all of them, even the most rigorously scholarly and specialized ones, have as their common denominator artistic beauty reflected in verbal structure that encapsulate the material revealed. But there is something subtler, something that is perceived with increasing clarity as we advance through a critical reading of Lydia's work, and that is that the author is not trying to bring us close to the black as something outside of and foreign to our culture, but as an integral part of it.

Julio Hernández Miyares. *Circulo.* 18, 1989,
p. 130

CALISHER, HORTENSE (UNITED STATES) 1911–

It is always gratifying to make the acquaintance of a writer of intelligence and feeling; it is these qualities which most clearly mark the work of Hortense Calisher, whose stories in the last few years have made their quiet, cogent bids for our attention. Miss Calisher is an eminently sober writer; without affectations or flashiness. . . . It is a pity that this long view does not take in lighter-hearted areas. Miss Calisher seems quite undisposed toward humor, except of a rather grim sort.

Gertrude Buckman. *The New York Times.*
November 18, 1951, p. 46

[*False Entry* is] the work of a writer who knows what she wants to do and how she wants to do it. The style, at least at first, seems rather mannered, and indeed it is involved and allusive, but the further one goes, the more one recognizes how beautifully it suits her purpose. . . .

Identity is not given us; it is something that we either do or do not achieve. That Miss Calisher can take this familiar truth and make of it something fresh and exciting is proof of her deep insight and her mastery of a most difficult method. Despite her unconventional method of telling her story, Miss Calisher knows how to make use of the traditional arts of the novelist. . . . If her aim is to explore deeply the mysteries of a particular person, she is able to bring minor characters on the stage in such a way that we can see them clearly. The novel rewards the closest possible reading, but it can give a more casual kind of pleasure, too.

Granville Hicks. *Saturday Review of Literature.* October 28, 1961, p. 17

The overall impression of [*Tale for the Mirror*] is that Miss Calisher has settled rather more comfortably and somewhat less excitingly into the mold which she set for herself ten years back. Then, as now, her concern was with the "knell of sadness for something that had been, that had never quite been, that now had almost ceased to be." And this singular concern often involves her in a melancholy sentimentalism that blurs the acuity of her vision by reducing all of life's problems to the lack of communication between human beings. Loneliness—and the inability of people to live in the present because of it—is her theme. . . . If Hortense Calisher's intimate vignettes seem strangely static in a world mad with motion . . . she has at the same time created some of the most discomfortingly vivid writing of this decade.

Gloria Levitas. *New York Herald Tribune.* November 4, 1962, p. 13

Hortense Calisher's second novel [*Textures of Life*] attempts, and pretty well pulls off, something of a *Golden Bowl.* This one could not be symbolized by the extravagant *objet d'art,* with its bizarre flaw, conceived by James. Miss Calisher's material is the American bourgeoisie at home, and the textures of the lives she interweaves are homely. Hers is a Golden Bowl in, so to speak, basketwork. But the working is Jamesian indeed in firmness of structure and subtlety of superstructure. Sometimes she uses the master's very idiom—not in pastiche but as legitimately and creatively as Tiepolo used Veronese's. . . .

In James's nexus the Prince is admittedly not up to the other three. Yet it is not simply as a weak character that he lets the dance down. Weak characters can be boldly portrayed; but James is too relenting towards the Prince to make him a Vronsky or a George Osborne; the weakness lies not only in the Prince but in James—where it is perhaps a weakness for Italian young men, or just for princes. Miss Calisher's construction has a comparable flaw, and again in the younger generation. *Jeune premier* parts are always the hardest to do. Her David may not properly exist—there is little to him but a trick of letting his glasses slide down his nose—but he is waved into being by adroit sleight of hand. It is Elizabeth, reacting against her mother's "taste," bohemianly disregarding material objects except such as she herself, as a sculptor, makes, in whom one suspects a lightweightness of character and a college-girl pretentiousness of intellect—which the author seems not to realize. With the older couple Miss Calisher can do no wrong. The vivid, invalid's life of David's father, the vaguer but penetrating vision of Elizabeth's mother—she splendidly creates both and superbly counter-poises them. Miss Calisher is not only that rarity, a talented novelist, but that double-blossomed rarity, a talented novelist who is serious about art.

Brigid Brophy. *The New Statesman.*
September 13, 1963, p. 326

Hortense Calisher's *Extreme Magic,* a novella and a number of short stories, is a collection remarkable for uneven achievement. The sensibility is extremely feminine—in the faintly pejorative sense—and the talent diaphanous. . . . The writing is sometimes skillfully evocative, the nuances suggestive, the imagery just; but then there are ornaments (many of them) as trashy as 'the river gave a little shantung wrinkle." . . . But there are two stories, "The Rabbi's Daughter" and "The Gulf Between," that are harmoniously true and moving—even substantial—because they rise from authentic experience: in this case cultivated, haute-bourgeois, upper-West-Side Jewish life, a little down on its uppers. Miss Calisher has a real sense of a past . . . she can show where things come from; what people really are; how they feel; how they affect one another; why what happens happens.

Eve Auchincloss. *New York Review of
Books.* June 25, 1964, p. 17

[In *Journal from Ellipsia*] Hortense Calisher expends a great many words on a sophisticated science-fiction theme, and these words are not cleanly bolted into clear but complex structures so much as—as though they were all made of some colloidal substance—allowed to stick into great lumps, like long-forgotten sweets shaken out of a paper bag. Admittedly her literary problem is the representation of communion between two worlds—one here, one *out there*—and the effect of cotton wool coming out of, or being stuffed into, desperately communicating mouths may be regarded, by some readers, as appropriate. But the book, besides being very long, is very hard to read, and one wonders whether it was all worth it. What happens in *Journal from Ellipsia* is this: an androgynous creature from beyond tries to break through into this world; it contacts Janice, a beautiful anthropologist, who now wants to break out of this world into the one beyond. Her story is told, as it were, posthumously—the unearthly talking machine, the top arguing scientists, the throwing of the ball of narration to different players (including the one from out there). There are British characters, and they tend to speak in what I call the toodle-pip idiom, an American invention. This, in a book about intergalactic communication, makes everything said seem more implausible than it ought to.

Anthony Burgess. *The Listener.*
April 21, 1966, p. 589

The New Yorkers is a miraculous novel in that it is exactly equal to its ambition. For the first fifty or even hundred pages its ambition is hidden or apparently denied. You think you are reading a futility—another perhaps wise but old-style novel "rich in texture," "closely worked," patient beyond easy disclosure, afflicted with the paradox of a choking capaciousness. Then begins the extraordinary glimmer of Design, and very rapidly there is evidence of something new—newly against the grain of expectation.

The miracle is not in the language, which, though controlled and self-aware, is occasionally formally florid, like porcelain. Sentence by sentence it does not always distinguish itself. Yet the method of its obliqueness, its internal allusions, echoes, and murmurings, all this is uncommonly cunning and thick with the ingenuities of discovery. The miracle is nevertheless not in the language but in the incredible spite—everything is spited, from literary fashion straight up to the existentially-perceived cosmos. If the anti-novel can be defined in part as spiting expectations, then Calisher's concept of it belongs with Nabokov's. Like other "New" novels, *The New Yorkers* is also about itself—which is to say it aspires to fool, to lead, to play tricks with its own substance. But unlike others, especially unlike the most intelligent—for what is more intelligent than a novel by, say, Susan Sontag?—Calisher's novel is *about* intelligence. Or, better yet, Intelligence.

Cynthia Ozick. *Midstream.* November, 1969,
p. 77

Hortense Calisher . . . is one of our most substantial yet elusive writers. By any narrow or literal definition, she is becoming less and less a strictly narrative artist. Her characters are boundless states of mind. Not does she structure books conventionally: *Queenie* doesn't move; it spins, pausing for scenes, pausing for ideas. Mrs. Calisher appears also to borrow imaginatively from the other arts, giving the reader the feel of the dance, of the mobile, of sculpture. In *Queenie,* probably the most light-hearted of her novels, she has made a tripping entry into the mind of a present-day young girl, and has with wit and spirit fashioned a kind of ballet around the story of Queenie's coming of sexual and intellectual age.

The story unwinds in the form of tapes addressed to various "interlocutors," including the admissions dean of "Hencoop College" in New York, God, a Hencoop professor in whom for a time Queenie reposes some faith, and finally the President of the United States. . . .

The book overflows with ideas, couched in sparkling aphorisms. Touching on the generation gap, the sexual gap, the abysmal political gap, the communication gap. As the device of the tapes suggests, the story is, among other things, about someone who wants to have a good talk with *Someone.*

Lucy Rosenthal. *Saturday Review of Literature.* April 3, 1971, p. 34

Like any good writer, Hortense Calisher keeps a reader on the move. She has a "style," though it worries her when people say that, because for some it implies surface, a glib veneer with nothing beneath it. But she needn't worry. Her intelligence shows without aid of italics and block capitals. To be "carried away" is not in her case to be swept off into rhetorical clouds of Chestertonian pomp, but to be led on by the imagination into fresh perception, awe and an occasional all-out celebration. . . .

Hortense Calisher is a creator of voices, moods, states of mind, but not of worlds. Her fiction, like her autobiography [*Herself*], sends us back into the world we know; it may refresh and enhance it, but it does not, even for a moment, obliterate or remake it. This is not to say that she is, in some old-fashioned sense, a realist. On the contrary, rather than fabricating reasonable facsimiles of "things as they are," she takes certain "scenes" for granted and lets her quick wit and marvelous imagination play over them. If we know a bit about the scenes she selects, we're likely to find her works beautifully agile and astute. If not, she is not about to hammer the parts together for us.

Robert Kiely. *The New York Times.* October 1, 1972, pp. 3, 20

Hortense Calisher is one of those writers whose books are more admired than read. . . . Now the joint publication of her autobiography and her fifth novel may finally bring Calisher the recognition and readership she deserves. . . . *Herself* is Calisher's personal statement about her art—and it is nothing less than a vertiginous guided tour through the mind of a wise and witty woman of sixty who since her childhood knew she would be a writer. . . . Her literary and social criticism is provocative. The comments about Turgenev and Yukio Mishima (whom she admires) and Hemingway, Mailer and literary critics (whom she doesn't) are especially penetrating.

Arthur Cooper. *Newsweek.* October 16, 1972, p. 110

Calisher is a shrew observer of our social ills—displacements of youth, futilities of the rich—but she is more than a naturalist noting easy details, cataloging crimes or sins. She is a maker of fictions; she insists on private consciousness—even when this consciousness is extreme, obsessive, and "poetic." [*Eagle Eye*] is a powerful indictment of social wrongs by an odd hero who may see less (or more) than he believes . . . Calisher stuns us with the "magic forbidden leaps" of her imagination. She forces us to enter—and withdraw from—her narrator's mind; she offers few clues to his ultimate condition. But by testing us with her sharp vision she emerges here as a true creator—an eagle of fictionmakers.

Irving Malin. *The New Republic*. May 3,
1973, p. 26

Like many a beginning writer, Hortense Calisher drew first on her own life history, but, as she relates in her memoir *Herself,* "suddenly after less than a dozen close-to-autobiographical stories, their process is over; I want out, to the wider world." However much the stories, novellas, and novels that followed this change in direction differ from the early stories in their subjects and styles, the rites of passage theme proved to be an enduring and ever developing one. The Hester Elkin of the autobiographical stories is the first of many Calisher protagonists to come out into a world in which change is the only constant.

Three of Calisher's novels, though stylistically worlds apart from one another, dramatize young people's initiations into adulthood. *Textures of Life* (1963) is Calisher's most quietly conventional novel; *Queenie* (1971), an exuberant comedy of manners that blends the real and the surreal; *Eagle Eye* (1973), one of Calisher's most demanding works, plunges the reader into its protagonist's circuitous stream of consciousness.

Central to all three, however, is a movement (a recurring one in Calisher's fiction) from the heights—in *Textures of Life,* of a smugly superior perspective; in *Queenie,* of ingenious theorizing; in *Eagle Eye,* of emotional distancing—to an active grappling with mundane, problematic realities. Typically, in Calisher's works, the thematic emphasis is on both the movement *from* and *toward,* on the protagonists' rites of both extradition and initiation. Appropriately enough, all three novels conclude with an open-ended journey about to begin.

Kathleen Snodgrass. *Texas Studies in*
Literature and Language. 31, Winter, 1989,
p. 554

CAMPOBELLO, NELLIE (MEXICO) 1909–

In the chapter of Spanish American literature labeled the "Literature of the Mexican Revolution" there generally appear well documented cases for calling this body of literature novel, biography, memoir, chronicle, regional fiction and a host of other terms. Clearly, this is an effort to appraise and define what was the literary outgrowth of the social and political upheaval known as the Mexican Revolution of 1910. Despite the varied manifestations of this body of writing as reflected by the author as participant or observer, by the author's partisanship for or against a particular revolutionary figure, by the author's attitude toward the success or failure of the Revolution, by the author's stress on social problems, or by the realistic or poetic depiction of the Revolution's violent aspects, there seems to be general agreement that there was a substantial body of writing that can be attributed to the Mexican Revolution of 1910.

The list of writers and works, of varying length and quality, includes a wide spectrum of Mexico's most prominent "novelists" and "novels." Among those writers mentioned in most histories of Spanish American or Mexican literature, in studies of the literature of the Revolution, or in works limited to the novel or short story, there appears the name of Nellie Campobello with a line or two about her publications and their place in the literature of the Mexican Revolution. Generally brief mention is made of her two "novels"— *Cartucho* (1931) and *Las manos de mamá* (1937)—both episodic evocations of scenes witnessed in her childhood in the north of Mexico.

Where does Nellie Campobello fit into that group of writers and writings that emanated from the Revolution? Certainly not a major figure nor a prolific writer like Mariano Azuela or Martín Luis Guzmán, Campobello is nevertheless representative of one of the typical manifestations of the literature of the Revolution—the *memoria* or *estampa*—that both primitive and poetic literary form that captured the Revolution the way its artists depicted it with their pencils and brushes. This new art form, as Luis Leal so accurately points out in his study of the short story of the Mexican Revolution had to and did create its own norms, thus developing a new technique coupled with a new use of language and rhythm. Just as the year 1910 marked the beginning of the twentieth century in Mexico, so it did for its literature. The stuff of this writing is the armed struggle of the Revolution and later on its social reforms. Since the Revolution went through so many phases and suffered so many conflicts among its various factions, the material it offered its writers was almost inexhaustible. The themes they treated ran the entire gamut of life and death, although the balance tilted more to death than to life. The Mexican Revolution was violent and much of its literature dwells on the many variations of this theme. There is cruelty and greed, daring and disillusion, duty and patriotism, injustice and sacrifice, heroism and stoicism.

Nellie Campobello is frequently associated with Rafael F. Muñoz and Martín Luis Guzmán, generally considered the masters of the short story of the Mexican Revolution. All three concentrated on the struggles in the north of Mexico between the *villistas* and the *federales* and between the *villistas* and the *carrancistas*. . . .

Nellie Campobello's contribution to that "genre," on the one hand so difficult to define and on the other so rich in volume and variety, is the personal testimony of the writer as observer or bystander. For it should be pointed out that the two publications that represent her major literary contributions . . . are the works of a woman born on the eve of the Revolution in 1909, that also capture the period of her adolescence. . . . The reader is struck by the stark realism of the episodes of *Cartucho*. Life and death, violence and bloodshed, march across its pages like the soldiers and generals off to the war depicted. The author as child observer and narrator witnesses death and destruction as only the very young and the very old can—either too innocent to really comprehend or too old and too worn to care.

How then can one interpret Nellie Campobello's *Cartucho?* To this reader, more than evocations of impressions of her childhood, these stories are stylized versions of some recollections and also of some episodes told to the writer and recreated by her to fit a particular style. These *estampas* that on the surface seem cold and indifferent, brutal and primitive, cruel and childish, are deliberate prose creations so designed as to shock the reader with the normality of the absurd, with the casualness of the cruel, and with the ordinariness of the horrible. This style, so simple and yet so complex, was elaborated by Nellie Campobello whose experience as a writer before the publication of *Cartucho* was limited to a volume of poetry, *Yo, por Francisca* (1929) and some newspaper articles. She herself alluded to her search for an appropriate framework for her stories when she said: "Me propuse, desde aquel momento, aclara, hablar las cosas que yo sabía, y así lo expuse a mis amigos. pero quererlo no me hacía capas; necesitaba yo una disciplina." The term *disciplina* with its connotations of strictness, rigor and form is the essence of *Cartucho's* style.

What holds *Cartucho* together either as a "novel" or as a collection of short stories is the fabric that Campobello weaves of the brutality of a struggle that pits Mexican against Mexican and that in its immense scope sucks in its civilian population. Page after page and episode after episode appear putting into words, very few words indeed, what it is like to live with war and with its dead and dying as part of one's everyday existence. . . .

In addition to the named and the nameless, thee are two figures whose presence one feels throughout *Cartucho*—Francisco Villa and Nellie Campobello's mother. They are the two heroes of Campobello's writings. . . .

Campobello's mother, her person and her spirit, permeate the pages of *Cartucho* so that the more lyrical *Las manos de mamá,* published six years later, seems like a natural outgrowth of the earlier work. . . .

Las manos de mamá is a kind of hymn or eulogy to Nellie Campobello's mother. In this work she is the central figure who occupies the entire stage. Whereas in *Cartucho* she is seen as strong, proud and brave in the face of civil war, here she is evoked as gentle, tender, loving and playful. Campobello refers to her throughout as "Ella" with a capital E who infused her children with her beauty and her youth. . . .

Nellie Campobello occupies a unique place in the literature of the Mexican Revolution. She is the only woman of her generation . . . to dedicate herself to a career in both arts and letters. Campobello combined two professions, dancing and writing. . . . *Cartucho* and *Las manos de mamá* stand on their own merits. In both "novels" the writer has juxtaposed horror and

tenderness, beauty and ugliness, chaos and tranquility, capturing in her own way the Revolution as it was lived by the men, women and children of Mexico.
Gabriella De Beer. *The American Hispanist.*
4:34–35, March–April 1979, pp. 14–16

Nellie Campobello's *Cartucho* (1931) is the most unusual novel of the Mexican Revolution. Like its counterparts, it is characterized by an episodic structure, an autobiographical format, and an epic vision of the revolutionary experience. But unlike the other novels of this subgenre, stylistic consciousness and effect are central to the novel's theme and experience. As many critics have pointed out, *Cartucho* is paradoxically both the most poetic and the most violent novel of the Revolution. The key to this paradox is the stylistic technique of subtle understatement and indirect expression. By poeticizing violence and brutality, the narration shocks the reader, causing the emotional impact of horror, compassion, and sorrow to penetrate deep into the reader's consciousness. The same is true of the novel's narrative point of view, which shifts between that of a child and that of an adult. The child's point of view, which dominates throughout the novel, presents the Revolution from a coldly objective and emotionally aloof perspective. The adult's point of view, which is more subtle and indirectly expressed, evokes, on the other hand, a profoundly human emotional reaction towards the everyday experiences of the Revolution. The contrast between the two points of view functions again to understate surface emotions, which in turn deepens their internal impact. In no other novel of the Revolution is the meaning of this historic event more vividly portrayed in terms of human suffering, brutality, and death.

Cartucho's subtitle, "Relatos de la lucha en el norte," suggests the novel's content. The narration consists of fifty-six brief sketches or vignettes of local figures or events from the violent war years of the Revolution. The majority of the vignettes relate a single incident which usually ends in the violent death of the figure who is the subject of the passage. Not all the vignettes deal with death, however; some are even comical, such as the passage in which Pancho Villa steals a boxcar full of watermelons. Others produce an effect of sadness or melancholy, such as the story of Bartolo Santiago and his sister who love each other dearly but can never be reconciled because of the sister's erring ways. The vignettes are presented randomly so that from episode to episode there are abrupt changes of tone and mood. Consequently, the reader perceives a composite view of life under extreme circumstances in which humor, sadness and, most prominently, death are all intermixed. . . .

Cartucho's narrative technique is based on understatement and indirect expression. Most critics emphasize the novel's cold, aloof, emotionless narrative tone and demonstrate considerable shock that the narrative point of view is that of a female child. Campobello intends, however, to elicit the reader's emotional involvement and identification with her fictional world. Throughout the apparently objective narration, there are a number of subtle suggestions of the narrator's true emotions, which are dominated by a profound sense of pathos. The key to the novel's narrative technique is the continuous shifting of perspective between the child's and the adult's contrasting views of reality.

Dennis J. Parle. Kentucky Romance
Quarterly. 32:2, 1985, pp. 201–2

Campobello's name is familiar to readers of literature of the Mexican Revolution; her blood-chilling yet tender evocations of a war-torn childhood are known under the title *Cartucho* (1931). Very few of her readers, however, are aware that she also wrote poetry or that her very first publication, which appeared in 1929, was a modest collection of fifteen poems entitled simply *Yo* whose author was identified as "Francisca," a quasi-pseudonym.

Its publication passed unremarked, which is not surprising in view of the fact that confessional verse by young women of the upper classes was hardly considered a noteworthy literary genre in Mexico at the time. The poetic debut of an aspiring female was generally confined to a local readership, and, if relatives and "proper society" could possible help it, such talent was nipped in the bud. . . .

Yo is therefore an apt title for Campobello's modest collection of early poems, as is her decision to identify herself simply as "Francisca;" the urge toward self-revelation is countered by a need for self-concealment. It is also possible that she chose to use her second name, Francisca, through identification with her hero, Francisco (Pancho) Villa. . . .

Two years after *Yo*, Campobello published her major work, *Cartucho*. These prose memoirs of the Revolution had been gestating in her mind and on paper for some time. We know this thanks to a lengthy autobiographical prologue that Campobello wrote to a 1960 edition of her collected works of *apologia pro vita sua*—in itself, a valuable document.

In the writing of *Yo*, Campobello established the primacy of the subjective experience. Through the articulation of her own inner turmoil and her refusal to relinquish autonomy, she achieved what might be called a higher level of psychological insight and sensitivity. De Beauvoir mentions this as a positive corollary to the suffering of the adolescent female, for "this complexity enriches her, and her inner life develops more deeply than that of her brothers. . . ; [s]he can give weight to the revolts that set her against the world." It was this heightened subjective awareness together with her commitment to moral principles that led her to the literary structure of *Cartucho*. . . .

The divided self of *Yo, por Francisca* is transcended in *Cartucho,* the work of a more mature artist. The young female, no longer asking pardon for her transgressions, has become a primary witness of history; Campobello had found her place, her literary *raison de être.*

Doris Meyer. Revista de Estudios
Hispanicos. 20:2, May, 1986,
pp. 51–52, 59–62

Nellie Campobello published *Cartucho: Relatos de la lucha en el norte* in Ediciones Integrales in 1931, yet of all the novelists of the Revolution she is the one who gets the least notice. In a *macho* world, she is not taken into account, and—give me a break—what's woman doing at the shotgun orgy, anyway? That's all we need; Nellie's too amusing, Nellie's too descriptive, Nellie's too "clever," so she is relegated to giving impressions, brilliant images seen from the balcony: a curious creature leafing inadvertently through a ghastly book that has nothing to do with her. And that's how she tells it, naïvely, with the candor of childhood: scenes that astonish in their cruelty and because they are witnessed by a little girl.

Ever since, Nellie writes as if she were firing bullets. Her sentences always hit the bull's eye, scorch with their directness, their absolute lack of elaboration. Unlike other writers of the Revolution, Nellie never criticizes it; on the contrary, she maintains almost as much devotion for the Revolution as she does for her mother. She feels no mistrust; everything it does is well done, everything can be justified, everything has its reason. She is still the little girl who sees a group of ten men take aim at one young man on his knees, badly wounded, his hands outstretched toward the soldiers, already dying from fear. She notices with interest how the body gives a terrible leap as the bullets hit it, how the blood gushes from numerous holes. It lies three days next to her window and Nellie gets used to the scrawny pile; when someone or other carries it off in the night, she misses it. "That dead body really belong to me."

Accustomed to violence, to cruelty, Nellie's familiar world is the world of executed men. They are a part of her childhood. In *Las manos de Mamá* she bequeathes us memorable pages about her mother, the real one and the other one: the Revolution. Her mother is a heroine who, as well as sewing on her machine to support her children, runs out to save people dear to her, and runs back in again to hem petticoats, turn up cuffs for little girls of school age. But "What was the poor little noise of that machine compared with the shouts of the cannon? . . . How many pounds of flesh would they come to in total? How many eyes and thoughts?" Strange little girl who thinks of heavy gunfire as a song and talk of the pounds of flesh made up by the dead bodies.

Elena Poniatowska. Introduction to Nellie Campobello. *"Cartucho" and "My Mother's Hands"* (Austin: University of Texas Press, 1988), pp. ix–xiv

In her two novels, Nellie Campobello deals with her themes in a most original fashion. The epic-choral structure of *Cartucho,* with the multiple characters and narratives, eliminates the vision of the individual, unique, unconquerable hero, putting the collectivity first, the people who made the Revolution. Appropriately, the central character of *Las manos de mamá,* viewed from different perspectives, yields a complex being, worthy of affection, admiration, and imitation, a mother who bears no resemblance to her traditional Mexican image, a mother building the future of her children and her nation. *She, I, You,* what a difference there is between these people and at the same time how much similarity; for, as the narrator says, "One hand fine and white, the other toasted and hard. They are two separate hands, yet they are the same."

Laura Cázares H. In Aralia López-Gonzalez
et al, eds. *Mujer y literatura mexicana y
chicana: Culturas en contacto,* vol. 1
(Mexico City: Colegio de Mexico, Tijuana:
Colegio de la Frontera del Norte, 1988),
pp. 168–69

CAMPOS, JULIETA (CUBA–MEXICO) 1932–

Fiction for Julieta Campos marks the apotheosis of a writing that fills the irrepoachable and silent void caused by two existential fatalities: love (Eros) and death (Thanatos). In her essays on literary theory collected in *La imagen en el espejo* (The mirror's eye) and *Función de la novela* (The novel's function), Campos has provided us with the keys to her own narrative. She notes that writing "never knows what it is seeking, ignores what it has to say; it is invention, the invention of the world and of man, constant invention and perpetual challenge." Concerning the irreproachable void, the discloses, "I always knew, secretly, that writing was a way of filling what I kept on experiencing as a void, despite all the true gratifications of real life." And furthermore, she compares writing to the attempt of Orpheus to save Eurydice, the object of his love, from death: "Faithful to the urgent need to bring to light the obscure object of that desire, Orpheus reclaims Eurydice every time a text emerges from silence." Campos's novels are an attempt to confront with art the inadequacies of life. They are a means of facing personal crises such as illness, of exorcising feelings about the nature of time and death, and of inhabiting the interstices of a reality rent by her aspirations for something more than the world can offer.

Muerte por agua (Death by water), her first novel, published in its third and definitive version in 1978, was a reaction to her mother's bout with cancer, an attempt to fill with words the distance that separated mother and daughter living in different countries. In *Muerte por agua* Campos established several constants in her narrative style and discovered a few points of contact with the French "new novel." In her intimate and detailed narrative the constants that emerge are a minimal plot; imperceptible physical motion; the failure of the characters to act decisively; the characters' sensitivity and great receptivity to internal voices of conscience and to their surroundings, which are sharply contrasted with the banal conversations sustained between them; their self-reflexive natures circumscribed by a specific physical setting; situations and thoughts devoid of logical relations to each other which, as a result, force the reader to supply the missing links; time as a corrosive element—symbolized by water, rain, termites, and even man-eating plants—that dilutes, devours, invades, and finally takes possession of city, house, body; and the presence of blinding light, ships and shipwrecks on the high seas, shells, paintings, and photographs. In connection with the French "new novel," *Muerte por agua* features the similar protagonist-narrator who subjectively selects and obsessively zeroes in on certain objects; the absence of the dynamics inherent in a traditional plot; and, above all, a subliminal dialogue similar to that found in Nathalie Sarraute's novels, like "a muted battle in which a true sense of life and death vie to emerge amidst commonplaces."

It appears that these links between Campos's first novel and the French "new novel" have led some critics astray in their judgment of her second novel, *Tiene los cabellos rojizos y se llama Sabina* (A redhead named Sabina), a work in which an artist depicts herself during the creative process and renders a work similar to Velázquez's painting *Las Meninas* (1656) and Picasso's *Carnets de la Californie* (1955). . . .

Sabina's outstanding accomplishment does not lie in the exploration of its own genesis but rather in its fusion of theme and novelistic structure, a unified, defiant challenge to the inexorable flow of time in the novel, which progresses towards no conclusive outcome. . . .

Plural meanings emerge in an unceasing dialogue sustained by author, text, and reader. *Sabina's* polysemous structure seems to defy reorganization into ordered, sequential episodes in time, thus denying the reader a traditional plot and a traditional reading. In doing this, Campos challenges the flow of time toward forgetfulness, toward the novel's end, toward the deaths of the protagonists. The entire novel takes place during the moment the main character, Sabina, looks out at the sea at five o'clock in the afternoon on the last day of her vacation in Acapulco.

While the steady, slow rhythm of the rain in *Muerte por agua* emphasizes the successive and unbearable plodding of time victorious, *Sabina* is a spell conjured against time. By unleashing an unceasing and implacable flood of memories, hopes, mirages, and fantasies, Campos attempts to meet and hold off the inexorable flow of time. The closed spaces—city, house, garden—of the short stories in *Celina o los gatos* (Celina or the cats) explode in *Sabina* into magical realms of imagination and creativity shaped by the multiple meanings of a text which Campos describes as "a propitious meeting place of confluent magnetism."

In Campos's novel *El miedo de perder a Eurídice* (Fear of losing Eurydice), water continues to prevail as a "two-edged symbol: at once, life and death." As in *Sabina,* the absence of a plot and the presence of an immobilized protagonist persist in *Eurídice:* a professor of French, seated at the Palace of Minos café in Mexico, reads a novel by Jules Verne, draws an island on a napkin, dreams of adventures and shipwrecks, and writes a diary that coincides with a love story. "Everything that happens, happens as he waits there, at the moment when writing comes between fantasy and reality." In *Eurídice* that moment becomes populated almost exclusively with the artistic heritage of Western cultures. . . .

El miedo de perder a Eurídice sublimates human love; art rescues love from death. The novel is the desire, the eternal search for a utopia, transformed into writing about writing and, by extension, about Western cultures.

Evelyn Picon Garfield. *Women's Voices*
(Detroit: Wayne State University Press,
1985), pp. 76–79

For some critics, the Cuban novel exists only insofar as its subject or its author is in some relation to the Revolution. This is not only the case for those critics who work on the island. The many studies published outside Cuba in the past twenty years also seem to corroborate this statement. In none of the serious recent works about Cuban literature is the work of Julieta Campos discussed. Nonetheless, neither her status as a Cuban nor a distinct place in Latin American letters can be denied to this writer, a notable essayist and novelist.

The failure of her work to achieve resonance in the critical studies of Cuban literature is not owing to any denial of her Cuban-ness on Julieta Campos's own part. On the back of her books, it always states that she was born in Havana in 1932. We also know that after graduating from the Faculty of Philosophy and Letters of the University of Havana, she left Cuba and now lives in Mexico. Julieta's Cuban roots go back several centuries. . . .

Criticism has seen the original of her narrative forms, her system of writing, in Julieta's work. But it has not stopped to consider its deep significance. . . . In Julieta Campos's narrative, Cuba is profoundly present. The Cuban quality is not in her prose, nor in patriotic emotion, nor the reflection of the political and social vicissitudes of the island. Her books do not conceal a manifesto. Her narrative work "is characterized by the abolition of boundaries between discursive prose and poetic thought." And it is this lyrical side of Julieta Campos that makes her recreate the Cuban quality and try to translate the ineffable climate of that Cuban quality, the nostalgia and homesickness, the customs, the narrow circle of the family, what Cinthio Vitier has called "the sound" of Cuba, the wind, the sea. Julieta Campos approaches Cuba with a love born of distance. We should remember that it was also from Mexico that "Heredia began the Cuban poetic englightenment out of the nostalgia of an exile. . . ."

In the work of Julieta Campos, there are many examples to confirm what Cinthio Vitier states about "our true telluricity" being "marine and aerial." Sea and wind are repeated as obsessions. . . . All of Julieta Campos's work shows a constant integration of the Cuban quality because Julieta, as Cinthio Vitier de Avellaneda has said, "in Cuban inside, inside her sensibility."

Martha Martinez. *Revista Iberoamericana.*
51, 1985, pp. 793–94, 796–97

Campos structures *She Has Reddish Hair and her Name is Sabina* so that multiple narrative possiblities can come into play. She takes as her point of departure the ineffable vision of her protagonist, Sabina. She integrates into the novel's structure this incomplete, albeit privileged, perspective on reality. She contrasts the works of the woman with the rock maple desk and the novel projected by Sabina with that of the man in "the labyrinth." In this way, she shows us the female novel in gestation, which is paradigmatic of the principal creative stages for Julieta Campos herself, as well as of the literary and social condition of women. Ultimately, *She has Reddish Hair and her Name is Sabina* reveals that Julieta Campos is a competent author, highly aware of her job and of the situation of the woman who writes literature, the woman who must seek her own mode of expression, as Campos has done in her text, in order to be able to affirm and realize herself through literary creation.

Alicia Rivero Potter. Revista ibero-
americana. 51, 1985, p. 907

The reader or audience that demands anything resembling a defined plot or sequence of action will be bewildered by *Jardín de invierno,* which completely abandons such concepts to explore the creation of theatrical mood and the ambiguities of memory. The play's affinities are with such authors as Beckett or such nondramatic works as Fuentes's *Cumpleaños* or the novels of Robbe-Grillet. Dialogue and action are highly ritualized and do not really convey an accessible content as such. Rather, the play functions on the double levels of conscious memory and metatheater. These are represented by the two physical levels of staging, one above the other, and by the characters who inhabit them: la Mujer del Piso Alto, who vanishes for much of the play: and the presumably more concrete characters la Mujer de Edad Indefinida, la Mujer del Sombrero de Paja de Italia, and el Hombre, who are apparently on the liner *Mauretania.*

Jardín de invierno is above all a visual play with strong cinematographic overtones, as though it had been influenced by the surrealist films of the 1920s. The difficulty in reading a text of this nature is that it cannot begin to suggest the potential for live production. A skilled director could give it a shape which is not easily visible in the printed version, and with a good cast—such as the 1986 production boasted—Juliet Campos's play could be a powerful theatrical experience.

Frank Dauster. World Literature Today. 64,
1990, p. 80

Un heroísmo secreto offers a compilation of reviews, reflections, and observations published between 1975 and 1982 in such Mexican journals as *Vuelta* and *Plural.* . . . The questioning of the uniqueness of the woman writer's experience will please some readers, whereas others may ask if the author is antifeminist. There are several pieces on Campos's travels, for reasons related to her profession. While en route, she frequently allows her attention to be distracted, turning inward to a private landscape.

Also an author of fiction (*Tiene los cabellos rojizos y se llama Sabina, El miedo de perder a Eurídice*), Campos reveals in her journalistic writings as much of her own esthetic perspective as she does of the writers and realities she evokes. As she herself indicates in the introductory paragraph: "A silent, secret heroism marks the act of writing, the commitment of the writer with the truth of her imagination and the freedom of her dreams." In compiling the volume, then, she is undoubtedly searching both for self-understanding and for the way in which this inner self can be revealed to the public. The chronological ordering resembles the ordering of an autobiography, and readers are asked to read through the lines to an understanding of Julieta Campos, she herself being ultimately the *Isla* or "Island" she consistently mentions: ubiquitous yet never truly anchored, always the focus in this search for a hero's secret. As she writes of her own geography, she guides us toward and into it, and her writing becomes her space: "Writing, that space created by desire." *Un heroísmo secreto* is a eulogy to the craft of literary creation; readers may react more or less favorably to specific evaluations by Julieta Campos, but they will not doubt the sincerity of her intent.

Kathleen N. March. *World Literature Today.*
64, 1990, p. 81

CAPÉCIA, MAYOTTE (MARTINIQUE) 1928–53

The intial situation in Mayotte Capécia's work *La négresse blanche* (The white negress) . . . metaphorically expresses the ambiguous situation of the woman of color in the French West Indies of the 1940s. She is a figure of tragic *déchirement,* torn in two. As the novel opens, Isaure, the "white Negress," finds herself locked in a room, her own bar, with three white men, two officers and a sailor, whom she says she despises but is forced (or chooses) to serve as customers. Outside the door, in the night, are *négres* whom Isaure scorns and fears and whom she refuses to admit to her establishment. The situation is symbolic of the colored woman's, (in the original "femme de couleur"), psychological and social incarceration and her dilemma: Assertive, fiercely proud, desirous of being financially independent, Isaure is nevertheless dependent on her white clients and remains a prisoner of her fears and prejudices against blacks, as Clarisse Zimra says, a pawn and a go-between, between two traditionally hostile groups. Capécia's protagonists as well as Lacrosil's, isolated in their own land, choose to abandon their society and for them the journey to France is peceived as the only means of escape from an intolerable, untenable situation.

The journey to France, like the journey to Africa in Maryse Condé's and Miriam Vieyra's novels, thus becomes at once a physical and a psychological voyage, the journey of an alienated, homeless individual in search of the motherland, of a people in exile who have three potential "homelands": the Caribbean, Europe and Africa; of a people deprived of their identity who have a triple heritage: African, European, and Antillean. Caribbean woman, the *assimilée* (a French term for an educated French subject or citizen born into a foreign culture but steeped in the values and traditions of French "culture"), like her male counterpart, is tragically exiled from herself. She is caught in a bind. Isaure locked in her bar and Sapotille in her cabin on the ship are imprisoned, yet paradoxically safe. By isolating themselves, by fleeing, they do not need to, and indeed cannot, rid themselves of their distorted values and point of view.

> Elizabeth Wilson. In Carole Boyce Davies
> and Elaine Savory Fido. *Out of the Kumbla:*
> *Caribbean Women and Literature.* (Trenton,
> New Jersey: Africa World Press, 1990),
> pp. 47–48

By the twentieth century, the female mulatto character had fused both higher and lower strains; not unexpectedly, since structuralism has taught us that a symbol is always contaminated by its opposite referent. In Capécia's novels, the heroine could be both the self-sacrificing *doudou,* little more than a pet animal whose affections do not run deep (and who can, therefore, be easily discarded since she's expected to recover just as easily); or the conniving Circe who gets what's coming to her and whom it behooves any self-respecting gentleman to discard after use. But dutiful or not, Massa's daughter still was being defined exclusively in terms of the white, male, scale of values.

Precisely because Mayotte Capécia was a second rate writer (and there subsist doubts as to her authorship), she exhibited rather nakedly in her work the racial strictures of her colonial society, what Fanon has decried as the neuroses of the lactification complex. Kept in the comfort she could not afford by a Frenchman who will eventually leave, the empty-headed high yellow woman of *Je suis martiniquaise* (1948) consoles herself with the idea that her son will at least (and at last) look whiter and climb farther than she. The formula was successful and turned up again, barely amended, in a second novel. World War II had just ended in a Gaullist victory. Here was a colonial making points in the *mé*tropole by writing a "true" story deprecating "false" Frenchmen. Her pseudo-autobiographical heroine sailing away to the land of *liberté-égalité-fraternité* vindicated an offical policy which was refusing, in a carrot and stick fashion, to grant the islands autonomy. Although she became a tad politicized in *La Négresse blanche* (1950), standing up to her white, Martinique-born mother-in-law, her heroine never really shook off her own prejudices. It was this naked cynicism about bartering sex for material survival that angered Fanon so.

If to recover the past it is necessary to throw out the false fathers, Fanon's career was exemplary. But the writer who, with Sartre, argued that the "cracker" creates the "nigger" much as the anti-semite creates the jew, contradicted his own logic when he put the blame full on the rump of the fundamental Other, the whoring accomplice in Massa's bed. Fanon's outrage jolted a whole generation out of complacency but overlooked. . . . more poignant questions. While *Black Skins, White Masks* devotes plenty of space to the unjust humiliation of the black man, little is spent on the corresponding degradation of the black female. As a good Marxist, Fanon must have known that systemic oppression acts dialectically. Could it be that a double patriarchy left its women no choice but to trade sex for safety?

> Clarisse Zimra. In Carole Boyce Davies and
> Elaine Savory Fido. *Out of the Kumbla:*
> *Caribbean Women and Literature*
> (Trenton, New Jersey: Africa World Press,
> 1990), p. 149

In *Je suis martiniquaise,* Mayotte must confront the consequences of her choices after her lover leaves her with a child, sending a check as his farewell, ironically accompanied by a request that she speak to her son about him having been "un homme supérieur" [a superior man]. The check, which she rightly sees as a measure of his disdain, shatters the false dream of placid domesticity that she had accepted as the height of happiness and for which she had given up a life of work which she must now resume. The lover's departure, however, signals an openness to a reconciliation with her father, a reintegration into a life she left behind to pursue the elusive dream of a white man's love and bourgeois respectability. Her return to her village is presented as a period of penance or her "betrayal of her race" in having had a white man's child and allows Capécia to explore the changing attitudes towards race in Martinique after the war, attitudes characterized by a more militant celebration of blackness and a growing repudiation of all liaisons with whites, both of which deepen Mayotte's alienation. Ultimately, the character's own development is limited, however, and she continues to state her desire to marry a white as she prepares to leave for France; but, in her distress and her penance, she has salvaged important aspects of her dignity and has achieved a reconciliation with her dead whom, in a glimpse of hope in the text, she carries within her as she sails away.

> Lizabeth Paravisini-Gebert. *Callaloo.* 15,
> 1992, pp. 70–71

CARDINAL, MARIE (FRANCE) 1929–

A woman may, as a writer, not feel the necessity of showing herself to be a woman in her work. But can she be unaware of the existence of a different reading of the words? Isn't the author also the first reader? An affirmative answer to these questions lies in the choice of a "bisexual-neuter" writing. For Cardinal, technical language, which is specialized, is read in the same way whether it is used by a man or a woman. The latter, in choosing it, would immediately be taken seriously; the combat would be nonexistent. This often hermetic and incomprehensible language, used principally by thinkers and philosophers, should, however, as in the past, be written for a privileged audience, an elite. Now, these days these people have a great wish to reach a wider audience than that of the specialists; for this reason they publish with well-known and nonspecialist houses like Grasset, Seuil, Gallimard. Cardinal interprets this "acte manqué" as the result of an internal censorship that favors the use of technical language. This language, she explains, not only has no sex, but *lets nothing of the body of those who use it get through.*"Are they [Barthes, Deleuze, Foucault, Dolle, Poulantzas] so afraid of their *bodies* that they no longer have any *voice?* What are the real words that they are hiding under those of their erudition?" . . .

We know the position of Marie Cardinal: not to justify nor to explain oneself, "to write brutally and disrespectfully." Women writing must no longer excuse themselves nor put on makeup to please. We have to finish with the ornamented, image-laden, lacy, disguised writings, which are delightful but don't have "the brutal and simple power of fine male writing." To avoid shutting ourselves off in the female ghetto once more, it is important to use the same language without paying attention to the prohibitions of usage, without adapting it, without retouching it, and force, by this disrespectful usage, help the reader to open up towards the meaning of the words. . . .

Let us trace Cardinal's trajectory on this subject. All her demands seem in fact to limit a disengagement of women from the *past* and an equality in the *established* use of words. A woman's "I want to be free" must have the same "grandeur" and "beauty" as a man's "I want to be free." Cardinal ostensibly aspires to a writing whose "brutal and simple strength" would be the equivalent of a man's. Desire for paternity? Inevitable recourse to the seal of approval of male authority? Not exactly. Cardinal wants, through the unchanged use of the material, to denounce the lacks in existing language and its failure to translate the truths of woman. For that, she says, we must "put ourselves into our bodies, to express the unexpressed."

Trinh T. Minh-ha. *French Forum.* 8:1,
January, 1983, pp. 48–52

In 1966. . . . a little-known French writer named Marie Cardinal published *La Souricière,* a novel about a young mother who deteriorates into a prolonged state of physical and mental inertia and ultimately commits suicide. The book made little impact at the time of its publication, although its author had received the Prix International du Premier Roman in 1962 for her first novel, *Ecoutez la mer,* and scattered critical acclaim for her second work, *La Mule de Corbillard,* in 1964. Cardinal was to wait another ten years before *Les Mots pour le dire* attracted widespread literary praise and established her as a leading spokeswoman for the female condition.

Les Mots pour le dire was a "thundering success," selling 320,000 copies in its first two years. Cardinal's readers, predominantly female, were attracted by the compelling voice of a middle-aged woman who found "the right words" to describe her seven years of psychoanalysis and whose release from debilitating forms of depression could be their own. Cardinal came to represent for her public a success story wrought by the mysteries of psychoanalysis, a form of treatment that did not become fashionable in France until the 1970s. Few have read her earlier work on madness, *La Souricière,* which presented a grimmer reality.

La Souricière and *Les Mots pour le dire* are two radically different examples of the psychiatric novel written by the same person on the basis of the same experience. The first is predominantly a work of anguish and defeat, culminating in the triumph of insanity. The second, "the book of an adventure that takes place through psychoanalysis," describes the author's rebirth into sanity. Together, like the two halves of *The Bell Jar,* they constitute the story of breakdown and recovery.

La Souricière is not, however, the literary equal of *Les Mots pour le dire.* Whereas the latter work displays the hard-won authority of the mature woman and author, the earlier book exhales the tremulous and disquieting breath of adolescence. Its psychological interest derives primarily from viewing it as an early, partially successful attempt to transpose mental illness into the familiar fictive form of the novel of the individual, with the ironical twist that it entails an apprenticeship into madness. . . . A young woman is removed from the South of France by marriage and installed into Parisian domesticity where instead of sensual freedom she experiences the deadening effects of three successive pregnancies. In less than five years the marriage of Camille and François—she a young Provençal who had scarcely passed her baccalaureate and he a Sorbonne professor fifteen years her senior— breaks apart. Camille closes into herself, into a terrifying world of obsession with her body and physical decay. As Camille becomes further imprisoned in morbid images of bodily decomposition, avoiding her husband and children as much as possible, he turns to the conventional outlet for married men: other women. At twenty-nine Camille feels that she and her marriage are finished," that only death could deliver her from such a life, and she had an appalling fear of death. She felt like a prisoner caught in a sordid mousetrap." . . .

Maternity had been the agent that brought to Camille's consciousness an awareness of her own mortality, and this terrifying awareness makes "normal" activities impossible. For years she is paralyzed by death anxiety and even when she makes a cosmetic cure, she is unable to sustain her recovery because it has not been built upon a confrontation with the true sources of her illness. . . .

Marie Cardinal suggests . . . *because* women produce babies, because they learn through childbirth that the body has a will of its own, that it moves implacably toward the generation of new bodies at the expense of the old, they become tragically aware of their own impotence in the face of biology, aging and death. Some women cannot tolerate this knowledge within the bonds of sanity. Why some women experience maternity as the gateway to insanity and others as the gateway to salvation does not lend itself to easy answers.

In *La Souricière* Cardinal was trying not to understand "why" but, rather, to describe in the conventional literary form of the third-person novel what it feels like to be in the grip of madness. Despite the novel's obvious failings—its adolescent self-absorption, its lack of fully developed characters, its sometimes unconvincing plot, its uneven style—it has the merit of successfully translating the mad woman's underworld into a terrain accessible to the uninitiated. . . .

Of the many psychiatric novels written by women during the past two decades, *Les Mots pour le dire* presents a remarkable example of female specificity. Speaking in the voice of the first person, the author recounts her history of a mental illness that took the form of an abnormality in menstruation—a menstrual period lasting for more than three years. . . .

What the blood masks is the true subject of the novel: a woman living in perpetual fear, afraid of falling down, of dying, of decomposing; haunted by the sense of her inner darkness; given to the hallucination of a "living eye" that follows her about; and fearful that others will notice her psychic warp. This is the clinical picture she presents at the onset of a psychoanalysis that lasts seven years.

The problem of Cardinal the analysand, as for Cardinal the writer, is contained in the title of the book: how does one find "the words to say it"? For the patient vis-à-vis her doctor, the dilemma is "how to find the words that would flow from me to him? How to construct the bridge. . . ." For the artist, how to find the words that will transmute interior monologue and psychoanalytic dialogue into literature? Words, in this context, have an extra dimension because, as Cardinal tells us, "for the mentally ill, words and objects are as much alive as people or animals." The author's mandate was to convey the emotional charge that deranged individuals perceive in words—to convey their living quality and their magical force. It is exactly this word-power that Cardinal acquired in the ten years between the writing of *La Souricière* and *Les Mots pour le dire*—two books that tell a similar story, though with distinctly different styles and outcomes. . . .

Cardinal's contribution to the literature of madness is to have expressed the most elemental realities of life and death as lived through the female

body. Her work records not only her personal idiosyncratic history and crucial aspects of the female condition in general, especially around the nexus
of maternity, but it also crosses the line of gender at the intersection of
madness and mortality so as to speak to all human beings who are sensitive
to the genesis of life and the obdurate fact of death.

Marilyn Yalom. *Maternity, Mortality, and
the Literature of Madness.* (University Park:
Pennsylvania State University Press, 1985),
pp. 36–37, 47–50, 69

Words articulated in the course of analytic treatment are not merely the
servants of confession or catharsis; they are signifiers in a chain which constitutes our social being. The ties that bind us to the reality which pre-exists
us and to the reality we create can, however, also be broken, as demonstrated
in Marie Cardinal's autobiographical text.

In *The Words to Say It* Cardinal offers a powerful account of her seven-
year analysis, an account which Bruno Bettelheim's Preface claims to be the
best we have. What Cardinal inscribes here is the story (or history) of her
psychic experience which, like the process of analysis itself, moves in and
out of the past, erratically. With other autobiographies by women, Cardinal's
shares that "reaching towards the possibility of saying 'I'" described by Linda
Anderson. In Anderson's view, women's autobiography involves "a continual
fracturing of its own surface, a breaking into disorder and uncertainty, as a
way of searching behind the formal structure, the accepted patterns of order
and significance." Accordingly, the "I" in Cardinal's first-person narrative has
a problematic status; it is a point of identification which shifts with the author's gaze and which comes into being only at the point of inscription. The
power of this particular instance of life-writing lies in Cardinal's difficult
relationship to language, a relationship which reveals her problematic position
as a subject in language.

The Words to Say It exemplifies the intricate connection between language and the unconscious, and between written (or spoken) articulation and
subjectivity. These are connections that psychoanalysis describes but rarely
succeeds in illustrating so effectively. My reading will focus on the second
connection, specifically on an analysis of the mother-daughter bond and of
the psychic structure of "abjection" as defined by Julia Kristeva. Before
embarking on this analysis, however, something must be said of the first
connection between language and the unconscious. It was only by transforming her relationship to language (through her analysis and through writing) that Cardinal was able to reposition herself as subject within it.

Patricia Elliot. *Mosaic.* 20:4, Fall, 1987,
pp. 71–72

Cardinal's *venue à l'écriture* was a slow and painful task. Beginning in 1962,
she wrote five slim novels before she was able to come to terms with her

mother, an implacable and ultimately tragic maternal figure who becomes the center of her much acclaimed book *Les Mots pour le dire* (1975). Her earlier books, in comparison, are all timid, sometimes aborted attempts at exploring the rich and powerful personal experiences which inspired Cardinal's later novels. Strangely enough, none of these earlier books deals significantly with the themes of madness or the mother. However, Algeria, the country of the author's childhood, is vividly present in those works. Together with the sea, traditionally associated with maternal imagery as reflected in the title of Cardinal's very first book *Ecoutez la mer,* they seem to work as metonymic representations of the mother of whom Cardinal is yet unable to write. The fifteen years during which the writer was forging her language and gathering strength to face the main issues, came to an end with *Les Mots pour le dire.* This novel constitutes Cardinal's pivotal work. It illuminates not only her later books but also her earlier novels by revealing the sources of her creative impulses: the hate and love relationship with her mother. This autobiographical novel is the story of a painful rebirth from the depth of madness. At the age of forty, having explored through psychoanalysis all the taboos and fears that fettered her, the narrator discovers her identity. She discovers also her creativity and her own language liberated from the restrictions imposed on it by her family and a male-dominated society.

Her first task, though, is to unmask her mother and to plunge herself into the depths of a daughter's hate for her mother. This *descente en enfer* follows the steps of the narrator's analysis she underwent for seven years in order to understand the severe psychological troubles she was experiencing. In the process, rapidly eroded by the power of analysis, the image of the virtuous but impervious mother is replaced by that of a frustrated woman who poured on her daughter her anger and bitterness, and vented her madness on her. . . .

Writing becomes an act of gestation and of purification at the end of which a new woman emerges. The frightening, almost unbearable task of rejecting her mother and all that she stands for is achieved. The narrator has freed herself and her discourse from the maternal influence and power: "Then I understood there was an entire area of my body that I have never accepted and which somehow, never, belonged to me. The zone between my legs could be expressed only with shameful words. . . ." At the age of thirty-six, she discovers her body, her "ass," her vagina, and the words to say it.

In her subsequent novels, *Une Vie pour deux* (1979), *Au Pays de mes racines* (1980), and *Le Passé empiété* (1983), Cardinal has truly found a voice of her own to express women's reality. She uses a vigorous and open language to write about subjects hitherto kept silent: women's bodies, women's experiences of child-bearing, menstruation, and love-making. Unlike Cixous and Irigaray, Cardinal is opposed to the creation of a separate female language for she fears it would further alienate women from society. Instead, she advocates the use of a transformed traditional language to give visibility to women's experiences. Furthermore, in her latest novel, *Le Passé empitété,* she claims the right for female writers to re-interpret the myths of our culture from a woman's perspective. Her book culminates into the moving figure of Clytemnestra, described not as a blood-thirsty adulteress of history but as the devastated mother of Iphigenia sacrificed to the gods by her father Agamemnon. In emphasizing the female point of view in Clytemnestra's story, Cardinal makes the image of the queen into a powerful metaphor of bonding. It symbolizes the reconciliation between the mother and the daughter, which Cardinal has envisioned at the end of *Les Mots pour le dire*. Clytemnestra, who visits the narrator day after day, becomes the projection of the narrator's mother as well as of the narrator herself. Mother and daughter, using Clytemnestra as mediator, discover their commonalities as women—as mothers and wives—in a male-dominated society. They are now united by bonds that transcend their personal history and link them to women throughout the ages. Cardinal has found the words to create "her-story," a story which brings her back to her origin: her mother.

Colette Hall. In Michel Guggenheim, ed.
Women in French Literature. (Saratoga,
California: ANMA Libri, 1988), pp. 234–37

CARTER, ANGELA (GREAT BRITAIN) 1940–92

Angela Carter has now been charting the unconscious processes of Western society for a number of years, principally in her series of novels but latterly also in the form of a kind of psychoanalytic journalism and in *The Sadeian Woman* (1979), a major history and interpretation of sexuality and its acculturation. I propose here to try to identify a principal shift of attention in this body of texts which occurred in the 1970s, through an examination of two of her novels, *The Infernal Desire Machines of Doctor Hoffman* (1972) and *The Passion of New Eve* (1977). That change can be expressed in plain terms, although these do not do justice to the convolutions of the psyche which structure the two texts. Both novels, and indeed all Carter's work, are to do with the unconscious and its shapes, and thus to do with sexuality, and in *Doctor Hoffman* this concern reaches a peak in the interplay of Freud and Reich which forms the underpinning of the text. But that peak is also a point of division, and what is new in *New Eve* is that the issue of sexuality is linked directly to the different issue of gender; that is to say, *New Eve* speaks— and, indeed, helps to form—a language in which it is impossible to conjugate the pure term "sexuality," for the questions of ownership, agency, and power which surround our use of language have been made manifest, and now there is "male sexuality" and "female sexuality," without an assumed bridge. The intensity of focus on hermaphroditism is present in both texts, but to different purpose: in *Doctor Hoffman*, hermaphrodites are merely the object of the gaze, the Platonic linked double to be worshipped and admired in *New Eve,* the structures of hermaphroditism operate within the perceiving subject itself, so that the gaze is dislocated at source. And the dislocation of the gaze entails also a primary dislocation of plot; it is significant that *Doctor Hoffman* is intensely reliant on literary models, from the picaresque pretensions of the hero (in some of his phases) to the conventionality of the love plot in which he is enmeshed. *New Eve,* of course, is not without models; but the relation between plot and character is more twisted, if only because of the further depths to which Carter has taken her exploration of the construction of the subject.

For both novels are dramatizations of the constructed subject, and they relate to each other precisely along the lines of the development of recent theoretical debate about such construction, and specifically about the exact point at which gender enters as a structuring principle. "You could effectively evolve a persona from your predicament, if you tried," Desiderio is admonished in *Doctor Hoffman* at one point, although Carter does not here go in for easy answers. Indeed, the "answers" with which she presents us are exceedingly difficult, rather in the manner of the metaphysical speculations of Flann O'Brien, and thus the question of the reality status—or, perhaps, varying reality statuses—of the "phantoms" which Hoffman unleashes on the city remains to the end a matter for conjecture. That conjecture is simultaneously a metaphysical one, about the concept of the symbol; what we might term a semiotic one, about the relation between the sign and its referent; and a sociosexual one, for it raises the questions of the ontological location of desire and of the arbitrariness of change.

David Punter. *Critique.* 25, Summer, 1984,
pp. 209-10

In the concluding pages of Angela Carter's *Nights at the Circus* a seriocomic incident occurs in which the central protagonist Fevvers, Cockney Venus and bird woman, gives an enthusiastic if cliché-ridden speech heralding the new age of women's liberation. She looks forward to the era when "all the women will have wings, the same as I. . . . The dolls' house doors will open, the brothels will spill forth their prisoners, the cages, gilded or otherwise, all over the world, in every land, will let forth their inmates singing together the dawn chorus of the new, the transformed—." Fevvers's flight of fancy remains incomplete, since her words are sharply interrupted by a cynical comment voiced by her foster mother Lizzie: "It's going to be more complicated than that. . . . You improve your analysis, girl, and *then* we'll discuss it." The episode is an important one, not just in terms of the novel in which it appears but in terms of Carter's fiction as a whole. The conversation between Fevvers and Lizzie illustrates a key area of tension in Carter's writing, by juxtaposing two antithetical impulses which inform it. While, on the one hand, a reference to celebratory and utopian elements is introduced, on the other, there is an equally strong emphasis on the analytic and the "demythologizing." In certain passages, such as the one quoted above, the two impulses interact. However, each is of interest in its own right and may, in fact, be identified with a particular stage of Carter's fiction. In her "early" texts (those published prior to 1978), it is the analytic and "demythologizing" impulse which is to the fore. These include *The Magic Toyshop* (1967), *Heroes and Villains* (1969), and *The Passion of New Eve* (1977). The themes which occupy her at this stage are: gender and its construction, the cultural production of femininity, male power under patriarchy, and the myths and institutions which serve to maintain it. The image which she frequently adopts to represent woman's role in society (man's too, on occasion) is the *puppet*. As well as carrying Hoffmannesque associations of the fantastic the image has connotations of the "coded mannequin," the metaphor employed by Hélène Cixous to represent the robotic state to which human beings are reduced by a process of psychic repression. The focus on the celebratory and utopian is something of a new departure in Carter's fiction. It does not fully emerge until the texts published in the late 1970s and 1980s, *The Bloody Chamber* (1979) and *Nights at the Circus* (1984). Here she treats themes relating to liberation and change, in the organization of personal life and the social formation. Acts of resistance against patriarchy are represented. The deconstruction of femininity and masculinity is explored and in keeping with the shifts in contemporary feminist thought, the perspective becomes increasingly woman-centered. A reevaluation of female experience takes place and the emergence of a female counterculture is celebrated. The image of the puppet is no longer central to the text. It is replaced by the images of Fevvers's miraculous wings which, she observe, make her body "the abode of limitless freedom," and the egg from which she claims to have been hatched. These images represent ideas of liberation and rebirth; they evoke, in Cixous's words, "the possibility of radical transformations of behavior, mentalities, roles, and political economy."

Paulina Palmer. In Sue Roe, ed. Women Reading Women's Writing (New York: St. Martin's, 1987), pp. 179–80

That the narrative grip of Oedipus is difficult to break free from is evinced, certainly, by the tenacity of those revered fairy tales which have hooked into our cultural ideology, and also by what in the past has been a marked absence of narratives which work to disrupt the status quo. Yet such resistant, cross-grain rewriting is precisely the task of Angela Carter, whose feminist revisionary rewriting of some of those classic fairy tales is, as Lorna Sage has described her work, more concerned with "myth-breaking" than "myth-making"—rewriting which "take[s] myths and turn[s] them inside out."

In *The Bloody Chamber,* Carter proffers two versions of the classic tale "Beauty and the Beast." One version, "The Courtship of Mr. Lyon," a hip, contemporary 1960s-style parody featuring a cigarette-smoking Beauty, is an overt expose of the contrived gender differences and positionalities that inform the original tale. In the companion piece, "The Tiger's Bride," Carter takes her revisioning a crucial step further, subverting "that old story" by repositioning and redefining woman's desire on her own terms. Carter's imaginative conceptions and formulations of what sorts of possibilities are available to women through cultural myths are a far cry, certainly, from those of Oedipus, which are, as de Lauretis explains, "honed by a centuries-long patriarchal tradition." In fact, these iconoclastic, tradition-breaking tales— especially "The Tiger's Bride"—do precisely what de Lauretis argues feminist writing and rewriting must do to subvert the continued predominance of the pattern of the Oedipal narrative: Woman—Beauty—is imagined/imaged as "mythical and social subject" in her own right, providing her own referential frame of experience, writing her ending to her own story.

"To a certain extent," Carter acknowledges regarding the foregrounding of a political agenda in her work, "I'm making a conscious critique of the culture I was born to." And to the extent that we read her narrative revisions as critiques of the dominant culture's inscriptions of sexual difference and desire, it is interesting and illuminating to read Carter's "Beauty" stories against Jean Cocteau's classic 1946 film text, *La Belle et La Bête*, which has always been studied as an experimental, avant-garde venture into the possibilities of cinematic production, yet which is nevertheless as familiar a rendering of the fairy story as Carter's versions are de-familiar ones.

Sylvia Bryant. *Criticism*. 31, 1989,
pp. 441–42

Carter's "Lady of The House of Love" demonstrates that, even when the text appears crystalline in its artfulness, evidently hostile to "real" human issues, such as history and temporality, there will be conclusions for the contextualist to draw. Once the right questions have been posed, the narrative shows that it is about more than the sad fate of vampires, more even than the sad fate of empires and armies. It is also about the fate of women in a patriarchal world. It is about power, and who, in such a world, normally possesses power. The wedding dress, seen from a contextualist perspective, becomes more than a pathetic element in the theatrical setting of rot and decay, more even than a crafty allusion (salient in the intertextual welter, Miss Havisham mysteriously smiles) to other texts. Once the narrative's feminist preoccupations and concerns have been identified, the wedding dress emerges abruptly as the most poignant motif of all: the symbol of women's voicelessness, subordination and narrowly limited expectations, their une-lected social roles handed down, in a patriarchal society. One may certainly argue that Carter uses history in a "destabilizing" manner, problematizing without interpreting, as Hutcheon writes of *The Infernal Desire Machines of Doctor Hoffman,* equally a positive or a negative textual property (depending upon the archive), but it is also the case that a genuine concern for human deprivation, what has not found fulfillment in history, pervades the text.

Postmodernism designates a nexus of intersecting discourses, constituting separate archives, each largely blind to opposed discursive formations.
It exemplifies the fruitfulness of poststructuralist metaphors that project
splintered, instable textual mosaics in which all categories, both genres and
periods, will display the decay of boundaries and, inevitably, their degeneres-
cence. It also shows the relevance of those other metaphors about boundaries
that characteristically play important roles in Bakhtin's thinking: metaphors
in which alien languages confront each other in public fora, in which different
speakers, bearing with them dissimilar axiological worlds, exchange utterances, seeking meanings that will never reside exclusively in either's speech.
Mocking the duplicitous "fiction of sharp distinctions" (behind, or beyond,
the ineluctably fuzzy borders of which stuff falls, and then falls again), postmodernism offers the opportunity to read both texts and culture with "parted
eye" in which, as Hermia exclaims in *A Midsummer Night's Dream,* everything "seems double." It is an opportunity, and neither a catastrophe nor a
punishment for the fallen *gerede* that one must speak, since the possibilities
for reflexivity, for self-consciously inscribing the problematic of one's own
explorations, are always exciting. For the time being, it may be the most
provocative, splendidly liminal specimen of what Howard Felperin calls the
"slippery grounds of discourse" available. And, as a discursive nexus, it continues to open toward multiplex investigations.

Robert Rawdon Wilson. *Ariel.* 20, 1989,
pp. 112–13

In her last three novels, Angela Carter has used the device of a journey, the
traditional symbol of a quest, to structure her narrative. Desiderio's travels
in *The Infernal Desire Machines of Doctor Hoffman* are explicitly referred
to as a "quest"; in *The Passion of New Eve* Evelyn's restless flight over the
North American Continent is called the search for "that most elusive of all
chimeras, myself"; and Fevvers in *Nights at the Circus* is convinced that
she has been "feathered out for some special fate" that will manifest itself in
the course of her travels. The adventures these characters encounter on their
journeys in the fantastic realm of the imaginary and the symbolic mediate a
discussion of the making of the subject in the light of philosophical, psycho-
analytical, and feminist ideas. All three novels are complex and multifaceted,
yet each of them deconstructs essentialist, humanist notions of the subject
and, as I will show in this essay, explores the constitution of the subject in
relation to one dominant aspect, which is at the same time representative of
cultural ideas about the subject in the 1960s, 1970s, and 1980s, respectively:
desire in *Hoffman,* gender in *Eve,* and free womanhood in *Circus.*

Carter uses the mask of the fantastic picaresque story in *Hoffman* and
Eve to dissect fashionable and commonly held conceptions of the subject. In
Hoffman the hero's journeys serve to dismantle the alluring progressive ideas
of the 1960s that individual and social freedom could be achieved if the social
repression of desires were lifted. These ideas are shown as an illusion founded

on the mistaken view that human beings are good by nature. The unconscious, in which nothing can be negated or destroyed, contains "good" and "evil" desires. The novel vindicates Freud's thesis that civilization cannot do without coercion and renunciation of instinct. It leads to the sober position that a certain amount of alienation, of unfulfilled desire and of sublimation, must constitute part of the formation of the subject in modern civilization, that desire must coexist with rationality.

In *Eve* Carter consciously explores the function of gender in the constitution of the subject. Eve/lyn learns during his/her journey that gender is not a natural category. The symbols of femininity are revealed as reflections of male desire. Yet although femininity does not correspond to any essence, women's subjectivity is shown to be de-formed by the social power of patriarchal stereotypes of femininity. A return to the mythical times of matriarchy is rejected as a dead end in *Eve,* but androgyny flickers up as a vision of a way out of the present gender division—thus grounding the novel in ideas developed by the Anglo-American women's movement in the 1970s.

In *Circus* Carter switches from the analysis of the formation of the subject, i.e., from the deconstruction of the subject as good and natural, to the construction of a fantastic subject, the free woman. The author envisages a fantastic woman's creative conception of free womanhood, and by means of adventures, difficulties and misfortunes on the heroine's journey, Carter explores its interdependence with the "Other," whose recognition is vital for the constitution of the subject. The comic form of this novel ensures that the utopian enterprise can find a happy ending without being reduced to facile propaganda or deceptive wish fulfillment. It is the increased self-confidence of women in the 1980s and their deeper theoretical understanding of patriarchy and the constitution of the subject that have made this light-heartedness and humor possible.

Ricarda Schmidt. Textual Practice. 3, 1989,
pp. 56, 73–74

CASSIAN, NINA (RUMANIA) 1924–

Rumanian poets have had no choice but to be political, since even to conform was in a sense a political act, while not to conform could be suicidal. . . .

Nina Cassian. . . . was forced into exile and lost the entire contents of her house (books, writings, letters, family mementos) together with everything else that exile takes away. One of the most uninhibited poems by this passionate and often anguished poet is a lament for the loss of her language:

> Please God take pity
> on the roof of my mouth,

on my tongue,
on my glottis,
on the clitoris in my throat
vibrating, sensitive, pulsating,
exploding in the orgasm of Rumanian.

This selection, *Life Sentences,* is said to span forty-five years, although it does not appear to include any of the 1950s poems which Cassian now rejects. The poems are undated, which makes it difficult to place them chronologically in the pattern of her life's work. The arrangement is roughly thematic: a group of poems referring to childhood and to elements in her Rumanian past—legends, folklore, cryptic and surrealistic allegories; two groups of love poems, displaying a passionate greed for experience and poised between celebration and violent despair, with images of bloodshed and physical cruelty gradually giving way to an almost calm acceptance of death and old age; a section of nightmarelike pieces using metaphors for imprisonment, mutilation, pain, and fear (a caged bear, a labyrinth, a rabbit's dying shriek); and a final section focusing on aspects of language, writing, and Nina Cassian's view of herself as a poet and a woman. This includes the famous early poem "Self-Portrait" in which she describers her "odd triangular face," the "ugly head" which worried her for so long. She is a self-conscious poet, personal without being precisely autobiographical; images interest her more than the factual details of everyday life (Rumanian poets don't much go in for the low mimetic), but her emotions are laid out on the page with uncompromising nakedness. "The Blood" begins: "Ah, how well I remember that pain! / My soul taken by surprise / jumped about like a chicken with its head cut off. / Everything was splashed with blood."

A total of twenty translators are listed. Most are American, but they include Cassian herself and the English/Rumanian partnership of Brenda Walker and Andrea Deletant, in poems taken from their Forest Books volume *Call Yourself Alive* (1988). I should confess that they also include me, with one very short version taken from the same collection. The resulting mixture of styles can be distracting. William Jay Smith's contributions are slickly metrical and smartly rhymed; other translators tend towards more neutral, less mannered renderings: Laura Schiff's smoothly fluent but nonrhyming versions work particularly well. Cassian used rhymed and metrical forms frequently and to brilliant effect, but naturally it was often not possible to reproduce these in English, and we are left to guess how far the form and style of any one translation reflect those of the original. Whatever the packaging, though, the nature of the contents is unmistakable: this is rich, vigorous often startling poetry.

Fleur Adcock. *Poetry Review.* 80:2, 1990,
p. 22

Nina Cassian comes to us, even in translation, as a poet of tremendous range and vitality. We are at once aware of her antecedents: a modernist, nurtured on those French poets who, through T. S. Eliot and Ezra Pound, helped to change the shape of twentieth-century poetry in England and America, she is at the same time very much a product of Rumania. Her poetry has something of the clear line and the strikingly simple texture of her countryman, Brancusi, and, like him, her sophistication is grounded in folklore. There is great variety to her work and a comic spirit that recalls the theater of the absurd of her other countryman, Ionesco. Her themes are eternal—love and loss, life and death—and they are communicated with an immediacy as rare as it is compelling. Hers is a passionate commitment in the greatest tradition of lyric poetry. For this poet, life is indeed a tragic sentence. But the sentence that she composes in answer to life is made up of clean Latin vowels, with rational syllables "trying to clear the occult mind." Only in poetry does she reach "the word, the inhabited homestead." And in poetry she takes her reader with her. . . .

For all the immediacy of Nina Cassian's poetry (and this immediacy and sensory appeal have made her a brilliant writer for children), her tone is never confessional but rather intense and direct and without self-pity.

William Jay Smith. *American Poetry Review.*
January–February, 1990, p. 23

Nina Cassian is a prolific poet with a large number of verse collections (*On the Scale 1/1, Songs for the Republic, The Ages of the Year, The Daily Holidays, Outdoor Show, Parallel Destinies, The Discipline of the Harp, Chronophagia, Ambitus, Lotto-Poems, Counting Backward,* et cetera) and with a definite place in the generation of Rumanian poets who began publishing at the end of the last war. Her poetry takes shape at the intersection of lucidity ("the platinum scalpel with which / I attempt the surgery of truth") with the games of imagination, the enticing, wonderfully shocking metamorphoses and mutations of words and feelings, of people and objects.

Taking the latitude and longitude of Cassian's work is no simple matter, however; for just as the charmed reader believes he is holding the map of the poet's passions and problems, she makes an about-face, scorns his admiration with an ironic grin, eludes him, reappears as fury, feline lover, murderess, buffoon, or ship's figurehead bringing in a new cargo of inventions, offering new projects and proposals. She may undertake "an anthology of hand motions" or, to punish her lover, decide to unscrew his head: "From now on—that's where you start—at the knot in your tie." Ready for tumultuous celebrations and longed-for communions, she may arrive bearing fantastic gifts but would also smuggle in the threat of "adamant truths." Her ironic list of temptations, drawn for a reluctant lover, offers life at an altitude and an intensity of giant dimensions, her hunger for living and experiment unsatiable: "Call yourself alive? I promise you / you'll be deafened by dust falling on the furniture / you'll feel your eyebrows turning to two gashes / and every memory you have—will begin / at Genesis." . . .

How much of Cassian's tumultuous and original voice is made available to the English-speaking reader by *Call Yourself Alive?* Definitely some of it. The collection offers sixty poems translated by the same Deletant-Walker team which so far has given us six books of Rumanian verse, and once more the work is done sensitively and respectfully. The problems of finding English correspondences for the rhymes and rhythms of Rumanian poetry, where the "discipline of the harp" is rigorous and rhyming is a tradition informed with culture, remain to be discussed elsewhere. A good many of Cassian's poems are games delighting in words and language and show her Meistersinger's virtuosity. They had to be eliminated from consideration. In exchange we are offered a number of her latest poems; they open a new cycle in the work and life of the poet, who in 1985 left Rumania and now lives in New York. The time of Cassian's exquisite games is receding, lacerated by memories of love and death, under the growing shadow of aging, in alien cities ("it is Christmas in mid-America"), like a Christmas decoration: "I rotate but without air / without delicate tinkling, hung from the ceiling." Still, her poetry remains indomitable. Wounded by time, by the loss of country and language, impatient with such absurdities as consolation and reasonableness, she challenges God the way she would challenge one of her reluctant lovers: "If you really exist— show up / as a bear, a goat, a pilot / come with eyes, mouth, voice / —demand something from me, / force me to sacrifice myself, / take me in your arms, protect me from above, feed me with the seventh part of a fish, / hiss at me, reanimate my fingers, / refill me with aromas, with astonishment / — resurrect me."

Marguerite Dorian. *World Literature Today.*
64, 1990, pp. 92–93

Nina Cassian's poems in *Life Sentence* go up like rockets to flower and burst in showers of sparks against a universal night sky. Sent up from blood-soaked earth like signals of transcendence into poetry's pure atmosphere, they are fueled by the pulse of a single human heart compelled by love of it to celebrate a tragic world.

First, then, momentum. Second, variety. Cassian's subjects occur at any and every instant of her terrifically aware existence, as these randomly chosen opening lines attest: "The lighthouse there at Cape Crepuscular / sends out signals: the weather is getting rough" (from "The Troubled Bay"); "The orbit I describe in my environment, / cautiously, so as not to strike birds with my forehead" (from "Orbits"); "I wake up and say: I'm through" (from "Morning Exercises"); "The word was uttered: let us break its neck" (from "Game Mistress")—open *Life Sentence* anywhere and electrifying images coruscate on the page. Not that the poems are all whoosh and glitter. Many are so quiet that the breaking of a heart may be heard:

Ready for goodbye, although the moon is rising.
Ready for goodbye, although the tea is boiling.
Ready for goodbye, although the wind is pouring
its triumphant notes into the air.
Ready for goodbye, although my sister's mother
carries in her womb a lovely daughter.
Ready for goodbye.

But always they breathe out the sense of an ascending spirit. . . .

What might be called the principle of metamorphosis is found throughout *Life Sentence. . . .* Cassian seems to have inspired in all of her translators here the passionate respect that poets give to a superlative practitioner of their shared art. Thus they are able to approach her work with their own best strengths. Poets will often turn to translating as a spur to or refreshment of their own work; the translators of *Life Sentence,* however, uniformly show unusual devotion to revealing and illuminating the unique forces which propel Cassian's living forms. Although some of the poems initially chosen to be presented in this selection had to be omitted because, as Smith has it in his Introduction, "the resonance and the allusions of the original[s] could not be carried over" into English, the recognition of these difficulties speaks excellently for the sensitivity of editor and translators alike. Smith goes on to report that Cassian, herself a translator of note, "has permitted, and even encouraged, her translators to take considerable liberty as long as they did not violate the spirit of her work." Thus such interpreters as Richard Wilbur and Dana Gioia have been able to keep their translations in strict accordance with Cassian's rhyme schemes, others have been able to approximate them, and still others have elected to emphasize meaning rather than arrangement. The list of translators is also a list of distinguished American poets, among them Stanley Kunitz, Ruth Whitman, and Carolyn Kizer; by investing their own talents in *Life Sentence,* they have produced a treasure. As Cassian has said elsewhere concerning what may be lost in translations of her poems, "I'm not limited to my own music. . . . I'm open to all the tunes in the world."

Constance Hunting. *Parnassus.* 16, 1990,
pp. 382–83, 386–87

CASTELLANOS, ROSARIO (MEXICO) 1925–74

The novel *Balún Canán* has suddenly elevated its author to the position of one of the best novelists of Mexico. The talent Rosario Castellanos had shown in the cultivation of her poetic art is prominently and decisively present in the prose of *Balún Canán.* . . .

The action of *Balún Canán* touches on violent themes but is contained within the passive rhythm of the narrative. These themes . . . form part of the nucleus of the relationship between the country gentlemen of the region and the peasants in their service. Together with these relationships, she treats the subjective conflicts of the characters and the objective ones resulting from the impact on the people of the social goals realized by the Revolution. . . .

The dialogue of the characters is adequate and clear, and everyone speaks in accord with his cultural station. In general, there is a predominance of expressions that reflect the idioms of the region, enriched by words taken from popular speech.

Rosario Castellanos comes off well in this first test in the realm of the novel. She has given to *Balún Canán,* the former name for the site where Comitán now stands, a novel that captures between its pages a moment in its history and a portrait of its landscape, its customs, and its beliefs.

Mauricio de la Selva. *Cuadernos Americanos.* 97, January–February, 1958, pp. 272–73

Rosario Castellanos is a young Mexican woman writer who combines passionate sensitivity with social history to make an arresting if not altogether satisfactory blend of novel. *Balún Canán* is a vivid, disorderly chronicle of landowning family life in a remote part of south Mexico during the late 1930s. It was a disturbed period when the local Indian peasantry, stimulated by Cárdenas's agrarian reforms and the official current of anti-clericalism, were beginning to kick in their own sullen sporadically violent fashion. They fire César Argüello's sugar plantation at Chactajal, and shoot his bastard nephew, Ernesto, a strange picaresque satyr of a character, disdainful of the Indians and the new threatening regime, resentful of the Argüellos to whom he doesn't quite belong.

After the fire the family moves back to Comitán, the little town near the Guatemalan border, where the novel opens. Here the curious interpenetration between Mexican Indian and Spanish Catholic superstitions is neatly illustrated when the little boy, Mario, falls ill and his mother, Señora Argüello, more than half believes the Indian nurse's warning that his spirit is being eaten by sorcerers. If only Señora Castellanos had been able to solve her story-telling problem she might have written a masterpiece. Unfortunately she puts most of it into the mouth of the seven-year-old Argüello daughter—herself, presumably—who narrates away in the breathless historic present, like an all-seeing eye. There are occasional monologues by adults and patches with no narrator. The effect is inevitably one of maddening dissociation. Even so, the vividness of the background is most impressive. This, you feel, is as near Mexico as you can get in print. And despite the extreme subjectivity, strict impartiality is preserved as between peasants and landowners. Nothing could be more tellingly detached than the laconic account of the odd masculine Aunt Francisca's brutality to her peasants.

Maurice Richardson. *The New Statesman.*
July 25, 1959, pp. 115–16

Still in her twenties and generously endowed as poet and novelist, Rosario Castellanos is almost unique among Mexican writers for the respect her work inspires among the embattled cliques of both Left and Right. *Balún Canán,* her first novel to reach us in translation, shows why.

Written during a period when she was employed as an anthropologist by the Indian Bureau in Chiapas, it deals with the social upheaval of the Cárdenas period in such a way as to give little comfort to either the diehard *hacendados* or the sentimental *indianistas.* Though never explicit, the author's sympathy for the sufferings of both parties is always felt. Bedeviled by the hatreds, fears and superstitions of a five-hundred-years-old unnatural relationship, the inevitable clash of peasant and landlord was bound to end in horror; yet the reader never feels that horror is being exploited for mere literary advantage. Only in the first few pages, as a matter of fact, is one conscious of anything highly wrought: poetical descriptive passages and characters vibrating with exquisite sensibility. And this is the more remarkable in a literary tradition that is apt to strike us as excessively style-conscious. . . .

What saves this Faulknerian tale from being merely a case history in degeneracy, is the degree to which the author (like Faulkner) manages to invest the degradation of the present with a brooding sense of the meaningfulness of the past. But this, unfortunately, she does too subtly, or ambivalently. The reader unversed in the Maya background or the Cárdenas foreground would never guess that any spirit of illuminating aspiration had ever crossed this dark terrain.

Selden Rodman. *The New York Times.*
June 5, 1960, pp. 4–5, 26

The Mexican Revolution, which began in 1910 and continued, more or less, until 1940, is only now becoming, as it were, externalized in its country's literature. While the Revolution was happening, outsiders such as D. H. Lawrence or Graham Greene could travel in the country, observe, comment, and cavil or commend, but Mexicans themselves were too deeply and traumatically involved to do so. Now the process of assimilation into art is going on apace, and there is in Mexico City a group of young novelists, several of whom are already being translated and appreciated abroad as well as at home.

Rosario Castellanos, whose *Balún Canán* was voted best work of fiction in Mexico for 1957, grew up in the high Chiapas country she describes. The central conflict of the novel is between the Mexicans of Spanish descent and the Indians. . . .

The seven-year-old girl who narrates part one of *Balún Canán* is from the first aware of the hostile dichotomy: her beloved Indian nurse has a wound her own people have given her because she loved the child and her brother. "Is it wicked to love us?" the youngster asks, and Nana, replies, "It's wicked to love those who give orders and have possessions. That's what the law says." . . .

It would have been a still better novel had it been all written from the child's viewpoint: the sudden change of narrator takes away from both the pace and the pathos of the story; it is almost as if the author felt she couldn't keep it up, that relating a whole revolution, even as experienced by one family, on one hacienda, from a seven-year-old's point of view, was too complex an undertaking.

Anne Fremantle. *Saturday Review of
Literature.* June 11, 1960, p. 38

In less than fifteen years, Rosario Castellanos has produced a considerable oeuvre of appreciable artistic quality, including seven books of poetry . . . two novels . . . a volume of stories . . . and a theatrical piece. . . . Her poetry, together with that of Jaime Sabines, a comrade-in-arms from the same area, has captured the attention of the most astute critics and the enthusiasm of the reading public. Among the work of younger writers, the poetry of Rosario Castellanos and Jaime Sabines perhaps constitutes the two points between which our lyric tradition moves: an intelligence that orders appetites and tempers the perceptions of the senses, and an emotionalism that challenges the elaborate products of reason and rebuilds the real world in its own way. (The marks of both writers are more-or-less perceptible among the poets who have recently "arrived.") Among the prose writers of her generation, Rosario Castellanos has produced the best constructed and the most ideologically sound work. In her essays and literary criticism, activities which she engages in sporadically, she reaffirms the gifts that we all recognize in her: sagacity and irony.

Professionally committed to literature, Rosario Castellanos demonstrates that inspiration and talent can be complemented by patience and hard work. . . .

In her most recent work, *The Guests in August,* she reveals similar purposes and reflects characteristics that marked her previous work, but, at the same time, she follows paths she has never before traveled. Perhaps this is her best work of narrative prose, for various reasons. First, it does away with any anthropological preoccupation: her characters are no longer Indians or white men; they are human beings. Second, realism does not exclude imagination: the anecdotes allow us to see the "verified facts" and the "possible happenings." Third, the style is a rejection of poetic prose and follows the canons of narrative prose. Fourth, the writer, in telling her story, reduces the field of her observations and abandons the omniscient point of view . . . letting [her characters] act, think, and feel with a certain amount of independence. . . .

Emmanuel Carballo. *Diecinueve
protagonistas de la literatura mexicana del
siglo XX* (Mexico City: Empresas
Editoriales, 1965), pp. 411, 424

As in her two earlier works of fiction, *Balún Canán and Royal City,* [Castellanos in *Business of Thunder*] analytically lays bare the pattern of relations between Indian and *ladino* ["white"] which influences all aspects and levels of life in traditional San Cristóbal Las Casas, provincial center of highlands Chiapas. . . .

Preoccupied with the relationship between reality and myth, the work is constructed on two contrasting temporal planes. The action unfolds in a clearly historical framework—the period of the 1930s and just after, the epoch of Cárdenas and high point of the Mexican Revolution. In contrast, time for the Tzotzil Indian has the ahistorical quality of Indian legend. The opening paragraphs set the scene in San Juan Chamula, Tzotzil religious and political center, in terms of a Christianized myth, recounted in the language and images of the *Popol Vuh,* Mayan version of the creation. At the novel's end, the defeated Indian rebellion is synthesized, not in terms of battles won or lost, but in the form of newly fashioned myth. . . .

The winds of reform, in the view of Rosario Castellanos, have been blocked from reaching the valley of San Cristóbal, as though the surrounding mountains had been erected to serve the prejudices of the controling class of aristocratic *ladino* landholders. In effect, her novelistic interpretation indicts the Revolution for having succumbed to easy compromise at Indian expense, rather than do battle with the entrenched conservative forms, including the church, which conspire to retain centuries-old semifeudalism.

Unlike earlier views of the Indian, Castellanos's vision does not gloss over the negative effects of blind superstition, of ritualistic alcoholism, of daily, relentless humiliation. But there is also consistent affirmation, especially in the hope that springs up in each generation, and in the grim, almost subconscious determination to survive the buffetings of a hostile fate, all of which form part of the Tzotzil mentality. . . .

The determinant in Indian life is the presence of the dominant society, presented in *Business of Thunder* through a series of *ladino* characters of various social classes. Most interesting are the traditional landholder and his embittered wife, their unhappy daughter, a guilt-ridden bishop, and an ambitious priest. The most striking common characteristic in all these individuals is the degree to which their entire system of values has been corroded by a blend of hatred and fear of the Indians, upon whom they depend but whom they regard as inferior, distasteful, and essentially unredeemable. In a manner reminiscent of Faulkner, Castellanos dramatizes the human equation of prejudice: perpetration of injustice upon a vulnerable cultural group can be achieved only at the expense of corrupting and deforming the institutions—social, religious, political—of the exploiters.

Joseph Sommers. *After the Storm*
(Albuquerque: University of New Mexico
Press, 1968), pp. 167–69

The new approach toward the Indian in the Mexican novel, inspired by narrative-type works coming from some anthropologists, finds its ideal exponent in Rosario Castellanos. Raised in the midst of the Tzotzil culture in Chiapas, she began to realize in the mid-1950s her rather unique opportunity for providing a new interpretation to the long-stereotyped Indian theme. The happy result can be seen in four works she published between 1957 and 1964, two volumes of stories and two novels. The first of these was *Balún Canán*, a novel which marked the beginning of the new trend. Here she treats the Indians as humans rather than as types, and she recognizes—and makes excellent use of—the value and force of the cultural heritage of the Tzotzil tribe. Because of this her Indian novels are more complex, less superficial, decidedly more natural and convincing than [B.] Traven's. . . . Not that she solves the Indian problem any more than Traven did, but she puts it into clearer focus and, by revealing the Indian capacity for absorbing the present into the myths and traditions of the past, she shows how he can look through his eternal role as the exploited and still have the strength to survive.

This is Rosario Castellanos's special contribution to the literature of her land, yet it is but one of the reasons for saluting this rather remarkable lady. We recall the distinct merits of her other literary efforts—poetry, essays, criticism, and fiction—and add the edifying effect of her many personal qualities—serenity, peace, love, leadership—and we reach the happy conclusion that Rosario Castellanos is easily one of the most important and admirable figures in the current Mexican literary scene.

> Walter M. Langford. *The Mexican Novel*
> *Comes of Age* (Notre Dame: University of
> Notre Dame Press, 1971),
> pp. 184–85

[*Family Album*] by Rosario Castellanos, Mexico's leading woman author and presently her country's ambassador to Israel, comprises three short stories and one novelette, all of which portray feminine characters in more or less typical contemporary situations, "Cooking Lesson," the best of the collection, records the interior monologue of a young, career-minded housewife whose thoughts wander in phenomenological patterns as she inadvertently burns a steak she is preparing her tradition-bound husband. The meat, shrunken and toughened through overexposure to heat, appears to symbolize the couple's marriage, which is constantly being eroded by friction and rapidly approaching the inevitable breakdown. Here form and content fuse, the protagonist's fleeting psychic digressions reflecting not only the deterioration of her emotional life but the accelerating momentum of change in the physical and social environment as well.

"Sunday" depicts the sterile, frivolous world of an upperclass woman anticipating her next amorous adventure while giving an informal reception, and "Little White-Head," focuses on an aging widow's extreme loneliness, the direct product of an absurdly sheltered and not atypical Latin upbringing. The protagonist of "Family Album," the book's most extensive narration, is a renowned poetess who has just returned to her native Mexico after winning an international literary award. Ironically, however, her escape from a hostile environment into the realm of art, instead of liberating her, has driven her to the point of paranoia.

Rosario Castellanos's hallmarks include linguistic precision, psychological penetration, and wry humor. Her vivid portraits of females groping vainly for identity through a maze of crumbling traditions in a male-dominated society dramatize the plight of today's alienated woman and help explain the mounting incidence of communication failures.

George R. McMurray. *Books Abroad.* 46,
Spring, 1972, p. 275

In 1973 . . . [a] Mexican woman, Rosario Castellanos, published a booklet entitled *Mujer que sabe latin . . .,* the first words of a well-known proverb which continues: *ni tiene marido, ni tiene buen fin* (a woman who knows Latin neither gets married, nor comes to a good end). In it she also upholds the intellectual equality of women and their right to pursue a career of learning, without having to feel that their lives are compromised, as the proverb referred to in the title suggests. It is interesting that, following the example of Sor Juana, to whom she refers, Castellanos also strengthens her arguments with portraits of women whose life achievements are evidence of that very equality. The list includes, among others, Virginia Woolf, Simone de Beauvoir, Doris Lessing, Betty Friedan, Penelope Gilliat, and Mary McCarthy.

Rosario Castellanos, who died tragically not many years ago in Israel, is also the author of poems, two novels, which can be classified as close to the intention of the "*novela indigenista*" and several collections of short stories. Many are the facets of society represented in her work, but the one dominant aspect is her portrayal of female characters and of their situation. Whatever the social level to which they belong, their life constitutes a denunciation of a system which thwarts their nature and victimizes them.

The life of "Modesta Gomez" is one of the many stories of poverty and exploitation which recur in the narrative of Latin American authors. Sent to serve in a rich family at an early age (so young that her legs, as yet unformed, are bowed by the strain of carrying the young master), raped and pregnant, she is thrown out of the house after many years of service. Now a widow, with three children to feed, she remembers with a certain nostalgia the husband who often beat her, yet loved her enough to make her a "señora" and give a name to her illegitimate child. It is a well known plot but for the climax and conclusion of the story, which add a novel aspect to this kind of narrative. Modesta Gomez increases her meager earnings as a shop assistant by working as an "*atajadora.*" This is an established "profession" which consists of going out early in the morning, meeting the Indians who come down to the towns to sell their few products in the markets, and "attacking" them (hence the name "*atajadora*") in order to steal from them whatever they can. The fatalism with which the Indians regularly face these encounters and the behavior of the women rolling on the ground and fighting tooth and nail for a jug or a sweater are the signs of the despair and the animal aggression which extreme poverty and injustice create. Having fought for nothing—since another "*ata-jadora*" gets the shawl she was after—Modesta nevertheless looks with satisfaction at her nails encrusted with blood of her victim, a young woman, in fact. Such is the distortion of human values and the elimination of compassion that society operates on its members! Far from seeing in the Indian girl an image of her own predicament, Modesta rejoices at the pain she has inflicted on her. In the scale of social misery it is comforting to know that there is always someone who suffers more than you.

Others of Castellanos's stories, such as those from *Convidados de agosto,* depict a different social setting, yet their insight into the mentality and situation of its female characters is equally striking. On the one hand, the pathetic picture of loneliness and frustration of those women who, in order to maintain that distance and those standards which man-dominated society demands of them, are unable to break out of the environment in which they are caged and remain unfulfilled like "faded petals"; on the other, satirical sketches sharply portraying the literary poses and the rivalries of pseudo-intellectual women and the hypocrisy of their excuses for not being able to live outright what they theoretically profess.

The stories of a later collection, *Album de familia,* are equally characterized by a subtle insight into the feminine mind and by a style of writing whose feminist intent overrides any other connotation. . . .

Considerably more argumentative are the essays of the book I have already mentioned: *Mujer que sabe Latin.* . . . Many of them are centered on the myths of women; the myths that men have created about them. The aura of mystery surrounding a woman, her reputed unpredictability and contradictions which enable man to place her outside the range of his understanding, and so despise her and enslave her when he no longer desires her. The myth of female purity which she must guard as repository of man's honor, which forces the woman into a position of "*espera,*" waiting for man to make the first move in love, and depending on him to arrive at a full awareness of her sexuality. The taboos which surround her feminine functions relating to conception and maternity once again emphasize the unknown element of her nature and increase the gap which separates her from man. Thus she is pushed into a position of subjugation and into the necessity of having to use devious methods in order to achieve her ends for "hypocrisy is the answer of the oppressed." . . .

We see then how, as well as being aware of the necessity of renovating Spanish, making it the Latin American language, Rosario Castellanos reveals also this aspect of the problem: how to transform a symbol of tyranny into the manifestation of identity and freedom. An experience not unlike that of the women who first ventured into writing adopting the language of men, to establish their position and assert their point of view.

Psiche Hughes. In Mineke Schipper, ed.
*Unheard Words: Women and Literature in
Africa, the Arab World, Asia, the
Caribbean, and Latin America.* (London:
Allison and Busby, 1985), pp. 229–32

I believe that Rosario Castellanos was a great Mexican writer: great in her aspirations, if not in her achievements. And great above all for the love she inspired and continues to inspire in us. Before her, no woman other than Sor Juana really embraced this vocation. There was no woman who lived to write. Rosario is proudly that, a creator, a maker of books. Her books—poetry and prose—are the diary of her life. And her life was marked for death. She had within herself, as in Greek tragedy, half of a smiling mask and half of a weeping one. Her effort, for the length of forty-nine years of life—a moral effort—makes her accessible to us. Rosario completed her work with her life and between the two—life and work, laughing mask, crying mask—lie the gifts that she left on earth, as a resplendent inheritance. Writing was her job, but from the beginning she lived her double condition: woman and Mexican, woman and Latin American, woman and marginal person, and this is just as bad as being black, Jewish, and cuckold all at once. As the witness to her own isolation and powerlessness, she wanted to make them visible as authentically as possible. She never lied, she never faked; she always safeguarded her inner truth.

Elena Poniatowska. ¡Ay vida, no me mereces! (Mexico City: Planeta, 1986), p. 96

Throughout the many individual volumes which make up Rosario Castellanos's collected poetry *Posesía no eres tú,* the poet returns again and again to the same sources: to the Bible, to pre-Columbian (particularly Mexican) history and myth, and to Greek mythology. Castellanos seeks in these ancient sources from both the old world and the "new" a sense of what is permanent in the past—a sense of purpose and meaning in the unfolding of the drama of human history. She seeks as well, a sense of her own identity, both collectively and individually, as a Mexican, a woman, and a unique human being. She seeks, as Beth Miller has noted, "un sentido de raigambre en la lengua y en el pasado." . . .

Castellanos's very early work (*Apuntes para una declaración de fe,* 1948, *Trayectoria del polvo,* 1948, *De la vigilia estéril,* 1950) draws its mythical and historical material mainly from the Bible. Throughout these volumes there are allusions to the Creation, Eden and the Fall, the Exodus, the fall of Jerusalem and the Babylonian Captivity. The poet uses these stories and historical events concerning the spiritual history of a people as a background against which to uncover the significance of her own history and that of her own people and time.

Beginning with the volume *El rescate del mundo* (1952), the source of myth and history shifts from the Bible to pre-Columbian civilization. Castellanos recreates many of the ancient Indian myths: leaving Aztlán, spiritual home of the early peoples of Mexico, the exodus period, the wandering in the wilderness, the legendary founding of the city of Tenochtitlán, and the awaiting of a messianic figure. These allusions acquire double significance through the obvious parallels between the two traditions that the poet has chosen to emphasize. In her attempt to interpret her own present (as an individual and as a part of Mexican society), she has fused the double roots of her cultural heritage. She has superimposed the pattern of the myth-history of the ancient peoples of Mexico on that of the Judeo-Christian tradition in order to integrate her own experience and to reveal the universal in human history.

Castellanos seeks through the recreation of collective memory not only the identity of her people or the meaning of individual existence, but the significance of her identity as a woman—of what it means to be female. Throughout her work, the poet tries to identify the specific destiny of woman in the history of man: to find in myth and history a sense of meaning and purpose in the unfolding of woman's tradition.

> Nancy Mandlove. In Elizabeth and Timothy Rogers, eds. *In Retrospect: Essays on Latin American Literature* (York, South Carolina: Spanish Literature Publishing Company, 1989), pp. 68–69

CASTILLO, ANA (UNITED STATES) 1953–

Ana Castillo's *Women Are Not Roses* (1984) rejects the worn-out stereotype of the delicate female whose purpose is to inspire, not act. Her poetic voice proclaims women's sexuality and freedom. . . .

One of the most promising [Mexican-American] novelists is Ana Castillo, whose *The Mixquiahuala Letters* (1986) is an epistolary novel consisting of forty letters sent by Teresa, a poet, to her artist friend Alicia. At the beginning of the book Castillo informs the reader that the letters are not to be "read in the usual sequence. All letters are numbered to aid in following any one of the author's proposed options." She provides a reading order for three types of people—the conformist, the cynic, and the quixotic—and adds that each letter can also be read separately as a piece of short fiction. Castillo's dedicatory note quite appropriately pays homage to Julio Cortázar, the Argentine author of *Rayuela* (Hopscotch), a 1963 novel that provides the reader with two separate orders in which to read. Castillo takes Cortázar's strategy for creative reading a step further by forcing the reader to assume an identity and participate in the game with a "personality." None of the three approaches allows for a reading of all the letters: the conformist sees twenty-nine, the cynic thirty-two, and the quixotic thirty-four. Twenty-three "core" letters are read by all three, while only the quixotic reads the first chapter and the conformist the last. Each type reads either one or two letters out of the 1–40 numerical sequence in which they are printed.

The Mixquiahuala Letters chronicles the lives of two women from the United States, beginning with their first meeting in Mexico and continuing over the course of a decade to a tragic event in one woman's life. Since all the documents are products of Teresa's pen, the reader sees only her viewpoint and her interpretation of those written by Alicia. Many letters deal with their Mexican travels together and the events in their lives as they visit several large U.S. cities. This novel is about relationships: among women and between women and men. It is an innovative, compelling, and captivating book which reveals a great deal about male-female relationships, both in Mexico and in the United States, while it explores the modern woman's attempts to change her role and status in traditional, male-dominated societies.

Carl R. Shirley and Paula W. Shirley.
Understanding Chicano Literature
(Columbia: University of South Carolina
Press, 1988), pp. 48, 138–39

Ana Castillo, a native of Chicago, first made an impact on the Chicano writers' community with the publication of her chapbook, *Otro Canto* (1977). Written mostly in English (as is almost all of Castillo's work), it ensured her reputation as a "social protest" poet at a time when it was difficult to be anything else. As a result, some of the ironic tones already present in the early work have been easily overlooked in favor of the protest message, which in fact is redoubled by irony. It can be argued that irony is one of Castillo's trademarks. Irony often appears when experience is viewed after-the-fact or in opposition to another's subjectivity. . . .

Notwithstanding the recent involvement of women in revolutionary struggles (i.e., Cuba and Nicaragua), it is still the case that in opposition to the erotic, a revolution or a war is especially marked with a traditional male subjectivity that awaits analysis. In order for a female speaker to recover the full meaningful impact of herself, she still must address how that self figures in the "heterosexual erotic contract," revolutions not excepted. Within this contract, the female body continues to be the site of both reproduction and the erotic; despite class position, a speaker and her gendered social experience are imbricated in that age-old contract. Thus, "A Counter-Revolutionary Proposition" may now be understood as a call to explore the politics of the erotic. Let us actively explore the neo-revolutionary implications of erotic relations that have been constantly displaced, undervalued, and even erased by masculine-marked militancy, or at best rendered passively by the male poet, with the woman as the muse, the wife, the mother. . . .

In *The Invitation* (1979), a chapbook-length collection of erotic poems and vignettes, Castillo's speaker no longer requests that her interlocutor forget that "everything matters" but pursues, instead, a sustained exploration of her erotic, at times bisexual, desires. The appropriation of the erotic for the female speaker is again a motivating force. The emphasis, however, is not so much on the speaker's uneasy conjunction with "proletarian politics" as it is with "textual politics." That is, the appropriative process resonates respectively against, and with, two important books of our time: Octavio Paz's *The Labyrinth of Solitude* (1950), and Maria Teresa Horta, Maria Isabel Barreno, and Maria Velho da Costa's *The Three Marias: New Portuguese Letters* (1975). Consider, for example, that in the second chapter of his book, Paz affirms women's dormant and submissive sexuality that awaits discovery through male efforts, while "The Three Marias" reject this view throughout their book and protest women's political bondage that, at the core, is based on their sexuality. Notwithstanding the different approaches that each of "The Three Marias" would take to liberate women, there is very little doubt that they agree that male perception of women's sexuality pervades all levels of women's existence.

The erotic thematics of *The Invitation* openly declare the influence of those two books. Castillo's text, when viewed in their light, becomes a purposefully glossed negation of Paz's view and an extension of the authors' own erotic vision. It is as if the relative absence of any sociopolitical debate of the Chicana/Mexicana's sexuality had made it imperative that Castillo explore instead her speaker's desire in the light of a textual milieu. Moreover, reading Castillo's work in this fashion enables us to clarify her struggle to place her erotic thematics and voices in the interstice of both her sociopolitical and textual experiences. In other words, if, due to her social position, the underclass female is called upon to address her class oppression with a readymade, class struggle rhetoric, attempting to address her sexual/erotic oppression forces her to see it in relation to texts.

Norma Alarcón. In *Breaking Barriers:
Latina Writing and Critical Readings*
(Amherst: University of Massachusetts
Press, 1989), pp. 94–97

[Bakhtin's] concept of the novel's central flexibility, its multilanguaged engagement with both literary and non-literary discourse, and its open contact with living reality, can assist in the reading of Ana Castillo's *The Mixquiahuala Letters,* a text which, like other Chicano novels, resists the purely social documentarian reading commonly applied to Third World literary narrative. Castillo's text emphatically declares itself to be a novel within the scope of Bakhtin's definition, and to recognize its dialogues with and commentary on Western, and especially Hispanic literary traditions, while at the same time seeing its commentary on social customs, is to unlock several doors into the themes of the work.

The text embraces an indeterminant reality beginning with the first (unnumbered) letter of Castillo's epistolary novel. This letter begins with the salutation "Dear Reader" and insists that "this is not a book to be read in the usual sequence." Instead, Castillo proposes three different possible groupings of the text's forty letters, all written from Teresa, a young Chicana student and writer, to her contemporary and friend Alicia, a half Hispanic and half Anglo artist. . . . The differences between each of these proposed readings lie primarily in their separate resolutions of the story of the protagonists Teresa and Alicia. The stated problems and conflicts remain essentially the same, but the outcomes shift dramatically between the three readings. In addition to the three suggested ways to read this novel, as prescribed by its author, there is also another, implied reading, which for the purposes of this essay I shall label "For the Conventionalist." This reading, for a conventional reader, is the linear reading of each of the forty letters in numerical order, which most readers might execute as purely a matter of habit. The open-endedness of the text then, in the case of Castillo's novel, lies in its open rejection of a single fixed outcome. Instead, we are led to three possible endings, and to a fourth complete reading of the text which contains all three endings at the same time and which questions them in light of each other. . . .

The success of Ana Castillo's *The Mixquiahuala Letters* lies in that it does precisely what Bakhtin recognized that the novel by its very nature must do: to represent the open-ended and dynamic nature of culture and ideology, and not merely to echo an artificially closed world. . . . In displaying the diverse cultural and social perspectives of our era one against the other, Castillo takes great leaps toward articulating a new, and emphatically Chicana world view. Castillo's text, in its refutation of established literary and social order, subverts conventionality of various stripes, and by lining it up against her portrayal of social reality, makes it display its own flaws and inconsistencies, thereby carving out a cultural space for a new and highly dynamic discourse.

Curiel. Discurso Literario. 7, 1989,
pp. 12–13, 22

CATHER, WILLA (UNITED STATES) 1873–1947

Willa Cather's best work is satisfying because it is sincere. In her books, there is none of the sweet reek that pervades the pages of so many "lady novelists." Love, to her, is "not a simple state, like measles." Her treatment of sex is without either squeamishness or sensuality. She loves the west, and the arts, particularly music, and she has sought to express feelings and convictions on these subjects. She tried, failed, and kept on trying until she succeeded.

Latrobe Carroll. The Bookman. May, 1921,
p. 215

Miss Cather's mind is basically static and retrospective, rich in images of fixed contours. . . . The characteristic quality of her mind . . . is not its puritanism or its idealism, but something deeper in which these are rooted. She is preeminently an artist dominated by her sense of the past, seeking constantly, through widely differing symbolisms, to recapture her childhood and youth. A sort of reverence for her own early years goes, hand in hand, with her Vergilian ancestor-worship; and out of this has flowered her finest work.

Clifton Fadiman. *The Nation.* December 7,
1932, pp. 564–65

A Lost Lady, Miss Cather's most explicit treatment of the passing of the old order, is the central work of her career. Far from being the delicate minor book it is so often called, it is probably her most muscular story, for it derives its power from the grandeur of its theme. Miss Cather shares the American belief in the tonic moral quality of the pioneer's life; with the passing of the frontier she conceives that a great source of fortitude has been lost.

Miss Cather's turn to the ideals of a vanished time is the weary response to weariness, to that devitalization of spirit which she so brilliantly describes in the story of Professor St. Peter. It is a weariness which comes not merely from defeat but from an exacerbated sense of personal isolation and from the narrowing of all life to the individual's sensitivities, with the resulting loss of the objectivity that can draw strength from seeking the causes of things. But it is exactly Miss Cather's point that the Lucretian *rerum naturae* means little; an admirer of Virgil, she is content with the *lacrimae rerum,* the tears of things.

Lionel Trilling. In Malcolm Cowley, ed.
After the Genteel Tradition (New York: W.
W. Norton, 1937), pp. 55, 61–62

Miss Cather's style, grave, flexible, a little austere, wonderfully transparent, everywhere economical, is wonderfully apt for her purposes. There are certain things, to be sure, it cannot do. It cannot register wit or amusement or even humor, save rarely; it never rises to passionate indignation; it lacks earthiness, despite Miss Cather's profound belief in a normal relation with the earth. Dialogue, as she reports it, is seldom more than adequate. But within its boundaries it is beautiful writing, liquid to the ear, lucent to the eye. . . . There are few to whom the adjective "classic" can be more truly applied, for beneath the quick sympathy there is a Roman gravity, a sense of the dignity of life which contemporary fiction . . . has mainly lost.

Howard Mumford Jones. *Saturday Review of
Literature.* August 6, 1938, p. 16

Willa Cather's traditionalism was . . . anything but the arbitrary or patronizing opposition to contemporary ways which Irving Babbitt personified. It was a candid and philosophical nostalgia, a conviction and a standard possible only to a writer whose remembrance of the world of her childhood and the people in it was so overwhelming that everything after it seemed drab and more than a little cheap. Her distinction was not merely one of cultivation and sensibility; it was a kind of spiritual clarity possible only to those who suffer their loneliness as an act of the imagination and the will. . . . Later, as it seemed, she became merely sentimental, and her direct criticism of contemporary types and manners was often petulant and intolerant. But the very intensity of her nostalgia had from the first led her beyond nostalgia; it had given her the conviction that the values of the world she had lost were the primary values, and everything else merely their degradation.

> Alfred Kazin. *On Native Grounds*
> (n.p.: Reynal, 1942), pp. 250–51

From beginning to end, the Cather novels are not stories of plot, but chronicles, given a depth and significance lacking in the merely historical chronicle by that "sympathy" which leads to a perfect interplay of environment and character.

Her art was essentially a representation of this reaction between the soul of man and its environment. That is why the best of her stories are told against the land. . . . Her own absorption in her people and her land creates the suspense that she herself has felt. . . . She is preservative, almost antiquarian, content with much space in little room—feminine in this, and in her passionate revelation of the values which conserve the life of the emotions.

> Henry Seidel Canby. *Saturday Review of
> Literature.* May 10, 1947, pp. 23–24

A Lost Lady reflects a curious "sunset of the pioneer"—a prismatic sunset, an almost mythical pioneer. Admirable as the story is with reference to its human relationships and emotional values, and remarkable for its creation of an atmosphere, it is still a kind of touching fairy tale of the more beneficent robber barons, or their second or third cousins. It is a reflection not of a society but of a point of view that, increasingly narrow, selective, and fanciful, is actually retreating further and further from society. . . .

From the whole range of Cather's values, standards, tastes, and prejudices, her tone is that of an inherent aristocrat in an equalitarian order, of an agrarian writer in an industrial order, of a defender of the spiritual graces in the midst of an increasingly materialistic culture. . . . Selecting and enhancing the most subtle effects of wealth, she has, rather like Sam Dodsworth's wife, either looked down upon or ignored the whole process of creating wealth. Writing so discreetly about the age when business was a personal adventure, she has neglected to mention the most typical forms of the adventure.

> Maxwell Geismar. *The Last of the
> Provincials* (Boston: Houghton Mifflin,
> 1947), pp. 183, 217–18

Mr. Maxwell Geismar wrote a book about her and some others called *The Last of the Provincials.* Not having read it I do not know his argument; but he has a case: she is a provincial; and I hope not the last. She was a good artist, and all true art is provincial in the most realistic sense: of the very time and place of its making, out of human beings who are so particularly limited by their situation, whose faces and names are real and whose lives begin each one at an individual unique center. Indeed, Willa Cather was as provincial as Hawthorne or Flaubert or Turgenev, as little concerned with aesthetics and as much with morals as Tolstoy, as obstinately reserved as Melville. In fact she always reminds me of very good literary company. . . . She is a curiously immovable shape, monumental, virtue itself in her work and a symbol of virtue—like certain churches, in fact, or exemplary women, revered and neglected.

Katherine Anne Porter. *The Days before*
(New York: Harcourt Brace, 1952),
pp. 72–73

Miss Cather's central theme is that of people who pull themselves up by their bootstraps. . . . The inner voice of the early novels of Willa Cather suggests this fascination with, and need to describe, various forms of success—but also certain forms of failure. The drive to power in these books is overriding, with the result that the novels contain no complicated plots, no complexity of human relationships, no love affairs that we can take seriously. Her heroines, those women with feminized masculine names, Alexandra, Ántonia— and the name Alexandra itself reminds us of one of history's greatest conquerors—have tenacious wills and an extraordinary capacity for struggle.

Leon Edel. *Willa Cather: The Paradox of
Success* (Washington, D.C.: Library of
Congress, 1960), p. 8

Willa Cather's principal symbol is the vast panorama of an untamed land. But it is a functionally complex symbol, accommodating several thematic levels, all inherently united. Note, for instance, that she sees the land as a meeting place for her idealistic pioneers, who find here both common cause and spiritual sanctuary. Yet she is impressed that the land or nature is an overwhelming force, often capable of exacting rigorous submission even while it may offer protection. But above all, she ever reminds us that the land is the manifestation of a divine, supersensible force.

Edward A. Bloom and Lillian D. Bloom.
Willa Cather's Gift of Sympathy
(Carbondale: Southern Illinois University
Press, 1962), p. 27

The country has shrunk, and our sense of the weight and relevance of Willa Cather's observation of Nebraska has shrunk with it. Nebraska is no doubt still there, but as a distinct imaginative possibility it has for the moment simply disappeared. As in so many other cases we are left confronting the artist who has been abandoned by his ostensible subject. The artist we now see is one whose energies are largely lavished on defensive maneuver, on masquerade. The power she now exercises is a measure of the degree to which the masquerade is itself something American. It is a small power when compared with Whitman's, but it is, despite the shell-work of fictional convention, a power of the same kind which engages us in "Song of Myself": a delighted absorption in the capacity of the self to embrace the world. In Whitman this play is overt; in Willa Cather it is masked. . . . Whitman's acceptance of his role was not open to a woman; instead Willa Cather carried on a masquerade which made it appear that she was accepting the conditions of adulthood while actually rejecting them. It was a shrewd woman of forty who published *O Pioneers!,* and discovered the terms of her disguise.

Quentin Anderson. *The New Republic.*
November 27, 1965, pp. 28, 31

All of what Willa Cather wrote, it seems to me, is ultimately a metaphor of the conflict which Miguel de Unamuno referred to as an "inward tragedy," the conflict "between what the world is as scientific reason shows it to be, and what we wish it might be, as our religious faith affirms it to be." For Willa Cather, this conflict was most broadly expressed in terms of the world she knew in her childhood—the pioneer era which she clearly idealized and ennobled in her fictional recreation of it—and the post-World War I wasteland she so thoroughly repudiated. It is easy to lose sight of the essentially symbolic nature of this conflict and to read it too narrowly in terms of literal pasts versus literal present. Her theme was not the superiority of the past over the present, but, as Henry Steele Commager has observed, "the supremacy of moral and spiritual over material values, the ever recurrent but inexhaustible theme of gaining the whole world and losing one's soul."

Rather than being irrelevant to the modern world, the moral thrust of Willa Cather's art, her concern with pioneers and artists as symbolic figures representing the unending human quest for beauty and truth, places her among the number, not of the backward-looking (which she saw herself as being one of), but of the true spiritual pioneers of all ages in whose lives or work other men continue to find inspiration.

Dorothy Tuck McFarland. *Willa Cather*
(New York: Frederick Ungar, 1972), pp. 4–5

It is love's partner, affection, that warms the life in [Cather's] work, and love's opposite, hate, that chills it. We meet pity and reconcilement there, and we meet obsession, and the hunger for something impossible. But what her characters are most truly meant for, it seems to me, is to rebel. For her heroines in particular, this is the strong, clear, undeniable impulse; it is the fateful drive. It is rebelling not for its own sake so much as for the sake of something a great deal bigger—that of integrity, of truth. It is the other face of aspiration. . . .

The desire to make a work of art and the making of it—which is love accomplished without help or need of help from another, and not without tragic cost—is what is deepest and realest, so I believe, in what she has written of human beings. Willa Cather used her own terms; and she left nothing out.

Eudora Welty. *The New York Times.*
January 27, 1974, p. 20

In . . . much of her fiction, Cather connects sexual passion with self-destruction; this remark suggests that the creator's passion, by contrast, thwarts death. The artist may "die of love" in the process of creation, but he is "born again." Cather's romantic apostrophe to the Nebraska soil in the concluding paragraph of *O Pioneers!* also promises rebirth for Alexandra, the novel's artist, after she has "faded away" into the land: "Fortunate country, that is one day to receive hearts like Alexandra's into its bosom, to give them out again in the yellow wheat, in the rustling corn, in the shining eyes of youth!" . . .

In speaking of *O Pioneers!* Willa Cather provided support for those critics who have found the novel's structure loose, insisting that she made no effort to impose form on her material: the book formed itself without her conscious intervention. The "cold Swedish story" had simply "entwined itself" with the Bohemian story, she told Elizabeth Sergeant, and "somehow she had on her hands a two-part pastoral." She struck a similar note in her preface to the second edition of *Alexander's Bridge* (1922), explaining that when the artist found "his own material" (as she had in *O Pioneers!*) he would have "less and less power of choice about the molding of it. It seems to be there of itself, already molded." But to trust the tale rather than the teller is to find that the two parts of Willa Cather's pastoral are carefully intertwined; these contrasting and counterpointed explorations of creative and sexual passion with their opposed heroines give the novel both thematic and structural unity. Willa Cather quite likely believed her statement that she did not consciously shape *O Pioneers!,* but in drawing on creative and psychological energies beneath consciousness she produced a novel whose structure may even seem overly controlled and balanced.

Sharon O'Brien. *Studies in American
Fiction.* Autumn, 1978, pp. 168–69

My Ántonia (1918), Willa Cather's celebration of the American frontier experience, is marred by many strange flaws and omissions. It is, for instance, difficult to determine who is the novel's central character. If it is Ántonia, as we might reasonably assume, why does she entirely disappear for two of the novel's five books? If, on the other hand, we decide that Jim Burden, the narrator, is the central figure, we find that the novel explores neither his consciousness nor his development. Similarly, although the narrator overtly claims that the relationship between Ántonia and Jim is the heart of the matter, their friendship actually fades soon after childhood: between these two characters there is only, as E. K. Brown said, "an emptiness where the strongest emotion might have been expected to gather." Other inconsistencies and contradictions pervade the text—Cather's ambivalent treatment of Lena Lingard and Tiny Soderball, for example—and all are in some way related to sex roles and to sexuality.

This emphasis is not surprising: as a writer who was also a woman, Willa Cather faced the difficulties that confronted, and still do confront, accomplished and ambitious women. As a professional writer, Cather began, after a certain point in her career, to see the world and other women, including her own female characters, from a male point of view. Further, Cather was a lesbian who could not, or did not, acknowledge her homosexuality and who, in her fiction, transformed her emotional life and experiences into acceptable, heterosexual forms and guises. In her society it was difficult to be a woman and achieve professionally, and she could certainly not be a woman who loved women; she responded by denying, on the one hand, her womanhood and, on the other, her lesbianism. These painful denials are manifest in her fiction. After certain early work, in which she created strong and achieving women, like herself, she abandoned her female characters to the most conventional and traditional roles; analogously, she began to deny or distort the sexuality of her principal characters. *My Ántonia,* written at a time of great stress in her life, is a crucial and revealing work, for in it we can discern the consequences of Cather's dilemma as a lesbian writer in a patriarchal society. . . .

In order to create independent and heroic women, women who are like herself, the woman writer must avoid male identification, the likelihood of which is enhanced by being a writer who is unmarried, childless, and a lesbian. In the case of *My Ántonia,* Cather had to contend not only with the anxiety of creating a strong woman character, but also with the fear of a homosexual attraction to Annie/Ántonia. The novel's defensive narrative structure, the absence of thematic and structural unity that readers have noted, these are the results of such anxieties. Yet, because it has been difficult for readers to recognize the betrayal of female independence and female sexuality in fiction—their absence is customary—it has also been difficult to penetrate the ambiguities of *My Ántonia,* a crucial novel in Cather's long writing career.

Deborah G. Lambert. *American Literature.*
January, 1982, pp. 676–77, 690

Willa Cather's novels champion the warrior hero, noble mother-women, the values of hard work, thrift, self-sacrifice, and the American family. A less likely modernist would be hard to find. And yet Willa Cather was a master of disguise. When she was in high school in Red Cloud, she cleared and wallpapered the closet in the attic bedroom shared by her brothers. She furnished the tiny space with a bed, a chair, and an elegant glass-shelved, glass-enclosed dresser. Thus she had at eye level several conch shells, whose outer spikes and curled overlip cradled creamy-pink lush insides. These prongs and their inner succulence together form a metaphor for Cather's craft—a facade of defended beauty that shielded hurt, desire, rage, and a need to hide.

Such prickly defenses are evident in Cather's essay "The Novel Démeublé," published in 1936 in the *New Republic*. This essay has clear connections to Virginia Woolf's "Modern Fiction," "The Russian Point of View," and "The Novels of Turgenev." While Woolf insists that genre and form may be wrenched to fit the extremes of post–World War I consciousness, "The Novel Démeublé" appears to turn its back on what is now called early male modernism—fiction that is experimental, audience-challenging, language-focused rather than story- or character-focused. Male modernism, however, gained its permission from the same sources Cather used for the self-validation evidently infusing "The Novel Démeublé." That is the fin-de-siècle deification of the male artist, whose rage at society elevated him above the ordinary and whose superior aesthetics freed him from moral restraint. Although as a young woman Cather claimed to abhor the aesthetic movement and decadence *(The Kingdom of Art),* she believed in the primacy, the religion, of art and its ruthless emotional imperatives as fervently as Verlaine or Wilde or Joyce *(The Kingdom of Art)*. Male modernism's obsessive centering on language rather than persons harkened back to Flaubert just as much as did Cather's insistence on impeccable prose and laconic use of detail. But the centrality of traditional fictional forms—supple prose that deliberately calls no attention to itself, an omniscient author, and seemingly realistic characters and narratives—are in Cather's work as much disguises as are the wrenched syntax and Homeric epic parallels in James Joyce's work. The desire for fame and honor to be obtained through her writing burned in Cather certainly as much as they did in Pound, Eliot, and Joyce, but Cather knew better than to despise money and her audience. To make an abundant living from an American reader's market while expressing the author's deepest childhood secrets, her rages, and her adult sexuality required subtle subterfuge. Under the furniture covers of the missing sofas and chairs of "The Novel Démeublé" is a clear implication about Cather's choice of disguise, argues Sharon O'Brien. . . . Extending her argument further, I suggest that, for Cather, seemingly traditional realism became a method to render the safely obvious devious and obscure.

> Jane Lilienfeld. In Bonnie Kime Scott, ed.
> *The Gender of Modernism*. (Bloomington:
> Indiana University Press, 1990), pp. 49–50

[Willa Cather] was a very intense woman. She herself said that she always wanted to hang garlands on people or else put them to torture, and this tendency was so strong in her that it evidently rubbed off on those whose paths crossed hers, for all her life people seem either to have liked her greatly or else felt repelled by her. She made Thea Kronborg say that there was such a thing as "creative hate"; a good example of this in her own writing is her review of D'Annunzio's *Il Fuoco,* which she resented for its treatment of Eleonora Duse. . . .

[Cather] liked what was "real," honest, straightforward, clean by the standards of common, decent humanity. As early as her first trip to Europe in 1902, she turned with relief from Monte Carlo, where she even felt that the artificial activities carried on corrupted nature herself. In the *Archbishop* she would deplore the replacement in the churches of the Southwest of the original, crude, hand-made art created by the people themselves with cheap purchased images, factory-made, and imported from the East. Even in Nebraska itself, once the generation of the pioneers had passed, a new breed came in that was more interested in driving into town in an automobile to buy something instead of staying on the farm and making it.

Edward Wagenknecht. *Willa Cather*
(New York: Continuum, 1993), pp. 139,
143–44

CEDERNA, CAMILLA (ITALY) 1921–

[In] 1945, Cederna was one of the founders of the weekly *L'Europeo* and continued to work as a professional journalist for this magazine for eleven years. Since 1956, she has been part of the the staff of *L'Espresso,* for which she has written as both a domestic and foreign correspondent, doing interviews and also a column, "The Weak Side." A brilliant and well-informed writer, Cederna exercises her sharp spirit of observation and her sense of the ironic in exploring a discourse where all the linguistic manifestations of a gradually updated lexicon are pleasantly respected. Behind her apparent frivolity, there is hidden a serious moral commitment, as witness the position she took on the political affair of the attack at the Banco d'Agricultura of Milan in December of 1969.

Enzo Ronconi, ed. *Dizionario della
letteratura contemporanea italiana,* vol. 1
(Florence: Vallecchi, 1973), p. 215

Considered one of the most daring writer-journalists of the past forty years, Cederna has always remained faithful to her gay, luminous, untrammeled—almost frivolous, as some criticism has insinuated—style. It is a style that has succeeded in evolving and, at the same time, always adhering to the "various changes that have taken place over the years," without betraying her own principles, but rather basing her writing on the search for and discovery of the truth. . . .

In this [latest] collection [*The Best of . . .*] the impression it gives has the bold and lucid attraction of something that has been set on fire, in which the eye of the reporter observes people and events from the political, cultural, and entertainment worlds without reverence. What they do or what has made news—described by Cederna in the pages of newspapers and magazines— are mixed with minor characters ranging from a cabinet minister to a sexpot, from the famous man of letters to fictional characters (like the Countess Pellettier de Belminy, invented by Cederna herself around the end of 1945 for the just-born *Europeo*)—each one with its story—that replicate prototypes from the world in which we live. A society, in short, that is more like one of Barnum's circuses: from Andreotti and Pella to Khruschev and the Kennedys, to Callas and Tebaldi, to Coppi, to Faviola the Queen of the Belgians and her brother Jaime de Mora. Among others, there are Milva, Pertini, Gadda, the DeFilippos, Orio Vergani, Toscanini, Pietro Valpreda, Montale, Elizabeth Taylor, Leopardi, Arturo Benedetti, Michelangeli, Fellini, Flaiano, Mina, Sbarbaro, Savino, Wanda Osiris, Lucio Piccolo and Tomasi di Lampedusa, Carla Boni, Carducci, Ava Gardner, D'Annunzio, the Counts Calvi di Bergolo, Giancarlo Menotti, Pinelli, Anna Magnani, Don Backy, Celentano, and Milena Cantu. Notably missing is the name of Giovanni Leone, although it was one of the key issues to which Cederna has devoted so many revealing pages. But, as the author herself states in an introductory note, it is a question of a choice of articles in which she preferred to privilege her activity as a chronicler of manners over the key battles of her life. And this is perhaps the reason that the characters, although so varied, are joined to one another . . . by a sort of infallible gaze on the part of the author who observes—passionately, but without rhetoric—the very variety of existence, from its apparently vaguest and most mundane expressions to the most atrocious ones. Rather, displacement from the social to the private, from the collective to the individual is an operation that permits her to define the character of people at all levels (including their way of dressing, speaking, moving). . . . In this sense, even people from the world of literature are captured with a characteristic reality, outside the usual conventional schemas. . . .

There are also unforgettable portraits . . . in which Cederna succeeds in distilling delicious falvors and corrosive poisons. . . .

But what is most striking in this very fine collection of articles written between 1948 and 1982 is that in some way they have scanned the life of Italians from the immediate postwar years to the 1980s. . . . And even though her articles on public issues are not included in the collection, some of the battles in which Cederna was the central figure are nonetheless recalled. Among them are the struggle to prevent the coverup of the case of the anarchist Pinelli, the defense of Pietro Valpreda, as well as a number of courageous crusades (the death of Feltrinelli, the Seveso tragedy). . . .

Written with great skill and centering on issues and events seen in depth throughout the author's career as a journalist and correspondent, the texts collected in this volume are at one and the same time a document and a piece of literature and of social history. A sort of diary of an intellectual that, sustained either by an authentic and delicate moral sensitivity or by a personal sense of humor, keeps watch over and interprets the malaises of our time and of a society in a constant state of transformation.

Pietro Frassica. *Gradiva*. 4:2, 1988, pp. 66–69

Camilla Cederna's literary production has reflected the manners and customs of influential segments of Italian society for four decades. In the 1950s and 1960s, her newspaper columns provided insight into the country's cultural, social, and political life; her work in the 1970s implicated the highest offices of government in scandalous activities; books written in the 1980s return to her earlier orientation and again expose the inner dynamism of a nation. Her first books, *Noi siamo le signore* (We are the ladies), *La voce dei padroni* (Voice of the big bosses), and *Signore e signori* (Ladies and gentlemen), contain ironic, pungent descriptions of the upper middle-class in Milan, as well as lively, humorous, and penetrating portraits of important personalities. Although Cederna depicts Italian life in an acute and nonconforming manner, she also exposes truth, especially in those instances when government officials try to camouflage it with cover-ups, payoffs, and continuous lies. Cederna's thirst for justice provides Italian readers with such powerful denunciations of corruption that Cederna may be compared to Bob Woodward and Carl Bernstein, whose *All the President's Men* publicized the Watergate scandals. . . .

Cederna's most recent volume, *De gustibus* (1986), consists of all the articles published by the writer between 1979 and 1986. Once again, she deals with trends, issues, and events but particularly highlights the language of advertising and fashion, commenting specifically on Americanisms and their general use by the Italian public. "Made in Italy" is a passage on style written as a mixture of the two languages. This perceptive rendition includes such expressions as *il nuovo look* (the new look), *respirare un feeling* (to breathe a feeling), *lo stile casuale* (casual style), *effetto hand-made* (hand-made effect), *la giacca con i taschini a patches per un look country* (the jacket with patched pockets for a country look), and *"fa" country la flanella* (flannel gives a country look). A few pages define what the writer refers to as *lessico pervertito* ("perverted sayings") and list such unbelievable neologisms found in the press as *si beve, si snacka* (people drink and snack) and *Managerialità* (manageriality). In addition, Cederna quizzes readers on misused clichés: "Who is seriously ill? 'Tourism.' What disease do parliamentarians suffer from? 'Disaffection.' Who risks having a paralysis? Any kind of public service and transportation, the political system, trade unions, and, even worse, the country's 'governability.'" Cederna devotes much of her attention to changes in language and analyzes the reasons for the rise and fall of new idioms. When she writes about a trendy adjective, she examines how the press uses it and what it really means. When, on the other hand, certain words decline in usage, she carefully lists their replacements. *Non male* (not bad) substitutes for *bello* (beautiful) or *bellissimo* (very beautiful). She criticizes journalists and writers who, misusing words, act "as if an invisible laziness or a collective infectious disease had suddenly struck them."

As a journalist, Cederna asserts her belief in an informative and instructive press. The integrity of her convictions teaches her to recognize problems, to report them, and to seek just solutions. Nevertheless, her great strengths remain an unshakable, positive outlook on life, an unfailing sense of humor, and the capacity to transform indifference into a firm commitment. In the concluding pages of *Il mondo di Camilla,* she identifies with Voltaire's comment on frivolity. "If nature had not made us a little bit frivolous, we would be very unhappy; most people do not hang themselves precisely because they are frivolous." Indeed, Cederna succeeds in incorporating the many and varied dimensions of her nation's life into her writings. This ability to portray Italian cultural and social history vividly, humorously, and truthfully in her reporting not only imbues her work with both literary and journalistic qualities but also serves to highlight creatively the heartbeat of contemporary Italy.

> Giovanna Bellesia. In Santo L. Aricò, ed.
> *Contemporary Women Writers in Italy: A*
> *Modern Renaissance* (Amherst: University
> of Massachusetts Press, 1990), pp. 185,
> 195–96

CERVANTES, LORNA DEE (UNITED STATES) 1954–

Emplumada, the first published collection by Lorna Dee Cervantes, is poetry that defines a Mexican-American identity and so carries an "ethnic" denomination. As ethnic poetry it is art that does not dwell in the region of purely detached art, "art for art's sake," but that necessarily attempts to establish its integrity in a particular territory and time. However, for Cervantes, the role of the ethnic writer intent on affirming a personal and group identity within a clearly defined temporal and spatial context is complicated by the fact that her sense of self as a woman does not conform to the traditions of her ethnic heritage. Together, the poems of *Emplumada* tell the story of a coming-of-age in which time-honored "great expectations" are necessarily altered. The rites-of-passage of a Mexican-American woman will not fit the formula of the nineteenth-century *Bildüngsroman,* nor will her rites be consonant with stereotypic sex roles in Chicano coming-of-age novels. As long as the achievement of an identity through a temporal process in which the child struggles to adulthood is male-identified, a discussion of the struggle toward an autonomous female identity will be viewed as feminist; and within the closely held values of ethnicity "feminism" is likely to be equated with subversion. Thus the poems of *Emplumada,* speaking as they do of a Chicana coming-of-age, heighten awareness of human as well as artistic complexities.

Cervantes establishes the spatial dimension of her poetry within a Mexican barrio of San José, California, where she grew up; and, though the poems of *Emplumada* identified with feathers and winged birds are poems of flight and of freeing, they are poems of place-centeredness. The ultimate liberation is not measured in distance but rather in the ability to stay on the scene where one has fought and won her/his sense of integrity. The poem "Crow" speaks of women as expert at keeping places clean and recalls the fact that Cervantes received her "literary education" as a little girl who, while her mother cleaned the houses of well-to-do families, read their volumes of Shakespeare. . . .

Cervantes is doubly admirable for not being caught in a double bind. Mythic imagery might speak of these poems as a source, a confluence where streams converge. Such metaphors of flowing and feeding have for a long time been assigned to woman. However, in Cervantes's poems nothing is washed away but rather what is and has been is defined and understood in human terms; and it is this clear definition derived from the art of the writer who represents a dual minority identity, that of woman and that of Chicana, that gets it all together. What might have been the bottom is the final line, the last definitive word. What might have been a double loss is a double gain.

Revelations of the woman who is not a blushing bride but a human being with scars and expectations, accomplishments and potentials, a woman who finds her roots in tradition and enters history, move her toward selfhood across a background of traditional gender configurations. *Machismo,* the cult of masculinity that sets women apart from an existential process of becoming something in the world, draws sharp images associated with Latin culture but not peculiar to it. In this context, the picture is most clearly seen. Definitions are without ambiguities so that the woman who exercises a right to choose knows what she is choosing. "Lorna Dee Cervantes," as Susan Mernit puts it, "is a writer who knows exactly who she is and how she got that way."

Lynette Seator. MELUS. 11, Summer, 1984,
pp. 23, 37

With regard to a number of fundamental issues, (Bernice) Zamora and Cervantes are not so far apart. . . . Both use their first book to announce a sort of *ars poetica* and . . . even considering the differences, each writer's process and the dynamic of her position's development with respect to her world and society men and poetry, reflects a similar paradigm. And, in both cases, the implicit aesthetic has a feminist character.

Zamora's *Restless Serpent* and Cervantes's *Emplumada* both begin with a poem about the patriarchal system, particularly about a ritual through which men try to structure society and life. . . . In each case, the text provides a feminist alternative as another, oppositional possibility, not just because it can be posed as something different, but rather as a way to confront the masculine paradigm with a protest, critique, and negation, and because it has its roots and strength in women themselves, whose experiences the poetry seeks to give a voice to. . . .

Cervantes feels no nostalgia for any sacred order, perhaps because she has never lived in a rural area where the old faith was practiced. For her, masculine rituals are not noble and do not commemorate any glorious figure. In the first poem in *Emplumada,* "Uncle's First Rabbit," she evokes the violent man, the killer, the hunter. The ritual is the boy's apprenticeship as he has to kill a rabbit for the first time, has to prove that he is a man who can kill in order to make his mark on the world. Men, Cervantes tells us, practice the same way of controlling their surroundings all through their lives, especially with respect to women at home or against other nations in their international relations. The patriarchal order is about imposing one's will through violence and death. . . .

Cervantes associates the woman with nature through the identity of a victim that she shares with animals. . . . Nature in Cervantes is the other violated by man. . . .

Cervantes makes her poetry into the affirmation of love and creativity in harmony with nature. During her apprenticeship, she faces many enemies who attack her, who try in some way to kill her, and who are avatars of the same enemy-ally. Her mother will guide her to be hard, hateful, and negative. . . . Each time, Cervantes survives, using the lessons to become strong and wise. Ultimately, she offers us the text itself as proof that she has made it through.

> Juan Bruce-Novoa. *Revista Ibero-americana.* 51, 1985, pp. 565–67, 573

Another poet who adds significantly to *flor y canto* is Lorna Dee Cervantes, a Chicana who invigorates her skillful verses with the rich resonance of womanhood, a state of being she perceives as large and expansive enough to circumscribe the diversity of human experience. Concerned with capturing the manifold quality of personal experience, including its most private aspects, Cervantes textures her work with vivid details from everyday life. Her verse also reveals a powerfully evoked *Chicanismo* comprehended as both a literal part of her self-identity and as an external source of metaphor. . . .

Cervantes usually develops a distinct subjective I-persona in each of her poems to achieve an intimacy reminiscent of Confessional Poetry. . . . A review of the individual titles in *Emplumada* discloses several poems with emphatically personal points of view—as the following titles indicate.

> Uncle's First Rabbit
> For Edward Long
> For Virginia Chavez
> From Where We Sit: Corpus Cristi

> Poem for the Young White Men Who Asked Me How I,
>   an Intelligent, Well-Read Person Could Believe
>   in the War Between Races
> To My Brother
> For All You Know
> Como lo siento
> [Etc.]

Accordingly, Cervantes's treatment of nature partakes of this subjectivity in interesting, powerful, and often unusual ways.

In "Emplumada," the book's last poem, the poet moves from a consideration of nature as *a mirror of the passage* of time to a representation of nature as *a means of escaping* time. To mirror the decay that time brings, Cervantes employs floral imagery. . . .

That this piece is both the volume's title poem and the last one in the book evidences a specialness that relates to the book's central theme. The poem conveys the fragility and transitoriness of lived experience and suggests that art—poetry here—is the only real way to gain "distanc[e] from history." The book's lexical inscription ties these two qualities together aptly. . . .

Lorna Dee Cervantes's "Visions of Mexico . . ." in the volume *Emplumada* incorporates some of these same concerns enunciated by Sánchez. She, too, finds that the "sense of [Mexico] can only ripple through my veins / like the chant of an epic corrido"—that is, a song—and she, too, is alert to the popular caricature that "Mexico is a stumbling comedy." In addition, Cervantes uses a contrasting *hay* as backdrop for "that far south" just as Sánchez employed Alaska to place Mexico in topographical and cultural perspective. She uses "Port Townsend, Washington" as the dissimilar locus, a place too "far north" where she doesn't "belong" and which lacks "pueblos green on the low hills" and "all those meadows: Michoacan/ Vera Cruz, Tenochtitlan, Oaxaca." Although when she's "that far south" her "own words somersault naturally as my name," speaking her joyful ease there, she is not impervious to the privations of the people. . . .

The same sort of affirmation that grows out of pain in the "lots" pieces weaves through "To My Brother," but in this poem the poet locates the center of agony in socioeconomic deprivation. Even the sun underscores the absence of money in "that dreary setting" of barrio poverty through the speaker's description of the round, copper "sun" as "scarred penny." Nevertheless, the "smog-strewn avalanche" of their squalid lives cannot destroy their minds and imagination. . . .

Just as the poet cannot understate the misery of their poverty, she cannot exaggerate the importance of thought and imagination in helping them—and, possibly, other poor—escape "the sullen skyline" of their objective reality. What saves the speaker and her brother from being overwhelmed by despair is the light of their "dreams" like "flying embers" which "glow in the heart all night." Thus, Cervantes matches the diamond brightness which closes

"Lots: II" with the fire brightness at the end of "To My Brother." The affirmation produced out of agony at the end of these pieces reveals an essentially biblical interpretation of suffering. It is biblical in its view of human pain as a prerequisite for growth and, possibly, transcendence. . . . While Cervantes does not make the biblical ethos explicit, it is implicit in her poetry's phoenix-like transformation of agony into affirmation.

Cordelia Candelaria. *Chicano Poetry*
(Westport, Connecticut: Greenwood Press,
1986), pp. 156–57, 182–83, 188–89, 217,
224–26

Cervantes is a great definer of terms. At the very beginning of *Emplumada,* she devotes a whole page to defining her title, according to a binary opposition.

> *em-plu-ma-do* [adj.] m., feathered; in plumage, as in after
>   molting
> *plu-ma-da* n.f., pen flourish

My reading of this pairing is that the act of writing has to do with coming into one's own, being empowered for flight (the colorful image of plumage is linked to the Chicano heritage).

The book is divided into three sections. Each has a headnote or short title. Each of these consists of two terms, either stated or understood. The headnote of the first section is ominous: "Consider the power of wrestling your ally. His will is to kill you. He has nothing against you." The pairing around the image of "ally" introduces the contradiction of malign will versus moral indifference. The second section, with the headnote "This world understands nothing but words and you have come into it with almost none," concerns the acquisition of a language necessary to survive in the world. Language has now become the ally with which one must wrestle in order to succeed. The third section is titled simply "Emplumada," referring us back to the pairing "feathered; in plumage" and "pen flourish." This would appear to speak to some synthesis, where the dangers of the world are confronted by a language appropriate to their expression, resulting in the freeing of the writer for an as yet unspecified task.

As the binary terms of each section of *Emplumada* suggest, the book is always in a state of development. The first section, governed by the image of "wrestling your ally," treats the poet growing up in her single-parent household of mother and grandmother, mediating images of "hardness" and "softness" to understand how she will confront the world. . . . The second section, governed by the problem of language, shows the poet cast out into the world, unable to recover her Mexican heritage and seriously challenged by the harsh world of the Anglo dominant culture. The third section attempts a reconciliation of tradition and modernity. The persona of the poet develops in each case. In the first section a myth of the past is brought into place, showing formative influences on the girl growing up in the barrio. The second section shows the poet in transaction with Mexican and Anglo culture. In the third section she speaks in her own voice. The identity of the poet Lorna Dee Cervantes and the persona of the book become more marked as the book progresses. . . .

Following Quiñonez's observation that Chicana poets are "creating new symbols, new images, and synthesizing all of those aspects into new myths," I would take *Emplumada* as a fabulous narrative of development in which we see simultaneously the autobiographical figure of the young poet, the spiritual figure of the artist taking flight, and the social figure of the Chicana struggling to find a language appropriate to deal with reality. After the crafted "family" poems in the first section come more social pieces where the lessons of the world are treated in a vivid way that still allows for a certain didacticism (you must learn to survive in a place full of danger). The increasingly lyrical and personal poems of the last section appear to announce the poet's emergence in her own voice, no longer looking back to family mythology or the "stage" she has passed through of learning how to deal with the world. Cervantes is portraying her own development in the form of a "portrait of the artist as Chicana." Of necessity, she will return to her origins and her social concerns in subsequent writings, with different strategies and seeking different results in the poetry.

> John F. Crawford. In Marie Harris and
> Kathleen Aguero. *A Gift of Tongues:*
> *Critical Challenges in Contemporary*
> *American Poetry* (Athens: University of
> Georgia Press, 1987), pp. 170–71, 179–80

[A] Chicana poet who has added a significant work to the body of Chicano literature is Lorna Dee Cervantes. *Emplumada* (1981) is a highly sophisticated collection of poems that manifest the concerns of the feminist poet. Subjects are wide-ranging and include domestic violence, identity, social oppression, nature, time, death, and poetry. One of Cervantes's most beautiful poems from this volume is "Beneath the Shadow of the Freeway," a narrative of three generations together forming "a woman family." The grandmother's quiet nurturing contrasts with the mother's cynicism. Their daughter/granddaughter listens to them both as the new freeway under construction gets ever closer to their home. The concluding stanzas state that the interloping freeway is now "across the street" as the girl now reflects her mother and grandmother in dress and actions. In another poem, "Freeway 280," the poetic voice describes the neighborhood apparently destroyed by the freeway, but the speaker has returned in hopes of finding part of herself that was lost with her neighborhood. The refusal of plant life to die and the return of the people to gather food suggest the indomitability of the *Raza* who persist in the face of technological blight. When this poem is read in the context of the previous one, "Beneath the Shadow of the Freeway," its meaning is enhanced by its association with the vivid picture of the women who used to live in the neighborhood.

"Poem for the Young White Man Who Asked Me How I, an Intelligent, Well-Read Person Could Believe in the War between Races" is a rebuke of the smug notion of a casteless society. The speaker describes a violent, war-like world, then contrasts it with the wounds of oppression:

> . . . my stumbling mind, my
> "excuse me" tongue, and this
> nagging preoccupation
> with the feeling of not being good enough.

The tone of Cervantes's "revolutionary" poem ("I am not a revolutionary./ I don't even like political poems") is one of quiet outrage, which is quite different from that of Movement poetry, which is generally hortatory and appeals to the indigenous past. . . .

Lorna Dee Cervantes displays a sophisticated refinement in her work which, paradoxically perhaps, also appears earthy. Even when she deals with subjects that have been written about many times in Chicano poetry, she infuses them with new meaning through her polished style. As one of the editors of a widely respected chapbook series, *Mango,* she has contributed to a growing body of outstanding poetry by Chicano and Chicana writers. Bruce-Novoa's appraisal of *Emplumada* as "among the best Chicano books ever published" is justly deserved.

Carl R. Shirley and Paula W. Shirley.
Understanding Chicano Literature
(Columbia: University of South Carolina
Press, 1988), pp. 45–47

CESPEDES, ALBA DE (ITALY) 1911–

Alba de Cespedes . . . is a kind of feminine knight-errant, tilting her literary lance in behalf of women. But it is not against their economic, political, or social plight that she tilts so much as against the plight of their psyche, the anguish of their hearts. Yet in this novel, *The Best of Husbands . . . ,* the author reveals, almost unwittingly, that no bridge crosses the psychological abyss between men and women. Her lance breaks against the stubborn facts of human nature. . . . This tale of an unresigned Cinderella . . . moves toward its climax of violence with emotional power and a certain genuine sensitivity. But the climax itself is somehow incredible. The lament for wives which underlies the story and appears to justify it is somehow absurd and immature, when we all know that the earth would cease to turn on its axis if men were to stop adventuring and crusading and grow so concerned with domesticity that they remained to coddle their wives at home.

Virgilia Peterson. *New York Herald Tribune.*
November 2, 1952, p. 14

There are many good things in this book [*The Best of Husbands*]. . . . But . . . other aspects of the work are dwarfed by the main theme which can be stated simply as the tragic failure of men to understand women. The title in the original *(Dala parte di lei—Her Side of the Case)* brings out its feminism very clearly. . . . Alessandra . . . is not abnormal among sensitive and intelligent women of today in wanting from her husband not so much protection as comradeship, not so much privilege plus disregard as respect and interest. Tragedy comes about not because her best of husbands doesn't understand her but because he simply doesn't see that there is anything to understand.

Thomas G. Bergin. *Saturday Review of Literature.* November 8, 1952, p. 52

[*The Secret*] is by far the most profound yet the simplest of Alba de Cespedes's books, written with the powerful insight that only a sensitive, highly intelligent woman could bring to the basic problem of Western woman: how to use the freedoms she has won, how to play the manifold roles of wife, mother and professional woman, yet still retain the essential touchstone, the self.

Signora de Cespedes is one of the few distinguished women writers since Colette to grapple effectively with what it is to be a woman. Her brilliant handling of Valeria's moral hegira places her in the forefront of contemporary novelists.

Frances Keene. *The New York Times.*
September 28, 1958, p. 5

Between Then and Now is a short novel written with a disciplined, restrained intensity that makes its effect in depth. It has a circular shape like a well-constructed play. . . . The way in which . . . a simple domestic incident is made to link present and past, and illustrate the speed of contemporary social flux is formally satisfying. The author has been compared with crashing ineptitude to Colette. Though her writing touch is light she is full of lofty ideas, like one of those noble souls that so delighted Stendhal when he first arrived in Italy.

Maurice Richardson. *New Statesman and Nation.* September 2, 1959, p. 328

Alba de Cespedes, one of Italy's most popular woman journalists, writes well. It is not her style, but her subject matter that leaves one unimpressed. Writing in the first person, she tells of the main character's years of young womanhood, lived during a war, and in a country which not only was a main battlefield, but found itself simultaneously fighting on both sides; she speaks of at least two love affairs and one broken engagement, and one wonders that so many currents of history, drama, and mankind brought to bear on one person could have resulted in so little feeling, understanding, or compassion. In this, *Between Then and Now* has the aroma of the Deux Magots, the Paris school of this-is-how-we-are-how-did-we-get-this-way.

When the reader reflects that this novel was written in sunny Rome, city of immemorial life and loud and vigorous living, he cannot but conclude that it may have been written in the wrong place, at the wrong time, and in the wrong original language.

John H. Secondari. *Saturday Review of
Literature.* March 26, 1960, p. 28

Cespedes's narrative centers on recurrent themes, most of them relating to the female condition. Her evolution means that as her readers move from one novel to the next, they find an increasing sense of the writer's individual maturation and her sense of the problems she is involved with. The language used by Cespedes to deal with these themes, whether in the vocabulary employed or in the logical structures that connect her various statements, functions such that the message can be readily grasped by a wide audience.

The center of such a narrative develops around the search for identity, initially presented through the realities of the most varied female characters; once attention is focused on the most representative character, on themes that are appropriate to a single model protagonist, the author follows the various ramifications of the themes themselves and the evolution of a female model henceforth defined as the bearer of the narrative sense.

This happens in such a way that every female character in search of identity goes through stages that are always the same, almost obligatory, from which is may deduced that every woman, as she grows up, has these necessary and unavoidable passages.

The female characters who carries Cespedes's narrative message is one who succeeds in separating herself from the social and familial fold in which she works out her fate. The female subject matter, once it is fully anatomized, makes way in the last novel, for the male point of view; it is no accident, in that an exploration of the female point of view would not be exhaustive without a direct contrast with the male one. . . .

To say that the title of a novel embodies its main theme or at least focuses attention on a major element, would be a mere tautology, but insofar as de Cespedes's narrative is concerned, it suffices to look at her titles to trace their thematic evolution.

From *No Turning Back,* which examines the fate of individuals at a precise moment of choice the passage from adolescence to maturity, to *Her Side of the Case,* a novel clearly centered on the destiny of being a woman, to *Forbidden Notebook,* in which the prohibition laid on the protagonist is a role that is already fixed but susceptible to being reopened, *Before and after,* which sums up in this adverbial contraposition a narrative constant embraced by Cespedes's entire output, to *Remorse,* the novel in which the protagonists take stock of their common sense of guilt, from which some of them succeed in freeing themselves, to *The Big Doll,* in which the physical attribute is central as a direct result of the male gaze privileged in the novel.

In Cespedes, the initial source of the process of self-analysis in private reality, with consequent opening to the social, always follows from an event, which may be a banal one, that places the "before" of the character's life in opposition to the "after." Cespedes's protagonists see their lives split in two: into an already fixed before that they analyze and an after represented by the new choices for the present. The constant connection between before and after creates the condition such that, given certain premises, certain consequences and choices are necessary and become immutable, in spite of the desire for change.

The fact is thus axiomatic that happiness in the traditional sense does not correspond to a life choice that safeguard's one's own identity; and, correspondingly, the possession of consumer goods and ordinary satisfactions corresponds to the acceptance of a foreordained role.

The conflict between reason and happiness is concretized from the first novel on in terms of these two opposing models of life.

> Maria Assunta Parsani and Neria DeGiovanni. *Femminile a confronto* (Manduria: Lacaita, 1984), pp. 15–17

CHACEL, ROSA (SPAIN) 1898–

Though she has written numerous critical articles in such journals as *Sur* (Buenos Aires) and *Nueva Estafeta* and has published two books of poetry, three collections of short stories, and two book-length essays, she is best known for her novels. After *Estación, Ida y vuelta* (1930), her next novel, *Teresa,* a biographical novel about Teresa Mancha, Espronceda's lover, was published in 1941 in Buenos Aires, where *Memorias de Leticia Valle* was also published in 1945. Her most ambitious novel, *La sinrazón* appeared in Buenos Aires in 1960. The second edition, published in Spain in 1970, won the 1977 Premio de la Crítica. Her latest work, *Barrio de Maravillas,* won the same literary prize in 1976. It is the first volume of a trilogy project. . . .

The proposed titles of the last two volumes are *Escuela de Platón* and *Ciencias naturales.* Recently an excerpt from her latest work, *Novelas antes de tiempo,* appeared in *La Nueva Estafeta.*

Unlike so many writers of the generations of 1927 and 1936, Chacel chooses to ignore the Spanish Civil War in most of her novels. Only in *La sinrazón* is that war presented and then only from the perspectives of two outsiders. One view is that of a young Spanish man who emigrated to Buenos Aires at the age of eighteen and who is concerned about the situation of Spain only because his uncle remains in Spain. The second point of view is a personal one: that of a young woman who joins the republican cause in order to find the man she loves. Editorial comment on the Civil War is, therefore, minimized. This lack of vehement protest can be attributed to Rosa Chacel's apolitical view of that tragedy of Spanish history. She explains that society is a moral, religious and intellectual structure whereas the political structure, for her, does not exist because she is not interested in ephemeral things. Therefore, the importance of the war was moral, religious, and cultural—not political. Spain adopted a way of life that she did not wish to live.

Rosa Chacel, then, is an apolitical person whose main interest is the aesthetic: that is to say, she finds pleasure in studying literature and art and in creating them. An overview of her novels can be gained by an examination of her first novel as a seminal work that manifests certain prevalent influences from the past and which contains themes and techniques that are used with greater maturity and success in her later novels.

Estación, ida y vuelta is, indeed, a novel of apprenticeship in two senses. First, it is the initial work of a young writer and, second, it is a type of *Bildungsroman*. This first novel is a learning process with many weaknesses which Chacel later acknowledged. . . .

Chacel's first novel is . . . a novel of initiation of the artist *(Kunstlerroman)* as well as an initial novel of apprenticeship for Chacel—a first novel that reflects the influence of several important European authors. In addition to this dependence upon the past, however, Chacel's work also has originality. Themes and techniques that are introduced in her first novel are developed and perfected in subsequent novels. One technique that is used in all her novels, except *Teresa,* is first-person narration, exploring the psyche of her protagonists through everyday occurrences. This technique, which is typical of the "novela de tempo lento" . . . eliminates authorial intrusion through the use of a diary or memoir. In *Memorias de Leticia Valle,* for example, a young girl writes in her diary about her feelings upon being sent away from Spain and her family during the Spanish Civil War. Social commentary is minimized because the girl does not understand the political reasons for her departure. Similarly, in *Barrio de Maravillas,* an adolescent describes her friendships and her everyday life in a first-person narrative. Chacel's narrator is usually a young female; in fact, only in *Estación* and *La sinrazón* is the principal character a man.

These two novels are similar in several other ways, especially in plot and tone. Rose Chacel explains that she began *La sinrazón* in the 1940s, developing ideas first expressed in *Estacion.* . . .

Rosa Chacel's novels, including her first novel of apprenticeship invalidate critical rejection of all the novels of the generation of 1927 as . . . ["dehumanized."] Though they lack the bigger-than-life events and climaxes

experienced by the nineteenth-century heroes, they bring a more . . . perceptive view of man or woman as an individual with half-understood dreams and
faults. Rosa Chacel's contribution to Spanish and world letters is a sensitive
and thorough exploration of the psyche, while . . . [avoiding] the frigid clinical analyses often found in other modern works.

Eunice Meyers. *Hispanic Journal.* 4, Spring
1983, pp. 78–79, 82–83

In 1925, with all the innocence and enthusiasm of youth, Rosa Chacel under-
took, in her first novel, *Estacion, Ida y vuelta,* the formidable task of creating
a novel purely Ortegian in form and content. Following Ortega's assertion
that "thought is a vital function, like digestion or the circulation of the blood,"
she sought a narrative form in which to develop "vital reason." The result is
a novel that reveals for the reader the thought of a young protagonist during
a series of extremely banal events, eliminating all the traditional functions of
narrative (in the first as well as the third person), to present actions and
thoughts retrospectively with an implicit or explicit interpretation. In this
way, it becomes a sort of invertebrate novel, a series of acts of attention
without the chronological armature that even pure stream of consciousness
novels have in their repetitive achronology.

Roberta Johnson. In Fernando Burgos, ed.
Prosa hispanica de vanguardia (Madrid:
Origenes, 1986), p. 201

To speak of Rosa Chacel is to speak of the prose of 1927 and, thereby, of its
highest point as a pretext to clear the way for those who, with an intelligence
equal to the poets', decided to effect the renewal of Spanish prose. When
Rosa Chacel published her first novel, *Estación, Ida y vuelta,* this group of
writers that Ortega was to sponsor in his *Revista de Occidente* and that was
to play the role of realizing in practice their mentor's ideas about the novel
or "dehumanized" art in general, was in process of coming together. . . .

Rosa Chacel's work demands that we make the effort of understanding
that the descent to nothingness or to the abysses of guilt or to a conscious
childhood or a frustrated hope requires a ruthlessly personal reading. . . . In
the very beautiful prologue to *Novela antes de tiempo,* Rosa Chacel makes
an entire declaration of principles which, in addition to being a magnificent
theoretical digression on the workings of narrative, is also a magnificent introduction to reading her. . . .

Also in *Novela antes de tiempo* . . .she indicates how the literary formula
that is ideal for her purposes is the *interior dialogue.* And Rosa calls upon
the *interior dialogue,* she says, when it is impossible to define "the ultimate,
secret, personal course of thought and the . . . sediment of life as a succession
of acts, emotions, situations, events." Ultimately, it is a question, as she has
stated elsewhere, of becoming deeply involved with one's own life. And here
we come to the other aspect that we are going to address: What is memory?

Memory is transformed by literary elaboration, it is formalized on the basis of the subjective and takes a preexistent reality . . . to unsuspected heights, submerging itself in the multiplicity of its consequences, it turns literature into a multi-voiced object. . . .

This has always been Rosa Chacel's method of narration, in her most strictly autobiographical books, as well as in those with other motivations. . . .

Luis Suñén. *Quimera*. 84, 1987, pp. 24–26

Chacel has often said that Mnemosine is the goddess who has inspired the philosophy underlying all of her novels, beginning with the Ortega-smitten *Estación, Ida y vuelta,* the manifesto for and root of all her later work. . . .

If we view the intention of autobiography as a provocation of memory, then Chacel displays an awareness of this phoenixlike task constantly. Peculiar to Chacel within her conceptualization of memory is the withholding of facts, which she usually refers to as "intringulis." She continually provides wafts of memory within her story, yet suddenly interrupts them with a secret she refuses to tell. Perhaps this "intringulis" device is Chacel's method for protecting her memory from completely revealing the most intimate details of her life. Chacel's memory is therefore more authentic than a strict autobiography which proposes to tell the truth. She deliberately lets us know that memory is the murky substance that activates her prose. Yet it does not compromise her imagination, just as her imagination does not compromise her memory.

Shirley Mangini. *Letras Peninsulares*. 3,
Spring, 1990, pp. 27–28

In 1985, Chacel published her *Novelas antes de tiempo* (Novels before their time). The title implies that the narratives included there were in fact seeds for possible novels, stories that had been incubating in her mind as she worked on *La sinrazón* and other lengthy novels. Although her latest novel, *Ciencias naturales,* appeared in 1988, three years after *Novelas antes de tiempo,* it is obvious that she was motivated to print the latter "before their time," fearing that she would not have enough time left to develop them into novels.

This worry is reflected even more noticeably in the shift in the format of the stories. The book consists of a preface and six stories. The first three are much longer than the rest, comprising more than two-thirds of the work, and each having two parts preceded by an introduction. The first segment of the first two stories, "Suma" and "La fundacion de Eudoxia," had been published earlier in *La Nacion* (Buenos Aires) and in *Revista Mexicana de literatura,* respectively. Even though the third story, "Margarita (zurcidora)," was entirely new, Chacel repeated the formula of the addition of a supposedly later conclusion and the two prologues. The last three stories, however, are not only considerably shorter, but they lacked a second part. The author herself takes over and provides her own commentaries. The pace of her writing quickens, and, in the fifth story, "Yo soy Bot," which tells of a professor of physics about to retire reluctantly, she seizes the character's "monodi-alogue." . . .

The stories tell of mysterious characters and obscure circumstances in their past, but the realistic style in which they are delivered defies the fantastic. Chacel is the narrator—there is no authorial distance from the story. She constantly establishes her authorial presence and authority addressing the reader directly. This "formula" disrupts the reader's identification with the characters and their world, and thus, dispels the effect of the fantastic.

Mercedes M. de Rodriguez. *Letras
Peninsulares*. 3, Spring, 1990, pp. 77–78

CHANG AI-LING (EILEEN) (CHINA) 1921–

In Chang Ai-ling's fiction of the war period there is frequently a turn of phrase, an allusion, a setting, that deliberately recalls traditional Chinese fiction and its love of the supernatural. Sometimes these allusions are overt, sometimes suggestive. When the Parisian prostitute in "Red Rose and White Rose" lifts her skirt above her head she seems to undergo a transformation, like the demon of "Huap'i (The painted skin) in *Liao-chai chih-i*. There are moments when the widow Liang in laying her snares recalls Madame White Snake, and Wei-lung her slave girl. Chinese fiction and drama had for centuries amassed a chaotic, vast world of supernatural creatures, and whether the authors took their work seriously or not, it testifies to the persistent interest in the irrational experience outside the Confucian heritage and a collective imagination that refused a systematic explanation of its vision. One of Chang's achievements lay in gathering this rich heritage into a thoroughly modern portrayal of human desire and vanity.

Twentieth-century writers, on the whole, looked at this tradition as merely the social phenomenon of an ignorant fascination with superstition rather than the uninformed expression of a fundamental aspect of the human psyche. Although some writers themselves remained superstitious, the majority dismissed this part of their cultural heritage in favor of a fascination with the new (or the advent of the new) society. As regards this oft-noted preoccupation with the new society, it is worth recalling T. A. Hsia's brief but trenchant comment on two major currents of modern Chinese literature: the romantic May Fourth literature of "New Youth" and the tradition-bound Saturday School of "Mandarin Duck and Butterfly literature." The writers of the former group were concerned only with affirming their ideals and passions, while the latter could only find an eye for the manners and concrete details of the new. Each group lacked and disregarded the better qualities of the other. If we look at Chang Ai-ling's work in the light of this statement, we find that she represents a strong departure from their work. Her concern is neither to gather comforting visions of an old society nor to extol visions of a new one. Her settings are sometimes antiquated, sometimes quite modern, but they are always peopled with characters within whose interior lives lies a world that has not outstripped the old society. Nor will it be liberated in the new. The characterization of both manners and passions, then, is disengaged and ironic.

Edward M. Gunn. *Unwelcome Muse:
Chinese Literature in Shanghai and Peking
1937–1945* (New York: Columbia University
Press, 1980), pp. 230–31

[Chang's] earliest published stories were first collected as *Ch'uan-ch'i* (1944; Romances) and later as *Chang Ai-ling tuan-p'ien hsiao-shuo chi* (1954; Collected short stories of Chang Ai-ling). Fine, ironic studies of love and courtship set in Shanghai and Hong Kong, the stories offer skeptical portraits of Europeans, Eurasians and Chinese trapped by circumstance and self-delusion. Their sensuous imagery and their diction recall traditional Chinese literature, yet the style is controlled by symbolic technique and modern psychological vision. The most representative of these stories is "Chin-suo chi" (The golden cangue, 1971).

The desolateness Chang reveals at the core of her characters' experiences is accentuated in the first novel she wrote following her return to Hong Kong, *Yang-ko* (1954; The rice-sprout song, 1955). As a depiction of peasants balking and rioting at excessive Communist demands to aid the Korean War effort, the novel is a dissident's work. The thematic continuity with her earlier stories is evident, however: time and circumstance are triumphant over the characters' attempts to transcend them through appeals to love or revolt, whether those characters be Communist cadres or peasants.

Similarly, in Chang's second major novel, *Ch'ih-ti chih lien* (1954; Naked Earth, 1956), Communism appears as the vehicle for more permanent themes in Chang's writing. Insofar as Maoist thought is fiction and simplification of reality, its actual implementation requires that party cadres perpetrate a callous charade in order to survive and to enjoy shallow rewards as the new elite of society. As prisoners of this system, two disillusioned cadres paradoxically face their first true freedom of choice as prisoners of war in Korea. In seeking to evoke the complexity of her characters and their careers during the founding years of the People's Republic, the novel does not always maintain the degree of control over setting and imagery evident in Chang's best work.

Chang has belonged to no school or major trend in modern Chinese literature, but she has had imitators. As a young writer she showed little of the concern for China's political fate that dominated the work of so many of her contemporaries, yet her treatment of love stands in marked contrast to that of other love literature of the time. Elements of the social protest in her later works correspond to the dissent of writers within China as well as outside, but her novels bear only superficial resemblance to the run of anti-Communist fiction in Chinese. To date, Chang's use of imagery, by turns compelling and subtle, remains unsurpassed.

Edward M. Gunn. In Leonard S. Klein, ed.
Far Eastern Literatures in the 20th Century
(New York: Ungar Publishing, 1986),
pp. 23–24

"The Golden Cangue" may be readily considered in terms of traditional Western characteristics of fiction. It is a long, novella length, work of the imagination, a portrait of a whole complete world, which may be approached through a study of character, narrative point of view and structure. Qiqiao's brilliance, cruelty and insecurity are uniformly present throughout the story, marking her as a "flat" static character, whereas her daughter, Chang'an, is a "round" dynamic personality. Initially an innocent naive girl with a capacity for selfless love, she emerges as the "spit and image" of her mother who manipulates others to maintain her own security. The narrator enjoys the vantage point of an omniscient being who reveals the thoughts and feelings of characters and who occasionally is wont to inject an editorial explanation, e.g., "solace is purely spiritual but is used here as a euphemism for sex." More rarely, the narrator is no longer an outside effaced observer with a privileged view but becomes a dramatized "I," a participant with a restricted view as in the novella's opening sentence with its enigmatic teasing emphasis on "we:" "Shanghai thirty years ago on a moonlit night . . . maybe we did not get to see the moon of thirty years ago." Structurally, "The Golden Cangue" enjoys parallels with a work of traditional Chinese fiction, the *Dream of the Red Chamber,* about which Eileen Chang has written critical studies and in fact imitates in "The Golden Cangue." Qiqiao reminds us of the brilliant cruel Wang Xifeng (Phoenix) of the *Dream,* and the story's movement from outer to inner circles, from the discussion of servants of the household to that of family members, parallels the structure of the *Dream* whereby the reader moves from the creation myth to Lin Dai-yu's entry into the inner sanctum of the Jia family household. Or, we may view the structure of "The Golden Cangue" in Western terms: a set piece of dialogue between servants introduces the major character who is then revealed sequentially as the novella progresses.

We think of "The Golden Cangue" as an autobiography, of course, partly because we are shaped by the *Dream* and the reading experience of a tradition which insists that that novel is a disguise of a real life and that fiction is historically and biographically accurate if only we read correctly. But we should not wish to search "The Golden Cangue" for Eileen Chang's personal life. We do suggest that formally in its exploration and spatiality this novella may be read as a counterpart to autobiography.

Lucien Miller and Hui-chuan Chang. In
Michael S. Duke, ed. *Modern Chinese
Women Writers* (Armonk, New York:
M. E. Sharpe, 1989), pp. 27–28

CHAUVET, MARIE (HAITI) 1916–73

More than other fictional traditions, the Haitian novel invites a sociocritical reading. The constant, insistent presence of social reality as background, the repeated manifestations of collective consciousness, the interweaving of individual destinies into a national destiny make it the site of a sociocritical analysis of *content*. One Haitian critic, moreover, described this novel, with a bit of irritation, as "an embryo of social and political scrutiny." . . . A genetic structuralist critique appears especially effective when it is applied to the masterpieces of literature. We hope to demonstrate here that this same approach may function in the case of a work of lesser status, like Marie Chauvet's *Amour.*

However, before approaching the analysis of it, let us stop for a moment at the notion of content to underline the importance, in Haitian literature as a whole, of two themes: that of violence and that of color; two themes that Marie Chauvet makes equal use of in the novel with which we are concerned. It will not be surprising to find this double subject matter, which reflects a historicosocial context belonging more to Haiti than to other Caribbean islands to which it is tempting to compare it, in the novel. . . . In contrast to other Caribbean islands, economic structures and power structures have not always resided in the same hands and have not been concentrated in the same group. In particular, the early seizure of political, if not economic power by the blacks may partially explain the ambiguous relations that Haitian consciousness has with negritude. The Haitian must accommodate to a double myth: on the one hand, that of the Black ancestor, the liberator, on the other, that of the African ancestor, savage and violent. The references to voodoo in particular, which is much resorted to in novels, those of Marie Chauvet among others, are a good illustration of the double movement of attraction and repulsion, toward what may be considered as the manifest survival of the "African" heritage. Marie Chauvet has her heroine's father say in *Amour:* "Ours is an undisciplined race and the blood of former slaves in us calls for the whip."

But it is not on the level of sociological content that we will locate a reading that will very readily point up the importance of this characteristic subject matter: violence and color. Rather, we will be concerned with an analysis of the structures of the narrative so as to point up a double design. We shall demonstrate that there exists, on the one hand, a clear and manifest design that may be assumed to be the author's conscious project; according to this design, *Amour* is the narrative of a victory, a double victory, individual and collective, of liberation achieved through violence, presented, in this case, as positive, revolutionary life-force. But, on the other hand, at a deep level, perceptible upon reflection, a second design appears, according to which the novel becomes the narrative of a failure, an illusory liberation which is, in actuality, nothing but a mutilation. Individual mutilation, which then seems to be the deep, unconscious meaning of the dénouement, takes on a symbolic collective value. It has been said that all novels are about failure. It must be understood what that means. Demonstrating that Marie's novel fails in its intention is not *our* intention. Showing that it is the narrative of a failure is not interesting—for us—except to the extent that, precisely, this constitutes a latent structure. This sub-textual counterpoint seems to us to illustrate dramatically the dialectic and the ambiguity of Haitian consciousness towards itself, its origins and its future.

Madeleine Cottenet-Hage. Francofonia. 6,
Spring, 1984, pp. 17–19

In her pathbreaking study, *Divine Horsemen: The Living Gods of Haiti,* anthropologist Maya Deren describes Erzulie Freida, a crucial loa in Haitian Voudoun, in the following way: "Voudoun has given woman, in the figure of Erzulie, exclusive title to that which distinguishes humans from all other forms: their capacity to conceive beyond reality, to desire beyond adequacy, to create beyond need. In Erzulie, Voudoun salutes woman as the divinity of the dream, the Goddess of Love, the muse of beauty. It has denied her emphasis as mother of life and of men in order to regard her . . . as mother of man's myth of life—its meaning. In a sense, she is the very principle by which man conceives and creates divinity." In Marie Chauvet's tri-partite novel *Amour, colère, folie* the principal Haitian female characters, Claire in *Amour,* Rose in *colère,* and Cécile in *folie,* are empowered by their metaphoric and symbolic relation to the female loa, Erzulie Freida. This special relationship is rendered by Chauvet's narrative strategies and her representation of the women. Her recreation of the female loa reinforces and cultivates, in Haitian literary discourse, the power of Haitian women to create new life. Like Erzulie, Claire, Rose and Cécile are mulatto, bourgeoise, beautiful and childless; they aspire to power, inner strength, and courage—qualities attributed to the Haitian Goddess of Love. The metaphoric representations of the three dominant female voices are also symbolic because Claire in *Amour,* Rose in *colère* and Cécile in *folie* reify, respectively, the mind, body and soul. Together they embody the female self.

Chauvet's females give life to the historical and cultural ambience of the period following the American occupation of Haiti (1915–34). The novel is set during the embattled times associated with the presidency of Elie Lescot. Issues regarding race and class, power struggles between the black and mulatto elite, and conflicts between the mulatto bourgeoisie and black elite are paramount. The policies of the Lescot government seemed to increase the social and political tensions prevalent in Haiti after the American occupation. For example, there was the government's contradictory anti-Nazi stance internationally and its ultra-conservative political practices nationally. Chauvet's recreation of these chaotic times illuminates dilemmas evolving from the experiences of Haitian women. In this context of turmoil, women change from uninvolved observers of social action to involved participants, and emerge as heroines empowered to create, like Erzulie, their own destinies.

Each woman is developed according to how she resolves the questions, "What is self love?" and "What is (are) the source(s) of my oppression?" This process of self-examination and self-actualization is the center of each text. Chauvet employs definable narrative strategies to control, or at least strongly influence, a reading of what she regards to be the sources of a Haitian woman's self-love and oppression. Viewed from this ideological perspective, these literary techniques reveal social and political problems faced especially by Haitian women and generate meanings about the complex nature of their lives.

Chauvet accents the Haitian mulatto bourgeoises who suffer in psychological, physical and spiritual ways, and who because of their multidimensional pain are forced to reassess the meaning of their privileged place in Haitian society. Indeed, the writer's imaginative handling of class and racial conflict, political and social injustice, sexual abuse and male-female relations authenticates the agonies of an entire society. Yet, the manner in which Chauvet uses specific characterization as metaphor for Erzulie's attributes and limitations conveys the idea that women's personal and political oppression co-exist, and social change therefore depends on their self-empowerment and conscious involvement in creating new life.

Just as Erzulie operates spiritually and materially in the configuration of Haitian Voudoun, Cécile, Rose and Claire are figured into a complex cosmic and material world. Chauvet shows each woman's different attempt to strike a balance between these worlds. The Haitian woman's active resistance to political and personal oppression determines her notion of self-love and guides her vision to effect change. Chauvet's construction of each heroine, based on a literary configuration of the Haitian female loa, is symbolic of the development of a politicized female consciousness that is nurtured by its relation to Erzulie. . . .

For Chauvet, the self-love and oppression of Haitian women are not opposites. The pain and the joy, the fears and hopes, the strength—all these have roots that lie deep in the Haitian soil and psyche. This grounding is symbolized in Chauvet's metaphoric representation of the complex character of Erzulie Freida, the divine celebration of unifying love: "She subsumes both the carnal and the spiritual; in her, eroticism and spirituality are one. Mistress of all elements, muse of earthly fecundity and divine spirituality, she gathers in herself the most potent and universal emotions. And her symbol is the heart, most often the pierced heart . . . the incorporation of a spiritual force into life and its manifestation in living form." Erzulie Freida is at work, our argument would conclude, in *Amour, colère, folie* where Marie Chauvet creates in fiction her own terms of critical inquiry.

Janis A. Mayes. *Journal of Caribbean Studies.* 7, Spring, 1989, pp. 81–82, 88

It is generally thought that the first break with tradition was Guadeloupe's Maryse Condé whose *Hérémakhonon* came out in 1976. There had been precursors. As early as 1957, a full three years before Césaire's *Toussaint,* Haiti's Marie Chauvet had written *La Danse sur le volcan.* For Haitians, the reference was clear, "dancing on a volcano" had been the words Toussaint had thrown in Leclerc's face. Still, with a talented high yellow heroine in the throes of unrequited love, it was more a romance than a historical novel; although it highlighted, with a meticulous attention to historical detail, the comings and goings of a theatrical company in San Domingo on the eve of upheaval. *Volcan* also had a fine psychological study of race relations in the portrait of a free man of color, heir to a white man's plantation, who, consumed by self-hate, treated his slaves with a cruelty which few of his white neighbors could match. True to form, *Volcan* had been preceded by *Fille d'Haiti* (1954), Chauvet's own romp through the negrophobic narrative convention, that self-indulgent side of the mulatto convention usually dealing with a (barely) colored woman too beautiful and too intelligent to be content with her inferior station. One can measure the force of the negrophobic tradition when one realizes that in Haiti, if anything, a high mulatto complexion should have been deemed desirable, rather than the reverse, particularly for a female. It seemed that Chauvet was trying her hand at all the conventional plots before trusting to her own instincts. *Fille d'Haiti* had one saving feature; it was the first systematic depiction of a love/hate relationship between a colored mother and her daughter, a plot which Lacrosil would radicalize further by using, instead, a white mother. In 1968 came *Amour, colère et folie,* a surrealistic work . . . [that] obliquely introduced the question of history in the text; sexual madness being its ruling metaphor, blood its ruling imagery. It consisted of three novellas set in a provincial city under siege, victimized by the forays of the *tontons-macoutes.* Their chief, an ugly black man from the lower classes, wracked by self doubt and usually impotent, took his racial and sexual revenge by torturing and raping the virginal mulatto daughters of the upper classes. Chauvet controlled the tendency toward voyeurism inherent in such a plot by presenting the counter picture of the pristine daughters of the Haitian bourgeoisie as sex starved, sex obsessed and religion mad. The sadistic behavior bordering on madness which bonded master and slaves in *Volcan* now reappeared, more finely tuned. In *Amour, colère et folie,* sexual deviancy, the hidden side of race wars, was presented as the metaphor for unnatural social conditions. Chauvet never had time to confront history directly, her logical next step.

Clarisse Zimra. In Carole Boyce Davies and
Elaine Savory Fido, eds. *Out of the
Kumbla: Women and Caribbean Literature*
(Trenton, New Jersey: Africa World Press,
1990), pp. 145–46

CHEDID, ANDRÉE (FRANCE–LEBANON–EGYPT) 1921–

With her roots in Egypt and Lebanon, Andrée Chedid has been settled in Paris since 1946. From having lived and studied there, she knows the West and the Middle East intimately, and the two cultures mark her entire work. A graduate of the American University in Cairo, Chedid published her first collection, *On the Trails of My Fancy* (Cairo, 1943) in English.

Although relatively little known in the United States, Andrée Chedid occupies a choice place among contemporary French authors. A novelist, short story writer, playwright, and, above all, poet, she has published numerous books several of which have earned important literary awards, such as the Mallarmé Prize in 1976 and the Goncourt Short Story Prize in 1979. . . .

At a time when there is a proliferation of books signed by women, the voice of Andrée Chedid counts among the most eloquent, for its genuinely human resonances as well as by the announcement of a renewal of forms and images.

"To advance, to retake joy, to defy obstacles, perhaps to overcome them, then to go forward again: these are what is possible to us." This is how Andrée Chedid expresses herself in a sort of *ars poetica* (and guide to life) entitled *Land and Poetry*. . . . And it is she who, during an interview, spoke of an eternal quest, the search for a humanity, I would say, a humanism.

Hers is a ceaseless quest, for the "Grail" of brotherhood is not to be found once and for all. It is in the process of the quest, and not in its termination that brotherhood is achieved and renewed. For man, "Tomorrow is always further ahead and there is no arrival."

This "journey," however, is not approached the same way for everyone. Chedid's trajectory, in particular, will be marked by feminitude and poetry. If I chance the word "feminitude," it is to avoid misunderstandings that might be aroused by "femininity" or "feminism," the pathetic quality of the first, the militant echoes awakened by the second, both of which are quite far from what, for the author, embodies the true nature of woman. It is thus to avoid all misunderstanding in advance that I had chosen "feminitude" with respect to Chedid, for her writing has nothing in common with the well-bred refinements of the literature called "feminine," nor is it a listing of complaints and demands. In the sense that I mean it, "feminitude" applies to women as sexual identities and social agents. In Chedid's work the presence of women within human cultures is affirmed and flourishes. By her own originality, woman enters the movement of solidarity of the contemporary world, as she is embodied in the realities of another time. It is "a new conception of the human being, accenting this aspiration which is not limited to one sex in particular, but at the basis of being." The term "feminitude" may appear to be inspired by fashion; perhaps, however, this notion will prove useful in the case of an author who happens to be a woman, but whose writing escapes this enclosed space of gender within which it would be improper to confine it.

Chedid's universe has no borders; whether we are talking about her poems, her novels and stories, or her theatrical works, in all her texts, poetry is the privileged means of communication. In her books, she declares, poetry dominates everything: "I always come back to poetry, as if it were an essential source." In fact, the quest for brotherhood and the quest for the perfect poetic form go hand in hand; the poet is "he who . . . pursuing to the ends of the earth and of men / the unity stripped of their name." To live poetry, according to Chedid, is to keep oneself "at the boundary between the apparent and the real." Poetry fills life with all its content; it is a presence, an appeal which asks to be heard; it reveals its earthly side to us, which is love. Thus, in *Land and Poetry,* Chedid expresses her aesthetic credo, inseparable from an ethic that remains closely connected to it.

Chedid's quest, poetic song and assertion of feminitude, is manifested in certain major lines characteristic of her whole oeuvre. Three aspects are especially worthy of attention: cosmic vision, liberation, vital energy. Each of these elements has a part in the quest as such and they act on and with one another.

Renee Linkhorn. *French Review.* 58,
March, 1985, pp. 559–60

Andrée Chedid's first book, *Delivered Sleep,* which was brought out by Stock in 1952, is certainly her most somber book, the least hopeful. The very young woman Chedid was at that time describes the tenor of existence of a young provincial Egyptian girl, married against her will, at the age of fifteen, to a husband of forty-five who is especially repugnant and hateful, forced on her according to tradition deeply embedded in Egyptian life then and now, whom she will end up killing fifteen years later.

This book, however, in no way makes use of the most melodramatic vein of its story, but rather, with great sobriety, makes us participate in that slow suffocation of hope, makes tangible to us the horror, the intolerable quality of those lives without exits, where, from the beginning, from earliest childhood, the forces of repression wall people up. . . .

House without Roots plunges us into the total absurdity and underlying horror always ready to rise to the surface of the Lebanese situation, as it was, in any event, in 1975, that is, at a time when, since there was still a semblance of order, a fraction of the population could try to pretend that everything was going to work out or, on the other hand, that nothing serious was really happening. *House without Roots* thus studies a situation in crisis, that instant where nothing is really working anymore, but when all hopes are still permitted and when the forces of life and death face one another in an orchestration increasingly precipitated by violence. Dealing with all this, nothing but some women and a little girl of good will who will be quickly swept away, eliminated, as once more those (and they are of the male sex) who have been courting death since time immemorial are the victors.

As with *Delivered Sleep, The Sixth Day, the Survivor,* an immemorial, primordial drama (in the specific case of *House without Roots,* that of the rise of violence) is replayed. The specifics of the Lebanese situation are rapidly surpassed, while the characters of the women, leaving their long patience or their circumstantial lethargy again, come forward to kill hatred and achieve their generous dreams of women. And here the fictional work, to the very extent to which it departs from the specificity of a precise and dated narrative, comes together with the poetic work, particularly the very beautiful texts of *Ceremonial of Violence* and *Brotherhood of the Word.* . . . In any event, it is interesting to note that these two poetic texts precede the novel by ten years—although the symbolic walk of Ammal and Myriam (who decide to cross the no-man's land of the square separating the Christian and Muslim quarters), this choice and this faith in peace and understanding, this simple extrapolation of friendship of children who refuse to hate, even if they must die for their love, has already been the subject of a short story that appeared in *Theme and the Body.* Which is to suggest how much the inevitable involvement of women who finally step out of their long patience is an essential theme for Chedid and how much hope she places in those women. . . .

Brotherhood of the Word, as its title indicates, returns to one of Andrée Chedid's fundamental themes. The author is concerned once more with the mystery of the Word, follows its genesis and rise in the individual, and, in so doing, rediscovers the profound unity, the undeniable brotherhood that should have marked human communities through the ages and at this precise moment. A reflection on the human condition, *Brotherhood of the Word* describes the cycles and alternations of a continual rebirthing and fiercely denounces those who oppose it. *Ceremonial of Violence,* an unbearably sharp cry of suffering, brings out man's tragic face—that which pushes him, as he is doing right now in martyred Lebanon (in a ceremonial also repeated throughout the ages) to choose death, which he takes on himself and whose propagating agent he becomes. To the liquid balm of the Word is opposed the continually reopened wound of violence. . . .

If her fiction captures moments of realization so well, this inexorable rise of the inevitable act, the poetic work relocates this crisis situation in a much wider basic movement which telescopes the human condition across the ages. The exemplary act can only return indefinitely to take up the torch of survival.

Nicole Trèves. *Dalhousie French Studies.*
13, Fall–Winter, 1987, pp. 80, 84, 86–87

Chedid's *Return to Beirut* is operating on an entirely different level to *The Little Mountain*—it skates on the surface while Khoury comes up through the depths. It is the novel of an outsider rather than an insider and Chedid substitutes symbolism for verisimilitude. A central story line of the novel is the attempt by two women from different religious communities, dressed identically, to embrace in a main square in Beirut, thus signalling to the warring communities that they should abandon the fight and choose peace. Although one woman is shot, they both survive to carry on the cause of peace. This is no more credible outside the novel than it is within it—the enormity of what has happened in Lebanon capsizes this oversimplified symbol, leaving Chedid clinging to the wreckage of ahistoricism and naivety. . . .

Less than ten pages into *The Return to Beirut,* the central character Kalya witnesses a quarrel between two taxi drivers who have just swerved to avoid each other. Both men draw pistols, but within minutes are slapping each other on the back and blessing each other. "Involved in every incident," we are told, "in every quarrel, in every reconciliation, God has appeared center stage." This comes over as a kind of literary anthropology, a foreigner's guide to the natives, which sets the tone of the novel and reduces the conflict to a clash of religions both equally armed and equally irrational. We have all read this story before. . . .

Because the weight of what Chedid is writing about cannot be supported by the form of her novel, the war in Beirut seems no more than an adjunct to descriptions of the past lives of her characters, which were led in grand hotels. She leads the reader myopically up blind alleys of oversimplification.

Chris Mowles. *New Statesman and Society.*
November 17, 1989, p. 38

CHEN JO-HSI (RUOXI) (CHINA) 1938–

These are the two major directive forces in Chen Jo-hsi's creative life: a sense of history—an acceptance of the total historicity . . . an author inherits from her culture and society—and a sensitivity to some of the extreme strains a person is put through in this strange and yet familiar world of ours. Her sensitivity has contributed to her being scarred emotionally by her experiences in 1966–73. Her sense of history has guided her from an adolescent of humble family origin (her father was a handyman in rural Taiwan) who aspired to be a Chinese Kafka or Joyce, to a seasoned writer who faces squarely her responsibility to her fellow human beings, a category much more broadly defined than the Marxist "people."

Chen Jo-hsi's stories are more than incisive commentaries on the tumultuous social and political phenomena in the People's Republic of China, though the timely significance of such commentaries is not to be denied. The art of her fiction has attained an admirable height, and the evolution of her art can be readily traced in her stories. . . .

Chen Jo-hsi's sense of history tends often enough to let her absorption in social criticism overpower her artistic restraint. The seven nightmarish years in the PRC have brought her closer to the Chinese people. "Only after those seven years," she said, "have I come to see the Chinese people, not merely as a racial accident, but as loveable and respectable members of humanity with tragic and heroic grandeur. Even in the most ordinary Chinese person we find the crystallization of several thousand years of culture and history, with his own dignity never to be subdued by any political tyranny." She admitted that "The Old Man" was something surging in her chest which she had to spit out. What she spit out in choked voice and between gnashing teeth were severe indictments of the system: "The self-styled 'Great Glorious and ever Righteous Party' only harbors opportunists and shameless scoundrels"; "political and Party leaders, yielding to their urge for new conquests, publicly abandoned their first wives under the euphemism of 'reorganizing the family'—Lieu Shao-ch'i himself thus reorganized his family no less than five times." The indictments are seriously intended, but with their editorializing tone they detract from the stories. Could Chen Jo-hsi have modified the editorializing passages in "The Old Man" and some other stories, including the masterfully drawn "Keng Erh in Peking"? There must be times when the author's anger and sorrow break loose from and explode under the "black, bloated thing" that has become a dead weight "like iron sinking deeper and deeper into my heart." . . .

Chen Jo-hsi is unwilling to justify her existence in this world with the integrity of her art alone. She sees herself "transform into the bridge" that Hsin-mei wants to build between those outside and those within China who equally love and are equally determined to work for China's bright future.

Kai-yu Hsu. In Jeannette L. Faurot, ed.
Chinese Fiction from Taiwan (Bloomington:
Indiana University Press, 1986), pp. 226–27,
231

Chen Ruoxi's collection *The Old Man and Other Stories* (some of which have appeared elsewhere in translation) is of uniformly high standard although the content and style of the stories vary considerably from the delicate everydayness of "The Old Man" with its light touch of tragedy to the Roald Dahl twist at the end of "The Tunnel" and the bitterness of "Ding Yun." No one writes more tellingly about life in China than Chen Ruoxi; her simple tales are beautifully written and painfully true. The last story, "Another Fortress Besieged," is a terribly funny satire on the lengths to which "outsiders" (in this case Chinese-Americans but we must blush with them) go to ingratiate themselves with visiting Chinese in order to gain access to China. Paradoxically, all the visitors want is to gain access to the United States.

Frances Wood. *China Quarterly.* 114, June,
1988, p. 307

Chen Ruoxi [Ch'en Jo-hsi] has described herself as "a native Taiwanese writer who is concerned about politics and society" and "who writes for the sake of conscience." Known in the English reading world as the author of *The Execution of Mayor Yin* [Yin xianzhang] she has become one of the most prolific and important overseas Chinese writers of the last decade. She occupies a unique position among modern Chinese writers due to the fact that she can speak with authority concerning three of the "worlds" that are of most concern to Chinese readers: the People's Republic, Taiwan, and North America. . . .

Chen Ruoxi's literary corpus to date represents a king of serial *Bildungswerke* in the literal sense of a "work of self-education" and is a report to her readers on what she has learned about a complex question that has been of primary importance in her life and thought, at least since her early twenties. All of her works seem to me to revolve around the central question of the relationship between the individual Chinese (usually Chinese intellectuals), Chinese society, and the history of China as a nation. Her ultimate concern with the fate of the Chinese nation and individual Chinese people (wherever they may reside throughout the world) and her consuming desire to comment upon and be a part of the unfolding of these two interlocking fates provide the primary motivation for her vocation as a creative writer. In the past ten years she has employed a large cast of literary personae—concrete and specific characters and an all-pervasive authorial presence—to make significant thematic statements about the ever-changing situation of the Chinese nation and the people caught up in the maelstrom of modern Chinese history. . . .

There is too little sense of "the amplitude that information lacks" and too little "productive imagination" in most of Chen Ruoxi's works to date. Year by year, as Chen has written her stories and novels, her characters, her situations, and her fictional societies are so close to the characters, situations, and real societies she has lived in that her fiction may someday be considered of merely "historical significance," a euphemism meaning of no literary significance. Perhaps Chen Ruoxi herself will be satisfied with historical significance, but I believe she should be able to do better.

Genuine historical significance is, however, something that most readers of modern Chinese fiction admire very much; and Chen's works as a whole offer them a sense of recent Chinese history from the pen of one who lived through one of its most critical eras. For this reason, although she may never become a great writer, Chen should continue to be an important figure in contemporary Chinese letters. Her works will probably continue to be read because, through them, she offers her readers an interpretation of the varied meanings that Chinese society has for Chinese individuals and uses her depictions of Chinese society to delineate what Chinese men and women are, singly and communally, and what they may become in the future. Readers of modern Chinese fiction will continue to read Chen Ruoxi's works for what they ultimately find there: imitations and intimations of modern Chinese life.

Michael S. Duke, ed. *Modern Chinese*
Women Writers (Armonk, New York: M. E.
Sharpe, 1989), pp. 53, 55, 72–74

CHEN YUAN-TSUNG (CHINA) n.d.

"This story is fiction," writes Yuan-tsung Chen in a foreword to her autobiographical novel, "but it is true." With elegant simplicity, she tells of life in the very first years of the People's Republic of China, providing a thoughtful, finely textured look at experiences few in the West have ever glimpsed.

The novel opens in Shanghai in 1949, just as the civil war between the Communists and the Kuomintang forces of Chiang Kaishek is coming to a dramatic close. The narrator, seventeen-year-old Ling-ling, has been raised by an aunt and uncle (her parents died when she was a child) in bourgeois opulence. Educated at a missionary school, taught to paint, dance, serve tea and flirt, she listens to the adults discuss politics at a dinner party ("Would a peasant appreciate all this?" asks one guest, waving toward the fine rugs, chandeliers, paintings and jewels). When her relatives leave for Hong Kong, Ling-ling decides to stay on, "eager to join the revolution."

At first, she works in a library as a cadre (the word—*ganbu*—means "doer"), helping to organize meetings for artists, writers and actors to discuss the role of art in the new society. Then, in 1950, she goes north to help carry out the new land-reform laws—to confiscate land held by feudal landlords and redistribute it among the peasants. . . .

Assigned with her to the tiny village of Longxiang in the far northwest province of Gansu are "Malvolio" Cheng, a comedian nicknamed for his brilliant performance in "Twelfth Night," and Wang Sha, a leading party official who gave up writing because the people needed "food, not plays or poetry." They travel on the Old Silk Road, now "poverty-stricken, worn out, and dilapidated." Longxiang has no phone or bicycle; the only food is a grayish paste called *pian-er-gruel;* people bathe only at birth, marriage and death, and clean themselves by picking off lice. Accustomed to suffering, they believe that everything is "predestined, all their hardships and subjection," and make no distinction among emperors, landlords and the Communist rulers of China.

Chen is no hearty socialist realist sketching a happy army of cadres marching off to a brave new world. Through Ling-ling's eyes, she shows all the harshness and conflict, the problems, ironies and tragedies of China's monumental effort to liberate three hundred million peasants from thirty centuries of feudalism. When a district leader addresses the villagers as "comrades," an old woman asks, "Who is Comrades?" "You are," says the man beside her. "My name is not Comrades." "We are all comrades now." Writes Chen, "This needed thinking over. The old woman lapsed into befuddled silence.". . .

Ling-ling works mainly with the women, who have accepted the ancient Confucian teaching that "the sovereign guides the subject, the father guides the son, and the husband guides the wife." She befriends a bright young girl, a tough old one-eyed widow and the town whore. Feeling alien, afraid and angry by turns, she helps the villagers cope with rape, murder, childbirth and famine in addition to land reform and local elections. She gets a letter from her aunt saying, "Eat well . . . Don't get your feet wet." She falls in love, wonders about her revolutionary commitment, can't imagine resuming her old life. Above all, she learns—about these people and this political experiment. She sees that "the more she strove for her ideal, the more problems she would have," but she does not give up. Sharing that vision, Yuan-tsung Chen (who worked [on various land-reform campaigns] in the People's Republic for twenty years and emigrated to California in 1972) has painted a vivid personal portrait on the canvas of modern history.

Jean Strouse. Newsweek. May 5, 1980,
pp. 88–89

By describing itself as an "autobiographical novel," a book sets itself a double task: it lays a claim to the authenticity of personal involvement which it must justify, while transposing personal experience into fictional terms. *The Dragon's Village* does communicate the flavor of life in these curiously opposite ways, but it remains less than satisfying for two reasons: the personality of the heroine is explored in less depth than is necessary to reveal adequately exactly when and why she changes. The second reason lies in the point at which the story stops: this is at the high point of successful agrarian reform, though the heroine is already dissatisfied with both the means and the aims of the Revolution. Surely the most fascinating material lay in the way that dissatisfaction developed into disillusionment, and in how she came to be able to accomplish the feat of actually leaving China. But perhaps Yuan-tsung Chen has reserved that part of her story for her next book.

Prabhu S. Guptara. World Literature Today.
55, 1981, pp. 725–26

This autobiographical novel describes the efforts, in 1951, of an enthusiastic troupe of young Shanghai cadres, proudly sporting their new "soldier-style" jackets and caps, to carry Mao's theory of land reform to a remote village in a northern province. The story of their trials and errors features several fine portraits of the village's womenfolk (including an aging virgin, widowed on her wedding day, and a woman of ill repute nicknamed the Broken Shoe) and some striking scenes in which the cadres discover that the rural proletariat has never heard of Marx, Abraham Lincoln, or Chiang Kai-shek. From the start, the narrator (a teen-age girl who graduated from a Catholic missionary school) is wary of the village's "unexpected strain of anarchism and violence," and when it erupts in vicious attacks upon young girls and old men, she fears that she and her comrades are largely to blame. This is an unusually frank and perceptive chronicle, marred only by monotony toward the end, when Miss Chen . . . begins to give equal weight to every recollection.

The New Yorker. May 12, 1980, p. 161

One of my colleagues, a scholar of modern Chinese literature, has deplored the capture of that writing by social scientists in the West, scholars who judge it by socio-political rather than literary standards. He is right, of course; it is rather as if Dickens and Trollope were the province of historians like Kitson Clark, or Hemingway and Faulkner the province of Arthur Schlesinger. Yet there is little doubt that most readers who turn to Yuan-tsung Chen's *The Dragon's Village* will do so not so much because of their interest in its literary merits, but rather because they are interested in the subject. It deals with the first stages of land reform under the Chinese communists, one of the most momentous acts of the new regime and one which, it seems safe to say, marks a genuinely secular change in what many used to imagine to be the endlessly cyclical pattern of history in China. . . .

We see how the reform was carried out in one particular corner of China. . . . Dragon's Village (Longxiang) . . . [in] a desperately poor region in the northwest, which had been a border outpost under the Han and Tang dynasties, and which remains a cultural and economic backwater today. Chen's narrator is Guan Ling-ling, a young girl who—like Chen—was born to wealth and privilege in Shanghai, and who—like Chen—threw in her lot with the new regime after the Communist victory. . . .

[Despite initial problems,] there is a happy ending—the land reform team holds a successful election, and the land is parceled out to the peasants. But there is an individual triumph too. Ling-ling wants to be a writer, and must make the decision not to allow herself to be frightened away from this calling by either the landlords or her Communist superiors. After the senior cadre suggest that keeping a diary may be dangerous, she has a dreadful nightmare in which nameless men search her room. "I could not care less what they called themselves," she writes of them, "Guomindang or communist, rightist or leftist, counterrevolutionary or revolutionary. They were the same people." She wakes, and tries desperately to burn her diary, only to catch sight of the flames consuming a favorite passage. It is then that she saves the rest of the pages from the fire, sits herself down, and spends the rest of the night writing down her experiences in Longxiang. Whether or not Chen went through such an episode herself is beside the point; this book is presumably built in large part on her memories of those years in the Northwest.

Nicholas R. Clifford. Commonweal.
October 10, 1980, pp. 570–72

CHOPIN, KATE (UNITED STATES) 1851–1904

No writer of the period was more spontaneously and inevitably a story teller. There is an ease and a naturalness about her work that comes from more than mere art. She seldom gave to a story more than a single sitting, and she rarely revised her work, yet in compression of style, in forebearance, in the massing of materials, and in artistry she ranks with even the masters of the period. . . . She was emotional, she was minutely realistic, and . . . used dialect sometimes in profusion; she was dramatic and even at times melodramatic, yet never was she commonplace or ineffective. She had command at times of a pervasive humor and a pathos that gripped the reader before he was aware, for behind all was the woman herself. She wrote as Dickens wrote, with abandonment, with her whole self. There is art in her work, but there is more than art.

> Fred Lewis Pattee. *A History of American Literature Since 1870* (New York: Century, 1915), pp. 364–65

Kate Chopin belongs to the artistic realism of today, as well as to her own generation. This generation sees life, or reality, differently from any generation before it. The literary artist in his absorbing process is no longer a discoverer, no longer a refiner, still less a dictator, but an observer at best, with an impulse to state his impressions clearly. And if one were to ask in what way after all Kate Chopin differs from a pastmaster in the short story art, say, de Maupassant, the answer may be that she blesses while he bewailed the terrible clearsightedness which is the strength and the anguish of every good writer. . . .

The Awakening follows the current of erotic morbidity that flowed strongly through the literature of the last two decades of the nineteenth century. The end of the century became a momentary dizziness over an abyss of voluptuousness, and Kate Chopin in St. Louis experienced a partial attack of the prevailing artistic vertigo. The philosophy of Schopenhauer, the music of Wagner, the Russian novel, Maeterlinck's plays—all this she absorbed. *The Awakening* in her case is the result—an impression of life as a delicious agony of longing.

In *The Awakening* under her touch the Creole life of Louisiana glowed with a rich exotic beauty. The very atmosphere of the book is voluptuous, the atmosphere of the Gulf Coast, a place of strange and passionate moods.

> Daniel Rankin. *Kate Chopin and Her Creole Stories* (Philadelphia: University of Pennsylvania Press, 1932), pp. 170, 175

In the work of Kate Chopin . . ., it is not the glamour of the Creole past but the emotional life of a passionate people with which she is concerned. Her work is significant indeed not in terms of quantity but of quality. Her output was not large, but she carried the art of the short story to a height which even [George Washington] Cable did not surpass. . . . Mrs. Chopin's last novel, *The Awakening* . . ., caused a storm of unfavorable criticism. . . .The reality of the book is striking, in its revelation of the shifting moods of a passionate woman, and it is told with admirable economy. But the basic fault

lies in Edna's utter selfishness, which deprives her of sympathy. The standards are Continental rather than Creole, and the novel belongs rather among
studies of morbid psychology than local color.

> Arthur H. Quinn. *American Fiction* (New
> York: Appleton-Century, 1936), pp. 354–57

But there was one novel of the 1890s in the South that should have been
remembered, one small perfect book that mattered more than the whole life-
work of many a prolific writer, a novel of Kate Chopin, who wrote Creole
stories, like one or two others in New Orleans who carried on the vein of
George W. Cable. *The Awakening* was more mature than even the best of
Cable's work, so effortless it seemed, so composed in its naturalness and
grace was this tragic tale of Grand Isle, the fashionable New Orleans summer
resort where the richer merchants deposited their wives and children. There,
with the carelessness and lightness of a boy, the young Creole idler Robert
awakened, with sorrowful results, from the dull dream of her existence the
charming young woman whose husband adored her while he made the sad
mistake of leaving her alone with her reveries and vague desires.

> Van Wyck Brooks. *The Confident Years:*
> *1885–1915* (New York: Dutton, 1952), p. 341

In detail, *The Awakening* has the easy candor and freedom appropriate to its
theme. It admits that human beings are physical bodies as well as moral and
social integers and that spirit acts not only by sublimation but directly
through the body's life. Not many English or American novels of the period
had come so far. And its successive scenes—of household, country place,
cafe garden, dinner party, and race track—are vividly realized. Kate Chopin
seems to have paid some attention to the recently translated *Anna Karenina*
and its extraordinary clairvoyance of observation. (Her short stories . . .
are less successful, relying excessively on Maupassantesque twists of ironic
revelation on the last page. But the people in them are real physical presences; invariably they strike us as having actual body, breath, color and
temperature.)

> Warner Berthoff. *The Ferment of Realism:*
> *American Literature, 1884–1919* (New York:
> Free Press, 1965), p. 89

There are two respects in which Mrs. Chopin's novel [*The Awakening*] is
harder than Flaubert's [*Madame Bovary*], more ruthless, more insistent on
truth of inner and social life as sole motivation. Edna Pontellier has her first
affair out of sexual hunger, without romantic furbelow. . . . And, second,
Mrs. Chopin uses no equivalent of the complicated financial maneuvers with
which Flaubert finally corners his heroine. Edna kills herself solely because
of the foredoomed emptiness of life stretching ahead of her. It is purely a
psychological motive, untouched by plot contrivance.

The patent theme is in its title (a remarkably simple one for its day): the awakening of a conventional young woman to what is missing in her marriage, and her refusal to be content. Below that theme is the still-pertinent theme of the disparity between woman's sexual being and the rules of marriage. And below *that* is the perennial theme of nature versus civilization.

Stanley Kauffmann. *The New Republic.*
December 3, 1966, p. 38

Greater attention, it seems to me, has to be given to the integral relationship between local color in [*The Awakening*] and the development of its theme, as well as to Kate Chopin's use of related symbolism. There is no doubt a certain irony in suggesting a new reading of *The Awakening* in terms of its local color. It was precisely because of diminished interest in regional literature that many commentators feel it was so long ignored; there is the obvious implication that regional literature is somehow incompatible with universal appeal. In exploring both local color and related symbolism more fully though, it seems to me that critics will do greater justice to the profundity of Kate Chopin's theme. For the novel is not simply about a woman's awakening need for sexual satisfaction that her marriage cannot provide; sexuality in the novel represents a more universal human longing for freedom, and the frustration that Edna experiences is a poignant statement about the agony of human limitations. . . .

There is a wealth of sensuous imagery in the novel, and this has been noted consistently by the critics; but what has not been noticed . . . is that sensuousness is a characteristic feature of the setting, a product of climate and the Creole temperament. And thus it must be considered primarily as constituting the new environment that Edna marries into, and not as directly supporting a preoccupation with sexual freedom. It is this environment that becomes the undoing of the American woman.

John R. May. *Southern Review.* Fall, 1970,
pp. 1032–33

It does not seem probable that [Kate Chopin] will burst into glory with the reissue of her complete works . . . but she is deserving of a good deal more attention than she has received, partly because she was long before her time in dealing with sexual passion and the intricate familial and personal emotions of women, and partly because she is an uncommonly entertaining writer. The stories, a good many of them only a page or two long, are frequently no more than anecdotes or episodes or even tricks; but, like Maupassant, whom she translated and by whom she was much influenced, she usually embedded her skeleton in sufficient flesh and musculature to conceal the joints. . . .

Mrs. Chopin's landscapes and her interiors, metropolitan or rural, are animate and immediately perceived; there is no self-indulgent clutter in them, just as her characters rarely are cartoons, generally recognizable as they may be. She is sparing and precise whether she is dealing with simple folk or people of elaborate construction, and she seems to have known and to have comprehended fully a great variety of people in a variety of strata.

Jean Stafford. *New York Review of Books.*
September 23, 1971, pp. 33, 35

Edna Pontellier's daring in asserting her will, striving to gain control over her life, and recognizing her relationship to the world would not be so remarkable were it not for the evidence throughout *The Awakening* of the multiple constraints that are part of her existence. In many ways, the novel chronicles Edna's growing awareness of the nature of those claims on her autonomy; hence, the title refers not only to the rousing of her erotic, individual, and spiritual impulses but to the entire series of awarenesses that culminate in her sleepless certitude about her position in the universe. Thus, *The Awakening* shares with the greatest dramatic art that most dramatic of themes, painful self-recognition. Although Chopin tells us that Edna "had abandoned herself to Fate, and awaited the consequences with indifference," nowhere does the author suggest the sort of omnipotent decree which determines Oedipus's destiny. Neither does Edna suffer the humiliations and griefs of Lear. Nevertheless, she does come to a similar kind of knowledge; she finally perceives herself within a world that while apparently open to her potentialities, remains closed to her deepest wishes and her will. . . .

Unlike Oedipus and Lear, this protagonist is Mrs. Pontellier, wife and mother, defined by her relationship to husband and children. Oedipus and Lear begin by ruling and learn the limits of their power. Edna begins by discovering the urge to rule her own life. Only in that process does she, like her famous forebears, learn the limits of her power, of the many differences separating Mrs. Pontellier from the great tragic heroes is precisely her nonregal status. She must begin her process of perception not from a position of power, but, quite basically, from a recognition, gained in a small instance of physical triumph, that she alone can accomplish something she thought impossible. Oedipus, confident because of his solving of the riddle, and Lear, sure of the affection of Cordelia, begin from thrones of authority. Edna starts hesitantly, fearfully, but increasingly resolved to act for herself.

Like the tragic hero, Edna fully engages her own yearning, her strengths, and her destruction. There is a magnificent calm, almost a stoicism, in Edna's acceptance of the limitations in her life. In full knowledge and recollection of her hopes, stripped of illusions, she swims in the milieu that expresses most openly a quintessence of her confinement.

Dorothy H. Jacobs. In Lynda S. Boren and
Sara de Saussure Davis, eds. *Kate Chopin
Reconsidered: Beyond the Bayou* (Baton
Rouge: Louisiana State University Press,
1992), pp. 80–81, 94

At the 1988 Modern Language Association conference, Elizabeth Fox-Genovese asserted that Kate Chopin had "little patience with the woman question." In underscoring this argument by writing that Chopin had "scant interest in social problems," she misleads us. Her argument that Chopin tried "to treat sexuality independent of gender relations" overlooks the texual evidence in *The Awakening*. Close analysis of the novel reveals that Chopin examines the interdependence of female sexuality and gender roles to challenge cultural assumptions about women. Even though she was not an advocate or unequivocal reformer, *The Awakening* reveals the influence of late-nineteenth-century feminists and their search for a new kind of heroine on whom women could model their lives. . . .

With sensuous imagination, irony, and acute sensitivity to the climate of thought about women in her time, Chopin patterns a medium fully appropriate to her realistic, insightful message. She does not warn women to conform, but implicit in her imagery and her story is the idea that without fulfilling work and the collaboration of men, female freedom may be destined to frustration. Edna's broken wing is caused by the snare of her illusions and by the winds of social expectations. Although, as Leonce says, she does have "some sort of notion in her head concerning the eternal rights of women," she falls short of daring Shavian liberation. A diagnostic and a cautionary tale, Chopin's narrative subjects Shavian argument and feminist thought to the corrective of her imagination. Without compromising her aesthetic principles, Chopin created a work of "destruction," like Ibsen's problem plays, one that exposes the domestic lies people live by. According to Shaw, "Every step in morals is made by challenging the validity of the existing concept of perfect propriety of conduct."

Chopin's novel is such a challenge. It illustrates Shaw's belief in works of "destruction," for "the advantage of the work of destruction is that every new ideal is less of an illusion than the one it has supplanted; so that the destroyer of ideals, though denounced as an enemy of society, is in fact sweeping the world clear of lies." In questioning the conventional lies about women, *The Awakening* is quintessential Chopinism. With uncompromising realism, wry irony that exposes the gulf between the illusions and realities of her characters, and sensuous symbolic detail that communicates theme without presenting it, the novel tests society's assumptions about women. It effectively gives Shavian argument fictional form.

Martha Fodaski Black. In Lynda S. Boren
and Sara de Saussure Davis, eds. *Kate
Chopin Reconsidered: Beyond the Bayou*
(Baton Rouge: Louisiana State University
Press, 1992), pp. 95, 112–13

Part of the impact of *The Awakening* lies in its skillful handling of economics. Chopin provides a text rich in monetary allusions that complement her heroine's quest for independence; in so doing, she establishes economics as a vital element of her characters' milieu. We are always aware of the economic pursuits in the novel—the business transactions of Mr. Pontellier, the Lebruns, and to some extent the Ratignolles. And we watch Edna in her pursuit of economic independence. But however much Chopin may have been intrigued by the financial world, she refrains from creating a Carrie Meeber in Edna Pontellier. Dreiser may enlist our concern for a character who struggles to acquire, but in *The Awakening* Chopin reverses the process, providing a protagonist who willingly strips herself of economic status. Edna's voluntary relinquishment of economic security results in an underlying tension in the novel and ultimately ensures a more sympathetic reader.

> Doris Davis. In Lynda S. Boren and Sara de
> Saussure Davis, eds. *Kate Chopin
> Reconsidered: Beyond the Bayou* (Baton
> Rouge: Louisiana State University Press,
> 1992), p. 143

Edna's choice—and Chopin's tone in its description—gives *The Awakening* perhaps the most ambivalent conclusion in all American literature. Clearly, Edna is defeated in her quest for a self, but just as clearly, she is victorious. She does achieve and preserve a self—the essential, which women are categorically denied—and she *is* a woman who acts selflessly in giving up her life for her children.

But in the ambivalence of this ending Chopin affirms the difficulty of the dream of female selfhood in a society that defines women as selfless. More importantly, perhaps, Chopin also reveals the limits of the late nineteenth century's definitions of selfhood. At its base, such a self affirms an ego, an I, that is only and always in control. Such a self is ever subject, never subjected to its responsibilities and relations to others, as women inevitably are. In Edna's dilemma Chopin exposes the dream itself, the fantasy of male selfhood that is epitomized by Huck Finn: the dream that we can escape the definitions of our community, our language, the others about us.

In revealing the tragic impossibility of that dream for women, who are *other,* she underlines its illusoriness for men, who have created that otherness to deny their own—a convenient raft on which to avoid the responsibilities and contingencies that shore-born creatures must sometimes find disconcerting. At the same time, however, in Edna's triumph Chopin suggests the hope of a self that is also selfless, one not wholly defined by others or wholly careless of the responsibility of others, neither wholly object nor subject of desire. In that ambivalent triumph, then, lies a revolutionary image of the dream of female selfhood.

> Barbara C. Ewell. In Lynda S. Boren and
> Sara de Saussure Davis, eds. *Kate Chopin
> Reconsidered: Beyond the Bayou* (Baton
> Rouge: Louisiana State University Press,
> 1992), pp. 164–65

CHRISTENSEN, INGER (DENMARK) 1935–

"The ABC's of Life and Death" is what one critic called Inger Christensen's *alfabet* (alphabet) upon its publication in late 1981. "Victory for Poetry—Make her Prime Minister," suggested another reviewer; "To Heaven with Inger!" proclaimed a third. Several years in the making, *alfabet* is at once basic as a child's ABC and complex as a Bach fugue, crystallizing into words both the beauty and the potential for destruction that permeate our world and our times.

Popular response to *alfabet* has matched the critical response; the book has been widely read during the months following its publication. This combination of critical and popular success is not unusual for Inger Christensen. During the twenty years since the publication of her first volume, she has won the Danish Academy's prize for literature, has been made a member of the Academy, and has had her work quoted by politicians as well as protesters, used as slogans by various groups, and set to both popular and "serious" music, Christensen is, overall, one of Denmark's most respected living writers.

One of the hallmarks of her work is the invention of new structures, structures that both complement and further the content of her writings in such a way that, in her work, form and content cannot be separated. For *alfabet* Christensen chose to combine two structures: the poems follow an alphabetical order, and the number of lines in each is determined by Fibonacci's mathematical series (1, 2, 3, 5, 8, 13 . . .), in which each number is the sum of the two previous numbers. The first poem in *alfabet,* then, focuses on "a"-words and has one line; the second focuses on "b"-words and has two lines, etc. In addition, the first line of each poem recurs after a given interval. The result is a group of poems that can also be seen as one long poem, constantly returning to its beginnings and growing from them anew in widening spirals, a work whose helical structure echoes the course of history, the motions of planets and stars, the coiling of our own genes. . . .

If Christensen had not expected bombs or chemicals to creep into her poetry, she was probably even less prepared to make a mathematical discovery in the course of writing *alfabet.* When she got to the seventh poem, the *g*-poem, she found the required 21 lines too unwieldy to present in an unbroken block, and began casting about for a system for dividing the longer poems into verses. It was then she discovered that Fibonacci's series is not only infinite, but, within itself, infinitely repeating. That is, 21, the seventh number in the series, can be broken into $1 + (2 + 2) + (3 + 3) + (5 + 5)$; 34, the next number in the series, can be broken into $2 + (3 + 3) + (5 + 5) + (8 + 8)$, and so on. She worked out the series' inner repetitions through $u(17,711)$, at first wanting to be sure the pattern held, then simply enjoying the beauty of the systems-within-systems, covering sheets of paper with vertical lines of figures like chains of small, black flowers.

Ultimately, though, the *alfabet* poems stop at *n*. The final section of the book paints a future destroyed, poisoned, underscoring a plea from one of the earlier poems:

> . . . let
> things be; add
> words, but let
> things be; see
>
> . . .
>
> how easily they tiptoe
> into your ear
> and whisper
> to death to go away

It is up to us whether the alphabet of all creation will continue.

Susanna Nied. *Scandinavian Review.* 70:4,
December, 1982, pp. 24–26

In *Det,* [It], Inger Christensen's important collection of poems from 1969, she has subdivided each of the three main chapters, "Scenen," "Handlingen," and "Teksten," into eight sections of eight poems each. The names of these sections are identical in each of the three chapters and are taken from the relation-types in [Viggo Brøndal's] *Præpositionernes Theori:* symmetries, transitivities, continuities, connections, variablities, extensions, integrities, and universalities. . . .

The use of these relation-types in the collection can be interpreted in two ways. *First,* one can claim that it is the notion of relation *as such* that is important, whereas the *specific* relations Inger Christensen chooses to include are unimportant. Thus it is not easy to see how the different relation-types could give a precise characterization of the sections they name in *Det.* The different types of relation can therefore be said to be used as a whole as a *metaphor* for the relations' numerously varied, but constant, presence in Inger Christensen's fictive universe.

This use is in fact characterized by two things: first, the knowledge, constantly present, that human reality is a language-based universe of meaning. That awareness pervades *Det* from the principal lines of composition to the smallest linguistic detail, in which minimal syntactic and morphological transformations, often in a structure of repetitions, dictate the progress of the poems. . . . Central, too, is the often repeated motif of the inseparable connection between the world and the description of the world. . . .

The second characteristic feature of the collection's universe, is the presence of a series of repeated motifs for which the notion of relation functions as a condensed metaphor: reciprocity between at least two parties (man and man, man and nature, man and society); connection and solidarity; structural interdependence; the priority of functional and positional definitions as opposed to substantial and "eternal" definitions of man. These motifs and the adduced metapoetical linguistic awareness give Inger Christensen's poems a hard constructivism, a sensitive openness, and a down-to-earth sense that are completely in the spirit of Brøndal. When this duality results in a synthesis, as in *Det,* she creates a great poetry. When this does not happen, there is a shift between a schematic and a romantic resonance. Similar borderline cases can also be found in Brøndal's writings.

With this outlined specification of motifs and with reference to Inger Christensen's particular preoccupation with the relation-type "universality," I have indirectly pointed to the possibility that her use of relation-types need not, as I have assumed thus far, have only an unspecified metaphorical function. One can in fact *secondly* propose that the individual relation-types are chosen precisely because they contain specific meanings (reciprocity, cohesion, effect, etc.). These meanings are bound up with the motifs in the work and at the same time allow them to be part of a system, whereby a progression can be established from the simplest relation (symmetry) to the most complex (universality), such that the connection between the individual stages in the process is maintained. In this way the relation-types selected serve as *practical* bases for the construction of *Det*'s universe, with its many internally linked elements and levels.

Sven Larsen. Scandinavian Studies. 60,
1988, pp. 331–32

Two [earlier] volumes anticipate Inger Christensen's principal work, and the greatest poetic achievement of Danish literature of the 1960s, the epic *Det.* Structured strictly symmetrically, like a musical composition or a chemical experiment, the work stages its own creation, reaching back to the beginning of time, a modern cosmogony, and simultaneously it absorbs the political and social questions of the period. Shaped in a flowing verbal creativity with rhymed stanzas, prose, and song lyrics, *Det* concludes with a stirring exploration of the human being's existential conditions. Only the creative self is able to overcome the dominant split between language and experience and thus make possible a movement from initial chaos to an increasingly more refined differentiation within human life, a movement that is mirrored in the text itself. On the external, social level Christensen shows an obvious sympathy with the outsider, the rebel; on the textual level she defends openness and the determination to break up and venture into the unknown. Both levels meet in an overpowering tribute to the individual's integration to the fellowship of all human beings as well as into the cycle of nature, which is perhaps only Utopia: "I have attempted to tell about a world that does not exist in order to make it exist."

Linguistic experimentation as well as the analysis of creation and creativity was anticipated in Christensen's two novels *Evighedsmaskinen* (1964; The eternity machine) and *Azorno* (1967; Azorno), but here it is seen in relation to the experience of love. The first is a Christ allegory about the incarnation of love in human beings and in society; the second is an epistolary and diary novel, in which various women try to explain their relationship with the man who has given the novel its title—a poet and Kierkegaardian seducer. Filled with jealousy, they all manipulate what they write down, whereby reality is turned into fiction. In her novel *Det malede værelse* (1976; The painted room), about the Italian Renaissance painter Mantegna, related to the fantastical story in the tradition of Isak Dinesen, Christensen attempts to maintain a synthesis of art and reality, image and life. Through three different narrators Christensen seeks to reach an understanding of the world as a creative process, of which art is a highly integrated part, but without ever reaching a final answer to the question of reality as being a form of art and art being a form of reality.

Det malede værelse concludes by letting one of the narrators, the ten-year-old son of the painter, walk into his father's painting as a symbol of the child's ability to transgress the borders by which the adult is confined. This unspoiled ability to experience life both in its mythic and basic form is illustrated in the poetry volume *Brev i april* (1979; Letter in April). Externally Christensen describes a journey to southern Europe with a child, whose precise observations of the surrounding world open up new and unexpected perspectives for the first-person narrator, the writing self, which in its turn provokes creative wonder and change. A related awareness of death is found in the collection *Alfabet* (1981; Alphabet), now directly connected with linguistic awareness. . . .

Christensen's entire oeuvre, which also includes a series of radio plays, published in *En vinteraften i Ufa* (1987; A winter's evening in Ufa), must be read as one single comprehensive linguistic and philosophical experiment to capture an elusive reality. Christensen is unquestionably the most prolific and distinguished Danish representative of the so-called systemic poetry, the theory that proposes that poetry is a linguistic construction guiding the author as a means of cognition by searching for reality in the words—between and outside the words—but always captured with the help of words. For a writer of less stature than Christensen such attempts could have approached a mathematical problem. However, Christensen is eminently successful in reaching far beyond such mechanical constructions through her visionary insights into the human mind and spirit, her enthralling mythic associations as well as an overwhelmingly fertile metaphoric imagination.

Sven Hakon Rossel. In Steven R. Serafin
and Walter D. Glanze, eds. *Encyclopedia of
World Literature in the 20th Century* (New
York: Continuum, 1993), p. 140

CHURCHILL, CARYL (GREAT BRITAIN) 1938–

Whether Caryl Churchill writes about frighteningly familiar middle-class life, seventeenth century witches, Levellers and Ranters of the 1640s, or 1960s burnouts, her plays challenge our most basic assumptions, those that make it possible for us to function in the most mundane and necessary ways. Forcing us to take a second look at our usually unshaken premises, Churchill's plays won't allow us the regular comfort of supposed truths about human nature, Western values, social organization, or historical progress.

But Churchill's plays do not occupy a safely distant metaphysical stratosphere. Their issues confront us in terms of human, earthly existence. Churchill's questionings insinuate themselves into our experiences of her plays. Her plays do not assault their audiences, affording us the chance to erect barriers against their thorny uncertainties. They fascinate and entertain; their challenges are sneaky. . . .

Churchill is one of several women who have been making significant contributions to the body of political playwriting in England. . . . Their work often addresses feminist issues related to the lack of regard, fearful misunderstanding, and condescending wonder with which their work is received. But just as there is no single party line shared by leftist writers, it would be a mistake to lump these women together as representing the unified feminist voice of England. . . .

Her stage plays, beginning with *Owners* in 1972 question the values of bourgeois life and the conditions necessary for the few to enjoy it. When Churchill focuses on society's oppression of women, she is not engaging in any single issue sloganeering. She explores this situation as one example of the oppression and alienation of people that she sees as an unavoidable effect of capitalism.

Churchill's characters' psychic, emotional, and ethical experience are the inexorable result of their socio-political organization—their social being determines their thought. Churchill questions that organization and reveals our tendency to mistake the systematic structures that determine our thought for the necessities of human nature. And she asks us to question the mechanisms by which we apply our schematized thinking to experience. But Churchill is not presenting treatises scrambling to disguise themselves as drama. She has no a priori ideological tenets to drape like plastic furniture covers over her art. Rather, the political values she examines are intrinsic to the writing.

Alisa Solomon. Theater. 12, Spring, 1981,
pp. 49–50

The more prominent Churchill's work becomes, the more it is caught in a variety of critical traps. Her plays have provoked far less public recognition than those of a dozen male playwrights with comparable, but lesser, bodies of work. Nothing of hers has thus far been produced on the West End or at the National Theater, measures of "success" that, while as dubious as a Broadway production in the United States, nevertheless provide access to both audiences and financial support. Yet, in contrast to the plays of some other British women playwrights, Churchill's work has been consistently produced and a number of her plays have been published. The support Churchill has received from Max Stafford-Clark and the Royal Court Theater, as well as from publishers, sometimes provokes unease rather than applause or relief, both because it is unique and because it implies a continuing dependence on men.

Churchill's work and its reception also raise complicated questions about the relationship of a playwright—especially a feminist playwright—to companies with whom she collaborates. Although Caryl acknowledges in interviews and published texts her debts to the companies with whom she has created many of her plays, is that sufficient distribution of "credit" since playbills and publications still bear only Churchill's name? And is it convention, entrenched social-aesthetic structures, or the playwright which is responsible for whatever injustices may thus occur?

Helene Keyssar. Massachusetts Review. 24,
Spring, 1982, pp. 198–201

Crisis of identity, its causes and consequences, produces the comic critique in Caryl Churchill's *Cloud 9* . . . her two-act play that follows a Victorian family into a twentieth-century setting. In the farcical sex tangles of act 1, an adult male actor plays a Victorian woman and an adult female plays a male child, making the point that sexual identity in the hallowed institution of the Victorian family is not "natural" but is constituted by prevailing gender codes. To problematize sexual identity in this way is of course to challenge the theatrical apparatus which dictates unitary representation of the individual. But Churchill makes cross-gender casting a result of sexual politics, as shown in the characters' first speeches, thumbnail autobiographies in comic doggerel. . . . Betty is the perfect Lacanian female victim, a consequence of patriarchal structuring. However, Churchill is concerned to represent Betty's status concretely, for "what [we] can see" is a walking contradiction of the verbal and the iconic. When Betty utters the confused clichés of the oppressed Victorian wife, we laugh not only because they are consistent with the stereotypes we have of that figure . . . but because the stage image is radically disorienting. We see a man representing a woman, mouthing her inanities, making typically female fluttering gestures with distinctly male arms. There is no transvestism here—that is, we are meant to see Betty included in the symbolic order only insofar as she is male. The point is not that the male is feminized but that the female is absent. What remains is a dress, a palpitation, a scream, all encoded female behaviors adding up to a trace denoting absence. The *woman* Betty is not represented; *she* lacks symbolization in culture.

Worse, this man-made woman is contrasted with the sexually aggressive Mrs. Saunders, who humiliates her, and the frustrated lesbian Ellen, who adores her. The same actress plays both characters, the only example of double casting in act 1. Of course, ironic doublings abound in *Cloud 9,* but the particular instance of Mrs. Saunders/Ellen has special significance. Despite their obvious differences, they are two versions of female marginality, virtual doubles. Sharing the same body they must never meet—the theatrical convention (of double casting) abets the coercive narrative of female subjugation. Churchill's message is painfully clear: in patriarchy women are divided not only from other women (in this case the "woman" Betty) but from themselves.

A more radical critique of patriarchy comes with the time shift in act 2 in which Churchill violates the theatrical convention that character time will be coterminous with the time frame of the text. In act 2 time has advanced a hundred years but for the characters it is only twenty-five years later. By disturbing diachronic time Churchill lays bare the problematic of history and female identity. No longer the period setting for the zany actions of act 1, the Victorian era can now be read as a set of coded practices that continues to bear pressure on the contemporary characters of act 2. The radical feminist rhetoric by which Vicky tries to live cannot fully lift her out of the past when she was, we recall, a doll-child, spearated from life. The lesbian Lin, confused about child care, gender markings, even jobs, is as marginalized as Ellen, the governess and closet lesbian of the first act. Because of the time shift, the fears and indecisions we witness in act 2 are lifted out of the causality of personal history and become evidence of the sociosexual configurations we saw represented in act 1. Churchill thus succeeds in semiotizing, making readable, the narrative of history in which the parts for women are written by patriarchal law.

The time shifts in *Cloud 9* also challenge audience narrativity, our desire to construct a coherent narrative from events presented in sequence. . . .

In act 2 Churchill presents an image of reassembled female identity, no longer positioning her female protagonist as a victim of history but as a heroine in her own narrative of liberation. In a monologue near the end of the play Betty tells how she has learned to touch herself and in the final image of the play she embraces her Victorian male incarnation while rock music blares, "It'll be fine when you reach Cloud 9." The fact that the audience is happily consuming this moment of female transcendence makes it even more suspect. The signifiers put into play in act 1 with the cross-gender casting are too neatly tied to the signified of self-acceptance, the unity of self. One might say that Churchill opts here for comic closure and narrative teleology rather than decentered play. Her historicist critique has become ahistorical romance.

Elin Diamond. *Theatre Journal.* October,
1983, pp. 277–79

For a decade now, deliberate confusion of dramatic roles and playfulness about otherwise serious concepts of gender and history have distinguished Caryl Churchill's plays from the work of mainstream playwrights in Great Britain and the United States. For instance, six performers in *Light Shining in Buckinghamshire* play twenty-four different *dramatis personae* with individual role assignments which vary from scene to scene and are unrelated to the performers' actual sexes. In the finale of *Vinegar Tom,* her "sequel" to *Light Shining,* two female performers portray two seventeenth-century theologians in the top hat and tails of music hall entertainers, singing with great irony the song "Evil Women." In a prefatory note to *Traps,* Churchill describes the play as an "impossible object," like an Escher drawing: "In the play, the time, the place, the characters, motives and relationships cannot all be reconciled—they can happen on stage, but there is no other reality for them. . . . The characters can be thought of as living many of their possibilities at once." The cast of seven performers in *Cloud Nine,* Churchill's first *bona-fide* commercial hit, play thirteen roles in varying age, gender, and race. . . . In *Top Girls,* an all-female cast of seven play a total of sixteen different characters, five of whom do not exist in the present. Even more recently, in *Fen,* five women and one man play twenty-two characters in an ambiguous setting which is simultaneously interior and exterior: in Annie Smart's 1983 stage design, "a field in a room." . . .

The theatrical inventiveness of Churchill's comedies suggests, in particular, that the individual self, as the audience recognizes it, is an ideological construct and the "real world," the world as it is recast by the performers, klieg lights, and chicken wire on the stage, consists of people and events which are individual only insofar as they are rhetorically defined in contrast to others. Her plays conceive character and event as paradoxes. People in her plays are not whole, though sometimes they are ignorant of their own fragmentation; they exist only in tension with their environment (time and space), the other people in the environment, and with the "others" who they themselves used to be at an earlier age (their former "selves"). Churchill describes the condition more vividly in dramatic terms in the closing image of *Cloud Nine,* when a character in act 2 confronts the version of herself from act 1: "BETTY *and* BETTY *embrace.*"

In performance, the plays assume obvious political importance, espousing the social concerns of contemporary feminism: gender stereotyping, the division of labor according to sex, the proprietary family, the oppression of sexual variety through compulsory heterosexuality, class struggle, ageism, and ethnocentrism. The dramatic events raise the audience's consciousness about social principles through the actions depicted and, more importantly, through the actual events of the performance: woman playing man, man playing woman, one person playing two (or more) persons, two persons playing one, the deconstruction of history and geography (and the related unities of time, place, and action) in order to dramatize the cyclical progress of political and social events in history. What the audience experiences during the performance, then, is defamiliarization of the ordinary (alienation effect) and the subversion of positive ideologies about gender, social hierarchies, and chronology. The comedies are parodic enactments and satires of prevalent, middle-class belief-systems and values, i.e., mythologies.

Joseph Marohl. *Modern Drama.* 30,
September, 1987, pp. 376–77

CIALENTE, FAUSTA (ITALY) 1898–

This second edition of the hitherto impossible to find novel by Fausta Cialente, *Courtyard to Cleopatra* (Cleopatra is a suburb of Alexandria, Egypt), will renew for a number of readers the joy of their first encounter with one of the finest Italian narrative works of the past three decades. For other readers, perhaps a great many, it will be an absolute surprise. I would place myself not that far from this latter group because, for whatever reason, I did not happen to make the book's acquaintance until some years after its first appearance, in 1936. But from then on, I have always been astonished, whenever our recent narrative is discussed, if *Courtyard to Cleopatra* did not come in for the highest praise. I would not wish to deny the fact that it may be said that novels and stories by other authors reflect a greater insistence on Significance or that their commitment to art was more conscious and sustained. But I do not know how many of them would have been able to show such indelible freshness. . . .

How solid and secure is the basis of Mediterranean exoticism in *Courtyard to Cleopatra!* An exoticism so authentic, so colorful, and at the same time so familiar. . . .

Guided by an infallible sympathy and ethnic faithfulness that must have been stupendously repaid by the success of her novel, Cialente preferred a modest choice. . . . She remained in a suburb of Alexandria . . . in a mixed neighborhood of Jewish small shopkeepers and Greek and Arab workers. She shared the life of these people, listened to their confidences, divined their passions and their secrets. And the fact is that nowadays, when I think of the beaches and harbors of the Mediterranean East, with their mixture of races, their poverty, their loves, all these things imbedded with the sound of words, the violence of odors, the quality of light, they all refer me back to the pages of *Courtyard to Cleopatra.*

The narrative proceeds with generous naturalness so intertwined with symmetries never insisted upon yet suggestive, with a taste for pictorial composition whose figurative and landscape themes and whose spatial pauses cut across the course of time and the development of the drama. . . .

With this edition, a new season deservedly opens up for the book. We envy those who will be reading it for the first time.

Emilio Cecchi. Preface to Fausta Cialente.
Cortile a Cleopatra (Milan: Mondadori,
1978), pp. 5–7, 10

Only in the novel *Courtyard to Cleopatra* does the author succeed in effectively expressing the collection of experiences that she brings to her writing; in the other books, the initial emotional impetus gives way to a content-oriented search and a narrative technique in a state of evolution.

In fact, in reading three novels of Cialente's, there is an obvious passage from themes belonging to an exotic and distant reality to others involving the reader's own daily reality more closely. The narrative distance also reflects flexibility, especially with respect to the way characters are presented. In the first book, the protagonist relies on a foundation of characters whose presence we devine as choric; in *Levantine Ballet* other figures begin to emerge beside them who, by no means incidentally, provide the titles for the book's various sections; and in the final book, *A Very Cold Winter,* various characters are granted their own space, through which the reader gets inside the characters.

Thus, it may be stated that the choral novel determines a constant in Cialente's narrative technique that is in evolution with respect to the space granted the protagonist. This change in structure may be noted macroscopically in the last novel, which, again not incidentally and in contrast to its predecessors, contains numerous points of view corresponding to the motivations of the various characters. . . .

To this flexibility within female heroism is opposed a constant model of male heroism, even if it takes different forms in the economy of the different novels. We are referring here to a certain apolitical, free character who embodies autobiographical qualities. If, with the figure of Marco in *Courtyard to Cleopatra,* this character was the privileged protagonist, in *A Very Cold Winter,* the character of Enzo comes across as marginal with respect to his surroundings, although still autonomous.

On the thematic level, a recurrent element places love and death together as a contrapositive element reflected through the presence of the liquid or water, bringing the discourse into the Lacanian terms of regression. To the image of water, to the liquid, according to Lacan, may be attributed the author's unconscious desire to return to the maternal womb, as protection from the world. But at the same time this means a renunciation of life, thus dying a little. The desire for protection, symbolized by the water-uterus, is projected in the narrative macrostructure in a nuclear family in which life is lived quietly, but renouncing the social, thus dying to the life outside. . . .

Even Camilla in *A Very Cold Winter,* who takes on the role of mother-martyr, achieves an identity when she leaves her home in Milan, but at the cost of conflicts and the loss of secure family affection.

Remaining within the family then, is at the cost of the loss of identity, but in exchange there are secure affections; by contrast, by going away one reacquires an identity, but the price is so high (uncertainty, conflict, sense of guilt) that the urge to return is very strong. . . .

The three novels present a gradation of tones in their setting, as well. In fact that the first book takes place entirely in Egypt, in Alexandria, the second between Egypt and Italy, and the third in Italy. This gradual displacement with the writer's country of origin all take place in the same historical period, the immediate postwar years.

> Maria Assunta Parsani and Neria
> DeGiovanni. *Femminile a confronto*
> (Manduria: Lacaita, 1984), pp. 65–67

Fausta Cialente belongs to a small group of Italian writers who, by choice or necessity, lived part of their adult life outside Italy. Although her family's nomadic life prevented her from establishing strong ties with any Italian regional culture or even with the national literary tradition, it fostered in her a European outlook. She is probably most similar to the Triestine Italo Svevo, who was also detached from the mainstream of Italian literature. Both authors communicate in an unadorned style of writing and portray restless, introspective, and autobiographical characters. Among European writers, Cialente emulates Gide and Proust in her extensive use of memory and of characters living in a specific environment at a particular moment in time. Her narrative work consists of six novels and several short stories. Three of her novels are set in Egypt: *Cortile a Cleopatra* (Courtyard to Cleopatra), written in 1931 and published in 1936, *Ballata levantina* (The Levantines) (1961), and *Il vento sulla sabbia* (Wind on the sand) (1972); the other three take place mainly in Italy: *Natalia* (1929), *Un inverno freddissimo* (A very cold winter) (1966), and *Le quattro ragazze Wieselberger* (The four Wieselberger girls) (1976).

A chronological examination of Cialente's fiction highlights the author's gradual progress toward self-revelation and her interpretation of the relationship between art (the world of the intellect) and life (the realm of social and political activism). In addition, the writer's measured disclosure of personal truth parallels her analysis of a woman's place in marriage and society. In her first stories, for instance, characters inhabit a magic or exotic world; thus, details about personal circumstances are few. Her later novels, on the other hand, portray individuals who are aware of their importance in historical situations and social settings; the writer relies more on real events and her own life story than on pure fiction. Her last work, which incorporates a significant amount of autobiographical information, blends the main themes of her narrative oeuvre; an exploration of the role of art in society merges with an examination of a woman's role in the world as she describes the author-protagonist, Fausta Cialente, heatedly engaged in the struggles of her time.

> Paola Malpezzi Price. In Santo L. Aricó, ed.
> *Contemporary Women Writers in Italy: A*
> *Modern Renaissance* (Amherst: University
> of Massachusetts Press, 1990), pp. 109–10

CISNEROS, SANDRA (UNITED STATES) 1954–

In some recent essays collectively titled "From a Writer's Notebook," Sandra Cisneros talks about her development as a writer, making particular references to her award-winning book, *The House on Mango Street*. She states that the nostalgia for the perfect house was impressed on her at an early age from reading many times Virginia Lee Burton's *The Little House*. It was not until her tenure at the Iowa Writers Workshop, however, that it dawned on her that a house, her childhood home, could be the subject of a book. In a class discussion of Gaston Bachelard's *The Poetics of Space*, she came to this realization: "the metaphor of a house, *a house, a house*, it hit me. What did I know except third-floor flats. Surely my classmates knew nothing about that." Yet Cisneros's reverie and depiction of house differ markedly from Bachelard's poetic space of house. With Bachelard we note a house conceived in terms of a male-centered ideology. A man born in the upper crust family house, probably never having to do "female" housework and probably never having been confined to the house for reason of his sex, can easily contrive states of reverie and images of a house that a woman might not have, especially an impoverished woman raised in a ghetto. . . . Cisneros inverts Bachelard's nostalgic and privileged utopia, for hers is a different reality: "That's precisely what I chose to write: about third-floor flats, and fear of rats, and drunk husbands sending rocks through windows, anything as far from the poetic as possible. And this is when I discovered the voice I'd been suppressing all along without realizing it."

The determination of genre for *Mango Street* has posed a problem for some critics. Is *Mango Street* a novel, short stories, prose poems, vignettes? . . .

The focus . . . on compression and lyricism contributes to the brevity of the narratives. With regard to this generic classification, Cisneros states:

> I said once that I wrote *Mango Street* naively, that they were "lazy poems." In other words, for me each of the stories could've developed into poems, but they were not poems. They were stories, albeit hovering in that grey area between two genres. My newer work is still exploring this terrain.

On a different occasion, Cisneros had called the stories "vignettes." I would affirm that, although some of the narratives of *Mango Street* are "short stories," most are vignettes, that is, literary sketches, like small illustrations nonetheless "hovering in that grey area between two genres." . . .

Mango Street is a street sign, a marker, that circumscribes the neighborhood to its latino population of Puerto Ricans, Chicanos and Mexican immigrants. This house is not the young protagonist's dream house; it is only a temporary house. The *semes* that we ordinarily perceive in house, and the ones that Bachelard assumes—such as comfort, security, tranquility, esteem—are lacking. This is a house that constrains, one that she wants to leave; consequently, the house sets up a dialectic of inside and outside: of living *here* and wishing to leave for *there*. . . .

The realization of the possibility of escape through the space of writing, as well as the determination to move away from Mango Street, are expressed in "Mango Says Goodbye Sometimes." . . .

I do not hold with Juan Rodríguez that Cisneros's book ultimately sets forth the traditional ideology that happiness, for example, comes with the realization of the "American Dream," a house of one's own. In his review of *Mango Street,* Rodríguez states:

> That Esperanza chooses to leave Mango St., chooses to move away from her social/cultural base to become more "Anglicized," more individualistic; that she chooses to move from the real to the fantasy plane of the world as the only means of accepting and surviving the limited and limiting social conditions of her barrio becomes problematic to the more serious reader.

This insistence on the preference for a comforting and materialistic life ignores the ideology of a social class's liberation, particularly that of its women, to whom the book is dedicated. The house the protagonist longs for, certainly, is a house where she can have her own room and one that she can point to in pride, but, . . . it is fundamentally a metaphor for the house of storytelling. Neither here in the house on Mango Street nor in the "fantasy plane of the world"—as Rodriguez states, does the protagonist indulge in escapism.

We can agree, and probably Cisneros on this occasion does, with Bachelard's observation on the house as the space of daydreaming: "the places in which we have experienced daydreaming reconstitute themselves in a new daydream, and it is because our memories of former dwelling places are relived as daydreams that these dwelling places of the past remain in us for all time." The house that Esperanza lives and lived in will always be associated with the house of story-telling—"What I remember most is Mango Street"; because of it she became a writer. Esperanza will leave Mango Street but take it with her for always, for it is inscribed within her.

Julián Olivares. In María Herrera-Sobek and Helena María Viramontes, eds. *Chicana Creativity and Criticism* (Houston: Arte Publico, 1988), pp. 167–69

Writing is central in Sandra Cisneros's work of fiction *The House on Mango Street,* [which is characterized] by a deceptively simple, accessible style and structure. The short sections that make up this slim novel, . . . are marvels of poetic language that capture a young girl's vision of herself and the world she lives in. Though young, Esperanza is painfully aware of the racial and economic oppression her community suffers, but it is the fate of the women in her *barrio* that has the most profound impact on her, especially as she begins to develop sexually and learns that the same fate might be hers. Esperanza gathers strength from the experiences of these women to reject the imposition of rigid gender roles predetermined for her by her culture. Her escape is linked in the text to education and above all to writing. Besides finding her path to self-definition through the women she sees victimized, Esperanza also has positive models who encourage her interest in studying and writing. At the end of the book, Esperanza's journey towards independence merges two central themes, that of writing and a house of her own: "a house as quiet as snow, a space for myself to go, clean as paper before the poem."

Esperanza's rejection of woman's place in the culture involves not only writing but leaving the barrio, raising problematic issues of changing class:

> I put it down on paper and then the ghost does not ache so much. I write it down and Mango says goodbye sometimes. She does not hold me with both arms. She sets me free. One day I will pack my bags of books and paper. One day I will say good-bye to Mango. I am too strong for her to keep me here forever. One day I will go away. Friends and neighbors will say, what happened to Esperanza? Where did she go with all those books and paper? Why did she march so far away?

But Esperanza ends the book with the promise to return: "They will not know I have gone away to come back. For the ones I left behind. For the ones who cannot get out."

The House on Mango St. captures the dialectic between self and community in Chicana writing. Esperanza finds her literary voice through her own cultural experience and that of other Chicanas. She seeks self-empowerment through writing, while recognizing her commitment to a community of Chicanas. Writing has been essential in connecting her with the power of women and her promise to pass down that power to other women is fulfilled by the writing and publication of the text itself.

Yvonne Yarbro-Bejarano. In María Herrera-
Sobek and Helena María Viramontes, eds.
Chicana Creativity and Criticism (Houston:
Arte Publico, 1988), pp. 142–43

If ideological and economic considerations structure Moraga's and Lizárraga's rape narratives, it is the theme of loss of innocence that predominates in Sandra Cisneros's short story "Red Clowns." In this vignette we encounter Esperanza, the innocent and naive protagonist who is accompanying her older and street savvy friend Sally to the carnival. Sally disappears with her boyfriend and Esperanza, alone in the amusement park, is attacked by a group of boys. The narrative begins with the bitter recriminations of a disillusioned and traumatized Esperanza after the sexual transgression has occurred where, in a monologue full of hurt and despair, she mourns her loss of innocence: "Sally, you lied. It wasn't what you said at all. What he did. Where he touched me. I didn't want it, Sally. The way they said it, the way it's supposed to be, all the storybooks and movies, why did you lie to me?" The diatribe is directed not only at Sally the silent interlocutor but at the community of women who keep the truth from the younger generation of women in a conspiracy of silence. The protagonist discovers a conspiracy of two forms of silence: silence in not *denouncing* the "real" facts of life about sex and its negative aspects in violent sexual encounters, and *complicity* in embroidering a fairy-tale-like mist around sex, and romanticizing and idealizing unrealistical sexual relations. . . .

The theme of the silent, voiceless victim, the woman that is afraid to denounce her attackers, is reiterated in Cisneros's story: "Sally, make him stop. I couldn't make them go away. I couldn't do anything but cry. I don't remember. It was dark. I don't remember. I don't remember. Please don't make me tell it all." This response to block out the rape scene and, to become silent and withdrawn is common in victims of sexual assault.

María Herrera-Sobek. In María Herrera-Sobek and Helena María Viramontes, eds. *Chicana Creativity and Criticism* (Houston: Arte Publico, 1988), pp. 177–78

Besides the double marginalization that stems from gender and ethnicity, Cisneros transgresses the dominant discourse of canonical standards ideologically and linguistically. In bold contrast to the individualistic introspection of many canonical texts, Cisneros writes a modified autobiographical novel, or *Bildungsroman,* that roots the individual self in the broader socio-political reality of the Chicano community. As we will see, the story of individual development is oriented outwardly here, away from the bourgeois individualism of many standard texts. Cisneros's language also contributes to the text's otherness. In opposition to the complex, hermetic language of many canonical works, *The House on Mango Street* recuperates the simplicity of children's speech, paralleling the autobiographical protagonist's chronological age in the book. Although making the text accessible to people with a wider range of reading abilities, such simple and well-crafted prose is not currently in canonical vogue.

The volume falls between traditional genre distinctions as well. Containing a group of forty-four short and interrelated stories, the book has been classified as a novel by some because, as occurs in Tomas Rivera's . . . *y no se lo tragó la tierra,* there is character and plot development throughout the episodes. I prefer to classify Cisneros's text as a collection, a hybrid genre midway between the novel and the short story. Like Sherwood Anderson's *Winesburg, Ohio,* Pedro Juan Soto's *Spiks,* Gloria Naylor's *The Women of*

Brewster Place, and Rivera's text, Cisneros's collection represents the writer's attempt to achieve both the intensity of the short story and the discursive length of the novel within a single volume. Unlike the chapters of most novels, each story in the collection could stand on its own if it were to be excerpted but each attains additional important meaning when interacting with the other stories in the volume. A number of structural and thematic elements link the stories of each collection together. . . .

On the surface the compelling desire for a house of one's own appears individualistic rather than community oriented, but Cisneros socializes the motif of the house, showing it to be a basic human need left unsatisfied for many of the minority population under capitalism. It is precisely the lack of housing stability that motivates the image's centrality in works by writers like Cisneros and Rivera. For the migrant worker who has moved continuously because of job exigencies and who, like many others in the Chicano community, has been deprived of an adequate place to live because of the inequities of income distribution in U. S. society, the desire for a house is not a sign of individualistic acquisitiveness but rather represents the satisfaction of a basic human need. . . .

Unlike many introspective writers, Cisneros links both the process of artistic creation and the dream of a house that will enable this art to social rather than individualistic issues. . . . She conceives of a house as communal rather than private property; such sharing runs counter to the dominant ideological discourse that strongly affects consciousness in capitalist societies. Cisneros's social motifs undermine rather than support the widespread messages of individualized consumption that facilitate sales of goods and services under consumer capitalism.

Cisneros touches on several other important women's issues in this volume, including media images of ideal female beauty, the reifying stare of male surveyors of women, and sex roles within the family. In an effort to counter the sexual division of labor in the home, for example, Esperanza refuses one instance of women's work: "I have begun my own quiet war. Simple. Sure. I am the one who leaves the table like a man, without pulling back the chair or picking up the plate." Although this gesture calls critical attention to gender inequities in the family, Cisneros avoids the issue of who, in fact, will end up performing the household labor that Esperanza refuses here. This important and symbolic, yet somewhat adolescent gesture merely touches on the surface of the problem and is likely, in fact, to increase the work for another woman in Esperanza's household.

The majority of stories in *The House on Mango Street,* however, face important social issues head-on. The volume's simple, poetic language, with its insistence that the individual develops within a social community rather than in isolation, distances it from many accepted canonical texts. Its deceptively simple, childlike prose and its emphasis on the unromanticized, nonmainstream issues of patriarchal violence and ethnic poverty, however, should serve precisely to accord it canonical status. We must work toward a broader understanding among literary critics of the importance of such issues to art in order to attain a richer, more diverse canon and to avoid the undervaluation and oversight of such valuable texts as *The House on Mango Street.*

Ellen McCracken. In Asunción Horno-
Delgado et al, eds. *Breaking Boundaries:
Latina Writings and Critical Readings*
(Amherst: University of Massachusetts
Press, 1989), pp. 63–64, 66, 70–71

From the moment of its publication, *The House on Mango Street,* by Sandra Cisneros, has attracted critical interest for various reasons. Some critics do a feminist reading of the work, as do Erlinda Gonzalez-Berry and Tey Diana Rebolloedo or Julián S. Olivares; others deal with the problem of literary genre, as does Pedro Gutierrez-Revuelta; and others are concerned with ideology, like Gutierrez-Revuelta, again, or Juan Rodriguez. . . . I am going to analyze the work as an act of discourse, a speech act, inscribed in a communicative literary situation, through which its author narrates a series of real or imaginary experiences with the intention of establishing a dialogue with an unknown audience and creating certain effects with her communication.

From this point of view, the change in the book's title that I suggest [*The Book on Mango Street*] is justified in two ways. First, externally, because as readers we confront The Book *of* Mango Street, that is, the literary text that creates the fictional space that is Mango Street. The other, internal, because in one of its symbolic possibilities, the house represents the book. . . . Moreover, the book is one of the preoccupations that Sandra Cisneros reveals in her critical essays. . . .

As a writer, Sandra Cisneros approaches the writing of *The House on Mango Street* as a cross between poetry and fiction: she wants to write narratives that individually have a unity in themselves but that, at the same time, could be brought together to form a larger work. . . .

As an act of discourse, *The House on Mango Street* must be understood in two ways: one, on the level of the characters' discourse, the other as a connection between the author and the group of readers who receive the work. In the first case, we encounter a multiplicity of voices coming, for the most part, from the barrio in which Esperanza, the narrator, lives. In the second, it is the voice of the author that we perceive through the text as we apprehend the work, which makes us conscious that we are dealing with a literary text produced by the author as such. . . .

Nonetheless, the representation of the community's voice should not be confused with the community's own voice expressing itself. In this sense, *The House on Mango Street* is an individual speech act, product of a concrete author. This author's intention, as she indicates in "Notes to a Young(er) Writer" was to speak about what others barely mention, the reality of the barrio and of the women without voice and without access to the world of books. . . .

The book thus takes on the importance of an object capable of achieving certain effects, particularly in recording the voices of those silenced beings or, at least, channeling their stories through the voice of a central narrator. In this sense, it belongs to the category of speech acts that J. L. Austin has called illocutionary.

Manuel M. Martín Rodriquez. In Aralia
López Gonzalez et al, eds. *Mujer y
literatura mexicana y chicana,* vol. 2
(Mexico City: Colegio de Mexico; Tijuana:
Colegio de la Frontera del Norte, 1990),
pp. 249–50, 252–53

In Sandra Cisneros's autobiographical prose poems, *The House on Mango Street,* the child protagonist Esperanza has a mystical experience of solidarity. Three elusive aunts, like fairy godmothers, admonish the aspiring young writer, "You will always be Mango Street. . . . You must remember to come back. . . . For the ones who cannot leave as easily as you." Although Esperanza dreams of "a house quiet as snow, a space for myself to go, clean as paper before the poem," her girlfriends reiterate, "Like it or not you are Mango Street and one day you'll come back too." Cisneros, the "About the Author" tells the reader, "reaffirms our belief that art and talent can survive even under the most adverse conditions."

This meeting of a history, in this case a multiethnic history, that will not be past and the distinction of the writer who nonetheless sees herself as somehow different, separate, from it, is one of the most sensitive issues of feminist autobiography. For students of autobiography per se, it has historical resonances. In nineteenth-century working-class writers, one often sees a similar struggle to distinguish oneself from the anonymous, unindividuated "masses" in order to establish a position from which to present oneself as a distinctive "I." Yet, like Cisneros, these workers separated themselves from history only the better to objectify and ultimately reclaim it: "What I remember most is Mango Street, sad red house, the house I belong but do not belong to."

Cisneros's artistic distinction, although similar in some respects to that of earlier working-class writers, echoes another tradition about which feminists might be more ambivalent. . . . Cisneros's autobiography gives rise to a tension between an ethos of artistic distinction (the privileged creative imagination) and the kind of gender and ethnic solidarity Cisneros seeks.

Regenia Gagnier. *Feminist Studies.* 17:1,
Spring, 1991, p. 137

In *House on Mango Street,* Esperanza herself is the narrative medium and the bridge. The narrative itself is a series of vignettes joined by the consciousness of Esperanza, whose role as medium and go-between is signaled by her doubled name: "In English it means hope. In Spanish it means too many letters. It means sadness, it means waiting." The very titles of the vignettes suggest the conversation of voices the narrative represents: "Cathy Queen of Cats"; "Alicia Who Sees Mice"; "Edna's Ruthie"; "Elenita, Cards, Palms, Water"; "Rafaela Who Drinks Coconut and Papaya Juice on Tuesdays." Esperanza becomes a writer who will tell these stories: "I put it down on paper and then the ghost does not ache so much." Esperanza can tell these stories because she is the one between, the one who has "gone away to come back. For the ones I left behind. For the ones who cannot get out."

In *The House on Mango Street,* "los espiritus" visit the kitchen of the wise woman Elenita. Holy candles burn on the top of her refrigerator; "a plaster saint and a dusty Palm Sunday cross" adorn the kitchen walls along with a "picture of a voodoo hand." Elenita, the "witch woman" who "knows many thing" tells the protagonist's fortune with the tarot, while in the next room Elenita's children watch Bugs Bunny cartoons and drink Kool-Aid on the plastic slipcovered furniture. Esperanza sees her "whole life on that kitchen table: past, present, future" and tries to feel on her hand the cold of the spirits, while a part of her mind is turned to the favorite cartoon she hears from the other room. Waiting for the spirits at the kitchen table is made no stranger nor more unfamiliar here than sitting in the living room drinking Kool-Aid.

> Wendy K. Kolmar. In Lynette Carpenter
> and Wendy K. Kolmar, eds. *Haunting the*
> *House of Fiction* (Knoxville: University of
> Tennessee Press, 1991), pp. 245, 239

CIXOUS, HÉLÈNE (FRANCE) 1937–

In violent images, Hélène Cixous has repeatedly underscored the revolutionary power of *l'écriture féminine*. Whereas speech *(parole)*, like our own existence, is inevitably caught up in the dominant system of discourse, writing *(l'ecriture)* "is precisely the very possibility of change, the space that can serve as a springboard for subversive thought, the precursory movement of a transformation of social and cultural structures." Woman must thus write herself: it is the essential act by which she can mark "her shattering entry into history which has always been based on her suppression. To write and thus to forge for herself the antilogos weapon. To become at will the taker and initiator, for her own right, in every symbolic system, in every political process." For Cixous, *écrire* is synonymous with *voler,* "to rob" and "to fly," to reappropriate and to soar. In particular, writing represents the most forceful weapon for reappropriating the female body, which man has confiscated as his property: "It will give her back her goods, her pleasures, her organs, her immense bodily territories which have been kept under seal." Like Madeleine Gagnon, who affirms the need to examine "my body in writing," as she entitles her essay in the collective volume, *La Venue à l'écriture* (1977), Cixous emphasizes the impact of articulating the forbidden aspects of female sexuality. "Let her speak of her sexual pleasure [*jouissance*], and God knows that she has enough to say, in such a way that she manages to unblock both female and male sexuality, and to dephallicentrize the body, deliver man from his phallus.

The determined effort to speak female sexuality pervades Cixous's most recent works—*La* (1976), *Angst* (1977), *Le Nom d'Oedipe: Chant du corps interdit* (1978), *Préparatifs de noces au delà de l'abîme* (1978)—and Irigaray's *Ce Sexe qui n'en est pas un* (1977). . . .

For Cixous and many of her contemporaries, the act of speaking and, even more, of writing as a female represents a fundamental birth drive which will destroy the old order of death, not merely its material, economic, social, and political manifestations, but the generative system, which determines the production of meaning. From this perspective, some French women regard the pragmatic empiricism of American feminist criticism as fundamentally doomed. They claim that our critical enterprise aims for equality within the Logos, for an equal share of existing symbolic systems, and thus that it essentially reconfirms the dominant phallologicentric order. In one of the first attempts to confront this contradiction, the troubling dis-connection between the French and the American theory and practice of feminist criticism, Cixous asked in her preface to the translation of Phyllis Chesler's *Women and Madness,* whether American women would ever locate repression in the realm of speech acts and in the essence of binary thinking that underlies the very discourse promoting women's liberation. In so doing, Cixous brought into sharp focus the problem explored by Shoshona Felman in the "Textual Politics" issue of *Diacritics* (1975), as she outlined the differences between Chesler's empiricist preoccupation with a clinical history of the institutionalized female on the one hand, and, on the other, Irigaray's investigation of the logic of female repression in *Speculum de l'autre femme.* Although neither critic had concrete proposals for repairing this dis-connection, Cixous urged both French and American women to valorize the female's difference, her otherness as the repressed, the missing signification, in order to undermine the traditional logocentric oppositions between masculine and feminine, intelligence and sensuality, reason and poetry.

> Donna C. Stanton. In Hester Eisenstein and
> Alice Jardine, eds. *The Future of Difference*
> (Boston: G. K. Hall, 1980), pp. 76–78

Because of the importance of Lacanian thought in the intellectual context in which they operate, feminist theorists in France have felt very keenly the need to engage directly with its arguments about sexual difference; many of their critiques of Lacanian theory in fact started out as criticisms from within. Feminist psychoanalysts (Luce Irigaray, for one) have been highly skeptical of the attribution of a negative value to woman's relation to language and of the sexism implicit in the elevation of the phallus to the place of Transcendental Signifier.

This is the background against which we have to understand the general preoccupation of French feminists with phallocentrism, and also their specific critique of the privileged place accorded the phallus in psychoanalytic accounts of language and sexual difference. In line with this critique, Hélène Cixous in *Castration or Decapitation?* aims a blow at "phallologocentric" culture where it hurts the most, and attacks it for marking woman as "other," as difference and negativity. She says no to the fathers, cheekily reminding them of the very thing they have most to fear—the threat of castration posed by the female body. As she says in *The Laugh of the Medusa*: "Let the priests tremble, we're going to show them our sexts! Too bad for them if they fall apart on discovering that women aren't men, or that the mother doesn't have one. Here Cixous is suggesting that certain aspects of feminist/feminine practice may constitute a challenge to phallologocentrism. Her specific concern is with the "feminine" approach to writing (or writing/reading) that is implied by the neologism "sexts": she wants to write, and to write about, a "writing that inscribes femininity.

When *Castration or Decapitation?* first appeared in 1976, the author's primary concern was to open up the question of the "repression of the feminine" in culture, and at the same time to challenge that repression by provocatively questioning the structures of masculinist language and thought—its dualisms, its hierarchical orderings, and so on. To these structures, the feminine comes as "other," a riddle that is finally insoluble within the terms of a masculine (libidinal) economy. Freud's unanswered question "What do women want?" articulates the puzzle that the feminine poses for a patriarchal order. For Cixous, female sexual pleasure (*jouissance*) constitutes a potential disturbance to that order, and a "woman-text"—a text that inscribes this *jouissance*—is a return of the repressed feminine that with its energetic, joyful, and transgressive "flying in language and making it fly" dislocates the repressive structures of phallologocentrism. And Cixous's own work offers an *écriture*—a practice of writing—that aims to do this by posing plurality against unity: multitudes of meanings against single, fixed meanings; diffuseness against instrumentality; openness against closure.

At the same time, however, despite its intent to question phallocentric discourse by means of a writing that subverts it, *Castration or Decapitation?* like other writings by Cixous of the same period, perhaps still constitutes a yearning toward, rather than a grasping of, an alternative practice: "There has not yet been any writing that inscribes femininity." Her more recent writings seem to pose something of a break in this respect. The vocality, tactility, resonance, and exhilaration to be found in *Castration or Decapitation?* are still there, but because the direct challenge to phallocentrism is no longer an explicit focus, these qualities structure the texts in a more thorough-going manner; meanings and readings are denser, more complex, more focused.

Vivre l'orange, for example, echoes with voices and resonates with textures. Its central image of the orange that the writer/reader ("I") reaches toward and grasps condenses and generates an almost infinite number of personal and cultural associations. The orange's juiciness, sensuousness, texture, and brightness are present in the writing itself, which is as tactile as the fruit being held and weighed in the hand. The sound association with Oran, the writer's birthplace, implies a return to sources, but the shape of the orange, the O, tells us that the route will not be a linear one. The shape also suggests the roundness of femininity, the shape and weight of a breast, a full and positive sign of sexual difference to replace the Lacanian Lack.

Annette Kuhn. *Signs: Journal of Women in Culture and Society.* 7, 1981, pp. 37–39

Hélène Cixous, one of the most prolific writers involved in French thinking about the feminine, maps out the binary oppositions that structure the phallocentric system as follows:

> *Where is she?*
> Activity/passivity,
> Sun/Moon,
> Culture/Nature,
> Day/Night,
> Father/Mother,
> Head/Heart,
> Intelligible/sensitive,
> Logos/Pathos.
>
> Form, convex, step, advance, seed, progress.
> Matter, concave, ground—which supports the step, receptacle.
>
> Man
> ———
> Woman

> Always the same metaphor: we follow it, it transports us, in all of its forms, wherever a discourse is organized. The same thread, or double tress leads us, whether we are reading or speaking, through literature, philosophy, criticism, centuries of representation, of reflection.

Cixous, a prolific practitioner of the *écriture féminine* she was among the first to call for, has the most ambitious and explicit programme for it.

Rejecting Freudian and Lacanian theories of woman as lack, she calls for an assertion of the female body as plenitude, as a positive force, the source simultaneously of multiple physical capacities (gestation, birth, lactation) and of liberatory texts. She concentrates on an erotics of writing, to be derived from a feminine unconscious shaped by female bodily drives:

> Write your self. Your body must be heard. Only then will the immense resources of the unconscious spring forth. . . .

Her own writing, she explains, proceeds from a kind of ego loss followed by attentiveness to the rhythms and images of her unconscious, which she fleshes out into an ongoing text-as-process. Metaphors of abundant maternity—composition as childbirth, ink as milk—accompany her portraits of woman as writer.

Cixous has produced over twenty texts since the mid-1960s. They range from studies of the breakdown of language and logic in Lewis Carroll and James Joyce through recitations by man-oppressed speakers, manifestos for feminine writing, lyrical celebrations of the evolution of a woman's subjectivity and, recently, collage-like representations of collaboration among women, such as *Vivre l'orange* (1979) and *With, ou l'art de l'innocence* (1981). *Vivre l'orange* is a poetic essay dramatizing and reflecting upon Cixous's discovery of a Brazilian poet and novelist, Clarice Lispector. Its multiple modes typify Cixous's invocations of feminine subjectivity—in this case, her belief that women have a pre-conceptual, non-appropriative openness to people and to objects, to the other within and outside them. She breaks down contradictions by juxtaposing meditation and narrative, literal and fantastic images, past and present, concrete detail and incantatory flow.

Ann Rosalind Jones. In Gayle Green and
Coppélia Kahn, eds. *Making a Difference*
(New York: Methuen, 1985),
pp. 81–82, 88–89

Sexual and linguistic difference is a guiding principle in the feminist project enunciated by Hélène Cixous. Cixous is the major advocate and practitioner of what is known as *écriture féminine*—feminine writing, which represents for Cixous the most propitious means for dismantling patriarchal language, and, through language, the social and cultural oppression of women. Cixous's 1975 text "Le Rire de la méduse" serves as a manifesto of *écriture féminine,* elaborating the link between the body, sexual difference, and language. For Cixous, women have historically been silenced: made to assume the role of physicality and materiality as a counter to masculine reason and discourse, women have been denied access to language and writing. They are, for Cixous, more fully physical than men; they more fully and furiously inhabit what she calls "ces corps somptuex;" "plus que l'homme invité aux réussites sociales, à la sublimation les femmes sont corps." At the same time, however, women have been divorced from their bodies by what they have been told about them, and about their sexuality. Thus, Cixous claims in "Le Rire de la méduse," the urgent imperative is for women to "s'écrire," to "write their bodies." . . .

The specificity of *écriture féminine* is thus squarely lodged, for Cixous, in the physical bodies of women. In an interview published in 1976, she states: "It is beyond doubt that femininity derives from the body, from the anatomical, the biological differences, from a whole system of drives which are radically different for women than for men. But none of these exists in a 'pure' state: it is always, immediately, 'already spoken,' caught in representation, produced culturally." Although Cixous seems to preclude here the possibility of getting back to woman's natural state—the state woman enjoyed before culture intervened to represent it to her—the majority of Cixous's texts reinforce the impression that it is the specificity of the female body and the diffuse, polymorphous nature of female desire which will, through a new order of writing, change the old order of life. . . .

Cixous's own texts provide examples of this new writing. Her style has been characterized as "stream of the unconscious," flowing in long sentences full of hyperbolic metaphors about wombs and mother's milk, which is generally equated with the "encre blanche" of *écriture féminine*. Cixous has written on James Joyce, and she shares with him an emphasis on extravagant punning in several languages and tones, a writing aimed at dislodging the Aristotelian logic of dominant syntax and determinate meaning. Cixous's insistence on plurality of tones and voices as a form-breaking device has also occasioned comparisons with Bakhtin's notion of a bawdy carnival of language. Perhaps her most insistent theme is the call to women to write their own bodies, to "nurture" a new type of text. Thus she describes her 1975 text, *Souffles,* as "A la fois texte-mère et texte-enfant, texte-amour: espace des genèses. Laisse couler le lait! Laisse voler l'écriture!" *Écriture féminine* for Cixous is both a celebration of the female body—she recuperates Freud's term "dark continent"—and a product of that body's libidinal and generative drives. . . .

In 1969 Cixous was awarded the prestigious Prix Médicis for a fictional text entitled *Dedans. Dedans* provides a lengthy meditation on and challenge to the Oedipal conflict from "within" the perspective of the family, and specifically of the girl child.

Cecile Lindsay. *French Review.* 60:1,
October, 1986, pp. 47–49

Portrait of Dora is the flip side of Freud's scientific-perverse-male presentation of the Dora "case." As it turns out, though, the reverse of perversity is not as symmetrical as Freud would have foreseen. Cixous's repetition of a male narrative from the other side, her actual quotations of Freud in her own text, have the effect of setting Freud's writing loose from its origin in the supposed author "Freud" and demonstrating that "his" words might belong to anybody—even to a woman.

Cixous might have yielded to the "temptation of writing a satire" on Freud. He would have made as easy a mark as the "respectable gentry" Freud himself disdained to attack. But to yield to such a temptation would have been to make a comic figure of Freud, to dismiss him as he finally dismissed Dora when she returned a year and a half later to ask Freud to treat her. Cixous does not merely turn the tables on Freud; she does not reverse his discourse against him, as he reversed Dora's against her. Nor, surprisingly, does Cixous write from the "real" Dora's point of view, since her sickness lay precisely in a failure of speech. This is the writing of a deferred Dora: a second, symbolic Dora. It is the writing of a hysteric whose world includes both Dora and Freud, whose language has been shaped both by the preemptive filter of male discourse and by female silence.

Cixous speaks in the void created by Dora's aphonia, in the space of meaning vacated by her body's symptoms. But although Cixous's reparation of Dora's speech appears to resemble Freud's "constructions," it differs in two important respects: first, she attempts to recover the worlds of both Dora and Freud by experiencing them specifically in a hysterical mode; second, Cixous's writing is not a strategy of opposition or mastery with respect either to Freud or to Dora.

This case history and its publication, so marked with gaps and lapses, is now punctuated by the greatest lapse of all: a period of seventy-five years between its representation in a text written by a man and its reliving in a text written by a woman. Cixous writes, then, in a double gap: the one between Dora and herself and the one between male and female writing. . . .

Portrait of Dora stands not only at the juncture of dreams and hysteria but also at the point where the discursive logic of written language and the recursive logic of speech (fail to) meet in a play text. The very title of the play emphasizes the doubleness of its project: it is a portrait, a line drawing of written language. It is not, however, *a* portrait or *the* portrait, but simply "portrait"—undefined, unpositioned—a drawing forth into the immediacy of presence. . . .

The word "door," interestingly enough, inhabits the title of the play both in French and in English; *porte-portrait,* door-Dora. And doors are everywhere in the play, opening and closing, in reality, in metaphors, and in dreams. . . .

We can see that the opening and closing of doors is a metaphor for both emotional receptiveness and sexual availability. It soon becomes clear, however, that doors have a different significance for men than for women, and that for the men all other references of this metaphor are subordinated to the expression of the sexual availability of women. In their parlance, doors are female genitals, and according to the logical law of the exclusion of opposites, doors must be either open or closed. . . .

A door closed on Freud is an opening of another kind. As Dora leaves his office at the end of the play, he says to her, making a significant slip: "I'd like to hear from me. Write me." And Dora answers, "Write? . . . That's none of my business." Dora could not write because, in the closed society she left Freud's office to join, her language could only have been the echo of his story.

Cixous is able to write; she is able to write because Freud's Dora and the world she lived in have become a memory. . . .

While Freud's text shut out women's desire in its homosexual appeal to other men, this mouth opens a new space in language undreamed of by men, a space where women, rather than canceling each other out, can love and dance together as they do in Dora's dream, where they can begin to feel "an overwhelming tenderness." This new mouth speaking from the midst of Freud's text tells the story of all the silent, abandoned patients, daughters, governesses, wives moving in a new rhythm, shedding the numbness of their symptoms as they don the fullness of their own sumptuous feelings.

Cixous's writing is this hysteric's dream.

> Martha Noel Evans. *Masks of Tradition:*
> *Women and the Politics of Writing in*
> *Twentieth-Century France* (Ithaca: Cornell
> University Press, 1987),
> pp. 165–66, 168, 176–77, 182, 184

CLIFF, MICHELLE (JAMAICA–UNITED STATES) 1946–

Set in the Jamaica of the 1950s, *Abeng* is a novel by a young woman writer who grew up in that complex West Indian society. Written in 1984, this third major work by Michelle Cliff—earlier writing includes *Claiming an Identity They Taught Me to Despise* and a shorter piece of fiction in the Lillian Smith edited *The Winner Names the Age: A Collection of Writings*—explores the search for racial, historical, and personal self-definition.

The underlying plot of *Abeng* traces the story of Clare Savage's coincidental understanding of her place in Jamaican society and her physical maturation into womanhood. Through the eyes of the light-skinned Clare, the summer of 1958 reveals the inconsistencies and complications that arise from belonging to a colonial society that exalts and imitates the English, on the one hand, and shows such imitation to be empty mimicry, on the other, when it is juxtaposed to the vestiges of mythological and folkloric customs retained by islanders. Thus Clare is caught between two drastically opposed points of view: her father's glorification of his British heritage and his pride in being light-skinned versus her mother's sympathetic understanding of and respect for the culture and tradition of her black Jamaica.

Clare struggles internally to understand the differences established by color gradations which limit and determine a person's worth. She reads *The Diary of Anne Frank* and finds similarities between anti-Semitism and racism. As a result, she reasons to herself that "just as Jews were expected to suffer in a Christian world, so were dark people expected to suffer in a white one." This is Clare's conclusion after having tried to come to terms with her own racial identity, but as Cliff describes her at this point in the novel, "She was a colonized child, and she lived within certain parameters which clouded her judgment."

If *The Diary of Anne Frank* gives the protagonist, Clare, some understanding of her identity, then Michelle Cliff's discovery of Zora Neale Hurston (a woman writer of the Harlem renaissance who went to Jamaica in the 1930s to do field work for one of her books) probably brought the writer to a closer comprehension of her own reality. In the novel *Tell My Horse* (1938), Hurston presents a study of Jamaican customs and traditions and acknowledges the fact that in Jamaica "there is a frantic stampede whiteward to escape from Jamaica's black mass." But the reference to the Hurston novel leaves the haunting question of whether Michelle Cliff's knowledge of Jamaica comes principally from her own early childhood experience or from her reading of Hurston's books and other later research. But regardless of which one the author draws most heavily upon, both vital experience and research are legitimate sources, and Cliff seems to have used both in the development of her novel.

At times Cliff intermixes more universal, political, and racial statements with *Abeng's* plot which digress from and hamper the narrative of the novel. But even these inconsistencies of narrative do not mar the book's worth. The depiction of the multifaceted Jamaican society through the eyes of a twelve-year-old girl is a sympathetic portrayal of a pathetic reality that hovers over much of the Caribbean. The novel's worth lies not so much in Cliff's commitment to presenting the inconsistencies and contradictions within Jamaican society, but in the more universal theme of awakening and self-definition. It is in this latter context that Michelle Cliff's *Abeng* will be most appreciated.

Daisy Santos Guzmán. *Sargasso.* 1:2, 1984,
pp. 65–66

Jamaican-born Michelle Cliff's latest novel, *No Telephone to Heaven,* touches on some of the themes of *Summer Lightning.* Cliff herself has lived outside of Jamaica for many years, and she writes knowingly about life in the "borrowed countries"—as she calls them—of American and England, about classism, and the clash of generations as it exists in Jamaica. This novel focuses, however, on what may be termed the pre-emptive concern of the entire region's literature; the question of a Caribbean identity.

The main character, Jamaican-born Clare Savage, is a divided person, as her name aptly signifies. ("Clare" or "clear" means light skin.) Her family has moved to Brooklyn, New York, where her father passes for white while her darker-skinned mother desperately grasps at tokens of the culture she has left behind. Eventually the mother returns home, taking one daughter with her and leaving Clare with her father. The duality is made overt: two sisters, the darker one in Jamaica and the lighter one in New York.

Clare is taken for white wherever she goes, but as a non-white Jamaican, proud of her homeland, her life becomes a tightrope, filled with perceived slights, self-imposed silences and an overriding sense of hypocrisy. As she travels in Europe and eventually enrolls at university in London, she is lonely and isolated: "I feel like a shadow . . . like a ghost . . .," she admits, "like I could float through my days without ever touching . . . anyone . . . Locked off." . . .

The narrative passes back and forth in time as it details the experiences of two generations. The novel begins with a group of men and women, dressed in khaki, riding in a truck to an unknown destination, then moves to describe the violent machete murder of a wealthy Jamaican family by their yardboy. We learn of Clare's family, and the events that ultimately place Clare on that moving truck, and of the yardboy's poverty-stricken, inhuman existence. Finally, the two narratives mesh into a unified whole. Even the narrative structure works towards Cliff's intended point: the need for wholeness.

While this highly literary novel focuses on Clare Savage's personal dilemma, it also confronts the political future of Jamaica. Colonial exploitation is symbolized by the rape of Harry/Harriet by an English officer, which also parallels the rape of Harry/Harriet's black mother by his/her white father. At another point Clare thinks she may be pregnant by Bobby, an American Vietnam deserter who, significantly, has a sore that refuses to heal. She has a possible miscarriage and later finds an infection has made her sterile. Images of sterility, barrenness, impotence—the inability to create and sustain life—are all here and all speak for the political situation Cliff vividly and terrifyingly describes.

The abundant symbolism and obvious erudition—quotations from European and Caribbean sources open each chapter—are impressive, but the novel's general appeal may suffer as a result. While there are evocative sections filled with strong rhythmic language and passages of insightful description ("Like his labor, his connections to other people were casual," is the description of the yardboy), dialogue is at times stilted. It is hard to think of the characters as flesh and blood. But Cliff's use of Jamaican patois is perfect. She deftly uses it to reveal the deep understanding between Clare and Harry/Harriet and moves in and out of the vernacular with unselfconscious ease. (She provides a glossary of Jamaican terms.)

As the title implies, *No Telephone to Heaven* provides no easy answers to the serious problems which confront Jamaica and its peoples, and other colonized peoples as well. What Cliff does offer is a provocative novel, rich in both story and substance.

Erika J. Smilowitz. Women's Review of
Books. 5, November, 1987, pp. 13–14

Michelle Cliff's *Abeng* is quite brisk, and various, in its illustrations of the dangerous seduction of a world-making but female-dismembering Word. Her versions of the inexorable logic of the Same suggest a condition of being taken (out) for which Judith Fetterly has coined the term "immasculation." For in Clare Savage we are shown in one instance, and it is an early one, the unresisting reader as daughter: "Clare's relationship with her father took the form of what she imagined a son would have, had there had been a son." And in another instance her female-ness is seductively contained in the mastering plot of a world-view in which dis/membering of the female is romance—this being the view that we get when patriarch Savage becomes, perhaps involuntarily, high priest and sacrifier in paternal clothing. Clare Savage's father, we learn, was no commonplace dreamer and teller of visions. His were of Atlantis, Stonehenge, and Pyramids; of magic and the extraterrestrial; of Armageddon and God's own time. He also dreams of the Aztecs. And through them he reaches back for that affect of power which comes from (dis)membering the female body: "[Mr. Savage] tried to pass these ideals on to his elder daughter—calling her an Aztec princess, golden in the sun. 'Clare, you would have certainly been a choice for sacrifice—you know the Aztecs slaughtered their most beautiful virgins and drank their blood.' It did not occur to Clare to question her father's reading of history—a worldview in which she would have been chosen for divine slaughter." . . .

Cliff's *Abeng* (re)calls out of and into connections and disconnections. . . .

Under such circumstances, it is significant that Michelle Cliff's call to (re)member with the *a-beng* (the conch shell used for passing messages *for and against* enslavers) ends both heuristically and in dense ambiguity.

Lemuel A. Johnson. In Carole Boyce Davies
and Elaine Savory Fido, eds. *Out of the
Kumbla: Caribbean Women and Literature*
(Trenton, New Jersey: Africa World Press,
1990), pp. 118–21

Michelle Cliff's *Claiming an Identity They Taught Me to Despise* (1980) deals head-on with the identity issue even to the expressive titling of her book. It is a lyrical, somewhat autobiographical exploration into identity with gender and heritage comprising this identity. Landscape, history, family, events, places, all become features of her exploration. The movement of the book mirrors the migratory pattern, beginning in the Caribbean and childhood and moving to adulthood and America. The sections entitled "Obsolete Geography" and "Filaments" particularly typify this theme. In the first, we get an extended catalog of Caribbean fruits, vegetation, details of day-to-day experience like the waxing of parlor floors, the burying of umbilical cords, the slaughtering of domestic animals. Much of the identification with "home" comes from the rural grandmother who maintains continuity with homeland and whose entire being conveys the multi-faceted composition of Caribbean society. We see her, however, caught up in the conflict of being privileged, yet poor, white-skinned but culturally Caribbean. Her mother is a distant, intangible, liminal presence in her life. The contradictions of surface appearance versus reality, of camouflage and passing are explored. For this reason she feels affinity with Antoinette of *Wide Sargasso Sea.* The hybrid creoleness that is essentially the Caribbean, the necessity of accepting all facets of experience, history and personhood in the definition of a self become integrated in her consciousness of her own identity. Personal history, family history and a people's history and culture all converge.

Cliff, like [Audre] Lorde, makes even more explicit her connections in her polemical essays. "If I Could Write This in Fire, I Would Write This in Fire," in *The Land of Look Behind* (1985), is definite about the politics of Caribbean identity. Color and privilege are held up and examined. British colonialism and American colonialism are juxtaposed. *Sula* is recalled, as is *Brown Girl, Brownstones,* and Ama Ata Aidoo's *Our Sister Killjoy,* so too are W. E. B. DuBois's concept of "Double Consciousness" and Bob Marley and the Rastafarian response. For Cliff as for Lorde and [Paule] Marshall, connectedness becomes a reality, "filaments" toughen and expand:

> The Rastas talk of the "I and I"—a pronoun which they combine themselves with Jah. Jah is a contraction of Jahweh and Jehova, but to me always sounds like the beginning of Jamaica. I and Jamaica is who I am. No matter how far I travel—how deep the ambivalence I feel about returning. And Jamaica is a place in which we/they/I connect and disconnect—change place.
>
> Carole Boyce Davies. In Carole Boyce
> Davies and Elaine Savory Fido, eds. *Out of*
> *the Kumbla: Caribbean Women and*
> *Literature* (Trenton, New Jersey: Africa
> World Press, 1990), pp. 63–64

A nun avenges seventy-five years of abuse by torching her family's Winnebago; a black woman bleaches herself into a checkerboard sideshow freak; a Vietnam vet wearing a hat of yesterday's news wanders in a forest of shell-shocked men: such is Michelle Cliff's landscape of fragmented souls in her short story collection, *Bodies of Water.*

Jamaican-born Cliff has shifted her focus from the West Indian setting of her outstanding novel *No Telephone to Heaven* (1980) to America. Just as Cliff herself has relocated to and "adopted" the U. S., her characters move as visitors in a strange land, not quite at ease with their surroundings or understanding their circumstances. The ten stories in *Bodies of Water* show remarkable range both in geography and tone, but they all share a common theme—the struggle to define the self in an essentially incomprehensible world.

Many of the stories feature abandoned children and disoriented adults, somehow set apart by a deeply wounding experience. Operating on a continually shifting foundation, where broken homes are more the rule than the exception, the characters often violate traditional social mores in their restless search for validation and wholeness. Rich intertextual references enliven the stories and illustrate how an individual's history can encompass many lives, as references from one "life" intrude into another. In "A Woman Who Plays Trumpet Is Deported," set in the 1930s and '40s, an African-American female musician travels to Paris, where "They pay her to play. She stays in their hotel. Eats their food in a clean, well-lighted place. Pisses in their toilet. . . . No strange fruit hanging in the Tuileries."

The narrative voices in *Bodies of Water* are quietly scattered, carefully avoiding certain disclosures, and Cliff's writing not only accommodates but even simulates this quality. Her sentences are choppy prose-poems, alternatively flowing with the ease of free association and halting as pain becomes too sharp for conscious articulation: the effect is a soft or syntactical breakdown reflecting the internal state of her characters. If the reader is often puzzled and must struggle to piece together these narratives, it is a confirmation of Cliff's success at portraying characters who mystify even themselves.

The penultimate story, "Bodies of Water," brings several of the characters from previous stories together in the form of an epistolary dialogue between a brother and sister. The recognition that there is some sort of connective tissue, however tenuous, among these lives, is a relief, and ultimately affirmative. Even if there are no triumphs, no dazzling epiphanies, even if these characters' lives only touch one another rather than interlock, it is somehow enough.

Laura Frost. Review of Contemporary Fiction. 11, 1991, pp. 317–18

COLETTE (FRANCE) 1873–1954

Mme Colette Willy is a lively woman, a *real* woman, who dares to be natural and who resembles a little village bride more than she does a depraved woman of letters.

Read [*Seven Animal Dialogues*], and you will see how much truth there is in what I am saying. Mme Colette has chosen to take all the fragrance of gardens, all the coolness of meadows, all the warmth of the local roads, and all the emotions of man and to place them in two charming little animals. All the emotions: I avow that through the schoolgirl's laughter resounding in the forest I can hear the sobbing of a spring. You cannot bend toward a poodle or a tomcat without a muted anguish filling your heart. When comparing yourself to animals, you feel everything that separates you from them and everything that brings you close to them. . . .

Toby-Chien and Kiki-la-Doucette know very well that their mistress is a lady who would not harm a piece of sugar or a mouse; a lady who, to our delight, walks on the tightrope she has woven with words whose bloom she never ruffles, whose fragrance perfumes our air; a lady who, with the voice of a pure French stream, sings of the sad tenderness that makes animals' hearts beat so quickly. [1905]

Francis Jammes. Preface to Colette, *Sept dialogues de bêtes* (Paris: Mercure de France, 1927), pp. 11–14

The Vagabond . . . confirms the originality of [Colette]. The novel consists of memoirs arranged with a great deal of skill and undoubtedly a great deal of imagination, related in a confidential tone that gives them a great deal of charm. This novel transports us to a higher region: there are passages of truly Nietzschean detachment, concerning the pulling away from happiness because of a love for freedom. These passages contain the highest, most feminine, and truest philosophy. What a peculiar book, with its mixture of acrobatics, sensuality (perhaps something more than sensuality), painful melancholy, and haughty bitterness! There is no modesty—but all of woman's sensitivity. No hypocrisy—but all the mysteries of an enigmatic soul in which pleasure can be stifled by will.

The Vagabond may not be a work of art, but it is surely a treatise on feminine psychology. It is woman stripped bare, shown in her eternal situation of wanting what she does not want, of no longer wanting what is offered to her and what she desires, of pulling herself away from life out of a pride in living. . . .

Although one is entitled not to enjoy this book, one should not reject an entire work in which there are such beautiful and moving things.

Rémy de Gourmont. *Promenades littéraires* (Paris: Mercure de France, 1912), vol. 4, pp. 96–97

Colette came late to the true novel—that is to say, the objective novel. . . . Her wish to focus on herself and her tendency always to write confessions seemed to justify the severe critics who claimed that women writers know only how to reveal themselves. But after *Mitsou* in 1919, Colette published a series of objective novels: *Chéri,* in 1920, *The Ripening Seed,* in 1923, and *The Last of Chéri* in 1926. She thus won the place she had been denied among creative novelists; and, just as [her earlier character] Claudine had become a social type, often cited in any classification of women, so Chéri immediately assumed an equivalent importance as the embodiment of the romantic gigolo. . . .

Chéri is no banal story of a liaison of an aging woman and a young boy. It is something infinitely more complex, something that should not repel any reader. . . . Freud's books try to teach us that the attraction of the adolescent male to the maternal woman is the most natural thing in the world. . . . Colette has given a definitive fictional treatment to this subject. Through restrained emotion and tender understanding, she is able to make us feel almost a sympathy for these somewhat ambiguous characters.

All the critics hailed this novel as an event, although they were divided into two camps: the admirers, and the indignant ones. But very few failed to perceive the vital force of a work about which Henry Bataille could say, in a striking phrase, "The last twenty pages of *Chéri* are Dantesque."

Jean Larnac. *Colette et son œuvre* (Paris:
Simon Kra, 1927), pp. 148–49, 162–63

Reading Colette, it is not difficult to understand why nature, especially human nature, can be seen as a skein of the animal sense. The opposing concept, the classic view of life, seeks to establish nature as a pattern of reason, whether mathematical or organic. Colette's invariable theme is: nature, man, and animal are identical. She is primarily the artist of profound and subtle sensations translated into a medium that is a strict expression of what the eye beholds and the hand touches. Even her landscapes are animal in the sense that they are reflected in her style as sensory and ever in motion. Always in her work there is a longing, as she says somewhere, "to possess the wonders of the earth with my eye." Her women and her cats are inter-changeable; her men can be scarcely told apart except for their oddities of physical make-up. And yet, although she is outstandingly a poet of volup-tuousness, she uses no vulgar tricks to bring off her effects.

Pierre Loving. *The Nation.* August 23, 1933,
p. 222

Colette is "authentic." She has the kind of style one would prefer not to call "style," because so many untalented writers . . . have gotten us into the habit of thinking of style as a self-conscious, artificial means of expression, one that even smells of the midnight oil. Colette writes the same way she thinks, feels, and speaks. Between what we read and what she has thought, felt, or spoken *there is no distance.* Hers is a natural style. I am not saying that the only great writers are those with natural styles: exceptions can be found. But let me say, let me proclaim, and let me repeat that a writer with a natural style is the only miracle in literature. . . .

The literary clique that claims to set the fashion in France . . . expresses its scorn for Colette by its silence. They do not tear Colette apart; no, they ignore her. Or else they praise her only to indicate her limitations: "She is the queen of the kingdom of the senses." Which means, of course, that matters of the intellect are closed to her. But thirty volumes in which all her notations are true and human, thirty volumes without a trace of the literary or the artificial, so much overflowing poetry of simplicity and well-being, so much imperceptible finesse, nothing excessive and nothing insufficient, never any-thing "foolish," such a perfect lack of pretentiousness—does not all this constitute intelligence, *genuine* intelligence, active intelligence, the kind that does not have to isolate itself to contemplate and admire itself, the only kind of intelligence needed for living?

There is perhaps a more valid reason for the half-silence of the intellectuals about Colette. . . . Critics do not know how to approach her works, because there is nothing to explain, nothing to criticize; her works need only be admired. [1934]

Henry de Montherlant. *Carnets 1930–1944*
(Paris: Gallimard, 1957), pp. 165–66

In Colette's sensitivity I can detect that of all French women, my female companions. This sensitivity consists of a desire for clarity, a constant struggle for physical pleasure, and a way of saying things very quickly, with a minimum of means and a maximum of music. Her traits, which one can discern from among a thousand writers—her style, with its spontaneous and ambiguous tendernesses; her love, so just and moderate even in its passions; her fondness for images, for verbs, and for a well-placed inflection in a sentence—all these elements are feminine and French. It is easy to understand why, in small-town libraries, at the home of a doctor, a wine merchant, or a horticulturist, it is Colette's books that look the most read, and the most carefully read. Indeed, whole passages from her books have been engraved in the memory of many an ordinary housewife, who is dazzled by Colette's ability to say things she herself might have said if it were not for the few meters, the little something, the invisible abyss that separates the housewife from the genius.

And Colette's genius, which French women feel is so close to their minds, of the same nature and essence, lies precisely in her answering all the questions about the inner life in the strictest way, like a generous oracle. She is infallible. . . .

A few critics thought they had raised an insurmountable objection by writing that Colette, although an incomparable artist, is not a great poet because she does not give answers, even tentative answers, to the harsh, tragic problems of the human condition; these critics claimed that she never participates in any contemporary quarrels or conflicts. But this is why French women praise her. For there are no problems! All problems have already been raised, all have been settled. Only the circumstances change, and Colette knows that well, better than anyone else.

Léon-Paul Fargue. *Portraits de famille*
(Paris: J. B. Janin, 1947), pp. 21–24

We are formed in the hours when we hardly know we are being formed. In Colette's warm but discreetly limited mind the flower, the animal, the human being live together in sensuous design. The observation of diurnal happening is extraordinary and marvelously conveys the strange hold that the tedium of life has on us. We feel the hours are our true "familiar spirit," the indissoluble intimate. But the marking of lost hours is not an occasion for the imaginative sensibility such as one sees in another very feminine writer like Virginia Woolf. Colette's pagan mind never leaves the surface of life, never ceases as it were to touch the skin; yet the effect is not trite nor arid. It is moving. She has the direct eye of an older civilization.

V. S. Pritchett. *New Statesman and Nation.*
August 11, 1951, p. 160

Having no knowledge of psychology, which had not been popularized when she began to write and has never been taken seriously in France, Colette never learned how a novelist was expected to build up her characters. She merely put them together as a painter composes a still life from objects lying about in his studio. She could not invent characters, she could only describe herself and the people she knew or heard about, adding a few extra traits here and there. This is the weakness, and at the same time, the strength of her work. It is weakness because a novelist is expected to be inventive, and Colette is not. It is strength because the people she produces are real people, and fiction should presumably have a link with life in one way or another if only because it is intended to be read.

Margaret Crosland. *Colette* (London: British
Book Centre, 1954), pp. 229–30

In the first half of the twentieth century, Colette became an institution for many literary connoisseurs. That she was the finest French prose writer alive was an unchallenged opinion. Expert as she is as a stylist, exquisite as her chiseling of words and images can be at times, we believe that her prose is too ornate and too remote from the naturalness and simplicity of the very great works of art for her to rank with the truly eminent masters of French prose. Her mannerisms soon pall on the fastidious reader. Her characters are too monotonous and they wander complacently in an atmosphere of venal loves, carnal concerns, and gigolos, without rising to the stature of Proustian lovers or Toulouse-Lautrece's mournful seekers of joy.

Henri Peyre. *The Contemporary French
Novel* (New York: Oxford University Press,
1955), p. 282

Born with talent, she achieved style. . . . She was at her most gifted in her descriptions of what she noted through any of her five senses, all abnormally alert—through her large gold-flecked, feral eyes; through her flaring nostrils; through her ears which heard small, far-off, distinguishing sounds; through her palate which held intact its own memories and judgments of ruddy wines, pink flesh or fine fruits eaten only in season since, being a gourmet, she disapproved of edibles falsely matured at the wrong time of year; and through her strong hands which in touching objects or bodies sent a series of tactile images and news rushing to her writer's brain. All she wrote in these realms read like precise, sensual, human records such as had not been seen in French literature. Only a woman could have compassed them for they were physically female, as different as a woman's voice is from a man's.

Janet Flanner. Introduction to *Seven by*
Colette (New York: Farrar, 1955),
pp. vi-vii

Few writers have ever been less engaged. This does not mean merely that she has no political or social ideas and no ethical convictions beyond those which an unthinking generosity and kindliness suggest. It means also an intro-version so complete that she is a prisoner of herself and unaware of things outside herself except insofar as she can make them part of that self. As blind as a child to everything not part of her own experience she is also childishly alert to and absorbed in everything which is. . . . She is so intelligent and so shrewd while remaining so completely unintellectual that inevitably she suggests the gamin—one would even be tempted to say the guttersnipe if the connotations were not so unfavorable and, what is more important, if her passionate interest in country life did not carry a constant reminder that an important part of the child she remained was the child who had grown up in a provincial garden.

Joseph Wood Krutch. *The Nation.* March
26, 1955, p. 268

She absolutely had to know the name of anything she was contemplating, whether animate or inanimate, and if this name was unfamiliar to her, or escaped her, she never could rest until she had found it. This was not so much to store it in her memory, but because the name completed the identity of the thing in question, and was inseparable from it. . . . She even loved certain words for themselves, quite apart from the idea which they represent. She loved them for their music, but still more for their graphic aspect, their design. Had she not spoken somewhere of the letter *S* "standing on end like a protecting serpent"? During periods of intense work she would dream of words. "I've had a typographical dream," she sometimes said to me in the morning.

Maurice Goudeket. *Close to Colette* (New
York: Farrar, 1957), p. 20

During her lifetime Colette had received and accepted as much official recognition as any other French writer of the first half of the twentieth century. She was a member of the Académie Royale Belge, a member and president of the Académie Goncourt, and in 1953 she was made *Grand Officier* of the Légion d'Honneur. . . .

It is difficult to believe that if Willy had not suggested that Colette write recollections of her school days, she would probably never have written at all. The fact is that a year or so after their marriage, Monsieur Willy, always in need of money, did make the suggestion, and so Colette, having bought notebooks which resembled those she had used in school, began to set down her girlhood memories. Willy read the finished product, decided that it wasn't what he wanted and put it away in a desk drawer. Two years later, while arranging his papers, he rediscovered the manuscript, reread it and concluded that with a little spice added to it the novel would sell. In 1900, *Claudine at School* was published and signed "Willy." Its immediate success was such that Monsieur Willy ordered another novel and another, locking his young wife in a room for four hours every day to make sure that she would work. Coerced into writing, Colette slowly discovered that it could be a means of earning money (the 300 francs a month which Willy gave her as pocket money), and also that it was habit forming; soon she deliberately chose to spend certain hours of each day with pen and notebook. Thus one of France's most prominent writers began as a slave to literature and ended as an addict. French literature owes an unpayable debt to Monsieur Willy.

Colette has been accused of not dealing, in her works, with the important political and human problems of her time, and of concentrating too much on her own small and particular domain of love and lovers, of nature and its manifestations. And to this accusation is always appended the reproach that Colette is indifferent to questions of morality, that she is incapable, perhaps, of dealing with them. But in her aimless "promenade," and "meditations," her constant evocations of the past, are the evidences of Colette's long dialogue with the real, with those things—love, a flower, an animal—which held her attention as intensely as her mother's was held by the rose cactus. Nothing is more "real" or more important to Colette than this contemplation of the actual, than this relationship which the human being establishes in solitude, with the world of living things. The implicit moral imperative is again, *"Regarde,"* and the accompanying aesthetic imperative and the key to her style is also *"Regarde";* "Look"—and, prepared to struggle with words, faithfully reproduce the object, the sensation.

Elaine Marks. *Colette* (New Brunswick,
New Jersey: Rutgers University Press,
1960), pp. 4, 36–37, 224

Certainly nothing ever replaced love for her as a subject for fiction. What other subject possibly could in her particular conception of the novel as a poetic condensation of emotional crisis in the life of ordinary people? Power, ambition, greed? She, like many other women, was just not interested. . . . But in her nonfictional work it was a different matter. Here there was no need to choose a subject which would engender the drama of emotional conflict, or charge a tightly-knit plot with the explosive qualities of suspense and irony and shock, no need even to create characters outside herself. She could, with her charmed pen, explore herself, and what she knew about life, write of all the myriad things that absorbed and delighted her—love, of course, among them, but so many others as well that her later works can be regarded as manuals in the art of enjoying life.

Margaret Davies. *Colette* (New York: Grove
Press, 1961), pp. 69–70

I remember her strong hands—serious writing is a manual labor!—and her fine feet in sandals, perhaps larger than most, rather like the feet of Greek goddesses. I remember her slightly frizzly hair fetched forward almost to her eyebrows, because (as she has told her readers) she has a square boyish or mannish forehead. I remember her delicate nostrils and her painted thin lips.

Glenway Wescott. *Images of Truth* (New York: Harper & Row, 1962), p. 88

[*The Blue Lantern*] is a brave and gay performance by an old woman in pain, a kind of unaffected tribute to herself. . . . She writes about the progressive fading of the senses, accepts it, and values what remains behind: sights, sounds, smells, animals, and old friends. She speaks with love of Jean Marais, of Cocteau and [Marguerite] Moreno and the dying Fargue; she is charitable to the most egocentric of the young, remembering her own youthful "shudder of repugnance at the touch of old people." She watches children at play in the garden beneath her window, and writes of them with the unillusioned toughness she showed in the music-hall stories of long before. She writes of animals with an unsentimental anthropomorphism we Anglo-Saxons may have trouble understanding, because our culture precludes the unsentimentally anthropomorphic. . . .

On the whole, then, one sees *The Blue Lantern* as an agreeable act of self-indulgence, a cultist tribute to a writer whose notoriety has merged into her fame, whose grossness time and the worshippers have sublimated into a unique delicacy. . . . The major Colette is tragic, and *The Blue Lantern* is strictly not so; it is brave, amused, charming. Yet the aged hedonist, almost happy in her pain, experiences the last stirrings of that spirit of rebirth which is the other side of tragedy.

Frank Kermode. *New York Review of Books.* December 12, 1963, pp. 3–4

A comparison between Colette and George Sand is inevitable at a superficial level at least because no other French women writers have known such fame and been so closely identified with their own work. . . .

In France, until 1900, and to some extent afterwards, all women writers were members of the aristocracy or like George Sand brought up by survivors from the *ancien régime*. Women have always been valued in France but only in relation to men, not in their own right. . . .

Colette seems to have been the first French woman writer who belonged uncompromisingly to the middle class, and the provincial middle class at that. It is here that the comparison with George Sand breaks down, for Colette never had the dash and authoritative attitude of her predecessor, *la dame de Nohant*. Colette was taught how to write, and it was a long time before she dared speak with her own voice. George Sand had less training, if more education, and her "collaboration" with Jules Sandeau was brief. Both writers affected men's clothes or manners for a time, one from romantic eccentricity combined with a wish to compete with men, the other from resignation and a temporary renouncement of men. . . .

[For Colette] happiness was hard to find and hard to keep. Colette seemed not to trust it and she lacked confidence because her personality and work, for all the naturalness they showed on the surface, were not natural at all, they had been organized by methods of various kinds, some haphazard, some controlled, but in any case somehow artifiessentially a comedy of manners performed by a cast of stereotyped characters. As is true of any good comedy of manners, *Gigi* is a triumph of style.

Robert D. Cottrell. *Colette* (New York:
Frederick Ungar, 1974), pp. 113–14

I would like to propose an approach to the psychological study of *Chéri.* The choice of the novel is motivated, not only by its incontestably superior quality, but above all because its theme, paradoxically, obliterates its unconscious content. . . . The approach is equally paradoxical. Colette's autobiographical texts are so fed by psychoanalytic themes—the fixation on childhood, the nostalgia for the lost paradise, love for the mother—that one tends to forget their symptomatic status: too attached to what is *said,* critics take them *at their word* and not sufficiently literally and, doing this, ignoring the flagrant contradiction between the *said* and the *not-said,* autobiography and fiction, whose key symptoms are the predominant presence of the mother, in the one, her absence, her defects, or her ridicule in the other. Starting with this symptom, I propose to invert the usual perspective, and to start with the hypothesis that her mother is a burden or weight on her. That is to say that it is the position of the child opposing or competing with the mother, sometimes represented by the woman, sometimes by the man, that is the thematic center of her novels, and *Cheri* is no exception.

Mieke Bal. In Bernard Bray, ed. *Colette:
Nouvelles approches critiques* (Paris:
Librairie A-G Nizet, 1987), p. 16

It seems to us that Renée Nérée [in *The Vagabond*] ends up finding a certain peace in renunciation to the extent that she reconnects with her calling as a writer. She is "a woman of letters who has turned out badly." This is the way her friends approach her. The author of three novels, she has stopped writing. She can no longer or no longer wants to. . . . Her inkwell is "powdery" and "pen dry." Now, the essential thing for her—she ends up being aware of it— is to "look for words" to express the beauty of the world, to "possess the marvels of the earth." . . . This belated raising of consciousness is accomplished precisely at the moment where, for the first time, she forgets Max. Can we not formulate the following hypothesis: the break becomes possible, not because Max stayed in Paris, but because Renée is writing again—she is *editing* her letters. Or rather, the distance would not suffice if it did not provide the occasion for Renée to rediscover her real reason for living: the writer's calling which, abolishing and transforming all forms of distance, makes it possible at iast for her to belong to herself and to the world, and to conquer a certain unity. *The Vagabond* is, in the last analysis, a novel that traces the destiny of a writer saved by writing. *Writing,* after all, is not a vagabond. It knows where it is going.

Michel Baude. In Bernard Bray, ed. *Colette:*
Nouvelles approches critiques (Paris:
Librairie A–G Nizet, 1987), pp. 115–16

Colette's life is an open book. If very few other writers have inspired as much biographical commentary and even prurient curiosity, it is perhaps in part because so much of Colette's work appears to be straightforward autobiographical statement, written in the first person and citing real people and places; indeed even the most fictional of her works often seem to be *romans à clef,* asking to be deciphered. Colette's writing thus unfolds at the boundary between life and the literary text.

But in spite of the amount of attention devoted to her life and work, until recently Colette seems to have remained an underappreciated literary figure. For decades, to be sure, she has been the *grande dame* of French letters, touted as the great feminine storyteller of the *Belle Epoque,* author of charming tales of female adolescence and titillating stories of bohemian life (the cover of a recent paper edition blazons, "she knows a woman's heart and mind, body and soul"). She has also been praised for her sensuous depictions of nature and her entertaining portraits of domestic animals. Yet although acknowledged as peerless stylist, Colette has only relatively recently begun to receive the kind of serious theoretical reading long granted to such a figure as Proust, that other celebrated *Belle Epoque* poet of society and memory. (Even the best-known French theorists of *l'écriture féminine* have largely neglected her work, perhaps because she has always been accepted by the literary establishment.) We should perhaps begin then by forgetting what we know about Colette—taking a cue from Freud and lending a kind of "free-floating attention" to her text.

While some feminist critics have already undertaken a reevaluation of Colette's writing—drawing upon psychoanalytic, sociological, and linguistic concepts to analyze the role of gender in her work—they too have often tended to focus on the autobiographical axis of her writing, in order to examine her experience working within and against the constraints of patriarchal society. As important as the feminist critic's emphasis on the life of the woman writer may be in the analysis of sexual politics, however, such an emphasis may risk relegating the text itself to the status of artifact, evidence about patriarchal society. And it is after all the textualized "Colette," the fictionalized persona, who motivates our curiosity about the real-life woman who produced the work.

Of course a textual focus need not (indeed should not) neglect biography, but it will necessarily foreground issues such as the gender of Colette's *textual* persona and the modernity of that textual voice, which at times bears a strik-ing resemblance to that of other great moderns such as Proust and Woolf. For Colette is a pioneer in techniques that anticipate the genre of "fictional autobiography" prominent today: the modernity of her work is manifest in the use of interior monologue and oblique characterization; the organization of autobiographical narratives by random associative memory (here she is a co-pioneer with Proust and with Breton); and in the tendency to intertwine herself with her own fictions, playing a game of hide-and-seek with her reader and creating a highly original brand of ironic humor in the process. Any rereading of this too-well-read author needs to pay attention to the intellectual importance of her contribution to the modern novel, forgetting the all-too-familiar notions about her femininity, spontaneity, and charm. For in addition to being profoundly modern, Colette's texts are often disturbing, unsettling, even uncanny in Freud's sense of the term, suggesting that perhaps more is at stake in rereading Colette than the rehabilitation of an undervalued writer.

I suggest that a combination of psychoanalytic and feminist perspectives may prove helpful in reconsidering the radicality of Colette's work and its uncanny impact on the reader. In weaving these approaches we will inevitably encounter the question of the nature and specificity of women's writing—if Colette is not simply "feminine," is she nonetheless a "woman writer"? Might her work answer the riddle that has haunted intellectual history in our cen-tury, first as the recurring refrain of psychoanalysis (what *does* woman want?) and more recently as the enigma of feminist criticism (just what is a woman writer)? Rereading Colette means confronting these two questions—woman's nature, and her desire—at the crossroads, at their intersection: What does woman (as writer, as subject of her text) want?

> Jerry Aline Flieger. *Colette and the Fantom Subject of Autobiography* (Ithaca: Cornell University Press, 1992), pp. 1–3

COLLINS, MERLE (GRENADA) n.d.

This first novel [*Angel*] by a Caribbean poet relates a familiar story: thanks to her mother's determination and sacrifices, the daughter of an impoverished provincial family receives a college education and returns to her family alien-ated by her inevitable politicization, her own growth mirroring the struggles of her country (in this case, Grenada) to gain political autonomy. What distin-guishes this work is its lyrical rendering. Collins's characters think and speak in patois: "People like you an me so, the harder we work in people kitchen and in people lan, the more we kill weself out and bring riches, is the poorer we get while we sweat goin in other people pocket." The initial strain imposed by the singular language quickly abates, and the technique enables the reader to share the perspectives of the protagonists and implicitly challenges the hegemony of "standard" English. In spite of the feminist and political themes, the characters are never reduced to mere mouthpieces; their dignity lies in their remaining conflicted even as they struggle with oppression. When America invades Grenada, the title character says, "We wrong. But that don make dem right." The combination of artistry and objectivity will commend this book to many readers.

Sybil Steinberg. *Publishers Weekly.*
July 22, 1988, p. 52

Set on the Caribbean island of Grenada, this first novel vividly portrays the harshness of life in the Third World. It is centered on two women, Doodsie and her daughter Angel, whose lives are played out against the rise of a dictatorship and its overthrow by a socialist government, which led to the American invasion of the island. Angel escapes poverty through education but returns home to teach, entering the struggle against the dictatorship and eventually the American invaders. Although the West Indian dialect makes this book slow reading (a short glossary of terminology helps), perseverance is rewarded. An enthralling look at women's lives in a developing country; highly recommended.

Christine King. *Library Journal.*
October 1, 1988, p. 100

I welcome the demotic sweep and hard-edged characterization of the thoroughly engaging novel *Angel,* which ought to establish its author's position among the best of West Indian novelists who have excelled at writing in the Creole (Roger Mais, Samuel Selvon, Lindsay Barrett, Merle Hodge, et alia) and delivering a consummate, artistic folk experience to the delight and appreciation of readers far outside our home area. I welcome too the essential social and political layering of the story line, which contributes a truthful and resonant verisimilitude to the gradually unfolding historical panorama of the narrative.

A Bildungsroman in our own specific West Indian cultural terms, *Angel* tells the story of the eponymous rebel's progress through her Grenadian childhood, her three years at the University of the West Indies in Jamaica, and her return home before the U.S. invasion of her island, which puts an end to her cherished hope of continuing political change for her society, the central challenge of her life up to that time. However, Angel's postinvasion sentiments at the close of the novel, as the long-past colonial *status quo ante* is restored, are: "The spirits gone, you know. The candle not goin out. They either gone, or they sympathetic. Nothing to fraid." The reader takes this as a clear signal that Angel expects a resumption of her revolutionary fervor, this time to be reborn of a crucial loss of fear.

With *Angel* Merle Collins joins the distinguished vanguard of a handful of politically persuasive West Indian novelists such as George Lamming, John Hearne, Jan Carew, V. S. Reid, and Marion Glean, and she does so with a novel whose language and characters are exceptionally sensitively devised and poignantly memorable.

Andrew Salkey. *World Literature Today.*
63, 1989, p. 151

COMPTON-BURNETT, IVY (GREAT BRITAIN) 1892–1969

Brothers and Sisters is one of the most remarkable and original novels I have read for a very long time. It is necessary to say so emphatically, because I fancy that it may easily be overlooked both by the reviewers and readers, not being a book whose value is immediately apparent on a cursory glance, nor even after reading the first score of pages. Every word must be read, for it is thick and packed, and consequently the reward is rich. A strange story, related almost entirely in dialogue, it is so bare, economical, and dryly terrible as to suggest comparison with the more painful of the Greek domestic stories, yet the ironic humor gives it a twist which constitutes its own peculiar quality. It is like biting a sloe between the teeth. As sardonic as Jane Austen, as bleak as Emily Brontë, *Brothers and Sisters* stands on its own feet, queer, angular, deliberate, ungainly, impressive. Its fate will be interesting to watch. Will it pass unnoticed? Will it find a crowd of imitators? The most that the reviewer can do is to draw attention to a book which should appeal to everyone interested in the possibilities of fiction.

Life and Letters. June, 1929, pp. 404–5

There can be no doubt that from the publication of *Brothers and Sisters* in 1929 to the present day, Miss Compton-Burnett has been more widely and consistently praised than most writers of her time. . . . She came to her highest and most decisive critical success in 1947, with *Manservant and Maidservant.* This headed all the review columns, and *The Times Literary Supplement* devoted to it a full-page "middle" article. The novel, under the title of *Bullivant and the Lambs* had a great *succès d'estime* in America, and sold more widely in that country than anyone could have anticipated five years before. . . .

There is no book of Miss Compton-Burnett's that has not its violent shock, as trim and tidy as a hand-grenade, and as destructive potentially.

The dazzle of her books, the cruel, incisive wit, usually prevents these shocks from being fully felt at a first, or even at a second reading. They are as strewn with epigram as a lawn with daisies, or a fakir's couch with nails. They have an extraordinarily good effect upon the literary critic, because they enforce his entire attention. It is absolutely essential to read every line of a Compton-Burnett novel, because to miss a single one turns the whole book to gibberish. Every sentence is extraordinarily dependent upon the other; the last few words of every book are the direct descendants of the first.

Writing of a dying age (it dies hard), she stands apart from the mainstream of English fiction. She is not an easy writer nor a consoling one. . . . Miss Compton-Burnett's great strength lies in the fact that we cannot place her; and so also does her weakness. She is strong in her own time. It may be harder for the future to deal with her.

Pamela Hansford-Johnson. I. Compton-Burnett (London: British Council/ Longmans, 1951), pp. 37, 39–43

The real objection to the author's method is not that her books are held together by melodramatic, or improbable, or reduplicated events, but that they are not so held together. . . .

A couple of comments on the policy of rigorous limitation and exclusion in dialogue. The first one is just that it takes an almost overweening audacity to discard at the outset the most powerful card in the hand of the novelist interested in character-drawing, that of differentiating by mode of speech. . . . My second comment is just that the danger in stylizing the procedure of dialogue in this way, and in thus tending inevitably to reduce the status of the individual character, is that of turning the whole thing, not indeed into a solemn game but into a frivolous game. Loss of seriousness is for some reason the dragon that lurks in the path of the writer who opts for other modes than a selection of the language really used by men. To read almost any piece of Compton-Burnett's "communal dialectics" is to experience a pleasure as intense as most available literary pleasures, and yet page after page, sometimes scene after scene . . . is marked by the triviality inseparable from fantasy.

Kingsley Amis. The Twentieth Century. August, 1955, pp. 172, 174

The degree of articulateness displayed by everyone—from servants and children to the tyrant of the household (an invariable figure)—seems alleged, until it is realized that this is a stylistic convention such as every artist has the right to adopt. That everyone in these novels employs the same tone and the same large and scholarly vocabulary does not, strangely enough, impair the vigor of the characterization, except in a few instances where the dimness of the outline is also due to other causes. Like any other artistic convention . . . this is a means which is amply justified by the end achieved—in this case the illumination of family life. . . .

But it is her zeal for measuring the *temperature* of emotion—the graph described from moment to moment by the action of the plot on the alert sensibilities of her characters—which is responsible both for the continuously witty surface of her writing, and the deeper truth of her picture. Like Henry James, Miss Compton-Burnett is much concerned to preserve an amusing surface, as well as a polite one; and this remains true of the most tragic passages in her books.

Edward Sackville-West. *Horizon* (London).

June, 1946, pp. 371, 374–75

Miss Compton-Burnett has dated her novels between 1885 and 1901—with the exception of the sketch, *Pastors and Masters,* where the events must have taken place later than 1918. One or two of the books are given no precise date, though the action evidently takes place at the end of the nineteenth century. She has chosen the end of the age of isolation and leisure and, though we may feel that this was the last age in which we would have chosen to live, she shows us that it was the one age really propitious for the rearing of the strange family growths in which she delights. Perhaps it was not altogether a free choice on her part. It is natural for an artist to revert to the age of his own childhood, and she has written: "I do not feel that I have any real or organic knowledge of life later than about 1910. I should not write of later times with enough grasp or confidence. I think this is why many writers tend to write of the past. When an age is ended, you see it as it is."

This does not at all mean that her novels are "dated"—their action is set in a period when family life could be lived and studied in isolation better than it can at present, when the impact of public life is often so close and so cruel. But her facts are eternal: every year still adds abominable tortures to the annals of the Family, even if they are fewer, and this will go on to the consummation of time. . . .

Few authors have used less summary, have made fewer comments on their people and happenings, have more completely excluded their own personalities from their work.

A comic writer often loses credit for realizing "the hopelessness of things" and for knowing that "truth is so impossible." It is not surprising that Miss Compton-Burnett has been ignored or passed over with a slighting reference by that school of critics who, for all their discernment, have made the mistake of finding Congreve shallow and heartless; their initial mistake has perhaps been due to the fact that, with their imperfect sense of humor, they have not been able to find either of them really comic. . . .

There are some authors, and she is one, who, in addition to their outer circle of readers and admirers, have also an inner circle to whom they seem to speak more intimately. There are people whose special author Miss Compton-Burnett is—to us, her work is no private religion or snobbery—it is a source of intense and peculiar intellectual excitement and pleasure.

Robert Liddell. *The Novels of I. Compton-*

Burnett (London: Gollancz, 1955),

pp. 23, 87, 13–14

It is Miss Compton-Burnett's daring—and to most of her readers, success-ful—convention to carry the psychological data, as opposed to the physical, to its [sic] furthest possible limits; not only does she leave us to guess about the location, appearance, "history" of her characters and plots, but she expects us to believe in the world she has imagined with no guarantee of credi-bility whatever—no narrator, no explanation, virtually no narrative of any kind. Using our detective common sense, a quality Miss Compton-Burnett pays her readers the compliment of assuming they possess, we can in fact piece together a lot more background detail than at first appears. . . .

Stilted and precocious as Miss Compton-Burnett's children may seem, there is no living novelist who has better understood what violent or sophisti-cated emotions an unhappy child can have; the fearful incantations of the children in *Elders and Betters* are as convincing, and moving, as the fantasies described by such writers as Henry James, Mr. L. P. Hartley, or Miss Iris Murdoch. . . .

In choosing to escape our particular workaday world, Miss Compton-Burnett has not contracted out of realism: she has merely ignored its transi-tory particularities in order to emphasize "realities of life" that will continue to plague us all, however "democratized" we may imagine our artistic ideals to be.

(London) *Times Literary Supplement.*
October 7, 1960, p. 645

Miss Compton-Burnett's novels have much in common with one another, far more than most writers' have. They have appeared fairly regularly at two- or three-year intervals, and the titles themselves have had a gnomic, often alliterative familiarity as novel has followed novel. Each title has told us something about the contents of the novel—*Brothers and Sisters,* for exam-ple, has six sets of brothers and sisters in it (the eldest pair of whom are also man and wife), while *A Family and a Fortune* concerns the effects of a large and unexpected inheritance which a dependent member of the household receives. In general the titles are not interchangeable, although *Men and Wives,* the climax of which is the murder of Harriet Haslam by her son Matthew, could with equal aptness, it would seem, be called *Mother and Son,* and *Mother and Son,* which is in part an account of courtship among certain middle-aged and elderly people, might almost as well be called *Men and Wives.*

Such similarities as exist among the titles are multiplied when we come to the novels proper. These similarities are what is initially most striking about the novels—similarities of mechanics and subject, what might be called veneer: what the novels look like. Every novelist adopts a set of conventions to serve as vehicle for his meaning—he chooses his settings, his point of view, characters, etc.—or, more accurately in most cases, they choose him. Miss Compton-Burnett's set of conventions varies much less from novel to novel than do other novelists'; to find a parallel, one would have to go to the drama, particularly the neo-classic drama, whether French or English, or perhaps the *pièce bien faite* of the late nineteenth century in France and in England. . . .

Rarest of all, especially in the later novels, is any physical description of action longer than an adverb or a phrase. When it does appear, it can be so effective that one marvels the more that a writer of such gifts should subjugate them to her greater aim. It is often what the classical author does not do that makes us admire what he does. . . .

Within the central house there is almost always a power figure like Sophia Stace—mother, father, aunt, grandmother, grandfather—and critics have agreed to call this figure the tyrant. His will is challenged, without much success, by his dependants. The first round of the battle may take place at the breakfast table, where more than half the novels open. The events proper may begin with an arrival, as stories always have; later in the events one or more members of the family may leave the household; they always return.

Charles Burckhart. *I. Compton-Burnett*
(London: Gollancz, 1965), pp. 25–26, 28–29

It has long been known to admirers of Ivy Compton-Burnett that she published a novel called *Dolores* when in her twenties, fourteen years before the first volume of the recognized canon, *Pastors and Masters*. Most of her interviewers tried to draw on her to speak of this early work; many enthusiasts visited the British Museum Reading Room especially to read it, for it had long been out of print.

Dame Ivy herself preferred to ignore it as having no part in the long, homogeneous (though each subtly very different) line of novels which she saw as standing for her unique achievement. The novels of her maturity, which came late, after, it would seem, a good deal of personal tragedy and the finding of a fulfilling personal happiness, are so marked, despite their varying successes, by an absolute certainty of aim both in method and in meaning, that it is hardly surprising that she should have preferred to omit a single juvenile essay, the chief feature of which is its dependence upon the styles of other novelists and a marked conflict between the various levels of its moral teachings. . . . Its interest lies largely in showing what paths Dame Ivy did not follow in her maturity, only a little in its intimations of the one she did. . . .

The Last and the First, splendidly put together by Livia Gollancz from penciled notebooks, is the last novel she left behind (her twentieth). Here we see her special powers pared down to their essentials, in part perhaps from weakness, in part from lack of time to revise (which for her must have meant to fill out), but, in fact, surely from a growing desire to present her theme without any of the trappings of realism. Description and action (even in her own peculiar interpretation of those terms) have gone: she simply gives us the stylized dialogue of a series of witty discussions of set themes among two families and their servants. . . .

The book is notable because it declares openly the compassion for wrong-doing that she asserted again and again in interviews. . . .

Angus Wilson. The Observer.
February 7, 1971, p. 26

The confident structures of nineteenth-century fiction certainly collapsed with the First World War, as did those of English society; the protean form of [D. H. Lawrence's] *Women in Love* or [Virginia Woolf's] *To the Lighthouse* are responses to the moral and social instabilities of their time. The symmetry of Ivy Compton-Burnett's novels is, on the contrary, a rigorous forcing of pattern and order to the surface: "Real life seems to have no plots. And as I think a plot desirable and almost necessary I have this extra grudge against life. But I do think there are signs that strange things happen, though they do not emerge."

Far from succeeding Lawrence and Virginia Woolf, Ivy Compton-Burnett in many senses precedes them. Her novels deliberately detach the reader from twentieth-century expectations; they are not only set in the nineteenth century, but conceived in its terms. It is no accident that her work should recall Jane Austen from the century's beginning, both by its confined canvas and the homogeneity of the novels, which seem facets of a single crystal. At the century's end her dialogue is often reminiscent of Chekhov, a dramatist she predictably admired: voices float in Chekhov, and reverberate; in Ivy Compton-Burnett they echo and intertwine. *Dolores* apart, however, "indebtedness" is no more the word for her writing than it is for Eliot's *The Waste Land*. If a nineteenth-century literary presence is felt in her work, it is there for comment, not as imitation. Her novels are *fin de siècle* in the decadent sense, not advanced or daring as Shaw and Wilde once seemed, but concerned with decay in art, in society and in the individual life. It would not have been possible to write these novels in a period of Edwardian complacence. Retrospect affords her the ultimate chill of objectivity: she composes the corpse of the nineteenth century for burial. The nature of her contribution to the English novel may therefore be best understood as the decisive severance of certain threads traceable through nineteenth-century fiction.

Philippa Tristram. Studies in the Literary
Imagination. Fall, 1978, pp. 28–29

Brothers and Sisters is the first mature work of I. Compton-Burnett. She has dismissed her first published book, *Dolores* (1911), as a "piece of juvenilia" which had been "meddled with" by her brother. It is a turgid and melancholy piece, differing drastically in vision and technique from her other works and illuminated only rarely by flashes of the talent which was later to emerge. While *Pastors and Masters: A Study* (1925) shows a radical change in outlook and writing technique, it is but "a Compton-Burnett novel in embryo"—the witty conversations lack the "bone foundation" of the works that follow. Unlike *Dolores* and *Pastors and Masters, Brothers and Sisters* is a fully realized novel, with the bone of plot and the flesh of narration and conversation complementing each other in a unified and harmonious design.

The prime actions in *Brothers and Sisters,* the concealments of the elder Andrew and Sophia, grow out of their characters as previously presented. Both the narrator's account and Andrew's conversation with his family and servants create a portrait of an old man, arrogant and overweening, likely, because of his pride in his reputation as well as in his judgment, to hide from Christian the secret of his parentage. Similarly, narration and conversation provide us with a picture of Sophia as "a feminine edition of her father," a young woman who masks great strength of will under a complaisant exterior. It is entirely plausible that she would conceal an unfavorable will, especially a will which, because of her ignorance of her father's motive, she believes may be the work of a senile mind. The actions of the various sets of brothers and sisters in becoming engaged to one another also have their roots in situation and character. While the double pairings and re-pairings are an instance of shaping and heightening—so many double engagements *are* improbable—they work organically in the chain of events set off in Moreton Edge by Andrew Stace's need to preserve his reputation and yet have his son inherit his lands. . . . The engagements between the Langs and the Wakes are also made plausible; the varied motives of each of the four are hinted at in the course of the novel.

In order to reveal the inextricable nature of human relationships Compton-Burnett has placed her characters at such close quarters that an event causes ripples in many lives. Compression of circumstances (in terms of geography, heredity, and social conventions) permits compression of events. This enables one component of her design, the action, to work on more than one level: action grows out of character and in turn provokes action, but action is also a figuring-forth of the novel's main subject. As they function structurally and thematically, incest and double engagements become an organic, indispensable element of the work. Some critics have described Compton-Burnett's characters as "wooden" or "cardboard" or "flat." The people in *Brothers and Sisters* elude such categories.

Mary Dalton Rowsell. *Twentieth Century
Literature.* Summer, 1979, pp. 207, 211–12

The novels of Ivy Compton-Burnett present intriguing problems of content and structure. They are distinctly not popular novels; yet, like many popular novels, they are written according to a few simple, undistinguished formulae. Scenes that are almost identical occur in several of the novels. The characters in one novel are often almost indistinguishable from those in another, and the crises that these characters encounter are often very similar and handled in the same ways. The locales of the novels might as well be the same, since they are usually described only specifically enough to be recognizably rural, English, and late Victorian.

Despite what may sound like the repetitious, monotonous, and unimaginative qualities that these novels have in abundance, they are, in fact, works of substance, fascinating in themselves, and lead the reader to think closely about human nature and human existence.

The major subject that runs throughout Dame Ivy's novels is egotism. The most odious characters are those who impose their egotistical views of the world on others who may be no less egotistical but who are less demanding, or who are in such dependent positions that they must restrain their egos lest others shatter them. Because the same basic characteristics appear throughout these novels in the personalities of children, men and women of every age, and occasionally in a cat, the reader may see the novels as creating a continuum: the amiable self-centeredness of the three-year-old in one novel becoming the murderous destructiveness of the adult in another and the dictatorial egotism of the family patriarch in a third.

All these conflicting wills and desires must coexist in a very narrow world where egos are in continual collision and from which escape is almost impossible. A human being knows few people well during a lifetime, and many of those he does know cause him trouble because they come into his life or he into theirs before he is capable of making judgments about good and evil or anything else. He and his life are bound up with the personalities and the lives of these few people in a manner and to an extent that he never is again with other people. This narrowness is emphasized in Dame Ivy's novels because she keeps the crucial events of life—birth, marriage, death—within the confines of a very small, claustrophobic circle related by blood and/or propinquity; and all the ramifications and consequences of actions are minutely explored within this circle.

Constance Lewis. *Twentieth Century
Literature.* Summer, 1979, pp. 224–25

Many readers initially find Compton-Burnett's style daunting because of her unorthodox technical devices: (i) the unobtrusive, non-judgmental narrative voice; (ii) the formal diction and sentence structure that characters employ in speaking; and (iii) the high proportion of dialogue to exposition. Cicely Grieg correctly surmises that a major reason that many readers are not drawn to Compton-Burnett's work is that she is a twentieth-century writer writing in the idiom of another era. Her characters' formal and epigrammatic speech reminds us of an earlier novel whose characters' viability was criticized because they spoke too formally—Samuel Johnson's *Rasselas.* Yet her style is much more accessible than the style of many modernist and post-modernist writers. Her sentence structure is most often simple, straightforward and declarative. Her choice of vocabulary is not at all abstruse, and she rarely resorts to metaphor. When her characters wax metaphorical, they quote the commonest of clichés, which are often challenged by other characters as inaccurate carriers of meaning. Precision, rather than complexity or obfuscation, is the hallmark of her diction. Attentive characters challenge any statement that pretends to authority and through their perpetual dialectic reveal that the assumption of authority is often without legitimate or logical support.

The criticism that her works contain too much dialogue and not enough exposition, that her works are closer to drama than to novels, again stems from preconceptions about the limitations of the genre. She has described her books as being "something between a novel and play," and several of her novels have been successfully dramatized on radio. By its nature drama is more intense and iconoclastic than fiction, although Compton-Burnett has explained her preference for the novel form as giving her more scope. By adapting dramatic principles to the novel, Compton-Burnett, in effect, eschews the expositional baggage of the nineteenth-century novel and disdains the often clogged and meandering stream-of-consciousness technique developed by her great contemporaries for a streamlined and direct method of delineating reality. Her technique, which on several occasions she described as "condensed," compresses and intensifies the effect of language, especially as it directly connects and brings characters into relation with each other.

Kathy Justice Gentile. *Ivy Compton-Burnett*
(London: Macmillan, 1991), pp. 21–23

CONDÉ, MARYSE (GUADELOUPE) 1937–

Hérémakhonon is the first novel of Maryse Condé, a Guadeloupean writing in Paris; her two plays, *Dieu nous l'a donné* (1972) . . . and *Mort d'Oluwémi d' Ajumako* (1973) have attracted serious, favorable attention. The novel, like the plays, is concerned with a serious theme; it involves revolution and the development of formerly colonized black peoples into a new "nation." It asks whether such a "good revolution" can occur, and if it can, what conditions it will require.

Like Armah's title, *The Beautyful Ones Are Not Yet Born,* Condé's *Hérémakhonon (on doit attendre le bonheur)* implies that though the good may arrive, it has not arrived as yet. *Hérémakhonon* is based upon the conviction that a single leader does not make a revolution; revolution can come only when a whole people moves. Leaders may be influential, of course, but they may also be tragic, futile, demagogic, tyrannical or absurd. *Hérémakhonon* does not deal with this large theme in a heavy-handed way, however. It tells a story by means of a rather simple device and draws its reader into its central character, Veronica, to see and to speculate upon events unfolding in a country unidentified but obviously in French West Africa of the Senegal-Mali-Upper Volta region, where baobabs, marabouts, and the Peul language exist. But the reader also reflects upon Veronica's past in the Antilles and in Paris, where she went to school. An internal dialogue intermingles the three time periods throughout the novel, as Veronica attempts a journey into her self to find whether a métisse has roots and ancestors in Africa.

The novel is not a treatise, however. Although it clearly shows Condé's impatient rejection of all clichéd thinking on the subject of Negritude, Maoism, democracy, et al., and although it clearly shows her hatred of exploitation, hypocrisy, and cant of all sorts as well as her sympathy with people, it does so by means of involving the reader in a dominantly personal story. Veronica is quickly attracted to Ibrahima Sory and takes him as her lover. Sory, whom she thinks of half-facetiously as *un Oronoko,* is a strong man in the new order under the figurehead leader Mwalimwana. Veronica also becomes the affectionate and beloved friend of Saliou, the revolutionary school director who sees Sory and Mwalimwana as tyrant-traitors to the new nation. Birame III, a young student-martyr, and a number of the members of Saliou's household emerge as sharply drawn characters who engage Veronica's affection in spite of herself. To her dismay, she is unable to stay out of the political struggle, and yet she is aware that she does not know enough to understand what is happening.

The novel ends, properly, with Veronica's return to the West—*her* world insofar as she has one. It provides no illuminating answers to the serious questions which abound in the Third World, nor does it clarify the tragic events in the "known" but not shown fates of Birame III and Saliou. But it does reveal a great deal, honestly and often harshly in personal conflicts, about a dozen characters. It introduces types of people and situations which are clear and recognizable as part of political life generally, and at the same time it denounces the practice of thinking in types and reifying one's general concepts. The "types" introduced are, after all, more individual than typical, as the reader sees through Veronica's eyes.

The novel is fascinating and fast-moving. It is also embellished with wit and wry allusions which delight the reader. When the school children, in public, take the oath of allegiance to Mwalimwana and are restored to good standing, "après chaque serment, l'assistance répond gravement. *Amin!*" One is tempted to reply to Condé: "An *i* for an *e,* that is to say?"

David K. Bruner. *World Literature Today.*
51, 1977, p. 494

Maryse Condé's heroine in *Hérémakhonon* (1976) is Véronique, who lives in West Africa and teaches philosophy at the Institut National. Véronique was born in Guadeloupe, studied in Paris, and came to Africa in order to compare her idealized concept with the reality of Africa. Her choice of a lover, however, places her in the same sort of isolation as before, when she was forced to leave Guadeloupe for bringing disgrace upon her black "bourgeois" family. Her friend then was a member of the wealthy mulatto middle class, who refused to marry her when the two of them were "caught in the act." In Paris Véronique lived for a time with a Frenchman, Jean Michel, which elicited the fury of her militant Caribbean compatriots. And now in Africa she is again in disfavor, not because of a difference in skin color but because she has a relationship with a minister, who comes from an influential family. Her students resent this because they consider themselves progressive and "critical," and are against corruption and favoritism. Intuitively Véronique agrees with them, but there is little she can do and she is fond of her lover. Her "Negro with ancestors" has a typical African marriage: his wife lives elsewhere with the children and in his official residence Hérémakhonon, he is free to receive his mistress. The name of his villa, which means "wait for happiness," does not apply to Véronique. As the political situation escalates she feels that there is nothing positive that she can do in this land and she returns to Paris.

In the course of events her recollections of her family in Guadeloupe and the years she spent in Paris all influence the way in which the heroine undergoes the reality of Africa. This is equally true in Maryse Condé's second novel. The Marie Hélène of *Une saison à Rihata* (1981) also comes from Guadeloupe and also studied in France, where she met her husband. For seventeen years she has lived in Africa and after all that time she is still considered *celle qui vient d'ailleurs,* a stranger. She has not been able to adjust to the way of life of the African women around her. They are obedient, never contradict their husbands and consider unfaithfulness on the part of the wife a "crime." In the eyes of her mother-in-law Marie Hélène is guilty of many a misdemeanor, and her marriage is not a happy one. And yet there are positive sides to her life in Rihata, such as her husband's sense of responsibility towards all those he considers his family. Daily life is dominated by political intrigue and there are several tragic deaths in the family. But in spite of everything the book ends on a positive note. After six daughters Marie Hélène finally has a son, whom she calls Elikia, which in the language of the country means *hope*. This suggests that there is a better future somewhere, in a still distant future.

In the works of [the] writers from Guadeloupe the present situation on the island is of little or no importance. . . . Maryse Condé's heroines have mainly negative memories of the cramped atmosphere of their childhood in the land of their birth. They look for the consequences of political decolonization in Africa rather than "at home," where such developments have not yet made themselves felt.

Ineke Phaf. In Mineke Schipper, ed.
*Unheard Words: Women and Literature in
Africa, the Arab World, Asia, the
Caribbean, and Latin America* (London:
Allison and Busby, 1985), pp. 190–91

Condé's dramas *Dieu nous l'a donné* (1972) and *Mort d'Oluwémi d'Ajumako* (1973) also are concerned with the manipulation of social mores and myths by individuals seeking political power and influence. Her three novels *Hérémakhonon* (1976), *Une saison à Rihata* (1981), and *Ségou* (1984) attempt to make credible on an increasingly larger scale the personal human complexities involved in holy wars, national rivalries, and migrations of peoples. . . .

Condé, in her fiction as well as in her criticism, reflects her concern for the art of writing. Though her characters are not self-portraits, their remarks appear often to echo her experience and her critical opinions. . . .

Condé has also stated the Véronica of *Hérémakhonon* is not a self-portrait and is perhaps even an *antimoi*. Nonetheless, Véronica's black bourgeois family in Guadeloupe somewhat resembles Condé's, cherishing blackness and white cultural values all at once. Véronica is also like Condé in that French, not the local Creole, is her first language. A product of a classical education, Véronica sprinkles her speech with epigrams ("Life is a bitch with a bum leg"), with puns, and with allusions to Pascal and Marivaux as well as to Césaire, Fanon, and Simone de Beauvoir. Condé's erudition and wit, and her fascination with history and the Middle Passage, are reflected in Véronica's assertion:

> After all, where would we be if Christopher Columbus hadn't crossed the Atlantic with his ship's hold full of sugarcane plants taken from the Moslems in Cyprus? We ought to make it our emblem, our standard. If man is a (thinking) reed [Pascal's *roseau*], the West Indian is a stalk [*roseau*] of sugarcane.

"I have the unfortunate habit of seeing symbols everywhere," Véronica wryly remarks. . . .

It is not that there has been a change in Maryse Condé's basic understanding, nor even in her narrative skills, that one is impelled to view *Ségou*, her latest novel, as a truly remarkable book, a work to be considered according to the same criteria one applies to *God's Bits of Wood, The Grapes of Wrath,* or *War and Peace.* Indeed, the ability to make the truth of fiction compatible with the data of historical events is discernible in all her writing. In her early plays, like *Dieu nous l'a donné* or *Mort d'Oluwémi d'Ajumako,* as well as in her novels *Hérémakhonon, Une saison à Rihata,* and *Ségou,* her management of fact and fiction would satisfy most Aristotelians. She is unwilling to accept a popular belief or to reject it just because it is popular, she is willing to refrain from drawing inferences and theorizing on the basis of inadequate or confusing evidence, and she has a persistent curiosity which sharpens her powers of observation. . . .

The telling of the narrative [of *Hérémakhoun*] is most effective: the reader believes in the characters and tends to see them as rather ordinary people occupying positions of extraordinary power and having somewhat distorted perceptions of themselves. Justly or not, one gains a comprehension of what a revolution is like, what new African nations are like, yet one is aware that this comprehension is nothing more than a feeling. The wise reader will go home as Véronica does—to continue more calmly to reflect, and to observe.

Une saison à Rihata, like *Hérémakhonon,* presents a revolution in progress toward failure in a West African nation. It involves a fairly large family of characters whose ethnic and social foci are Africa, Paris, and the Antilles. There is a difference in the telling of the story, however, which is noteworthy. The main character is not a visitor-woman, but an indigenous man whose birth and position have thrust social obligations upon him which he, however, has not accepted. Much of what the reader sees is seen through this man's eyes, but not all. The reader is permitted into the thoughts and feelings of other characters also, and the narrative becomes more a family chronicle than a spectator piece. The major actors in the chronicle are two sisters, two brothers, various children, a powerful father in the background, and a number of political activists. As the family drama of conflicts, loves, hates, and betrayals unfolds, the social implications in the abortive attempt at political overthrow move into the foreground. Here also, as in *Hérémakhonon,* Condé draws upon her real-life experience: she makes use of her knowledge of Guadeloupe, West Africa, and Paris to create credible people in a credible social environment. It is not herself she writes about—except, of course, in that limited sense that Flaubert recognized Emma Bovary with his "C'est moi." As a matter of fact, when asked about the autobiographical elements in *Hérémakhonon,* Condé said flatly: "Mais l'histoire de Véronica n'est pas la mienne et je n'ai aucune envie de raconter ma vie." That attitude seems still to hold with respect to *Une saison à Rihata,* and with respect to *Ségou.*

Upon reading *Ségou,* at least one difference from the two previous novels is immediately clear: its magnitude. The magnitude is not wholly one of the number of pages (nearly five hundred), but also of the years covered (sixty to eighty), of the localities involved (perhaps a dozen different nations or kingdoms), of the number of major historical and fictional characters extensively developed (over a dozen), of the major historical events integrally involved (the march of Islam over north central Africa, the later years of the slave trade, the "repatriation" in West Africa of Brazilian slaves, et cetera).

With such an overwhelming mass of data and with so extensive a literary objective, the risks of writing a *roman à thèse* (a genre not favored by Condé) or of producing a heavy, didactic treatise are, of course, great. The main reason that Condé has done neither is, perhaps, because she has written here essentially as she did in her two earlier novels: she has followed the lives of the fictional characters as individuals dominated by interests and concerns which are very personal and often selfish and petty, even when those characters are perceived by other characters as powerful leaders in significant national or religious movements. . . .

The great historical matters like the slave trade, the governance of women, and the conflicts of nations and religions, which are in the background of the story of the Traoré family in *Ségou,* are similarly dealt with. Condé avoids the intrusion of her own voice, directly or indirectly. In such areas of judgment, she feels that the reader should be permitted to act *tout seul.*

> Charlotte and David Bruner. *World Literature Today.* 59, 1985, pp. 9–13

Maryse Condé's novel, *Une Saison à Rihata,* set in a fictitious African country, opens with a description of the protagonist's house: it is cut off from the rest of the town, a picture of neglect and decay, damp, mildewed, a crumbling reflection of its former colonial glory. The appearance of the house offers a striking parallel to the situation of the family and in particular to that of its *Antillaise* mistress, Marie-Hélène—a stranger in exile and at odds with her surroundings in an alien and hostile society. A brilliant, middle-class woman, married to an African, she had hoped to heal the divisions in herself by a return to her ancestral homeland. Marie-Hélène's life in Africa, however, is characterized by shattered hopes and unfulfilled dreams. She finds herself banished to an isolated and stagnating provincial town and responds to being rejected by Africa by withdrawing from life and from those around her. The journey back has not recovered the lost mother, the mythical Africa, the ancestral homeland. Like Césaire's poet, the Antillean heroine fails to find what she expected. She becomes more cut off, more exiled from herself. The rejection of Africa leads to a corresponding withdrawal from all everyday reality, expressed metaphorically by her physical isolation: Her room becomes her refuge where she rejoins her rejected West Indian homeland through the medium of the dream and the imagination.

> Elizabeth Wilson. In Carole Boyce Davies and Elaine Savory Fido, eds. *Out of the Kumbla: Caribbean Women and Literature* (Trenton, New Jersey: Africa World Press, 1990), p. 48

Hérémakhonon (the title is a Malinké word meaning "to wait for happiness") is the story of a Guadeloupean teacher who goes to an unnamed West African country resembling Sekou Touré's Guinea as a *co-opérante* for the French government. While French West Indian bourgeois men had of course gone to Africa for many generations as members of the French colonial bureaucracy, Véronica is part of a distinctly modern world in which women, particularly foreign women, have moved beyond traditional roles; she teaches philosophy, to male students. She also expects a kind of sexual freedom usually denied to African women. Ambivalently, she wants to find a place for herself in the country and yet to remain apart. She refuses for some time to be involved in politics, even after her favorite pupil and the head of the school where she teaches are imprisoned, tortured, and eventually killed for opposing the regime; indeed, she starts a love affair with a government minister responsible for the torture of her friends. Finally, however, she decides to return to Paris and possibly to her white French lover.

Hérémakhonon is an exploration of the various boundaries Véronica has experienced and the ways in which they intersect. Specifically, she is concerned with defining her identity as a woman, a native of the Caribbean, a black for whom Africa is largely mythical, and a member of an intellectual elite within the French tradition. Véronica describes her childhood experience as having taught her to be proud to be black; her family's way of life, however, was completely shaped by French customs and by a middle-class scorn of the poor black community. Consequently, her search is partly for a community not divided by class considerations. But it is also a search for a black man who can be free; as she puts it, she wants to sleep with a black man who has never been branded. Véronica's attempts at moral and intellectual honesty are often at odds with her psychological need to find a strong man.

Condé treats with irony the tensions resulting from the various roles into which Véronica tries to fit. She does not, however, leave Véronica without hope. *Hérémakhonon* is a bildungsroman in which, at the end, there is real moral and intellectual development, as well as a chance for a new start.

Adele King. *College Literature.* 18:3,
October, 1991, p. 97

Maryse Condé's latest novel, entitled *Traversée de la mangrove,* explores the question of gender and formal structures in light of the author's attempt to define a narrative center that would effectively subvert not only patriarchal discourse but also the colonial discourse within which it is inscribed. It is relevant to note that there is no single authoritative voice in *Traversée de la mangrove* and yet one notices in the use of varied points of view, the voice of an implicit author who prudently guides the reader to reflect upon the notion of identity as a cultural construct whose limits and boundaries define the individual self. The premise of a narrative center here is not to be confused with a single vision or narrative voice. Condé's text defies, or, more accurately rejects this notion since the varied points of view would have us redefine the center as a homogeneous entity. It would be more appropriate to speak of a multiple individual whose divergent perspectives challenge the assumptions of a particular representation of reality. . . .

A careful reading of *Traversée de la mangrove* allows the reader to discover the tension between the semiotic and the symbolic as they relate to one's identity as a cultural and linguistic construct. The oscillation between the first and third person narrative in the text is indicative of the implicit author's intention to differentiate and problematize the narrative voices of her characters. From this intention emerges the search for a style or a form capable of reflecting and refracting impressions and perceptions of reality, a reality that Condé seeks to evoke rather than legitimize. . . .

Traversée de la mangrove invites the reader to play a dynamic role in the process of signification. Condé's manipulation of the conventions of detective plots (the identity of the mystery man; the particulars of the crime) underscores the importance of the act of reading within and outside the parameters of the text. Conscious of the levels of reference and symbolic interplay within which Sancher's identity can be explored, the implicit author purposely situates him outside the narrative, thereby directing the reader in and out of the text by the use of narrative and discursive strategies. Denied a concrete referential existence, Sancher's story is mediated by the perception and images that others have of him. But the author encounters two main difficulties: How does one balance the emphasis on male representation against an emphasis on a female mode of perceiving and interpreting? Since Sancher is at the source of the text as language, how does one reconcile the overdetermined meaning of the text with the perspective and discourse of the implicit author, who refuses to validate any attempt to fix or objectify reality? By the author's constant modification of them, distances and narrative voices serve as markers to guide the reader through. . . .

[T]he crossing of the mangrove, the understanding of the text as language, is meaningful only if the reader is willing to relinquish the notion of a single perspective or a unified perception of reality as the sole basis of knowledge and truth.

Susanne Crosta. *Callaloo.* 15:1,
Winter, 1992, pp. 147, 154–55

Contrary to the novel bearing the same title within *Traversée de la mangrove* which its mysterious author, Francis Sancher, will never complete, Maryse Condé's novel bears thoroughgoing witness to the stories of twenty individuals. Some become entangled and drown in the mangrove thicket, a metaphor for present-day Guadeloupe; others move toward an originative sun illuminating the way home to personal truths that they must discover by themselves. On another level this complex narrative, comprised of ten first-person and ten third-person accounts intricately interwoven between a narrative introduction entitled "Le serein" (dusk) and a closing chapter named "Le devant-jour" (dawn), furnishes the reader with a metaphoric map detailing all the death-inducing traps in the mangrove thicket and ways to avoid them. The path to life and freedom stretches out unencumbered to welcome the reader at book's end. The passage through the thick forest which surrounds us all has already claimed Francis Sancher's life when the novel begins; at least six of the characters whose stories surface during the night of Sancher's wake slip further into their figurative graves. Other characters, however, succeed in extricating themselves from the obstacles that have thus far choked off life, and they move toward the light of a new day and the promise of collective salvation.

The inner life of another person seldom corresponds to the person we perceive in social intercourse. Not one of the individuals in *Traversée de la mangrove* is transparent to the larger community. The continuous flow of inner experiences and the fluidity of intersubjective experiences in the novel reproduces in all its complexity the process that happens constantly in human interaction. Translating that experience into fiction, immersing the reader in the character's spoken and unspoken feelings, juxtaposing the character's inner life with his or her impressions of the other characters in the novel, moving back and forth from first person to third-person self-effacing narration in which the character's thoughts and feelings are privileged—Maryse Condé accomplishes no less in this novel. The reader recreates these relationships, weaving together all the threads in this infinitely complex yet simple tapestry of the heart. "We," the narrator and the reader, become empathically attuned to all the characters, including the omnipresent Francis Sancher. . . . These are the unspoken words we have read and heard, the map we have been given to navigate toward the light.

Ellen W. Munley. *Callaloo.* 15:1,
Winter, 1992, pp. 156, 165–66

CONSTANT, PAULE (FRANCE) n.d.

First came Negritude literature with its cry for the *prise de conscience* against a white world which reduced the black to an *en-soi*. Next comes the literature of the postcolonial period with the colonizer's regrets and helplessness. The white master becomes a Hegelian master, an impotent administrator with nothing to administer but the daily boring existence. He feels that he is living in a no-man's-land, a wasteland, which spells despair, anguish, loneliness and emptiness.

This [*Ouregano*] is the existential arena where the reader meets the Muranos (chief of medical staff), the Bonenfants (the judge), the Duboises (the chief administrator), the Refons (the private school directors) and Beretti, an outcast who found refuge in Ouregano, having murdered a black man elsewhere. Each family has come to Ouregano to begin a new life away from France. Away from home, from the theater houses, from the Sunday afternoon walks in busy parks, from the latest styles and coiffures, each character has to play his role in Ouregano—a microcosm of Pascalian loneliness and solitude. Each one becomes a psychological cannibal, out to destroy the other for the sake of passing time.

Of course, the game is safe as long as each one knows the limits. Unfortunately, these hollow human beings unleash their frustrations onto innocent children, who become their scapegoats. Tiffany Murano, an eight-year-old, suffers and carries with her the heavy memories of a decadent world, of harsh and uncaring parents, of unconcerned teachers who enjoy ridiculing her and ultimately drive her to despair. In fact, Paule Constant's *Ouregano*—

the author's first novel—portrays an unhappy world, largely seen through the eyes of Tiffany. The author's brisk sketches of characterization permit the reader to penetrate a world still pervaded by racism and alienation.

However, if Constant's convincing *style rapide* attempts to draw the reader into sharing the empty existence of this administrative circle, only those who have led such an existence could identify with the characters. I would like to think that Constant's aim is much broader, for Ouregano is the microcosm of our decadent world, a world devoid of grace and respect, a world of gladiators metaphysically fighting existence itself. Our consolation is that Tiffany is at last allowed to leave Ouregano for a private school in France. A better life? Perhaps not, but it is at least a change.

With this positive tone the novel ends. The reader forgives the author for any omniscient analytical narrative at times disturbing. *Ouregano* is a novel to be read, and we hope that Constant continues to share with us her keen insight into human nature.

Victor Carrabino. *World Literature Today.*
55, 1985, pp. 424–25

White Spirit is a spirited novel, brisk, loaded with corrosive satire, showing, in a matter-of-fact way, blacks and whites squirming in unison in a cruel, absurd world, somewhere in black Africa today. Its author sumptuously weaves many different threads together, in a baroque proliferation of silhouettes and subplots, with characters larger than life but taken from life, viewed by a critical eye and a sharp mind. Its action and locale are closely linked to Paule Constant's earlier novels *Ouregano* (1980) and *Balta* (1983). Chronologically, it inserts between the two, since *White Spirit,* initially planned as *L'enfance du singe,* narrates circumstances surrounding the birth and early years of the chimpanzee that Balta frees from the zoo in "la Mégalo," Monsieur Alexis. Several characters from the earlier novel reappear, such as Beretti and le Père Jean. Thus the three novels, jointly, amount to a new, contemporary *Comédie humaine* or, more specifically, a *comédie africaine,* wherein neither colonial nor neocolonial whites are spared.

White Spirit displays a large cast of grotesque puppets in Ubuesque settings, from Port-Banane with its import-export warehouses and its Hollywoodian brothel of Barbie dolls installed in the former governor's palace, "the Sunset," to "the Devil's banana" plantation inland and its "Village-Modèle" (an oxymoron), the site of the store to which Victor has been assigned, a branch of "A la Resource de l'Africain," selling nothing but junk, including the fatal "White Spirit" of the title. This mysterious household product is the overall link among the characters, and it has many connotations on different levels, from the literal to the symbolic; these are left to the reader's own interpretation but definitely carry, under the guise of illusory hopes, a strong message of danger and destruction. Expressions in English are used freely throughout the novel with a purpose that seems to underline global artificiality and acculturation.

Recognition of actual *faits-divers* as a possible source for some episodes (such as a mystical mass suicide) or of several literary reminiscences as homages or pastiche is discreetly left to the reader's intuition. The brilliant first chapter, "La volonté de Dieu," introducing the nonhero Victor and his doting grandmother in Bordeaux, may be a new version of Félicité and her nephew (also called Victor) from *Un cœur simple* of Flaubert. Like Flaubert, but in her own way, Paule Constant is notable for the quality of her writing, impeccable in structure and style. Behind all the barbs of irony and satire, *White Spirit* shines with creativity, verve, and intensity of feeling. A touch of class in the contemporary French novel.

Danielle Chavy Cooper. World Literature
Today. 64, 1990, pp. 437–38

Who or what is "le grand Ghâpal" referred to in the bizarre title of Paule Constant's fifth novel? The puzzled reader will soon learn from the Duke of C. and his seven-year-old daughter (who is writing her memoirs at that early age!) that "le grand Ghâpal" is the mystical insignia of the abbesses of the ancient convent of C. The *Ghâpal* is none other than the "Stone of Paradise" brought back from Mesopotamia by Alexander the Great. It goes back to biblical times and Moses's parting of the Red Sea. As *l'escarboucle de la licorne,* it is a mystical, magical, mythical stone. It has been the prized possession of the abbesses of C. since the foundation of their convent. The present abbess is Sophie-Victoire, the beloved sister of the duke. To wear the *Ghâpal* one day is the goal of Emilie-Gabrielle: this is why she yearns to become the next abbess and makes three wishes granted by her doting father, as in a fairy tale.

The whimsical story takes place in the early eighteenth century, with all the charm and naughtiness associated with the Regency. It is in many ways a pastiche of eighteenth-century French novels, with highly improbable episodes, written in formal, classical prose, elegant, refined, iconoclastic, tongue-in-cheek—a novel Paule Constant must have had fun writing, and one which readers will have fun reading, so outrageous is it.

As for the cast of a play (or a puppet show?), the author begins by listing the characters in order of importance. Besides the seven protagonists—all belonging to the highest nobility, with family names replaced by initials—there are seven associates, each of whose names is replaced by that of his or her social function, whether religious (the Panegyrist, the Prioress, the Cardinal, the Confessor) or domestic (the Nurse, the *Demoiselle de Paris*). The only name given is that of Suzanne, suggesting hereby the maid of the lady, such as Suzanne of *The Barber of Seville* fame. Unexpectedly, there are also seven animals listed, each one with a fancy name; such animals were all the rage at the time, often seen in eighteenth-century portraits of lords and ladies: a falcon (Brutus), a lap dog (Zelmire), a clothed monkey (Venus), and four greyhounds (Courage, Peace, Justice, and Mercy). This gives the tone of what is to come.

The novel itself is structured with perfect symmetry, in four parts of five chapters each, corresponding to the four seasons, starting with winter and ending with autumn, but obviously not the seasons of a single year, since Emilie at the start is seven, but turns twelve and fifteen in spring and summer. As to the unity of place, it is respected inasmuch as the novel starts and ends at the castle, with the central episodes at the convent in Paris/Paradise, a convent as grand and as worldly as Versailles.

Expect the unexpected in *Le Grand Ghâpal*. After the black-and-white in living color as seen in Constant's previous novels . . . *Le grand Ghâpal* provides fireworks.

Danielle Chavy Cooper. *World Literature Today.* 67, 1993, pp. 145–46

COOPER, ANNA JULIA (UNITED STATES) 1858–1964

Anna J. Cooper was not concerned with merely narrating the experiences of black women in her book; she was also advancing the idea that black women need to speak up for themselves and not allow black men always to speak for them. As she exclaimed in the opening pages of her work,

> Our Caucasian barristers are not to blame if they cannot quite put themselves in the dark man's place, neither should the dark man be wholly expected, fully and adequately to reproduce the exact voice of the Black woman.

Her reference to black males was not an attempt to indict them but an expression of her belief that no one else could "more accurately tell the weight and fret of the long dull pain than the open-eyed but hitherto voiceless black woman of America." Her book was intended for the eyes of black males as well as females, since the former were partially to blame for the low status of women. She spoke and wanted other black women to speak about their true position in society so that a clearer and more accurate picture of their real status would be known.

In promoting the cause of women's rights, Cooper's major concern was to see that higher education was made more readily available to black women. She held that whenever women sought higher education or had aspirations to higher goals in life, they were usually discouraged by those who considered these attainments to be solely male prerogatives. Cooper believed that most women had no real goals of their own or desire for education, since they thought that their only value was to please men. Thus, it was not surprising to Cooper that the average woman gloried in her ignorance. . . .

Cooper believed that some educated black men, too, held negative views of women, and she partially blamed them for not encouraging women in educational endeavors and for not making themselves aware of the depressed conditions of women, although they were aware of other developments in the world. She therefore maintained that the principal issue in the relation between the sexes was no longer a question of how women could stifle their growth and ignore their interests in order to make themselves more acceptable to men, but how men could adjust to the demands of women.

> Sharon Harley. In Sharon Harley and
> Rosalyn Terborg–Penn, eds. *The Afro-*
> *American Woman: Struggles and Images*
> (Port Washington, New York: Kennikat
> Press, 1978), pp. 88–89

In the captivating title of her first published work, *A Voice from the South: By a Black Woman of the South,* a collection of essays written between 1886 and 1892, we recognize the two major concerns of her life—the race problem and the role of women, in particular black women, in its solution. We sense here the younger Anna Cooper with memories of Oberlin still fresh after seven years back in the Southland. Her self-confidence and earnestness now and then have a youthful ring suggestive of a recent college graduate. Superabundant illustrations from literature and history at times show more breadth than depth; her style is rather florid even for that day, the tone rhetorical, sometimes satirical, but not without a refreshing sense of humor.

Nevertheless her understanding of the plight of her people as well as of their psychology has an authentic quality born of first-hand experience. As we recall, the early 1890s saw a marked deterioration in the status of blacks throughout the South, an ominous resurgence of lynching which, for example, called forth a vigorous campaign of protest led by her contemporary Ida B. Wells. Anna Cooper could not be a silent spectator. Her carefully considered recommendations for dealing with these problems, which would gain force with the passage of time, are already vividly present. . . .

Anna Cooper from the very outset of her career viewed education for blacks as a human concern as well as a racial one; at its core were the individual's aptitude and bent. At the time she was writing *A Voice from the South* she deplored the prevalent craze for Latin and Greek as a status symbol among newly freed blacks, and admired Booker T. Washington's remarkable achievements in vocational training. A decade later, as we have seen, when the tables were turned, she resisted to the last ditch the efforts of the "Tuskegee Machine" to close the doors to higher education for blacks.

For a number of years the demands of her teaching and related school duties as well as other activities limited Anna Cooper's writing to magazine articles, addresses, etc. The picture of her life in Washington during part of this period was not forthcoming until the late thirties in her volume on the Grimké family. Not surprisingly, this work, despite its main purpose as a biography of her closest friend, is one of the few from her pen possessing the characteristics of autobiography as well.

Leona C. Gabel. *From Slavery to the Sorbonne and Beyond: The Life and Writings of Anna Julia Cooper* (Northampton, Massachusetts: Smith College Department of History, 1982), pp. 73–74, 77

In her collection of essays, *A Voice from the South,* Anna Julia Cooper, like W. E. B. Du Bois a decade later, identified the conflict of race as being the central American dilemma. It was the question of the "colored man's inheritance and apportionment" that Cooper saw as "the perplexing *cul de sac* of the nation." Cooper felt that the dominant white power structure existed in "sublime ignorance" of the needs or desires of blacks. She drew a parallel with the ignorance of men of the needs and desires of women which formed her initial premise and the occasion for the book. As white voices could not adequately speak to the black experience of oppression, "neither should the dark man be wholly expected fully and adequately to reproduce the exact Voice of the Black Woman." My intention is not to provide a detailed analysis of each of the essays that form *A Voice from the South* but rather to consider the overall trajectory of Cooper's argument, focusing on three areas: the social status of women and the importance of education, the nature of imperialism and racism as hegemonic ideologies, and the critique of the white women's movement.

Cooper referred to a number of historical definitions of womanhood, juxtaposed them with a political indictment of the oppression of blacks within the United States, and emerged with a particular analysis of the position of the black woman that effectively challenged the terms of contemporary debate about gender and about race. Cooper's initial argument was based on the assumption that a civilization should be measured by the way its women are treated. . . .

Cooper's analysis of the position of women, both white and black, was more than a demand for female access to social institutions; it was also a complex analysis of social, political, and economic forces as being peculiarly masculine or feminine in their orientation and consequences. Unlike Frances Harper but prefiguring the concerns of Pauline Hopkins, Cooper identified the intimate link between internal and external colonization, between domestic racial oppression and imperialism. Her critique of imperialism and racist attitudes is a particularly good example of how she developed her theories of masculine and feminine practices and spheres of influence. When considering this critique, it is important to recognize that Cooper's categories are not biologically dependent concepts referring to the physical differences between males and females, for she made it clear that women could conform to masculinist practices and attitudes and men could display what she called "womanly virtues."

Cooper recognized the imperialist or expansionist impulse, with its ideology of racial hierarchies, as a supreme instance of patriarchal power and confronted her readers with a series of rhetorical questions to force a reassessment of the history which produced

> the self-congratulation of "dominant" races, as if "dominant" meant "righteous" and carried with it a title to inherit the earth? Whence [came] the scorn of so-called weak or unwarlike races and individuals, and the very comfortable assurance that it is their manifest destiny to be wiped out as vermin before this advancing civilization?

Cooper condemned the increasing imperialist expansion to Asia and the Pacific with its contemporary appeal to a manifest destiny to civilize the uncivilized as justification for consigning "to annihilation one-third the inhabitants of the globe." This impulse to conquer defined the predominant male influence, an influence which was compared to the beast from the Book of Daniel, devouring all before it and demanding its worship as an incarnation of power. The possible counteracting force, the female influence, was powerless to mollify or restrain "the beast," in Cooper's terms, and the pervasiveness of the rampant will to dominate and despise the weak was evident in the racist attitudes of women who were otherwise thinking beings. The example that Cooper used was a familiar one for black women and illustrated how the movement for women's rights was consistently compromised by racist attitudes and practices. For Cooper wanted to remind her readers that the women's movement and its leadership did not escape patriarchal influences or the "worship of the beast." But, despite this knowledge, Cooper felt that the only counter to patriarchal abuse of power was the feminine factor, which had to be developed through the education of women. Education, she argued, would empower women so that they could shape an alternative course to a future society which would exercise sensitivity and sympathy toward the poor and oppressed. Power in the hands of women, however, Cooper knew was not in itself the answer, for, as she had experienced, the power that white women were able to gain was rarely exercised in sympathy with their black sisters.

Hazel Carby. *Reconstructing Womanhood:
The Emergence of the Afro-American
Woman Novelist* (New York: Oxford
University Press, 1987), pp. 97–99, 101–2

A Voice from the South, which has recently been reissued in Gates's superb series, includes a fully formed theory of canon set forth in the context of a clearly recognizable feminism and antiracism. "Can any one conceive a

Shakespeare, a Michael Angelo, or a Beethoven putting away any fact of simple merit because the thought, or the suggestion, or the creation emanated from a soul with an unpleasing exterior?" Cooper asks, leaving the reader no doubt as to the acceptable answer. She proceeds to distinguish two motives for writing. In the first category she places

> those in which the artistic or poetic instinct is uppermost— those who write to please—or rather who write because *they* please; who simply paint what they see, as naturally, as instinctively, and as irresistibly as the bird sings—with no thought of an audience—singing because it loves to sing,—singing because God, nature, truth sings through it.

She goes on to say that for these writers, "to be true to themselves and true to Nature is the only canon." Such writers "cannot warp a character or distort a fact in order to prove a point." Shakespeare heads her list of these writers, with George Eliot second.

The second group she calls, not disparagingly, "the preachers." They "have an idea to propagate, no matter in what form their talent enables them to clothe it, whether poem, novel, or sermon,—all those writers with a purpose or a lesson, who catch you by the buttonhole and pommel [*sic*] you over the shoulder till you are forced to give assent in order to escape their vociferations." At the head of this list she puts Milton "in much of his writings," with Thomas Carlyle in "all of his." She proceeds to warn that although the first class "will be the ones to withstand the ravages of time," the others risk having their day and passing away. She cannot, however, leave Milton there. Thus she distinguishes Book Three of *Paradise Lost,* "in which Milton makes the Almighty Father propound the theology of a seventeenth century Presbyterian," from the first stirrings of consciousness in Eve (a passage she quotes in full), where "Eve with guileless innocence describes her first sensations on awaking into the world." Such passages as these, she says, "will never cease to throb and thrill." Apparently unaware of Wollstonecraft's *The Female Reader,* she is nevertheless drawn to the same passages. Cooper is also steeped in the Bible, which she often quotes in her book, although— as one would expect even from what little I have said about her—she resists any narrow doctrine, whether of Christianity or of anything else.

Michael Payne. *College Literature.*
18:2, June, 1991, pp. 15–16

CORTI, MARIA (ITALY) 1915–

Maria Corti occupies a position at the highest level of Italian literary studies. . . . In the fields of linguistic history, philology, criticism, and literary theory, and most recently, in Dante studies, her works are the kind that leave their mark—either because they open up new paths or because they bring closure to complicated tales left hanging by others; moreover, they have the power of writing modeled on the creative experience. In fact, the writer's gift coexists with the scholar's talent in her ("really two souls in one body"): three books of narrative published hitherto (the two novels, *L'ora di tutti,* 1961 (Otranto), reprinted several times and translated into various languages; *Il ballo dei sapienti,* (The wise men's ball) 1966—two reprints and a Bulgarian translation—and the most recent "American tease," *Voci dal Nord Est* (Voices from the North East), 1986, containing various tales and a clutch of unpublished material). . . .

L'ora di tutti [is] the disturbing historical and imaginative fresco of the desperate resistance of the inhabitants of Otranto, besieged and then massacred by the Turks in the fifteenth century—a set of emblems suspended between the precariousness of existence and the persistence of memory. And *Il ballo dei sapienti* [is] a work whose narrative center, human involvement and subtle irony have not been sufficiently recognized; its protagonists are from the student world of the early 1960s, [and the novel deals with] academic customs, and, over it all, the function of culture, among the limitations and compromises of daily life.

> Bice Mortara Garavelli. In Ada Testaferri,
> ed. *Donna: Women in Italian Culture*
> (Toronto: Dovehouse, 1989), pp. 39, 44

Sirens, who in ancient Greece assumed the form of birds of prey with the head of a woman and throughout the ages gradually changed into mermaids, have always been symbols of intellectual seduction. Their enchanting voices lead to the sure destruction of anyone who succumbs to their charms. The episodes in *Il canto delle sirene* represent for the most part various versions of how the sirens, in different disguises, manage to seduce and destroy their victims. It is an entertaining work, if not a very memorable one.

In the episode "Silence of the Siren" the idea is that a man might save himself from the siren's song but certainly not from her silence. If he thinks that he has successfully resisted her appeal by his own strength, the sense of pride and self-satisfaction that follows undoes him, and this no mortal can resist. During the Middle Ages in the region of Otranto in southern Italy young Basilio, a painter of frescoes, wooden boxes, and vases, is enamored of Cosima, the attractive girl who is his constant companion. His great loves are painting, Cosima, and his boat. He often takes Cosima sailing, but one day he goes out alone and fails to return. He falls overboard and is sucked under, the victim of his siren. The next day his body is found in the Bay of Malepasso, known also as the Bay of the Sirens.

In another episode we are moved to nineteenth-century Norway, where one of the sirens surfaces in an icy fjord. She goes ashore to await the melting of the ice and chooses for her first night a hut where she hears the strains of a flute. It is the home of a young fisherman, blond, with eyes the color of midnight. He welcomes her, but during the long hours of the Scandinavian night they fail to become friends mainly because the lady, despite her beauty, is without a heart. One day she leaves and returns to the sea. Back in the cabin the fisherman awakes and begins to wonder if it was all a dream. He decides to leave his native village and goes to the big city, where he becomes a famous musician. His friends back home lose track of him until one day a rumor reaches them that he had been lost in a shipwreck while traveling to fulfill a concert engagement. Once again the siren claims her victim, this time by delayed action. It is a touching story with a new twist on an old theme.

In another story the siren is Celestina, a lady of the 1980s who, after earning her university degree in medieval literature, continues to do research in her chosen field. She is twenty-nine years old and spends most of her time in libraries—that is, until she meets Marco, a physicist. They go to the mountains for a vacation and fall in love. They plan to marry, but in the end Celestina returns to her research, abandoning her man and claiming, we presume, one more victim.

At the novel's conclusion the sirens are reminiscing. Men seem to have learned nothing throughout the ages, since they are now trying to destroy themselves and the world with their scientific inventions. Science is an ocean, and men do not know that just below the surface the sirens are waiting. The shipwreck of old is replaced by dead fish and polluted water. The majority of men are insignificant novices who fall into the most obvious traps. At this propitious moment the sirens indulge in a "dance of insignificance," a ritual to celebrate the destruction of the world.

Maria Corti, a Milanese who writes lovingly of her native city, teaches at the University of Pavia. Among her earlier works are two novels, *Il ballo dei sapienti* (1966) and *Voci dal Nord Est* (1986), the latter the winner of the Premio Caserta.

Rufus S. Crane. *World Literature Today.*
64, 1990, p. 290

In 1981 director Ermanno Olmi gave us *L'albero degli zoccoli,* a tender, moving fresco of epic proportions, the portrait of northern Italian farmers in a changing, slowly industrializing society. In halting vernacular his actors documented the dramatic transformations the poor farmers in the foothills around Bergamo witnessed at the turn of the nineteenth century. The same area, a few miles to the southeast, and roughly the same people, fifty years later, are featured in Maria Corti's *Cantare nel buio* (Singing in the Dark). They are still poor, but farming is no longer sufficient to their needs. Every morning they take the five-o'clock train to Milan, the city where they work mostly as masons, carpenters, or—the lucky ones—in factories. They all take the same train, a *carro bestiame* (cattle wagon), in which they sit on the dirty floor in the early-morning darkness, a shapeless, sleepy mass of tired, cold bodies, singing at times to give one another courage and warmth. Every night, once more in the darkness, their daily pilgrimage is reversed, and they are dumped at the local train station, to go home to their bowl of soup. Italians call them *pendolari,* for their daily commute is as regular as the dreadful swinging of a pendulum.

Corti, a well-known professor at the University of Pavia, editor of the scholarly journals *Autografo* and *Strumenti critici,* and author of many volumes of literary criticism, has written several novels. . . . She knows and loves the farmers of the *campagna* around Brescia. *Cantare nel buio* is certainly a work of devotion and respect. It is well written and sets the reader nicely into the life of the village, sharing with its residents their dreams and . . . [disappointments,] their first attempts to unionize and the subsequent repression by the *carabinieri.* There are no main characters in the novel. It is, in a way, the diary of a village itself. The only dissonant element is the speech patterns of the villagers. Corti's attempt to reproduce their linguistic features and traits does not seem to go far enough. Their speech sounds always unnatural and contrived, too literary and affected.

In spite of a handful of picturesque interjections in the local vernacular, the gap between reality and Corti's novel appears too wide. Even without opting for a total vernacular, the author should have given the language of the speakers much greater leeway. The result would have been far more dramatic and lively. This is certainly a long-debated question, however, one that is still unresolved in the linguistic complexity of contemporary Italy, well after the efforts of Manzoni, Verga, Gadda, and many, many other postwar writers.

Luigi Monga. *World Literature Today.* 66,
1992, p. 703

This vivid and beautifully written novel [*Otranto*] uses different voices to relate the days in 1480 when Turks attacked the small southern Italian fishing village of Otranto. Simple Colangelo describes how he and his fellow fishermen were enlisted to protect their home and reminisces about meeting with his future wife in secret. When Francesco Zurlo arrives to govern Otranto, he has to deal not only with unfriendly subjects but also with a stubborn son who dreams of fighting the Turks, and his only friend's infatuation with a much younger woman named Idrusa. Idrusa also speaks. The young widow of a fisherman she never loved, she carries on an affair with a Spanish officer under the watchful eyes of her neighbors. Another narrator, Nachira, hides out in a wine cellar to avoid the conquering Turks and then is threatened with death if he does not convert to Islam. A year later, Aloise de Marco describes the inhabitants of Otranto as they celebrate their liberation. A flawless translation maintains the individuality of each voice, and in an informative preface Bright cogently explains the choice to use modern speech in a tale that reverberates in the twentieth century on different levels, making observations about class, gender and politics.

Penny Kaganoff. *Publishers Weekly.*
September 27, 1993, p. 58

COURTHS-MAHLER, HEDWIG (GERMANY) 1865–1956

An examination of the image of women in the novels of Courths-Mahler does not make sense unless one reflects on the problem of emancipation as well. In fact, the hypothesis exists that both issues stand in relationship to one another. Light romance novels delude the female reader by promising a happy ending as the end result of conformity, ignoring her disadvantaged position in the real world. The right and the necessity of emancipation remain concealed as a result. From this viewpoint, light romance novels present a means of obstructing emancipation. The test of this assumption requires a dual approach:

First, one must assess the degree to which the analysis of the images of women yields information about the relationship between the image of women and of society to the realities of the period in which the novels appeared.

The books by Courths-Mahler—and the genre of light fiction on the whole—rank as "worlds of wish and escape" which share no relation to reality. Courths-Mahler's own statements substantiate this opinion: "Nothing I did was different from what film did later: I showed hard-working people the kind of life that they had always yearned for, that they would nonetheless never get to know. I devised fairy-tales for big children."

An examination must reveal whether this statement is true. Despite denials of any connection to factual reality and regardless of any claims to a "falsification of the image of the world and society," the novels themselves construct a new reality. This reality ultimately brings into play thoughts and fantasies about the reality outside the novel, even if these connections are perhaps merely distorted and fragmented. What is then the relationship between these and the period in which the novels are composed? Do the problems women had faced since the middle of the previous century find expression there, and are there indications of a solution? Do the novels by Courths-Mahler (and similar objects of cultural production) support the claim that the content of mass media messages serves to stabilize the contemporary social and cultural structure rather than to confront it and foster change? "Consumer goods within the industry of culture inject and stabilize social behavior according to the dictates of those in power."

Second, one must analyze the contribution the novels make to the as of yet unsolved problems of emancipation, or rather, one must assess whether the key images presented serve to hinder necessary social change, and if so, how. . . .

Hedwig Courths-Mahler herself deemed her novels "harmless fairy tales." In fact, they are harmless only for those who advocate social stagnation. The fundamental world view presented in the novels reveals tendencies that stand in total opposition to a society whose interests lie in the right to individual development and human equality. The people whom the author hails as "complete" or "noble" are actually deformed creatures in a hermetically sealed world. Because of their fear and dependence, they cannot function as free individuals. The beautiful and virtuous female figures, too, are merely lifeless apparitions made up of randomly exchangeable attributes. Their diligence and self-sacrificial helpfulness to others, repeatedly hailed as positive, do not appear believable. Examined in relation to the constant and persistent subordination to fate and male domination, they take on an almost threatening aspect: "To be virtuous means here self-denial and obedience, repression of individuality rather than its fullest realization."

The light romance novels prove themselves a means of side-tracking the right of the individual to self-fulfillment through the manipulation of his/her consciousness. Courths-Mahler's novels confirm "the self-contradictory nature of the Enlightenment, which elevates the freedom of man to a principle, while at the same time providing man the intellectual and technological means for man's subjugation of his fellow man."

> Ingrid Müller. *Untersuchen zum Bild der Frau in die Romanen von Hedwig Courths-Mahler* (Bielefeld, Germany: Pfeffersche, 1978), pp. 12–13, 56–57

During the 1920s Hedwig Courths-Mahler established a solid reputation as Germany's most popular "Volksautorin," churning out stereotyped romantic novels for the increasing number of lending libraries and the growing army of blue-collar and white-collar workers whose lives are so vividly portrayed in Siegfried Kracauer's pioneering study, *Die Angestellten.* Her reputation was not without its critics; one of the earliest was the Leipzig cabaret artist Hans Reimann, whose parody, *Hedwig Courths-Mahler, Schlichte Geschichten fürs traute Heim,* carried the ironic inscription "geschmückt mit reizenden Bildern von George Grosz." Where artists and writers such as Grosz, Tucholsky, and other members of the left-wing intelligentsia regarded art as a critical weapon and used satire, parody, and argument as means of alerting their public to discordant elements in their contemporary society, Courths-Mahler practiced an idealizing, moralistic art which looked back to the cozy world of the mid-nineteenth century *Gartenlaube*. Gibes from the avant-garde did nothing to disturb her popularity with the masses, and her system of production was so streamlined that she could turn out eight or ten novels a year.

In the last ten years a large number of these novels have once again been reprinted and widely distributed in Germany, and in the secondary literature which has grown up around them it has become something of a commonplace to insist on the "innocence" of Courths-Mahler's works. This "innocence" rests on the claim that her conservative romantic idylls lift the characters out of historical time into the timeless world of the fairy tale.

By being treated as simple folk myths, without any precise historical setting, they are thus supposedly freed from association with the "völkisch" and nationalist literature which acted as the carrier of extreme right-wing political and social ideology from the turn of the century right through until 1945. I want to challenge this viewpoint, and to argue that Courths-Mahler belongs securely within this "völkisch" tradition. Some years ago, Gertrude Willenborg persuasively demonstrated the prevalence of authoritarian personality structures in Courths-Mahler's works and suggested that her popularity during the period 1918–1930 could be taken as an indication that such attitudes—whether conscious or unconscious—had gained widespread acceptance long before the political triumph of fascism in 1933. I suggest that there are also historical elements within her fiction which support this reading and account for her continuing popularity in the period 1933–1939. National Socialism drew upon the "völkisch" and nationalist tradition for many elements of its ideology, and Courths-Mahler did not have to change direction after 1933 to retain her readership.

A 1936 novel, *Lissa geht ins Glück,* contains quite precise historical comments which portray a strongly nationalist, anti-feminist, and anti-modernist viewpoint which is wholly compatible with Nazi statements of the same period. Moreover, the blurring of the real time of history with the timeless world of myth within this novel is a further feature which links the fictive world of Courths-Mahler with a common ideological practice of the Third Reich. I have found no evidence to support Henry Pachter's statement that "in her off hours she was a courageous pacifist and feminist." Her novels all point in the opposite direction—in *Die Kriegsbraut* (1915) a jingoistic tone is unmistakable, and her novels constantly uphold the view of women as dependent beings. In the 1920s, as indeed in the 1980s, her works tend rather to support an anti-feminist lobby. But she was certainly outspoken in defending the validity of popular literature, and the arguments she used in her own defense are still appealed to by supporters of her work today. . . .

The tradition of which Courths-Mahler . . . became a part genuinely believed, no doubt, that the profoundly conservative and anti-feminist views it propagated were without political content or consequences. In the opening statement of *Die Gartenlaube* in 1853, Ernst Keil had written (like a pale echo of Schiller's *Die Hören*), that the journal would cultivate "das Gute" and "das Edel," promote "gutdeutsche Gemütlichkeit . . . die zu Herzen spricht," and remain "fern von aller räsonierenden [sic] Politik und allem Meinungsstreit in Religions- und anderen Sachen." In part, this repudiation of politics sprang from a naive sense that politics had nothing to do with everyday life. In addition, apparent retreat from the political sphere, as Dahrendorf has shown, was, in fact, a way of asserting the priority of domestic and moral virtues over the public sphere of external politics, where the petty-bourgeoisie still felt excluded from power. The "völkisch" novel of Courths-Mahler and others was certainly promoting cultural attitudes and a distinctive ideology of women, the family and marriage, but—in spite of left-wing warnings—such values were not widely perceived as having a political bearing until after 1933, when the Nazis openly declared the triumph of the "conservative revolution." . . .

The dream life of a nation may be composed of myths, but it is also a powerful ingredient in the history and in the historical consciousness of that nation. Hedwig Courths-Mahler produced popular literature—a literary dreamlife—for the masses which promoted a strict moral code, rigid demarcation of sexual roles and unquestioned acceptance of male authority, and a nostalgic view . . . a retreat from modernity and the divisiveness of industrialism: the secure conservative world of rural life. An adequate literary sociology cannot be content with arguing that such fiction is as it is because it is simply "following the market." It is also shaping that market, and keeping it tied to its present attitudes. In short, it is an historical element in the shaping of public opinion, and inevitably plays its part in the constant struggle between opposing ideologies. . . .

Courths-Mahler's enormous readership in Germany, both in the 1920s and 1930s should be seen, not as evidence of the timelessness of her myths, but rather as an historical factor which served the cause of the "conservative revolution." Similarly, her resurgence in the 1980s helps to preserve the gulf between the avant-garde and popular literature and continues to act as an agent retarding social change.

M. Kay Flavell. *German Studies Review.*
8, 1985, pp. 65–67, 71–74, 86–87

CRAIG, CHRISTINE (JAMAICA) 1943–

It is always a cause for celebration when a Caribbean woman publishes a new creative work: we are still hopeful that at some time in the near future we shall see a burgeoning of female literary achievement in the islands comparable to that which is going on in other countries. . . .

Christine Craig's work has been becoming better known outside her native Jamaica for some time now and her new work, *Quadrille for Tigers,* is both a welcome extension of her published poetry and a further demonstration of her commitment to women and of course, her creative work.

Quadrille for Tigers is a collection of fifty-two poems which range over a variety of themes. . . . She is aware of color (especially silver, which is a frequent element in important images in her poetry), sound, touch, shape, and the natural world. This sensuous quality and the detailed observation of gardens, houses, personal relationships, motherhood, and friendship delineate the borders of Craig's poetic world as the familiar confines of a women's world. Yet this is not to demean her work in any sense, for the immense importance of the woman's work in building human aspiration and providing the foundation for human effort is recognized in her poems in a way which reveals both her sympathy for woman and her anger at the social fabric which undermines her strength. . . .

[The poem "All Things Bright"] is a particularly forceful and effective comment on the way in which the stoic hopes of mothers for the advancement of their children are constantly threatened by the women's powerlessness in the broader social context, where "the men prey upon us." The "us" here is an aspect of Craig's explicit identification with women. Her poetry, while not exclusively concerned with being woman, has a very clear statement to make. Craig's awareness, consciousness of the place and experience of women in her society is a major element in her work.

The particular condition of the black woman is a major theme. "Prelude to Another Life" which seems rather prosaic in form, and which obviously has a relation to Derek Walcott's autobiographical poem *Another Life,* deals with a grandmother and sisters, two of the influences which make a woman whatever she is. Here again, the motherly hope of the grandmother's youth is that education will save her pupils and her relatives. . . .

The texture of this poem, with its golden bees and yellow dogwood, daffodils, the golden E of education, sunny morning and golden bridges of childhood is reminiscent of Walcott's poem, which also has yellow and gold as major emotional tones.

Culturally, aesthetically, Craig's work rests on a foundation of black writing, black consciousness as well as a woman's awareness which reaches out over all society.

Craig's poetic development is demonstrated in this volume, in the sense that she is clearly still experimenting with various influences and forms, trying to find her own voice. Sometimes she relies too much on abstractions, conventional images and pretty colors or concepts, "Wet leaves, white blossoms/quiver a tremulous clarity," "liquid mirror of today's truth." But she is more often than not a very definite, interesting poet, whose turns of thought are challenging and whose language reflects her determination to be honest and to argue her points within a subtle poetic pattern. She is a precise poet, choosing mainly short forms, dealing with moments of perception in a controlled but lively poetic style, "The Causeway," a poem about the divisions in Jamaica seen through white and black images, is confined cleverly within four stanzas which interweave the black/white concepts with direct comment on social tensions. Her portrait poems, her delicate accounts of intimacies and the difficulties of loving, her social and political comments on women and on the black experience in Jamaica are all facets of her poetic personality.

This volume has given me great pleasure. . . .

Craig's warmth and willingness to express the moments of doubt and pain which constantly afflict those of us trying to have good relations with men and to change society's dislike of women to something better is as important as her carefully chosen words and patterns of words. We await her next volume.

Elaine Savory Fido. *Caribbean Contact.*
November, 1984, p. 15

Quadrille for Tigers is attractive, accomplished, important. Christine Craig, a significant poet with a pleasing individual voice, often contrives to sound casual, but her poems are craftily layered. Her publishers accurately note that the poems in this collection are informed by the poet's "womanhood as well as her Jamaican roots" and that "her imagination extends over a wide range of human experience, brilliantly picturing its struggles as well as its joys."

Many of the poems are intimately Jamaican in reference—"Sunday in the Lane," for example, "The Causeway," or the painterly "St Ann." But their resonances echo wide. In "Lost from the Fold," for example, we have Death scuffling his adidas, using macka to pick his teeth, while his dread friend Hunger skanks; but the poem's protest can readily be shared by anyone willing to respond to poverty or neglect, and to the loss of faith. The neglected woman on the street is lost from the fold, apparently forgotten. The persona is impelled to turn away from faith. The consolations of the Son of Heaven are bitterly implied to be unavailable under the blaring "hot sun of this hell." As in many of the poems, there is also a gender element in the perception: the victim observed is a woman; the God who seems to have absconded is male, as are "Death the certain friend" and his accomplice Hunger. But the claim on our sympathies is not restricted by the poem's local habitation or its play of gender.

Some of the pieces, more explicitly, speak for the condition of woman. ("Poor woman, the man's truth/is an empty yabba for you.") But they are often gentle in their address to man, as in "Poem for a Marriage," "Love Poem," "For Klaus or John or Pierre." There are poems of love, of longing, of friendship; poems of friendship with other women; poems of family affection. The general tendency is towards love and reconciliation. . . .

If the woman is determined to be "a free black woman" and to shape her own journey, she is also keen that she and the man—brother, lover, friend—should "make something new together."

The movement towards reconciliation is not confined to man/woman relationships. It is there also in other potential polarities: black/white, rich/poor, Old World/New World, for example. Like gender, history, race and class need not necessarily divide. Art can reconcile, can transcend; and the human person traffics in a range of possibilities. . . .

At the center there is a tension, emphasized in the title of the volume, between control and energy.

The association of quadrilles and tigers hints also at the poet's Jamaican base (quadrille is an emblem of Jamaican culture) and her involvement beyond Jamaica (literal tigers do not leap in Jamaica, though there may be one in the zoo—the tigers, literary and universal, symbolize psychic energies).

In every single human house there are two people living uneasily: "one Says life is rational," "The other says, life is the crazy/whirling baton of some cosmic conductor." . . . The artist tries to reconcile "These two, trying to make one song." The reconciliation is not necessarily fusion; it may be achieved, as also in this volume, by movement between the tendencies. No one poem says it all. Ultimately the statement is incomplete, dynamic; is moving still. . . .

Christine Craig includes us all. She speaks (with quiet eloquence) not just for the woman, the free black woman, the struggling artists, but also for anyone who has ever recognized in him or herself "a store of locked up life."

Mervyn Morris. *Jamaica Journal.* 18:4,
November 1985–January 1986, p. 62

[In Christine Craig's *Quadrille for Tigers,* "All Things Bright" exemplifies] the effect present in a great deal of her work, namely a presentation of different elements each in an intersecting relation with the other. Craig often writes from that crossroads center, her poems taking creative energy from a juxtaposition of factors in an experience which she creatively perceives. In this poem, the central persona is a mother, trying to bring up a daughter, concerned with the small details of appearance ("you not going anywhere/in those dirty shoes") but emotionally hurt by the violence in Kingston through which she must go "Eyes mussed with tears" to take her daughter to school. The daughter, whose sensitivity to the violence in the city is a mark of sharing values with the mother, is also hurt by the world outside the home and her face is "sad,/just at the edges." Good mothering is frustrated by the social chaos, in the sense of not being able to protect the child against all hurts in the environment (and the child's vulnerability is a sign of being able to care). In the poem, we are made to realize how all human relations are enhanced or damaged by the state of society:

Women's lives shot to stillness
in small, hot rooms. Men
bought and sold, holding death bold
in the gleam of guns,
a deadly phallic power against the impotence of poverty.

Here Craig does not quite say that economic tensions create sexual tensions, but she shows how one interacts with the other, how the need to be traditionally female and withdrawn (as the daughter in the poem wants to withdraw), and the need to be traditionally male and keep potency through aggression, are both dangerous in the circumstances of extreme economic exploitation. . . .

In another poem in the same volume, "Lost from the Fold," where Craig focuses on a derelict woman who has died in the street, there is a juxtaposition of the woman with the rhetoric of religion. . . .

The poem is subtle in its anger, but very definite, and again, the interaction of gender issues with economic circumstances which affect everyone in the city (Rastafarianism as the cult of the poor and oppressed is very present here but is redefined in relation to the dead woman) is a strong characteristic of the creative identity of the work.

But the poem which most clearly identifies this interaction of interests is Craig's well known "Crow Poem." The "crow" is a woman whose voice "wants to say things/ about blue skies, blond sand," but this Caucasian tourist poster imagery is rejected. Instead, a "rasping carrion croak/jets from my beak/sharp edged." The wordplay ("Illsuited"; "jets") contains the double-layering which informs the poem: again there is a delicate touch to the dilemma and a wry playfulness:

> Perhaps there is out there
> one crow, wheeling over the city dump
> convinced she is a woman.

The clichéd image of the crow is thus reassembled and revived here by the female consciousness which pervades the poem: at one level it works as a statement about woman's constant sense of physical inadequacy in the face of male desires for "pretty" images and of course, in this case, for "white" tourist clichés of attractiveness, but then the poem shifts and realigns. It is a much more awkward self which becomes the basis of a tentative contact with a loved other:

> I want so much to put
> my arms around you but
> extended they are feathered
> vanes, snapped, tatty things
> no longer curving.

The creative power of "Crow Poem" comes from the delicacy of this brave facing of an alienated self.

Elaine Savory Fido. In Carole Boyce Davies
and Elaine Savory Fido, eds. *Out of the
Kumbla: Caribbean Women and Literature*
(Trenton, New Jersey: Africa World Press,
1990), pp. 32–33

CUNARD, NANCY (GREAT BRITAIN) 1896–1965

One of the most astonishing facts about *Negro* is its existence; another is its author. Both have been accorded legendary status. Before the publication of *Negro* in 1934, Nancy Cunard, daughter of Sir Bache Cunard, of the shipping family, and of a generation that produced Edith Sitwell, Gertrude Stein, Kay Boyle, and Margaret Anderson, had been a poet, an adventurous publisher of avant-garde books, a creative and commanding figure among the Montparnasse literati, and an eager student and collector of African art. From early youth she had shown a dramatic capacity to stir controversy, but it was *Negro,* compiled primarily for the black race and dedicated to "one of them," that brought her career to an explosive climax. . . .

Negro was the first comprehensive documentation that supported the black man's claims and demands for equal treatment. It stated and demonstrated the thesis so widely accepted today, that creatively and culturally the black man is the white man's equal. Although its very name may now evoke a bygone era, it must nonetheless be accorded a prominent place in that past which, in its shaping influence, is immutably linked to the present. . . .

But *Negro* does more than recall a past that gave shape to the present. And it can certainly claim to be much more than a repository of old ideas and attitudes, interesting as they may be. *Negro* has had, and continues to have, a proclamatory career. Its pages ring with the challenge of contemporary black demands: for equal educational facilities and opportunities, for studies in black history and black literature, for integration into the white student movement, for black separatism, for the use of massive force as a means of countering repression, for pride in blackness. Their modernity sustains the catalytic role Nancy had foreseen for *Negro* in always encouraging a belief in probability rather than prophecy. "Prophecy is of no use," Nancy wrote at the time she compiled *Negro.* "The inner sense of probability, forerunner of accomplished fact, is the guerdon. No light word—Probability. It links conviction with instinct, is almost instinct itself, is the feeling of coming things."

> Hugh Ford. Introduction to Nancy Cunard.
> *Negro* (1934; abridged edition, New York:
> Frederick Ungar, 1970), pp. xi, xxvi–xxvii

Negro is the most ambitious anthology on blacks ever attempted. It covers practically every aspect of black life: history, literature, education, law, racial injustice, theater, art and music. It examines not only black life in the United States, but also in the West Indies, South America, Europe and Africa. At the time when the book first appeared, 1934, the inferiority of blacks was still an unquestioned assumption among whites, except for a small minority of artists and intellectuals. Nancy Cunard was one of the latter, and her purpose in compiling, editing and publishing this anthology at her own expense was to prove "that there was no superior race, merely cultural differences, that racism has no basis whatsoever." The result is a book that is unashamedly didactic and, in great part, polemical, exposing the persecution of blacks through reportage on chain gangs, lynchings and the case of the Scottsboro boys, and proving the equality of blacks through essays on their intellectual and artistic accomplishments. It is a book that was valuable and necessary for its time. Today it is a historical artifact, but a fascinating one. . . .

The list of contributors is quite impressive and includes William Carlos Williams, Theodore Dreiser, Ezra Pound, Langston Hughes, Samuel Beckett (who translated most of the French articles into English), W. E. B. Du Bois, Alain Locke, Jomo Kenyatta and George Padmore. But, as in any anthology, the quality of the articles varies. Many of the contributions by whites are paternalistic and patronizing. . . .

Fortunately, many of the essays are free of racism and Communist dogmatism. There are five brief, but excellent essays by Zora Neale Hurston on black speech, religion and music, an analysis of the still-neglected black poet Sterling Brown (one of the editors of "The Negro Caravan") by Alain Locke, W. E. B. Du Bois on "Black America" and George Padmore on Africa.

Negro tried to present a world view of blacks and considering that it was compiled and edited by a white, it was a good try, despite its defects. The book is also a mirror of a fascinating woman. A daughter of the Cunards of shipping line fame, Nancy Cunard was born in England in 1896, but lived in France during much of her life. On two occasions she visited the United States during the preparation of *Negro,* staying in Harlem hotels and creating a stir among the New York press. Until her death in 1965, she remained intensely interested in the causes that had dominated her life. Hugh Ford writes a very informative introduction, capsuling her life and the history of this anthology, though Mr. Ford is guilty of his own benevolent racism when he informs us that Miss Cunard was a champion of "true 'black power.'" He makes her sound more like the Great White Mother than the dynamic woman I have the feeling she was.

Most important, *Negro* reflects a period of Western history when a few whites were beginning to regard blacks with a certain sympathy. This sympathy was more akin to pity than compassion, a feeling that allowed whites to continue regarding blacks as inferior. Still, it was an important departure from the hatred and brutality commonly accorded blacks. Today, it is easy to look back and see that the Nancy Cunards were using blacks to free themselves from the caparisons of Western civilization as much, if not more, than they were trying to help blacks. And, it is too easy to be harsh with them because of this. They did what they could with what they had and, in the end, that is all that can be asked of any of us. *Negro* is the summary of a generation of black and white intellectuals and artists who groped toward a dialogue. This book does not meet the needs of today, but by so vividly showing us where we have been, it can help us to more closely define where we are and where we must go.

> Julius Lester. *New York Times Book Review.*
> August 30, 1970, pp. 7, 24

Read about Michael Arlen's *Green Hat,* read about Ezra Pound, or about the Spanish Civil War, and you are bound sooner or later to stumble against a reference to Nancy Cunard. Man Ray photographed her; so did Cecil Beaton. Brancusi made a sculptural portrait of her and Oskar Kokoschka painted her. . . . Nancy Cunard was serious about lost causes, serious about the plight of the poor and the downtrodden. Today she appears to us as a relic of romantic rebellion, as a person it would have been nice to know, as a person— whatever her personal charm—flung to the edges of the reeling 1920s and 1930s by the centrifugal force of great aesthetic and political energies. . . .

[P]erhaps the important thing to be said about the least of what we find here is what the noted black author Julius Lester has said: "They did what they could with what they had and, in the end, that is all that can be asked of any of us." And it must be noted that there is much of enormous value in this collection, much that anticipates intuitions that are only today in general circulation. One of these is a stunning essay by René Crevel, translated into English by Samuel Beckett, called "The Negress in the Brothel," that develops with elegant clarity the thesis of Kate Millett's *Sexual Politics:* "Man in the middle, obedient to God, obeyed of women—chaplet of subordinations."

Nancy Cunard herself was subordinate to nothing but her eccentric will. During the time she was assembling many of the pieces collected here she lived in Harlem, her life-style scandalizing her peers in England—whom she violently disavowed—and providing lurid copy to the yellow press. (She only managed to pay the high printing cost of *Negro* by the grace of a British libel judgment in her favor that brought her a settlement of 1,500 pounds.) But if she was no mistress to any single man or cause, she was quick—too quick for her intellectual good—to grab a solution from the ready-to-wear rack, and her pieces here suffer from her untutored celebration of the Communist cause, from her readiness to bandy such dull-witted locutions as "imperialist lackeys" and her tin-eared sloganizing: "Up with an all-Communist Harlem in an all-Communist United States!"

Never mind. She put the book together, and she lived its radical hope.

> Geoffrey Wolff. *Newsweek.* October 5, 1970,
> p. 102

In 1925, the Hogarth Press published Nancy Cunard's *Parallax.* In 1928, Cunard herself had decided to set up a hand press in France, and she wrote Leonard and Virginia Woolf to seek their advice. Surprised, and perhaps alarmed at Cunard's temerity, they exclaimed, "Your hands will always be covered with ink!" . . . Like Virginia Woolf, however, Nancy Cunard enjoyed having her hands covered with ink and admitted that "the smell of printer's ink pleased me greatly, as did the beautiful freshness of the glistening pig-ment"; she too quickly mastered the technical skills and found release from tension in the physical exertion demanded by the press. For Cunard, the operation of a hand press was an aesthetic experience: she delighted in choos-ing typefaces and paper stock and designing covers and bindings.

The Hours Press was not conceived as a commercial publishing firm, but neither did Cunard think of it as a hobby. Her decision to open the Hours Press constituted commitment to experimental poetry, and she was willing to risk financial loss in order to publish the best verse she could find. As Hugh Ford explains, she wanted to publish good work by young writers and to reward them "in a manner more generous than that to which they were accustomed." . . . Many of the writers she published, however, were well known (George Moore, for instance, was in his late seventies when Cunard published his *Peronnik the Fool*), her only "discovery" being Samuel Beckett, who won the Hours poetry prize for "Whoroscope" in 1930. She also pub-lished a "poem-fresco" by the Chilean painter Alvaro Guevara; a French translation by Aragon of Lewis Carroll's *The Hunting of the Snark;* the cata-logue for a Paris exhibition of work by the American painter Eugene Mac-Cown (who had made the cover designs for Cunard's long poem *Parallax*); poems by Robert Graves, Laura Riding, Richard Aldington, Roy Campbell, Brian Howard, Bob Brown, and Harold Acton; a portion of Pound's *Cantos;* an essay by Havelock Ellis, *The Revaluation of Obscenity;* and a collection of six songs by Henry Crowder—who was Cunard's colleague at the press—based on the poetry of Beckett, Aldington, Acton, and Walter Lowenfels. Cunard's association with Crowder, a black American jazz musician, would lead to her interest in compiling the anthology *Negro,* her political involvement in the black cause, and the publication in 1931 of her pamphlet *Black Man and White Ladyship,* a public attack on Lady Emerald Cunard's racist attitudes.

Anne Chisholm has suggested that the decision to open the press may have been occasioned by Cunard's sense of dissatisfaction with her own ca-reer as a poet: "she kept on writing and publishing occasional poems, but she needed to try a more practical outlet for her energies." The three years Cunard spent at the Hours Press, however, led to highly productive years of writing and publication: *Negro,* her anthology on black politics and culture, was published in 1934; she served as a journalist for the *Manchester Guardian* during the Spanish Civil War, while writing war poetry and publishing com-mentaries on the war; later, she served in England as a translator for the Free French during World War II, often monitoring Ezra Pound's broadcasts from Italy. In 1944, she completed an anthology of French translations of British poems about France *(Poems for France)* and had completed a collec-tion of war poems entitled *Man-Ship-Tank-Gun-Plane.*

Cunard's decision to establish a small press marked the moment in which she turned away from her own self-interest to a commitment to others in col-laborative efforts. As Hugh Ford has suggested, the story of the Hours Press is one "of close personal relationships and co-operation between . . . Cunard and the authors she published, which made possible the most fruitful sort of collaboration." . . . This story is also one of an emerging political identity.

Shari Benstock. *Women of the Left Bank:*
Paris 1900–1940 (Austin: University of
Texas Press, 1985), pp. 389–90

Cunard's monumental anthology, *Negro,* published in 1934, was conceived in 1930 out of the love she felt for African and Afro-American art, the rage she felt as she learned about racism, and her relationship with [Henry] Crowder. Her dedication of *Negro* to Crowder demonstrates the inseparability for Cunard of the public and the private, the personal and the political, the sociological and the aesthetic. With 150 contributors from many countries, the book included articles on African art; Afro-American and West Indian poetry and music; the institutionalization of racism in the United States; the history of blacks in the Americas; communism and race; and African, West Indian, and South American histories and ethnographies. Ambitious in scope, the book had 855 pages, with 385 illustration. About two-thirds of its authors were black, the rest white—including stellar names of the Harlem Renaissance and white modernism. No publisher would touch such a big and politically volatile book manuscript. Cunard gleefully used the 1,500 pounds she received from the British press in a settlement of her libel suits to publish the book. "Poetic justice," she exclaimed to friends.

The events surrounding the compilation of *Negro* were stormy and personally difficult for Cunard. To begin the collection of materials, she went openly with Crowder to London, where they lived in the flat of a friend. Lady Cunard was very upset with her daughter's public liaison with a black man. In December 1930 they fought it out, never to meet again. After Cunard traveled to New York with Crowder to collect materials in Harlem, Lady Cunard cut her daughter's allowance, first by a quarter, then in half. Cunard retaliated in 1931 by publishing the pamphlet *Black Man and White Ladyship,* a public exposure of her mother's Anglo-American bigotry and hypocrisy. The essay, which created an enormous scandal, narrates her confrontation with her mother and reveals the racism of Lady Cunard and all her "liberal" friends (such as George Moore) in all its specificity. Not merely a diatribe against her mother, the essay publicizes Cunard's repudiation of class and race privilege, advocacy of racial justice, and critique of British imperialism. She celebrated African art and Afro-American music; she insisted that white Europeans were no more "civilized" than black Africans. Cunard broke the taboo of privacy—she washed the dirty linen of her race and class in public. She demonstrated with vicious wit and brutal honesty the disease of racism. The conflation of matriphobia and political radicalism is breathtaking, raising troubling questions about the mother-daughter bond within the psychodynamics of gender, race, and class. She shocked even her friends, people like Richard Aldington, who had been more than a little in love with her. Crowder himself though the pamphlet "a most idiotic thing to do." . . .

The essay "Scottsboro—and Other Scottsboros" presents a detailed history of the case, prefaced by the caveat that the case is not unusual, that "the same capitalist oppression and brutality" are "at the root" of many other cases, including the "murder-by-law of Sacco and Vanzetti." In "The American Moron and the American of Sense—Letters on the Negro," printed below, she astutely analyzed the intersection of racism and sexism in the titillated hounding she had received from the press. "Jamaica—The Negro Island" surveys the history and culture of Jamaica and anticipates her later career as a journalist. Her poem "Southern Sheriff" adapts the Browning dramatic monologue to her political purposes: in dialect, a white southern sheriff reveals the extent of his bigotry as he defends it. Her essay "Harlem Reviewed" . . . is a verbal tour through various aspects of Harlem life—its vibrancy and its slums, its creativity and its oppression, its religion and its politics. She worked hard in the essay to avoid the white fascination for black Otherness that characterized many whites who went "slumming" in Harlem; at the same time, she did not hide behind a screen of color-blind objectivity. She made clear that she was a white woman in a world different from her own. She ended with a messianic call to communism as an idea that could end racial prejudice. . . .

The rise of fascism in Spain, Italy, and Germany became her next focus. While Pound was increasingly enthralled by Mussolini and was formulating his anti-Semitic economic theories, Cunard first condemned the Italian invasion of Ethiopia and then went to Spain to support the Republicans against the Fascists. As a reporter for the *Manchester Guardian,* she wrote many stories about the appalling plight of the refugees, as well as the events of the Spanish Civil War. Canvassing over a hundred writers for their position on the war, Cunard published the pamphlet *Authors Take Sides on the Spanish War,* which reported that 126 replies were pro-Republican, five were for Franco, and sixteen (including Eliot and Pound) were neutral. For Cunard: "It is unthinkable for any honest intellectual to be pro-Fascist as it is degenerate to be for Franco, the assassin of the Spanish and Arab people. . . . Above all others, the writer, the intellectual, must take sides. His place is with the people against Fascism." . . .

Cunard's notes for a memoir she never wrote capture the steadfastly moral and political vision of her stance: "When of SELF writing: Re the three main things. 1 Equality of races. 2 Of Sexes. 3 Of classes." Her friend Sylvia Townsend Warner said in a related vein: "Her temper was notorious, her life was willful and erratic—and she was compellingly respect-worthy."

Susan Stanford Friedman. In Bonnie Kime
Scott, ed. *The Gender of Modernism: A
Critical Anthology* (Bloomington: Indiana
University Press, 1990), pp. 65–67

Given her indifference to feminism, it would be ironic if the chief cause of the loss of Nancy Cunard's presence as a radical intellectual was her gender.

She was not the kind of role model usually offered to aspiring young crusaders for social justice. She'd be a failure as a heroine in a "Lives of Great Women" series, and feminists will not find a long-lost champion of women's rights when her achievements are reviewed. Her life was not a happy one, nor was it stable in any sense. Women are supposed to live stably and provide stability for others. Nancy Cunard was a revolutionary, dedicating her life to political upheaval, committed to changing the world. . . .

[S]he was not a hostess or a lady with a salon, as a historian of women surrealists who had never heard of her assumed when she asked contemptuously, "Did she *do* anything?" Nancy Cunard was primarily what we used to call in the civil rights and antiwar movements, a full-time political organizer. She was a living network, a one-woman permanent walking demonstration against racism and fascism, and a celebrant of black culture in all its forms. She had a voice in shaping all the competing and conflicting discourses of modernism, but in their histories there is only the marginal trace of a husky whisper, a smudge like a streak of kohl across those hooded piercing eyes remembered in a malicious footnote. She was an autodidact, a self-made intellectual and political organizer. And she was very successful at her work. She produced an enormous amount of knowledge to combat racism and to invite Europe and the West to see Africa and Negro cultures as civilizations. Her work and the work of those she organized to produce the monumental *Negro* anthology, an international body of progressive intellectuals and artists of all races working together to produce and disseminate knowledge about black culture, was ridiculed, lost, dismissed, made fun of, ignored—and then it was done all over again. This is what gives me a chill. The case of the loss of the *Negro* anthology is an example of what happens to the histories of all oppressed groups when they have no institutions—universities, libraries, museums, art galleries—to protect and value, cherish and circulate them. . . .

Belittled by histories of the Harlem Renaissance, Nancy Cunard was left out altogether from the story of the culture she did so much to shape, the story of the Communist Party in Harlem in the 1930s; she is basically a missing person in Valentine Cunningham's history of British writing in the 1930s, barely mentioned in the histories of the English expatriates and the Spanish Civil War, ignored as a journalist and war-correspondent, marginalized as a modernist poet, erased from her role as organizer of the international protest movement on behalf of the Scottsboro boys, her Hours Press listed on the fringe of the small press and avant-garde publishing world (discovering Beckett, printing Pound's *Cantos*), reduced to a footnote in the biography of her lifelong friend Langston Hughes or demonized or left out of the lives of her former lovers like Louis Aragon, so that, incidentally, her role in the Paris Left as well as in Surrealism itself is summarily cut. Her role in collecting and showing African art in Paris early in the century and her pioneering of the revaluation of ethnic objects as art for museums and private collectors changed art history. Roger Fry is remembered, but even he is excluded from recent studies of primitivism. Where is Nancy Cunard?

Her work for the *Negro* anthology revitalized the field of anthropology and introduced fieldworkers and ethnographers to each other's work as well as to positive ideas about Africa as civilized rather than savage cultures and had a major influence on French ethnographic practice, as Michel Leiris says in his memoirs. . . .

Only an autodidact could have imagined such a grandiose intellectual scheme (requiring immense amounts of research in primary documents in libraries all over the world) as Nancy Cunard's *Negro* anthology. Only a committed left-wing activist could have called up the worldwide ideals of cross-racial brother-and-sisterhood to bring such a project into being. Only a mad surrealist poet would have thought that its dynamite collections of artistic power and beauty would blow up in the face of bourgeoisies of all nations and colors and that the scales of prejudice would fall from their eyes at once. Only an intrepid Englishwoman in exile would have believed that she could bring it off, commissioning, cajoling, editing, revising, dealing with bruised egos and suspicious intellectuals, underground leaders, separatists and photographers and professors and anthropologists, folklorists and politicians, discovering new voices, letting controversial voices be heard, publishing manifestoes and always having the last word—editing the conservative Du Bois, arguing with Marcus Garvey, proclaiming in her fellow-travelling footnotes that the way and the only way of racial freedom was the Communist Party. . . .

There is a great deal of work to be done on the history of the making of the *Negro* anthology and all of Nancy Cunard's writing on race. Nancy Cunard's route out of the hypocrisy and racism of her class is not to be easily dismissed. One cannot despise a woman who devoted herself to the cause of black liberation. Sex and race are dangerous subjects and very complex, especially when tangled in a woman's political life, as she and her friends lived and as we read their lives.

Jane Marcus. In Mae Henderson, ed.
Borders, Boundaries and Frames (New
York: Routledge, 1994), pp. 34–35, 37, 39, 60

DABROWSKA, MARIA (POLAND) 1889–1965

Relativism seems closely related to Bergson's philosophical doctrine of time. . . . In the popular mind, these ideas confirm the meaninglessness of the passage of time, the relativity of all things that never return, doomed to inevitable evanescence. Using this general approach, we can examine two related literary trends. One is a hasty attempt to grasp the whole subject of time, which leads to the complete decomposition of human values, including the style of writing itself. The other attempt is to weave character development and human values into a fabric of perpetual flux; this is the still-fashionable relativism.

Dąbrowska belongs to this second school of thought: she is above all concerned with constant change, with the relationship between man and his world, which he knows is in perpetual motion, in light of which knowledge only the totally blind remain ignorant.

Barbara's problem [in *Noce i dnie* (Nights and Days)] can thus be clearly stated: her whole struggle with reality, her constant anxiety, is simply her inability to adapt to the changing stream of life. Her behavior is contrasted with Bogumil's attitude toward life. However, the constant flow of time that Dąbrowska points to is not to be confused with the concept of time as all-powerful, which dissolves all desires and thoughts into one wave. She does not reduce all human desires to one common denominator of irrational confusion in time, but rather gives human passions and desires an autonomous existence of their own, as things arising from the depths of human consciousness. Her characters are portrayed in terms of their values and desires, which do not become fused with the eternal flow of time. . . .

[Dąbrowska] has this deep sense of the passing of time, without which it would be difficult for people to understand each other. But she also has the will to resist this force; she speaks not of twinkling flashes of light on the water, of people-dragonflies. She does not let herself be hypnotized by the knowledge that everything passes with time. . . . Not only does she accept the course of life; she loves it.

Kazimierz Wyka. Kultura (Warsaw).
May 8, 1932, p. 2

The novelists of the preceding period indulged in re-creating subconscious processes, and in this analytical procedure individuality was often lost. In Dąbrowska we have the return to the novel of individuality and character. With deep consciousness of their interrelationship Dąbrowska brings these two aspects together, thus finding the proper attitude toward life and individuality. The typology of her characters is based on the principle of antithesis: those who have a distinct individuality and can find themselves and the right approach in the world, and those who are "empty," who cannot find their place in the world. This typology is one of the most complete and clear and perfect of artistic creations. . . .

[*Noce i dnie*] seems a real innovation, mainly due to the return to the old postulate of the wisdom of life, which has been forgotten lately by our writers. This return is associated with a shift in philosophical outlook from the purely scientific toward a more general world view. The epic attitude, the combining of the right attitude toward life and individuality with the intellectual element, finds harmonious unity in her art.

Reflections and aphorisms do not destroy the epic character. A complete elimination of subjectivity is not an absolute requirement for an epic writer; what is important is that the role of narrator be limited to very discreet remarks. Philosophical reflections on life expressed impersonally realize Goethe's theory that the narrator must speak in epic words as if from behind a screen. Reflections organically interwoven into the stream of the narrative make the characters and the events less ephemeral, elevate them to the level of epic time, and lend them the glory of universal importance. Dabrowska is thus able to imbue her characters with the aura of metaphysical mystery and the deep meaning of life. [1935]

Stefan Kolaczkowski. In *Polska krytyka
literacka* (Warsaw: Państwowe
Wydawnictwo Naukowe, 1966), pp. 443–44

If one were to dare to have an opinion on literary currents when one is so close to them as to have no perspective, he might venture to state that Maria Dąbrowska's *Nights and Days* represents the climax of a reaction from poetry, the natural expression of a confident and youthful generation like that of the 1920s, in favor of the novel form. Poetry is opposed to reality, and the late 1920s and our own 1930s cry out for the solid, homely fare of reality.

Nights and Days is the fruit of long years of labor. Its first volume was published in 1931 and its final, the sixth, appeared only in 1934. To go about reading it seems like a large undertaking, but once in it, once caught in the web of the doings of its characters, one hates to have it come to an end, as one does with all long, monumental works . . . with *The Forsyte Saga,* or *The Magic Mountain, The Peasants* or *The Seven Pillars of Wisdom.*

Arthur P. Coleman. *As I Look at the New
Polish Books.* 20, 1936, p. 1

Na wsi wesele (A village wedding) is a work of a special kind, an account-settling work. A classic example of this genre in our literature was once [Żeromski's] *Przedwiośnie* (Before the spring). Lately, in a similar way *toutes les proportions gardées*—public opinion in our countries was aroused by Ilya Ehrenburg's *The Thaw.* Such works have their own laws, are totally subordinated to the intellect. This often perverts the style even of outstanding artists, as can be observed in the case of the uncontrolled journalistic character of *The Thaw*. It is an artistic achievement of a high level that Dąbrowska did not let this happen in *Na wsi wesele,* although even here there is a mutation of style, a departure from Dąbrowska's customary way of writing. Condensations and certain exaggerations do not destroy the high artistry. The work is far from a verbatim report; even the smallest details ultimately contribute to the total effect. *Na wsi wesele* is so packed with the details of current life that, although fully accessible to contemporaries, it will require commentary in the future.

In *Na wsi wesele* Dąbrowska struggles with the problems of social revolution, and she does it on this large a scale for the first time in her career, since *Trzecia jesień* (The third autumn) is much more modest in this respect. Many important issues enter literature belatedly, but truly great artists cannot remain deaf to them. This is the mark of their greatness. Dąbrowska confronted these issues in *Na wsi wesele* with the full power of realism and with the full richness of her philosophy.

Tadeusz Drewnowski. *Nowa kultura.*
March 4, 1957, pp. 6, 7

Maria Dąbrowska composed *Noce i dnie* according to principles that subconsciously utilized techniques of the writers of "folk" epics. It is not difficult to find in her work the basic pattern on which the *Odyssey* or *The Song of Roland* were founded. We see here the same basic motifs that lead to the glorification of the hero. To be sure, many centuries have passed; the hero has been pulled down to earth, and instead of encounters with gods or angels he faces the daily reality of the twentieth century. His attitude, nevertheless, remains heroic in the sense that he has been created by the writer according to the same universal principles that can be found in all geographical locations, in all places in which people have sung the glory of the best among them.

Charles Hyart. In *Pięćdziesiąt lat twórczości
Marii Dąbrowskiej* (Warsaw: Państwowy
Instytut Wydawniczy, 1963), p. 107

Dąbrowska's novel entitled *Noce i dnie* is actually a whole cycle, a monumental tetralogical structure, the two last parts of which each consist of two volumes. The first and second parts, *Bogumil i Barbara* (Bogumil and Barbara) and *Wieczne zmartwienie* (Eternal worry) appeared in 1932, followed by *Miłość* (Love, two parts, 1933) and *Wiatr w oczy* (Wind in the eyes, two parts, 1934).

The novel belongs to the genre of "family chronicle," and the influence of novels such as Thomas Mann's *Buddenbrooks* and John Galsworthy's *Forsyte Saga* is clearly noticeable. But the influence is largely formal; Dąbrowska's ideological perspective, her grasp of contemporary reality, and her insight into individual psychological problems make her work completely independent.

On the ideological level the main difference is that while both in *Buddenbrooks* and in *The Forsyte Saga* the stress is on the gradual decline of the respective families when they deviate from those traditional principles on which their wealth and importance had grown, in Dąbrowska's novel the emphasis is rather on the problem of creating new values for the landless and hard-working former land-owning class.

In actual fact the whole problem is more complicated. The ideals of Bogumil, the main hero of the novel, are still to a certain extent the same as those of his predecessors, and his attachment to worldly possessions is quite strong. Only at the very end, on the eve of his death, does he free himself from these bonds, and this happens on the moral rather than economic level. It is the daughter, Agnieszka, who is the real seeker of new ideals completely free from the traditional attachment to private property.

Zbigniew Folejewski. *Books Abroad*. 38,
Winter, 1964, pp. 11–12

Establishing the influence of one writer on another does not explain much. There is no work of literature read by a sensitive writer that would not leave some trace on him. It also happens that more visible traces can be left by works other than those the writer himself considers most important. *Les Thibault* [by Roger Martin du Gard] was certainly among books read by Dąbrowska at the time of her writing *Noce i dnie*. . . . But also on her reading list was clearly Thomas Hardy, and his sharp drawing of provincial characters left a deep mark on her memory, at least as deep as that left by Dickens.

But Dąbrowska's element is not urban life; it is not the provincial-town characters who come to life under her pen. The countryside, however, floats like a boat on the surface of mighty, mysterious, inscrutable, cruel, yet generous nature, a nature that is in some mysterious way similar to Joseph Conrad's sea. Life with nature, life with the earth, demands heroism. Fate remains very close to the people, because man is not protected from it by various forms of civilization. Man remains close to his fellow man even when he fights him, just as on Conrad's sea. Unexpected ties of brotherhood arise, as between the "master" and his coach driver Peterka in "Szklane konie." Strange love affairs also arise, as between Bogumil and the maid Felicia (in *Noce i dnie*).

The earth is, then, the main element, the main force, especially for people who have to claim the earth foot by foot from the forest, the rocks, and the sea. It has thus been made an object of worship in the literature of the north (Knut Hamsun's *Growth of the Soil*). On the Polish plains, where there was enough soil but not enough for everybody, the cult of the earth arose from the inequities of distribution, from social and economic causes, from the desire to possess. Thus, it is desired by the landless family Karczmarek in the story "Najdalsza droga" (The longest road), and likewise by Bogumil, a former landowner. The idolatry of Bogumil's gesture of kissing the earth derives from a Nordic, Hamsunian inspiration.

Andrej Kijowski. *Maria Dąbrowska*
(Warsaw: Wiedza Powszechna, 1967),
pp. 113–15

DANE, CLEMENCE (GREAT BRITAIN) 1888–1965

In the world of the representative and interpretative imagination all reasonableness and all convincingness is derived from the artist's perfect control over the various strands of moral and physical causality that weave the tragic web. To resort to accident, that is, to the frankly obscure and unexplained, is to sacrifice the intellectual seriousness of your action at once. That is why Clemence Dane's *A Bill of Divorcement* does not, despite its earnestness and power, impress me as being of a tragic character. It may be that after fifteen years of hopeless insanity a man can suddenly regain his reason. But the proof of an action or event must be, as David Hume pointed out long ago, strong in direct proportion to its improbability. Miss Dane has not troubled to supply that proof. That, finally, the suddenly recovered man should wander into his old home on the very Christmas day on which his wife has at last determined to end her long solitariness, is to precipitate a tragic crisis not from within its natural elements but from an alien and extraneous source. Some allowance must indeed be made for the conventionalization of time and space which the drama demands. But it is the unwise playwright who accentuates this unavoidable artifice by the use of festivals and anniversaries and coincidences so perfect as to challenge belief at once.

Ludwig Lewisohn. *The Drama and the Stage* (New York: Harcourt, Brace, 1922),
pp. 99–100

A Bill of Divorcement has been called a propaganda play by people who are unable to distinguish sociological thought from political axe-grinding. But if propaganda, what does it propagate? Miss Dane draws no conclusions about divorce reform, either for or against. Rather, she studies human nature under certain postulates; and her play's "message," if it has a message, seems to be that human nature in 1933 will still sway between desire and convention. For the rest, it is a melodrama of the emotions, with mother and daughter as the vital figures and the others as types. . . . Pity is the mainspring of Miss Dane's creation (you remember *Regiment of Women?*). Dramatically it is her trump card. . . .

With Miss Dane, pity springs deep-rooted from a sense of cruelty which is more keenly developed in her than in any contemporary dramatist. One thinks of Galsworthy: she is more personal than he, being less confined to types. She is as cruel instinctively as Barrie, and in effect more so: for the man's cruelty is obscured and cloyed by sentiment, the woman's cored with a steel whip of indignation which keeps it supple and true; Barrie hides his sense of cruelty, Miss Dane exploits hers to the utmost. Let me be very clear on this, lest in so stressing her cruelty I seem to do Miss Dane an injustice. For I believe this sense of hers, this sharpened susceptibility to the cruel side of life, to be her finest quality. Some natures strangely lack it; we have all known good-natured folk—the sort who "wouldn't hurt a fly"—who are cruel both to animals and men in a way which would horrify them could they perceive it. Others are ultra-sensitive, intensely aware of cruelty even where none was meant—like Mrs. Fairfield [in *A Bill of Divorcement*], you remember, who hated those rat hunts in the barn. And in such finer natures springs, as it were by compensation, a divine and unplumbed pity which goes far beneath sentiment and places them in a class apart. Virgil, first of the great romantics, had this double sense; it is what makes his battle scenes so haunting and memorable. Villon had it, warped towards the macabre by his peculiar circumstances. Shakespeare had it too: and one may notice that Miss Dane fastens instinctively on this in her study [*Will Shakespeare*] of him, even though she misses his yet bigger side, his enormous laughter. Herself, she has it pre-eminently: so that in her work, always so subtly imaginative, her sense of pity for one character often leads her to elaborate the most delicate refinements of cruelty in another.

Graham Sutton. *Some Contemporary Dramatists* (n.p.: Leonard Parsons, 1924), pp. 48–50

A curious case, Miss Clemence Dane's. It is a long while since I read *Regiment of Women,* but I believe it really was an interesting novel. In any case, the writer made it out of very accurate observation, and it was rather improved than otherwise by the fact that she had not, one suspected, the faintest idea of what she was really talking about. Then she started writing plays, and revealed herself to be one third a Sardou, and the rest a sentimentalist and feminist of the most aggressive, not to say, pestilential, order. I think she would now do well to stick to the stage, for which she obviously has an uncommon gift. . . . Her new novel [*Wandering Stars*] is hysterical, and as far as my eyesight carries, worthless.

Raymond Mortimer. *New Statesman and Nation.* April 26, 1924, p. 68

One turns to a play by Clemence Dane with a feeling that both structure and content and theme will be sincere and not chosen and handled for the flim-flam trick of catching the superficial interest. *Mariners* failed as a stage play, and the reading of it—which is profitable—shows the reason why. The intensity of Miss Dane's characterization, the strength of her plea for the younger generation, put out of focus the invention of her situations, which rattle in an otherwise excellent piece of stage writing. And, besides, the American theater-going public will take pot shots at any amusement that has a "sad ending."

Montrose J. Moses. *The Bookman.*
March, 1928, p. 109

The Moon Is Feminine is a tragic fantasy of Brighton in Regency days. I thought that Henry Cope at twenty-six had thoughts old for his age, but a far ancestress of his came from St. Martin's Land—that is, she was a green fairy, and one never knows how people with fairy blood in them will behave. . . . The significance [of this work] may be obscure, but the manners of the Regency are well caught by Miss Dane's distinguished writing, and this novel is as important and as unimportant as something painted by Conder on a fan.

Harold Brighouse. *Manchester Guardian.*
April 26, 1938, p. 7

In *Naboth's Vineyard* Miss Clemence Dane has written a spectacular drama of vigorous opulence. . . . The gorgeous paraphernalia and crowding minor persons do not smother the action. . . . This is less a play than an attractive *tour de force:* it has the swarthy richness of *Salammbô* and something of that slow resistless impetus which marks Victor Hugo.

Gilbert Norwood. *The London Mercury.*
July, 1946, p. 326

DANGAREMBGA, TSITSI (ZIMBABWE) ca. 1958–

I am delighted to recommend this remarkable novelist from Zimbabwe to American readers. One feels that her voice—cool, sardonic, wise—is not simply that of a contemporary African woman, but of an ancient one. Perhaps it is an echo of the early African priestesses: those women who were called to speak to the people about themselves and did not bite their tongues. A voice that is done with charlatans. A voice of a woman who learns to love, as Adrienne Rich advises, "with all her intelligence." A voice that says, with nary a genuflection in any direction, that if Africa is to survive it must transform itself from the hearth outward.

Alice Walker. *Ms.* July–August 1990, p. 61

Tsitsi Dangarembga's first novel, *Nervous Conditions,* provides a fresh and original treatment of themes common to some earlier African novels. A village girl is drawn to the city seeking a salaried job and colonial Western ways. A bright student seeks betterment through education. A "been-to" scholar cannot readjust to home cultural conditions. Dangarembga's somewhat fictionalized autobiography of her early teen years in the 1960s is, however, no stale stereotype. She portrays Tambu, the village poor relation, and Nyasha, her cousin who had spent five years in English schools abroad, as sensitive, bright adolescents. With considerable humor and insight, she makes their crises of self-fulfillment in today's Zimbabwean world the focus of her novel: "This story is how it all began . . . my own story."

Tambu at her village home was better off than her neighbors but lacked most amenities. She was somewhat undernourished, scantily clad, and accustomed at age thirteen to hunger and hard agricultural work. Her schoolmaster uncle decides to bring her to his mission-home school in town for a better education. She shares a room with his daughter Nyasha. Now, perhaps, she can lighten "the poverty of blackness on one side and the weight of womanhood on the other." Many surprises mark her initiation into her new life. She sees flower beds planted, not for utility, but for joy. She first thinks the garage is her new home and is disappointed, but afterward daunted, by the real house, "worried because it wasn't." Passing the packed coat closet, she thinks, "These people . . . never get wet or cold." She is both fascinated and repelled by her outspoken Anglicized cousin. They do learn to communicate despite Tambu's halting English and Nyasha's rusty Shona.

The novel develops with the growing friendship between the two girls. They share their need for education to bring them status, power, and liberation. The relatives and teachers who both heed and hinder their progress are sympathetically and realistically portrayed. Rather than concluding, the story stops shortly after Tambu graduates to a distant mission college and Nyasha survives a nervous breakdown caused by cramming for examinations. Dangarembga takes her title from Fanon's line "The condition of native is a nervous condition." Her excellent style and power of characterization make the book outstanding. We can hope for a continuation of the author's fictionalized autobiography, for as she states, "It was a long and painful process for me, that process of expansion . . . would fill another volume."

Charlotte H. Bruner. *World Literature Today.* 64, 1990, pp. 252–53

Tsitsi Dangarembga's *Nervous Conditions*—a remarkable first novel, winner of the African regional prize in the 1989 Commonwealth Writers' Prize competition—details the hysteric in the colonized's house in Rhodesia on the eve of intensified guerilla struggles in 1969. The hysteric takes several forms: most spectacularly, anorexia nervosa; more banally, angelic housewifely submission, the horizontal violence of naming women witches, the repression of loss which manifests itself in obsessively repeated justifying myths which entrench colonial rule, and "bad nerves" which accompany playing the part of the "good kaffir" of the colonizer's imagination. Dangarembga's epigraph—"'The condition of native is a nervous condition'"—is from Jean-Paul Sartre's Preface to Frantz Fanon's *The Wretched of the Earth,* referred to here simply as "an introduction" to Fanon's text. In the Preface Sartre discusses the repressed sources of the horizontal violence—violence directed at the sister or fellow oppressed—which precedes the vertical violence of wars of independence from colonizing powers. . . .

Western culture, he says, bewitches the "carefully selected unfortunates" of Fanon's black colonial elites: "Our enemy betrays his brothers and becomes our accomplice; his brothers do the same thing. The status of 'native' is a nervous condition introduced and maintained by the settler among colonized people *with their consent.*" The hysteria in *Nervous Conditions* is a product of precariously repressed rage at patriarchal and colonial domination; it is "a defiance through excess, through *overcompliance*" with domination, which "(psychically) mutilates" the self to prevent "brutalization at the hands of others—hence the tragic self-defeat entailed by hysterical resistance." Hysteria is "the *symptomatic acting out* of a proposition the hysteric cannot articulate" within bewitching master narratives or the justifying narratives by which the hysteric is mastered. Dangarembga works to "re-insert" into the histories of "consent" to patriarchal and colonial domination "acts and figures" of resistance under the spectacular and banal signs of the hysteric.

These "acts and figures" bespeak two principal things: the manners in which the sexualities of native men and women are contained and mortified by colonialism and by Shona and Western patriarchy respectively; and the nature and scope of masculine and feminine investment in that libidinal continence and mortification. Dangarembga implicitly qualifies Fanon's argument that "consent" to racial domination is a sign of an inferiority complex, reinforced by material privilege. She extends and "writes back" to Fanon's canonical "master narrative" of post-colonial psychiatric thought and literary criticism. Her "burden" is to "dis/spell," or to use Woolf's metaphor for bloodletting, to "throw the inkpot" at the hysteric by sharply and compassionately representing the justifying myths and narratives which support it. . . .

Dangarembga uses many of Frantz Fanon's key concepts—the creation of a black colonial elite as a means of pacification; the distinctions between physical, structural and psychological violence; the early elaboration but not naming of horizontal violence; the psychological damage wrought by a colonial system of domination; and the need to liberate repressed anger at domination. She extends these concepts significantly, though, by implicitly structuring her critique of the Shona patriarchal system of domination—for Shona women a parallel system of repressive authority to the colonial English—within their terms. Her subtle and discriminating awareness of the causes and processes of libidinal investments which ensure consent to domination and of the operation of hysterical resistance marks an original, important and far-ranging revision of Fanon's work on domination, which as Homi Bhabha rightly observes does not adequately theorize, even implicitly, the question of gender difference.

Sue Thomas. *Journal of Commonwealth Literature.* 27, 1992, pp. 26–27, 34–35

Nervous Conditions . . . provide[s an] indictment of imported educational structures that are totally unsuitable to the African . . . social contexts, particularly as these affect women. Although Tambu makes great efforts to assimilate mission education, and succeeds so well that she wins a scholarship to the prestigious Sacred Heart Convent, she is forced, through her relationship with Nyasha, to recognize the alienation resulting from this. Tambu's family regard education as the key to material prosperity and "emancipation," with Babamukuru, Tambu's uncle and Nyasha's father, representing an object lesson in the cash value of education: "He didn't need to be bold any more because he had made himself plenty of power. Plenty of power. Plenty of money. Plenty of everything." When Tambu performs so brilliantly in the entrance exam that she "thereby earn[s] the privilege of associating with the elite of that time, the privilege of being admitted on an honorary basis into their culture," Nyasha says sarcastically that this would be a "marvelous opportunity" to forget:

> To forget who you were, what you were, and why you were that. The process, she said, was called assimilation, and that was what was intended for the precocious few who might prove a nuisance if left to themselves.

Tambu rejects Nyasha's advice, not because she is fooled by the glamour of the opportunity, but because she sees it as a way of arming herself against patriarchy and poverty. Her determination is fueled by a memory of how her brother had tried to prevent her from continuing her education by destroying the mielie crop which she was hoping to use to finance her own schooling, and the humiliation suffered by her mother when she is forced by their benefactor Babamukuru to participate in a ridiculous charade of a Christian "white wedding."

While the young Tambu defers to Babamukuru on almost every occasion, seeing him as holding the key to her "emancipation," the older narrating Tambu reveals not only the injustices of the patriarchal system, but also how her education enables her to expose it. Unlike Nyasha who no longer knows where she belongs, it is clear that Tambu has not forgotten "who she is and where she comes from" because she is still bound to the rural homestead where her peasant farmer parents live.

Miki Flackemann. *Journal of Commonwealth Literature*. 27, 1992, pp. 41–42

DARK, ELEANOR (AUSTRALIA) 1901–85

A superior piece of craftsmanship [*Return to Coolami*], its approach is indirect and its subject-matter subtle. Indeed, technically the book is a praiseworthy accomplishment, using the stream-of-consciousness method with great ability. The scene is Australia and the occasion of the story an automobile trip of a family of four from a Sydney suburb to the sheep ranch of Coolami some three hundred miles away. The reader is permitted to observe the thoughts of each of the four travelers, and insofar as they do become distinct it is in each other's thoughts rather than in their own. The difficulties of Susan, the young wife, are the substance of the story, but she is so much a spoiled and willful neurotic that the reader is hard taxed to give her problems sufficient sympathetic attention. That is where Miss Dark, for all her technical dexterity, fails in the task of providing entertainment.

Love also triumphs in *Return to Coolami:* it is love between the sexes. This provides the dominant emotion for all the characters; their intellects grasp no other certainty, there is nothing more powerful to move their faiths. It is a common heresy in the modern world and the modern novel.

Geoffrey Stone. *Commonweal.*
October 16, 1936, p. 592

In the first novel [*Slow Dawning*] naturally [Dark] shows her hand most clearly and is most openly romantic; but in all [three], though in ever stronger doses, she uses the same astringents. She uses as a counterblast to herself an insistent frankness and realism in detail, but never allows it to go too far. Just as the leading traits in the three heroines are courage, honesty and candor, which save them from any accusation of being "pretty dears," so a certain realism is imported into the structure of the stories. Life is faced. The heroines face it, but they never go too far. . . .

It is in her technique rather than in her matter that Eleanor Dark has added luster to Australian fiction. The criticism that is most frequently brought against Australian fiction in the mass is that it is bald, crude and ingenuous. Such books as *Prelude to Christopher* and *Return to Coolami* do something to redress the balance. They have a technical subtlety to delight the heart of the craftsman. It is in the elaboration of her technique that Eleanor Dark shows the development of her talent and the virtuosity of which she is capable; it is curiously separated from both the matter of her novels and the premises which lie behind them.

M. Barnard Eldershaw. *Essays in Australian
Fiction* (Melbourne: Melbourne University
Press, 1938), pp. 193–95

Mrs. Dark, to her credit, saw [in *The Timeless Land*] that the very unworthiness of so many of [Governor Arthur] Phillip's associates brought out in him qualities of exceptional vision and nobility. One cannot perhaps credit the British Navy with producing quite such a contemplative Marcus Aurelius as the author paints the Governor. But Phillip's letters prove him to have been an unusually wise administrator, and in any event this study of the inner struggles of a man of fine sensibilities shouldering his heavy responsibilities in a situation of extraordinary loneliness is a fine literary achievement that is its own justification. . . .

If anything stands in the way of *The Timeless Land* taking rank as an Australian classic, it is the preponderance of interest devoted to the natives in an account of a primitive existence that is largely drawn from purely conventionalized impressions of bush life. Nevertheless, Mrs. Dark has found new things to say about Australia. She avoids all the over-reiterated detail of the Australian scene and introduces masses of fresh and interesting material in a mature style that breaks entirely with the old romantic frontier medium of the Adam Lindsay Gordon order that has governed so much of Australian literature hitherto.

H. J. S. *Christian Science Monitor.*
January 17, 1942, p. 10

Eleanor Dark has produced a rich, tidy opus [*Storm of Time*] that has to do with the early colonization of Australia. She dexterously manages the chaotic events that range from 1799 to 1808 by dividing the novel into three sections corresponding to the terms of the three governors sent by the Crown to rule New South Wales during that time. By the bye, the third governor is Bligh, who eighteen years or so before his governorship was captain of the *Bounty*. He is not painted as the Hollywood ogre. A stern and quick-tempered man, yes, but there is sufficient to rouse him in a clique of ruthless, land-rich colonial exploiters.

The author gives a comprehensive view of the greedy owners, the ignorant natives, the swarm of exiled convicts and the confused officials. She gives cohesion to the novel by carrying through it such characters as the convict Finn, the imperious landowner Mannion and his gentle Irish wife, and the young renegade Johnny who lives as a native. A highly readable, expertly balanced novel.

Catholic World. May, 1950, pp. 153–54

We can trace in [Eleanor Dark] a development from a preoccupation with the humanist utopia on a level, in terms, shared by Furphy and O'Dowd, to a preoccupation with the primal integrity of Australia as a place—a preoccupation not very far removed from the primitive animalism of Jindyworobaks. In *Prelude to Christopher,* there is a constant preoccupation with the failure of the Lane experiment in Paraguay, rather dimmed by a somewhat colorless mist of eugenics; and it is a preoccupation with failure that, at crucial moments, opens up discussion on the possibilities of the experiment so that we are left in the end with Eleanor Dark's attitude remaining unsolved as an attitude, remaining as an intellectual dilemma. This is a kind of honesty we should not have found entirely unexpected in her, for she is Dowell O'Reilly's daughter.

In *Return to Coolami,* what draws the tense and emotionally burdened family through the dangerous details of their drive is the attraction of Coolami, the cleansing, heartening quality of the place, and the ethos of comforting nature which it embodies. At one moment we think the attraction is mere nostalgia, at another we are persuaded of its capacity really to heal and hearten. . . .

Eleanor Dark is far from being a negligible writer; and I can't help finding something greatly significant in her journey, even if, or rather especially since, it ended in what I consider imaginative failure. The search for the significance of the utopia of Furphy and O'Dowd, influenced surely by Furphy and O'Dowd, has ended in a nostalgic re-reading of pre-history, which puts utopia in the past and makes it inaccessible to the European consciousness. The line of influence is there; the idea of utopian humanism has had its long-term effect. The result is failure.

Vincent Buckley. Quadrant. 3:2, 1958–59,
pp. 45–46

Eleanor Dark is far from being defeatist in the sense that Vance Palmer can be, and she is hardly a fatalist in her historical novels, but in her other novels accidents often play a decisive role, so that it may be said that they abound in fatalism. This constant employment of accident as a *deus ex machina* has been labeled melodramatic, but I suspect that it is probably a form of realism coming naturally to the wife of a doctor who may be concerned with accidental death and injury day by day. On the other hand, I feel that there is very little somberness of fatalism, little sense of man as victim, since the accident seems created, not by fate, but by the firm shaping hand of Eleanor Dark the skillful craftsman. . . .

It was surprising when Eleanor Dark, whose novels had been marked by seriousness and dignity, emerged as a genuine humorist with the delightful drollery of *Lantana Lane,* which combined touches of satire and wit with comedy of character and the humor of misadventure. One sketch, "Sweet and Low," as vulgar as Chaucer, triumphs as one of the funniest stories in Australian writing.

T. Inglis Moore. Social Patterns in
Australian Literature (Berkeley: University
of California Press, 1971), pp. 154–55, 193

In her early novels Eleanor Dark approached women's experience from three perspectives. *Slow Dawning* deals with the difficulties of maintaining oneself as an autonomous intellectual and sexual being. *Return to Coolami* attempts to isolate the nature and experience of love and *Prelude to Christopher* focuses on maternity and the psychology of motherhood. *Slow Dawning,* written early in the 1920s, is her most explicit feminist statement; she wrote it in the early 1920s with an eye to make money, but it was not published until 1931 and she later disowned it as a "potboiler." . . .

Slow Dawning openly discusses women's sexual feelings with scanty reliance on the range of euphemism usually found in women's fiction of that period. Eleanor Dark acknowledges women's sexual needs and in exposing the double standard of sexual morality makes the quite extraordinary statement that there are no facilities like brothels for women. Despite this audacious suggestion, she is not seriously advocating brothels for women, for informing every discussion of sexuality, waiting in the wings, is love; it is love, ultimately, that is the powerful force in women's lives. . . .

In *Slow Dawning* there is no attempt to make any analysis of the class nature of Australian society or the economic and political conditions underpinning these "tragedies." The solutions Eleanor Dark envisaged are based on a bourgeois conception of the family and bourgeois expectations of work. . . .

Yet *Slow Dawning* remains interesting because, of these early novels, it alone offers a hint of collective political action by women, even though this hint is overridden by its reliance on individual solutions.

In *Prelude to Christopher*, Eleanor Dark experimented with techniques and devices that were being taken up in Europe between the wars. She used a compressed and shifting time-scale, interior monologue and stream of consciousness to present a peculiarly intense psychological analysis of a woman whose sanity is under threat. These experiments, which continued in all her fiction, except the historical trilogy, set her apart, in technique. . . .

While *Slow Dawning* had criticized the tyranny of unwanted maternity and the birth of children into poverty and disease, *Prelude to Christopher* points to motherhood as the fundamental experience for women through which they lay claim to their social influence. It is a claim made through the relationship between femaleness and nature. There is a long history in fiction, and even more in poetry, of metaphors from nature being used for womanhood and for female sexuality. This is a tradition that women writers have inherited but with which, yet again, they find themselves in an ambiguous relationship. Eleanor Dark does not use the symbolism of flowers, so frequently used for femaleness with undertones of frailty and delicacy. She uses the much tougher, even phallic, image of trees. It is because of their maternity that women are "rooted like trees"; it is because of this connection that women represent "the fundamental laws of humanity." Social conflict and imbalance, even war, are explained by the absence of this connection with nature, by the domination of the masculine principles—power, aggression and "the laws of science"—to the exclusion not only of women themselves but the humanity they represent. In *Return to Coolami*, the third of Dark's early novels, Marjorie warns that as the "feminine brain starved and hampered through the ages is fighting at last into its own," women will put their price on maternity. They will not continue to bear children "into a world not fit to receive them" and the world will become fit only with the full integration of the female intellect and female humanism into the ordering of society, that is when "nature" and "society" are brought together. This idea of striking against childbirth, while polemically arresting, was of course totally impracticable. Yet it was put up seriously by women who were acutely sensitive to the symbolism of motherhood. Such a suggestion indicates the difficulties women writers faced once they moved off the safe terrain of personal resolutions in their fiction. With no theoretical or political backing in which they could ground their feminism, they were forced into rather awkward metaphors.

> Drusilla Modjeska. *Exiles at Home:*
> *Australian Women Writers, 1925–1945*
> (London: Angus and Robertson, 1981),
> pp. 215–20

DAS, KAMALA (INDIA) 1934–

The . . . ability to remain entirely true to a certain viewpoint characterizes Kamala Das's writing . . . . But if this ability gives Mamta Kalia's work originality and freshness, it gives Kamala Das's power. This is reinforced by Kamala Das's concentration on what amounts to virtually one theme in her two books, *Summer in Calcutta* published in 1965 and *The Descendants* published in 1967. She writes about love, or rather, the failure of love or the absence of love with the obsessiveness of a woman who can realize her being fully only through love. . . .

But in her best poems, it is impossible not to be moved by and involved in the passionate urge and drive of the rhythm, the haunting images of sterility *(Dance of the Eunuchs),* the ultimate resilience in the face of any relationship that threatens to devastate her vital and potential self.

> Eunice De Souza. In Saleem Peeradina, ed.
> *Contemporary Indian Poetry in English*
> (Bombay: Macmillan, 1972), pp. 85–86

Almost all the critics of Kamala Das have been quick to notice that part of the strength of her poetry emanates from her powerful personality. But while the vigor of her personality seems to operate rather transparently, and on the surface as it were, it does not detract from the complexity of the woman's ambivalence which is the core of her recurrent theme of the certitude and the precariousness of sexual love. . . .

The obvious elemental force of Kamala Das's poetry might tempt one to over-simplify the complexity of her work, and, no doubt, the phrase "virgin whiteness" (which she herself uses in "The Fear of the Year") provides the necessary clue: interpreting the phrase not in the conventional sense of undefiled purity or piety but, rather using the sexual analogue which Kamala Das so often suggests through her imagery, in the sense of a raw, unsophisticated concentration of impulses and reactions to situations. Whiteness suggests, in the first place, this complex but intense concentration of psychological gestures under the almost presiding agency of the images of heat, especially that of the sun; and secondly, the absorptive, all-devouring sensibility of the poet. Here is the "unending lust, the ocean's tireless waiting": first, the woman's sexual lust, and then the poet's lust for experience for sights as well as insights. While the former is explicitly treated only in poems such as "A Relationship" and significantly tangled with other considerations in others, the latter is more suggested than realized, more a devouring of sights and sounds than an organic synthesis of these into an evolving and consistently sustained vision of life, despite her avowed "love for this gift of life more than all." True, there is a sense in which the theme of the woman's "unending lust" seems to swell into a larger, more symbolic lust for life. . . .

Kamala Das is essentially a poet of the modern Indian woman's ambivalence, giving expression to it more nakedly and as a thing-in-itself than any other Indian woman poet. The reason for this is, I think, that she seems to have a good deal of the conventional woman in her makeup, so that not only is she able to speak of the common woman and her basic need for love and security with inside knowledge, but cannot help, in addition, expressing an ambivalence proceeding from her own duality, proceeding from, that is, the combination in herself of a need for domestic security and the desire for an independence, an independence consistent with a non-domestic mode of living. Married at the age of fifteen, and finding herself tied to a hollow relationship which she could not untie, Kamala Das's story, despite its sensationalism which seems partly contrived, makes poignant reading and in essence strikes one as representative of a not so uncommon social phenomenon in India. Marriage and love are not and need not be mutually exclusive, but for Kamala Das, as she tells us time and time again, they have proved to be so. When Kamala Das speaks for love outside marriage she is not really propagating adultery and infidelity, but merely searching for a relationship which gives both love and security. Thus it is not without significance that she should give a mythical framework to her search for true love, and identify it with the Radha-Krishna myth or with Mira Bai's relinquishing of the ties of marriage in search of Lord Krishna, the true lover.

Devindra Kohli. Kamala Das (New Delhi:
Arnold-Heinemann, 1975),
pp. 15, 23–24, 27–28

Kamala Das is one of our few significant poets writing in English today. She is pre-eminently a poet and has truly made a mark for her poems rather than her prose writings with variegated interests. It is not improper to assert that she has a paucity of experience which allows her but little scope to comprehend the varieties of life and also that now she has nothing new to say or say anew. What strikes a reader is not this paucity of experience but her compelling originality and freshness as also her command over the verse technique and the English language which has long been, duly and unduly, called an alien medium with respect to our poets writing in this language. . . .

Kamala Das made an instant appeal with her first collection *Summer in Calcutta* (1965) As a poet, she explores her psychic geography with an exceptional female energy and achieves the capability to express her inimitable vision through the technique of sincerity. She has shown through her promise and fulfillment the mark of redoubtable poetic genius. Whatever the form and value of her poetry, her poetic stance is genuine and she has nearly achieved the discipline of form.

With her *self* as the central myth, Kamala Das has shown large human catholicities and acquired the technique of sincerity to express the intangible in experience. It is natural that we find her saying: "I myself had no control over my writing which emerged like a rash of prickly heat in certain season." The season she means is obviously the season of her basic, irremediable self which is the poetic nucleus of the confessional poets. All poetry is basically a confessional act though the label identifies particularly the poets like Robert Lowell, Theodore Roethke, Anne Sexton, John Berryman, Sylvia Plath in America and Kamala Das in India. But Kamala Das, among all the poets in the confessional genre, stands in splendid isolation owing to her eminently personal note. Shaking the pan-Indian feminism, she writes of her private anguish in an effortless manner. This may adequately be called her expressive form. . . .

What is more remarkable in Kamala Das is that her poetry mirrors her life in all its nakedness—the oft-experienced horrors and the rare joys of love. Her life itself violate the chiseled, systematic and traditional norms and values and she affirms to a form of life which is characterized by the unconventional and extremely modern point of view. This form of life is truly reflected in the form she achieves in her poetic practice. There is no conventional metrical form but free verse, a harvest of imagery with which she identifies herself, rather exclusively, a choice of diction, usually envenomed and pointed. It is appropriate to say that Kamala Das creates a free form, shaking all the established norms of life and art.

Anisur Rahman. *Expressive Form in the Poetry of Kamala Das* (New Delhi: Abhinov, 1981), pp. xi, 1–2

Kamala Das's *Summer in Calcutta* (1965) appeared at a time when English poetry by Indian women had moved on from such colonial and nationalist themes as the rewriting of legends, praise of peasants, and from general ethical statements to writing about personal experiences. While outmoded diction and sentiments were at last overtaken in favor of a more contemporary and less artificial manner, the subject matter of the women poets was often limited to well-meaning platitudes about romantic love, which were treated without depth, complexity, interest or even the projection of much emotion. By contrast the poems of Kamala Das when focused on love treat it within a broader ranges of themes, more realized settings and with deeper feeling, bringing to it an intensity of emotion and speech and a rich, full complexity of life. Das's themes go beyond stereotyped longings and complaints. Even her feelings of loneliness and disappointment are part of a larger-than-life personality, obsessive in its awareness of its self, yet creating a drama of selfhood.

Having started writing verse in school and having early published in *Indian PEN* (1948), Kamala Das evolved from a rudimentary poet using traditional verse methods to someone with a highly personal voice but without strong awareness of technique or theory. She is a natural poet with an excellent feeling for sound, rhythm, phrasing, image, symbol, word play, and drama. The prosody of her early poems is mostly a matter of counting syllables in a regular rhythm. Later, as her versification and sense of form became freer and looser, her style changed but did not necessarily improve. Always a hit-or-miss poet, who wrote regularly but trusted the muse more than revision, she began to miss more often.

Her early poems are primarily concerned with her marriage, love life, desire for intimacy and the various results—including guilt—and her fame as a writer. . . .

Alongside Das's unfilled need for love, another prominent subject of her poems is the need to assert, to conquer, to dominate. There is, for example, her obsession with an older man who "hurt" her in her teens and whom she obsessively feels she must capture as her lover. In her poetry love and hate are often neighbors, just as an assertion of sexual freedom sits near feelings of self-disgust expressed through depression. The theater of Das's poetry includes the revelations, the confessions, the various contradictory bits and pieces. While the poems describe a longing for a man to fill her dreams with love, she is also proud of her conquests, and ability to make men love her. Having taken a lover she will mock him. Rather than the seduced, she often appears the seducer, the collector, especially of those men known as lady killers. Driven by a need for an all-encompassing love to fill her days, she is also someone involved in the game of sexual triumph with its trophies. . . .

If many poems speak of unhappiness and the desire for an all-absorbing love, others are filled with Das's discovery of the life around her on the streets and in bedrooms. While marriage has hurt her ego, leaving her unfulfilled, her poems also record a woman enjoying the newness of the world as she wanders the streets and pursues her own interests. The poems in *Summer in Calcutta* and even the later, sometimes more somber, depressed verses, written after serious illness, reveal someone younger, more questing, more sexually driven than the author of *My Story* with its claim that being treated brutally led to adultery and its self-apologetics and spiritualist conclusion. The poems show that through her sexual confessions her writing has made her a self-conscious celebrity; and she plays up to it, often bragging and celebrating. . . .

Writing is a means of creating a place in the world; the use of the personal voice and self-revelation are means of self-assertion. Das opened areas in which previously forbidden or ignored emotions could be expressed in ways which reflect the true voice of feeling; she showed how an Indian woman poet could create a space for herself in the public world. She brings a sense of locality to her poems. There are the rooms in which she lives, the homes she has left, the bedrooms, restaurants and streets in which she meets her lovers, the rides in cars, the people she visits or notices, the people she addresses in personal terms. . . . Das's poems assume their location, create their space by being set in situations rather than by observing or alluding to their environment.

Kamala Das's most remarkable achievement, however, is writing in an Indian English. Often her vocabulary, idioms, choice of verbs and some syntactical constructions are part of what has been termed the Indianization of English. This is an accomplishment. It is important in the development of a national literature that writers free themselves from the linguistic standards of their colonizers and create a literature based on local speech; and this is especially important for women writers. Such a development is not a matter of national pride or a linguistic equivalent of "local color"; rather it is a matter of voice, tone, idiom and rhythm, creating a style that accurately reflects what the writer feels or is trying to say instead of it being filtered through speech meant to reflect the assumptions and nuances of another society.

Bruce King. *Modern Indian Poetry in English* (New Delhi: Oxford University Press, 1987), pp. 147–53

Kamala Das lends a new dimension to her love poetry by revealing her kinship with an anterior Indian tradition which has its roots in Indian epics. Apart from this, her Nayar background not only provides a suitable background but also strengthens the confessional streak of her poetry. Thus the significant aspect of her love poetry is the merger of two traditions—the Indian and the Western. It is in this light that an attempt is made here to examine Kamala Das's love poetry.

Search for love is the principal preoccupation of Kamala Das's poetry. She confesses with utmost candor that she "began to write poetry with the ignoble aim of wooing a man." As a result love becomes the pervasive theme and it is through love that she endeavors to discover herself. As she concerns herself with various facets of love, her love poetry can be divided into two phases. While in the first phase her obsessive concern with physical love is quite prominent, in the second, her drift towards ideal love can be discerned. By ideal love she means the kind of relation that exists between the legendary Radha and Krishna. She yearns for such a love which does not impede her impulse to freedom. . . .

In the narcissistic phase, the lovers do not outgrow their egos which stand as hurdles preventing their merger. They are chained in self-admiration.

But it is not a permanent phase as it undergoes mutations seeking "total freedom." It is in the second phase of ideal love that the lovers transgress the boundaries of their egos or narrow selves to merge with each other, as such merger ensures total freedom. The poet beholds such an exemplary relation in the love between Radha and Krishna. She surmises herself as Radha who goes in search of Krishna, the ideal lover, in spite of her marriage. This brings into her poetic context the *Abhisarika* tradition of Sanskrit poetry. Besides this her uninhibited treatments of love and sex reminds one of *Sahaja* tradition.

But in Kamala Das the element of *bhakti* is absent. Her relation with Krishna is purely human. She confesses, "I was looking for an ideal lover. I was looking for the one who went to Mathura and forgot to return to his Radha." Thus the poet lives simultaneously in two worlds, the actual world, where love usually is a synonym for lust—in her words "skin communicated love," and the mythical world of Vrindavan.

While there is so much in her poetry which seems to draw from earlier Indian traditions, there are also various shades of physical love described in the confessional mode. This mode of expression suits her as she ventilates her personal experiences and humiliations and also the intensity of her experience. In conformity with the confessional tradition, she talks in poetic terms about her unpleasant sexual experiences. Inevitably her poems are autobiographical. This lends a kind of authenticity to her poetry which is found lacking in much of love poetry written today. . . .

Kamala Das's love poems stand apart as they fruitfully combine the indigenous traditions such as *Abhisarika* and *Sahaja* and the confessional tradition which is western. Her love poetry is a fine blending of the two different literary traditions.

P. Mallikarjuna Rao. *Kakatiya Journal of English Studies.* 8, 1987–88, pp. 60–62, 66–67

Kamala Das as we meet her towards the end of her story is not the same Kamala whom we met in the beginning of her story. The change that her being has undergone is manifest at several levels. Besides the physical changes that she has undergone, one can perceive the psychic change too. The last few chapters reflect a phoenix-like emergence of a new being from the ashes of the past, the changing relations between the Being and the Other. The evolution of her ideas from hedonism to altruism to mysticism is evident. The senses are cleansed and humbled, the self has surrendered itself, its individuality and its will. No longer a narcissist concerned with her own self, she is now concerned with the problems of man's situation in the world. She can now participate in the "great life of the All." The inward journey ends up with the realization of the self. The one who was dark and had always lived in darkness seems to have come to light, to wisdom.

She is obviously a restructured whole now. From "I" consciousness, she moves on to the cosmic consciousness. She has developed an attitude of compassion. Her all-embracing love is characteristic of the illumination. The one who was a great egoist, a narcissist, seems to have arrived at the truth that "Blessed are the poor in Spirit, for theirs is the Kingdom of Heaven." The individual ego, no longer deludes her. She is no longer ignorant about the true nature of man's existence and the universe in which he lives. Now she feels that the cosmos belongs to her and she to it. So, the boundaries of self are extended. She lacked knowledge about reality. This ignorance was the cause of her anguish. When she attains knowledge, she attains freedom from all suffering. After the death of her ego (Hankara) she tries to look for her original relation to herself, to the world and the Other, in the unity of internal relations and of a fundamental project.

Iqbal Kaur. *Untying and Retying the Text:*
An Analysis of Kamala Das's My Story
(New Delhi: Bahri, 1990), pp. 257–58

DELBO, CHARLOTTE (FRANCE) n.d.–1985

For two thousand years, we have lamented the death of Christ, Mrs. Delbo tells us, but he agonized (according to her) for only three days and three nights. We pass over her interpretation of the Agony of Christ. What tears will we have for those who agonized more than three hundred nights? The repetition of "trois cents nuits et beaucoup plus de trois cents journées" twice in the same sentence reinforces the length of time. The bitterness is apparent. "Ils ne croyaient pas à la résurrection dans l'éternité / Et ils savaient que vous ne pleureriez pas." This is a dominant theme, not only of *Aucun de nous* but also of *Qui rapportera ces paroles:* none shall cry for those who suffered. This phenomenon is beyond understanding. It is easier to accept that one man suffered on the cross and died to redeem humanity than it is to accept the *"inconcevable,"* that six million died and four million returned after a trip to the other end of the earth. The futility of their suffering is contained in "Et ils savaient que vous ne pleureriez pas." If their suffering would change nothing, would bring about nothing new, then they were suffering for nothing, and they were aware of the futility of their suffering.

The leitmotif of those who "know" is one of the dominant themes of *Aucun de nous.* We are surprised that there are so many things that can be learned from life in camp: that hunger brightens the eyes, that thirst dims them, that one's eyes can stay dry at the death of the mother that one loved, that in the morning one wants to die, that at night one is afraid, that a day is longer than a year, that a minute is longer than a life, that the heart, the eyes and the nerves are the most durable parts of the body, that stones do not cry, that there is only one word for terror and one for anguish.

Here, Charlotte Delbo is illustrating part of her technique. If there is only one word for terror and one for anguish, then there is no need to look for synonyms. The repetition of the same word conveys the repetitions of a suffering that never changes, of a terror that never relents and that never is metamorphosed. Familiar words do not have the same meaning because the frame of reference from which they are being drawn is so different. The author will therefore recreate this frame of reference, at the same time fully realizing that she cannot at any time leave it to our imaginations because life in Auschwitz is beyond imagination.

> Cynthia Haft. *The Theme of the Nazi*
> *Concentration Camps in French Literature*
> (The Hague: Mouton, 1973), pp. 133–34

Charlotte Delbo's *Auschwitz et après* was published by the Editions de Minuit in 1970 and 1971. The three-volume series, *Aucun de nous ne reviendra, Une Connaissance inutile,* and *Mesure de nos jours,* constitutes her memoirs of the twenty-seven months of imprisonment in Nazi concentration camps to which her Resistance activities in France had condemned her. On the surface, *Auschwitz et après* is an extremely literary organization of prose and poetry; its episodes are presented for the most part achronologically, with juxtaposition and flashback the dominant means of transition between them. It is perhaps by reason of the nightmare effect produced by such an organization that [Alvin] Rosenfeld includes *Auschwitz et après* among the "surrealist" responses to the Holocaust, while for Cynthia Haft, whose study of French literature on the camps gives a privileged position to Delbo, the series represents "perhaps the purest and most sensitive *chants tragiques* about concentration camps.

> Yet such categorization, even by one so wary as Rosenfeld of calling Holocaust literature "literature," and the apparent literariness of the trilogy itself, should not mislead us into thinking that *Auschwitz et après* is the solution posed by Delbo to the problem of language as representation of atrocity. The substantial time interval separating the memoirs from the events they recount suggests, rather, that for Delbo as for other Holocaust writers, the experience of atrocity has rendered language suspect, if not entirely meaningless.

In Delbo . . . it is not only the problem of referent, that is, the experience of atrocity, of deeds too horrible to recount in words, that threatens the verbal representation of that experience; it is, rather, the loss of faith in the process of signification itself, begun and completed at Auschwitz. Critics, such as Langer and Haft, have suggested that the choice of the writer willing to confront and convey the horror of the Holocaust, is between factual narration and imaginative reconstruction. Although Delbo's earlier *Convoi du 24 janvier* is a painstaking exercise in biography and the establishment of the facts concerning the fate of the 230 deportees in her transport, in *Auschwitz et après,* more directly centered upon the conditions of existence in the camps, she maintains the choice between recollection and reconstruction as a perpetual tension between *l'histoire* and *des histoires,* between history and stories. Such tension is all the more problematic, of course, for disbelief in the possibility of signification undermines Delbo's obligatory representation of the experience by which that belief was lost. . . .

In place of these codes . . . these groundless fabrications that she inherits on her return to culture, Delbo opposes a narration that steadfastly refuses to accept invention, that points out its own embellishments the better to represent, paradoxically, the absolute inability to represent that defined the camps. . . .

Other Holocaust writers besides Delbo, acutely aware that their context and codes are no longer those of their readers, have shared the concern for credibility evident in her appeal to an eyewitness, in her despair at the characteristics of fiction thus appropriated by history. "We'll have the thankless job of proving to a reluctant world that we are Abel, the murdered brother," says Dr. Schipper in *The Holocaust Kingdom.* How can it not seem to the reader that Abel's voice is an invented one? The women in *Auschwitz et après* and in Delbo's plays as well repeatedly lament this catch-22 of the murdered brother that they know undermines all they can ever say about the camps. . . . How can the stories even begin to sound like history when the narrator admits that by rights they *ought* to be fiction and that she herself ought not to exist?

Rosette Lamont has suggested that Delbo's return to the theater after *Auschwitz et après* marked her rejection of discursive and even lyrical narration in favor of the stark visual imagery and communal (theatrical) experience that might begin to close the contextual gap between the speakers from the camps and their audience. In theater or in memoir, however, there remains always in Delbo the oxymoron that marks the "revenante" as semiotic outcast in her own culture, unwilling heiress to the inhuman and anti-humanist legacy of Nazism. Reading *Auschwitz et après,* one wonders with Charlotte Delbo just how it can mean anything that one has "survived a death camp," and so ponders the chilling question buried at the heart of her work; if, inevitably, *cela devient une histoire,* might it not have been better for the sake of coherence if no one had ever come back at all?

Renée A. Kincaid. French Forum. 9:1, 1984,
pp. 98–99, 105–8

Words have so often been used for lies, for propaganda, that it has become difficult to believe. Charlotte Delbo, a graduate of Auschwitz, a poet of the Holocaust *(Aucun de nous ne reviendra, Une connaissance inutile, Mesure de nos jours),* became a dramatist partly because she realized that words were not sufficient to convey the truth she bore. She had to concretize this truth in images. There, the ghosts, her dead companions, came back to life. And yet, one must not think for a moment that Delbo is a realist. "All is true, but the dramaturgic means are entirely free of realism," she said to this writer on the night of "La Générale" of *Qui rapportera ces paroles?* (March 18, 1974).

The latter is a dramatic poem enacted upon a bare stage, tilted up to suggest a grotesque world where not only work is hardship, but the mere act of standing still. The women, dressed in the same colorless, sack-like tunics, a kerchief on their heads, do not resemble prisoners as much members of a Greek chorus. No structure attempts to reproduce the blockhouse, but as we see them lie down, huddle together to keep close for warmth, we know that they are "inside." No clear difference is made, between inner and outer space since all physical space is that of imprisonment. Only the space of the text can take us out of that condition, in the telling of dreams, the occasional exchanges of hopes, the planning of lives in some future of found freedom. We do not need to see the barbed wire fence, the dogs, the guards, to know what is happening. The women tell us: their lips whisper, their eyes, wide with horror, convey the murder of a friend, her throat torn by police dogs, her brain spilling under the blows of a guard, or the removal of one of them from the ranks as, unfit for work, her legs swollen, she is conveyed to the death house. Are we like those who listen to the stories of the survivors without having witnessed the events'? Not so. The miracle of the stage is that we cannot disbelieve these faces pale with fatigue, with fear, even as we tell ourselves that the pallor is stage makeup. The life on the stage is real life, or rather it is life intensified. It convinces us in a way that documentaries and photographs do not. There is a surfeit of horror when we are faced with the records of the real, but the truth of art involves us directly since the tragic events presented in its mirror send us back our own image, that of the fate of humankind.

Delbo's Aeschylean tragedy, with the chorus of women as the main actor, opens with Francoise's prologue wherein she states that she has come back from "the place of no return." It ends with the spoken duet of the same Françoise, now accompanied by one of the youngest of the prisoners; the two of them are the survivors of the group. Within the closed circle of Francoise's and Denise's dirge, the play, divided into three acts but performed without an intermission, falls into that single action which constitutes the essence of classical drama according to Aristotelian definition.

Charlotte Delbo's *Qui rapportera ces paroles?* is closer to Aeschylus and to Dante's *Purgatorio* than to Sophocles or to Aristotle's theory of Greek dramaturgy. Like the author of the *Commedia,* Charlotte Delbo keeps an eye on "the tragic moving of the psyche itself." Although the Christian signs of Faith, Hope and Charity are no longer on the horizon, the camp inmates exchange their impressions of the day, communicate to one another some of their dreams and nightmares, some of their fears and aspirations. Like all great tragedies, Delbo's play is not only a contemplation of dissolution, but a celebration of life even in the face of death.

Rosette C. Lamont. *L'Esprit Créateur.* 19, 1979, pp. 68–69

In her own writing Delbo uses the first person singular sparingly. Most of the time she will speak through a collective "nous." This is not to be taken as "a self-effacing style," as is suggested by Marlene E. Heinemann in her recently completed but still unpublished study, *Women Prose Writers of the Nazi Holocaust.* Rather one ought to view the collective pronoun as a self-conscious attempt to transmit what the Russian dissident writer Andrey Siniavsky calls "A Voice from the Chorus." The great writers who have emerged from "l'univers concentrationnaire" are natural classicists, and moralists: they do not seek individual expression; they are the sacred interpreters of the dead and the survivors.

Delbo does not wish to write a personal memoir, but to create a series of prose poems that will speak for all those who were with her. She addresses the universal consciousness of today, and that of thinking people in the centuries to come. "Il faut donner à voir," she says with passionate intensity. Her purpose is to raise the image of the camps for all to see.

Delbo's style is clear, pure, well-balanced. She needs to do little or even no rewriting. By the time a text pours out of her it seems to have assumed its final form within her wonderfully lucid mind. This does not mean, however, that it is ready for publication. In the case of *None of Us Will Return (Aucun de nous ne reviendra),* Charlotte had the supreme courage, self-control, and strength of purpose to hold on to it for twenty years in order to put the text to the test of time. If surviving is part courage, part instinct, the determination to convey, or crystallize the unforgettable image of camp life without being hasty, vengeful, or simply didactic, takes a wrenching kind of honesty.

Each one of Charlotte Delbo's prose poems is a quintessential concentrate of an extreme situation or condition: nudity (the result of forced public disrobing), hunger, thirst, fear, powerless pity, bloodless exhaustion, illness, a slow dying. As Elie Wiesel once stated in the course of a public lecture: "Words, simple, every day words such as 'bread,' 'water,' 'sleep' did not signify the same thing in camp as they did and do outside. Nor can they ever mean the same to those of us who have issued from *l'univers concentrationnaire.*"

The Holocaust writer faces a dilemma: to compose a tragic work, classical in its intention to address each and every one, and yet raise the image of what Dante could only paint in Hell. In the work of Wiesel, Semprun, Delbo, the incidental, the contingent evaporate leaving in the alchemical *vas* of literary language something so powerfully direct and physical that it becomes, paradoxically, metaphysical. This can only happen when the intention of the writer is to produce a work of art, something beyond bearing witness. . . .

When Delbo describes her companions, she sees them as both tragic and strangely comical. They wear their long coats backwards in order to carry in the stretched out bottom part the earth and stones needed to create a garden at the camp's gate. This additional work, mortal to those already weakened, was performed on the day of the Lord, Sunday. The women, Charlotte notes, particularly the Jewish prisoners who had no special aprons, looked like penguins. It was impossible to preserve a feeling of one's humanity, to recall a world in which one had used a toothbrush, purchased a piece of soap, reached for a breakfast croissant, and—most unthinkable of all—applied perfume as a kind of floating, invisible dress, a veil of scent. Women tried to remember they had once been women, and people, but this was almost beyond the reach of their memory. They had become beasts of burden, and the cogwheels of the immense, and senseless technological machinery of the Nazi state. . . .

The women of Delbo's trilogy *(Aucun de nous ne reviendra, Mesure de nos jours, Une conaissance inutile)* seem to move in a dream dreamt by some evil force that holds them in thralldom, a nightmare from which they cannot awaken since they are not the dreamers, since the evil dreamer is out of reach.

Within this unreality which had become their only reality, a light remained—for some—a memory of the other life. It came from words, from literature. For Charlotte who knew that literature, drama, theater were all aspects of life, a deeper, more intense kind of life, this universe of art held the real. They (her captors) could imprison her, send her to forced labor, plan to end her life, but they could not take from her that world peopled by characters she knew as well if not better than her family and friends.

In her novella, "Phantoms, My Companions" ("Spectres mes compagnons"), Delbo evokes what it means to be in touch with these vivid ghosts, literary characters. . . .

Who will endure the horror of camp life? What literary character might share this extreme form of exile. Charlotte is certain at first that she is now irretrievably alone. But, at that very moment, she catches a glimpse of Electra. Delbo writes: "She stood at the edge of a line formed by reeds, and it seemed to me that she wore a proud, resolute smile."

Electra heralds in other "resurrections": Giraudoux's Ondine, Molière's Don Juan, even Proust's Oriane. These ghosts made of words will live side by side with women whose flesh is melting from their bones, turning them into ghostlike creatures. Words can be as palpable as flesh; they can lend dignity to those who have been stripped of pride and hope.

Charlotte Delbo tells her readers that the books we peruse, the plays we see, are not "irrelevant" art objects, but friends who can assist us in the hour of our greatest need. . . .

When we study the literature that has issued from the camps, we realize with a special intensity that great art helps people survive because survival in dire circumstances can be a matter of spirit. Hope cannot cure malnutrition, but for a young, basically strong person the desire to live was often stirred by memory, that of one's personal past, and that of the collective past we find in works of art. Only memory makes it possible to envision shaping a future.

By upholding literary values, by believing in literature, Charlotte Delbo made her apprenticeship as a poet; she became one of the living voices of the Holocaust. Her companions in camp—the other phantoms, soon to become wispy ghosts—begged her to remember, to be their voice if she survived. Charlotte took her mission as a sacred trust. If she waited to publish her first book it was not negligence on her part, but the imperatives of her demanding spirit. If she was "self-effacing," it was only in this sense; she effaced the self in order for the world to glow.

Heroic in the Resistance, heroic in the camps, it is as a literary artist that Charlotte Delbo proved herself a true hero.

> Rosette C. Lamont. In Alice Kessler-Harris
> and William McBrien, eds. *Faith of a*
> *(Woman) Writer* (1984; Westport,
> Connecticut: Greenwood Press, 1988),
> pp. 248–49, 251–52

DELEDDA, GRAZIA (ITALY) 1875–1936

Though she is not a first-class genius, she belongs to more than just her own day. She does more than reproduce the temporary psychological condition of her period. She has a background, and she deals with something more fundamental than sophisticated feeling. She does not penetrate, as a great genius does, the very sources of human passion and motive. She stays far short of that. But what she does do is to create the passionate complex of a primitive populace. . . . Sardinia . . . [is] an island of rigid conventions, the rigid conventions of barbarians, and at the same time, the fierce violence of the instinctive passions. A savage tradition of chastity, with a savage lust of the flesh. . . . It is the human instinct still uncontaminated. . . . It is this old Sardinia, at last being brought to heel, which is the real theme of Grazia Deledda's books. . . . The old, blind life of instinct, and chiefly frustrated instinct and the rage thereof, as it is seen in the Sardinian hinterland, this is Grazia Deledda's absorption. . . . She can put us into the mood and rhythm of Sardinian life like a true artist, an artist whose work is sound and enduring.

> D. H. Lawrence. Introduction to Grazia
> Deledda. *The Mother* (London: Jonathan
> Cape, 1922), pp. 7–13

It should be stated emphatically that the book is written without the least offense to any creed or opinion whatsoever, and touches on no question of either doctrine or Church government. It is just a human problem, the revolt of primitive human nature in distress against man-made laws it suffers from and cannot understand.

Mary G. Steegmann. Translator's preface to
Grazia Deledda. *The Mother* (New York:
Macmillan, 1923), p. xii

Sardinian she is, Grazia Deledda, in every trait of her art. Her realistic observation admits of the poetic fatalism and symbolism dear to primitive people; her style has the unconventional abruptness of a rough literature, and her conception of the great principles of morality are those of her people.

She has avoided the two opposing currents in the Italian literary world, humanitarian socialism and aesthetic individualism. Ignoring all transitory social relations, she depicts that first essential, irreducible nucleus—the family. The sacredness of the family is the basis of the Sardinian code of morals, and the protection of the family the ideal of Sardinian honor.

Joseph Spencer Kennard. *Italian Romance
Writers* (London: Brentano, 1922), p. 351

In *The Mother*, . . . action . . . is presented with a classic simplicity that can well afford to leave to the force of clearly conceived character and situation the effect of tragedy upon the reader. . . . [The characters] are made wonderfully distinct and articulate in a few words of dialogue and description. The skill with which they are made to live is the same that makes the novel, as a whole, a masterpiece of artistic economy, and it is so fine that one begins to realize it only after the enthusiasm that the book inspires is subjected to afterthought and the dubious supererogation of analysis. . . . It is deeply moving as a familiar tragedy of common experience and it is a thoroughly expert literary performance.

Edward T. Booth. *New York Evening Post.*
December 29, 1923, pp. 403–4

When seen in the perspective of the entire roll of [Nobel] Prize winners, Grazia Deledda's name will not appear to be so inglorious as in the isolated announcement of the fact that the Committee had again selected a writer who meant little or nothing to the average reader. To say the least of it, she is as good a novelist as Pontoppidan and Gjellerup, and, if Selma Lagerlöf had not written one masterpiece, . . . it might be argued that she and Grazia Deledda are of more or less equal standing, and rather similar in their simplicity of mood and matter. . . . Efforts to acclimatize Grazia Deledda in England and America met with the same fate as had been the lot of her master Giovanni Verga, . . . [for] not even the endorsement of D. H. Lawrence could induce much enthusiasm here for the regionalist school of which Verga was the acknowledged leader. . . . If one were to seek for an American figure of comparable importance, the name of Sarah Orne Jewett would suggest itself.

Grazia Deledda is a conscientious craftswoman in a minor *genre,* at home only with her own people, an unpretentious and vivid story-teller.

Ernest Boyd. *Saturday Review of Literature.*
December 3, 1927, p. 380

She is a writer of considerable dramatic power, exact and logical in the delineation of her characters; and along with these qualities there is a third—a remarkable power of description. People, places and scenes are drawn with great clarity and skill. . . . Her prose, which has many graces, has at times a poetic ring. The Sardinian scenes are so well depicted, so faithful, that the reader is projected into the daily lives of those who dwell in one or other of the smaller towns and villages. . . . It is a life of primitive simplicity in which the very soil seems alive and imbued with a personality for good or evil. . . . Grazia Deledda has received unstinted praise for her skillful delineation of character and for the idealism which informs all her work. But it is seldom that she lets her "fancies run in soft luxuriant flow," and wit and humor are not generally to be sought for.

John Mifoud. *New Statesman and Nation.*
February 25, 1928, p. 623

Grazia Deledda was born just when the old medieval life, which lasted to within living memory in the remoter districts of Italy, was breaking down before the advance of the modern world. . . . In this transition period she passed her impressionable young days. . . . And something of the atmosphere of the popular story-teller seems to pervade her novels with their pictures of the life of a primitive people, whose passions are violent and elemental, their virtues and vices almost those of patriarchal days. . . . She has made this primitive world so completely her own, it is so much a part of herself, that for her it becomes genuine tragedy. . . . [The] rough, racy peasant humor, which Grazia Deledda has obviously caught from the life around her, is the only relief of the kind she allows herself in some of the best of her novels. The suddenness with which it flashes out is almost disconcerting in its effect. We have heard young Italians speak with dislike of the gloomy, Nordic character of her books, and she has been compared to the Russians. There is little of the brightness of the south about them. Fate seems to brood over them as does the mountain Orthohene over Nuoro. Nature too is no mere setting, but in close relation with man and his moods . . . ; and her leading characters are haunted by a dream world, which is as real to them as the world in which they live, and seems to deepen the mystery of existence.

Lacy Collison-Morley. *Edinburgh Review.*
April, 1928, pp. 353–56

Deledda has received unstinted praise for her skillful delineation of found faith in the forces of nature and a glowing enthusiasm for the richness and beauty of the earth. The different forces of life live in her spirit in a harmony that is never disturbed by ascetic aspirations or spiritual problems. She considers these aspirations and problems intellectual and arbitrary creations of man. Life, in its fatal unity, does not know how to separate nor isolate. Religious feeling and spirituality, however, live closely interwoven with human passions and they, too, are reduced to a form of instinct. Love, too, assumes in her a cosmic character, as the individual lives in a flux of nature; he is part of it, although rebellious to society and to any external force that may stand between him and nature.

This cosmic unity constitutes the raw material out of which Deledda fashions her novels. She sketches with a hand that is moved by the same passion for life that creates the hunger and thirst of the creatures of her fancy.

Domenico Vittorini. *The Modern Italian Novel* (Philadelphia: University of Pennsylvania Press, 1930), pp. 58–59

She wielded a vigorous brush, splashing her colors upon the canvas, showing a complete mastery of the technique of chiaroscuro; for her high lights she has the delight of her characters in the world about them, a world of color and fragrance, of brilliant sunshine, of granite-like mountain peaks and rushing mountain streams; for her shadows, storm and tempest, passion fostered by solitude, the torment of the man scarcely higher in the scale than the brute. . . . Clarity of thought and of expression distinguishes every book. . . . We are spared interminable analysis, the psychology is the psychology of action, the dialogue is crisp, the characters explain themselves. It is a strange blossoming of a remarkable talent, a veritable flower of the soil.

Mary Fraser. *The Bookman.* August, 1932, pp. 239–40

[In] this last of her books . . . *Cosima,* we read Deledda's story from her earliest years, and see the places and atmosphere in which her precocious appetite for story-telling developed. The book is alive with the immediacy of the dreams, the obstacles, the candor and the moral experiences which were the source and strength of her talent. This young Cosima, seen by herself through the veil of memories, is the last and somehow fading flower of Deledda's moving and colorful masterpieces.

Anacleta Candida Vezzetti. *Books Abroad.* Spring, 1940, p. 202

All of Deledda's best narrative has as its subject the crises of existence. Historically, such a crisis is the result of nineteenth-century cultural unity, with its faith in historical progress, the secular sciences, and juridical guarantees to defend civil liberties. For this reason, the writer appears to participate fully in the decadence movement climate. Her characters represent the bewilderment of perplexes and shadowed consciousness, assailed by the rising of opposing instincts, open to all experiences for which life offers opportunity and stimulus. A hypertrophy of sensibilities is thus developed, and irresistibly attempts to measure itself against all the conventions, the fetishes of our daily mediocre normality. Whence the extreme pathos of great confrontations of souls that we witness in *Canes to the Wind* and other novels of the same period.

But the bewilderment does not go so far as total loss of conscience, so the revolt against social institutions does not lead to their definitive rejection. The spirit of stability is offered from a vision that we may call Christian-stoic, that . . . offers the possibility of affirmation of the individual. For this reason, in the pages of our author, the individual "I" remains the undisputed protagonist. . . . And also for this reason the novel's structures retain a classical symmetry based on the articulated system of relationships among the characters.

At first glance, Deledda's entire narrative appears suspended between old and new, between the urgent temptations of iconoclastic anarchy and the obstinate anchoring into a tradition from which it is too sad and threatening to detach oneself. . . . Captivated by the magic of the images, the reader may be induced not to go too deeply into their ambiguity wherein, however, lies their true richness. In order to appropriate them fully, you have to identify analytically the terms of the conflict taking place in the writer's soul. But ultimately you will have to conclude that it is precisely in the refusal or reluctance before logically unopposable responses that the permanent *raison d'être* of Deledda's work lies. Born of anti-intellectual impulses, it configures artistic experience as a form of direct and total apprehension of reality.

Vittorio Spinazzola. Introduction to Grazia
Deledda. *La madre* (Milan: Mondadori,
1967), pp. 17–18

For most critics, the most important tensions in *Cenere* arise in the clash between old and new, tradition and modernity, myth and rationality, provincial Sardegna and the continent. Transgression of the limits imposed by destiny, poverty and unconsciousness bring condemnation on the heads of those who dare be different; rebellion is ruled out. This view of *Cenere* and of Deledda's novelistic production is quite widely diffused. . . .

First of all, Anania's desire to find his mother and to overcome the painful internal divisions in his own personality sets him to study fervently and creates ultimately the aggravated sense of class conflict that unsettles him even more. . . .

In this novel the reader is confronted by a social and psychological problem which is quite foreign to many American readers, particularly at the university: the idea that education and social mobility might provoke true crises in individuals, because education and social mobility, despite their promise of social enlightenment, may also sever an individual from his social, intellectual, and psychological past. Yet the solution attempted by the protagonist, and by other characters, is not so foreign. Resolution of class conflict (and by extension moral conflict) is viewed in *Cenere* as a tendency to return to childhood, or in terms of a child's relationship—unequal but equal—to his parents. This is yet another reason that Anania's undertaking is doomed from its inception. Childhood appears an attractive (but impossible) solution because it presents the alternative of making choices that do not really count, giving answers that have no weight, having (apparently) infinite liberty which is limited only by the presence of a parent and "truncated" definitively with the acceptance of responsibility that is so traumatic for some.

Marilyn Migiel. *Stanford Italian Review.*
5, 1985, pp. 58–61

After trying to explain Deledda's work by useless recourse to the various "isms" of the moment, criticism is now in agreement in recognizing as the salient characteristic of the Sardinian writer her inability to commit herself completely to any of the literary-cultural movements of the time. Deledda, in fact, seems rather to absorb the culture that she lives surrounded by, transforming it immediately into very personal schemas and thus appropriating it to herself according to imperatives that are entirely her own.

The central topos of her copious narrative oeuvre is love, and this is seen as a totalizing experience. The initial situation, in Deledda's narrative, is generally negative, thereby following the narrative schema of Verga, and inheriting from realism a good dose of conceptual pessimism. The Eros erupts all-powerful and passionate, but is manifested above all as a force that divides, that isolates. The controlling force of Eros, the desire for the other, operates in Deledda's narrative as an element of profound schism, not only because it opposes the individual to society, but also because . . . it means separation from the object itself of desire and, above all, internal division. . . . In fact, the initial situation in Deledda's narrative is often doubly negative in that in it the subject lives love experience as both infraction and as sin. The direction of a social and hence historical order, places the character in the condition of disobeying, because he is subject to the time and to a law that predates the society itself that in the story is understood as tradition.

Ada Testaferri. *Donna: Women in Italian
Culture* (Ottawa: Dovehouse, 1989), p. 109

DESAI, ANITA (INDIA) 1935–

Mrs. Desai brings something new to the Indo-Anglian novel. Instead of portraying character in terms of the environment, or defining an individual in terms of his social or caste functions, Mrs. Desai creates character and the environment is important only insofar as it enables the reader to understand the character. Moreover, the true artist that she is, Mrs. Desai presents each individual as an unsolved mystery. Her first two novels present numerous memorable characters, major as well as minor, characters who are unique individuals living in their separate worlds of problems and passions, loves and hates. An unexpected glimpse is offered into the heart of a character. . . .

Unlike many of the other Indians writing in English Mrs. Desai is not interested in merely telling a story. Her technique is not that of a mere narrator who subordinates character to the main business of telling the story. She is more interested in her characters and the story is of secondary importance. This makes her work something very unusual in Indo-Anglian fiction. It gives to the Indo-Anglian novel a poetic depth, a psychological sophistication which were lacking. Most of the other Indo-Anglian novelists are not interested in their characters. Too often, they present an outsider's view of human nature.

The interaction between the poetic texture and the narrative structure in her first two novels raises the Indo-Anglian novel to a higher level of artistic success. It is no longer necessary to justify Indo-Anglian fiction on non-literary grounds. There is no need to apologize for the immaturity of this literature. The moment the novel acquires the depth, the dimension, and the mystery of true poetry it can be said to have come-of-age. A novel like *Cry, the Peacock* is a perpetual pleasure since on every page of the book we have the rich imagination of the author presenting the glory of the world of nature, its beauty and its colors and these become dramatically relevant since it is the poetic sensibility of the heroine that is transmuting the world in her thirst for life and hanger for living a FULL life.

Similarly, the minor characters, each an island unto himself, understood and frequently misunderstood by the other characters, give a new depth and dimension to the Indo-Anglian novel.

Each novel by Mrs. Desai is a marvel of technical skill. Everything irrelevant or superfluous is pruned out. So carefully is this pruning done that we have little masterpieces which possess formal perfection and poetic richness. This perfection is not the mere skill of a novelist obsessed with technique. It is the product of a mature artistry which fuses the different and differing elements into a remarkable unity. The sense of form which is late to develop is the sign of the maturity of a literature and Mrs. Desai's first two novels are a happy example of the fusion of form with content, of texture with structure.

B. Ramachandra Rao. *The Novels of Mrs. Anita Desai* (New Delhi: Kalyani, 1977), pp. 61–62

With all her attempts at variety, Anita Desai remains primarily a novelist of moods, of persistent states of mind or psyche. Most of her novels are extended narratives of states of "Being" which do not cohere into plot or structure in the conventional sense. Anita Desai sees the world in terms of experience as it emerges from the encounter of the experiencing self with the world outside. Her primary emphasis is, thus, on sights and sounds, on movements and patterns both physical and mental as they impinge on the consciousness of her protagonists. Her protagonists are usually sensitive women who, haunted by a peculiar sense of doom, withdraw into a sequestered world of their own. Anita Desai dwells on the variety and complexity of this limited world with the sensitivity and imagination of a poet. She observes every sight and sound with an intensity that not only amazes but also baffles us. Nothing escapes her eyes, not even the leg of a spider! This intensity and density of texture compensates for the absence of a strong plot or story line in her fiction. One reads her novels like long poems drawn mostly from those corners of life where no poetry seems to exist. This also accounts for the absence of humor in her writing though she can occasionally create a humorous character like Miss Moffit.

Behind her exquisite prose passages, however, there lurks a horrifying, almost macabre, sense of fatality which she renders in equally macabre and near-morbid detail. This strain is a disturbing but still unaccounted for element in her fiction. Anita Desai seems to be struggling in her art towards the mastery of a violence which seems to threaten not only her protagonists but also her own self. Right from *Cry, the Peacock* this violence has persisted in her work as a kind of inevitability, forcing one to conclude that it has some kind of metaphysical or psychological significance not yet explored and analyzed.

Anita Desai's gifts as a prose stylist are now acknowledged. What is perhaps overlooked in the process is the fact that most of her problems as a fiction writer begin with her insistence on too much style on too small a canvas. Her limited canvas forces her to strategies which are not always conducive towards highly convincing fiction. It often takes her away from the human context which is the primary substance of all fiction. Her fiction seems to doubt this very assumption for it is the "non-human" rather than the human which is its primary focus. Here one can see the true significance of Anita Desai's artistic endeavor. She seems to be working towards a kind of fiction which in conventional terms will be categorized as anti-fiction. In her novels, conventional elements do not seem to exist. They simply grow out and are not observed till they have grown out. This unexpectedness is perhaps the only fictional element in her fiction. Gautama's murder, Adit's reversal, and Raka's fire on the mountain come to us as totally unexpected events and shock us into the recognition of a reality which we had all along ignored. In this technique of powerful reversal, Anita Desai has acquired a peculiar mastery though sometimes the effect is quite contrary to the one intended. Her reversals . . . linger on in our consciousness like the impact of a powerful explosion and leave us disturbed. In this, Anita Desai's novels, perhaps, achieve the true function of art which is to disturb us and to make us aware of realities we have always ignored. Anita Desai seems to be moving towards a greater and greater mastery of this art.

R. S. Sherma. *Anita Desai* (New Delhi:
Arnold-Heinemann, 1981), pp. 166–68

Anita Desai is not a writer of epics—indeed, few women are. Instead, she works within a narrow range, showing the impact of forces on one individual. In *Cry, the Peacock* she deals with a narrow aspect of Indian culture, setting, etc. Were it not for the fact that Maya accompanies Gautama's visiting relatives on a shopping trip to Delhi, we would not even know where she lives. Though for practical purposes she lives in a house, not a city—and indeed, in the most basic sense she lives not in a house, but in her own mind. Still, although the author has disposed of many of the "essentials" of plot, setting, and characters, this does not mean that *Cry, the Peacock* lacks Indianness. Maya is an Indian, and her thoughts have an Indianness about them, despite their disturbed state. She reflects on Indian weather, Indian flora and fauna, Indian religious and mythical figures (especially Shiva and the dance of death), and traditional folk/religious elements (as personified by the astrologer). She takes for granted a pampered way of life, but she seems not to view it as related to modernity or to the West even though the amenities have been provided by her father and husband, both lawyers and, therefore, men who travel in highly westernized circles. If we take Maya's attitude toward the cabaret-goers as emblematic of her more general perception of the West, she is not much impressed or influenced by it.

Desai's language is more than uniquely Indian; it is uniquely her own. She uses the normal Indian English vocabulary for weather, food, clothing, etc., but she heightens it by inventing interesting, even shocking, combinations of words. Unusual juxtapositions and arresting metaphors constantly assault the senses of readers, almost demanding that they feel the way Maya herself feels. In no other way could the inner life of such a woman be described or conveyed.

Anita Desai is in the vanguard of a new generation of Indian writers who are experimenting with themes of inner consciousness. She makes significant contributions to Indian literature, and to world literature in English; at the same time, she gives her readers valuable insights into the feminine consciousness through her memorable protagonists.

Ann Lowry Weir. *Journal of South Asian
Literature.* 16, 1981, p. 4

Fire on the Mountain cannot be understood merely in terms of the plot or in terms of the actual events that happen. In fact, very little of moment actually occurs in the novel. Indeed on a first reading, the sudden violent eruptions of the last two chapters almost seem inexplicable in the context of the work as a whole. In order to understand the meaning, one has to go back and read the novel through the images and make them work for us as one might a poem. It is only then that one begins to see the organic quality of the work. The house, the landscape do not function merely as settings or backdrops for the action, but as extensions of the characters themselves. In fact, this is one of Desai's achievements here. Though she uses the technique of inner narration much in the way that Virginia Woolf does, she is able to break the quality of sameness that the outer world assumes in most of Woolf's novels, in *The Waves* especially. Carignano, Kausali, the Simla landscape is an utterly different thing in the eyes and to the beings both of Nanda Kaul and Raka . . . .

All three of the characters have been victims of various kinds. Nanda, if not a victim of violence, has certainly been a victim of her husband's indifference and of the family that has taken her for granted all her long life. Ila Das, of course, is the most obvious victim of violence in her own death by murder. There is as well a suggestion of the way she has become a scapegoat in the scene with the schoolboys when Ram Lal manages to rescue her umbrella from them and it is "now as maimed and crooked as a hunchback, a witch of olden times tied and readied for the fatal dip in the pond." The boys virtually pillory Ila Das; their mean and cruel behavior is almost worse than the final rape and murder. Raka is a victim of the world of her parents that she is born to, through no fault of her own. In turn she is the one person in the novel who is aware of the violence perpetuated on others. When she hears Ila Das also playing the "game of old age" with Nanda, she feels revolted:

> Lately her great-grandmother had bored her with it, played it with such theatrical ardor as to make it as unreal as theatre. It made her ache for the empty house on the charred hill, the empty summer-stricken view of the plains below, the ravine with its snakes, bones and smoking kilns—all silent, and a forest fire to wipe it all away, leaving ashes and silence.

Raka's final act to set fire to the mountain, then, is not merely an act of violence, but also an act of purification as if she might burn away the lies and deceit of Nanda's portrayal of her childhood as well as the violence of her own.

Francine E. Krishna. Indian Literature.
25:5, 1982, pp. 164, 168–69

Anita Desai is one of our known writers who has published a substantial body of prose-fiction—four novels *(Cry, the Peacock, Voices in the City, Byebye Blackbird, Fire on the Mountain),* and a collection of short stories titled *Games at Twilight.* Since her work raises certain basic issues about imaginative writing, particularly the relationship between art and experience, between form and content, I wish to explain why she fails to engage the reader's interest. . . .

What strikes the reader on his first encounter with her writing is her overzealous concern with the medium of communication, regardless of the nature of experience embodied in each story. Often she seems to pack an abundance of trivia into each sentence till the words groan under the pressure of overwrought syntactical langeurs. . . .

The writer weaves her cocoon of labored prose (often lapsing into clichés) around mere vacuities, seldom offering the reader any real climactic moment of suspense or stimulation. . . .

The overall impression of reading Anita Desai's stories and novels is one of a senile, spinsterish sensibility lashing inanities into excitement. For instance, her novel *Fire on the Mountain* (even the melodramatic title fails to redeem the banality of the narrative), portrays an old woman, Nanda Kaul, who beguiles the tedium of her hours by reading, "in small sips, bits and pieces from *The Pillow Book of Sei Shonagon*," as she lies tucked away in the seclusion of Carignano, amidst the Simia hills. She finds her privacy disturbed by the arrival of Raka, her great-granddaughter whom she babysits all through the forty-four chapters, and 145 pages, only to be shocked into hearing, on the very last page of the novel, that the child has set off a blaze.

> "Nani, Nani," whispered Raka, shivering and crouching in
> the lily bed, peering over the sill. "Look, Nani, I have set the
> forest on fire. Look, Nani, I have set the forest on fire. Look,
> Nani—look—the forest is on fire."

If the writer has here tried to offer the reader a wisp of action, she has failed lamentably because the "fire" comes upon him too suddenly, with no relevance, symbolic or otherwise, to the central plot.

Dullness broods over this narrative as it does over most of Anita Desai's prose fiction. Wooden, sexless characters stalk across her pages, chasing dark shadows at twilight. Nothing profound or soulful ever falls within the range of her aesthetic experience—it is just words, words, in tangled sentence structures, forcing the reader into a sort of insensateness. In a very perceptive contribution to an "International Symposium on the Short Story," Herbert Gold asserts "that the storyteller must have a story to tell, not merely some sweet prose to take out for a walk." But when even the prose is bittersweet and stilted, the writer may have trouble in coaxing his readers "out for a walk."

Shiv K. Kumar. In S. N. A. Rizsi, ed.
*The Twofold Voice: Essays in Honor of
Ramesh Moher* (Salzburg: Salzburg Institut
für Anglistik und Amerikanistik, 1982),
pp. 190, 193–94

Of all the contemporary Indian-English novelists, Anita Desai, avowedly "an essentially subjective writer," is indubitably the most powerful imagist. Setting great store by imagery in the novel as an art form, she regards its use as an effective technique for the articulation of her sensibility and handles it superbly. Demonstrating her fictional strategy and underscoring her essentially tragic vision of life, Desai resorts generously to imagery to vivify psychic states as well as the distinctively individual consciousness of her highly sensitive, introverted characters and the complexities of human relationships, scenes and situations, resulting in a remarkable textural density. Indisputably, her novels would have meant much less to us were it not for the transforming presence of imagery.

All six novels by Desai teem with various meaningful, functional images. On closer scrutiny, we notice that botany, zoology, meteorology, nature and color predominate as sources, and occasionally she also employs certain other stray images that, though answering immediate artistic experiences, operate on a minor level, focusing on the moods of certain characters and forming a sort of tonal chord in her novels. These minor images do not arise from what has gone before, though they do generally suggest a prefigurative pattern. . . .

Never otiose, Desai's imagery, which is chiefly anticipatory, prefigurative or demonstrative in nature, is always highly functional. Botanical, zoological, meteorological and color images are central to her fictional strategy and spotlight the tragic vision of life to which she, like Kamala Markandaya, is essentially committed. Her artistic image patterns, singularized by subtle interrelatedness and continuity, act on our imagination with tremendous cumulative force. Creating a mosaic of textural density in almost all her novels, Desai's imagery is wedded to rich lyricism. She is basically a powerful imagist-novelist but is also a remarkable lyrical novelist as well, and there is a subtle interaction between her imagery and lyricism. In sum, Anita Desai is the only Indian-English novelist who exploits imagery to such an extent and to such an artistic end. Certainly this is her unique achievement.

Madhusudan Prasad. World Literature
Today. 58, 1984, pp. 363, 369

In *Where Shall We Go This Summer,* Sita retreats to her childhood home, but returns after having realized that a woman's situation cannot be improved by escaping from life, but through positive commitment and through personal and social responsibility. Nanda Kaul in *Fire on the Mountain,* retreats very late in life only after her widowhood when she could acquire her husband's money. This is a common feature in the life of Indian women who are denied any financial freedom in their lives. Her disgust with her past is so intense that she refuses to have any connection with the outer world. However, Desai has made Nanda painfully aware of the consequences of total withdrawal at the end of the book.

Seema Jena. Carving a Pattern out of Chaos
(New Delhi: Ashish, 1990), pp. 67–68

In *Fire on the Mountain,* as in most of Desai's work, atmosphere and landscape are intricately linked. These two elements are used symbolically and are associated with human emotions and sensations, thus enabling the reader to form a more complete picture of the characters because the world around them is directly connected both to their inner being and actions. Kasauli's atmosphere holds an emblematic quality for those who meet there, each perceiving the place and its atmosphere differently and each seeking solace in it: Nanda Kaul attracted by the barrenness and silence; Raka, her great-granddaughter, drawn to its wilderness; Ila Das enthralled because it is "a little bit of the past come alive."

The novel culminates with the forest burning. Although surprising in some ways, it is clear, in retrospect, that the event has been foreshadowed throughout, beginning with the title, *Fire on the Mountain.* Both Nanda Kaul and Raka have been obsessed with the element of fire, Nanda Kaul first showing Raka the ruins from previous fires, then Raka being drawn back to them again and again. The fire alluded to in the middle of the novel, which then seemed unreal—"It was far away. . . . It was like a fire in a dream—silent, swift and threatening"—has now been brought close and into reality. Raka, who stole a box of matches from the kitchen and set ablaze the forest around Carignano, calls at the window to her great-grandmother: "'Look, Nani, I have set the forest on fire. Look, Nani—look the forest is on fire.'"

By starting the fire, she destroys in a symbolic way the illusions with which Nanda Kaul has lived; she burns the life of dreams that Nanda Kaul had built up around her to make her life bearable and to avoid facing reality. But once the fantasies are reduced to ashes, truth survives. It is apt that Raka should be the agent of destruction, for earlier when Nanda Kaul talked about her childhood, the girl detected that the old lady was making up the stories. And when Nanda Kaul and Ila Das dredged up the past as they imagined it, Raka became restless and bored, again aware of their lies. Thus, Raka's act cannot be regarded as one of gratuitous violence and destruction, but one powerfully symbolic.

Through the characters of Nanda Kaul, Raka, and Ila Das, each experiencing a different kind of alienation, Anita Desai explores, with the subtlety and artistry that have become the hallmarks of her work, those themes constituting her fictional preoccupations: lack of human communication and the devastating effect of spiritual isolation. And she grafts on yet another human conflict, one that dominates her work: the discrepancy between the inner being and the outer world.

Diana Libert. In Robert L. Ross, ed.
*International Literature in English: Essays
on the Major Writers* (New York: Garland,
1991), pp. 571–72, 578

DESSAULLES, HENRIETTE (pseud. FADETTE) (CANADA) 1860–1946

The teenage girl who keeps her diary while waiting for marriage: this stereotype appears rather often in the novels of the nineteenth century. In Quebec,

Laure Conan made use of it in *Angeline de Montbrun* in 1882. The cover of Francoise Van Roey-Roux's book about intimate literature in Quebec is illustrated by the picture of a young girl that could be Henriette Dessaulles. Henriette Dessaulles's journal, written between 1874 and 1889 at Saint-Hyacinthe, is the only example of a female intimate journal of the nineteenth century cited in this work. However, Henriette mentions that all her girl friends were writing their diaries. . . . It is surprising to observe that despite the great number of journals which were written and the power of this stereotype in fiction, there exist very few actual journals from the period to illustrate how a young girl wrote and what she talked about. Henriette's was not published until 1971. In France, only one has become well known, but its author is far from being typical. She is a young Russian expatriate, Marie Bashkirtseff, born the same year as Henriette Dessaulles, who wrote her journal from 1870 until her death in 1884 at the age of twenty-four years. The first paradox as concerns the journal of Henriette Dessaulles is thus that it represents the best example, to my knowledge, of a genre normally fated for oblivion and which, while being typical, is exceptional because it survived. . . .

As Henriette develops as a character in her journal, there is a corresponding modification in the role of the narrator. At first, she is writing for herself, the journal serves as a confidant, replacing a mother who would console and help her. Sometimes she uses "tu" in addressing herself, in the tone of a mother who would encourage her daughter. She wants to justify herself and needs approval. In the second phase, the journal becomes her confessor, in place of Mr. Prince whom she detests. She would like to confess directly to God like the Protestants, but she admits having trouble praying. The journal becomes her judge, the "tu" form sometimes taking the tone of a paternal scolding.

From the beginning of her journal, she excludes those around her, even Maurice, as confidants. But to the extent that she becomes increasingly attached to him, as his opinion matters more, she begins to address him in the journal. He becomes its narrator. Thus, in the course of the journal, the narrator undergoes a change of sex. At the beginning, it is herself, her dead mother, or the stepmother whose love she desired; passing subsequently through her father, the priest, and God, it is eventually Maurice whose approval she wants. To the extent that she renounces the role of judge for herself, it is a man who assumes it. However, it is not all that simple: the features that she does not like in her stepmother (she is authoritarian, violent, brutal) are rather masculine; those that give her confidence in Maurice are his delicacy, his tenderness, his affection—his feminine side, as she observes.

Maurice will become the reader of the journal, shortly before the marriage. This journal will already have become "a somewhat cumbersome friend whose usefulness has ceased." Once she can speak freely to Maurice, the taste for writing diminishes. The journal is interrupted following the marriage: the other pages of the notebook will be blank. . . .

If it were a story, this would be the ending. They got married and had lots of children. (Henriette wanted to learn about contraception, but whom to ask?) But it is a real journal. Thus the story goes beyond the narrative. We can ask a question that makes no sense for fiction: "What happened afterwards?" Henriette relates in her journal a dream that was to come true; it is about Maurice's death. He did die, in fact, after fifteen years of marriage. During that time, Henriette apparently wrote nothing. Left a widow (at the age of thirty-four), she would return to writing, not a personal journal, but as a journal*ist*. This is the proof that the identity formed in the course of adolescence can evolve. She returns to her original idea of making her own life. When she became a journalist, she acquired a new identity, that of Fadette, a pen name with which she would sign a weekly column in *Le Devoir* from 1910 to 1945. She will thus recapture two concerns of her teenage diary: the short story—she will publish two collections of tales for children—and graphology, the study of handwriting. She gave a lecture at the first Congress on the French Language in Canada, on woman's literary mission. Always fascinated by the relations between the subject and writing, Fadette, in Quebec in 1946, the year of her death, is not so far from the women writers of contemporary Quebec.

> Valérie Raoul. *French Review.* 59, 1986,
> pp. 841, 844–45, 848

At the end of the nineteenth century, Henriette Dessaulles, a young girl belonging to the liberal French Canadian upper class at Saint-Hyacinthe, keeps her journal in order to capture her life better. Why did this teenager have recourse to a private form of writing, knowing at first, no other "rule" than that of the *"obsessive 'I'"* which scrutinizes and interrogates itself in the perspective of the diaristic space? . . . The expression of the "I" in the *Journal of Henriette Dessaulles* functions as a transitory phenomenon and thus gives form to a love novel being written by the "I". . . .

Secret, enclosed, and transitory, the writing of the intimate diary for Henriette Dessaulles "appears as the birthplace of a new identity that seems bizarrely not to have preexisted in her." This placement onstage of the self thanks to which the narrator imagines, discovers, and constructs her character is also motivated by the appeal to the other, by the search for a substitute for the mother. The search for a new love object is incarnated in a form at once typical of women's writing—the hourly expression of the intimate diary—and of literary fiction—the lack, the trials, and the happy ending of the love story or novel—for Henriette works daily at the "ultimate reorganization of her psychic space" by reinventing the family romance already fixed in her memory. If the happy ending of this literary, psychological, and amorous adventure seems to put an end to Henriette's "childhood" where she might "find a little joy once again," this denouement masks as well the mourning of the intimate "I" and the entrance of the woman into the "known and recognized forms" of the institution as bourgeois morality of the late nineteenth-century required.

Lise Ouellet. *Francofonia*. 14, 1988, pp. 53, 61

Henriette Dessaulles's *Journal* poses a paradox: it is about an evolution, but, by assuming the form of the development of love, the evolution is abolished by its own very achievement. Literally and symbolically, the *Journal* ends with marriage. The other aspect of the paradox, connected to this one, but not necessarily, resides in the fact that, by the presence of a recipient, the fact that it becomes communication, the writing ceases to be a transgression in itself. From the moment that Henriette turns her notebooks over to Maurice, the journal prefigures the silence where it will be abolished. From that point on, it is no longer a process of becoming but one of waiting: it is no longer written, it is read. [Fadette's] *Letters* already doubly sets itself up in opposition to the journal: by the predominance of a public audience, for this is journalism properly so called, by the intermediary of the pseudonym that what she writes in the pages of the newspaper *Devoir* outside the bounds of writing. From the *Journal* to *Letters from Fadette;* it is less a question of distance than of inversion: from the intimate to the familial.

Beyond the most varied functions and justification, the *Journal* is a site of writing: it becomes text and as such bears in itself its meaning and its function. All the better if historic knowledge is assisted by it, but the *Journal* is accountable to a different truth: it is above all a listening to oneself, holding itself within its wording as in its irreducible singularity.

At the time when literature was part of good works, Fadette enjoyed wide renown. Shortly after 1945, her memory was no longer kept up except in some circles where edification still had literary value. If, for a number of years, her career was evoked and her writing studied in literature courses for convent schools and their male equivalents, her name no longer even figured in the postwar textbooks and works of literary history.

It is in her capacity as author of the *Journal* that Henriette Dessaulles reenters Quebecois literature and that she remains forever young within it. For us today and perhaps for generations to come, she illuminates the end of the nineteenth century. Even more. . . in her destiny as in her writing, she prefigures the twentieth century.

Jean-Louis Major. Introduction to Henriette Dessaulles. *Le Journal* (Montreal: Presse de l'Université de Montréal, 1989), pp. 66–67

DEVANNY, JEAN (AUSTRALIA) 1894–1962

Most of Jean Devanny's novels are thinly disguised political tracts with stagey plots, flimsy characters and plenty of proletarian heroics. Even so they are important for their feminism which was fierce and uncompromising. While Jean Devanny saw fiction as an effective political weapon offering palatable propaganda, the use of this form gave her a certain protection. While she was fighting on women's issues as a woman rather than as a writer, she was vulnerable to attack on personal grounds. Without strong theoretical or political backup, it was hard to keep the debate away from personal recriminations by her and sexist accusations against her. This was, of course, exacerbated by the fact that part of the impetus to her feminism came from personal experience. She had legitimate grievances. In fiction, however, she could use her characters as a veil; she could vent her anger through them; she could show the injustices she herself smarted under through her heroines while ensuring that their personal and political credentials were impeccable, and seen to be impeccable.

The best of Jean Devanny's novels of this period is *Sugar Heaven,* a detailed report of the 1935 sugar strikes around Innisfail in North Queensland, encased in fiction. The fictional structure of the novel is well enough formed to carry her lapses into political rhetoric. *Sugar Heaven* was well received and is still remembered by the people who lived through the strike. It is also an angry novel in which Jean Devanny engages directly with the Communist Party over its treatment of women. The documentation of the strike is the major focus of *Sugar Heaven* and the narrative structure is used primarily to demonstrate the nature of women's political consciousness. Dulcie comes to North Queensland as the young bride of a sugar worker. She has no political consciousness; in the past, she had even supported scab labor. She had done so innocently, of course, and this adds poignancy, rather heavy-handedly, to her gradual political awakening and triumph as a successful women's organizer. The point *Sugar Heaven* makes is that women, tied to the home, worried about the next meal and "weeping for fear of the unknown," have to be brought around slowly. The political lessons they need to learn have to come through the reality of their situation. Abstract political rhetoric will not do for women; but once they see the importance of socialism for themselves as women, for their children, for their families, they will fight with a determination that will leave men gasping. Women are portrayed as natural militants. The Communist Party is chastized for ignoring a pool of militancy that could be tapped simply by cadres taking their problems seriously; but as Jean Devanny knew only too well, more often than not the dominant party attitude was to dismiss or discount women.

The character used against these attitudes is Eileen, a woman with talent, intelligence, superb political consciousness, and considerable influence among the local women. She insists on her right to sexual autonomy and refuses to pretend that she is other than she is. Her major crime is a love affair—of the very highest caliber—with an Italian, and on these grounds she is refused entry into the Communist Party. This is Jean Devanny at her furious best. Here is a woman who has it over all the men in every possible way; yet simply because she loves openly and without apology a man who is Italian she is kept out of the party. The injustice is heightened by the fact of Eileen's purity on every other count and by the party's racism in the face of large settlements of Italians in the cane-cutting areas and the prominence of Italians in the strike. *Sugar Heaven* accuses Communist men of racism, willing to accept Italians on strike committees, but not in their houses and far less in their women's beds. The final feminist statement in *Sugar Heaven* is that, despite her mistreatment Eileen stays in Queensland to work with the women, refusing her lover's tempting invitation to go to Italy, preferring "love of the class" to love for a man. Thus the point is made, and not subtly, that women's political consciousness is enduring and self-sacrificing, the traditional female qualities.

In *The Virtuous Courtesan,* Jean Devanny addresses herself to the conjuncture of class and sex, one of the few novels of the time to do so. Who is the prostitute, the novel asks, the respectable woman who marries for property, and grants her favors for prestigious associations, or the professional with a heart of gold who whores to keep her family together? Poppy, honest and generous on the streets, is contrasted with Inez, the mean, manipulative woman of the bourgeoisie. *The Virtuous Courtesan* shows how women are exploited by men regardless of class, but emphasizes the variation in class response. More often than not the middle-class women are sycophantic and parasitic, while the working-class women work and live hard, making what they can of their situation. At least the bourgeois men in the novel work, whereas the women make no social contribution. Central to the novel is a love affair between a working class man and a middle class woman. While Jack defends Sharon as "our kind if . . . not our class," ultimately her class background dominates and the affair is a disaster, ending in disillusionment and bitterness for poor honest proletarian Jack. While marriage and sexual relations are a game for the bourgeoisie, a way of maximizing and maintaining class privilege, for the working class marriage is either serious, entered for love, or simply a means of survival.

Drusilla Modjeska. *Exiles at Home:*
Australian Women Writers 1925–1945
(London: Angus and Robertson, 1981),
pp. 227–29

It was in the mid-1930s that Devanny produced *Sugar Heaven,* the work that she claimed later was "the first really proletarian novel in Australia." It is also relevant to a reading of the novels as documents of class struggle that both writers [Devanny and Prichard] were members of the Communist Party which, at this period, was centrally involved in many of the struggles of the

Australian working class. Other aspects of the Party's politics which had a decisive impact upon both Devanny and Prichard (as well as Frank Hardy, Dorothy Hewett, and others later) were the Party's particular prescriptions for artistic production (socialist realism), its sexual puritanism, and its hostility to "intellectuals." Membership of the Party had a decisive impact upon the literary production of both writers as well as on its reception both within and outside the Party. . . .

[The] notion of "authentic" presentation of the working class is a complicated and difficult question. It is still an issue in, for example, recent discussions of popular culture and how far authentic working-class values are present within it. Though Devanny asserted in 1942 that her *Sugar Heaven* was "the first really proletarian novel in Australia," its "proletarian" quality includes the presentation of "false consciousness" as well as development toward a revolutionary understanding of their situation in the course of the strike. . . .

Between *Sugar Heaven* (1936) and her sugar industry trilogy (only two volumes of which were completed, the second, still unpublished volume entitled *One Can't Have Everything*), Devanny moved away from the immediate present of the canecutters' strike of 1935 and back to the 1890s, as had Prichard for *The Roaring Nineties,* her first goldfields novel. *Cindie* (1942), the first volume, opens on the Queensland canefields and deals with the transition from the period of the farmers' use of press-ganged Kanaka labor to the time when most of the Kanaka workers were repatriated as a result of the White Australia policy favored by the labor movement. . . .

With her novel *Cindie,* Devanny encountered a problem for socialist realism; she was depicting the owning class with a degree of sympathy: while her heroine starts out as a maid in the family, she marries the boss's son by the end of the novel. These chickens came home to roost, and Devanny was unable to find a publisher for the second volume of the trilogy, *One Can't Have Everything.* . . .

Devanny had always been concerned with overcoming racial prejudice; her second novel, *Lenore Divine* (1928) has two carefully developed Maori characters, and *Sugar Heaven*'s presentation of an Italian as the lover of Eileen, a central figure in that novel, aroused deep concern for the "authentic" in one leading north Queensland Party member who, according to Devanny's autobiography, commented: "No Australian woman would have an affair with an Italian"; though as Devanny pointed out, "the prototype of the woman in the book was his own wife." Eileen analyzes her own public approach to her relationship with Tony as an attempt to attack these attitudes which, as Menghetti shows, were widely prevalent in the bourgeois press. . . .

The question of "'literary value" is a contentious one in the discussion of writers such as Devanny and Prichard. Even sympathetic socialist feminists such as Modjeska and Turner have reservations about Devanny's technique—the novels of Richardson or Dark, for example, are considered much more "finished" products than *The Butcher Shop* or *Sugar Heaven.* Effective characterization, lyrical narrative passages, and symbolic structuring are more effectively executed in a novel like *Working Bullocks* than in *Sugar Heaven,* and this does have a bearing on the pleasure produced in reading the text. But notions of aesthetic pleasure do also have a class basis—Devanny said of *Sugar Heaven* that her central intention was not to produce an aesthetically pleasing work but an "authentic" and agitational one for a working-class audience: "Not that the book was an important 'literary' document. By no means. Its value lay in that it reflected truly the heroic conduct of the strikers, the capabilities of their leadership, and was written in fiery agitational style. 'It's written like you speak,' a cane-cutter told me." . . . Both Devanny and Prichard (as Hardy and Hewett later) were attempting to make an essentially bourgeois form—that of the novel—accessible and popular, while maintaining commitment. Their work not only was an inspiration to Hardy and Davison but was perceived as pioneering by other of their contemporaries. Franklin stresses what she sees as the originality of Devanny's achievement in *Sugar Heaven:*

> Mrs. Devanny sacrifices literary art to fervor for political ideology as she deals with the incidence of strikes, disease and bad times, as well as the difficulties of several languages among non linguists, and other problems brought by our later settlers in lush places among serpents and stinging plants and ants; but she is vivid, valiant, temerarious and, like the man with the machete, is hacking her way into new literary territory.
>
> Carole Ferrier. *Gender, Politics and Fiction: Twentieth Century Australian Women's Novels* (Brisbane: University of Queensland Press, 1985), pp. 102–7

In 1929 Jean Devanny arrived in Sydney and had every resource stretched by the harshness of the depression. By this stage the author of numerous books (*The Butcher Shop,* 1926; *Lenore Divine,* 1926; *Old Savage and Other Stories,* 1927; *Dawn Beloved,* 1928; and *Riven,* 1929), she had no hope of being able to give her attention to her writing because she was locked into the struggle to find sufficient food and shelter for herself and her family. In the search for a social/political solution to such widespread suffering and misery, Jean Devanny turned to the Australian Labour Party: convinced that they had no remedy, in 1931 she joined the Communist Party—and like Katharine Susannah Prichard, she too visited the Soviet Union during the early 1930s. . . .

In her life and her writing, Jean Devanny persistently challenges patriarchal authority: this is one reason why she was so shamefully and shabbily treated by the Communist Party—and one reason why I find her writing so stirring and strong. I do not always endorse her values, although my reservations are not associated with the pretext that her work was primarily propaganda and therefore "beyond the pale": rather I am critical of *The Butcher Shop,* for example, which in its brave and bold assertion of women's right to sexuality, seems to give sex and satisfaction too much significance as a solution. But some of her political novels (and there are more than twenty novels in all from which to choose), such as *Sugar Heaven* (1936) and *Cindie* (1949), set in the Queensland canefields, were for me a salutary introduction to the political/social/racial—and misogynist—history of Australia. I would recommend Jean Devanny's fiction to all alert, intellectually active individuals who cherish the dream of a just world: I would be delighted to teach a course on the view of Australia, its people and traditions, as encoded within the work of Jean Devanny. Such representations would match little with the prevailing perspective, but the literary heritage, and society, could be all the richer for the inclusion of Jean Devanny's views. Which is why I so much regret her exclusion from the valued literary tradition.

> Dale Spender. *Writing a New World: Two Centuries of Australian Women Writers* (London: Pandora, 1988), pp. 259–61

DIDION, JOAN (UNITED STATES) 1934–

As melodramatic as [her] material may appear . . . it is not at all so as Joan Didion handles it. She is, above all, cool, and an impressively skilled writer. Even in this first novel [*Run River*] there seems to be nothing technically that she cannot do. . . . Her reader suspects that the author, with all of her power—to present character, to manipulate time, to suggest significance through detail and symbol, to be aware—might herself not know what she wants, or might not see life, as Philip Roth does, as possessing a tang.

> Robert Maurer. *New York Herald Tribune.* May 12, 1963, p. 10

Joan Didion is one of those brilliant new-breed journalists who wander sadly and watchfully across the United States as if touring a disaster area. . . . The subjects [of *Slouching towards Bethlehem*] are conventional, given Miss Didion's temperament: Las Vegas weddings (an essay on American vulgarity); San Francisco hippies (the American dream gone to pot); backstage Hollywood à la Lillian Ross; Joan Baez ("a girl who might have interested Henry James"); Howard Hughes (subversive hero of the middle-class underground). A substantial element of spiritual biography is present in these pieces of wary skepticism. Though she has a journalist's weakness for converting her themes into "myths," "dreams," and "folk" symbols—she is an original observer and even better, an original thinker. Has anyone ever written a better treatment of that overexposed topic of the year—hippies?

Melvin Maddocks. *Christian Science
Monitor.* May 16, 1968, p. 11

There hasn't been another American writer of Joan Didion's quality since Nathanael West. She writes with a razor, carving her characters out of her perceptions with strokes so swift and economical that each scene ends almost before the reader is aware of it; and yet the characters go on bleeding afterward. A pool of blood forms in the mind. Meditating on it, you are both frightened and astonished. When was the wound inflicted? How long have we to live? . . .

It is the condition of a woman's mind that is her subject; it is the "nothingness" after one has been used as an object that she explores; it is the facts beyond "answers" or "explanations" that she plays with.

John Leonard. *The New York Times.*
July 21, 1970, p. 33

To read Joan Didion is to worry about her. There is in most of her work the terrible feeling that this latest pained and painful examination of whatever is on her mind right now is only the freshest installment in some epic suicide note to the world. The premonition of personal loss is apocalyptic. . . .

Here, in her second novel and first departure in almost a decade from the first-person reportage she does so excruciatingly well, are both disappointment and relief. Disappointment, because [*Play It as It Lays*] is nothing like the gorgeous caterwauling tour de force that might have been expected; relief, a personal relief, because at the end she explicitly rejects suicide as an alternative—for her—to the miserable goings-on so sparely chronicled. . . .

Familiarity with her autobiographical work makes it impossible to read this novel without recalling on almost every page the other memories, the real ones.

It doesn't seem important finally, whether this is a good book or not. Those who care about Joan Didion will have to read it. For one thing, it is a compelling exercise in literary pathology; but, most of all, it is a matter of devotion.

Nicholas A. Samstag. *Saturday Review of
Literature.* August 15, 1970, p. 27

Nullity, nothingness, human negation, *nil*—these are merely variants of the same phenomena, the essential emptiness of experience, that great hole at the middle of things. Single as the phenomena may be, the characters in novels can make varying approaches to it, as novelists themselves can have various feelings about it. It can be seized in a kind of hungry embrace, in the fashion of the moral idiots who people the world Miss Didion creates in [*Play*

It as It Lays], a novel written with such bitter wit that the reader feels at the end that it must have been acid that he has been drinking. . . .

I am tempted to say that this novel is a triumph not of insight as such but of style, meaning by *style,* of course, the linguistic embodiment or, rather, actualization of imagination. . . . If Miss Didion had made one false move, the whole thing would have collapsed like a pricked balloon. But she didn't.

Mark Schorer. *American Scholar.*
Winter, 1970–71, pp. 168, 174

Didion's great talent lies in her ability to evoke the stunning abstractness of southern California "dying in the golden light." Her images of people alone on freeways, beside mansion pools, in supermarkets at three in the morning, at despairing beach parties, on blistering streets with curlers in their hair and wedgies on their feet are remarkable and compelling. And indeed, much of this sense of things pervades *Play It as It Lays.* . . .

I could not escape the sensation, as I read *Play It as It Lays,* that Maria's language was not her own: that her telescoped responses and significant silences had been placed in her mouth and behind her eyes by a generation of literary references created by an experience that was not the primary experience of the author. Thus, the story of Maria's life fails to become a convincing portrait of emotional removal; on the contrary, the story *itself* becomes an act of emotional removal. One feels oneself in the presence of a writer who believed it good to be told she wrote like a man, and has—with the tools of talent and intelligence—knocked that belief into place: a shield between herself and her work.

Vivian Gornick. *Village Voice.*
May 31, 1973, p. 32

Play It as It Lays depends upon an intimate connection between setting and theme; but also . . . its overriding thematic concern is man's relationship with himself and with existence in general. Didion's novel is neither primarily a sociological commentary on the values of contemporary American society nor a psychological case study of its heroine. It is, rather, a picture of personal dread and anxiety, of alienation and absurdity lurking within and without. For although Hollywood is her setting, nothingness is Didion's theme. . . .

The facts of Maria's life are the basic material of thousands of soap opera situations. What saves *Play It as It Lays* from degenerating into banality is Didion's control over her material, her skill in focusing attention not on the events in Maria's life so much as on her cumulative response to them. The real action of the novel takes place in the mind and heart of Maria as she is forced to deal with her experiences. Viewed from a medical point of view, she might well be classified as a near schizoid personality whose experiences have precipitated a severe emotional crisis resulting in the loss of an integrated personality. In a more profound sense, however, her sickness is neither emotional nor psychological; it is ontological. She is suffering not from a nervous breakdown, but from the breakdown of a world around her which threatens to engulf her whole being with nothingness. . . .

With relentless attention to telling detail, a perceptive eye for sharply-etched characters, an unerring ear for the absurdities and non sequiturs that pass for daily conversation, and a diamond-hard unsentimental style, Joan Didion has fashioned a remarkable novel which never misses in its portrayal of a modern woman caught in a mid-twentieth-century crisis. She has cast anew, in her unique idiom, one of the prevailing concerns of modern literature: confrontation with the void. Despite its preoccupation with death, suffering, boredom and despair, *Play It as It Lays* is always fresh and alive. The novel not only touches the heart of its reader through its sensitive treatment of Maria Wyeth but also assaults the mind in its investigation of the heart of darkness too often discovered lurking behind the fundamental questions about existence in the modern world.

David J. Geherin. *Critique.*
16:1, 1974, pp. 64–65, 78

All of Didion's heroines have trouble with history, personal and otherwise, and each of her novels is an attempt at traveling backwards in search of various historical explanations. It is a tentative operation—she only grudgingly appreciates "all the opiates of the people, whether they are as accessible as alcohol and heroin and promiscuity or as hard to come by as faith in God or History." A willingness to seek explanation in the past, and to invite disappointment, is the impetus of each of her novels, as well as the basis for their narrative structures. All three books open immediately after a disaster—Everett's murder of Ryder Channing and his subsequent suicide in *Run River* (1963); Maria's breakdown and hospitalization in *Play It as It Lays;* Charlotte Douglas's death in a Central American revolution in *A Book of Common Prayer*—and then take the reader backwards in time to show him what triggered the catastrophe. The effect of the technique is not only to erase immediately any grounds for optimism in the reader—he knows that the book can only take him back to the bad end he has already glimpsed—but to prepare him for an historical test: is the view of the past he is about to get sufficient explanation of the disaster he has already witnessed? This question is one that Didion repeatedly asks of history in these books. Her faith in her own exploration and method is much tried and ultimately very limited, but her looking backwards remains compulsive.

The heroines of all three novels share an unusual number of similarities. Physically, each has what is called for Lily Knight McClellan in *Run River* a "compelling fragility" or for Charlotte an "extreme and volatile thinness." An inability to cope with the day-to-day, a dreaminess, forms a large part of their sexual attraction.

Thomas Mallon. *Critique.*
21:3, 1980, pp. 43–44

In both her essays and her fiction Didion seeks to render the moral complexity of contemporary American experience, especially the dilemmas and ambiguities resulting from the erosion of traditional values by a new social and political reality. To this end, she violates the conventions of traditional journalism whenever it suits her purpose, fusing the public and the personal, frequently placing herself in an otherwise objective essay, giving us her private and often anguished experience as a metaphor for the writer, for her generation, and sometimes for her entire society.

In her fiction, on the other hand, Didion has found that a traditional form and structure better suit her purpose. Unlike many other contemporary novelists, she creates real settings, characters that behave with some consistency, plots that have a beginning, middle, and end. In her few pieces of literary criticism Didion defends these traditions against the "new fiction" of Kurt Vonnegut, Joseph Heller, and Bruce Jay Friedman. Lacking plot, structure, or consistent point of view, the new fiction, Didion feels, allows the author to abnegate his responsibility to make a moral statement. . . .

Implicit in Didion's view of the writer's responsibility is her conviction that, however multiple and ambiguous it may be, truth exists and can be approached by the writer with the courage and skill to project a coherent, realistic vision. Her own vision reveals to us the moral condition of contemporary Americans, living by illusions as fragile as fine china, clinging to shards of broken dreams, yet often redeemed by an immense potential for love and commitment.

Katherine Usher Henderson. *Joan Didion*
(New York: Frederick Ungar, 1981),
pp. vii–viii, 143, 146–47

No contemporary writer has more successfully carved the symbolic properties of emotional inertness into a territory of her own than has Joan Didion, and nowhere more so than in the style she has pursued with a discipline wholly to be admired. Of her work it can truly be said its substance is the sound of the author's voice. . . .

In Didion the insistence on atmosphere over character in transparent. People are given liquid injections of attitude and placed firmly on a monochromatic landscape the prose insists is the color of interior light. No Didion character will ever surprise either the author or the reader. . . .

In Didion, the antisocial and the spiritually malevolent have been given metaphoric meaning. Her people are not dangerously lost and damaged; rather they are the holy scraps of existential survival. Her men are nihilists whose sexual brutality is an inverse mark of Cain: sensitive souls mangled by murderous life. Her women are thin, crushed-mouthed, silent: Magdalene-madonnas pushed willingly around by the nihilists for whom they suffer gladly because they, too, know living is an alien business. These nerveless, hollowed-out, childlike women stare wide-eyed into the joyless Don Juanism of their men, and they do not turn away. Floating in unanchored space, arrested in emotional time, they are in thrall to spiritual loss.

For Didion, modern life is a wound from which there is no recovery. In her novels, abortion, infant mortality, and cancer are symbolic inflictions. Because there is no escaping fatal loss, nothing matters. Nothing mattering is a recurrent assault on a woundedness as undefended as a child's. We who, accidentally and only apparently, survive the siege of life understand this. Deeply. We walk through our meaningless days and nights, mad and battered, our cruel, corrupt behavior the stigmata of the permanent hellishness that is the only condition we will ever know.

Didion's contribution to the literature of the walking wounded is a rhythmic use of ellipsis devoted to capturing the taste and feel of this ultimate piece of understanding. Volumes of unspoken message are trapped inside her sentence repetitions, her broken-up paragraphs, her tight-lipped juxtapositions. She inserts repeatedly, endlessly, throughout her novels, in puzzling, inappropriate silly places, certain sentences that carry the burden of her insistence. . . .

She gives texture to the prose of nothingness, enriches the distance, lends dimension to the etherizing numbness, and insists on the legitimacy of the Corrupt Innocents in the Alien Promised Land with a relentlessness no other American writer can equal. . . .

Yet skilled as this writing is, it does not feel genuine. There is a space between the pain it alludes to and the expression of that pain. That space seems occupied by a stylish kind of American hip, derived from Hemingway and adopted by an adolescent camp culture, an existential macho swagger whose characteristic economy of expression is duplicitous.

Vivian Gornick. *Village Voice.*
February 18–24, 1981, pp. 36–38

Joan Didion's finest novel to date, *A Book of Common Prayer* (1977), is by no means easy to understand or interpret, but two sets of analogies help to clarify the book's complex intentions. One is to the distinctively "feminine" variant of the contemporary identity quest as written, for instance, by Ruth Prawer Jhabvala, in *Heat and Dust,* Doris Lessing in *Memoirs of a Survivor* and especially Christa Wolf, in *The Quest for Christa T.* These women, and several others, write the sort of artist-parable which presupposes that the narrator can, and should at least attempt to, "find" herself through the act of writing a book, the overt subject of which is the search for the true biography of someone else—a feminine alter ego. The other analogy . . . is to the almost exclusively "masculine" genre of the elegiac romance. . . .

Didion's book, . . . is a masterpiece of artist-parable as well as of elegiac romance. Like *The Quiet American, A Book of Common Prayer* is a story of self-discovery through a gain in moral awareness, but it is also, like *The Quest for Christa T.,* an account of the problematic nature of any attempt to ascertain, let alone convey, the truth of Self or Other by way of a text: "I have not been the witness I wanted to be." Though theme and detail are much closer to Greene's, Didion might well have picked up some hints from Christa Wolf's book on how to persuade a genre to change gender.

Patricia Merivale. In Judith Spector, ed.
*Gender Studies: New Directions in Feminist
Criticism* (Bowling Green, Ohio: Popular
Press, 1986), pp. 140–41

The pervasiveness of the theme of the tragic mutilation of the white American soldier in Vietnam has driven such skeptical and ironic versions of soldiering from the field. It has also distracted our attention from the men, the policies, and the cultural presumptions that sent American soldiers to Vietnam. The fall of Saigon, for example, is the event around which Joan Didion's *Democracy* circles, but its narrative is not about the American soldier "trapped by history, dragged down" etc., etc., but about the politicians, businessmen, and shady government officials—white American men too, just about every one of them—who devised and executed the policies that put the American soldier in the mud. Didion's is not a tale of innocent young men surprised (and why, *still,* so surprised?) by their capacities for violence and brutality and blinding fear, but of ripened war mongers, grown familiar and easy with their ways and means. War is the profession of the American men Didion depicts in *Democracy* and, by the end of the novel, our hearts do not bleed for them. . . .

Like most women novelists, Joan Didion has been inclined to avoid any wars she can walk around. Her early thoughts about Vietnam are located in Haight-Ashbury. *Slouching towards Bethlehem* records not the war in Asia but the culture that war spawned at home. World War II fills her mind in the intense silence of the "19,000 graves in the vast sunken crater above Honolulu." Her first two novels feature neurotic, well-heeled West Coast women whose brushes with the nuclear peril or the wars around the world are rare, accidental, and unexamined. In the last decade, however, in a voyage that began with *A Book of Common Prayer* and ended with *Salvador,* Didion has forced herself to stand where a war is going on.

"You have to pick the places you don't walk away from," Leonard Douglas tells his wife, Charlotte, in *A Book of Common Prayer* when she informs him of her decision to remain in Boca Grande, a thinly disguised portrait of El Salvador in the mid-1970s. The necessity that draws Didion to any war zone is perhaps more urgent and interesting than the necessity that dictates her particular choice of Central America; still, El Salvador is not the choice of most contemporary American novelists. Descended from members of the party that chose not to attempt a crossing of the Sierras in winter, and born and raised in the center of California's Central Valley, Joan Didion has a map of the world that does not correspond to those of East Coast and European intellectuals. Haunted by World War II, she does not look toward Europe or Russia. She looks west at Hawaii and the Pacific. Didion is drawn toward

Central America by the same map of the world that makes Hawaii the appropriate place for thinking about World War II. The war zones in Central America are, for her, the ones closest to home. If her family history, her place of birth, her respect for heat do not fully account for her interest in El Salvador, the kind of war being fought there may. The "unpleasantness" in El Salvador does not immediately threaten nuclear extinction or global conflict. It is a small war in a small country, a war that is overlooked because it never stops, a war that engages the attention of the Super Powers only sporadically and usually unofficially. More crucially, it is a war being waged by identifiable men: husbands, fathers, brothers, lovers, the men sitting at the next table at the Escalon Sheraton. . . .

For the reader who comes to *Salvador* from *A Book of Common Prayer,* the effect of an awakening not from but into terror, of a shocking encounter with the actual in the apparently fictitious, is intensified by the repeated discovery that the fictions of Boca Grande are the facts, even the facts "improved," of El Salvador.

Lynne Hanley. *Writing War: Fiction,
Gender, and Memory* (Amherst: University
of Massachusetts Press, 1991),
pp. 107, 84–88

DIKE, FATIMA (SOUTH AFRICA) 1948-

Can a play in which somebody says, "Before we were so close; now you put all these walls around you, around me" be any good, even if, as here, it is said by Linda Black, a South African white woman, to Phumla Hlophe, the daughter of the dead black family retainer, with whom (Phumla, that is) Linda grew up as all but sisters? The answer is "No!" If Fatima Dike, the author of *Glasshouse,* had put the line into the mouth of a crazed Kaffir addressing the prime minister, it still would be a piece of stale, shopworn goods, as is "We forgot—our ambitions drowned by our whiteness," and almost everything else.

Actually, the basic situation of *Glasshouse* has possibilities. Old Mr. Black (who, you will recall, was white) has been killed by rebellious blacks; he has willed his house to both Linda and Phumla. Even though Phumla refuses to identify the killers, Linda loves her enough to share the house, and living, with her. But because apartheid does not permit such an arrangement, Phumla can stay only if she pretends to be Linda's servant, which she agrees to do. This is where the play ends. It is where, in my opinion, it should start. What does this enforced role playing do to black-and-white sisterhood?

But, of course, even then it would only be interesting if written by someone with a talent comparable, say, to Athol Fugard's rather than Fatima

Dike's. Miss Dike, for example, gives us flashbacks to the women's childhood, which seem to serve absolutely no other purpose than to show how embarrassing it is for an adult actress to pretend that she is a candy-gobbling youngster. Again, Miss Dike has Linda, from time to time, donning a grotesque white male mask in order to impersonate in a low voice this or that representative of repressive South African authority. This device is cribbed from Genet's *Les Noirs,* but there, much more effectively, it is the blacks who put on such white masks. Although Maggie Soboil, the South African actress playing Linda, struggles heroically with this transsexual imposition, the device is fairly ludicrous and distinctly adscititious.

Both Mary Alice (Phumla) and Miss Soboil have good moments, and both of them, even when not playing children or men, have poor ones. Mary Alice, for instance, is unsuccessful with monologues relating atrocities, and rather too old for Phumla; she is, however, often wryly funny and can make the irrational stubbornness of the persecuted come to believable life. Miss Soboil is slow to warm to her role, and has some awkward scenes; she does get steadily better and ends up powerfully persuasive. . . . *Glasshouse* is full of makeshift plot devices that are either incomprehensible or unconvincing; it takes some doing to write uncompellingly of South Africa's tragedy, but Miss Dike has achieved the near-impossible.

John Simon. *New York.* April 6, 1981,
pp. 54–55

Fatima Dike shows in her first play, *The Sacrifice of Kreli,* that her aim is less to reconcile the races than to proclaim pride in the black man's past. It was performed by the Sechaba Players in Cape Town and Johannesburg in 1976. She told Stephen Gray why she chose a part of history as her theme:

> Now, what made me write this play is that one day I realised there were eighteen million black people in this country who had no past, because whatever past we had as a nation was oral history, and it was wiped out by the history which the white people in South Africa had written against what we had to say. Here was a part of my history, my past. From then onwards I felt that if I had a past and a present, I could also have a future.

She chose the story of the fate of the Gcalekas after the Ninth Frontier War. Kreli the King led an army of 12,000 men against the British army. At the end of the war 500 men were left but still they refused to surrender and decided to go into exile in a natural fortress called The Hole. The play takes place seven years after the end of the war. The women and children are elsewhere and the men feel they cannot continue to live under such conditions. The ancestors are to be propitiated by a sacrifice. During the ceremony a white reporter arrives and Kreli interrupts the sacrifice to receive him, because otherwise "They will think we are pagans." The sacrifice fails through his subservience to the possible opinion of an outsider. The men blame their diviner, Mlanjeni, and condemn him to death by being sewed up in the skin of a bull slaughtered that morning for the sacrifice, and then put out in the open for three days. Through the heat of the sun the skin shrinks and crushes him. Mlanjeni, however, lives long enough after the skin is opened to give a message to his people from the ancestors. "They say there is a way." Kreli sends his warriors to spread the message of hope and survival among his people:

> Go and tell our people that our sun is rising . . . go and tell our
> people to plow their burnt fields and build their fallen walls . . .
> go and tell our people we will work and grow.

"And now," he says to the last one, "my son, go and tell our people we will defend the honour of what we are." Dike first wrote the play in Xhosa and then translated it herself, keeping to the idiom for authenticity in dialogue.

In her second play, *The First South African,* written in 1977 and produced at the Space Theatre in Cape Town in that year, Dike turned to a modern theme. It is about a young man, Ruben Zwelinzima Jama, known as Rooi, whose mother was black and his father white. Dike says of the play that it is based on a true story. "Through some fate of the genes he was born white physically, blonde hair and blue eyes. He grew up in Langa, spoke Xhosa fluently and was classified as colored when he was old enough. Here was a man who looked like a white, who had the heart of a black, and was colored. My question was: what is that man?" . . .

The play ends tragically. Dike shows that there is no room in South Africa for a man who does not carry a recognizable racial stamp. Rooi is eventually accepted by no-one and becomes insane.

In her last play to date, *Glasshouse,* Dike goes back to exploring the possibilities of bridging the gap between the races. Her theme is a doubly ironical one. Linda's father is killed by a rioting mob while trying to rescue Phumla, the daughter of his black employees. Phumla knows who are the people that killed him but will not speak. The man's will, in what his daughter calls a "sick joke," leaves his house to the two girls who have grown up together. Under the group areas act it would only be possible for them both to live in it, as they wish to do, if Phumla pretends to be Linda's servant, but this both girls refuse to do. *The Glasshouse* is a microcosm of South African life in which two young people try to find a way of living together. Rambling, discursive, and far too long, this is the least successful of Dike's plays. Since it fails to grip the audience, it cannot make its point.

Ursula A. Barnett. *A Vision of Order: A*
Study of Black South African Literature in
English (1914–1980) (Amherst: University of
Massachusetts Press, 1983), pp. 242–43

Fatima Dike is regarded as an important black South African playwright. Although she has not been as prolific as [Athol] Fugard, her plays have also met with wide acclaim. Especially in *The First South African* (1977), . . . Dike faithfully represents and utilizes the "languages" of her world, i.e., of modern township life. . . . [In contrast] to her more traditional play, *The Sacrifice of Kreli* (1987), *The First South African* displays a greater variety of languages, including traditional language, and is also more accessible than *The Sacrifice of Kreli*. . . .

The First South African is worked out in terms of three distinctive social strata as they are manifested in township life in general and in the main character's life in particular. This ties in with the structure of the play which largely expresses and embodies the development of the main theme and operates on three levels with the suggestion of a fourth, weakly defined level. These represent different social strata. Firstly, there are the customs and traditions of the Xhosa; on this level the main character goes by the name Zwelinzima. Secondly, there is the playful yet precarious life of a tsotsi; on this social stratum he is called Rooi. Thirdly, the alluring borderlife of the white man beckons; here he is called Ruben James. . . .

Code-switches in *The First South African* are very much dependent on the relative status of the participants and the formality of the relationships. This is closely linked to the three different social strata that exist in the play: Xhosa traditional life, tsotsi life and the white man's world.

The characters reveal not only their knowledge of social strategies in that they alter their speech to fit the social situation, but also communicative competence in that they know when and where to switch, in whose presence to switch and what code to use. Since they are aware of the different codes, they are also eager to point out the aptness of a code-switch or the lack thereof. . . .

In *The First South African* all characters have an awareness of the different codes, as well as of the social value and range of applicability of each code. In the tsotsi scenes, Rooi and Max use four languages at once. English serves as the basis; Afrikaans, Xhosa and tsotsi language are then grafted onto the basis in the form of entire sentences or syntactic units. In these scenes a feeling of intimacy and confidentiality is created. However, complete switches from one language to another also occur. In the Bantu Administration office scenes both Freda and Rooi make use of a mixture of Xhosa, English, and Afrikaans when talking to the black clerk. However, when they talk to the superintendent, they switch from this mixture to English exclusively. Their switches are intentional and have strategic value, because they want to achieve a desired goal or effect, be it to attain the goodwill of the whites or to acknowledge the superiority of the whites by regarding English or Afrikaans (depending on the specific situation) as the more important language. By thus recognizing a code-switch as a social strategy, the characters apply code-switches effectively to their own benefit.

Esmé Grubler. *South African Theatre Journal*. 1, 1990, pp. 39–41, 44, 47–48

DIMITROVA, BLAGA (BULGARIA) 1922–

At the end of [the translation] process, the poems seemed to be falling into three groups, and so the book [*Because the Sea Is Black*] took shape in sections.

The first consisted of poems from Dimitrova's book *Forbidden Sea,* a collection in which thematic variations are worked on the poet's meditations at the Black Sea, after her cancer diagnosis; throughout these pieces, the doctor's prohibition against swimming is metaphorically extended to convey other demarcations—those dividing definition from definition, world from world, being from being (old from young, man from woman, living from dead). The paradoxes that everywhere engage Dimitrova's attention (the colors of our human blindness, the doubleness of human nature) are clearly visible here. And it is the horizon, ultimately, emblem of all distinctions, that turns out to have been the protagonist of this series.

The second grouping is of poems in which the poet's identity as a woman (mother, daughter, lover) is central. A painfully honest series about the illness of an aging mother reveals the woman's dual role as suffering and suffered; the mother's fate is one the poet takes for legacy.

It is in the last section that one sees Blaga Dimitrova's project in its broadest terms. The perspective engages metaphysics as politics, interiority as outer space, history as a future. Here her characteristic gifts seem clearest: her love of language and adventures in it, her steadfast focus on the human community in the face of its daily and perennial annihilations, her reverence for the brave and solitary human gesture, her refusal of any command to kneel, and, throughout, her faith in a transcendent understanding.

> Heather McHugh. Translator's introduction
> to Blaga Dimitrova. *Because the Sea Is
> Black* (Middletown, Connecticut: Wesleyan
> University Press, 1989), pp. viii–ix

"Heretical ethics—*herethics*—may just be that which makes life's bonds bearable, that which enables us to tolerate thought, and hence the thought of death. 'Herethics' is *à mort, amour,*" writes Julia Kristeva; I can imagine no better introduction to the work of her compatriot the Bulgarian poet and heretrix Blaga Dimitrova. For more than four decades, Dimitrova has been the conscience of Bulgarian poetry, its reconstructor of mind and innovator of language, its voice of comfort and courage, aiming to accomplish, in what has by and large remained a solitary effort, a revolution in sensibility that took several generations in the West.

Schooled in the modernist poetries of Europe and in the classics, Dimitrova emerged as the foremost Bulgarian woman poet in the 1950s and 1960s when her once-powerful predecessor, Elisaveta Bagryana, had strayed into strained superficialities. Dimitrova's poetry, too, had passed through a stage of political acquiescence, but when Stalinism fell into disfavor and a chorus of male voices preached self-congratulation, she showed a will to emancipation and a resolve to probe the changing dilemmas of human life. She was quick to discern that women in the Bulgarian tradition have been subjected to many sentimental distortions, behind which stand the figures of individuals in pain and silence; she saw that the social and psychological dislocations in Bulgarian society were deeper and more problematic than many were led to believe. Her preoccupation with women's lives and concerns often provoked critical dismay. (Indeed, it is still the custom of critical officials to dismiss her bolder experiments as feminine idiosyncracy, or as un-Bulgarian.) Read in its proper cultural context, the poetry and prose she started writing was not only a passionate plea for extending the nominal emancipation of women by shedding proscriptive patriarchal morality, especially sexual morality; it was, above all, an assertion of individual experience as the ultimate measure, even when self-knowledge and personal integrity meant loneliness and homelessness. It was a call for cultural openness against the ideas and values of a complacent provincialism.

Her moral imperatives led her, in the late 1960s, to a passionate concern about the Vietnam War. Her two prose books and many poems on the subject go beyond strictly political confrontation, founded as they are on a humanitarian concern for men and women under physical pain and metaphysical anguish, irrational violence and rationalist assault. It was natural that in those years of bewildering turmoil in both West and East, her campaign for human freedom would not confine itself to the Vietnam War. Ever more intently since her powerful novel *The Avalanche* (1971) (which was denounced by the establishment as "existentialist"), Dimitrova has grappled with human realities that have been marginalized in Bulgarian poetry and prose. She focuses on the body, on death, and on language. Precariously poised between dogmatism (and the concomitant snuggeries of social and artistic conformity) on the one side and personal bereavement and the harrowing experience of the cancer ward on the other, her art transcends its narrower national context. Her novel *Face* in defiance and in humor (which orthodox zealots like even less) challenges totalitarian practices of aesthetic and academic coercion. Her recent books of poetry, *Sea Forbidden, Spaces, Voice,* and *Labyrinth,* move far ahead of local developments and ever deeper into the interior of a perceptive, generous, and compassionate mind.

Dimitrova's battle with boundaries has won her a popularity bordering on adoration in her native country, and her poetry and prose have already been translated into many European languages. As a Bulgarian, I am happy to acknowledge my debt to her, and hope that her voice, coming from the other Europe and in translation, may speak to the American audience with the force of the genuine.

Niko Boris. Translator's introduction to
Blaga Dimitrova. *Because the Sea Is Black*
(Middletown, Connecticut: Wesleyan
University Press, 1989), pp. xi–xiii

With the publication of *Because the Sea Is Black* Wesleyan University Press has provided American poetry lovers with a long-overdue introduction to one of Bulgaria's finest living authors and certainly of its most respected. Poet, novelist, playwright, and publicist, Blaga Dimitrova has been translated into numerous European languages and has gained recognition as one of Eastern Europe's outstanding writers. . . .

Up until the events of November 1989, when the old communist political and cultural structures began to crumble throughout Eastern Europe and a younger generation of social activists began to make itself known, Dimitrova was a rarity on the Bulgarian literary scene: a writer with a conscience. Few other writers of her generation (or any other for that matter) managed to retain their moral and creative integrity throughout he decades of the Zhivkov regime. Despite the oppressive influence of the officially imposed tenets of socialist realism and a seductively effective . . . policy that rewarded writers with innumerable privileges for toeing the party line, Dimitrova and a handful of her colleagues refused to become the literary "yes men" of the Zhivkov regime and sought whenever possible to reflect in their works a true picture of the individual and society.

Because the Sea Is Black represents a selection of poems originally published in Bulgarian . . . the most recent ones coming from the collection entitled *Laberint.* . . . The poems have been felicitously selected and translated by the American poet-translator Heather McHugh in collaboration with a talented Bulgarian colleague, Niko Boris. . . .

Dimitrova's verse will say many things to many people: her themes and concerns are both universal and specific. Love (and the failure to communicate it) between mother and daughter or man and woman, a preoccupation with time, and the search for an independent identity true to itself (whether a woman's, a nation's, or even a language's) are among the recurrent themes. Those poems treating women, whether the poet's memories of a relationship with her mother or the general plight of women in a male-dominated society, are, for me, among her most evocative for their power to communicate through imagery. Through her striking manipulation of image and language, the descriptions of such mundane household routines as hanging out the wash becomes a metaphor for the mother's (woman's) sacrifice of self and identity: "I still remember her against a patch/of sky washed laundry-blue, and caged by balconies out back, the gallows/of the clothesline overhead."

McHugh and Boris have done an excellent job of selecting and translating some of the finest examples of Dimitrova's poetry. Their versions reveal a remarkable sensitivity to the linguistic contours and metaphorical texture of the originals. Dimitrova has always had a fascination for language—its use and abuse—and it is to the translators' credit that the poems they present here manage to convey the flavor and spirit of the poet's linguistic experiments. *Because the Sea Is Black* is an elegant and intimate introduction to Bulgarian poetry at its best and to one of the most respected writers in Eastern Europe today. Although it will certainly have only limited appeal for the American reading public, we can only hope that its appearance will inaugurate a more active interest in one of the more eloquent representatives of one of the lesser-known literatures of Eastern Europe.

Micaela S. Iovine. World Literature Today.
65, 1991, pp. 140–41

Dimitrova began publishing shortly before World War II, and her early poems demonstrate both her lyric gift and her orientation toward the everyday; they are also traditional in form. Her attitude toward the terrible times of 1943 already demonstrated that she had a deep understanding of historical catastrophe but nevertheless affirmed that life was good.

Although never a party member, Dimitrova sympathized with certain communist objectives at the beginning. In 1950, after the death of the communist prime minister Georgi Dimitrov (no relation), Dimitrova brought out a small volume, *Stikhove za vozhda* (verses on the leader), a cluster of chronologically arranged biographical lyrics on Dimitrov, clearly influenced by Mayakovsky in their fabricated enthusiasm for the new political order. In recent years, however, Dimitrova has avoided mentioning this collection.

In 1952–1954 Dimitrova spent two years as a construction worker in the Rhodope mountains, an experience that found romanticized expression in the moderately modernist novel *Putuvane kum sebe si* (1965; journey to oneself), a story of a woman who wishes to do a man's work in this world without ceasing to be a woman.

Putuvane kum sebe si was the first of several novels, generally relatively short and as modernist in their approach as they could be under Bulgarian circumstances. They include *Otklonenie* (1967; Deviation), *Lavina* (1971; Avalanche), and *Litse* (1981; Face), a book literally "imprisoned" by the authorities until the end of the decade. Dimitrova also traveled to Vietnam on at least five occasions during the course of the Vietnam War, describing her experiences in *Podzemno nebe: Vietnamski dnevnik* (1972; Subterranean heaven: a Vietnam diary) and using them as material for lyric poems describing the admirable behavior of ordinary people confronting the adversities of war.

For years Dimitrova wrote in the shadow of Bulgaria's best-known twentieth-century woman poet, Elisaveta Bagryana. When the latter effectively withdrew from the literary scene, Dimitrova not only succeeded her as the country's leading woman poet and literary intellectual, but also became one of her chief interpreters through such volumes as *Mladostta na Bagryana* (1975; Bagryana's youth), written in collaboration with her critic-husband Yordan Vasilev; it contains reminiscences, portraits, and detailed poetic analyses of which perhaps only another poet is capable.

Still, it is as a lyric poet that Dimitrova has made her mark in Bulgarian literature. For most of her career she has been a consistent modernist, thought not an extreme one. She is very much aware of language as a medium, but also of language as an artifact created by an entire culture over many centuries. She has visited western Europe on several occasions, and values its cultural achievements, but her strongest commitment is to her own people's roots, both distant and more to hand. She pays explicit tribute to the older generation of Bulgarian poets—including Bagryana and Atanas Dalchev—who helped create the more immediate culture in which she moved. And she honors her father and mother, whose declining days she has recorded in moving lyrics. She is sustained, not constricted, by her links with past generations. She incorporates the legacy of the past into her own personality, which she will transmit to others in its entirety only when she dies.

In recent years, as Bulgarian cultural constraints have loosened, Dimitrova's writing has become progressively more complex and difficult, as it deals with some of the deepest issues of human existence. In 1968 she wrote: "The guilty feeling of a transit passenger— / this never deserts me." In 1990 she published a long poem, *Tranzit* (transit), an allegory of her country's contemporary difficulties cast in the form of reflections of an airline passenger delayed by bad weather. "But we shall certainly take off!" are her final words.

Dimitrova is now something of an elder "statesman" of Bulgarian culture. In the past she was not a hero, but neither did she commit any actions of which she need be deeply ashamed. She has publicly admitted her earlier shortcomings and, more important, paid eloquent tribute to those few who, unlike her, at critical points raised protesting voices. A bout with cancer in addition to recent political developments has made her resolve to write each of her poems "as if it were her last," and not to distort the truth as she perceives it. This moral determination, coupled with her linguistic mastery, has made her perhaps the foremost literary figure of contemporary Bulgaria.

Charles A. Moser. In Steven R. Serafin and
Walter D. Glanze, eds. *Encyclopedia of
World Literature in the 20th Century* (New
York: Continuum, 1993), p. 181

DINESEN, ISAK (pseud. KAREN BLIXEN) (DENMARK)
1885–1962

If, as Dorothy Canfield lets fall, the pseudonymous author of these tales is a continental European "writing in English although that is not native to his pen," we have here a linguistic triumph for which there is probably no precedent. Barring a few slips from idiom which are so attractive as to seem premeditated, the English of the book is such as I for one have never seen written by a foreigner to the language, and none too often by those in the grammar born. And if, as rumor has it, the author is a Danish woman who never wrote a book before, we have a phenomenon so astonishing as to be incredible. Not that I disbelieve it, for of a person, man or woman, Dane or Albanian, who can write like this I am willing to believe any miracle.

The time of the tales is the nineteenth century, usually before 1850, and the place is Europe—Denmark, Italy, France, or Switzerland, though the prevailing skies are northern; the people have such names as Nat-og-Dag, De Coninck, Pellegrina, and Pozentiani. As for the stories themselves, they are mad after a peculiar fashion which gives the most modern possible meaning to the second word in the title [*Seven Gothic Tales*]. . . .

Isak Dinesen is a twentieth-century Zélide who manifests all the sensibilities and despairs of the time. One of her people, Mira the story-teller, regrets that he has grown silent as he has lost his fears. "When you know what things are really like you can make no poems about them. . . . I have become too familiar with life; it can no longer delude me into believing that one thing is much worse than another. The day and the dark, an enemy and a friend—I know them to be about the same." Yet something is left to Mira. "Every night, as soon as I sleep I dream. And in my dreams I still know fear." So Isak Dinesen can be supposed to have dreamed these tales; they sound like that, they are both luminous and plastic, both phosphorescent and marmoreal; and they would appear to be the final expedient of one who had no other way of proving that the world still is, or within a century was, no less exciting than it used to be. Episodes are piled upon episodes, or wrapped around the body of a tale like so many bands of silken leopard hide; personalities, announced at the start as perverse, grow to heroic stature as swift sentences develop an appropriately astonishing prose theme. Everywhere the prose is cool, certain, comprehending, disenchanted. Morten De Coninck, returning as a ghost to his father's mansion, declares: "We have been amateurs in saying no, little sisters. But God can say no. Good God, how he can say no. We think that he can go on no longer, not even he. But he goes on, and says no once more." Cardinal Hamilcar, or rather the man in bloody bandages whom we take to be the Cardinal, knows how to speak of a civilization which seems to him to have lost the glory of an ancient time when there were other and better gods: "No human being with a feeling for greatness can possibly believe that the God who created the stars, the sea, and the desert, the poet Homer and the giraffe, is the same God who is now making, and upholding, the King of Belgium, the Poetical School of Schwaben, and the moral ideas of our day."

The time has come, they say, when we must look with abhorrence upon a novelist who wastes any more talent upon characters who are laws unto themselves. May there be a moment, however, for these utterly graceful and outrageous people of Isak Dinesen. It is possible that we shall never see their like again.

Mark Van Doren. *The Nation.*
April 18, 1934, p. 449

Isak Dinesen has the straight-out gift for performing illusion, and the resources of mind and heart of a great lady who has lived for a good many

years in many different parts of the world. In her tales, one of the extraordinary things is that the spell—for they lie in the realm of magic and romance—
gets done by the speed of wit, takes its turn within the circle of morality, and
keeps its hold through irony, which usually attends on learning and experience, not enchantment. But I haven't found anything out, for the spells work,
too, through the pure delight of the senses.

Isak Dinesen a long time ago made herself master of the tale. Austerely
objective in their execution, true to her credo of the story teller's story, her
tales are also extremely personal in their point of view, in their great style.
They have a vigor which persuades us that vigor perfectly solves the secret
of delicacy, for her stories are the essence of delicacy. She has a marvelous
gaiety, and what makes it more marvelous still are its transpositions, true
gaiety's other key. Her tales are glimpses out of, rather than into, an extraordinary mind. Sometimes one feels that Isak Dinesen's stories come toward one
like the flashes and signal-beams from a lighthouse on a strange and infre-
quently sighted coast—a coast beautiful and precarious, for it may be the
last outreach of magic, but resting on bedrock.

Like all her tales, these twelve are like no other tales. They range from
country to country, the north to the south—from point to point in time, from
here to there in reality. There are tales joined onto other tales, tales inlaid in
tales, and one long, disturbingly beautiful, unfinished Gothic tale called "The
Caryatids." . . .

Isak Dinesen's tales are not written for children. They are far too sophisticated, too psychologically subtle, too philosophically speculative for any
but a child genius. This, however, may help to assure them against the skepticism for a down-to-earth age now threatened by a new despotism—that which
Dwight MacDonald has brilliantly diagnosed as "The Triumph of the Fact."
Isak Dinesen's stories belong to another realm—the realm of the court ball,
of the carnival, of the masquerade. They belong somewhere out in literary
space in a constellation brightened by the stars of Shakespeare, Plato, and
Guy de Maupassant. These are her torch-bearers at the banquet-table to
which, in the mask of Hoffmann, she bids us sit down with Socrates and talk
about eternity.

Eudora Welty. *The New York Times.*
November 3, 1957, p. 5

Seven Gothic Tales is a great book about Europe, because Isak Dinesen's
experience of Africa stands behind it; and Europe stands, in the same way,
behind every word of *Out of Africa.* That is why *Out of Africa* (1937) is
literature and not just another memoir of an interesting life.

While a great deal of *Seven Gothic Tales* was "thought of," as Isak
Dinesen says in the foreword to the Danish edition, "and some of it written
in Africa," *Out of Africa* was, as she made clear to me, entirely conceived
and written after she got back to Europe. In assuring the Danish readers of
Seven Gothic Tales that the parts about Denmark "have to be considered

more as the fantasies of a Danish emigrant than as an attempt to describe reality," she is saying that a Denmark conceived from the standpoint of Africa is not everybody's Denmark. But the apologetic tone is an attempt to forestall hostile criticism; for the imagination works by just such reconciliation of opposites, and there is no doubt that she considers her imagined Denmark more real than the Denmark of ordinary observation.

Her Africa is not everybody's Africa either. I have already suggested that it is an Africa of certain romantic expectations come true—expectations as to the possibility of recovering in primitive places that unity of man with nature which yields psychological and social unity as well: expectations as to the possibility of recovering a kind of life that prevailed in Europe before the Industrial Revolution, that unique event, cut Europeans off from nature and the past, and consequently from all other civilizations. Her Africa is also seen retrospectively, as something already lost even to her. It is seen in a way she herself could not have seen it while she was in the midst of the experience and did not know it was to end. It is because Africa figures as a paradise lost—both in Isak Dinesen's life and in the life of Europe—that *Out of Africa* is an authentic pastoral, perhaps the best prose pastoral of our time.

Robert Langbaum. *Isak Dinesen: The Gayety of Vision* (London: Chatto and Windus, 1964), pp. 178–179

Dinesen's re-creation of her experiences in Kenya, overtly structured by a metaphor equating Kenya with Paradise, falls within the mainstream of an established tradition that depicts eastern and southern Africa as secular utopias. "The Africa of this [tradition] is beautiful, open, sun-drenched—a golden land that preserves ways of life now but a memory in Britain—a nostalgic fantasy that, born of a distaste for the present, glorifies the past." Yet there is a religious aspect of Dinesen's experience and metaphor that transcends the secular implications and that constitutes, as we shall see later, the truly mythic character of her autobiographical works. The religious facet, however, derives from the secular one, and therefore cannot be appreciated without an elaboration of the latter. . . .

From the point of view of the *African* context of Dinesen's experiences, the politics are superficial; Kenya and its indigenous people provide the stage and the props used to enact the drama conceived in Europe. The desires to preserve certain romantic values and to flee or fight the values of industrial civilization are acted out in a conveniently idyllic setting in Kenya. However, Dinesen's more substantial interactions with the Africans gradually, but profoundly, alter some aspects of her personality and values and eventually influence her art. Her assimilation of various elements of the indigenous cultures has a significant effect on the religious component of her Edenic metaphor and on the structure of her autobiographic works. Yet the intellectual and aesthetic changes are to a great extent determined by the nature of the social, political, and economic interaction between Dinesen and the Africans. . . .

Dinesen's sense of omnipotence, her view of herself as a god, and her transformation from empiric to mythic consciousness together constitute the substantial, religious component of her metaphor of Kenya as a paradise. Whereas the secular aspect of the latter is based upon the social freedom that the feudal structure of the colony affords its aristocratic immigrants, the religious element derives from the transfiguration of Dinesen's consciousness through her interaction with the natives. The cultural differences between the Africans and Dinesen as well as the specifically modified feudal relationship between them permitted her a series of religious experiences that establish the basis of the metaphor. Her acceptance and the use of mythic conscious-ness constitute the practical formalization of the religious experience.

> Abdul R. JanMohamed. *Manichean*
> *Aesthetics: The Politics of Literature in*
> *Colonial Africa* (Amherst: University of
> Massachusetts Press, 1983),
> pp. 49, 52, 65–66

Critical discussion of Isak Dinesen's *Out of Africa* has centered on the ques-tion of whether it can be called an "autobiography." Noting the way Dinesen rearranged, blurred, and omitted details of her experience managing a coffee plantation in Kenya from 1914 to 1931, critics have found it to be more myth than history, calling it a pastoral, a tale of sojourn, a travel book, a memoir, and "not quite an autobiography." This confusion is understandable because *Out of Africa* is neither a chronicle of the times nor an account of Dinesen's private experience; it is comprised of anecdotes, character studies, medita-tions, descriptions, and information about the farm. In addition, Dinesen portrays herself as a figure without the interiority we might expect from a speaker who says she will "write down as accurately as possible my experi-ences on the farm." Nevertheless, the disagreement about what to call *Out of Africa* raises questions both about what meaning we give to the term "autobiography" and about what we assume constitutes a "life."

Out of Africa can be called an autobiography if we remember that as a theoretical construct "autobiography" names texts in which we cannot make a simplistic distinction between the protagonist and the author, as we might be able to in speaking of, say, autobiographical fiction. In fact, *Out of Africa* confronts us with the paradox central to the study of autobiography: the protagonist both is and is not the author. An autobiographer does not create a persona that can be defined simply as imaginary or historical, nor does s/he create a life that can be interpreted as either fiction or documentary. Rather, s/he creates another life, one that is analogous to the life lived, not a transcription of it. The crucial problem in reading autobiography is not the accuracy of the account, but the basis upon which the author chose to include some details and exclude others.

If we read *Out of Africa* as an autobiography, we assign ourselves the critical task of deconstructing, if you will, the difference between the author and the protagonist. The form Dinesen has given to the information about her experience constitutes a "mask," and our understanding of the life she represents depends not upon "unmasking" the speaker but in closely examining the lines and contours of that mask. Two related questions must be addressed: what mythos, or underlying narrative pattern, determines the form of the life Dinesen has created? And what idea provides the basis for Dinesen's use of that mythos? Before turning to the text itself, we shall first establish that Dinesen used the myth of Lucifer's rebellion as a paradigm for her experience as a woman, and that she used this paradigm to develop an idea of her life that was in harmony with Kierkegaard's definition of tragedy.

Judith Lee. *Prose Studies.* September, 1985

The qualities that have led to Karen Blixen's literary fame are the first ones to strike the readers of her stories. The exquisite and refined narrative manner and the mysterious and fantastic elements of their plots have given her readers a somewhat intimidating impression of her: Karen Blixen as the aristocrat and sybil in Danish literature, the great anachronism who manages to combine old culture with archaic unculture. But this portrait reveals only half the truth, and it suffers a bit from banality. There is much spirit in Karen Blixen's writings, but not so much witchcraft as people have tended to impute to them; she enchants without bewitching. And her aristocratic manner never outweighs her piety.

One of the chief reasons why Karen Blixen has a dazzling and disorienting effect on her readers is because they take for literary sophistication what is basically her personal viewpoint. In her tales, stories and anecdotes are arranged in layers, one on top of the other and the innermost kernel of any of her tales is never a moral principle but rather another smaller story or an image. Compositional lines never meet in a point but come together to form a figure. This is a consistent characteristic in everything she has written—including her book of memoirs, *Out of Africa.* It was in the light of an image or through a symbol that she attempted to understand her situation in Africa when she encountered adversity. This means that for her it is not the concept but rather myth and portent that are the primary spiritual entities capable of revealing humanity's basic conditions.

Aage Henriksen. *Isak Dinesen/Karen
Blixen: The Work and the Life* (New York:
St. Martin's, 1988), pp. 18–19

That Dinesen's vision of the world is deeply and fundamentally androcentric is . . . an inescapable conclusion. Women in Dinesen's world can possess power only through a severely delimited series of choices: as wife, mother, or lover, as artist within one of the "feminine" arts, or as older woman. In no case, it is possible for them to be sexual, independent, and powerful.

Indeed, female sexuality and independence appear to be mutually exclusive concepts in Dinesen's view. Thus, it is difficult, at least on this point, to grant Dinesen the "overbærenhed" (indulgence) she requested, for she does not portray "menneskets højeste, guddommelige muligheder" (humanity's highest, divine possibilities) but only man's possibilities and, as such belongs to "nutidens litteratur" (the literature of today) not because of her depiction of women, but rather in spite of it.

Marilyn Johns Blackwell. Scandinavian
Studies. 63, 1991, p. 63

[D]espite her increasing inclusion in feminist analyses, she has been overwhelmingly represented as a type of Athena, quintessentially her father's daughter, devoted in her work as in her life to a constellation of values supremely androcentric—a psychological and textual as well as a sociohistorical ancien régime. Hence two remarkably different, mutually exclusive "Isak Dinesens" stand before us, as in a double exposure—a divided figure poised between ex-centric feminist reconceptions and the perdurable law of the Same. Thus "reading Isak Dinesen" might serve as a synecdoche for the kinds of epistemological crisis the question of gender provokes for contemporary criticism.

Yet even Dinesen's feminist critics tend to overlook what I take to be the most salient and revolutionary quality of her writing: the radical discursive practices that undermine what appears to be, in Eric Johannesson's phrase, "a neat and orderly structure." Dinesen's complex, self-reflexive texts brilliantly anticipate not only feminist concerns with women's historical experience in androcentric societies, but also conceptions of language and subjectivity more recently articulated by continental writers like Cixous, Kristeva, and Irigaray, who focus primarily on semiotic systems, reading "woman" as both a psychosexual being and a discursive category. Implicit in my rereading of Dinesen is an attempt to negotiate the gap between these two discourses on woman, often characterized as mutually exclusive. Yet I use these dual designations only provisionally and heuristically, as general indices of the theoretical positions I would traverse, for whatever their divergences, both perspectives pose fundamental questions about the cultural construction of gender and the gendered construction of culture, questions that compel a massive revision of received notions of subjectivity, authorship, and representation. Thus rather than reject either approach. I prefer to draw on their different strengths, allowing each to open up textual implications that might otherwise remain obscured—and indicating, by the way, the degree to which each presupposes and inflects the other. A writer as playful as Dinesen (who attributed inconsistency not only to femininity and divinity but to inspired authorship) demands flexible, eclectic reading practices capable of dwelling in apparent contradictions, setting theoretical differences in dialogue, and suggesting the ways such oppositions may themselves be called into question.

While the traditional view of Dinesen holds that "the writer begins where the woman ends," I want to suggest that where the writer begins, the "woman" goes underground, constituting a dynamic of disruption and recreation that undermines the surface structures of the text. In one of her lectures on the status of women in Western culture, Dinesen herself addressed the question of woman's "double-voiced discourse," maintaining that women in a patriarchal society might best subvert the "ancient citadels of males, the strongholds of the church, science, and law," by *acting*—"as in their time the Achaeans did in Troy, by going within the walls in a wooden horse. That is, [by making] their entry in disguise, in a costume which intellectually or psychologically represent[s] a male."

Susan Hardy Aiken. *Isak Dinesen and the Engendering of Narrative* (Chicago: University of Chicago Press, 1990), pp. 7–8

Isak Dinesen's writings constitute a very special world of their own within twentieth-century fiction. And it is far from coincidental that to readers as well as to critics they appear as an illuminated island. One reason of course is the indisputable mastery of her narrative constructions; those in themselves will guarantee her a front-rank position. But moreover it is perhaps the peculiar state of non-contemporarity in Dinesen's work which is the main reason for their ability still to appear as open, inviting, attractive—and still mystically indefinite. This "non-contemporarity" is not only what characterizes the immediate relationship between the very form of Dinesen's works and their time (her contemporary world literature is signed with names such as Joyce, Proust, Virginia Woolf—and appears *somewhat* different). No, the noncontemporarity, the clash between times (or the clash between discourses, to be semiotically more precise) is also inherent in the works. What we have in mind here is not the thematic transmission of the action into landscapes of the past, although this transmission indeed is an important feature of the constructions. No, the clash takes place above all between on the one hand the narrative construction which (seemingly) is in charge, and which even at the time of publication was emphatically *outdated,* and on the other hand a theme which on a closer look is tremendously modern. Any reader of Dinesen's narratives, professional or amateur (or the rare combination of both), is thus simultaneously thrown in several different directions. Within one register she is thrown back into an almost premodern discourse not only because of the concrete rooms of action and the obviously old-fashioned olympic, narrative construction, but also qua the critique of the individuals' project of controlling reality which, apparently rooted in a feudal-absolutist state of thinking, is emphatically and repeatedly exercised in the points of the intrigues as to attitudes. At the same time, however, behind the apparent "naturalness" of these narrative constructions, this critique is indeed surprisingly modern. And, finally, is perhaps already (modally) "postmodern" qua its relaxed and virtually self-ironical *accepting* embodiment of the emphatically importunate undecidability of the problem of enunciation; this is remarkably different from the way contemporary modernism felt itself more or less involuntarily prisoned by a tragic feeling of loss of substance, evoked by the very same experience.

These clashes of discourse include and point out the problem of discursive change in the works, and this is no doubt one reason why Dinesen's works are still able to fascinate.

Morten Kyndrup. *Framing and Fiction: Studies in the Rhetoric of Novel, History, and Interpretation* (Aarhus, Denmark: Aarhus University Press, 1992), pp. 297–99

Isak Dinesen's most famous work is her memoir, *Out of Africa,* called by Truman Capote one of the most beautiful books of the century. What perhaps gives *Out of Africa* its power is a sense that its tellings act as sacred text, where the generative word is supreme; where the self is exalted until it touches the divine. Throughout *Out of Africa* Isak Dinesen is always the imaginative being—the divine I—who creates and makes possible the life throughout. About a native African, Jogona Kanyagga, Isak Dinesen writes: "I had created him and shown him himself: Jogona Kanyagga of life everlasting," comparing herself to the Lord "when He formed him [Adam] out of the dust."

Within the silences and between the linguistic hesitations of the text, colonialism's power is felt, if compassionately administered. One might say, then, that Isak Dinesen herself interferes with recent readings of *Out of Africa* as a text subverting colonialism. While on her African farm, Isak Dinesen scribbled into notebooks (in what appear to be the beginnings of a story) the names of people working for her, referring to them as slaves. It was a gap she did not leap in *Out of Africa.* Instead, the exaltation of self made possible by colonialism is felt here. Critics such as Jan Mohamed and Ngugi wa Thiong'o have opened the charge on *Out of Africa* as a work born in the colonial experience, pressing away from the admiring view of *Out of Africa* as modern pastoral, shifting the focus to the problematic text of colonialism it is. Despite its author's intentions, *Out of Africa* has become a political text. Indeed, Martin Green has suggested that *Out of Africa* is an implicit warrior's call to expand the empire, Isak Dinesen's description of the Masai issuing from someone "associated particularly with the military caste."

If Isak Dinesen's reputation continues to unfold and her romantic tales to fascinate us as we near the end of the twentieth century, perhaps it is because we ourselves feel the same unsettling of meaning conveyed in the breathless structure of *Seven Gothic Tales* and *Last Tales,* the same precariousness of *being* rushed along perched atop the icy rush of words in *Winter's Tales.* Yet we cannot but continue to hope for relief, for a cosmos where destiny—anecdotal utterances of the universe—is written as ultimate syllabic intent, and words wrap us in meaning and truth. Perhaps in that still, cold stretch of the cosmos as we seek to re-imagine Isak Dinesen, we rediscover ourselves and emerge with the astonishing revelation that we can imagine each other.

For Isak Dinesen, who delighted in the engagement with destiny her pseudonym and role-playing allowed, Africa may have permitted her to sound an imaginative note in Denmark when she took the name of *Isak,* a probable borrowing from the Somali family name of Isaak. For this player of the imagination, watching herself continually appropriated and reinvented within different forms of critical discourse may have finally become an amusement and distraction. For us, it is a reminder that literary works and their authors must yield gracefully to each new critical shaping and pummeling for a literary reputation to take on an ever larger life of its own; to watch the unfolding of a reputation under such continual reinvention becomes cause for high literary spectacle.

Olga Anastasia Pelensky. Introduction to
Isak Dinesen: Critical Views (Athens: Ohio
University Press, 1993), pp. xvi–xvii

DING LING (CHINA) 1907–86

Ding Ling began her career as a highly personal author rather than a dedicated propagandist. In her first phase (1926–29) she was primarily interested in probing the meaning of life in unabashedly feminine and autobiographical terms: the stories in her first collection, *In the Darkness* (1928), notably "Meng K'o" and "The Diary of Miss Sophia," all flaunt the sexual restiveness and impotent fury of a warm-hearted girl in the sinister powers of the city. Apparently lonely and confused. Ding Ling pours all her resentments and exasperations in the diary mold of her fiction. Her next work, *Wei Hu* (1930), a long story noted for its frank descriptions of sex, is an exercise in the romantic-revolutionary manner: its theme is the incompatibility of a couple when one member advances beyond the other in revolutionary behavior and outlook. In two companion pieces, "Shanghai, Spring 1930," Parts I and II, Ding Ling continues with her probing of the dilemmas of a bourgeois intellectual when confronted with proletarian experience.

In 1931 Ding Ling joined the Communist party and turned resolutely into a proletarian writer. "The T'ien Village," a transitional piece, depicts a city-bred Communist working among Hunan peasants; the long story *Water* describes a peasant uprising under the provocation of famine. From that story on, even though she returned briefly to her despondent, nihilistic mood when she could no longer hide her disgust with the Communist regime at Yenan in the early 1940s, Ding Ling has written about little else but peasants, soldiers, and Communist cadres, with this work culminating in her novel about land reform, *Sun over the Sangkan River* (1949). . . .

The reputation of Ding Ling during the 1930s was mainly sustained by her early stories, which are supposedly "modern" in their attitude toward sex and therefore superior to the more decorous fiction of Ping Hsin and Ling Shu-hua. When Ding Ling turns to proletarian fiction in 1931, she is stripped of even that youthful nihilistic candor, revealing her essential triteness as a propagandist. *Water,* generally regarded as one of the proudest exhibits of Communist fiction, may serve as an example. Though in style and intent it differs little from the earlier proletarian stories, it can be taken as a forerunner of socialist-realist fiction. . . .

There is nothing wrong with the basic situation depicted in *Water.* Chinese peasants have time and again suffered from famine and received no succor from the well-to-do and government agencies. The theme is of crucial human importance, and properly handled, the story should become a moving tragedy, irrespective of the point of view of the author. But intent on illustrating her Marxist thesis and beautifying her language, Ding Ling has apparently forgotten the all too apparent physiological reality of people under famine. This blindness to physical reality, and to psychological and social reality, constitutes the one fundamental weakness of Communist writers, though ideally there is no reason why they should be so unobservant. Perhaps the type of mind which takes to the oversimplifying formulas of Marxism is naturally of an abstract order, incapable of much interest in the fascinating concrete phenomena pertaining to human existence. . . .

A conscientious attempt to tell the party truth, *Sun over the Sangkan River* is for the most part a very dull book. A novel of about 460 pages, it has actually fifty-eight chapters, most of which are short sketches of the villagers and of the cadres who come to work among them. As sociological case histories, however, some of these sketches contain a surprising amount of material for the documentation of fear. Whether out of her mistaken zeal to grasp the dialectic of history in all its complexities or out of her latent hostility toward the Communist regime—even in 1942 Ding Ling was voicing her discontent with the Yenan bureaucrats—we cannot know; but she did devote space to the disquiet and suffering of the persecuted minority, though always careful to establish beforehand their reactionary or feudalist character. The novel therefore does have some interesting moments in its depiction of a village cowering under the fear of land reform.

Sun over the Sangkan River is at its best when it delineates the shifting social alliances following the intrusion of the cadres upon the placid village. Communism abolishes the old privileged class but creates in its place a new one. Tacit snobbery, and diplomacy play about the same roles in human relations as in the old regime. Occasionally Ding Ling forgets about her land reform to probe this social drama.

C. T. Hsia. *A History of Modern Chinese Fiction* (New Haven: Yale University Press, 1971), pp. 262–63, 268, 271–72, 488, 490

Because of Ding Ling's belief in the interdependence between the man/
woman and the writer, between experience and art, she will often—indeed,
feels it is part of her obligation to do so—refer to real persons and events in
her life or treat personal experiences, sometimes in their raw immediacy, in
her fiction. She does not hold back from confronting herself in her writings
even in moments of pity and agony, from exposing herself to the public in all
her emotional vulnerability. In this impulse toward literary soul-barring Ding
Ling was hardly alone—it was a typical phenomenon among May Fourth
writers. But her techniques for making over the autobiographical into the
fictional were both diverse and markedly her own. The two stories ["A Certain Night" and "From Night Till Daybreak"] that take as their starting point
the same traumatic event, the execution of her husband Hu Yepin, provide
a contrast in narrative methods; significantly, both are also turned into occasions for demonstrating the importance of literature as a response to life. . . .

It is striking to note how many of Ding Ling's stories conclude in the last
paragraph with the main character physically picking up a pen or composing
sentences. He or she has overcome despair, has resolved a conflict, is making
a fresh start, or has reached a state of acceptance or awareness. The act of
writing asserts a new sense of order imposed on the chaos of reality. In
presenting this image of the writer, Ding Ling provides a very concrete example in her own practice of what much of modern Chinese literature was trying
to do. Great historic crises may not always produce literature adequate to
their times, but for the generation of Chinese writers of the May Fourth
movement, caught in the crisscross of literary, political, and social revolution,
literature was their response to the horrors of what was happening around
them. The crumbling of the old order, the humiliations of imperialism, the
savagery of civil war, police terror, massacres, even when they were not, like
Ding Ling, direct victims, were part of their personal internal experience.
Writing would be their answer to the insoluble problems of their times, their
attempt to grapple with the fearful intangibilities of their existence.

Yi-tsi M. Feuerwerker. In Merle Goldman,
ed. *Modern Chinese Literature in the May
Fourth Era* (Cambridge: Harvard University
Press, 1977), pp. 283–84, 287

I do not know of another woman writer in the world like Ding Ling who,
after having been reported to have died twice as a result of repeated persecutions, is still very much alive and writing again at the age of seventy-five. . . .

Ding Ling, however, is still alive after having disappeared for twenty
years, and her story *Du Wanxiang* published recently signals her reappear-
ance. With the help and encouragement of Ye Shengtao, a writer of the older
generation, Ding Ling published her first works *Meng Ke* and *The Diary of
Miss Sha Fei* in Beijing in the bitter winter of 1927. These works electrified
the literary world and reading public, winning her the reputation of a new

woman writer in China. Since then, her position in the literary field has in fact remained steadfast, despite several attacks on her.

During the past fifty years, Ding Ling has published about 140 novels, stories and essays, totalling nearly one and a half million words. But during the three years of her imprisonment in a Kuomintang jail and the period from 1955 to 1976, she was unable to write or publish any work. . . .

In artistic creation, Ding Ling pours her feelings into her main characters, totally honest in regard to them. Thus her readers are moved and enter into her feelings, often catching glimpses of her innermost thoughts and sometimes even suspecting that certain characters or episodes describe the author herself. This is of course a misjudgement, but from it we can see Ding Ling's sincere love and the truthfulness of her writing. Although with the passage of time her feelings have deepened so that her themes have altered and new characters keep appearing in her works, this fundamental sincerity which distinguishes her writing remains unchanged.

Ding Ling's style is meticulous yet bold, vivid yet simple, profound yet not ornate. According to her, she always puts herself in the place of the characters she is depicting, entering into their feelings and analyzing them repeatedly. She does not begin to write until she feels each detail is reasonable and satisfactory. This is why the characters she portrays are so vivid, with highly individual characteristics, and we sense that they are speaking from their hearts.

In general, Ding Ling is not too particular about composition and form whether in writing a short story or a novel. Still less does she seek for fantastic plots. What she stresses is the portrayal of the characters, the dissection of their inner world and depiction of the atmosphere in which they live. So, superficially, her writings are like a stream flowing smoothly past, like stars scattered in the sky, but what readers actually find in them is profound meaning, beautiful prose and a lyrical quality.

But the most important theme that runs through all Ding Ling's writings is her love for the people, especially her love for China's unhappy women. This love leads her to weep and laugh, to curse and pray, to suffer and rejoice.

Feng Xiaxiong. *Chinese Literature*. 1980:1,
pp. 3–4, 8–9

The Sun Shines on the Sanggan River showed, in its sweeping vision of China in revolution, the vast distance, in both ideology and technique, that Ding Ling had traversed in her writing since her early stories about young women involved in lonely crises of love, sex, and identity. Although this literary development confers interest and complexity on Ding Ling's works, it did not assure her continuing status in a volatile revolutionary society. Her prestigious position lasted but a few years. In 1957 she was the prime target of the antirightist drive and denounced in a nationwide campaign. She was attacked for her superiority complex, for her sexual immorality, for ideological failings, for maligning the peasant masses in her fiction, and for traitorous conspiracy

against the party. She was further charged with setting up literature in opposition to party leadership, by subscribing to the bourgeois view that the
achieved literary work was an individual creation that could secure for its
author profit and fame, a view referred to by her critics as her "one-bookism."
The party saw it as necessary to wage the struggle against her to "protect
the socialist line in art and literature."

Yi-tsi Mei Feuerwerker. *Feminist Studies.*
10, 1984, p. 75

Ding Ling's early stories and novels (1927–30) are noted for their bold depictions of youthful love and the conflict between body and mind. The short
story "So-fei nü-shih ti jih-chi" (1928; "The Diary of Miss Sophia," 1974) is
an outcry of the agonizing soul of a "new woman" fighting for emancipation
from the rigid traditional conventions governing relationships between the
sexes in China. Its frank revelation of the protagonist's passionate sexuality
startled the Chinese literary world of that time. The conflict between love
and revolution is the theme of the novels *Wei Hu* (1930; Wei Hu) and *I-chiu
san-ling nien ch'un Shang-hai* (1930; Shanghai, spring 1930), in both of which
the young protagonist sacrifices love for the revolutionary cause.

The novella *Shui* (1931; The flood, 1936), first published in *Pei-tou,* a
literary organ of the League of Leftist Writers edited by Ding Ling herself,
marks the beginning of her second phase (1931–36), the main goal of which
was to present the life of the peasant masses. *Shui* is a powerful story of the
struggle during a devastating flood of a group of destitute villagers, who later
turn into a revolutionary force "fiercer than the flood." The work has no
outstanding individual characters but portrays the masses as a composite
protagonist. Since Ding Ling had no actual experience and contact with the
peasants, however, her descriptions and characterizations are superficial, and
she was criticized for her brand of romantic revolutionism.

This failure in her early attempt at Socialist Realism Ding Ling remedied
in *T'ai-yang chao tsai Sang-kan-ho shang* (1948; The Sun Shines over the
Sangkan River, 1954), the major novel of her third period (1937–57). Living
among the peasants in Communist-controlled areas in north China, Ding Ling
personally witnessed and actively participated in land-reform work in 1946
and 1947. The novel, which won the Stalin Prize, is a realistic presentation
of the class struggle between peasants and landlords in a farming village, the
breaking up of the feudal landowning system in Chinese society on the eve
of the Communist victory, and the vital role of the Party cadres in land
reform. Here again the protagonists are groups of peasants and Party workers. For its successful creation of new heroic images, for its fidelity to life,
and for its artistry, the novel has been hailed by Communist critics as an
"epic of our great land reform."

Liu Wu-Chi. In Leonard S. Klein, ed. *Far
Eastern Literatures in the 20th Century*
(New York: Ungar Publishing, 1986),
pp. 48–49

Ding Ling, who died four months ago at the age of 82, led a colorful life. She came from an upper-class background, and she shocked literary circles in the late 1920s with "Miss Sophie's Diary" and other stories that revealed the private ruminations of female protagonists, including frank admissions of sexual desires. In the 1930s she became increasingly political, first addressing conflicts of love and ideology among urban intellectuals and then describing the peasant revolution. Her private life was flamboyant; she joined a ménage à trois with two male writers, the famous Shen Congwen and her common-law husband, Hu Yepin, who was shot for Communist activism in 1931.

After joining the party and then suffering three years of incarceration by the Nationalists, Ding Ling eventually found her way to the Communist guerrilla base in Yanan, where her criticism of bureaucratic attitudes and male chauvinism brought her into conflict with none other than Mao Zedong. In the early 1950s, she served as the chief editor of the *Literary Gazette,* the party's organ of literary politics. In 1955 she was abruptly denounced for having "bourgeois" attitudes (and because she challenged the power of the literary commissar Zhou Yang) and disappeared into the great north wastes for two decades of labor reform. Returning in the late 1970s, she advocated the strange view that writers should not complain so much (hardly her own record!), thereby drawing the ire of young writers who now labeled her a Communist conservative.

Her fame rests on this remarkable life, and rightly so. It rests less securely on her fiction. To be sure, "Miss Sophie's Diary" served an interesting purpose, and the mature stories of the early 1940s (represented by "When I Was in Xia Village") are considerably more complex and sensitive than other modern Chinese war fiction. But what came between, in the 1930s, was largely unconvincing and dull. Ding Ling's peasants speak and act less like peasants than what young urban revolutionaries imagine them to be. Her tin ear for dialogue is also evident. Two revolutionaries are about to be shot at dawn: "Courage, comrade," one says. "It's not that. I'm rather worked up," the other replies. After 1949 Ding Ling abandoned creative writing.

Perry Link. *New York Times Book Review.*
July 6, 1986, p. 16

Ding Ling's stories appeared in English language collections in the 1930s but they have been newly translated [*Miss Sophie's Diary and Other Stories*] by the prolific and evercompetent Bill Jenner. The collection covers 1928–41, from the stories describing the fashionable and progressive youth of Shanghai to those set in the cave-villages of Yan'an. It was in Yan'an that Ding Ling challenged the male-chauvinist world of the Chinese Communist Party (and lost). In her stories, strong-willed women dominate those around them, Miss Sophie's febrile struggles may be the result of her own domination by the tuberculus bacillus but Miss Tertia who arrives in a small village in men's clothing, is a figure in her own right. Ding Ling is perhaps most successful when describing the young in Shanghai, some attracted by the glamour of city life, others attracted by political causes, but the background to the some-what self-indulgent world of the young is described very powerfully in *Rushing*, one of her better straightforwardly political stories.

China Quarterly. 109, March 1987, p. 141

Mother shifted Ding Ling's discursive focus from the individual female personality to the shared identity of the revolutionary sisterhood, from woman as a sexed identity to identity as a restoration of conventional, familiar, voluntarily politicized kinship connections. It was a significant movement for a number of reasons. First, it disassociated the question of female identity in modern China from the metonymic exclusionary tactics of Western sexual universalism. Second, while it relinked the "woman problem" to specified elements of inherited convention, it also unsettled certain received notions about femininity. Third, it supplied new genealogical resources to Ding Ling's project of self-invention.

Mother restored the question of female identity to a concretely Chinese cultural framework. Ding Ling's previous fiction about Chinese women had always included references to foreign ways of being female. An obvious example is her use of foreign names like "Sophia," "Mary," "Vicky," and "Elsa" for Chinese protagonists. Another is the importance of literary prototypes in her earliest fiction, primarily Emma Bovary and Marguerite of the Camellias. In the novel *Wei Hu* the metaphor of femininity had already shifted from the eroticized demimonde to the new Russian "soviet woman." Yet until *Mother* Ding Ling's fiction simply assumed a universal sexually designated category—woman—into which Chinese, like Russian, Japanese, and English women were naturally and hierarchically (depending on degrees of liberation) fitted.

Mother challenged this "deadly metonymic play" through which an imported, universalizing, "feminism" suppressed its cultural specificity. It overtly connected the question of women's liberation to foreign imperialism.

Ding Ling's rediscovery of the political sisterhood made it possible to separate personal identity away from reproductive physiology ("there is no natural sexual identity of women") but also to divest kinship of its biological referent. In *Mother* the relationship of the fictive political sisters outweighs even the reproductive bond of daughter and mother. (Thus the fantasy that "Xiao Han" is her mother's sister.) This movement is reconciliatory, because it regrounds the whole problem proposed by the discovery of women—mechanisms of engenderment, the relation of personal identity and sexual morality, origins and operation of subordinating systems—very neatly in the discourse of kinship.

Although deeply implicated in specific local codes and systems of sexual differentiation, *Mother* confounds our expectations of the natural identity of all women. That is its importance to Western feminist criticism. It now remains to reconstruct the context where kinship rhetoric acts as the dominant code, incorporating and subordinating sexual differentiation to its own purposes.

Tani E. Barlow. In Michael S. Duke, ed.
*Modern Chinese Women Writers: Critical
Appraisals* (Armonk, New York: M. E.
Sharpe, 1989), pp. 15–16, 22

With the 1928 publication of "Miss Sophia's Diary," Ding Ling became a nationally recognized writer. She continued producing "bourgeois" fiction for several years, narratives with no formal political coding, focused exclusively on the matter of female subjectivity, touching the extraordinarily sensitive issues of sexual repression and expression, homoeroticism, female Don Juan-ism, sexual politics, and the generally "dark" quality of female consciousness. She appeared to blame women's undisciplined subjectivity in part upon male society and in part upon the victims themselves. And since she borrowed heavily from her own experience—Wang Jianhong's life in particular became an icon to what she cast in retrospect as the wasted efforts of their anarcho-feminist years—readers, especially critics, understood the short stories col-lected in the volumes *In Darkness, A Woman, Suicide Diary,* and the novel *Wei Hu,* to be unmediated confessional autobiography. This critical reading of her work made her angry and defensive. Even publishing in the country's leading progressive literary journal, *Short Story Monthly,* failed to reassure her that her work had intrinsic merit beyond its power to shock and her own freak value as a woman writer who had raided the "male" subject matters of sexuality, power, death, and despair. . . .

The early 1930s . . . marked a shift in the way Ding Ling represented herself. She displaced her older project of realizing herself as a woman. Over the ensuing decade, she identified herself first as a writer, and furthermore, as a certain kind of writer. Drawing on her previous experience with Hu Yepin and Shen Congwen, editing their experimental literary magazine *Red and Black* in 1928, Ding Ling used the *Dipper* assignment as a means of personal transformation, as a publishing outlet for her own explorations in critical realist narrative, and as a forum from which she discussed the need for literature and literary culture to respond to political crisis. Her grueling efforts at self-discipline she chronicled in fragmentary writings like "Not a Love Letter," "Miss Sophia's Diary, Part 2," and "From Dusk to Dawn," Her struggle to reframe her narrativity inside a referential code largely deter-mined by revolutionary politics gave rise to "Water," a pathbreaking story that combined Qu Qiubai's insistence that writers focus on the life of the masses with an attention to panoramic representation, probably influenced by film. "Net of Law," "Flight," "Songzi," and other so-called proletarian pieces followed. In each, the representation of "objective reality" dominated the process of narrative. Ding Ling's subject was thus the present stage of history rather than any specific internal conflict of human consciousness.

This breakthrough suddenly made her a leading pioneer in explicitly ideological left-wing fiction. . . .

The real question is how Ding Ling, a sexual, literary, and cultural radical, could have committed herself to the statist project of revolutionary Chinese Communism. . . .

Ding Ling appropriated the [Party's trope of] literary rape. She used rape narratives to redefine and focus upon the question of representation of women in statist discourses. "When I Was in Xia Village" particularly questions the conjuncture of women and literary representation—to what effect, on whose terms, under what inscription of femininity, for what eventual political good.

> Tani E. Barlow. Introduction to Ding Ling. *I Myself Am a Woman: Selected Writings of Ding Ling* (Boston: Beacon Press, 1989), pp. 25, 29, 31, 36

The title *I Myself Am a Woman* is from Ding Ling's famous essay "Thoughts on March 8"—i.e., International Women's Day 1942, an occasion on which she considered it appropriate to evaluate critically the plight of women in communist Yan'an and air their grievances: "I myself am a woman, and I therefore understand the failings of women better than others. But I also have a deeper understanding of what they suffer." She was referring to the contempt and misery that women were subjected to in Mao's male-dominated wartime stronghold, where theoretically women were supposed to be emancipated. In the essay Ding Ling argued for the need to construct "woman" as a social and political category, just as "proletariat" is. The official position of the communist leadership, however, was that feminist concerns must yield to the larger interests of proletarian solidarity. Ding Ling's views were ill taken, dismissed as the unwelcome expression of "narrow feminism." As a result of her article, Mao convened the Yan'an Forum on Literature and Art to impose discipline on all writers and artists.

Perhaps the most famous modern Chinese woman writer of essays and short stories, Ding Ling lived an eventful life touched by great moments in modern Chinese history. . . .

The first and last stories in Tani Barlow's compilation reflect Ding Ling's journey from feminist "bourgeois" fiction to final solution of her feminist concerns via the socialist road: Du Wanxiang (literally "Du the Late Fragrance") in the final 1978 piece bearing her name is a woman who has totally identified herself with the party and achieved liberation without ever leaving the New Democratic family. Ding's early fiction "Miss Sophia's Diary" (1928), on the other hand, dwells on the "dark" quality of female consciousness and subjectivity, touching on the sensitive issues of sexual repression and expression. Between these two stories one finds a gray area in "Shanghai, Spring 1930," where the characters are beginning to shift to a more socialist orientation. In my opinion, these early stories show Ding Ling the artist as a most careful observer of human nature, a faithful painter of the female psyche. Among the thirteen selections in *I Myself Am a Woman* are several National Defense narratives structured around a central opposition between the state and the family (a major source of women's oppression) and sharing a concern with the problem of rape and justice. Conspicuously absent is Ding Ling's 1947 novel about land reform, *The Sun Shines over the Sanggan River.* Barlow provides an excellent introduction, though the general reader will have to struggle with quite a few less common collocations such as "indigenous narrativity" and "hybridizing her genre."

K. C. Leung. *World Literature Today.* 64,
1990, p. 696

[In her introduction to *I Myself Am a Women*] Barlow claims that "Maoism transformed 'woman' into a subordinate ideological category." Sensitive to the way in which western theorists are re-evaluating feminism and even criticizing it as an "instrument of Western imperial control," Barlow seeks to understand the category of "woman"—customs, textual representations, ideological framework—in its uniquely Chinese terms. This means searching for the "social construction of gendered subjects" within kinship relationships and *yin/yang* epistemology, both systems which assign meaning through relative relationship rather than absolute essence. Thus although cultural revolutionaries advocated "individualism" as a means of fighting the power of kinship relations determining existence and action, they often could not envision what an individual woman would be like outside kinship definitions.

Those who have tried to teach Ding Ling's stories to American students will immediately grasp the importance of placing her work within Barlow's historical and theoretical framework. American students often read "Miss Sophia's Diary" as a boring, repetitive meditation on a selfish, self-indulgent woman; when we realize that in several of her early stories, Ding Ling is investigating the question of "what modern Chinese women would be in the absence of Confucianism," however, the story becomes profound social commentary. Without understanding that rape stories were politically sanctioned National Defense narratives, we cannot see the significance of Ding Ling's challenge to the way in which rape produced meaning: "Who assigned meaning to the loss of female chastity? Was it the rape victim? Was it the signifying system in the village patriline, which joined the sexual organs of women to civic virtue?" Reading Ding Ling's work, beginning with the 1927 "Diary of Miss Sophia" and ending with the 1978 "Du Wanxiang" as a long-term investigation of "woman" in Chinese society forces us to look more closely at the constructions which take place through the process of textual representation.

Wendy Larson. *Journal of Asian and
African Studies.* 25, 1990, p. 244

DJÉBAR, ASSIA (pseud. FATIMA ZOHRA IMALAYEN)
(ALGERIA) 1936–

North African writers of French expression have long had an ambivalent relation to language, for the medium that history forced upon them also happened to carry the ideology of the colonizer. To some, the alien language became the instrument of such radical alienation that they stopped writing altogether. Among those who deliberately gave up their craft is Assia Djébar of Algeria.

Although critics have examined the writers' attitude to language, none, so far, has addressed the question from the standpoint of sex. Since North African literature was born of the social fact of colonialism, might not the response of women writers, socially alienated by reason of sex as well as language, be different from that of the men? Assia Djébar is a good case in point because her decision to give up writing had primarily to do with her self-image as a woman and a writer. This essay proposes to examine the conflict between language and the feminine self at the symbolic center of her fiction and the circular narrative structures that express it. In Djébar's novels, space is sexualized because language is.

Her first novel, *La Soif,* was published in Paris in 1957. The twenty-year-old was immediately hailed as the new Françoise Sagan. This not altogether unwarranted comparison was to embroil Djébar in the ideological quarrel so symptomatic of colonial literatures, her more nationalistic readers condemning her for wasting her talents on bourgeois concerns instead of singing of the glorious struggle of the masses. Then came *Les Impatients* (1958), *Les Enfants du nouveau monde* (1962), and *Les Alouettes naïves* (1967), books which showed increasing social concerns. What all four novels shared, however, was a single obsessional theme: woman's quest for identity. Undertaken first as the purely personal and individualistic venture of *La Soif,* it gradually became the communal revolutionary adventure of heroines fighting by the side of men, redefining their role in a changing society. In the new Algeria, a new woman was being born.

This optimistic interpretation of Djébar as a writer increasingly committed to social realities and of her heroines as increasingly autonomous women represents, by and large, the critical consensus on her work. I wish to argue here that all is not what it seems. For if one looks at the symbolic structure, the progressive implications of plot and theme disappear and a radically different meaning emerges. If is the fable (in the Hoffmanian sense) of the francophone writer as Woman. . . .

In Djébar's work, the drama of the traditional world and the tragic love affair that underlines the conflict between tradition and modern life belong to the surface story. The real drama and the hidden story have to do with what goes on between women. Both *La Soif* and *Les Impatients* depict the impossible quest for a prelapsarian world of female symbiosis. The narrator's actions must be read as symbolic attempts to recreate woman's perfect universe. Homoerotic wholeness before the fall, which is to say, before the intrusion of man, sex, and language.

In contradistinction to the plot, the symbolic structure makes this clear. The images of narcissicism, emptiness, and solitude characteristic of the autoerotic sequences now reappear to describe the heterosexual relationship. Such a relationship is marked by the narrator's obsessive compulsion to recreate the original female relationship for which man's love is but a poor alternative. . . .

Djébar's fiction and her attitude to it cannot be separated. It is through writing that she discovered her commitment to other women; yet through such commitment she arrived at the impossibility of writing "in order to give women their voice." Her first novels present a world of women alienated from one another and therefore, from themselves by language, the instrument through which the fragmented narrative consciousness discovers both the gap and the impossibility of bridging it. Their circular narrative structure, metaphor for the impossible quest, enclosed other symbolic circles, hieratic spaces of female desire through which, like a *mise en abyme* the text obliquely calls attention away from its surface, deep into its symbolic structure, the fable of the writer as Woman.

Clarisse Zimra. *Research in African*
Literatures. 11:2, Summer, 1980,
pp. 206–7, 212–15, 218–19

Within [the] group of Algerian women writers, Assia Djébar stands out as the most prolific and versatile. She has published four novels, a volume of poetry, and most recently, after a hiatus of thirteen years during which she has been working primarily on films, a book of short stories. Djébar's work reflects a serious commitment to her craft and to feminist issues. Studying her work produced over a twenty year period provides us with important perspectives on her development as a writer committed to feminism.

Djébar's nation, Algeria, which cast off colonial rule after a bitter seven year struggle against France and gained independence in 1962, has been forced to face an increasing number of problems in the post-independence era; the issue of women's rights in society is not the least of them. Moreover, it is a problem that has received considerable attention in Algeria. . . .

Djébar probes the psychological and sociological complexities of woman's position in a Muslim society in transition. . . .

Djébar's literary career began in 1957 with the publication of her first novel, *La Soif.* This novel was followed by *Les Impatients* (1958), *Les Enfants du nouveau monde* (1965) and *Les Alouettes naïves* (1967). In 1969, she published *Poèmes pour l'Algérie heureuse* as well as a play, *Rouge l'aube,* written in collaboration with Walid Garn (her ex-husband). A collection of short stories, *Femmes d'Alger dans leur appartement* appeared in 1980. . . .

By choice of subject and decor, *La Soif* is a European rather than an Algerian novel. However, the work does foreshadow themes that will assume greater importance in later writings. *La Soif* presents a moving description of the disintegration of a marriage as witnessed by the protagonist, Nadia. She becomes attracted to a couple who gradually draw her into their intense and somewhat neurotic relationship. Each of Djébar's heroines formulates ideas of marriage, and most experience partial if not total failure in that relationship. Nadia, who is trying to find her way in the world, finally recognizes her egotism. In the place of love, she discovers solitude within her own marriage.

The heroine of *Les Impatients,* Djébar's second novel, is the counterpart to Nadia. Dalila belongs to the Algerian bourgeoisie as it existed prior to the outbreak of the Algerian war. Dalila expresses the impatience of the young generation trying to free itself from an atrophied society and its hypocrisy.

Whereas *La Soif* deals with the dissolution of a marriage as witnessed by the heroine, *Les Impatients* centers upon the dissolution of a potential marriage between the heroine and her fiancé. . . .

Taken together, *La Soif* and *Les Impatients,* both anchored in the pre-revolutionary Algeria of the early 1950s, form a whole. *La Soif* depicts a modern European-oriented Algeria and a heroine who moves from relative freedom as a single woman to the constraints of marriage. *Les Impatients* presents traditional Muslim Algeria and a heroine who travels the road in reverse, moving from bondage to liberty. It is the concept of choice, no longer available to Nadia, now a reality for Dalila, a concept alien to the traditional Arab woman, that is now more clearly expressed in Djébar's last two novels, *Les Enfants du nouveau monde* and *Les Alouettes naïves.*

With *Les Enfants du nouveau monde,* Djébar passes from the individual to the collective identity of Algerian women, from psychological intrigue to the harsh reality of a nation at war. Djébar presents the novel as a *tèmoignage,* a chronicle of events written in the immediate post-war period. For Djébar, the account of the independence struggle must center upon Algeria's women, newly discovered heroines unaccustomed to political action.

Djébar's style in this novel is more complex. Abandoning the first person narrative and short sentences, she now uses a rapid, nervous prose and long intricate sentences. The power of this novel lies in the descriptive passages, particularly those which transmit the immediate effect of the war upon the populace. . . .

Les Alouettes naïves brings us to the last few months of the Algerian liberation struggle, the summer of 1962. This novel reflects the same thematic and stylistic preoccupations of *Les Enfants du nouveau monde.* Djébar presents a multiplicity of sketches, places emphasis upon daily life experiences, and returns again to lyrical prose. She succeeds once more in presenting a fresco of a nation in combat, but creates a more personal world by focusing upon the life of a young couple: Nfissa and Rachid.

In *Les Alouettes naïves,* the novelist experiments with chronology. Dividing the novel in three time segments—*Autrefois, Au delà* and *Au-*

jourd'hui—Djébar begins with a flashback. The protagonist, Nfissa, just released from prison, tells her family about her previous experiences in the *maquis* and in prison. Her account is interspersed with childhood memories. *Aujourd'hui* centers upon her relationship with Rachid, an Algerian journalist she has married in Tunisia where she is a social worker aiding Algerian refugees.

In a sense, Nfissa is Lila, the emancipated protagonist of *Les Enfants du nouveau monde,* who has matured further. She has been through the prison experience, has taken part in the revolutionary activity, and has experienced exile in Tunisia. After losing her first lover who was killed in battle, Nfissa is in the process of forming an important and meaningful relationship with Rachid. . . .

In 1980, Djébar published a collection of short stories, *Femmes d'Alger dans leur appartement.* The three-part structure of *Les Alouettes naïves* with its lyrical erotic chapter, *au-delà,* has become condensed. Only two remain; yesterday and today, *hier* and *aujourd'hui.* Hence, the communication which existed in the former novel now disappears. Djébar's position has shifted towards sisterhood. Her heroines discover one another, recognizing one another's courage, suffering, sacrifices, and nobility. Equally important, they view themselves as having been bypassed by history. In independent Algeria, a new generation, exclusively male, holds office, makes speeches, and writes the new rhetoric. . . .

Djébar views Delacroix's painting, "Femmes d'Alger dans leur appartement" as a valid symbolic representation of the Algerian woman today. Thus, she has borrowed the title of the painting for her collection of short stories written and edited over a period of two decades. Delacroix had composed the painting from memory after a Muslim official had allowed him a privileged look at the cloistered women in 1832. This was the western artist's first look at cloistered Arabic women, exotic in appearance, mysterious in the obscurity of their chambers; they appeared as decorated, mute objects. In the painting, three of the women gaze at one another enveloped in their private sealed universe. The fourth looks ahead, beyond the viewer; she is lost in reverie. For the public, the painter, the master of the harem, these women were objects—decorated and lovely, yet objects. In addition, they are in their place, bound to a traditional enclosure. . . .

Djébar clearly fears that women's contribution to the liberation effort and therefore to the process of building a nation goes unrecognized, and she likewise sees the dialogue between men and women in serious difficulty. As a mature literary artist committed to giving her mute sisters a voice, Djébar commands a unique position in Maghrebian literature and is worthy of considerable praise.

Mildred P. Mortimer. In Hal Wylie et al.,
eds. *Contemporary African Literature*
(Washington, D.C.: Three Continents, 1983),
pp. 7–14

Assia Djébar (the pseudonym of Fatima Zohra Imalayen) is the first Algerian writer to study the plight of her sisters. Her novels describe the mental and physical frustration of Algerian women from a fictional female perspective. After the publication of *Soif* (1957) and *Les impatients* (1958), Djébar was rebuked by literary critics because her work was not rooted in the war of independence and because she wrote about the kind of women's problems that only affected upper middle-class society. She retired to Tunisia, later Morocco, where she came into contact with Algerian refugees, and for the first time understood what her people were thinking and feeling. In her next novels *Les enfants du nouveau monde* (1962) and *Les alouettes naïves* (1967), her heroines are conscious of their political role in the reconstruction of their country. But at the same time she shows that Algerian women are still the victims of patriarchal standards and traditions:

> Yes, it is almost easy to forget, he thinks as he comes home in the evening and looks at this wife whom the all-powerful oppressor out there will never know. People say she is "imprisoned," but her husband thinks "liberated,"

and later on in the same passage "a body that submits without response, because the dialogue of mutual contact is missing."

In 1970 the Algerian radio put on an adaptation of her play *Rouge l'aube* (1969), but cut out all passages which referred to the part women played in the struggle for liberation. And for a long time after that Djébar wrote nothing. It was not until 1979 that her next novel *Femmes d'Alger dans leur appartement* was published in Paris by the feminist press Editions des Femmes. At present she is involved in filmmaking, because this enables her to reach women who are illiterate. Djébar's work is regularly imported into Algeria. Younger women see her as the symbol of their emancipation.

Lourina de Voogd. In Mineke Schipper, ed.
*Unheard Words: Women and Literature in
Africa, the Arab World, Asia, the
Caribbean, and Latin America* (London:
Allison and Busby, 1985), pp. 94–95

The opening scene in Djébar's *L'amour, la fantasia* sets in motion the conquest of space and language. Djébar's fifth novel begins with the scene of a little girl being walked to school for the first time. The day that Assia Djébar's father escorted her to school . . . he set her on a bilingual, bicultural, indeed an ambiguous journey that freed her from the female enclosure but sent her into a form of exile away from the majority of her sisters. . . . In this novel Djébar studies the journey, unique at a time when few Algerian girls had access to school, and brings to it the perspective of four decades of bicultural apprenticeship.

L'amour, la fantasia is composed of two narratives. One is the autobiographical journey; the other is the history of Algeria at two dramatic and painful historical periods: the conquest of 1830 and the independence struggle of 1954–62. In search of women's contributions to Algerian history, Djébar makes use of official French documents and French correspondence of the colonial period. She does indeed find traces of women's participation in history, thus giving credibility to the struggle of the *soeurs disparues*. In addition, Djébar uses oral history to give voice to surviving heroines, the *porteuses de feu* of the Algerian revolution, and allows them to tell their own stories. Djébar insists that just as space has been sexualized in traditional Algeria—inner space, the home, reserved to women; outer space, the workplace and the government, reserved to men—so too has history. The written account of the conquest of Algeria that she unearths from the archives is French and male; the oral account that she puts together from interviews with participants is Arabic and female. Most important, in this endeavor *écriture* and *kalaam* are unknown and unintelligible each to the other. Djébar uses her language skills, translating, transcribing, interpreting, to bridge the gap between the two. The result is a documentary that bears witness to the violence and destruction inflicted by the invading armies of the colonizer upon the indigenous populations.

Mildred Mortimer. *Research in African Literatures.* 19, 1988, pp. 302–3

A servant in three-quarter rear view uses an arm to open a curtain on three women with enigmatic expressions. Two of these women are in front of a water pipe. The third is seen reclining, leaning on some cushions. This is *Women of Algiers in their Apartment,* a masterpiece by Delacroix, painted after a short visit the artist made to a harem in Algiers in 1832. In 1955, Picasso reinvented *Women of Algiers,* stripped Delacroix's women naked and opened the field.

Women of Algiers in their Apartment is also the title of a collection of ten short stories by Assia Djébar published in 1980. Starting from an aesthetic reflection on the pictures of these two great painters, Djébar was able to open up a militant discourse. This discourse Djébar refuses to make polemical. It is rather the search for a personal discourse. She does not wish to speak "in the name of . . ." but make a study of a female reality as the gaze of the two great painters captured it. This collection, according to the author, consists of "some eavesdropping from 1958 to 1978."

Through these two rapid looks, Delacroix and Picasso recovered a female presence. From 1832 to 1955, there is a parenthesis of a century and a half in which the entire drama of segregated Algerian society was posed. Within this society there is a closed and locked grotto, that of the Arab woman.

Twenty years after the war of independence, what is the fate of the women whose revolutionary role cannot be challenged. What are the walls against which they "beat"? Such are the questions that Djébar's books asks.

The stories are organized into two sections: "Today" and "Yesterday." The inversion of order emphasizes the disappointment the author feels with regard to the condition of women which has not changed; with some exceptions, they are today as they were yesterday. A second version of Delacroix's painting, dating from 1849, accentuates, by means of the color and light used, the feeling of loneliness, enclosure, and isolation of the three women. Djébar concludes that Delacroix's women have not moved for a century and a half. These pictures, unfortunately, remain contemporary. . . . Taking the point of view of the painter, Djébar adds a new dimension to North African literature. In her turn, she presents a picture of Algerian society. Her work is articulated around several themes, starting from the relation of women with one another, from the eye of "the other" upon their enclosed space which has always forced them to keep mouth and eyes in the dark.

These women have not left their apartments. Their voices are silenced, relegated to the shadows. Assia came to them, listened to them, and transmitted their underground words . . . For each female word that comes out of the silence of the harem becomes a transgression. The author's undertaking is to restore language to these women accustomed to whispering or keeping quiet; to bring to light the "words of the veiled body, a language, that also, in its turn, took the veil long since," she says in her introduction. . . .

Djébar's work sets up a bridge between the tradition, that prison with a locked door, chained shut, and Picasso's hope of a wide open door, opened to mobility, and full participation on the part of the Algerian woman.

Nadia Turk. *Constructions.*
4, 1989, pp. 89–91, 98

DOMIN, HILDE (GERMANY) 1912–

Hilde Domin, born in Cologne, lived a long time in Latin America and in the United States, from where she returned in 1954. . . . [She] has preserved unharmed the sound, fragrance, and color of Latin-American poetry in her own verse and has merged it with her own destiny. . . . "Only a rose for Support": in this constantly recurring motif of feminine lyric poetry, the mellowness of the south is legitimately combined in Hilde Domin's work with modern thought, in which, since Mallarmé, the rose is the most valid symbol of the word—the word in which Eros still lives.—In some instances her work is disturbed by genitive metaphors, which unfelicitously combine the concrete with the abstract ("kitchen of time," "sieve of pain"). The abstract here operates like a foreign element. Feminine poetry is always most powerful when it says what it has to say through the roses.

Wieland Schmied. *Wort und Wahrheit.*
1960, p. 212

Rückkehr der Schiffe [Return of the Ships]. . . . a very astonishing volume of excellent poetry. Truly this poet is a virtuoso. It may sound trite but seems worth saying: she has lived and experienced and suffered, she has seen and heard a great deal and thus has something to tell us. Her message is not very comforting. The ray of hope . . . is certainly no brighter than that famous last "g" at the end of *Doktor Faustus*. But it is very visible.

Richard Exner. *Books Abroad*. 1963, p. 180

When we read her volume of poetry, we don't remain without an inner joy, emotion, and spiritual gain. It is generally a matter of real verbal art—often only very concise, clear images, in which the humanistic content rests concealed as though in a core. Hilde Domin once characterized herself as a "walker"—a walker, however, who in no way "roams romantically in countries at the edge of the world," but feels obligated to the "here." Profanely expressed, that could mean to man, to the present, to her homeland, to nature, to love—that is, to all that grows, ripens, and develops into a higher existence. Her dreams too are related to this. Roaming about in distant regions does not allow the "area that love makes into a place" to be forgotten. Moreover, "adventures have become questionable." An unquenchable longing points homeward, into safety. From "exile," from "the night," from "anxiety," from "the distances," the poet flees back to the "littlest thing," to the vegetative and creatural, although the pain of exile, the "homesickness for farewell long after the return" will probably remain imprinted forever on this poet.

René Schwachhofer. *Neue deutsche
Literatur*. July, 1965, p. 175

In the later poem Hilde Domin says in an authentic poetic phrasing, reduced to essentials, what matters to her and, fundamentally, to all poetry: finding the magic word. . . .

One repeatedly encounters in these poems the theme of art, the possibilities of creation. What is striking is the simplicity of statement, its unpretentious boldness; here there is no joining and entanglement of epochs, of mythological references, no new words are coined. Instead, there is understatement, almost commonplaces. . . . No reference work is necessary to comprehend these lines. A magically inspired speaking tone seems desired to name what is visible "here." . . .

No moan of despair, no doubt in the possibility of expression, not even silence as an answer (as in Rilke's elegy fragment) is proclaimed here; but rather, in the sense of the *Sonnets to Orpheus* (a paean to the immortality of art), the everlasting capacity for expression. In this doubtless belief in the poet's unbroken capability despite all to sing about the "here" is where Hilde Domin's poems touch those of Robert Frost and Jorge Guillén. In the arduous restriction to the simple and natural, which also have the power to grasp the world's chaos and complexity, lie this poet's talent and ability.

Edgar Lohner. *Neue Rundschau*.
1965, pp. 340, 344–45

Das zweite Paradies (The second paradise). . . . It's a love story. And its language can reflect anything: fright, pain, preparation for the saving suicide, and the magnificent inanities of lovers' conversations.

But what is told here is not a suspense story. The book's real suspense lies in the strong emotional charge of the experience it describes and in the lucid awareness of the artistic presentation. For the story is not simply told, but thought through logically and carried out consistently as a literary problem. The style changes in keeping with the tasks to be performed. Pain and sorrow call for short, terse sentences. These short sentences slow up the action. They make slower reading than the long periodic sentences that, so to speak, carry the reader along through the action. But the reader is not to be carried—he is to be shocked. Point by point, he is slowed down and compelled to collect himself for the next sentence. Remembered images, descriptions of persons or interiors require longer sentences; at once the mood changes, the gaze that rests on things becomes objective.

The concentrated emotion, however, lies in the dialogues. . . . Just as the woman tries to hide her thoughts, and just as the man sees through her and lets her know it, just so the matter is transacted a thousand times a day. Everybody's destiny.

Christa Reinig. *Die Zeit.*
March 25, 1969, p. 13

Das zweite Paradies (The second paradise). Hilde Domin, poet and literary critic, has now published her first novel. As in her poetry and literary criticism, we find a portrait of modern man, threatened by a society full of pragmatism and worship of technical progress. Two approaches dominate: one considers the poem as its own justification; the other sees it in its relationship to society, as a dialogue between the poet's vision and reality.

The novel is very personal, with the intensity of a confession; yet never can we forget that it takes place within German society. There are constant references to it. . . . There are also inserts of quotations from the newspaper *Der Spiegel,* adding a grotesque element. . . .

It is not only the multidimensional quality that makes the novel so interesting, but also the fresh, authentic tone and the limpid, simple, at times very informal style, full of intensity and sparkle, that charm the reader.

Anna Otten. *Books Abroad.* 1969, p. 256

For more than a decade, literary scholars have studied prose and poetry written by authors who left Germany as the National Socialists increased their power. Despite widespread and keen interest, however, research has generally proposed inconclusive answers to its fundamental question: Do the themes and structure of these exiles' works set their art apart from literature created in their homeland during this time? It would be impossible to treat the whole case properly by examining Hilde Domin's work alone; yet, if they are representative of the character of other emigrants' work, the subjects and perspective she adopts suggest that some German literature written abroad differs negligibly from that produced at home during and after the Third Reich. Indeed, although fear of the National Socialists' persecution forms a theme important to her writing, Domin's literary structures and frame of reference seem, as a whole, to be firmly rooted in the intellectual atmosphere of the Weimar Republic. Moreover, the anxiety and sense of alienation they betray, their concern for the inadequacies of language and predilection for the neo-Romanticism which partially characterized much of the literature of this period—her formative years—had already become part of an international tradition. During her years abroad, these concepts nourished her until the poet found her own voice. Meanwhile, some of the Germans who had remained at home continued to write in this tradition. Thus, Hilde Domin's novel and her poetry are, in salient aspects, virtually indistinguishable from works composed by Germans who had never experienced exile. Of course, international influences discernible in her writing relate Domin's work, as well, to literature by such authors as Ingeborg Bachmann, never an exile from the Third Reich, and Paul Celan, whose complex personal history precludes classifying him in any of the existing scholarly definitions as an exile from Nazi Germany.

It is important to note, too, that Domin herself strove to strip her particular experiences of their historical elements. Thus, speaking of persecution by the National Socialists as only one example of abuse which has existed since the beginning of time, the poet concludes that all human beings are exiles on the earth: her exile is only an extreme manifestation of this universal phenomenon. Still, it would be wrong to decide that Hilde Domin's works are not autobiographical, for inclusion of details drawn from her life adds much depth and beauty to them. Looking closely at the interplay between experience and art exhibited in her writing, let us seek to delimit the influences bearing on Domin's literary structures and perspective. . . .

Domin's notion of the poet's primary task . . . seems rooted in early twentieth-century literary theory. The poet should, she holds, portray the disparity between circumstantial "reality" and essential reality. . . . Affirming that the split can be overcome in a poem, Domin echoes a belief common to the international literary generation of James Joyce, Hermann Hesse, T. S. Eliot, and Rilke. Another conviction shared by many of them, that freedom from time may be achieved in an "autonomous aesthetic world," finds expression, with her claim that a poem is itself a utopia, in one of Domin's later essays: "Der Lyriker bietet uns die Pause, in der Zeit still steht." This desire for timelessness recurs suggestively in two atemporal structuring principles Domin uses in *Das zweite Paradies*. The novel consists of segments which are not ordered according to the chronology of the narrator's life and, in the section named with the novel's title, changes from past to present in narrative tense occur where no proper motivation is given in the account. . . .

Other aspects of Domin's novel center it in the traditions of early twentieth-century literature. The work belongs to the subgenre of the lyrical novel, which, as Ralph Freedman defines it, may be exemplified best by Rilke's *Malte Laurids Brigge* in the early twentieth century, and characterizes, among many others, the works of André Gide and Virginia Woolf. Both German novels take death, love, and alienation as their major themes, and, in each, what seems a loosely constructed plot focuses on an artist's soul; both employ lyrical prose characterized by parataxis, short sentences, sentence fragments, alliteration, internal rhyme, similes, and metaphors in abundance. In an effort to "transcend the impasse of language," Hesse and his contemporaries used the archetypal image, which "evokes a timelessness," to connect "the character in the present and a mythical figure from the past." Domin's novel joins the archetypes of Adam and Eve with the fate of the narrator and her husband to break down temporal divisions and deepen meaning.

Dagmar C. Stern. *Hilde Domin:*
From Exile to Ideal (Bern and Frankfurt:
Lang, 1979), pp. 11–15

In the literature of the exiles' return, the oeuvre of Hilde Domin forms a rare counter statement. While most works by or about repatriated exiles echo Thomas Wolfe's regretful conclusion that one "can't go home again," Hilde Domin intones a paean or love song, sometimes muted, always tentative, to her once and present homeland. . . .

Because of the centrality of this theme in her work and its sensitive and fastidious treatment, the appellation "Writer of Return," first coined by Hans-Georg Gadamer in 1971, has recurred in critical writings about Domin. This article proposes to explore the implications of this label and the motivation for her cautious optimism. In the face of her—by objective measurements—Spartan exile experience and of her fellow returnees' often expressed reluctance to reintegrate, her more sanguine outlook compels attention.

The metamorphosis of Hilde Domin into a different kind of woman during her exile has only rarely received scholarly attention. Her highly individualistic attitudes, as Eva Zeller notes quite correctly, seem to preclude her participating in or advocating suffragette-like group activities; her public statements, for example her denial that literature can be divided into female and male literature—she only recognizes good or bad—may have diverted attention from her frequent civic espousals of women's rights. But Domin is the author of a fervent, yet understated series of epigrams entitled "Über die Schwierigkeiten, eine berufstätige Frau zu sein." In this polemic she strongly demurs from the well-intentioned, but patronizing compliment from a male colleague that she ranks "unter Poeten ein Mann." Obviously she had reached equal status as a woman and as a writer undeterred by chauvinistic comparisons. Given that attainment, it seems to be no accident that the marital rift her novel describes follows the heroine's declaration that she can no longer sustain, either in exile or after returning home, the role of mother-protectress she had initially assumed vis-à-vis her lover and husband. . . .

What finally destined Hilde Domin to write positively of her return is the conciliatory attitude toward Germany she was able to muster. She forgot nothing of the past horrors—her open letter to Nelly Sachs attests to her continued loathing of them and fear of their recurrence—but she portrays, in her novel, scenes of inhumanity taken from other times and places, e.g., a pogrom in Russia. They signify that the Germany of the Nazi period had no monopoly on evil. Without such insights, without a sublime sense of conciliation, Domin could not have gone back to Germany.

Guy Stern. Germanic Review. 62,
1987, pp. 136–37, 140

H.D. (HILDA DOOLITTLE) (UNITED STATES) 1886–1961

The poems of H.D. do not lend themselves to convenient classification, as Poems of Passion and Emotion, Poems of Reflection, Poems of the Imagination, and Poems Descriptive, and so on. In all of them, passion, emotion, reflection, and the image, the sharp, vivid image that does the work of description, are fused together in the burning unity of beauty. . . . H.D. invariably presents her subtlest, most metaphysical idea under some living sensuous image solid enough to carry the emotion. The air we are given to breathe may be rarefied to the last degree, yet we are moving always in a world of clear colors and clear forms.

May Sinclair. The Dial. February, 1922,
p. 203

It has been said of H.D.'s earlier poetry that it was perfectly wrought but cold and passionless, and that it was concerned rather with the loveliness of a perished age than with the modern world of everyday emotions. . . . Perfectly wrought the poems are: the rhythms swoop in and out of the head as birds perch and flutter in and out of apple-branches. Lines haunt the ears as the sound of rain in the South. The use of some simple but unexpected syllable brings all the fragrance into a mood that Ionian roses suddenly awaken after some swift storm. But they are not cold, they are not passionless; and apart from the color of some Attic names how are these songs anything but the expression of the emotions and desires of an extremely present age?

Winifred Bryher. Poetry. March, 1922,
pp. 334–35

Her special form of the mode of Imagism—cold, "Greek," fast, and enclosed—has become one of the ordinary resources of the poetic language; it is a regular means of putting down words so that they will keep; and readers are mistaken who confuse familiarity with flatness or who think facile imitation of the form emulates the perception that goes with the mode. She has herself made sharply varied use of her mode, but she has not exhausted it; she has only—for present changing purposes of a changing mind—partly broken it down into the older, perhaps primary mode of the distich. The relatively long uncoiling of a single spring of image, unpredictable in its completeness, now receives a regular series of impulses and arrests, of alternations and couplings.

R. P. Blackmur. Language as Gesture
(New York: Harcourt, 1952), p. 352

H.D. has herself abandoned the "Imagist" effects of her early poems, the best of which suggest the clean line of Greek vase-paintings and, for all the passion they assert, have a lapidary quality about them. In her later work the old vehemence, if subdued, is present, and the phrasing recalls the familiar cadences. Yet is differs from what went before in carrying a far heavier weight of symbolic meaning and in being overtly subjective. . . . Again and again, turning the pages of this quondam Imagist, the reader hears a melody not only in the lines themselves but suggested by them, as it were, hovering just beyond the expressed sounds for some musician, not a maker of verse, to capture and realize.

Babette Deutsch. The New York Times.
September 22, 1957, p. 37

"Invisible," "most proud," in love: these are the strength of the poet throughout the work of H.D. Ardent and clear, her lyrics show us that an everpresent devotion to the art of the poem sustains passion. The strength of the poem lies in her command of words so that they call up sensual immediacies (as images) and are themselves sensual immediacies (as elements of a most skilled tonal structure), and, increasingly in the later work, in her knowledge of words, their roots and histories, their lore and powers. Her trilogy written during the Second World War (The Walls Do Not Fall, Tribute to Angels, and The Flowering of the Rod) stands with Ezra Pound's Cantos, Eliot's Four Quartets, and William Carlos Williams's Paterson as a major work of the Imagist genius in its full.

Robert Duncan. Poetry. January, 1958,
p. 256

She gives us the best glimpse we have today of classic poetry, an English poetry so nearly Greek in concept and execution as to be remarkable. She gives us that stasis in the poem which keeps a perfect tension between emotion and reason, between fact and idea, between sensitized perception and elegant restraint, between the brute world and art. . . . She gives us, in rare poems, the early poems, a glimpse and capture of an ideal world of eternal poetic values, crystal-bright, hard and pure, clean and fine. H.D. has the impersonal height from which streams a radiant purity.

Richard Eberhart. *Poetry.* January, 1958,
p. 265

H.D.'s strength lies in her rendition of detail: her weakness is in structuring those details into a poetic, characterological, or, still more acutely, fictional whole. Poems, fiction, even essays like *Tribute to Freud* or *By Avon River* become a series of isolated images or events linked by free associations, often through mythological themes. At the very sentence level, her boundaries tend to be ill-defined. A sentence modifier from one sentence will seem to apply to the next. Lists (of which H.D. uses many) will be oddly broken between sentences. The word to which a pronoun or adjective refers may be one or two sentences back; the reference itself may be twinned or multiple. Often, for structure, she will resort to a series of parallel structures to be summed into a totality. Sometimes she will use negations—a series of *not*'s or *nor*'s to strip off the extraneous and come to the final, finely rendered residue as a climax.

Doubtless no small part of H.D.'s propensity for myth is a quest for similar organizing structures. If one can see present people, events, and feelings as projections or continuations of a simpler, more structured mythic past, they become more manageable and, for H.D. at least, somehow more real. She uses for living people the image of a palimpsest or a series of old photographic negatives on top of one another; the sign one sees on the surface implies a deeper reality underneath. She seeks to turn herself, her very body, into an hieroglyph or emblem—as in the use of her initials for a seal or sign. Her poetry, like the myths she emulates, manifests that which is spiritual, abstract, and timeless by the hard, the real, the objective, the exact.

Norman Holland. *Contemporary Literature.*
Autumn, 1969, p. 475

The poems in this new book [*Hermetic Definition*] date from circa 1960, when [H.D.] was seventy-four. She had been inserted into literary history at twenty-six, when Ezra Pound invented "Imagism" to supply a context for five poems of hers. A normal context would have been a book of poems, but Pound sensed that book's worth would be a long time getting written. He had didactic uses for a "movement" anyhow, and "Hermes of the Ways," "Orchard," a few others might as well exemplify it as wait for an *oeuvre*.

Unhappily the invented movement that was meant to float her reputation encapsulated it, and though she lived many more decades and extended her self-definition through many volumes, she has remained totally identified with the very little she had done when she was first heard of. It is as though five of the shortest pieces in *Harmonium* were to stand for the life's work of Wallace Stevens.

Her psychic life was contorted. Freud himself analyzed her, and she lived her last years at Küsnacht on Lake Zurich under care that was partly psychiatric, partly directed toward the corporeal needs of an old woman who had broken her hip and walked only with difficulty. She kept resin and pine-cone burning in her room, and pondered books of hermetic symbolism. . . .

These poems are "about" her phantasmagoric self, in part her sense of having become a myth prematurely. . . .

Hugh Kenner. *The New York Times.*
December 10, 1972, p. 55

Why is her poetry not read? H.D. is part of the same literary tradition that produced the mature work of the "established" artists—T. S. Eliot, Ezra Pound, William Carlos Williams, D. H. Lawrence. She in fact knew these artists well; she had known and almost married Pound while the two were students in Philadelphia (H.D.'s intensely absorbing recreation of their life-time friendship, *End to Torment,* is being prepared for publication); her friendship with Williams goes back to those student days; but most important, she was an active member of the London literary circle that spun out the dazzling succession of artistic "isms"—imagism, dadaism, vorticism, futur-ism—before the catastrophe of the First World War smashed this coterie into the confusion of a spiritual wasteland. Like these artists, H.D. began writing in the aestheticism and fascination for pure form characteristic of the imag-ists; and like them, she turned to epic form and to myth, religious tradition, and the dream as a way of giving meaning to the cataclysms and fragmenta-tion of the twentieth century. Her epic poetry should be compared to the *Cantos, Paterson,* the *Four Quartets,* and *The Bridge,* for like these poems, her work is the kind of "cosmic poetry" the imagists swore they would never write.

The pattern of her poetic development not only paralleled that of more famous artists, but it was also permeated by major intellectual currents of the century. In 1933 and 1934 she was psychoanalyzed by Freud an explora-tion deep within her own unconscious that ultimately linked for her the per-sonal with the universal, the private myth with the "tribal" myths. At the same time that she studied with Freud, the convinced materialist, she was a student of comparative religion, of esoteric tradition, and, like Yeats, of the occult. The forces perpetually at work to bring a directionless century to war were a constant preoccupation in her work. Consciously rejecting the mechanistic, materialist conceptions of reality that formed the faith of the empirical modern age, H.D. affirmed a "spiritual realism" and the relevance of a quest for intangible meanings. Her growth into a poet exploring the psyche or soul of humanity and reaching out to confront the questions of history, tradition, and myth places her squarely in the mainstream of "estab-lished" modern literature. But still, outside of a few poets like Denise Lev-ertov, who wrote "An Appreciation" of H.D., Robert Duncan, and the aficionados who circulate a pirated edition of *Hermetic Definition,* few people read her poetry. . . . H.D. was a serious prolific poet exploring the same questions as her famous counterparts and thus inviting comparison with them. It is something of an understatement, I think, to say that in our profession artists do not have to wear the badge of greatness in order to have articles and books written about them. The simple relevance of her work to the issues and experiments of modern poetry demands that it be studied. . . .

The answer is simple enough, I think. It lies biographically and factually right in front of our critical noses—too close perhaps to be seen easily. It lies in what makes H.D. and her work different from a long string of more studied poets like Eliot, Pound, Crane, Williams, and Yeats. And it lies in the response of her critics. She was a woman, she wrote about women, and all the ever-questioning, artistic, intellectual heroes of her epic poetry and novels were women. In the quest poetry and fiction of the established literary tradition (particularly the poetic tradition), women as active, thinking, individual human beings rarely exist. . . . Women are dehumanized, while the quest of the male poet is presented and understood as the anguished journey of the prophet-seer for the absolute on behalf of all humankind. For "mankind" they may be the spokesmen, but for "womankind" they are not. As a woman writing about women, H.D. explored the untold half of the human story, and by that act she set herself outside of the established tradition.

Susan Friedman. *College English.*
36, March, 1975, pp. 802–3

Helen in Egypt is an epic poem of great depth and beauty; it is H.D.'s finest achievement. . . . As an impersonal poem *Helen in Egypt* is a meditation upon the cause of war. War takes place, says H.D., because someone (or some group or culture) will not bend to the will of someone else (or some other group or culture).

H.D. sees the war between the sexes as primal and believes all wars follow the same logic. A person or culture attempts to enforce his will on another person or another culture. Who, then, is to be blamed? The one who attempts to force his will on another or the one who refuses to submit? In H.D.'s experience men had attempted to force their will upon her; resistance leads to strife. Do we then blame the woman for resisting? Or do we blame her for provoking the attack? Or, suggests H.D., is it not the case that men ought to take responsibility for war? They are, after all, the aggressors. Why should women be blamed for simply existing? These are some of the larger questions that prompt the strophes of *Helen in Egypt*. . . .

While it is true that H.D.'s vision was informed by far more than Aldington, Pound, and Lawrence, she was always deeply aware that the particular traumatic events involving them had precipitated her coming to consciousness. Her work with Freud enabled H.D. to bring these events into consciousness on an epic scale and to understand the transpersonal nature of her experience. The Helen-Iphigeneia realization is not a mere metaphor for a personal event; rather, the event was the efficient cause, the precipitating occurrence from which the conception was realized. But the efficient cause is not the sufficient cause. The conception was informed by the entire body of circumstances of the poet's life and mind.

Janice S. Robinson, *H.D.: The Life and
Work of an American Poet*
(Boston: Houghton Mifflin, 1982),
pp. 362, 369, 378–79

By a tremendous output of prose fiction, H.D. extended her range and challenged her continuing "canonization" as imagist saint (miracle worker and icon) which had been solemnified in a young *Collected Poems* in 1925, only twelve years after her first publication as H.D. In this second period alone (1920/25–1933/34), there are three groups of novels: a *Magna Graeca* set (*Hedylus* and *Palimpsest*); the "Madrigal cycle" (*Paint it To-day, Asphodel, HERmione,* and the later *Bid Me To Live* (*A Madrigal*)); and a Borderline group.

One project of this prose is to unify such female experiences as (lesbian, bisexual, heterosexual) sexuality and motherhood with creative power. H.D. struggles to assume the authority of Otherness so that female-centered experiences and ties are the source of theme and character, narrative and resolution, language and rhythm. This is not achieved without a struggle with negative evaluations of female situations, especially the mother-daughter tie, but also the trustworthiness of some lesbian relations. A related project of H.D.'s prose is to elide the Otherness of women with the otherness of both visionary and artist. So many of the novels—certainly the three discussed here—offer the overlapping stories of *Bildungs-* and self-reflexive *Kunstler-roman* about the repeated formations of a woman artist who must "create her creativity" given the social, psychic, ideological and political events reverberating with her femaleness: the conditions in which she writes as a woman, the politics of gender. H.D. begins to claim herself in Otherness by ceasing to be the perfect poet and becoming-something else; writing, as Mary Jacobus has tersely indicated, "elsewhere, elsehow," . . .

The presence of desire and the erotic defines the final phase of H.D.'s literary career, from 1949 to 1961. After her self-exploratory *Notes on Recent Writing* (1949), and throughout the last decade of her life, beginning when she was well over sixty years old, she experiments with placing various kinds of female desire (sexual/erotic, maternal) at the heart of narrative and language—in the production of texts and in the analysis of culture. In treating sexualities in an autobiographical fashion, H.D. claims a consummate gender authority: to speak of female sexuality from a personal center, to consider sexuality as part of her identity, to play with forms, stages, forces and structures of sexuality, and to reread the role of sexuality in history. In so doing, she plays with fantasies, with the fictive and with the frank, including fictive frankness, frank fantasies, fantastic fictions.

Rachel Blau DuPlessis. *H.D.: The Career of
That Struggle* (Bloomington: Indiana
University Press, 1986), pp. 31–32, 102

Far from escapist and sentimental, H.D.'s transformed romanticism drew upon the romantics' preoccupation with the split between eros and spirituality projected in the dialectical landscapes of romantic quest romance. As with the romantics, H.D.'s search for a "lost land" she called "Hellas" signifies the inward quest for a reconciliation of sexuality and spirituality: the quest pattern of her psychic landscapes imitates the structure of romantic quest romance, as described by Harold Bloom, which frequently recounts a journey through "crisis" and despair in the "lower paradise" of sexual thralldom to a regenerate paradise of love where eros and creative autonomy are triumphantly reunited. However, both the fallen and regenerate paradises of romantic tradition assume a poetics of male desire, which H.D. necessarily transformed, I suggest, to express the obstructed or liberated forms of desire within the female imagination. The sensuous trap or "Venusberg" typified by such poems as Keats's "La Belle Dame Sans Merci" or Swinburne's "Laus Veneris," in which the knight is doomed to endure the embrace of Venus for all eternity, projects specifically male anxieties about female domination. The moment of "crisis" for the male quester occurs when he becomes "feminized," and surrenders his sexual and imaginative freedom to a female principle of manipulative power; decadents such as Swinburne were labeled "effeminate" by male modernists Eliot and Yeats for their fascination with the overflowered love bower and its resident dominatrix. Male modernists were more tolerant of the early romantics who reasserted sexual difference and male privilege in regenerate bowers of love such as Shelley's Hellenic paradise in *Epipsychidion,* where Shelley's quester projects a union with his beloved Emily. Bloom's description of the consummated romantic quest as "a dialectic of love . . . uniting the imagination with its bride" envisions a hierarchical relation between the sexes in which the quester is male and the object of his quest is female. While the romantic tradition provided H.D. with a form for her own debate about the possibilities of achieving a union of erotic fulfillment and creative autonomy, it inadequately expressed that conflict within the female imagination. . . .

H.D.'s unique transformation of romanticism may account for the uncharacteristic exuberance of her modernist poetics. Struggling to break with the "effeminate," "escapist" tradition of the past, H.D.'s most anti-romantic contemporaries preoccupied themselves with the urban wasteland, while the several forms of H.D.'s Hellas continued to generate new fictions from romantic explorations of gender and sexuality.

Cassandra Laity. In Susan Stanford
Friedman and Rachel Blau DuPlessis, eds.
Signets: Reading H.D. (Madison: University
of Wisconsin Press, 1990), pp. 111, 125

I suggest that *Sea Garden* is a consciously crafted whole, with studied consistency in landscape, voice, and theme. The landscape is a sufficiently constant feature among the poems that we get the sense of a finite place: desolate

sandy beach strewn with broken shells, large promontories and rocky head-
lands; inland, a barren stretch of sparse but hardy vegetation beyond the
beach, and low wooded hills nearby; deeper inland, the marshes and places
of luxuriant or cultivated growth. The voice in these poems also possesses
consistency. All the speakers have a similar tone and intensity, even in poems
dealing with specific dramatic situations and appearing to have sometimes
male and sometimes female speakers. This voice is similar to that in H.D.'s
translations of Euripidean choruses. Though few of the poems speak of "we,"
the collective voice is suggested; the "I" dissolves within the pervasive sense
of generalized suffering and exaltation, like the single voice in the chorus of
tragedy. The poems are often addressed to another person or to a god, and,
in a few instances, they are simple meditations. But the most representative
address, occurring in more than a third of the poems, is the apostrophe, the
vocative voice. It seems in part to function as prayer or supplication, sum-
moning presences, as do some of the poems in the *Greek Anthology*. More
than this, the apostrophe, as Jonathan Culler points out, serves to create "a
detemporalized immediacy, an immediacy of fiction." The "apostrophic"
force is central to lyric power, creating "a fictional time in which nothing
happens but which is the essence of happening." The voice of these poems,
then, is hermaphroditic, collective, and atemporal. The poem is, in a sense, a
liminal state without ordinary determinations of gender, person or tense. . . .

Sappho's "emotional wisdom," as H.D. saw it, rested in her capacity to
love and to transfigure the mortal gesture within the lucid, uncompromising
light of imagination. Such wisdom, too, H.D. possesses. In *Sea Garden* Sappho is "She [who] watches over the sea," moving one inward to her severe
salt domain. H.D., serving this mortal Muse, makes of the ephemeral rose
the durable substance of rock. Like Meleager she shapes and gives a "sweet-
speaking garland" to initiates who wish experience of the common mysteries.

> Eileen Gregory. In Susan Stanford Friedman
> and Rachel Blau DuPlessis, eds.
> *Signets: Reading H.D.* (Madison: University
> of Wisconsin Press, 1990), pp. 139, 151

Palimpsest, like a number of H.D.'s works, is a trilogy, a form that was highly
attractive to her throughout her career. There is, for example, the work finally
called *Trilogy,* composed of *The Walls Do Not Fall* (1944), *Tribute to the
Angels* (1945), and *The Flowering of the Rod* (1946); there is *Helen in Egypt*
(1961) structured as "Pallinode," "Leuké," and "Eidolon"; there is the tripartite *Hermetic Definition* (1973) written as "Red Rose and a Beggar," "Grove
of Academe," and "Star of Day." All of these published works consciously
use a tripartite structure as a controlled and controlling device. Among the
unpublished work, however, there are trilogies less intentional, more obsessive, generated by the impulse to retell "the story," to do it right or more
clearly wrong, to reveal it finally or to disguise it more completely. These
series are more triptychs than trilogies, perhaps, as they do not move forward

from the initial telling but rather back inside it, altering the landmarks but never leaving the original "scene." One might group, for instance, the three novels surrounding *Palimpsest—Paint It To-Day* (1921), *Asphodel* (1921–22), and *HERmione* (1981; written as *HER* in 1927)—which process and reprocess H.D.'s pre-1920 relationships; one might also take as a unit *The Sword Went Out to Sea* (1946–47), *White Rose and the Red* (1948), and *The Mystery* (1949–51), novels that, according to Janice Robinson, H.D. "conceived of . . . as a prose trilogy" (343). I would suggest rather that H.D. *recognized eventually* the connections among these novels, for in her prose, H.D. does not "conceive" trilogies. She conceives such structural strategies in the poetry, but in the novels she discovers them after the fact just as she discovered in analysis that she functioned psychologically in triangles. This is perhaps part of the reason she was drawn to the trilogy as form—because it acted out early relationships in a kind of prose compulsion which she did not get control over, understand, or use to her real advantage until the poetry after analysis. Suffused also with mystical, numerological, and Delphic associations, the trilogy accommodated both emotional triangles and arcane trinities, offering H.D. the textual space in which she could work both the psychic and spiritual aspects of her vision.

> Deborah Kelly Kloepfer. In Susan Stanford
> Friedman and Rachel Blau DuPlessis, eds.
> *Signets: Reading H.D.* (Madison:
> University of Wisconsin Press, 1990), p. 187

HER deserves publication in its entirety. It is important to an understanding of H.D.'s entire canon as well as to the literary history of the modernist novel in general and the lesbian novel in particular. *HER* concerns a quest for identity which centers on the interrelated questions of vocation, marriage, and sexuality. . . .

[H.D.'s] exploration of the socially condemned category—the lesbian—was defiantly revisionist throughout her life and art; her erotic "difference," in whatever aspect of her life it found expression, served as a center of identity from which she could create. She consistently renamed and reclaimed the female, the spiritual, the lesbian within the context of a hostile world that valued the male, the material, the heterosexual. But she never adopted that "difference," particularly her sexual difference from a heterosexist society, as her whole identity. The dilemma which the open ending of *HER* illuminates is one that H.D. continued to address in different forms for the rest of her life. H.D. forged her oeuvre in persistent and profound struggles with cultural and narrative questions concerning sexuality and the domains of gender.

> Susan Stanford Friedman and Rachel Blau
> DuPlessis. *Signets: Reading H.D.* (Madison:
> University of Wisconsin Press, 1990),
> p. 209, 227

In April 1920, while staying with her friend Bryher in a hotel on the island of Corfu, H.D. had a vision which marked and measured the rest of her life. It set the aims, announced the means, and disclosed the dimensions of her great work, the visionary epics *Trilogy* and *Helen in Egypt,* and it seemed to guarantee her gift as seer and prophet. It would be twenty years from the Corfu vision to the poems that first grasp its promise, however, years of drift and anxiety in which H.D. would write and rewrite the story of her vision. By the time the event achieves final formulation in the first part of *Tribute to Freud,* it is clear that, however charged the vision's imagery, the plot we are to follow, the *mythos* of the matter, is its method: the miraculous projection of the images.

As H.D. explains in *Tribute to Freud,* the images she witnessed had the clarity, intensity, and authenticity of dream symbols and yet took shape not inside her mind but on the wall between the foot of her bed and the washstand. Because it was late afternoon and their side of the hotel was already dim and because the images were outlined in light, the shapes that appeared could not have been cast shadows. Neither accidental nor random, they formed with a stately, steady purpose, one after another, and seemed inscribed by the same hand. Their abstract, impersonal, rather conventional notation—a head in profile, a chalice, a ladder, an angel named Victory or Nike—made them appear part of a picture alphabet or hieroglyphic system, a supposition reinforced by their orderly succession, their syntax. For these reasons and because of the eerie, miraculous portentousness of the moment, H.D. calls this experience the "writing on the wall."

> Adalaide Morris. In Susan Stanford
> Friedman and Rachel Blau DuPlessis, eds.
> *Signets: Reading H.D.* (Madison: University
> of Wisconsin Press, 1990), p. 273

My topic is a dimension of H.D.'s writing which is of the deepest importance and without which we would not be reading her at all: the beauty of her poetic music; that mysterious, exquisite, "crystalline" yet fluid movement of her versification; her ear. And our ears, listening. For poetry is first of all and most magically a tissue of sound. . . .

We cannot confine the significance of discoveries in prosody merely to literary history. If poets need new ways to make sound run in the listening ear, it is because they find themselves taking a new stance toward reality, toward society. "When the music changes, the walls of the city tremble," says Plato; the reverberations of prosody are inevitably political as well as aesthetic. I hope to suggest, then, that the uniqueness of H.D.'s versification is inseparable from her radical stance as visionary and modernist poet.

> Alicia Ostriker. In Susan Stanford Friedman
> and Rachel Blau DuPlessis, eds. *Signets:*
> *Reading H.D.* (Madison: University of
> Wisconsin Press, 1990), p. 336

In more ways than one, H.D. was in a unique position to recognize the special relation that exists between women and images. Born, or rather baptized, Hilda Doolittle, she was rechristened "H.D." by her friend Pound, who appended this signature to her earliest publications along with the fashionably French epithet that—until recently—defined her reputation: *Imagiste*. Following Pound's cue, critical legend made "H.D." "the perfect Imagist," not only *an* example, but *the* example, the exemplar, the veritable Image of Imagism. And since *Imagisme* has itself long been recognized as what T. S. Eliot called "the *point de repère* for the beginning of modern poetry," "H.D." was accorded a certain place in the history of literature—but only to the extent that she embodied, perfectly, fully adequately and with nothing left over, a certain *theory* of the Image, which was not her own. For as one historian of imagism remarks, "H.D. was no theorist."

"H.D." was no theorist—only an example of a theory, an image, her images, presented in evidence for a male-authored truth. In this way a naive reading practice reinscribed as history what was, after all, only a theory: that the poetic Image, in a timeless moment of aesthetic perception, could effect an adequation of seeing and knowing, appearance and reality, outside and inside. But just as feminist criticism has dislodged "H.D." from her place of (no) honor in the literary history of men, so has feminist theory analyzed the Imaginary logic that put her there in the first place.

Elizabeth A. Hirsh. In Susan Stanford
Friedman and Rachel Blau DuPlessis, eds.
Signets: Reading H.D. (Madison: University
of Wisconsin Press, 1990), p. 430

DOVE, RITA (UNITED STATES) 1952–

Most recent poets' treatment of the languages which write us as public (as well as private, to perpetuate the familiar but ideologically charged dualism) is usually delicately carved, but somehow quietist. Take the recent volume by the finely sensitive poet, Rita Dove, *Museums.* Making a great improvement on her earlier volume in the same series, *The Yellow House on the Corner,* Dove's poems focus on the intersection of the "individual" and the history that has brought her into being. Learning, travel, cultural comparison all bring the enculturated self—here Black, American, Woman—into self-contradictions. . . .

[The] confrontations are finely evoked, and are all the more interesting precisely because the ideological tensions speak through these crisp, replete poems. Once again the subject is interpolated through the conflicting discourses which speak her. But imprisoned in the contradiction of American ideology, she fails to realize that she herself is "spoken," constituted by the fissures, contradictions, and deformities that speak through her words. Like Hass's poetry, Dove's opens up for critical commentary the language of the cultural unconscious repressed by a poetic that has divided the world into observant, neurotic "self" and an inert world of "objects." Such a dualism— seemingly so characteristic, almost "material" to American writing since the Puritans—is revealed as deeply scarred by the dominant ideology. The subject is interpolated as alienated, dispersed infinitely in the words by which it struggles to locate itself in an endless world of absence. But in that dispersion, we are pointed beyond the text, in the way that Pearl in *The Scarlet Letter* or the green light at the end of Daisy Buchanan's pier points us, to a different text, present, in Althusser's words, only "as a necessary absence in the first."

It may be objected that there is a whole area of criticism neglected by my approach to these few contemporary poets, however representative they may be of the best work by the poets of the 1970s and 1980s. It is true, certainly, that Dove's work is finely chiselled, varied in tone, witty, provocative, but it is interesting how Milosz, himself such a celebrated craftsman, should also ignore the "workshop" aspect of poetry to concentrate on writing as the bearer, or refuser, of desire and power. The best poetry—if we can risk an absurd generalization—is not that which triumphantly solves or closes the formal problems which brings it into being. It is those poems which refuse complicity or reluctantly accede to the power of ideology, making the struggle perceptible, betraying into textuality the gaps and silences of its apparently replete presence, bringing to the surface—in the way I suggest Hass's poems do, or Dove's or Forché's—the contradictions that striate the whole social formation. Such poems, regardless of their surface concerns, make us see the ideological struggles from which they are born and from which they detach themselves as art.

Gary Waller. Denver Quarterly. 18:3,
Autumn, 1983, pp. 135–37

Thomas and Beulah, Rita Dove's newest book, . . . engages history, in this case, personal history. In *Museum,* . . . she moved easily through more modern history as well. *Thomas and Beulah* refers obliquely to twentieth-century American history, but from the family album snapshot on the cover through the appended "Chronology" (first item: "1900: Thomas born in Wartrace, Tennessee"), we read this book as a family chronicle. However, the poems themselves are not about an individual's *relationship* to her history, nor about the weight of history. They are, more, history allowed to speak for itself. The title page tells us that the "poems tell two sides of a story and are meant to be read in sequence." The history contained in *Thomas and Beulah,* indeed, is found in the unfolding story—or juxtaposed stories—told of the youth, marriage, lives and deaths of two people. We even forget that the poems are historical, in part because they mix past and present tense, in part because of the frequent use of the past and present progressive, and in part because of the vividness of the characters revealed.

There is no editorializing, and no morals are drawn; the lives stand only for themselves, although through image and sound—one could say through the poetry—the reported lives are enriched and given meanings articulated more fully than they could be by the people described. For example, "Straw Hat" describes Thomas, who at age twenty-one arrives in Akron from Tennessee after a few years on riverboats where he sang to his friend Lem's mandolin playing. "Straw Hat" reads: "He used to sleep like a glass of water / held up in the hand of a very young girl." The language is simple, but the image and alliteration capture the sense of a now-gone childhood and, by contrast, the water in which Lem drowned. The image of the girl also leads the reader into Thomas's courtship of Beulah in the next poem "Courtship." . . .

Given such apparently sparse language, a surprising amount is said. Thomas's youthful cockiness is captured (in the phrase, "King of the Crawfish," as much as in the description of his clothes). We are also given Thomas's point of view; the parenthetical aside seems almost his stage whisper, telling us that the scarf is more a sign of his well-being than of love; the same is suggested when we see he is willing to use a chance encounter with a gnat to his advantage. At the same time, though, the fact that the scarf is "still warm from his throat" comments on more than Thomas's ability to talk a good line; it suggests he *is* sharing something of himself, as well.

"Courtship" gains in meaning from the gathering sense of Thomas's character in the first half of the book, and it also resonates with the poem, "Courtship, Diligence," in the last (Beulah's) half of their volume. "Courtship, Diligence," opens: "A yellow scarf runs through his fingers / as if it were melting." We think of the phrase, "butter wouldn't melt in his mouth," and also of how, from Beulah's perspective, Thomas's feeling he has money (and scarfs) to throw away seems more like mismanagement, or emotional miscalculation, than financial success. . . . Helen Vendler has suggested that Dove offers us a poetry of "the disarticulated," of those whose lives, and therefore histories, are fragmented . . . it is worth adding that most of the language in *Thomas and Beulah* could have been spoken by the people whose story is told, which is to say that the poems do not seem to impose on their subjects. Rather, they slowly build a context for the objects, images, and scraps of reported speech and song that appear and keep reappearing. This is an impressive achievement, although it also means that the poems have more power taken together than individually. To give one more example: when Thomas watches the "shy angle of his daughter's head," sees his son-in-law swallow, and feels for the first time "like / calling him *Son*" ("Variations on Gaining a Son"), attentive readers confronted only with this poem will recognize the oblique reference to fishing and to the commonplace, "hooking a man." But it is only in the context of the other poems about Thomas, about his own marriage, about his more literal fishing trips (in "Lightnin' Blues" and "One Volume Missing"), and about his desire for a son that these lines have their full impact. This is, of course, an appropriate way to reimagine and re-present the lives traced in the book, since they are lives not fully examined by those who live them. The marriage of Thomas and Beulah, in particular, is clearly one where communication is tacit, contained precisely in repeated phrases and motions that have gained meaning over the years. The poems reenact both the accretion of meaning and the taciturnity, perfectly right for this subject, although, given other subjects, one might want more.

Lisa M. Steinmann. *Michigan Quarterly Review.* 26:2, Spring, 1987, pp. 433–35

Rita Dove's *Thomas and Beulah.* . . . winner of the 1987 Pulitzer Prize, has a distinctive, ambitiously unified design. It traces the history of two blacks who separately move North, to Ohio, meet and get married in the 1920s, and go on to raise four girls, enduring many vicissitudes before their deaths in the 1960s. Arranged serially and accompanied by an almost essential chronology, the poems, we are told in a note beforehand, are meant to be read in order. Much as Michael Ondaatje has done in his poem-like novel, *Coming through Slaughter,* Dove reconstructs the past through a series of discontinuous vignettes which enter freely into the psyches of the two main characters.

It is important that the poems are arranged chronologically because we often need all the help we can get in clarifying many of the references. Even with chronology as a guide, the poems sometimes seem unnecessarily obscure and cryptic. More often, however, the difficulty of the work is justifiable because the insights are exactly as subtle as they are oblique. In exploiting the virtues of ellipsis, Dove evidently has faith we will have gumption enough to stare a hole in the page until our minds leap with hers across the gaps . . .

One of the great strengths of this book is the depth of Dove's sympathetic understanding not only of Beulah but also of Thomas; she manages to convey the inner savor both of Thomas's early ebullience and of his later frustration and despair at not being allowed a part in the world equal to his considerable sensitivity. The mandolin provides him with a creative outlet, but it becomes the bittersweet outlet of the blues. As Dove's narrator puts it in "Straw Hat:"

> To him, work is a narrow grief
> and the music afterwards
> is like a woman reaching into his chest
> to spread it around.

The diction of this passage, which includes the elegant phrase "narrow grief," is a good indication of how Dove manages to use the more abstract resources of English to telling effect, without sacrificing the credibility of her account.

In her forays into the black vernacular, Dove chooses not to be phonetic; instead, she concentrates on diction and speech rhythm and does so with dialectical pizzazz. . . .

[T]he poems appeal so directly to the five senses that we're convinced of their authenticity before, and after, we've had time to plumb their artfulness.

Consider, for example, with what resourcefulness and immediacy Dove dramatizes Beulah's reluctant attraction to the wild mandolin player, Thomas, during their courtship. . . .

Beneath its sensuousness, the passage conceals a delicately comedic irony. Beulah may snobbishly prefer a pianola to the mandolin, but snobbery is no defense against the flamboyant appeal of Thomas's scarf and "cool" hands, whatever "cool" may mean, and it may mean many things, from graceful to calculatingly seductive. Thomas lives long enough to be worn down by time and by the lack of meaningful work, but in his prime, especially in his courtship of Beulah, he was a prodigy to behold, the "King of the Crawfish." And no less remarkable is Dove's portrayal of Beulah herself, whom we first see as an elegant woman, fending off Thomas in "pleated skirt [that] fans / softly, a circlet of arrows"; we follow her into a dignified, though sadly reduced widowhood, where the best she can say, in retrospect about her marriage is *we were good, / though we never believed it.* The psychic cost of suffering makes itself keenly felt in *Thomas and Beulah,* a blues book.

Peter Harris. Virginia Quarterly Review.
64:2, Spring, 1988, pp. 270–72

The sequence of *Thomas and Beulah* resembles fiction more than it does a poetic sequence—Faulkner's family chronicles in particular. Dove's modernist narrator stands back paring her fingernails like an unobtrusive master or God. The cover shows a snapshot, of Thomas and Beulah presumably, and the volume may be considered as a photo album, or two albums, with only the date and place printed underneath each picture. Thomas and Beulah are probably Rita Dove's grandparents; the book is dedicated to her mother, Elvira Elizabeth, and the third child born to Thomas and Beulah is identified in the chronology as Liza. But whether the couple is actually Rita Dove's grandparents is less important than the fact that all evidence of their relation has been removed. Any choice of genre involves an economy of gains and losses. Objective, dramatic narration—showing rather than telling—has the advantage of letting the events speak for themselves and the disadvantage of dispensing with the problematics of narrative distortion and a camera-eye or God's-eye view. *Thomas and Beulah* tells it like it is and assumes it is like it tells us.

The most surprising thing about *Thomas and Beulah* is the severance not between narrator and story but between story and story. In "Wingfoot Lake," Beulah's in-laws take the widow to a segregated Goodyear picnic: "white families on one side and them / on the other, unpacking the same / squeeze bottles of Heinz, the same / waxy beef patties and Salem potato chip bags." The "two sides of a story" are similarly segregated in Dove's volume, cordoned off by the roman numerals I and II. *Thomas and Beulah* tells no joyous love story, as we might expect, nor even a tragedy of love lost. The lives of Thomas and Beulah rarely intersect: There are few common events in their stories and no Faulknerian climax in which their worlds collide. They rarely think about each other (Beulah's name does not even appear in Thomas's side); and when they do, it is with an absentminded fondness. Their lives' desires lie elsewhere. . . .

Beulah also explodes the fiction of her own story by denying the existence of the omniscient, absentee Narrator who relates it—the rest is ellipsis. In "One Volume Missing," Thomas buys a used encyclopedia: "for five bucks / no zebras, no Virginia, / no wars." And no Zion, as in the "A.M.E. Zion Church," which sold it. *Thomas and Beulah*—with its gaps, divisions, and deletions—comes also as an incomplete set. But that is Dove's bargain. For us to read any of her fragmentary alphabet, the never-never Volume that would integrate the Goodyear Picnic, Thomas and Lem, Thomas and Beulah, the main clauses and their absolutes, Beulah and Beulah, the narrator and her stories, must remain missing.

John Shoptaw. In Henry Louis Gates, Jr.,
ed. *Reading Black, Reading Feminist* (New
York: NAL–Dutton, 1990), pp. 375, 381

The discipline of writing *Thomas and Beulah,* a family epic in lyric form, required Rita Dove to focus, as never before, her talent for compression. How to get years of her grandparents' joy and anguish into spare lines without presuming to sum up for them; how to telescope distances of place, background, dreams, without narrating—these were some of the problems she solved so brilliantly in that book. The past shed its patina as bits of voice and image shone through to bespeak whole epochs and regions. The book moved us by its understatement, the major ally of compression, and by its sympathetic imagination, that refused to make Thomas and Beulah stereotypes, the mere objects of our pity or nostalgia.

In *Grace Notes* Dove returns to the range of subjects and settings that characterized her first two books (she is remarkably broad in the scope of her references without ever being showy). All the features we have grown to appreciate in this poet arise here in their finest form: descriptive precision, tonal control, metaphoric reach within uncompromising realism. Moreover, she has brought these talents to bear upon a new intimacy and moral depth, served by memory and imagination working together . . .

It is to the cast-off, the "truly lost," the "lint" of the world that Dove turns in the final section of *Grace Notes.* What vitality is left for Genie, "born too late for *Aint-that-a-shame?*" Quite a lot, it seems, dream of "a breezeway and real nice wicker on some AstroTurf." For Billie Holiday and women like her, caged canaries, the bitter message is: "If you can't be free, be a mystery."

In a volume of poems full of resistance, offering ways of coping with and transcending wounds, these last poems have the eerie placidity of surrender; they remind us that our vulnerabilities are real and often untranscendable. The volume which began with black American adolescence, its fears and aspirations, ends in an Old Folks Home in Jerusalem, ancient, mythical desert place where the pangs of difference, worldly hope, even survival are no longer in question. "So you wrote a few poems" almost cuts the wing, coming as it does from the scene of Jews enduring their final suffering. But the last words of the volume are not simply bleak: "Everyone waiting here was once in love." The invisible wings of the human spirit continue to flutter.

Bonnie Costello. Callaloo. 14:2, Spring,
1991, pp. 434, 437–38

DRABBLE, MARGARET (GREAT BRITAIN) 1939–

A Summer Bird-Cage (quotation from Webster) is a sad but funny little tale about the breakup of a marriage. Louise, a notable beauty, marries for his money a rich but nasty novelist; the story is related by her less beautiful sister, Sarah, in a colloquial, unpretentious, yet stylish prose which is perfectly fitted to the narrative. The characters and setting are entirely "contemporary," but Miss Drabble is neither a beatnik nor a young-angry, and her pictures of girlhood have a charm and tenderness which recall the novels of Rosamond Lehmann; yet the book is without a trace of sentimentality. Its moral might be expressed in the words of the heroine in the last chapter: "What fools middle-class girls are to expect other people to respect the same gods as themselves and E. M. Forster."

To call a first novel "promising" always seems a bit unfair, implying as it does that the author might have done better if he had tried a little harder. Miss Drabble may write better novels in the future, and I hope she does, but *A Summer Bird-Cage* seems to me a noteworthy achievement and, considering Miss Drabble's age (she is twenty-four), remarkably mature.

Jocelyn Brooke. The Listener.
April 11, 1963, p. 645

If a romantic novel is a novel that is essentially about the romance of love, then Miss Margaret Drabble writes romantic novels: and the point about her new one *The Waterfall* is that a harsh voice demands to know if every word within her romantic framework is the truth, and in the end rejects the framework itself. Her heroine is Jane, who like Rosamund and Clara before her, is refreshingly far from being open-legged for sex at the drop of a fly-zip. In creating Rosamund Stacey in *The Millstone,* Miss Drabble offered us a girl whose feelings about the prospect of sexual intercourse were more natural and more typical than the heroines of so much contemporary fiction—created by women as well as by men—have us believe. Rosamund, you may recall, had two boyfriends, each of whom assumed, as was her intention, that she was going to bed with the other: she remained, until she wished otherwise, a wise virgin. Clara in *Jerusalem the Golden* was more obliging, but she did have a way of keeping a book or two under her pillow to tide her over anything she might not care for.

Jane of *The Waterfall* is very similar to Rosamund and Clara, except that in her case Miss Drabble has delved more ruthlessly. . . . The dense introspective style that accompanies Jane when she's being truly honest sometimes reads like an argumentative thesis, but this is hardly a fault because Jane is a girl whose mind operates like that. Only once or twice does introspection seem unduly bothersome in this brilliant novel, and that's when it's too long indulged at a dramatic moment. Otherwise, *The Waterfall* seems to me to be a skillful, subtle achievement, a woman's novel that should be read, above all, by every man who's ever likely to have love for a woman on his mind. Contained within the limits of an everyday adulterous *affaire,* it is evenly perceptive and revealing throughout, and if it makes less compelling reading than some of Miss Drabble's earlier novels, that lack is more than compensated for by the greater riches of a greater truth. Miss Drabble's strength is that she never seeks to overreach herself or attempt what is alien to her imagination; and for that reason I believe it's unlikely that she has it in her to write a bad book. *The Waterfall* is built upon the foundations of all she has written before; what she builds upon *The Waterfall* may well be sheer magnificence.

William Trevor. *The New Statesman.*
May 23, 1969, p. 738

Margaret Drabble's *The Needle's Eye* is an extraordinary work: It not only tells a story deftly, beautifully, with a management of past and present (and future) action that demonstrates Miss Drabble's total mastery of the mysterious form of the novel, but it succeeds in so re-creating the experiences of her characters that we soon forget they are fictional beings (perhaps they are not . . .?) and we become them, we are transformed into them, so that by the end of the novel we have lived, through them, a very real, human and yet extraordinary experience. . . .

Each of Margaret Drabble's novels has been an extraordinary leap forward: from the well-written, entertaining, but not disturbing *The Garrick Year,* to the moral ambiguities of *The Millstone,* to the rather strange, disturbing *Jerusalem the Golden* and its remorseless "survivor," to the half-mad narrative of *The Waterfall.* Though I have admired Miss Drabble's writing for years, I will admit that nothing she has written in the past quite prepared me for the depth and richness of *The Needle's Eye.*

Joyce Carol Oates. *The New York Times.*
June 11, 1972, p. 23

Why, it may legitimately be asked, have critics of *The Millstone* been misled by Drabble's [Rosamund]?

The answer to this is twofold. First, Rosamund's sophistication is such that even her *partial* probings of her motives already impress the unwary reader as scrupulous. Her wit, along with the quasi-critical eye with which she regards herself, go far toward "seducing" us into approving her, toward helping us identify with her. On the level of the text itself, of the "plot," this identification is further encouraged by the presence of certain wishful elements which are never, to my mind, rationalized adequately: Rosamund's economic situation, her accommodations, her parents' willingness to stay abroad, George's absence for nearly two years, etc. So persuasive is the rhetoric, however, that these elements do not detract from the overall credibility of the novel.

But there is another, perhaps more compelling reason for the spell Rosamund has succeeded in casting over readers of *The Millstone*: she is the symbolic expression of our own resistance to truth, to the reality of unconscious motivations. By identifying with her, the ego of the reader succeeds in triumphing, in however illusory a fashion, over the dim yet fearful conflicts that are so much a part of our psychic makeup. In this sense, *The Millstone* has a fairy-tale quality to it, for Rosamund's claims to new awareness through pain strikes us as protesting a bit too much; she gets her wish, after all, without paying an exorbitant price. And this makes us feel, "at some level," as Rosamund would say, that we can get ours, too. *The Millstone* is by no means a milestone in mature moral fiction if we identify too quickly with its heroine. If we resist that temptation, however—and it is not at all clear Drabble intended us to do so—we are offered an admirable portrait of character the very "rightness" of which, in every detail of its execution, reveals its origin to be in Margaret Drabble's intuitive grasp of the workings of the unconscious.

Susan Spitzer. *Novel.* Spring, 1978,
pp. 244–45

Margaret Drabble is a novelist because she is a woman. Had she been a man, she would no doubt have been an actor, since she did more acting than writing as an undergraduate at Cambridge in the 1950s. After graduation, she joined the Royal Shakespeare Company, where she had a walk-on part in *A Midsummer Night's Dream* and understudied Vanessa Redgrave as Imogen in *Cymbeline.* She also had a baby, and discovered, as generations of women had before her, that "it rather cramped [her] style." So she turned from acting to writing, since "women had never been shut off from the materials of fiction. A pencil and a piece of paper . . . and all human life was there."

There are those who would question whether all of human life is there in Margaret Drabble's novels, at least in the early ones. For she is generally regarded not as a woman who writes novels but as a "women's novelist." This is a label she has recently been at some pains to shed. But, like most labels, it can be useful if read correctly.

If a women's novelist is someone whose subject is women, then there can be no question, I think, that the author of *A Summer Bird-Cage, The Garrick Year,* and *The Millstone* was a women's novelist. Her subject was what it was like to be a woman in a world which calls woman the second sex. For whatever biological accident may have determined Margaret Drabble's choice of a career, the real impetus for her first novel was provided by a book she read during her last year at Cambridge, a book she acknowledges affected her profoundly, Simone de Beauvoir's *The Second Sex.* "This seemed to me to be wonderful material and so important to me as a person. It was material that nobody had used and I could use and nobody had ever used as far as I would use it."

Ellen Cronan Rose. *The Novels of Margaret Drabble* (Totowa, New Jersey: Barnes and Noble, 1980), pp. 1–2

What interests me is how accurately, how richly, [Margaret Drabble] renders a particular mood, a particular state of mind. Further, though I am not sure that she would agree with me, I believe that her true strength as a writer is a lyric strength: what *happens* in her novels is not really the important thing. Indeed in this area her reader must be willing to tolerate a good deal of implausibility—implausible minor characters, implausible plots, and (especially) implausible endings. But if we do tolerate these things, we do so because we know how little they interfere with the essential pleasure of reading Drabble. The following pages are an attempt to define that pleasure, to isolate the special experience her fiction at its best has to offer us.

It is, at bottom, the same pleasure, the same experience, she herself finds in the novels of Arnold Bennett: "He always leaves me," she says, "with a sense that life is full of possibility." That phrase, I should say, describes more aptly the vital quality of her own work. And particularly of her heroines, for it's what preeminently they share—an eagerness, an ineradicable hopefulness about life. Not contentment: they're not particularly contented women. And certainly not complacency: if Drabble's heroines feel hopeful about life it's not because they are unacquainted with despair. It is the play of hope against opposing currents of emotion that defines the special atmosphere of Drabble's fictional world.

Ellen Z. Lambert. *University of Toronto Quarterly.* 49, Spring, 1980, p. 228

Indeed, to read Margaret Drabble specifically as a female writer allows the critic to isolate features of her texts that may suggest characteristically feminine narrative strategies.

Drabble's preference, then, as she concludes each of her novels, for affirmation rather than denial, for continuance rather than ending, seems striking enough to insist on an investigation of the effects of such a preference on the overall structuring of the narratives. Indeed, this preference must be recognized also as philosophical, a choice. Drabble does not naively ignore contemporary crisis, a perspective that would simply remove her novels from serious consideration. Apparently the more she writes, the more fascinated she becomes with the nature of apocalypse, with the ways in which apocalyptic thinking dominates people's lives and, therefore, narrative structures. Nonetheless, in spite of her acknowledgement of catastrophe, even her fascination with it, she refuses to make sense of an ending. On one level, her narrators and characters discuss this rejection as a structural one, questioning the convention that novels' endings are immanent in their beginnings. Of course, as all novels must, Drabble's end. But like the novels of John Fowles, a writer to whom she bears a number of similarities although her closeness to her female characters inevitably alters the stance and status of the narrative act, Drabble's novels emphasize arbitrary conclusions by their very structures. On another, possibly more important level, this privileging of the arbitrary rather than the necessary becomes a correlative for a philosophical or, perhaps more correctly, a psychological statement. Indeed, as Frank Kermode suggests, to be in the midst of a great crisis in human affairs "is what we all want, for it makes us more interesting, is indeed an aspect of our narcissism." Drabble's insistence on the continuance of the fictional universe she creates thus seems a refusal to celebrate "the great crisis" that feeds our narcissism, is, indeed, a questioning of the ethics of that narcissism. Furthermore, one of her major themes, the generating of children, emphasizes a cyclical recurrence that contradicts endings and that perforce focuses attention on a female sexuality that illustrates, to use a phrase from a poem by Margaret Atwood, the "long thread of red blood, not yet broken"—continuance.

Lorna D. Irvine. In Ellen Cronan Rose, ed.
Critical Essays on Margaret Drabble
(Boston: G. K. Hall, 1985), pp. 74–75

Margaret Drabble's *The Realms of Gold* is one of two modern women's novels that I would describe as pervaded by womb imagery and in which the womb is seen as the source of vast creative power. The other novel is Doris Lessing's *The Four-Gated City*. . . . The governing image of Margaret Drabble's *The Realms of Gold* is that of a hole, a large or small, real or symbolic vacuum or lacuna, which, like the womb, must be filled if life is to have meaning. Many of the chief characters engage professionally in probing various depths, in drawing meaning out of one abyss or another. Frances Wingate's mother is a gynecologist; her lover a historian; her cousin a geologist; she herself an archaeologist. While David, the geologist, pokes into huge volcanic craters, seeking meaning, finding "man's life too short to be interesting . . . [wanting] to see all the slow great events, right to the final cinder, the black hole," Frances herself, the remarkable hero of this robust and happy novel, is less ambitious, less cosmic. She explores smaller holes, archaeological excavations, and the historic past. Within her sphere, however, she is sufficiently powerful, energetic, and imaginative to will a whole civilization into being, as her meditation on Tizouk, the city she discovers and resurrects, makes evident. Tizouk is, she feels, the "city of the imagination," which she single-handedly has found and excavated: "I must be mad. . . . I imagine a city, and it exists. If I hadn't imagined it, it wouldn't have existed." Like a woman conceiving and giving birth, Frances finds a desert void which she thoroughly peoples and inhabits out of her own vast creative power.

Frances, the monolithic matriarch of the novel, succeeds where others fail; she seems possessed on every level—physical, intellectual, emotional—of a teeming fecundity. Unlike other characters in the book—her nephew Stephen especially, she can imagine only the destructive void, and not the void potential with new life, and who feels kinship with doomed Empedocles—Frances has enough creative energy and power for almost anything—and, more, she knows it. Life, for her, is largely a question of choosing the right channels for her abundant creative force. She is, she knows, an earth mother with the astonishing powers of a primitive goddess. . . .

The power to create, which Frances has in such prodigious amounts, is a tricky, dangerous power, Blakean in its ambivalence, as likely to destroy as to bring into being, conferring on its possessor great responsibility. Creative power is, as Drabble describes it, reminiscent not merely of Blake's Orc but also of Doris Lessing's ambiguous imp/demon of creative energy in *The Golden Notebook.* As any woman who has contemplated her own frightening ability to give birth to a child deformed or monstrous knows, this is a powerfully female vision of creation.

In *The Realms of Gold,* the power to create imaginatively is seen as an extension of the power to procreate physically, to beget offspring. At the beginning of the novel, Drabble shows us an octopus who dies immediately after serving her procreative function. For people, though, life goes on after childbirth. When, however, the human organism—Frances Wingate in this case—chooses to continue living after procreating, creation becomes self-conscious rather than merely biological.

Carey Kaplan. In Ellen Cronan Rose, ed.
Critical Essays on Margaret Drabble
(Boston: G. K. Hall, 1985), pp. 133, 135–36

[A] reading of Drabble's growing concern with the power of women to use their imaginations and in doing so to replace conditioned, passive, and dependent roles with a new capacity to accept responsibility and make choices provides us with a much-needed way into the apparently bleak, grim, male-centered world in her eighth novel, *The Ice Age.* So far, at least, most of Drabble's critics have maintained a puzzled distance from this chilling book. Overviews of her oeuvre tend to skip over the novel as quickly as possible; there are as yet no published studies devoted exclusively to *The Ice Age,* and in the only collection of Drabble essays published in this time, there are separate studies of each of the last five novels *except The Ice Age* (and two each on *The Realms of Gold* and *The Needle's Eye*). This unwonted scholarly reticence reflects, among other things, the centrality of "women"—as characters, and as an issue—to the best of Drabble's critics, and the subsequent bafflement when she writes a book whose "main character" or even perhaps "protagonist" and "hero" is a man. Two very different readers of Drabble, Ellen Cronan Rose and Elizabeth Fox-Genovese, are disquieted (in very different ways) by this development. In *The Ice Age,* Fox-Genovese sees the culmination of Drabble's "increasingly harsh repudiation of female being," an unambiguous refusal on her part to deal with "the womanliness with which she no longer chooses to identify." While Rose is also clearly disturbed by her belief that Drabble has "to some extent endorsed" male values and feelings and that many of the female characters in the novel "accept and accede to the male point of view," she discerns a critique of "patriarchal visions" in *The Ice Age* (as in the preceding two novels) that Fox-Genovese has either discounted or failed to perceive. I suggest that the "feminist censure" Rose finds just "not wholly absent" in the book carries in fact much greater weight than she has given it, and that the novel—leaving aside the questions of authorial intentions altogether—strongly indicts male (ab)uses of the imagination and mythologizes an alternative that Drabble has been interested in from the beginning of her career: the female imagination.

Elaine Tuttle Hansen. In Ellen Cronan Rose,
ed. *Critical Essays on Margaret Drabble*
(Boston: G. K. Hall, 1985), pp. 152–53

The Waterfall is Margaret Drabble's most literarily allusive novel, a complex metafiction that draws attention to problems of finding a style and of making an ending. Jane Gray, the first-person narrator, is writing a novel about herself in the third person in an attempt to understand her passion for James, her cousin's husband; and she intersperses her stylized, romantic fictionalization with a critical, analytical first-person commentary. In the same way that Anna Wulf, the protagonist of Doris Lessing's *The Golden Notebook,* is writing a novel in order to understand her feelings for her lover, so too does Jane write in order to "comprehend" her experience; and just as the conventional novel Anna writes demonstrates Lessing's sense of the limits of conventional form, so too does Jane's novel express Drabble's commentary on novelistic convention. Drabble has referred to Lessing as "both mother and seer," and nowhere is her indebtedness more apparent than in the metafiction of *The Waterfall.* Though most readers of *The Waterfall* have approached the novel—in the way critics usually approach Drabble's fiction—as social realism significant for what it reveals "about life," Drabble's manipulation of novelistic convention here is as revolutionary as Lessing's, representing no less than a renegotiation of the "contract" of the realist novel. In this tale of adulterous, slightly incestuous passion that leaves its heroine thriving, Drabble repudiates "the old novels" in which "the price of love was death" and creates a new "system" and morality. Drabble's deliberate dialogizing makes this a "polyphonic" text (so termed by Julia Kristeva in her discussion of M. M. Bakhtin) which "transgresses" "linguistic, logical, and social codes" and is therefore "subversive." By making the reader part of the production of meaning, by drawing him/her into the processes of creation and revealing the contradictions involved in those processes, she makes *The Waterfall* a *scriptible* or "writerly" text that disturbs—in Roland Barthes's terms—the ideologically complicit contract between writer and reader.

Gayle Greene. *Novel.* 22,
Fall, 1988, pp. 45–46

The Gates of Ivory begins as Liz Headleand—familiar from *The Radiant Way* and *A Natural Curiosity,* the preceding novels of the trilogy that Margaret Drabble here completes—receives a curious package in her post one morning, a package containing part of a human finger bone. It arrives from Stephen Cox, last seen at the end of *The Radiant Way,* on his way to Cambodia to write a play about Pol Pot; it contains fragments of a prose manuscript and a play, some journals, postcards, sketches, and a booklet of "Atrocity Stories," but no message of instruction. As Liz and various other friends of Stephen try to piece together the meaning of this "text"—is it a joke, an S.O.S., a novel, or evidence of "craziness on a grand scale"?—the reader contemplates the tragedy of Cambodia. The novel engages us, simply, as a missing persons story, and more deeply as a mystery on a "grand theme."

Drabble's canvases have become larger in the course of her thirty-odd-year career. She began in the 1960s with works that associated her with "women's issues" (e.g., *The Millstone, The Waterfall)* and moved, in the 1970s and 1980s, to large-scale works that offer vast panoramas of English society and analyses of the condition of England *(The Ice Age, The Middle Ground, The Radiant Way).* In *The Gates of Ivory,* she reaches out to bring England into a global context. This final installment in the unnamed trilogy is in some sense the most ambitious of her eleven novels to date. . . .

The Gates of Ivory is about the attempt to comprehend Bad Time from within the comforts and complacencies of Good Time. As such it is an appropriate sequel to *A Natural Curiosity,* which concerned the fascination of Alix (Liz's best friend) with the serial murderer and decapitator Paul Whitmore; only here we contemplate serial murder gone big, gone political, and are asked to take in the "Big numbers. Mass destructions. Mass graves"—the twentieth century. What is the cause, what can account for such atrocities? characters repeatedly ask. Like Alix contemplating Paul Whitmore, they ask whether men like Hitler, like Pol Pot, are born wrong or driven wrong by wrongs done to them. Is it nature or nurture that makes such hard hearts? Alix unearths a bad mother and a childhood trauma in Whitmore's history, yet she knows this does not finally explain him—"he is as incomprehensible, as opaque as he ever was." Alix—like those drawn to the bridge—is asking a question to which there is no answer. . . .

This novel is not only about the impossibility of comprehending Bad Time from the perspective of Good Time, it is also about the ambiguity inherent in the attempt: "It would be easy to say that we grow fat and greedy, that we thrive on atrocities, that we eagerly consume suffering," but "it is not as simple as that." Drabble reveals the horribly mixed motives of human action, the intermingling of heroism, despair, idealism, and delusion, the fine line between battening off atrocity and attempting to alleviate it.

Besides questioning the morality of art, Drabble questions the truth of art, approaching these age-old issues from new angles. *The Gates of Ivory* is about the difficulty of distinguishing "true" from "false" representations of experience—representations we can trust from representations that "deceive," messages that come through the gates of horn from those that come through the gates of ivory. The gates of ivory, as Drabble's epigraph (from the *Odyssey*) tells us, "deceive us with false images of what will never come to pass," whereas the gates of horn "speak plainly of what could be and will be." But in this postindustrial, postcolonial, postmodern age, our experience is so thoroughly mediated—in the literal sense of being shaped by the media and by technological methods of information dissemination—that it is difficult to know which is which, which is "real." "Stephen Cox meets a Kampuchean refugee who is playing the role of a Kampuchean refugee in an American semi-fictionalized documentary about Kampuchean refugees. He meets extras who have worked on *The Killing Fields,* some of them survivors of the killing fields. . . . The gates of ivory, the gates of horn. The shadow world." . . .

What I love about this novel is what I love about the best of Drabble's works—it's rich and complex and allusive and textured and intertextual and takes on the big questions: life and art, representation and responsibility, the possibility of political action, the question of human nature. It's a novel of ideas at a time when most fiction seems deliberately lobotomized; it's major in an age of minimalism. What I find disturbing is perhaps built into a project that takes on the unknowable, the unthinkable, the impossibility of conceiving of Bad Time from the perspective of Good Time, of understanding and expressing "the horror" within novelistic form; though I also have a sense, which I wish the novel had explored, that specific political factors, such as the U.S. bombing of Cambodia in the 1970s, had something to do with unleashing "the horror" onto this land. Yet, I do think that this novel is doing something important politically. After Liz receives Stephen's package, she becomes obsessed with "the unfolding retrospective horror story of skull landscapes and killing fields" and sees Cambodia everywhere; she feels that Stephen has "posted" Cambodia to her. So too, did I feel Drabble had posted Cambodia to me: The novel is an act of commemoration, a story to pass on—to tell and remember.

Gayle Greene. *The Nation.* August
31–September 7, 1992, pp. 217–20

DRAKULIĆ, SLAVENKA (CROATIA) 1949—

I warn you. There is not much laughing in this book [*How We Survived Communism and Even Laughed*]. Originally commissioned as an essay in the U.S. feminist magazine *Ms.* Slavenka Drakulić, one of Yugoslavia's founding feminists, has written one of the first insider accounts of what it was like to be a woman under eastern European Communism. It is neither a comprehensive nor an academic study; more, a set of connected allusions, observations and recorded conversations.

For anyone used to those fictional and journalistic accounts of eastern Europe that concentrate on the shadowy state censor, the *samizdat* press, the professor-forcibly-turned-window-cleaner, Drakulić's resolutely domestic frame of reference is both shocking and exhilarating. Most of her action takes place not in the street or the office but in the post office queue, and, of course, the kitchen. Her first bold chapter heading says it all: "The Trivial is Political."

Above all, this is a book about *things*: about nylon stockings and soap, telephones and fur coats, tumble driers and toilet paper. (There is a whole chapter on the changing quality of toilet paper under communism.) It is also about food; people's dreams and glimpsed memories of proper pizzas, creamy chocolate, strawberries, that American bubble gum with the comic wrapping paper.

Drakulić is militant about the meaning of such items for those who have been deprived of them. She must be the first and only person to have begun a speech at a U.S. Socialist Scholars' Conference by holding a tampon and sanitary towel aloft. "I have just come from Bulgaria where you cannot get these. Nor are they available in Poland or Czechoslovakia. Just think about it," she said. The audience was startled into applause, but, being mostly men, were more puzzled than roused.

It is implicit in her account that women are, literally, the guardians of longing. When her grandmother died, her wardrobe was crammed with white tulle and rancid oil, shampoo and outdated insulin, each of them a reminder of a shortage endured. Hers is a story reproduced a hundred thousand times.

Yet, in both east and west, a desire for the good things of life is too commonly called envy and emptied of political content. There is a wonderful description of how it feels, in this world of shortages, to hold a copy of *Vogue* in your hands. It is not just the images that wound—the impossibly beautiful women with their wondrous clothes—but the paper itself, the thick silkiness of it. "I hate it," says her Hungarian friend, Agnes. "It makes me so miserable I could almost cry."

Traditional socialists will find this book very difficult indeed, precisely because it explores the problem of shortages, the material world, in experiential terms. This was always feminism's fraught gift to "wider" politics; so be it. Where Drakulić fails to make the experiential leap herself is in a certain inability to imagine that western women might have a *Vogue* problem; that they, too, might have lived long lives of barely suppressed individualized rage and envy.

More than once, Drakulić's argument reminded me of the work of British feminist Carolyn Steedman, in particular a passage in her *Landscape for a Good Woman*. Steedman, writing of her mother's longing for the good things of life, says that there is in Britain, as yet, "no language of desire that presents what my mother wanted as anything but supremely trivial . . . and yet the borders of her exclusion were immense; her loss resolutely material."

Melissa Benn. *New Statesman and Society.*
January 24, 1992, p. 39

In [*How We Survived Communism and Even Laughed*] Drakulić, a highly regarded novelist and journalist, writes around, under and outside the crisp categories of theory. Her essays—stories, really—shift and mutate, full of emotion and contradiction. Ironically, this anti-Communist's a bit of a Brechtian—she alienates us from conventional feminist and leftist notions, she believes that truth is concrete, and claims as her leitmotif "the trivial is political." . . .

Such "trivia" unfold within the larger framework of political repression. The Yugoslavia Drakulić paints is not a landscape of torture or death squads, but of bugged offices, unctuously threatening censors and demanding bureaucracies. The outward repression creates an inward one—the imagination grows numb, the memory of different times fades. The will to act is stripped away "by our conviction that somebody else—the government, the party, those 'above'—is in charge of it." Whatever "it" may be, from a dress design to a university job to industrial policy. . . .

The book is completely clear about women's position in Yugoslav society. This is a male supremacist world, from the double sexual standard to the double day. Most of the women we hear about are professionals, but it's not hard to extrapolate to industrial workers, peasants, poor Moslems. That women were in many ways, in many cases, better off under Communism than before World War Two isn't discussed but is also clear. You can't lose a right to abortion you haven't been given. Yet while the situation varied from republic to republic—Slovenia is "European," Montenegro is pure tribal Balkan—nowhere was it free, or fair, or good.

As so often happens, the political situation defused, and still defuses, women's resistance. . . .

In the same mess, men and women suffer unequally. Now that the mess has changed from Communist to nationalist, both men and women will still be in it, and still unequal. Indeed, more unequal. Drakulić's current writing confirms an ever-increasing hostility to women's rights, as does the recent spate of vicious attacks on her by the Croatian press (which is heavily censored, worse than before). Can women afford solidarity forever?

If *How We Survived Communism* were simply the first feminist report on women's lives in Eastern Europe, it would be essential reading in every women's studies program. The beauty and precision of Drakulić's writing make it much more than that: we can feel these lives, walk into their rooms, smell their soup. We can get under the skin of her fear as war enters her city. Never underestimate the need for such particular knowledge, our need to grasp the ambiguity, hesitation and conflict at the roots of theory.

Erika Munk. *Women's Review of Books.*
9:8, May, 1992, pp. 3–4

It's too soon for books on what's happened in [the former Yugoslavia in] the last year and a half.

Slavenka Drakulić has one worth reading, though: *How We Survived Communism and Even Laughed.* . . . A Croatian journalist and feminist who writes occasionally for such U.S. magazines as *Ms.* and *The Nation,* she published this nonfiction collection in English last March. All the pieces were written before the outbreak of hostilities, some before the demise of the central communist government. But they reveal a great deal about everyday life in what was the least repressive, most prosperous nation in Eastern Europe until it collapsed overnight into barbarism.

I suspect Drakulić might choose a different title for this book if she were naming it today—her people are uncertain of survival and you wouldn't expect many to be laughing. But they laughed through forty-five years of communism, didn't they? Why is it worse now?

One answer: "Within the iron embrace of the Communist Party, the wounds of nationalism were not healed. Instead, they were ordered to disappear."

Linda Rocawich. *Progressive.*
December, 1992, pp. 38–39

Slavenka Drakulić's collection of autobiographical essays [*Balkan Express*] about the effect of the Yugoslavian war on everyday life is named after an excruciating train trip the author took from Vienna to Zagreb. She shares a compartment with two Yugoslavs. No one will speak for fear that their accent will disclose their ethnic origin, no one can take a newspaper out of their bag without revealing their allegiance. Even if the travellers did feel chatty, there is nothing to talk about except the war—an impossible, unacceptable subject for conversation between strangers.

So, as the train bumps along, the three passengers sit, knees jostling, looking out the window mutely. Yet, Drakulić observes, the silence which "verges on a scream" is a "good sign, a sign of our unwillingness to accept the war, our desire to distance ourselves and spare each other, if possible."

From a war that has been so noted for its brutality and horror, this approach may seem unexpectedly mild-mannered, almost drawing-roomish. There are no eyewitness reports of floating corpses in the river, no dens of torture, no barrels of babies' eyes—little of the common currency of war reporting.

Instead, Drakulić chronicles the smaller events which, between April 1991 and May 1992, illustrate the gradual shedding of normal life, the slow slipping into war. She notices that the word "slaughter" now slips off the television anchorman's lips with ease. She sees a gun tucked in the belt of a man at the bus stop. At the grocery store she hears a woman order: 16 kilos of oil, 20 kilos of flour, 20 kilos of sugar, 10 of salt.

Real life is always slightly at a slant for our expectations. When Drakulić opens a magazine and sees a photograph of a couple lying dead on the ground she finds she is fascinated, above all, by the crumpled, yellow packet of yeast by the woman's head. When the first bomb falls near Drakulić's flat in Zagreb, she freezes in her seat, and, overcome with a sense of heaviness, wonders why on earth she has just redecorated the bedroom with Laura Ashley wallpaper.

Just as in Anne Frank's diary, despite the Holocaust, the teenager is obsessed with family squabbles and homework, Drakulić's attention to seemingly mundane matters accounts for the writing's verisimilitude. But there is also a self-conscious message: "Look, I'm one of you. I have an unexceptional urban, middle-class life—children, newspapers, visits to the cinema, shopping trips, television programmes. Now watch as I become something else. . . . Let me show you the changes as the dark pressures of war take over." . . .

Inevitably, war also undermines our trust in the power of language, and the writer trying to convey this heightened internal reality must call on enormous powers both of expression and of restraint. That Drakulić accomplishes this balance—her "ice over a treacherous river"—is probably the greatest achievement in this wise, profound and original book.

Amanda Mitchison. *New Statesman and Society.* January 29, 1993, p. 47

No mystery seems more urgent or more difficult to fathom than the riddle of how a society as seemingly civilized as our own—one in which children play video games and babies loll in high-tech strollers while their parents browse in bookstores and drink cappuccino in cafes—could erupt in an orgy of savagery, murder, and rape. Certainly that is a question we ask ourselves about the Balkans, even though the photographers only got to Sarajevo in time to catch the fires, the rubble, the corpses, the scorched holes in buildings—and so have mercifully spared us images of the beautiful city it used to be.

Slavenka Drakulić, a Croatian journalist whose previous books include *How We Survived Communism and Even Laughed,* knows precisely how lovely and how complex the former Yugoslavia was, and how deeply the fighting has scarred the newly independent republics. The essays that make up her latest collection, *The Balkan Express,* read like notes on learning how to survive in a land at war and how to absorb the successive shocks of violent change and disruption.

Written between April 1991 and May 1992 and assembled in roughly chronological order, these mostly short pieces form a loose narrative. . . .

One is thankful for Ms. Drakulić's intelligent and brave refusal to descend to polemic, or to xenophobic finger pointing. Wisely, she avoids blaming the brutal ethnic Other for the war and looks for the true culprit—forces in the communal and political history of the region. "But finally," she writes, "there must and does come the question why, which is the hardest to answer because there are hundreds of answers to it, none of them good enough. No graphics, drawings or maps can be of any genuine help, because the burden of the past—symbols, fears, national heroes, mythologies, folk songs, gestures, and looks, everything that makes up the irrational and, buried deep in our subconscious, threatens to erupt any day now—simply cannot be explained."

No one can fault Ms. Drakulić for failing to explain the inexplicable or for voicing the contradictions that one hears so frequently: everyone saw the war coming, but no one believed it would come; ethnic antagonisms had simmered for centuries, yet "nationality . . . wasn't an issue." Such "inconsistencies" are, she says, "precisely what I wanted to write about." Even so, her thoughts on the war can seem muddled and bewildering. . . .

Still, one is glad that *The Balkan Express* was written, and hopeful that Ms. Drakulic's essays will inform and touch her readers. Ideally, her impassioned eyewitness account of the Balkan conflict may make the war more real to those who have somehow managed to distance themselves from the appalling television news footage of rape victims, cadaverous prisoners, and the ruins of once-gracious cities. One thinks of the historic English law that made it a punishable offense to witness a murder or discover a corpse and not raise a "hue and cry." Judged by that standard, Slavenka Drakulić is one of the very few innocents.

Francine Prose. *New York Times Book Review.* May 23, 1993, pp. 9–10

Slavenka Drakulić is a mapper of fraught and forbidden territories. Having chronicled the recent Eastern European crises in her essay collections, *Balkan Express* and *How We Survived Communism and Even Laughed,* the Croatian writer has turned to fiction to explore the more intimate terrain of the female body. Her second novel, *Marble Skin,* marks her courageous foray into the literary no-man's land of the sexual mother, a compelling figure of desire rather than maternal love. Crossing the frontiers of taboo, Drakulić plunges into the heart of incestuousness to expose the female psyche in its darkest and most fleshy aspects.

At the center of the drama lies the marble mother, carved in erotic self-absorption and exposed to the gaze and the sticky fingers of the public. It is a labor of love and hatred, sculpted by a daughter desperate both to reach her elusive mother and to escape the tyranny of her perfect beauty by trapping it in marble. The real mother sees the sculpture and, recognizing the years of sexual conflict and stifled communication etched in its contours, tries to kill herself. With the force of her chisel, the daughter has broken through the marble skin to touch her mother and to wrench out a retribution for the incest and rape she once endured at the hands of her mother's husband.

First published in Yugoslavia in 1989, the book's scandalous subject-matter earned it an explosive reception. More provocative than the literal incest, however, is the shocking incestuousness of the writing, which melts the fine line between pleasure and pain, love and disgust, to reveal their disturbing closeness. The daughter is at once violent and tender in her yearning for the mother she finally kills in art. . . .

Wielding more subtlety than force, . . . Drakulić insinuates us into a heady realm of sensuous and sensual perception that blends touch, look, taste and smell. Searching the recesses of female sexuality, *Marble Skin* uncovers a breathtaking, subcutaneous world of knowing that is compelling if claustrophobic.

Andrea Ashworth. (London) Times Literary
Supplement. July 30, 1993, p. 20

"The title of my book feels wrong," writes Slavenka Drakulić in the introduction to *How We Survived Communism and Even Laughed.* "We have not yet survived communism and there is nothing to laugh about it." Since the war in Croatia broke out when Drakulić had just finished writing her book, she is right. Her mentioning the war in the beginning, however, should not make us expect to get an elucidation of the Balkan wars. She lumps Yugoslavia with Eastern Europe—not the Balkans or the Mediterranean—although Yugoslavia, strictly speaking, has not been behind the Iron Curtain, nor a part of Eastern Europe; moreover, she never distinguishes among the totalitarian socialisms of Eastern Europe, calling them all simply communism, and she never defines communism. Theory does not interest her: but that may be an advantage since she can freely concentrate on people's lives. . . .

[E]ven if it is not clear that the author has suffered much under the system, she does convincingly portray many women who have, which makes for a worthwhile reading, although the author's obsession with women's problems makes her neglect the key problem of Yugoslav and Soviet politics: nationalism. Perhaps sexism, with which she deals, is pretty much the same thing as nationalism and chauvinism. That parallel has not been pursued in the book, in which the "We" means women, and therefore, "we," men and women, should not expect more than the book sets out to tell us.

As a spokeswoman for the women of Eastern Europe, she relates complaints she has heard in most East European countries: "Look at us—we don't even look like women. There are no deodorants, perfumes, sometimes even no soap or toothpaste. There is no fine underwear, no pantyhose, no nice lingerie. Worst of all, there are no sanitary napkins." And she asks:"-What is the minimum you must have so you don't feel humiliated as a woman?" I am puzzled. Here in the West feminists struggle to free women from the cultural tyranny that treats them as objects that should be wrapped in lingerie, pantyhose, makeup, perfume, and there, feminists struggle to have all that jazz!

Drakulić tells us that we should not apply the standards of post-consumer awareness to a pre-consumer society. "What do we care about the manipulation inherent in the fashion and cosmetic industries? To tell us that they are making a profit by exploiting our needs is like warning a Bangladeshi about cholesterol." . . .

[The] journalistic mentality, of course, is similar to spying mentality, which Drakulić describes in a post office where a man peered over her shoulder at her bills. "In fact he really can learn a lot about my own and everyone else's lives just by waiting in post office, bank, or any other institution that involves standing in line, paying bills, or acquiring money or some kind of documentation." Now, in the new democracy in Croatia, Drakulić says, one of the first decrees the Croatian parliament has issued was that each post office should draw a yellow line, far from the counter, to protect people's private spaces, and to prevent people from scrutinizing other people's lives. (Incidentally, Drakulić uncritically calls the present Croatian government a democracy just as she has uncritically called the previous government communism). It should not surprise us that, after living like that—scrutinized and trained to scrutinize—Drakulić has become a good journalist. The surprising thing is that there aren't thousands of them. But let's wait and see. Just as nuclear physicists from the Soviet Union will crowd the American physics departments, books written by women from excommunist countries might crowd American bookstores. Let's welcome them.

Josip Novakovich. Prairie Schooner. 68:1,
Spring, 1994, pp. 157, 160, 162

DREWITZ, INGEBORG (GERMANY) 1923–86

Thematically and in terms of content, the novel [*The Carrousel*] is reminiscent of Gerd Gaiser. There are a flood of books which confront the fate of man during the Hitler regime and the Second World War, and so does Ingeborg Drewitz in *The Carrousel*. She introduces us to Berlin between the years 1938 and 1953. Here she foregrounds three decisive turning points, each guided by the fate of this city's people: the Berlin of 1938, that is, the Berlin with its marching columns before the outbreak of World War Two; the Berlin of 1945 at the time of collapse, and finally, Berlin as the divided city. Here it is a great success. Ingeborg Drewitz possesses a good talent for observation,

a special sense for inner connections, and understands full well how to translate these into vivid lyrical language. The problems and concerns are often
merely implied, and there is no clear separation of plot and reflection. . . .

A strong book that testifies to a great talent while at the same time
delivers a warning to those who continue—even in the seriousness of the
hour—to fail to see the light.

Kasper Schoretits. *Wiener Bucherbriefe.*
4, 1963, n.p.

The book's title [*October Light*] signals the mood and the situation in which
the main character finds herself. The novel is simply yet carefully constructed; using first-person narration, Ingeborg Drewitz has told the story of
a failure. The run of events is reported in a conventional manner, and the
author does without literary finesse and formal experiments. Her single concession to modern technique are the flashbacks, in which perceptions and
memories confront one another. Through abrupt splicing, the narrator sets
up stirring moments from the present alongside stiff moments from the past.
Her skeptical and realistic attitude enriches the genre of the woman's novel
by setting it in a new key.

In her own words, the author wanted to depict "the tension between
action and effect, between hope and the bit of banality that comes out of it."
Therefore, she draws a sketch of average figures and commonplace conflicts.
The heroine vacillates between dream and resignation, expectation and conformity, and the path she follows reveals a fate typical for our times. The
recapitulation of decisive moments in her life makes it clear that today's
everyday tragedies follow a format almost like that of classical antiquity.

Karlheinz Schauder. *Deutsche Post.*
22:1, January 5, 1970, p. 17

Yesterday Was Today—One Hundred Years of the Present: a crafty title that,
on first glance, appears inappropriate when one considers the timespan actually covered by the plot: 1923 through 1978. Still, when one allows oneself
to think back on one hundred years of German history, one runs into an
event which can only be meant by an author as politically sensitive as Ingeborg Drewitz (an assertion further substantiated by a reference to an attempt
on the Kaiser's life which resulted in a family's flight): the Socialist Laws of
1878, enacted by Bismarck. These laws, coupled with a conservatism in both
domestic and foreign policy, set into motion one of the numerous historically
documented persecutions of the German Left. Thus, already the title alone
parenthetically states that the family history and personal history of a woman
does not play themselves or free themselves of political reference.

Angelika Mechtel. *Die Zeit.* 43,
October 20, 1978, p. 10

Yesterday Was Today is a "women's book," but it is far from the fashionable flightiness that distinguishes so many products in our age of favorable economic trends. There is a lot of experience and work put into Ingeborg Drewitz's novel. Both are rare.

Three women—Susanne, Gabriele, and Renate—stand in the middle of this family chronicle, which embraces five generations. The novel begins, programmatically, with a birth that is described with more precision than I have ever read anywhere else. Only someone who has experienced it herself could have written it like this. And it ends with a birth," as if that were all there is: starting out, loving one another, no doubts, no memories of the old, yet the suffering of so many that is ever so new."

The old, yet ever so new suffering: for Ingeborg Drewitz, that is the suffering of the last one hundred years of German history, the ongoing flight for a more just life; but it is also the suffering of women, and their so very realistic "fear of abandonment."

Margret Eberths. Deutsches Volkszeitung.
48, November 30, 1978, p. 18

Childhood, youth, student years under Nazism, marriage, motherhood, emancipation and a career after war's end—How does a woman use her own generation's bitter experiences to fight her way through and make it in this society? With this question in mind, Ingeborg Drewitz develops reflections of herself in female "playing pieces" which she constructs out of her own potentialities, her own history and experience. Thus, her women are ideal types in terms of . . . integrity and inner strength: uncompromising in their search for self-realization, while at the same time extending beyond their own boundaries and sacrificing themselves for their life partner, their children, those near them who are socially weaker, and those who are physically or psychologically disadvantaged. The woman in *October Light* is still someone who waits "without knowing whatever for," a radio journalist, who, upon running into her former husband, now an unsuccessful actor, reminisces about their times together, times when they "had drawn up the world afresh" and a "theater, in which the audience itself joined in the play." The heroine, Katrin Lambert, is thus a fighter who, lonely yet dogged, commits herself above and beyond her duties as a social worker and dies in the process. Still, the narrator—in her function as the first-person reporter in search of Katrin Lambert's life—not only adopts the cause of her wrecked protagonist, but also slips into the role of her novel's heroine by assuming a care-taker position regarding her charge.

Yesterday Was Today is the story of a woman who comes increasingly to consciousness, and steadily learns how better to say "I" in self-declaration. The novel tells the story of the life of the radio journalist Gabriele M., whose birthdate coincides with the author's. It tells of her childhood in the 1920s, which again bears the stamp of her mother and grandmother, tracing National Socialism, war, reconstruction, the Cold War through the New Left generation of her daughter, who continues striving for that for which her mother had striven at that same younger age. At times in first person narration, at other times from the perspective of the narrator and accompanied by observations about the individual and historical times, Gabriele M. makes the search for her self her main point in life. . . .

Against the backdrop of her attempts to deal with the past, Drewitz's literary works—regardless of which genre or medium she used in writing—may be viewed as variations which derive from a basic model: from the collective failure within a historical situation, as well as from the individual failure within private events. The fundamentally resigned tone of her texts is the object of frequently recurring criticism which is unjustified, in my opinion. If it is true that the average citizen is witness to his own failure, this does not make him despicable, but rather serves to strengthen his potential for resistance. . . .

For Ingeborg Drewitz, literature serves first and foremost a socio-pedagogical mission: "The author writes for the masses, who remain insignificant due to their consumer habits, in order to raise their consciousness of their situation, and to allow them recognition of their dependencies." Historically, her novels are "great" because they are not removed from everyday reality, and it is from this perspective that they must be viewed. The scene is set in Berlin. The actors are middle-class citizens. The depiction is critical, yet free of prejudice.

Barbel Jäschke. In Heinz Puknus, ed. Neue
Literatur der Frauen: Deutschsprachige
Autorinnen der Gegenuart
(Munich: Beck, 1980), pp. 69–74

Ingeborg Drewitz had not written for the theater since the 1955 premiers of her two dramas *All Gates Were Guarded* and *The City without a Bridge*. But in 1983, during her stay as a "writer-in-residence" in Austin, Texas, she got to work. A piece evolved that deals with reality to such a great extent that its content consumes itself with cliches. With all her claims to reality, she works here as if life were a dress pattern book: in black-and-white.

It deals with the generational conflict between a mother and daughter, and it deals with the conflict between political consciousness and personal advantage. From little Jewish boys to members of the RAF [Red Army Faction], from square fathers to helpless mothers, it runs the gamut.

It will and cannot be denied that the family's story, displayed in all its incorrigibility, has happened in this or some such similar manner in many a place. Still, in her efforts to offer moral instruction, Ingeborg Drewitz falls victim to the same errors as the playwright Rolf Hochhuth does on repeated occasions: everything remains merely a surface imprint. The reality that is sought proves evasive. It behaves insidiously. The image of the world remains

a stereotype. Identification becomes overidentification. A self-indictment becomes a didactic play, and a didactic play becomes a school text book.

Verena Auffermann. *Suddeutsche Zeitung*.
27, February 1, 1985, p. 50

Perhaps this novel [*Prometheus, Atomic Physicist*] presents an early outline
version of a multivolume narrative work. Unremitting dissatisfaction could
rise up in the reader; the critics strike an impasse: doctors, physicists, social
officials, etc. The social reformers find themselves up a blind alley: Communists, Maoists, New Leftists. Prometheus is chained to the soft bed of an
institution. Jesus is not nailed to a cross, but rather is torn apart between
the announcement and accusations.

Ingeborg Drewitz works with displaced parts out of which emerges a
collage. Pieces of the collage join in friendship, and find hope in one another
through mutual confession of their defeat. Words, combinations of words,
and wordings *experience* defeat, also in the act of writing.

"Prometheus' passion for freedom and his degradation" have preoccupied her since early on, says Ingeborg Drewitz in an Afterword. But so has
the goodness of Jesus. For her now, at the age of sixty-six, the thresholds
between madness, truth and necessity have been the most painful themes in
all of her works: escape from the norm, courage to be oneself, and if need
be, at the cost of all others, including one's friends. "I was not free of guilt.
I was a part of the team. A piece of an 'us.'"

This, Prometheus's self-accusation, transforms itself into a question:
Take courage—but from where? Not beating, not killing, those are self-
evident. But how can one bear such degradations, such acts of disregard?
Such nearness and distance, when words have gone dull before deaf ears?

A book of large scale which deals with commitment and grief, disruption,
failure, and the helplessness of language that wastes away, just as the characters waste away.

Christa Daricum. *Suddeutsche Zeitung*.
99, April 30–May 1, 1986, p. iv

Of all the novels by Drewitz, feminist literary criticism has devoted the most
attention to *Gestern war Heute (Yesterday was today)*, due to its emphatically
autobiographical bent and to the fact that this novel depicts the development
of a woman from birth through her fifty-fifth year, centering around the main
character's quest for self-realization. Sigrid Weigel chooses this work as well
for her collection of autobiographical novels, which she calls *Women's History—Women in History*. She compares it to Christa Wolf's *Kindheitsmuster*
(Model for a childhood), examining both works, and the central theme of the
self, within the broader context of the vastly differing political conditions in
the societies in which the two women authors respectively live. Both novels
voice a critique of their nations' existing situations; Christa Wolf's does so
by conceptualizing the self purely as utopia, while the novel by Ingeborg

Drewitz confronts the Western ideology of individuality with the perception that "without arrogance the SELF cannot assert itself."

When asked by Elaine Martin whether she considers herself a feminist writer, and whether it bothers her when feminist critics classify her as such, Ingeborg Drewitz responded: "I do not write literature according to a particular program." "Of course I am interested in women's problems, and some of them are addressed in my works. It's just that I would consider it erroneous for my work to be adopted by the feminist cause." As Sigrid Weigel's analysis emphasizes, Drewitz's novel *Gestern war Heute*—and, in fact, all her novels—cover a significantly broader complexity of themes than does feminism. As a result, examinations should not concentrate on the parallels between her biography and her novels, but rather should seek to understand the novels as creations of poetic imagination. Thus, though the themes of the feminine self and the emancipation of women do make up a partial aspect of the thematic discussion of human problems, they are to be understood only within this broader context.

Not a single critic disputes the contention that the unifying characteristic of all of Drewitz's novels is their common anchoring in historical events. In a time span ranging from the 1920s to the immediate present, the novels depict individual fates that serve a representative function for the survival of large portions of the German population during these critical years. The historical component holds a particular urgency because it is always Berlin that sets the stage for all that occurs, a city which remains the focus of political debate between East and West and which defines the lives of its inhabitants in an utterly unique way. . . .

An analysis of Drewitz's novels in terms of their narratological construction yields information about the reception of these novels. As Stanzel himself emphasizes, it is precisely the figural narrator—whose insight is incomplete and fragmented—which characterizes the literature of the twentieth century. Like the figural, the first-person narrator too has only limited knowledge. Primarily relying on these two narrational modes, while employing an authorial voice to relay factual but no interpretive information, Drewitz's novels place central emphasis on the dualities and contradictions in life.

> Gerhild Bruggermann Rogers. *Das Romanwerk von Ingeborg Drewitz* (New York: Peter Lang, 1989), pp. 10–11, 213

DREXLER, ROSALYN (UNITED STATES) 1926–

This vital, intense "diary" [*I Am the Beautiful Stranger*] of one Selma Silver, who was growing from ages thirteen to sixteen in the 1930s, is swift, complete, individual, and universal. You can mock its occasional sillinesses, but you're left holding its truths. For Selma is wholly convincing even when you can hardly believe her. . . . Back then, when "teenager" hadn't yet been invented, I don't think anybody talked the way Selma sometimes does. But nobody back then (except maybe Saroyan) wrote as spiritedly as Mrs. Drexler does, either.

> Maggie Rennert. *Book Week.*
> June 27, 1965, p. 22

Rosalyn Drexler's plays suggest, more than anything else, the early Marx Brothers. Wayward, full of lip, fantastic yet anchored in domesticity, they work at reordering all those matter-of-fact details, from the date on the calendar to the necessity of putting on one shoe after another, which obstruct us in our pursuit of significant whim and appetite. . . . All her dialogue issues from an imagination which has previously discovered the uses of language for new guise, for bluff, feint, decoy and red herring—all necessary properties and instrumentalities of the crucial game that goes on in most of her work. The game might be called "keep them guessing" or "never give a sucker an even break." For Mrs. Drexler's imagination holds that the world is forever trying to impose roles and identities upon us which it is our duty and pleasure to resist and repudiate by outwitting the identifiers and the casting directors.

> Richard Gilman. Introduction to Rosalyn
> Drexler. *The Line of Least Existence* (New
> York: Random House, 1967), pp. ix–xi

In addition to writing plays, the libretto for *Home Movies* which won the off-Broadway award known as the "Obie," and two successful novels, Rosalyn Drexler is a successful painter. This visual orientation may explain her highly untraditional view of theatrical language, a quality evident in all her plays. Like Koch, she conceives of language as most engaging when least eloquent, and closest to a state of pure "flatness." In *Hot Buttered Roll* the dialogue is in the prose style of the girlie magazine. The play is about a certain Mr. Corrupt Savage, whose most passionate wish is to go on spending his days in contemplation of the supposedly inspiring pictures and text characteristic of this genre. . . . In Drexler's reality, the eternally flesh-contemplating Corrupt Savage is the nearest thing to a true saint, or hero. It is the cold calculators who surround him, those contemptuous of human fantasies however odd or pathetic, who are the real villains of the piece.

> Michael Benedikt. *Theatre Experiment*
> (Garden City, New York:
> Doubleday, 1967), p. 197

The Line of Least Existence is a joy to read, as are all Rosalyn Drexler's plays in the collection recently published by Random House. Few contemporary playwrights can equal her verbal playfulness, fearless spontaneity, and boundless irreverence; few in fact, share her devotion to pure writing, preferring their language functional, meaningful, or psychologically "real." Whether her plays amount to anything, whatever that means, is hard to say: hers is obviously an up-to-date sensibility, and I read considerable off-hand, tough, supercool wisdom about human relationships into her fantastifications, knowing all the time that they may be as frivolous as they look.

Michael Smith. *Village Voice.*
March 28, 1968, p. 50

The new literary voice comes from some odd and perilous psychic area still being charted, some basic metabolic flashpoint where the self struggles to convert its recurrent breakdowns into new holds on life and reality. It is the voice of writers like Donald Barthelme, Thomas Pynchon, and Rosalyn Drexler. In her new book [*One or Another*], Mrs. Drexler monitors the voice of Melissa . . . married to Mark. . . . In these lives madness is no longer a possibility—it is a note in their chord of being that automatically sounds with every breath they draw. . . . What counts now is the delicate new apotheosis, a new transcendence that accepts the mad world as the only human habitat, while plotting shrewdly against its madness. Few writers have been able to suggest this new transcendence. Mrs. Drexler is one of them: funny, scary, preternaturally aware, she is at the exact center where the new sensibility is being put together cell by cell.

Jack Kroll. *Newsweek.* June 1, 1970, p. 87

One or Another is a very funny book; moreover, it is both funny "ha-ha" and funny "weird," an observation Melissa Johnson, the novel's heroine-narrator, would be likely to make herself. In *One or Another* reality and unreality are merged; the borderline between dreams and actual events has been erased; shadows are indistinguishable from substance. Obviously, a novel of the interior is not concerned with plot. Mere sequences of events hold no interest. Style alone sustains *One or Another*. With careful economy and wit (that rare commodity bludgeoned out of so much of contemporary literature), Miss Drexler guides the reader through the tortured dreamscape in which Melissa Johnson finds both refuge and exile.

William Hjortsberg. *The New York Times.*
June 28, 1970, p. 5

[In *To Smithereens*] the relaxed sleaziness and community of the lady wrestling world alternates with the frantic, tired chic of the plastic New York art scene, in which here-barely-disguised New York artists and hangers-on act out their own fantasies of power, success, and grandeur. Does it all sound slightly sick, weird, ugly/sad, and obsessed-with-violence? It's exactly the opposite. . . . [Rosalyn Drexler] has a marvelous talent for taking this kind of material and imbuing it with qualities of great warmth and wicked satire, pathos, and a haunting aura of nostalgia for a world most of us have never known. . . . She's an absolute original who can take all the ingredients that usually characterize "serious fiction" . . . and use them with inventiveness, playfulness, and even hilarity.

Sara Blackburn. *Book World.*
March 19, 1972, p. 5

The scene of [*To Smithereens*] is less a time and a place—New York, mainly in the late 1960s and early 1970s—than a condition of consciousness. New York becomes a name for a brand of hysteria, for a circus of crazies, comically seen and perfectly human and manageable as it turns out. Paul and Rosa, individual and well-defined as they are, tend to disappear into this collective portrait. Paul is the twitchy, ruined modern male from an R. Crumb comic ("the *universal* Paul," Rosa thinks), and Rosa is the resurgent female, all immediacy, innocence, and half-nelsons.

"You're not as crazy as you seem, are you?" a character says in Rosalyn Drexler's play *The Line of Least Existence.* "None of us is. We're all rational people." The specific context of the words makes them sound like a desperate pleading lie; we are just as crazy as we seem, if not crazier, but please let's not admit it. But the play itself, and in particular the character of the woman speaking the lines, suggests that what the words say is literally, drably true. We are dull people, and any semblance of vivid craziness we may present is an illusion. Mrs. Drexler knows that we really are crazy, and in very bad shape; but she also knows that the forms of our craziness have a conformity, a banality all of their own. Between madness and grayness, or out of a gray madness, we have to put something together.

Michael Wood. *New York Review of Books.*
August 10, 1972, p. 14

The raunchy and the ridiculous are Drexler's home territory—you feel she spends a lot of time in all-night cafeterias. Her word-play is like sword-play—with rubber swords that still deliver a stinging slap. Her set-pieces—newspaper clippings, radio interviews, beauty advice—are among the delights of [*The Cosmopolitan Girl*]; her one-liners are memorable. . . . She weaves a seamy web of parodies that covers the situation perfectly. Moving back and forth between the absurd and the everyday Drexler puts both in their place—on the same plane. *The Cosmopolitan Girl* is a send-up and send-off for the New Woman.

Sara Sanborn. *The New York Times.*
March 30, 1975, p. 4

Drexler's plays are conceived as musicals, with characters freely breaking out into song or dancing their way through the plays *(Home Movies, The Line of Least Existence, The Writer's Opera).* Full of energy, and forever embroiled in farcical encounters and manic chases, Drexler's people let loose an anarchy on stage that is both blatantly comical and mildly threatening at the same time *(The Bed Was Full).*

The excessive theatrical physicality and irreverence of her plays is complemented by a highly individualistic and precise use of language, comprised mostly of puns, *bons mots,* and a sharp wit that brings to mind the playwrights of the Ridiculous, particularly Ronald Tavel. But unlike that school's use of nostalgia—invoking old movies and popular entertainments—Drexler's works do not allude to a world outside the plays. Self-sufficient in terms of character and plot, they exist in a hermetic world where the only laws applicable are those of the playwright herself *(The Line of Least Existence).*

Although many of her plays come close to being campy and parodic *(Home Movies),* they refuse to align themselves with any single sensibility or point of view. There is nothing which is not parodied, undercut, vilified, or grotesquely degraded in Drexler's oeuvre *(Hot Buttered Roll).* Characters exist merely to bounce off others, serving for the most part as foils to the unending barrage of puns and language.

Except for a single attempt at realistic drama *(The Investigation),* and a linearly constructed mytho-historic re-creation *(She Who Was He),* Drexler's plays, with their deliberately anarchic and obtuse structures, belong to the absurdist vein of playwriting. At times her work relates to humanistic themes that go beyond the world of the plays (loneliness and despair in *Softly, and Consider the Nearness*; alienation and tragic separation in *Skywriting*).

In all instances, however, the emphasis is less on characterization and inner reality than on surface detail and stagecraft. Skillfully manipulating entrances and exits, and juggling with the unending series of masks that her characters wear, Drexler assumes the air of a ringmaster employing her skills to create entertaining spectacles for the stage. . . .

Although equipped with biting wit, a diabolically effective use of stage language, and a satiric pen ever poised to cut down accepted social mores, Rosalyn Drexler's structural weaknesses minimize the impact of her plays. Since they exist merely as the aftermath of an imagination gone wild, and are usually denied the benefit of even a barely discernible plot, her plays lack the purpose and direction of farce. There *is* no desire to reach a goal—they end as abruptly as they begin, for no reason other than to create mayhem and a brief span of orgiastic revelry.

Even her characters are mostly without history, a past to direct them. Like paper cut-outs, they are set into motion by the chance configurations into which they fall. Assuming odd and delightful shapes at the end of a kaleidoscope, they create new forms. But like all such shapes, they begin to tire after a while. The need is not so much for greater variety but for a theatrical experience that offers both laughter and food for thought. At best, Drexler's plays are theatrical jokes, a carnival where reality is submerged so that all may revel in a drama of illusion or partake in the line of least existence.

Gautam Dasgupta. In Gautam Dasgupta and
Bonnie Maranca, eds. *American
Playwrights: A Critical Survey* (New York:
Drama Book Specialists, 1981),
pp. 209–10, 218

DUNBAR-NELSON, ALICE (UNITED STATES) 1875–1935

Alice Dunbar-Nelson's contributions to American literature are unique, and she herself is distinctive for four major reasons: (1) she was a frequently published Black writer at the turn of the century; (2) she was married to the most gifted Black writer of his age, Paul Laurence Dunbar; and was, as Eugene Metcalf accurately says, "eclipsed by her husband's fame"; (3) she was an early and vocal advocate of women's rights; and (4) most significant for this study, she was, like Kate Chopin and George Washington Cable, an explorer of and writer about the New Orleans area and the peoples found there.

Alice Ruth Moore was only 20 when she published her first collection of short stories, *Violets and Other Tales,* in 1895. In the year after her marriage to Paul Laurence Dunbar she published another collection, *The Goodness of St. Rocque and Other Stories* (1899), under the name Alice Dunbar. She became Alice Dunbar-Nelson after Dunbar's death in 1906 and her subsequent marriage to Robert J. Nelson in 1916, and her later works include books "on race," such as *Masterpieces of Negro Eloquence* (1914) and *People of Color in Louisiana* (1916–17), and poetic and prose contributions to such magazines as *Lippincott's, Crisis, McClure's, Age, Women's Era, Monthly Review,* and *Colored American.* Alice Dunbar-Nelson was, in short, a prolific regional writer who has been almost completely overlooked. . . .

Mrs. Dunbar-Nelson's New Orleans stories fall generally into four categories: those treating unsuccessful love, those dealing with quietly tragic heroism, those dealing with women's rights, and those outlining ethnic portraits. . . .

Alice Dunbar-Nelson's literary achievements are, to be sure, somewhat modest ones. The issues in her stories—and some of the pieces are, in fact, sketches—do not always have substantial depth, and some seem designed for quick dramatic impact that might have been provided a bit more legitimately with somewhat slower working out of plot. But for all of that, those who call her stories of New Orleans charming, with careful detail and good dialect, and with an accurate capturing of ethnic rituals (and prejudices), are quite right. And although she has remained almost completely unknown, she has deserved better.

Roger Whitlow. In Emily Toth, ed.
Regionalism and the Female Imagination
(New York: Human Sciences Press, 1985),
pp. 109–10, 124

Dunbar-Nelson adhered to a basically romantic concept of poetry, and really did wish—as she told Dunbar years earlier—to maintain separation between race and imaginative literature. This is almost as obvious in her poems of the New Negro 1920s as it was in her short stories at the turn of the century.

"April Is on the Way," which was published in *Ebony and Topaz* in 1927, is ostensibly the monologue of a hunted man who is seemingly about to be lynched for protecting his beloved from violation by white men. However, the situation is so obliquely handled and so enmeshed with contrasting scenes, philosophizing, and nature description that it is almost lost. (Dunbar-Nelson may have believed, though, that the counterpointed contexts would serve to add poignancy.) The net result is a rather confusing work.

Counterpoint was one of her favorite techniques in these late 1920s poems. In fact, ironic juxtaposition seems to be her way of handling social commentary. . . .

Dunbar-Nelson did not write very much poetry. What she wrote improves markedly from her juvenile verse to the mature work of the 1920s. Overall, she is a fairly good poet who is particularly competent in rhymed and metered forms and is at her best when these forms are combined with traditional, yet sincerely felt, poetic subjects. Dunbar-Nelson's bent as a writer was more discursive than poetic, especially if "poetic" is viewed in the modern sense as abbreviated concentration of expression. Her facility with language fostered in her a torrential habit with words. For example, diction of all kinds—from colloquial to learned to literary—sprang easily from her huge vocabulary. . . .

It seems that had Dunbar-Nelson devoted more time to her poetry, she would have produced even better work, but apparently it did not absorb her to that extent. In addition to not being her predilection, deliberate concentration on writing a poem did not accord with her concept of poetry. Essentially romantic, it caused her to reserve poetry for intense emotion and other special occasions. Given how she hoarded the "Dream Book," it is apparent that she sometimes saw poetry as too private to be publicly shared. This dichotomy helped to foster her attraction to the ideal versus real, natural versus artificial theme that she used as the base for both the content and form of many of her poems. Her romantic concepts also account for her stock of nature imagery. That she wrote poetry—even to the degree that she did— ultimately proved to be a boon for Dunbar-Nelson. It suited the Harlem Renaissance emphasis on verse and found space in the books and magazines of the period, thus helping to ensure her niche in literary history. . . .

Her diary was the only place where Dunbar-Nelson could even begin to discuss her sexual relationships and other personal privacies. She kept it from July 29 to December 31, 1921, then from November 1926 to December 1931, and probably also for additional months that have been lost. Of necessity, this work became a repository for psychological clues and other general information about her. It serves, especially, to illuminate what it meant to be a black woman/writer in earlier twentieth-century America, while providing the accompanying background and contexts. Finally, Dunbar-Nelson's diary is one of her most significant writings, a literary document that may be her . . . enduring one. She expressed a prescient knowledge of its worth when she wrote in it on September 21, 1928: "Put in most of the day at the office making up my diary. Seemed an awful thing to do just to spend that time, but my diary is going to be a valuable thing one of these days." This diary is only the second book-length one available by an Afro-American woman. Because of Dunbar-Nelson's sophisticated literary background, she was familiar with the form and traditions of English diary-keeping, which somehow suited her needs. She used her journal as a place to vent her thoughts and emotions and disrobe her inner self. Clearly, it was important to her. She railed against it as a weight on her heart and could barely find the time that it required, but she managed to keep it up. The diary charts the contours of her life over the years that it covers, revealing in its style and type of entries her kaleidoscope of moods and activities.

The diary also presents Dunbar-Nelson's strongest and most distinctive voice. . . . Viewed as literature, Dunbar-Nelson's diary is not like the self-consciously and laboriously written documents of Virginia Woolf and Anaïs Nin. Kept in the ordinary way, it has the expected virtues (spontaneity, daily disclosure, etc.) and limitations (flatness, repetition, loose writing, etc.) of the prototypical—not to say classic—diary form. Even though she never regarded the journal as a vehicle for creative literary expression, its style has interest, merit, and tonal variety. However, in terms of its posthumous value, the diary (like her journalism) was an unfortunate genre in which to pour so much time and effort. Such noncanonical forms are not highly prized, and neither are the many women who write in them.

Gloria T. Hull. *Color, Sex, and Poetry:*
Three Women Writers of the Harlem
Renaissance (Bloomington: Indiana
University Press, 1987), pp. 80–82, 97–99

A good deal of her fame springs from her authorship of the Creole sketches and stories contained in *Violets* and in her second volume, *The Goodness of St. Rocque* (1898). Replete with local color, these pieces are correctly described as charming and well-written. They are also devoid of any significant references to the murkier aspects of racial identity and prejudice, even though history and sociology confirm that color, caste and race were deadly, daily realities for the mixed blood inhabitants of southern Louisiana who people her stories. A few isolated allusions can be found—to Black longshoremen during a strike, to the blond versus dark attractions of two rival heroines, to an orphan girl obliquely described as a little "brown scrap of French and American civilization" whose "glorious tropical beauty" makes her so vulnerable to racial-sexual exploitation that she consigns herself to the convent.

In contrast to this work, other of Dunbar-Nelson's lesser-known writings present a more complex picture of race and the Creole, especially the Creole with immediate or identifiable Negro ancestry. . . .

[Still] it must be said that Dunbar-Nelson's shying away from race as a literary theme can be partially explained by market conditions, by what agents, readers and publishers wanted. They bought her slight and charming stories, but backed away from serious explorations of the color line. Given the constraints of Dunbar-Nelson's own personal ambivalence and authorial credo, plus the limitations of the marketplace, we must be grateful that any stories like "The Pearl in the Oyster" and "The Stones of the Village" exist. They help us to understand the psycho-racial-social forces which shaped— both negatively and positively—Dunbar-Nelson as a writer, and enlarged the field of her art. She is no longer simply a female regionalist producing safe, run-of-the-mill local color stories, but a Black Creole woman writer who also tried to bring these hidden complexities into literary light.

Gloria T. Hull. *New Orleans Review.*
15, 1988, pp. 34–35, 37

When Alice Dunbar-Nelson, then Alice Moore, published her first volume of short stories entitled *Violets and Other Tales* in 1895, she had few if any literary predecessors. Published when she was just twenty years old, Dunbar-Nelson's little "potpourri" of poetry, short stories, essays, and reviews was only one in a small handful of printed works then in existence by African-American women. She completed *The Goodness of St. Rocque and Other Stories,* a second volume of short stories, four years later, after her marriage to celebrated poet Paul Laurence Dunbar. Although Dunbar-Nelson wrote prolifically—newspaper columns, essays, articles, and reviews identified her as a writer in her own right—these two were the only collections of her work published in her lifetime. They are particularly important, as Gloria T. Hull suggests in her introduction to *The Works of Alice Dunbar-Nelson,* because they helped, in their way, to "create a black short story tradition for a reading public conditioned to expect only plantation and minstrel stereotypes."

Featured prominently among the narrative structures Dunbar-Nelson employed in both her published and unpublished fiction was the romance plot. In the published stories in which this plot was utilized, it was formulated in much the same way as it was in the works of her white counterparts. In "The Goodness of St. Rocque," from which the second book takes its title, the female protagonist's ultimate concern is securing the affections of her wandering lover, and she turns to the mystic arts to do so. In "Little Miss Sophie," the heroine is a poor creole who, despite the fact that her wealthy lover has jilted her, continues to wear his ring. The ring turns out to be a family heirloom, and at the end of the tale Miss Sophie dies (conveniently) so that the ring may be returned to him, saving him from financial ruin. These stories, aimed at an integrated audience, are not racially specific (creole is the only racial characterization offered; in many stories the race of the characters is never mentioned or alluded to), and they seem primarily to reflect the concerns of the wider culture.

It is with some of the later, unpublished works that Dunbar-Nelson begins to depart from the prevalent formula to express a narrative vision generated by other sources. In particular, her short story "Ellen Fenton" stands out as a marked departure both from her earlier works and many of those of her white contemporaries. Written for inclusion in *Women and Men,* projected around 1902 (the same year she separated from her husband) but never published, "Ellen Fenton" is noteworthy for the way in which it handles the romance plot, combining, rather than separating, the feminine quest with the heterosexual love motif. . . .

Rather than to isolation and separation, the quest for self-actualization in "Ellen Fenton" brings the hero to a new sense of connection with her community. Even though Ellen does not occupy the position she once held in her town, she is clearly more connected to the people around her, particularly Herbert. No longer cold, she is capable of feeling things deeply and genuinely. And because her real self is inviolate, she can assume any number of roles—even those which are constrictive and limiting to others—without losing herself. The quest, as Dunbar-Nelson offers it, is circular in nature, eventually bringing the questor back into the community she was forced to leave in order to find herself. And because the result of the quest is a codified and clearly identifiable self, relationships (whether heterosexual or homosexual) prove no threat to her independence. Indeed, one of the pleasant surprises of Dunbar-Nelson's treatment of the quest is that it seems to encourage the union of the hero with an equally self-sufficient companion at the end. . . .

And yet, that Dunbar-Nelson, herself in the midst of bitter separation from the husband she had once adored, could nonetheless envision such an ending for a hero so like herself, makes the notion of a naive ending impossible. That her mind and heart could imagine for another what she herself had not known is the ultimate testament to her spirit and to the grandeur of her imagination. "Ellen Fenton" stands as touchstone for the modern reader, one of the many examples of the ways women artists, white and African-American, envisioned change for one another and for future generations.

Alisa Johnson. *Studies in American Fiction.*
19, Autumn, 1991, pp. 165–67, 173–74

DUNCAN, SARA JEANNETTE (CANADA) 1860–1922

There are some challenging elements of qualification in Sara Jeannette Duncan's rendering of personal and public life in Canada at the turn of the century. This qualification is implicitly registered in the mere facts of her career. Duncan spent most of her adult life outside Canada. Of her twenty or so novels only three deal to any great extent with Canada, and even in her earlier journalism her interests are often directed beyond her own country to the United States and the wider English-speaking world. She referred to *The Imperialist* as "my Canadian novel," suggesting that her attention to Canada was indeed an aspect of a wider view (by the time of its writing, she had in fact published several novels, of varying degrees of seriousness, set in England, the United States, and British India). Yet Duncan is of special interest to students of Canadian writing precisely because her experience and interests went beyond the borders of Canadian thought and geography in her day. If *The Imperialist* remains finally ambiguous about the prospects of its hero and his community, that might be the most significant comment the novel makes on Canada at the end of the nineteenth century. It is very clear that Lorne's imperialism cannot provide a basis for that more complete national existence he is concerned to promote. His policies have been too thoroughly discounted by indifference and scepticism, even more devastating in such a case than outright hostility. And there is real doubt about the actual soundness of Lorne's policies, on the practical level where they must finally be tested. Yet it is far from clear, in Duncan's account, that anything else in Elgin can spark the livelier and fuller national life which Lorne alone seems to think is necessary. This reasonable aspiration, both generous and moderate, is harshly frustrated. Duncan's final word on Elgin, and on the outlook for her protagonist within his society, is ambiguous: either the fuller community life to which he has dedicated his personal virtues is forming and will affirm itself one day, in "the enduring heart of the new country already old in acquiescence," or it is already too late for its development: "for that it is too soon, or perhaps it is too late." The country has shown both signs of endurance and of acquiescence; by an ironic twist of fate, which Lorne understands and which he seeks to break free of, it has endured largely by acquiescing. It is the mixed consequences of this shared history that Duncan explores in *The Imperialist,* and she leaves us at the end with an unanswered question about the shape of the future. In an early essay entitled "Colonialism and Literature," Duncan declared that "a national literature cannot be looked for as an outcome of anything less than a complete national existence." This rather stringent equation between a youthful nation's politics and its imaginative life may help to explain why, in Duncan's "Canadian novel," imaginative idealism is obliged to take a political turn, and lays itself open to a discouraging setback.

Francis Zichy. *English Studies in Canada.*
10, 1984, pp. 340–41

Cousin Cinderella (1908) is one of Sara Jeannette Duncan's most conspicuously "Jamesian" novels. The plot is an "international" one in which two Canadians visit London in an attempt to establish some kind of relationship with Old World culture. Thomas Tausky notes a further similarity in the "fine, even Jamesian" characterization of the heroine, Mary Trent. But *Cousin Cinderella* is not simply a general recreation of a Jamesian context; several points establish the relationship of *Cousin Cinderella* to a specific novel by Henry James: *Roderick Hudson* (1876). Duncan uses the points of reference provided by *Roderick Hudson* to delineate the differences between the U.S. and Canada, and their relationship to European culture. . . .

If the resemblances between *Cousin Cinderella* and *Roderick Hudson* are intentional, then they bear upon one of the important themes of the novel—the difference between the American and the Canadian experience of Europe. Both Roderick Hudson and Graham Trent partially devalue their own culture and their own gifts in their emulation of European values; they act as colonials in the heart of empire. When Europe rejects the American, he has nothing to fall back on because he has deprived himself of his own strengths. But in *Cousin Cinderella* Europe learns from Canada, for when Barbara Pavisay rejects Graham Trent she does so, in effect, for his own good. The representatives of England realize that the kind of union between Canada and the Empire that would require Canadians to give up their own strengths is false. But the union between Canada and England may still take place through the genuine love of Mary Trent and Barbara's brother, Peter Doleford. The Pavisay family fortunes are saved by the Trent money, but without the loss of Trent independence and initiative. Mary Trent, who has struggled to maintain the perspective of Minnebiac ("a small town in Ontario with the accent on the 'bi'") offers Lord Doleford the chance to utilize the gifts of his British heritage in the backwoods of Canada. Their union under-lines the message of the novel—that the Empire must be held together by sentiment rather than by submission.

Misao Dean. *Studies in Canadian
Literature*. 11, 1986, pp. 96–98

Social change was a direct and unavoidable result of the ending of pioneer society in Ontario, and Sara Jeannette Duncan's *The Imperialist* (1904) illustrates some of the major issues and dilemmas that were confronted by Ontario women at the turn of the century. To cite one example, in *The Imperialist*, Duncan defends the new career options which were becoming increasingly available for women in a post-frontier society. Her protagonist, Advena Murchison, has a university education and supports herself by working outside the home. Yet Duncan is also a traditionalist in her portrayal of female characters in *The Imperialist*. Advena's mother resembles the ideal pioneer woman as this woman was described by Catharine Parr Traill in *The Backwoods of Canada* and *The Canadian Settler's Guide*. But Advena and her mother are surprisingly similar, despite their vastly different career choices. Advena is, in fact, a new version of the pioneer woman, a pioneer woman on a new frontier. Through her characterization of Advena Murchison, Duncan redefines the frontier and the frontier woman to suit a new set of social circumstances. Thus, while Advena Murchison is undoubtedly a new, independent woman, she can still be defined as a pioneer: a feminine ideal, like her mother before her, Advena faces and seeks to change a frontier landscape. . . .

Advena's frontier in *The Imperialist* is one which is composed of social attitudes and issues, a frontier which she could have chosen to avoid, as do her peers, Abby Murchison Johnson and Dora Milburn. Abby and Dora choose to emulate the circumscribed, outmoded roles of the women in their mothers' generation while Advena moves confidently into a new frontier region. At a time when few women worked for a living, and fewer still had acquired a university education, Advena has done both, making her something of a pioneer feminist. The perception of the development of women's rights as a pioneering process and the portrayal of feminists as pioneers are, in fact, common in Canadian social history. The portrayal of feminists as pioneers was, moreover, a logical step in the evolution of the perception of the pioneer woman as a feminine ideal. When the physical frontiers had been conquered, Canadian women were obliged to look elsewhere for proof of their competence or, as the case may be, their superiority. As a result, the definition of a woman's proper role changed somewhat. The major emphasis was shifted from her contribution towards changing a hostile physical frontier to her participation in the process of improving an unfriendly or even unjust social ore. Feminist crusaders in Canada were optimistic about their efforts and perceived themselves as powerful agents for positive social change. Theirs was a global point of view in many cases, and they anticipated the advent of the millennium. Evidently the definition of the frontier had expanded far beyond small backwoods farms to include humanity in general. It is important to note, however, that none of this process of the expansion of woman's proper sphere of activity involved a rejection of what were then seen as traditional feminine values in Canada. The precedent of a capable, active pioneer woman who could overcome any obstacles in her path had been established by women such as Traill. Many of the qualities possessed by the original pioneers—for instance, activity in the face of an emergency, a cheerful acceptance of adverse circumstances, the courage and pragmatism necessary to begin to effect positive change on the frontier—were seen as useful tools on the new social frontier, and a relatively easy transition was made from a physical landscape to a social arena.

> Elizabeth Thompson. *The Pioneer Woman: A Canadian Character Type* (Montreal and Kingston: McGill and Queen's University Press, 1991), pp. 61–62

Applying ideas drawn from James and other modern writers to her Canadian experience, Sara Jeannette Duncan envisaged a collective colonial point of view, created by the colonials' experience of living in, and of commitment to, life on the margins of Empire. Suspicion of British and American imperialist assumptions and respect for colonial independence were her Canadian inheritance; born at the height of the British Empire, Duncan herself had witnessed many examples of inflexible British administration as well as the first flowering of American militaristic belligerence. Duncan's marriage in 1891 to Everard Cotes, an Anglo-Indian civil servant, and her subsequent experience of life in Calcutta and Simla had shown her the connections between her Canadian experience and that of other colonials, and had confirmed her view that the colonial point of view on international affairs, while often overlooked by centrist legislators, usually offered the most practical solutions to local problems. Yet as a professional journalist (for *The Week,* the *Montreal Star,* and *The Globe,* among other newspapers), and later as a novelist, Duncan also saw herself as part of a monologic idealist tradition of literature in English that included Matthew Arnold and Thomas Carlyle. A vigorous and witty controversialist, she made no bones about her commitment to the future of the Empire and her personal identification with British history and British mission. Like many of her contemporaries, she saw the Empire as a bulwark against the destructive social effects of materialist capitalism; an effective check on U.S. militarism; and a preserve for the ideals of justice, disinterested debate, altruism, and community which were threatened by the conditions of modern life. Her work speaks to the contradiction, as common among Canadians of her day as of ours, between commitment to the ideals of our European heritage and suspicion of its imperialist motives, to the difference that is the Canadian point of view.

Duncan's view of her position as a Canadian was intimately related to her view of her role as a woman. The nationalism of the 1880s that fostered Duncan's understanding of the colonial point of view coincided with the first organized feminist movement, in favor of women's suffrage (a coincidence that has been repeated in more recent history with the revival of both feminism and nationalism in the 1960s and 1970s). Duncan's early declaration in favor of women's suffrage, like her belief in the legitimacy of Canada, again placed her on the margins of centrist ideology. As a woman, created and defined as "other" by malestream ideology, Duncan was aware that social, political, and literary conventions imposed artificial limitations on women, just as British colonial stereotypes placed artificial limits on Canadians. Moreover, her comments on the role of the heroine in the modern novel clarify her view that to write as a colonial in an international context is to write in a feminine voice. . . .

Feminist polemics provided a standpoint from which Duncan regarded the traditions of fiction, and the artistic innovations that resulted are themselves political statement. The women in Duncan's novels are not consciously feminist, and the novels contain few of the crusading social reform passages that characterize the works of marriage reformers such as Grant Allen (*The Woman Who Did*). Rather, the feminist impulse that is evident in Duncan's early journalism is transformed into an artistic problem: how to confront the reality of women's lives in an artistic form whose traditions have been molded by men to whom that reality was, to a large extent, unavailable. One of the defining aspects of women's writing is the portrayal of a new kind of heroine, substituting an active, thinking subject for the passive, instinctual object of romance fiction. Literary feminism, as Ellen Moers defines it and Duncan carries it out, is an attempt to construct new patterns for women's action in novels. . . .

Duncan's creation of the new kind of heroine who attempts to gain self-definition through travel, love, and the vocation of the artist demonstrates how her artistic vision is shaped by the feminist principles that she elucidates in her journalism. The novels evoke and then challenge both the social and the literary conventions that limit women's actions; they question stereotypes of female behavior, be they traditional or feminist, and allow the female characters to develop individually. Duncan's depiction of women parallels her representation of political colonialism; she reveals the singular point of view available only to those who have experienced life beyond the definitions imposed by the center, and she looks to ideals to help create the unity that will allow men and women to continue to work together and to mitigate the increasing focus on the pragmatic, material aspects of life.

Misao Dean. *A Different Point of View: Sara Jeannette Duncan* (Montreal and Kingston: McGill and Queen's University Press, 1991), pp. 4–5, 64–65

DURANTI, FRANCESCA (ITALY) 1935–

Translators are (g)host writers, intermediary creators constrained to embody another's spirit. For aristocratic Fabrizio, the translator-hero of *The House on Moon Lake,* this shadow status becomes inescapably metaphysical, a fount of identity, a source of clues and portents.

Displaced by lack of money from a class unused to making its own way in life, of Milan's literary world but not fully in it, he is a dissatisfied outsider, living at a paranoid remove from the reality of life's demands and his own needs, and wary of commitment: to his lover, the independent Fulvia; to Mario, the childhood friend who has helped him find his feet. It is the betrayal of them implicit in his furtively guarded pursuit of an ambition that opens the fictional prospect of lessons to be learned and, by whichever tortuous route, a homecoming.

But the novel swerves gradually and unexpectedly from this apparent course, so that the mishaps and encounters nudging Fabrizio's secretive search for the lost novel—"The House on Moon Lake"—of a little-known Viennese writer, become truly sinister only in retrospect: not the random dark mockery of the innocent abroad that their tone first implies. This is disconcerting. What starts out as a sophisticated urban fairytale twists into a literary ghost story and a psychodrama of male neurosis.

The twist is Faustian. Found and translated, the novel brings success, capped by a biography of the author which locks Fabrizio into a final act of duplicity. Ineluctably drawn by his estrangement from the materiality and materialism of modern life into a fatal empathy with the long-dead writer, he finds himself trapped in a kink of the past. Under the silky skin of her writing Duranti develops a careful central characterization, its lurking complexities turned provisionally in the light with each graphic shift of atmosphere.

Seasons are also marked by the women whose apposite names divide the book in its three parts: radiant Fulvia; idealized, imaginary Maria; the bloodless Petra. This ambiguous tale of a man's neurotic evasions from the present—taking him from the mutual generosity of love towards a thralldom that echoes the threatened vampire landscape of the *fin-de-siècle* male imagination—refracts troubled, passive perceptions of women.

Liz Heron. *The New Statesman.*
March 6, 1987, p. 38

The *effetti personali* (personal possessions) are the center of Francesca Duranti's novel of ideas and self-search, a work cast in the form of a spy story and written by one of the most successful "liberal" Italian women novelists today. Trained as a lawyer, Duranti has been publishing prose since 1976 and established an international reputation in 1984 with her most successful novel thus far, *La casa sul lago della luna,* (The house on Moon Lake), which won no fewer than three literary prizes and was translated into fifteen languages. . . .

The protagonist of Duranti's newest work, Valentina Barbieri, who lives in the "postfeminist" era, must deal with the bitter realization that her ten-year marriage to the writer Riccardo Prini has been a failure. Although his successful series of popular biographies on the patriarchs is largely due to her ideas and her research, once he has become a television personality he leaves her for another woman without even acknowledging her contribution to his success. Valentina compares her experience with that of her mother, who coped more successfully with similar problems during the heyday of feminism: critical of her own passivity but also of her mother's *savoir vivre,* she leaves Western capitalism behind for a visit to "Yuri Gagarin's country." She is a specialist in Slavic languages and wants to interview her favorite author, the eminent novelist Miloš Jarko, who is well known in the West.

Upon her arrival, Valentina finds that Jarko is away and that no one wishes to talk about him and his childhood or knows of his whereabouts. Seeking help at the local writers' union, she is soon enveloped in a net of lies and contradictions, sees her time and efforts wasted, and is even spied upon. Her isolation helps her examine her own life more objectively, however, and shedding her former passivity, she initiates a relationship with a young and idealistic writer, Ante Radek. A recurrent topic of discussion between the lovers is the desire for material possessions, greed in all forms—apparently a basic human trait. Valentina eventually decides against marrying Ante, but not before learning from him that her search for Jarko cannot possibly succeed: Jarko is a fictitious figure, created through a series of misunderstandings by Western journalists during a PEN Club conference in New York and perpetuated (with official blessings) by Ante and two other Eastern authors, who supply Jarko's novels to the West for the glory of the party and the fatherland.

The fifteen chapters of *Effetti personali,* written in lucid prose, are each prefaced by a Latin quotation from the patriarchs (with accompanying Italian translation) concerning traditional leading ideas of Christian dogma, vices, virtues, character traits, and also on the role of women: "companions of man," in the words of Ugo da San Vittore. Valentina returns to the West and to her few possessions, having realized that even ideology cannot completely transform human nature. She has yet to find herself, but she at least has learned that she possesses a distinct personality that she can defend even in confrontation with such an obvious "beautiful soul" as Ante represents. Duranti's novel is a fine, intelligent analysis of past and present values regarding women's roles and offers insight into the difficult future role of independent women: "Io devo comportarmi—a modo mio."

Maria Luisa Caputo-Mayr.
World Literature Today.
64, 1990, p. 448

Francesca Duranti is one of the most acclaimed modern Italian novelists, having already been awarded several prestigious Italian literary prizes. Her latest novel, *Lieto fine* (Happy ending), is in many ways a latter-day fairy tale that centers on Aldo, a fifty-five-year-old Peter Pan who divides his time between his ivory-tower existence surrounded by his perfect art collection in an exquisite villa and spying through binoculars on the inmates of the other villas on the same estate. He also manages to find time to write books on art just as the aged matriarch Violante, owner of the estate finds time to publish recipe books when she is not projecting grandiose plans for her "kingdom." It is a strange irony that the heir she has decided on to replace her as "queen" should be her daughter-in-law Lavinia (Goldilocks), a middle-aged adolescent wallowing in a mire of misery of her own creation. (She has still not managed to come to terms—twenty years later!—with her disastrous marriage to Violante's elder son.)

A potentially interesting character, the beautiful youth Marco, who casually enters the lives of these lotus eaters and acts on them as a catalyst, turns out, alas, to be a boring young man, "not worse than many others," whose main concern in life is keeping up to date with the most expensive fashions. The one moment of realism in the novel occurs when Aldo, looking round the family gathered together at lunch, thinks to himself: "Oh lo spreco di quella tavola! La noia di quella conversazione! L'imbecillità di quelle vuote regole!" It is a short-lived realism, however.

In true fairy-tale fashion the novel has a happy ending, but without, needless to say, any necessity on the part of the characters to struggle against apparently insuperable odds—as in the great genuine fairy tales—before attaining the true reward of virtue. The only meager consolation is that the characters deserve each other.

Gabrielle Barfoot. *World Literature Today.*
62, 1988, p. 645

One of the new Italian novelists who write in the manner of Umberto Eco, Duranti won international success with her 1984 novel *The House on Moon Lake.* Her latest book [*Happy Ending*] offers reading pleasure similar to some of Muriel Spark's books. Together with Aldo, a famous art dealer with a shady past, Violante, the reigning matriarch of a mismatched family, works on a plan to distribute her responsibilities among her family members. Her son, her two daughters-in-law, and Aldo are spending a weekend on her country estate when a young man unexpectedly arrives and becomes the catalyst of change in everyone's lives and relationships. Except for the radiant Violante, the characters are not all that attractive, but one ends up liking them anyway. This is a beautiful novel, lively and intelligent, written in graceful, sensual prose, inviting the reader to reflection and aesthetic enjoyment.

Ulla Sweedler. *Library Journal.*
January, 1991, p. 147

As the title [*Happy Ending*] implies, Ms. Duranti's novel is a romantic comedy. It concerns a group of rich aristocrats on a Tuscan estate where they inhabit the big house, the lesser house, and the least house, leading one character to mention the three bears. Over the wall is a freakish building with a tower from which their dear friend and admirer observes proceedings through binoculars. Most of these people are gently daft and seemingly as fixed in their absurd positions as the patio paving stones. Then Goldilocks, in the shape of a young man of ethereal good looks and no conversation at all, turns up and shakes them all loose. This pleasant tale is told with intelligence and grace that lift it above the saccharine level to which it might easily have fallen.

Phoebe Lou Adams. *Atlantic.*
March, 1991, p. 132

After ten years of marriage, Valentina Barbieri has been jilted by her husband, a monster of appetite. Riccardo "wants everything": fame, designer clothes, an expensive car, a fancy address, a summer retreat, swanky friends, experimental sex and, above all, money. And he gets it—gets a radio talk show and a showpiece girlfriend too, an economist, appropriately enough. He does all this by writing smart-alecky and irreverent biographies of the church fathers. These biographies succeed, however, because of Valentina's research and editing, for which she has received no recompense, material or emotional. One day she hears furtive scratchings on the door of her apartment, formerly theirs, and through the peephole discovers her ex-husband removing the brass plaque on which is engraved his name, formerly theirs. "As of that moment," Valentina says, "I ceased to exist."

So begins *Personal Effects,* the Milanese writer Francesca Duranti's third novel, elegantly translated by Stephen Sartarelli. Her first, the prize-winning, *House on Moon Lake,* was published in Italy in 1984, shortly before her fiftiethth birthday; her second, *Happy Ending,* appeared just a few years later. Yet all three books read as if they were written by an old master after years of turbulent creativity: by a Knut Hamsun, a Max Frisch, a George Sand. Ms. Duranti's novels are assured and spare and pure, as if all self-indulgence and argumentativeness had been burned away by old creative fires, a humane lucidity rising from the ashes. But maybe Ms. Duranti's other careers as a translator and lawyer are behind her self-effacement and her feel for both sides of any case. . . .

Ante [Radek] is a meek lover, but he believes in terror, the police state, forced labor, executions. He is to our time what the church fathers were to theirs. He does, however, finally tell Valentina all there is to know about Milos Jarco—and thereby deepens the mystery, which is of the existential kind that facts cannot dissipate. And his revelation is a wry commentary by Ms. Duranti on how literary celebrity—not to mention fiction, writers and even readers—is created.

It is not that Valentina learns nothing. She learns, for example, that there is no point of balance, no stable course, between domination and submission, between "ravenous greed" and a breaking of "the pact between man and things." Better yet, she learns that "where the last illusion falls, comedy begins." And the reader learns that Ms. Duranti's kind of novel, like the kind Milos Jarco writes, is "not a copy of reality, but unexpectedly, magically, its archetype." That's what we have here: not an account of something that might happen, but of something that always happens, finely rendered.

George Stade. *New York Times Book Review.* June 20, 1993, p. 22

DURAS, MARGUERITE (FRANCE) 1914–96

In *A Dam against the Pacific* Marguerite Duras revealed an original and bold talent. I admired that novel a great deal. I find the same gifts in her new book, *The Sailor from Gibraltar,* but not her own authentic personality. . . .

[Anna] has loved only one man, a sailor from Gibraltar. . . . She loved him; he left her; she pursued him, waited for him; two or three times they met again and "rekindled the flame." Then he fled again, or rather he vanished one evening, and she has never stopped waiting for him. She pursues him by boat, from port to port, from country to country. . . . Anna will never again reach the mysterious place in which the Sailor from Gibraltar has undoubtedly found refuge from love and from the police. And her strange lover of the moment, Anna's confidant, shares the delights of this pursuit with as much unsatiated ardor as Anna. The Sailor from Gibraltar looks very much to me like the symbol of happiness.

The reader, somewhat worn out by so many voyages, by disillusions, and intoxications of every variety, closes the book with a sort of relief. But he will not forget it. . . .

Gérard d'Houville. *Revue des deux mondes.*
December 15, 1952, pp. 728–30

Nothing could be more misleading than the title *Moderato Cantabile.* The novel sings, yes, but in Marguerite Duras's works the emotions are never moderate. Often at the beginning of her books her central characters are established in a misleading equilibrium, as if in a lethargy. Then a break—an awakening—takes place, and the awakening is always spectacular. This is what happens in the extraordinary love scene in the automobile in *A Dam against the Pacific,* in the drunkenness of the minor bureaucrat who is about to change his ways in *The Sailor from Gibraltar,* in the mother's sudden entrance into the night club in *Whole Days in the Trees.* In *Moderato Cantabile,* the occurrence of a crime sets everything in motion. . . .

The whole story is not narrated, or even suggested. Instead the woman in the story makes a discovery, and the reader, if he is up to doing so, is invited to make the same discovery. Undoubtedly the details of interpretation matter little, and errors are permissible. The main thing is to feel the power of the dialogue, to feel the electric charge that magnetizes every phrase, every word. That charge is so great that the actions and words can be reduced to a minimum. One hand placed on another hand becomes more erotic than a ten-page bedroom scene in a book by another writer. The simple description of the long boulevard by the sea along which the woman must walk at night, dragging her tired child behind her, when she has had too much to drink and is running out of time, conveys with every repetition the weight of her burden and the courage necessary for escape.

I would be tempted to call *Moderato Cantabile* an extremely interesting experiment if I did not know that for Duras there are never any experiments. She throws herself wholeheartedly into every new book as if into a battle, with an intrepid courage. This time she has clearly won a victory.

Roger Grenier. *La table ronde.*
July, 1958, pp. 122–23

She was aiming, obviously, at a definition of existence as Western man experiences it today, in this particular moment of the mid-twentieth century. . . . The fictional world of Madame Duras is the movement of time, at once creating and isolating personality: the tilting of time toward a past which a second later is transformed into an empty nothingness. . . . These are strange lives, in which all memory of the past, all the accumulations of experience, shriveled up into the expressions uttered at that very moment. The fictional curve of temporality coils, like a planetary eclipse, around the two poles of memory and the instant, each of which defines the other.

Armand Hoog. *Yale French Studies.*
Summer, 1959, pp. 70–72

The Square is a very short novel, mostly in dialogue, with hardly any description or supports like "he said" and "she said." It is a conversation between a couple sitting in the late afternoon on a bench in a Paris square. He is a hawker, she is an overworked servant girl. They each have a philosophy of life, which is what the novel is about. . . .

This novel was, I believe, praised by Beckett, whose own characters the two nameless and, largely, faceless people on the bench resemble. By its very simplicity the idea of the book is highly ambitious. Ingredients: a man and a girl in a public square, never moving, only talking—what ingenious possibilities for a novel! But I do not think *The Square* has succeeded; it seems to me an interesting and sophisticated exercise-piece.

I am the last person to object to any movement which aims at the elimination of clutter from the novel, or to anybody's larking about with the novel form. But in order to practise economy you have to have some substance to practise it upon. The only excuse for presenting a novel in an abbreviated form is that it should convey a lot more than it says; the effect should be compressed, dynamic. My objections to *The Square* are therefore not directed against its intentions but against the book itself. These objections are as follows:

(1) It reeks of art.

(2) Short as it is, it is too long. That is to say, its action and development would justify a short story of not more than 2,000 words. Its present length of, say, 30,000 words is monotonously drawn out with repetitious talk.

(3) The dialogue is insufficiently differentiated. (This may be partly the translators' business.) Consequently it is sometimes difficult to see who is speaking.

(4) The experiment of an almost total dialogue-novel has almost succeeded in changing the genre, so that it looks and sounds like a radio script.

Muriel Spark. *The Observer.*
July 19, 1959, p. 11

Marguerite Duras does not describe her characters: they are before us and they talk. More or less we learn in the course of their conversation something of their physical appearance since they mention it. But they speak, as we speak, each for himself and for the others, at times indifferent and at times careful about making themselves understood. Just as with dramatists, this novelist appears not to direct the dialogue of her characters, to let them express themselves freely and that it is circumstance and not the author which links remark to remark. But the situations in which the conversations occur are hers; in the secret resemblances from book to book one finds clues to the problematical personality or, one might say, to the profound obsession of the writer.

Serge Young. *Revue générale belge.*
April, 1960, p. 134

Her novels are written to be sipped, slowly, until one really feels giddy, just as the characters themselves become intoxicated. . . . The style has the slow and repetitive obstinacy of a drunkard's comments and thoughts. And it is that very drunkenness that persuades the reader and gives the work the value of revelation. Essentially, Duras's novels are like alcohol or like a poem. Drunkenness and its truth can only be "understood" if one is drunk, just as a poem is, in the last analysis, its own explanation. . . . Each novel moves ahead with the specific unity of some systematic inebriation. There is the cognac-manzanilla "style," just as there was the Campari bitters style and, before that, the whiskey style.

Jacques Guicharnaud. *Yale French Studies.*
Spring–Summer, 1961, p. 112

Whether on a farm, a yacht, or a beach, the persons Mme. Duras describes play out the entire drama of human existence. They are all seeking something—meaning of life, fulfillment, or happiness—but their will is a fragile bark soon surrendering to the great currents and waves which carry them on according to plans that are not of human making. As in Simon's novels, time goes on, destinies are accomplished, and life is perhaps over before these nameless persons are fully aware of what has been happening. Their reactions have nothing of Promethean grandeur, but are feeble whinings or petty mutual brutalities.

All this is forcefully presented chiefly by means of dialogue. The novels are full of conversation—a bumbling, inexplicit flow of words that through its very incoherence and fortuity reveals the pathos of these starved lives.

Laurent Le Sage. *The French New Novel*
(University Park: Pennsylvania State
University Press, 1962), pp. 85–86

These words which are said in this work which nears the limit of speechlessness by men and by women foundering, with dulled senses, hypnotized, and almost paralyzed, slowly, in night, are words which traverse a space which is pale sea-green and like gelatin; they look for themselves hesitatingly in order to form sentences but they come always against an insurmountable wall. The word, with Mme. Marguerite Duras, is not communication, but solitary incantation; it fills silence like the most doomed cry for help.

Philippe Sénart. *Mercure de France.*
June, 1962, pp. 311–12

In my opinion, Marguerite Duras's work should be linked to that collection of widely varying attempts that is called the "new novel." The primary reason is the importance given to tempo in her work, the role that duration constantly plays in her writing. While all her works deal with passion (its development, its dangers, and its inevitability), passion is almost always . . . seen in terms of time, in terms of its essential relationship with the contradictory and complementary effects of duration. Time and passion: to be sure, this is not a new coupling. What *is* new, however, is the shift of emphasis, the importance given to a particular aspect of duration (which is stressed to the point of making it the protagonist of the story) and the constant concern with communicating the ambiguity of perceived duration to the reader.

The almost obsessive preoccupation with time, and the discovery of the novelistic possibilities of subjects that have their own time (or dislocated time, like the world of memory)—these are undoubtedly among the most prominent features in the "new novelists," all of whom have read Proust, Joyce, and Faulkner. It is worth noting, however, that the "new novel" is often the story of a man, more precisely, of a narrator, who tries to come to terms with time, a story of how difficult it is to account for past time (Butor, Simon), a story that sometimes gives up or deliberately rejects any temporal perspective (Robbe-Grillet). But for Duras, duration and its effects are not technical problems . . . but theme. And her very personal interpretation of this theme is what gives this novelist her special place in the French novel of today. What . . . characterizes her contribution (and is also the sign of her success) is undoubtedly the durable memory she leaves her readers of having been for the space of a reading, subjected to a unique tempo. . . .

Jean-Luc Seylaz. *Les romans de Marguerite Duras* (Paris: Archives de Lettres Modernes, 1963), pp. 40–44

The Afternoon of Mr. Andesmas hardly contains a story. Practically nothing happens in the afternoon described. An obese old man simply sits on the balcony of his mountain cottage and, from time to time, casts a glance on the village below. His solitude is absolute, painful, and poignant, and the gay musical fragments which sporadically reach his ears from down below emphasize his spiritual and physical loneliness. . . .Life is thus construed to be neither absurd, nor unjust, but simply terribly mediocre. Sometimes one falls in love, one marries, one has children or a clandestine affair. Impossible passions and calamitous dramas occur, incarnation and superiority seem within reach, only to fade quickly and plunge the victims into the antechamber of hell where neither hope can animate nor desire can stop the onrush of permanent acquiescence.

The lesson of *The Afternoon of Mr. Andesmas* crystallizes Mme. Duras's previously exposed views on the mediocrity of life. In her twenty-year-old career as playwright, film writer, and above all novelist, she has succeeded in synthesizing the qualities of what is generally called the "American Novel" with the engaging aspects of the New Novel now raging throughout Europe. She has managed to become neither so famous as Hemingway, for example, nor so notorious as Alain Robbe-Grillet. But her ability to combine the forces of the old with the lucidity of the new seems to assure her place in modern French literature. Her middle-of-the-road position represents, perhaps, the writer's own tacit assent to the inferiority of existence. Marguerite Duras, then, already widely known and appreciated by war-torn European readers who, more than others, have cause to question our "best of possible worlds," deserves a greater reception among the American intelligentsia, indeed among all *aficionados* of better writing.

Alfred Cismaru. *Dalhousie Review.*
Summer, 1967, pp. 210–11

Duras's plays are all based on the aim at an absolute break or its realization. They are probing examinations of the leap into something other, a leap by which the characters invent or rediscover their authentic destinies. . . .

"The love that flows between them, stifling," at the end of *Suzanna Andler,* is beyond expression; it is a dazzling and radically new fact. . . . The "flow" of love at the end of *Suzanna Andler* has some resemblance to the denouement of *La Musica.* A marriage has fallen apart and ended in divorce. The husband and wife have both taken lovers, and they can thus remake their lives according to a bourgeois pattern. Instead of such a mediocre solution, Duras has husband and wife meet again for a few hours and discover a new form of love for each other—a new beginning, absolute but sublimated, for they will separate again, forever. Although they go on to their respective lovers, they have made the leap into a legendary situation—that of impossible love. The passion between them will grow, but it is beyond realization and beyond language, for it both unites and separates them.

At the end of these two plays something radically new has been initiated. The bourgeois stagnation of people who are bound socially, but isolated psychically, explodes. The beginnings of true communication are effected, which, for want of anything better, is called love. A clearer and more comprehensive explanation of things would no doubt destroy the absolute novelty of the event or, more precisely, the advent. A kind of private apocalypse is anticipated, which is both desired—for through it the characters come out of themselves to make contact with others—and dreaded, for, like all apocalypses, it can take place only if everything that exists is destroyed.

In Duras's works increasing emphasis has been placed on the necessary phase of destruction, an explosion of the present state of things, ranging from a rejection of bourgeois conventions to actual murder.

Jacques Guicharnaud. *Yale French Studies.*
46, 1971, pp. 114–16

Duras has been writing since childhood, but it was not until 1944, when she was thirty, that she published her first novel. Since then her work has branched out in many directions: fifteen short novellas—or we might best call them prose narratives—the last entitled *Love*. Her work has become increasingly strange and hard to read, but it obsesses and fascinates those readers who have once entered Duras's world. She has written a book of short stories, two volumes of plays, and film scenarios, of which the best-known is *Hiroshima, My Love*, the film for which she wrote her first script. Lately, fascinated by the medium, Duras has started to produce her own films.

There is a kind of fluidity or plasticity in her writing that allows a narrative to become a play or scenario; indeed, her works sometimes go through the three media—narrative, play, script. Technically, Duras's narratives have tended toward musical forms, modulating basic themes that occur hauntingly throughout her work: madness, suffering, solitude, but also love. Her prose narratives set up highly stylized, simple scenarios in which characters, identified only by name, embody the buried unconscious needs and frustrations that, in Duras's view, haunt modern lives, blocked by the orderly mechanical patterns of bourgeois existence. Because they embody these emotional needs and deprivations, they enter into strange dialogues, encounters, and relationships. But whatever the characters and scenario, underlying them all is the theme of love—love as a mode of perception and total dispossession of the self, a love that includes the sexual as *one* of its modalities, but which does not exclude different modalities breaking with bourgeois patterns of exclusivity.

Germaine Brée. *Women Writers in France*
(New Brunswick, New Jersey: Rutgers
University Press, 1973), pp. 66–67

A number of Duras's books are written indifferently as plays, film scripts, or novels. In at least two of these texts, *India Song* and *Détruire, dit-elle,* there is an enigmatic passage: if these texts were to be staged in a theater, declares a peremptory editorial voice, "il n'y aurait pas de répétition générale." This apparent distaste for dress rehearsals is strange, but revealing. Behind it lies a paradox. If no dress rehearsals may be allowed for these texts, it is most likely so that the continuity between rehearsal and performance may be preserved. Performance itself becomes a rehearsal, or, since the French word, "répétition," cannot distinguish between a rehearsal and a repetition, it becomes a rehearsal as well as a repetition. The act of repeating in Duras's texts turns towards the future as well as facing into the past. From the very beginning, performance repeats a loss of origin, it is a circular event having no originating moment.

But even before the question of dress rehearsals arises, self-reflexive repetition and circular self-rehearsal are already the preferred terms of reference of Duras's fictions. In the context of her work, the borderline between what is and what is not fundamentally a repetition becomes difficult to draw, and the idea of repetition or rehearsal can take in phenomena as diverse as self-adaptation (the reworking, for instance, at a distance of some twenty-five years, of the novel *Un Barrage contre le Pacifique* into the play *L'Eden Cinéma*), self-quotation (as in the figure of Anne-Marie Stretter, who, "différemment toujours," travels across texts, as a name, at any rate, from one fiction to another), structural circularity within narrative and the ritualistic re-enactment of plot events (as, for example, in *Moderato cantabile,* or *Le Ravissement de Lol V. Stein*), and the use of various echoing leitmotifs both within and between texts. Here, the phenomenon of textual repetition is more than a simple consequence of the entropy of the signifier. The questions which arise from repetition can be extended to apply in principle to all Duras's films, plays, and novels, and it becomes clear that the use of repetition as a structuring device is central to her whole strategy as a writer and filmmaker.

Leslie Hill. Modern Language Review.
84, July, 1989, p. 601

What force is this that surges so violently, like the Pacific, in the writings of Duras?

One is tempted to respond: Love. Love seems to be the incandescent center of Duras's fiction. All of her books, *Le Marin de Gibraltar, Le Ravissement de Lol V. Stein, Hiroshima mon amour, L'Amant,* to name a few, are stories of love encounters. Marguerite Duras wrote in 1987, in *La Vie materielle:* "A book is the story of two people who love. That's it: who love without being forewarned."

But the element that surges in the novels of Duras is not love, even if the text is the story of a love encounter that opens a dialogue between a man and a woman. The structure of her writing is complex: the discovery of love . . . between a man and a woman takes place in the eyes or memory of another who observes it and tells of it; this "other" is always a woman. The simple dialogic relation is transformed into a complex triangular relation: the event that is as powerful as the Pacific is not love, but love as it is lived through the eyes and the silence of a woman. Marguerite Duras's writing is a woman's writing in this sense: "For thousand of years, silence has been synonymous with woman. Therefore, literature *is* women. It's women whether it speaks of women or is created by women." Women, in Marguerite Duras's work, are the witnesses of a love that happens to others; or even to themselves as others, witnesses, martyrs in the etymological sense, women are subjected to the passion of seeing, a passion in which they lose their identity. The woman's gaze is the absence of self in which her own image is not reflected, but the love of two other people. "All the women in my books regardless of their age, spring from the character of Lol V. Stein, that is, from a certain self-effacement." The "V signifies the tearing apart of the subject, the loss of her identity, as she stands before the window where she loses herself in the contemplation of the couple outside the window, this mirror that reflected nothing and before which she could only see with delight the eviction of her being that she so desired."

Marguerite Duras places silence, literature, and women together as components of the same equation. The writing of Marguerite Duras is a written silence: things are not said explicitly but suggested in short sentences where abstract nouns replace adjectives, producing a theatrical effect which dramatizes her writing. This sober and silent writing is the event (ex-venire) of a woman: a woman leaves the social, masculine world where she is condemned to silence and enters into "la folie," madness, the fascination with the spectacle of the Other. Nevertheless, men are not absent from the narratives of Duras: on the contrary, they play important roles as narrators, as in *Le Ravissement de Lol V. Stein,* or at least as partners of a dialogue, as in *Moderato cantabile.* They are themselves fascinated by the mystery of feminine madness and attempt to approach and read it, to make it speak the masculine voice is necessary to give shape to this silence, this specifically feminine emptiness. Madness is a feminine illness par excellence. . . . In the mesmerizing contemplation of what happens to another or to oneself as "other," an enormous vacuum is created in which the loss of subjectivity occurs; this loss is at the same time absolute subjectivity and the beginning of literature.

Catherine Cusset. *Yale French Studies.*
76, 1988, pp. 62–63

Lol V. Stein is not readily approached. By a somewhat surprising enunciative strategy, it's only one-third of the way through that the reader is permitted to learn that the narrator who knows so many things about her is also a character whose fate is henceforth connected to that of the heroine. This technique has the effect of separating her even more from visibility, to make her retreat further towards mystery. This strange narrator character, Jacques Hold, thus speaks of himself as of a third party, treating himself like a character among other characters, as if to join the no less floating enunciative status of Lol who can also speak of herself as of a third person. The narrator thus seems to have been conquered by the dispossession that affects Lol, to be seriously infected by the dichotomy inherent in the personality of the heroine, she who tries to contemplate her drama from without, to relive it as a theatrical piece is played. Thus Lol V. Stein is not apprehended directly: seizure of the heroine is hindered by this doubly complex enunciative strategy which doubly ravishes her in real life and also somewhat in novelistic life. This project of "ravishment" of the heroine is what the author pursues, in various ways, all through the work. . . .

Lol V. Stein is thus not a character in a novel. Taking an additional step towards unreality, she touches myth. She is a theatralized fantasy. And the key words of the novel "ravish" individuals and places to serve no other ends than their own pure sonorous existence which sets up a fantastic reality around Lol whose mad name designates and calls at once to unreason, the dance, and music, in the fixity of a place whose obsessive name serves to structure her waking dream.

Bernard Albert and Marie-Thérèse Mathet.
French Studies. 44, 1990, pp. 416, 422

EBNER, JEANNIE (AUSTRIA) 1918–

In 1954, author Jeannie Ebner—at that time thirty-six years old—published her first novel . . . under the title *Sie warten auf Antwort* (They're waiting for an answer). Despite numerous and in part very positive reviews in Austria and Germany, the novel never went beyond a first edition. And of this first edition, a total of just five hundred and seven copies were sold by the end of 1955, that is, in the time period in which its reception by the literary world could have influenced its market sales. The novel brought its author renown within literary circles and transformed the writer into an author to be taken seriously, for it revealed Ebner's characteristic tendency to speak in parables, allegories and myths. It also demonstrates relatively compactly a narrative tone from which the author increasingly strays, in her later works, in the direction of a more realistic narrative style, but to which she finds her way back time and again, particularly in key passages.

The author offers this brief summary of her own experience: "At sixteen I spent my days in an office. Evenings, in bed, I spent reading Karl Marx and Rilke. The former I did not understand, the latter awakened in me the wish to die of consumption." There no trace of these influences in the first novel, which, right up until it reached print, had the working title "The Helpless Ones." A kinship appears, however, to Musil and Kafka, though the author did not, or at least not consciously, draw from their work. . . .

Revolt as a permanent process is what the novel offers as an alternative, revolt as an expression of life. The permanent act of meaningful, methodical, and just change, or in other words, life offers itself to the helpless as a possibility for survival, but only insofar as they grasp the possibility of this solution, and keep at a distance any absolute version of this form of existence.

Thus, the representation of helplessness appears to make the possibility of its mastery reasonable, after all.

August Obermayer. *Modern Austrian Literature*. 14, 1981, pp. 63, 78

"Enough with futile appeals directed at the Surveyor's Office. We must take a step toward self-help," so implores the second flier's text, composed by Dr. Förlich, a character in the novel *They're Waiting for an Answer*. Outraged over the silent response of the architect, symbolizing God, and over the ruin of the house, which forms the centerpiece of the novel, and some of its inhabitants, he tries within the framework of his "Society for Self-help" to battle human powerlessness. . . . He acknowledges the people's personal responsibility and sense of authority, something that they, and their fathers before them, had denied themselves as a result of misunderstanding the Christian doctrine of unconditional obedience.

Another society is founded in Jeannie Ebner's third novel—*Figures in Black and White*—the "Society for Saving Europe." Its goal is to lay the leadership of the nations in the hands of the intellectuals, because career politicians have proven their lack of conscientiousness. For Antonia, one of the spokeswomen, this leads naturally to the triumph of magic and female intuition over the cool logical male mode of thought, and so, in the last analysis, to the political involvement of women, as beings superior to men. . . .

Jeannie Ebner's work on the whole is determined by emancipatory efforts. Her chief concern is not so much the fundamental affirmation of equality between the sexes, though this is indeed a component, as the previous examples from *They're Waiting for an Answer* and *Figures in Black and White* suggest. She is much more concerned with human emancipation, that is, with a clear integration of the individual in world history, the search for a human-affirmative meaning in earthly existence, and a positioning of man, who has been left since expulsion from paradise to helplessly fend for himself: in short, his relationship to God. Moreover, there appears on almost every page of Jeannie Ebner's work the opposition between the individual and the community, which bears on the characteristically antithetical mode of her thinking and writing, and is thus representative of it. . . .

While Jeannie Ebner's heart belongs first and foremost to poetry, she has gradually switched over to more broadly constructed epic forms. She herself says in jest, but not without an element of truth: "I always say that lyric poetry is the great love of every writer, while one's relationship to short prose is a sleazy one, and the novel is marriage. That is to say that it brings out the joys of love, the joys of intuition and inspiration, but it also requires work, diligence, discipline. And what is really beautiful about that is the fact that one can work on writing a novel for a year's time. Besides, the intellect, thoughts about the world and life, are strongly developed within me alongside a certain realism and logic. One can express that much better in a novel than in a poem." . . .

Jeannie Ebner is not actually a feminist, because she views the problem of the oppression of women merely as a partial aspect of the general human problem of lack of responsibility and personal authority. She is a committed individualist.

Carine Kleiber. In Carine Kleiber and Erika
Tunner, eds. *Frauenliteratür in Osterreich
von 1945 bis heute* (Bern: Lang, 1988),
pp. 79–80, 82–86

Jeannie Ebner, who otherwise demonstrates a marked leaning toward speculative considerations, reacts to questions regarding the process of literary creation with annoyance. Statements about her own work are also few and far between. With the exception of "The Threads," her only theoretical work to date, most of her remarks about this topic are worked into her last two works, *Three Tones of a Flute* and *Aktäon.*

Jeannie Ebner does not wish to broadcast a message. She neither possesses a clearly defined ideology nor believes in the compatibility of literary quality and didactic concern. But clearly, the act of writing contributes to her own method of coping with life, in that it allows her to write herself free, directly promoting day-dreaming and game-playing with potentialities. Jeannie Ebner expresses this in *Aktäon* when she calls for the right to "fabulize." . . . She also establishes here a parallel between herself and God: "God has decreed it so. He alone writes his text, and perhaps even He does not know how the whole thing will end.". . .

Desentimentalization of the theme of sexual relations, reached by Theres in *Figures in Black and White* through the help of her lover Stieglitzer, paves the way for a positive attitude of women toward relations between the sexes in Jeannie Ebner's later books. Erotic intimacy becomes a matter of course in *Three Tones of a Flute* and *Aktäon* without excluding conventional morality in a provocative manner, and it is the result of a mutual affection that does not necessarily develop into love. . . .

Figures in Black and White is not only pioneering in the field of sexual emancipation of woman, however, but also in that of her socialization. Women are valued only when they engage in a career and lay claim to their intellectual capacities, which in no way lag behind those of their male counterparts; or in other words, when they shape their state of being into an existence.

Carine Kleiber. *Jeannie Eber: Eine
Einfürung* (Bern: Lang, 1985), pp. 29–30,
45–46

The first chapter of *Sie warten auf Antwort,* explicitly titled "Introduction," deals expressly with matters of narration: "A story always begins with the fact that from a state of total equilibrium suddenly energy is set free, gets into motion without any apparent external cause but from inner necessity. This is how the action starts. The plot of which the story consists cannot be stopped anymore. It starts with a deed." Thus the position of the narrator is established. It is in spite of all emotional concern a position of distance, an intellectual analysis of creative activities, a description of these activities. Thus it is possible that consciously created characters seem able to escape the narrator's control and manipulative power, but at the same time the narrator is fully aware of that happening. There is a certain degree of freedom for the character and therefore for the narrator, but once this freedom has been exercised and a decision has been taken, the events take over: "The net has caught him, he cannot escape from the course of the story, cannot find his way back, cannot free himself. The story progresses and sweeps him away like a boat without steering on the high sea. All that is left for him to do is to have trust in a star and fight for his life."

Ebner thus provides two categories for the comprehension of the narrative act. There is the conscious, purposeful and planned arrangement on the part of the narrator on the one hand, and the accidental, fateful, and metaphysical occurrence taking over the narration on the other hand. These two extreme positions, the manipulative intellect and the unpredictable intuition, are always evoked within Ebner's work. They are frontiers, poles of human endeavor which, according to Jeannie Ebner's conviction, have to be brought together somehow in order to enable men to catch a glimpse of the truth. This approximation to the truth, if it occurs at all, takes place in a mysterious in-between region *(das Zwischenreich)*. Although this is a spatial metaphor, it denotes a mental condition. . . .

Although Ebner evokes catastrophes and disasters of apocalyptic proportions, there remains always a glimpse of hope, an opening into a possible future. Ebner's characters are not caught by the absolute finality so frightening in Kafka's world. Her allegories, symbols, and metaphors are not totally hermetic; she always keeps open a small window on reality. It is therefore not surprising to observe a development toward a more realistic mode of presentation. Ebner wrote a considerable number of short stories in the style of her first novel, but by 1958, when her second novel, *Die Wildnis früher Sommer* (The jungle of early summers), appeared, a definite development had taken place. The emphasis has changed from a symbolic and mythological mode of presentation, to a psychological exploration of the characters; a more realistic style has therefore emerged. This development is not surprising, for Jeannie Ebner has always aimed at projecting her messages into figures, at creating characters who by means of their behavior and actions communicate the narrator's comprehension of the world and consequently fulfill the author's intention.

August Obermayer. In Donald Daviau, ed.
*Major Figures of Contemporary Austrian
Literature* (New York: Peter Lang, 1987),
pp. 146–49

EDGELL, ZEE (BELIZE) 1941?–

For Beka Lamb [in the novel of that title] educational achievement is something that strengthens the relationship she shares with her paternal grandmother. When Beka wins the essay contest at her convent school and when she successfully passes First Form, after failing the previous year, Beka's sense of self-worth and accomplishment grows immensely. The relationship between her and her Granny Ivy grows to a new level also.

Granny Ivy is the family matriarch who is Beka's link between the present and "before time." The view of Belizean society that Granny Ivy presents to Beka is one that is colored by her position as a poor, hard-working Black woman who has lived in colonial Belize all her life. She is outspoken, has an independent spirit, and she takes an active role in the political battles of her community because she is a fierce nationalist and wants to see her country free. Granny Ivy wishes for political change, but the reality of colonial politics and the entrenched class divisions which are exacerbated by the various racial mixtures and prejudices in the society, continually informs her that achieving independence will be a serious battle within her country.

Beka goes to the PIP's (People's Independence Party) meetings with Granny Ivy and actively discusses the issues with her. Only after Beka becomes absorbed in her schoolwork and the essay contest do they realize that their political discussions are a vital part of their bond. Fear of losing Beka to schools which teach Belizean youth "to look outside instead of in" prompts Granny Ivy to lash out at Beka when she shows no interest in the political happenings anymore. "Who ever heard about any black girl winning so much as a pencil at that convent school? Do you see any black nuns?" Although Granny Ivy wants change in the society and wants her granddaughter to succeed, she sees that education, especially the Catholic centered education of the convent school, alienates the youth from their roots which leads many of them to become condescending toward their kin or exiles from their land. In order to compensate for her own fear and frustration, Granny Ivy continually calls forth one of the primary contradictions in the Belizean educational system and Catholicism in general, namely, their practice of discrimination against Belizeans of African descent.

Interestingly, Beka understands and believes Granny Ivy. Nevertheless she wants to "try" because that is what her mother teachers her and that is also the way of the younger generation of Black Belizeans. At fourteen, Beka already knows that the prospects for life as an educated Black woman are limited since Black people there are seldom allowed to reach their potential. She transposes these feelings into feelings of identification with her best friend Toycie. Toycie, who was once the brightest student in the convent school, is victimized by the sexism of the school's head nun who expels her because she is pregnant and by the class prejudice which mandates that her pettibourgeois "pania" boyfriend jilt her because she is poor and Black. The smallness and prejudice of the community that leaves no avenues of escape for Toycie and lead to her madness and subsequent death are things that Beka wants to bar from her life. They are part of the ways that Granny Ivy accepts as life "before time." They cause a great amount of insecurity and self-doubt in Beka which she tries to explain to her grandmother. . . .

That Beka does try to win the essay contest and does have hope for winning is a direct result of her relationship with her mother. It is Beka's mother who castigates Granny Ivy for continually discouraging Beka with her stories of "before time." The two women constantly disagree on matters of politics and culture, but Lilla Lamb's weak manner and temperate spirit assure that she and Granny Ivy never come to hostile argument. In her role as an upwardly mobile housewife, Lilla offers Beka the view of the future. She encourages her husband to give Beka a second chance at the convent school, although she would abide by any decision he made in the matter. She also wishes to abandon any and all of the folkways which she considers superstitious because she feels that "the old ways will poison the new."

Objecting to the necessity of having a traditional wake for her grandmother, Lilla explains to Granny Ivy that abandoning the old ways amounts to progress. Lilla knows that adapting to the European customs brings more favor from the colonial hierarchy and helps facilitate social mobility. She is therefore willing to relinquish all the traditional rituals in favor of "progress."

Beka's mother also knows that education is a means to social mobility. She believes, much more than Granny Ivy, that "things are changing." Because her father would not pay for her to finish high school and because her husband never got a chance to go at all, Lilla dreams of Beka's graduating. The same day that she tells Beka "you might as well learn kitchen work, because it seems like that's all you'll be good for," is the same day that she gives Beka a new exercise book and pen. She never wavers in her faith in Beka's ability to pass. This is a special aspect of the relationship she has with her daughter which helps Beka to overcome her habit of lying whenever she fails her family's expectations of her.

As Beka's self-avowed mission to conquer her habit of lying and to pass First Form is told in flashback, it becomes clear that the bond she has with her mother and grandmother aids in her achievement of a more positive selfhood. Beka gains self-confidence and realistic insight into the social outlines and conflicts in her society. This helps her academically, but it also helps her to understand and deal with the social and psychological implications of her best friend's victimization and death. Granny Ivy's fear of change is counter-balanced by Lilla's insistence on change. And Lilla's fear of indigenous cultural ritual is counter-balanced by Granny Ivy's explanations of the importance of keeping some of the "old ways." Therefore, Beka gets both views in more or less equal portions. She weighs both and tries to create a balance that is useful for her young life.

Yakini Kemp. SAGE. 2, 1985, pp. 25–26

Set within the framework of a colonial society, a society aspiring to independence, *Beka Lamb* examines the dialectical relationship between that society and the individual. The personal stories of the girls Beka and Toycie are used in ways of examining the colonial society. The relationship between Toycie and Emilio in particular suggests the exploitative colonial one. And Beka's journey to self-assurance compares with her country's move to independence. In addition, the traditional ways are shown in conflict with the values promoted by the Church and educational institutions. The result is dramatic change whose impact, emphasized by the constant references to "befo' time" and "tings bruk down," is seen in the disintegrating society, its former wholeness and stability eroded by the colonial experience. But disintegration is only part of the life cycle. Edgell's heroine learns this truth, and by implication independence is therefore a real possibility for her country.

The more important emphasis, however, is on the highly personal odyssey of Beka from early adolescent dependence and uncertainty to self-definition and integration. The novel begins in the present, revealing Beka's success and achievement. It then moves to the past, recalling the major events of her life in order to explain and give meaning to the present. Edgell appropriately uses a folk ritual—The Wake—to place this journey. The Wake operates on two levels: it is a way of mourning what is gone; it is also an attempt to discover and celebrate what has been gained. So Beka, in having a private Wake for Toycie, is paying her respects to the dead and allowing herself to grieve; but in recalling Toycie's life, she is also gaining insight into her own life and that of her society. The Wake is essentially a medium through which the events of the past are recounted, sifted for their fine truths, and appropriated. In doing so, Beka is engaged in ordering through memory the fragments of the past, finding its patterns and recreating self. Like Hagar in Margaret Laurence's *The Stone Angel,* another novel carefully organized around the act of remembering, she comes to a new understanding of self and community. Beka learns truths necessary for her survival as an integrated person. The Wake, as Miss Ivy points out, is "a help to the living." Moreover, the Wake is a symbol of past traditions which Edgell shows Beka must retain if she is to have an awareness of her community and her race. . . .

In *Beka Lamb,* Edgell portrays the importance of adolescent girls' private relationships. And while she admits to the tension that society creates she demonstrates that finally it is the girls' personalities and their means of resolving conflicts that determine their growth. The mother-daughter relationship in its various forms also provides central support for the adolescent. There is a direct relation between its presence and the adolescent's definition of self. In addition, Edgell examines stereotypical female means of coping—emotional and passive. Such ways are shown as negative: heroines who practice them fail to attain wholeness. In contrast, there are strong and independent women who through an active creativity impose their will on their world. Edgell has affirmed emotionality and passivity are not the only feminine ways of coping.

Beka Lamb offers us a more complex picture of the female adolescent. Through Toycie and Beka, Edgell examines the conflicts she faces with her awakening sexuality and society's increasing expectations. Such expectations are often ambiguous. They acknowledge her visible growth and supposed maturity but not her sexuality. Beka and Toycie are thus most vulnerable in that area. Miss Flo makes oblique references to Beka's sexuality and Miss Ivy's confession helps her. But generally, the adult women remain silent about their daughters' sexuality. And while Edgell does not claim that biology controls a girl's perception of self and the choices she makes (that is, that biology is destiny), she does take into account the pressure society exerts on a woman to conform to its image of femininity, especially during adolescence.

Like other women, Beka must confront and surmount these pressures to achieve selfhood.

Lorna Down. *Ariel.* 18, 1987, pp. 39–40, 50

Zee Edgell's *Beka Lamb* (1982) deals with a "normal" adolescent whose best friend Toycie becomes severely mentally ill and does not recover. . . .

[A]lmost universally, female children are socialized into "good behavior"—meaning compliant, obedient, submissive. behavior. Toycie, as we learn in *Beka Lamb,* was a model child, as she's a model young lady; her anxiety to please and to conform is obviously informed by her vulnerable and precarious position in the world as an orphaned, and thus economically dependent woman. . . .

In *Beka Lamb* . . . education offers an alternative for girls to "the washing bowl underneath the house bottom"; but to graduate, the black Belizean students must conform to the model imposed by white, foreign educators, must "leap through the hoops of quality purposely held high by the nuns." For many, there is a clash between the norms and expectations of their traditional creole society, which they are expected to deny, and those within the convent gates.

Ramesh Deosaran calls attention to the rapidity of modernization in the Caribbean and notes that while new opportunities and prospects arise as a result, they are often accompanied by an "anti-tradition" attitude which has long-term negative effects on society. In the case of Toycie, whose culture permits sexual indulgence and unmarried motherhood, but whose rise up the social ladder involves emulation of the Virgin Mary, we may see the result of the type of psychological conflict detailed above: the harsh judgment of Toycie is also a judgment of traditional values, seen as backward and immoral by the modern, foreign educators. . . .

To identify with the witch/whore stereotype is to incur the wrath of Christian morality, to become, in effect, no better than the prostitute National Vellour, in *Beka Lamb,* a scorned and feared outcast.

The choice between these polarities is dramatized in the case of Toycie. Father Nunez lectures schoolgirls on the choice between the model of the Virgin Mary and that of Eve, who has the power "to unleash chaos upon the world." Like her own mother and many women in her neighborhood, Toycie becomes pregnant out of wedlock. Her nausea, causing her to vomit on the chapel floor, establishes her in the eyes of the nuns as a fallen woman, a source of contamination to be removed from the school before her sins infect others. The message she must learn is that to rise socially, it is necessary not only to break with her creole class but also with its morality—or suffer the consequences.

Evelyn O'Callaghan. In Carole Boyce
Davies and Elaine Savory Fido, eds. *Out of
the Kumbla: Caribbean Women and
Literature* (Trenton, New Jersey: Africa
World Press, 1990), pp. 89, 95–96

EDMOND, LAURIS (NEW ZEALAND) 1924–

In Middle Air . . . appeared in 1975 and won the PEN Best First Book Award. Five more books followed before her *Selected Poems* containing a selection from her previous books and thirty-five new poems, came out in 1984.

Her publishers [Oxford University Press,] submitted it for the British Airways Commonwealth Poetry Prize and it won first the Area Award and then the overall prize.

The chairman of the judges, the poet Peter Porter, describes the poems as "written very much from a woman's point of view," but if this implies domestic preoccupations it is rather unfair. Lauris Edmond is well aware of life outside the walls of the home. She may write one poem about sitting up late stitching small girls' dresses, but in another a bush fire rages to within three or four yards of the house.

"I am interested in the intricacies of relationships," she says. "Although I respond to the country there are people in my landscapes. Nowadays I am enormously aware of the passing of time, the temporariness of experience. The world itself seems beset by temporariness."

She does not regret giving up so much time and energy to the personal, but her new work is moving away from this and looking towards wider questions and issues—affected by politics even if not yet actually about political issues.

Although she now lives in Wellington, her observation of nature remains as acute as when she lived in the country, and the ecological issue is one that deeply concerns her. She sees the physical world as under threat, and firmly supports Prime Minister David Lange's stand on the *Rainbow Warrior* affair.

Gillian Mawrey. *Commonwealth.*
28:4, 1986, p. 156

The New Zealander Loris [*sic*] Edmond has written seven books of poetry and a novel in the space of a decade. This selection won the British Commonwealth Prize given by British Airways in 1985.

It is a remarkable tour de force, even more remarkable when it is remembered that Loris [*sic*] Edmond began to publish at an age when some writers have laid down their pens for good. Living in a remote place with few intellectual contacts, and faced with personal difficulties, her urge to write went underground. It has emerged in this fine poetry, mature in style and substance.

Which of these poems could have been written by a young poet? "Boy," perhaps, and some of the more descriptive pieces, but the poems radiate as a whole a mature experience. They do not, however, admit to age, but to a full life, still packed with ideas, events, people, her main concern the adjustments we continually make in relationships. She can be very plain, in dressing gown and slippers in a "mucky, mild domestication," turned suddenly to bloody encounters by a newspaper paragraph. She can be lyrical, leaping, as in "September"; she does ecstasies well (very hard to do), in "Camping" and "Epiphany".

What will return to the reader again and again, however, is the truth and exactitude of poems which tell of daily living, of human shifts and means, expressed with graceful clarity, with wit and sharp observation. She is not afraid to "grab" the reader with emotion shared, but she is not "confessional." We receive the full strength of feeling only by a kind of osmosis. "I cannot chronicle our love," she says, "nor yet keep silent, I am so entangled in its conjuring nets." The death of a child she refers to obliquely, only once saying flatly, "One of you is dead." The "Wellington Letter," addressed to a "gentle ghost," tells of life, not death, and seems to invoke more than one ghost.

Barbara Giles. *Overland*. 103, 1986,
pp. 74–75

New Zealand poetry is an instructive case for those post-colonial literatures, such as West Indian, which are trying to develop an appropriate language and subject matter in English, a language in origin foreign to them, to express a modern cultural identity. Before this century, New Zealand poets, like their Caribbean counterparts, were mostly a faint echo of mainland English writing, with a tendency towards the nostalgic pastoral. When this began to be supplanted in the earlier part of this century, the dilemma for New Zealand writers was particularly acute because, as well as feeling culturally secondary as a colony, there was a sense of settlers' guilt, extending back to the seventeenth century and the first displacement of the Maoris.

Among the new group of radical poets who expressed this heritage in the 1930s, the leading figure was Allen Curnow. . . .

Following Curnow has proved as daunting a weight for New Zealand writers as 'Yeats as an example' has been for Irish (and for strikingly similar reasons). Most of the male poets (James Baxter is the most striking exception) have tended to secularize somewhat desperately towards a kind of Barry Humphries philistinism. The women, by refusing the anxiety of influence, have fared better. Lauris Edmond was past fifty when she published her first volume; *Seasons and Creatures,* eleven years later, is her eighth. She is a predominantly personal, rather than public, poet, and her most memorable successes (such as "Epitaphs") are about family tragedy or happiness. The new book, like its predecessor, has three sections but they all have the same insistent themes: the Ages of Woman, illness and human resolution. There are some marvelous poems here: "Tempo" which reaches out with both tenderness and exhilaration for metaphors for the stages of pregnancy; "Hymns Ancient and Modern" is another haunting child elegy, like "Epitaphs":

in All Saints Sunday School
at a death we sang Abide With Me

in our effortless thin voices
and looked out the window
savouring all the Sunday dinners
still to come.

The images of liberty and the everyday in the last three lines deepen under the influence of the double meaning of effortless ("easy" and "not trying"). "The Noh Plays" is another poem with a metaphorical resonance that extends Edmond's range. Her previous book, *Catching It,* had an air of mandarin quietness that approached complacency; this one returns to the spirit of her earlier work and is her most impressive achievement so far.

Bernard O'Donoghue. *Poetry Review.*
78:1, 1988, pp. 34–35

Lauris Edmond is [an] internationally known New Zealand poet, winner of the 1985 Commonwealth Poetry Prize. *New and Selected Poems,* her most recent and most representative collection, gives opportunity to assess nearly twenty years of publication. What gives the volume its special interest is the strong impression of a poetry and a poet in stasis.

This is traditional romantic poetry. It focuses upon the perceptions and emotions of the writer, the honeydew eater. It is a poetry of observed nature and landscape and of straightforward feeling, as the titles suggest: "Waterfall," "Six Poplar Trees," "Before First Light," "Going to the Grampians," "The Night Burns with a White Fire," "Composition with Window and Bulldozer," "To a Grandson." Image after decorative image, word after word, epithet on "poetic" epithet could, allowing for semantic and syntactic drift, have flowered from quills two hundred years before: "Resonant harmonies," "Rapacious wind . . . the brilliant booty of the leaves," "morning's tender sky," "a dark lake bruised by the winter trees," "the moving pageant of the universe," "feel how the world rolls in its rind of mountains and seas." It is a poetry where voice is crucial, and dialogue or monologue is a favored device. And though Edmond does not employ traditional prosody—apart from a fondness for set numbers of lines to a stanza—there is seldom the echo of colloquial speech or the idiosyncratic freedom of line or sentence or the interleaving of topic or register of much contemporary verse. It is a poetry whose theme is essentially "the natural intermittent light of" the unique self, each living "in the body differently." The highest courage is to face the extinction of that self. And in a late-twentieth-century absence of search for Sublimity or Divinity in what is perceived, the perceptions and the consequent feelings of the observing-reporting-performing self are the centering, the unifying, concern.

There is, however, a second kind of stasis here. Neither Edmond's kind of poetry nor the attitudes it embodies nor the subjects it treats have developed, transmuted, or deepened over the years. She deals with the same topics in the most recent as in the earliest poetry: "Lake Idyll," "Moonshine Valley;"

"Brian," "Boy"; "Midwife," "Two Birth Poems"; "The Affair," "Pas de Deux." She employs the same diction, displays the same desire to signal meaning and to impose response upon readers with the same devices.

Of course, poets may have their particular topics and voice; but the Edmond of 1992 is to a quite remarkable degree the Edmond of 1975, as if her talent, her interests, her responses, her poetic forms and language were determined at the outset of her writing career. And perhaps fittingly, the best work in the collection is one of the oldest, the sequence "Wellington Letter," where the ruminating voice movingly recollects the lost loved one. Little new material is included, only some twenty poems not contained in previous volumes, few of those unpublished. This, then, is an excellent introduction to Edmond's poetry—and to the poetry she has yet to write.

Bernard Gadd. *World Literature Today.*
67, 1993, pp. 680–81

In *Hot October* the poet Lauris Edmond gives us her own childhood, unfictionalized: the subtitle "An autobiographical story" seems less an indication that she has tampered with the facts than a comforting protective gesture towards people who appear in the later pages under false names but could no doubt, New Zealand society being so small, be readily identified. She begins with a wonderfully immediate description of the Napier earthquake of October 1931, in which the small Edmond sisters escaped death by minutes because it happened to be playtime when their school suddenly collapsed.

The book is in three sections, two largely of narrative and a long central one consisting of letters to her mother from the young Lauris Edmond when she was a student in Wellington. The comparison with Sylvia Plath's *Letters Home* is irresistible—and unfair: apart from lively enthusiasm and occasional bursts of effusiveness Edmond's letters have little in common with Plath's. For one thing, she scarcely mentions her writing; she was a full-time student at the Teachers' Training College and a part-time one at the university, and her other energies went into drama productions, music lessons, dancing, social life and tramping—long wet treks into the mountains and rowdy, innocent nights in remote bush huts with crowds of fellow students. It was an innocent era: no sex is reported, even outside the letters to Mother, and even though it was wartime; male students went from college into the army, and on week-end leaves from their training camps took Lauris and her friends to dances or, even more to her taste, for sophisticated black coffee at the French Maid and a browse in Modern Books.

She sounds like a sensible and mature young woman; in between the agonizings and giggles over boyfriends, clothes and exams there is serious discussion of politics and ideas (a family habit: her parents were devotees of Social Credit, which she herself gradually abandoned). There are, of course, two people speaking in this book: the eager teenager and the wise, drily witty older woman who can look back with slightly bemused sympathy at her younger self, knowing what was to become of the marriage with which this account ends. There is to be another volume; I look forward to it.

Fleur Adcock. (London) Times Literary
Supplement. February 2, 1990, p. 123

EKMAN, KERSTIN (SWEDEN) 1932–

Kerstin Ekman began her literary career employing a genre generally considered devoid of artistic pretensions, the detective story. The plots of two of her first three novels, *30 m mord* (Thirty-Meter Murder), *Han rör på sig* (He's Still Alive) and *Kalla famnen* (Cold Embrace), published in rapid succession in 1959–60, draw on her association with the film industry as a writer and producer during the late 1950s. These works served to introduce Kerstin Ekman to a wide reading public and established her as the Swedish "Queen of the Detective Story," a reputation that continued to haunt her long after subsequent novels demonstrated the breadth and depth of which she was capable.

The next novel, *De tre små mästarna* (The Three Little Masters; 1961), taking its title from a Mah-Jongg configuration that provides an important twist in the plot, is in an entirely different class. When asked to what she attributed this sudden improvement in quality, Kerstin Ekman replied, "The earlier novels were so bad that I realized if I was going to continue writing I had to start taking my work seriously."[2] The story, set north of the Arctic Circle in a remote hamlet, is simple enough: while investigating a mysterious death, two outsiders, one a policeman and the other a friend of the deceased, must attempt to penetrate the silence, the collective feeling of guilt and the solidarity against intruders that they encounter among the villagers. The strength of the novel does not derive primarily from its carefully worked-out plot. What is striking, however, is the evocation of mood stemming from a nuanced, detailed attention to the natural setting and an incisive portrayal of group psychology. The style also demonstrates an abrupt departure from previous works: it is lyrical, occasionally rhapsodic. *De tre små mästarna*, which won a prize as the best Swedish detective story of 1961, was Kerstin Ekman's debut as a serious writer. . . .

Kerstin Ekman's descriptions of the labors that occupied women's lives in previous generations, descriptions unique in Swedish literature, also provide a unifying element. Largely through the detailed portrayal of a series of physical tasks, the author traces the gradual improvements in the lives of her characters and thus indirectly the betterment of the Swedish standard of living in general. Two chapters near the beginning and end of the novel respectively furnish a framework for the illustration of this process. . . .

The selection of Kerstin Ekman to fill Chair Fifteen in the Swedish Academy, left vacant by the death of Harry Martinson in 1978, was especially appropriate. Although Martinson's artistic production embraces a formal experimentation, particularly in his poetry, that is far removed from Kerstin Ekman's straightforward yet supple prose style, the two writers share both a deeply-felt empathy for those outside the mainstream of society and a sensitive rapport with the natural world.

Rochelle Wright. *World Literature Today.*
55, 1981, pp. 204, 208–9

The contemporary novelist Kerstin Ekman (b. 1932) is often seen as an heir of the realistic, socially aware vein of Swedish literature that had its origins in the Modern Breakthrough and again came to the fore in the 1930s with the epic novels of the working-class writers. In the view of some critics, her primary contribution is to have enriched the genre of the historical novel by focusing on female characters. She thereby provides an alternative perspective on events that counterbalances the male point of view that traditionally has dominated both history and fiction. . . .

The series of four novels Kerstin Ekman published between 1974 and 1983—*Häxringarna* (Magic Circles), *Springkällan* (The Spring), *Änglahuset* (Angel House), and *En stad av ljus* (A City of Light)—are, to be sure, associated with the reflowering of the traditional narrative in Sweden during the 1970s and '80s, when a number of other distinguished writers—Sven Delblanc, Sara Lidman, and Per Anders Fogelström among them—published multi-volume series with historical and provincial settings. Especially in the first two novels, Kerstin Ekman, like her contemporaries, reveals close ties to the epic tradition of the 1930s, both with respect to subject matter and style. However, in the third volume of the series, *Änglahuset,* there is a gradual displacement of documentary realism in favor of subjectivity and introspection, and in the final volume, *En stad av ljus,* external action recedes largely into the background as the first-person narrator, Anne-Marie Johannesson, explores a complex of issues having to do with the creation of a coherent self through the very process of narration. Though one can argue that this is precisely what August Strindberg, the most prominent Modern Breakthrough author and the great self-dramatizer of them all, does in his various autobiographical novels, the central concerns of *En stad av ljus* are very far removed from those of *Häxringarna*, or for that matter any novel by Moa Martinson, the only woman among the major figures of the 1930s generation. The emphasis on the transforming power of narration instead hearkens back to the transitional novel *Pukehornet* (Devil's Horn), in which Kerstin Ekman, by deliberately flaunting the conventions of the detective genre that first established her reputation, proclaims her true interests and demands to be taken seriously as a writer of fiction. . . .

Although there is little in the tetralogy that may be characterized as directly polemic, Kerstin Ekman makes it clear that society's historical failure to recognize women as full individuals with many varied capabilities and interests or to encourage them to develop to their full potential, and the continuing tendency to relegate them to their supposed biological function and the domestic sphere, are both class and gender-related issues. . . .

By choosing a nonrealistic and unconventional approach to historical subject matter in *Rövarna i Skuleskogen,* Kerstin Ekman subverts the reader's expectations of factual accuracy or narrative continuity. She does not so much present historical events from an unusual perspective as use a historical backdrop to explore fundamental issues of the human condition. History itself is a series of stories, but . . . the author distinguishes between exciting external events and adventures of the mind, preferring the latter. *Rövarna i Skuleskogen* is not a historical novel, she has commented, but rather a novel about history—about how we write our own personal narratives and how we construct a collective narrative of our shared past.

Even in her most conventionally realistic works, Kerstin Ekman periodically reminds the reader that without a story-teller, neither stories nor history can exist. In the earlier volumes of the tetralogy, the function of the narrator is to rescue from oblivion the stories of those history has forgotten. In *En stad av ljus* and *Rövarna i Skuleskogen,* the perception of the central importance of the narrative role expands to become both subject matter and theme. Without dismissing her earlier attempts to provide an alternative history, these recent works reveal her awareness of the limitations of the documentary method. Literary critics who persist in classifying Kerstin Ekman as an epic realist do an injustice to the true range of her imaginative concerns.

Rochelle Wright. *Scandinavian Studies.* 63,
1991, pp. 293–94, 297, 303

In her prose poem *Knivkastarens kvinna* (The knife-thrower's woman) Kerstin Ekman makes use of the raw specificity of the title. The insecurity of a woman at a shooting gallery, ducking and running, "without trust either in her living or her dying," is compared to a woman's infinite trust in the man at the carnival who is throwing knives aimed close to her body.

When I got this book in my hand, I was stunned. I had enjoyed Ekman's series of novels that portray three generations of women growing up, working, hating and loving one another, becoming indifferent to one another. Her new work, depicting life in a small Swedish town (Katrineholm, Ekman's hometown) from the perspective of women, does not deny that life can be mean and merciless; but the reader gets no feeling that the author has a chip on her shoulder or wants merely to score points. On the contrary, Ekman's feminist perspective seems natural and avoids underlining "the sad lot of women." With obvious delight in storytelling, she describes how women act and react to an abundance of phenomena, and it is all refreshing and stimulating—and somehow tender.

This is different. The poems narrate a story of abortion and hysterectomy, precisely the kind of things that only happen to women's bodies and which throw many women into the dark night of disgust and despair. For some the aftershock is violent self-destruction. That is the case with the knife-thrower's woman: "She has been living under The Great Above and never glanced at The Great Below. She has lived here in the lively and noisy layer of life. Now she must journey." In the hospital and later in the asylum she feels stripped of everything, even her name: "On the wall the white rectangle shines without a picture." The poem continues: "Descend, descend, in this sea / step slowly / to life or death. / Let·one wave take you / or the other. / You are on your way home / to your name."

"Descended into hell," it says in the apostolic creed. In a marvelous book, *Nedstigning: Texter kring en myt,* (Descent: Texts Around a Myth), another author, Maria Bergom Larsson, tells how, during a crisis of life and death, she got hold of the five-thousand-year-old Sumerian myth about the descent of the goddess Inanna into the kingdom of death, a myth that has many similarities with the Christian, except that here a woman is the subject. In Ekman's book we again encounter the Inanna myth, depicting the descent from The Great Above to The Great Below until the self is dead and extinguished, and then the painful journey back from suicide. "Why did you come back?" she finally asks, and her answer is deceptively simple: "I returned because I wanted to live." For both authors the myth proves adequate for interpreting horrendous experiences of life-threatening crises.

To conquer despair does not mean to get rid of despair. That cannot be done. One must learn to live with depression and to create a life like that of the knife-thrower's woman, who lives in trust: "The goddess has returned. She had allies." One quiet morning at the seashore, she is standing on a pier. The sea is breathing calmly: "Once it happens The water heals / The air is cleansed The fire is burning out / and earth begins to gather in a crevice."

Brita Stendahl. *World Literature Today.*
65, 1991, pp. 722–23

EMECHETA, BUCHI (NIGERIA) 1944–

Another writer and I were discussing the difficulty of working immediately after the birth of our children. "I wrote nothing for a year," I offered, "that didn't sound as though a baby were screaming right through the middle of it." "And I," she said, leaning forward, "was so stricken with melancholia whenever I tried to think of writing that I spent months in a stupor. Luckily," she added, still frowning at this dismal memory, "I always had full-time help." Having had a sitter only three afternoons a week, I thought she had a nerve comparing her hard time to mine.

What this woman and I needed to put our lives in perspective was a copy of Buchi Emecheta's book *Second Class Citizen.*

It was the dedication page of this novel that made me read it, because it is exactly the kind of dedication I could not imagine making myself.

> To my dear children,
> Florence, Sylvester, Jake, Christy and Alice, without whose sweet background noises this book would not have been written.

What kind of woman would think the "background noises" of *five* children "sweet"? I thought the dedication might camouflage the author's unadmitted maternal guilt, but Emecheta is a writer and a mother, and it is because she is both that she writes at all.

Adah, the central character of *Second Class Citizen,* has no memory of her existence before the age of eight. She is not positive she was eight, because, "you see, she was a girl. A girl who had arrived when everyone was expecting and predicting a boy. So, since she was such a disappointment to her parents, to her immediate family, to her tribe, nobody thought of recording her birth." Adah's "tribe" are the Ibos of Nigeria, and among the Ibos a woman's only function is to work hard around the house and have countless children, preferably boys.

It is her brother, Boy, who is routinely sent to school, while Adah is left home to learn the duties of a wife. Bright and intensely interested in learning to read, Adah sneaks off to school: because her desire to be educated is as pathetic as it is obvious, she is allowed to stay. Her parents are reminded by her teachers that, since Adah will be educated above the other girls in her age group, her bride price will be higher. In short, they will be able to make money off her.

The years pass in dreams of going to England (which Adah thinks is a kind of heaven), in hard work at home, and in study, which Adah loves. When it is time to apply to the university, however, Adah—who is now orphaned—discovers that because she has no home she will not be allowed to take the necessary exams. Because women who live alone in Ibo society are considered prostitutes, and because she needs a home to continue her education, Adah marries Francis, a lazy and spoiled perennial student who considers her his property. (And in Ibo society, she is.) Eager for elevation among her clan (a woman who has many sons eventually reaches the rank of man), Adah has two children in rapid succession, impressing everyone with her ability to reproduce as well as hold down a high-salaried civil-service job at the American consulate. When she follows Francis to London she discovers such speedy reproduction is not admired there. With children in tow and a husband who has accommodated himself to being a second-class citizen, resigned to living in a hovel (almost no one, English or otherwise, will rent to "Africans with children"), Adah must adapt to a country that is overwhelmingly racist, and to people who seem incapable of decent behavior toward their former subjects.

Ignoring her husband's advice that she too is now a second-class citizen and must accept work in a factory with the other African wives, Adah applies for a better job, in a library. To her husband's discomfiture, she gets it, but must soon give it up because she is pregnant again.

The horrors of Adah's life are many: Francis is physically abusive out of frustration at not passing the exams he came to England to study for; Adah's countrymen and women are rude and unhelpful because they consider Adah, with her first-class job, a show-off; Adah's pregnancies are hard, and her children often sick. But through it all she manages to view her situation from a cultural perspective that precludes self-pity. Early on, she makes a distinction between her husband and her children: "But even if she had nothing to thank Francis for, she could still thank him for giving her her own children, because she had never really had anything before."

And it is here that Adah makes the decision that seems to me impressive and important for all artists with children. She reasons that since her children will someday be adults, she will fulfill the ambition of her life not only for herself, but also for them. The ambition of her life is to write a novel, and on the first day she has her oldest child in a nursery and her youngest two down for their naps, she begins writing it. Since this novel is written to the adults her children will become, it is okay with her if the distractions and joys they represent in her life, as children, become part of it. (I agree that it is healthier, in any case, to write for the adults one's children will become than for the children one's "mature" critics often are).

In this way, she integrates the profession of writer into the cultural concept of mother/worker that she retains from Ibo society. Just as the African mother has traditionally planted crops, pounded maize, and done her washing with her baby strapped to her back, so Adah can write a novel with her children playing in the same room.

The first novel that Adah writes is destroyed by her husband. It would shame his parents, he claims, to have a daughter-in-law who writes. Adah leaves him and begins another book. To support herself she works in a local library, where she amuses herself listening to what are for her simplistic woes, which her British and American colleagues insist on revealing to her. She writes her novel in bits and pieces while her children are still asleep or not so quietly playing.

The book jacket makes clear the similarity between Adah's life and that of the author: "Buchi Emecheta was born in 1944 near Lagos, Nigeria, and she went to school and later married there. In 1962 she went to London, where, with her five children, she still lives, working among the black youth in Paddington. She finds time for writing by getting up at four every morning, before the demands of children and job take over."

The notion that this is remotely possible causes a rethinking of traditional Western ideas about how art is produced. Our culture separates the duties of raising children from those of creative work. I have, myself, always required an absolutely quiet and private place to work (preferably with a view of a garden). Others have required various versions of any ivory tower, a Yaddo, a MacDowell Colony.

Though *Second Class Citizen* is not stylistically exciting and is no doubt heavily autobiographical, it is no less valid as a novel. And a good one. It raises fundamental questions about how creative and prosaic life is to be lived and to what purpose, which is more than some books, written while one's children are banished from one's life, do. *Second Class Citizen* is one of the most informative books about contemporary African life that I have read.

Alice Walker. *Ms.* January, 1976, pp. 40, 106

Of all the women writers in contemporary African literature Buchi Emecheta of Nigeria has been the most sustained and vigorous voice of direct, feminist protest. . .

In Emecheta we detect . . . an increasing emphasis on the woman's sense of self, as the writer has matured and as that maturity enables her to deal more and more adeptly and convincingly with the subtleties of characterization and private introspectiveness. With Emecheta the fervor and rhetoric of protest— that is, the explicit and unequivocal denunciation of the sexual status quo— have not diminished. If anything, she has become a more effective protest writer precisely because she has been increasingly successful in blending rhetoric of impassioned protest with her maturing talent for characterization. . . .

The effectiveness of Emecheta's protest is often undercut by her short-comings as a writer. All three works suffer from lapses into banal statement and into what is, quite simply, sloppy writing that deserves more careful editing than it apparently received. . . .

Even more self-defeatingly, her criticisms of African men are often marred by generalizations that are too shrill and transparently overstated to be altogether convincing. Thus, when Adah hears that an African student is about to abandon his pregnant English girlfriend she "cursed all African men for treating women they way they do" [in *In the Ditch*]. The indictment fails to be convincing, especially in a work devoted to the disadvantages of women in *English* society, precisely because the example of male callousness which Adah chooses to attribute to African men in some special way is so patently shared by non-African men in this work and throughout Emecheta's writing as a whole. In the circumstances, the generalization seems to be merely spiteful rather than really illuminating.

In addition to these lapses in style and tone, Emecheta's rhetoric of protest often betrays symptoms of an uncritical response to Western modes of perceiving, and describing Africans. Africans appear too often as "natives" in her works, and there are the familiar Western contrasts between "civilization," on the one hand, and Nigerian "superstitions" or crudeness, on the other. This acceptance of the old Eurocentric standards is all the more disconcerting, and self-defeating, in a writer who is so obviously preoccupied with inequality and oppression as they are manifest in both language and social custom. . . .

In the final analysis, entrenched notions of male privilege and female inferiority are galling to Emecheta, not so much as questions of moral principle but as barriers to survival and self-improvement among poor women in England and emerging or developing countries like Nigeria. Her ambiguity on the subject of sexual injustice, reflects a certain ideological fuzziness, or a certain degree of naiveté, about middle-class status as a key to the unquestionable fulfillment of women as individuals and free persons. However, that very ambiguity flows from one of her significant achievements in describing the lives of British and Nigerian women: by linking the disadvantages of women with the handicaps of poverty, Emecheta places the experiences of her women within a broad context of social injustices in Great Britain, the West as a whole, and the Third World. Curiously enough, Emecheta has tried to minimize the degree to which her work links the woman's experience with other social and economic issues.

Lloyd W. Brown. *Women Writers in Black Africa* (Westport, Connecticut: Greenwood Press, 1981), pp. 35–39

The profound upheaval effected in women's lives by changes [in contemporary Africa] is the particular territory of one of the most gifted and prolific of the African women novelists, the Nigerian writer Buchi Emecheta. In less than seven years Emecheta has produced five novels: *In the Ditch* (1972), *Second Class Citizen* (1974), *The Bride Price* (1976), *The Slave Girl* (1977), and *The Joys of Motherhood* (1979). The first two autobiographical books recount the near heroism of Emecheta's performance. Through the struggles of their central character, Adah Obi, we learn how Emecheta began writing in a tiny council flat in North London, somehow carving out enough time to write from her hectic life as a university student, British Museum librarian, and single parent of five small children. An awareness of the hardships surrounding their genesis, however, is not necessary for an appreciation of Emecheta's novels and the totality of their achievement. For though they are not inter-related installments of one encompassing work, it is revealing to look at the five novels as parts or "chapters" of a larger whole—a single, continuous narrative which amounts to a kind of epic of female experience in twentieth-century Africa. Taken together, in fact, Emecheta's novels compose the most exhaustive and moving portrayal extant of the African woman, an unparalleled portrayal in African fiction and with few equals in other literatures as well. The entire realm of African female experience can be found in these books, from birth to death, with all the intermediate steps of childhood, adolescence, marriage, and motherhood. And Emecheta's historical and social breadth in the novels is equally impressive: covering a period from 1910 to the present and moving from the small Nigerian village of Ibuza which figures in all the books to westernized, urban Lagos, and finally to London, the promised land of Emecheta's Adah.

Apart from the largeness in scope, Emecheta's account of African womanhood is an unapologetically feminist one. She exposes and repudiates the feminine stereotypes of male writers such as Achebe Amadi and others, and reveals the dark underside of their fictional celebrations of the African woman. She explores the psychological and physical toll on women of such things as arranged marriages, polygamy, perpetual pregnancy and childbirth, and widowhood. The female figure hovering in the wings and background or burdened with symbolic cargo in male-authored African fiction are brought center stage by Emecheta and an entirely new drama emerges as a result of this radical change in sexual perspective.

Taken on its most stark terms, this drama involves three inter-related but also conflicting issues or problems: the oppression—sometimes tantamount to slavery—of African women; their education; and the effect upon their lives of westernization or "development" (the familiar traditional or rural versus Western or urban conflict from a new, female point of view). It is the clash among these three forces and a faltering by persistent desire for female autonomy and fulfillment that gives rise to the central dilemma posed by Emecheta's fiction. A tragic because seemingly irresolvable dilemma: the African woman, far more than the Western woman or African man, is caught in a terrible bind. In order to be free and fulfilled as a woman she must renounce her African identity because of the inherent sexism of traditional African culture. Or, if she wishes to cherish and affirm her "Africanness," she must renounce her claims to feminine independence and self-determination. Either way she stands to lose; either way she will find herself diminished, impoverished. It is Emecheta's growing awareness of the futility of attempting to resolve this dilemma that accounts for the growing bitterness we can trace in the development of her novels. Indeed, there is an almost retrogressive movement in the fiction, moving from the qualified optimism of her first book, *In the Ditch,* to the unrelieved despair of her last, the ironically entitled *Joys of Motherhood.*

The feminist narrative that we can discern in Emecheta's five novels would seem to conclude with the liberated, self-sufficient heroine of her first and second books whom we leave on the brink of successive authorship in England. With each succeeding novel Emecheta moves progressively backward, and this retreat proceeds on several levels. In *Joys of Motherhood, The Bride Price,* and *The Slave Girl* we move backward historically from the 1960s of the first two books through the fifties, forties, thirties and finally to the early decades of the century. We also retreat to the beginning of the African woman's life cycle, to her infancy and childhood in *The Slave Girl* and her adolescence, marriage and motherhood in *The Bride Price* and *Joys of Motherhood.* And finally we backtrack culturally from England to Lagos to Ibuza, the traditional village that despite the incursions of white missionaries remains relatively immune to colonial invasion. Not only, then, does Emecheta explore the plight of the contemporary woman torn between her African culture and her feminist aspiration, she also searches the past, the traditional worlds of her mother and grandmother, in order to fathom the origin of her current entrapment between two visions, two worlds, two destinies. . . .

[I]t is significant that Adah's promise is never fulfilled in Emecheta's later work. As Emecheta's gifts as a novelist developed from the awkward, diffuse autobiography of her first two books to the lyricism of *The Bride Price* and finally to the tragic dignity of *The Joys of Motherhood,* her vision of African womanhood steadily darkened. In her first novel she exhausted her imaginative vision of the African woman's struggle for freedom—an unfinished and only vaguely adumbrated struggle as it turns out. In all her subsequent novels she explored not her own success or the possibility and forms of female fulfillment, but rather the social, cultural, and historical reason why each fulfillment should seem so tenuous and problematical.

Thus Emecheta now seems to be at a crossroads in her career. She has exhaustively and definitively recorded the reality of life for African women at every stage of their lives and in all possible social and cultural contexts. Her five novels are no less than an epic account of African womanhood. The question now is whether, having explored the present and cast a searchlight back on the past, Emecheta will be able to look ahead and imagine a future for African women—a future which can embrace and integrate their African and female identities and bestow a measure of wholeness on lives that have been so fragmented and incomplete.

Katherine Frank. *World Literature Written in English.* 21, Autumn, 1982, pp. 477–79, 493–96

Buchi Emecheta has several novels and children's books to her name. In what is perhaps her best-known novel, *The Joys of Motherhood* (1979), which has been translated into many languages, the main character is Nnu Ego, the daughter of an Ibo chief in the first half of this century. Her story begins in a village in Iboland, where the life of the people is predetermined by the rules which govern their society. A woman's position depends first on her father and later her husband. Nnu Ego's first marriage fails because she is childless. Her husband's reaction is: "I am a busy man. I have no time to waste my precious male seed on a woman who is infertile." Later she is married off to a second husband, Nnaife; she despises him but has no say in the matter. It is only after she becomes pregnant that Nnu Ego manages to resign herself to her fate. She lives in the slums of Lagos, where she raises a great many children under difficult conditions, in a spirit of loving sacrifice. In the course of the book the title acquires ironic overtones, though the author recounts with considerable humor the experiences of an African woman in her relationships with men, with children and with other women. . . .

In 1980 Buchi Emecheta returned to Nigeria after an absence of many years. Her sojourn as guest lecturer at the University of Calabar in 1981 provided the inspiration for her novel *Double Yoke* (1982). The title refers to the impossible double burden which African women must bear in a modern, rapidly changing society. They must meet the demands of tradition as well as those of contemporary society. The author put both lines of thought, male and female, as she discusses such topics as the myth of virginity, the idealization of the traditional mother role, etc. In doing so she obviously flew in the face of tradition, for this was the first time the women's standpoint had been presented with such a degree of frankness. The generally accepted views always favored men. A woman who was not a virgin when she married was called a whore. Men were free to have illegitimate children, but it was a disgrace for a woman to have a child out of wedlock. Emecheta's novels are extremely popular in Nigeria and elsewhere, but they have sometimes been coolly received or even been ignored by African critics.

> Mineke Schipper. *Unheard Words: Women
> and Literature in Africa, the Arab
> World, Asia, the Caribbean, and Latin
> America* (London: Allison and Busby, 1985),
> pp. 45–46

In *The Joys of Motherhood,* the protagonist Nnu Ego, had given all her life to producing and cultivating her children, had made no friends nor taken care of herself. She had followed all the traditional guidelines concerning motherhood and care of children but she realizes too late that she had all but wasted her life. As her children begin lives of their own, and she has, as yet, no grandchildren, she feels totally dislocated. . . .

The novel starts with Nnu Ego's agony at the loss of her four week old son. She is about to commit suicide because her life is already so tied to conception and motherhood. Emecheta ironically calls this chapter "The Mother" for we realize that Nnu Ego is no longer a mother. In fact we realize in Chapter Three that she was unable to conceive in her first marriage, that she was divorced for nursing her co-wife's child with her dry breasts. The symbolism of breasts for motherhood is evident here for when we first see Nnu Ego we feel the agony of her loss as we witness her breasts oozing milk which goes to waste for her child has died. . . .

Ona, Nnu Ego's mother, is worthy of some discussion here. Ona provides another societal alternative to marriage but it is still male defined and therefore a limited alternative. Her father and her lover Agbadi strike a bargain over ownership of her unborn child based on its sex. Nnu Ego is female so she goes to her biological father Agbadi. Unfortunately the author lets Ona die during the birth of her second child and Agbadi ignores her dying wish that her daughter's life not be circumscribed by society's regulations on marriage and female roles. Ona would have been a dynamic character had she been developed by the author.

But the author's purpose is clearly to show the tragedy of woman's existence when it remains circumscribed by motherhood alone. The only reward for Nnu Ego is a good funeral and a shrine in her name. The latter is the only distinction between the slave woman and Nnu Ego. . . .

Yet the lesson of her life and death remain misunderstood by the rest of her community:

> Stories afterwards, however, said that Nnu Ego was a wicked woman even in death because, however many people appealed to her to make women fertile, she never did. Poor Nnu Ego, even in death she had no peace. Still many agreed that she had given all to her children. The joy of being a mother was the joy of giving all to your children, they said.

For the reader, however, the irony of Nnu Ego's life and death is a forceful lesson in the pains of motherhood.

Emecheta has consistently dealt with those traditional attitudes to women, including those which the woman herself accepts, which tend to enslave her. For this reason, the slave woman is a fairly common Emecheta emblem. Motherhood, therefore, is just one of the routes to woman's potential enslavement. Her other novels, *The Bride Price* (1976) and *The Slave Girl* (1977) play on this "slave to tradition" theme. Her two painful autobiographical novels *In the Ditch* (1972) and *Second Class Citizen* (1975) deal with the personal race, class and sex oppression which came out of her experiences in Nigeria and London as girl-child and woman.

Carole Boyce Davies. In Carole Boyce
Davies and Anne Adams Graves, eds.
Ngambika: Studies in African Literature
(Trenton, New Jersey: Africa World Press,
1986), pp. 252–54

Double Yoke is a love story told in the blues mode. The story laments a loss; yet it sings a love song. Its theme of the perilous journey of love, is a major preoccupation in author Buchi Emecheta's dramatic work. On an equally fundamental level, *Double Yoke* describes the tragic limitations of Nigerian women in pursuit of academic excellence and the anxiety of assimilation. Similar to her earlier novels, *Double Yoke* assesses the predicament of women in Africa. By describing the sexual and cultural politics in Nigerian society, Emecheta again campaigns against female subjugation and champions her case for female emancipation. Nko, the author's intellectually oriented heroine, provides some insight into the psyche of modern African women who are encumbered by traditional African misconceptions attached to the university-educated female.

Firstly, *Double Yoke* is a love story but with tragic implications. Buchi Emecheta is at her best in describing the anxiety lovers often experience because of mutual distrust at one time or another and the inability to reconcile their difficulties. According to the author, love, if betrayed, is directly responsible for the misery that afflicts the human soul. The tale of the terrifying journey of the possibilities and failures of love is then at the dramatic center of *Double Yoke*. . . . In *Double Yoke,* the female psyche emerges as an important quarry for concern. From multiple female voices such as Nko's, Mrs. Nwaizu's, Miss Bulewao, and Nko's roommates, emerge pertinent questions that put the nature of the female's well being at the heart of traditional African social organization. . . .

A sub-theme in *Double Yoke* is the exploration of the dilemma of men and women positioned between modernization and traditionalism in this instance on university campuses in Nigeria. Young adults become disoriented by conflicting standards of morality and the role of men and women in a changing society. . . .

Apart from Ete Kamba's inability to throw off the precepts of traditional African society which give certain prerogatives to men and deny them to women, author Emecheta points out that today's modern female is also torn between two worlds and unable to function properly in either. Nko is confused about the actual role the educated female should play in Nigerian society. The title of the book, *Double Yoke,* then is symbolic. According to the author, because educated Nigerian women are expected to play both the role of the submissive, gentle, docile female and the modern, sophisticated individual, there is confusion about which values to adopt: those of traditional African society or those of the west. Both African men and women are therefore in bondage. Living in two different cultures brings too much tension. Hence, they must live with a "double yoke" for daring to walk where angels fear to tread.

> Marie Linton Umeh. In Carole Boyce
> Davies and Anne Adams Graves, eds.
> *Ngambika: Studies of Women in African*
> *Literature* (Trenton, New Jersey: Africa
> World Press, 1986), pp. 173, 177–78

Buchi Emecheta is to date the most important African woman writer. Not only the extent of her output but also the centrality of her subject matter—the role of women in present day Africa—has put her in this position. In her treatment of her subject, she shows courage in challenging traditional male attitudes to gender roles; anger and iconoclastic contempt for unjust institutions, no matter how time honored or revered they are; and a willingness to seek new ways to subvert what she sees as the unjust subjugation of women in the name of tradition. . . .

The role of women continues to be Emecheta's main subject [in her later work] but within this unity of subject matter two of her novels depart stylistically and conceptually from the main body of work. Emecheta has described *Destination Biafra* and *The Rape of Shavi* as "imaginary works, based on ideas and ideals" (*Head above Water*). As the subject matter of *Destination Biafra* is war, the imaginative backdrop of the book is on a larger scale than her previous, mainly domestic settings. Emecheta tries to cope with army movements, war atrocities, and political deliberations and deceptions. . . .

With *The Rape of Shavi,* Emecheta leaps into fantasy but keeps a firm grip on the didactic purpose that runs through all her work. An allegory about the relationship between Europe and Africa, the novel begins in an unknown place some time in the future after a rumored nuclear holocaust, but in the course of events the action moves very much into the present and into known localities. It also sums up the history of the European conquest of Africa. . . . The idealization of pre-contact African society is a countercurrent in Emecheta's writing. In her previous books, the emphasis has been on the negative aspects of traditional African (Ibo) culture, gender roles, and slavery in particular, and Britain, despite its racism, was seen as offering the freedom of social mobility through individual initiative and effort. *The Rape of Shavi* cannot be said to moderate this view, as it is in too sharp a contrast to it. Emecheta seems to be searching for the best values in the world views of her two civilizations, but as they appear stubbornly incompatible, she lands, so to speak, in mid-culture.

Mid-culture is also the center of *Gwendolen,* but in this novel, which represents a return to the social realism of the earlier books, Emecheta tackles the problems of converging and conflicting values in a much more direct manner and with a clearer vision of her own position. . . .

The book starts off in Jamaica, where Gwendolen is left behind with her grandmother as first her father, and later her mother, leave for "Moder Kontry" and settle in London. While in her grandmother's care, Gwendolen is molested sexually by Uncle Johnny, who misuses his position as an old family friend and supporter of grandmother in difficult times. This is an important aspect of the concept of incest, for it shows the vulnerability of children in adult relationships. Although the grownups in the village condemn Uncle Johnny when Gwendolen finally tells her secret, her grandmother is annoyed at losing his support, and the village casts Gwendolen, here called June, as a wicked girl. She is given a second chance when her family sends for her, not entirely out of love, but to help look after the three younger children, born in London. Her arrival there gives Emecheta the opportunity to describe immigrant slum conditions through Gwendolen's eyes, which are innocent of the social meaning of her observation. Slowly these observations situate the family at the very bottom of the social scale, illiterate and unable to cope with the complexities of British society, like getting a council flat, but surviving and gaining pleasure and support from a primitive church community.

Her grandmother dies and her mother goes back to Jamaica. During her mother's absence her father starts an incestuous relationship with Gwendolen, who at sixteen has stopped going to school and is looking after her brothers and sister. She becomes pregnant, but at the same time she meets a white boy, another departure in Emecheta's work; she starts a sexual relationship with him, much to her father's relief, as he hopes that the boy friend can take the blame for the baby.

On her return, her mother harbors uneasy but unspoken feelings, which evolve into hatred toward Gwendolen who leaves home and is taken into care after a brief spell in a mental hospital. The outcome is optimistic, if slightly confusing. The father commits suicide, the mother is forced to acknowledge the paternity of the baby when she is confronted with it—it is black, not colored, and looks like her husband—and she turns her anger toward her husband, still not completely reconciling with her daughter. Gwendolen lives with the baby in a council flat and is happy, and her boy friend remains a friend in spite of the shame of the baby's paternity. This ending is seen as "modern": A new set of relationships emerges, formed on the basis of personal choice in opposition to blind adherence to the inherited patterns of race and family relationships. There seems to be an implicit suggestion that this alternative social organization might prevent a repetition of Gwendolen's experiences.

This willingness to search for new ways of social and sexual organization and to change views when social circumstances alter, combined with forthright anger, makes Emecheta a controversial writer. Her criticism of aspects of African tradition invites the charge of traitor to her culture; and her feminism, which viewed through Western eyes is mild (she refuses to be called a "feminist"), has enraged critics—mainly African and male—who have made vitriolic attacks on her books, claiming that they misrepresent Ibo society. Some of that criticism makes one suspect that her books are indeed true and of vital importance.

Kirsten Holst Petersen. In Robert L. Ross,
ed. *International Literature in English:*
Essays on the Major Writers (New York:
Garland, 1991), pp. 283, 287–90

ENCHI FUMIKO (JAPAN) 1905–86

The name Enchi Fumiko is already familiar to Western readers from *The Waiting Years,* the translation of her work *Onnazaka* (1957), in which Tomo the stoic heroine endures long years of humiliation by her husband, who not only keeps her and his two mistresses all under the same roof, but even seduces his young daughter-in-law. The combination of a minutely thought-out development of the story, fine psychological depiction of many characters, and a powerfully effective conclusion has brought deserved praise to this work. Interestingly, however, not all her novels and short stories are like

Onnazaka. For example, while she has continued to write realistic novels, she has also written several works that combine realism and fantasy. Also, while the women in *Onnazaka,* with the possible exception of Tomo's daughter-in-law, abide by the old feudal morality imposed upon them, many other women portrayed by Enchi freely violate that code, committing adultery and seducing young men. Indeed, one of the recurrent elements in these works is overt female sensuality expressed by an eroticism quite distinct from that found in *Onnazaka*.

This difference is quite intentional. Enchi says that a writer should experiment with new styles, new themes, or whatever, at each decade of the writer's life in order not to fall into a predictable set of mannerisms. In an interview, she reveals that it was only after her position as a writer had been established, with *Onnazaka* in 1957, that she became more confident and felt bold enough to write what she really wanted to write, without being concerned with readers' negative reactions. Presumably, then her subsequent works should provide a more accurate reflection of Enchi's true preference of theme. This paper will examine her depiction of female sensuality in narratives that combine both realism and fantasy. . . .

First, her genuine erudition takes her readers very naturally to a fascinating world of classical literature. Secondly, the lovemaking in these works is more ethereal than real, and this unrealistic treatment of sex brings, rather than harsh realism, a soft and delicate eroticism, particularly in the latter two works. Thirdly, Enchi's interest is more in the sexual impulse than in the act itself. For example, no matter how many men Yukiko may sleep with, Enchi's concern is not the comparison of sex among them, but rather the special power Yukiko possesses to attract all those men. Fourthly, although Enchi often uses older women who are in love with much younger men, she gives them a stoicism and common sense that they have acquired through age. And, by doing so, she maintains the dignity of the novel.

Lastly, we should add a brief reference to Enchi's minute attention to literary style, using her own words.

> I don't use the words which sound distasteful to my womanly sense . . . even though this strict selection may narrow down my vocabulary. In Tanizaki's work, there are lots of scenes in which one relieves oneself in the bathroom. But one notices that because of the nature of the description, he is all the more careful to use the right words, and the reader is never left with a foul aftertaste. That is what I call aesthetic eroticism in style.

One can say then that Enchi has succeeded in her effort to create erotic literary works on an aesthetic level.

Yoko McClain. *Journal of the Association of Teachers of Japanese.* 15, 1980, pp. 32–33, 44

In Japanese Buddhist tradition as seen in the masked play of the Noh, woman's fate lies in the fact that love leaves her with jealousies and resentments which tie her to the abyss between *yume* (dream) and *utsutsu* (reality), an abyss from which she struggles to be liberated into the realm where all is one. This classic theme has been carried into the modern novel by Fumiko Enchi, who is often said to be Japan's finest woman novelist. In her novel of 1957, *Onnazaka* (translated as *The Waiting Years* in 1971), she tells the story of Tomo Shirakawa, who hides her *honné* of jealousy and resentment under a mask of *tatemae;* Tomo masks herself as the perfectly obedient wife who finds agreeable maids to serve the household and to be the concubines of its master. The serene mask worn by Tomo Shirakawa is reminiscent of the masks worn by the actors who play the wives in the "woman play" cycle of the Noh repertoire. Like theirs, Tomo's mask reveals her true feeling about her husband in her shocking deathbed demand that her ashes be scattered rather than buried with his in the family vault. In Japan this is the ultimate insult to the bloodline of the husband. Tomo's final victory over him completes the circle of her struggle. As in the Noh, enlightenment arrives for the woman who has battled her passions and been tortured by them.

But it is in *Onna men,* of 1958 (literally, "Women's Masks"), that Fumiko Enchi develops most thoroughly the metaphor of women's veiled actions compared with the masks of the Noh "woman plays." Divided into three parts, each with the name of a Noh mask as a title to indicate an aspect of woman's character, *Masks* tells the story of a woman who is tormented by resentment after her husband's mistress, a maid in the house, trips her, causing the wife to miscarry. The wife's struggle to regain her own independent identity by repaying her husband's infidelity in secret, again by insulting his bloodline, results in her becoming a masked woman who manipulates others to achieve her revenge. But her revenge is her victory, and her skill in keeping her *honné* hidden until all is accomplished shows her woman's burden of sin, and her ability to endure much suffering as well as the mystery of femininity. . . .

Fumiko Enchi is fascinated with the classic Japanese theme of the feminine obsession with jealousy, resentment, revenge, and an attachment to things of this world that can endure beyond the grave. In her novel the poses, the veiled actions symbolized by the mask reveal both the true self of the heroine and the true nature of woman. The three Noh masks Enchi uses as the three chapter headings in her novel are not meant as metaphors for individual characters, but as symbols for different aspects of woman's character itself. The qualities embodied in these masks are quite specific: Ryo no onna (literally, "spirit woman") "represents the vengeful spirit of an older woman tormented beyond the grave by unrequited love"; Masugami (showing the face of a young woman in a state of frenzy), portrays repressed sexuality, a state in which the cold contours of the mask conceal an attraction to violence; and Fukai is the mask of the "deep well," the deep woman. The masks portray types; the women, actresses who wear them in turn. Mieko, for example, is described as "a quiet mountain lake whose waters are rushing beneath the surface toward a waterfall." Hers is "the face on a Noh mask, wrapped in her own secrets," but she is clearly drawn as an individual masked woman rather than a representative of a specific mask.

> Catherine Broderick. In Sharon Spencer, ed.
> *Anaïs, Art, and Artists* (Greenwood,
> Florida: Penkevill Press, 1986), pp. 180–87

Enchi's autobiographical trilogy, *Ake o ubau mono* (1957; One who steals red), *Kizu aru tsubasa* (1962; The injured wing), and *Niji to shura* (1968; Rainbow and carnage), is probably more representative of her work. In these novels she depicts a woman's loveless, acrimonious marriage and her relationships with other men. The heroine's intense frustration as a novelist undoubtedly parallels Enchi's own experience before she established herself as a writer. She received the fifth Tanizaki Jun'ichirō Award for the trilogy in 1969.

It is in many of her short stories that Enchi often exhibits her profound knowledge of classical Japanese literature by weaving elements from it into contemporary settings, which become fascinating combinations of reality and fantasy, actuality and apparition. For example, in "Nise no enishi: shūi" (1957; The conjugal ties: Gleanings), she borrows the theme of a mysterious tale with the same title by Ueda Akinari (1734–1809), in which a man long dead returns to life, to create a bizarre story about a woman who gives herself over to wild fantasies.

One of Enchi's latest accomplishments is the translation into modern Japanese of *The Tale of Genji,* the long eleventh-century tale by the court lady Murasaki Shikibu; Enchi succeeds well in reproducing the sensitivity of the original.

Now in her mid-seventies, Enchi is highly respected by critics for her profound knowledge of classical Japanese literature, her careful choice of words, and her literary versatility. Yet her work is also loved by the general public for being neither overintellectual nor too theoretical.

> Yoko McClain. In Leonard S. Klein, ed. *Far*
> *Eastern Literatures in the 20th Century*
> (New York: Ungar Publishing, 1986),
> pp. 92–93

The ultimate revival of the feminine voice in fiction had to wait until a few years after Ichiyō's death.

The revival was accomplished by Enchi Fumiko (1905–86), who in 1985 became only the second female author to receive Japan's highest award—the Bunka Kunshō, or the Order of Cultural Merit. Enchi personifies what I see as the three crucial contributions of female writers to contemporary Japanese writing. She is, to begin with, the first woman to establish a clear, sustained literary voice for herself in almost seven centuries. Second, while she was not what we today might consider a feminist, Enchi was one of several writers who were instrumental in the overthrow of the narrow, narratorially strangled genre of autobiographical fiction (the *shi-shōsetsu* or "I" novel) created by male writers in the first decade of the twentieth century. Enchi's work is the most powerful challenge to the male-dominated "I" novel that has been produced in Japan until very recent times.

The third element of Enchi's work that I find compelling is the direct link that she has to classical Japanese women's literature—to *The Tale of Genji,* in particular, but also to other works from the traditional canon. It is primarily through this link that Enchi has been able to find her own literary voice and to view herself in some respects as a literary reincarnation of the female authors of the eleventh century. Enchi's fiction is populated with ghosts, spiritual mediums, scholars who study spirit possession, and all manner of characters who travel back and forth between past and present, between life and death, between body and soul. This constant movement has the effect of closing the gap between the Heian period, when women still had a literary voice, and the present, where Enchi struggles to establish hers.

Reading works such as *Onnazaka* (The waiting years, 1957; trans. 1971) or *Onnamen* (Masks, 1958; trans. 1983), one gets the strong impression that the living ghost (the *ikiryō*) of a Heian woman writer has found lodging within the withered, tormented body of a contemporary shamaness, and that the voice which speaks to us through Enchi's narrators is filled with strength, passion and fury. The contrast between the calm, socially acceptable exterior of Enchi's women—often described in terms of masks, of heavily concealing makeup, or as actresses playing dictated roles—and the hot emotions bubbling beneath the surface create dynamic tension in her writings. Enchi takes decaying forms—physical bodies now beyond actual sexual contact—and classical literary images and infuses both with a new, terrifying, cynically modern compulsiveness.

In Enchi's story "Nise no En—Shūi" (A bond for two lifetimes—gleanings, 1957; trans. 1982), a vibrant, widowed woman serves as scribe for a physically debilitated scholar as he translates a seventeenth-century Ueda Akinari tale into modern Japanese. Enchi has produced a masterpiece in this story, and one of its strongest qualities is the superb irony that pervades it. The female scribe in the story is the only character who is truly alive: The professor whose words she records on paper is shriveled and impotent and needs help using his bedpan, but even in that condition, he and all the other men who appear are depicted as slaves to lust. The relations between men and women, Enchi suggests, are the only bonds that last for more than one lifetime—bonds that are stronger than religious devotion or anything else. By the end of the story, the scribe is able to accept and forgive what she describes as the "inevitable sexual aggressions of men" and feels an "unsettling agitation" that "warms her heart" when she fantasizes herself as the object of that passion.

It is perhaps inevitable that when Japanese women sit down to write, to create, they become immediately aware of the irony of their situation: In the external world, they are considered to have no power, no influence. Their public task is to stay out of public. Privately, however, they can tap enormous resources of power and control, enjoying all manner of victories on the hidden, emotional underface of society. That, I would suggest, is the social origin of irony in women's literature; but whatever it comes from, an author such as Enchi embodies both the power and the frustrations of a woman in the contradictory tangle of Japanese male-female relationships. Her characters are midwives in the creation of culture and literature.

Van C. Gessel. Japan Quarterly.
35, 1988, pp. 411–12

Fumiko Enchi. . . is widely and justly acclaimed for her skills as a storyteller, for the social issues regarding women that she raises, and for the atmosphere of otherworldliness that she so effectively creates. There seems, however, to be little discussion of her talents in structuring a narrative. That may result partly from the fact that *Onnazaka* (1957; *The Waiting Years*), for all its fine qualities, betrays some fundamental weaknesses in its structure and mode of narration, and that the more mature work, *Onnamen* (1958; *Masks*), is still more distinguished for the atmosphere of horror and spirit-possession that it invokes than for any particularly dazzling narratorial effects.

The aim of this essay is to study Enchi as a creator of narrative structures through an examination of the novel which is most impressively shaped, her 1965 work *Namamiko monogatari* (A tale of false oracles). Despite its central position in Enchi's oeuvre and its likely status as her masterpiece, it has been little discussed by Japanese critics, and few of their comments have touched directly on the techniques of narration in the novel. This is unfortunate, since it is likely that Enchi intended *Namamiko monogatari* to take its place alongside *The Waiting Years* and *Masks* as a kind of informal trilogy echoing aspects of her lifelong attraction to the *Tale of Genji*. For if *The Waiting Years* is in some sense a view of a modern, fallen *Genji* world as seen through the eyes of a long-suffering Lady Aoi, and if *Masks* can be regarded as a shift to the perspective of Lady Rokujō, then *Namamiko monogatari* is to a certain degree a re-creation of the ideal, a reenshrinement of the Shining Prince as seen through the eyes of the faithful, loving Murasaki. . . .

It is this quality of falseness that I find most intriguing in the narrative construction of *Namamiko monogatari*. There is such a burden of falsehood in the work that one begins to question every item of information that is related. Clearly the story itself is false: Enchi has fabricated the existence of a previously undiscovered classical narrative, and she has added fictive elements to a historical tale already slightly shaky in its claims to total historicity. The frame in which the story is set is bogus, despite Enchi's exaggerated claims to the contrary. Virtually all the characters in the story are duplicitous in their dealings with one another, even though many of them are claimed in the tradition to be paragons of refinement and virtue among the court aristocracy.

In the midst of all this fraudulence Enchi plants an innocent, idyllic, purportedly "true" love story involving Ichijō and Teishi. They are presented as cranes on the dungheap, paragons of simple virtues that are being trampled all around them. I suppose it is possible to focus one's attention upon the beautiful, moving harmony of that relationship and regard it as Enchi's central thrust in the novel, but she has applied so many of her authorial energies to the creation of the spurious frame into which this love story is cast that I cannot help but wonder what her true concerns really are. . . .

Enchi as narratorial medium has possessed a segment of her readers and spoken to them in the voice of Teishi, declaring the purity of her intentions and the spotlessness of her love. Others of us, however, have been inhabited by the *ikiryō* of the false shameness Kureha, and the voice that speaks to us from the text suggests that every human communication is a mixture of truth and falsehood, that history in the red is only one of several tales that could be told about the course of human events, and that the apparatus to sort out the voice of the true oracle from those of the many sham mediums is not available to us mere mortals. Enchi's tale, with its mingling and scrambling of pure and false intermediaries—in a manner effectively reminiscent of Tanizaki in *A Portrait of Shunkin* (1933) or Akutagawa in "Hell Screen" (1918) or "In a Grove" (1922)—successfully communicates only one truth: that no form of narrative message can be regarded as the final word.

Van C. Gessel. World Literature Today.
62, 1988, pp. 180–85

Enchi Fumiko's *Onnamen,* translated by Juliet Winters Carpenter as *Masks,* was published in Japan two years before Ōhara's work. That Western readers had to wait twenty-seven years for their own version of this extraordinary work is one of the crimes of the century. *Masks* is a chilling, literate, challenging novel, one of the best of several works in which Enchi details the phenomenally destructive power that gushes from the soul of a woman scorned. Complementing a convoluted plot of revenge carefully orchestrated by the female protagonist is a web of associations which Enchi weaves between her narrative and the Lady Rokujō sections of *Genji.* Mieko is like a pressure-cooker set on high, the destructive energy relentlessly mounting within an enclosed space until it cannot but explode, destroying everything around her—friend and foe, and ultimately the encasement of her own vengeful soul. It is, my students frequently claim, a "weird" book, but one with the power to enchant and seduce the reader in the same way that Mieko takes over the minds and bodies of her daughter and daughter-in-law. It is a book that cannot be forgotten.

Van C. Gessel. Journal of Japanese Studies.
15, 1989, pp. 446–47

ENGEL, MARIAN (CANADA) 1933–85

In *Bear,* Canadian novelist Marian Engel's heroine finds her identity and learns how to live her life through an encounter with reality in the form of the wilderness. The meeting is archetypal, reminiscent of the confrontation with the "night of first ages" experienced by Marlow and Kurtz in Conrad's *Heart of Darkness.* Although there are important differences between Engel's and Conrad's handling of this theme, the parallels in plot, setting, concepts, and symbolism in these works suggest that Engel, perhaps without being aware of it, found in *Heart of Darkness* an inspiration for *Bear.*

S. A. Cowan. *Ariel.* 12, 1981, p. 73

Marian Engel's *Bear* has received a good deal of popular attention, part of it from readers who are attracted to the sort of thing promised by the blurb on the cover of the paperback edition: "The shocking, erotic novel of a woman in love." The promise, one notes, is, for the most part, kept, but the novel is likely to be of interest for a good deal longer than most books of this sort because it is much more than the story of a woman in love with a bear. In fact, the novel can be read on several levels, and there is much in it to delight the academic critic as well as the casual reader.

One starting place for the academic critic is the classification of a work, the attempt to see it in relation to other works. If we start in this way with *Bear,* we must say that it is a romance, and that the conventional action of romance—the quest in search of treasure which is guarded by a monster—lies behind the action of this novel. "I don't suppose you found any buried treasure," Joe King says to Lou, and Lou herself is aware of the pattern when she thinks of the word "Treasure" in going through the trunks in the basement. Here we have a realistic version of that romance action: a journey undertaken by an archivist to catalogue the contents of a house, material which may be valuable for historical or literary reasons; the only inhabitant of the estate is a bear. But this external action is not the novelist's main concern. Indeed, Lou finds little of lasting value in the house, and, contrary to expectations when the chief setting is an old and mysterious house, there are no surprises to be discovered. At the end, the house is "empty" and "enormous": "She had not found its secrets. It was a fine building, but it had no secrets."

More important than outer events is the inner action. The story is an account of the renewal of Lou herself, a rebirth, or (in psychological terms) the achievement of an integrated personality. At the beginning of the novel, Lou is a fragmented individual, with dried-up feelings and a barren intellect; at the end, she is healed and whole, and she feels "strong and pure." We are alerted to this pattern, perhaps too obviously, by Lou's first postcard to the director: "'I have an odd sense . . . of being reborn.'" But if the reference to the nature of the action is obtrusive, the patterns by which it is worked out are satisfyingly subtle and complex. . . .

The fact that the house is central may perhaps be traced back to Engel's first concept of the book. It was, she told an interviewer in the *Toronto Star,* to be a short story for an erotic anthology to be published by the Writers' Union of Canada:

> I thought, "All pornography takes place in an isolated palace," so I built my isolated palace—the white octagonal house—then in walked a bear. I don't know where he came from, just from somewhere in my psyche.
>
> Well, it was no good as a pornographic story, but the idea was too good to waste, so it became a novel.

The "isolated palace" in pornography represents the fulfilment of sexual desires, its isolation providing the freedom to act out such desires without the usual social or moral restrictions. The "white octagonal house" retains the character of its pornographic predecessor, but goes considerably beyond it to suggest the fulfilment of desires that are wider in scope and more admirable in character.

Bear is an unusually good novel. The patterns . . . are woven together in a subtle and complex way. We have no sense that actions are forced or details thrust upon us. Everything is carefully observed and fully realized. If, as Margaret Avison has said, the devil is etc., there is no devil in this book. We live "sweetly and intensely" with Lou and her bear, exploring, like her, the infinite richness of simplicity.

Donald S. Hair. *Canadian Literature.*
92, 1982, pp. 34–35, 44

Response to Engel's *Bear* indicates that the average reader sees the novella in much the same way as Lou initially sees Cary's notes on bears. The truncation of Lou's character, and the cryptic nature of the book's style, are suggestive of an elusive inner logic which is as informative, and as mystifying, as the fragmented notes. In the same way that the notes seem trivial, irrelevant glosses on more "significant" works, the novella has struck many (critics as well as casual readers) as trivial, a badly-executed exercise in symbol-mongering, demanding, as the notes do, an effort of faith and I-Ching to release a dubious significance. But in the same way that the notes and the bear are necessary qualifiers of the Victorian vision embodied in house and library, the novella is a valuable extension of the world of articulated human experience right here in the twentieth century.

Michelle Gadpaille. *Canadian Literature.*
92, 1982, p. 154

Bear won the Governor General's Award for the best Canadian novel of 1976 and rightly so, I think, because it is quintessentially Canadian. It is a Canadian pastoral about landscape and wilderness, about a quest, about a bear, about the relation between civilization and savage nature. Like *Surfacing* it is a pastoral written by a woman, but it offers even more radical alternatives to the conventions of pastoral and animal stories, for what *Bear* does is attempt to inscribe female sexuality on the wilderness. A curious mixture of tradition and innovation, *Bear* erects a complex structure of pastoral, pornography, and myth in its exploration of desire and our unattainable dreams of communion and transcendence through sex, through wild nature, through mystic vision. Inevitably dreams have to confront real possibilities of limits and transgressions and in the end can have their fulfillment only in fantasy and myth. This is the territory of *Bear* as it traces a woman's experiences on an island in Northern Ontario in the late 1970s. . . .

There has always been a bear on the estate; bears are part of the Cary family's history, for the first Colonel Cary, following the model of Lord Byron whom he had met at Malta, had a tame bear, and there is a bear there still. It is this bear whose massive presence comes to pervade the novel, taking possession first of the house and then of Lou's consciousness and fantasy life. The story develops as a summer idyll of her love affair with the bear, which is for Lou a regenerative experience releasing imaginative energies and allowing her to make vital connections with her own hidden nature and with the natural world outside herself. It might be seen as a process of "de-creation" where Lou gets rid of her socially acquired persona and pushes to the very demarcation line between humanity and nature or animality. But with the end of the summer comes the end of the idyll: Lou's work is finished, the bear, obeying its natural rhythms, is getting ready to hibernate; finally it is the bear who draws the demarcation line between them and shows her what is forbidden by natural law. As Lou attempts to copulate with him, the bear reaches out one paw and rips the skin on her back from shoulder to buttock. Only then does she realize the gap between the animal and the human and retreat to her side of the line, dismissing the bear and waving a burning stick at him. She gets ready to leave; the bear is taken away by an old Indian woman, and having made her farewells, Lou starts her drive back to Toronto. She is the same yet not the same, her old self but "at last human," in transition between the wilderness and the city, between old patterns and new possibilities—and comforted as she drives at night by the constellation of the Great Bear in the sky.

In this final transformation sexual longing dissolves by the light of the stars into a vision which is close to mystical communion. *Bear* emerges as a feminized version of the Canadian wilderness myth, a quest for unity of being through loving connection between the human and the natural worlds. Such desires have their realization only in fantasy or myth, though as Jay Macpherson remarks, "the power to dream is not mere passivity or escape, but is creative and transforming, a kind of art."

Coral Ann Howells. *Ariel.* 17, 1986,
pp. 105–6

ERB, ELKE (GERMANY) 1938–

In 1978, the East German poet Elke Erb published a collection of fifty-nine short poetical texts, entitled *The Thread of Patience* (*Der Faden der Geduld*). Fifteen of these texts had already appeared in an earlier volume, *Reports* (*Gutachten*), published in 1975. To the reader's surprise, the collection "The Thread of Patience" begins with a poem by the Dadaist Hans Arp: "I am once again a real house. / I am not like the other houses / a pigtail with two legs / an egg with wings / a pyramid goiter." The Arp poem establishes the tone, signaling that what will follow are experiments in form, new linguistic formulations, and new and confusing ways of lending meaning, if that is even still possible. Luckily, tacked onto the end of the little book is a "Conversation with Elke Erb," conducted by Christa Wolf, in which the reader learns that there is good reason for his or her inability to understand most of these texts. Christa Wolf becomes the reader's advocate, in that she articulates what the reader him(her)self has already noticed: "[The] new texts [are] disobliging; unaccommodating; incomprehensible; encoded. I believe," continues Wolf, "a good number of these defy understanding. I feel myself an incompetent, not even in a position . . . to intervene with questions." Socialist Realism is a concept that scarcely allows itself to be clearly defined anymore; such is the extent to which the personal-private sector has invaded the social, and to which new structures and forms of expression have pushed aside the old hackneyed clichés. Yet despite this great alteration in artistic forms and themes, a generally applicable fundamental gesture—a recognizable concern—still makes itself apparent, which aims at communication. . . .

Such literature, it is clear, must have a provocative and inflammatory effect within the context of a cultural program that orients itself toward social engagement. It is almost completely devoid of social-political themes, and when they are present, their appearance is muddled. In comparing the new texts from *The Thread of Patience* with the texts from Erb's earlier volume *Reports,* we detect a clear tendency toward cryptic obscurantism, and a tone of coldness, distance, but also of rebellion and anger. In reference to her own randomly manipulated linguistic formulations, she writes in her essay "The Physicists" about the technical language used by scientists that is completely incomprehensible to the lay population: "It's all right if they do that," which implies: It is not all right if I do. What stands out is the fact that her least accessible texts, those which are pure experiments in form, were composed after the Biermann Affair of November 1976. Erb was one of the many who stood up for the expatriate political singer Wolf Biermann in a written request directed at the GDR government authorities. In an essay written in February of 1977 entitled "Coincidences and Patience" ("Zufälle und Geduld"), Erb warns in a striking formulation: "Patience. What does patience have to do with violence? It is hard. It is as hard as it is soft. It endures and it waits. It is good. It tolerates no last word. This is not my last word." Are Erb's texts a rebellion against regimentation, a rebellion that manifests itself in linguistic experimentation and provocative hermetics? "At some point, over a long period of time," the poet reflects, "I dissembled my presuppositions and destroyed them within me: that certain way of being trapped, wanting to follow, wanting to be led, wanting and having to believe." Is the issue here a complete loss of illusions? Let us remember that the roots of the Dada Movement, too, lay in a loss of illusions. The volume *The Thread of Patience* was characterized by Christa Wolf as a "retreat from the joy of communication, retreat from any recognizable 'concern.'" Obstinacy and a feeling of pulling back within oneself are the apparent sponsors of the little book. Nowhere is this made clearer than in a short "dadaist" witticism made by the poet on February 21, 1977, entitled "The Visit": "Bashfulness in the countryside: If someone knocks, say 'the door' instead of 'come in!'"

Christine Cosentino. *Germanic Notes.*
13, 1982, pp. 5–6, 8

Elke Erb is a critic—Sarah Kirsch scholars will know her Kirsch article, which is included in *Erklärung einiger Dinge;* she is an editor, with several editions to her name—the Kirsch article, for example, is the afterword to her 1977 Reclam (Leipzig) edition of Kirsch's poetry, *Musik auf dem Wasser;* she is a translator of Russian poetry and prose (Gogol, Blok, Bedny, Pasternak). And, last but not least, she is a poet. Two collections of her work have appeared thus far in the GDR: *Gutachten* (1975) and *Der Faden der Geduld* (1978); a third volume is scheduled for publication in 1983 (by Aufbau). In the West, Wagenbach published a sampling from the two GDR collections, entitled *Einer schreit: Nicht!,* in 1976; and a selection of Erb's new texts, *Trost,* was published by Deutsche Verlags-Anstalt in 1982. In spite of these publications, however, Elke Erb the writer is relatively unknown—unfortunately, for especially her more recent work, her unconventional striving for immediacy in her writing, and her experiments with language are worthy of attention. . . .

Characteristic of the texts included in *Gutachten*—and of Erb's poetic signature in general—is the exact describing of objects or events. Many of her poems and miniatures—not only in *Gutachten* but, in spite of changes in form and poetic philosophy, in *Faden der Geduld* and *Trost* as well, the discussion of which we can anticipate in this regard—are portraits: physical and psychological portrayals of people in everyday situations. With a few succinct phrases—and with no attempt to provide a background or to explain why this should be so—she sketches their essential being. . . .

Elke Erb's attempt to exclude the auctorial voice, to present uninterpreted reality to the reader, is at odds with the official socialist view of art and the function of the writer (according to which the writer is expected to be an interpreter of reality). It is also contrary to most literary practice in the GDR. No matter whether counted among the officially favored or among the "dissidents"—or somewhere in between—GDR writers tend to preserve the editorial voice of the author; the author directs and guides the reader—whether in feigned omniscience or as one engaged in a personal struggle for truth in which the reader is invited to participate. As a rule, GDR writers are intermediaries—and consciously so—between the reader and "reality." Elke Erb, on the other hand, makes no special effort to be understood by her readers; she hopes that the reader will somehow comprehend what it is that she is trying to convey—"in einem günstigen Augenblick."

> Margy Gerber. *Studies in GDR Culture and
> Society, 3* (Lanham, Maryland: University
> Press of America, 1983), pp. 251, 253, 258

ERDRICH, LOUISE (UNITED STATES) 1954–

Set in North Dakota and depicting the lives of the sometimes loosely connected, sometimes over-connected members of the Kashpaw and Lamartine families (Chippewa Indians interbred with white trash), *Love Medicine* is a novel about survival, about going home (both locally and metaphysically), about true and false spirits (gods, demons, powers). With seven narrators and an occasional word from the authorial voice, Louise Erdrich covers fifty years (1934–84) of her characters' on- and off-reservation lives. The narratives overlap; they are composed of memories and current events. Each narrator is innocent about, while contributing to, the wider significance of the book. So, Nector Kashpaw, in his forties in 1957, tells how the priest at his high school "would teach no other book all four years but *Moby-Dick*," and of how he identified with Ishmael. . . .

Erdrich also borrows Melville's symbol of the crushing opponent, the omnipotent enemy. The monster's whiteness is significant, for, while this is a novel that concentrates on individuals, the politics of being an American Indian are not forgotten. . . .

Death, rather than doom, pervades the novel. While the characters do keep bouncing to the surface in their coffins (and, like the original Ishmael, they are all, of course, outcasts) when their lives are obsolete, they have the capacity to embrace oblivion like their old tribal forefathers; Henry Lamartine sits in his car on the railroad track; Henry Junior dives into a swirling river; Nector purposely chokes to death; and June Kashpaw begins an epic march "home":

> Even when it started to snow she did not lose her sense of direction. Her feet grew numb, but she did not worry about the distance. The heavy winds couldn't blow her off course. She continued. Even when her heart clenched and her skin turned crackling cold it didn't matter, because the pure and naked part of her went on.

Death for the Indian, like the Catholic, is not the end, but, while Sister Leopolda, the terrifying "saint" who had fought the young Marie's demons with a window pole, a poker, a bread fork and scalding water, looks forward only to a transfigured afterlife, many of the Indian characters experience timeless moments in their earthly lives. They recognize, heathenishly, the forces of nature; they have a sense more of mutability than of salvation: Lipsha, for instance, on the dandelion (and the Indians), "The spiked leaves full of mother's milk. A buried root. A nuisance people dig up and throw in the sun to wither. A globe of frail seeds that's indestructible."

This richly complex first novel is an expert combination of teller's tales, family saga, tribal consciousness, and of reportage on the anomalous position of the Red Indian in modern society. While the threads (with the book's shifts in time and voice) are initially hard to follow, there is a real sense for the reader, at the end, of having acquired much more than a sum of the book's parts.

Linda Taylor. (London) *Times Literary Supplement.* February 22, 1985, p. 196

Love Medicine, a first novel by Louise Erdrich which recently won the National Book Critics Circle Award, is very much a poet's novel. By that I mean that the book achieves its effect through moments of almost searing intensity rather than through the rise, climax, and closing of a sustained action, and that its stylistic virtuosity has become almost an end in itself. The prose indeed has remarkable energy and sensuousness. But I found *Love Medicine* a hard book to penetrate. The episodes, most of them dramatic monologues, are loosely strung together and the relationships of the various narrators and characters are so confusing that one must constantly flip back to earlier sections in an effort to get one's bearings. The reader who perseveres will undergo an imaginary adoption into a nearly forgotten American Indian tribe.

The subject has much documentary interest. Louise Erdrich, who is herself of Chippewa descent, has created a scroll-like account of the often squalid, demoralized, but at times rhapsodic lives of the Kashpaws, Lazarres, Lamartines, Nanapushes, and Morrisseys—Indian and part-Indian families living on a Chippewa reservation in western North Dakota. The novel begins in 1981, moves back to 1934, and then forward by stages to the present. . . .

On the face of it, the factual details presented by Louise Erdrich combine to give an appalling account of the lives of contemporary Indians on a reservation—impoverished, feckless lives far gone in alcoholism and promiscuity. Bitter pride alternates with shame; away from the reservation some of them try to account for their dark complexions by claiming to be "French" or "Black Irish." By implication, *Love Medicine* delivers an irrefutable indictment against an official policy that tried to make farmers out of the hunting and fishing Chippewas, moving them from the Great Lakes to the hilly tracts west of the wheat-growing plains of North Dakota. But the author's intentions are more lyrical or rhapsodic than polemical. The pervasive sadness of the Indian condition is offset by proclamations of joy, wisdom, and reconciliation that might go a long way toward making the account more palatable to a sentimental reader. . . .

Alas, the love medicine does not always work, though Louise Erdrich applies it thickly to the wounds and abrasions that her characters suffer. At times the language becomes overwrought to the point of hysteria or else so ecstatic that the reader may feel almost coerced into accepting a romanticized version.

Robert Towers. *New York Review of Books.*
April 11, 1985, p. 20

Louise Erdrich's rough-hewn poems [in *Jacklight*] view the American West they inhabit under two contrary aspects: as wild, demonic nature or as landscape of human loneliness, whose physical correlatives are on the one hand forest and plain, and on the other roadside and small town. In the former mode, she seeks what was once called the "deep image," a logically inexplicable but archetypally resonant cluster of language meant to liberate an elementally powerful emotional response. While her reading has probably included W. S. Merwin and Galway Kinnell, she may have gone back beyond those practitioners of the style to some of its sources; the quest for the deep image was significantly informed by the poetry of oral cultures, and Erdrich (as the book jacket informs the reader) "belongs to the Turtle Mountain Band of Chippewa." Erdrich achieves some fine, spooky effects; "The Woods," with chilling terseness, rewrites the Daphne myth in the terms of a Native American animism: "Light bleeds from the clearing. Roots rise. / Fluted molds burn blue in the falling light, / and you also know / the loneliness that you taught me with your body." But this is an inherently chancy mode, which depends heavily on the poet's "ear," her ability to distinguish the genuinely striking from the merely portentous. Erdrich at times is betrayed by the speed with which the mysteriously evocative language of one moment flattens into the cliché of the next; when she writes "Husband, by the light of our bones we are going," one reflects that bones have already shed rather too much light on the landscape of American poetry, and that no one is likely to find much new ground by that source of illumination.

More frequently, Erdrich takes as her subject everyday life, though the everyday life of those who are in some way marginal, exploited, isolated. A colloquial plain style, enlivened by an eye for irony and a sense for speech-rhythms, serves these poems well. The series of dramatic monologues gathered in the sequence "The Butcher's Wife," written in the personae of various inhabitants of a small town in the early twentieth century, stand out as probably the volume's best work. Erdrich dwells on the loneliness of the characters she creates, their double estrangement in a vast, empty landscape and in their isolation from one another. . . .

As a sequence, "The Butcher's Wife" relies less on Erdrich's uncertain talents as a coiner of epithets and more on her ability to build a fictional world through an accumulation of vignettes. While the notion of a sequence like this might seem alarmingly like another cruise up Spoon River, Erdrich shows a flair for imagining the texture of other lives. One is not surprised to find out that she has also published a novel recently. Variety and scope are goals as worthy as compression and power; Erdrich pursues the former a good deal more comfortably and effectively than the latter. Indeed, her gifts seem to lie more in narrative than in lyric, and her growth as a poet will likely depend on her finding ways to embody in poems her talents as a narrator.

Vernon Shetley. *Poetry*. April, 1985, pp. 40–41

The Beet Queen is a Dickensian story, an angry comedy about abandonment and survival, pluck and luck (ambition and coincidence), common sense and pretension, and wise children and foolish adults. The book is structured in an almost classical manner. It opens with a sudden, unpredictable disaster that tosses an orderly world into terrible disarray. It then follows the paths of the half-dozen affected lives through three generations of small triumphs and reversals, long digressions and quick returns, until at last, in a ceremonial event that reunites and reorders the scattered elements of the tale into symmetrical, benign relations, it circles back to where it began, with everything the same only different—which in classical comedy, as in Dickens, is almost always the point. It's a form that in the hands of lesser artists than Louise Erdrich often affirms the status quo and lends itself to sentimentality. When, however, the story is played against a view of history in which decent folks are victimized not by their dopey and amusing gullibility but by economic and social forces too powerful to overcome with wile or guile, then the story has a divine rage, and one sees the radical power of the old form—renewed.

The story of *The Beet Queen* is the story of the entwined fates of three generations of women whose men orbit around them like distant planets, necessary to the system as a whole but taking all their heat and most of their momentum from the women at the center. The book is divided into sixteen chapters narrated by the main characters and covering four decades in the lives of Mary Adare, one of the most memorable women in recent American fiction; her beleaguered mother, Adelaide; her narcissistic cousin, Sita Kozka;

her lifelong friend, the half-Chippewa Celestine James; and Celestine's daughter, Dot. There are three men of note—Mary's older brother Karl, who fathers Dot; Dot's godfather, Wallace Pfef; and Celestine's half brother Russell Kashpaw, a shattered war hero. There is also Omar, a barnstorming stunt pilot, who, in the opening chapter, flies off with Adelaide, permitting her to abandon her three children on the fairgrounds below. This is the desperate, sad act that initiates the tangled actions of the book. . . .

The Beet Queen is the second of a projected quartet of books dealing with the same cluster of families and events. *Love Medicine,* widely praised for its energy, inventiveness and compassion, was focused more directly on the lives of the Indians, and might for that reason seem more explicitly political than its successor. Yet it's evident from *The Beet Queen* that Erdrich has quite as much compassion for the white inhabitants of the small town of Argus, North Dakota, and environs as for the Chippewas. . . .

Erdrich has been able to give each of her characters their own tone, diction, pitch and rhythm, without letting go of her own. The effect is to deprive the book of a single hero, one character against whom all the others are defined, and to replace it with something like a community. Although this was also true of *Love Medicine,* it is more successful in *The Beet Queen,* where the multiple voices are orchestrated more elegantly and the structure of the narrative is more rigorously formal. A number of recent books with similar ambitions come to mind—Carolyn Chute's *The Beans of Egypt, Maine,* Joan Chase's *During the Reign of the Queen of Persia,* John Edgar Wideman's *Damballah,* for instance. It's as if these authors have chosen to eschew, on principle, a single central consciousness—an individualized sympathetic norm that, like the reader's consciousness, has found itself set in the center of a world gone wacky—and have instead attempted to make a family or a village or tribe, that is, a people, into the protagonist. They seem to be struggling to discover, or perhaps rediscover, a narrative form equal to a social and political vision radically different from the one we inherited from the modernists. Such books are proposing profound changes in the way we read fiction and, as a consequence, in how we see the world.

Russell Banks. *The Nation.* November 1,
1986, pp. 460–63

Winner of the National Book Critics Circle Award for fiction, this wondrous saga [*Love Medicine*] set in North Dakota, tells the multigenerational history of two Native American families. A brilliant, haunting insight into life for today's Native Americans, on and off the reservation, it should remind every generation of Americans of the legacy of our historical role, if we are to face the reality of living in a multicultural world.

Arthur I. Blaustein. *Mother Jones.*
December, 1988, p. 49

Tracks, Louise Erdrich's new book, is more somber, its North Dakota palette a starker black and white than Rosca's reeling tropical landscape [in *State of War*]. But if its poetry is more controlled, it is equally powerful and elegant.

It begins as a dirge for a vanishing people:

> We started dying before the snow, and like the snow we continued to fall. It was surprising there were so many of us left to die. . . .
> But the earth is limitless and so is luck and so were our people once.

The speaker is Nanapush, tale-spinner, tribal chairman (against his better judgment) and survivor: he is the voice and the epitome of his people, and he is passing on the story of their death in the bitter winter of 1913 to the young woman who is among the last of his tribe. "Granddaughter," he tells her, "you are the child of the invisible, the ones who disappeared."

The annals of how he rescues Fleur, the young girl's mother and the last of the Pillager family, and how her life touches on his over the years, alternate with a story in another voice, that of Pauline, whose half-Indian soul fights with her yearnings to be white, to be Christian and to be good. She too knows Fleur, whom she meets when they are both briefly employed at a slaughterhouse, and her long, contorted relationship with the other woman wavers between idolatry, envy and loathing. The social brutality of the world of the slaughterhouse, the drunken, denatured life there, contrast with the harsh, clean struggle for survival on the tribal lands. Bit by bit, these are lost to white duplicity and Indian greed. The old values are corrupted like Pauline herself, who, having no talent for life, finds her place caring for the dying and develops an obsessive vocation for histrionic Christianity. Her masochistic stabs at sainthood are about equally grim and hilarious, as, allowing herself to urinate only twice a day, wearing her shoes on the wrong feet, and hallucinating sweetly destructive messages from her Savior, she descends into a state of medieval madness.

Meanwhile, Nanapush, with his makeshift, dwindling family of survivors, nurtures the worthier parts of any religion quite unconsciously in the daily habits of his life and lives with nature in a dangerous but honorable relationship. A spirit world surrounds him and the members of his community; it is in all things, magical and tangible, a part of ordinary existence. Nanapush is wonderfully biased, and his tribal bigotries about the inexorable traits of each individual family are in blessed contrast to our contemporary mode of finding all peoples, all nations and all sexes equal and indistinguishable in all things. His humor is bawdy, dry and omnipresent: even dying of starvation he notes that it's lucky now that he's reduced to eating his moccasins, that at least they aren't storebought dyed leather. "Those can kill you," he remarks.

The chronology of *Tracks* is earlier than that of either of Erdrich's previous novels, *Love Medicine* and *The Beet Queen,* which share some of the same characters and are part of the same fictional cycle. Its documentation of the death of the Chippewa people and the destruction of their world, and its affirmation of the survival of their spirit, is exemplary of everything a novel should be to justify fiction as a still-living art.

Edith Milton. *Massachusetts Review.*
30, 1989, pp. 118–19

Louise Erdrich is a contemporary writer of German–American and Chippewa heritage. Like many literary works by Native Americans, her novels, *Love Medicine* (1984), *The Beet Queen* (1986), and *Tracks* (1988), reflect the ambivalence and tension marking the lives of people, much like herself, from dual cultural backgrounds. Erdrich's novels feature Native Americans, mixed-bloods, and other culturally and socially displaced characters whose marginal status is simultaneously an advantage and a disadvantage, a source of both power and powerlessness. . . .

Erdrich's concern with liminality and marginality pervade all levels of her texts. It affects not only characterization but also thematic and structural features. Semiotic analysis reveals Erdrich's preoccupation with marginality beyond the thematic level. . . .

Although no text could ever have completely homogeneous encoding, Erdrich's texts represent extreme cases of code conflict. Frustration of narrativity produces the reader's own liminal experience and thus underscores Erdrich's primary theme.

Conflicting codes in Erdrich's texts fall into two large categories—codes originating within Western-European society and those originating within Native American culture. Conflicting codes involve

—Christianity versus shamanic religion;
—mechanical or industrial time versus ceremonial time;
—the nuclear family versus tribal kinship systems;
—main or privileged characters versus characters of equal status;
—privileged narrative voices as opposed to dialogical or polyphonic narrative development.

Stylistic and rhetorical effects in Erdrich's work often result from these various code conflicts; such effects register most emphatically in the text's symbolic field.

As novels depicting the lives of socially marginal figures, Erdrich's books are rife with conflicting cultural codes to which the reader must respond. . . .

All of [the] conflicting codes in Erdrich's text produce a state of marginality in the reader, who must at some point in the reading cease to apply the conventional expectations associated with ordinary narrativity. The reader must pause "between worlds" to discover the arbitrary structural principles of both. This primary value—epistemological insight—which Erdrich's text associates with marginality might then be adopted through a revision of narrativity. Stranded between conflicting codes—deprived of "a stable point of identification" within the world evoked by the text—the reader is temporarily disempowered. However, such disempowerment or "alienation" leads to another kind of power. The reader must consider a possibility forcefully posited in all of Erdrich's works (as well as in those of other contemporary Native Americans): the world takes on the shape of the stories we tell.

Catherine Rainwater. *American Literature.*
62, 1990, pp. 405–7, 422

A widely read novelist *(The Beet Queen, Love Medicine),* Louise Erdrich as poet continues to draw on her Native American and Roman Catholic heritage for meditations on the claims of sexuality. Images of snakes, apples, hair, cats, roses, and bodies populate the poems of *Baptism of Desire* in celebration of Eros. Written, she tells us, in the night hours during pregnancy, the poems range in attitude from a fearful and cautious relationship to God in the opening "Fooling God" to warm parental love surrounding a newborn child in the short and beautiful "Birth": "When they were wild / When they were not yet human . . . / I was on the other side ready with milk to lure them, / And their father, too, each name a net in his hands." In dramatic narrative poems reappear characters from Erdrich's first collection, *Jacklight* (1984): Potchikoo, Otto, Mary Kroger, Rudy J. V. Jacklitch. We reenter the world of the reservation and its tales and culture, part Indian tradition, part modern American. At the center of the five sections stands a single long poem, "Hydra," as a brilliant centerpiece: "Snake of the heat seeking venom . . . / Snake of the hard hours, you are my poetry."

Doris Earnshaw. *World Literature Today.*
64, 1990, p. 645

The Crown of Columbus is difficult to read without remembering that the [Michael] Dorris-Erdrich team got some $1.5 million to turn out a book from their Indian perspective for the Quincentenary. Put that aside, though, and there is a fair bit of entertainment—discounting some dreary chapters depicting the life of the dreary man who is a central character, and an interminable free-verse poem about Columbus recited by that same leaden man—and there are as well some neat interspersings of debunking and demythifying along with some artful presentations of Indian-angled perceptions of the Columbian legacy. Columbus, insofar as he matters at all, is rightfully treated as a "naïve innocent" in a world he could never understand, even as he set about laying waste to it.

A few minor historical errors occur, and there's a peculiar confusion of Columbus's mistress, Beatriz de Arana, with the ruler of Gomera, Beatriz (or, in some accounts, Ines) Peraza, but what undermines the basic conception of the book—even given that it is a novel, for it otherwise pretends to verisimilitude—is a historical flaw so glaring that at first I presumed it intentional. You see, the plot turns on the idea that there was a crown that Columbus gave to an Indian chief on his first voyage, a gift long lost whose existence is confirmed in parts of his log and a letter that has been missing for centuries. Then pages from the log and the letter come to light in the present, discovered by an Indian woman who teaches at Dartmouth, and that sends her off on an adventure that eventually leads, in a most improbable way, to the crown itself.

The trouble is that the page from the letter, as translated into English, a facsimile of which is printed on page 145 of the book, ends with Columbus writing, "Given in the settlement of Isabela on the twenty-eighth of January in the year fourteen hundred and ninety-two." Well, Isabela was the name of the settlement that Columbus established on his *second* voyage, not his first, in January *1494,* not 1492, and indeed in January 1492 Columbus was still in Granada, Spain, trying to get his voyage approved. So this is clearly not an authentic document, one would suppose, and I assumed that eventually this would be revealed, so we would know that there was skulduggery afoot and the crown referred to didn't really exist. Except that no mention of this mistake is ever made, the page is taken throughout to be genuine, and in the end there really is a crown. It is a mistake not merely incidental but crucial, and for me fatal to the plot. Erdrich and Dorris, who write so convincingly elsewhere from their own experience, seem here to have been a little hasty in trying to exploit Columbus's.

Kirkpatrick Sale. *The Nation.*
October 21, 1991, p. 488

One of the dominant motifs in the fiction of American Indian writers is the vision quest, whose goal is the integration of inner and outer being through knowledge gleaned from nature. Louise Erdrich has explored this territory in *Love Medicine, The Beet Queen* and *Tracks,* and she revisits it in her moving new novel, *The Bingo Palace.* Set, like the others, on the North Dakota plains, this latest book shows us a place where love, fate and chance are woven together like a braid, a world where daily life is enriched by a powerful spiritual presence.

Her story comes to us in the alternating voices of the inhabitants of the Chippewa reservation—the novel's chorus—and of Lipsha Morrissey, the central character, who is sometimes laconic, frequently passionate and, through painful experience, increasingly insightful. Presented in a counterpoint that is by turns colloquial and lyric, all these voices reveal how inescapably Lipsha's fate is inscribed within his heritage. To emphasize this connection, Ms. Erdrich begins and ends *The Bingo Palace* with the chorus, thus bracketing both Lipsha's good luck and his misadventures within a broader view of the world that binds the past to the present while looking uncertainly toward the future.

As the novel's title implies, gambling is a major force on the reservation; but while this may initially suggest that life there has been reduced to a game of chance, it soon becomes clear that luck, which means nothing in the world of contingency, is actually design in the realm of the spirits. . . .

The Bingo Palace . . . eventually return[s] to its strengths, ending with a beautiful evocation of the spirit world. Part eulogy, part coda, the last few pages bind together the living and the dead in an elegiac choral voice. Here, as in most of the book, Ms. Erdrich's sympathy for her characters shines as luminously as Shawnee Ray's jingle dress. We leave this brightness aware of the complex pattern that links Lipsha, Fleur, Shawnee Ray and all the rest of the characters to both their community and their land.

Lawrence Thornton. *New York Times Book Review.* January 16, 1994, p. 7

ESPINA, CONCHA (SPAIN) 1879–1955

As a technician [Concha Espina] seems supremely gifted. She is unusually articulate and sensitive enough to echo the subtle moods of the earth and the sky as well as the petty sufferings of her puppets. . . . Her theme [in *Mariflor* (i.e., *The Sphinx of Maragata*) and *The Red Beacon* (i.e., *Sweet Name*)] is poverty, which drives the sentimental wants of the individual to a conflict with the interests of the family and of established custom. Poverty circles over her creatures with the ever-nearing flight of a hawk, finally clawing them down to submission. It is here that she fails. Her understanding of life is too tenuous to make us feel that the failure of her victims to triumph over poverty is the tragic dénouement of what might have been a nobly successful life. Her heart's desire is vulgar. There is no difference between her idea of happiness and that of the shopkeeper. This world would be, for her, the best possible if we could manage to eliminate poverty from it. Then the beautiful girl would be able to marry the sensitive young poet, rather than sell herself to a rich elderly man who can save her family from its dire needs. Confronted with the possibility of such a Utopia we cannot help feeling grateful that human stupidity perpetuates so mean a thing as poverty, for it occasionally lends the only glimmer of meaning to human life.

It is true that Concha Espina is "the foremost novelist of Spain today," as she has been called. But it should be remembered that since the death of the Countess of Pardo Bazán there has appeared no woman writer capable of doing work of permanent human significance. The fact that she is the recipient of a prize from the Academy merely attests to her ideologic and artistic respectability.

Eliseo Vivas. *The Nation.* August 13, 1924, p. 168

Concha Espina's novel, *The Woman and the Sea* . . . belongs to the type of literature—rhetorical, sentimental and silly—which characterized and reigned supreme during Echegaray's period and up to the European War. . . . Mr. Boyd assures us [in the introduction] that Concha Espina is "an interpreter as highly to be esteemed as Pérez de Ayala, Pio Baroja and Ramón del Valle-Inclán." . . . Concha Espina sold her books because she had become a symbol, the woman writer, *la escritora,* and because, I must admit, she was liked by young girls and their pure mothers. But the serious reader and the discriminating critics respectfully kept at a distance from her sugary tracts and from those heroines of hers, beautiful she-wolves, voracious readers of Nietzsche and Schopenhauer, whose indoor sports seem to have been the wrecking of happy homes.

Angel Flores. *New York Herald Tribune.*
August 5, 1934, p. 7

Spain's greatest contemporary woman writer and one of her greatest literary artists of all times is Concepción Espina y Tagle, known to the world as Concha Espina. . . .

Most of Concha Espina's novels are realistic and are based on actual experiences of the author, on documentation that she made "on the ground," so to speak. But it is not the photographic realism of a Zola. It is, rather, the artistic realism of a Cervantes; a reality viewed with the eyes of the soul. Concha Espina seems to be the living counterpart of other great Spanish women of the past, such as Isabella I and St. Theresa, for example, whose life and works exemplified one of the most characteristic traits of Spain: that combination of idealism and realism which found such beautiful expression in the paintings of El Greco, in the novels of Cervantes and in the plays of Lope de Vega. It is this combination which in Concha Espina becomes a power to see reality projected to a higher and more beautiful plane.

In many of the works of this author, and particularly in her first novel, *The Girl from Luzmela,* and in her subsequent works, such as *The Sphinx of Maragata . . ., The Rose of the Winds, Sweet Name* . . . and in her latest novel, *Rear Guard,* the dominant note is Concha Espina's extraordinary understanding of the psychology of women, and particularly of their attitude in the face of failure, failure to realize what they most desire after intense suffering. In these novels, as in all her works, as far as style is concerned, Concha Espina excels in description, in description of Nature, especially. It is in these descriptions that she is at her very best, and that one fully appreciates her charming artistry. Her art is imbued with Spain's glorious traditions and is, at the same time freshly modern. Finding, as she does, deep inspiration in Spanish tradition, she transcends time and space and rises to the universal, just like the great writers of Spain's Golden Age, Cervantes, Lope de Vega, Calderón, Gracián, and so many others.

Ralph J. Michaels. *Mark Twain Journal.*
Spring, 1938, pp. 5–6

The novels of Concha Espina resound in our ears like a melody played on a cello behind the curtains of a room in which jazz can be heard. It is not that one is the enemy of the other—it is a question of distinct aims—but rather it is that the excitement of what is happening now attracts us.

We have esteemed Concha Espina less than she deserves. I know for certain that she, an exceptional spirit, would pay this apparent disdain little mind. She would pay this disdain little mind—let us make it clear—as soon as she knew that the alienation of so many young people was not the fault of her work. Moreover, she realized that there were not many who were able to penetrate to the sense—the sense of form, the most problematic aspect of a work because it was the obvious one—of a classical, luminous and well-ordered creation. She would feel sorry more like a mother who sees her child keeping bad company. She knew very well that clarity ultimately becomes artistic integrity, for nothing is stronger than truth. The prodigal son whom we all have become will eventually return to the paternal home. . . .

From *The Girl from Luzmela* to *A Valley in the Sea,* passing on to *The Sphinx of Maragata, The Nature of the Dead,* and so on, you can follow the passage of a life, of a woman. This is precisely what we look for today in literature: a man or a woman. We contemplate an exemplary life, of needs and struggles, of constant activity. . . .

[Concha Espina's] work is for those of us who are accustomed to pass each other on narrow staircases in today's buildings without ever letting the other person go first, while we remember the old, wide staircases on which four people could pass at one time, and on which, nevertheless, people did allow the other person to go by first. The gesture of yesteryear seems to us totally useless. But we are in the process of learning that courtesy, like beautiful and serene forms in art, can be a thing of primary necessity. This process requires that the spirit be civilized and the sensibility purified.

When this occurs, Concha Espina will occupy the place that is fitting for her in Spanish letters.

José Hierro. Revista de Literatura.
September 1955, pp. 100–103

In none of Concha Espina's creations are there dark or schismatic solutions. Spirituality is imposed with a providentialism that is inherited, perhaps, from classical taste. In any case, the plasticity—the careful, well-worked, and artistic composition—is one of the characteristics that can be appreciated as the common characteristic in all the novels of Concha Espina. Colors are kept pure; situations are not besmirched; there are no blots on anyone's honor nor any exposés; there are only delicate ranges of colors, pale shades, fugitive wisps and oblique lights of great academic craft. . . .

[In *The Girl from Luzmela,*] Concha Espina's first novel, one of [Spain's] finest and most humanistic pens is to be found in embryo, a pen with the most delightful powers of observation that are connected by moving descriptions and, also, by landscapes. They have that rare quality of being able to distance reality while at the same time embracing it as the only thing that really directs human destinies. . . .

Alicia Canales. *Concha Espina* (Madrid: ESPESA, 1974), pp. 21, 93–94

For many critics, Carmen [in *The Girl from Luzmela*] typifies Concha Espina's women protagonists. However, Carmen's experience of life as well as her reaction to it are markedly different. Her tragedy hinges on externally imposed conditions which lead her to temporarily embrace suffering. As the novelist comments on several occasions, her passive resignation implies a rejection of the beauty of life as incompatible with moral perfection. Like Saint Teresa of Ávila, Concha Espina stresses that spiritual and moral values cannot supersede our human condition; they must enable us to confront our reality without denying it, enhancing our appreciation of life and our ability to enjoy it. In this respect Carmen's asceticism is clearly deficient and should be distinguished from the constructive self-denial presented in other novels. Possibly because she herself has not yet fully come to terms with the need for women to transform their inevitable suffering into a positive experience of life, Concha Espina sidesteps the issue in this first novel, creating a character whose suffering depends on external obstacles eventually circumvented. Thus the optimistic ending to *The Girl from Luzmela* reflects the lack of a fully elaborated vision in the developing novelist.

Mary Lee Bretz. *Concha Espina* (Boston: Twayne, 1980), p. 31

Between April and July of 1937, Concha Espina wrote her novela *Retaguardia* (Rearguard). Luzmela (province of Santander), the writer's usual summer residence, has remained (in the strict geographic division imposed by the war) within the republican zone, and Concha Espina, with an ideology contrary to that of her rulers, considered herself a prisoner; foreseeing possible risks, she hid the written pages in a leadlined box buried in the family garden; this painful situation lasted until the very end of August.

The "images of the living and the dead" that make up *Retaguardia* are strewn throughout the nine days that neither correspond exactly with so many other days nor are successive time or without gaps in their continuity; such days deserve, considering their unusual character, the label days "of danger and passion."

José María Martínez Cachero. *Bulletin Hispanique*. 85, 1983, p. 284

As compared to [Emilia] Pardo Bazán, Concha Espina is in all respects more traditional. *El jayón* (1918), her first and best known play, takes place in rural northern Spain. The . . . characters are largely local types, but the main characters are generally free from determinateness. Their [nature] is in no way specific to the area or to the contemporary period. . . .

Espina's *La tiniebla encendida* was written in 1940 and, like *La otra* and *Moneda blanca* (1942), was never staged. All three of these works typify the literature of the years immediately following the Spanish Civil War, with minimal conflict, moralistic resolutions, nationalistic rhetoric, and emphasis on plot complexity over other aspects of drama.

El jayón remains Concha Espina's major contribution to Spanish drama. In Keir Elam's terms, it is a play that emphasizes code observing, with little modification of conventional factors. Here the code-breaking occurs because Espina combines two codes that are not normally concurrent, the classic-tragic and the naturalistic.

Mary Lee Bretz. *Estreño: Cuadernos de Teatro Español.* 10, 1984, pp. 44–45

ESTEVES, SANDRA MARIA (UNITED STATES) 1948–

We may conclude that the poem ["To Julia and Me"] is what Bloom calls "an act of creative correction." The anxiety of influence has led Esteves to read into Burgos's poetry a posture that is not militant enough. This leads her to go beyond the positions taken by de Burgos in her poems. Esteves's speakers says "I viewed a saint and saw myself instead." Contemplating Julia not only facilitated the speaker's vision of herself but leads her to self-recognition of her ability to go beyond the other poet's words: "she dances around with your words / she springs new life from your roots dried and seasoned." The words "dried and seasoned" indicate how closely Esteves's speaker sees her poetry linked to that of her predecessor. Esteves creates with this the . . . aversion, if you will, between herself and de Burgos. Esteves's will have to draw new life from the dry roots of Julia's words—she will go further than her predecessor.

The "purple hymn" that was how Esteves's speaker describes Julia's poetry, turns into "the beat of an Afro-Cuban drum," a description of Esteves's own poetry. If the poetry of Julia de Burgos has traditionally been seen as the standard of the creative work for committed women on the island in this century and, therefore, as a symbol of culture, in revising Julia's position as committed woman and poet, Esteves indicates the way that both efforts can be taken a step further. The "neo-Rican" woman writer in this poem seeks inclusion in the Puerto Rican cultural tradition represented by de Burgos in order to take that cultural trajectory beyond the parameters that it has reached up to now on the island.

Luz Maria Umpierre. *Revista Chicano-Riqueña.* 11, 1983, p. 142

Sandra Maria Esteves has written the majority of her work in English, probably because English is her first language. Sandra Maria, daughter of a Dominican mother and a Puerto Rican father, was born in the South Bronx, in an immigrant community. She has published poems in various anthologies and periodicals; and as of now I am aware of two of her published collections of poems, *Yerba buena* (1980) and *Tropical Rains: A Bilingual Downpour* (1984). Generally, her poems bear witness to her individual and collective experience in a society that, like North American society, discriminates against her group: Latinos, Dominicans, and Puerto Ricans. It is a poetry in which this condition is protested and denounced. Sandra Maria's poetry participates in two tendencies already identified by Efrain Barradas in his commentaries on the poetry written by Puerto Ricans in the United States: they are heretics and mythmakers. Sandra Maria makes a myth, for example, of the Latin woman to differentiate her from the rest and exalt her cultural expression in the face of the dominant power.

But Sandra Maria also participates in heresy about a myth. . . . Everyone knows that the experience that Julia de Burgos had as a Puerto Rican emigrant to the United States left empty gulfs in her life that we can perceive in her poetry. For many Puerto Ricans of both sexes, Julia de Burgos has been converted into a venerated image. Women in particular are able to feel close solidarity with her sensual poetry that bears witness to the experience of love in poetic discourse new to Puerto Rican poetry. But in the United States her figure is all the greater because of the solidarity aroused by her immigrant experience. Together with Lolita Lebron, she is one of the most venerated of Puerto Rican women. Sandra Maria also admires her, but in her poem "To Julia and Me" she pays critical homage to the vision of life that Julia de Burgos reflected. Starting from her experience, Sandra Maria constructs "heresy": She has identified with and learned from Julia's experiences and poetry, but she asks: "but why did you let the dragon slay you / why did your vision suffocate / in suicidal premonition you could not die / within the flesh beat the heart / and my child need no image of despair; or too much poetry of this and that but not enough / to rise above the clouded cross." And she also confesses that the generations after her have needed, in addition to poetry, other forms of affirmation. . . . But later she returns to remind us of the solidarity that as Puerto Rican and woman she has felt with Julia's poetry. . . .

This so-called heresy has its historic reasons, as the narrative voice of the poem explains to us. This world, like the one that Julia experienced, continues to discriminate against women: "It is the same world that has not moved / but an inch from your suffrage / women still tend fires that men burn / and lovers still imprison dream." For this reason—and learning from Julia's experience—the female vision of the world that is offered is a very different one from Julia's. . . .

This also happens in the other poem of Sandra's that I wish to comment on and that in my opinion presents that other side of the coin that Efrain

Barradas pointed out: myth-making. The poem is entitled "To the Borinquen Woman." The poem's general tone is one of exaltation of the woman who, although born in the Barrio has succeeded—within the context of discrimination—to continue to transmit the values of her Latin culture. It is then that these values are exalted. The woman is admired because it is she that teaches our men "to be strong." But, on the other hand, she assumes a submissive posture before tradition and before her relations with men: "I respect their ways inherited from our proud ancestors." She accepts, then, the tradition and the division of labor that that tradition assigns to woman: "I do not complain about cooking for my family / because abuela taught me that women is the master of fire." . . . But there is also denunciation and protest because the Puerto Rican woman of the Barrio is the victim of discrimination. And in the face of that discrimination she must oppose, as an alternative, as a source of strength, her origins and cultural tradition: "My eyes reflect the pain of that which has shamelessly raped me / but my soul reflects the strength of my culture."

Yamila Azize. Cupey. 4:1, 1987, pp. 20–21

The switch [in "To Julia and Me"] from Spanish to English underscores the sources of learning behind the formation of the feminist consciousness. The images of nature and moods, so frequent in the poetry of Julia de Burgos, are presented in Spanish because they are the product of a cultural legacy in Spanish. The verses in English summarize the new experiences and resolutions that have molded the contemporary Latina woman as an immigrant in the United States. . . .

[Esteves's "A la mujer borrinqueña" suggests that] women will play a fundamental role in the struggle for cultural and national affirmation but also continue to assume those typical roles to which they have been subordinated in the patriarchal society: the house, the kitchen, the education of the children. The mystique presented in this poem contrasts with the vision in the previous poem, which insisted on women's active participation in the struggle for social change. If the "heresy" towards the Julia-myth presents other possible options for the Caribbean woman immigrant, the myth of Latin femininity suggests the acceptance of those models that perpetuate women's submission. However, the defense of Latin cultural values does not necessarily justify those traditional models.

Yamila Azize Vargas. In Asunción Horno-
Delgado et al, eds. Breaking Boundaries:
Latina Writing and Critical Readings
(Amherst: University of Massachusetts
Press, 1989), pp. 54–57

ETCHERELLI, CLAIRE (FRANCE) 1934–

In this novel [*Elise ou la vraie vie*] everything happens as if the written word had replaced the spoken word. This can come as a surprise just at first, since we are not dealing, here, with those who, in our society, always seem to hold the privilege of written expression. Henri is the only bourgeois intellectual in the story. But once you enter the prison house of this novel, you start to look at things differently. These creatures dehumanized by work and poverty all nonetheless have a certain image of themselves. It is as if they had some dim awareness that they should express themselves is in a fashion "higher" than their condition of robot or beast of burden. Expressing themselves is in a sense to affirm that they are no longer merely poor slobs, dirty and despicable, to deny that they are only "that," to create conditions for dialogue. (Do you talk to a robot? A beast of burden?) All these sub-humans—all, without exception—feel the need to go beyond themselves. Each will do so according to his or her means. Some of them remain very close to their usual situation of poor creatures, that is, they have recourse to a mode of expression that they believe appropriate to promoting a prettier picture of themselves, that would express their human dignity, but that only further identifies them, albeit at a higher level, with their condition as reified beings. This recourse is essentially the fate of the women who are, of course, the least accustomed to expressing themselves, because they are the most alienated. . . .

Seeing and the gaze play a large role in *Elise ou la vraie vie*. It seems that, in this universe of poverty, the word itself is a luxury. The force of circumstances equips the workers to use the gaze better than the word. The gaze is not only a means of expression and communication, it is also a source of pleasure and pain.

For Elise and Arezki, who are, nonetheless, the most adept at expressing themselves verbally, the gaze also plays a preponderant role. . . .

What if Elise felt the need to write what she had experienced? A still inchoate but understood need? You don't go from the assembly line to writing, just like that. . . . Why would Elise write? To free herself from her sad memories? She would have chosen writing as a means of deliverance because she considered it the most painless. . . . Rescuing that experience from randomness, giving it shape and value, wouldn't this mean a passage to what would then be "real life"? "Real life" would no longer be made up of inconsistent dreams about a vague future, nor of meaningless suffering, but would be constituted by a human act that was truly human because undertaken lucidly and responsibly.

Could Elise write? Why not? Isn't she accessible to the world and to others, "virgin" and skeptical toward falsified words and prefab behaviors?

She has looked around her, she has withdrawn into herself. She could write.

Anne Ophir. *Regards féminins: condition féminine et création littéraire* (Paris: Denoël-Gonthier, 1976), pp. 161–62, 191, 234

Elise ou la vraie vie deals with a young woman working in a Paris car factory who develops a relationship with an Algerian worker during the early part of the war before the collapse of the Fourth Republic. Etcherelli gives a powerful account of the weight of racism in French society. She shows the images of the North African that are dominant in the media:

> This evening their newspaper would report "North Africans attack a grocer's wife." And further on, beneath an edifying picture, "French Muslims greet the Resident Minister." In both cases dogs. Either good faithful, affectionate, petted dogs, or mad dogs.

For Etcherelli, the fact that French workers accept these images is to be understood first and foremost in their conditions of work. It is the alienation of the work process, the isolation and atomization, and above all the sheer physical fatigue that makes workers unable and unwilling to oppose the racism foisted upon them:

> I wasn't too sure how a life passes by as you watch it pass. But here, in Paris, with all its legends of suburbs and barricades, I wondered why and how. Work, weariness, lack of time, but also a revolting, almost ancestral passivity, a gregarious instinct dried up a life in which the local cinema and the pub represented the supreme disalienation.

This passive alienated racism, Etcherelli shows, is fed by the more active racism of the factory supervisors, who deliberately incite contempt and hatred for the Algerian workers, and by the systematic brutality of the police. But the racism of the state and the employers is distinct from the racism of the workers. The former is a deliberate ideological weapon; the latter is the product of social and economic oppression; it could be changed.

Etcherelli shows clearly that the existing forms of political consciousness and organization leave a huge barrier between French and Algerian workers. When Elise meets some Algerian militants, one of them complains that even those French workers who oppose the war do so out of self-interest:

> And you know why they're against the war? Because it costs money. Not because of us, and our wives and kids. Because it cuts their living standards.

But when the union in the factory calls a meeting to discuss its demands, none of the Algerians turn up. A worker says to Elise: "And where are your pals the Arabs?"

An authentically internationalist politics would have to combine solidarity and self-interest. Without it Elise is trapped helplessly between the two communities.

Ian Birchall. In Francis Barker et al, eds.
Europe and Its Others, vol. 2 (Colchester:
University of Essex Press, 1985), pp. 166–67

Claire Etcherelli, "Ecrivain solitaire" (Isolated writer) and contemporary female novelist, has been able, in her limited literary production, to deal with demanding and difficult subject matter. She has been able to create a new but always up to date universe, inserting herself into the central currents of her era and, at the same time, maintaining her own distinct individuality. In fact, while presenting us in her novels with numerous elements reminiscent of naturalism and the existentialist movement, she is basically a writer who cannot be confined to any one specific literary movement. The universe that she powerfully creates in her works contains elements closely related to the French literary tradition and is a part of another sphere, that is, the world in which what counts most are the highest and most worthy values of humanity. These elements, which can be traced in each of her novels, are altruism and generosity, understanding and forgiveness, tenacity in struggle, the most complete giving of oneself and the dignity of the human individual. Now, it is worth considering how Claire Etcherelli has dealt with such themes and what causes determined such a sincere, powerful, and profound treatment of them. . . .

[Some time after her experience working on the assembly line at Citroën] she began to write a novel in which she recorded her hard and at times cruel experience at the auto plant. She was profoundly marked by it and for this reason made a very fine book out of it, one that is not, however, simply an autobiographical novel but that is at the same time an indictment of the racism that had become disturbing in the working class after the influx of foreign labor. This book, *Elise ou la vraie vie,* deservedly awarded the Prix Fémina in 1967 and followed by a resounding success among a wide reading public, is a plea, a diatribe (though very contained and serene) against injustice, the exploitation of the poor, the alienating work of the factory, in short, against "man's inhumanity to man." . . .

Claire Etcherelli sees Elise's . . . problems. . . . Hers is a direct and unhappy experience that has imposed significant sacrifices on her. Despite everything, though . . . Claire Etcherelli continues her noble struggle unperturbed. The author's altruism, reflected through the character of Elise, shows the most absolute understanding toward whoever needs it, toward those, that is, that she herself called the wretched on the earth. This approach, even more altruistic and generous on the author's part, is presented to us in her second novel, *A propos de Clémence* (About Clemence), again through the principal character (Clémence, in fact). It is a work dedicated once more to the difficult life, the precarious existence of maladapted individuals. The protagonists are creatures brought low by society and their own miserable social condition. . . .

Like Milie, the heroine of her third book *(Un arbre voyageur)* (A traveling tree), Claire Etcherelli has been able to preserve some of that generosity and that profound love for others. . . . [The third novel] is a book full of elements that bear witness to the will to live and to struggle indefatigably on the part of Milie who, in an irrepressible movement of life, tries to mount a defense against all that can impede her natural course, her ever growing sense of the absurd, her exuberance, her energy.

Fabiola Occhetti. *Quaderni di Filologia e*
Lingue Romanze. n.s. 1, 1985, pp. 275–78

Elise ou la vraie vie was published in 1967, was awarded the Prix Fémina and received much public attention for a first novel. This story of the love affair between a French woman and an Algerian man, both workers in a car factory in Paris, and set during the Algerian War of Independence, was widely praised for its damning portrayal of racism and of the conditions of work endured in the factory. The author Claire Etcherelli was also the center of attention in articles and interviews which focused particularly on her own experience as a worker and her non-literary background. This success has lasted through time, outshining Etcherelli's other novels, to the extent that, if a recent issue of *L'Evénement du jeudi* is to be believed, *Elise* appears to have become a modern icon of poverty and oppression and disillusion. The political promises of a former Socialist Prime Minister are dismissed as "la vraie vie d'Elise." *Elise* had also been hailed as a precursor of the women's writing which appeared from the early 1970s in France, given the central importance it ascribes to women's experience and its political denunciation of sexism at work and at home.

Elise ou la vraie vie is a novel of many things: of class and poverty and the difference between them; of the effects in France of the Algerian war, especially on Algerian workers; of women; of the impossible nature of the quest for romanticism in the modern world; of the city. But also, and very importantly, it is a novel of identity. Although it could by no stretch of the imagination be termed experimental fiction, this first-person narration, while respecting the conventions in order to successfully construct the story of the character/narrator as authentically lived experience, nonetheless raises questions about the way the coherent continuous self of realist fiction coexists with its de facto dispersal across narrative structures. Autonomy and unity are themselves fictions elaborated on the basis of otherness and belief. This is all the more acute in a text which thematises the importance of identifications and knowledge to consciousness of self. Both thematically and structurally, *Elise* helps us to see the heterogeneity of the self, the disparate and contradictory nature of the political and cultural discourses which traverse it. In more ways than one, it is written under the sign of Beauvoir and Sartre, in its insistence on the social construction of femininity, and the dialectical relationship of subject, other and action in the world. . . . I believe that the awareness of subjectivity in this novel is inseparable from the political consciousness of the protagonists, the coming to political awareness of the narrator Elise, and the nature of class politics and social positioning; that this fragmentation is built into the mode of narration, namely the first-person autobiographical account; and that important categories of feminist analysis such as experience, writing, otherness, can be tied together in realist fiction in a political way, challenging the reader's naive identifications at the level of characterization. . . .

The political discourse of gender and race (or rather sexism and racism) fragments the discourse of class; sexism politicizes the nonpoliticized narrative of home/poverty/charity; class and the factory politicize the social. *Elise ou la vraie vie* is a political realist text which places its readers in the position of critical awareness of the complexity of politics, identity, social and cultural codes. It transcends, not only naive identification with victimized characters, but also the naive morality of many well-meaning didactic social texts.

Realism is founded on visual metaphorization, on a rhetoric of representation, and many feminist critics have hesitated over its value. "Ecriture féminine" and other theories of writing otherness, which could be seen as founded on a rhetoric of action—though I at least have a sneaking suspicion that the connection between writing differently and difference outside that particular writing means that representability has not quite been shown the door yet—argue the patriarchal, logocentric nature of realism. Not to contest the alignment of man, reason, rationality, and representability is, sheeplike, to repeat and perpetuate it. And, by its nature, this is what realism is condemned to do. A different tradition within feminist criticism argues that realism, with its illusory world of people, life, and experiences, evades politics. Telling it like it is, becoming truly oneself, one's own person, is thus to wade around in the garbage of (sexist) ideological givens, naive beliefs in "direct true experience," the "real world," nature masquerading as culture, with no critical political purchase on ideological processes.

Elise ou la vraie vie suggests that realism's potential for a feminist *prise de conscience* remains considerable.

Margaret Atack. In Margaret Atack and Phil
Powrie, eds. *Contemporary French Fiction
by Women: Feminist Perspectives*
(Manchester: Manchester University Press,
1990), pp. 56–57, 67–68

ETCHEVERTS, SARA DE (ARGENTINA) n.d.

In 1930 . . . Nestor Ibarra placed Sara de Etcheverts's novel in his *"ultraista"* catalogue. Ultraism was the only avant-garde movement within the range of Argentinean literature in the period between the two World Wars. Other innovative schools—surrealism, for example—did not find a way of reaching their audience. . . .

There was no choice other than to include Sara de Etcheverts's novel in Ultraism and Nestor Ibarra did so. We take this sponsorship into the school for granted, but an examination of the book forcefully draws our attention to wide areas of prose that escape beyond the boundaries that Argentinean "avant-guardists" set up from 1921 on. *El constructor de silencio* (The sculptor of silence) was certainly erected under the sign of Ultraism, but certain of the premises of Italian Futurism also had a decisive influence. . . .

The work of Sara de Etcheverts presents itself to us as a curious exception to the general lack of influence of Futurism in Argentina at this period, insofar as she selected the most generic of the fundamental points of the Futurist program and mixes and unmixes them in her novel. . . .

Let us examine separately the two aspects—Ultraist and Futurist—of *El constructor de silencio.*

From Ultraism, Sara de Etcheverts adopts the poetic conception of prose, fragmentariness, non-linear construction, and accumulation of metaphor. What is more, certain passages taken separately constitute genuine Ultraist poems. . . .

The elimination of verbal articulations, the mere juxtaposition of dry images and metaphors, recall, if not the best Ultraist poems, at least the movement's most common mannerisms. . . .

We believe that the Futurism of *El constructor del silencio* may be summarized in certain aspects of the third, fourth, and fifth points of the First Milan Manifesto:

> (3) Since literature hitherto has glorified the immobility of thought, ecstasy and the dream, we will exalt aggressive movement, febrile insomnia, etc.

> (4) We are not ashamed to declare that the splendor of the world has been enriched with a new beauty, the beauty of speed. A racing car . . . is more beautiful than the *Victory of Samothrace.*

> (5) We want to sing to the man who dominates the wheel whose ideal radius crosses the earth, launched into the circuit of its orbit.

This could be Sara de Etcheverts's *ars poetica.*

Alfonso Sola Gonzalez. *Capitulos de la novela argentina* (Mendoza, Argentina: Gral), 1959, pp. 50–53, 55–56

Sara de Etcheverts, whose fictions have received little attention either in her native Argentina or abroad, provides a valuable summary of these ambivalent feminist perspectives in Argentine literature. Her five novels, published between the late 1920s and 1944, offer lessons in literary history as they mark phases of transition in a changing aesthetic sensibility. While Argentine writers of the 1920s were divided into disputatious camps of social realists and avant-garde esthetes, identified respectively as the Boedo and Florida movements, Etcheverts follows an independent course that at once absorbs the experimental tendencies of the cosmopolitan mode and projects a social awareness of the inequities of modern Argentine life. The first stage of her writing reflects the disengaged aesthetic principles of *belle époque* art, which was formed by audacious formal games and language play. Etcheverts's attraction to futurism is unmistakable: a strident resurrection of Marinetti's cult of the machine, velocity, and violence gives radical energy to her narratives. Etcheverts follows not only the principal tenets of futurism as conceived by Marinetti but also leans upon those writers who actively shared the European modernist fever: references [to] and parodies of Lawrence, Montherlant, and D'Annunzio punctuate the pages of her fictions. Etcheverts's texts reveal an uncritical absorption of European modernism; in fact, she even uses—not ironically—the misogynist declarations of those writers to describe her supposedly independent female characters. This pattern is especially evident in Etcheverts's first novels, *El animador de la llama* (The flame bearer) and *El constructor del silencio* (The sculptor of silence) in which she exalts the artist as iconoclast and innovator. Etcheverts's heroes—artists, actors, and alienated wanderers who roam the streets of Buenos Aires—generate a series of discussions on aesthetic sensibility and posit to the reader modes of interpretation of contemporary reality. Characters meet in literary salons and thus construct a textual situation that invites debate on modes of representation in art and the possibility of self-discovery through fiction. Through structured inquiries of this kind, Etcheverts presents the contradictions of the modern intellectual who at once is seriously attracted to the contrivances of the avant-garde and genuinely believes in her own originality. Revealing the writer's indebtedness to a foreign discourse, Etcheverts's characters invariably act out the prescriptive declarations of European literary manifestoes, as if to announce a clear dependence upon distant models. In her later books, *El hijo de la ciudad* (Child of the city), *Una mujer porteña* (Buenos Aires woman), and *Convivencia* (Convivial life), she turns to a deliberately essayistic prose that forcefully questions the failures of Argentine liberalism and revaluates the productive conditions of the artist and her obligations to society. In her search for literary solutions for the problems of everyday life, Etcheverts fills her narratives with contradictory assertions about culture and feminism: a forced amalgam of borrowed ideas again mediates her understanding of national political alternatives. National identity, the essence of Argentine character, and the future of national democracy are resolved by the artist amidst the clatter of the automobile and the wonders of modern aviation. Although immigration, colonization, and the dissonant perspectives on life that separate the metropolis from the provinces occupy much of the narrative discussion of her later fictions, Etcheverts makes it clear that the solution for Argentina's problems will not come from the popular sectors but from the artist qua innovator who promises democratic restoration through literary invention and machinery. Technology (of the futurist brand) provides adventure for her narrative heroes while it paradoxically denies them their claims to uniqueness. Etcheverts examines problems of individual alienation and provides questionable solutions through the strategies of imported literary lessons. Her five novels project the common themes of the Argentine writer of the 1930s while they offer the reader a mode of reconsidering modern literary history. . . .

Sara de Etcheverts's novels serve as an apprenticeship for the larger aesthetic and political problems of the modern Argentine writer. Protecting the interests of the intellectual in a hostile and commercialized society, Etcheverts allows her heroes to elaborate plans for self-redemption. She locks her protagonists in the comfortable structure of the intellectual coterie wherein all dialogue and actions are generated. This bohemian group creates a private world for Etcheverts's characters, insulating them from contemporary Argentine realities. At the same time, it permits them a comfortable space in which to nurture an esoteric spiritualism or the illusions of utilitarian reform. Argentine history, then, becomes a pretext for literary discussion. Characters never engage directly in the major events of their day but, instead, take advantage of historical data to serve the interests of debate and meditation. Etcheverts introduces foreign literary models in order to legitimize the role of the artist in society, but the presence of writers such as Marinetti and Montherlant only serves to reinforce the intellectual dependency that characterizes Etcheverts's heroes and especially dominates the female protagonists. The borrowed European project fails in each of the novels because of the dissonant cultural perspectives that separate Argentina from the cultural centers abroad and serves as a metaphor for the dependent ideological formulations that emerged from Argentina in the decades of the 1920s and 1930s. In no case do Etcheverts's heroes—male or female—compensate for their inadequacies as fallen gods in a technological age. Instead, their specious analyses only point to the false consciousness that informs the artist in a world of questionable values. Etcheverts offers no solutions for her characters; like her contemporaries, she projects in fiction the writer's despair before the crisis of modernity.

Francine Masiello. In Beth Miller, ed.
*Women in Hispanic Literature: Icons and
Fallen Idols* (Berkeley: University of
California Press, 1983), pp. 247–49, 258